# MICHIGAN
## *at the Millennium*

**A Benchmark and Analysis of Its Fiscal and Economic Structure**

EDITED BY

Charles L. Ballard • Paul N. Courant
Douglas C. Drake • Ronald C. Fisher
Elisabeth R. Gerber

Michigan State University Press • *East Lansing*

Copyright © 2003 by Michigan State University Press

⊚ The paper used in this publication meets the minimum requirements of ANSI/NISO Z39.48-1992 (R 1997) (Permanence of Paper).

Michigan State University Press
East Lansing, Michigan 48823-5245

Printed and bound in the United States of America.

09  08  07  06  05  04  03    1  2  3  4  5  6  7  8  9  10

LIBRARY OF CONGRESS CATALOGING-IN-PUBLICATION DATA

Michigan at the millennium / edited by Charles L. Ballard . . . [et al.].
p. cm.
Includes bibliographical references.
ISBN 0-87013-668-2 (acid-free)
1. Michigan—Economic policy. 2. Michigan—Economic conditions.
3. Fiscal policy—Michigan. I. Ballard, Charles L.
HC107.M53M5323 2003
330.9774—dc21
2003006913

Book design and layout by Sharp Designs, Inc., Lansing, MI

Visit Michigan State University Press on the World Wide Web at
www.msupress.msu.edu

# Contents

# Figures

# Tables

# Preface

*Charles L. Ballard, Paul N. Courant, Douglas C. Drake,*
*Ronald C. Fisher, and Elisabeth R. Gerber*

The State of Michigan has undergone significant economic, social, and political change over the last two decades. The chapters in this volume examine numerous aspects of this change—and continuity—in the Michigan economy and fiscal structure. This work follows in the footsteps of a number of important previous studies of the Michigan economy and fiscal system. The current volume received much inspiration from and loosely follows the organization of *Michigan's Fiscal and Economic Structure*, edited by Harvey E. Brazer (1982). It also looks back to Brazer's "Michigan Tax Study Staff Papers" (1958). Both of the Brazer volumes helped set the standards for comprehensive studies of state economies and tax structures. While now dated, both still offer valuable historical data and insights.[1]

Realizing that the 1982 Brazer study was in need of a general update, the state's three major research universities joined forces to establish a team of editors. The editors compiled a preliminary list of topics for the study in 2000 and 2001, and then the editors approached colleagues at universities, at research organizations, and in government to solicit their participation in the study. Several topics were added, and generous financial support was received from the Charles Stewart Mott Foundation, Michigan State University, the University of Michigan, and Wayne State University.

Each author or team of authors was asked to take their "best look" at the general topic they had accepted. Authors were asked to review the most similar chapter in the 1982 Brazer study, and to analyze the changes since that time in Michigan, the Great Lakes region, and the United States. Authors were encouraged to speculate on the challenges facing Michigan in the immediate future, and to outline some policy options that might be worthy of consideration to address those challenges. Finally, authors were asked to produce chapters based on professional-quality research, presented in a style suitable for a general audience.

The contributors took slightly different tacks as they steered along this general course. Some of the chapters in this volume are more analytical than others. Some are more descriptive in tone and approach. However, all of the chapters are suitable for the general reader. A few contain footnotes and brief sections that require some knowledge of basic statistics, but the main body of each chapter should be accessible to all.

The editors sought to guide the authors, not to dictate either the style or the content of their work. While some common themes emerge, and will be discussed in the next section of this preface, each chapter stands on its own.

The editors may or may not agree with the conclusions and recommendations offered in each chapter. We do agree that the research chapters offer information and analysis that are worthy of consideration by policymakers and others concerned about Michigan today and over the next decade. We hope that an expanding understanding of some of the basic structural issues addressed in this volume will help build the broad political and social consensus necessary for Michigan to adapt and respond to those pressures. We do know that each of us has learned a great deal about Michigan in the process of putting together this book, and we believe that our readers will as well.

## Organization

This volume is organized into three broad sections. The first group of chapters examines the demographic and economic makeup of Michigan, with chapters focusing on some specific sectors of the state economy. The second group of chapters considers state and local government expenditures in Michigan, including specific areas of expenditure and public policy. The third group of chapters focuses on state and local revenues. This third section begins with an overview of major revenue sources for state and local governments and public schools in Michigan. The section includes chapters on the state's major revenue sources, as well as on public borrowing and the impact of the "Headlee" Amendment.

This structural organization is particularly well suited for a reader who wants information about one or two specific topics. For the reader who would prefer to begin with a review of this volume from a more thematic perspective, some common themes across the chapters are discussed in this preface and in chapter 1.

## Common Themes

A number of common themes emerge from the contributions of our authors. First, the size and roles of state and local governments in Michigan, and the relationships between them, have changed in important ways over the last two decades. Second, the state has invested heavily in human and physical capital. Third, conflicts over tax policy have played a central—though evolving—role throughout this period. Fourth, Michigan's economy has become more diversified over the last two decades, although the automobile industry still

plays a very crucial role. Fifth, economic change has created significant new challenges for many parts of Michigan, especially its aging central cities. Sixth, changes in the state's population also create current and future challenges for policy makers. Among the more important demographic issues are the aging of the population and the major role that race continues to play.

## The Size and Roles of State and Local Governments

One theme that emerges from the chapters to follow is that there have been important changes in the size and roles of state and local governments in Michigan, and the relationships between them, over the last two decades. Perhaps most significantly, there clearly has been an increasing relative role for the state government in Michigan compared to that of local governments. Many of these changes resulted from the adoption of the Proposal A school finance reform by voters in 1994. Effective 1 July 1994, this reform dramatically reduced both the local property tax burden and the local role in financing K–12 education.

Proposal A increased state taxes, but by a lower amount than it reduced local taxes, thereby producing a net tax cut overall. With state-collected taxes now providing roughly 80% of nonfederal funds for K–12 education, Proposal A was largely responsible for a major expansion of the state budget. Between Fiscal Year 1983 and Fiscal Year 2002, the rate of growth of state spending was higher for school aid than for any other category except prisons. As noted in chapter 15, "K–12 Education in Michigan," by Julie Cullen and Susanna Loeb, this financing shift has produced a significant equalization in per-student expenditures across school districts in Michigan. Because Proposal A had a dramatic effect on the state budget, it also earns a prominent role in chapter 12, "Overview of State Government Expenditures in Michigan," by Gary Olson.

This trend toward a greater role for the state government relative to local governments manifests itself in other ways as well. With the state's increasing involvement in financing K–12 education has come a growing role for the state in evaluating and controlling the production of local education as well, including MEAP testing, new state educational standards, increased publication of data about local schools, and even direct state government takeover of districts.

As mentioned previously, the only category of state expenditure that grew more rapidly than school aid was expenditures on prisons. In chapter 24, "Issues in Crime and Criminal Justice," Sheila Maxwell, David Martin, and Christopher Maxwell show that corrections expenditures hold the dubious honor of increasing by 627.2% from 1983 to 2002, without any change in the nature of financing or responsibility for housing prisoners. Instead, this increase resulted from a set of policy decisions that resulted in the incarceration of more people. The number of inmates rose from about 13,000 in 1982 to nearly 49,000 in 2002, and it is still growing. Still, expenditures on corrections account for only 4% of total state spending.

Expenditures related to health care represent another major and increasing component of the state budget. According to John Goddeeris's analyses in chapter 9, "Health Care in Michigan," health spending consumed nearly a quarter of the gross state budget for Fiscal Year 2002. Furthermore, that total represents only the expenditures of the Department of Community Health, and does not include the indirect health care costs faced by state and local government, including health care for inmates, health care for active employees, and health care for retired employees. Those costs may be compounded in the next two decades, as the aging baby boomer generation translates into an aging corrections population in addition to an aging general population.

Moderating the pressures of health care costs and corrections on the state budget during the 1990s was the significant reduction in expenditures for welfare-related programs. The state-funded General Assistance program was eliminated in 1991. The welfare reform of 1996 also contributed to major budget savings from reduced caseloads, as did the economic expansion of the late 1990s. (See chapter 17, "Michigan's Welfare System," by Kristin Seefeldt, Sandra Danziger, and Sheldon Danziger, and chapter 19, "Income Replacement and Reemployment Programs in Michigan," by Stephen A. Woodbury.)

Michigan's role in electric power generation and regulation is evolving as well, as Michelle Wilsey discusses in chapter 23, "Restructuring and Deregulation of the Electric Power Sector in Michigan." A greater share of electric power generation is now coming from private, nongovernmental generators, but with continued state regulatory oversight.

Other examples of the increase in state government's role relative to that of local governments can be seen in state-local fiscal relationships. Michigan localities depend heavily on state aid, relative to their counterparts in other states. Or, to put it another way, Michigan localities have little revenue autonomy. In chapter 13, "An Overview of Local Government Expenditures," authors Earl Ryan and Eric Lupher emphasize that a large portion of the services delivered by local governments are financed by the state. As a result, Michigan ranks very low nationally in the percentage of services delivered by local governments with "own-source revenues," that is, with revenues they raise directly. Indeed, only 48.6% of the financing for local governments in Michigan comes from own-source revenues. Michigan ranks forty-eighth among the states in this regard, with only Vermont (40.7%) and New Mexico (44.3%) showing smaller shares. This is a major part of the reason why *state-government* taxes in Michigan may appear to be high relative to those of a number of other states with a similar service mix. Further, local property tax options are greatly limited by state law, local income tax options are even more limited, and there is no local sales tax (save for selected local targeted excises). Similarly, the state greatly controls local government borrowing. These fiscal relationships between state and local governments in Michigan are further discussed in Ronald Fisher and Jeffrey Guilfoyle's chapter 31, "Fiscal Relations among the Federal Government, the State of Michigan, and Local Governments in Michigan."

State and local governments in Michigan have tremendously increased the amount of their borrowing over the last two decades. Jay Rising and Thomas Clay's chapter 30, "Borrowing by Michigan Governments," summarizes these changes, most of which have been in concert with national trends. In terms of state government debt, both general obligation and revenue debt, Michigan ranked thirty-sixth in debt per capita in 1980, remained at thirty-sixth in 1990, and rose to twenty-second in 2000. A major contributor to this increase was the School Bond Loan Fund (SBLF). The SBLF had very low levels of debt in both 1980 and 1990, but its debt level is significantly higher currently, due to a large increase in the amount of local school construction. (See chapter 30 for more information on how the SBLF provides state support for local capital costs.) Other major increases in general obligation debt came in the area of environmental protection.

Much of the growth in state government debt has been for non-general obligation or "revenue" debt. Revenue and grant anticipation borrowing for transportation programs more than doubled from 1980 to 1990, and then tripled from 1990 to 2001. Similar major expansions occurred in many other areas, such as those handled by the State Housing Development Authority, the State Hospital Finance Authority, and the Higher Education Student Loan Authority.

In sum, Michigan state government has become increasingly responsible for financing education and health care and for delivering prison services over the last two decades. Both state and local governments have increased their borrowing. The state plays a smaller part in providing welfare benefits, both because of changes in program responsibilities and because of reductions in caseloads. Local governments provide a wide range of services, but rely heavily on state and other revenue sources.

## Public Investment in Human and Physical Capital

A major role for state and local government is to provide or encourage public investment in both physical and human capital. The research reported in several chapters in this volume suggests that there has been an increase in some types of investment and a decrease in others. As discussed in chapter 24, "Issues in Crime and Criminal Justice" by Maxwell, Martin, and Maxwell, the state has invested heavily in criminal justice infrastructure. But as Kenneth Boyer shows in chapter 16, "Michigan's Transportation System and Transportation Policy," Michigan's transportation capital infrastructure is lacking relative to that of other states, while Gloria Helfand and John Wolfe show in chapter 21, "Michigan's Environment," that the state's physical environment has improved in some ways but has declined in others.

With regard to human capital, there certainly has been an increase in resources for K–12 education over the last two decades (see chapter 15, "K–12 Education in Michigan"), although those additional resources have been allocated more to some schools than to others. Districts that traditionally have been "low spending" certainly have seen a substantial increase in resources, while the highest-spending districts have seen increased limitations and restrictions. As discussed by Stephen Woodbury in chapter 19, "Income Replacement and Reemployment Programs in Michigan," Michigan has also invested signifi-

cantly in worker retraining and reemployment programs.

## Tax Revolt, Tax Reduction, and Tax Reform in Michigan

When Michigan voters adopted the "Headlee" Amendment to the state constitution in 1978, they put Michigan at the forefront of the national "tax revolt" movement, and in some ways, the state has remained there—certainly at least until the 1994 adoption of Proposal A. Tax changes, coupled with attempts to limit the state's taxing and spending powers, played a major role in state and local politics during the first decade of the period we examine. Tax reduction has been a dominant theme of the second decade.

*The Headlee Amendment.* Chapter 33, "Tax Limitation in the Michigan Constitution: The Headlee Amendment," looks at the tax revolt movement nationally, and at Michigan's long constitutional history of limiting government's powers to tax and spend. Chapter author Susan Fino argues that in the context of Michigan's history of such limitations, the adoption of the Headlee Amendment may be reasonably thought of as an evolutionary change rather than a revolutionary one. Headlee's provisions include (1) creation of an overall limit on state revenue collections, (2) a comparable spending limit, (3) a requirement that a fixed share of the state budget be expended on behalf of local government, (4) a requirement that local property taxes be rolled back if growth on a community-wide basis exceeded inflation, and (5) a requirement for the state to fund new requirements mandated upon local governments. These were significant changes, but were not far out of line with prior limits and requirements.

What was new in the Headlee Amendment was its comprehensiveness in imposing so many changes at once. Perhaps the most restrictive portion of the Headlee Amendment for state government has been the state requirements, or "mandates" provision. This has been the basis of the long-running "Durant" litigation over state funding of local special education programs and other requirements. This litigation continues today, now twenty-five years since the adoption of the amendment, with no clear end in sight.

*Property Taxes.* From the perspective of property owners, one of the most significant aspects of the Headlee Amendment was the section allowing for "millage rollbacks." This provision may have slightly slowed the growth of local property taxes through the 1980s. However, as noted by Naomi Feldman, Douglas Drake, and Paul Courant in chapter 28, "The Property Tax in Michigan," the rollback provision was limited in its delivery of tax relief. Ongoing dissatisfaction with rising property taxes was a large contributor to the pressure for school finance reform that ultimately resulted in Proposal A. Both chapter 28 and chapter 15 ("K–12 Education in Michigan") speak to the pressures and issues of property tax reform and school finance reform.

One of the principal selling points of Proposal A was its provision for a cap on the increase in taxable value of each individual parcel of property. This feature, popularly known as the "assessment cap," in some ways made Michigan's property tax limits more like those adopted by California in its Proposition 13 in 1978. The assessment cap limits the assessment on each parcel to an increase no greater than the rate of inflation, until it is sold. When the property is sold, it is reassessed at its full market value.

The K–12 portion of Proposal A added still more limiting provisions to the Michigan Constitution. Local school districts now have virtually no discretion in the amount of local mills they can levy for school operating purposes. Indeed, the state constitution now requires a three-fourths vote of the legislature to increase any of the property tax levies that can be used by the local districts.

If limitations on taxing powers and government spending have been one dominant theme of our period, so too have been issues of tax reform and tax reduction. The combination has produced a period that can best be summarized as one of dramatic change, especially at the state level.

The early 1980s saw major increases in income tax rates, as revenue collections were driven downward by strong economic downturns. Income tax rates were elevated from 1982 to 1986, before returning to the rate of 4.6% that had been in effect from 1974 to 1982. The 1990s told a different story. Even though Proposal A brought about a major increase in *state* taxes, it reduced *local* taxes, resulting in a net tax cut (and was marketed as such). It has been followed up throughout the decade with dozens of minor exemptions and exclusions. Beginning in 1999, continuing rate reductions were legislated for both the individual income tax and the Single Business Tax.

*The Single Business Tax, the Sales Tax, and the Income Tax.* The Single Business Tax was originally designed as a kind of value-added tax. However, in chapter 29, "Michigan's Flirtation with the Single Business Tax," author James Hines notes that the SBT has been so eroded that it is far from a pure value-added tax today. The two largest taxes at the state level (the income tax and the retail sales tax) have also been subject to significant base erosion over the last twenty years. Some of that erosion has resulted from legislated policy changes. However, in the case of the retail sales tax, much of the narrowing of the tax base has been due to the changing nature of the economy. The ongoing shift in the state from a goods-producing economy to a service-producing economy has already had profound effects in terms of narrowing the sales tax base (see Joel Slemrod's discussion in chapter 27, "Michigan's Sales and Use Taxes"). This trend toward a shrinking tax base is likely to increase in the future. It may be exacerbated by the increasing role of the Internet in commerce. Internet sellers, and other remote sellers such as catalog firms and firms using "800" numbers, are often not required to collect sales taxes because they lack the legal "nexus" in the state where the buyer resides.

Chapter 26, "Michigan's Personal Income Tax," also addresses the question of long-term base erosion. Author Paul Menchik notes the significant and growing tax preferences given to senior citizens under the Michigan income tax. Menchik's chapter raises concerns about the demographics of this growing population group. He argues that through public policy, the state is exempting a rapidly growing number of people from the state's income tax base, many of whom have relatively high incomes. As the size of the elderly population increases, the revenue loss from these tax preferences will put increasing strain on the state's finances.

*Other Taxes.* Chapter 32, "Miscellaneous Taxes in Michigan," by Lawrence Martin, explores Michigan's reliance on tobacco and alcohol taxes and gambling profits, among other revenue sources. Tobacco offers a particularly perplexing perspective on public policy: Michigan has come to rely more and more on a revenue source that is utilized in part to reduce the consumption of the product. Gambling has also become an increasing source of public revenue in Michigan, both from the state lottery and from casino gaming in Detroit and on Indian lands.

During the 1990s, the Michigan Inheritance Tax was changed to a "federal pick-up" estate tax. Barring legislative action to decouple it from the federal tax, that tax will be effectively repealed in Michigan with the end of the federal credit for state taxes on estates of decedents after 2004.

The tax revolt has also played itself out in the degree to which state revenues are dedicated, or "earmarked," for use in specific ways. Some of this earmarking is done constitutionally, some by statute, and some by other actors, such as the federal government. When one set of funds is earmarked, it is still possible to offset earmarking by shifting to the use of other funds. However, when larger and larger shares of state revenues are limited to specific purposes, the governor and the legislature may have reduced budgetary flexibility, unless explicit action is taken.

Significant earmarking of taxes for specific purposes has always been a part of Michigan's fiscal tradition, and has become more so in the last decade. Proposal A contributed major changes with its package of taxes earmarked for school aid. The recent increase in the tobacco tax produced additional earmarking. The same is true of the rate reductions in the individual income tax, which were accompanied by an increase in the percentage of income-tax revenues earmarked for school aid. Ironically, the taxes that were recently repealed or are scheduled for repeal (Intangibles, Estate, and Single Business Tax) are among the few taxes with no earmarking.

## The Movement toward a More Diversified Economy

Michigan's economy has become more diversified over the last two decades, and therefore has in some ways become more similar to the national economy. However, the state continues to rely heavily on the auto industry, and will likely do so far into the future.

In chapter 2, "Overview of the Michigan Economy," authors Joan Crary, George Fulton, and Saul Hymans note that prior to 1980, Michigan had long been regarded as a highly cyclical, highly prosperous state dominated by the automobile industry. Compared to its neighboring states, Michigan began the period under study with much higher unemployment, but also with higher wages. By the end of the 1990s, the state's income and unemployment levels were essentially equal to the average of its Great Lakes state neighbors.

Michigan is now much closer to the national average in terms of income. Michigan's economy also appears to be less cyclical than before.

*Changes in the Labor Force.* In chapter 4, "The Evolution of the Michigan Labor Market from 1970 to 2001," author George Johnson reports that wages in the state, while still somewhat above the national average, have dropped dramatically over this period relative to those of the rest of the nation. Johnson suggests that a portion of the change is attributable to a drop in union membership in Michigan, from roughly 40% of the workforce in the 1970s to roughly 20% in 2000. Interestingly, the relative decrease in real, inflation-adjusted wages has not been as severe as the relative decrease in nominal wages, because prices have not grown as rapidly in Michigan as they have in many other parts of the country.

Of the differences that remain between Michigan and the rest of the nation, a large portion can be attributed to the state's mix of industries and employment. Michigan is still far more concentrated in automobile manufacturing than the nation as a whole. Chapter 2 reports relative "location quotients" that compare Michigan's industrial concentration to that of the nation. Michigan's economy is eight times more concentrated in automobile manufacturing than is the national economy. Thus, the high productivity and high wages in the auto industry play an important role in keeping the state's income levels at or slightly above the national average.

*Manufacturing Industries.* Other chapters take different approaches to the issue of diversification. In chapter 8, "Automotive and Other Manufacturing Industries in Michigan," authors Richard Block and Dale Belman report that in 1977, motor vehicle manufacturing represented 45.6% of total state manufacturing, while all manufacturing was 35% of total Gross State Product (GSP). By 1999, manufacturing as a whole had declined to 26.2% of GSP, and the motor vehicle sector was 33.5% of that.

Despite this decline, Michigan manufacturing in 1999 represented the same share (5.4%) of total U.S. Gross Manufacturing Product that it did in 1980. This is because manufacturing's share of output declined nationwide. Consequently, Michigan remains the third-largest manufacturing state in terms of value of shipments, ranking behind only California and Ohio. By two other measures, Michigan has actually moved up in the rankings: from sixth to third in production employment between the 1977 and 1997 Censuses of Manufactures, and from seventh to fourth in number of production hours.

*Connections to the International Economy.* Michigan has consistently been a leading export state. In chapter 6, "Michigan's Stake in International Trade and Investment," Alan Deardorff reports that Michigan ranks fourth nationally in terms of exports. Exports grew strongly through the 1990s, both from Michigan and from other states.

Michigan's leading export is automobiles, or "transportation equipment" as reported in the official national data. Chapter 6 shows that transportation equipment represents over half of Michigan's total exports, with machinery a distant second, and other sectors essentially negligible.

*Agriculture and Tourism.* Other sectors of the state's economy have seen some diversification over the period under study as well, but their economic impact is much less than that of manufacturing. In Chapter 10, "Michigan's Agricultural, Forestry, and Mining Industries," authors Arlen Leholm, Raymond Vlasin, and John Ferris find that these sectors are declining in importance by most measures, and rank far below sectors such as manufacturing, services, trade, education, health care, and government in terms of employment and income. Land acreage in Michigan farms has declined consistently since its peak of 19 million acres in 1920. The current level of 10.4 million acres compares to the level of 1870. Employment in agriculture has also declined.

One potential area for diversification is tourism. However, in chapter 22, "Michigan Tourism," author Donald Holecek discusses why this sector is unlikely to have a significant impact on Michigan's movement toward a more diverse economy. Despite growth in tourism expenditures over the past twenty years, Michigan actually appears to have increased both its net domestic and international travel deficit over the period. A large portion of the travel in the state is by Michigan residents visiting other residents or vacationing within the state. This localized travel severely limits tourism's potential as an economic growth area. Michigan's geography, climate, and lack of a large number of headliner destinations probably mean that expansion and diversification of tourism as an export industry is unlikely.

*Economic Development and the High-Technology Economy.* Chapter 14, "Economic Development Policy in Michigan," comes at the question of diversification and change from the perspective of Michigan's state-supported efforts at economic development. Authors Timothy Bartik, Peter Eisinger, and George Erickcek note that Michigan has frequently been considered a national leader in innovative development programs. Michigan was one of the first states to target "high technology" as part of its recruitment and diversification strategy. However, the authors argue that changes in political leadership and priorities and restructuring of programs have limited the impact of these initiatives. They conclude that Michigan could benefit from greater continuity in its economic development efforts. A case can also be made for Michigan to build in better systems of evaluation for its efforts, in order to identify the most effective development tools.

In chapter 7, "High Technology in Michigan's Economy," authors Abel Feinstein, George Fulton, and Donald Grimes look explicitly at how far the state has moved toward cultivating a "modern" high-technology economy. The authors conclude that Michigan has become the world center for research, engineering, and design of motor vehicles. They note that, while Michigan has the largest number of motor-vehicle production workers of any state, it also has a large share—56%—of the industry's technology-oriented workers. Michigan has a greater proportion of workers in high-technology occupations than the national average, and these high-tech occupations are growing faster in the state than in the nation as a whole. Michigan's involvement in automotive manufacturing extends far beyond the Big Three, because many of the foreign-based manufacturers also have research facilities in Michigan. Of the $18 billion of automotive research and development spending in the United States in 1999, an estimated $13.5 billion was spent in Michigan.

However, in other ways, Michigan's transformation to a high-tech economy is less impressive. In the category "Information Technology" that many of us most directly associate with the concept "high-tech," Michigan has a smaller concentration than the nation, and is growing at about the national rate. In the category of "Biotechnology," Michigan has grown substantially from a small base, but has lost relative share to other states.

Relative to its Great Lakes neighbors, Michigan has the second-highest *number* of high-technology workers, behind Illinois, despite the fact that

Illinois has a larger population. Also, Michigan's high-tech employment is increasing at a more rapid rate. Among the Great Lakes states, only Minnesota has a higher *share* of high-tech employment (at 5.8%, compared to Michigan's 5.6%).

In addition to contributing to the diversification of the state's economy, strength in high-tech industries has another important economic benefit: the jobs pay well. The average weekly wage for all occupations in Michigan over the period 1997–2001 was about $625. The average for all high-technology occupations was almost 70% higher, at about $1,050.

Chapter 7 concludes with an analysis of some of the factors that may contribute to the growth of high-technology industries and employment. These include the availability of venture capital; the role of higher education; tax factors; agglomeration, or the achievement of a critical mass that leads to further expansion; and the overall attractiveness of a state and region. The authors note that Michigan faces critical labor force shortage issues. In a world where high skill is increasingly critical to workforce success, Michigan's well-educated labor force is already essentially fully employed. Retirements will become a critical workforce issue around 2010.

*The Low-Skill Labor Force.* To the extent that Michigan has a surplus of workers in any segment of the labor force, it exists in that portion of the population with less than a high school education. In chapter 18, "The Less-Skilled Labor Market in Michigan," author Rebecca Blank shows that the unemployment rate is much higher for these workers than for the rest of the workforce. Even among those who are working, many are what Blank calls very-low-wage earners—those earning wages at a level less than the twentieth percentile nationally. In 1979, one-third of these workers had no high school diploma. By 1989, those with no high school diploma were 45.5% of the very-low-wage workers. By 2000, they were 52% of the group below the twentieth percentile.

While the relative position of these workers improved in the boom years of the late 1990s, they still face limited opportunities to move on to more skilled positions. Blank notes that the problems faced by these workers are especially challenging during an economic slowdown. She recommends consideration of a number of policy options, especially for younger workers. These options include continued improvement in the public education and job-training systems, consideration of adoption of an earned income tax credit, and/or actions to make health insurance coverage available to these workers, to help keep them in the workforce.

Additional testimony to both the need for and the value of workforce development comes from chapter 17, "Michigan's Welfare System," by Seefeldt, Danziger, and Danziger. That chapter describes a study of Michigan women that looked at characteristics of those in the workforce and those who remained reliant on welfare. Some of the most striking differences between the two groups were that 48% of the welfare-reliant lacked a high school diploma, while only 20% of the wage-reliant did. Another striking difference: Some 57% of the welfare-reliant experienced transportation difficulties when working, while only 19% of the wage-reliant did so.

In sum, Michigan, its businesses, and its people exist in a fully interactive and international economic system. The state is still highly dependent on the automobile industry, but that industry is far different than it was even ten or fifteen years ago.

## Michigan's Cities and the Changing Economy

As Michigan's economy evolves, many of the state's older central cities and inner-ring suburbs, built around the economic foundation of manufacturing in general, and motor-vehicle manufacturing in particular, are experiencing significant difficulty. In chapter 11, "Economic Performance of Michigan Cities and Metropolitan Areas," authors David Crary, George Erickcek, and Allen Goodman find that Michigan's older central cities have experienced loss of population, loss of jobs, and an increasing degree of racial segregation and poverty. These changes, however, are not isolated to Michigan or to the auto industry. While most *metropolitan areas* in the Midwest and Great Lakes regions grew in population over the last two decades, their *central cities* all declined. Analysis in chapter 11 shows that population declined significantly from 1970 to 2000 in Buffalo, Chicago, Cleveland, Milwaukee, Pittsburgh, St. Louis, and Toledo. St. Louis experienced percentage declines greater than those of Detroit or Flint. Buffalo, Cleveland, and Pittsburgh had similar population declines to those of Detroit and Flint. The metropolitan areas of Buffalo, Cleveland, and Pittsburgh experienced significant declines as well.

Michigan's nine metropolitan areas represent 82% of the state's total population, and their viability is obviously critical to the economic, social, and fiscal health of the entire state. Between 1980 and 2000, all of the state's metropolitan areas except Ann Arbor and Grand Rapids lagged the United States in population and income growth. All experienced significant degrees of out-migration from the central city to suburban areas. All have a significant manufacturing base. While total employment grew in all metropolitan areas except Flint, each area had significant job losses in manufacturing in the 1990s.

Flint provides a stark example of the concept of "diversification by subtraction." Flint began the 1990s as the Michigan city with by far the greatest concentration of employment in the automotive industry. Over the decade, Flint bore the brunt of job losses: a net decrease of 900 jobs over the decade, with a loss of 20,500 jobs in manufacturing (17,800 of those in the automobile industry) more than offsetting growth in other sectors. Chapter 8, "Automotive and Other Manufacturing Industries in Michigan," provides further evidence of this sectoral decline, with a 68.1% decline in automotive industry jobs in Flint from 1980 to 2001, moving Flint from 15% of the Michigan total during most of the 1980s to 5.6% of the Michigan total in 2001. Largely due to these automotive industry losses, two other industries have increased in their local concentration and relative economic importance: Local Government Medical (especially Hurley Hospital) and General Merchandise Stores.

The movement of population, jobs, and resources from Michigan's central cities to the suburban fringe has created other public policy challenges as well. In chapter 5, "Land Use," author Gary Sands notes that while Michigan still has significant amounts of undeveloped land, there is growing pressure on suburban fringe areas. In chapter 21, "Environment and Natural Resources in Michigan," Gloria Helfand and John Wolfe note that these changes have been met with some environmental successes in terms of more effective pollution abatement and control, but also with new challenges, such as land fragmentation and habitat loss.

## Michigan's Changing Population

Michigan's share of the total U.S. population has been declining since 1970 (see Kenneth Darga's chapter 3, "Population Trends in Michigan").

Although Michigan's population is growing, and in fact the state has experienced net in-migration in recent years, that growth is slower than the growth of the nation as a whole. There has also been an enormous shift in residential location from central cities to the outlying suburban and rural fringes of the state's metropolitan areas.

Michigan's population is aging as well, and it is likely that the percentage of the population over the age of sixty-five will grow dramatically in the next twenty years. Although the population of the state is aging as a whole, Michigan's communities are aging at different rates. The rate of aging is more rapid in the state's central cities. This aging population is likely to create a greater strain over time on the state's public resources, especially the state's public pension system, although Leslie Papke, author of chapter 20, "Public Pensions and Pension Policy in Michigan," notes that these pension plans are currently in sound financial condition.

The racial distribution of Michigan's population indicates that the state is significantly whiter than the nation as a whole. Michigan has a slightly larger proportion of blacks than does the nation as a whole, but significantly fewer Hispanics and Asian/Pacific Islanders, and about the same share of Native Americans.

The racial realities of Michigan present both a challenge and an opportunity for the future of our cities and schools. While Benton Harbor, Detroit, and Flint are the only three large cities in the state with African American majorities, nearly all of the major cities have experienced a significant growth in the concentration of African American population since 1980.[2] Michigan schools are among the most segregated by race in the nation.[3] The basic cause is white flight from urban areas, especially Detroit, since the 1950s.

These patterns of residential segregation are well illustrated in the case of Flint and the rest of Genesee County. Seventy-five percent of the African Americans in the county live within the Flint city limits. There are striking differences in income levels and poverty rates between the city and county as well.

Population dispersion has had significant effects on infrastructure costs in both the developing areas and the central cities: the developing areas face pressures for construction of new infrastructure, and the central cities are now beginning to face the need to update and modernize infrastructure that is often fifty or more years old. For example, chapter 5, "Land Use," cites a study by the Southeast Michigan Council of Governments that estimated a need of $41 billion for road and bridge work in southeast Michigan, plus another $14 to $26 billion for sanitary and storm water systems. In chapter 16, "Michigan's Transportation System and Transportation Policy," author Kenneth Boyer notes that the state's highway systems show some of the worst conditions of any in the nation. Thus, Michigan is presented with a major challenge by the need to repair, maintain, and improve its infrastructure. The challenge is even greater in view of the increasing geographical dispersion of the population.

We now invite our readers to continue with the remaining chapters of this volume, which present a detailed portrait and analysis of the Michigan economy at the beginning of a new millennium.

■

## REFERENCES

Brazer, Harvey E. 1961. Taxation in Michigan: An appraisal. The Institute of Public Administration, University of Michigan.

———, ed. 1958. Michigan tax study staff papers. Special Legislative Tax Study Committee.

———, ed. 1982. *Michigan's fiscal and economic structure.* Ann Arbor: University of Michigan Press.

Cline, Denzel C., and Milton C. Taylor. 1966. Michigan tax reform. Institute for Community Development and Services, Michigan State University.

Haber, William, Eugene C. McKean, and Harold C. Taylor. 1959. *The Michigan economy: Its potentials and its problems.* Kalamazoo, Mich.: W. E. Upjohn Institute.

McCracken, Paul, ed. 1960. *Taxes and economic growth in Michigan.* Kalamazoo, Mich.: W. E. Upjohn Institute.

## NOTES

1. Other volumes worth reviewing for a look at Michigan's fiscal history (and this is by no means a comprehensive list) include: *The Michigan Economy* (Haber, McKean, and Taylor 1959); *Taxes and Economic Growth in Michigan* (McCracken 1960); *Taxation in Michigan* (Brazer 1961); and *Michigan Tax Reform* (Cline and Taylor 1966).

2. We know from the Census of 2000 that Michigan also has the whitest large city in the country: Livonia. The exception of increasing concentration was Battle Creek, but that apparently was due solely to its annexation of Battle Creek Township in 1982. The African American share of Battle Creek's population thus declined in the 1990 Census, and while still below the 1980 level, it increased significantly once again in the 2000 Census.

3. "Schools Divided by Race Lines," *Detroit Free Press,* 20 January 2003, B1, citing "A Multiracial Society with Segregated Schools: Are We Losing the Dream?"

# An Overview of Michigan's Fiscal and Economic History

*Douglas C. Drake*

## Introduction

Michigan has been shaped by a variety of historical influences. Those influences include geology, climate, exploration, and settlement. They also include the fiscal, economic, and political histories and traditions that have developed around the evolving role of government in society and the changing relationships of state and local governments in response to both fiscal crisis and fiscal reform. This chapter will briefly explore a number of these influences.

Geologically, Michigan is both protected and blessed by abundant water resources. Those same water resources put the state off to the side of major cross-continent transportation routes. Another influence is the climate, which seems to be a negative factor in the attraction of both industry and immigration.

The legacy of human settlement represents yet another set of influences, beginning with the era of a prewritten history that at a minimum still shapes the concept of place in Michigan. The Chippewa, the Huron, the Menominee, the Ottawa, and the Wyandotte tribes gave Michigan more than place names. Today's Michigan also still reflects the legacy of European discovery and settlement. This includes a legacy of some of the traditions that linger in social and political culture just as the names linger on communities and thoroughfares: Aubin, Baraga, Brulé, Cadillac, Charlevoix, Chene, Dequindere, and Marquette are just a few of the names reflecting this varied heritage that can be found within the state. Furthermore, if we now know the place as Detroit, this does not change the legacy of the place that was once known as d'etroit.

Some of the early Europeans came to Michigan in the search for the fabled Northwest Passage, but perhaps just as many came out of curiosity and the sheer joy of discovery, to seek whatever it might be that lay just beyond the next bend of the river or the next point of land on the big lakes. Some also came on a quest for fortune.

Bruce Catton's bicentennial history of Michigan notes that Michigan has a long tradition of boom and bust economic cycles. These began with the fur trade (Astor House on Mackinac Island is as much a symbol of a once dominant industry as is any automotive assembly plant). In later years the boom and bust pattern would be exhibited by mining, then lumbering, and then by the automobile industry.[1]

Sweat and steel marked Michigan's economic progress through the first centuries of its history. Perhaps silicon, biology, chemistry, and physics will mark its progress through this century.

## The Changing Nature of Fiscal Policy and Reform

Michigan's fiscal and economic history and tradition represent a set of influences that continue to shape our present and future. This chapter will now turn to a number of these issues. Michigan's long-term fiscal history mirrors that of many other states. For much of its history state government played a subordinate role to local government. The property tax was one of the primary sources of financing for state services, as it was for local government. That ended in 1933, when Michigan joined a number of other states in adopting a retail sales tax to fund public services (see chapter 27).

As pressures grew for more public services, Michigan state government expanded in size. Michigan's tax structure continued to evolve through the 1930s and into the present as pressures mounted to finance the demands for public services and for reform in the financing and delivery of those services.[2]

Over time the pattern of those policy discussions shifted back and forth in emphasis between adequacy and fairness or equity, with the question of the tax burden a constant in the debates. Michigan has experimented with a number of significant and innovative tax and fiscal reforms over the decades. A strong tradition developed for "earmarking," or restricting certain revenue sources to specific uses, removing legislative discretion. In 1946, for example, Michigan voters amended the state constitution to earmark roughly three-fourths of the state sales tax collections. This tradition continues today.

Michigan's tradition of reform and innovation in tax policy includes the following major policy

---

**TABLE 1.1**

### A Selected Chronology of Key Dates in Michigan's Fiscal History

| | |
|---|---|
| 1932 | Voters approve fifteen-mill property tax limit amendment to constitution. |
| 1933 | Michigan adopts a 3% sales tax, PA 167 of 1933. |
| 1934 | Michigan cedes use of property tax to local governments. |
| 1937 | Michigan adopts a 3% use tax, PA 94 of 1937. |
| 1946 | Sales tax diversion amendment earmarks over 70% of sales tax revenues. |
| 1953 | Adoption of Business Activities Tax "temporarily" in effect for nine months of FY 1954, but made permanent for the next fiscal year and beyond. |
| 1954 | Voters modify sales tax diversion amendment in constitution and cap rate at 3%. |
| 1959 | "Payless payday" in May 1959 (pay for state workers delayed one week). |
| 1960 | Voters approve sales tax rate increase to 4%. |
| 1967 | Repeal of Business Activities Tax, adoption of Individual Income Tax at 2.6% (PA 231 of 1967, effective 1 October 1967, or nine months of fiscal 1967-68), Corporate Income Tax at 5.6%, and Financial Institutions Income Tax at 7.0% (business taxes effective 1 January 1968). |
| 1970 | UAW strikes General Motors, mid-September through November. |
| 1971 | Income tax rates increase: Individual to 3.9% (PA 76 of 1971, an increase of 50%), Corporate to 7.8% (an increase of 39.2%), Financial to 9.7% (an increase of 38.6%). |
| 1972 | Adoption of district power equalizing school aid formula. Voters approve constitutional amendment authorizing lottery. |
| 1973 | Adoption of circuit-breaker property tax relief program; income tax personal exemption increased from $1,200 to $1,500 (PA 20 of 1973). Fiscal Year 1973 has partial year of lottery sales. |
| 1974 | Voters exempt food and drugs from sales tax; individual income tax rate increased from 3.9% to 4.6% to offset (PA 19 of 1975, effective 1 May 1975). |
| 1975 | July collections of sales, use, and withholding taxes accrued back to 30 June, year end of FY 1975. Executive Orders 1974-11 and 1975-2 impact FY 1975. |
| 1976 | August 1975, Single Business Tax adopted, to be effective 1 January 1976 (PA 228 of 1975); corporate income tax, corporate franchise fee, local personal property tax on business inventory, business portion of intangibles tax, financial institutions income tax, and other smaller taxes repealed. Executive Order 1975-12. Creation of fifteen-month fiscal year, 1 July 1975 to 30 September 1976. Fiscal year now runs from 1 October to 30 September. |
| 1977 | Budget Stabilization Fund created (PA 76 of 1977). |
| 1978 | Voters approve "Headlee" Amendment to Michigan constitution. |
| 1980 | Executive Order 1980-3, first use of Budget Stabilization Fund. |
| 1981 | Executive Order 1981-8. |
| 1982 | Executive Orders 1981-9, 1982-4, 1982-6, 1982-13. Income tax increase: to 5.6% for six months, effective average of 5.1% for both tax year and fiscal year (PA 155 of 1982). Tobacco tax raised from 11 to 21 cents per pack. |

actions. The Business Activities Tax, a type of value-added tax, was enacted in 1953, but was repealed in 1967 with the adoption of personal and business income taxes. In 1975 the business income taxes were themselves repealed and replaced with a different type of value-added tax, the Single Business Tax, effective 1 January 1976. To date, Michigan is the only state to have experimented with value-added taxation.

School finance reform figured prominently in public debate in the late 1960s and early 1970s. That debate subsided for a time after 1972 with the replacement of an uncapped foundation grant system with one of district power equalizing in 1972.[3] That debate began again in the late 1980s and early 1990s, culminating in the 1994 voter approval of Proposal A.

Food not intended for immediate consumption and prescription drugs were exempted from the state sales tax by voter-initiated petition in 1974.

Ferment against taxes in general and the property tax in particular flared up periodically over the years. In the mid to late 1970s it manifested itself in a number of voter and legislated ballot issues that culminated in voter approval of the "Headlee" Amendment to the Michigan constitution in 1978.[4]

The 1970s produced a mix of economic and fiscal fortunes for Michigan. There were both lean years and full years, and both had impacts on the state's fiscal structure. Income taxes were increased dramatically in 1971 in response to a sluggish national economy and a lengthy auto-worker strike. The increased tax rates produced strong revenue growth as the economy recovered that was used in part to finance tax reductions for low- and moderate-income taxpayers.

---

|  | |
|------|---|
| 1983 | Executive Order 1983–5. Income tax increase, tax year 1983 = to 6.35 %, for FY 1983 to = 5.91% (PA 15 of 1983). |
| 1984 | Income tax increase still in effect, but reduced by PA 221 of 1984. Tax rate for tax year 1984 = to 5.85%; for FY 1984 = to 6.15%. |
| 1985 | Income tax increase still in effect, tax rate for tax year 1985 = to 5.35%; for FY 1985 = to 5.35%. |
| 1986 | Income tax increase, retroactively ended as of 1 January 1986. Effective tax rate for tax year 1986 = to 4.60%; for FY 1986 = to 4.79%. Large tax amnesty program. |
| 1988 | Tobacco tax increase from 21 to 25 cents per pack for "Health and Safety Fund." |
| 1990 | Ends in deficit. |
| 1991 | Executive Order 1991–17. |
| 1992 | Executive Order 1992–13, General Assistance program eliminated effective 1 October 1991 (beginning of FY 1992). |
| 1993 | Legislature acts to eliminate the property tax as a funding source for local school district operations after 31 December 1993. Search begins for alternatives. Two reform packages are adopted 25 December 1993, for submission to voters in March 1994. Inheritance tax replaced by Estate Tax (PA 54 of 1993). |
| 1994 | Voters approve Proposal A plan financed primarily by sales tax increase. New system of financing for local schools begins 1 July 1994. Taxes effective 1 May 1994. Sales and use taxes increase to 6 cents, tobacco tax |

|  | |
|------|---|
| | increases, and new state property tax and real estate transfer tax are added. Income tax is reduced from 4.6% to 4.4%; tax rate for tax year 1994 = to 4.47%; for FY 1994 = to 4.52% (PA 328 of 1993). Single Business Tax is reduced from 2.35% to 2.30% (PA 247 of 1994). |
| 1995 | First full year of Proposal A school financing. Intangibles tax begins four-year phase-out (PA 5 of 1995). |
| 1999 | Income tax phase-down from 4.4% to 3.9% enacted (PA's 2–6 of 1999). Single Business Tax phase-out enacted, from 2.30% to 0.0% over a twenty-three-year period (PA 117 of 1999). |
| 2000 | Income tax phase-down accelerated (PA 40 of 2000). Tax rate for tax year 2000 = to 4.20%; for FY 2000 = to 4.25%. |
| 2001 | Budget Stabilization Fund withdrawals and other uses of one-time funds. Both fiscal and tax year income tax rate is 4.20%. |
| 2002 | Budget Stabilization Fund withdrawals and other uses of one-time funds. Executive Order 2001-9. SBT phase-down paused by formula in act: Budget Stabilization Fund balance drops below $250 million. Tax year income tax rate is 4.10%; FY 2002 rate = to 4.13%. |
| 2003 | Budget Stabilization Fund withdrawals. Executive Orders 2002-22 (Governor Engler) and 2003-3 (Governor Granholm) reduce FY 2003 spending. Tax year income tax rate is 4.00%, and FY 2003 rate = to 4.03%. |

SOURCES: State of Michigan Executive Budget documents, various years; State of Michigan Comprehensive Annual Financial Reports, various years; Senate Fiscal Agency, Statistical Reports, various years. Some data for older years from Harvey Brazer, "Taxation in Michigan: An Appraisal," Ann Arbor: Institute of Public Administration, University of Michigan, 1961; Harvey Brazer, ed., Michigan Tax Study Staff paper, Special Legislative Tax Study Committee, 1958; Denzel C. Cline and Milton C. Taylor, "Michigan Tax Reform," East Lansing: Institute for Community Development and Services, Michigan State University, 1966.

### TABLE 1.2

**Years Requiring Extraordinary Actions to Complete Balanced Budgets since 1979**

| | |
|---|---|
| 1980 | Budget Stabilization Fund (BSF) withdrawal, Executive Order 1980-3. |
| 1981 | BSF withdrawal, Executive Order 1981-8. |
| 1982 | Income tax increase (5.10% for tax year and fiscal year); Executive Orders 1981-9, 1982-4, 1982-6, and 1982-13; also tobacco tax increase from 11 to 21 cents a pack to finance accounting deficit (Working Capital Reserve Account). |
| 1983 | Income tax increase (6.35% for tax year, 5.91% for fiscal year), Executive Order 1983-5; portion of income tax increase (.25) also dedicated to accounting deficit (State Accounting and Fiscal Responsibility Account). |
| 1984 | Income tax increase (5.85% tax year, 6.15% fiscal year). |
| 1985 | Income tax increase (5.35% for tax year and fiscal year). |
| 1986 | Income tax increase (4.60% for tax year, 4.79% for fiscal year); amnesty program provides one-time $89.5 million to GFGP budget; transfer of unneeded balances from Working Capital Reserve account to GFGP is another one-time source. |
| 1988 | Cigarette tax increases from 21 to 25 cents per pack for "Health & Safety Fund." |
| 1990 | Ends in deficit. |
| 1991 | Ends in deficit, Executive Order 1991-17. |
| 1992 | Executive order 1992-13. |
| 1993 | Executive order 1993-6. |
| 2001 | BSF withdrawals, other one-time funds. |
| 2002 | BSF withdrawals, other one-time funds. Executive Order 2002-9. |
| 2003 | BSF withdrawals, other one-time funds. Executive Order 2002-22 (Governor Engler), Executive Order 2003-3 (Governor Granholm). |
| 2004 | Major reductions prior to executive recommendation. |

SOURCES: State of Michigan Executive Budget documents, various years; State of Michigan Comprehensive Annual Financial Reports, various years; Senate Fiscal Agency, Statistical Reports, various years.

NOTE: Extraordinary actions include such actions as the BSF withdrawals and budget-cutting executive orders noted previously, but also include significant uses of other one-time revenue sources or one-time funding reductions, "negative" supplementals. Most budgets are "tight," in that all requests are not funded and many are not fully funded. These years presented problems that were clearly greater than normal.

## Fiscal Crisis and Fiscal Reform

Michigan has begun both the current decade and the new political administration in the same way that it began the 1990s, the 1980s, the 1970s, and the 1960s: with either a state budget crisis of significant proportions, a major disruption in the state economy, or both (see tables 1.1 and 1.2). The 1960s began with a constitutional amendment to increase the state sales tax rate from 3% to 4%, to provide more adequate funding of public services, especially education. The decade was dominated by tax reform discussions focused on revenue adequacy and growth to finance growing demands for public services. Those discussions resulted in the adoption of state corporate and personal income taxes in 1967.

The 1970s began with a record automobile industry strike that had a devastating impact on Michigan's tax receipts. One result was a dramatic increase in the rate for individual and business income taxes. By 1973 a strong national economy and a rebounding auto industry helped drive major increases in state revenues. This led to major tax reform and reduction that significantly increased the personal exemption on the state income tax and created the "circuit-breaker" property tax relief program in Public Act 20 of 1973 (See chapters 26 and 28). The tax reductions came just in time for the OPEC oil embargo, which had especially adverse effects on the United States automobile industry, dominated by the three companies headquartered in Michigan.

The ensuing fiscal crisis fostered a number of responses. First, Michigan changed accounting practices to accrue revenues collected after the close of the fiscal year in 1975. Second, the economic fluctuations of the early 1970s demonstrated the volatility of the corporate income tax. This led state government and businesses to explore business tax reform. The result was the adoption of the Single Business Tax (SBT) in August of 1975, to be effective for a portion of FY 1976. The first quarterly estimated payments of the new tax overlapped the final annual payments for the major state taxes it replaced (the corporate income tax, the corporate franchise fee, and the business portion of the intangibles tax). This overlap generated about $200 million in one-time revenues critical to balancing the state budget.

Fiscal Year 1976 stands out in Michigan fiscal history for two other important reasons:

First, when it became apparent that additional efforts were going to be necessary to balance the budget, the state changed its fiscal year. Fiscal Year 1976 became a fifteen-month year, ending on 30 September rather than the traditional 30 June. The state budget gained another $200 million of one-time revenues, largely because of incorporating three months of revenue in a period that included only one state payment to K–12 schools. Second, recognizing the fiscal shock, Michigan political leaders sought new tools to manage what was widely viewed as an extremely volatile state economy, with the auto industry specifically and manufacturing in general contributing to wide positive and negative swings. One of those tools, enacted via Public Act 76 of 1977, was what is now known as the Budget Stabilization Fund (also commonly called the "Rainy Day Fund").

The decade of the 1970s ended with strong economic performance. FY 1979 is often anecdotally remembered by long-time Capitol observers as the last really "good" year for the General Fund, General Purpose (GFGP) budget, in the sense that it produced exceptionally strong revenue growth and comparable strong increases in most spending areas, with little or no difficulty in achieving balance. Expenditures increased by 11.0% over the FY 1978 level. It was not to last.

The early 1980s are the beginning point for many of the chapters in this volume, and the end point for the 1982 Brazer volume. The decade began with a deep recession and double-digit inflation.

The new Budget Stabilization Fund was essentially emptied in FY 1980 with a $263.7 million withdrawal. FY 1980 also saw one budget-cutting executive order.[5] FY 1981 also saw the state switch back to cash accounting for Medicaid and empty the remaining balances of several other small funds. In FY 1982, Governor Milliken proposed and the legislature approved a series of four consecutive executive orders. Still another executive order was used in FY 1981. The FY 1982 budget was finally balanced by increasing the state income tax from 4.6% to 5.6% from 1 April 1982 to 30 September 1982, the end of the fiscal year. This succeeded in balancing the state budget for FY 1982, but it meant that the ongoing spending base had been supported by a large influx of *temporary* revenue. As a result, any optimism for FY 1983 and beyond depended upon a strong national and Michigan economic recovery.

While there have been a number of strong economic years over the last two decades, they were not sufficient to avoid recurring difficulties in financing public services and balancing the state budget. Starting with FY 1980 and running to what has been projected by many observers for FY 2004, fifteen of these twenty-five fiscal years have required or will require extraordinary action to resolve some degree of fiscal crisis.[6]

This volume primarily looks at a period of Michigan history marked by just two governors: James Blanchard and John Engler. By many accounts they were two of Michigan's strongest governors, yet their politics and approach to policy were strikingly different. Both took office in the midst of fiscal crisis and both left with the state in or on the cusp of yet another fiscal crisis. Both made major contributions in many policy areas, and those changes will be discussed in detail in the following chapters of this volume.

James Blanchard took office as governor in January 1983, amidst a developing realization that the national economic recovery would not be strong enough to forestall more state budget difficulties. Blanchard's administration faced a GFGP budget deficit for the then three-month-old fiscal year that was estimated at $701 million, plus an accumulated deviation from Generally Accepted Accounting Principles (GAAP) of $762.3 million, for a total potential deficit of nearly $1.5 billion. The operating deficit of $701 million was equal to about 16% of FY 1982 GFGP spending.[7] Blanchard's response proposed both budget cuts and an increase in the state income tax from 4.6% to 6.35%. The total 1.75 percentage point increase included an earmarked rate of 0.25% dedicated to restoration of Michigan's accounting integrity by accumulating sufficient cash to reverse accounting differences from the use of Generally Accepted Accounting Principles (GAAP), such as the change to Medicaid cash accounting and others.[8]

The proposed tax increase became a partisan issue, ultimately passing both the House and Senate on essentially straight-party voting, with one Republican senator crossing the line for the decisive Senate vote. However, at one point in the Senate debate, nearly all of the Republicans voted for an amendment to the governor's plan that, if adopted, would have raised more revenue over the four years than the enacted increase actually remained in effect.[9] Neither Governor Blanchard nor most legislative Democrats supported that amendment because of concern that the economic downturn and budget crisis could last for an indeterminate period. Seeking to avoid another future tax increase vote, they opposed the time-limited Republican amendment.

The 1983 income tax increase did resolve the budget crisis, and more quickly than expected. The recovery after 1983 proved to be stronger than projected, and thus produced stronger revenue growth, even in the face of pressure on the automobile industry.[10] Even so, the income tax increase was not fully phased out until FY 1986. In addition, sufficient revenue was collected to enable Michigan to adopt consistent GAAP accounting practices effective with the book closing for FY 1986.

The political universe of Michigan changed in 1983, just as the fiscal universe did. In response to the income tax increase, voters in two state Senate districts recalled the incumbent Democratic state senators. The Republicans subsequently elected to replace them created a majority in the Senate that selected John Engler as Majority Leader. Democrats continued to control the Michigan House, and the 1990 election saw John Engler step forward to challenge Governor Blanchard's re-election.

The economy deteriorated throughout 1990, jeopardizing the budgets for FY 1990 and FY 1991. As the election approached, however, it seemed as if FY 1990 would end in precarious balance, with a major challenge looming in balancing the enacted FY 1991 budget for whomever won election as governor.

After losing his bid for re-election, but prior to leaving office, Governor Blanchard proposed an informal book closing for the fiscal year ending 30 September 1990. Contained in the state's Monthly Financial Report dated 28 December 1990, the proposal showed a balanced budget by virtue of a number of one-time actions. The principal one-time action was a recommendation to appropriate the liability for property tax credits in the current budget year, rather than accrue the liability to the year being closed. On the basis of this recommendation, the unofficial balance for the General Fund, General Purpose (GFGP) budget was $7.8 million.[11]

Upon taking office in January 1991, Governor Engler rejected the use of the proposed one-time actions and directed that the FY 1990 books be closed without them. Engler argued that the proposed change in the accounting treatment of the property tax credits required statutory authority that could not properly be granted after the end of the fiscal year. The result was a GFGP deficit of

$310.4 million. The Comprehensive Annual Financial Report for FY 1990 also showed a positive balance in the Budget Stabilization Fund of $385.1 million.[12] Rolling the operating deficit forward to FY 1991 (as required by the state constitution) meant that Michigan faced a deficit for that year estimated from as low as $1.1 billion to as much as $1.7 billion. While the problem was not entirely solved in FY 1991, Governor Engler then set about closing that deficit by budget cuts and one-time actions (including some of those originally proposed by Governor Blanchard) that put Michigan's budget back in balance by the end of FY 1992.

Fiscal Years 1990 and 1991 are thus the only years since the adoption of the 1963 Constitution where Michigan has officially closed its books in deficit on both a "statutory/budgetary" basis as well as a GAAP basis.[13]

The budget cuts that helped achieve that balance also profoundly changed the shape of public services in Michigan, most notably by the elimination of the state's General Assistance program. For a more in-depth discussion of the end of General Assistance and the impact of welfare reform in general, see chapter 17 of this volume.

The direct and politically difficult actions taken by both of these governors, one addressing a budget crisis by a combination of budget cuts and significant tax increases and the other addressing this issue largely by budget cuts alone, produced major improvements in the state's credit rating. Both instances were also followed by an extended period of relatively strong economic growth. Ultimately, however, both periods of extended growth were followed by periods of new fiscal crises.

### The Size and Scope of Government

The following discussion turns to a brief look at several broad measures of the size of state and local government, the size of the Michigan economy, and their relationship to each other.

One simple measure of the size of state government is the number of state employees. The following charts summarize several measures of average annual state civil service employment.

Figure 1.1 shows Civil Service employment levels peaking in FY 1980, at the beginning of the period addressed by this volume. From that peak, employment began to decline in the last two years of the Milliken administration as a result of the

**FIGURE 1.1**

### Civil Service Classified Employment, 1969–2002 (annual averages)

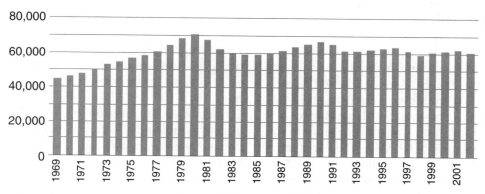

SOURCE: State of Michigan, Civil Service Commission, Annual Workforce Reports, various years.

recession. By the end of the Blanchard administration in 1990, civil service employment had bounced back up by 4,704, or 7.6 %, but was still 3,116, or 4.5 %, below the 1980 peak.

In FY 2002 (the last full year of the Engler administration), average annual state civil service employment was down 6,644 from Blanchard's 1990 level, and 9,760 from the 1980 peak. However, the data for FY 2002 somewhat understates the change, since it is based on fiscal year average employment levels. In particular, this understates the impact of a massive early retirement program that was not completed until 1 November 2002, a full month after the end of FY 2002.

Under this plan, employees were eligible to leave as early as 1 July, and had to leave by 1 November (except for a few hundred who were granted short extensions). The first payroll of FY 2002 on 13 October 2001 had 61,401 employees.

The 22 June payroll, just prior to the first departures under the plan, showed only a small decline in civil service employment to 61,275. The next payroll, on 6 July, showed that civil service employment had dropped to 59,796 as the early retirement program began to take effect. Small drops in the number of employees were then recorded on each subsequent payroll, with the fiscal year–ending payroll on 28 September showing 58,113 employees. Small declines resumed until the 9 November payroll, which showed an employment drop to 53,735 employees, nearly 8,000 less than at the beginning of the fiscal year.

Annual changes in employment also serve as one measure of the existence of budget pressures/fiscal crises. Figure 1.2 shows that most of the negative changes match up with periods of fiscal crises (the shaded bars indicate approximate periods of national recessions). One major

**FIGURE 1.2**

### Annual Percentage Change in Civil Service Employment, 1969–2002

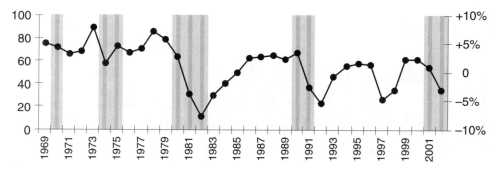

SOURCE: State of Michigan, Civil Service Commission, Annual Workforce Reports, various years.

exception is the dip in 1997 and 1998, when nearly 5,000 employees left the state workforce in another early retirement program.

One of the major changes in state government in the last two decades has been the growing trend toward using incarceration as the primary means of punishment for crime. This trend is not represented in either figures 1.1 or 1.2. Figure 1.3, however, shows that excluding employment in the Department of Corrections, little net hiring was done over the last twenty years. Indeed, from the average annual peak of 69,907 in 1980 (including 5,052 Corrections employees), the 2002 totals represent a fiscal year average of 60,147 employees, of which 17,821, or 29.6%, worked for the Department of Corrections. This was an increase of 12,765 Corrections employees from the 1980 level. All other employment fell from 64,855 to 42,375 (see chapter 24 for a review of corrections policies).

This decline of 22,560, or 34.74%, in the noncorrections workforce reflected major changes in the type, level, and method of service delivery by state government. Much of the change (19,378) came via reductions in the former Departments of Mental Health and Public Health (now combined in the Department of Community Health), and in the former Department of Social Services (now the Family Independence Agency). The Medicaid program, formerly in the Department of Social Services, was also moved to the Department of Community Health.

The significant declines in noncorrections employment represent the results of budget pressures, to be sure, but they also represent some trends that cannot be specifically quantified. First, a portion of the reduction in employment in the human services agencies is related to the policy of deinstitutionalization of most mental health patients. Responsibility for care of the majority of those receiving publicly supported mental health services now rests with local Community Mental Health Boards. These services are largely funded by state and federal dollars, but the employees work for local governments, not the state government.[14]

Second, some portion of the reduction in employment in what is now the Family Independence Agency is clearly due to declines in caseloads.

Third, some portion of this change also represents a trend toward contracting out certain services. For example, some of the functions once performed by the Department of Public Health are now performed under contract by the nonprofit Michigan Public Health Institute. Other changes involve experiments in privatizing highway maintenance contracts. The size of this trend is especially difficult to measure, but is likely to be in the hundreds of jobs, rather than the thousands.

It is also likely that expansion of service delivery for other programs may have come at the local level rather than the state level, and often with state funding. While there has been an ebb and flow over the years, one of the recurring themes of Michigan's political and fiscal history has been the delivery of services by local governments, supported by state funding.

Michigan has a large number of local governments: 83 counties, 1,114 general law townships, 128 charter townships, 273 cities, 213 general law villages, 49 home rule or charter villages, and 277 noneducation authorities of one type or another.

**FIGURE 1.3**

**Changes in Major Sectors of State Civil Service Employment**

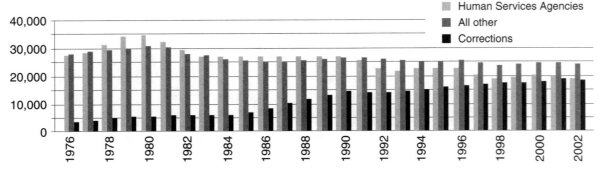

SOURCE: State of Michigan, Civil Service Commission, Annual Workforce Reports, various years.

In addition, there are 27 community college districts, 57 intermediate school districts, and 524 K–12 districts. Another 31 districts offer only a K–6 or K–8 program, and 210 public school academies or charter schools offer a range of programs from K–3 to K–12. The relationships between state and local governments, and among local governments, have changed over time and are still changing. The emergence of the charter township as a significant vehicle for public service delivery has changed a number of local-to-local and local-to-state interactions.

For some public services, Michigan governments operate similarly to the governments of other states. However, Michigan differs from other states in the way in which it delivers a number of services. One specific area of difference regarding service delivery and accountability is clearly in the transportation finance system, with county government playing a larger role than in most other states.[15]

## The Size and Scope of State and Local Government

The Gross State Product (GSP) represents an estimate of the total value of goods and services produced by the Michigan economy. As such it provides a good benchmark for measuring the size of state government by tracking the changes in the percentage of state taxes as a share of GSP. State personal income provides a measure of the total resources of the citizens of Michigan. Figure

1.4 tracks the changing share of total state taxes as a share of both GSP and personal income over the last two decades.

Figure 1.4 shows periods of relative stability, but with some discernible changes. For example, it shows the share of state taxes as reflected by both measures declining in the recession years of 1980 and 1981. This is followed by the separate 1982 and then the 1983 tax increases (the latter of which was phased down but remained at least partially in effect through 1986), along with the economic recovery. The tax increases took visibly larger shares of both GSP and personal income. The share of GSP and personal income absorbed by taxes peaks again around 1990 before declining slightly in yet another recession, and then jumps up dramatically in 1994 and 1995, to stabilize again on a higher plateau. This latter increase reflects the Proposal A school finance reform. It is important to note here that while state taxes did increase, local taxes were reduced dramatically. The entire Proposal A reform package was a net tax cut, so this look at state government taxes tells only part of the story relative to both state and local government taxes as a share of GSP and of income.

When local taxes are added to state taxes in figure 1.5 the level of taxes as a percentage of personal income is obviously higher. However, the picture is still one of a good degree of relative stability, with most differences due to major policy changes. For example, the effects of the creation of the state income tax in the late 1960s are still visible in a clear increase in the share of personal

---

**FIGURE 1.4**

**Total State Taxes as Share of State Personal Income and Gross State Product**

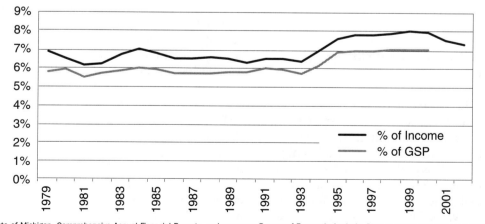

SOURCE: State of Michigan, Comprehensive Annual Financial Reports, various years; Bureau of Economic Analysis. Please note that the state personal income data is available on a more current basis than the gross state product data, which is why two more years of data are reported for this series.

## FIGURE 1.5

**State and Local Taxes as Percentage of State Personal Income**

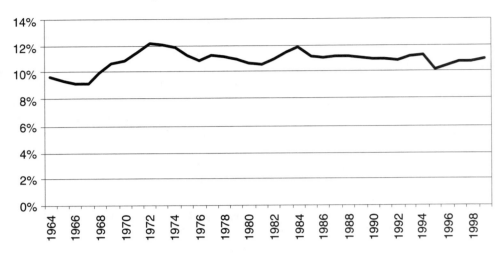

SOURCE: Bureau of the Census, State and Local Finances, various years. Please note that the availability of the local tax data lags considerably, so that 1999 is the most recent year available for both state and local government.

income taken by taxes. The increase in income tax rates in the early 1970s is also visible. From 1974 forward, however, there is a considerable stability, with only one year with taxes above 11.5% of personal income (1984), one year below 10.5% (1995), eleven years between 11.0 and 11.5%, and twelve years between 10.5 and 11.0%, with all years since Proposal A (implemented in 1994), below 11.0%. The late 1990s show a slow growth in combined taxes from the Proposal A reduced level, but this figure appears to have stabilized again. It is likely that when data is available for local revenues for years after 1999 that a slight additional decline will be noticeable as a result of further state tax cuts and the effects of the recession. This decline is already visible in the state tax data for 2001 and 2002 displayed in figure 1.4.

### Limits on the Size and Flexibility of Government

Figures 1.4 and 1.5 also reflect changes in the way government has approached tax policy over the last few decades. In combination with table 1.1, these latter two figures tell a story of a Michigan that through the 1960s and 1970s focused most of its tax policy discussions primarily on adequacy as it wrestled with increasing pressures for expansion of state services. The pressure for new taxes or significant increases in taxes continued into the early 1980s, as noted earlier, but the tax policy

discussions began to also address questions of fairness and stability. The circuit-breaker property tax credit created in 1973 and the adoption of the Single Business Tax (SBT) in 1975 were clear examples of this change in the content of tax policy discussions. Concern for flexibility in finance also played a role in these two decades. When the Lottery was adopted in the early 1970s, it was a new GFGP revenue source, with no restrictions or earmarking. To a limited extent, the adoption of the SBT and the income tax increases of 1982 and 1983 reversed the long-time Michigan policy trend of earmarking most state revenue sources for specific purposes.

Nevertheless, the Michigan tradition of earmarking has had tremendous staying power. By 1981, public pressure to address a popular perception that the Lottery was supposed to have gone to education became so strong that its funds were earmarked for the School Aid Fund. Other significant limitations on both the size and flexibility of state government came via the adoption of the "Headlee" Amendment in 1978 (see chapter 33).

Rightly or wrongly, one of the history lessons that became "common wisdom" about the income tax increase of 1983 and the subsequent recall elections has been that tax increases are a politically dangerous tool to address budget crises. This fiscal and political iteration of common wisdom seems to be that tax increases can be politically viable only if they have one or more of the following characteristics: (1) They are

FIGURE 1.6

**Earmarking of Michigan Taxes and Total Direct Revenues, FY 1980 to FY 2002**

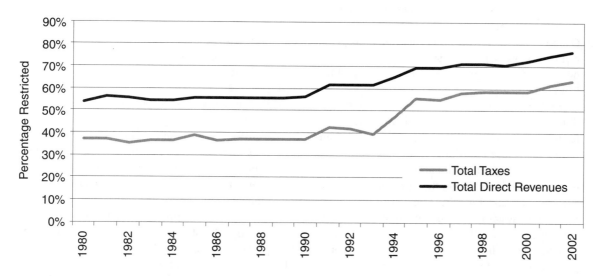

SOURCE: State of Michigan, Comprehensive Annual Financial Reports, various years; Wayne State University State Policy Center, "Research Resources"; author's calculations.

significantly restricted or earmarked (as in the case of Proposal A); (2) They are part of a net tax cut (once again as in the case of Proposal A); (3) They are presented to the voters for their approval (as with Proposal A); or (4) They are utilized to avoid budget cuts in very popular programs, such as the tobacco tax increases in 2002, which helped avoid major additional cuts in state grants to local governments.

In combination with the tax rate and tax base reductions that were prevalent in the 1990s, Michigan also acted to repeal the largely unrestricted Intangibles Tax. The pending elimination of the Estate Tax will mark the end of another significant unrestricted revenue source. The rate reductions and ultimate phase-out of the Single Business Tax that is now current law will end the largest completely unrestricted state revenue source.

The net result of all of this is that larger and larger shares of state taxes and other revenues are limited to specific uses, leaving the governor and the legislature discretionary control over an ever-shrinking portion of the revenue pie, as shown in figure 1.6. The lower line indicates the share of *state taxes* that is restricted to specific uses. The top line indicates the share of *all state revenues* that is restricted. This line includes the restricted taxes, but also includes federal funds and many licenses, fees, permits, and other miscellaneous sources of revenue that are restricted to a specific

use by constitution or statute. In FY 2002, nearly four out of every five dollars in the state budget were subject to some kind of limitation on the discretion of the legislature regarding their use.

### Some Concluding Thoughts on Michigan's Fiscal and Economic Structure

The preceding discussion has noted some major trends in Michigan's fiscal structure over the last several decades. Many changes to those trends occurred in response to shifts in attitudes about public policy. Other changes clearly responded to the state economy as it evolved. Both the economy and public attitudes toward government will continue to change. These changes will produce challenges equal to or greater than those already faced. These challenges are similar to those of other states but with emphasis rooted in Michigan's own fiscal, economic, social, and political history and traditions.

Michigan will resolve the latest in its long series of fiscal crises. In the process, policymakers may wish to consider adding more tools for long-range planning and budgeting to Michigan's already strong system of fiscal management to better enable state government to minimize the recurrence of future periods of fiscal crisis.

## NOTES

1. Bruce Catton, *Michigan, A Bicentennial History* (New York: W. W. Norton & Co., 1976).
2. Chapters 12, 13, 15, and 31 of this volume provide numerous examples of state-financed, locally delivered services and how Michigan may differ from other states.
3. "Foundation grants" provide a basic grant or foundation amount to individual districts. In most foundation systems, individual districts are then required to raise additional resources from local taxes. An "uncapped" foundation means that local districts have no limits on the amount of revenue that can be raised locally. Michigan's post–1994 foundation system is a "capped" foundation, with very strict limits on locally raised revenues. A district power equalizing formula guarantees an equal yield of revenue for equal effort despite local differences in property values.
4. See chapter 33 for a thorough discussion of the Headlee Amendment. It is also discussed in chapter 28 regarding property taxes.
5. All references to executive orders in the text and tables 1.1 and 1.2 refer to executive orders issued under the governor's authority to cut the budget.
6. "Extraordinary action means going beyond the normal discipline of putting a budget together, even in good times. Each of these fifteen years was marked by significant budget cuts, either in budget development or after enactment by executive order, supported by significant general tax increases, withdrawals from the Budget Stabilization Fund, uses of other one-time resources, or all of the above.
7. Michigan Financial Crisis Council, Report to Governor James J. Blanchard, 21 January 1983, various pages.
8. In addition to the small portion of the income tax increase dedicated to the accounting deficit, a ten-cent increase in the cigarette tax had been enacted in 1982 for the same purpose. Together they ultimately allowed for the accounting changes to be made with the FY 1986 book closing.
9. The tax rate for calendar year 1983 was 6.35%. It dropped twice in 1984, to 6.10% in January, and then to 5.35% on 1 September, and then retroactively jumped back to 4.6%, effective 1 January 1986.
10. The mid-1980s were marked by strong import competition, the beginning of "transplant" or foreign-based automobile manufacturing in the United States, and a number of traditional "Big 3" plant closings, many of them in Michigan.
11. Shelby P. Solomon, director of the Department of Management and Budget, to Harry Gast, Jr., chair of the Senate Appropriations Committee, and Dominic Jacobetti, chair of the House Appropriations Committee, 28 December 1990.
12. Patricia J. Woodworth, director of the Department of Management and Budget, letter to the Michigan State Senate and House of Representatives, 30 January 1991, cover letter transmitting a preliminary closing report to the legislature, and State of Michigan Comprehensive Annual Financial Report for Fiscal Year 1990, various pages.
13. State of Michigan, Comprehensive Annual Financial Reports for Fiscal Year 1990 and 1991. The FY 1991 deficit was reported at $169.4 million. "Statutory/budgetary" basis accounting refers to deviations from GAAP authorized by state statute. FY 1997 was technically in deficit as well, but the conditions that created the deficit did not surface until after the books were closed. As a result, the beginning balance for FY 1998 was restated to reflect the correction. See State of Michigan, Comprehensive Annual Financial Report for Fiscal Year 1998, 27n. 4.
14. Chapter 13 can provide some indications of local government spending trends in this area.
15. Chapters 13, 15, 16, and 31 discuss and explore these relationships in greater detail.

# 2

# Overview of the Michigan Economy

*Joan P. Crary, George A. Fulton, and Saul H. Hymans*

## Introduction

On a visit to Moscow in the mid-1970s, one of the authors responded to a "Where in America are you from?" query with "Michigan, Detroit."[1] "Ah," said the Muscovite, "where they make cars." Michigan was and is much more than just "where they make cars," but there's clearly a great deal about the state's society and economy that derives from the inveterate dominance of the motor vehicle industry in Michigan.

For three decades after World War II, it was accepted conventional wisdom that the Michigan economy

- exaggerated the nation's cyclical movements—rising relative to the national economy during cyclical expansions and falling harder during cyclical contractions—but,
- enjoyed a higher level of real income per capita than the nation, when averaged out over the ups and downs of the business cycle.

Michigan, in other words, was long regarded as a highly cyclical, but also highly prosperous, state. By the early 1980s, however, the U.S. manufacturing sector, in general, and the motor vehicle industry, in particular, were feeling the effects of increasingly dynamic global competition, and the

Michigan economy seemed to be impacted disproportionately.

Most of this chapter deals in broad-brush terms with what has happened to the Michigan economy since the early 1980s, since the publication of the now-classic *Michigan's Fiscal and Economic Structure*, edited by Harvey E. Brazer and Deborah S. Laren, which recognized within the first sentence of its preface that "the State of Michigan was passing through a period of difficult economic adjustment," and, further, that it seemed to be "more basic than the typical cyclical movements that had characterized the economy of the State of Michigan in the post–World War II era."

What do we think, two decades later? Was Michigan really losing out relative to the national economy throughout the 1980s? To what extent did Michigan share in the prosperity of the 1990s?

These issues are stated in *relative* terms. They question the status of the Michigan economy in the context of its position within the U.S. national economy, which is a quite natural way to think about the state's economic fortunes and is the perspective that is adopted in most of this chapter. Yet the state's residents face many absolutes, including the strength and stability of the job market, growth in the standard of living, and the like. We begin in the next section, therefore, with a brief look at how Michigan's economy has progressed over the past two decades in absolute terms, irrespective of how strong or weak that might be relative to the nation as a whole. Following that, we take a quick look at Michigan in the context of the Great Lakes economic region, and then return to the *Michigan and the nation* perspective.

## The Michigan Economy, 1979–2000

We focus this brief survey of Michigan's economic absolutes on the behavior of the key aggregate indicators: employment, income, and economic growth. The relevant data are contained in table 2.1, covering selected individual years and four consecutive five-year intervals during the period from 1979 to 2000.

The years 1979–82 represent the very difficult period with which the Brazer-Laren book ended. During that period, the state's unemployment rate nearly doubled, shooting up from a 7.8% average for calendar 1979 to 15.5% for 1982. The percentage of the state's sixteen-and-over population holding jobs fell from 59.2% in 1979 to 53.5% in

1982 as the job market weakened dramatically.[2] Real personal income (measured in chained 1996 dollars[3]), a measure of pre-tax purchasing power, fell absolutely from $19,469 per person in 1979 to just $18,056 per person in 1982, a sharp drop of 7.25% in three years. Two years later, in 1984, as economic recovery was taking hold nationwide, the unemployment rate in Michigan edged down to 11.2%, the employment/ population rate recovered to 57.3%, and purchasing power, on the rise again, moved up to $19,782, more than $1,700 above its 1982 level and more than $310 above where it had been in 1979.

Michigan's economic fortunes improved markedly during the 1984–89 interval. The unemployment rate dropped from 11.2 to 7.1%, the employment/population rate climbed above 61%, and real income per capita rose by an average of 2.4% per year to reach $22,326 for calendar 1989.

The early 1990s produced a stall in economic activity in the state as well as the nation, and the period from 1989 to 1992 sent all the economic indicators in reverse. However, economic recovery was under way again after 1992, and Michigan's economic fortunes were heading upward once more. By 1994, the unemployment rate had fallen to 5.9%, marking Michigan's first full year of unemployment below 6% since 1973. Real income had marched up to $23,856 per person, enough to bring the 1989–94 rate of growth of real per capita income to an average of 1.3% per year, despite the need to make up for an absolute decline in income during the 1989–92 period.

Then came the second half of the 1990s, which achieved so many macroeconomic milestones. By 1999, Michigan's unemployment rate had fallen to an average of just 3.8%, then the lowest on record since 1966 and among the lowest in the entire post–World War II period. Simultaneously, the employment/population rate soared to just under 66%. Purchasing power also grew rapidly, with real income per capita rising at 2.2% per year on average during the 1994–99 period and hitting a level of $26,598 for 1999.

The great boom of the 1990s peaked in the year 2000. That year, Michigan's unemployment rate fell to a 3.6% average, a record 66.4% of the sixteen-and-over population were employed, and real income per capita topped $27,000, nearly 40% above its value in 1979. This implies a growth of (pre-tax) purchasing power averaging 1.6% annually over the entire twenty-one-year interval shown in the table.[4]

**TABLE 2.1**

**The Michigan Economy, Selected Years, 1979–2000**

| Year | EMPLOYMENT | | INCOME |
|---|---|---|---|
| | Unemployment Rate (%) | Employment/ Population Rate (%) | Real Personal Income per Capita (1996 dollars) |
| 1979 | 7.8 | 59.2 | 19,469 |
| 1982 | 15.5 | 53.5 | 18,056 |
| 1984 | 11.2 | 57.3 | 19,782 |
| 1989 | 7.1 | 61.1 | 22,326 |
| 1992 | 8.9 | 59.7 | 22,112 |
| 1994 | 5.9 | 62.7 | 23,856 |
| 1999 | 3.8 | 65.9 | 26,598 |
| 2000 | 3.6 | 66.4 | 27,090 |
| **5-Year Interval** | | | **(% Growth per Year)** |
| 1979–84 | | | 0.3 |
| 1984–89 | | | 2.4 |
| 1989–94 | | | 1.3 |
| 1994–99 | | | 2.2 |

SOURCE: U.S. Department of Labor, Bureau of Labor Statistics (June 2002); U.S. Department of Commerce, Bureau of Economic Analysis (June 2002); Michigan Employment Security Commission (1996), updated by Michigan Department of Career Development.

## Michigan and the Great Lakes Region, 1979–2000

As noted previously, we are focusing primarily on Michigan as a part of the national economy. We recognize, however, that Michigan is also commonly thought of as a part of the Great Lakes region, comprised of Indiana, Illinois, Michigan, Ohio, and Wisconsin. It is worthwhile, therefore, to place the Michigan economy into the Great Lakes context, both for the information it will provide and, as well, to ease possible concerns over our decision to adopt a national rather than a regional perspective in the balance of the chapter.

Table 2.2 provides data on unemployment, real income, and economic growth for the aggregate of the other (excluding Michigan) Great Lakes states, which we denote as the OGLS.[5] We can use tables 2.1 and 2.2 to provide direct comparisons of Michigan and the OGLS for the 1979–2000 period.

What stands out immediately is that the period began with Michigan experiencing a much higher unemployment rate than the rest of the region, 7.8% unemployment in Michigan in 1979 versus just 5.6% unemployment for the OGLS. On the other hand, Michigan's resident population enjoyed somewhat higher ($341 or 1.8%) real personal income per capita in 1979 despite the higher unemployment rate.

The 1979–82 period produced roughly a doubling of the unemployment rate in the OGLS, as it did in Michigan. Yet that translated to an unemployment rate increase of 6.1 percentage points in the OGLS, compared with a much larger 7.7 percentage points in Michigan. Correspondingly, real income per capita fell by about $1,400 in Michigan over the period, compared with just over $500 in the rest of the region. By 1982, Michigan's real income per capita had fallen behind that in the rest of the region.

The cyclical upswing during 1982–89 produced an 8.4 percentage point drop in the Michigan unemployment rate, compared with only 6.3 percentage points in the OGLS. The bigger loss in Michigan of the early 1980s was followed by a bigger gain in the subsequent expansion. This cyclical expansion took income in Michigan back up above that in the OGLS, but not as much above as in 1979 (0.4% above in 1989, compared with 1.8% above a decade earlier).

In contrast to the early 1980s, when recession impacted Michigan with particular severity, the unemployment effects of the economic stall of the

### TABLE 2.2

**Other Great Lakes States, Selected Years, 1979–2000**

| Year | EMPLOYMENT Unemployment Rate (%) | INCOME Real Personal Income per Capita (1996 dollars) |
|---|---|---|
| 1979 | 5.6 | 19,128 |
| 1982 | 11.7 | 18,622 |
| 1984 | 8.9 | 19,926 |
| 1989 | 5.4 | 22,234 |
| 1992 | 7.0 | 22,728 |
| 1994 | 5.3 | 23,540 |
| 1999 | 3.9 | 26,572 |
| 2000 | 4.0 | 27,142 |
| **5-Year Interval** | | **(% Growth per Year)** |
| 1979–84 | | 0.8 |
| 1984–89 | | 2.2 |
| 1989–94 | | 1.1 |
| 1994–99 | | 2.5 |

SOURCE: U.S. Department of Labor, Bureau of Labor Statistics (June 2002); U.S. Department of Commerce, Bureau of Economic Analysis (June 2002). Calculations by authors.
NOTE: States considered here are Illinois, Indiana, Ohio, and Wisconsin.

early 1990s were more nearly equal in Michigan and the rest of the region. Between 1989 and 1992 the unemployment rate rose by 1.8 percentage points in Michigan, compared with 1.6 percentage points in the OGLS. Michigan did, however, continue to fare much worse in terms of income, suffering a *decline* of more than $200 during the period from 1989 to 1992, compared with an *increase* of nearly $500 in the rest of the region.

The expansion of the 1990s turned out to be especially favorable to Michigan, at least in employment terms. At the economic peak in 1979, Michigan's 7.8% unemployment rate had been 2.2 percentage points in excess of that in the OGLS; in 1989 it was still quite high, but above the rest of the region by a slightly smaller 1.7 percentage points. A decade later, however, in 1999, Michigan registered a 3.8% unemployment rate, virtually the same as the OGLS unemployment rate of 3.9%. A year after that, in the cyclical peak year of 2000, Michigan's unemployment rate, at 3.6%, had actually slipped below the OGLS unemployment rate of 4% (which happened to match the national average for that year).

Michigan's closing of the gap in the labor market over the twenty-one-year interval from 1979 to 2000 was not accompanied by a commensurately

**FIGURE 2.1**

**FIGURE 2.1**

**Relative Income and Employment, 1956–2001**

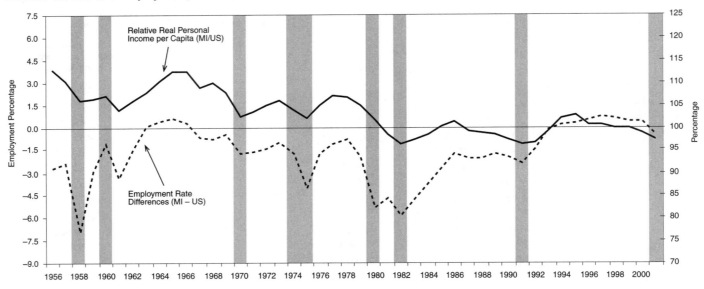

SOURCE: U.S. Department of Labor, Bureau of Labor Statistics (June 2002), U.S. Department of Commerce, Bureau of Economic Analysis (June 2002). Calculations by authors.

positive movement in income, or purchasing power. The favorable 1.8% income differential that Michigan had enjoyed in 1979 was replaced by virtual equality of real income per capita in Michigan and the rest of the Great Lakes region in 1999 and 2000.

This end-point-to-end-point trend in income did not proceed smoothly over the two-decade interval. As the growth rate data in the tables show, Michigan lagged relative to the OGLS in real per capita income growth during the first and last five-year intervals, 1979–84 and 1994–99, and gained during the intermediate decade from 1984 to 1994. Yet the gains during the middle period were outweighed by the losses on either side. This suggests the possibility of a relative deterioration in the income-quality of jobs in Michigan over at least parts of these two decades. In fact, this same issue will arise in our comparisons of Michigan and the nation, which follow.

### The Cyclical Behavior of Relative Income and Employment: 1956–2001

To the question, "How does Michigan fare as a part of the U.S. economy?" Figure 2.1 suggests a number of bottom-line responses; that is, suggestive answers without reasons. Yet it is a good place to begin.

The figure shows two series plotted annually

for the years 1956 through 2001, with nine of the years in that interval shown as *shaded*. These shaded years—1958, 1960, 1970, 1974–75, 1980, 1982, 1991, and 2001—are the years of economic recession in the national economy.[6] This figure compares the Michigan and U.S. economies in terms of two critically important macroeconomic variables: employment and income. Relative employment behavior is represented by the line marked with circles, which plots, year by year, the value given by the Michigan employment rate minus the U.S. employment rate. The negative value, –2.8%, shown for 1956, for example, comes from:

- Michigan employment rate in 1956 = 93.1%
- U.S. employment rate in 1956 = 95.9%
- Michigan rate – U.S. rate = 93.1% – 95.9% = –2.8%

Thus, a negative number indicates that Michigan's employment rate is lower than the national average, while a positive number indicates that Michigan's employment rate is higher than the national average. When the curve rises, Michigan's employment rate is rising relative to the national average; when the curve falls, Michigan's employment rate is falling relative to the national average. In short, high or rising rates signify *strong* or *improving* employment conditions for Michigan relative to the nation as a whole; low or declining rates signify *weak* or *deteriorating* conditions for Michigan relative to the nation as a whole.[7] What does the relative employment curve show?

In general, the employment curve is low or declining in and around a period of recession, and then rises during the economic recovery and expansion that follow recession. The long expansions, such as those that occurred during the 1960s, 1980s, and 1990s, show clearly that Michigan's employment market tends to improve sharply relative to the nation as a whole for at least the first half of the expansion period. It then stabilizes for a time, and it may weaken slightly toward the end of the economic expansion. As the economic expansion gives way to recession, Michigan's employment market weakens quite sharply relative to the national economy, and the relative employment curve plunges, making room for a sharp recovery in the next economic upswing.

Notice that this is saying something much more than: "Michigan's economy cycles with the national economy." That would be shown by a flat line indicating that Michigan's employment rate moved up and down exactly with the nation's. Rather, the employment curve in figure 2.1 shows that *Michigan's economy is more cyclical than the national economy*. When employment prospects in the national economy fall during recession, Michigan's employment prospects fall even more; when employment prospects improve during economic recovery, Michigan's employment prospects improve even more. At least in terms of employment, Michigan's economy is cyclical relative to the national economy.

The other curve in the figure shows relative per capita personal income; that is, for each year, we calculate real personal income per capita in Michigan divided by real personal income per capita in the United States, and multiply by 100. Thus, the value 112.8 shown for 1956 signifies that in that year Michigan's real personal income per capita exceeded the corresponding national average by 12.8%. What is perhaps most noticeable about the two series shown in the figure is the extent to which they are alike: for the most part, the highs and lows match, the ups and downs match.[8] When Michigan's employment market is strong (or improving) relative to the nation's, Michigan's real per capita income is high (or improving) relative to the nation's. Thus, *Michigan's economy is cyclical relative to the national economy in terms of real income, or purchasing power, as well as employment.*

## Discerning Trends in Relative Income and Employment: 1956–2001

There is more than cyclical behavior to be seen in figure 2.1. One can also attempt to discern any long sweep, or trend, that emerges over the near half-century covered in the figure. The impressions that are suggested by the relative employment series would seem to be as follows. The 1958 recession and the 1980–82 period were particularly severe and drove Michigan's employment market to extreme weakness compared with the nation as a whole. Abstracting from those episodes, however, there appears to be nothing in the way of a discernible net movement, or trend, in Michigan's relative employment during the 1956–82 period. When not beaten down by the most severe recessionary conditions, Michigan's employment rate ran, on average, about 1.5 percentage points *below* the nationwide employment rate.[9] Note that during this 1956–82 period there was but one subinterval when Michigan's employment rate ran stronger than the national average, and that was during the boom years of the 1960s, 1963–66.

The relative employment picture appears to have gotten much stronger for Michigan since the bleak days of the early 1980s. By the mid-to-late 1980s, Michigan's relative employment conditions had strengthened enough to bring its relative employment deficit down to about 2 percentage points (compared with an employment rate deficit of nearly 6 percentage points in 1982). The 1991 recession caused but a small dip in the curve, and thereafter Michigan's relative employment picture improved to its best position of the entire near half-century. For a seven-year stretch from 1994 through 2000, Michigan's employment rate ran above the nation's, on average by more than four-tenths of a percentage point.[10] The 2001 recession produced a small dip in the relative employment curve and took Michigan's employment rate half a percentage point below the national average, while leaving the curve still very high in historical terms.

Has the period since the late 1980s brought Michigan's employment picture permanently to approximate parity with the nation? Will Michigan's employment rate now cycle around approximate equality relative to the national average, instead of a deficit of some 1.5 percentage points, as in the 1956–82 period? That depends on the conditions that brought Michigan to par in the 1990s, and whether those conditions will persist.

It is difficult to answer these questions while still in the grip of cyclical economic weakness. The answer will have to await the passage of time.

Now let us turn to the longer sweep in the behavior of Michigan's relative income, or purchasing power. The relative income curve in figure 2.1 seems to suggest some particularly strong statements. From 1956 to 1982, real per capita income in Michigan appears to have been on a clear downward trend relative to real per capita income in the nation as a whole. Abstracting from the cyclical ups and downs, Michigan income fell from 13% above the national average in 1956, to 10% above in 1968, to just 5% above in 1979. The 1980–82 period then produced a cyclical drop, which took the purchasing power of Michigan's population to nearly 4% *below* the national average in 1982.

The long downward trend in Michigan's relative income, which persisted from 1956 to the early 1980s, appears not to have continued since then. Indeed, there appears to have been little if any net movement in Michigan's relative income position since 1983. *The double-digit income premium that Michigan enjoyed in the mid- to late 1950s had disappeared by the early 1980s.* Since then, however, the relative income curve has been roughly flat and close to 100%, indicating that *the purchasing power of Michigan's residents has been roughly on par with the national average since the mid-1980s.*

This visual impression from figure 2.1 of a persistent downward trend in Michigan's relative income from 1956 to 1982, followed by the apparent absence of any such trend during the past twenty or so years, is so important a notion that its statistical integrity ought to be checked out. Statistical analysis (explained in the endnote to this paragraph) confirms that during the period 1956–82, Michigan's relative income declined by a statistically significant 0.28% per year, independent of cyclical ups and downs. In other words, with Michigan's real personal income per capita being 12.8% above U.S. real personal income per capita in 1956, it would be expected that Michigan's income would be 12.52 (12.8 – 0.28)% above U.S. income in 1957, 12.24 (12.52 – 0.28)% above U.S. income in 1958, and so on, losing 0.28% per year. Such a loss in relative income per year would cumulate to 2.8% every decade, or 7.3% over the entire period 1956–82, independent of the cyclical ups and downs in Michigan's relative income. On the other hand, the same statistical analysis confirms that from 1983 on there has been no fur-

ther statistically significant year-by-year loss in Michigan's relative income position, independent of cyclical ups and downs. The visual impression of, on average, a stable relative income position during the past twenty or so years is, therefore, indeed statistically significant.[11]

There is an especially important implication to all of this. From 1956 through the early 1980s there was no net trend in Michigan's relative employment position, but its relative income position was losing ground at about 0.28% per year. This implies a trend decline in the *income-quality* of employment in Michigan, relative to the nation. This deterioration in the income-quality of Michigan's jobs appears to have come to an end in the latter half of the 1980s, when relative employment and relative income both seemed to stabilize. The early 1990s produced an improvement in Michigan's relative employment position and apparently some improvement in relative income as well, seeming further to confirm approximate stability in the income-quality of state employment in the current period, a development worth trying to understand.

## The Industrial Composition of Compensation and Employment: 1979–2000

It is well understood that Michigan's economy is heavily industrial, compared with the nation as a whole. Surely that has an impact on the generation of Michigan's relative personal income and should help us to understand the latter. Unfortunately, the data do not permit a decomposition of aggregate personal income by industry of origin.

On the other hand, aggregate employee compensation (wage and salary payments plus other labor income) accounts for about two-thirds of personal income and turns out to be an extraordinarily good indicator of the latter, especially in the *relative* metric on which we are focusing. This is established quite clearly by figure 2.2, which compares relative real personal income per capita and relative real employee compensation per capita for the period 1979–2000. The correlation between these two series is 0.97. Relative personal income and relative compensation are virtually parallel, and their movements are virtually identical.

Another point of comparison between the two series is the fact that relative compensation per capita is uniformly above relative personal income per capita. For the period 1979–2000, their annual differences average 4.6%. Michigan

**FIGURE 2.2**

**Relative Income and Compensation, 1979–2000**

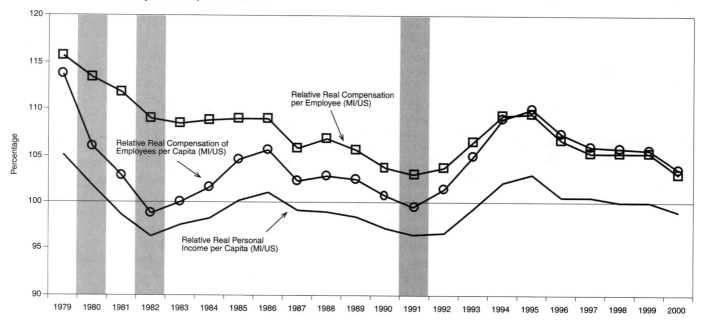

SOURCE: U.S. Department of Commerce, Bureau of Economic Analysis (June 2002). Calculations by authors.

has retained a compensation premium relative to the nation as a whole, even while the personal income premium it used to enjoy has been wiped out.[12] This does not, however, alter the conclusion of the preceding section. The issue of the relative income-quality of employment in Michigan remains to be understood.

Finally, figure 2.2 contains a third series: compensation *per employee* in Michigan relative to compensation *per employee* in the United States. The compensation per employee series are the ones that can actually be disaggregated by industry. The major difference between the relative compensation per employee series and the relative compensation per capita series is that the latter was even more dramatically impacted by the economic doldrums of the difficult 1980–82 period. That is because compensation per capita is the product of compensation per employee and employees per capita;[13] and, as was noted in the context of table 2.1, the 1980–82 period produced a huge decline in employment relative to population. As a result of this extreme behavior in the early 1980s, the relative compensation per employee series is not as highly correlated with the personal income per capita series; the correlation is 0.64, as opposed to 0.97 for the relative compensation per capita series. Nonetheless, it is clearly evident that studying the movements in

the relative compensation per employee series will also reveal a great deal about Michigan's relative personal income per capita.

For purposes of the analysis by industry, we have disaggregated compensation and employment into six sectors: motor vehicle manufacturing (SIC 371), other (non–motor vehicle) manufacturing, services, retail trade, all other private industries, and government.[14] We can think of statewide compensation per employee as a weighted average of the compensations per employee in each of the industries of the state, with the weights being the shares of statewide employment in each industry; and similarly for nationwide compensation per employee. Michigan's relative compensation per employee can be denoted, symbolically, as: (*MI pay* × *MI shares*) ÷ (*US pay* × *US shares*).

As an example, suppose a state has just two industries, A and B, and industry A pays $20,000 per employee and accounts for 30% of state employment, while industry B pays $50,000 per employee and accounts for 70% of state employment. In that case, *statewide* compensation per employee would be: (0.3 × $20,000) + (0.7 × $50,000) = ($6,000) + ($35,000) = $41,000.

The state and the nation could have different overall levels of compensation per employee if they had different compensation rates per industry,

**FIGURE 2.3**

**Decomposition of Relative Compensation per Employee, 1979–2000**

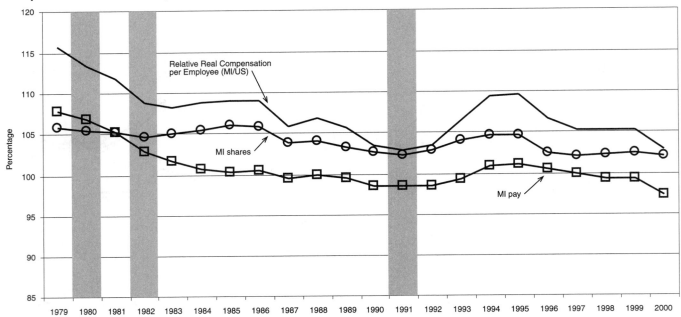

SOURCE: U.S. Department of Commerce, Bureau of Economic Analysis (June 2002). Calculations by authors.

different employment shares per industry, or, of course, a combination of the two. Thus, to continue the example, suppose that in the nation as a whole industry A pays $30,000 per employee and accounts for 40% of national employment, while industry B pays $45,000 per employee and accounts for 60% of national employment. In that case, *nationwide* compensation per employee would be: (0.4 × $30,000) + (0.6 × $45,000) = ($12,000) + ($27,000) = $39,000, and the state's *relative* compensation per employee would be: ($41,000 ÷ $39,000) × (100) = 105.1.

In this illustration, the state enjoys a 5.1% compensation premium by virtue of having relatively more of its employment in the higher-paid industry, which the state happens to pay even more highly than the nation.

One way to begin to analyze Michigan's relative compensation per employee is to see whether the differences between Michigan and the United States might be due primarily to differences in industrial employment shares, or primarily to differences in industrial compensation (pay) rates. In other words, suppose we calculate two counterfactual relative compensations:

a. What Michigan's relative compensation per employee would be, year by year, if Michigan's

industrial employment shares were exactly the same as the nation's, while the compensation rates per industry were the actual Michigan compensation rates (denoted "MI pay"),[15] and

b. What Michigan's relative compensation per employee would be, year by year, if Michigan's compensation rates by industry were exactly the same as the nation's, while the industrial employment shares were the actual Michigan employment shares (denoted "MI shares").[16]

Each counterfactual relative compensation can be compared with the state's actual relative compensation. If the counterfactual in (a) looks pretty much like Michigan's actual relative compensation, then the employment shares are pretty much irrelevant and it's Michigan's industrial pay scale that dominates. If, on the other hand, the counterfactual in (b) looks pretty much like Michigan's actual relative compensation, then pay scales are pretty much irrelevant and it is Michigan's employment shares that dominate.

Figure 2.3 allows us to make a judgment as to whether either the state's pay scale or the state's employment shares dominate, or explain, its relative compensation per employee. The solid series is the actual relative compensation per employee, as shown in figure 2.2. The series labeled "MI pay"

**TABLE 2.3**

**Employment Distribution by Industry, Michigan and United States, 1979–2000**

| | Average Real Compensation[a] per Employee (1996 dollars) 2000 | Distribution of Employment, Michigan (%) | | | | | | Location Quotient | | | | | |
|---|---|---|---|---|---|---|---|---|---|---|---|---|---|
| | | 1979 | 1984 | 1989 | 1994 | 1999 | 2000 | 1979 | 1984 | 1989 | 1994 | 1999 | 2000 |
| Motor Vehicle Manufacturing | 87,572 | 10.8 | 9.6 | 7.4 | 6.7 | 6.3 | 6.3 | 9.79 | 10.52 | 9.28 | 8.43 | 7.95 | 8.12 |
| All Other Private Industries[b] | 51,974 | 17.5 | 16.7 | 17.6 | 17.3 | 18.0 | 17.9 | 0.76 | 0.72 | 0.78 | 0.80 | 0.82 | 0.82 |
| Other (non-371) Manufacturing | 50,727 | 21.1 | 18.9 | 17.4 | 16.2 | 15.1 | 14.7 | 0.95 | 0.96 | 1.01 | 1.06 | 1.11 | 1.11 |
| Government | 39,725 | 17.1 | 16.8 | 15.9 | 15.4 | 14.6 | 14.6 | 0.96 | 0.99 | 0.96 | 0.92 | 0.93 | 0.93 |
| Services | 35,398 | 17.2 | 20.9 | 23.3 | 25.9 | 27.7 | 28.2 | 0.90 | 0.95 | 0.93 | 0.94 | 0.91 | 0.92 |
| Retail Trade | 18,701 | 16.2 | 17.1 | 18.5 | 18.4 | 18.3 | 18.4 | 0.97 | 0.98 | 1.03 | 1.03 | 1.03 | 1.04 |
| Michigan | 41,454 | 100 | 100 | 100 | 100 | 100 | 100 | | | | | | |

| | | Distribution of Employment, United States (%) | | | | | |
|---|---|---|---|---|---|---|---|
| | | 1979 | 1984 | 1989 | 1994 | 1999 | 2000 |
| Motor Vehicle Manufacturing | 64,267 | 1.1 | 0.9 | 0.8 | 0.8 | 0.8 | 0.8 |
| All Other Private Industries[b] | 53,189 | 23.1 | 23.0 | 22.6 | 21.6 | 21.9 | 21.8 |
| Other (non-371) Manufacturing | 48,437 | 22.3 | 19.6 | 17.2 | 15.3 | 13.6 | 13.3 |
| Government | 44,635 | 17.8 | 17.0 | 16.5 | 16.8 | 15.7 | 15.7 |
| Services | 36,261 | 19.1 | 22.0 | 24.9 | 27.7 | 30.3 | 30.7 |
| Retail Trade | 20,343 | 16.7 | 17.5 | 18.1 | 18.0 | 17.7 | 17.7 |
| U.S. | 40,282 | 100 | 100 | 100 | 100 | 100 | 100 |

SOURCE: U.S. Department of Commerce, Bureau of Economic Analysis (June 2002); U.S. Department of Labor, Bureau of Labor Statistics (June 2002).
(a) Wage and salary payments plus other labor income.
(b) Private industries excluding manufacturing, retail trade, and services.

is the counterfactual in the (a) comparison above. The series labeled "MI shares" is the counterfactual in the (b) comparison above.

Quite clearly, for all but the first three years, 1979–81, it is the "MI shares" series that is very much closer to the actual relative compensation per employee series. This implies that, *at least since the early 1980s, it is the industrial distribution of employment in Michigan that most accounts for the* level *of its relative compensation per employee;* that is, for Michigan's compensation premium relative to the nation as a whole, which has averaged 4.3% since 1985. Michigan's industrial pay scale may differ from the national average, but that's far less important to Michigan's roughly 4.3% average compensation premium than is the fact that Michigan's *employment distribution,* "MI shares," differs from the national average.

On the other hand, Michigan's pay scale is not entirely irrelevant to understanding Michigan's relative compensation per employee. While Michigan's employment distribution explains the current *level* of relative compensation, *it is the* *pattern of pay scales in Michigan that accounts for the* downward trend *in Michigan's relative compensation per employee that persisted until the mid-1980s.* These findings, in turn, suggest that we should look for what is unique in Michigan's industrial employment shares in order to understand Michigan's relative compensation premium —that is, why Michigan's average compensation level is where it is these days. Furthermore, we should look at Michigan's relative pay scales industry by industry in order to understand why the average income-quality of Michigan employment lost ground during the years prior to the mid-1980s. The data in tables 2.3 and 2.4 will help us in these matters of industrial detail.

Table 2.3 presents Michigan and U.S. employment distributions by industry, covering the period 1979–2000. The years shown are every fifth year: 1979, 1984, 1989, 1994, 1999, and the final year 2000. This choice of years provides substantial time detail while avoiding the recession years and permitting us to concentrate on the longer-term movements. The industries are the six that underlie the series in figure 2.3, and are listed in order of real compensation per employee in Michigan in the year 2000. The ordering would be the same for compensation per employee in the United States as a whole. The upper-left portion of the table shows the industrial distribution of employment in Michigan; the lower-left shows the same for the nation. Thus, 10.8% of Michigan's (establishment-based) employment was in motor vehicle manufacturing in 1979, 17.5% was in the all other private industries category, and so on, down through 16.2% in retail trade. For the nation as a whole in 1979, only 1.1% of employment was in motor vehicle manufacturing, 23.1% was in the all other private industries category, and so on, down through 16.7% in retail trade.

Perhaps the easiest way to compare the state and national employment distributions is to compute what are known as *location quotients,* which we do in the upper-right portion of table 2.3. Each figure there is the ratio of Michigan's employment share to the nation's employment share, for the industry and year in question. Thus, the 9.79 location quotient for motor vehicle manufacturing in 1979 is given by 10.8 ÷ 1.1 (calculation based on more decimals) and indicates that Michigan's employment share in vehicle manufacturing was 9.79 times the nation's in 1979.

Three conclusions emerge easily from perusal of the location quotients for the employment distributions.

1. Michigan is relatively highly concentrated in motor vehicle manufacturing, these days about eight times more than the United States as a whole, though this is not quite as high as was the case a few decades ago. Furthermore, motor vehicle manufacturing is the highest-paid industry of the six: in real terms $87,572 per employee in Michigan in 2000 versus $41,454 for the statewide average.
2. The biggest relative *under*-concentration of employment in Michigan is in the all other private industries category, the second-highest-paid category, where Michigan's employment concentration is only about eight-tenths of the national average.
3. In the other four industries, Michigan's employment concentration is comparatively close to the national averages: no more than 10% below, no more than 11% above.

Since we have already concluded that Michigan's employment distribution, called "MI shares" in the preceding and in figure 2.3, is the

key determinant of its relative compensation premium, it clearly has to be the relative employment dominance of motor vehicle manufacturing in the state that is being reflected in that compensation premium, which has been running at 4.3% on average since the mid-1980s.

To understand the dynamics of the relative income-quality of employment in Michigan—the downward trend through the mid-1980s and approximate stability since then—figure 2.3 suggests that we concentrate on the industrial pay scales, as shown in table 2.4.

The layout in table 2.4 is basically the same as in table 2.3, except that the body of the table contains the industrial pay scales—specifically, average real compensation (wage and salary payments plus other labor income) per employee—for Michigan in the upper left and for the United States just below that. Thus, real compensation per employee in motor vehicle manufacturing averaged $66,828 in Michigan in 1979, rose to $71,611 for 1984, and wound up at $87,572 for the year 2000. The corresponding U.S. real pay scales for motor vehicle manufacturing were $56,873, $60,782, and $64,267, respectively. The ratio of the Michigan to the U.S. pay scale in motor vehicle manufacturing is shown by the statistics on relative compensation per employee in the upper-right portion of the table: beginning with 117.5 [($66,828 ÷ $56,873) × 100] in 1979, and ending with 136.3 [($87,572 ÷ $64,267) × 100] in 2000.

We want to examine the relative compensation statistics in table 2.4 to identify the dynamic movements in Michigan's relative compensation premium. The relative compensation numbers display the income-quality of employment in Michigan, by industry and year. Why did the income-quality of employment in Michigan decline from 1979 to the mid-1980s? Because it fell in five of the six industries shown: by as little as 4 percentage points for employment in the government sector, to as much as 9 percentage points in the services sector. The exception is motor vehicle manufacturing, where the income-quality held about constant, with Michigan holding nearly an 18-percentage-point premium over the nation as a whole.

After the mid- to late 1980s, the pattern of relative compensation changed sharply. The income-quality of employment in motor vehicle manufacturing in Michigan moved up from a premium of about 18% to more than 30% by the

**TABLE 2.4**

**Average Real Compensation per Employee by Industry, Michigan and United States, 1979–2000**

| | Compensation per Employee, Michigan (1996 dollars) | | | | | | Relative Compensation per Employee | | | | | |
| | 1979 | 1984 | 1989 | 1994 | 1999 | 2000 | 1979 | 1984 | 1989 | 1994 | 1999 | 2000 |
|---|---|---|---|---|---|---|---|---|---|---|---|---|
| Motor Vehicle Manufacturing | 66,828 | 71,611 | 74,693 | 95,568 | 88,713 | 87,572 | 117.5 | 117.8 | 125.6 | 131.5 | 137.6 | 136.3 |
| All Other Private Industries[a] | 44,542 | 42,298 | 44,546 | 46,822 | 51,327 | 51,974 | 108.3 | 100.5 | 101.7 | 101.3 | 99.6 | 97.7 |
| Other (non-371) Manufacturing | 45,505 | 45,455 | 46,085 | 49,566 | 50,111 | 50,727 | 119.6 | 113.2 | 110.7 | 113.1 | 107.3 | 104.7 |
| Government | 33,508 | 35,608 | 36,738 | 39,589 | 39,875 | 39,725 | 92.1 | 88.3 | 87.0 | 92.0 | 89.9 | 89.0 |
| Services | 28,554 | 28,424 | 30,394 | 31,695 | 35,172 | 35,398 | 108.1 | 99.0 | 98.9 | 98.6 | 100.5 | 97.6 |
| Retail Trade | 20,241 | 18,345 | 17,361 | 17,443 | 18,728 | 18,701 | 104.4 | 97.8 | 93.7 | 94.2 | 93.7 | 91.9 |
| Michigan (MI pay × MI shares) | 38,564 | 37,577 | 37,469 | 40,087 | 41,378 | 41,454 | 115.7 | 108.7 | 105.6 | 109.3 | 105.4 | 102.9 |

| | Compensation per Employee, United States (1996 dollars) | | | | | |
| | 1979 | 1984 | 1989 | 1994 | 1999 | 2000 |
|---|---|---|---|---|---|---|
| Motor Vehicle Manufacturing | 56,873 | 60,782 | 59,461 | 72,686 | 64,469 | 64,267 |
| All Other Private Industries[a] | 41,112 | 42,079 | 43,787 | 46,217 | 51,544 | 53,189 |
| Other (non-371) Manufacturing | 38,037 | 40,166 | 41,649 | 43,827 | 46,707 | 48,437 |
| Government | 36,387 | 40,317 | 42,206 | 43,030 | 44,378 | 44,635 |
| Services | 26,405 | 28,706 | 30,722 | 32,143 | 35,010 | 36,261 |
| Retail Trade | 19,398 | 18,767 | 18,529 | 18,515 | 19,997 | 20,343 |
| U.S. (US pay × US shares) | 33,340 | 34,560 | 35,466 | 36,661 | 39,264 | 40,282 |

SOURCE: U.S. Department of Commerce, Bureau of Economic Analysis (June 2002); U.S. Department of Labor, Bureau of Labor Statistics (June 2002).
NOTE: Average Real Compensation includes wage and salary payments plus other labor income.
(a) Private industries excluding manufacturing, retail trade, and services.

mid-1990s and more than 36% most recently. The income-quality of employment in services and all other private industries stabilized at about parity with the nation (relative compensation at about 100%). Income-quality of employment in government and retail trade stabilized at deficits of about 5–10%. Only other (non–motor vehicle) manufacturing continued to experience a falling income-quality of employment from the mid-1980s to the present. On balance, these movements ended the decline in the income-quality of employment in Michigan and netted out to an approximate stability.

This analysis has enabled us to identify *where* the movements in income-quality occurred, but not *why*. Neither does this overview permit us the opportunity to dig deeper to find out. We can, however, offer a few hypotheses for others, perhaps, to explore. The near-universal decline in income-quality of employment in Michigan from the late 1970s to the mid-1980s may well have been an economic response to the particular structural (microeconomic) difficulties faced by the Michigan economy during the 1980–82 period, though it did not start then. The doubling of the income-quality premium in motor vehicle manufacturing most likely reflects the rationali-

zation of employment in that sector in recent years. That is, production employment has been spread more broadly across the nation, especially among the foreign nameplate, or *transplant*, producers, and employment in headquarters and research functions has become more concentrated in the state of Michigan. These tendencies are entirely consistent with the combination of rising relative compensation in the motor vehicle sector, in conjunction with declining location quotients in motor vehicle sector employment.

## Michigan's Productivity Performance, 1979–2000

In periods such as the late 1990s, when a very large proportion of the population is participating in the labor market and the unemployment rate is very low, the major source of economic growth is rising productivity. Indeed, in the long run, improvements in our standard of living derive largely from increases in productivity.

Much has been made in recent years of the strong gains in national productivity during the second half of the 1990s, following the sluggish performance during the 1970s and 1980s, and of

**FIGURE 2.4**

**Relative Productivity (MI/US), 1979–2000**

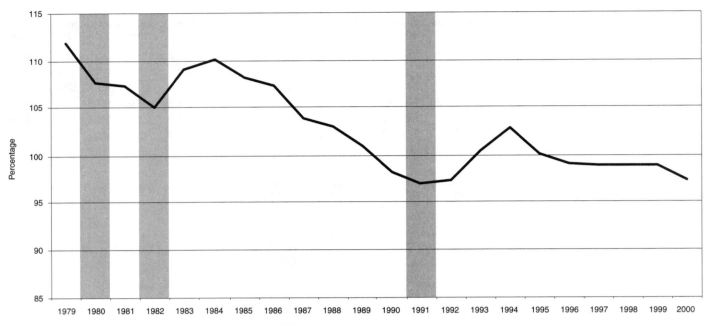

SOURCE: U.S. Department of Commerce, Bureau of Economic Analysis (June 2002). Calculations by authors.

the importance of productivity in facilitating wage gains without igniting inflationary pressures. To what extent has Michigan participated in the recent productivity surge?

The usual measure of productivity at the national level is output per labor hour. At the state level, however, labor hour data are not readily available. The following analysis, therefore, will focus on output per worker rather than the more common output per hour.[17] Output is represented by inflation-adjusted gross state product (real GSP) measured in 1996 dollars.[18] Employment is the total full-time and part-time employment by industry series as reported by the Bureau of Economic Analysis (BEA).[19]

We plot relative productivity in figure 2.4; that is, for each year we calculate output per worker in Michigan divided by output per worker in the United States and multiply by 100. The figure covers the period 1979–2000, with the recession years shaded. From 1979 to 1989, Michigan's output per worker exceeded its national counterpart. Michigan began the period with a 12% productivity premium but lost ground throughout the 1980s except for a cyclical rebound following the 1980–82 recession. Thus, during the years of slower national productivity growth, the state's productivity gains were even smaller. After the 1990–91 recession, the downward trend in relative

productivity is less clear. Although the state's productivity level has hovered just below parity since 1995, it has stayed above its low of 96.9% of national productivity recorded in 1991, and it remained steady over most of the period of strongest national performance, 1996–99.[20]

To understand the sources of the changes in relative productivity performance, we turn to an industrial decomposition of average statewide productivity similar to the one used to interpret relative average compensation per worker. In this instance, productivity can be expressed as a weighted average of productivity in each industry in the state, with the weights being the shares of statewide employment in each industry; nationwide productivity can be expressed similarly. Using the methodology employed in the decomposition of average compensation, we can construct two counterfactual relative productivity series—"MI productivity," which retains Michigan's productivity rates but uses the national industrial employment shares, and "MI shares," which retains Michigan's industry mix but uses national productivity rates—to compare with the actual relative productivity series.[21]

Figure 2.5 shows the actual relative productivity series (from figure 2.4) along with the two counterfactual series. The "MI shares" line is relatively flat and remains above 100% over the entire

**FIGURE 2.5**

## Decomposition of Relative Productivity, 1979–2000

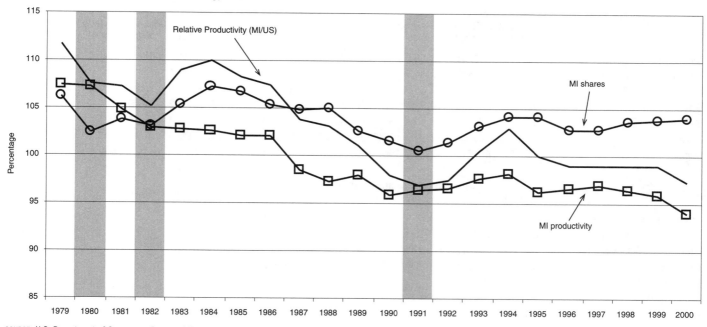

SOURCE: U.S. Department of Commerce, Bureau of Economic Analysis (June 2002). Calculations by authors.

period, suggesting that *Michigan's employment mix contributes a bonus in output per worker relative to the national average.* The size of the bonus due to industry mix falls into two regimes—the 1979–89 period, when the Michigan employment mix adds an average 4.8% premium; and the 1990–2000 period, when the premium averages only 2.9%.

The "MI productivity" line falls below the actual relative productivity line over the entire period and drops below parity beginning in 1987. Its overall contour is similar to that of the actual series, with a downward slope prior to 1990 and a nearly flat trend thereafter. This suggests that *much of the deterioration in Michigan's overall relative productivity during the 1980s was due to relatively weaker productivity growth, at least in some industries, rather than to the state's industrial employment mix.*

Table 2.5 presents national and state productivity data for the same six industry groupings used earlier. Again, the period covered is 1979–2000, with every fifth year and the final year, 2000, shown. The industry groupings are ordered by productivity in Michigan in the year 2000. The upper-left portion of the table shows industrial productivity for Michigan; the lower-left shows the same for the United States. The upper-right portion contains relative productivity measures

(Michigan productivity divided by U.S. productivity and multiplied by 100) for each industry grouping.

If we compare the industrial productivity rates, it is easy to see why Michigan's industry mix ("MI shares") provides a productivity bonus relative to the nation. Over the 1979–2000 period the motor vehicle industry generates between 1.6 and 2.4 times the average output per worker each year for both the state and the nation (in 1984 in Michigan, for example, 118,836 ÷ 49,775 = 2.4). That relatively high productivity, however, gets a much greater weight when Michigan employment shares are used in the calculation. Recall from table 2.3 that, compared with the nation, Michigan has 8 to 11 times as high a concentration of employment in motor vehicle manufacturing.

The measures of relative productivity by industry on the right side of table 2.5 provide some guidance as we look for the source of the 1980s' slide and the 1990s' stability in industry-wide relative productivity exhibited by the "MI productivity" line in figure 2.5.[22] The nonmanufacturing sector accounts for all of the deterioration during the 1980s. In each of the four nonmanufacturing industry groupings, the state's relative productivity declined between 1979 and 1989, and in three out of four groupings, relative productivity in Michigan slid from a productivity premium in

**TABLE 2.5**

## Average Productivity by Industry, Michigan and United States, 1979–2000

| | Productivity[a], Michigan (1996 dollars) | | | | | | Relative Productivity | | | | | |
|---|---|---|---|---|---|---|---|---|---|---|---|---|
| | 1979 | 1984 | 1989 | 1994 | 1999 | 2000 | 1979 | 1984 | 1989 | 1994 | 1999 | 2000 |
| Motor Vehicle Manufacturing | 88,451 | 118,836 | 94,587 | 111,490 | 99,193 | 100,158 | 100.8 | 107.7 | 104.3 | 101.3 | 88.5 | 87.4 |
| All Other Private Industries[b] | 72,591 | 72,895 | 72,369 | 76,794 | 81,162 | 80,775 | 114.3 | 109.4 | 100.3 | 97.0 | 94.4 | 92.6 |
| Other (non-371) Manufacturing | 34,844 | 42,466 | 53,338 | 64,917 | 77,797 | 79,274 | 92.7 | 94.4 | 98.7 | 106.2 | 99.8 | 97.0 |
| Government | 45,939 | 43,296 | 42,448 | 43,885 | 43,649 | 43,250 | 106.8 | 100.2 | 96.9 | 100.0 | 97.2 | 95.9 |
| Services | 38,727 | 34,404 | 33,733 | 32,220 | 32,648 | 32,813 | 105.3 | 98.4 | 95.4 | 95.1 | 95.1 | 93.7 |
| Retail Trade | 22,991 | 23,359 | 22,838 | 23,571 | 30,154 | 31,433 | 104.6 | 96.4 | 92.1 | 93.1 | 95.9 | 94.9 |
| Michigan | 48,462 | 49,775 | 48,108 | 50,883 | 53,802 | 54,101 | 111.7 | 110.0 | 101.0 | 102.8 | 98.9 | 97.3 |

| | Productivity[a], United States (1996 dollars) | | | | | |
|---|---|---|---|---|---|---|
| | 1979 | 1984 | 1989 | 1994 | 1999 | 2000 |
| Motor Vehicle Manufacturing | 87,734 | 110,356 | 90,694 | 110,044 | 112,055 | 114,598 |
| All Other Private Industries[b] | 63,516 | 66,629 | 72,153 | 79,176 | 85,976 | 87,268 |
| Other (non-371) Manufacturing | 37,579 | 44,971 | 54,039 | 61,113 | 77,926 | 81,703 |
| Government | 43,025 | 43,215 | 43,804 | 43,867 | 44,925 | 45,098 |
| Services | 36,763 | 34,979 | 35,346 | 33,898 | 34,320 | 35,009 |
| Retail Trade | 21,988 | 24,234 | 24,793 | 25,324 | 31,457 | 33,122 |
| U.S. | 43,385 | 45,241 | 47,644 | 49,481 | 54,422 | 55,619 |

SOURCE: U.S. Department of Commerce, Bureau of Economic Analysis (June 2002).
(a) Real GSP per worker.
(b) Private industries excluding manufacturing, retail trade, and services.

1979 to a deficit by 1989. The slippage ranged from a 14 percentage-point decline (100.3 – 114.3 = –14.0) for other private industries to a 9.9 percentage-point drop for government and services. Relative productivity in motor vehicle manufacturing, as well as for the rest of manufacturing, moved counter to the statewide trend and improved during the period.

The improvement in relative productivity during the 1990s was widespread across the nonmanufacturing industries. After declining in the earlier period, relative productivity for each of government and services was little changed from the late 1980s to the late 1990s. The relative productivity for the other private industries sector continued to fall, but the 7.7 percentage-point decline was only about half the drop from the earlier period. In contrast to stability or a lower rate of decline, retail trade actually produced a moderate increase, 3.8 percentage points, in relative productivity from 1989 to 1999. Productivity growth was particularly strong for retail trade during the 1990s both for the nation and the state, much of it related to the use of computers for pricing, inventory control, and scanning equipment at checkouts.

Motor vehicle manufacturing experienced a substantial decline in relative productivity during the 1990s, as its productivity premium, 4.3% in 1989, turned into a substantial deficit, –12.6% in 2000. This may be a function of the growth of transplant auto facilities outside of Michigan over this period.[23] The sharp drop in relative productivity within this sector was substantially muted in the "MI productivity" series, where it was weighted by the sector's extremely small share of national employment (see table 2.3).

*Michigan's relative productivity, which declined during much of the 1980s, appears to have leveled off during the 1990s and held steady even during the latter part of that decade.* This improved productivity performance likely contributed to the stability, which we noted earlier, of real personal income per capita in Michigan compared with the nation.

## Michigan's Income Distribution 1992–2000

The size of aggregate income for a region and its rate of growth over time are valuable indicators of the region's economic standing and performance. These statistics do not provide us with any insight, though, on how this income is distributed across the population or how the distributions change as total income expands or contracts over time. To

## TABLE 2.6

### Distribution of Families by Income Category, Michigan and United States, 1992–2000

| Income (1996 dollars) | 1992 | | 2000 | | 1992 (%) | | 2000 (%) | |
|---|---|---|---|---|---|---|---|---|
| | **MI** | **U.S.** | **MI** | **U.S.** | **MI** | **U.S.** | **MI** | **U.S.** |
| $10,000 or less | 241,571 | 7,546,467 | 174,151 | 5,350,257 | 9.4 | 10.6 | 6.5 | 7.0 |
| $10,001–20,000 | 315,823 | 10,094,849 | 244,066 | 9,237,745 | 12.2 | 14.1 | 9.2 | 12.2 |
| $20,001–30,000 | 346,449 | 10,075,875 | 289,307 | 10,040,193 | 13.4 | 14.1 | 10.9 | 13.2 |
| $30,001–40,000 | 364,361 | 9,373,438 | 300,344 | 8,822,810 | 14.1 | 13.1 | 11.3 | 11.6 |
| $40,001–50,000 | 315,740 | 8,346,349 | 233,774 | 7,951,182 | 12.2 | 11.7 | 8.8 | 10.5 |
| $50,001–60,000 | 236,480 | 6,823,451 | 256,723 | 7,053,497 | 9.2 | 9.5 | 9.6 | 9.3 |
| $60,001–70,000 | 200,625 | 5,474,003 | 263,777 | 6,051,166 | 7.8 | 7.7 | 9.9 | 8.0 |
| $70,001–80,000 | 176,822 | 3,766,091 | 196,709 | 4,632,654 | 6.9 | 5.3 | 7.4 | 6.1 |
| $80,001–90,000 | 101,079 | 2,673,347 | 158,750 | 3,553,062 | 3.9 | 3.7 | 6.0 | 4.7 |
| $90,001–100,000 | 78,841 | 1,896,473 | 120,888 | 2,929,867 | 3.1 | 2.7 | 4.5 | 3.9 |
| $100,001–110,000 | 46,739 | 1,440,724 | 103,865 | 2,089,547 | 1.8 | 2.0 | 3.9 | 2.8 |
| $110,001–120,000 | 56,551 | 1,216,348 | 83,946 | 1,686,064 | 2.2 | 1.7 | 3.2 | 2.2 |
| $120,001–130,000 | 36,039 | 765,600 | 38,940 | 1,174,109 | 1.4 | 1.1 | 1.5 | 1.5 |
| $130,001–140,000 | 16,361 | 547,296 | 41,395 | 921,446 | 0.6 | 0.8 | 1.6 | 1.2 |
| $140,001–150,000 | 11,117 | 358,923 | 16,592 | 753,738 | 0.4 | 0.5 | 0.6 | 1.0 |
| $150,001–160,000 | 8,308 | 298,750 | 27,632 | 601,587 | 0.3 | 0.4 | 1.0 | 0.8 |
| $160,001–170,000 | 8,890 | 229,396 | 10,381 | 351,779 | 0.3 | 0.3 | 0.4 | 0.5 |
| $170,001–180,000 | 8,954 | 134,078 | 17,953 | 284,138 | 0.3 | 0.2 | 0.7 | 0.4 |
| $180,001–190,000 | 1,364 | 112,525 | 13,589 | 247,627 | 0.1 | 0.2 | 0.5 | 0.3 |
| $190,001–200,000 | 2,238 | 73,576 | 4,615 | 179,558 | 0.1 | 0.1 | 0.2 | 0.2 |
| $200,001–210,000 | 1,698 | 60,710 | 1,818 | 94,909 | 0.1 | 0.1 | 0.1 | 0.1 |
| $210,001–220,000 | 0 | 56,619 | 2,058 | 89,143 | 0.0 | 0.1 | 0.1 | 0.1 |
| $220,001–230,000 | 2,735 | 39,154 | 4,505 | 80,953 | 0.1 | 0.1 | 0.2 | 0.1 |
| $230,001–240,000 | 0 | 31,323 | 0 | 54,508 | 0.0 | 0.0 | 0.0 | 0.1 |
| $240,001–250,000 | 0 | 14,428 | 0 | 34,071 | 0.0 | 0.0 | 0.0 | 0.0 |
| Over $250,000 | 1,701 | 73,557 | 56,796 | 1,657,050 | 0.1 | 0.1 | 2.1 | 2.1 |
| | 2,580,486 | 71,523,350 | 2,662,574 | 75,922,660 | 100 | 100 | 100 | 100 |

SOURCE: Compiled from the Current Population Survey March Supplement, 1993 and 2001. Expressed in 1996 dollars, using the personal consumption expenditures deflator.

develop a more complete profile of the Michigan economy, we would like to know how aggregate income has been distributed across the population in recent times—and in particular, what can be said about whether the poor are becoming more or less poor relative to the rich.

Information on income distribution is not as readily available for regions of the country as it is for the country as a whole, but the March supplements to the Current Population Survey from the U.S. Census Bureau do provide state estimates of the number of families by level of family income. From the Census Bureau data, we assembled estimates of Michigan family income for 1992 and 2000. For comparison purposes, similar information was compiled for the country as a whole.[24]

The data for Michigan and the United States for 1992 and 2000 are arrayed in table 2.6. The first column lists family income categories in $10,000 intervals from zero to $250,000. Families receiving more than $250,000 form an open-ended category; that is, all family incomes from $250,001 to the income of the richest family are represented in this single category. The values in the next four columns of the table represent the number of families in each of these income categories. The last four columns indicate each category's percentage of the total. For example, the first row of the table shows that the 241,571 families in Michigan with an income of $10,000 or less in 1992 constitute 9.4% of the 2,580,486 families in Michigan in 1992 (total shown at the bottom of column 2); the 7,546,467 families in the United States with the same income constitute 10.6% of the 71,523,350 families in the nation in 1992; and so on.

## TABLE 2.7

**Distribution of Families by Aggregate Income Category, Michigan and United States, 1992–2000**

| Income Category (1996 dollars) | % of Families | | | |
| --- | --- | --- | --- | --- |
| | 1992 | | 2000 | |
| | MI | U.S. | MI | U.S. |
| $20,000 or less | 21.6 | 24.7 | 15.7 | 19.2 |
| $20,001–40,000 | 27.5 | 27.5 | 22.2 | 24.8 |
| $40,001–60,000 | 21.4 | 21.2 | 18.4 | 19.8 |
| $60,001–100,000 | 21.7 | 19.4 | 27.8 | 22.7 |
| Over $100,000, excluding top 2.5% of families | 5.3 | 5.2 | 13.6 | 11.0 |
| Top 2.5% of families | 2.5 | 2.5 | 2.5 | 2.5 |
| **Summary Comparison Ratios of Family Distribution among Categories** | | | | |
| Lowest vs. 2 highest categories | 2.8 | 3.2 | 1.0 | 1.4 |
| 2 lowest vs. 3 highest | 1.7 | 1.9 | 0.9 | 1.2 |

SOURCE: Compiled from the Current Population Survey March Supplement, 1993 and 2001. Expressed in 1996 dollars, using the personal consumption expenditures deflator.

To better understand this table and some of the limitations of the data in it, it is important to know how it was assembled. First, nominal family incomes were deflated by the personal consumption deflator prior to assembling the table, so that the income categories all refer to real income in 1996 dollars. This permits us to determine whether a family had an increase in purchasing power, and in that sense, in its economic standard of living, between 1992 and 2000. To illustrate: Take the case of a family earning, say, $92,106 in nominal dollars in 1992 (its actual dollar income in that year) and $125,454 in nominal dollars in 2000. Both of those amounts are equal to $105,000 in inflation-adjusted 1996 dollars, and therefore that family would have had no increase in its purchasing power between 1992 and 2000 and would appear in the $100,001–$110,000 row of the table in both years. The entire increase in nominal income was absorbed by increasing consumer prices. Thus, the rows in the table represent incomes in terms of purchasing power rather than actual reported incomes.

A second detail on the table is that the number of families in each cell was determined by surveying a sample of the population. These samples were then inflated by statistically derived weights to represent the population. For Michigan, some of the samples were very small, particularly in the higher income categories for 1992. For instance, no family in the survey reported income in the

$240,001–$250,000 category, and thus the population estimate of this category was also zero (zero times the weight equals zero). Since this zero is undoubtedly an inaccurate representation of the entire population, the small sample sizes restrict our ability to draw highly detailed inferences from the data shown in table 2.6.

There is a wealth of information in table 2.6, but its very detail makes it cumbersome to cull out its basic messages. Because of this, and the sample size problems with some of the individual cells, we combined the detailed income divisions to form the six summary income categories shown in table 2.7. We took care to select the broader categories so that the key characteristics in the detail were not masked. For 1992, the most striking characteristic of the distribution of families by income is the much greater proportion of families in the lower end of the income categories, compared with the higher end. For both Michigan and the United States, there were approximately three times as many families receiving under $20,000 as there were receiving over $100,000. Precisely, in Michigan there were 2.8 times the proportion in the lowest category (21.6%) as there were in the highest two categories (5.3% + 2.5% = 7.8%), as shown by the summary ratio at the bottom of the table. The discrepancy for the nation was somewhat larger, with a corresponding ratio of 3.2 [24.7% ÷ (5.2% + 2.5%)]. If the bottom *two* income categories are compared with the top *three* for either area in 1992, there are nearly twice as many families in the lower income categories, but again, proportionately a bit more in the lower income categories in the nation than in Michigan. In 2000, the discrepancy between lower and upper income remains somewhat larger in the country as compared with Michigan, as shown by the summary ratios.

The most dramatic characteristic of the distributions for 2000, however, is not the comparisons between Michigan and the United States, but rather the differences for either area between 1992 and 2000. For both Michigan and the United States in 2000, the number of families in the lower income divisions has declined and come much closer to the number of families in the higher divisions. As shown by the summary ratios, Michigan's number of families in the lower versus the higher income categories has moved from two to three times greater to about par; the U.S. ratios have also improved dramatically, but remain above one. Even after taking into account any difficulties in making comparisons between years because of sampling variations, it seems apparent that for both the state and the nation there has been a substantial upward gravitation in the proportion of families receiving higher real, inflation-adjusted income during the 1990s.

To make a more direct assessment of comparative income equality, we need to convert the distributions of the number of families to income distributions. The format of the original data in table 2.6 requires two adjustments for this conversion. First, we assume that the midpoint of each $10,000 income interval represents the earnings of each family in the interval. Thus, in Michigan in 1992, all 315,823 families earning between $10,001 and $20,000 are assumed to receive $15,000, so that the income of the entire category is $4,737,345,000 (315,823 × $15,000). Second, since our uppermost income interval is open-ended, we cannot identify a midpoint for this group. For the purpose of calculating summary income equality statistics, we have removed the families receiving the very highest income from further analysis. The most convenient cutoff involved removing the 2.5% of the families earning the highest real income from each area in each year. The effect of this adjustment to the data is to remove the highest income category shown in table 2.7. Although we thereby retain the vast majority of the families for our analysis, our findings may not be strictly comparable to calculations elsewhere that do include this group.

After calculating the total income per category using the midpoint formula (adjustment 1 above), and removing the highest income families (adjustment 2 above), the distributions across categories of total income as well as total families can be compiled. For expository purposes, the resulting distributions of families and income are summarized in table 2.8 using the same real income categories as in table 2.7, with the highest income category now removed.

The distribution of families across income categories shown in the top panel of table 2.8 is slightly different from that in table 2.7, strictly due to the absence of the highest-income category in table 2.8. As would be expected, with the same number of families in each of the remaining categories between the two tables, and a smaller total number of families in table 2.8, the proportion of families in each category is a little higher in table 2.8. For example, those families receiving under $20,000 in Michigan in 1992 formed 21.6% of all families in Michigan, but a somewhat larger 22.2% of the smaller group, which excludes the

## TABLE 2.8

**Distribution of Income by Aggregate Income Category, Michigan and United States, 1992–2000**

| Income Category (1996 dollars) | 1992 | | 2000 | |
|---|---|---|---|---|
| | MI | U.S. | MI | U.S. |
| | % of Families[a] | | | |
| $20,000 or less | 22.15 | 25.30 | 16.11 | 19.71 |
| $20,001–40,000 | 28.25 | 27.89 | 22.71 | 25.48 |
| $40,001–60,000 | 21.95 | 21.75 | 18.90 | 20.27 |
| $60,001–100,000 | 22.15 | 19.80 | 28.52 | 23.19 |
| Over $100,000 | 5.50 | 5.26 | 13.75 | 11.34 |
| | % of Income[a] | | | |
| $20,000 or less | 5.27 | 6.33 | 3.03 | 4.25 |
| $20,001–40,000 | 18.99 | 19.43 | 11.87 | 14.39 |
| $40,001–60,000 | 24.14 | 25.15 | 16.48 | 19.17 |
| $60,001–100,000 | 37.59 | 35.03 | 38.05 | 33.95 |
| Over $100,000 | 13.99 | 14.07 | 30.58 | 28.25 |
| **ADDENDUM** | **Modified Gini Coefficient[b] of Income Inequality** | | | |
| | 0.362 | 0.375 | 0.364 | 0.386 |

SOURCE: Compiled from the Current Population Survey March Supplement, 1993 and 2001. Expressed in 1996 dollars, using the personal consumption expenditures deflator.
(a) Excludes the top 2.5% of families with the highest income.
(b) Computed from the detailed data (table 2.6) underlying the distributions summarized in this table.

top 2.5% of families. The relative proportions across each of these groups, however, do not change.

The distribution of *income* across income categories is presented in the lower panel of the table. When the income data are viewed this way, it becomes clear that income is concentrated in the upper income categories. For instance, only 5.3% of the income received in the state and only 6.3% of the income received in the nation goes to those earning under $20,000 in 1992, versus about 14% to those earning over $100,000 (but again, not including the richest 2.5%). The spread is even more dramatic in 2000, when the proportions between the highest and lowest categories range from 6.6 times greater for the nation (that is, 28.25 ÷ 4.25) to 10 times greater for the state (30.58 ÷ 3.03). Again, between 1992 and 2000 there appears to be a shift into the higher real income categories for families both in Michigan and the United States.

A direct comparison of the distributions in the top and bottom panels creates a few general impressions. First, in each area and year, the family and income distributions are most similar in the middle of the distribution, and become more dissimilar moving in either direction toward the ends of the distribution. The deviations are particularly acute at the lower end, where there are a relatively large number of families compared with their total income. Second, from scanning the table, in either year or across years there appear to be no substantial differences between Michigan and the United States in the relationship of the family distribution to the income distribution.

To make a precise statement about how the family distributions summarized in the top panel of table 2.8 line up with the income distributions summarized in the lower panel, we can compute a single summary measure on our sample data known as the Gini coefficient. The Gini coefficient is a number between zero and one that measures the degree of equality (or inequality) in the distribution of income, with a value of zero representing perfect equality and a value of one representing maximum inequality.[25] To obtain as informative a calculation as possible, we use the detailed income categories that underlie the summary information in table 2.8. In practice we see Gini coefficients calculated on U.S. income distributions ranging roughly between 0.3 and 0.5, depending on the time period and the exact income concept measured. The Gini coefficient is most useful as a comparative measure, comparing several income distributions or the change in a distribution over time.

*The coefficients for both 1992 and 2000 support our informal observation that the income distributions for Michigan and the United States are not substantially different; if anything, Michigan's distribution, yielding the smaller Gini coefficient, is a little closer to equality.* The coefficients for the nation suggest a small increase in inequality from 1992 to 2000, but not a change that should be regarded as large in the absolute. As a matter of fact, the official Gini coefficients for the United States based on household measurements, compiled by the U.S. Census Bureau on denser and more complete data sets, and *including the highest-income categories*, can be characterized in much the same way: the national income distributions have not gotten any closer to equality over the period, and may have moved slightly toward greater inequality.[26]

In summary, the information in tables 2.6–2.8 indicates that there has been a substantial gravitation of families into the higher real income categories over the 1990s, that is, even after accounting for inflation. For both 1992 and 2000, the income distribution for Michigan is at least as close to equality as that of the nation. Indeed, the indication of a somewhat greater degree of equality in Michigan compared with the nation is even stronger for 2000 than it was for 1992. It will be interesting to see how these income distributions change over the next few decades, when the age distribution of the population will have moved dramatically toward the more elderly categories, which may cause even greater changes in income distribution than we have seen over the past decade.

## Summary

It proves convenient to summarize our findings under five headings: relative employment, relative real income, income-quality of jobs, relative productivity, and income distribution.

*Relative employment.* Except for a few severe contractionary episodes, Michigan's unemployment rate ran about 1.5 percentage points above the national average during the period 1956–1982. The state's relative employment performance improved dramatically during the 1990s. Indeed, throughout 1994–2000, the state's unemployment rate ran below the national average.

*Relative real income.* In the years prior to the 1980s Michigan enjoyed a level of real income per capita that was above the national average. Yet this income premium, as high as 13% in 1956, dwindled to 5% by 1979 and then disappeared entirely in the early 1980s. That deterioration has not continued, and since the mid-1980s, the real income of Michigan's residents has been roughly on par with the national average.

*Income-quality of jobs.* These patterns of employment and income suggest the possibility of a relative deterioration in the income-quality of jobs in Michigan. Our findings imply that this deterioration, manifest as a decline in average compensation per employee in Michigan relative to the nation, ended in the mid-1980s. Since then, average compensation in Michigan has run parallel to the national average.

*Relative productivity.* Michigan's relative productivity, output per worker in Michigan compared with the nation, declined during much of the 1980s. Relative productivity leveled off during the 1990s and held steady even during the latter part of that decade when the national productivity trend improved dramatically.

*Income distribution.* The 1990s produced a substantial gravitation of families into higher real income categories in Michigan as well as the nation. The income distributions for Michigan and the United States are not substantially different. Compared with the nation, however, Michigan does appear to have moved toward somewhat greater equality in its distribution of income during the 1990s.

We close with an important and sweeping generalization. It is indisputably true that the Michigan economy has long been and remains more cyclical than the national economy. This is the case whether relative performance is measured in terms of employment or real income. The data of the 1990s suggest that Michigan's excess cyclical sensitivity may be less extreme than it was a few decades ago, but it is much too soon to regard that as a firm conclusion.

■

## REFERENCES

Beemiller, Richard M., and Clifford H. Woodruff III. 2000. Gross state product by industry, 1977–98. *Survey of Current Business* 80(10): 69–90.

Brazer, Harvey E., and Deborah S. Laren. 1982. *Michigan's fiscal and economic structure.* Ann Arbor: University of Michigan Press.

"Current Population Survey March Supplement" U.S. Department of Labor, Bureau of Labor Statistics, and U.S. Census Bureau. 1993. *www.bls.gov/cps.*

"Current Population Survey March Supplement" U.S. Department of Labor, Bureau of Labor Statistics, and U.S. Census Bureau. 2001. *www.bls.gov/cps.*

Harbour and Associates. 2002. *The Harbour report: North America 2002.* Detroit: Harbour and Associates, Inc.

Michigan Employment Security Commission. 1996. *Michigan statistical abstract–1996 edition.* Ann Arbor: University of Michigan Press.

U.S. Census Bureau. 2001. *Money income in the United States: 2000.* Washington, D.C.: Government Printing Office, September.

U.S. Department of Commerce, Bureau of Economic Analysis. 2002. *www.bea.doc.gov.* [cited June].

U.S. Department of Labor, Bureau of Labor Statistics. 2002. *www.bls.gov/data.* [cited June].

## NOTES

The authors would like to express their gratitude to Didem Bahar Ozgun for her exceptional research assistance in preparing the data, figures, and tables.

1. "Michigan, Ann Arbor" would have been more accurate, but was presumed to have been less informative to the average Muscovite.

2. The employment rate, which is 100 minus the unemployment rate, measures the percent of the labor force that is employed. The labor force is restricted to those age sixteen and over who are actively seeking jobs (both the successful and the unsuccessful). When the labor market is strong, more of the sixteen-and-over population tend to seek jobs; when the labor market is weak, some tend to become discouraged, with the result that fewer of the sixteen-and-over population wind up actively seeking jobs. When the latter occurs, the drop in the numbers actively seeking jobs buoys the employment rate, and thereby understates the full weakness in the labor market. The percentage of the sixteen-and-over population holding jobs (labeled the *Employment/Population Rate* in table 2.1) is based on a cyclically stable denominator and is therefore a more reliable indicator of strength in the labor market, especially in conjunction with the unemployment rate itself.

3. Throughout the chapter, nominal income is deflated by the personal consumption deflator published in the national income and product accounts. The result is real income measured, in the technical language of the U.S. Department of Commerce, in *chained 1996 dollars.* In the balance of this chapter we drop the word *chained.*

4. The corresponding indicators for the United States are: 4% unemployment, 64.5% employment/population rate, $27,389 real personal income per capita, and 1.9% per year growth of real personal income per capita.

5. We have, literally, added employment over the four other Great Lakes states, added labor force, added income, added population, and so on, to aggregate Illinois, Indiana, Ohio, and Wisconsin into a single region, which we abbreviate as OGLS.

6. Recessions are *official* when declared so by the National Bureau of Economic Research (NBER). These recession periods are dated in terms of months and quarters, however, not years. The NBER declared a recession for the months August 1990–March 1991, inclusive, and the two quarters 1990q4 and 1991q1. Thus, the years 1990 and 1991 are *involved* in that recession. Shading both 1990

and 1991 in figure 2.1, however, might suggest, misleadingly, that the recession lasted two years. We made the decision that a year involved in a recession would be shaded if it satisfied either one of the following two criteria: (a) at least half the year, whether measured as six months or two quarters, was in recession, or (b) real GDP growth was negative for that calendar year. The negative growth criterion became operative only twice, in 1975 and 1991. All other shaded years were selected for having been in recession for at least six months or two quarters. The year 2001 is a special case. April 2001 is officially the first month of the latest recession, but the official endpoint has not, as of this writing, been declared by NBER. We have assumed that September 2001 would be the *earliest* possible month that could be labeled as the bottom of the recession. If so, that would qualify 2001 to be shaded on the criterion of at least six months in recession.

7. Since the *Em*ployment rate is just 100 minus the *Unem*ployment rate, the same numerical information, with opposite sign, would be shown by the Michigan unemployment rate minus the national unemployment rate. But we wanted a *high value* to signify *strength in Michigan* (relative to the nation) and a *rising curve* to signify *Michigan improving* (relative to the nation), so we chose to difference the employment rates.

8. After removing a linear time trend from each of the series (relative income and relative employment) in figure 2.1, the resulting de-trended series have a correlation of 0.77.

9. This is equivalent to saying that during 1956–82 Michigan's unemployment rate ran, on average, about 1.5 percentage points *above* the national unemployment rate, when not stressed by severe recessionary conditions.

10. Equivalently, Michigan's unemployment rate ran, on average, more than four-tenths of a percentage point below the national unemployment rate during 1994–2000.

11. The results cited in the text derive from using the relative income variable in figure 2.1 (*Rel Inc*) as the dependent variable in the following multiple regression (fit period 1956–2001, t-statistics in parentheses):

$$Rel\ Inc = 110.53 - 15.51 \times D83on - 1.82 \times [UNEM^{US}$$
$$\qquad (151.3) \quad (-5.1) \qquad\qquad (-6.1)$$
$$- UNEM^{US}(-1)] - 0.72 \times [UNEM^{US}(-1)$$
$$\qquad\qquad\qquad (-3.7)$$
$$- UNEM^{US}(-3)] - 0.28 \times TIMEpre83$$
$$\qquad\qquad\qquad (-6.0)$$

$$+ 0.09 \times TIME83on$$
$$\qquad (1.2)$$

$$\bar{R}^2 = 0.85$$

where $D83on = 0$, prior to 1983; 1, 1983 and thereafter; $UNEM^{US}$ = U.S. unemployment rate in percent, yearly; $X(-n)$ = variable $X$ lagged $n$ years; *TIMEpre83* = time trend variable with values 1, 2, 3, $\cdots$, 27 from 1956 through 1982; and zero after 1982; *TIME83on* = time trend variable with values 28, 29, 30, $\cdots$, 46 from 1983 through 2001, and zero prior to 1983.

The U.S. unemployment rate changes are used to capture the effects of the national business cycle on Michigan's relative income position (rising U.S. unemployment is expected to be associated with lower relative income for Michigan). This allows the trend variables to measure any persistent changes over time in relative income independent of cyclical ups and downs.

12. This implies that for some component(s) of personal income, Michigan must be generating a deficit relative to the U.S. average. Apparently, the component that most accounts for the 4.6 percentage-point gap between relative compensation and relative income is proprietor income. Michigan's proprietor income per capita is only about two-thirds of national proprietor income per capita. We've no special understanding of why this is so.

13. Compensation per capita = (compensation ÷ population) = (compensation ÷ employees) × (employees ÷ population).

14. This decomposition was settled upon after some experimentation. We began with the full one-digit distribution of industries and then experimented with various higher levels of aggregation that attempted to keep industries with similar pay scales together. The six-sector breakdown we chose kept things manageable without sacrifice of content in terms of what we were trying to learn about Michigan's relative compensation.

15. That is, we replace (*MI pay × MI shares*) ÷ (*US pay × US shares*) with (*MI pay × US shares*) ÷ (*US pay × US shares*) to arrive at a counterfactual relative compensation that we refer to, symbolically, as "MI pay" because the only component of the counterfactual that refers to Michigan is its pay scale.

16. That is, we replace (*MI pay × MI shares*) ÷ (*US pay × US shares*) with (*US pay × MI shares*) ÷ (*US pay × US shares*) to arrive at a counterfactual relative compensation that we refer to, symbolically, as "MI shares" because the only component of the counterfactual that refers to Michigan is its industrial

employment shares.

17. At the national level we constructed both an output per labor hour series and an output per worker series for the private sector over the period 1977 to 1998. The two series were very highly correlated, with a correlation coefficient of 0.996.

18. Gross state product (GSP) is often viewed as the state equivalent to the national gross domestic product (GDP). For a brief discussion of the similarities and differences, see Beemiller and Woodruff (2000, 69).

19. The BEA series is a broader measure of employment than the Bureau of Labor Statistics nonfarm establishment employment series used earlier, but it still provides industrial detail. It includes farm and agricultural industries and covers proprietors as well as wage and salary employment.

20. Note the broad consistency in the contours of the relative productivity curve in figure 2.4 and the relative real personal income curve in figure 2.2.

21. In the terminology used in the discussion of the decomposition of average compensation, relative productivity can be defined as ($MI\ productivity \times MI\ shares$) ÷ ($US\ productivity \times US\ shares$) and the two counterfactual series are $MI\ productivity = (MI\ productivity \times US\ shares) \div (US\ productivity \times US\ shares)$ and $MI\ shares = (US\ productivity \times MI\ shares) \div (US\ productivity \times US\ shares)$.

22. These data need to be interpreted with caution. Although we believe the lack of hours data at the state level has little impact on the interpretation of industry-wide productivity trends, we do not have evidence to support or refute the same conclusion at the industry level.

23. The conventional wisdom that the transplant facilities have higher productivity performance (lower total hours per vehicle) is supported by measures compiled by Harbour and Associates (2002, 142–43).

24. The authors would like to acknowledge Donald R. Grimes and Stanley A. Sedo of the University of Michigan for their assistance with these data.

25. If the distribution of families in the top panel of table 2.8 matched the distribution of income in the lower panel, the Gini coefficient would equal zero; if one group of families received all of the income in the population, the coefficient would equal one.

26. U.S. Census Bureau (2001, 7–8).

# 3

# Population Trends in Michigan

*Kenneth J. Darga*

Economic and social trends are closely linked with demographic trends. Population changes affect the availability of labor, the demand for particular categories of goods and services, the number and types of crimes committed, the level of tax revenues, the need for social services, the amount of federal funding received by the state, and the nature of challenges faced by economic, political, financial, and administrative systems. Economic trends also influence the three fundamental demographic variables: birth rates, mortality rates, and migration rates.

Important population trends that affect Michigan's economy include the following:

- Although Michigan's population grew faster in the 1990s than in the 1980s, Michigan continues to grow more slowly than the United States as a whole.
- Many Michigan cities and villages lost population during the 1990s while many townships grew very rapidly.
- The northern Lower Peninsula continues to be the fastest-growing region of the state in percentage terms, while the most rapid absolute growth is on the periphery of the major metropolitan areas.
- The median age of Michigan's population continues to rise. The number of middle-aged per-

sons has increased and the number of young children has decreased.
- Further changes in Michigan's age structure should make the first decade of the twenty-first century more favorable than the 1990s were for the growth of major cities.
- Although Hispanic immigrants represent a smaller percentage of the population in Michigan than in the United States as a whole, the state's racial and ethnic composition continues to become more diverse.

## Growth of Michigan's Population

Michigan's population grew by 6.9% from 1990 to 2000. As shown in table 3.1, this healthy rate of growth represents a significant increase over the 0.4% growth of the 1980s, when a severe recession affected the availability of jobs in Michigan. The increase of Michigan's population in the 1990s was also higher than that of the 1970s, when Michigan gained fewer residents through international migration and lost more residents through domestic migration.

Nevertheless, Michigan's rate of growth was far lower in the 1990s than in many previous decades. Michigan's growth had been fueled by industrialization in the first three decades of the twentieth

## TABLE 3.1

### Population of Michigan and the United States, 1900–2000

| Year | United States | | Michigan | | MI as % |
|------|--------------|--------|----------|--------|---------|
| | Number | Growth | Number | Growth | of U.S. |
| 1900 | 76,212,168 | | 2,420,982 | | 3.2% |
| 1910 | 92,228,496 | 21.0% | 2,810,173 | 16.1% | 3.0% |
| 1920 | 106,021,537 | 15.0% | 3,668,412 | 30.5% | 3.5% |
| 1930 | 123,202,624 | 16.2% | 4,842,325 | 32.0% | 3.9% |
| 1940 | 132,164,569 | 7.3% | 5,256,106 | 8.5% | 4.0% |
| 1950 | 151,325,798 | 14.5% | 6,371,766 | 21.2% | 4.2% |
| 1960 | 179,323,175 | 18.5% | 7,823,194 | 22.8% | 4.4% |
| 1970 | 203,302,031 | 13.4% | 8,881,826 | 13.5% | 4.4% |
| 1980 | 226,542,199 | 11.4% | 9,262,044 | 4.3% | 4.1% |
| 1990 | 248,718,291 | 9.8% | 9,295,287 | 0.4% | 3.7% |
| 2000 | 281,421,906 | 13.1% | 9,938,444 | 6.9% | 3.5% |

SOURCE: U.S. Census Bureau, Censuses of Population and Housing, 1900 to 2000.

century and by the demand for labor in Michigan's factories during World War II. Growth in the 1950s and 1960s was primarily caused by the Baby Boom.

As shown in table 3.1 and figure 3.1, Michigan's share of the nation's population increased from 1910 to 1960, but it has decreased during each decade since 1970. Several factors contribute to this decrease:

- The long-term trend toward settlement of the West has continued. In the nineteenth century and the early twentieth century, westward movement of America's population helped to fuel Michigan's growth. In more recent

decades, however, westward movement has drawn population from Michigan to rapidly growing states such as Arizona, Colorado, Texas, and California.

- The prevalence of central air conditioning has helped to make southern climates more attractive in recent decades. This has facilitated employment growth in the South and Southwest and it has helped reverse the flow of migrants between those regions and the Midwest.
- Southern climates attract retirees from Michigan. Some retirees move to the south on a year-round basis. Others are counted by the census at their southern addresses in March, even if they spend much of the year in Michigan.[1]
- Michigan has attracted less than its share of international immigrants, particularly from Hispanic countries. Although Michigan's foreign-born population grew significantly in the 1990s, the national foreign-born population grew even more.[2] Michigan's rate of growth through migration from Latin American countries was less than one-sixth as high as the national rate.[3]
- Military service draws population from Michigan to other states. Because the U.S. Census counts military personnel at their place of current residence rather than at their state of origin, nearly all Michigan natives in the armed forces are counted as residents of other states. Michigan had less than its share of military population even before the closure of the K. I. Sawyer Air Force Base and Wurtsmith Air Force Base in the early 1990s. The percentage of adult Michigan residents reported as being on active military duty in 2000 ranks last among the fifty states.[4]

The effects of these factors can be seen in figure 3.2, which shows Michigan's estimated residual net migration by age during the 1990s.[5] Michigan had a net loss of approximately 22,500 people who were age fifty-three to seventy-five in 2000. This largely represents Michigan residents who migrated to Sun Belt states or were counted by the census at seasonal residences in Sun Belt states. Michigan also had a net loss of approximately 59,600 people who were age twenty to thirty-one in 2000. Without the absence of roughly 54,600 residents for military service, along with their children and spouses in many cases, Michigan would have gained population in this age range.[6]

## FIGURE 3.1

### Population of Michigan as Percentage of United States, 1900–2000

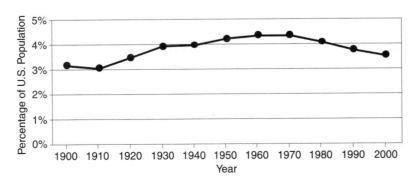

SOURCE: U.S. Census Bureau, Censuses of Population and Housing, 1900–2000.

Michigan did gain population in several age groups during the 1990s. The state had a net gain of approximately 8,200 people who were age seventy-six to eighty-four in 2000. This may represent return-migration of former residents in order to be close to family members. Michigan also had net gains of approximately 74,400 people who were age thirty-two to fifty-two in 2000, and also 114,600 people under age twenty. These gains reflect the eventual return—often with spouses and children—of many people who had previously left Michigan for military service, school, or employment in other states. They also reflect significant immigration to Michigan from foreign countries as well as the net effects of other migration in and out of Michigan for economic or personal reasons.

Future changes in Michigan's share of the nation's population will depend upon several factors. A nationwide decrease in the rate of international immigration would tend to slow the decrease of Michigan's population share, since Michigan and other Midwestern states tend to attract less than their share of new immigrants. Recessions, on the other hand, have generally tended to accelerate the decline of Michigan's population share. It must be noted, however, that not all recessions have an equal effect. The recession of the early 1980s caused a significant drop in Michigan's population share because it reduced employment more severely in the Midwest than in much of the rest of the country.[7] The recession of the early 1990s, on the other hand, had less effect upon migration out of Michigan because Michigan's rate of unemployment remained close to the national rate. The recession of the early 2000s appears to be similar; in October 2002, Michigan's unemployment rate of 5.6% was very close to the national rate of 5.7%.[8]

## Geographic Distribution of Michigan's Population

More than half of Michigan's population—54.7% in 2000—lives in cities and villages, which are represented as white areas in figure 3.3. The remaining 45.3% of Michigan's population lives in the portions of townships outside village limits. After growing in the first half of the twentieth century, the percentage of Michigan's population in cities and villages has declined since 1960, and even the absolute number of people in cities and villages has declined since 1970. (See figure 3.4.) The total

**FIGURE 3.2**

**Estimated Residual Net Migration by Age for Michigan, 1990–2000**

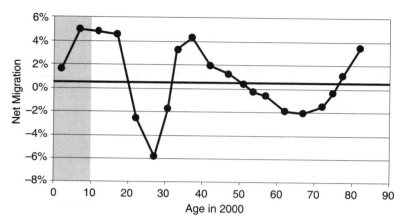

SOURCE: Calculations are based on data from the U.S. Census Bureau (modified age/race/sex counts from the 1990 Census, and Summary File 1 from the 2000 Census), the Michigan Department of Community Health (quarterly counts of births for April 1990 through March 2000) and the National Center for Health Statistics (life table for 1990).

NOTE: Residual migration rates for children under age ten are based on less than ten years of migration, and they are therefore not fully comparable to rates for other age groups. For example, net migration for children born in the twelve months prior to the census tends to be very low because there has been little time for migration to occur.

**FIGURE 3.3**

**Michigan Cities and Villages, 2000**

SOURCE: Center for Geographic Information, Michigan Department of Information Technology.

## FIGURE 3.4

**Population Inside and Outside City and Village Boundaries, 1960–2000**

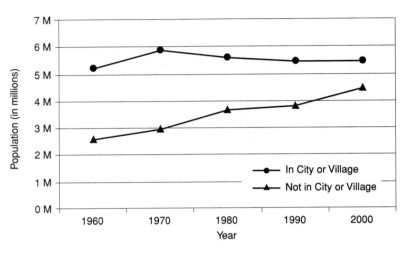

SOURCE: U.S. Census Bureau, Censuses of Population and Housing, 1960–2000.

## FIGURE 3.5

**Categories of Metropolitan and Nonmetropolitan Counties in Michigan (as defined for 2000 based on the 1990 Census)**

SOURCE: Center for Geographic Information, Michigan Department of Information Technology.

population of Michigan's cities and villages decreased by 0.4% in the 1990s, following decreases of 2.0% in the 1980s and 5.7% in the 1970s. Out of 535 cities and villages in Michigan, 216 declined in population from 1990 to 2000 and another 115 grew by less than 5%. In contrast, the total population outside city and village boundaries increased by 17.4% during the 1990s. Several factors contribute to these trends:[9]

• Limited-access highways, affluence, and movement of jobs from central cities to suburbs have combined to make it feasible for more people to move a greater distance from major urban cores.

• Many cities and villages do not have vacant land for residential development. People who wish to build a new house must then seek building sites outside the city or village limits.

• People are attracted to townships by the prospect of less congestion, larger lots, lower land prices, rural lifestyles, and better schools.

• Household size has decreased in most communities, as families have fewer children and as a larger percentage of the population reaches an age where children have moved out of the house or householders live alone. In communities that have little or no vacant land for development, such decreases in household size result in decreases in population, since they cannot be offset by people moving into new housing.

• There was a decline between 1990 and 2000 in the number of people in key age groups that tend to live disproportionately in cities—young adults and their preschool children. This will be discussed further in the section of this chapter on age distribution.

Population distribution can also be analyzed in terms of the metropolitan classifications of counties. Based on population density and commuting patterns in the 1990 Census, Michigan has twenty-five metropolitan counties and fifty-eight nonmetropolitan counties. As shown in figure 3.5, metropolitan counties can be divided into "central" and "fringe" categories, depending on how much of their population is located in cities that have been designated by the Census Bureau as "central cities."[10] Nonmetropolitan counties can be distinguished according to location in the southern Lower Peninsula, northern Lower Peninsula, or Upper Peninsula.

Despite the movement of population from

cities, 50% of Michigan's population still lives in the thirteen metropolitan counties that contain central cities. (See figure 3.6.) This represents a gradual decline from a peak of 65% living in the same counties in 1950. (See table 3.2.) Another 32% of Michigan's population lives in twelve "metropolitan fringe" counties, for a total of 82% in metropolitan areas as a whole. This is a slight decrease from the peak of 85% living in the same counties in 1970.

The thirteen central metropolitan counties grew fastest from 1900 through 1930, as Michigan was becoming a major industrial state. (See figure 3.7.) These counties grew much more slowly during the Great Depression, but rapid growth resumed from 1940 to 1950 as World War II brought new workers into Michigan's factories. Growth then tapered off as population shifted from central cities to suburbs. The central metropolitan counties declined somewhat in size from 1970 to 1990, but growth resumed in the 1990s. The twelve metropolitan fringe counties follow a similar pattern, except for a higher rate of growth since 1930 and peak growth rates that occurred ten years after the peaks for the central counties.

The remaining 18% of Michigan's population lives in fifty-eight nonmetropolitan counties. As shown in table 3.2 and figure 3.8, the population of the nonmetropolitan counties of the southern Lower Peninsula has increased at a fairly steady pace since 1930, rising to 8% of the state total in 2000. The nonmetropolitan counties of the northern Lower Peninsula have followed a similar pattern, but with a higher level of population loss prior to 1930 and a higher level of growth in recent decades. Since 1970, this group of counties has had a higher rate of growth than any of the other four groups. Nevertheless, these twenty-seven counties still represent only 6.4% of Michigan's population, up from 4.2% in 1960. These counties had accounted for over 12% of Michigan's population in 1900, before industrialization drew much of their population to urban communities in the southern portion of the state. It was not until after 1960 that this group of counties finally surpassed the population level it had reached in the census of 1910.

Factors contributing to growth of the northern Lower Peninsula include the following:

- Low land and housing costs in most communities.
- Less crowding than in metropolitan areas.
- Scenic beauty and outdoor recreational resources.

**FIGURE 3.6**

**Population Distribution by Category of County, 2000**

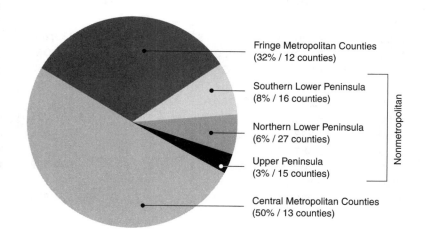

Fringe Metropolitan Counties (32% / 12 counties)

Southern Lower Peninsula (8% / 16 counties)

Northern Lower Peninsula (6% / 27 counties)

Upper Peninsula (3% / 15 counties)

Nonmetropolitan

Central Metropolitan Counties (50% / 13 counties)

SOURCE: U.S. Census Bureau, 2000 Census, Summary File 1. County classifications are based on geographic location, metropolitan status in 2000, and percentage of 1990 population in designated central cities.

**FIGURE 3.7**

**Growth of Central and Fringe Metropolitan Counties, 1900–2000**

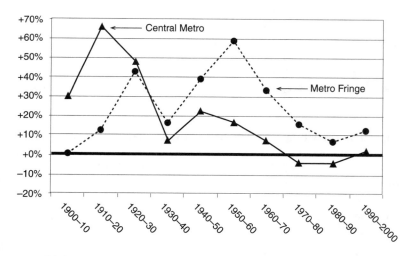

SOURCE: U.S. Census Bureau, Censuses of Population and Housing, 1900–2000. County classifications are based on geographic location, metropolitan status in 2000, and percentage of 1990 population in designated central cities.

- Improved employment opportunities relative to previous decades.
- Return-migration by people who had left northern Michigan in prior decades.
- Permanent in-migration by people who had previously been seasonal residents.

**TABLE 3.2**

## Population Counts by Category of County, 1900–2000

| Year | STATE Total | METROPOLITAN Subtotal | Central | Fringe | NONMETROPOLITAN Subtotal | South L.P. | North L.P. | U.P. |
|---|---|---|---|---|---|---|---|---|
| 1900 | 2,420,982 | 1,424,263 | 993,977 | 430,286 | 996,719 | 438,694 | 296,663 | 261,362 |
| 1910 | 2,810,173 | 1,720,587 | 1,289,538 | 431,049 | 1,089,586 | 435,414 | 328,544 | 325,628 |
| 1920 | 3,668,412 | 2,628,946 | 2,146,196 | 482,750 | 1,039,466 | 424,817 | 282,093 | 332,556 |
| 1930 | 4,842,325 | 3,857,254 | 3,168,967 | 688,287 | 985,071 | 415,649 | 250,746 | 318,676 |
| 1940 | 5,256,106 | 4,204,933 | 3,404,891 | 800,042 | 1,051,173 | 444,286 | 283,343 | 323,544 |
| 1950 | 6,371,766 | 5,279,388 | 4,172,367 | 1,107,021 | 1,092,378 | 487,972 | 302,148 | 302,258 |
| 1960 | 7,823,194 | 6,631,977 | 4,877,149 | 1,754,828 | 1,191,217 | 556,763 | 328,502 | 305,952 |
| 1970 | 8,881,826 | 7,565,309 | 5,231,147 | 2,334,162 | 1,316,517 | 628,205 | 383,965 | 304,347 |
| 1980 | 9,262,044 | 7,718,795 | 5,028,893 | 2,689,902 | 1,543,249 | 726,779 | 496,713 | 319,757 |
| 1990 | 9,295,287 | 7,697,653 | 4,836,456 | 2,861,197 | 1,597,634 | 745,185 | 538,534 | 313,915 |
| 2000 | 9,938,444 | 8,169,466 | 4,944,586 | 3,224,880 | 1,768,978 | 816,894 | 634,468 | 317,616 |

## Population Shares by Category of County, 1900–2000

| Year | STATE Total | METROPOLITAN Subtotal | Central | Fringe | NONMETROPOLITAN Subtotal | South L.P. | North L.P. | U.P. |
|---|---|---|---|---|---|---|---|---|
| 1900 | 100.0% | 58.8% | 41.1% | 17.8% | 41.2% | 18.1% | 12.3% | 10.8% |
| 1910 | 100.0% | 61.2% | 45.9% | 15.3% | 38.8% | 15.5% | 11.7% | 11.6% |
| 1920 | 100.0% | 71.7% | 58.5% | 13.2% | 28.3% | 11.6% | 7.7% | 9.1% |
| 1930 | 100.0% | 79.7% | 65.4% | 14.2% | 20.3% | 8.6% | 5.2% | 6.6% |
| 1940 | 100.0% | 80.0% | 64.8% | 15.2% | 20.0% | 8.5% | 5.4% | 6.2% |
| 1950 | 100.0% | 82.9% | 65.5% | 17.4% | 17.1% | 7.7% | 4.7% | 4.7% |
| 1960 | 100.0% | 84.8% | 62.3% | 22.4% | 15.2% | 7.1% | 4.2% | 3.9% |
| 1970 | 100.0% | 85.2% | 58.9% | 26.3% | 14.8% | 7.1% | 4.3% | 3.4% |
| 1980 | 100.0% | 83.3% | 54.3% | 29.0% | 16.7% | 7.8% | 5.4% | 3.5% |
| 1990 | 100.0% | 82.8% | 52.0% | 30.8% | 17.2% | 8.0% | 5.8% | 3.4% |
| 2000 | 100.0% | 82.2% | 49.8% | 32.4% | 17.8% | 8.2% | 6.4% | 3.2% |

## Population Growth by Category of County, 1900–2000

| Interval | STATE Total | METROPOLITAN Subtotal | Central | Fringe | NONMETROPOLITAN Subtotal | South L.P. | North L.P. | U.P. |
|---|---|---|---|---|---|---|---|---|
| 1900–10 | 16.1% | 20.8% | 29.7% | 0.2% | 9.3% | –0.7% | 10.7% | 24.6% |
| 1910–20 | 30.5% | 52.8% | 66.4% | 12.0% | –4.6% | –2.4% | –14.1% | 2.1% |
| 1920–30 | 32.0% | 46.7% | 47.7% | 42.6% | –5.2% | –2.2% | –11.1% | –4.2% |
| 1930–40 | 8.5% | 9.0% | 7.4% | 16.2% | 6.7% | 6.9% | 13.0% | 1.5% |
| 1940–50 | 21.2% | 25.6% | 22.5% | 38.4% | 3.9% | 9.8% | 6.6% | –6.6% |
| 1950–60 | 22.8% | 25.6% | 16.9% | 58.5% | 9.0% | 14.1% | 8.7% | 1.2% |
| 1960–70 | 13.5% | 14.1% | 7.3% | 33.0% | 10.5% | 12.8% | 16.9% | –0.5% |
| 1970–80 | 4.3% | 2.0% | –3.9% | 15.2% | 17.2% | 15.7% | 29.4% | 5.1% |
| 1980–90 | 0.4% | –0.3% | –3.8% | 6.4% | 3.5% | 2.5% | 8.4% | –1.8% |
| 1990–2000 | 6.9% | 6.1% | 2.2% | 12.7% | 10.7% | 9.6% | 17.8% | 1.2% |

SOURCE: U.S. Census Bureau, Censuses of Population and Housing, 1900–2000. County classifications are based on geographic location, metropolitan status in 2000, and percentage of 1990 population in designated central cities.

The population of the Upper Peninsula has been remarkably stable since 1910, with decades of modest population gain alternating with decades of modest population loss. (See figure 3.9.) Although the Upper Peninsula's population count changed by only 2.5% from 1910 to 2000, its percentage of the state's population declined from a peak of 11.6% in 1910 to only 3.2% in 2000. In addition to the factors listed previously in connection with the northern Lower Peninsula, the population of the Upper Peninsula is affected by:

- Fluctuations in the level of mining and lumbering activity.
- Migration of young people to other areas for education and employment.
- Low numbers of births, reflecting past out-migration of young adults to other areas. In 2001, eleven of the fifteen counties of the Upper Peninsula had fewer births than deaths.

Although the difference between 18% growth in the northern Lower Peninsula and 1% growth in the Upper Peninsula seems dramatic, it should be noted that the 1980s and 1990s were only the second and third decades since 1900 in which the highest and lowest growth rates among the five county groups differed by less than 30 percentage points. The 1990s were only the third decade since 1900 in which none of the five groups of counties experienced a population decline.

## Trends in Age Distribution

Changes in age distribution have very important effects upon public institutions and the economy. The demand for K–12 education, higher education, jobs, prisons, health resources, income maintenance programs, and housing are all influenced by changes in the number of people in different age groups. Because these changes tend to be slow and fairly predictable—the people who will be ten years of age and older in 2010 were already born by 2000—we can learn a lot about the future by studying Michigan's current population and the pattern of changes in its age structure over time.

## Michigan's Current Age Structure

The distribution of Michigan's population by age and sex in 2000 is illustrated by the "population

**FIGURE 3.8**

**Growth of Nonmetropolitan Counties of the Lower Peninsula, 1900–2000**

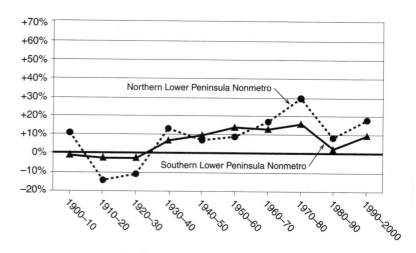

SOURCE: U.S. Census Bureau, Censuses of Population and Housing, 1900–2000. County classifications are based on geographic location and metropolitan status in 2000.

**FIGURE 3.9**

**Growth of the Upper Peninsula, 1900–2000**

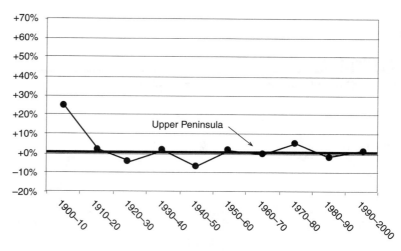

SOURCE: U.S. Census Bureau, Censuses of Population and Housing, 1900–2000.

pyramid" in figure 3.10. The youngest age groups are shown at the bottom of the pyramid, males are on the left, and females are on the right. This figure reflects the demographic history of the entire twentieth century—some of the people in the top bar for 2000 were in the bottom bar of the population pyramid for 1900—and the shape of the pyramid reflects changes in the pattern of births, deaths, and migration over the past one hundred years. Michigan's pyramid for 2000 had

**FIGURE 3.10**

**Michigan Population by Age and Sex, 2000**

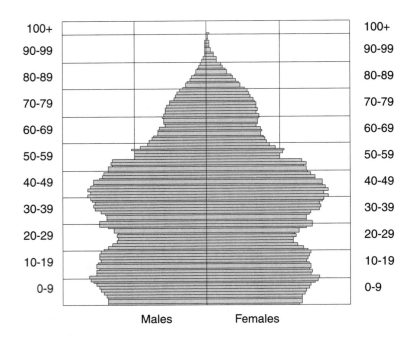

SOURCE: U.S. Census Bureau, 2000 Census, Summary File 2.

**FIGURE 3.11**

**United States Population by Age and Sex, 2000**

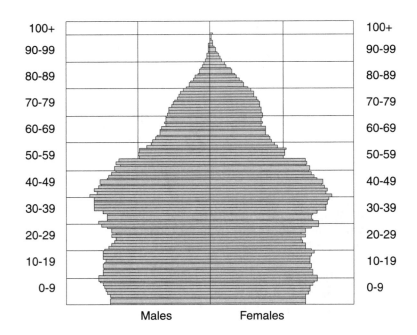

SOURCE: U.S. Census Bureau, 2000 Census, Summary File 2.

two major bulges, representing a large number of school-age children and a large number of middle-aged persons born during the Baby Boom. There were also three significant constrictions of the pyramid. The relatively small number of preschool children and the small number of young adults are obvious, and the number of people age fifty-four to sixty-nine was also relatively small. Michigan's age structure is very similar to that of the nation as a whole, which is shown in figure 3.11.

## Aging of Michigan's Population

The most important trend with respect to Michigan's age distribution is that the population is getting older. The percentage of Michigan residents over age sixty-five has increased throughout the past century, and it is projected to increase considerably in the first decades of the twentieth century as well. (See figure 3.12.) There are many misconceptions and misunderstandings about this aging trend. In order to understand what is happening, why it is happening, and what it will mean, it is essential to examine changes in age structure from a historical perspective.

Figure 3.13 shows the growth rate of Michigan's population over age sixty-five for each decade from 1900 to 2020. This chart shows that, contrary to a popular misconception, rapid growth of the elderly population is not a new phenomenon. In fact, the number of people over age sixty-five grew faster in each of the preceding nine decades than in the 1990s. The rate of growth for this age group was even higher from the 1920s through the 1950s than it is projected to be between 2010 and 2020, when the first half of the Baby Boom turns sixty-five. This provides an important clue for understanding Michigan's aging population. We obviously need to look beyond simplistic explanations—such as "people are living longer now"—in order to understand the aging of Michigan's population.

## Historical Changes in Age Structure

Figure 3.14 illustrates changes in Michigan's age structure from 1900 to 2000. The triangular shape of Michigan's population pyramid for 1900 is typical of rapidly growing areas. It reflects all three of the basic demographic variables:

- As each age group becomes older and moves up the pyramid over time, mortality tends to make it a little bit smaller. Although this contributes to the overall triangular shape of this population pyramid, it is not the primary explanation. Even in the years leading up to 1900, when maternal mortality, infant mortality, and deaths from infectious diseases were much more common than they are today, mortality was a dominant factor only at the top of the pyramid, where high death rates reduce the number of elderly people.

- High birth rates are a much more important explanation for the overall shape of this pyramid. Over a long period of time in which the average woman has more than two children, the number of children born each year tends to be higher than the number born the year before. This causes the entire pyramid to take on a triangular shape.

- The most important factor explaining the shape of this pyramid is migration. In the years leading up to 1900, Michigan had been receiving a large number of immigrants from other countries as well as migrants from eastern states. Each year, migration would primarily increase the number of young adults and children in the bottom half of the pyramid. Then, when everyone grew older and moved up a notch in the pyramid, the bottom half would increase again. Over a long period of time, this also caused the entire pyramid to take on a triangular shape.

The shape of the pyramid for 1930 is quite similar. The broadening at the base of the pyramid is somewhat less pronounced than in 1900, reflecting somewhat lower rates of birth and immigration. Nevertheless, these demographic forces were still causing Michigan to grow at a rapid rate and to increase its share of the nation's population. Although all of the population pyramids are the same overall size, since they are based on percentages of the total population, it is important to note that the pyramid for 1930 represents twice as many people as the pyramid for 1900. The large age groups toward the bottom of the 1900 pyramid—augmented by new immigration—moved up six slots by 1930 to displace the smaller age groups ahead of them. At the same time, the bottom six bars were replaced by even larger numbers of people born between 1900 and 1930.

Thus, the large increase in the population over age sixty-five from 1900 to 1930 cannot simply be

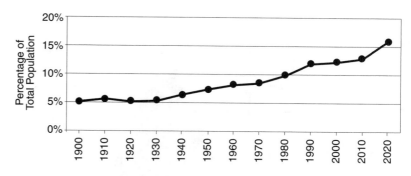

**FIGURE 3.12**

**Population over Age 65 as Percentage of Total: Michigan, 1900–2020**

SOURCE: U.S. Census Bureau: Censuses of Population and Housing, 1900–2000; *Population Projections for States by Age, Sex, Race, and Hispanic Origin: 1995–2025*, Report PPL-47, October 1996.

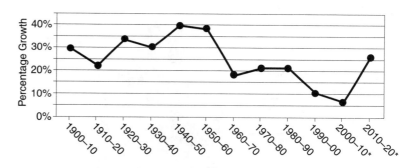

**FIGURE 3.13**

**Intercensal Growth Rates of Population over Age 65: Michigan, 1900–2020**

SOURCE: U.S. Census Bureau: Censuses of Population and Housing, 1900–2000; *Population Projections for States by Age, Sex, Race, and Hispanic Origin: 1995–2025*, Report PPL-47, October 1996.

attributed to people living longer. Rather, it reflects the upward movement of large bars from the bottom of the pyramid. In other words, it reflects more births between 1835 and 1865 than between 1805 and 1835, as well as many decades of net immigration by young people who subsequently turned sixty-five by 1930. This same principle also explains subsequent fluctuations in the growth rate of Michigan's elderly population.

The shape of the pyramid for 1960 reflects dramatic demographic events that will continue to affect Michigan's age distribution for many decades to come. The Great Depression in the 1930s caused a sharp decrease in the number of births and a very sharp decrease in the level of immigration from foreign countries.[11] The Depression was followed by World War II, which also

**FIGURE 3.14**

## Population Pyramids for Michigan, 1900–2000

### 1900

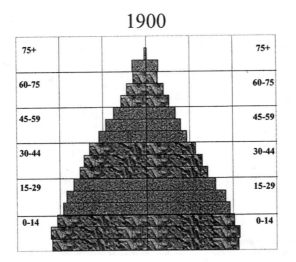

### 1930

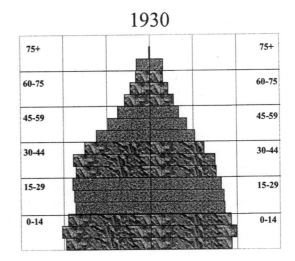

### 1960

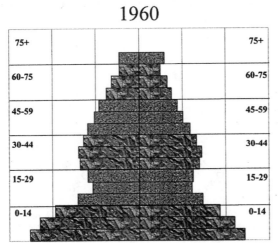

### 1990

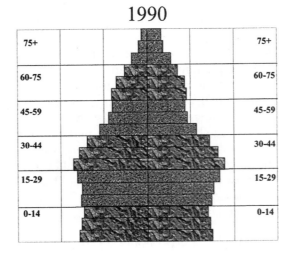

### 2000

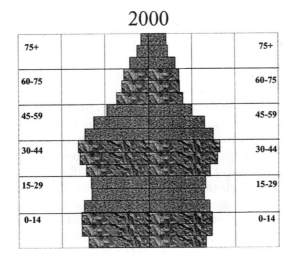

SOURCE: U.S. Census Bureau, Censuses of Population and Housing, 1900–2000.

depressed levels of birth and immigration. People born from 1930 to 1945 are represented by short bars in the population pyramid, and they were age fifteen to thirty in 1960. World War II was followed by the Baby Boom, which lasted roughly from 1946 to 1965. In addition to older couples having children that had been postponed during previous years, young people tended to marry at an earlier age and desire larger families during this period. The first fifteen years of the Baby Boom are represented by the long bars for ages zero to fourteen in the pyramid for 1960.

This population pyramid for 1960 helps to explain some of the major economic trends of the 1960s and 1970s. The small number of people who were born during the Depression and World War II—people who were age fifteen to twenty-nine in 1960 and twenty to thirty-four in 1965—contributed to a fairly tight labor market and low unemployment during the 1960s. This demographic situation was reversed in the 1970s, however, when people born in the Baby Boom entered the labor market and the participation of women in the labor force increased. Because of these rapid increases in the labor force, unemployment rates were generally higher in the 1970s than in the 1960s, even though the number of jobs rose rapidly during the 1970s.

The Baby Boom was followed by a Baby Bust, which can be seen as a constriction in the population pyramids for 1990 and 2000. In addition to reflecting a later age at marriage and lower desired family sizes, the transition from Baby Boom to Baby Bust was an echo of the decline in births during the Great Depression and World War II. By 1965, the population in the reproductive years consisted largely of the small generation born during that era. The Baby Bust then continued as the average age at marriage decreased further and members of the Baby Boom generation did not fully replace themselves. In addition, a significant portion of Michigan's Baby Boom generation moved to other states as young adults during the recession of the early 1980s. This also contributed to a low number of births in the 1980s. Effects of the Baby Bust were generally the opposite of the effects of the Baby Boom. When this small generation entered the job market in the late 1980s and the 1990s, low levels of unemployment became easier to achieve and labor shortages eventually began to develop.

The Baby Bust was followed by an echo of the Baby Boom, which can be seen as a small bulge in the number of children in the pyramids for 1990 and 2000. This bulge also reflects a substantial number of immigrants and children of immigrants. At the very bottom of the pyramid for 2000 is a new decrease in the number of children—yet another echo of the Great Depression and World War II.

## Implications of Michigan's Current Age Structure

Due primarily to high levels of birth and migration prior to the Great Depression, the number of people over age seventy in 2000 was higher than the number of people over age seventy in previous years. As these people continue to age, they will contribute to the demand for health services, social services, and assisted living situations.[12] At the same time, however, the small generation born from 1930 to 1945 will have a moderating effect on the demand for such services. Since this generation was age fifty-four to seventy in 2000, the number of people turning sixty-five has been relatively low since 1995, and it will remain low until 2010. In addition to holding down the demand for health-related services, the small size of this generation is temporarily reducing pressure on retirement systems and reducing the number of job vacancies due to retirement.

The large generation age thirty-five to fifty-three in 2000 will continue to have a powerful effect upon the economy as they grow older during the first decade of the twenty-first century. They will continue to be a large component of the workforce and make a large contribution to consumer spending and saving. They will also contribute to an increase in the demand for health services and related services, particularly after 2010, but their impact at that time will be offset to some extent by the small generation that will then be displacing a larger generation in the oldest age groups. They will also begin to increase pressure on retirement systems after 2010.

In addition to contributing to an extended period of generally low unemployment as they entered the workforce, the relatively small size of the generation age twenty to thirty-four in 2000 helped contribute to lower crime rates and lower demand for some categories of social services during the late 1980s and the 1990s.[13] However, they are being replaced after 2000 by a somewhat larger generation that was age five to nineteen in 2000. On the one hand, this is tending to alleviate labor shortages as more new workers begin to make a contribution to the labor force. Availability of

FIGURE 3.15

**Population Pyramids for Selected Counties**

## Midland County, 2000

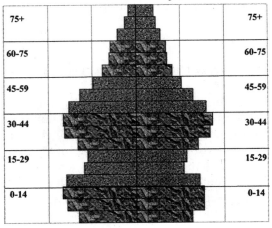

## Roscommon County, 2000

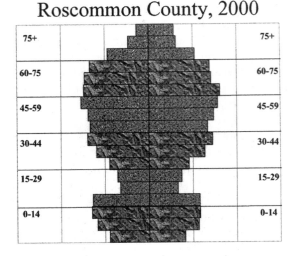

## Ionia County, 2000

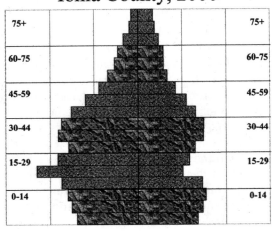

## Ingham County, 2000

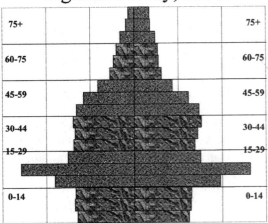

SOURCE: U.S. Census Bureau, 2000 Census, Summary File 1.

workers is likely to be a particularly important issue after 2010, when Baby Boomers begin to retire in large numbers. On the other hand, increases in the number of young adults are likely to have negative effects upon unemployment, crime, and demand for certain social services during roughly the first fifteen years of the century.

The relatively small number of children under age five in 2000—which reflects the small number of young adults at that time—has contributed to a relatively low demand for social services and other services aimed at young children. This will cause downward trends in school enrollment as this small cohort passes through the K–12 educational system after 2000, and it may affect college enrollment after 2013.[14] However, it should be noted that the number of births may not remain at this very low level for long. When the somewhat larger generation that was age five to nineteen in 2000 passes through its prime child-bearing years over the coming decades, it is likely to cause another small echo of the Baby Boom.

### Local Variations in Age Structure

Age structure varies considerably from one city or county to another. Some counties have an age structure similar to that of the state as a whole, as illustrated by the pyramid for Midland County in figure 3.15. Other counties—particularly in the northern half of the state—have a preponderance of older people. This reflects many decades of losing young people to metropolitan areas for jobs and education, coupled with several decades of attracting many middle-aged people and retirees. The age pyramid for Roscommon County in figure 3.15 is typical of many such counties.

Several counties are strongly affected by special population groups, such as prisoners or college students. For example, the preponderance of adult males in Ionia County reflects the presence of several state prisons, and the large number of young adults in Ingham County reflects enrollment at Michigan State University. (See figure 3.15.)

There are important differences in age structure between central cities and many of the suburbs and fringe areas that surround them. Central cities tend to attract many young people who are finding their first full-time jobs, having their first children, and living in rented housing or buying their first homes. However, central cities tend to lose somewhat older residents who move to outlying areas in search of different schools, newer and larger homes, or larger parcels of land. Cities therefore tend to have a relative preponderance of young adults and preschool children, while older adults and older children are often underrepresented.

The population pyramids for Lansing and Flint are fairly representative of central cities. The light pyramids in figure 3.16 represent local age distributions, and the statewide pyramids are shown in dark shading for purposes of comparison. When the statewide pyramids are placed on top of the local pyramids, as shown on the right side of figure 3.16, the light tips on some of the bars indicate age groups that are overrepresented in the local area. When the statewide pyramids are placed behind the local pyramids, as shown on the left, the dark tips on some of the bars indicate age groups that are underrepresented in the local area.

As would be expected, many suburban and outlying communities follow the opposite pattern. Young adults and young children tend to be underrepresented relative to the statewide pattern, while middle-aged adults and older children tend to be overrepresented. Figure 3.17 compares the statewide age distribution to that of Ada Township (a community east of Grand Rapids), DeWitt (a small city north of Lansing), and Hamburg Township (a rapidly growing community in

Livingston County). All of the local pyramids in this figure have bulges and constrictions at the same ages as the statewide pyramids, but the magnitudes of those bulges and constrictions are much greater.

These patterns have important implications for the growth rates of central cities and their outlying suburbs. The age groups that gravitate toward central cities were relatively small statewide by 2000 while the age groups that tend to live in outlying suburbs were large. This age distribution favored growth of outlying areas at the expense of central cities in the years leading up to the 2000 Census. That situation will gradually reverse during the decade after 2000. The relatively large number of people who were age five through nineteen in 2000 will be reaching ages when they will be having their first jobs, their first children, and their first homes. In many cases, this will involve moving from outlying communities to central cities. At the same time, there will be a drop in the number of people who will be reaching middle age or school age. Thus, there will be fewer people to move out of central cities and fuel growth of outlying areas.

## Racial and Ethnic Diversity

Both Michigan and the United States as a whole became more racially diverse during the twentieth century. This trend is largely attributable to international and interstate migration. Differences in fertility rates have also played a significant role—since the early 1970s, fertility rates for whites have been below replacement levels.[15]

Statistics about racial and ethnic background are not absolutely precise. Major shortcomings of the data in the early twentieth century include lack of information on the small Hispanic population, incomplete coverage of American Indians and other race groups by the census, and underreporting of American Indian race by those who did participate in the census. A major limitation of the data for 2000 is the uncertainty introduced by the option of reporting more than one race.

Non-Hispanic whites have gradually declined from 99% of Michigan's population in the 1910 Census to 79% or 80% in the 2000 Census.[16] Throughout this period, nonwhites and Hispanics have comprised a larger percentage of the population for the nation as a whole than for Michigan. Nationwide, non-Hispanic whites decreased from somewhat less than 89% of the population in 1910

FIGURE 3.16

**Age Structure of Selected Central Cities Compared to Statewide Age Structure for 2000**

## Central Cities (total)

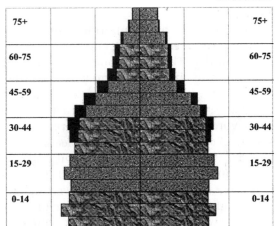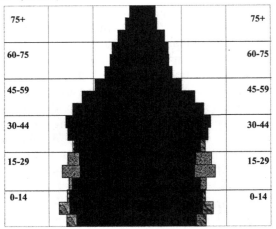

## Lansing

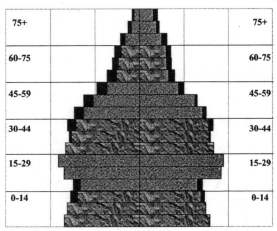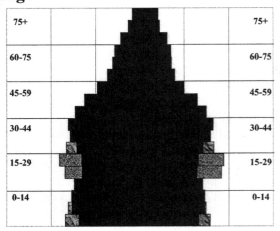

## Flint

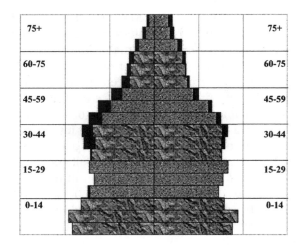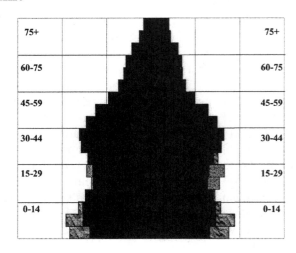

SOURCE: U.S. Census Bureau, 2000 Census, Summary File 1.

**FIGURE 3.17**

**Age Structure of Selected Communities Outside Central Cities Compared to Statewide Age Structure for 2000**

## Ada Township

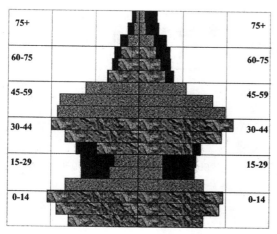

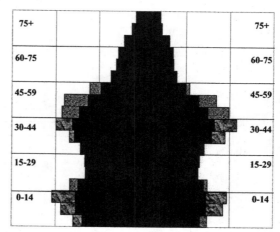

## Dewitt City

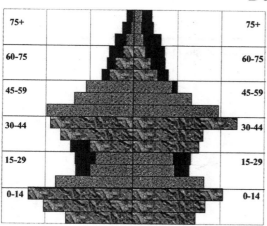

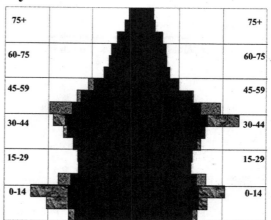

## Hamburg Township

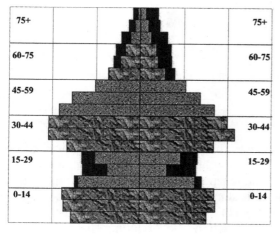

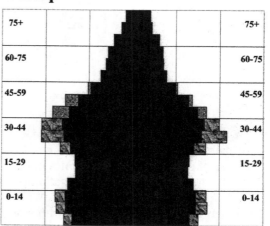

SOURCE: U.S. Census Bureau, 2000 Census, Summary File 1.

**FIGURE 3.18**

**Non-Hispanic Whites as a Percentage of Total Population in Michigan and the United States, 1900–2000**

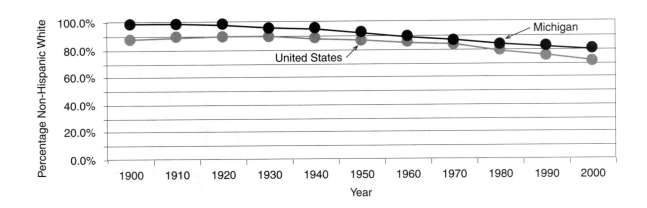

SOURCE: U.S. Census Bureau: Census 2000 Modified Race Data Summary File; Modified Age, Race, and Sex Data from the 1990 Census; Historical Census Statistics on Population Totals By Race, 1790 to 1990, and By Hispanic Origin, September 2002, Working Paper Series No. 56.

**FIGURE 3.19**

**Distribution of Michigan and U.S. Population by Race and Hispanic Origin in 2000**

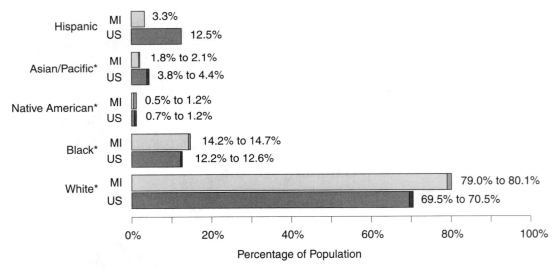

SOURCE: U.S. Census Bureau, Census 2000 Modified Race Data Summary File.

to approximately 70% in 2000.[17] The combined percentage of nonwhites and Hispanics in Michigan in 2000 was about equal to the national percentage for 1980. (See figure 3.18.)

Michigan ranks first in the nation with respect to the percentage of its population reporting Dutch ancestry (4.8%) and its percentage reporting Arab ancestry (1.2%). The state's percentage reporting Polish ancestry (8.6%) ranks second in the nation.

People in these ancestry categories would generally classify themselves as non-Hispanic whites. The state's percentage of residents reported as black is somewhat higher than the national percentage (14.2% to 14.7% in Michigan versus 12.2% to 12.6% nationwide, excluding Hispanic blacks). However, Michigan ranks much lower with respect to two of the fastest-growing minority groups. The percentage of the population reporting Hispanic

**FIGURE 3.20**

## Michigan Population by Race, 1900–2000

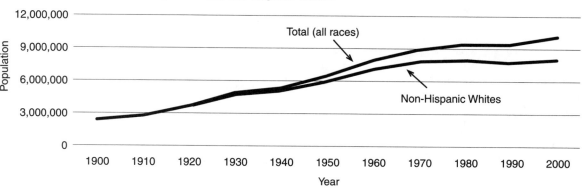

**Panel A: Total Populaton and Non-Hispanic Whites**

Total (all races)

Non-Hispanic Whites

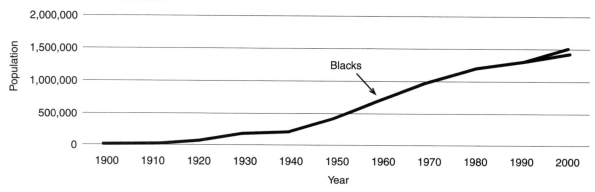

**Panel B: Blacks**

Blacks

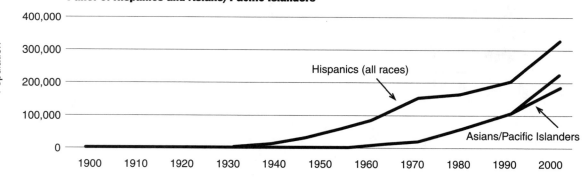

**Panel C: Hispanics and Asians/Pacific Islanders**

Hispanics (all races)

Asians/Pacific Islanders

SOURCE: U.S. Census Bureau: Census 2000 Modified Race Data Summary File; Modified Age, Race, and Sex Data from the 1990 Census; Historical Census Statistics on Population Totals By Race, 1790 to 1990, and By Hispanic Origin, September 2002, Working Paper Series No. 56.

origin is almost four times as high in the nation as a whole as in the state (12.5% nationwide versus 3.3% in Michigan). The percentage of the population reporting Asian or Pacific races is about twice as high in the nation as a whole as in the state (3.8% to 4.4% nationwide versus 1.8% to 2.1% in Michigan, excluding Hispanic Asians and Pacific Islanders). Figure 3.19 compares the population

shares of Hispanics and major race groups in Michigan and the United States.

Figure 3.20 illustrates the historic growth of Michigan's Hispanic population and selected race categories. In the top panel, the space between the "Total" line and the "Non-Hispanic Whites" line represents the growth of Michigan's minority population. The middle panel shows that Michi-

**FIGURE 3.21**

**Minority Population of Michigan Census Tracts, 2000**

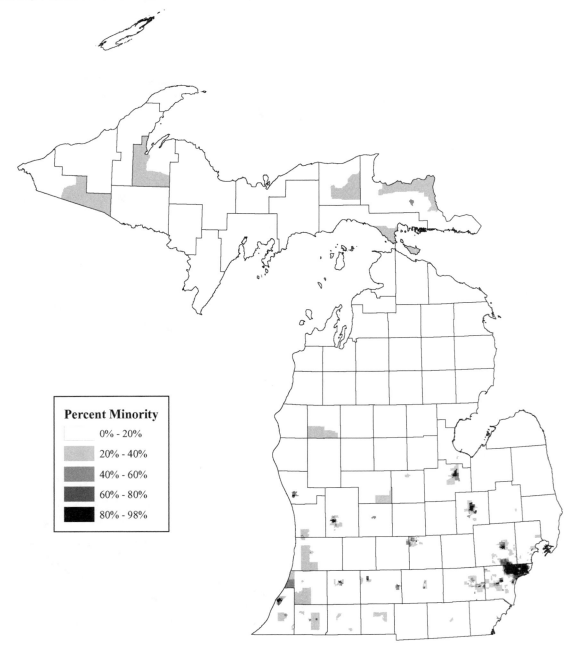

SOURCE: U.S. Census Bureau, Census 2000, Summary File 1, Table P4. Michigan Center for Geographic Information.

gan's black population grew fastest from 1940 to 1980, when many blacks were attracted from southern states to jobs in Michigan cities. The divergence at the tip of the line indicates the difference between including and excluding persons who reported in 2000 that they were black in combination with other races. The bottom panel shows the dramatic growth of Michigan's Hispanic and Asian/Pacific population. Michigan's His-

panic population grew by 61% during the 1990s, but it should be noted that such growth is not a new phenomenon. In fact, Michigan's Hispanic population grew faster in percentage terms during each decade from 1940 to 1970 than in the 1990s. Michigan's Asian/ Pacific population has been growing rapidly only since 1960, but since that time its growth has exceeded even that of the Hispanic population in percentage terms. Michigan's Asian/Pacific population grew faster than its Hispanic population in numeric terms as well in the 1970s and 1980s.

Divergence at the tips of the lines represents the difference between including and excluding persons reporting the indicated race in combination with other races in 2000.

Minority population groups are not distributed uniformly across the state. The shaded areas of figure 3.21 represent census tracts with higher percentages of minority population than the state as a whole. Although the term "minority population" is used here to refer only to non-whites and Hispanics, it should be remembered that several other ethnic groups can also be considered minorities. The Arab and Chaldean populations of metropolitan Detroit are important examples of minority groups that are classified as "non-Hispanic white." Such groups are not classified as races on the census, and data about them are limited and incomplete. They are therefore left out of most counts of the minority population.

Many of Michigan's minority groups—particularly blacks—tend to be concentrated in or near central cities. Nevertheless, there are significant concentrations of blacks in some non-metropolitan areas, such as Lake County and Cass County. Hispanics tend to be somewhat less concentrated around major cities, and significant concentrations of American Indians are located in rural areas of Michigan. Since individual state prisons tend to reflect the racial distribution of the entire state prison system rather than that of the communities in which they are located, concentrations of minority groups also appear in census tracts that contain state prisons. Out of 580 census tracts in which more than one-third of the population is non-white or Hispanic, only five are located outside metropolitan areas. Three of those five tracts contain state prisons.

The Detroit tri-county area has significant concentrations of many minority groups, as illustrated by figures 3.22 and 3.23. The shaded areas of these figures represent census tracts with higher percentages of the indicated races than the state as a whole. High percentages of blacks reside in most parts of Detroit itself and in down-river neighborhoods adjacent to Detroit, Inkster, Pontiac, southern Oakland county, and several other communities. Hispanics are the predominant ethnic group in the southern portion of Detroit, and there are also fairly high concentrations of Hispanics in northern Pontiac and adjacent townships. The Asian/Pacific population of

**FIGURE 3.22**

**Minority Population of Michigan Census Tracts in Detroit Tri-County Area, 2000**

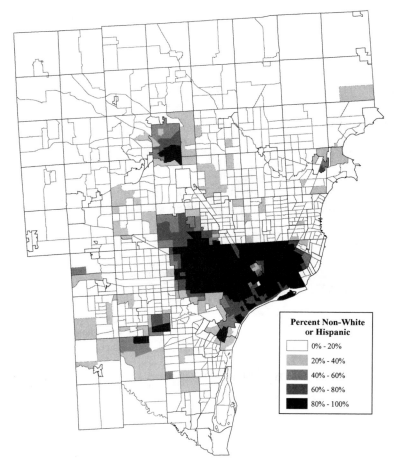

Percent Non-White or Hispanic
- 0% - 20%
- 20% - 40%
- 40% - 60%
- 60% - 80%
- 80% - 100%

SOURCE: U.S. Census Bureau, Census 2000, Summary File 1, Table P4. Michigan Center for Geographic Information.

the tri-county area tends to be concentrated in southeastern portions of Oakland county, northwestern portions of Wayne county, Inkster, Hamtramck, and several neighborhoods of Detroit. The American Indian population is widely scattered across the tri-county area, and it is below 6% in every census tract.

◼

**NOTES**

1. The intent of the census is to count people at their "usual residence." For seasonal migrants, that would be the address at which they spend the

**FIGURE 3.23**

## Geographic Distribution of Individual Races in the Detroit Tri-County Area, 2000

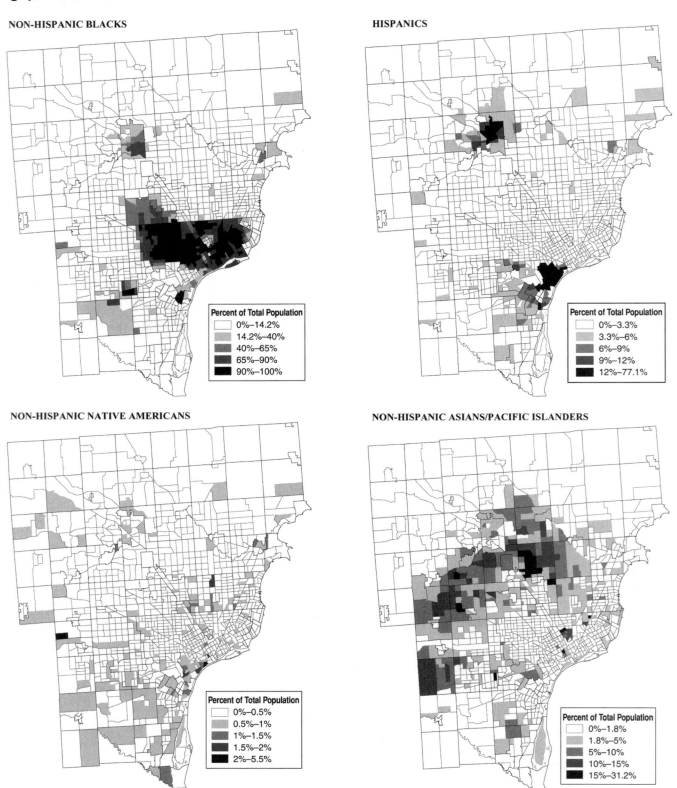

NON-HISPANIC BLACKS

HISPANICS

Percent of Total Population
- 0%–14.2%
- 14.2%–40%
- 40%–65%
- 65%–90%
- 90%–100%

Percent of Total Population
- 0%–3.3%
- 3.3%–6%
- 6%–9%
- 9%–12%
- 12%–77.1%

NON-HISPANIC NATIVE AMERICANS

NON-HISPANIC ASIANS/PACIFIC ISLANDERS

Percent of Total Population
- 0%–0.5%
- 0.5%–1%
- 1%–1.5%
- 1.5%–2%
- 2%–5.5%

Percent of Total Population
- 0%–1.8%
- 1.8%–5%
- 5%–10%
- 10%–15%
- 15%–31.2%

Shading patterns are based on data for census tracts. Percentages for the Black, Asian/Pacific, and Native American maps do not include persons for whom the indicated race was reported in combination with other races.

SOURCE: U.S. Census Bureau, Census 2000, Summary File 1, Table P4. Michigan Center for Geographic Information

largest portion of the year. However, in departure from previous practice, the census form for 2000 did not include a place for respondents to report that their usual residence was elsewhere, and the instructions did not discuss the concept of usual residence. Thus, some people who spend most of the year in Michigan were counted at addresses in different states where they received census forms in March.

2. Foreign-born residents increased from 3.8% of Michigan's population in 1990 to 5.3% in 2000, while the national percentage increased from 7.9% to 11.1%. Thus, growth in the number of foreign-born residents accounted for 1.5% of Michigan's population but 3.2% of the nation's population. See U.S. Census Bureau: 2000 Census, Summary File 3, table P21; 1990 Census, Summary Tape File 3, table P37.

3. See U.S. Census Bureau, profiles of selected demographic characteristics for Michigan and the United States in 1990 and 2000, table DP-2.

4. U.S. Census Bureau, 2000 Census, Summary File 3, table P39.

5. Michigan's residual net migration was computed as the difference between Michigan's census counts for particular age groups in 2000 and expected population levels that were calculated by applying mortality rates to Michigan's 1990 census counts by Modified Age, Race, and Sex (MARS) and births from April 1990 through March 2000. The resulting estimate is referred to as a residual because it is calculated indirectly as a difference between other estimates, and because it includes the effect of extraneous factors such as improvements in census coverage from 1990 to 2000.

6. Michigan accounts for an estimated 55,700 out of roughly 1.4 million active-duty military personnel, but only about 1,100 of those personnel are based in Michigan. See U.S. Census Bureau, *Statistical Abstract of the United States: 2001*, tables 501, 502, 503, and 504. The percentage of military personnel in 2000 who originated in Michigan is based on Michigan's percentage of the national population age ten to nineteen in the 1990 Census.

Other factors affecting net population change for this age group include international migration, people coming to Michigan for work or school, and people leaving Michigan to work or study elsewhere.

7. For example, Michigan's unemployment rate was 15.5% in 1982, compared to 6.9% in Texas and 9.9% in the United States as a whole. Although even Texas was affected by this recession, it was not affected as much as the Midwestern states. Bureau of Labor Statistics, U.S. Department of Labor, Local Area Unemployment Statistics, April 2002; annual average estimates from the Current Population Survey. See: *http://stats.bls.gov/cps/home.htm# annual*; *http://stats.bls.gov/lau/staa_7001.pdf*

8. Bureau of Labor Statistics, U.S. Department of Labor, "Regional and State Employment and Unemployment: October 2002," and "The Employment Situation: October 2002." See: *http://stats. bls.gov/news.release/pdf/empsit.pdf*; *http://stats.bls. gov/news.release/pdf/laus.pdf*

9. For more detailed discussion of land-use issues, see chapter 5 in this volume. For more detailed discussion of issues confronting Michigan's cities, see chapter 11 in this volume.

10. Central metropolitan counties include: Bay, Berrien, Calhoun, Genesee, Ingham, Jackson, Kalamazoo, Kent, Midland, Muskegon, Saginaw, Washtenaw, and Wayne. Although Pontiac and Holland are classified as central cities, they account for a small percentage of the population totals for their respective counties. Oakland and Ottawa are therefore classified as fringe metropolitan counties, together with Allegan, Clinton, Eaton, Lapeer, Lenawee, Livingston, Macomb, Monroe, St. Clair, and Van Buren.

11. See Immigration and Naturalization Service, U.S. Department of Justice, *2000 Statistical Yearbook of the Immigration and Naturalization Service*, September 2002, 18.

12. For further discussion of issues related to health services, see chapter 9 in this volume.

13. For further discussion of crime rates and related issues, see chapter 24 in this volume.

14. For further discussion of issues relating to K–12 education, see chapter 15 in this volume.

15. In order for a population to replace itself, women need to have an average of 2.1 children in the course of their lifetimes. This results in an average of two surviving children per woman. The fertility level for a particular year is measured by the "total fertility rate," which indicates how many births a hypothetical woman would have by the end of her reproductive life if, for all of her childbearing years, she experienced the age-specific birth rates measured for that particular year. The total fertility rate for white women fell from 3.3 in the final years of the Baby Boom to 1.7 in the mid-1970s, and then increased slightly to 1.8 by 2000. See U.S. Census Bureau, *Statistical Abstract of the United States, 1990*, table 84, and "Fertility of American Women: June 2000," Report P20-543RV, October 2001.

16. The higher figure for 2000 (80.0%) includes people who reported that they were non-Hispanic white in combination with other races. Those individuals are not included in the lower figure (79.0%).

Census statistics for 1910 reflect the total number of whites; the number of Hispanics in Michigan in 1910 was statistically negligible. Statistics for 2000 are based on the Census 2000 Modified Race Data Summary File, in which respondents who marked the "other race" category are reassigned to standard race groups.

17. Non-Hispanic whites represent from 69.5% to 70.5% of the national population, depending on whether individuals are included who indicated that they are white in combination with other races. The figure for 1910 represents the total white population, and the figure for 2000 does not include Puerto Rico. Statistics for 2000 are based on the Census 2000 Modified Race Data Summary File.

# 4

# The Evolution of the Michigan Labor Market from 1970 to 2001

*George E. Johnson*

## 1. Introduction and Summary

The purpose of this chapter is to investigate how the nature of the labor market in Michigan relative to the rest of the United States has changed from the 1970s to the present time.

If an economist were asked during the 1970s to list the major distinctive characteristics of the labor market in Michigan as contrasted to that of the rest of the United States, three stylized facts would come quickly to mind. These are as follows:

a. *The huge importance of the automobile industry in Michigan*—especially in the populous southeastern corner of the Lower Peninsula—in the determination of employment. Well over one in ten full-time jobs in the state during the 1970s resided in the three-digit manufacturing category "Motor Vehicles and Motor Vehicle Equipment," versus about 1.5% for the United States as a whole.

b. *The high level of wages in Michigan*—again, especially in the southeastern part of the state—relative to most other parts of the country.[1] This was, not surprisingly, true during the 1970s of blue-collar workers in the heavily unionized automobile industry. Quite surprisingly, however, it was also true of other groups of workers that would not be expected to be directly affected by developments in the automobile industry.

c. *The greater cyclical sensitivity and higher average unemployment rate of the Michigan economy.* During the 1970s the unemployment rate in Michigan averaged 7.9%, compared with just 6.2% for the entire United States. Between the peak year 1973 and the trough year 1975, the U.S. unemployment rate rose from 4.9% to 8.5%, but the Michigan rate rose from 5.8% to 12.5%.

It could be argued—up to a point—that stylized fact (b) followed from (a), and that (c) followed from a combination of (a) and (b). The highly concentrated automobile industry at that time had a strong (although, because of the energy crises of the 1970s, possibly tenuous) hold on consumer demand in the United States and thus very high profit levels per worker. Labor in that industry was represented by a very clever and aggressive union that was able to expropriate a significant share of the monopoly profits for the rank-and-file UAW members. Holding wages in other industries in Michigan constant, therefore, the high wage rates in the automobile industry would tend to make the average Michigan wage level relatively high.

That wages in the automobile industry are very high, however, will not necessarily mean that the *average* wage in Michigan (the average of wages in the automobile and other industries) will be significantly higher than the average wage elsewhere. The reason for this is that an abnormally high wage in one industry might be expected to serve as a magnet to draw workers to Michigan, to work temporarily in jobs in other industries (e.g., young men working in hardware stores) at wages that are lower than they are in those industries in other parts of the country.

Based on available macrodata from the 1970 U.S. Census and microdata from the Current Population Survey (CPS), I found (Johnson [1982] and [1984]) that, contrary to the reasoning of the preceding paragraph, non–auto industry wage rates in Michigan during the 1970s tended to be significantly *higher* than in most other parts of the United States. I called this a "fallout effect" of the high wage levels in the automobile industry. In terms of the labor/macroeconomics literature, there are two sets of reasons why this kind of behavior might occur. First, there is the possibility of a "threat effect," by which nonunion employers attempt to keep their wage rates close to the wages paid by unionized firms, so as to ward off unionization.[2]

A second potential explanation is the effect of a large union/nonunion wage differential on the average effort level of workers in nonunion firms. Nonunion firms may, accordingly, find it profitable to raise wages above what they could "get away with" in order to extract effort from their workers.[3]

For whatever the reason, employers of nonunion labor in many industries in Michigan were reluctant to offer wage levels that were as low as they could be in terms of the standard labor competition model. The results in my 1982 paper concerning the structure of wages in Michigan were

consistent with some sort of fallout explanation of the degree to which wage levels in Detroit and Michigan were high across the board, but they hardly *proved* it.[4] Further, I could find no evidence of fallout effects in other metropolitan areas of the United States with high degrees of unionization or a high-wage principal industry. To the extent that the fallout effect existed at all, it appeared to be a phenomenon peculiar to Michigan.

Stylized fact (c) flows from (a) and (b). First, if wage rates in Michigan are artificially set significantly above those in other areas of the country, potential migrants are willing to put up with a higher unemployment rate in Michigan.[5] The equilibrium unemployment rate in Michigan would be greater than the average in the rest of the United States so as to equate the expected utility associated with attachment to Michigan versus somewhere else.[6] As will be discussed in section 3, following, the estimated wage differential between Michigan and the rest of the United States during the 1970s varied between 6% and 14%.

The remainder of this chapter is an investigation of the degree to which stylized facts (a)–(c) still apply to the Michigan labor market. To summarize the major conclusions of this exercise, I find that stylized fact (a)—the great importance of the motor vehicle industry—appears to be as true in 2000 as it was in the early 1970s. However, wage rates in the Greater Detroit metropolitan area and in the rest of Michigan, which by stylized fact (b) were much higher than in comparable areas in the 1970s, appear to have fallen during the 1980s to levels that are very close to the national average, and have remained at that lower level through the 1990s. The reasons for the decline in Michigan's relative wage position, which is the subject of parts C–G of section 3, may include regional price level changes and the strong decline in union representation in Michigan.

Stylized fact (c) concerning the relative equilibrium value and cyclical sensitivity of the unemployment rate in Michigan relative to that of the rest of the country now appears to be only half correct. Since the early 1990s the Michigan unemployment rate has tended to be slightly less than the national rate (but not significantly so in a statistical sense). However, there is no evidence that the Michigan economy is less cyclically sensitive, relative to the rest of the United States, than it was before the 1990s. Neither of these facts is surprising, since (1) Michigan wage levels are no longer high relative to those of the rest of the country, and (2) the cyclically sensitive automobile indus-

---

**TABLE 4.1**

**Annual Growth of Population in Michigan, the East North Central Region, and the Rest of the United States, 1930–2000**

| Interval | Other U.S. (%) | Michigan (%) | E.N.C. (%) |
|----------|----------------|--------------|------------|
| 1930–50 | 1.1 | 1.4 | 0.6 |
| 1950–60 | 1.7 | 2.1 | 1.7 |
| 1960–70 | 1.3 | 1.3 | 1.0 |
| 1970–80 | 1.3 | 0.4 | 0.3 |
| 1980–90 | 1.1 | 0.0 | 0.1 |
| 1990–2000 | 1.3 | 0.7 | 0.7 |

SOURCE: *Historical Statistics of the United States*, table a-195, to 1970, and various issues of the *Statistical Abstract of the United States* for data after 1970.

try is still about as important in the Michigan economy as it used to be.

## 2. Changes in the Structure of Labor Demand and Supply

### A. The Data

An important fact about the labor market in Michigan is that population and employment have been relatively stagnant compared to the rest of the United States since 1970. Table 4.1 reports annualized growth rates for recent decades in Michigan, the non-Michigan East North Central region (which includes Ohio, Indiana, Illinois, and Wisconsin, in addition to Michigan), and the United States net of all the E.N.C. states. Michigan's population grew somewhat faster than that of the rest of the United States from 1930 to 1960, such that the fraction of the U.S. population residing in Michigan increased from 3.2% in 1930 to 3.6% in 1960. After 1970, however, Michigan's population grew much

**TABLE 4.2**

**Distribution of Full-Time Employment by Selected Characteristics for the United States, Michigan, and the East North Central Region (Net of Michigan), 1973–74, 1979, 1989, and 2000.**

| Characteristic | 1973–74 All U.S. | MI | ENC | 1979 All U.S. | MI | ENC | 1989 All U.S. | MI | ENC | 2000 All U.S. | MI | ENC |
|---|---|---|---|---|---|---|---|---|---|---|---|---|
| DEMOGRAPHIC | | | | | | | | | | | | |
| Women | .352 | .309 | .339 | .379 | .350 | .364 | .424 | .385 | .415 | .437 | .409 | .433 |
| Black | .086 | .073 | .074 | .089 | .097 | .081 | .096 | .099 | .087 | .104 | .120 | .109 |
| Hispanic | .048 | .012 | .021 | .050 | .014 | .022 | .053 | .010 | .031 | .107 | .031 | .063 |
| Age < 40 | .568 | .597 | .567 | .611 | .606 | .604 | .601 | .601 | .593 | .503 | .489 | .497 |
| Urban | .702 | .736 | .764 | .732 | .789 | .761 | .765 | .835 | .770 | .794 | .880 | .842 |
| | | | | | | | | | | | | |
| EDUCATION | | | | | | | | | | | | |
| < High school | .245 | .209 | .241 | .175 | .169 | .171 | .108 | .084 | .106 | .096 | .069 | .081 |
| High school | .410 | .447 | .452 | .410 | .440 | .455 | .397 | .410 | .437 | .325 | .328 | .349 |
| Some college | .172 | .178 | .152 | .209 | .226 | .186 | .234 | .266 | .228 | .286 | .318 | .379 |
| College + | .163 | .166 | .155 | .206 | .165 | .188 | .261 | .240 | .239 | .298 | .285 | .291 |
| | | | | | | | | | | | | |
| INDUSTRY | | | | | | | | | | | | |
| Agriculture | .015 | .009 | .007 | .017 | .008 | .009 | .015 | .010 | .008 | .016 | .009 | .009 |
| Mining | .010 | .003 | .007 | .014 | .003 | .006 | .009 | .001 | .004 | .007 | .001 | .003 |
| Construction | .065 | .052 | .048 | .060 | .051 | .051 | .058 | .044 | .049 | .065 | .057 | .054 |
| Non-Dur. Mfg. | .121 | .105 | .109 | .107 | .082 | .116 | .095 | .084 | .104 | .069 | .054 | .087 |
| Dur. Mfg. | .173 | .192 | .251 | .155 | .170 | .225 | .124 | .129 | .169 | .098 | .109 | .186 |
| Motor Vehicles | .017 | .115 | .032 | .015 | .156 | .030 | .014 | .128 | .030 | .012 | .123 | .022 |
| Public Utilities | .077 | .064 | .081 | .080 | .067 | .073 | .083 | .063 | .082 | .084 | .059 | .082 |
| Trade | .163 | .150 | .158 | .172 | .143 | .164 | .176 | .177 | .172 | .180 | .184 | .177 |
| Finance | .056 | .040 | .049 | .064 | .047 | .058 | .073 | .061 | .069 | .070 | .059 | .070 |
| Bus. Services | .028 | .025 | .027 | .030 | .021 | .026 | .052 | .051 | .047 | .065 | .065 | .062 |
| Pers. Services | .021 | .016 | .017 | .023 | .020 | .016 | .026 | .021 | .020 | .026 | .014 | .017 |
| Prof. Services | .184 | .177 | .161 | .188 | .171 | .173 | .203 | .171 | .181 | .237 | .216 | .228 |
| Ent. Services | .006 | .005 | .004 | .007 | .006 | .006 | .008 | .006 | .005 | .014 | .011 | .013 |
| Public Admin. | .065 | .046 | .048 | .068 | .055 | .047 | .062 | .055 | .045 | .058 | .038 | .046 |
| Union Membership | .269 | .405 | .363 | — | — | — | .200 | .314 | .257 | .145 | .232 | .191 |
| | | | | | | | | | | | | |
| Sample Size | 56,586 | 3,569 | 7,747 | 117,675 | 4,371 | 15,228 | 125,045 | 5,170 | 15,071 | 116,791 | 4,144 | 13,048 |

SOURCE: *Historical Statistics of the United States*, table a-195, to 1970, and various issues of the *Statistical Abstract of the United States* for data after 1970.

more slowly than that of the rest of the United States, and the Michigan/United States ratio fell to 3.0% in 2000. Michigan's population grew somewhat faster than that of the other E.N.C. states from 1930 to 1970, but has had roughly the same slow growth rates since.

In order to analyze what has been happening to the Michigan labor market during the past thirty years, I rely primarily on four different samples from the Current Population Survey (CPS). The first of these is a merge of the May Surveys for 1973 and 1974, and the other three are CPS samples from the Outgoing Rotation Groups, collected in March and November, for the years 1979, 1989, and 2000. Each of the years corresponds to a peak of the business cycle.

Because I am interested primarily in full-time workers, I restrict the samples to those respondents between the ages of eighteen and sixty-six (inclusive) who worked at least thirty-five hours during the sample week and reported weekly earnings of at least $76 in terms of the price level in 2000.[7] The resultant sample sizes—for the entire United States, Michigan, and the East North Central Region net of Michigan—are reported for each of the four CPS data sets in the last line of table 4.2.

## B. Relative Trends in Michigan

Table 4.2 reports some of the major trends from the early 1970s to 2000 in the composition of the labor force in Michigan versus the entire United States and the East North Central region net of Michigan. Some of these trends—notably the increase in the relative age of the Michigan full-time labor force[8]—follow from the fact that Michigan has been losing population in a relative sense. Some other notable trends apparent in table 4.2 are as follows:

a. There was a large increase, both absolutely and relative to the rest of the country, in the fraction of the full-time labor force in Michigan who are African Americans from the early 1970s to 2000. The large increase in the Hispanic population in the United States as a whole, from 4.8% in 1973–74 to 10.7% in 2000, was also experienced by Michigan. However, since there were so few Hispanics in Michigan in the early 1970s, the fraction of Hispanics in the Michigan workforce in 2000 was only about a third as large as the national proportion.

b. Although the fraction of full-time employees who are attached to the motor vehicle manufacturing industry declined consistently from the early 1970s to 2000 for the United States as a whole, the importance of that industry in Michigan was fairly consistent over the period. There were large declines in the fraction of full-time employees in Michigan associated with other manufacturing industries, but automobile employment remained strong.

c. The fraction of full-time employees who belonged to trade unions was very high in Michigan in the early 1970s—about 40%. Although unionism in Michigan was still higher in 2000 than it was in the rest of the United States, as well as in the surrounding East North Central states, the union proportion in Michigan had declined by almost one-half. This decline is explored much further in section 3-F below.

## 3. Changes in Michigan's Relative Wage Position

### A. The Empirical Earnings Function

In order to estimate the wage level in Michigan relative to other regions of the United States, observed labor quality and other characteristics held constant, it is necessary to utilize an earnings function with which to interpret the data.[9] The basic earnings function, which will be applied to microeconomic data for full-time workers in the United States, was formulated so as to form the basis for answering questions about relative wages in Michigan. The earnings function uses the statistical technique of multiple regression analysis.[10]

The regional variables that are included in each multiple regression are as follows:

- URB: Residence of the individual in a metropolitan area (MSA)
- MI: Residence in Michigan
- ENC: Residence in the East North Central region (Michigan, Ohio, Indiana, Illinois, and Wisconsin)
- BIG: Residence in one of twenty-one large metropolitan areas (New York, Los Angeles, Philadelphia, Detroit, etc.)
- DET: Residence in the Greater Detroit metropolitan area

The excluded category is those workers who are both outside any MSA and outside of the East North Central region. Estimates of several logarithmic earnings differentials can be calculated from these estimated parameters. For example, the estimated average relative earnings differential between the average non-Detroit MSA in Michigan and the average smaller MSA in the United States outside of the East North Central region is equal to $b_2 + b_3 + b_4 + b_5$.

The variables modified by the c coefficients are human capital variables represented by education and experience. $S_1$ is a one/zero variable for individuals who did not attend high school; $S_2$ represents high school attendance short of graduation; $S_3$ (high school graduates) are the excluded group; $S_4 = 1$ for those with some college, including an associate degree, but no bachelor's degree; the $S_5$s are those who received a bachelor's degree; and $S_6 = 1$ for all workers who claimed at least a year of graduate training. $X$ represents years of *potential* labor market experience beyond age eighteen, and its square is included to capture the diminishing (and eventually negative) effect of age on earnings. The interaction of experience and its square with a dummy variable for those with college or more ($H$) is included to allow for the possibility of different shapes of the age earnings profiles of highly educated labor.

The one/zero variables following the d coefficients, *BL* for African Americans, *HSP* for Hispanics, and *WOM* for women, are designed to pick up the effects of any labor market discrimination that may occur, and ethnic and gender differences in average levels of unobserved skill characteristics. The interactive variables *BL\*WOM* and *HS\*WOM* are included to allow for the possibilities that these ethnic effects may be different for men and women. The interaction variables between WOM and potential experience and its square, *WOM\*X* and *WOM\*X²*, are interpreted to reflect the historical fact that, *on average,* women, primarily because of child-rearing functions, acquired less actual experience per unit of potential labor market experience than men did. Consequently, we expect $d_4 < 0$ and $d_5 > 0$. Given the large increase in women's labor force participation rates, however, we would expect that the magnitudes of $d_4$ and $d_5$ would diminish over the period of our data (1973–74 to 2000).

It is also useful to run an additional set of earnings functions that control for the industry in which individuals work. We know that skill-adjusted wage levels in some industries, for example, mining and durable goods manufacturing, tend to be much higher than in other industries, such as trade and personal services. Whatever the reasons for these industry wage effects—explanations range from differences in the nonpecuniary attributes of employment in different industries (jobs in mining, for example, are dirty and dangerous and require extra compensation to attract workers) to the effects of unions and profit-sharing—it is informative to add a set of industry dummy variables to the basic earnings function given by (1). The dummy variable $I_j$ takes the value of one when a worker is employed in industry $j$, and $m_j$ is the average wage advantage (relative to the excluded industry).

More importantly, inclusion of industry dummy variables means that the estimated locational effects on wages are net of the effects of industry on wages. For example, the estimated wage level from (1) in non-Detroit urban Michigan relative to the average smaller urban area outside of the East North Central area is $b_{MI} = b_2 + b_3 + b_4 + b_5$. We might expect, however, that wages in urban Michigan (for example, in the Lansing MSA) would be higher than in urban areas in the United States (for example, in the MSA for Worcester, Massachusetts) because of the much greater presence of the high-wage motor vehicles industry in Michigan. The influence of industry composition on this wage differential can be discerned by comparing the estimated value of $b_{MI}$ from the basic model to its estimated value in a regression that includes industry dummy variables.

## B. Changes in the Structure of Earnings in the United States

Before launching into a discussion of the trend in the wage level in Michigan relative to the rest of the United States, it is useful to review some of the major trends affecting the structure of wages in the national labor market. The most important of the estimated parameters of the basic model for each of the four years are reported in table 4.3.[11] Table 4.4 gives the implied estimated average annual real (in 2002 dollars) earnings by gender for full-time workers with either high school or college (a bachelor's degree but no graduate study) completed for three different ages, and table 4.5 calculates the annual growth rates of real earnings by gender, education, and age.

These tables reveal some of the stylized facts

## TABLE 4.3

**Selected Estimated Parameters of the Basic Model, 1973–74, 1979, 1989, and 2000**

| Variable | 1973–74 | 1979 | 1989 | 2000 |
|---|---|---|---|---|
| $S_1$ | −.238 | −.257 | −.275 | −.356 |
| | (.006) | (.005) | (.007) | (.009) |
| $S_2$ | −.113 | −.117 | −.144 | −.221 |
| | (.005) | (.004) | (.005) | (.006) |
| $S_4$ | .106 | .106 | .161 | .131 |
| | (.005) | (.003) | (.003) | (.003) |
| $S_5$ | .279 | .264 | .457 | .490 |
| | (.009) | (.007) | (.008) | (.009) |
| $S_6$ | .409 | .412 | .646 | .681 |
| | (.010) | (.007) | (.008) | (.010) |
| $X$ | .0411 | .0429 | .0499 | .0385 |
| | (.0006) | (.0004) | (.0005) | (.0006) |
| $X^2$ | −.00077 | −.00076 | −.00084 | −.00063 |
| | (.00001) | (.00001) | (.00001) | (.00001) |
| $H*X$ | .0074 | .0049 | −.0009 | .0037 |
| | (.0012) | (.0006) | (.0009) | (.0010) |
| $H*X^2$ | −.00018 | −.00017 | −.00012 | −.00021 |
| | (.00003) | (.00002) | (.00002) | (.00003) |
| $WOM$ | −.262 | −.240 | −.135 | −.190 |
| | (.008) | (.005) | (.007) | (.008) |
| $WOM*X$ | −.0211 | −.0213 | −.0192 | −.0091 |
| | (.0009) | (.0007) | (.0007) | (.0008) |
| $WOM*X^2$ | .00040 | .00036 | .00028 | .00010 |
| | (.00002) | (.00002) | (.00002) | (.00002) |
| $R^2$ | .456 | .395 | .394 | .370 |
| $MSE$ | 0.37 | 0.40 | 0.43 | 0.46 |

SOURCE: *Historical Statistics of the United States*, table a-195, to 1970, and various issues of the *Statistical Abstract of the United States* for data after 1970.
NOTE: Estimated standard errors of regression coefficients in parentheses.

about changes in the wage structure in the United States from the 1970s to the present that have been the focus of a great deal of research (see, for example, Bound and Johnson [1992], Katz and Murphy [1992], and Katz and Autor [1999]). These major facts are as follows:

1. *The Effect of Educational Attainment on Earnings Rose Markedly after 1979.* After declining fairly sharply during the 1970s, the relative earnings of college graduates rose significantly during the 1980s, and this increase continued, somewhat more slowly, through the 1990s. This was true for both men and women, but the increase in the college/high school relative wage was greater for younger than for older cohorts.

2. Holding age and education constant, *the average wages of women relative to men increased*

*throughout the whole period.* For each subgroup in table 4.3, women did better than men throughout the 1973–2000 period, but women's gain was greater in the 1980s than in the 1970s or 1990s and was greater for older than for younger women. This means that the gender wage gap—the percentage advantage of men's over women's wages—declined during the last third of the twentieth century. For example, for forty-year-old high school graduates, the gap in 1973 was 100 × (60.7/34.9 − 1) = 74.0 percent, which means that this group of women earned, on average, 100 × (1/1.74) = 57% of what men earned. The estimated average wage gap for this group declined to 100 × (60.0/42.6 − 1) = 40.9% in 2000, which means that the average woman earned about 71% of what the average man earned. These figures imply that, between 1973 and 2000, approximately one-third of the gender earnings differential was eliminated.

3. *Real Earnings Adjusted for Gender, Age, and Education Were Relatively Static in the 1973–2000 Period.* A remarkable feature of the U.S. economy during the last part of the twentieth century is that, on average during the period of this study, the average earnings of most gender/age/education groups, adjusted by the Personal Consumption Expenditures (PCE) deflator, were relatively constant. In the case of young males without college degrees, average real wages actually declined over this time interval. For example, by table 4.4, the average twenty-five-year-old male high school graduate earned, in 2002 dollars, $33,500 in 1973 and just $28,500 in 2000, a decline of 0.6% per year, or about 15% over the twenty-seven-year interval. This is reflected in the aggregate statistics. Between 1973 and 2000, the real value (again adjusted by the PCE) of average hourly earnings of production and nonsupervisory workers in the private sector was essentially unchanged (an annual growth rate of +0.1%)—even though the average worker in this group was considerably older and more educated in 2000 than in 1973. By contrast, this real wage grew at an annual rate of 2.0% in the preceding twenty-seven-year period (from 1947 to 1973).

Because of product quality changes, substitution effects, and some other factors. the PCE may overstate the annual rate of growth of the cost of living by at least 0.5 percentage points (see Boskin et al. [1998]).[12] This means that approximately one-half of a percentage point should be added to the annual growth rates of real wages in table 4.5 in order to account for the "true" changes in real wages. It implies further that the young high school graduate in 2000 was, instead of being 15% poorer, approximately even with his counterpart twenty-seven years earlier. A long period of stagnant average real wages, however, is unprecedented in American economic history.

It is interesting to note that the relative earnings of workers with college degrees increased such that their real earnings over the 1973–2000 interval rose, although quite slowly by historical standards. Women's wages relative to those of men also rose significantly throughout the period.

4. *The Unexplained Variation in Earnings across Individuals Grew over the 1973–2000 Period.* One important feature of the analysis of wage determination is that individual earnings levels are affected by a variety of characteristics that are not observed in the analysis. These unobserved characteristics—innate ability, motivation, special skills, and the like—undoubtedly have an influence on individual earnings levels, but we cannot be sure which particular characteristics contribute how much to potential earnings. Most labor economists believe that there has been over the past twenty-five years a large increase in the return to these characteristics, and this has been manifested in the increase during this time of the proportionate variation across different workers in earnings rates after taking account of the observable variables (education, age, etc.).

Referring to the estimating equation in footnote 10, we can rewrite the basic earnings function as

$$\log E = vZ + e \qquad (1)$$

$Z$ is the set of variables (locational, human capital, etc.) included in the regression, and $v$ is the set of coefficients on these variables. $vZ$, therefore, is the value of $\log E$ predicted by the observed variables in the model, and $e$ is the effect of all unobserved variables (including, notably, individual skill that is not correlated with included variables such as education).

We can get an indication of the importance of these unobserved determinants by looking at the dispersion of $e$.[13] We know from past research (see Juhn, Murphy, and Pierce [1993] and Katz and Autor [1999]) that this has been growing since the early 1970s, meaning that there has been an increase in inequality among workers after adjusting for observable variables. This is reflected in our CPS data sets by the consistent rise in the root mean squared error (MSE) of the basic model from the 1973–74 to the 2000 results in table 4.4.

**TABLE 4.4**

**Estimated Average Annual Earnings (in thousands of 2002 $s) of Year-Round, Full-Time Workers by Gender, Age, and Education, 1973, 1979, 1989, and 2000**

| Year | at Age | Men | | Women | |
|------|--------|------|---------|------|---------|
| | | H.S. | College | H.S. | College |
| 1973 | 25 | 33.5 | 39.5 | 22.6 | 28.6 |
| | 40 | 44.4 | 60.7 | 25.5 | 34.9 |
| | 55 | 41.5 | 60.6 | 24.5 | 35.8 |
| 1979 | 25 | 33.4 | 38.3 | 23.1 | 28.4 |
| | 40 | 45.8 | 58.6 | 26.8 | 34.3 |
| | 55 | 44.6 | 59.1 | 25.9 | 34.5 |
| 1989 | 25 | 27.3 | 36.4 | 21.2 | 30.2 |
| | 40 | 40.2 | 56.3 | 26.5 | 37.1 |
| | 55 | 40.5 | 56.4 | 25.7 | 35.8 |
| 2000 | 25 | 28.5 | 41.2 | 22.2 | 33.2 |
| | 40 | 38.9 | 60.0 | 27.6 | 42.6 |
| | 55 | 40.0 | 59.9 | 26.9 | 40.4 |

SOURCE: *Historical Statistics of the United States*, table a-195, to 1970, and various issues of the *Statistical Abstract of the United States* for data after 1970.
NOTE: Estimated average salaries equal average weekly earnings, evaluated from the estimated basic regressions at the relevant education and experience levels for non-Black, non-Hispanic workers residing in the Detroit CSMA, multiplied by 52.

**TABLE 4.5**

**Annual Rates of Growth (Percentage) of Earnings Rates by Gender, Age, and Education Between Selected Time Intervals**

| Year | at Age | Men | | Women | |
|------|--------|------|---------|------|---------|
| | | H.S. | College | H.S. | College |
| 1973–79 | 25 | 0.0 | –0.5 | 0.4 | –0.1 |
| | 40 | 0.5 | –0.6 | 0.8 | –0.3 |
| | 55 | 1.2 | –0.4 | 1.0 | –0.6 |
| 1979–89 | 25 | –2.0 | –0.5 | –0.9 | 0.6 |
| | 40 | –1.3 | –0.4 | –0.1 | 0.8 |
| | 55 | –1.0 | –0.5 | –0.1 | 0.4 |
| 1989–00 | 25 | 0.0 | 1.1 | 0.4 | 0.9 |
| | 40 | –0.3 | 0.6 | 0.4 | 1.3 |
| | 55 | –0.1 | 0.6 | 0.4 | 1.1 |
| 1973–00 | 25 | –0.6 | 0.2 | 0.1 | 0.5 |
| | 40 | –0.5 | 0.0 | 0.3 | 0.7 |
| | 55 | –0.1 | 0.0 | 0.4 | 0.9 |

SOURCE: *Historical Statistics of the United States*, table a-195, to 1970, and various issues of the *Statistical Abstract of the United States* for data after 1970.

Under standard assumptions, we can calculate the ratio of the effect of unobserved variables on earnings for workers in different percentiles of the e distribution. These calculations indicate that in 1973–74 someone in the 66th percentile of the *e*

**TABLE 4.6**

**Selected Estimates of Relative Earnings Level Effects Involving Michigan and the Detroit CMSA for All Full-Time Workers, 1973–74, 1979, 1989, and 2000**

| Comparison | 1973–74 | | 1979 | | 1989 | | 2000 | |
|---|---|---|---|---|---|---|---|---|
| | Basic Model | Ind. Effects | Basic Model | Ind. Effects | Basic Model | Ind. Effects | Basic Model | Ind. Effects |
| (i) ENC MSA/US MSA | .055 | .048 | .043 | .035 | −.021 | −.027 | .005 | .001 |
| | (.005) | (.005) | (.004) | (.004) | (.004) | (.004) | (.005) | (.005) |
| (ii) MI MSA/ENC MSA | .016 | .010 | .067 | .048 | .072 | .064 | .041 | .034 |
| | (.011) | (.011) | (.012) | (.011) | (.013) | (.012) | (.014) | (.014) |
| (iii) MI MSA/US MSA | .071 | .058 | .110 | .083 | .051 | .037 | .046 | .035 |
| | (.010) | (.010) | (.011) | (.011) | (.012) | (.012) | (.014) | (.013) |
| (iv) US CMSA/US MSA | .091 | .092 | .094 | .090 | .148 | .142 | .111 | .107 |
| | (.004) | (.003) | (.003) | (.003) | (.003) | (.003) | (.003) | (.003) |
| (v) Det. CMSA/+ MI MSA | .151 | .142 | .105 | .098 | .111 | .104 | .098 | .093 |
| | (.015) | (.014) | (.014) | (.014) | (.014) | (.014) | (.016) | (.016) |
| (vi) Det. CMSA/US CMSA | .131 | .108 | .121 | .091 | .014 | −.001 | .033 | .021 |
| | (.011) | (.011) | (.009) | (.009) | (.009) | (.008) | (.009) | (.009) |

SOURCE: *Historical Statistics of the United States*, table a–195, to 1970, and various issues of the *Statistical Abstract of the United States* for data after 1970.
NOTE: Estimated standard errors of regression coefficients in parentheses.

distribution earned 110% more than someone in the 34th percentile. By 2000, someone in the 66th percentile of the e distribution earned 151% more than someone in the 34th percentile. This is, unfortunately, the case of the rich getting richer and the poor getting poorer.

## C. Relative Wages in Michigan

Estimates for 1973–74, 1979, 1989, and 2000 of six different regional wage effects, based on regressions on data for samples of all full-time workers in the United States, are reported in table 4.6. The regional wage effects in the table are as follows:

a. ENC MSA/US MSA: the average estimated wage differential between workers in smaller metropolitan areas in the East North Central region (Michigan, Ohio, Indiana, Illinois, and Wisconsin) and workers in smaller metropolitan areas in the United States $(b_4 + b_5)$;

b. MI MSA/ENC MSA: the differential between workers in smaller metropolitan areas in Michigan and workers in smaller metropolitan areas of other states in the East North Central Region $(b_2 + b_3)$;

c. MI MSA/US MSA: the differential between metropolitan areas in Michigan and non–East

North Central regions of the United States $(b_2 + b_3 + b_4 + b_5)$;

d. US CMSA/ US MSA: the average differential between workers in larger metropolitan areas (New York, Los Angeles, Chicago, etc., but excluding Detroit) and smaller metropolitan areas $(b_6)$;

e. Det. CMSA/MI MSA: the average differential between workers residing in Detroit[14] and those residing in other urban areas of Michigan $(b_7)$;

f. Det. CMSA/US CMSA: the average differential between workers in greater Detroit and other large metropolitan areas outside of the East North Central region $(b_2 + b_3 + b_4 + b_5 + b_7 - b_6)$.

The most important of the six estimated wage differentials are (c) urban Michigan versus other urban areas in the United States and (f) Detroit versus other large metropolitan areas. The estimated value of the first of these from the basic model indicates that, on average, workers in non-Detroit urban Michigan earned 7.4% more than the average U.S. worker in a metropolitan area of similar size in 1973–74. The estimated differential from the basic model increased to 0.110 in 1979, and then declined to 0.056 in 1989 and 0.046 in 2000. The decline of 0.064 log points from 1979 to 2000 has an estimated standard error of .018 (see table 4.10), so the estimated decline in the Michigan/Other differential is statistically significant. We would like to discern how much of this wage advantage is attributable to the fact that Michigan's industrial base is associated with high wage levels everywhere. When dummy variables for fourteen industries (including the three-digit industry motor vehicles) are added to the basic model, the estimate of the Michigan/Other differential falls by about a fifth to 0.058.

The estimated coefficients on the industry dummy variables in regressions on the entire sample (i.e., using all education and gender combinations) are reported in table 4.7. These coefficients are remarkably stable over the twenty-seven-year interval of our CPS data. However, between 1979 and 2000 there was a slight fall in the relative wage effect of the motor vehicles industry. This lowered Michigan's relative wage position, because of the large importance of that industry in the state. Further, there were increases in relative wages in finance and various service industries, all of which are relatively underrepresented in Michigan, compared to the rest of the United States. Consequently, the decline in the estimated Michigan/Other differential from 1979 to 2000 was only 0.048 log points when industry composition is taken into account, 0.016 less than the estimate in the basic model.

A rather more striking development is the change in the estimated average wage differential between workers residing in the Greater Detroit metropolitan area and those residing in large metropolitan areas outside of the East North Central region. For the basic model, this Detroit/Other Big differential was 0.131 in 1973–74 (workers in Detroit earning 14.0% more than workers in other big cities), was 0.121 in 1979, and then plummeted to 0.014 in 1989 and 0.033 in 2000. For the regressions with industry variables included, the estimated Detroit/Other Big differential falls from 0.131 in 1973–74 to 0.121 in 1979, and then falls sharply to essentially zero in 1989 and 2000. Thus, we can conclude on the basis of the global regressions (using all education/gender groups) that the average wage differential between Michigan and the rest of the United States fell significantly from 8–11% to 4–5% and that the Detroit/Other Big City differential fell from 9–12% to essentially zero.

Do these conclusions apply to all subgroups of workers? It might be supposed that regional wage differences—especially those involving Michigan, like the ones discussed previously—might differ by education and gender. In particular, it could be

## TABLE 4.7

**Estimated Industry Effects on Earnings (Relative to Wholesale and Retail Trade) in Global Regressions, 1973–74, 1979, 1989, and 2000**

| Industry | 1973–74 | 1979 | 1989 | 2000 |
|---|---|---|---|---|
| Agriculture | −.133 (.013) | −.099 (.009) | −.065 (.010) | −.069 (.011) |
| Mining | .330 (.016) | .422 (.010) | .456 (.013) | .403 (.017) |
| Construction | .273 (.007) | .235 (.005) | .249 (.006) | .198 (.006) |
| Non-Dur. Mfg. | .115 (.006) | .130 (.004) | .173 (.005) | .148 (.006) |
| Dur. Mfg. | .154 (.005) | .170 (.004) | .223 (.004) | .171 (.005) |
| Motor Vehicles | .280 (.012) | .280 (.010) | .320 (.011) | .251 (.013) |
| Public Uts. | .225 (.007) | .261 (.005) | .269 (.005) | .197 (.006) |
| Trade | .000 | .000 | .000 | .000 |
| Finance | .103 (.008) | .108 (.005) | .201 (.005) | .184 (.006) |
| Bus. Services | .045 (.010) | .049 (.005) | .102 (.006) | .127 (.006) |
| Pers. Services | −.240 (.011) | −.132 (.008) | −.119 (.008) | −.081 (.008) |
| Prof. Services | .054 (.006) | .044 (.004) | .090 (.004) | .051 (.004) |
| Ent. Services | .012 (.020) | −.027 (.013) | −.026 (.013) | −.007 (.011) |
| Public Admin. | .191 (.007) | .153 (.005) | .212 (.006) | .163 (.006) |

SOURCE: *Historical Statistics of the United States*, table a–195, to 1970, and various issues of the *Statistical Abstract of the United States* for data after 1970.
NOTE: Estimated standard errors of regression coefficients in parentheses.

argued that, because of high unionization and the industrial composition of the state, the relative Michigan/ Elsewhere wage would be higher for blue-collar workers than for other workers. To investigate this, I defined four dummy variables for the sample: Men with less than college (defined as sixteen years of schooling for the CPS data through 1989, and receipt of a bachelor's degree in 2000), women with less than college, men with college plus (meaning graduate work beyond the bachelor's degree), and women with college plus. First, table 4.8 reports the relevant sets of estimated regional effects for regressions run separately for each of the four gender/education groups (that is, a separate earnings function was estimated for each of the four groups). To see

## TABLE 4.8

### Selected Estimates of Relative Earnings Level Effects Involving Michigan and the Detroit Area by Gender and Education, 1973–74, 1979, 1989, and 2000

| Comparison | 1973–74 Basic Model | 1973–74 Ind. Effects | 1979 Basic Model | 1979 Ind. Effects | 1989 Basic Model | 1989 Ind. Effects | 2000 Basic Model | 2000 Ind. Effects |
|---|---|---|---|---|---|---|---|---|
| **Men < College** | | | | | | | | |
| (i) ENC MSA/US MSA | .055 | .048 | .043 | .035 | –.021 | –.027 | .005 | .001 |
| ENC MSA/US MSA | .072 | .063 | .068 | .054 | –.002 | –.013 | .026 | .021 |
| | (.007) | (.007) | (.006) | (.006) | (.006) | (.007) | (.008) | (.007) |
| MI MSA/ENC MSA | –.002 | –.006 | .051 | .036 | .075 | .074 | .009 | .002 |
| | (.015) | (.014) | (.016) | (.016) | (.019) | (.018) | (.021) | (.021) |
| MI MSA/US MSA | .070 | .057 | .119 | .090 | .076 | .061 | .035 | .023 |
| | (.013) | (.013) | (.016) | (.015) | (.018) | (.017) | (.020) | (.020) |
| Det. CMSA/MI MSA | .141 | .124 | .101 | .097 | .101 | .093 | .109 | .109 |
| | (.019) | (.019) | (.020) | (.019) | (.021) | (.020) | (.024) | (.024) |
| Det. CMSA/US CMSA | .143 | .109 | .153 | .117 | .048 | .028 | .061 | .049 |
| | (.015) | (.015) | (.013) | (.013) | (.012) | (.012) | (.015) | (.015) |
| **Women < College** | | | | | | | | |
| ENC MSA/US MSA | .034 | .030 | .014 | .011 | –.030 | –.035 | –.004 | –.010 |
| | (.009) | (.009) | (.007) | (.006) | (.007) | (.007) | (.008) | (.008) |
| MI MSA/ENC MSA | .051 | .025 | .115 | .085 | .041 | .033 | .054 | .040 |
| | (.020) | (.019) | (.019) | (.019) | (.021) | (.020) | (.024) | (.023) |
| MI MSA/US MSA | .085 | .055 | .129 | .096 | .011 | –.002 | .050 | .030 |
| | (.018) | (.017) | (.018) | (.018) | (.020) | (.019) | (.023) | (.022) |
| Det. CMSA/MI MSA | .152 | .181 | .068 | .066 | .101 | .104 | .060 | .070 |
| | (.027) | (.026) | (.024) | (.023) | (.024) | (.023) | (.027) | (.027) |
| Det. CMSA/US CMSA | .110 | .115 | .087 | .062 | –.051 | –.052 | .000 | –.005 |
| | (.022) | (.020) | (.016 | (.015) | (.015) | (.014) | (.015) | (.015) |
| **Men College+** | | | | | | | | |
| ENC MSA/US MSA | .025 | .026 | .028 | .025 | –.034 | –.037 | –.005 | –.012 |
| | (.018) | (.017) | (.012) | (.012) | (.012) | (.007) | (.013) | (.013) |
| MI MSA/ENC MSA | .013 | .019 | .002 | –.004 | .081 | .033 | .061 | .066 |
| | (.035) | (.035) | (.036) | (.036) | (.035) | (.020) | (.041) | (.040) |
| MI MSA/US MSA | .038 | .045 | .030 | .021 | .047 | .029 | .056 | .054 |
| | (.032) | (.031) | (.035) | (.034) | (.033) | (.032) | (.039) | (.038) |
| Det. CMSA/MI MSA | .175 | .154 | .212 | .182 | .154 | .143 | .135 | .109 |
| | (.047) | (.047) | (.045) | (.045) | (.039) | (.039) | (.045) | (.045) |
| Det. CMSA/US CMSA | .132 | .123 | .116 | .089 | .047 | .032 | .064 | .046 |
| | (.036) | (.037) | (.030) | (.031) | (.023) | (.023) | (.024) | (.025) |
| **Women College+** | | | | | | | | |
| ENC MSA/US MSA | .046 | .044 | .022 | .023 | –.046 | –.037 | –.012 | –.008 |
| | (.024) | (.024) | (.016) | (.016) | (.014) | (.012) | (.014) | (.014) |
| MI MSA/ENC MSA | –.010 | –.010 | .075 | .076 | .117 | .063 | .077 | .073 |
| | (.047) | (.046) | (.050) | (.049) | (.043) | (.034) | (.044) | (.042) |
| MI MSA/US MSA | .036 | .034 | .097 | .099 | .071 | .026 | .065 | .065 |
| | (.042) | (.042) | (.047) | (.047) | (.042) | (.032) | (.042) | (.042) |
| Det. CMSA/MI MSA | .258 | .276 | .085 | .091 | .097 | .101 | .087 | .062 |
| | (.070) | (.068) | (.063) | (.062) | (.049) | (.049) | (.050) | (.050) |
| Det. CMSA/US CMSA | .140 | .147 | .057 | .063 | .012 | .025 | .008 | –.023 |
| | (.057) | (.056) | (.042) | (.041) | (.027) | (.023) | (.031) | (.041) |

SOURCE: *Historical Statistics of the United States*, table a-195, to 1970, and various issues of the *Statistical Abstract of the United States* for data after 1970.
NOTE: Estimated standard errors of regression coefficients in parentheses.

if the estimated parameters on the locational variables for the four different demographic groups were different, I then interacted these dummy variables with all locational variables in the regressions (basic model and with industry dummies).[15]

Of particular interest are the estimated changes from 1979 to 2000 in the Michigan/Other differentials for smaller metropolitan areas and in the Detroit/Other Big City differentials for each of the groups, which are reported for the regressions with and without industry controls in table 4.9. For the results with industry variables included, there are two conclusions: First, the Michigan/Other relative wage differential appeared to decline by about 7% for noncollege workers of both genders, but, on average, the differential did not change significantly for either men or women college-plus workers.[16] Second, the estimated 1979–2000 decline in the average Detroit/Other Big City differential was about 7% for both men and women noncollege workers; but, due to sample size limitations, it is measured fairly imprecisely for college-plus workers.

From a purely definitional point of view, a fairly large part of the reason for the decline between 1979 and 2000 in the relative wage in Michigan and Detroit is the fact that the relative wage of the entire East North Central region fell relative to that of the rest of the United States during this period. For the results for all groups from the basic model, for example, the change in the Michigan versus Other U.S. MSA differential of –0.064 can be decomposed into the changes in the East North Central versus Other U.S. MSA differential, –0.038, plus the change in the Michigan versus East North Central differential, –0.026 (see table 4.9).

The general decline in the relative position of the East North Central region raises the question of which regions in the country were increasing and which were decreasing in the relative wage rankings. To answer this, regressions were run using the basic model and the industry effects model, but replacing the ENC, MICH, and DET variables with dummy variables for the nine major regions (with East North Central as the excluded group). These estimated coefficients are reported in table 4.10. Between 1979 and 2000, four regions (New England, Middle Atlantic, South Atlantic, and East South Central) experienced all else equal wage increases relative to the East North Central region; three regions (West South Central, West North Central, and Mountain)

**TABLE 4.9**

### Estimated 1979–2000 Changes in Selected Area Wage Effects

| Comparison | All | < College | | College + | |
| --- | --- | --- | --- | --- | --- |
| | | Men | Women | Men | Women |
| **BASIC MODEL** | | | | | |
| ENC MSA/US MSA | –.038 (.006) | –.042 (.010) | –.018 (.011) | –.033 (.018) | –.034 (.021) |
| MI MSA/ENC MSA | –.026 (.018) | –.042 (.026) | –.061 (.031) | .059 (.055) | .002 (.067) |
| MI MSA/US MSA | –.064 (.018) | –.084 (.025) | –.079 (.029) | .026 (.052) | –.032 (.063) |
| US CMSA/US MSA | .017 (.004) | .016 (.006) | .000 (.007) | .001 (.009) | .019 (.008) |
| Det. CMSA/MI MSA | –.007 (.021) | .008 (.031) | –.008 (.036) | –.077 (.064) | .002 (.080) |
| Det. CMSA/US CMSA | –.088 (.014) | –.092 (.020) | –.087 (.022) | –.052 (.038) | –.049 (.059) |
| **W/ INDUSTRY** | | | | | |
| ENC MSA/US MSA | –.034 (.006) | –.033 (.009) | –.021 (.010) | –.037 (.018) | –.031 (.020) |
| MI MSA/ENC MSA | –.014 (.018) | –.034 (.026) | –.045 (.030) | .070 (.054) | –.003 (.060) |
| MI MSA/US MSA | –.048 (.017) | –.067 (.025) | –.066 (.028) | .033 (.051) | –.034 (.059) |
| US CMSA/US MSA | .017 (.004) | .013 (.006) | .005 (.007) | .029 (.008) | .023 (.008) |
| Det. CMSA/MI MSA | –.005 (.021) | .012 (.031) | .005 (.035) | –.072 (.064) | –.029 (.078) |
| Det. CMSA/US CMSA | –.070 (.013) | –.068 (.020) | –.067 (.021) | –.043 (.040) | –.086 (.058) |

SOURCE: *Historical Statistics of the United States*, table a-195, to 1970, and various issues of the *Statistical Abstract of the United States* for data after 1970.
NOTE: Estimated standard errors of regression coefficients in parentheses.

stayed approximately even with the East North Central; and the wage level in the Pacific region, after rising in the 1980s, fell sharply relative to the ENC in the 1990s. On balance, the relative wage increases in the East and the South caused average wages in the Midwest relative to average wages in the United States to decline.

### D. Relative Wages within Michigan

The only wage differential *within* Michigan reported in tables 4.6 and 4.8 is that between workers in the Detroit Consolidated Metropolitan Area (which includes Ann Arbor and, in 2000, Flint) and those in other urban areas of the state.

**TABLE 4.10**

**Estimated Relative Wage Effects by Geographic Division for All Workers, 1973–74, 1979, 1989, 2000**

| Geographic Category | Basic Model | | | | Industry Effects | | | |
|---|---|---|---|---|---|---|---|---|
| | 1973–74 | 1979 | 1989 | 2000 | 1973–74 | 1979 | 1989 | 2000 |
| New England | −.042 | −.093 | .068 | −.002 | −.038 | −.090 | .071 | .004 |
| | (.008) | (.005) | (.005) | (.006) | (.008) | (.005) | (.005) | (.006) |
| Middle Atlantic | −.027 | −.049 | .031 | −.009 | −.022 | −.044 | .035 | −.004 |
| | (.006) | (.004) | (.005) | (.006) | (.006) | (.004) | (.005) | (.005) |
| East North Central | .000 | .000 | .000 | .000 | .000 | .000 | .000 | .000 |
| West North Central | −.082 | −.043 | −.044 | −.037 | −.072 | −.035 | −.032 | −.032 |
| | (.007) | (.005) | (.006) | (.007) | (.007) | (.005) | (.006) | (.006) |
| South Atlantic | −.063 | −.073 | −.003 | −.015 | −.059 | −.064 | .003 | −.010 |
| | (.006) | (.004) | (.005) | (.005) | (.006) | (.004) | (.004) | (.005) |
| East South Central | −.128 | −.079 | −.054 | −.037 | −.126 | −.084 | −.055 | −.036 |
| | (.008) | (.006) | (.007) | (.007) | (.007) | (.006) | (.007) | (.007) |
| West South Central | −.123 | −.059 | −.046 | −.054 | −.116 | −.056 | −.042 | −.054 |
| | (.007) | (.005) | (.006) | (.006) | (.006) | (.005) | (.005) | (.006) |
| Mountain | −.051 | −.018 | −.027 | −.028 | −.046 | −.010 | −.012 | −.019 |
| | (.009) | (.005) | (.006) | (.006) | (.008) | (.005) | (.005) | (.006) |
| Pacific | .007 | .050 | .080 | .006 | .005 | .063 | .090 | .015 |
| | (.006) | (.004) | (.005) | (.006) | (.006) | (.004) | (.005) | (.006) |

SOURCE: *Historical Statistics of the United States*, table a-195, to 1970, and various issues of the *Statistical Abstract of the United States* for data after 1970.
NOTE: Estimated standard errors of regression coefficients in parentheses.

This is because, with the exception of 1989, the other areas could not be identified within the CPS data (presumably for confidentiality reasons). The resultant Detroit/Other Michigan Urban wage differential is reported in row (v) of table 4.6, as well as for individual gender/education groups in table 4.8, and its average value for 1979 onward is about 10 to 11%.

In 1989, however, the data permit the identification of residence in other specific areas of Michigan, and these variables were added to the regressions using the entire sample of full-time workers in the United States. The estimated coefficients on dummy variables for ten non-Detroit MSAs in Michigan (including Toledo, which is in the Michigan orbit) are reported in table 4.11. For example, the coefficient of −0.114 on the Grand Rapids dummy in the basic model means that, adjusted for observed skill variables, wages in Grand Rapids are on average 0.892 of the wage level in Detroit, or 10.8% less than in Detroit. The estimated values of these specific Michigan effects vary from a statistically insignificant −0.040 for Lansing to −0.212 (a 19% disadvantage relative to Detroit) for Benton Harbor.

From a statistical point of view, one cannot be very confident that wage levels within Michigan

outside of Detroit vary significantly.[17] Part of the reason for the marginal significance of these results is that the sample sizes of individual areas are fairly small. It *appears* that the relative wage level in Michigan areas depends positively on the size of the area and negatively on the distance from the Detroit area, but we cannot be highly confident concerning this result.

### E. Relative Price Level Changes

A clear implication of the model of the determinants of the equilibrium wage in an area, set out in the appendix A of Johnson (2002), is that the equilibrium wage level in an area should, other things held constant, be proportional to the price level in that area. Unfortunately, data that indicate cost-of-living differences across areas are subject to serious conceptual and measurement problems, so it is not possible to test the implication of the standard economic model in appendix A that the elasticity of the area wage with respect to the regional price level is equal to one.

The most widely used such data are the American Chamber of Commerce Researchers Association (ACCRA) area cost-of-living indices, which have been collected quarterly since the early 1980s.[18] Examples of the calculation of these indices are shown in table 4.12. The average urban price level is equal to 100 at each point of time, so, according to the ACCRA data for 1999, cost-of-living for Detroit was 12.9% higher than for the average city, and cost-of-living for central New York City was a whopping 132% higher than for the average city.[19] One of the problems with the indices is that the weights for the six components (groceries 16%, etc.) that are reported on the first row of table 4.12 are the same for all areas. Thus, in terms of the dispute about the use of the CPI as an index of the true cost-of-living discussed in section 2-B, the ACCRA indices are subject to substitution effect bias. Further, there is also very likely a large bias due to outlet effects (e.g., a resident of Manhattan facing an expensive medical procedure could take a train to Baltimore and have the procedure performed at about half the cost). Also, the ACCRA indices refer to post-tax price differences between areas, for no attempt is made to adjust for differences in state and local income tax rates.

In an attempt to test the implication of the standard theory that the proportional effect of regional price levels on wage levels is equal to one, Dumond, Hirsch, and MacPherson (1999) added the logarithm of the ACCRA price index (log $P_{ai}$ for area $i$) to regressions similar to (2) and its augmented variants, say

$$\log E = \Theta \log P_{ai} + vZ + e \qquad (2)$$

Their estimates of the coefficient on the price variable, $\Theta$, range from 0.37 to 0.50 and are always

**TABLE 4.11**

**Estimated Wage Levels Relative to Detroit/Ann Arbor CMSA in Michigan MSAs and Related Summary Statistics, 1989**

| Metropolitan Area | Area Sample Size (1) | Percentage Employed in Auto Ind. (2) | Percentage Union Coverage (3) | Basic Model (4) | Industry Dummies Included (5) |
|---|---|---|---|---|---|
| Detroit/Ann Arbor | 2688 | 16 | 31 | .000 | .000 |
| Flint | 252 | 32 | 44 | −.063 (.029) | −.071 (.028) |
| Jackson | 90 | 8 | 31 | −.152 (.047) | −.143 (.045) |
| Toledo | 323 | 8 | 40 | −.084 (.026) | −.073 (.025) |
| Lansing | 226 | 15 | 36 | −.039 (.030) | −.041 (.029) |
| Saginaw | 255 | 19 | 38 | −.151 (.028) | −.154 (.028) |
| Battle Creek | 63 | 8 | 44 | −.136 (.056) | −.111 (.054) |
| Kalamazoo | 128 | 6 | 23 | −.099 (.039) | −.084 (.038) |
| Grand Rapids | 425 | 5 | 20 | −.114 (.023) | −.105 (.022) |
| Benton Harbor | 79 | 3 | 22 | −.212 (.050) | −.188 (.048) |
| Muskegon | 111 | 5 | 47 | −.116 (.042) | −.129 (.041) |

SOURCE: *Historical Statistics of the United States*, table a-195, to 1970, and various issues of the *Statistical Abstract of the United States* for data after 1970.
NOTE: Estimated standard errors of regression coefficients in parentheses.

**TABLE 4.12**

**ACCRA Relative Cost-of-Living Data for Nine Areas, 1999-III**

| Urban Area | All 100% | Grocery 16% | Housing 28% | Utilities 8% | Transportation 10% | Health 5% | Misc. 33% |
|---|---|---|---|---|---|---|---|
| Detroit | 112.9 | 106.2 | 137.6 | 107.7 | 103.0 | 109.6 | 100.0 |
| Lansing | 103.3 | 100.9 | 122.8 | 82.0 | 93.7 | 91.5 | 97.9 |
| New York (Manhattan) | 231.8 | 141.5 | 460.3 | 179.8 | 119.6 | 185.8 | 135.2 |
| New York (Long Island) | 143.5 | 124.5 | 177.8 | 160.0 | 116.4 | 153.0 | 126.5 |
| San Diego | 126.7 | 126.2 | 161.3 | 101.2 | 128.4 | 120.2 | 104.5 |
| Chicago | 109.0 | 109.3 | 109.6 | 110.7 | 115.8 | 112.4 | 105.5 |
| St. Louis | 97.3 | 99.6 | 95.9 | 96.1 | 99.5 | 105.7 | 95.7 |
| Baltimore | 97.0 | 97.2 | 92.4 | 121.0 | 97.1 | 94.0 | 95.5 |
| Houston | 94.5 | 93.3 | 83.8 | 100.0 | 105.8 | 110.7 | 97.1 |

Source: ACCRA Internet site.

### TABLE 4.13

**Union Membership of Full-Time Workers by Gender and Education and by Industry for Noncollege Men, 1973–74, 1989, and 2000**

| Group | 1973–74 US | MI | ENC | 1989 US | MI | ENC | 2000 US | MI | ENC |
|---|---|---|---|---|---|---|---|---|---|
| All Groups | 26.9 | 40.5 | 36.3 | 20.0 | 31.4 | 25.7 | 14.5 | 23.2 | 19.1 |
| Men < College | 37.6 | 50.3 | 49.8 | 25.3 | 40.6 | 35.7 | 18.0 | 28.8 | 26.8 |
| Women < College | 16.1 | 28.2 | 21.9 | 13.7 | 21.7 | 17.0 | 9.9 | 19.5 | 12.8 |
| Men College+ | 10.8 | 18.5 | 12.9 | 15.6 | 19.6 | 13.2 | 11.3 | 15.6 | 12.1 |
| Women College+ | 16.3 | 40.0 | 16.5 | 24.2 | 33.3 | 20.7 | 18.4 | 23.2 | 19.4 |
| **Men < College by Industry** | | | | | | | | | |
| % Mng. & Mfg. | 39.1 | 52.7 | 43.7 | 31.5 | 45.3 | 41.3 | 24.9 | 36.5 | 33.1 |
| % Union | 48.0 | 62.3 | 61.0 | 31.0 | 52.7 | 43.5 | 20.3 | 40.9 | 29.8 |
| % Con., Public Utilities | 28.3 | 20.2 | 24.4 | 29.2 | 22.0 | 25.9 | 30.5 | 23.0 | 27.2 |
| % Union | 47.9 | 62.7 | 59.0 | 38.4 | 51.0 | 51.3 | 30.4 | 41.5 | 45.2 |
| % Other Industries | 32.6 | 27.1 | 26.9 | 39.5 | 29.0 | 32.8 | 44.5 | 40.5 | 39.7 |
| % Union | 16.2 | 18.0 | 21.2 | 11.0 | 16.8 | 22.7 | 8.1 | 10.7 | 11.6 |

SOURCE: *Historical Statistics of the United States*, table a-195, to 1970, and various issues of the *Statistical Abstract of the United States* for data after 1970.

statistically significantly less than one. That the estimated value of $\Theta$ is less than its hypothesized value, however, is hardly surprising, given the fact that the ACCRA index is an imperfect measure—probably biased away from 100 as well—of the true cost of living in each area.

The Bureau of Labor Statistics reports price indices for large urban areas, Detroit being the only one in Michigan, but these are relative to a base period and are—correctly in the light of the problems associated with the ACCRA indices—not intended to provide comparisons across areas. We can, however, look at the change in the Detroit CPI relative to all other areas in the United States and relate this to estimated changes in area wage effects involving Detroit. In 1979 the value of the CPI in Detroit relative to the average for the urban United States was 1.009 of its value in the base year 1967.[20] In 1989 the relative price level in Detroit was 0.972, and in 2000 its value was 0.951. Thus, between 1979 and 2000, the CPI in Detroit changed by $\log(0.951 \div 1.009) = -0.061$, or a fall of about 6%.

Notice that the decline in the period 1979–2000 in the average (across all groups) relative wage level in Detroit (see table 4.9), either –0.088 for the basic model or –0.070 when industry effects are taken into account, is within two standard errors of the –0.061 decline in the relative CPI in Detroit over this period. This means that we cannot reject the null hypothesis that there

was no change in the relative real compensation level in Detroit (and, presumably, the rest of Michigan) versus other comparable areas of the United States. In other words, referring to the industry-adjusted estimates in table 4.6, the average worker in Detroit earned, other things equal, $\exp(0.091) = 1.095$ as much as the average worker in another large metropolitan area in 1979. The Detroit CPI in 2000 was $\exp(-0.061) = 0.941$ of its 1979 value. Assuming that Detroit had the same relative real wage in 2000 as in 1979, we would expect that the average relative wage in Detroit would have been equal to $0.941 \times 1.095 = 1.031$. In fact, the 2000 Detroit relative wage was $\exp(0.033) = 1.034$.

### F. De-Unionization

Perhaps the most prominent trend in the data on the Michigan labor market in table 4.2 is the sharp decline in the proportion of full-time workers in the state who are union members. This estimated unionization rate fell from 40.5% in 1973–74 to 31.4% in 1989 to 23.2% in 2000. This trend, however, is not peculiar to Michigan, for the percentage unionized also fell in the United States as a whole and in the non-Michigan states of the East North Central region over this period. The absolute change in unionization over the twenty-seven-year period was larger for Michigan than for the entire United States, –17.3 percentage points in Michigan versus –12.4 percentage points for the whole country, because Michigan was much more highly unionized initially. In proportional terms, however, the decline was slightly greater for the nation than for Michigan (46% v. 43%).

One feature of the economics of unionism is that the institution has very different effects on workers with different characteristics. There are two relevant aspects of this. First, as seen in table 4.13, the percentage of each gender/education group that is unionized varies considerably, with the highest rate for noncollege men, the lowest rate for college-plus men, and women in between (although college-plus women have higher rates than noncollege women in the most recent data). Accordingly, the fall in unionization rates from the 1970s to 2000 was sharpest for noncollege men.

Second, the estimated effect of union membership on earnings varies considerably across gender/education groups. To estimate this effect, consider an earnings function regression run separately for each gender/education group of the form

$$\log E = \mu_k U + v_k Z + e \qquad (3)$$

where $U$ is a one/zero dummy for union membership and $\mu_k$ is the estimated effect of union membership on log earnings. The estimated values of the $\mu_k$s for the four groups in 1973–74, 1989, and 2000—for the basic model and with industry dummy variables included—are reported in table 4.14. Referring to the estimates in the regressions with industry controls, the estimated value is

about 0.10 over the sample period (slightly higher in 1989) for noncollege men, meaning that union members earn—education, potential experience, race, industry, and region held constant—$\exp(0.10) = 1.105$ as much as workers who do not belong to unions. The estimate of $\mu_k$ for noncollege women appears to have fallen in the latter part of the sample period.

The significantly consistently negative estimate of $\mu_k$ for college-plus men points out the problems associated with estimating the relative wage effects of unionism. No one would believe that the true effect of unionization on the wages of the 10–15% of college-plus male workers who belong to unions is to *lower* their wages by 7% to 9%. Instead, the negative coefficient very likely reflects the fact that those college-plus men who are unionized are, on average, relatively low in terms of unobserved skill characteristics. The male CEOs, top lawyers, and so on who have the highest earnings in the sample would tend not to be union members. Thus, the estimated negative value of $\mu_k$ for college-plus men probably reflects a selection effect rather than the true effect of union representation on earnings. It is also possible that at least some of the positive estimated value of $\mu_k$ for noncollege men reflects selection effects rather than the true effects of unions on earnings—although one might expect, as did Lewis (1986), that the bias is in the opposite direction as that for college-plus workers.

Assuming that the selection problem is not very serious for noncollege men, one can test the fallout effect of union wages (the average level of which is $W_U$) on nonunion wages ($W_N$ on average), which was discussed in section 1. If the fallout

**TABLE 4.14**

**Estimated Proportional Union Relative Wage Effects by Gender and Education, 1973–74, 1989, and 2000**

| | < College | | | | College + | | | |
|---|---|---|---|---|---|---|---|---|
| | Men | | Women | | Men | | Women | |
| Year | Basic | w/Ind. | Basic | w/Ind. | Basic | w/Ind. | Basic | w/Ind. |
| 1973–74 | .138 | .094 | .175 | .124 | –.102 | –.083 | .147 | .125 |
| | (.004) | (.005) | (.008) | (.008) | (.016) | (.016) | (.018) | (.019) |
| 1989 | .181 | .135 | .199 | .151 | –.127 | –.091 | .056 | .073 |
| | (.004) | (.005) | (.006) | (.006) | (.010) | (.010) | (.010) | (.010) |
| 2000 | .138 | .100 | .120 | .086 | –.123 | –.092 | .002 | .037 |
| | (.006) | (.006) | (.007) | (.007) | (.011) | (.013) | (.010) | (.010) |

SOURCE: *Historical Statistics of the United States*, table a-195, to 1970, and various issues of the *Statistical Abstract of the United States* for data after 1970.
NOTE: Estimated standard errors of regression coefficients in parentheses.

**TABLE 4.15**

**Estimated Relative Wage Effect of Union Membership for Noncollege Men in Michigan and Non-Michigan United States**

| Year | Basic Model | | | with Industry Controls | | |
|---|---|---|---|---|---|---|
| | U.S. | MI–U.S. | MI | U.S. | MI–U.S. | MI |
| 1973–74 | .142 | –.055 | .087 | .099 | –.064 | .035 |
| | (.005) | (.017) | (.016) | (.005) | (.016) | (.016) |
| 1989 | .180 | .004 | .184 | .134 | –.012 | .122 |
| | (.005) | (.018) | (.018) | (.005) | (.018) | (.018) |
| 2000 | .139 | .065 | .204 | .103 | .047 | .150 |
| | (.006) | (.025) | (.024) | (.006) | (.025) | (.024) |

SOURCE: *Historical Statistics of the United States*, table a-195, to 1970, and various issues of the *Statistical Abstract of the United States* for data after 1970.
NOTE: Estimated standard errors of regression coefficients in parentheses.

effect is important in an area, an increase in the union wage will cause nonunion firms to raise their wages in an effort to avoid unionization. If the fallout effect were not applicable, there would be no direct effect of $W_U$ on $W_N$. In terms of the finding of Johnson (1982), the fallout effect in the United States applies only to Michigan. This means that for a regression of the form

$$\log E = \mu_k U + \omega_k U \times MICH + v_k Z + e \qquad (4)$$

we would expect—for the relevant skill groups, in particular noncollege men—that the estimated coefficient on the interaction between residence in Michigan and unionism would be negative. This means that, if the fallout effect is operative, the average relative wage effect of unionism in Michigan, $\mu_k + \omega_k$, would be smaller than its value for the rest of the United States.

Estimates of (4) for the Basic Model and that augmented with industry dummy variables are reported in table 4.15, for noncollege men in the three samples for which there are union membership data in the CPS. For both versions of the model in 1973–74, the estimated value of $\omega_k$ is significantly negative. For the results with industry controls, the estimated value of the average union relative wage effect in Michigan, 0.035, is on the margin of statistical significance. These results are consistent with the existence of a fallout effect *in Michigan at that time*. For the 1989 data, however, when the unionism proportion for noncollege men in Michigan had fallen from 50% to 40% (see table 4.13), the estimated value of $\omega_k$ had fallen to insignificance. Further, for the 2000 sample, at which point the fraction unionized was down to 29%, the estimated value of $\mu_k$ was posi-

tive although on the margin of statistical significance. By the reasoning of this model, the fallout effect operated in the earliest year, but it ceased to apply in the later years as unionism became less pervasive in Michigan.

Why did union membership in Michigan decline so markedly from the early 1970s throughout the period of this study? The decline in union representation in Michigan is, of course, consistent with national trends.

A good part of the decline in unionization in both the United States and Michigan is attributable to changes in the demographic (especially gender and education) and industry composition of employment. To see if Michigan's relative propensity to unionize has changed over time, we run a logistic regression of the form

$$\log[U \div (1 - U)] = gZ + u \qquad (5)$$

where $U$ is the probability that any full-time worker will be a member of a union and $Z$ is the set of explanatory variables. These explanatory variables include the educational attainment dummies, *WOM*, the interaction of *WOM* with a dummy variable for college-plus, and all of the regional dummy variables used in the earnings functions as well as a dummy variable for the three regions in the South.[21] The results for this model in the three relevant sample periods are reported in table 4.16 for the Basic Model, which includes the above variables, and for a model in which the major industries are controlled for.

To interpret the estimated parameters in table 4.16, consider the estimated coefficients on the dummy variable *SOUTH*. For the regressions that included industry controls, this coefficient was a highly significant –0.933 in 1973–74. This means that, holding education, gender, and industry constant, the log odds of a worker in the South belonging to a union compared to a worker elsewhere in the United States outside of the East North Central region was equal to –0.933. This means that a southerner was, other things held constant, 39% as likely as someone in the rest of the United States to belong to a union.[22] One of the interesting facts contained in table 4.16 is that noncollege women are much less likely than noncollege men to be union members, but the opposite is true of workers with college plus. An interesting change in the results over time is that men with very low levels of schooling were much more unionized than high school graduates in 1973–74 but much less so in 2000.

**TABLE 4.16**

Estimated Differences in Log Odds of Unionization by Location and Selected Characteristics, 1973–74, 1989, and 2000

| Difference | 1973–74 | | 1989 | | 2000 | |
|---|---|---|---|---|---|---|
| | Basic Model | Industry Effects | Basic Model | Industry Effects | Basic Model | Industry Effects |
| ENC MSA/USNS MSA | .180 | .083 | .100 | .066 | .051 | .049 |
| | (.032) | (.034) | (.025) | (.026) | (.027) | (.028) |
| MI MSA/ENC MSA | .236 | .181 | .310 | .288 | .239 | .198 |
| | (.063) | (.068) | (.065) | (.069) | (.075) | (.079) |
| MI MSA/USNS MSA | .416 | .264 | .410 | .354 | .290 | .247 |
| | (.059) | (.063) | (.062) | (.066) | (.071) | (.075) |
| Det. CMSA/MI MSA | .176 | .129 | .132 | .091 | .139 | .133 |
| | (.085) | (.092) | (.072) | (.078) | (.083) | (.088) |
| Det. CMSA/USNS CMSA | .465 | .220 | .369 | .220 | .292 | .216 |
| | (.065) | (.070) | (.042) | (.047) | (.048) | (.050) |
| SOUTH/USNS | −.868 | −.933 | −.728 | −.821 | −.729 | −.838 |
| | (.026) | (.027) | (.018) | (.019) | (.021) | (.021) |
| WOM<COLL/MEN<COLL | −1.172 | −.941 | −.591 | −.613 | −.688 | −.774 |
| | (.025) | (.027) | (.016) | (.019) | (.021) | (.023) |
| WOM COLL+/MEN COLL+ | .521 | .742 | .887 | .824 | .707 | .564 |
| | (.035) | (.039) | (.029) | (.031) | (.033) | (.038) |
| DROPOUTS/HIGH SCH | .327 | .249 | .048 | .100 | −.377 | −.212 |
| | (.033) | (.031) | (.028) | (.030) | (.038) | (.041) |

SOURCE: *Historical Statistics of the United States*, table a-195, to 1970, and various issues of the *Statistical Abstract of the United States* for data after 1970.
NOTE: Estimated standard errors of regression coefficients in parentheses.

With respect to unionism in Michigan, the linear combination of coefficients that compare unionization rates in urban Michigan with rates in urban areas outside of both the East North Central and the South are reported in the "MI MSA/USNS MSA" row of table 4.16. For the basic model without industry controls, Michigan's estimated log odds declined from 0.416 in 1973–74 to 0.290 in 2000, but this decline had a standard error of 0.092 and is not significant. For the regressions with industry controls, the positive effect of Michigan residence on the odds of union membership (about 30% greater) is fairly constant over the period, although there is a spike in the middle. The same conclusions apply to the observed higher rates of unionization in the Detroit area relative to other large areas in the United States (outside of the South and East North Central region).

It thus appears that the large de-unionization in Michigan was a reflection of trends in the rest of the United States. The absolute decline in the percentage unionized in Michigan was larger than in the United States as a whole, because the unionization rate started out much higher in Michigan.

## G. Unexplained Wage Dispersion

As pointed out in section 3-C above, a major development in the wage structure in the United States since the 1970s has been the large increase in the dispersion of wages—both with respect to observable variables like education and with respect to the residuals of earnings functions. The same phenomena apply to Michigan over this time interval. This is seen in table 4.17, in which the distributions of residuals for the earnings functions for noncollege men (see table 4.8) are reported. The interpretation of these numbers is as follows: For non-Michigan observations in the Basic Model for 1973–74, the difference in the value of the residual between someone in the seventy-fifth percentile of residuals and somebody in the twenty-fifth percentile is 0.456. This means that, holding right hand side variables constant, a person in the seventy-fifth percentile earned

**TABLE 4.17**

**Distributions of Residuals for Noncollege Males in Michigan and in the Rest of the United States**

| Year | Model | Non-Michigan U.S. | | Michigan | |
|------|-------|-------|-------|-------|-------|
| | | 75/25 | 90/10 | 75/25 | 90/10 |
| 1973–74 | Basic | .456 | .897 | .407 | .820 |
| | w/Industry | .430 | .851 | .401 | .776 |
| 1979 | Basic | .514 | .987 | .452 | .910 |
| | w/Industry | .488 | .948 | .436 | .865 |
| 1989 | Basic | .598 | 1.158 | .579 | 1.137 |
| | w/Industry | .577 | 1.122 | .560 | 1.089 |
| 2000 | Basic | .594 | 1.149 | .617 | 1.120 |
| | w/Industry | .573 | 1.118 | .581 | 1.074 |

SOURCE: *Historical Statistics of the United States,* table a-195, to 1970, and various issues of the *Statistical Abstract of the United States* for data after 1970.

$\exp(0.456) = 1.578$ times as much as a person in the twenty-fifth percentile. The ratio of the earnings of a person in the ninetieth percentile of the residual distribution to someone in the tenth percentile was $\exp(0.897) = 2.452$. These estimated ratios are, of course, somewhat smaller when variation in earnings associated with industry is accounted for. It is clear, however, that this unexplained dispersion increased from the early 1970s to 1989, such that it is much larger in 2000 than it was twenty-seven years previously.

Comparing the 75/25 and 90/10 ratios of the residuals for Michigan versus the rest of the United States, one sees that there was clearly a smaller dispersion of the residual variance in Michigan than elsewhere during the 1970s. For the 90/10 ratio for the regressions with industry controls, the 1973–74 relative wage was $\exp(0.851) = 2.342$ for the United States, but only $\exp(0.776) = 2.173$ for Michigan, and the 1979 values were 2.581 and 2.375 for, respectively, the non-Michigan United States and Michigan data. In 1989 and 2000, however, both the 90/10 and 75/25 relative values in Michigan were approximately the same as those for the rest of the United States. Whatever was unique about Michigan that yielded a somewhat lower degree of wage dispersion in the earlier years appeared to have disappeared in the 1980s, and stayed away to the beginning of the new century.

Table 4.17 is confined to the analysis of the residuals for noncollege males, but the same qualitative pattern applies to women and to college-plus workers—that is, the Michigan wage structure was characterized by less variation dur-

ing the 1970s, but has been characterized by roughly the same amount of variation as the rest of the United States since that time.

## 4. Changes in Michigan's Macroeconomic Structure

An important feature of the Michigan economy prior to a decade ago was the fact that the state's unemployment rate was usually much higher than the national rate—especially in periods in which the national economy was in recession. From 1994 through 2000, however, Michigan's unemployment rate was actually lower than the national rate. This leads to the question of *why* Michigan's relative unemployment position changed so markedly.

First, it is instructive to document the path of Michigan's relative unemployment rate. Column (1) of table 4.18 reports the coefficients of a regression of the form

$$\log(U_{mi} \div U_{us}) = a_0 + a_1 D93 + v \qquad (6)$$

estimated on annual data from 1971 through 2001, where $U_{mi}/U_{us}$ is the ratio of the unemployment rate in Michigan to that in the United States and $D93$ is a dummy variable for all years from 1993 on. The constant term is the average value of the logarithm of the relative Michigan unemployment rate before 1993, and its value is highly significant, $\exp(0.301) = 1.35$, which means that the unemployment rate in Michigan averaged 35% higher than the unemployment rate in the United States. The average value of the logarithm of the Michigan unemployment rate for 1993 onward is $a_0 + a_1$, which is negative but statistically insignificant.

Thus, the unemployment rate in Michigan tended to be a third higher than the national rate before 1993, but essentially equal to the national rate thereafter.

An expanded approach to the explanation of $U_{mi}/U_{us}$ is to recognize that (i) there is *persistence* in the time path of relative unemployment rates and (ii) because of its dependence on the motor vehicles industry, the Michigan economy is more cyclically sensitive than the national economy. This leads to the alternative estimating equation

$$\log(U_{mi} \div U_{us}) = a_0 + a_1 D93 \\ + a_2 \cdot \log(U_{mi} \div U_{us})_{-1} + a_3 SHOCK + v \qquad (7)$$

where the "−1" means the value of the variable in the preceding year and where *SHOCK* is the value of the change in the logarithm of the national unemployment rate if it is positive (otherwise *SHOCK* = 0). Estimates of the model without the *SHOCK* variable are reported in column (2) of table 4.18, and estimates of the full model in column (3). $a_2$ is significantly between zero and one, implying that $U_{mi} \div U_{us}$ is subject to persistence but tends to adjust toward some equilibrium value, and $a_3$ is significantly positive, implying that the Michigan economy comes down with pneumonia when the United States economy catches a cold. In the absence of an increase in the national unemployment rate (i.e., *SHOCK* = 0) and any disturbances to the determination of the relative Michigan unemployment rate (i.e., $v = 0$), the value of the logarithm of the Michigan/U.S. unemployment rate would tend toward its equilibrium value,

$$\log(U_{mi} \div U_{us})_* = (a_0 + a_1 D93) \div (1 - a_3) \quad (8)$$

The estimated values of this equilibrium log relative unemployment rate for the pre-1993 and 1993+ periods, as well as the difference between them, are reported in the last three rows of column (3) of table 4.18. The inclusion of the *SHOCK* variable causes the average *equilibrium* value of the pre-1993 Michigan/U.S. unemployment rate to fall from 35% to 25%. It also lowers the estimated 1993+ value, but that is still not statistically significantly different from one (the equality of $U_{mi}$ and $U_{us}$).[23]

An additional regression added an interaction variable between *SHOCK* and *D93*. The coefficient on this variable—say $a_5$—would, in principle, tell us whether the Michigan economy is still more cyclically sensitive than the national economy. If $a_5$ were significantly negative, we would conclude that Michigan is less sensitive in the 1993+ period than it was earlier. The point estimate of the value of $a_5$ turns out to be positive, which means, on the face of things, that the Michigan economy is more cyclically sensitive than it used to be. However, since it is based on only one observation (the rise in the national unemployment rate in 2001), we cannot make any sort of strong inference about whether Michigan's cyclical sensitivity with respect to the labor market has changed.[24] Given the continued relative importance of the automobile industry in the state economy, however, there is no reason to suppose that it has.

---

**TABLE 4.18**

**Determinants of the Michigan Unemployment Rate Relative to the Entire United States, 1971–2001**

| RHS Variables | (1) | (2) | (3) |
|---|---|---|---|
| $\log(U_{mi} \div U_{us})_{-1}$ | — | .534 | .509 |
| | | (.156) | (.134) |
| *SHOCK* | — | — | .479 |
| | | | (.141) |
| D93 | −.358 | −.167 | −.151 |
| | (.041) | (.066) | (.056) |
| Constant | .301 | .136 | .109 |
| | (.022) | (.052) | (.045) |
| $R^2$ | .712 | .787 | .845 |
| MSE | .103 | .090 | .076 |
| **Estimated** $\log(U_{mi} \div U_{us})$ | | | |
| pre-1993 | .301 | .292 | .223 |
| | (.022) | (.041) | (.045) |
| 1993+ | −.057 | −.067 | −.085 |
| | (.034) | (.061) | (.053) |
| Difference | −.358 | −.359 | −.308 |
| | (.041) | (.073) | (.064) |

SOURCE: *Historical Statistics of the United States*, table a-195, to 1970, and various issues of the *Statistical Abstract of the United States* for data after 1970.
NOTE: Estimated standard errors of regression coefficients in parentheses.

---

## 5. Conclusions

This chapter has dealt with the question of how the labor market in Michigan has changed over the last thirty years. The most significant changes are as follows:

1. Wage rates of full-time workers in Michigan relative to other states and in the Detroit metropolitan area relative to other large areas fell significantly during the 1980s, such that, by the year 2000, they were only slightly above the national average.
2. The motor vehicles industry is still extremely important in terms of the employment base in Michigan.
3. Trade union membership among full-time workers in Michigan declined sharply over the time interval of this study. The same trend applied to the entire United States. However, since unionization rates were so much higher in Michigan to begin with, the same proportionate decline in unionization in Michigan as in the United States yielded a much larger percentage point decline in Michigan.

4. Although it is tempting to conclude that the decline in trade union influence in Michigan caused the decline in the Michigan/United States relative wage level, the data examined in this study do not *prove* that number 3 *caused* number 1. The decline in Michigan's relative wage position is also consistent with a decline in the consumer price index of Michigan relative to the rest of the United States.

5. During the 1990s Michigan appeared to move from a position of having a significantly higher unemployment rate than the average for the entire United States to having an equilibrium unemployment rate equal to (or, perhaps, slightly less than) the national rate. This would be an expected consequence of the decline in the Michigan/U.S. relative wage rate.

■

## REFERENCES

Boskin, M., E. R. Dulberger, R. J. Gordon, D. Jorgenson, and Z. Griliches. 1998. Consumer prices, the consumer price index, and the cost of living. *Journal of Economic Perspectives* 12:3–26.

Bound, John, and George Johnson. 1992. Changes in the structure of wages in the 1980s: An evaluation of alternative explanations. *American Economic Review* 82:371–92.

Ciccone, Antonio, and Robert E. Hall. 1996. Productivity and the density of economic activity. *American Economic Review* 86:54–70.

Dumond, J. Michael, Barry T. Hirsch, and David A. MacPherson. 1999. Wage differentials across labor markets and workers: Does cost of living matter? *Economic Inquiry* 37:377–98.

Glaeser, Edward L., and David C. Maré. 2001. Cities and skills. *Journal of Labor Economics* 19:316–42.

Johnson, George. 1982. Wage rates in Michigan compared with the rest of the U.S. In *Michigan's fiscal and economic structure*, edited by H. Brazer and D. Laren. Ann Arbor: University of Michigan Press: 85–110.

———. 1984. Intermetropolitan wage differentials in the United States. In *The measurement of labor cost*, edited by J. E. Triplett. Chicago: University of Chicago Press: 309–32.

———. 2002. Evaluating labor market trends in Michigan: Technical issues. Mimeograph. University of Michigan, April.

Juhn, Chinhui, Kevin M. Murphy, and Brooks Pierce. 1993. Wage inequality and the rise in the returns to skill. *Journal of Political Economy* 90:410–42.

Katz, Lawrence F., and David H. Autor. 1999. Changes in wage structure and earnings inequality. In *Handbook of labor economics*, vol. 3A, edited by O. Ashenfelter and D. Card. Amsterdam: Elsevier: 1463–1555.

Katz, Lawrence F., and Kevin M. Murphy. 1992. Changes in relative wages, supply and demand factors. *Quarterly Journal of Economics* 107:35–78.

Kim, Bonggeun. 2001. The wage gap between metropolitan and non-metropolitan areas. Mimeograph. University of Michigan, September.

Lewis, H. G. 1986. *Union relative wage effects: A survey.* Chicago: University of Chicago Press.

Rauch, James. 1993. Productivity gains from geographic concentration of human capital: Evidence from the cities. *Journal of Urban Economics* 34:3–33.

Roback, Jennifer. 1982. Wages, rents, and the quality of life. *Journal of Political Economy* 90:1257–78.

Rosen, Sherwin. 1969. Trade union power, threat effects, and the extent of union organization. *Review of Economic Studies* 39:185–96.

Shapiro, Carl, and Joseph Stiglitz. 1986. Equilibrium unemployment as a worker discipline device. *American Economic Review* 74:433–44.

## NOTES

A more technical version of this paper is Johnson (2002). I am grateful to Jamila Stanton for excellent research assistance and to the editors of this volume for useful suggestions.

1. Michigan's relative wage position was widely recognized at the time. For example, an editorial in the *Detroit News* on 23 April 1982 concluded that "Michigan's high wages have long been a source of pride, for they represent a triumph of organized labor on behalf of the ordinary worker, and symbolize a high standard of living in the state. But what good are the world's highest wages if the jobs that pay them continue to evaporate?"

2. This hypothesis was most notably set forth by Rosen (1969).

3. The standard reference to the "efficiency wages" model of wage determination is Shapiro and Stiglitz (1986).

4. To get stronger evidence in favor of this interpretation, one would have to get microdata on wages by industry in Michigan and elsewhere in the United States before and after the unionization of the automobile industry in the mid- and late-1930s. My hypothesis is that the wage rates of

Michigan workers who looked nothing like auto workers (say, female clerks in doctors' offices) as well as the wages of less-dissimilar workers (e.g., young men working in hardware stores) increased much more rapidly during this period than they did in other parts of the United States. Such data, of course, are not readily available for the 1930s, so my hypothesis can be tested only on a partial basis. It should also be pointed out that an alternative interpretation of the evidence for the 1970s is that Michigan is simply an unattractive place to live and requires a compensating differential to all potential workers.

5. This is called "queue unemployment" in economics jargon, but it is a common sense proposition. For example, a little piece entitled "A Statistical Note" in the *Detroit News,* 9 January 1984, A-8, concluded that "Michigan workers have the third highest average annual paycheck in the nation, $18,809. That is behind only oil-endowed Alaska and the federally endowed District of Columbia; Michigan, however, has one of the highest unemployment rates. Is there a connection?"

6. The fact that the unemployment rate in Michigan tended to be significantly higher than that in the United States as a whole in the 1970s suggests that the interpretation of the Michigan/U.S. wage differential as reflecting poor nonpecuniary characteristics of Michigan (see note 4) is refuted.

7. For discussion of part-time employment, see chapters 17 and 18 in this volume.

8. Since younger workers are more likely than older workers to migrate, the heavy out-migration accompanying a large decline in relative population must necessarily lead to a "graying" of the population that remains in Michigan.

9. There are interesting economic questions concerning why the wage level in a particular area—observed and unobserved skill characteristics of workers held constant—might differ from the wage level in other areas. In the theoretical appendix in Johnson (2002) I go into these issues in some detail.

The traditional approach is to look for nonpecuniary differences between areas (see Roback [1982]). More recent papers have focused on unobserved quality differences as a major explanation of regional wage differences (see Rauch [1993], Ciccone and Hall [1996], Glaeser and Maré [2001], and Kim [2001]).

A third explanation focuses on price level differences among regions, a factor that is examined in section 3-E, following.

10. This basic function is as follows:

$$
\begin{aligned}
\log E = {} & b_0 + b_1 URB + b_2 MI + b_3 MI * URB + b_4 ENC \\
& + b_5 ENC * URB + b_6 BIG + b_7 DET + c_1 S_1 + c_2 S_2 \\
& + c_4 S_4 + c_5 S_5 + c_6 S_6 + c_7 X + c_8 X^2 + c_9 H * X \\
& + c_{10} H * X^2 + d_1 BL + d_2 HS + d_3 WOM \\
& + d_4 WOM * X + d_5 WOM * X^2 + d_6 BL * WOM \\
& + d_7 HSP * WOM + e, \quad\quad\quad\quad (1)
\end{aligned}
$$

where $\log E$ is the natural logarithm of earnings and $e$ is a statistical disturbance term. The logarithm of earnings, rather than its untransformed value, is used so that the estimated coefficients reflect *relative* rather than *absolute* differences. Throughout the text I will refer to differentials in proportionate terms. For example, the earnings of an urban relative to a nonurban worker from (1) is $\exp(b_1)$.

11. The regressions for 1973–74 also include a dummy variable for the latter year, which picks up (the considerable) wage inflation from 1973 to 1974.

12. The Boskin Commission argued that the Consumer Price Index (CPI) was upward-biased by about one percentage point per year. The average annual rate of growth of the CPI over the 1973–2000 interval was 0.5 percentage points greater than the rate of growth of the PCE. Thus, use of the PCE may involve a bias in the calculation of the average annual rate of growth of real wages equal to approximately 0.5%.

13. Specifically, we focus on the square root of the variance of $e$—the root mean squared error (MSE) of the regression—which provides an indication of the importance of these unobserved determinants of earnings.

14. Ann Arbor SMA is included in the Detroit Consolidated Metropolitan Statistical Area in all years. Flint SMA is also included in the Detroit CMSA in the 2000 CPS data.

15. I also performed tests of the null hypothesis that the interaction of these gender/education dummy variables and the five variables particular to Michigan (*MI, MI*URB, ENC, ENC*URB,* and *DET*) are zero. These coefficients are jointly significant—that is, we reject the hypothesis that the Michigan wage effect is the same across the four gender/education groups—for the 1973–74 and 1979 data sets, marginally significant for 1989, and, by and large, insignificant in 2000. Further, although there is less than one chance in a hundred that these different effects arose due to change in the earlier years, the value of the relevant $F$ statistics, which are reported in the technical version of this paper, are such that the estimated Michigan wage differentials across gender/education groups are not substantially different from each other.

16. These differences, however, are not statistically

significant. In other words, we cannot reject the null hypothesis that the changes in the relative wage position of the four groups were equal.

17. The null hypothesis that the estimated coefficients on the nine Michigan areas (that is, excluding Toledo) in the model with industry dummy variables included are equal yields $F = 1.88$ and $p = 0.051$. Eliminating Flint from this test yields $F = 1.75$ and $p = 0.082$.

18. These indices are described in the ACCRA web site, *www.accra.org*, but they are not available without charge.

19. The average value of the ACCRA indices for 1985 through 1994, reported in Dumond, Hirsch, and MacPherson (1999), was 114.4 for Detroit/Ann Arbor and between 100 and 108—an average of about 105—for the various other urban areas in Michigan they report. Taken at face value, this means that most ($\log[114.5 \div 105] = 0.085$) of the 0.098 to 0.111 log wage differential between Detroit and other urban areas in Michigan for 1989 is accounted for by the higher cost-of-living in Detroit.

20. All CPI data were taken from various issues from the statistical tables in the *Monthly Labor Review*, table 23 of March 1980, table 22 of July 1984, table 32 of July 1990, and table 29 of July 2001.

21. The South is included as a dummy variable in part because of "right to work" laws, which increase the cost of organizing and maintaining unionism, and, more generally, because Southerners tend to be more conservative politically.

22. Exponentiating, the relative odds of belonging to a union are $[(P_S \div (1 - P_S)] \div [(P_{US} \div (1 - P_{US})] = \exp(-0.933) = 0.39$ for a southerner, compared to a northerner.

23. The reason for the statistical insignificance is that there are only nine years of data since 1992. We will have to experience a few more full business cycles before we can be sure whether the equilibrium Michigan unemployment rate has fallen below the U.S. rate. My suspicion is that it probably has not, because the Michigan wage level has not fallen below the average for the nation.

24. To illustrate this point, assume that the average values of the unemployment rates for Michigan and the United States for the first half of 2002, 6.6% and 6.0%, respectively, hold up for the rest of the year. In that case, the estimated coefficient on the interaction between *SHOCK* and $D_{93}$ falls to 0.314 with a standard error of 0.327. Since we cannot (as of August 2002) know what the final values of those two unemployment rates will be, this is by no means a piece of evidence on the question of changes in the relative cyclicality of the Michigan economy. Instead, it merely shows how tenuous is any conclusion based only on data through 2001.

# 5

# Land Use in Michigan

*Gary J. Sands*

## Introduction

This chapter describes the patterns of land use across Michigan, with particular emphasis on developed (urbanized) land and the transition from open to urban uses. The way in which land is used and regulated contributes to the quality of life enjoyed by Michigan residents, as well as to the health of the state and local economies.

Land use and development issues have become much more of a public and political concern in recent years. The current patterns of suburban development, often pejoratively referred to as sprawl, are regarded negatively. The Sierra Club (2000), for example, has defined sprawl as "irresponsible, poorly planned development that destroys green space, increases traffic, crowds schools and drives up taxes." While this definition concisely summarizes what many people view as the detrimental consequences of growth, it does not recognize the positive aspects of growth and development. A more balanced perspective is essential.

## Recent Trends in Land Use Policy

This distinction between the positive and negative consequences of new development is at the heart of the Smart Growth initiatives. The American Planning Association (APA) defines "Smart Growth" as "planning, designing, developing, and revitalizing communities to promote a sense of place, preserve natural and cultural resources, and equitably distribute the costs and benefits of development" (American Planning Association 2002). Smart Growth differs from current practices in that it emphasizes channeling a larger proportion of regional growth to areas already served by existing infrastructure. Social equity, environmental protection, and fiscal efficiency are also important components of Smart Growth's efforts to enhance the quality of life in urban and suburban areas.

Sustainability is another concept that has gained prominence in recent years. According to one definition, "Sustainable development . . . meets the needs of the present without compromising the ability of future generations to meet their own needs" (Jacobs 1991). While sustainable communities advocate many of the same principles as Smart Growth and those opposed to sprawl, there is a greater sense of stewardship, with recognition that some limitations on current activities may be necessary to ensure the continued viability of our communities.

## Context: Current Land Uses and Trends

The State of Michigan has a land surface area of approximately 36,246,000 acres, or about 56,600

**FIGURE 5.1**

**Population per Square Mile, 2000, by Municipality**

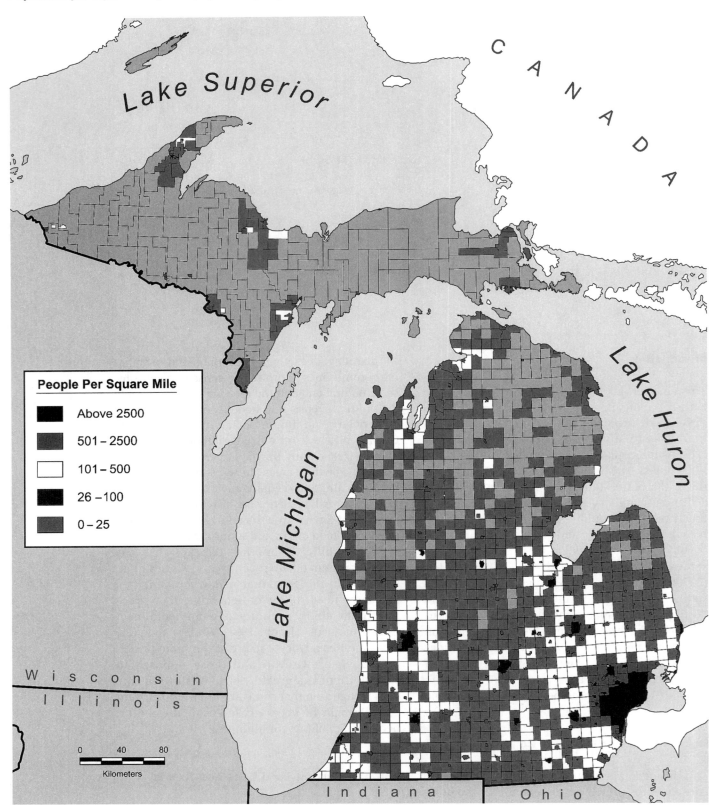

**People Per Square Mile**

- Above 2500
- 501 – 2500
- 101 – 500
- 26 – 100
- 0 – 25

SOURCE: Michigan State University Center for Remote Sensing and Geographic Science (*www.crs.msu.edu*).

square miles. (Inland waters represent an additional 1.1 million acres.) The majority (79%) of the land area is privately owned. (City streets and parks and other land owned by local governments within urban areas are included in this total as well.) The federal government owns 3.2 million acres, about 9% of the state. The State of Michigan is also a major landowner, holding about 4.3 million acres, or 12% of the total.

With almost ten million residents according to the 2000 U.S. Census, Michigan has an average population density of 175 persons per square mile. This is the fifteenth-highest population density among the fifty states, ranking between Virginia (179 persons per square mile) and Indiana (170 persons per square mile). (See appendix A.) There are about 3.6 acres of land for every Michigan resident.

The population is, of course, not distributed evenly across the state. Figure 5.1 illustrates that Michigan's population is concentrated in the southern third of the Lower Peninsula. There is a general correspondence between the population density (figure 5.1) and the distribution of developed areas of the state (figure 5.2).

Most of the land in Michigan is not developed. Developed areas consist primarily of residential uses, but also include commercial and industrial uses. In the early 1980s, just 8% of the 33 million acres of nonfederal land in the state were classified as developed (table 5.1). Over the next fifteen years, the amount of developed land increased by 30%. In 1997, they represented almost 11% of the total.

The nonfederal, undeveloped areas of Michigan are not necessarily idle but often are the location of important economic activities. Agricultural uses (crop and pasture lands) constituted about 37% of the total area of the state in 1982. Since that time, the amount of land actively used for agricultural purposes has declined by almost 1.5 million acres, or 12%. Cropland (including land enrolled in the Crop Reduction Program) has decreased by 582,000 acres, or about 6%. Pastureland has shrunk by 870,000 acres, a decline of almost 30%. (See also chapter 10 in this volume.)

Timber and forest uses are the largest category, constituting close to half of the total nonfederally owned land. Acreage in this category actually increased by 538,000 acres during the 1980s and 1990s, as a result of forest growth on former crop- or pastureland. The remaining 2.2 million acres of undeveloped land consists of farmsteads and other farm structures, barren land, and marshland. The amount of land devoted to these uses

**TABLE 5.1**

**Michigan Land Use Trends, Nonfederal Lands, 1982–97 (thousands of acres)**

| | Rural | | | |
| | Crop/Pasture[a] | Forest | Other | Developed |
|---|---|---|---|---|
| 1982 | 12,346 | 15,816 | 2,168 | 2,72 |
| *Percentage* | *37.4%* | *47.9%* | *6.6%* | *8.3%* |
| 1987 | 11,939 | 16,026 | 2,132 | 2,926 |
| *Percentage* | *36.2%* | *48.6%* | *6.5%* | *8.9%* |
| 1992 | 11,618 | 16,053 | 2,119 | 3,181 |
| *Percentage* | *35.2%* | *48.6%* | *6.4%* | *9.6%* |
| 1997 | 10,893 | 16,354 | 2,178 | 3,546 |
| *Percentage* | *33.0%* | *49.6%* | *6.6%* | *10.7%* |
| Change 1982–97 | –1,453 | 538 | 10 | 821 |

SOURCE: U.S. Department of Agriculture (2001).
(a) Includes Crop Reduction Program Acreage.

has remained relatively constant during the 1980s and 1990s.

Michigan has been endowed with significant mineral resources that make a substantial contribution to the state's economy. Michigan ranks fourth among the fifty states in terms of the value of nonfuel minerals produced. A 1980 inventory of surface land used for mining indicated that only a small area, approximately 129,000 acres, was devoted to mining (Wyckoff and Moultane 1995). This total does not include land used for oil and gas operations, however. Acreage under oil and gas leases totaled about 12.5 million acres, most under private leases. Mining activities are found throughout the state. Sand and gravel operations occur in all eighty-three counties, for example, while oil and gas operations are found in sixty-one Lower Peninsula counties.

Some types of development may be important even though they affect only a small portion of the undeveloped land. The introduction of recreational trails or mining and drilling activities through forests may impact the recreational and scenic values of a much larger area than that used for the new activity. (See chapter 21 in this volume.) New roads and power line rights of way may disrupt farming operations while having only a limited effect on the amount of land used.

## Land Use and Population Change

Changes in land use over the past two decades have affected about 2.8 million acres, or 8.5% of

**FIGURE 5.2**

**Michigan Land Use**

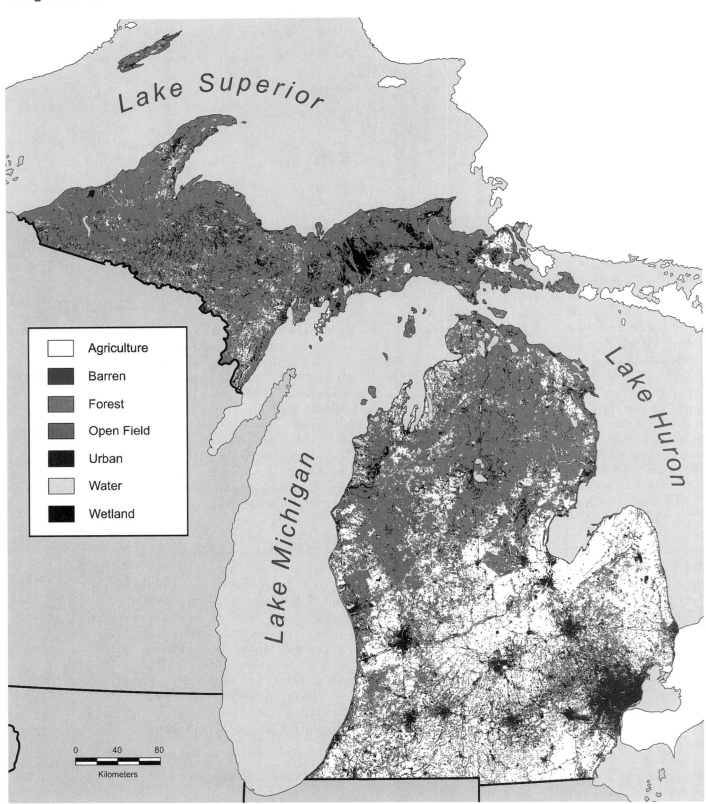

SOURCE: Michigan State University Center for Remote Sensing and Geographic Science (*www.crs.msu.edu*).

the total. Urbanization on the fringes of Michigan's urban areas accounts for about one-third of this total. Most of the reduction in cropland reflects public policies (in particular the Federal Crop Reduction Program) and individual responses to the market for agricultural and timber products.

The amount of developed land is, in part, a function of population. As indicated in table 5.2, which summarizes findings of the U.S. Department of Agriculture's National Resource Inventory (NRI), Michigan was the eighth-most populous state in 1982 and had the sixth-largest total of developed acres. The 30% increase in developed land between 1982 and 1997 accompanied a rise in the state's population of less than 4%. The amount of developed land per capita rose by nearly one-quarter. Yet development occurred at even lower densities in several other states. As a result, Michigan rose in the rankings of states by density (see appendix B).

An analysis of the NRI data for individual metropolitan areas (Fulton et al. 2001), found that most Michigan metropolitan areas were less dense than either the U.S. or the average for Midwestern metropolitan areas in 1997 (table 5.3). Between 1982 and 1997, the population of eight of the Michigan metropolitan areas (Grand Rapids being the exception) grew more slowly than the national average. Nevertheless, all areas experienced substantial increases in their urbanized land area, resulting in relative declines in urban density of between 12% and 28%.

An analysis by David Rusk (1999), utilizing Census data for a longer time period (1960 through 1990), compared the changes in urbanized land and population in fifty-eight metropolitan areas, including five in Michigan. The rate of increase in urbanized land was below average in four of the five Michigan metropolitan areas. Because of the slow population growth rates, however, the population density of the newly urbanizing areas was well below the central city density in the same metropolitan area The results of this analysis are summarized in table 5.4.

## Future Trends

According to the Michigan State University Land Transformation model's projections, as reported in the Michigan Land Resource Project Report (Public Sector Consultants 2001), the built-up areas of Michigan could increase from 2.3 million

**TABLE 5.2**

### Trends in Developed Land in Michigan, 1982–97

|  | 1982 | 1997 | Change |
|---|---|---|---|
| Total developed acres | 2,725,000 | 3,546,000 | 30.1% |
| *National rank* | *6* | *8* | |
| Population | 9,397,000 | 9,735,000 | 3.6% |
| *National rank* | *8* | *8* | |
| Developed acres per capita | 0.29 | 0.36 | 24.1% |
| *National rank* | *36* | *32* | |

SOURCE: U.S. Department of Agriculture (2001).

**TABLE 5.3**

### Changes in Density of Michigan Urbanized Areas

|  | Persons per Urbanized Acre 1997 | Growth 1982–97 | | |
|---|---|---|---|---|
|  |  | Urban Population | Urbanized Land Area | Urban Density |
| Battle Creek | 2.74 | –1.8% | 17.3% | –16.3% |
| Benton Harbor | 2.74 | –2.8% | 27.9% | –24.0% |
| Detroit | 4.27 | 5.0% | 29.0% | –18.7% |
| Flint | 2.97 | –0.6% | 21.4% | –18.1% |
| Grand Rapids | 3.32 | 26.9% | 45.2% | –12.6% |
| Kalamazoo | 3.52 | 9.7% | 30.2% | –15.8% |
| Lansing | 3.40 | 6.8% | 50.3% | –28.9% |
| Muskegon | 2.92 | 6.9% | 28.5% | –16.9% |
| Saginaw | 3.54 | –3.0% | 31.8% | –26.4% |
| MIDWEST AVERAGE[a] | 3.39 | 7.1% | 32.3% | –19.0% |
| U.S. AVERAGE | 3.55 | 17.0% | 47.1% | –20.5% |

SOURCE: Fulton et al. (2001).

(a) Based on seventy-six metropolitan areas in Illinois, Indiana, Iowa, Kansas, Michigan, Minnesota, Missouri, Nebraska, North Dakota, Ohio, South Dakota, and Wisconsin.

**TABLE 5.4**

### Growth and Density Changes, 1960–90

| Urban Area | Growth Rate | | Persons per Square Mile | |
|---|---|---|---|---|
|  | Population | Urbanized Land | New Growth | Central City |
| Detroit | 34% | 165% | 1,496 | 7,107 |
| Grand Rapids | 92% | 378% | 920 | 7,543 |
| Kalamazoo | 97% | 300% | 1,251 | 6,557 |
| Muskegon | 11% | 138% | 1,516 | 5,369 |
| Saginaw | 32% | 168% | 100 | 5,597 |
| AVERAGE (58 metro areas) | 80% | 305% | 1,573 | 7,504 |

SOURCE: Rusk (1999).

acres in 1980 to 6.4 million acres by 2040. These projections reflect the trends observed between 1980 and 1995, when the statewide average rate of urbanization was more than eight times greater than the rate of population growth.

This average conceals wide differences among the state's large urban areas. For example, urbanized land area in the Bay City metropolitan area increased twenty-seven times more rapidly than did population between 1960 and 1990; in the Saginaw area, the ratio was fourteen to one. Even in Lansing and Ann Arbor, where development patterns were relatively compact, the ratio of urbanized land to population growth was two to one.

There are other broad changes that may influence the shape of land use and urbanization in Michigan over the coming decades. One of these is the aging of the population. The U.S. population over the age of sixty-five is expected to double by 2030, to a total of seventy million (Howe 2001). The absolute and relative increase in the size of this population cohort (especially in those over the age of eighty) will strain not only the Social Security and health care systems, but also local transportation, housing, and social services delivery systems. This demographic shift may reduce pressures for large-lot housing developments. The low-density suburban development that has prevailed in recent years is generally considered to limit the mobility and independence of the elderly population.

In recent decades, Michigan's urban areas have been exporters of elderly residents, with many of their retirees choosing to move to northern Michigan resorts or warmer climates. Many of Michigan's suburbs and central cities have a lower than average proportion of their populations over the age of sixty-five. The continuation of this scenario is not certain, however. There is some indication that the elderly may elect to return to urban areas, to be closer to family or health care services and facilities.

A second major consideration relates to the implications of the growing importance of telecommunications. A significant increase in telecommuting may contribute to a greater dispersion of the population, with people living where they wish and transacting some or even most business electronically (Lincoln Institute of Land Policy 2001). The Bureau of Labor Statistics reports that some 3.6 million persons worked at home for pay in 1997 (Dearborn 2002). This figure is expected to increase in coming years. These trends could result in a significant reduction in the number of commuting trips and vehicles on the road during peak periods.

At the same time, the results may not all be benign. Reducing the number of work trips might encourage a more dispersed development pattern, with workers accepting longer commuting trips that are made less often. This, in turn, could contribute to a need for increased road capacity extending further from the central cities and metropolitan areas. The need for a more extensive public infrastructure could also include public water and sewer systems to serve the far-flung residential development.

This dispersion of the population could increase pressures on fragile environments. Changes may also have implications for the fiscal situation of some communities (Dearborn 2002). Municipalities levying income taxes on nonresidents could see their revenues from this source decline. State sales tax revenues might also be negatively affected.

There are other possible changes, far beyond Michigan's borders and its control, that will affect land use and development. Global warming, depletion of fossil fuels, and changing environmental standards are some of the factors that may have an impact on land use. These changes, however, are likely to be more gradual in their impact and more subtle in their implications. Moreover, there is often a lack of scientific consensus regarding the implications of these trends, let alone the best approaches to correcting the implied problems. Achieving this consensus is a prerequisite to the citizen education required before major alterations in established patterns of behavior are possible.

## Land Use and Development Controls

Most land use regulation occurs at the level of local government's within the framework of state enabling legislation (Wyckoff 1995). The rights of individual property owners, as well as the costs and benefits of development, are often of paramount concern at the community level. The state government is involved as a landowner, through regulation of some activities, by passing enabling legislation, as well as through investments in infrastructure. The federal government also plays an important role as landowner, regulator, and source of funds.

According to an analysis by the Sierra Club, Michigan was tied for last among the fifty states in terms of the quality of state land use planning and growth management (Sierra Club 2000). Generally, Michigan was found to be lacking in both the role state government plays in these areas and in the tools that were provided to local governments through enabling legislation. For example, Michigan statutes allow but do not require communities to adopt land use plans.

All municipalities in the state, including townships and counties, are authorized to develop master plans. Separate enabling legislation exists for cities and villages, townships and counties. State statutes do not mandate specific contents for the plans nor require communities to consider a broader area in developing their plans. Recently passed legislation (Public Acts 263, 264, and 265 of 2001) does, however, require local jurisdictions to communicate with their neighbors, sharing proposed plans and soliciting comments.

Other states are much more specific with respect to the nature of local plans (American Planning Association 1996). California and Florida, for example, require that local master plans include a number of specific elements, such as transportation, environment, and housing. Many states specify that the plans be reviewed on a periodic basis, typically every five years. Plans are coordinated with capital improvement activities. There may also be requirements for coordination or consistency between local plans and state goals and objectives. New Jersey has perhaps the most elaborate system in this regard.

The most common form of land use regulation is the local zoning ordinance. Michigan's zoning enabling statutes have not undergone a comprehensive update since the 1970s. Although recent amendments specify that many communities must provide a cluster option for residential developments, the use of many of the other modern tools for development control has not been authorized.

The state land division (plat) act has recently been amended (Public Act 591 of 1997). While these amendments have the positive benefits of increasing the certainty and efficiency of the land subdivision process, they also have the effect of removing the approval authority for the creation of large lots from local control.

Michigan has also adopted legislation to protect farming operations and agricultural land. Under Public Act 116 of 1974, owners of agricultural lands may apply for a development rights agreement that provides a covenant not to develop the property for a fixed term in exchange

for a reduction in property taxes. (See chapter 10 of this volume.) In addition, Public Act 93 of 1981, the Michigan Right to Farm Act, protects generally accepted agricultural and management practices from nuisance suits.

## State and Local Issues

There is increasing concern among a variety of interests (environmental and agricultural groups, as well as public officials and citizens) about the nature and rate at which land is being urbanized in Michigan (Larson 1994). Often this concern is expressed as a desire to stop "sprawl," without providing a clear definition of the term. The specific nature of the criticism of development patterns may include low densities, lack of form or structure (large single-use districts with no focus), increased traffic congestion, excessive infrastructure costs, discontinuous or "leap-frog" development, loss of valued natural areas, deterioration of older urban neighborhoods, or the isolation of population groups, such as the poor or minorities (Galster et al. 2001). Regardless of the definition that is used, the patterns of land use in developing areas have consequences for both the quality of life of the residents of Michigan and the fiscal health of the state's communities.

There is not, however, unanimous support either for changing land use patterns and regulations, or for the specifics of what the changes should be. Continuation of "business as usual," or something very close to it, is often encouraged by groups such as the development industry and property owners (Peterson 2002; Diamond and Noonan 1996). The development community is concerned that efforts to better manage or control development will, at best, make it more costly to develop, and at worst, lead to a total ban on growth. Property owners, ranging from speculators to family farmers, are concerned that they will be denied their anticipated capital gains. Many individuals equate the current pattern of suburban development with the American Dream of owning a large single-family home on a large lot. For others, property rights (and home rule for local governments) and market solutions are deemed preferable to increased regulation and government intervention.

These ideological conflicts are likely to continue unresolved. There are, however, a number of specific issues related to land use and development that many observers agree require attention.

Even though efforts to achieve a more comprehensive solution might be preferable, it is likely that problems of land use will be addressed more incrementally.

## Infrastructure Costs

The provision and maintenance of public capital facilities, including roads, water and sewer lines, and associated facilities, along with public buildings such as schools and fire stations, represent a large component of government expenditures. Financing of infrastructure for new development is often shared among the levels of government along with the private sector. For example, a developer may pay for the installation of local water and sewer lines serving a new residential subdivision, while the local government generally will have the responsibility for trunk water and sewer lines, as well as for major treatment facilities. Private utility companies (electric, gas, and telecommunications) will typically follow a similar cost-sharing arrangement.

Added costs for educational and recreational infrastructure, as well as public safety and traffic management, are not directly covered. Such costs typically do not emerge until some time after the development is built and the homes are occupied. (For public education, this situation is exacerbated by the fact that the public entity obligated to provide the facilities and services is not the same as the one responsible for approving the development.) Associated capital costs, as well as the higher operating costs, generally must be covered from local property tax revenues or other levies. With respect to education costs in particular, numerous studies have found that most residential development does not "pay its own way" in terms of tax revenues (Burchell et al. 1998).

In other states, provision has been made for impact fees or other exactions to offset the higher capital costs associated with new development. Particularly in California and states where property taxes are restricted, these fees have become an increasingly important source of funding for necessary improvements. These tools have not been used in Michigan, and in some circumstances may be subject to challenge under the so-called Headlee Amendment to the Michigan Constitution (Article IX, Sections 25–33) that requires voter approval of new or increased tax levies. (See chapter 33 of this volume.)

Some states, New York for example, assist in the cost of capital improvements for schools. While Michigan has shifted some of the burden of school operating costs from local districts to the state, the financing of new facilities continues to rely heavily on local voter approval and the local tax base. Only limited state subsidization is available through the School Bond Law fund. (See chapter 30 of this volume.)

Beginning with *The Costs of Sprawl* in the mid-1970s (Real Estate Research Corporation 1974), a number of studies have been undertaken to assess the fiscal implications of various types of new development. A review of some five hundred studies by Robert Burchell et al. (1998) found broad agreement that higher-density developments typically consume fewer resources per unit, while low-density development generated more miles of vehicle travel and more trips. The studies also found that low-density development was likely to have a greater impact on agricultural and other fragile land.

An analysis of costs for alternate forms of new development—both typical and compact—was undertaken by the Center for Urban Policy Research of Rutgers University for the Southeast Michigan Council of Governments (SEMCOG 1997). This study analyzed the costs of new development in selected Michigan municipalities utilizing two sets of assumptions. The first assumed that the projected population and employment growth would be accommodated at densities equivalent to the average for growth in the previous decade. Under the second scenario, half of the projected growth would be more compact, occurring within an urban growth boundary at densities 10% above the previous average. The analysts considered this level of increase in density to be negligible. The balance of the new housing would continue to occur outside of the growth boundary, but at densities 40% below average.

Overall, the compact growth scenario generated savings in all categories. The compact development patterns resulted in a savings of 12.7% in the amount of developed land, with comparable rates projected for the preservation of agricultural and other sensitive lands. Infrastructure requirements would be reduced by 12% to 18%. Compact growth could reduce average housing costs by about 6%.

The SEMCOG study further found that in fourteen municipalities in different regions of the state, the compact growth scenario was found to have a positive fiscal impact on the local government. (Table 5.5 and appendix C.) While new development generated less revenue than the attendant costs in both instances, the compact growth scenario generally had a more favorable cost-revenue impact. Local governments would realize an annual cost savings of $1.9 million (about 4.25% of the added costs) under a compact growth scenario. Total infrastructure expenditures by local and state governments would be reduced by $53 million for roads, $18 million for water, and $15 million for sewer improvements.

These findings are consistent with other recent research. The Canada Mortgage and Housing Corporation (1999), for example, found that a more compact development with a variety of different land uses (for example, residential and commercial) could save an average of $5,300 (16%) on per unit development costs and even more ($5,600) on operating and maintenance costs.

## Suburban Congestion

For much of its history, American city planning has been concerned with the problem of alleviating congestion in central cities and their business districts. In recent years, however, development patterns have shifted this concern to the suburban areas surrounding the cities. Traffic volumes have declined on many urban roads and freeways, while suburban traffic volumes have increased substantially.

The relatively low density of recent suburban development, along with the separation of land uses, makes public transit impractical and fosters reliance on individual automobiles for most trips (Cervero 1988). The average number of daily vehicle trips is higher in the suburbs because there are fewer destinations within walking distance. Many suburbs face high levels of congestion in the midday period, as well as during the morning and evening rush hours.

According to data compiled by the Texas Transportation Institute (TTI) Surface Transportation Policy Project (2001), problems resulting from traffic congestion have increased in metropolitan areas across the country. The rising congestion has resulted in significant costs, including time lost to delays, greater fuel use, and increased pollution. These costs have been increasing much more rapidly than have the number of vehicle miles traveled.

Figure 5.3 presents the trends in these measures for the Detroit area, the only Michigan met-

**TABLE 5.5**

**Annual Cost Revenue Impacts, Current vs. Compact Growth**

|  | Current | Compact | Difference |
|---|---|---|---|
| Added cost | $44,723,849 | $41,659,585 | $3,064,264 |
| Added revenue | $39,553,497 | $38,387,209 | $1,166,288 |
| Net cost | −$5,170,352 | −$3,272,376 | $1,897,976 |

SOURCE: Southeast Michigan Council of Governments (1997).

**FIGURE 5.3**

**Traffic and Congestion Indices, Metropolitan Detroit, 1982–99**

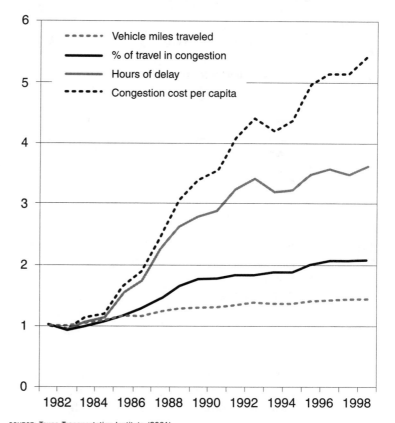

SOURCE: Texas Transportation Institute (2001).
NOTE: 1982 = 1.0.

ropolitan area included in the TTI database. Since 1982, Total Vehicle Miles (TVM) traveled in the metropolitan area increased by about 40%, and have remained relatively steady though much of the 1990s. During the last half of that decade, however, Detroit area drivers were twice as likely to encounter congestion as they were in the early 1980s. This increase is attributable to increases in both the number of vehicles and the TVM per

**TABLE 5.6**

**Per Capita Congestion**

| Metro Area | Population (000's) | Density pers/sq.mile | Per Capita Congestion Losses | | Congestion Index | |
|---|---|---|---|---|---|---|
| | | | Hours | Dollars | 2000 Value | Change 94–00 |
| **Very Large Areas (Over 3,000,000)** | | | | | | |
| New York | 17,090 | 4,205 | 23 | $450 | 1.16 | 14 |
| Los Angeles | 12,680 | 5,600 | 62 | $1,155 | 1.59 | 9 |
| Chicago | 8,090 | 2,915 | 27 | $505 | 1.31 | 14 |
| Philadelphia | 4,590 | 3,315 | 15 | $290 | 1.10 | 10 |
| San Francisco | 4,030 | 3,210 | 41 | $795 | 1.45 | 14 |
| Detroit | 4,025 | 3,060 | 25 | $475 | 1.22 | 7 |
| Dallas–Ft. Worth | 3,800 | 1,980 | 37 | $695 | 1.10 | 14 |
| Washington | 3,560 | 2,610 | 35 | $655 | 1.35 | 1 |
| Houston | 3,375 | 1,610 | 36 | $675 | 1.09 | 9 |
| Boston | 3,025 | 2,610 | 28 | $525 | 1.30 | 11 |
| VERY LARGE AREAS AVERAGE | 6,425 | 3,400 | 35 | $650 | 1.28 | 11 |
| | | | | | | |
| **Other Selected Large Areas** | | | | | | |
| Atlanta | 2,975 | 1,640 | 33 | $635 | 1.32 | 19 |
| San Diego | 2,710 | 3,590 | 24 | $480 | 1.32 | 16 |
| Phoenix | 2,600 | 2,320 | 28 | $525 | 1.27 | 23 |
| Minneapolis–St. Paul | 2,475 | 2,005 | 26 | $495 | 1.22 | 18 |
| Miami | 2,270 | 4,055 | 33 | $600 | 1.28 | 6 |
| Baltimore | 2,170 | 2,895 | 20 | $635 | 1.10 | 10 |
| St. Louis | 2,040 | 1,805 | 20 | $395 | 1.03 | 4 |
| Seattle | 2,000 | 2,285 | 34 | $660 | 1.23 | 14 |
| Tampa–St. Petersburg | 1,950 | 1,770 | 21 | $395 | 1.13 | –3 |
| Denver | 1,910 | 4,350 | 35 | $640 | 1.23 | 21 |
| Cleveland | 1,885 | 3,000 | 8 | $165 | 0.97 | 6 |
| Pittsburgh | 1,790 | 3,030 | 7 | $130 | 0.77 | 3 |
| San Jose | 1,675 | 1,525 | 33 | $635 | 1.34 | 1 |
| 75 AREA AVERAGE | 1,770 | 2,656 | 27 | $505 | 1.15 | 11 |

SOURCE: Texas Transportation Institute. 2001 Urban Mobility Study.

vehicle. The average number of hours of delay increased more than threefold and the congestion costs per capita increased more than fivefold.

The increasing use of the state's roads and highways requires increased expenditures on maintenance. The Michigan Department of Transportation estimates that, despite rehabilitation of an average of almost 1,500 highway miles annually since 1998, almost 2,600 of Michigan's 12,000 miles of the National Highway System were in poor condition in 2000 (Michigan Department of Transportation 2001). An additional 10,800 miles of county roads require reconstruction and 14,100 miles resurfacing, with over 90% of these existing needs unfunded. Furthermore, 21% of the 10,700 highway bridges are structurally deficient. (See also chapter 16 in this volume.)

## Case Studies

The significance of many of these issues is illustrated by the following case studies of urban areas around Michigan. The Southeast Michigan and Grand Rapids metropolitan areas are included because they are the two largest regions in the state and are following different approaches to regional development issues. Flint is prototypical of an aging industrial city. The Traverse City area is smaller but is coping with rapid growth that may affect important natural resources. Jackson County, experiencing substantial amounts of urban development despite limited employment and population growth, has embarked on a broadly based initiative to understand and manage development pressures.

## FIGURE 5.4

## Southeast Michigan Urban Development, 1980–2010

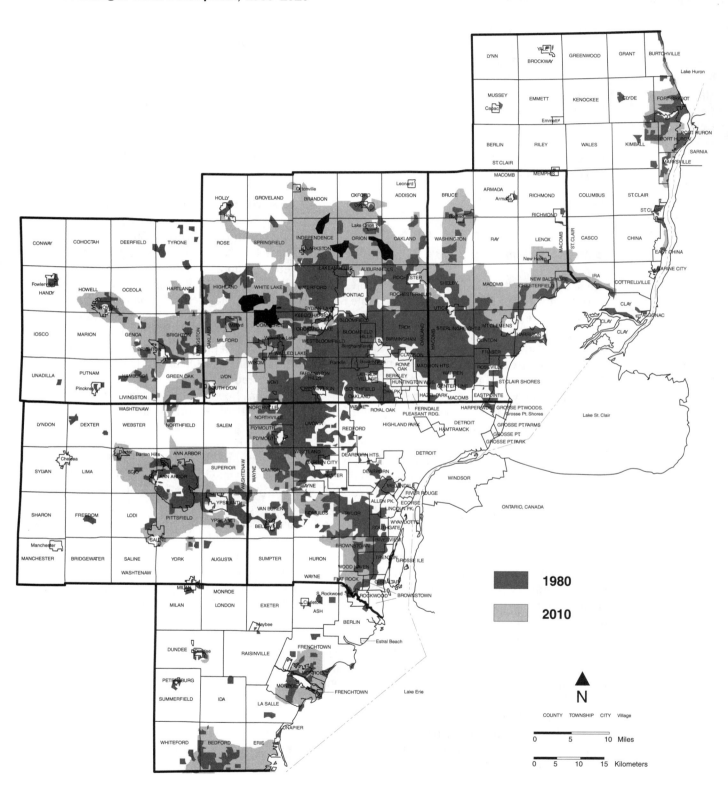

SOURCE: Southest Michigan Council of Governments (1997).

**TABLE 5.7**

**Metropolitan Detroit Population Trends**

|  | 1990 | 2000 | Change 1990–2000 | |
|---|---|---|---|---|
|  |  |  | Number | Percentage |
| Detroit | 1,027,974 | 951,270 | −76,704 | −7.5% |
| Balance Wayne | 1,083,713 | 1,109,892 | 26,179 | 2.4% |
| Macomb | 717,400 | 788,149 | 70,749 | 9.9% |
| Oakland | 1,083,592 | 1,194,156 | 110,564 | 10.2 |
| Lapeer | 74,768 | 87,904 | 13,136 | 17.6% |
| Monroe | 133,600 | 145,945 | 12,345 | 9.2% |
| St. Clair | 145,607 | 164,235 | 18,628 | 12.8% |
| TOTAL | 4,266,654 | 4,441,551 | 174,897 | 4.1% |

SOURCE: U.S. Census of Population.

## Southeast Michigan

The six counties that constitute the Detroit Primary Metropolitan Statistical Area (see table 5.6) included more than half of Michigan's total population from 1950 through 1970. Since 1970, other areas of the state have experienced higher population growth. By 2000, the Detroit PMSA population had increased to a total of 4.441 million, but represented only 44.7% of the state total.

The distribution of the population within the metropolitan area has also changed considerably. In 1950, Wayne County alone included three of every eight Michigan residents and, along with Oakland and Macomb, included 47 percent of the state's population. Between 1950 and 1970, the population of Wayne County rose by about 235,000 persons, while the combined total for Oakland and Macomb counties rose by almost one million, as growth shifted to these counties.

This trend continued between 1970 and 1990. Wayne County's population declined by about 560,000 persons during this period, primarily because of the continued steep decline of Detroit's population. Oakland and Macomb counties recorded gains of 176,000 and 92,000, respectively. The total population of the three counties fell by more than 290,000 between 1970 and 1990.

During the same period, the other three counties in the PMSA experienced considerable growth. Between 1970 and 1990, Lapeer, Monroe, and St. Clair Counties experienced an aggregate increase of about 63,000 in their population. This represents a gain of almost 18%.

Since 1990, the six-county PMSA has experienced a population increase of about 175,000, or 4.1% (see table 5.7). The population decline in

Detroit has slowed somewhat, while growth in the outlying counties has accelerated. In addition, the Census Bureau's definition of the Detroit Consolidated Metropolitan Statistical Area includes the Ann Arbor Primary Metropolitan Statistical Area (Washtenaw, Livingston, and Lenawee Counties) and the Flint Primary Metropolitan Statistical Area (Genesee County). With populations of 509,689 and 436,141, respectively, these two areas bring the Detroit CMSA's total population in 2000 to 5.46 million.

Despite the expansion of the urbanized area during a period of limited population growth, metropolitan Detroit as a whole remains relatively dense when compared to other large metropolitan areas. According to an analysis by the Texas Transportation Institute (2001), the six-county Detroit PMSA had the tenth-highest density among metropolitan areas with a population of two million or more in 1999. With just over 3,000 persons per square mile, metro Detroit was almost as dense as the San Francisco-Oakland urban area (3,200 persons per square mile), and was denser than other Midwest urban areas such as Chicago (2,900), Minneapolis (1,900), and St. Louis (1,800).

Even though the metropolitan population as a whole has been relatively stagnant, the area faces high costs for providing and maintaining infrastructure. The 2025 Regional Transportation Plan prepared by the Southeast Michigan Council of Governments (SEMCOG 2000) identifies $41 billion in road and bridge maintenance and improvement projects. Of this amount, funding has been identified for only $24 billion. These totals include costs of about $4 billion to operate and maintain the current public transportation system.

The estimated cost of maintaining and improving the regional sanitary and storm sewer system over the next thirty years is $14 to $26 billion (SEMCOG 2001b). (Inflation and interest charges could double the cost.) Most of these costs are associated with rehabilitating the existing facilities and remediating overflow/capacity problems. The total includes more than five thousand miles of new sewers.

These projected costs far exceed identified resources. In recent years expenditures on such projects have ranged between $700 and $900 million annually. Local planners attribute the relatively low level of current investment in part to a shift in federal funding patterns that has seen the federal contribution fall from $255 million in grants in 1976 to $68 million in loans in 2000. Competition for limited local resources from other capital projects will make it difficult to complete the already identified projects.

Other capital programs will also require substantial public investments, both in renewing existing facilities and in building new ones. The Detroit Public Schools, for example, are engaged in a $1.5 billion dollar program of renovation and new school construction. Some school officials and community members have stated that this amount only begins to address the total needs. A recent study estimated the cost of needed renovations and improvements to the City of Detroit's Belle Isle Park at $180 million (Bauza 2001). The city has commissioned a study of the capital needs of their other park and recreation facilities, with the expectation that the total for these projects will exceed the Belle Isle estimate.

Efforts to limit the development of new infrastructure are often frustrated by the need to provide adequate services to residents and businesses already at the urban fringe. New roads, water and sewer lines, schools, and other public infrastructure are required to meet the current needs of the population that has already moved to the periphery. For example, the discovery of arsenic in well water in a number of Oakland County communities has resulted in the approval of requests to extend public water service to new areas, despite the fact that the area already served by public water lines is more than sufficient to accommodate projected growth for years to come. Moreover, as infrastructure is extended to meet public health needs, the improvements open up new areas to easy development.

The size and complexity of the region make attempts to manage development difficult. The region is served by the Southeast Michigan Council of Governments, which provides a regional perspective on these issues. While SEMCOG functions as the Metropolitan Planning Organization for the programming of federal transportation dollars, and as the regional review agency for other federal programs, the agency lacks overall planning and implementation powers. Individual municipalities plan for their own needs, often with little regard for the likely effects on neighboring jurisdictions. Reliance on limited local capacity to raise revenue can contribute both to delays in implementing essential infrastructure projects and to encouragement of development in efforts to increase the local tax base. Individual households and businesses choose a location based on their own best interests, leaving aging infrastructure and high taxes to be dealt with by others.

With the exception of Wayne County, the Michigan Department of Transportation's projections anticipate that population growth in the Detroit PMSA counties will exceed that of the state. Oakland and Macomb Counties are expected to grow by 15% and 13%, respectively, by 2025, while higher rates will prevail in the outlying counties. SEMCOG's projections (2001a) show similar results, along with an increase of almost three hundred thousand jobs in the suburbs.

## Grand Rapids

The second-largest city and metropolitan area in the state, Grand Rapids has experienced a considerably different development history than has Southeast Michigan. The Census Bureau definition of the Grand Rapids Primary Metropolitan Statistical Area now includes four counties: Kent, Ottawa, Allegan, and Muskegon. In addition to Grand Rapids, the PMSA includes substantial urban populations around Muskegon and Holland. During the 1960s the City of Grand Rapids annexed considerable territory, providing opportunity for growth of both population and tax base over the next decade. By the 1980s, however, suburban Kent County began to exceed the central city on many indicators of growth and prosperity. More recently, growth has continued to shift outward, with the highest growth rates occurring in neighboring Ottawa County. About half of the metro area's growth has occurred in Kent County, with only about 6% of the total in the City of Grand Rapids.

Public policies have played an active role in shaping growth and development activity in this region. The City of Grand Rapids has pursued a number of policies to revitalize the core area and improve neighborhoods, with some success. Downtown development projects have brought not only businesses and recreational facilities, but also substantial numbers of residents. Businesses have been encouraged to participate in walk-to-work programs by offering assistance to their employees who buy homes in the area. This not only aids neighborhood revitalization efforts but also lessens the commuting requirements for workers.

Grand Rapids has been active in using economic development incentives. Industrial tax abatements have generated $441 million in investments and some four thousand jobs (Czurak 2001). The City of Grand Rapids has been the most active of the Renaissance Zone commu-

**TABLE 5.8**

**Grand Rapids Metropolitan Population Trends**

|  | 1990 | 2000 | Change 1990–2000 | |
|---|---|---|---|---|
|  |  |  | **Number** | **Percentage** |
| Grand Rapids | 189,126 | 197,800 | 8,674 | 4.6% |
| Kent County balance | 311,505 | 376,535 | 60,030 | 20.9% |
| Ottawa County | 187,768 | 238,314 | 50,546 | 26.9% |
| Allegan County | 90,509 | 105,665 | 15,156 | 16.7% |
| Muskegon County | 158,983 | 170,200 | 11,217 | 7.1% |
| TOTAL | 937,891 | 1,088,514 | 150,623 | 16.1% |

SOURCE: U.S. Census of Population.

nities designated by the state in 1997, with $84 million invested and over seven hundred new jobs in the zone.

Regional approaches have also played a role. In 1989, the Michigan legislature passed legislation that allowed all metropolitan areas in the state (except Detroit) to create a Metropolitan Council to undertake a number of planning and management functions at the regional level. The Grand Rapids area has been the only one to take advantage of this legislation. The Grand Valley Metro Council was created in 1990 and currently its membership includes Kent and Ottawa Counties, the City of Grand Rapids and thirty suburbs. The Metro Council has the ability to plan and provide public services on a regional basis, as well as the ability to levy property taxes to support its activities (Grand Valley Metropolitan Council 1993).

The Grand Rapids Water/Sewer Futures Project is a cooperative effort to manage development through the provision of public water and sewer service. This project created a Utility Service District where service would be provided and an Urban Utility Boundary, representing a reserve area. Outside of the boundary, the rate schedule is significantly higher. The boundaries and rules for expansion are set by a Utility Advisory Board, and a separate Urban Cooperation Board allows for pooling of funds for regional projects. Funds are provided by dues assessed on a per capita basis (Orfield 1999). Competition from the Wyoming water utility, which is more entrepreneurial it its approach and is not part of the Utility Advisory Board, has limited the effectiveness of this tool.

In recent years, significant highway costs have been incurred in suburban Kent County to accommodate suburban growth. Among the largest projects is the $75 million South Beltway

(M-6), which runs from Cascade Township to Ottawa County along the southern border of Kentwood and Wyoming. While this improvement addresses a real and significant need in terms of alleviating congestion, it also has the potential for contributing to increasing development well beyond the current limits of the urbanized area.

Over the next two decades, the population and economic growth of the Grand Rapids metropolitan area is expected to continue, but at a somewhat slower rate. Projections prepared by the Michigan Department of Transportation (2001) expect the region to add 210,000 to its population by 2025. Half of the total growth is expected to occur in Ottawa and Allegan Counties.

The Grand Rapids area is perhaps the most aggressive of Michigan's urban areas with respect to efforts to address development issues on a regional basis. The Metro Council and utility board represent growth management tools that do not currently exist in other metropolitan areas. There is also a strong initiative to provide public education and information regarding the impacts of growth. The West Shore Strategic Alliance is examining transportation issues on a multicounty basis.

The results of these efforts, however, are seen by some as less than satisfactory (Orfield 1999). Conflicting priorities, whether among water utilities or local governments, with respect to population growth will contribute to the continued dispersion of development patterns. While there is clearly a regional perspective on growth, little of this has filtered down to the local level to be incorporated in master plans or land use and development regulations.

## Flint

With a population of 436,000, the single-county Flint Primary Metropolitan Statistical Area is the fifth-largest in Michigan. The Genesee County population doubled between 1940 and 1980, when it peaked at 450,000. The City of Flint itself began to experience a loss of population in the 1960s, with its population declining from 197,000 to 130,000 at the 2000 Census.

Suburban Genesee County is not homogenous. It includes a total of thirty-one municipalities: ten cities, four villages, and seventeen townships. Flint Township was the largest suburb in 2000, with a population of 33,700. With the exception of the city of Burton, all of the other suburbs with populations of at least 10,000 are townships.

Genesee County includes a number of aging suburbs that are losing population. In addition to the City of Flint, ten other municipalities lost population between 1990 and 2000. Growth in the past decade has been concentrated in the southern part of the county, in the vicinity of Fenton and Grand Blanc. Much of this growth appears to be overspill from Oakland County.

The city of Flint differs from most of its suburbs in a number of measures. The city is home to 75% of the county's African American population. Income and educational attainment are substantially higher in the suburbs than in the city, while poverty rates, unemployment, and the incidence of single-parent households are each higher in the city. One-third of Flint's residents are under the age of eighteen, compared to one-quarter of the suburban population. The Genesee County suburbs have a higher proportion of elderly than the city does.

Much of the city of Flint's population decline is attributable to economic restructuring, in particular the loss of manufacturing jobs. General Motors, by far the largest employer in the county, had cut its employment in half by the mid-1990s, to 38,000. Employment at General Motors facilities in Flint has continued to decline and may be down to 15,000 by the end of the current decade. In its efforts to combat this decline, the City of Flint has utilized a wide variety of economic development incentives. Industrial tax abatements have been used to attract over $1 billion in investment and are credited with preserving almost forty thousand jobs. (See chapter 14 of this volume for a detailed description of these programs.) Despite these efforts, the city's population has continued to decline, both absolutely and relatively. The loss of population and economic activity has left the community with extensive areas of abandoned and underutilized property, some of it contaminated.

The Michigan Department of Transportation anticipates the rate of population growth in Genesee County to increase slightly over the next two decades. (Other sources are more pessimistic, projecting a steady or declining population for the county as a whole.) By 2025, the county population is expected to reach 455,000, a gain of 4.4%.

### Traverse City/Grand Traverse Bay

This northwest Michigan community presents a microcosm of the issues related to efforts to limit

**TABLE 5.9**

**Flint Metropolitan Population Trends**

| | 1990 | 2000 | Change 1990–2000 | |
| --- | --- | --- | --- | --- |
| | | | Number | Percentage |
| Flint | 140,761 | 129,943 | −10,818 | −7.7% |
| Balance Genesee | 289,698 | 306,198 | 16,500 | 5.7% |
| TOTAL | 430,459 | 436,141 | 5,682 | 1.3% |

SOURCE: U.S. Census of Population.

the negative impacts of growth on the community. Although the total population of the area is relatively small, about 115,000 in 2000, the rate of growth over the last few decades has nevertheless resulted in significant stress (Grand Traverse County 1996). Table 5.10 summarizes the population trends for this area.

The growth-related concerns are similar to those found in larger urban areas. Traffic congestion, especially during the summer tourist season, is considered a major problem. Urban development is perceived to be a threat to important agricultural land. Local regulations and high land prices make it difficult to provide new housing to meet the needs of the rapidly growing number of service workers. All of these concerns reflect commonly vocalized complaints about the impacts of rapid growth on local roads with limited capacity or on long-time residents and businesses (including agriculture) that may resist changes that are all too visible.

Residents and governments in the area have attempted to address these issues. *Focus 2020*, the current Master Plan for Grand Traverse County (Grand Traverse County 1996), incorporates two fundamental principles aimed at changing the "business as usual" pattern of land development

**TABLE 5.10**

**Grand Traverse Bay Population Trends**

| | 1990 | 2000 | Change 1990–2000 | |
| --- | --- | --- | --- | --- |
| | | | Number | Percentage |
| Traverse City | 15,155 | 14,522 | −633 | −4.2% |
| Gr. Traverse Balance | 49,118 | 63,132 | 14,014 | 28.5% |
| Leelanau | 16,527 | 21,119 | 4,592 | 27.8% |
| Benzie | 12,200 | 15,998 | 3,798 | 31.1% |
| TOTAL | 93,000 | 114,671 | 21,671 | 23.2% |

SOURCE: U.S. Census of Population.

## TABLE 5.11

**Jackson County Population Trends**

| | 1990 | 2000 | Change 1990–2000 | |
| --- | --- | --- | --- | --- |
| | | | Number | Percentage |
| Jackson City | 37,466 | 36,316 | –1,150 | –3.1% |
| County balance | 112,290 | 122,106 | 9,816 | 8.7% |
| TOTAL | 149,756 | 158,442 | 8,686 | 5.8% |

SOURCE: U.S. Census of Population.

that will occur as the county continues to experience population and economic growth. First, modest increases in density are encouraged. Second, the growth is to be directed to existing urban areas and the adjacent urban influence areas. While development controls will continue to be a local prerogative, the county may seek a more active role in managing growth.

The area provides a number of examples of effective initiatives to at least partially alleviate the stresses of growth. In Peninsula Township, a locally funded farmland preservation program has been used to address the loss of not only agricultural productivity but also scenic views on the Old Mission Peninsula through the purchase of development rights. Some 1,847 acres have been enrolled in the township's program, with state and private agreements covering an additional 1,573 acres. Local property tax millages are used to fund this program.

Brownfield redevelopment projects in Traverse City have also been encouraged. The redevelopment of a former ironworks just south of downtown has brought jobs and residents to the area. The redevelopment of the former state hospital has proved to be more challenging, with considerable difficulty being encountered in finding economically viable reuses for the facilities.

The current levels of traffic congestion have not resulted in acceptance of all road construction projects. The proposed highway bypass south of the Traverse City has been a focus not just of controversy but of careful study and analysis. With a price tag of more than $240 million, this highway has been identified by the Sierra Club as one of the fifty most wasteful roads in America (Sierra Club 1999) because of its high cost and potential for opening new areas to urban development. Local interests are concerned not only with the environmental and fiscal costs of the proposal, but also with how the project would impact the viability of established business districts.

An additional twenty-eight thousand persons are expected to be added to the regional population by 2025 (Michigan Department of Transportation 2001). About 60% of the growth will occur in Grand Traverse County. Although the absolute increase is expected to be smaller, both Benzie and Leelanau Counties are expected to have growth rates of close to 30% over the period, compared to 22% in Grand Traverse County.

### Jackson

The City of Jackson and Jackson County have not experienced the growth pressures to the same extent as some of the suburban Detroit or western and northern Michigan communities. Nevertheless, the past decade has witnessed an increase in population, and this trend is expected to continue in the coming years, in part as a result of growth pressures from adjacent counties. Table 5.10 summarizes the population growth trends in the county.

Because this growth has raised concerns about the impact of development on the county's quality of life, all of the local governments in the county—nineteen townships, seven villages, and the City of Jackson—have agreed to join with Jackson County in the development of a comprehensive master plan (Thomas 2002). An earlier goal-setting exercise involving a broad range of public officials and citizens, the Jackson Comm-Unity Transformation, raised concerns about issues such as improved intergovernmental cooperation, effective public participation in decision making, and commitment to sustainable growth policies. The continued spread of urban development, especially in an area experiencing little growth in population or employment, can result in conflicts between individual landowners or communities and broader interests.

The countywide master plan represents an attempt to create a mechanism to provide more accurate and timely information about the use of land resources, to alleviate intergovernmental conflicts that arise from development, and to support the better use of public funds for planned improvements. The planning process is based on long-term, equitable management and use of natural resources; policies will be formulated through the use of cutting-edge tools and techniques, including computer mapping and simulations, for impact assessment and visualization.

The county has hired a consultant to assist in

gathering input from township supervisors and city and village managers, organizing community input, and preparing a traditional land use document. Priorities being addressed in the master plan include preservation of farmland and rural character, transportation and traffic, residential development, utilities and public service, land use and economic development, recreation, and intergovernmental cooperation (Thomas 2002).

The second phase introduces an interactive decision support system called Smart Places®, a geographic information system (GIS)–based modeling program that answers the "what if" questions frequently associated with planning and zoning decisions (Thomas 2002). It allows nontechnical users to interactively review land use scenarios, sketch recommended changes, and evaluate these recommendations against local and state policies, objectives, and constraints. Greater understanding of the impact of proposed developments on the implementation of planning policies, zoning rules, public services, environmental management, and socioeconomic equity will be feasible. Important land use decisions can be made that are based on hard data in real time.

The capacity of this community-based partnership is accelerated by the MSU Alliance for Land and Water Decision Support. This university partnership involves the Department of Resource Development, the Victor Institute for Responsible Land Development and Use, and the Institute of Water Research. The MSU Alliance, along with the Jackson County Extension office, is developing the decision support system for the interactive component of the plan and will initiate a Citizen Planner program to provide training and outreach support to local governments in using the decision support system and developing their respective master plans.

## Public Policy Issues

These examples illustrate how different communities around Michigan are attempting to deal with the issues of growth and development. Several common threads exist in these efforts:

- Local governments are often leaders in terms of innovations, but their efforts may be hampered by a lack of clear statutory authority.
- Absent such authority, and with the difficulty of achieving consensus among local govern-

ments and their citizens, successful regional initiatives have been rare.
- Shared concern about quality-of-life issues, which include social and economic as well as environmental values, is key to building consensus.
- The most successful planning efforts appear to have the widest base of stakeholder participation, including interest groups, governments, and the public at large.
- The effectiveness of local efforts is limited by the voluntary, and potentially transitory, nature of cooperative agreements and the competition among jurisdictions for tax base and development.
- Regional planning efforts can be effective in providing information and a forum for public participation.

## Conclusions

Issues related to land use, especially land use change, will continue to affect every Michigan resident over the next decade and the years to follow. Despite relatively slow population growth over the past two decades, the state of Michigan has continued to experience high rates of land development. While the consequences have not always been as serious in Michigan as in faster-growing states, an increasing number of Michigan's citizens have come to view the current development patterns with concern.

Some view recent changes as diminishing the quality of life. Urbanization has impacted agricultural lands, wetlands, and other fragile environments. Others argue that, with a stagnant population, suburban growth is a "zero sum game," with new development at the periphery of metropolitan areas negatively impacting older communities. The fiscal problems of some older suburbs can be traced to the current land development patterns. Activities ranging from second home development to oil and gas operations and snowmobiling have disproportionate impacts on the state's rural areas. The public costs of maintaining and extending infrastructure are substantial. The continuation of current land use patterns will force state and local governments in Michigan to face difficult decisions about both resource allocation and development policies.

Although many find these trends to be undesirable, they continue, in part, because of a longstanding commitment to property rights and local government home rule. Throughout the United States in general, and in Michigan in particular, individual rights and freedoms are at the heart of government and public policies. This strong commitment to the ideal of private property makes government-imposed solutions difficult.

The notion of improved land use and more efficient development patterns (involving lower costs for providing and maintaining required infrastructure) is not incompatible with this attitude, however. Indeed, regulations that contribute to the preservation of individual choices, the more efficient use of public funds, and the overall quality of life of all residents would be consistent with American ideals.

Local problems are rarely solved by the imposition of solutions by higher levels of government. At the same time, however, individuals and individual communities cannot ignore their neighbors. Purely market solutions may be too shortsighted; communitarian solutions may be too difficult to organize and sustain. Within the broad framework of the marketplace, there is a role for government, but not one of imposing the perfect solution. The complexities of the externalities involved in land use decisions by individual governments seem to call for broader public participation.

Two things that are necessary are more flexible tools for managing the development process and better information on the consequences of development decisions. The first of these can be addressed by providing local governments with a range of tools that will allow them to provide property owners with development choices that will lead to more efficient land use. These could include transfer of development rights, expanded purchase of development rights, urban growth boundaries (which designate the area available for urban development), urban services districts (which identify areas where urban infrastructure will be provided), and regional revenue sharing. While these tools are not appropriate in every situation, authorizing their use through statutory authority will provide more and better tools to communities that wish to use them.

In addition, there is a clear need for more collaboration and coordination of public-sector decision making with respect to developments that have impacts beyond the boundaries of a single taxing jurisdiction. Extending the current requirements for information sharing on plan development to zoning changes and large-scale development proposals would facilitate this type of collaboration.

## Policy Options

There are clearly no easy solutions to the complex issue of how land use choices should be managed. Although there is no single best solution that is appropriate in all instances, state and local governments might work to build a framework for individual choices that ensures that the interests of each community, as well as the state, both short and long term, are protected. While from time to time the state may undertake direct actions that impact land use, its primary responsibility is likely to continue to be one of establishing the statutory framework for local decisions on land use. The following are some specific policy areas that should be addressed in the process of constructing such a framework:

- Encouragement of expanded housing choices for all residents. Should new developments and suburbs be required or encouraged to include a broader spectrum of housing choices that weave neighborhoods together rather than isolate them?
- Address the issue of transportation choices. Should the state restrict funding of road extensions in favor of repairs and transportation management? Should there be support alternatives to drivers commuting alone, including commuter lanes, dial-a-ride, small vanpools, and other forms of mass transit?
- Ask if owners of working (agricultural, horticultural, and forestry) land have enough viable choices with respect to how the land is used.
- Consider if current statutory authority and funding are sufficient to realize effective master planning at both the local and regional levels.
- Consider if requiring an assessment of the regional impacts of major projects supported by State funds would improve planning and reduce development conflicts.
- Consider if limiting the availability of economic development incentives to projects that are consistent with established regional development policies would help focus development without encouraging sprawl.

There is also a need to consider means to strengthen regional mechanisms that address growth and development issues. While basic decisions on land use and development are often best left to the local levels, there appear to be a number of functions that might be more effectively addressed from a broader perspective, including:

- Encouraging coordination of the planning for the provision of regional infrastructure, including roads, transit, water, sewer, and other facilities;
- Improving mechanisms for identifying sensitive lands and other critical natural resources that can affect development;
- Providing a land use information exchange to assist in the coordination of local decisions; and
- Promoting the objective analysis of the cost and revenue implications of development, both in general and for specific projects.

Local governments, in both urban and rural areas, could then take advantage of these land use tools to better address local problems, both those within their own communities and those with spillover impacts on their neighbors.

■

## REFERENCES AND ADDITIONAL READINGS

American Planning Association. 1996. *Getting to growing smart.* Washington, D.C.: American Planning Association.

———. 2002. *Policy guide on smart growth.* Washington, D.C.: American Planning Association.

Bauza, Margarita. 2001. Belle Isle boosters push rescue plan for Detroit gem. *Detroit News,* 24 August, 1B.

Burchell, Robert, Naveed Shad, David Listokin, Hilary Phillips, Anthony Downs, Samuel Seskin, Judy S. Davis, Terry Moore, David Helton, and Michelle Gall. 1998. *Costs of sprawl revisited: The evidence of sprawl's positive and negative consequences.* Washington, D.C.: Transportation Research Board, National Research Council.

Canada Mortgage and Housing Corporation. 1999. *Infrastructure costs associated with conventional and alternative development patterns.* Ottawa, Ont.: Queens Printer.

Cervero, Robert. 1988. Land-use mixing and suburban mobility. *Transportation Quarterly* 42(3): 429–46.

Czurak, David. 2001. Tax abatements fuel expansion projects. *Business Resource Guide 2001.* Grand Rapids Business Journal.

Dearborn, Philip. 2002. *Effects of telecommuting on central city tax bases.* Washington, D.C.: Brookings Institution.

Diamond, Henry L., and Patrick Noonan. 1996. *Land use in America.* Washington, D.C.: Island Press.

Fulton, William, Rolf Pendall, Mai Nguyen, and Alicia Hamilton. 2001. *Who sprawls most? How growth patterns differ across the U.S.* Washington, D.C.: Brookings Institution Center on Urban and Metropolitan Policy.

Galster, George, Royce Hanson, Michael R. Ratcliffe, Harold Wolman, Stephen Coleman, and Jason Freihag. 2001. Wrestling sprawl to the ground: Defining and measuring an elusive concept. *Housing Policy Debate* 12(4): 681–717.

Grand Traverse County. 1996. *Focus 2020: Grand Traverse County Master Plan.* Traverse City, Mich.: Grand Traverse County Planning Commission.

Grand Valley Metropolitan Council. 1993. *Grand Valley Metropolitan Region 2015 metropolitan development blueprint.* Grand Rapids, Mich.: Metro Council.

Howe, Deborah. 2001. *Aging and smart growth: Building aging-sensitive communities.* Translation Paper No. 7. Washington, D.C.: Funders' Network for Smart Growth and Livable Communities.

Jacobs, Michael. 1991. *The green economy.* Concord, Mass.: Pluto Press.

Larson, Naomi. 1994. *Land use issues identification. A Michigan's trend future working paper.* Rochester, Mich.: Michigan Society of Planning Officials.

Lincoln Institute of Land Policy. 2001. *The new spatial order? Technology and urban development.* Cambridge, Mass.: Lincoln Institute of Land Policy.

Michigan Department of Environmental Quality. 2000. *Michigan environmental quality report.* Lansing, Mich.: State of Michigan.

Michigan Department of Transportation. 2001. *Facts and figures.* Lansing, Mich.: State of Michigan.

Orfield, Myron. 1999. *Grand Rapids area metropolitics: A west Michigan agenda for community and stability.* Minneapolis, Minn.: Metropolitan Area Research Corporation.

Peterson, Jane. 2002. Viewpoints differ when it comes to dealing with growth. *Commercial, Inc.* March, p. 11.

Public Sector Consultants, Inc. 2001. *Michigan land resource project.* Lansing, Mich.: Michigan Economic and Environmental Roundtable.

Real Estate Research Corporation. 1974. *The costs of sprawl.* Washington, D.C.: GPO.

Rusk, David. 1999. *Inside game outside game.* Washington, D.C.: Brookings Institution.

Sierra Club. 1999. *Road to ruin report.* Washington, D.C.: Sierra Club.

———. 2000. *Smart choices of sprawling growth.* Washington, D.C.: Sierra Club.

Southeast Michigan Council of Governments. 1997. *Fiscal impacts of alternative land development patterns in Michigan: The costs of current development versus compact growth final report.* Detroit, Mich.:

SEMCOG.

———. 2000. *2025 regional transportation plan for Southeast Michigan.* Detroit, Mich.: SEMCOG.

———. 2001a. *2030 regional development forecast for Southeast Michigan.* Detroit, Mich.: SEMCOG.

———. 2001b. *Investing in Southeast Michigan's quality of life: Sewer infrastructure needs.* Detroit, Mich.: SEMCOG, April.

Staley, Sam. 1999. Effective sprawl solutions found in market, not regional planning. *Detroit News,* 24 October, 9C.

Surface Transportation Policy Project. 1998. *An analysis of the relationship between highway expansion and congestion in metropolitan areas.* College Station, Tex.: Texas Transportation Institute.

Texas Transportation Institute. 2001. *2001 urban mobility study.* College Station, Tex.: Texas A&M University.

Thomas, Michael. 2002. *The changing face of land use planning in Michigan.* Lansing, Mich.: MSU Alliance for Land and Water Decision Support.

U.S. Department of Agriculture. 2001. *National resource inventory 1997.* Washington, D.C.: USDA.

Wyckoff, Mark. 1995. *Institutional structure of land use decision making in Michigan. A Michigan's trend future working paper.* Rochester, Mich.: Michigan Society of Planning Officials.

Wyckoff, Mark, and Terry Moultane. 1995. *Mineral trends working paper.* Rochester, Mich.: Michigan Society of Planning Officials.

## APPENDIX A

**Population Density 2000: Selected States**

| | Population | Sq. Miles | Population/ Sq. Mile | Rank |
|---|---|---|---|---|
| California | 33,871,648 | 163,696 | 217 | 5 |
| Illinois | 12,419,293 | 57,914 | 223 | 11 |
| Indiana | 6,080,485 | 36,418 | 170 | 16 |
| **Michigan** | **9,938,444** | **96,716** | **175** | **15** |
| Minnesota | 4,919,479 | 86,939 | 62 | 31 |
| North Carolina | 8,049,313 | 53,819 | 165 | 17 |
| Ohio | 11,353,140 | 44,852 | 277 | 9 |
| Pennsylvania | 12,281,054 | 46,055 | 274 | 10 |
| Virginia | 7,078,515 | 42,774 | 179 | 14 |
| Wisconsin | 5,363,675 | 65,498 | 99 | 24 |
| UNITED STATES | 281,421,906 | 3,794,083 | 80 | —— |

SOURCE: U.S. Census of Population.

APPENDIX B

## Acres Developed by State, 1982–97

| State | Developed 1997 | | | Increase 1982–97 | | |
|---|---|---|---|---|---|---|
| | Acres (000) | Percentage | Rank | Number | Percentage | Rank |
| Alabama | 2,252.3 | 7.2% | 23 | 635.7 | 39.3% | 17 |
| Arizona | 1,491.4 | 3.5% | 43 | 402.8 | 37.0% | 19 |
| Arkansas | 1,409.1 | 4.7% | 33 | 265.7 | 23.2% | 33 |
| California | 5,456.1 | 10.3% | 17 | 1,318.1 | 31.9% | 25 |
| Colorado | 1,651.7 | 3.9% | 38 | 415.2 | 33.6% | 24 |
| Connecticut | 873.9 | 28.6% | 4 | 123.3 | 16.4% | 44 |
| Delaware | 225.5 | 18.6% | 6 | 58.5 | 35.0% | 22 |
| Florida | 5,184.8 | 16.9% | 7 | 1,913.4 | 58.5% | 3 |
| Georgia | 3,957.3 | 11.4% | 14 | 1,590.3 | 67.2% | 1 |
| Hawaii | 179.7 | 4.8% | 32 | 30.5 | 20.4% | 39 |
| Idaho | 754.9 | 3.9% | 37 | 204.7 | 37.2% | 18 |
| Illinois | 3,180.9 | 9.1% | 20 | 492.3 | 18.3% | 41 |
| Indiana | 2,260.4 | 10.1% | 18 | 425.6 | 23.2% | 34 |
| Iowa | 1,702.1 | 4.8% | 31 | 119.9 | 7.6% | 48 |
| Kansas | 1,939.9 | 3.8% | 39 | 221.4 | 12.9% | 46 |
| Kentucky | 1,737.5 | 7.2% | 22 | 592.2 | 51.7% | 7 |
| Louisiana | 1,623.8 | 6.2% | 26 | 389.9 | 31.6% | 26 |
| Maine | 712.0 | 3.7% | 40 | 202.5 | 39.7% | 16 |
| Maryland | 1,235.7 | 20.4% | 5 | 322.7 | 35.3% | 21 |
| Massachusetts | 1,479.2 | 30.4% | 3 | 445.2 | 43.1% | 10 |
| Michigan | 3,545.5 | 10.8% | 15 | 820.2 | 30.1% | 29 |
| Minnesota | 2,185.5 | 4.6% | 34 | 465.6 | 27.1% | 32 |
| Mississippi | 1,474.0 | 5.3% | 29 | 353.8 | 31.6% | 27 |
| Missouri | 2,517.4 | 6.0% | 27 | 433.5 | 20.8% | 37 |
| Montana | 1,032.3 | 1.6% | 49 | 153.7 | 17.5% | 42 |
| Nebraska | 1,205.9 | 2.5% | 44 | 94.4 | 8.5% | 47 |
| Nevada | 381.4 | 3.6% | 41 | 109.2 | 40.1% | 15 |
| New Hampshire | 588.6 | 11.9% | 11 | 209.6 | 55.3% | 6 |
| New Jersey | 1,778.2 | 39.1% | 1 | 512.7 | 40.5% | 14 |
| New Mexico | 1,152.7 | 2.3% | 46 | 371.7 | 47.6% | 9 |
| New York | 3,183.6 | 10.7% | 16 | 547.8 | 20.8% | 38 |
| North Carolina | 3,856.4 | 13.6% | 10 | 1,439.7 | 59.6% | 2 |
| North Dakota | 991.8 | 2.3% | 45 | 57.6 | 6.2% | 49 |
| Ohio | 3,611.3 | 14.1% | 9 | 828.5 | 29.8% | 30 |
| Oklahoma | 1,926.3 | 4.5% | 35 | 332.8 | 20.9% | 36 |
| Oregon | 1,222.3 | 4.1% | 36 | 266.7 | 27.9% | 31 |
| Pennsylvania | 3,983.2 | 14.3% | 8 | 1,164.4 | 41.3% | 12 |
| Rhode Island | 200.6 | 30.5% | 2 | 33.1 | 19.8% | 40 |
| South Carolina | 2,097.3 | 11.6% | 13 | 748.4 | 55.5% | 5 |
| South Dakota | 959.7 | 2.1% | 47 | 122.3 | 14.6% | 45 |
| Tennessee | 2,370.6 | 9.5% | 19 | 865.9 | 57.5% | 4 |
| Texas | 8,567.0 | 5.2% | 30 | 2,280.5 | 36.3% | 20 |
| Utah | 661.6 | 3.6% | 42 | 191.5 | 40.7% | 13 |
| Vermont | 317.5 | 5.8% | 28 | 74.8 | 30.8% | 28 |
| Virginia | 2,625.8 | 11.7% | 12 | 784.5 | 42.6% | 11 |
| Washington | 2,065.0 | 6.8% | 24 | 527.8 | 34.3% | 23 |
| West Virginia | 873.6 | 6.2% | 25 | 289.7 | 49.6% | 8 |
| Wisconsin | 2,417.9 | 7.4% | 21 | 428.7 | 21.6% | 35 |
| Wyoming | 643.7 | 1.9% | 48 | 93.8 | 17.1% | 43 |
| NATION | 98,251.7 | 6.6% | —— | 25,005.9 | 34.1% | —— |

SOURCE: U.S. Department of Agriculture (2001).
NOTE: Data for Alaska are not yet available.

## APPENDIX C

## Annual Cost and Revenue Impact of New Development

| Community | Current Added Cost | Current Added Revenue | Current Difference | Compact Added Cost | Compact Added Revenue | Compact Difference |
|---|---|---|---|---|---|---|
| **Southeast Michigan** | | | | | | |
| Harrison | $1,542,388 | $861,076 | −$681,312 | $1,490,966 | $820,540 | −$670,426 |
| Macomb | $5,091,515 | $4,379,449 | −$712,067 | $4,053,520 | $3,969,190 | −$84,330 |
| Bedford | $996,846 | $1,134,165 | $137,319 | $965,328 | $1,121,665 | $156,337 |
| Novi | $14,769,424 | $11,766,829 | −$3,002,594 | $14,653,446 | $11,807,116 | −$2,846,331 |
| Pittsfield | $3,719,980 | $7,490,948 | $3,770,967 | $3,734,848 | $7,514,031 | $3,779,193 |
| Canton | $9,275,327 | $5,419,323 | −$3,856,004 | $7,924,363 | $4,942,195 | −$2,982,168 |
| **West Michigan** | | | | | | |
| Kentwood | $3,572,526 | $1,998,102 | −$1,574,424 | $3,390,741 | $1,962,729 | −$1,428,012 |
| Allendale | $912,787 | $1,113,150 | −$200,363 | $845,180 | $1,058,339 | −$1,428,012 |
| Montague | $334,440 | $330,129 | −$9,311 | $327,076 | $309,401 | −$17,675 |
| Muskegon | $1,632,708 | $2,505,778 | $873,070 | $1,585,668 | $2,409,922 | $824,254 |
| **Northwest Michigan** | | | | | | |
| Bear Creek | $221,193 | $274,641 | $53,488 | $215,853 | $271,439 | $55,586 |
| Petoskey | $452,279 | $161,444 | −$290,835 | $430,191 | $153,176 | −$277,015 |
| Resort | $271,442 | $119,814 | −$151,628 | $265,515 | $121,504 | −$144,011 |
| Garfield | $1,925,993 | $1,998,648 | $72,655 | $1,776,888 | $1,925,961 | $149,073 |

SOURCE: Southeast Michigan Council of Governments (1997).

# 6

# Michigan's Stake in International Trade and Investment

*Alan V. Deardorff*

## I. Introduction

At first glance the state of Michigan appears geographically to be rather central to the United States, and certainly those of us who live here tend to think of ourselves as part of America's heartland. Yet true as this may be, it is also true that Michigan interacts extensively with the rest of the world, in part across our border with Canada, but also with many other more distant countries through international commerce. This chapter documents the extent of that interaction.

Although international economic interactions take many forms, there are two that are especially important in their implications for the Michigan economy: international trade and international investment. In trade, Michigan firms and consumers purchase many goods and services from foreign firms, and these imports provide a low-cost source of many of the things we depend upon for our standard of living, as well as essential inputs for Michigan's own producers. More distinctive, however, and perhaps more important for the health of the Michigan economy, are our exports. As we will see, Michigan exports more each year than all but three other states. In consequence, a significant portion of Michigan's economy, including its employment of labor, depends upon this access to world markets.

Section 2 of this chapter will use available data to indicate of what Michigan's exports consist, to which countries and parts of the world we export, how our exports have changed over time, and how Michigan compares with other states along these dimensions. It will also examine how important these exports are for employment in the Michigan economy, both directly and indirectly.

International investment includes both U.S. investment abroad and foreign firms' investment in the United States. Much of this investment is financial, but an important part of it, called Foreign Direct Investment (FDI), consists of the acquisition of real productive capital in another country, specifically the ownership by foreigners of establishments in the United States, and the ownership by U.S. firms of establishments abroad. Of these two, it is the former that has the most direct and obvious impact on the local economy, and fortunately there exist good data on the extent of such foreign ownership at the state level. This will be reported in section 3, where we will see how many firms in the Michigan economy are owned by foreigners.

These two sections constitute the bulk of the chapter, for two reasons. First, there is now a large amount of data at the state level, both on exports and on inward FDI. And second, these are the two forms of international transaction that relate

**TABLE 6.1**

**U.S. and Michigan Merchandise Exports to the World, 1993–2000 (billions of 2000 dollars)**

|  | U.S. | Michigan | Michigan Share |
|---|---|---|---|
| 1993 | 440.7 | 24.0 | 5.4% |
| 1994 | 480.6 | 34.5 | 7.2% |
| 1995 | 534.2 | 34.0 | 6.4% |
| 1996 | 585.8 | 35.9 | 6.1% |
| 1997 | 664.7 | 36.7 | 5.5% |
| 1998 | 679.0 | 39.2 | 5.8% |
| 1999 | 700.8 | 42.0 | 6.0% |
| 2000 | 780.4 | 51.6 | 6.6% |

SOURCE: Office of Trade and Economic Analysis (2002); deflated by price index for exports of goods from Bureau of Economic Analysis (2001, table 7.9).

**TABLE 6.2**

**States with Largest Levels of Merchandise Exports, 2000 (billions of dollars)**

| Rank | State | Level 2000 | % Change[a] 1993–2000 |
|---|---|---|---|
| 1 | California | 129.9 | 96 |
| 2 | Texas | 68.7 | 98 |
| 3 | New York | 53.0 | 35 |
| 4 | Michigan | 51.6 | 109 |
| 5 | Washington | 33.4 | 27 |
| 6 | Illinois | 32.2 | 64 |
| 7 | Ohio | 29.1 | 70 |
| 8 | New Jersey | 28.8 | 103 |
| 9 | Florida | 24.2 | 70 |
| 10 | Pennsylvania | 24.0 | 87 |

SOURCE: Office of Trade and Economic Analysis (2002).
(a) % Change is constant prices.

**TABLE 6.3**

**States with Largest Ratios of Merchandise Exports to GSP, 1999 (billions of dollars)**

| Rank | State | Percent 1999 | %pt Change 1993–99 |
|---|---|---|---|
| 1 | Washington | 17.6 | –2.2 |
| 2 | Vermont | 16.5 | –0.8 |
| 3 | Delaware | 14.0 | –0.5 |
| 4 | Michigan | 13.5 | 2.1 |
| 5 | Oregon | 10.2 | 1.3 |
| 6 | Texas | 9.0 | 1.1 |
| 7 | California | 8.4 | 0.3 |
| 8 | Minnesota | 8.3 | –0.3 |
| 9 | Indiana | 8.0 | 1.6 |
| 10 | District of Columbia | 7.8 | –2.3 |

SOURCE: Calculated from Office of Trade and Economic Analysis (2002) and Bureau of Economic Analysis (2001).

directly to economic activity in Michigan, especially jobs. Having documented the extent and nature of these international connections in sections 2 and 3, the chapter will conclude in section 4 by discussing how these connections may matter for residents of Michigan. To see this, we will look first at how much we gain from this international trade and investment, then turn to the extent to which these connections expose us to the effects of changes on international markets.

## II. Michigan's Exports

Table 6.1 reports the levels of merchandise exports, in real 2000 dollars, for Michigan and for the United States as a whole, beginning in 1993, which is the first year for which trade data are available in any form by state.[1] It is clear that over the period from 1993 to 2000, Michigan's exports grew substantially. Michigan's share of U.S. exports has hovered around 6% during this period, an amount that is almost twice Michigan's share of Gross State Product (GSP).[2]

This suggests, correctly, that Michigan is one of the country's largest exporting states. We can see this clearly in tables 6.2 and 6.3, which report the ten largest exporting U.S. states by dollar value of exports and by percentage of GSP, respectively. Michigan ranks fourth on both lists, surpassed by only California, Texas, and (barely) New York in terms of absolute exports, and by Washington State, Vermont, and Delaware in terms of the percentage of its gross product that it exports.[3] No state surpasses Michigan on both lists.

The tables also report how these values have changed over the span of available data. The value of Michigan's exports has grown by more than that of any other state in the top ten by export value. In addition, its exported share of GSP has grown by more than that of any other state in that top-ten list. Any way you look at it, it seems that Michigan is a major exporter of merchandise.[4]

These data include only exports of merchandise, and they exclude services, the trade in which is of increasing importance in the United States and the world. We will look in more detail at some of Michigan's service exports in the following, but we should say at the outset that Michigan's exports of services appear to be somewhat less important than its exports of goods. Data are available at the state level only for selected categories of services, but among these, even in the sector in which Michigan seems to export the most—professional, scientific, and technical services—Michigan ranks only thirteenth out of the fifty states.

The message, then, is that the state of Michigan is one of the largest exporters in the United States, with the bulk of these exports concentrated in merchandise, not services.

## What Does Michigan Export?

The answer here is easy and obvious: cars. Actually, the available data are not fine enough to identify cars per se, or even the more relevant category "road motor vehicles and parts." Instead, they aggregate these with other vehicles, such as aircraft, in the category of "transportation equipment."

Michigan's largest export categories are shown in table 6.4, while the available breakdown of these exports by industry is shown in table 6.5 for manufactures and table 6.6 for agriculture and other commodities. The tables also show the percentage change in exports over time for the available data, which unfortunately in this case is only from 1997 to 2000. This is far too short a time period to provide good evidence of trends, but it is all that we have.

From table 6.4, the dominance of transportation equipment in Michigan's exports is obvious, constituting well over half of total state exports and growing at close to the same rate as total exports. Second place among state manufactured exports is occupied by machinery, with exports less than a quarter as great as in transportation equipment. Outside of manufactures, in agriculture and other commodities, exports are essentially negligible. Possible signs of change in the future, however, can be seen in two sectors: chemical manufactures and computers and electronic products. Although the level of state exports of these industries is not much more than one-tenth of transport equipment exports, exports in both of these industries have been growing several times as fast as exports of the latter, at least in the few recent years for which we have data.

A more complete list of state manufactured exports is provided in table 6.5. Table 6.6 does the same for goods exports outside of manufactures. If there is a message here, it is that Michigan's exports are not only small but declining in sectors where the state lacks comparative advantage, such as labor-intensive apparel and leather products, and land-intensive agriculture and pro-

cessed food and beverages. It is perhaps interesting, in contrast, that recent export growth has been quite strong in several sectors, including animal production; fishing, hunting and trapping; and mining. However, the value of mining exports, especially, is very sensitive to price

**TABLE 6.4**

**Michigan Exports by Major Sector, 2000 (millions of dollars)**

| | Level 2000 | % Change 1997–2000 |
|---|---|---|
| TOTAL | 51,615 | 36 |
| AGRICULTURAL & LIVESTOCK PRODUCTS | 158 | −21 |
| MANUFACTURES | 50,782 | 37 |
|     Transportation equipment | 30,378 | 32 |
|     Machinery manufactures | 5,475 | 14 |
|     Chemical manufactures | 3,736 | 91 |
|     Computers and electronic products | 3,354 | 139 |
| OTHER COMMODITIES | 676 | 21 |

SOURCE: Office of Trade and Economic Analysis (2002).

**TABLE 6.5**

**Michigan Exports of Manufactures, 2000 (millions of dollars)**

| | Level 2000 | % Change 1997–2000 |
|---|---|---|
| MANUFACTURES | 50,782 | 37 |
|     Transportation equipment | 30,378 | 32 |
|     Machinery manufactures | 5,475 | 14 |
|     Chemical manufactures | 3,736 | 91 |
|     Computers and electronic products | 3,354 | 139 |
|     Fabricated metal products | 1,975 | 58 |
|     Plastic and rubber products | 1,092 | 77 |
|     Electrical equip., appliances and parts | 1,055 | 18 |
|     Primary metal manufactures | 1,024 | 39 |
|     Nonmetallic mineral manufactures | 662 | 32 |
|     Furniture and related products | 539 | 61 |
|     Misc. manufactures | 360 | 1 |
|     Processed foods | 329 | −22 |
|     Paper products | 249 | 38 |
|     Leather and related products | 103 | −59 |
|     Wood products | 94 | 33 |
|     Printing and related products | 91 | 5 |
|     Petroleum and coal products | 79 | 40 |
|     Fabric mill products | 77 | 31 |
|     Non-apparel textile products | 69 | 111 |
|     Beverage and tobacco products | 24 | −42 |
|     Apparel manufactures | 14 | −38 |

SOURCE: Office of Trade and Economic Analysis (2002).

**TABLE 6.6**

**Michigan Exports of Agriculture and Other Nonmanufactures, 2000 (millions of dollars)**

|  | Level 2000 | % Change 1997–2000 |
|---|---|---|
| AGRICULTURAL & LIVESTOCK PRODUCTS | 158 | –21 |
|     Crop production | 137 | –29 |
|     Animal production | 21 | 179 |
| OTHER COMMODITIES | 676 | 21 |
|     Waste and scrap | 165 | 54 |
|     Mining | 150 | 650 |
|     Spec. classification provisions | 149 | 47 |
|     Oil and gas extraction | 49 | 78 |
|     Used merchandise | 15 | 20 |
|     Fishing, hunting, and trapping | 13 | 262 |
|     Forestry and logging | 12 | 2 |
|     Goods returned to Canada | 123 | –56 |

SOURCE: Office of Trade and Economic Analysis (2002).

**TABLE 6.7**

**U.S. and Michigan Selected Service Exports, 1997 (millions of current dollars)**

|  | U.S. | Michigan | MI Share |
|---|---|---|---|
| Software publishers | 7,295 | 80.2 | 1.1 |
| Broadcasting and telecommunications | 4,450 | 31.6 | 0.7 |
| Information and data processing services | 634 | 4.1 | 0.6 |
| Professional, scientific, and technical services | 18,994 | 395.7 | 2.1 |
| Administrative, support, and waste management services | 2,390 | 34.1 | 1.4 |

SOURCE: Receipts from exported sales, reported in Coalition of Service Industries (n.d.).

**TABLE 6.8**

**States with Largest Exports of Transport Equipment, 2000 (millions of dollars)**

| Rank | State | Level 2000 | % Change 1997–2000 |
|---|---|---|---|
| 1 | Michigan | 30.4 | 32 |
| 2 | Washington | 21.0 | 7 |
| 3 | California | 10.0 | –18 |
| 4 | New York | 6.8 | 56 |
| 5 | Ohio | 6.3 | –1 |
| 6 | Texas | 5.3 | –12 |
| 7 | Indiana | 4.3 | 48 |
| 8 | Connecticut | 3.3 | 53 |
| 9 | Florida | 2.4 | 5 |
| 10 | Illinois | 2.2 | –16 |
|  | UNALLOCATED | 2.1 | 209 |
|  | U.S. TOTAL | 11.8 | 9 |

SOURCE: Office of Trade and Economic Analysis (2002).

changes, and all of these categories start from a very small base, so too much should not be made of these large percentage changes.

As noted previously, data at the state level on service exports are even harder to come by than data on goods exports, and there does not seem to be anything available that is at all comprehensive. What we do have are data for just a handful of service sectors, reported by the Coalition of Service Industries (n.d.). Table 6.7 shows these export data for five service sectors, for the United States as a whole, and for Michigan.[5] The largest of these, both in absolute terms and as a share of U.S. exports, is professional, scientific, and technical services, for which Michigan exports are approximately 2% of U.S. exports. Since Michigan produces more than 3% of U.S. output and exports more than 6% of U.S. goods exports, it is clear that service exports—at least those reported—are of relatively minor importance for Michigan.

Not included here are educational services, which are, of course, of special interest to many of us contributing to this volume. For example, in fall 2001 the University of Michigan enrolled 2,908 nonresident alien graduate students and 1,085 undergraduate students.[6] If these students spent $20,000 each on tuition, then the value of this education sold to foreign nationals, which is really also an export of services, would approximate $80 million dollars from the University of Michigan alone.[7] Adding tuition at other universities and educational institutions, plus the living expenses of these students during their stay in Michigan, these service exports could easily be comparable to the other categories mentioned in table 6.7.

Another category of services trade that is missing from table 6.7 is travel and tourism. International visitor expenditures in Michigan have been estimated at $600 million for 1999,[8] suggesting that if this category of services had been added to table 6.7, it might well have been larger than any of those reported. The United States is, of course, a large buyer as well as a seller of tourism services, and the estimate is that Michigan spends more than it earns in this category by an amount of $1.24 billion.[9] However, Michigan is an attractive tourist destination for visitors from abroad, and its exports of tourist services would appear prominently in a list such as that in table 6.7, if comparable data were available.

A clear and unsurprising message of this section is that, although Michigan's exports are diverse, exports of automobiles remain the largest and most important. This is emphasized further in table 6.8, which shows the top ten state exporters of transport equipment. Michigan easily leads this list, with exports almost one-third greater than those of the runner-up, Washington. Furthermore, Washington makes the list only because transport equipment includes aircraft. Table 6.8 also reports the percentage changes in transport equipment exports for these states over the period of the available data, 1997–2000. Here Michigan is surpassed by several states, but its recent export growth remains well above that of the country as a whole in this industry.

## To Whom Does Michigan Export?

The answer here is almost as easy as for the previous question: Michigan exports to Canada, and to a somewhat lesser extent, to Mexico. Table 6.9 shows Michigan's total exports to the major regions of the world, while table 6.10 shows exports to the top ten countries that import from Michigan.[10] Both tables also show Michigan's share of U.S. exports to these destinations, and the percentage changes in these export flows in recent years.

As mentioned, Canada gets the largest portion of Michigan's exports, with Mexico a close second. Together, these NAFTA countries receive more than three-quarters of total Michigan exports of merchandise. The European Union is the only region other than North America to get more than one-tenth of Michigan's exports, with the largest individual country flows going to the United Kingdom, Germany, and Belgium. Among individual countries, however, Japan is the third-largest destination for Michigan's exports.

These patterns are not that different from those of the United States as a whole, but they are more extreme in being focused on North America. This can be seen from the fact that Michigan's exports to North America are more than 13% of U.S. exports there, compared to Michigan's share of only 6.6% of U.S. total exports regardless of destination. No other large region gets such a disproportionate share of Michigan's exports, and among the individual countries listed in table 6.10, only Saudi Arabia and Austria receive comparably large shares of U.S. exports from Michigan.

These data are again available only since 1997, too short a time period to establish any meaningful trends. Nonetheless, it is notable that during

**TABLE 6.9**

### Michigan Merchandise Exports to Regions of the World, 2000 (millions of current dollars)

| | Level 2000 | % of U.S. Exports | % Change 1997–2000 |
|---|---|---|---|
| North America | 38,537 | 13.4 | 47.0 |
| European Union | 5,448 | 3.3 | 14.8 |
| Asia, Selected other[a] | 2,701 | 1.7 | 1.5 |
| South America | 1,622 | 4.4 | 9.4 |
| Middle East | 1,117 | 5.9 | –3.2 |
| ASEAN[b] | 793 | 1.7 | 64.4 |
| Africa, Subsaharan | 145 | 2.5 | 168.0 |
| Eastern Europe | 114 | 1.9 | –42.3 |
| Central America | 103 | 1.0 | 36.3 |
| Caribbean | 81 | 0.7 | 46.0 |
| Former Soviet Republics | 24 | 0.7 | –74.1 |
| World | 51,615 | 6.6 | 36.1 |

SOURCE: Office of Trade and Economic Analysis (2002)
(a) Asia, Selected other is China, Hong Kong, India, Japan, South Korea, and Taiwan.
(b) ASEAN is Brunei, Burma (Mayanmar), Cambodia, Indonesia, Laos, Malaysia, Philippines, Singapore, Thailand, and Vietnam.

**TABLE 6.10**

### Major Country Destinations of Michigan's Merchandise Exports, 2000 (millions of current dollars)

| | Level 2000 | % of U.S. Exports | % Change 1997–2000 |
|---|---|---|---|
| Canada | 22,046 | 12.5 | 11.6 |
| Mexico | 16,491 | 14.8 | 155.4 |
| Japan | 1,393 | 2.1 | 7.0 |
| United Kingdom | 1,371 | 3.3 | 0.6 |
| Germany | 1,059 | 3.6 | 0.2 |
| Belgium | 851 | 6.1 | –21.3 |
| Australia | 710 | 5.7 | 30.5 |
| Brazil | 644 | 4.2 | 17.0 |
| Saudi Arabia | 630 | 10.1 | 109.2 |
| Austria | 595 | 23.3 | –20.9 |

SOURCE: Office of Trade and Economic Analysis (2002)

that short period, Michigan's already large exports to Mexico grew by more than 150%. This is in marked contrast to our exports to the other NAFTA partner, Canada, where exports grew by only 11%. The reason is presumably that our trading relationship with Canada is more mature, having already grown large under the U.S.–Canada Free Trade Agreement that preceded NAFTA, as well as under the much older U.S.–Canada Auto Pact.

**TABLE 6.11**

**Michigan's Exports to Canada and Mexico in Its Top Export Sectors, 2000 (millions of current dollars and percentage of Michigan exports)**

| | Total | CANADA Level | CANADA % | MEXICO Level | MEXICO % |
|---|---|---|---|---|---|
| MANUFACTURES | 50,782 | 21,448 | 42 | 16,424 | 32 |
| Transportation equipment | 30,378 | 14,278 | 47 | 9,837 | 32 |
| Machinery manufactures | 5,475 | 2,414 | 44 | 1,743 | 32 |
| Chemical manufactures | 3,736 | 857 | 23 | 476 | 13 |
| Computers/elec. products | 3,354 | 650 | 19 | 1,697 | 51 |
| Fabricated metal products | 1,975 | 887 | 45 | 843 | 43 |

SOURCE: Office of Trade and Economic Analysis (2002).

**TABLE 6.12**

**Export Sales of Michigan Metropolitan Areas, 1999 (level, recent real growth, per income and per person)**

| | $ Million 1999 | % Growth 1993–99 | Per $1000 Personal Income 1999 | Per Person 1999 |
|---|---|---|---|---|
| Ann Arbor | 1,746 | −15.0 | 92.8 | 3,132 |
| Benton Harbor | 287 | −9.0 | 70.6 | 1,796 |
| Detroit | 28,008 | 73.2 | 198.9 | 6,259 |
| Flint | 1,165 | 27.8 | 109.1 | 2,664 |
| Grand Rapids/Muskegon/Holland | 3,256 | 97.2 | 112.0 | 3,094 |
| Jackson | 160 | 73.6 | 42.8 | 1,016 |
| Kalamazoo/Battle Creek | 1,052 | 68.0 | 91.9 | 2,352 |
| Lansing/East Lansing | 244 | 37.6 | 21.3 | 541 |
| Saginaw/Bay City/Midland | 1,831 | 120.4 | 175.6 | 4,569 |

SOURCE: Office of Trade and Economic Analysis (2002) and Bureau of Economic Analysis (2001).

**TABLE 6.13**

**Export Destinations of Major Michigan Metropolitan Areas, 1999 (millions of dollars and percent of total)**

| | Benton Harbor | Detroit | Flint | Gr. Rapids | Kalamazoo |
|---|---|---|---|---|---|
| TOTAL | 287 | 28,008 | 1,165 | 3,256 | 1,052 |
| Canada | 43.0% | 49.7% | 84.4% | 53.2% | 53.7% |
| Mexico | 5.2% | 26.3% | 1.2% | 7.1% | 5.1% |
| Caribbean/Central Am. | 0.1% | 0.4% | 0.2% | 0.7% | 1.0% |
| South America | 3.2% | 2.2% | 1.2% | 1.7% | 2.4% |
| Europe | 22.9% | 13.3% | 4.0% | 16.6% | 21.0% |
| Asia | 14.9% | 4.0% | 2.9% | 18.5% | 14.5% |
| Africa | 1.5% | 0.1% | 0.0% | 0.4% | 0.4% |
| Near East | 3.3% | 2.7% | 5.8% | 0.8% | 0.5% |
| Australia | 5.9% | 1.3% | 0.4% | 1.1% | 1.3% |

SOURCE: Office of Trade and Economic Analysis (2002).

The industry breakdown of Michigan's exports to its two largest trading partners, Canada and Mexico, is shown in table 6.11 for Michigan's top five export sectors. Exports of the top two sectors, transportation equipment and machinery, also dominate the exports to these two destinations, in roughly the same proportions as to the world as a whole, as can be seen by comparing the two countries' shares in these sectors to their shares in manufactures. Michigan's chemical exports, on the other hand, are rather smaller to Canada and especially to Mexico than they are to other parts of the world. At the same time, computer and electronic products are underrepresented in exports to Canada, while they are considerably overrepresented in exports to Mexico. Indeed, more than half of Michigan's total exports of computers and electronics goes to Mexico.

## Who Exports from within Michigan?

Limited data are available showing the exports of metropolitan areas within Michigan. Table 6.12 shows the levels of exports of nine metropolitan areas in 1999, together with their percentage growth since 1993 and comparisons to income and population. The largest exporter is, of course, Detroit, whose exports of $28 billion in 1999 constituted over two-thirds of Michigan's total exports in that year (see table 6.1). Far behind Detroit, the next largest exporting area was Grand Rapids/Muskegon/Holland, which exported more than $3 billion, followed in order by Saginaw/Bay City/Midland, Ann Arbor, Flint, and Kalamazoo/Battle Creek, each with exports of between one and two billion. In the period since 1993, most of these export flows grew substantially, with the fastest growth posted by Saginaw/Bay City/Midland. Exceptions to this growth were Ann Arbor and Benton Harbor, whose exports fell over the course of the period.

To put these export flows into perspective, table 6.12 also compares them to the areas' levels of personal income and population. Detroit continues to lead the list, with more exports in 1999 both per thousand dollars of personal income and per person of population. However, on these bases Saginaw/Bay City/Midland now comes a close rather than a distant second, and both Flint and Grand Rapids/Muskegon/Holland have exports of more than one dollar in every ten dollars of personal income. On a per capita basis, every one of these metropolitan areas except

Lansing has exports of more than $1,000 per person. Detroit exports more than $6,000 per person, and even Ann Arbor, whose exports trail the other metropolitan areas in many respects, comes in third among them on a per capita basis with over $3,000 in exports per person.

In interpreting these numbers, one should, of course, keep in mind that they reflect merchandise exports only, and do not include the services that we discussed previously. The latter include education, professional/scientific/technical, and tourism, all of which might add considerably to the exports of some of these metropolitan areas.

Available information on the destinations of these metropolitan-area exports is even more limited, as shown in table 6.13. This shows, for just five of the nine metropolitan areas in table 6.12, the percentage breakdown of their exports to selected countries and geographic regions of the world. The destinations of Detroit's exports are, of course, similar to those of exports of Michigan as a whole, with almost half going to Canada, and another quarter to Mexico. It is perhaps of some interest that the other largest exporting metropolitan areas send an even higher proportion to Canada, with Flint exporting almost 85% there. In contrast, however, these same areas export a much smaller percentage to Mexico, in spite of the NAFTA. What they do not export to Mexico, several of these areas seem to send to Europe, which gets more than 20% of the exports from both Benton Harbor and Kalamazoo. Asia, too, gets almost 15% of exports from these two metropolitan areas, and even more from Grand Rapids, in contrast to the only 4% of Detroit's exports that Asia gets. Thus there are substantial differences across locations within Michigan in the countries and regions to which they export. These differences almost certainly reflect differences in the industries that dominate these different metropolitan areas, but unfortunately we have no data on their exports at the industry level.

### Benefits from Exports

So far we have looked only at the exports themselves, but exports are only a means to various desirable ends, not an end in themselves. To an economist, the primary benefit from exports is the imports that they permit a country to purchase in return. If trade were balanced, one might think that since the value of imports would equal the value of exports, these export values would

**TABLE 6.14**

**Michigan and U.S. Jobs from Exports, 1997 (thousands of jobs)**

| | MI Rank | MI Jobs | U.S. | Max | Highest-Ranked State |
|---|---|---|---|---|---|
| Jobs tied to manufacturing exports | | | | | |
| Number (thousands) | 4 | 372.9 | 7,676.2 | 1,147.9 | CA |
| % of private sector jobs | 8 | 9.5% | 7.2% | 17.3% | NM |
| Manufacturing jobs tied to manufacturing exports | | | | | |
| Direct export related | 5 | 100.2 | 2,027.8 | 288.8 | CA |
| Indirect export related | 3 | 90.8 | 1,316.4 | 210.1 | CA |
| Total export related | 4 | 191.0 | 3,344.2 | 498.9 | CA |
| % of mfg. employment | 8 | 22.9% | 19.8% | 39.4% | WA |
| Nonmanufacturing jobs tied to manufacturing exports | | | | | |
| Number | 5 | 181.9 | 4,332.0 | 649.0 | CA |

SOURCE: Office of Trade and Economic Analysis (2001).

provide a pretty good measure of import values. However, the point of international trade is that a given value of exports allows us to buy goods and services that, because of comparative advantage and other sources of gains from trade, would have cost us more to produce ourselves. Indeed, it is this gap, between what we pay for imports and what it would have cost us to produce them ourselves, that measures the gains from trade, and the value of exports tells us little about that gap. For example, suppose arbitrarily that the goods we import would have cost us 10% more to produce ourselves than to import. Then each dollar of exports, when the revenue is spent on imports, would yield a sort of dividend of $0.10 in the gains from trade.

We have seen that in the year 2000, Michigan's exports came to $51.6 billion. If this 10% figure for the gains from trade were correct, then we could infer that Michigan's exports had generated, in addition to the revenue from the exports themselves, an extra five billion dollars worth of gains from trade. What does this mean? It means that, in addition to the over fifty billion dollars that we earned using resources to produce those exports, we also released an additional five billion dollars worth of resources from the need to produce goods that we could get more cheaply from abroad. These released resources, as long as they are employed, are being used to produce a kind of bonus: goods that we could not afford to produce if we did not trade.

The qualification just stated—"as long as they are employed"—raises a question that has long been a source of worry in the Michigan economy and elsewhere: what does trade do to employment? Here the concern is not so much the trade that Michigan itself enters into, which we have been examining here, but rather the trade—especially imports—of others in the United States that may have been at the expense of purchases from Michigan. This is not something that we can easily address, especially with data on the Michigan economy itself. However, there is one connection between trade and employment that we can address, and we turn to that next.

## Jobs Supported by Exports

The International Trade Administration (ITA) of the Department of Commerce reports the numbers of jobs that are supported by exports, including manufacturing jobs that are directly export related (producing the exports themselves), manufacturing jobs that are indirectly export related (producing inputs for exports), and nonmanufacturing jobs in several categories (business services, transportation services, wholesale and retail trade, and other nonmanufacturing sectors) that are "tied to manufactured exports" (also providing services to the industries that export). Results are reported and ranked by state. Table 6.14 identifies the states with either the highest number or the highest percentage of jobs tied to each of these sectors and lists that number or percentage. Thus, for example, while California has the largest number of jobs tied to manufacturing exports, 1,147,900, New Mexico has the largest percentage of its private sector jobs tied to manufacturing exports, 17.3%.

Thus, according to the ITA's calculations, 372,900 jobs in Michigan are tied to manufacturing exports. This number is exceeded in only three U.S. states, with California having the most jobs tied to manufacturing exports. These workers constitute 9.5% of Michigan's private-sector employment, and Michigan ranks eighth among U.S. states in terms of the percentage of private-sector employment that is tied to exports.

These figures include all three of the above-mentioned categories—direct, indirect, and non-manufacturing—and in fact those directly employed in producing for export, 100,200 workers, are not much more than a quarter of the total. Another 90,800 workers produce manufactured inputs that are used in producing exports, while almost half of the total export-dependent jobs are not in manufacturing at all. Some 181,900 work-

ers provide services to manufacturers that produce for export. Yet even though the connection is indirect, these workers are just as dependent on exports as those in the exporting factories themselves. These proportions are not atypical among U.S. states, as indicated by both the state's ranking on these indicators and the totals for the United States as a whole.

The main lesson from table 6.14 is that Michigan's jobs depend relatively heavily on exports. In the private sector as a whole, almost one in ten jobs is tied to exports, while in manufacturing, more than one in five workers produce either directly or indirectly for export. These numbers are somewhat higher than those for the United States as a whole, but not vastly so. Michigan's economy, as our data for exports have already indicated, is very much like the U.S. economy in its engagement with international trade, but it is even more heavily engaged.

It is customary to focus on the jobs that are lost when expanding imports cause domestic industries to cut back, and it is quite appropriate to do so in view of the economic hardship that such cutbacks cause. Yet we should not lose sight of the fact that, over the long term, exports and imports have expanded together, and exports create jobs at the same time that imports may displace them. The jobs that are identified here as being tied to exports would be lost if trade were to cease, and that also would cause hardship. Nobody, of course, is advocating that international trade should cease. Yet if barriers to trade were to increase, the effect would be a partial cessation of trade and a consequent partial loss, not only of the gains from trade but also of the jobs that depend on trade.

## III. Michigan's Foreign Ownership

The preceding section focused on Michigan's exports, which certainly constitute a major way that the Michigan economy interfaces with the world economy. We turn now to foreign direct investment (FDI), which also plays an important role in the state's economy. FDI goes both directions, of course, with Michigan firms owning subsidiaries abroad at the same time that foreign firms own subsidiaries here. However, data are available only for the latter, and that is what we will attend to in this section. While it would be desirable, of course, also to have data on Michigan's outward FDI, it is inward FDI that has the most direct effect on economic activity in the state, including the employment of Michigan workers.

To provide an idea of the size and importance of foreign ownership, table 6.15 shows employment in foreign-owned firms in Michigan and in the United States for 1997, which is the most recent year for which data are available.[11] It also compares these employment levels to both total employment and manufacturing employment tied to exports from table 6.14. Looking first at all (private) sectors, 4.37% of Michigan private-sector employment is in foreign affiliates, slightly less than the percentage in the United States as a whole. This is a bit less than half the number of workers whose jobs are tied to manufacturing exports. A disproportionate amount of foreign-affiliate employment is in manufacturing, however, so that over 10% of Michigan's manufacturing employment is in foreign affiliates. Thus, one in ten manufacturing-sector workers in Michigan are employed in foreign-owned firms. This is actually somewhat less than the comparable figure for the United States as a whole, but it is hardly negligible. On the other hand, it is also evident from table 6.15 that, while the fraction of Michigan employment in foreign affiliates is somewhat less than that of the United States as a whole, Michigan's fraction of jobs tied to exports is larger. Thus, exports are more important for Michigan employment than foreign ownership, both absolutely and relatively, in comparison to the rest of the country. Nonetheless, in absolute terms in 1997, 84,100 manufacturing workers were employed in Michigan by foreign firms.

We saw in the previous section that Michigan ranks high among U.S. states in terms of exports. Given this somewhat smaller role for foreign ownership, it is not surprising that Michigan's ranking based on that should be lower. Table 6.16 shows the top ten states ranked by manufacturing employment in foreign affiliates, and Michigan ranks ninth. The table also shows how these employment figures grew between 1987 and 1997. Michigan's manufacturing employment in foreign affiliates grew by 63% over this period, very similar to the rate of growth in these figures countrywide. It may be of interest that among the top ten states, two of Michigan's neighbors, Indiana and Ohio, posted the fastest growth in manufacturing foreign affiliate employment over this period, with Indiana's figure more than doubling during the ten years.

### TABLE 6.15

**Employment in Foreign Affiliates Compared to Employment Linked to Exports, Michigan and U.S., 1997 (thousands of jobs)**

|  | MI | | U.S. | |
|---|---|---|---|---|
|  | Number | % | Number | % |
| Total employment |  |  |  |  |
|   In foreign affiliates | 171.6 | 4.37% | 5,202 | 4.88% |
|   Tied to manufacturing exports | 372.9 | 9.50% | 7,676 | 7.20% |
| Manufacturing employment |  |  |  |  |
|   In foreign affiliates | 84.1 | 10.08% | 2,064 | 12.22% |
|   Tied to manufacturing exports | 191.0 | 22.90% | 3,344 | 19.80% |

SOURCES: Bureau of Economic Analysis (1997) and Office of Trade and Economic Analysis (2001).

### TABLE 6.16

**States with Largest Manufacturing Employment in Foreign Affiliates, 1997 (thousands of workers)**

| Rank | State | Level 1997 | % Change 1987–1997 |
|---|---|---|---|
| 1 | California | 185.3 | 47% |
| 2 | Ohio | 135.9 | 90% |
| 3 | Texas | 131.9 | 83% |
| 4 | North Carolina | 117.5 | 57% |
| 5 | Illinois | 104.4 | 59% |
| 6 | Pennsylvania | 102.8 | 17% |
| 7 | Tennessee | 86.8 | 67% |
| 8 | Indiana | 85.5 | 110% |
| 9 | Michigan | 84.1 | 63% |
| 10 | Georgia | 83.8 | 50% |
|  | UNITED STATES | 2,063.7 | 57% |

SOURCE: Bureau of Economic Analysis (1997).

### What Do Michigan's Foreign Affiliates Do?

Table 6.17 shows the breakdown of Michigan's foreign affiliates by major industry, together with the data for the United States as a whole and the growth over the 1987–97 period. Reported are both the value of property owned by affiliates and their employment levels. By both measures, somewhat more than half of Michigan's foreign affiliate presence is in manufacturing. This is somewhat higher than for the United States as a whole, as also indicated by the fact that Michigan's percentage of U.S. foreign affiliates is higher in manufacturing than in all other sectors except the smallest one, professional, scientific, and technical services.

Thus, foreign presence in Michigan is somewhat disproportionately attracted to manufacturing. On

**TABLE 6.17**

### Industry of Foreign Affiliates in Michigan and the United States

| | Value of Property[a] (millions of dollars) | | | Employment of Affiliates (thousands of employees) | | | | |
|---|---|---|---|---|---|---|---|---|
| | U.S. | MI | MI% of US | U.S. | Growth[b] | MI | Growth[b] | MI% of US |
| All industries | 877,568 | 21,170 | 2.4 | 5,201.9 | 61.3 | 171.6 | 78.2 | 3.3 |
| Manufacturing | 400,182 | 12,899 | 3.2 | 2,258.0 | 46.4 | 92.5 | 60.3 | 4.1 |
| Wholesale trade | 100,507 | 2,430 | 2.4 | 509.7 | 58.3 | 13.4 | 48.9 | 2.6 |
| Retail trade | 31,769 | 498 | 1.6 | 683.6 | 22.4 | 14.3 | 16.3 | 2.1 |
| Information | 64,587 | 596 | 0.9 | 292.1 | | 5.3 | | 1.8 |
| Finance[c] and Insurance | 38,563 | 220 | 0.6 | 225.1 | 31.4 | 4.1 | 127.8 | 1.8 |
| Real estate & rental/leasing | 94,385 | 567 | 0.6 | 39.8 | 17.4 | 0.3 | 0.0 | 0.8 |
| Prof., sci., & tech. services | 4,735 | 183 | 3.9 | 85.1 | | 4.1 | | 4.8 |
| Other industries | 142,841 | 3,777 | 2.6 | 1,108.6 | 481.3 | 37.4 | 434.3 | 3.4 |

SOURCE: Bureau of Economic Analysis (1997).
(a) Gross property, plant, and equipment of affiliates.
(b) Percent growth 1987–1997.
(c) Except depository institutions.

the other hand, the growth in foreign affiliation over the 1987–97 period, although substantial in manufacturing, has been fastest in other parts of the economy. Unfortunately, the available breakdown places most of this growth in "other industries," so we do not know exactly what it is.

We also do not have any breakdown of foreign affiliation within manufacturing itself. We are therefore unable to answer the obvious question of whether foreign affiliates are concentrated within the transportation equipment industry, as was the case for Michigan's exports. As a very

**TABLE 6.18**

### Country of Ownership of Foreign Affiliates[a] in Michigan, 1997, and Growth since 1987

| | Number of Affiliates | | | Employment of Affiliates (thousands of employees) | | | |
|---|---|---|---|---|---|---|---|
| | Level 1997 | Growth 1987–97 | % of MI | Level 1997 | Growth 1987–97 | % of MI | %Mfg |
| ALL COUNTRIES | 1,107 | 41 | 100% | 171.6 | 78.2 | 100% | 49 |
| REGIONS | | | | | | | |
| Africa | 6 | –14 | 1% | n.a. | | | |
| Asia and Pacific | 325 | 102 | 29% | 34.1 | 82.4 | 20% | 62 |
| Europe | 585 | 29 | 53% | 102.1 | 85.3 | 59% | 51 |
| Latin America & other W. Hemisphere | 22 | –4 | 2% | 2.3 | –28.1 | 1% | n.a. |
| Middle East | 20 | 67 | 2% | 3.7 | 1750.0 | 2% | 27 |
| SELECTED COUNTRIES | | | | | | | |
| Australia | 10 | –29 | 1% | 1.1 | –73.8 | 1% | 18 |
| Canada | 137 | 13 | 12% | 25.3 | 39.0 | 15% | 32 |
| France | 72 | 44 | 7% | 6.7 | –15.2 | 4% | 57 |
| Germany | 151 | 48 | 14% | 34.1 | 135.2 | 20% | 57 |
| Japan | 293 | 111 | 26% | 32.7 | 138.7 | 19% | 64 |
| Netherlands | 47 | 57 | 4% | 13.1 | 244.7 | 8% | 15 |
| Switzerland | 57 | 10 | 5% | 9.4 | 308.7 | 5% | 41 |
| United Kingdom | 159 | 10 | 14% | 29.3 | 65.5 | 17% | 56 |

SOURCE: Bureau of Economic Analysis (1997).
(a) Number of affiliates with property, plant, and equipment or employment.

crude indicator of that, we have obtained a listing of "Michigan Companies with Foreign Parents" from the Michigan Economic Development Corporation, and this listing includes for most of them a short description of their business. The listing includes 863 foreign-owned businesses in Michigan, of which 188 included the words "auto," "automotive," or "automobile" in their description. As a broader measure, we also counted all those whose descriptions included something that we recognized as relating to automobiles or to motor vehicles more generally, and found 264. Together, these results suggest that perhaps only one-third of Michigan's foreign-owned companies produce directly in or for the automobile industry, considerably less than the apparent share of that industry in Michigan's exports. Of course, the number of companies is of less interest than their value added or their employment, but comparable data on these are not available.

## Who Owns Michigan's Foreign Affiliates?

The single country that owns the most foreign affiliates in Michigan is Japan, by a wide margin, as shown in table 6.18. By number, Japan had 293 affiliates in Michigan in 1997, compared to 159 for the United Kingdom, 151 for Germany, and 137 for Canada. On the other hand, the German affiliates employed more workers than did the Japanese affiliates, with all four of these countries employing rather similar numbers, in excess of twenty-five thousand workers each. Collectively, on the other hand, Europe accounts for more than half of Michigan's foreign affiliates, both in number and in employment.

Japan also posted the greatest growth in number of affiliates during the 1987–97 period. At the same time, while the European affiliates were expanding both their numbers and their employment less rapidly than Japanese affiliates, employment in European affiliates grew almost three times as fast as their number, indicating that the European affiliates were growing substantially in average size.[12]

As for the industry composition of these affiliates, the final column of table 6.18 shows that the majority of foreign affiliates in Michigan employed most of their workers in manufacturing. However, Canada, Switzerland, and especially the Netherlands were exceptions, with only a minority of employment in manufacturing.

**TABLE 6.19**

### Size Distribution of U.S. and Michigan Foreign Affiliates by Value, 1997

| Size class[b] | Number of Affiliates[a] | | | |
| | U.S., by National Size | U.S., by State Size | MI | MI% |
|---|---|---|---|---|
| TOTAL | 8,602 | 31,257 | 880 | 2.8 |
| 0–$99,999 | 595 | 6,646 | 161 | 2.4 |
| $100,000–$999,999 | 1,262 | 7,032 | 218 | 3.1 |
| $1,000,000–$9,999,999 | 2,966 | 9,101 | 265 | 2.9 |
| $10,000,000–$24,999,999 | 1,268 | 3,435 | 100 | 2.9 |
| $25,000,000–$99,999,999 | 1,394 | 3,454 | 92 | 2.7 |
| $100,000,000–$249,999,999 | 569 | 976 | 27 | 2.8 |
| $250,000,000 and over | 548 | 613 | 17 | 2.8 |

SOURCE: Bureau of Economic Analysis (1997).
(a) Number of affiliates with property, plant, and equipment or employment.
(b) Property, plant, and equipment size.

**TABLE 6.20**

### Size Distribution of U.S. and Michigan Foreign Affiliates by Employment, 1997

| Employment class[b] | Number of Affiliates[a] | | | |
| | U.S., by National Size | U.S., by State Size | MI | MI% |
|---|---|---|---|---|
| TOTAL | 7,445 | 34,791 | 1,034 | 3.0 |
| 1–9 | 1,376 | 14,439 | 391 | 2.7 |
| 10–19 | 697 | 3,680 | 116 | 3.2 |
| 20–99 | 2,154 | 8,214 | 269 | 3.3 |
| 100–249 | 1,186 | 4,076 | 124 | 3.0 |
| 250–999 | 1,226 | 3,391 | 101 | 3.0 |
| 1,000–2,499 | 403 | 725 | 22 | 3.0 |
| 2,500 and over | 403 | 266 | 11 | 4.1 |

SOURCE: Bureau of Economic Analysis (1997).
(a) Number of affiliates with property, plant, and equipment or employment.
(b) Employees per affiliate.

## How Big Are Michigan's Foreign Affiliates?

Tables 6.19 and 6.20 show the distribution of Michigan's foreign affiliates by size, with table 6.19 reporting by value and table 6.20 reporting by number of employees. In both tables, the first row shows the numbers of affiliates in total for which the relevant information was available, while subsequent rows show numbers in various size categories. The first two columns show the numbers for the United States as whole, the first based on subsidiaries' size in the nation as a whole, while the second gives the number of state-affiliate combinations of the given size within individual states. Thus, for example, a single foreign-owned firm with a value in the whole United States of $500 million will contribute one unit to the last row of the first column of table 6.19. Yet if that firm has, say, subsidiaries in each of twenty-five states, each with a value of $20 million, then it will also contribute twenty-five units to the second column in the fifth row, $10–$25 million. Michigan's affiliate size distributions are shown in the third column, with its percentage of the second column shown in the final column.

From the two tables, it is clear that the size distributions of Michigan's foreign affiliates are quite similar to those of the nation as a whole, as long as size is measured at the state level. Of course, many affiliates are present in multiple states, so their sizes nationwide tend to be larger than their presence in individual states. Yet the fact that the percentages in the final column are all quite similar tells us that Michigan's affiliates are not all that different from the average of all other states.

There are a few small differences that may be worth noting, however. First, in both of the tables, Michigan's smallest percentage is in the smallest size category. Thus one could say that Michigan has somewhat less than its share of the very smallest foreign affiliate firms.[13] At the other end of the spectrum, Michigan has a disproportionately large number of foreign firms in the largest employment class, employing 2,500 or more workers. It has eleven of these firms, while it would have only eight if they were distributed alike in all employment classes. Thus there is a slight tendency for Michigan's foreign affiliates to be larger than the average of affiliates in other states.[14]

## IV. What Does It All Mean?

The preceding sections have quantified two aspects of the role of the international economy in Michigan: exports and foreign ownership. In simple terms, we have seen that Michigan is one of the nation's largest international traders, in terms of its volume of exports. Those exports are tied to one in ten of Michigan's jobs and one in five of its manufacturing jobs. Foreign ownership is somewhat less important than exports for Michigan, but even here, one in twenty private-sector jobs and one in ten manufacturing jobs are in firms that are owned by foreigners. Thus, a non-negligible fraction of the Michigan economy depends on world markets, either for sales, for ownership, or for both. To conclude this chapter,

we will discuss more carefully just what these and other interactions with the world economy mean for the livelihoods and well-being of Michigan residents. There are two aspects of this that we will discuss: the extent to which Michigan gains from its and the nation's international trade and investment; and the extent to which these international linkages make the state susceptible to economic shocks.

One topic that will not be discussed, in spite of its importance in much of the rest of this volume, is the impact of trade and investment on the budget of the Michigan state government. The reason for this omission is that the state budget is not obviously very much affected, positively or negatively, by international trade and investment. The state does not tax international trade separately from other transactions, and its taxes on operations within the state are for the most part no different for foreign-owned entities than for domestic ones. Likewise, state expenditures would seem to be driven almost exclusively by domestic concerns. Of course, the health of the state budget does depend on the health of the state economy, and that, in turn, depends in part on foreign sales. Yet this is really just a by-product of the role that trade and investment play in the broader Michigan economy.

## Michigan's Gains from Trade and Investment

Economists speak frequently of a country's "gains from trade," by which we mean the increased value of goods and services that become available to a country's consumers as a result of international trade, in exchange for its exports. The same concept applies to states, and it is reasonable to ask whether, and to what extent, Michigan gains from trade and investment. To define this question more concretely, we could ask whether Michigan would be worse off if it did not trade. The answer is clearly yes, but the size of this loss would differ depending upon the time horizon considered, since many who would lose immediately from an abrupt termination of trade would eventually recover at least part of their loss by changing to other activities. The gains from trade are usually considered on a long-run basis, after all such adjustments have been completed.

Michigan's gains from trade are without a doubt far larger for its trade with other states than for its trade with the rest of the world. In spite of Michigan's prominence as an international trader, we are much more fully integrated into the U.S. economy than into the world, and if that integration were interrupted, the cost to the state would be devastating. Indeed, it is hard to imagine how today's Michigan population could survive if it had to depend on itself and its own productive capacity for all of the goods and services that enter its consumption.

Compared to this, the effects of blocking only Michigan's international trade would be small, but they would be nonetheless significant. Using a standard partial equilibrium calculation of the gains from trade based on the export share reported in table 6.3, and using very approximate estimates of the responsiveness of supply and demand to price changes, Michigan's gain from trade in 1999 is estimated to be $2.5 billion, or 0.8% of gross state product.[15]

This underestimates the gains from all international trade to the state of Michigan, since it includes only the trade that Michigan itself enters into with other countries. Yet much of what Michigan buys from other states is available at current prices only because of international trade between other states and the rest of the world. Thus, if Michigan alone were to completely cease direct exports to and imports from the rest of the world, it would still share in the considerable gains that the rest of the country enjoys from such trade. These, too, are significant, but not huge, simply because the United States has such a large and diverse economy that it can provide reasonably well for itself without trade. Yet the fact of these additional gains does mean that the number given for Michigan's gain from trade in 1999 understates the benefits that Michigan derives from the existence of the global economy.

We saw in section 3 that foreign affiliates of firms in Michigan own over $20 billion worth of property here. To the extent that these foreign affiliates produce for export, they contribute to part of the gain already identified due to trade. Yet mostly they produce for the U.S. market, and the question arises whether Michigan gains from their presence. In one sense, the answer is clearly yes: These affiliates employed 171,600 workers in 1997, and if they were to shut down, these jobs would be lost. Yet that is only a short-run effect, and presumably after a period of perhaps painful adjustment, those workers would find jobs in other industries that would replace the foreign affiliates.

In the long term, these affiliates contribute things other than jobs to the Michigan economy. One of these is simply capital, which makes Michigan labor more productive and raises real incomes and real wages. Another is the particular expertise that foreign firms have and that they use as the basis for their expansion as multinational enterprises, including their business models, their patents, and their complementary interactions with their operations in other countries based on comparative advantage. Foreign direct investment is an alternative to trade for exploiting such comparative advantage and for generating other forms of gains from trade as well. For example, multinational firms use their knowledge capital to provide services such as research and development in one location that contribute to their productivity in all locations, and this source of economies of scale contributes not only to their own profits but also to the real incomes of the countries in which they operate. There is no easy way to estimate these gains from foreign ownership, and we therefore will not attempt to quantify them here. Yet we would expect them to approximate, in order of magnitude, the gains from trade noted previously.

## Michigan's Exposure to International Shocks

If the world were not subject to change, then the discussion so far of Michigan's gains from trade and investment would be the end of the story. Yet in fact, of course, both Michigan and the world are constantly changing. If Michigan were not engaged with the rest of the world, then it would be immune from changes abroad, both positive and negative. However by participating in the world economy, we subject ourselves to the effects of such changes, and these will sometimes help, sometimes hurt.

For example, Michigan is heavily influenced by the world price of oil. As in all economies that produce none of their own oil, people in Michigan suffer as consumers whenever the price of oil rises, and they gain when it falls. Even more important, perhaps, is the fact that the market for our largest industry, motor vehicles, is critically dependent on the price of oil as well. When oil prices rise, car sales fall, at least of the large gas-guzzlers in which Michigan has traditionally specialized. This represents a source of vulnerability in Michigan to foreign markets, but it is not one that we could escape by not trading. Without oil imports, oil would be far more expensive, and Americans might need to find other forms of transport, much as Europeans have done.

Michigan is also exposed to international shocks in the form of exchange rate changes. Because the Michigan economy bulks large in manufacturing of traded goods, both in the exports that we have documented here and in competition with imports, Michigan's markets are more sensitive than most to changes in exchange rates. We saw this dramatically in the early 1980s, when a large appreciation of the U.S. dollar put Michigan firms at a disadvantage relative to imports, and the recession that hit most of the country hit hardest here.

That vulnerability continues, although it has a flip side as well: when the U.S. dollar falls on international exchange markets, Michigan also benefits disproportionately. Until recently, the dollar has again been strong, and we have once again felt the pain of international competition during the recent recession. However, the weakness has been milder than it was in the early 1980s, perhaps indicative of the more diversified economy that we have today.

In addition to oil prices and exchange rates, the main other sources of international instability are the financial crises that periodically disrupt foreign markets. Though hardly new, these have hit with particular force during the last decade, starting with Mexico shortly after the NAFTA was implemented, hitting many East Asian economies starting in 1997, spilling from there into Latin America and Russia, and most recently afflicting Argentina. These crises have common features: (1) a loss of confidence in the government and financial system of the targeted developing or transition economy; (2) capital flight that drains financial resources from the country; culminating in (3) a devaluation of their currency and a resulting collapse of asset values and a rash of bankruptcies. These crises obviously inflict their greatest pain on the target countries, but they also spill over to other countries that have invested in them and that transact with them in international trade. The point for Michigan is that this is one source of international disruption that does *not* seem to be particularly salient for us. Although our trade with Mexico is very important, the peso crisis does not seem to have hurt us badly, and the harmful effects of the other crises have been felt more in other parts of the country that are specialized more in financial markets than in manufacturing.

Not all changes in the international economy take the form of shocks, and not all are bad. Over the last half century there has been more or less continuous growth in the world economy, and this has included gratifying rates of progress in an increasing number of previously very poor countries. This economic growth, although it has been occasionally interrupted by the sorts of crisis just mentioned, has for the most part produced a steady expansion of world markets for both goods and services, together with an increasing supply of ever more efficiently produced products for the world to buy. Michigan has, for the most part, prospered in this environment, producing ever more goods and also some services for sale on world markets, and, like the rest of the country, increasing standards of living by using the proceeds from these exports to buy an increasing variety of products from abroad. In the long run, the costs of temporary shocks due to changing oil prices, exchange rates, and financial crises have paled in comparison to the benefits of worldwide economic growth that we prosper from at home through the mechanisms of international trade and investment. One may hope and presume that this growth will continue into the future, and that Michigan will continue to take advantage of the opportunities that trade and investment provide.

■

## REFERENCES

Bureau of Economic Analysis. 1997. *Foreign direct investment in the United States, benchmark surveys.* U.S. Department of Commerce, *http://www.bea .doc.gov/bea/uguide.htm#_1_23.*

——. 2001. *Regional accounts data: Gross state product data.* U.S. Department of Commerce. *http:// www.bea. doc.gov/bea/regional/gsp/.* Released June.

Coalition of Service Industries. n.d. *In the national interest: The U.S. services industry case for trade promotion authority.* *http://www.uscsi.org/csi- services-statistics.pdf,* downloaded April 2002.

Office of Trade and Economic Analysis. 2001. *U.S. jobs from exports.* International Trade Administration, U.S. Department of Commerce. *http://www.export .gov/docTSFrameset.html.* February.

——. 2002. *State exports to countries and regions.* International Trade Administration, U.S. Department of Commerce. *http://www.ita.doc.gov/td/ industry/otea/state/preformat.html.*

## NOTES

I have benefited from conversations on the topic of this chapter with Joan Crary, George Fulton, Bob Lipsey, Dave Richardson, Bob Stern, and other participants in the *Michigan at the Millennium* project, as well as from detailed suggestions from the editors of the volume.

1. For the purposes of this chapter, it would obviously be valuable to have data on trade from earlier years, but unfortunately these do not seem to have been collected, even in forms that might be less useful than what we report here. Furthermore, as will become clear in the discussion to follow, while some of the available data start in 1993, other data are available only from 1997 onward. Therefore, throughout this section, we can provide only a tantalizing taste of how Michigan's trade may have changed over time.

   These and other data on state merchandise exports are from the Office of Trade and Economic Analysis (2002). The data are taken, in turn, from the Census Bureau, and are based upon "exporter location," that is, the state in which the exporting company is located, not where the exports happen to leave the country.

2. GSP is available from the Bureau of Economic Analysis (2001), but only through 1999. In 1999, Michigan's share of total U.S. GSP was 3.3%.

3. Such percentages can be somewhat misleading, since GSP, like national Gross Domestic Product (GDP), is a value-added measure while the value of exports is not. Thus it is possible for an economic unit to export more than 100% of its GSP or GDP, as indeed is the case for small countries like Singapore and Hong Kong, whose huge exports embody a large amount of imports. For comparison across economic units, such as is done here, this should not be a problem.

4. Trade data, such as are reported here, are far from perfect. The best are collected by customs officers who monitor imports, and the data can be presumed to be fairly complete in developed countries such as the United States and many of the countries with whom we trade. However, even here the values of reported trade may be subject to distortion, as importers seek to avoid paying customs duties. The export data that we use here, on the other hand, are more difficult to collect, since exporters do not pass through customs as they leave the country and are instead simply required to report their shipments to the government. In recent years, deregulation of trucking in the United States has meant that outward shipments have been increasingly carried by truckers who have failed to report, and the United States now collects much of its export data with the help of Canadian customs. These and other problems with the trade data pose some difficulties for econometric analysis and other uses, but should not matter much for the broader picture that we are trying to draw here.

5. Without data on other services, it is hard to know how representative these data are, but we can get some indication by comparing them to the service transactions included in the U.S. balance of payments accounts by the Bureau of Economic Analysis. For 1997, total exports of private services by the United States were $239 billion, of which only $33 billion, or about 15%, are included in table 6.7. Large categories of U.S. service exports that are missing from table 6.7 include travel, passenger fares, and other transportation, which together made up more than half of U.S. service exports in 1997, as well as royalties and license fees, affiliated services (within firms), education, financial services, and insurance.

6. Personal communication from Glenna Schweitzer of the University of Michigan registrar's office.

7. Many of the graduate students do not themselves pay tuition, as it is provided as part of their compensation as graduate student instructors or research assistants. That does not lessen the value of the education service being exported, however, but means that the state is also importing the services of these same graduate students as instructors.

8. Personal communication from Donald Holecek, based on data from the Travel Industry of America.

9. Calculated from data and assumptions by Donald Holecek. See chapter 22 in this volume.

10. It may be of some interest to know which countries do *not* import from Michigan, or at least are not listed in the available data, even though they show positive imports from the United States as a whole. There are thirty destinations with imports listed for the United States but not for Michigan. Most of these are very small, such as Niue and Tuvalu, but a few seem more important: Armenia, Libya, Sudan, Iran, Chad, Iraq, the West Bank, and Cuba (these in decreasing order of total U.S. exports to them). Their omission from the data for Michigan suggests that political concerns may interfere with the accuracy or completeness of the data here.

11. Note, therefore, that these data precede the 1998 merger of Daimler-Benz AG and the Chrysler Corporation. More recent data, if they were available, would include the United States and Michigan operations of Daimler-Chrysler among foreign affiliates, with obvious importance especially for

the industry composition of foreign ownership discussed in the following.

12. This was true also in Japan, but to a much smaller extent.

13. Not a lot less, though: If Michigan had the same percentage of the smallest size class that it has of all affiliates, then it would have 25 more of these small firms—186 instead of 161.

14. Strangely, although the largest employment class is overrepresented in Michigan according to table 6.20, the largest class by value in table 6.19 is not.

15. The welfare gain from trade in a single sector as a share of value of output in that sector is given by $(\frac{1}{2})s^2 \div [(1-s)E_D + sE_S]$, where $s$ is the fraction of output exported and $E_D$ and $E_S$ are the elasticities of demand and supply, respectively, in the sector. The number in the text is obtained by applying this formula to Michigan's merchandise exports, with elasticities $E_D = 1$ and $E_S = 2$, and interpreting the result as a fraction of gross state product.

# 7

# High Technology in Michigan's Economy

*Abel Feinstein, George A. Fulton, and Donald R. Grimes*

## Introduction

The concept of high technology is an enigma. Many people feel they know what it is, but concrete definitions are elusive. Often the industry is viewed, too narrowly, as being synonymous with the dot-com economy, the "cyber" world, or the information economy. These high-profile enterprises are an essential component, but they do not cover the whole field. Other views are too broad; there seems to be a competing perception that high technology is synonymous with the "new economy," that is, that advances in technology are responsible for everything that has changed in the world's economy. (In fact, the working title of this chapter was "Michigan and the New Economy," and in discussions among colleagues it became apparent that the topic was viewed as synonymous with high technology.) This is certainly not the case. There are a number of different sectors and trends coming into play as the economy evolves. Some of these trends are indeed driven by high technology, but many are not. Some reflect changes in business practices, and others are simple accelerations of trends that have been evident for decades.

Therefore, unlike other industry studies in this volume, the first task in this study is to determine what the industry is. Our definition needs to be operational rather than purely conceptual, as the next logical questions are whether Michigan has whatever the industry is, how much of it Michigan has relative to other states, and how well Michigan has performed compared with other states. This means that we need measures over time. High tech may be one of the most visible industries in terms of public awareness, but unfortunately, it is virtually invisible in the published data.[1] Thus, we had the formidable task of reformulating these data in order to calculate our own numbers.

Beyond measurement is an evaluation of performance. The general approach taken for many of the studies in this volume has been to update their analysis of the Michigan economy for the twenty years since *Michigan's Fiscal and Economic Structure* was published (Brazer and Laren 1982). Our analysis takes the late 1980s as the base from which movements are tracked, because much of the growth and interest in this area has occurred since then. One objective in assessing recent performance is to determine whether Michigan is doing the right things, and doing them right. Even if pursuing high tech is the right thing, which seems to be taken as a given, there is still the question, often asked, of whether we are focusing on the right kind of high tech. This question leads to the observation that high tech is not actually an industry, but rather is

**TABLE 7.1**

### Distribution of Industries among Various High-Tech Definitions

| SIC | Industry | BLS High-Tech Inclusive | BLS High-Tech Intensive | American Electronics Assoc. |
|---|---|---|---|---|
| 28 | Chemicals | • | | |
| 281 | Industrial inorganic chemicals | | • | |
| 283 | Drugs | | • | |
| 286 | Industrial organic chemicals | | • | |
| 291 | Petroleum refining | • | | |
| 348 | Ordnance and accessories | • | | |
| 351 | Engines and turbines | • | | |
| 353 | Construction-related machinery | • | | |
| 355 | Special industrial machinery | • | | |
| 356 | General industrial machinery | • | | |
| 357 | Computer and office equipment | • | • | • |
| 361 | Electric distribution equipment | • | | |
| 362 | Electrical industrial apparatus | • | | |
| 365 | Household audio and video equipment | • | | • |
| 366 | Communications equipment | • | • | • |
| 367 | Electronic components and accessories | • | • | • |
| 371 | Motor vehicles and equipment | • | | |
| 372 | Aircraft and parts | • | • | |
| 376 | Guided missiles, space vehicles, parts | • | • | |
| 381 | Search and navigation equipment | • | • | • |
| 382 | Measuring and controlling devices | • | • | • |
| 384 | Medical equip., instruments, supplies | • | | |
| 3844 | X-ray apparatus and tubes | | | • |
| 3845 | Electromedical equipment | | | • |
| 386 | Photographic equipment and supplies | • | | • |
| 481 | Telephone communications | | | • |
| 482 | Telegraph and other communications | | | • |
| 484 | Cable and other pay TV services | | | • |
| 489 | Communications services, NEC | | | • |
| 737 | Computer and data-processing services | • | • | • |
| 871 | Engineering and architectural services | • | | |
| 873 | Research, development, testing services | • | • | |
| 874 | Management and public relations svcs. | • | | |

SOURCE: Assembled by the authors from Hecker (1999) and American Electronics Association (2001).

stable. We consider whether that is true, and if so, how we go about getting more high tech. We certainly do not have all the answers, but we've made progress in fleshing out the high-tech picture for Michigan, and that gives us a basis for making better-informed decisions now, as well as a jumping-off point for further research on the subject.

## Identifying and Measuring High Technology

Before we can discuss the ramifications of high technology, we must first define it. It can be defined conceptually as the systematic application of scientific and technical knowledge, but that does not get us where we want to go. We need an operational definition so we can identify and measure the presence of high tech among the various elements of the economic structure, and at present there is no generally agreed-upon definition. Different analysts, statistical agencies, and industry groups have offered different measures. We will consider several alternatives that take either an industry or an occupational approach to isolating high tech.

### Industry Definitions of High Technology

Since there is no fixed definition of high tech, there is no "official" high-tech industry, or list of industries, for which standard economic data are developed—a fact that is often not recognized except by researchers in the high-tech field. Most of the definitions of high tech are industry-focused. That is, they use the industrial classifications designated by the federal government to identify sectors associated with high-tech business activity. The industries included on the high-tech list vary, each definition having different criteria for classifying an activity as high tech.

We have chosen to look at three of the most prominent industry definitions of high tech: two provided by the U.S. Bureau of Labor Statistics (Hecker 1999) and another from a list compiled by the American Electronics Association (2001). The industries that qualify as high tech under these criteria are listed in table 7.1, identified by the federal government's Standard Industrial Classification (SIC) codes.

Each of the Bureau of Labor Stastistics (BLS) definitions is based on two ratios: employment in research and development (R&D) as a percentage of total employment in the industry; and

a term that gathers a number of different ventures under its umbrella. To facilitate the analysis, we have partitioned high tech into three major categories that turn out to have distinct performance characteristics in Michigan.

The remaining issue has to do with what all of this means for policy. It seems that high technology has become the mantra of policy makers everywhere, who believe that with it their economies will be better off: they will grow faster, be richer, be more productive, be more cyclically

employment in technology-oriented occupations, also as a percentage of total employment in the industry. The broader BLS high-tech definition includes those industries where both percentages were at least *twice* the all-industry average. The threshold for the narrower high-tech-intensive industry subset is fixed at *five* times the all-industry average. The American Electronics Association (AeA) list is composed of industries in the electronics and telecommunications sectors. These are the sectors that encompass the business activities of AeA member firms.

Despite its prevalence, there are several fundamental problems with the industry approach to defining high tech used by both BLS and AeA. First, because all employment in a designated high-tech industry is included, the industry approach counts many workers not involved in R&D or technology. Using the industry-based approach, both the engineer responsible for computer-aided design and the office assistant in the same firm would be counted as high tech. This also creates the anomaly that workers with the same job functions are arbitrarily classified as high tech or not high tech depending on their industry. For example, the electronics technician at a computer chip factory *is* high tech, but the electronics technician at a potato chip factory is *not* high tech.

Another drawback of the industry approach, one that greatly limits regional analysis, is that an industry that qualifies as high tech at the national level may not be high tech at the state level. For example, a high-tech equipment-manufacturing facility is unlikely to show the concentration of R&D workers locally that is used to identify the high-tech sector nationally.

A particular difficulty with the AeA definition is its restricted scope. The AeA industry list does a very credible job of capturing those industries producing or directly tied to electronics and information technology. Electronics and information technology are undoubtedly major components of the high-tech universe, but they do not constitute all of high tech. The pattern of R&D spending, which is usually considered to be a good index of technological effort, makes this point quite clearly. The computer and electronics, communications, and software industries accounted for about one-third of total industry R&D in 2000. This is a large slice, but it still means that two-thirds of the economy's technological activity is occurring in other sectors. Plainly, the implication of these statistics is that high tech is a consider-

---

**TABLE 7.2**

**Michigan High-Tech Employment and Ranking among States, 2000, Comparing Various High-Tech Industry Definitions**

| | BLS High-Tech | | AeA |
|---|---|---|---|
| | Inclusive | Intensive | |
| Employment in high tech, 2000 | 568,168 | 122,613 | 108,554 |
| RANKING AMONG STATES: | | | |
| High-tech industry jobs | 4 | 17 | 18 |
| High-tech share of private sector jobs | 1 | 34 | 37 |
| High-tech job growth, 1990–2000 | 37 | 29 | 41 |

SOURCE: Derived from industry data in appendix A.

---

ably more extensive phenomenon than the tightly focused AeA concept.

Nevertheless, since these are the most prominent industry definitions of high tech, we developed estimates of high-tech employment for all of the states in the country, including Michigan, based on these concepts. This was done by applying the two BLS definitions as well as the AeA definition to industry employment data for all states (the designation "all states" herein includes the District of Columbia).[2]

Data were assembled by state for each of the definitions, and three measures were constructed: high-tech employment level in 2000, high-tech proportion of total state jobs in 2000, and high-tech growth rates between 1990 and 2000. The full details on all states are shown in appendix A.[3] The rankings for Michigan for each of the three measures and each of the three definitions are shown in table 7.2.

As shown in the table, application of these definitions yields widely varying measures of Michigan's high-tech performance. The measures are clearly affected by the industries included or excluded on the various high-tech lists. The BLS high-tech–intensive and AeA employment levels and shares are similar, but they are significantly different from the same statistics for the BLS high-tech inclusive definition. On the basis of the BLS inclusive definition, Michigan ranks among the top states in the country in high-tech employment (number 4) and high-tech employment share (number 1). On the other hand, the BLS high-tech–intensive industries and the AeA definition put Michigan in the middle of the pack for high-tech structure.

The largest difference is the inclusion of the auto sector (SIC 371) in the BLS inclusive definition, and its exclusion in the other two definitions

## TABLE 7.3

### High-Tech Occupational Definitions

| Current Population Survey Code | Title |
| --- | --- |
| | **Total High Tech** |
| 044–059 | Engineers |
| 213–218 | Engineering and related technologists and technicians |
| 064–068 | Mathematical and computer scientists |
| 069–083 | Natural scientists |
| 223–225 | Science technicians |
| 229 | Computer programmers |
| | **Industrial High Tech** |
| 044–054, 056–059 | Engineers except electrical and electronic |
| 214–218 | Engineering and related technologists and technicians except electrical and electronic |
| 065–068 | Mathematical and computer scientists except systems analysts |
| 069, 074–076, 079 | Natural scientists except chemists, agricultural and food scientists, biological and life scientists, and medical scientists |
| 224–225 | Science technicians except biological technicians |
| | **Information Technology** |
| 055 | Electrical and electronic engineers |
| 213 | Electrical and electronic technicians |
| 064 | Computer systems analysts |
| 229 | Computer programmers |
| | **Biotechnology** |
| 077 | Agricultural and food scientists |
| 078 | Biological and life scientists |
| 223 | Biological technicians |
| 073 | Chemists except biochemists |
| 083 | Medical scientists |

SOURCE: Technology groupings by occupation defined by the authors.

(see table 7.1). This illustrates the "classification mix" problem with the industry definition. The auto industry has a mix of workers, some who unambiguously have technology-oriented responsibilities, and others who do not. Michigan has by far the greatest number of autoworkers among the states, but it also has the lion's share—56%—of the industry's technology-oriented workers. Thus, the inclusion of the industry unduly inflates Michigan's high-tech credits, but to exclude it unfairly discounts these credits. The same could be said for other states that house an industry with a dominant presence; the aircraft industry in Washington would be an example.

In other words, table 7.2 does not provide a decisive characterization of Michigan's high-tech

standing, unless one of the definitions is considered to be compelling—and in our judgment, that is not the case.

Even if the issue of choosing a high-tech definition were resolvable, the industry approach remains problematic because we are dealing with technologies not well defined by industrial classifications. (In this context it is important to keep in mind that most economic data are categorized according to the U.S. government-defined standard classification system.) For example, one of the hottest new technology areas is nano-technology, which spans many industries (as typically defined) and cannot be isolated to even a cluster of industries, much less a single one. Analysis of high-tech activity by industry, therefore, may have limited utility for the policy maker.

### Occupational Definitions of High Technology

In our judgment, a more productive approach to understanding high tech may be to view it through an occupational lens rather than using the more standard industry perspective. There are several advantages to the occupational approach. First, the occupations more clearly identify the human capital endowments that are central to high-tech economic activity. This largely avoids the problem noted in the industry definition, where the "auxiliary" workforce is counted as part of the high-tech total.

Second, the occupational breakout would seem to provide a clearer, less contentious, and more intuitively appealing identification of technology-related workers. Broadly speaking, the high-tech occupations can be defined as engineering workers, scientists, and information technology (IT) professionals. These occupations are clearly and inarguably high-tech–focused. Indeed, they would appear to be virtually synonymous with the concept.

Third, the occupations cross those industry boundaries that can artificially impede our understanding of a region's high-tech qualities. For example, one of the most promising high-tech sectors is "wireless" technology, which is clearly encompassed by electronic engineering and IT occupations, but is not confined to a single industry.

Finally, it is possible to array the occupational data so as to distinguish a variety of technology areas. In other words, we have been able to add a technology dimension to the occupational perspective. In addition to total high tech, we have sorted the technology-related occupations into three categories: industrial high tech, information technology, and biotechnology. The occupational breakout we have chosen to define each of these categories is shown in table 7.3; the classification system for the individual occupations is the one used by the U.S. Census Bureau.

The *industrial high tech* group includes those occupations covering research, development, and engineering functions in the industrial manufacturing economy. It is not surprising, therefore, that engineers and engineering technicians make up the vast majority—86.4%—of the category, although a sizable number of scientists and science technicians are also included. This group has a longer history than the more fledgling, albeit more touted, information technology and biotechnology categories. In fact, our original label for the industrial high tech group was "traditional high tech." We became concerned that the label would be perceived as an oxymoron, even though by any reasonable criteria, including our own, the group qualifies for the high-tech designation.

Operationally, we define the *information technology* (IT) group as electronic engineers and technicians and systems analysts and programmers. The latter two occupational titles also cover those IT jobs that have emerged as a result of personal computers, networks, and the World Wide Web. The rationale for the IT category is self-evident. This grouping of activities is viewed by many as practically synonymous with high tech. (Obviously, we see the high-tech employment universe as being much larger. Given the importance and visibility of information technology, however, it is only reasonable to recognize it as a major high-tech category.)

For purposes of quantification and analysis, we define the occupational *biotechnology* category as consisting of life and medical scientists and technicians. Biotech is an emerging field that is widely recognized as having the potential for major scientific advance, and which is also becoming a hotly contested economic development prize. Michigan is now investing heavily in biotech research, and the state is being forcefully promoted as a center for biotech enterprises. For example, one of the University of Michigan's major new programs is the Life Science Initiative. The university has committed $230 million to the construction and operation of a Life Science Institute, and additional funding is to be provided by corporations and foundations. Envisioned as a centerpiece for the Life Sciences Corridor in southeast Michigan, this is a twenty-year project to invest in and promote life sciences research and business development.

This biotech "biopolis" includes the University of Michigan, Wayne State University, Michigan State University, and the Van Andel Institute in Grand Rapids. The State of Michigan has pledged approximately $1 billion from its share of tobacco settlement funds. The competition for biotech is fierce, because no state wants to be left behind. For instance, Pennsylvania plans on spending $2 billion of its tobacco money on biotechnology, and thirty-nine other states have some promotional program (Pollack 2002). The competition for biotech has, if anything, intensified recently, because the information technology sector has proven to be less recession-proof than previously believed (this will be discussed later). Economic developers are therefore shifting their attention to other high-tech ventures.

## Michigan's High-Technology Performance

Employment trend information for the various high-tech occupational clusters is presented in table 7.4 for Michigan and the United States as a whole. Data have been averaged for the 1987–91 and 1997–2001 time periods. Multiple-year intervals rather than point-in-time estimates were chosen for analysis because of sample size considerations. Care was taken to select multiyear periods that represent comparable phases of the business cycle. Different sets of years were evaluated, and the years selected were those found to offer the optimum combination of sample size, business cycle comparability, and recency of data. (The fundamental themes of the analysis were, in fact, consistent across all the data sets examined, regardless of the time intervals chosen.) The employment measure used is private sector plus public university employment. This measure was chosen in preference to total employment because after careful evaluation the private-plus-public-university cohort was found to more clearly articulate the high-tech regional analysis.

*Total high-tech* occupational employment in Michigan stood at 245,540 in the 1997–2001 time interval, as shown in table 7.4. This puts Michigan's high-tech employment in the same league as major local industry divisions such as construction, transportation-communications-utilities, wholesale trade, and finance (but smaller

**TABLE 7.4**

**High-Tech Occupational Employment Trends Summary, Michigan Compared with the United States, 1987–91 and 1997–2001**

|  | 1987–91 | 1997–2001 | % Growth |
|---|---|---|---|
| **Total High Tech** | | | |
| MICHIGAN EMPLOYMENT: | | | |
|    Engineers | 79,400 | 117,314 | |
|    Mathematical and computer scientists | 26,181 | 51,454 | |
|    Natural scientists | 8,529 | 12,414 | |
|    Engineering and related technologists and technicians | 33,262 | 34,926 | |
|    Science technicians | 7,867 | 8,861 | |
|    Computer programmers | 14,778 | 20,571 | |
| Michigan total high-tech employment | 170,017 | 245,540 | 44.4 |
| U.S. total high-tech employment | 4,071,665 | 5,651,917 | 38.8 |
| **Michigan location quotient** | **1.12** | **1.15** | |
| | | | |
| **Industrial High Tech** | | | |
| Michigan total industrial high tech employment | 108,485 | 142,186 | 31.1 |
| U.S. total industrial high tech employment | 2,027,690 | 2,187,863 | 7.9 |
| **Michigan location quotient** | **1.44** | **1.72** | |
| | | | |
| **Information Technology** | | | |
| Michigan total information technology employment | 52,377 | 89,651 | 71.2 |
| U.S. total information technology employment | 1,787,538 | 3,055,460 | 70.9 |
| **Michigan location quotient** | **0.79** | **0.78** | |
| | | | |
| **Biotechnology** | | | |
| Michigan total biotech employment | 9,155 | 13,703 | 49.7 |
| U.S. total biotech employment | 256,437 | 408,594 | 59.3 |
| **Michigan location quotient** | **0.96** | **0.89** | |

SOURCE: Compiled by the authors using a special tabulation constructed by David Macpherson, Florida State University, with unpublished data taken from the *Current Population Survey*, U.S. Bureau of the Census.

than manufacturing, retail trade, and the major service industry categories).

The upward trend in high-tech occupational employment has been very powerful both in the United States and in Michigan, although Michigan grew a bit faster. The Michigan rate of increase between 1987–91 and 1997–2001 was 44.4% versus 38.8% nationally. These high-tech employment gains were two and one-half times the aggregate employment increases of 17.5% in Michigan and 15.8% nationally.

Another way of comparing Michigan's performance relative to the nation's is through a statistical measure known as the location quotient. The location quotient is typically used as a measure of the concentration of an industry category regionally compared with its concentration in the United States. A location quotient of more than one

means that the industry claims a greater percentage share of employment locally than nationally. A location quotient of less than one signifies a lesser concentration locally; a location quotient of one indicates that the industry shares are equivalent.

In our analysis, we use a location quotient to measure the concentration of employment in occupations rather than in industries. Michigan's location quotient for total high-tech occupational employment was 1.12 in 1987–91 and 1.15 in 1997–2001. This means that the high-tech share of aggregate employment in Michigan was 12 to 15% higher than it was in the United States. The uptick in the location quotient over the decade suggests that Michigan's high-tech advantage actually increased somewhat during the 1990s.

As shown in table 7.4, high-tech employment can be more finely articulated by three classes of technology: industrial high technology, information technology, and biotechnology. Among the technology subsets, Michigan's advantage in the *industrial high tech* category is striking. Indeed, the concentration of industrial high tech employment in Michigan was about one and one-half times the U.S. share over the past decade. More precisely, the industrial high tech location quotients are 1.44 and 1.72 for the 1987–91 and 1997–2001 periods, respectively. Michigan is one of the leaders in industrial high tech employment. In 1997–2001, Michigan, with 142,186 workers, was third after California and Texas in industrial high tech employment. As a percentage of total employment, Michigan, at 3.3%, ranks first in the nation. Full details on the state comparisons are provided in appendix B.

Michigan's significant comparative advantage in industrial high tech reflects the fact that it is the "capital" of the U.S. auto industry. The importance of auto manufacturing in Michigan is, of course, well established and widely recognized. What is less well understood is the implication of this for technology activity in Michigan. Because the three largest U.S.-based motor vehicle companies are headquartered in Michigan, their research, engineering, and design functions are also centered here. In addition, many overseas auto producers have located their U.S. tech centers in Michigan. This results in a massive investment in technology resources in Michigan and the creation of a large technology-related employment base.

According to National Science Foundation (NSF) data, motor vehicle industry funding for research and development totaled nearly $18 billion in 1999. The auto industry would rank fourth in industrial R&D spending if broader industry groups were included, in particular the computer/electronics products and chemical sectors (see appendix C). On the other hand, autos would be ranked second if only the most detailed categories published by NSF were included. Regardless of the exact sorting procedure used, the basic point here is that the motor vehicle industry—which accounts for more than 11% of total company R&D in the United States—is one of the top industries for R&D. Of the $18 billion, three-quarters—$13.5 billion—is attributed to Michigan R&D.[4]

Beyond the impact on industrial high tech employment, it is worth noting the sheer magnitude of motor vehicle industry R&D spending in Michigan, and its prominence in the state's economy. The volume of motor vehicle industry R&D

expenditures in Michigan ($13.5 billion) is not much less than the $14.6 billion the industry spends on payroll for employees (excluding headquarters and technical center employees) in Michigan.[5] Granted, this figure is not complete because it does not include some suppliers, and total compensation will be larger than payroll. Nevertheless, the order of magnitude equivalence of R&D spending and payroll is striking.[6]

The data in table 7.4 also show that Michigan's already strong industrial high tech standing improved between 1987–91 and 1997–2001, the location quotient rising from 1.44 to 1.72. This means that industrial high tech moved from being 44% more concentrated in Michigan than in the United States to being 72% more concentrated over the period. The upward movement reflects some positive trends in Michigan's industrial high tech employment during the 1990s. There was also some weakness in other regions, which tended to push up Michigan's score relative to that of the United States as a whole.

One positive factor for Michigan was the growing importance of engineering and design as a strategic competitive factor in the motor vehicle market, which translated into a greater need for high-tech workers in the state. A second factor was the increasing transfer of engineering functions to parts suppliers by the major automobile manufacturers. For this to be successful, closer coordination was necessary between engineering staffs. This was accomplished by relocating supplier engineering facilities and personnel to Michigan. Also during the 1990s, overseas auto companies greatly expanded their North American operations and production capacity. Because of Michigan's depth of automotive engineering talent, the overseas producers have tended to locate their North American R&D facilities in Michigan.

While these favorable trends pushed up employment in Michigan, cutbacks in defense spending in the first half of the 1990s slowed industrial high tech employment growth in other states. The defense industries, particularly aerospace, are among the largest employers of industrial high tech workers. Since defense spending in Michigan is very limited, the national decline would tend to push up Michigan's industrial high tech location quotient. Large increases in defense procurement are now planned, however, which will likely operate to decrease Michigan's industrial high tech location quotient as defense-related high tech employment rebounds in other states.

*Information technology* employment in Michigan increased between 1987–91 and 1997–2001, from 52,377 to 89,651. Calculation of the location quotients yielded a figure of 0.79 in 1987–91 and 0.78 in 1997–2001. One view of IT in Michigan is that it stands at a 20% disadvantage compared with the nation. Although IT employment grew at a very strong rate of over 70% in Michigan during the 1990s, it still only just maintained its 20% disadvantage. IT in Michigan would have had to grow at an improbable rate of 120% to gain location quotient parity with the nation. That Michigan is much less concentrated in IT employment is not a terribly surprising result. There is a distinct regional twist to the location of the information technology industries. Computer and chip manufacturing and packaged software development tend to be concentrated in California, other western states, Texas, and the northeast. Defense electronics and software are concentrated in the same regions, plus the Mid-Atlantic states.

Perhaps the "man bites dog" story for information technology is that Michigan still does as well as it does in this sector. Michigan has its niches; it has a strong position in industrial electronics and computer services, and it is fairly well represented in systems design and programming and computer support services. In the 1997–2001 period, Michigan ranked number thirteen in the nation in information technology employment, on a par with Colorado and Washington. Furthermore, despite some competitive disadvantage in the IT category overall, the employment trend in Michigan has been very strongly positive, expanding by 71.2% in the 1990s, slightly above the U.S. growth rate.

The third-largest high-tech group in Michigan is *biotechnology*. Michigan employment in the biotech occupations totaled 9,155 during the 1987–91 period and increased to 13,703 during the 1997–2001 time span, a growth rate of 49.7%. Nationally, the rate of increase for the biotech occupations was 59.3%. Michigan's biotech location quotient stood at 0.96 in 1987–91 and 0.89 in 1997–2001.

Several inferences can be drawn from these statistics. The location quotients can be interpreted as indicating that Michigan has a competitive position in the biotech sector. The location quotients show the concentration of biotech occupational employment in Michigan to be a bit below the U.S. level, but the gap is not large, especially considering the small employment base.

Compared with the other states, Michigan ranks eighth in total employment and tenth in biotech employment. Again, this is not a large difference.

The growth rate numbers indicate that the biotech sector is rapidly expanding, both nationally and in Michigan. By any standard, Michigan's employment increase of 49.7% and the U.S. employment gain of 59.3% represent a strong growth pattern for both state and nation.

The final point to make about the biotech data is that the numbers involved are still relatively small. Nationally, the biotech occupations employ fewer than half a million workers and account for only about 7% of high-tech employment. The importance of biotech lies more in its potential, both scientific and economic, than in its current employment levels. Biotech is somewhat of an "infant industry" that is generally regarded as having excellent prospects for future growth. Based on trends over the past decade and economic development initiatives such as the Life Sciences Corridor, it appears that Michigan is positioning itself to share in this growth.

Michigan's high-tech performance, compared with that of its neighbors in the six-state Great Lakes region, is shown in table 7.5. Michigan's level of high-tech employment in the region is second only to that of Illinois, and it is a close second. Michigan's employment figure for 1997–2001 is 245,540, only slightly below the Illinois level of 261,690. With high-tech employment share as the gauge, the Michigan figure of 5.6% is comparable to Minnesota's 5.8% proportion, while the other Great Lakes states all have high-tech shares below 5%. Aggregate regional high-tech growth was about 40% over the decade. Employment in Michigan increased a bit faster, expanding by 44.4%. The Minnesota and Wisconsin growth rates were stronger yet, at 66.2% and 59.7%, respectively. Illinois, Indiana, and Ohio had growth rates in the 29–32% range. In summary, among the six states in the region, Michigan ranks a very close second in both level and share of high-tech employment, and is third in high-tech employment growth. These rankings put Michigan in a competitive position relative to its regional neighbors.

## Summary of High-Tech Performance

The introduction to this chapter posed a number of questions regarding Michigan's high-tech sector. With high tech, is the state's economy growing faster, is it richer, is it more productive, is it more cyclically stable? Broadly speaking, these questions address the issue of the economic importance of high tech. Our analysis indicates that Michigan does indeed have a large base of high-tech workers, and that high-tech employment has shown a strong growth trend. The total number of high-tech workers in Michigan in the 1997–2001 period was 245,540, making the high-tech sector as large as or larger than construction, transportation-communication-utilities, wholesale trade, and finance (but smaller than manufacturing, retail trade, and the major service industry categories). High-tech employment in Michigan grew by 44.4% in the 1990s, more than double the state's overall employment growth rate, and Michigan's high-tech employment growth rate was higher than the U.S. rate of 38.8%.

Another frequently cited issue is the wage level of high-tech workers. High-tech occupations tend to pay higher-than-average wages. Table 7.6 profiles the wage levels of high-tech workers and the relationship between high-tech wages and the average wage of all employees. More occupational wage details are shown in appendix E.

In the 1997–2001 period, high-tech occupations paid an average of $1,050 per week compared with $625 in all occupations, a 68% premium. The wage premium for industrial high tech and information technology workers is about the same, 69%, and biotech occupation wages are 50% above average. As might be expected, there is more variation in wages among the less-aggregated high-tech occupations. One occupation, science technicians, has a wage level below the all-employment average. The wage premium in the other occupations ranges from 27% for engineering technologists and technicians to 86% for engineers.

We used the statistical technique of multiple regression analysis to test the effect of high-tech employment on growth in productivity and wages across all states. The technical results are reported in appendix F. In addition to using high tech's employment share to explain movements in productivity and wages, a number of control variables were included as explanatory factors as well, to account for productivity and wage changes that were unrelated to high-tech employment.

The statistical analysis showed strong support for the hypothesis that a state's high-tech employment is beneficial to productivity and wage growth. We tested two effects on productivity and wages: the share of high-tech employment at the beginning of the period and the change in high-tech employment over the period (in our case,

**TABLE 7.5**

### High-Tech Occupational Employment, Great Lakes States

|  | Employment | | % Change 1987–91 to 1997–2001 | Share of Total Employment (%) 1997–2001 |
|---|---|---|---|---|
|  | 1987–91 | 1997–2001 |  |  |
| Illinois | 198,420 | 261,690 | 31.9 | 4.9 |
| Indiana | 78,882 | 101,852 | 29.1 | 3.8 |
| Michigan | 170,017 | 245,540 | 44.4 | 5.6 |
| Minnesota | 80,472 | 133,746 | 66.2 | 5.8 |
| Ohio | 168,825 | 218,177 | 29.2 | 4.5 |
| Wisconsin | 68,585 | 109,503 | 59.7 | 4.3 |

SOURCE: Derived from occupational data in appendix B.

**TABLE 7.6**

### Summary of Michigan Occupational High-Tech Wages

|  | Average Weekly Wage 1997–2001 | Ratio of High-Tech Wages to Wages in All Occupations |
|---|---|---|
| All occupations | $ 625 | 1.00 |
| Total high tech | 1,050 | 1.68 |
| Engineers | 1,160 | 1.86 |
| Mathematical and computer scientists | 1,095 | 1.75 |
| Natural scientists | 1,108 | 1.77 |
| Engineering and related technologists and technicians | 794 | 1.27 |
| Science technicians | 494 | 0.79 |
| Computer programmers | 944 | 1.51 |
| Industrial high tech | 1,056 | 1.69 |
| Information technology | 1,057 | 1.69 |
| Biotechnology | 937 | 1.50 |

SOURCE: Compiled by the authors using a special tabulation constructed by David Macpherson, Florida State University, with unpublished data taken from the *Current Population Survey*, U.S. Bureau of the Census.

1989–99). Each of these measures had a positive and statistically significant effect on both productivity and wage growth. That is, both the initial concentration of high-tech employment in an area and its change over time are significant factors underlying the growth of productivity and wages for the area.[7] We judge this to be one of the most significant findings in the chapter, particularly since the findings are applicable to all regions of the country; it seems that a region cannot go wrong with a skilled high-tech workforce. What this all adds up to is that the advantages to the economy—higher wages, faster wage growth, and greater productivity—are a major justification for pursuing high tech.

**TABLE 7.7**

**Growth Path of U.S. Real GDP and Its Investment Component for Information Equipment and Software, Fourth Quarter of 2000 to First Quarter of 2002 (seasonally adjusted annual rate)**

| Quarter | Real GDP | Information Equip. and Software Investment | Real GDP Excluding Information Equip. and Software |
|---------|----------|-------------------------------------------|---------------------------------------------------|
| 2000 Q4 | 1.1 | 1.6 | 1.1 |
| 2001 Q1 | –0.6 | –10.0 | 0.1 |
| 2001 Q2 | –1.6 | –18.6 | –0.4 |
| 2001 Q3 | –0.3 | –11.4 | 0.4 |
| 2001 Q4 | 2.7 | –1.2 | 3.0 |
| 2002 Q1 | 5.0 | 6.6 | 4.9 |

SOURCE: U.S. Department of Commerce, Bureau of Economic Analysis (2002).

High-tech activities have also been thought to be stable over the business cycle, but if the 2001 recession is any indication, high tech is not an exception to the rule after all. Although information technology was a major driver of economic growth in the 1990s, it was also a major contributor to the downturn of 2001. This is apparent in table 7.7, which shows that inflation-adjusted (real) investment in information-processing equipment and software declined in every quarter of 2001, registering a drop of more than 10% over the year. If this category is removed from real GDP, the resulting measure of output declines in only one quarter, and that at a modest annual rate of 0.4%. The growth path for real GDP absent IT would not qualify technically as a classical recession.

It is not surprising, then, that some of the geographic areas most associated with information tech suffered some of the largest increases in unemployment rates during 2001. Examples include: Silicon Valley, 5 percentage points (from 1.5 to 6.5); Austin, Texas, 2.9 percentage points (from 1.7 to 4.6); Boulder, Colorado, 2.5 percentage points (from 2 to 4.5); Seattle, Washington, 2.3 percentage points (from 3.5 to 5.8); and the Research Triangle (Raleigh–Durham–Chapel Hill, North Carolina), 2.3 percentage points (from 1.7 to 4). The comparable increase for the country as a whole was 1.5 percentage points (from 3.7 to 5.2). It turned out that high-tech employment, far from being recession-proof, was very sensitive to typical investment behavior.

In summary, our data and analyses confirm that there are many good reasons to attract high-tech firms to an area, including favorable growth prospects for employment, wages, and productivity. We did find, however, that the same claim cannot be made for immunity from business cycle downturns.

## Michigan's High-Tech Setting: Diagnosis and Prescription

So far we have established that high tech is worth having if you can attract and retain it (and not break the bank in the process)—at least as we have defined and measured the high-tech concept. Fortunately, Michigan has enough employment in high tech to regard it as a major division of the local economy. Michigan's current high-tech endowment varies by its major categories, but in each case, employment in these high-value-added enterprises has outperformed Michigan's overall job growth. Moreover, as we extrapolate from the recent past to the future, the productivity premium being delivered by high tech becomes an increasingly critical focus for regional economic development. As observed in chapter 2 of this volume, "in the long run, improvements in our standard of living derive largely from increases in productivity." We conclude, therefore, that sustaining and enhancing Michigan's high-tech endowment does seem to belong in the state's mission statement.

So, we return to one of the fundamental questions posed at the beginning of this chapter, "How do we go about getting more high tech?" To answer this question, we consider the possible options, analyzing their respective merits.

### Factors Fostering High Tech: A Statistical Analysis

It is not difficult to come up with a list of factors that are purported to foster the development of a high-tech environment; the components of such a list have made their way into the lexicon of high tech. Many of these factors pass the intuition test for inclusion, but there appear to be few examples of statistical analyses evaluating how these factors actually correlate with observed performance. And of course, there is no such analysis on the economies of states, since the measures necessary to monitor high-tech performance over time did not even exist prior to our study. To fill this analytical void, we make a first pass at assessing how well factors thought to promote high tech are able to explain regional movements in high-tech occupational employment since the late 1980s.

We used the statistical technique of multiple regression analysis to test how factors frequently cited as promoting high tech were related to high-tech employment performance across states between the 1987–91 and the 1997–2001 periods. Specifically, we investigated how the evolution over time of our four categories of high-tech occupational employment, expressed as a share of total employment, could be explained by variations in the following factors:

1. venture capital expenditures (provided largely to enterprises that are developing new ideas, products, or processes);
2. higher-education graduates in high-tech–related fields, by the most relevant degree category (associate's, bachelor's, master's, or Ph.D.);[8]
3. the difference in the number of higher-education graduates over time, by degree category;
4. state and local property, sales, and income (both corporate and personal) taxes as a proportion of state personal income;
5. the difference in state tax rates over time;
6. technology employment in the base period—included to capture the agglomeration or "clustering" effects of the established level of technology (i.e., the notion that "like attracts like"); and
7. the difference over time in total employment (excluding the technology occupations)—included to control for other factors that influence the general attractiveness of a state (for example, climate, scenery, and other amenities).

In order to represent these factors quantitatively in our analysis, we would need measures for all states over time. The paucity of such measures limited our ability to test the factors as comprehensively as we would have liked. Nonetheless, we were able to assemble a data set that provides some initial insight into what matters for the development of high tech.

The technical results of our analysis are shown in appendix G and summarized here. The overall explanatory power of the factors in combination was very significant statistically for the all technology, industrial tech, and information tech categories. The explanatory power for biotech was only moderately significant statistically, undoubtedly due to its much smaller size and shorter history.[9] Next we consider each of the factors in turn.

*Venture capital expenditures* were an extremely important factor across the categories of high tech, except for industrial technology. The effects were positive and significant for total technology and information technology, and highly significant for biotechnology. For industrial technology, the effect of venture capital was essentially zero, not surprising since this category of high tech is much more established and does not normally attract seed funding. As shown in appendix H, for the period 1995–2001, Michigan's ranking among the states for total venture capital expenditures is twenty-five, and for venture capital expenditures per employee it is a very weak thirty-five. Compared with the other five Great Lakes states, Michigan ranks fourth on both measures, behind Minnesota, Illinois, and Ohio. Michigan appears to be significantly undersubscribed in this strategic area.[10] Indeed, a local professional consultant in the venture capital business has characterized Michigan investors as "timid" in this area. We have no special knowledge on the accuracy of this statement, but at least for IT and biotech, we do have some evidence that venture capital matters and, as noted, Michigan is weak in this area. Of course, increasing the rate of spending is not enough to guarantee results; it has to be productive spending. During testing of our analysis for sensitivity to changes over time, we found that much of the boom in venture capital spending in 1999–2001 did not lead to the same increase in real activity as did investment in the 1995–98 period.

The *awarding of higher-education degrees in high-tech fields* had a consistently positive effect on high-tech employment. The effect of bachelor's degrees on information technology was significant, and on industrial technology it was moderately significant. For biotechnology, the Ph.D. degree dominated the other degrees, which is not surprising considering the advanced level of education required for many of the roles in this high-tech category.[11]

There are a number of reasons why there was not a stronger statistical relationship between education and employment. College graduates in a state are not captive; they can leave and seek jobs elsewhere. Also, there are foreign immigrants moving into high-tech jobs who are not included in the graduate count. On the other hand, many high-tech students do remain in Michigan after graduation, which means that there is some advantage to attracting promising students. Recent estimates show that Michigan retains 79% of its public university graduates who have gone on to work in high-tech jobs. More surprising is that 55% of students who come to Michigan from out of state to pursue education in high-tech fields remain here after graduation (Michigan Economic Development Corporation 2001). Nevertheless, there is much anecdotal evidence that job-matching activities have not been optimized. It is important to ensure that these high-tech graduates at least have complete and timely information on locally available job prospects that potentially match their skills and interests.

Our analysis does not account for the flow of graduates outside of a state to employment inside the state. Some of our recent research suggests that Michigan has enjoyed net in-migration during the 1990s of those with at least some college education, reversing the trend of the 1980s, which saw net out-migration of highly educated residents. It appears that when the opportunities are there, they will come—or at least some of them will.

The *tax rate* factors were included to measure the possible negative effect of high tax rates or growing tax rates on the location of high-tech enterprises. The tax rates had a consistently negative effect on high-tech employment, but were never even moderately significant. This result could suggest that taxes are less important than other factors in making high-tech location decisions. It could also indicate, though, that some of the influence of the tax factor was picked up by the catchall factor representing the attractiveness of an area.

The *agglomeration* factor seems to have the weakest correlation with high-tech employment growth. The measures used to proxy the clustering of like activities had an insignificant effect on employment in three of the high-tech categories, and the effect on industrial tech was contrary to our expectations. Here, the agglomeration effect was negative and statistically significant, suggesting that employment in industrial technology occupations has been spreading out among the states (disagglomeration). In fact, the majority of the twenty-five states with an above-average share of industrial technology employment in the 1987–91 period registered below-average growth during the following decade.

In this regard, Michigan is a major exception: a state with an above-average share of industrial tech employment showing above-average growth.

Indeed, Michigan was the biggest outlier among states in the regression analysis, with the greatest positive difference between its actual change in share of industrial tech employment and that predicted by the analysis. This statistical observation is consistent with our view that the high-tech component of the auto industry, that is, the engineering, research, and design functions, is becoming more concentrated in Michigan (for a similar view, see chapter 2).

The catchall proxy variable for the *attractiveness of an area* attempts to control for factors that would influence any industry in its location decision. The variable was positive and highly significant for all technology and industrial technology, and moderately significant for IT. It had virtually zero effect on biotech employment; in fact, three-quarters of the biotech companies formed in the past decade clustered in nine areas, all on the coasts and surely not exhaustive of amenities across the country (Pollack 2002). Some of the factors influencing an area's attractiveness are within the sphere of state government control or influence, and some are not. In the end, however, the market determines what matters and what does not.

There are a number of other factors influencing the high-tech setting that are not included in our statistical analysis, or are transparent elements of the analysis. For instance, such topics as site selection, infrastructure and telecommunications issues, energy, and environmental concerns merit detailed consideration. This overview chapter on such an expansive subject as high tech does not permit us to penetrate deeper into the large territory falling under its shadow. Since issues of labor quality are so compelling, though, and because universities are becoming the focal point for the nurturing of high tech, we chose to expand on these two topics by briefly considering university-based technology transfer and computer literacy.

### The Role of Universities in the High-Tech Setting

One of the primary contributions of the university community to the high-tech economy is the educating of students who then become the skilled workforce at the heart of the high-tech enterprise. To reflect this contribution, our statistical analysis included university degree recipients in high-tech-oriented disciplines as one of the factors posited to influence the evolution of high tech.

**TABLE 7.8**

**Computer and Internet Availability and Usage, U.S. and Great Lakes States, September 2001**

| | At School (Ages 6–15) | | At Work, Private Sector (Ages 25–60) | | Households | |
|---|---|---|---|---|---|---|
| | % Use Computer | % Use Internet | % Use Computer | % Use Internet | % with Computer | % with Internet |
| U.S. | 88.5 | 59.1 | 55.9 | 40.7 | 56.5 | 50.6 |
| Illinois | 91.0 | 59.4 | 57.3 | 41.3 | 53.0 | 46.9 |
| Indiana | 90.9 | 63.2 | 54.9 | 37.9 | 53.2 | 47.3 |
| Michigan | 92.8 | 68.8 | 56.0 | 40.2 | 58.3 | 51.2 |
| Minnesota | 91.0 | 69.2 | 64.5 | 48.9 | 64.6 | 55.6 |
| Ohio | 90.2 | 68.4 | 56.1 | 36.0 | 57.6 | 50.9 |
| Wisconsin | 91.4 | 68.1 | 60.0 | 41.0 | 56.4 | 50.2 |

SOURCE: Data on school and work from a special tabulation by David Macpherson, Florida State University; data on households from National Telecommunications and Information Administration, U.S. Department of Commerce.

For the major research universities, their contribution extends beyond teaching. The contributions in the research arena can also be fundamentally important to the high-tech economy, but they were not included in the statistical analysis because a suitable data set could not be assembled. Nevertheless, the topic is worth touching on, albeit outside of the context of the statistical analysis.

Research universities expand knowledge and create technology that can serve as a magnet for high-tech firms to locate in the vicinity. In Michigan, research in automotive engineering (industrial tech) is an established example, and the new Life Sciences Corridor (biotech) is intended to create the same synergies in the future. Research universities can also foster high-tech activities through technology transfer and other commercialization activities. In Michigan and most other states, these activities currently have only a modest impact on local economies. For example, recent survey results indicate that licensing income for university-developed technology received by Michigan public universities from licensees located in Michigan amounted to only $421,131 and twenty-eight licensees in 1999. In the same year, there were forty-seven Michigan start-up companies that spun off of university research, but all of the companies were small; they generated a total of $131,353 in licensing revenues. Michigan State University was the source of the largest number of start-ups, which generated about 475 in-state jobs (SRI International 2002).

The global impact of technology transfer activity at Michigan universities is much larger. In particular, the licensing income from licensees located in Michigan is only a small fraction of the income received from out-of-state licensing (especially at the University of Michigan). Much of this income is recirculated into the research process; the university administrations are, in fact, required by law to invest their share of this revenue in research, research infrastructure, and education (SRI International 2002).

The main attraction of technology transfer is its potential for much larger payoffs in the longer term, as well as the benefits that are expected to accrue both to universities and to private industry from their working more closely together. The conventional wisdom on the calculus of promoting these relationships is that the long-term payoffs greatly exceed their costs (SRI International 2002). The ultimate impact of technology transfer on Michigan's high-tech environment will be more easily determined in the future, when our assessments can be based on more experience than we have now.

**Computer Literacy in the High-Tech Setting**

The availability of a qualified workforce has consistently been viewed among seasoned economic development professionals as a primary, often *the* primary, factor in attracting industry to an area. For high-tech enterprises, knowledge is of the essence, and to meet that need there is no substitute for a strong educational system in the state. Also important is a basic level of literacy in the sciences, both for students who might pursue advanced education and careers in high tech, and for those who would benefit at work and at home from greater use of technology. Computer literacy is the most visible factor, as well as conveniently being the one for which we have some measures, so we are able to evaluate how Michigan compares with other states.

Data on computer usage for all states, drawn from Census Bureau surveys conducted in September 2001, are presented in appendices I, J, and K, and are summarized for the Great Lakes states in table 7.8. Appendices I and J show the rate of computer usage and Internet usage at school (primary and secondary students aged six to fifteen), and at work (private sector workers aged twenty-five to sixty), respectively. Appendix K provides information on the percentage of households that have computers and Internet connections.

The student group has the most forward-looking prospects, and perhaps holds the greatest interest for public policy analysts. The survey results on students are positive for Michigan. The state ranks fourth in computer usage and tenth in Internet usage among all states, although there is not a wide disparity in usage rates across many of the states. A reported 92.8% of Michigan students are using computers in school, and 68.8% use the Internet.[12] The equivalent national figures are 88.5% and 59.1%. Among the Great Lakes states, Michigan is first in school computer usage and second in school Internet usage.

In the workplace, Michigan occupies the middle ground among states, ranking twenty-eighth in computer usage (56.0%) and twenty-ninth in Internet usage (40.2%). Again, the dispersion across states is not great. Michigan private-sector workers are on par with their counterparts nationally, where 55.9% use computers and 40.7% use the Internet. In the Great Lakes, the rate of computer usage at the jobsite is quite similar in Illinois, Indiana, Michigan, and Ohio; the Wisconsin and Minnesota percentages are higher. Michigan's workplace usage of the Internet falls in the middle among the Great Lakes states. Among households, Michigan is a bit ahead of the nation in the availability of computer resources. The proportion of Michigan households with a computer, 58.3%, is a little above the U.S. average of 56.5%. Michigan households with an Internet connection are 51.2% of total households, compared with 50.6% nationally.[13] Among the Great Lakes states, Michigan is number two, after Minnesota, in both computer ownership and Internet connectivity.

We will not know, until economic historians address the issue, if it was the production or the use of the new information technology embodied in computers and the Internet that created the most benefit to society during the twenty-first century. If the widespread use of the new information technology eventually turns out to be the greatest good to emerge from the IT revolution (as opposed to actually manufacturing and developing the new technology), then Michigan's young citizens appear to be well situated.

### Prescriptive Summary

Since our analysis of what matters to high tech is far from comprehensive, our road map to high-tech prosperity outlines only a few major highways. Such a map does provide a sense of direction, however, and that is a good start. The following points are what stood out for us in conducting the study.

1. One major concern we have about the prospects for high tech in Michigan is whether there will be a sufficient pool of labor with the skills and education sought by firms in the technology business. In the second half of the 1990s, labor shortages were prevalent in Michigan across all educational categories, including college graduates, the educational category most in demand by high tech. This is shown in table 7.9, where the labor force participation rates and unemployment rates in Michigan for 1996 and 1999 are broken out by four different levels of educational attainment: not a high school graduate, high school graduate or GED, some college or associate's degree, and bachelor's degree or more. What is clear from the table is that most of the gains in labor supply over the period came from among those with less education. The gain of 6 percentage points in the participation rate (those residents employed or actively seeking employment)[14] and the drop of 2.5 percentage points in the unemployment rate among those with less than a high school education is especially striking. In the category of college graduates, on the other hand, labor force participation was unchanged between 1996 and 1999, remaining at the very high rate of 80%. Unemployment was also fairly static, settling in at very low rates under 2%. The reason this category shows so little change is that the participation rate is already so high and the unemployment rate is already so low that there is virtually no further room for movement. To compensate for the paucity of more highly educated workforce entrants from the resident population, Michigan has had some recent

**TABLE 7.9**

**Labor Force Statistics for Michigan by Educational Attainment, 1996 and 1999**

| Educational Level | Labor Force Participation Rate (%) | | | Unemployment Rate (%) | | |
|---|---|---|---|---|---|---|
| | 1996 | 1999 | Change | 1996 | 1999 | Change |
| Not a high school graduate | 41.2 | 47.3 | 6.0 | 12.8 | 10.3 | −2.5 |
| High school graduate or GED | 65.6 | 67.2 | 1.6 | 5.4 | 3.8 | −1.6 |
| Some college or associate's degree | 76.0 | 76.9 | 0.8 | 3.9 | 3.0 | −0.8 |
| Bachelor's degree or more | 80.0 | 80.0 | 0.0 | 1.8 | 1.6 | −0.2 |
| All | 66.5 | 68.9 | 2.4 | 4.9 | 3.8 | −1.1 |

SOURCE: Compiled by the authors from *Current Population Survey,* Census Bureau, U.S. Department of Commerce.

success in attracting migrants with postsecondary education, as mentioned earlier.

According to our current long-term economic and demographic forecast (Fulton and Grimes 2003), the echo of the baby boom will mute the effects of increasing retirements during the decade of 2000–10. After 2010, though, the effects of accelerating retirements will dominate. Michigan's prime working-age population (those aged sixteen to sixty-four) is forecast to show no growth between 2010 and 2030. By contrast, between 1990 and 2000, Michigan's prime working-age population grew by over 400,000 people. (This forecast suggests that by 2030, Michigan will have a higher percentage of residents over the retirement age than Florida has now.) Simply put: an aging population will ensure that tight labor conditions in the local economy are prevalent after 2010. Furthermore, Michigan is not an isolated case; other regions of the country will also face the growing problem of labor shortages. The competition for all workers will be fierce, and if the experience of the past decade is any indication, in no area will it be as fierce as in the highly educated end. This is precisely the domain of high-tech enterprises. Michigan *must* become more successful in educating, training, attracting, and retaining highly skilled workers in order to flourish in the high-stakes technology game.

2. High tech requires funding on a large scale. Our study indicates that venture capital expenditures have had a significantly positive influence on information technology and biotechnology. Our data, as well as discussions with venture capitalists, suggest that investors in Michigan have been relatively risk-averse in their support of these ventures. Therefore, another major concern is the availability of venture capital for Michigan's nascent high-tech enterprises. Although the recent dot-com bust confirms that some prudence is called for, it is a fundamental tenet that higher returns are associated with higher degrees of risk.

3. State governments have also been actively funding these initiatives. Over 80% of the states have some promotion program in biotech alone, for instance, and the stakes are high. The State of Michigan has pledged approximately $1 billion for the Life Sciences Corridor, and some state governments have committed much more to biotech. So, the cost is high and much of the benefit will not be seen any time soon. There are many competing calls on these scarce resources, and we as citizens are going to be continually reevaluating whether we are going to stay the course on funding these initiatives at the scale required for them to be effective. It is important to focus on the longer-term view, which is often difficult in the political arena.

4. Most of the public discussion on high tech has focused on the newer categories of IT and biotech. One of the prominent findings in this chapter, however, is how large a contributor the industrial tech category is to the Michigan economy, how rapidly it has been growing, and how much of a comparative advantage the state has developed over the rest of the country. Perhaps the economic question most asked by the popular press in recent years is whether Michigan has become more diversified, by which they mean, are we less auto-dependent? This interpretation of diversification and the auto industry's role in the Michigan economy misses a fundamental point. Michigan is quietly becoming the world center for automotive engineering, research, and design, presumably an activity worth having. Many of the opportunities we seek may be right in our own backyard.

## Conclusion

When we took on the task of assessing high technology in Michigan's economy, we immediately came up against a fundamental problem: beyond a rough conceptual understanding, we did not know what high tech was. That is, we did not have any measures of the industry (we eventually did not even view it as an industry), so we could not evaluate its structure or track its performance. Consequently, a considerable amount of our effort was devoted to appraising methods of data construction and then developing data series on high-tech occupational employment from the late 1980s to the current period. We did this not only for Michigan but also for all of the states in the country, so that we could assess the state in both absolute and relative terms. To further illuminate the analysis, we partitioned high tech into industrial tech, information tech, and biotech.

By our measures, Michigan has a good-sized high-tech workforce, nearly a quarter of a million jobs in recent years, which rivals the scale of some of the state's major industry divisions. Furthermore, all of the high-tech categories grew very rapidly over the 1990s, either outpacing the nation (industrial tech), keeping up with the nation's torrid pace (information tech), or staying close to the nation's vigorous pace (biotech). Fueled by Michigan's emergence as a world center for automotive engineering, research, and design, industrial high tech has developed a dominant presence in the state. Its share of employment locally exceeds its share in the nation by an impressive 72%. Information tech, on the other hand, is 20% less concentrated in the state than in the nation, although it has a strong position locally in industrial electronics and computer services, systems design, programming, and computer support services. Biotech is a little less concentrated in Michigan than it is in the country, but a substantial financial commitment is being made to this fledgling venture, especially in the Life Sciences Corridor. Biotech is emerging as the newest economic development battleground among states, at least among those able to stay in the high-stakes game.

One of the major findings on high tech's importance to an economy is that it makes an impressive contribution to productivity and wage growth, and what is more, this finding pertains to all regions of the country. Since improvements in an area's standard of living are derived largely from increases in productivity, the productivity premium that high tech delivers becomes a critical focus for regional economic development.

Having assessed the structure and performance of high tech, we next tried to tease out of the data how some factors touted as fostering the development of high tech fared when put to the statistical test. Assembling consistent data on these factors over time for every state was a daunting task, and the scarcity of information limited our analysis. It seems clear, though, that success in the high-tech arena depends heavily on whether the state can supply an adequate pool of highly educated workers and sufficient venture capital. As far as we can tell, that is what the high-tech market wants.

∎

## REFERENCES

American Electronics Association. 2001. AeANET: AeA's definition of the high-tech industry. *www.aeanet.org*.

Brazer, Harvey E., and Deborah S. Laren, eds. 1982. *Michigan's fiscal and economic structure*. Ann Arbor: University of Michigan Press.

Fulton, George A., and Donald R. Grimes. 2003. *Economic and demographic outlook for the counties of Michigan to the year 2030*. Ann Arbor: Institute of Labor and Industrial Relations, University of Michigan.

Hecker, Daniel. 1999. High-technology employment: a broader view. *Monthly Labor Review* 122 (6): 18–33.

Michigan Economic Development Corporation. 2001. Attracting & retaining the best talent to Michigan. Report prepared by the Partnership for Economic Progress, a collaborative initiative of the Michigan Economic Development Corporation and the Presidents Council, State Universities of Michigan. Lansing: Michigan Economic Development Corporation. November. *http://medc.michigan.org*.

National Science Foundation, Division of Science Resources Statistics. 1999. *Research and development in industry*, table A-32. Washington, D.C.: U.S. Government Printing Office.

———. 2000. *Survey of industrial research and development*. Washington, D.C.: U.S. Government Printing Office.

Pollack, Andrew. 2002. Cities and states clamor to be bio town, U.S.A. *New York Times*, 11 June.

SRI International. 2002. The economic impact of Michigan's public universities. Report prepared for Michigan Economic Development Corporation and Presidents Council, State Universities of Michigan. Project No. PDH 02–019. Menlo Park, Calif.: SRI International. *http://medc.michigan.org.*

U.S. Census Bureau. 2001. *County business patterns 1999. Michigan.* Washington, D.C.: U.S. Government Printing Office, April. *http://www.census.gov.*

U.S. Department of Commerce, Bureau of Economic Analysis. 2002. *Survey of Current Business* 82 (8). Washington, D.C.: U.S. Government Printing Office, August. *http://www.bea.gov.*

## NOTES

The authors would like to express their gratitude to Jackie Murray for her exceptional work in editing and processing the material in this chapter. We would also like to thank David Macpherson of Florida State University, who made an invaluable contribution to the enormous task of assembling data for the chapter, using the CPS microdata tapes.

1. The U.S. government uses the Standard Industrial Classification (SIC) coding system to define industry divisions. This system, developed in 1941 and most recently updated in 1987, does not isolate many of the high-technology enterprises that were in their infancy in the late 1980s. Statistical agencies in the United States are in the process of implementing an entirely new classification system, known as the North American Industrial Classification System (NAICS). When NAICS is fully implemented, it will better identify and track high-technology-related activities, although some deficiencies will remain.

2. The source of the employment data is the Covered Employment Statistics program (ES-202) operated by BLS. A significant operational issue was the disclosure restrictions in the ES-202, which reduced the availability of some industry cells in some states. To "patch" these empty cells, we adapted data from the Bureau of the Census, County Business Patterns, a very time-consuming process. County Business Patterns also restricts data release for confidentiality reasons, but unlike the ES-202, it provides a range of employment from which a midpoint estimate can be calculated.

3. The appendices to this chapter are included because most of them contain data that cannot be found in other sources. Much more detail on the measures that we constructed for this project can be found on the Internet at *http://www.ilir.umich.edu/lmr.*

4. Total spending on R&D by all industries in Michigan (from both private and federal sources) totaled $17.7 billion in 1999. This puts Michigan second only to California in industrial R&D (details on all states are provided in appendix D).

5. Payroll data is taken from County Business Patterns 1999.

6. The data are not available to make historical comparisons over time, but the auto companies report an expanding R&D function, and the opinion of industry analysts is that the growth is gravitating toward Michigan.

7. In the case of productivity, each additional percentage point in share of high-tech employment *at the beginning of the period* was found to be associated with a 1.94-percentage-point gain in productivity over the ten-year period from 1989 to 1999. In addition, a *change* of one percentage point in high tech's employment share over the period was associated with a 2.29-percentage-point increase in productivity over the period.

8. The number of degrees awarded by field of study, by state, were compiled by extracting information on the number of degrees awarded by all postsecondary institutions in the United States. This information is part of the Integrated Postsecondary Education Data System maintained by the National Center for Education Statistics.

9. In the terminology used in the text, "moderately significant" means statistically significant at the 10% level, "significant" refers to the 5% level, and "highly significant" refers to the 1% level.

10. Comparable data across states were not available to us for earlier periods. A longer series is available for the United States, and it shows that venture capital expenditures were an order of magnitude smaller a decade ago than they are now. This implies that most of the growth in venture capital over the decade is captured by the more recent data.

11. Due to limited degrees of freedom resulting from data restrictions, only the educational degree category (associate's, bachelor's, master's, or Ph.D.) that contributed the most explanatory power to an equation was included.

12. Statistically, both of these values are one standard deviation above the mean values across all states.

13. Statistically, both of these values are within one standard deviation of the mean values across all states.

14. Included in those not participating in the labor force would be people not working outside of the home, students, welfare recipients, and retirees.

## APPENDIX A

### Various Definitions of High-Tech Industry Employment by State

| State | BLS High-Tech Inclusive | | | BLS High-Tech Intensive | | | AeA | | |
|---|---|---|---|---|---|---|---|---|---|
| | Employed 2000 | % Growth 1990–2000 | High-Tech % of Total Emp. 2000 | Employed 2000 | % Growth 1990–2000 | High-Tech % of Total Emp. 2000 | Employed 2000 | % Growth 1990–2000 | High-Tech % of Total Emp. 2000 |
| U.S. | 10,804,208 | 18.9 | 8.3 | 5,631,696 | 20.9 | 4.3 | 5,526,770 | 39.1 | 4.3 |
| AL | 119,333 | 17.5 | 6.4 | 58,192 | 16.0 | 3.1 | 54,477 | 29.9 | 2.9 |
| AK | 8,502 | 42.2 | 3.1 | 1,899 | 82.8 | 0.7 | 5,488 | 102.1 | 2.0 |
| AZ | 186,244 | 41.6 | 8.4 | 126,354 | 26.7 | 5.7 | 109,648 | 36.5 | 4.9 |
| AR | 60,657 | 23.0 | 5.4 | 21,888 | 31.6 | 1.9 | 22,994 | 37.0 | 2.0 |
| CA | 1,544,211 | 11.7 | 10.4 | 1,049,763 | 12.0 | 7.1 | 985,561 | 36.3 | 6.6 |
| CO | 216,765 | 56.6 | 9.9 | 147,332 | 57.5 | 6.7 | 183,793 | 99.2 | 8.4 |
| CT | 180,488 | –11.7 | 10.8 | 113,774 | –11.7 | 6.8 | 81,524 | 18.4 | 4.9 |
| DC | 56,843 | 23.7 | 8.9 | 32,054 | 121.1 | 7.8 | 18,847 | 34.8 | 4.6 |
| DE | 45,194 | –15.1 | 11.1 | 20,117 | –21.7 | 3.2 | 10,970 | 123.2 | 1.7 |
| FL | 404,196 | 35.6 | 5.7 | 195,571 | 18.9 | 2.8 | 235,179 | 38.6 | 3.3 |
| GA | 253,558 | 62.4 | 6.5 | 128,643 | 97.7 | 3.3 | 170,716 | 98.2 | 4.4 |
| HI | 13,013 | 16.2 | 2.4 | 5,592 | 38.6 | 1.0 | 8,561 | 7.7 | 1.5 |
| ID | 46,775 | 66.3 | 8.3 | 34,818 | 59.6 | 6.2 | 28,750 | 109.9 | 5.1 |
| IL | 516,941 | 16.8 | 8.7 | 236,313 | 27.1 | 4.0 | 229,377 | 26.4 | 3.9 |
| IN | 276,595 | 18.3 | 9.4 | 77,280 | –1.7 | 2.6 | 67,922 | –7.1 | 2.3 |
| IA | 88,545 | 22.6 | 6.1 | 37,526 | 40.9 | 2.6 | 43,168 | 45.5 | 3.0 |
| KS | 121,853 | 25.1 | 9.3 | 74,292 | 30.5 | 5.7 | 48,484 | 99.4 | 3.7 |
| KY | 132,161 | 45.0 | 7.5 | 39,553 | 39.3 | 2.2 | 39,625 | 39.7 | 2.2 |
| LA | 95,607 | 10.1 | 5.1 | 37,253 | 14.4 | 2.0 | 28,079 | 39.8 | 1.5 |
| ME | 27,612 | 24.4 | 4.7 | 16,700 | 35.4 | 2.8 | 14,985 | 34.8 | 2.5 |
| MD | 215,930 | 20.4 | 9.0 | 127,290 | 21.6 | 5.3 | 116,728 | 23.2 | 4.9 |
| MA | 395,836 | 7.9 | 12.1 | 255,519 | 8.1 | 7.8 | 251,206 | 13.3 | 7.7 |
| MI | 568,168 | 14.5 | 12.4 | 122,613 | 23.1 | 2.7 | 108,554 | 24.6 | 2.4 |
| MN | 218,748 | 25.4 | 8.4 | 120,165 | 24.8 | 4.6 | 139,741 | 32.9 | 5.4 |
| MS | 48,250 | 14.9 | 4.2 | 13,355 | 53.5 | 1.2 | 17,583 | 38.7 | 1.5 |
| MO | 197,630 | 3.1 | 7.4 | 89,829 | –2.9 | 3.4 | 92,679 | 46.1 | 3.5 |
| MT | 15,916 | 153.6 | 4.2 | 5,287 | 139.1 | 1.4 | 6,367 | 103.5 | 1.7 |
| NE | 57,488 | 52.5 | 6.5 | 35,111 | 64.5 | 4.0 | 36,606 | 45.3 | 4.1 |
| NV | 32,323 | 35.2 | 3.2 | 15,270 | 18.5 | 1.5 | 19,833 | 112.1 | 1.9 |
| NH | 67,913 | 18.7 | 11.2 | 45,592 | 19.0 | 7.5 | 45,476 | 16.4 | 7.5 |
| NJ | 377,130 | –1.0 | 9.7 | 229,610 | 6.7 | 5.9 | 193,867 | 12.9 | 5.0 |
| NM | 52,267 | 25.6 | 7.3 | 32,023 | 16.9 | 4.5 | 26,288 | 71.7 | 3.7 |
| NY | 585,218 | –2.2 | 6.9 | 314,105 | 2.3 | 3.7 | 362,327 | 3.4 | 4.3 |
| NC | 302,500 | 40.3 | 7.8 | 145,729 | 51.6 | 3.8 | 141,421 | 56.0 | 3.7 |
| ND | 15,027 | 124.5 | 4.9 | 7,310 | 210.7 | 2.4 | 7,907 | 161.2 | 2.6 |
| OH | 484,245 | 9.5 | 8.8 | 166,735 | 11.6 | 3.0 | 150,363 | 28.8 | 2.7 |
| OK | 94,193 | 15.4 | 6.5 | 35,976 | 15.1 | 2.5 | 46,108 | 49.8 | 3.2 |
| OR | 125,943 | 83.3 | 7.8 | 80,468 | 82.1 | 5.0 | 85,264 | 79.4 | 5.3 |
| PA | 425,337 | 13.0 | 7.6 | 213,058 | 20.8 | 3.8 | 192,700 | 35.7 | 3.5 |
| RI | 25,849 | –2.9 | 5.5 | 15,247 | –2.4 | 3.3 | 16,614 | –3.6 | 3.6 |
| SC | 127,279 | 11.9 | 7.0 | 36,848 | –11.9 | 2.0 | 41,730 | 35.8 | 2.3 |
| SD | 22,251 | 96.8 | 6.1 | 12,963 | 205.9 | 3.6 | 15,112 | 173.3 | 4.2 |
| TN | 192,625 | 19.1 | 7.2 | 50,163 | 3.6 | 1.9 | 52,982 | 32.6 | 2.0 |
| TX | 783,036 | 33.1 | 8.4 | 449,550 | 29.7 | 4.8 | 462,593 | 68.6 | 5.0 |
| UT | 101,147 | 63.5 | 9.7 | 64,705 | 55.4 | 6.2 | 56,563 | 104.4 | 5.4 |
| VT | 23,066 | 12.3 | 7.8 | 14,880 | 0.5 | 5.0 | 14,244 | 3.6 | 4.8 |
| VA | 348,553 | 51.6 | 10.2 | 200,005 | 83.2 | 5.8 | 226,126 | 85.5 | 6.6 |
| WA | 289,582 | 33.2 | 10.7 | 222,080 | 24.9 | 8.2 | 134,428 | 119.8 | 5.0 |
| WV | 34,421 | 10.7 | 5.0 | 18,074 | 25.4 | 2.6 | 10,806 | 33.0 | 1.6 |
| WI | 203,149 | 20.3 | 7.4 | 63,705 | 65.1 | 2.3 | 71,147 | 36.5 | 2.6 |
| WY | 7,826 | 62.5 | 3.4 | 3,145 | 153.4 | 1.4 | 2,835 | 32.8 | 1.2 |

SOURCE: Compiled by the authors from Current Employment and Wages program, U.S. Bureau of Labor Statistics, and *County Business Patterns*, U.S. Bureau of the Census.

**APPENDIX B**

## High-Tech Occupational Employment by State, 1987–91 and 1997–2001

| State | Total High Tech Employed 97–01 | % Growth 87–91 to 97–01 | % of Total Emp. 97–01 | Industrial High Tech Employed 97–01 | % Growth 87–91 to 97–01 | % of Total Emp. 97–01 | Information Technology Employed 97–01 | % Growth 87–91 to 97–01 | % of Total Emp. 97–01 | Biotechnology Employed 97–01 | % Growth 87–91 to 97–01 | % of Total Emp. 97–01 |
|---|---|---|---|---|---|---|---|---|---|---|---|---|
| U.S. | 5,651,917 | 38.8 | 4.9 | 2,187,863 | 7.9 | 1.9 | 3,055,460 | 70.9 | 2.6 | 408,594 | 59.3 | 0.4 |
| AL | 73,170 | 56.6 | 4.1 | 32,881 | 29.0 | 1.8 | 35,583 | 84.8 | 2.0 | 4,706 | 135.1 | 0.3 |
| AK | 8,819 | 37.3 | 3.9 | 4,805 | 25.6 | 2.1 | 3,537 | 58.8 | 1.6 | 477 | 28.9 | 0.2 |
| AZ | 93,422 | 48.9 | 4.8 | 34,917 | 27.6 | 1.8 | 53,925 | 59.9 | 2.8 | 4,580 | 175.4 | 0.2 |
| AR | 28,368 | 52.5 | 2.8 | 12,106 | 16.0 | 1.2 | 13,294 | 81.7 | 1.3 | 2,968 | 247.5 | 0.3 |
| CA | 777,200 | 37.6 | 5.6 | 263,904 | 0.5 | 1.9 | 455,721 | 68.1 | 3.3 | 57,575 | 85.2 | 0.4 |
| CO | 146,901 | 100.3 | 7.6 | 48,138 | 34.4 | 2.5 | 90,520 | 169.8 | 4.7 | 8,243 | 107.8 | 0.4 |
| CT | 93,538 | 0.5 | 6.3 | 40,904 | −15.9 | 2.8 | 42,429 | 7.9 | 2.9 | 10,205 | 101.7 | 0.7 |
| DC | 8,828 | 20.2 | 4.7 | 2,699 | −3.9 | 1.4 | 5,559 | 31.1 | 3.0 | 570 | 91.3 | 0.3 |
| DE | 19,017 | 5.9 | 5.6 | 8,412 | −18.5 | 2.5 | 7,890 | 58.7 | 2.3 | 2,715 | 1.9 | 0.8 |
| FL | 227,899 | 40.2 | 3.7 | 81,968 | −0.3 | 1.3 | 132,283 | 87.5 | 2.1 | 13,648 | 39.2 | 0.2 |
| GA | 163,679 | 73.5 | 4.8 | 52,193 | 10.1 | 1.5 | 101,716 | 145.1 | 3.0 | 9,770 | 79.1 | 0.3 |
| HI | 11,367 | 13.3 | 2.4 | 4,117 | −23.3 | 0.9 | 6,529 | 76.5 | 1.4 | 721 | −25.4 | 0.2 |
| ID | 24,216 | 89.7 | 4.5 | 10,723 | 76.9 | 2.0 | 10,498 | 106.8 | 1.9 | 2,995 | 83.5 | 0.6 |
| IL | 261,690 | 31.9 | 4.9 | 87,163 | −0.4 | 1.6 | 155,046 | 63.7 | 2.9 | 19,481 | 20.1 | 0.4 |
| IN | 101,852 | 29.1 | 3.8 | 49,430 | 18.5 | 1.8 | 46,339 | 45.7 | 1.7 | 6,083 | 13.7 | 0.2 |
| IA | 57,349 | 80.0 | 4.2 | 21,738 | 40.5 | 1.6 | 29,469 | 121.5 | 2.2 | 6,142 | 99.0 | 0.5 |
| KS | 53,152 | 38.1 | 4.6 | 23,837 | 5.7 | 2.0 | 26,002 | 87.8 | 2.2 | 3,313 | 57.5 | 0.3 |
| KY | 56,156 | 73.9 | 3.5 | 24,904 | 28.9 | 1.5 | 27,920 | 147.7 | 1.7 | 3,332 | 94.6 | 0.2 |
| LA | 64,991 | 26.6 | 3.9 | 42,276 | 13.1 | 2.6 | 18,484 | 62.0 | 1.1 | 4,231 | 65.3 | 0.3 |
| ME | 18,857 | 32.3 | 3.3 | 9,811 | 15.0 | 1.7 | 7,774 | 65.6 | 1.4 | 1,272 | 24.1 | 0.2 |
| MD | 144,550 | 38.8 | 6.8 | 43,847 | 6.2 | 2.1 | 85,448 | 48.2 | 4.0 | 15,255 | 192.1 | 0.7 |
| MA | 194,140 | 19.1 | 6.9 | 64,645 | −2.1 | 2.3 | 108,545 | 23.2 | 3.9 | 20,950 | 136.5 | 0.7 |
| MI | 245,540 | 44.4 | 5.6 | 142,186 | 31.1 | 3.3 | 89,651 | 71.2 | 2.1 | 13,703 | 49.7 | 0.3 |
| MN | 133,746 | 66.2 | 5.8 | 43,200 | 23.4 | 1.9 | 79,119 | 94.2 | 3.4 | 11,427 | 142.3 | 0.5 |
| MS | 27,023 | 51.1 | 2.6 | 14,933 | 46.7 | 1.4 | 10,887 | 58.7 | 1.0 | 1,203 | 41.7 | 0.1 |
| MO | 100,509 | 26.7 | 4.1 | 42,414 | 7.5 | 1.7 | 48,255 | 52.0 | 2.0 | 9,840 | 20.8 | 0.4 |
| MT | 9,313 | 84.8 | 2.5 | 4,870 | 74.7 | 1.3 | 3,027 | 108.3 | 0.8 | 1,416 | 77.4 | 0.4 |
| NE | 26,707 | 68.2 | 3.4 | 8,413 | 17.7 | 1.1 | 15,977 | 104.6 | 2.1 | 2,317 | 151.3 | 0.3 |
| NV | 20,396 | 46.5 | 2.5 | 9,946 | 23.5 | 1.2 | 9,308 | 79.3 | 1.1 | 1,142 | 69.2 | 0.1 |
| NH | 37,692 | 9.9 | 6.5 | 13,242 | 11.0 | 2.3 | 22,333 | 4.7 | 3.9 | 2,117 | 103.6 | 0.4 |
| NJ | 226,575 | 24.2 | 6.5 | 66,273 | −13.9 | 1.9 | 138,781 | 59.5 | 4.0 | 21,521 | 17.1 | 0.6 |
| NM | 29,423 | 51.7 | 4.7 | 13,929 | 32.2 | 2.2 | 13,627 | 68.8 | 2.2 | 1,867 | 136.6 | 0.3 |
| NY | 283,626 | 1.4 | 4.0 | 101,537 | −21.8 | 1.4 | 165,508 | 27.2 | 2.3 | 16,581 | −15.4 | 0.2 |
| NC | 140,547 | 51.7 | 4.3 | 59,864 | 25.7 | 1.8 | 68,003 | 78.3 | 2.1 | 12,680 | 84.0 | 0.4 |
| ND | 7,021 | 59.6 | 2.5 | 2,694 | 11.4 | 0.9 | 3,617 | 126.9 | 1.3 | 710 | 83.5 | 0.2 |
| OH | 218,177 | 29.2 | 4.5 | 100,529 | 11.9 | 2.1 | 101,858 | 53.1 | 2.1 | 15,790 | 26.8 | 0.3 |
| OK | 47,689 | 1.3 | 3.6 | 19,844 | −17.7 | 1.5 | 23,987 | 11.9 | 1.8 | 3,858 | 152.8 | 0.3 |
| OR | 66,018 | 102.8 | 4.5 | 20,569 | 37.6 | 1.4 | 40,753 | 173.4 | 2.8 | 4,696 | 74.2 | 0.3 |
| PA | 239,481 | 23.4 | 4.7 | 101,017 | −8.2 | 2.0 | 113,874 | 65.2 | 2.2 | 24,590 | 63.0 | 0.5 |
| RI | 21,163 | 22.0 | 5.0 | 7,933 | −11.8 | 1.9 | 11,968 | 60.8 | 2.8 | 1,262 | 38.5 | 0.3 |
| SC | 62,262 | 22.8 | 3.9 | 33,929 | −0.3 | 2.1 | 25,244 | 64.2 | 1.6 | 3,089 | 141.3 | 0.2 |
| SD | 8,719 | 107.6 | 2.6 | 3,586 | 79.2 | 1.1 | 4,330 | 162.4 | 1.3 | 803 | 46.3 | 0.2 |
| TN | 81,464 | 85.6 | 3.5 | 35,535 | 46.8 | 1.5 | 37,664 | 125.0 | 1.6 | 8,265 | 179.5 | 0.4 |
| TX | 470,621 | 55.6 | 5.5 | 182,330 | 10.3 | 2.1 | 266,700 | 115.7 | 3.1 | 21,591 | 60.0 | 0.3 |
| UT | 45,461 | 72.6 | 5.0 | 16,634 | 22.1 | 1.8 | 26,064 | 144.2 | 2.9 | 2,763 | 35.0 | 0.3 |
| VT | 13,144 | 24.4 | 4.6 | 4,295 | −16.7 | 1.5 | 7,839 | 56.4 | 2.7 | 1,010 | 152.5 | 0.4\ |
| VA | 178,842 | 69.0 | 6.3 | 57,642 | 40.1 | 2.0 | 114,551 | 89.1 | 4.0 | 6,649 | 62.4 | 0.2 |
| WA | 147,937 | 45.7 | 6.0 | 55,247 | 9.9 | 2.2 | 86,242 | 89.3 | 3.5 | 6,448 | 13.1 | 0.3 |
| WV | 18,600 | 27.7 | 2.9 | 10,946 | 18.3 | 1.7 | 6,199 | 52.7 | 1.0 | 1,455 | 16.2 | 0.2 |
| WI | 109,503 | 59.7 | 4.3 | 45,609 | 38.1 | 1.8 | 53,944 | 89.7 | 2.1 | 9,950 | 39.6 | 0.4 |
| WY | 5,553 | 24.9 | 2.7 | 3,291 | 7.8 | 1.6 | 1,644 | 97.4 | 0.8 | 618 | 10.4 | 0.3 |

SOURCE: Compiled by the authors using a special tabulation constructed by David Macpherson, Florida State University, with unpublished data taken from the *Current Population Survey*, U.S. Bureau of the Census.

**APPENDIX C**

## Company and Nonfederal Funds for Industrial R&D Performance in the United States, by Industry, 1997–2000

| | NAICS codes | 1997 | 1998 | 1999 | 2000 |
|---|---|---|---|---|---|
| | | | (millions of dollars) | | |
| All industries | 21–23, 31–33, 42, 44–81 | 133,611 | 145,016 | 160,288 | 180,421 |
| Manufacturing | 31–33 | — | — | 99,865 | 110,750 |
| Food | 311 | 1,244 | 1,305 | 1,132 | 1,145 |
| Beverage and tobacco products | 312 | 447 | 384 | (D) | 417 |
| Textiles, apparel, and leather | 313–316 | 378 | 399 | 334 | 266 |
| Wood products | 321 | 26 | 55 | 70 | 105 |
| Paper, printing, and support activities | 322, 323 | 2,252 | 1,660 | 2,474 | 2,700 |
| Petroleum and coal products | 324 | 1,349 | 1,390 | (D) | 1,172 |
| Chemicals | 325 | 16,385 | 18,733 | 20,051 | 20,768 |
| Basic chemicals | 3251 | 1,840 | 3,467 | 2,648 | 2,050 |
| Resin, synthetic rubber, fibers, & filament | 3252 | 1,802 | 1,995 | 2,216 | 2,842 |
| Pharmaceuticals and medicines | 3254 | 10,213 | 9,601 | 12,236 | 12,793 |
| Other chemicals | 325 (minus 3251–52, 3254) | 2,530 | 3,670 | 2,951 | 3,084 |
| Plastics and rubber products | 326 | 1,480 | 1,625 | 1,785 | 1,675 |
| Nonmetallic mineral products | 327 | 546 | (D) | 595 | 845 |
| Primary metals | 331 | 754 | 588 | 457 | 598 |
| Fabricated metal products | 332 | 1,854 | 1,727 | 1,608 | 1,631 |
| Machinery | 333 | 5,470 | 5,831 | 5,658 | 6,539 |
| Computer and electronic products | 334 | 29,697 | 31,873 | 29,939 | 39,553 |
| Computers and peripheral equipment | 3341 | 7,718 | 8,276 | 4,126 | 5,162 |
| Communications equipment | 3342 | 2,751 | 8,456 | 5,797 | 11,183 |
| Semiconductor and other electronic components | 3344 | 14,033 | 9,072 | 10,624 | 12,787 |
| Navigational, measuring, electromedical, control instruments | 3345 | 4,659 | 5,483 | 8,632 | 10,114 |
| Other computer and electronic products | 334 (minus 3341–42, 3344–45) | 537 | 585 | 760 | 307 |
| Electrical equipment, appliances, and components | 335 | 2,580 | 2,139 | 3,820 | 3,390 |
| Transportation equipment | 336 | 21,713 | 20,677 | 23,928 | 22,917 |
| Motor vehicles, trailers, and parts | 3361–63 | 14,340 | 13,781 | 17,987 | 18,306 |
| Aerospace products and parts | 3364 | 6,961 | 6,521 | 5,309 | 3,895 |
| Other transportation equipment | 336 (minus 3361–64) | 412 | 375 | 632 | 716 |
| Furniture and related products | 337 | 240 | 211 | 248 | 284 |
| Miscellaneous manufacturing | 339 | 3,447 | 3,888 | 3,825 | 4,195 |
| Medical equipment and supplies | 3391 | 3,031 | 3,363 | 3,251 | 3,741 |
| Other miscellaneous manufacturing | 339 (minus 3391) | 416 | 525 | 574 | 453 |
| Other manufacturing | 31–33 (minus 311–16, 321–27, 331–37, 339) | (S) 23 | (D) | — | — |
| Small manufacturing companies | Fewer than 50 employees | 2,357 | 2,188 | 2,950 | 2,549 |
| Nonmanufacturing | 21–23, 42, 44–81 | — | — | 60,423 | 69,671 |
| Mining, extraction, and support activities | 21 | 447 | 458 | 2,352 | 822 |
| Utilities | 22 | 209 | 177 | 126 | 136 |
| Construction | 23 | 241 | 445 | 690 | 222 |
| Trade | 42, 44, 45 | 15,862 | 16,415 | 19,521 | 24,929 |
| Transportation and warehousing | 48, 49 | 662 | 253 | 460 | 277 |
| Information | 51 | 10,191 | 13,025 | 14,892 | 16,290 |
| Publishing | 511 | 7,535 | 9,522 | 11,253 | 12,926 |
| Newspaper, periodical, book, and database | 5111 | 340 | 334 | 371 | 365 |
| Software | 5112 | 7,194 | 9,188 | 10,882 | 12,561 |
| Broadcasting and telecommunications | 513 | 2,139 | 1,788 | 1,393 | 1,025 |
| Radio and television broadcasting | 5131 | (D) | (D) | (D) | (D) |
| Telecommunications | 5133 | (D) | 1,710 | (D) | (D) |
| Other broadcasting & telecommunications | 513 (minus 5131, 5133) | 12 | (D) | 18 | 59 |

| | NAICS codes | 1997 | 1998 | 1999 | 2000 |
|---|---|---|---|---|---|
| | | | (millions of dollars) | | |
| Other information | 51 (minus 511, 513) | 518 | 1,716 | 2,246 | 2,339 |
| Finance, insurance, and real estate | 52, 53 | 1,326 | 1,700 | 1,570 | 4,024 |
| Professional, scientific, and technical services | 54 | 9,380 | 11,440 | 14,379 | 17,949 |
| Architectural, engineering, and related services | 5413 | 1,152 | 1,405 | 2,402 | 2,232 |
| Computer systems design and related services | 5415 | 2,995 | 2,861 | 3,989 | 4,943 |
| Scientific R&D services | 5417 | 4,688 | 6,446 | 7,413 | 9,715 |
| Other professional, scientific, and technical services | 54 (minus 5413, 5415, 5417) | (S) 544 | 728 | 575 | 1,059 |
| Management of companies and enterprises | 55 | 309 | 417 | 72 | 49 |
| Health care services | 621–23 | 635 | 584 | 631 | 477 |
| Other nonmanufacturing | 56, 61, 624, 71, 72, 81 | 911 | 2,095 | 752 | 713 |
| Small nonmanufacturing companies | Fewer than 15 employees | 1,569 | 2,327 | 4,977 | 3,783 |

SOURCE: National Science Foundation (2000).

KEY: (D) = Data have been withheld to avoid disclosing operations of individual companies.  (S) = Indicates imputation of more than 50%.  (–) = Indicates data not collected.

---

## APPENDIX D

## R&D Performance by State, 1999 (millions of dollars)

| | Federal | Company | Total | Rank | | Federal | Company | Total | Rank |
|---|---|---|---|---|---|---|---|---|---|
| U.S. Total | 22,535 | 160,288 | 182,823 | | Montana | (D) | (D) | 33 | 47 |
| Alabama | 190 | 365 | 556 | 35 | Nebraska | 6 | 172 | 178 | 42 |
| Alaska | (D) | 3 | (D) | — | Nevada | (D) | (D) | 337 | 37 |
| Arizona | 224 | 4,210 | 4,434 | 11 | New Hampshire | (D) | (D) | 1,099 | 31 |
| Arkansas | 3 | 213 | 216 | 39 | New Jersey | 126 | 9,327 | 9,453 | 5 |
| California | 4,042 | 35,006 | 39,047 | 1 | New Mexico | (D) | (D) | 1,342 | 25 |
| Colorado | (D) | (D) | 3,136 | 15 | New York | 2,105 | 9,284 | 11,388 | 3 |
| Connecticut | 207 | 3,777 | 3,984 | 12 | North Carolina | 19 | 3,934 | 3,953 | 13 |
| Delaware | 9 | 1,252 | 1,261 | 28 | North Dakota | 0 | 75 | 75 | 46 |
| District of Columbia | 52 | 119 | 171 | 43 | Ohio | 1,148 | 5,366 | 6,514 | 10 |
| Florida | 706 | 1,991 | 2,697 | 16 | Oklahoma | 2 | 363 | 365 | 36 |
| Georgia | 178 | 1,649 | 1,827 | 20 | Oregon | 3 | 1,537 | 1,540 | 23 |
| Hawaii | 1 | 26 | 27 | 48 | Pennsylvania | 441 | 8,491 | 8,932 | 7 |
| Idaho | (D) | (D) | 1,210 | 29 | Rhode Island | (D) | (D) | 1,264 | 27 |
| Illinois | 41 | 7,674 | 7,715 | 8 | South Carolina | (D) | (D) | 665 | 33 |
| Indiana | (D) | (D) | 2,246 | 18 | South Dakota | 0 | 13 | 13 | 49 |
| Iowa | 6 | 553 | 559 | 34 | Tennessee | (D) | (D) | 1,768 | 21 |
| Kansas | (D) | (D) | 1,284 | 26 | Texas | 118 | 9,817 | 9,935 | 4 |
| Kentucky | 1 | 683 | 684 | 32 | Utah | (D) | (D) | 1,123 | 30 |
| Louisiana | 53 | 134 | 187 | 41 | Vermont | (D) | (D) | 318 | 38 |
| Maine | 52 | 88 | 140 | 44 | Virginia | 1,096 | 1,391 | 2,488 | 17 |
| Maryland | 455 | 1,246 | 1,700 | 22 | Washington | (D) | (D) | 7,231 | 9 |
| Massachusetts | 2,374 | 6,940 | 9,314 | 6 | West Virginia | (D) | (D) | 216 | 40 |
| Michigan | 134 | 17,580 | 17,714 | 2 | Wisconsin | 72 | 1,877 | 1,949 | 19 |
| Minnesota | 242 | 3,137 | 3,379 | 14 | Wyoming | 0 | (D) | (D) | — |
| Mississippi | 43 | 71 | 114 | 45 | Undistributed funds | 1,077 | 4,572 | 5,649 | — |
| Missouri | 21 | 1,367 | 1,387 | 24 | | | | | |

SOURCE: National Science Foundation (1999, table A-32).

(D) = Data withheld to avoid disclosing operations of individual companies.

## APPENDIX E

### Michigan Occupational High-Tech Wage Trends

| Occupation | Average Weekly Wage 1987–1991 | 1997–2001 | Occupation | Average Weekly Wage 1987–1991 | 1997–2001 |
|---|---|---|---|---|---|
| TOTAL HIGH TECH | | | Science technicians except biological | | |
| Engineers | $868 | $1,160 | technicians | 465 | 530 |
| Engineering and related technologists | | | *Industrial high tech occupations total* | *$776* | *$1,056* |
| and technicians | 575 | 794 | | | |
| Mathematical and computer scientists | 753 | 1,095 | INFORMATION TECHNOLOGY | | |
| Natural scientists | 833 | 1,108 | Electrical and electronic engineers | $815 | $1,180 |
| Science technicians | 440 | 494 | Electrical and electronic technicians | 501 | 747 |
| Computer programmers | 602 | 944 | Computer systems analysts | 723 | 1,120 |
| *High-tech occupations total* | *748* | *1,050* | Computer programmers | 602 | 944 |
| *All occupations* | *$424* | *$ 625* | *Information technology occupations total* | *$691* | *$1,057* |
| | | | | | |
| INDUSTRIAL HIGH TECH | | | BIOTECHNOLOGY | | |
| Engineers except electrical and electronic | $882 | $1,156 | Agricultural and food scientists | $519 | $1,036 |
| Engineering and related technologists and | | | Biological and life scientists | 761 | 749 |
| technicians except electrical & electronic | 592 | 810 | Biological technicians | 345 | 431 |
| Mathematical and computer scientists | | | Chemists, except biochemists | 885 | 1,370 |
| except systems analysts | 796 | 1,008 | Medical scientists | 800 | 876 |
| Natural scientists except chemists, | | | *Biotechnology occupations total* | *$748* | *$ 937* |
| agricultural and food scientists, biological | | | | | |
| and life scientists, medical scientists | 819 | 1,188 | | | |

SOURCE: Compiled by the authors using a special tabulation constructed by David Macpherson, Florida State University, with unpublished data taken from the *Current Population Survey*, U.S. Bureau of the Census.

**APPENDIX F**

**Relationship between Employment in Technology Occupations and Productivity and Wage Rate Growth, by State, 1989–99 (numbers in parentheses are standard errors)**

| Independent Variable | Change in Real GSP Per Employee, 1989–99 | Change in Average Wage, Nominal Dollars, 1989–99 |
|---|---|---|
| Intercept | 0.05119 | 0.30245[b] |
| | (0.03441) | (0.03157) |
| Change in tax rates | −1.68498 | NA |
| | (1.38225) | NA |
| Total technology employment 1987–91 | 1.94349[a] | 1.77068[b] |
| | (0.76830) | (0.65095) |
| Change in total technology employment | 2.29113[a] | 1.89964[a] |
| | (1.04342) | (0.86574) |
| Change in real GSP per employee | NA | 0.26648[a] |
| | NA | (0.10950) |
| Percent union | NA | 0.00182 |
| | NA | (0.00128) |
| Alaska dummy | −0.38176[b] | −0.19772[b] |
| | (0.07034) | (0.06661) |
| Louisiana dummy | −0.14543[a] | NA |
| | (0.06856) | NA |
| Number of observations | 51 | 51 |
| R-square | 0.529 | 0.586 |
| F Value | 10.12 | 12.71 |

SOURCE: For GSP: *http://www.bea.doc.gov/bea/regional/spi*; for average wage and employment used in GSP per-employee calculation: table SA30, *http://www.census.gov/govs/www/estimate.html*; percent union and employment in total technology occupations compiled by the authors using tabulations constructed by David Macpherson, Florida State University, with unpublished data taken from the *Current Population Survey*, U.S. Bureau of the Census.
(a) Significant at the 5% level.
(b) Significant at the 1% level.

**APPENDIX G**

## Regression Results for Change in Occupational Employment, by State, 1987–91 to 1997–2001 (numbers in parentheses are standard errors)

| | All Technology | Industrial Technology | Information Technology | Biotechnology |
|---|---|---|---|---|
| Intercept | 0.00379 (0.00987) | 0.00316 (0.00410) | 0.00698 (0.00708) | 0.00274[a] (0.00140) |
| tax91 | −0.01087 (0.08498) | −0.02556 (0.03342) | −0.00493 (0.06486) | −0.01734 (0.01350) |
| chtax | −0.21172 (0.16486) | −0.05918 (0.06729) | −0.15945 (0.12346) | −0.00695 (0.02494) |
| vc95 | 0.00681[b] (0.00293) | −0.00001 (0.00106) | 0.00496[b] (0.00232) | 0.00109[c] (0.00037) |
| tottec87 | −0.03409 (0.10401) | | | |
| indtec87 | | −0.18799[b] (0.08064) | | |
| inftec87 | | | 0.02616 (0.13961) | |
| biotec87 | | | | −0.12493 (0.12266) |
| chtottot | 0.03872[c] (0.01141) | | | |
| chtotind | | 0.01724[c] (0.00375) | | |
| chtotinf | | | 0.01517[a] (0.00883) | |
| chtotbio | | | | 0.00027 (0.00148) |
| totbac90 | 2.47625 (1.90904) | | | |
| chtotbac | 7.51853 (5.44107) | | | |
| indbac90 | | 3.68893[a] (1.91085) | | |
| chindbac | | 6.21893 (7.03668) | | |
| infbac90 | | | 6.38911 (3.87089) | |
| chinfbac | | | 29.13719[b] (11.8738) | |
| biophd90 | | | | 5.72468 (5.10468) |
| chbiophd | | | | 2.30893 (13.1217) |
| No. of observations | 51 | 51 | 51 | 51 |
| R-square | 0.492 | 0.466 | 0.484 | 0.238 |
| F Value | 5.95 | 5.35 | 5.76 | 1.92 |

SOURCE: Employment in total technology occupations compiled by the authors using a special tabulation constructed by David Macpherson, Florida State University, with unpublished data taken from the *Current Population Survey*, U.S. Bureau of the Census. Tax rates derived from data found at *http://www.census.gov.govs/www/estimate.html*. Venture capital figures calculated by the authors using data from "Cyberstates 2002," American Electronics Association, Washington, D.C., 2002. Number of education graduates by degree and field of study were derived from data found at *http://nces.ed.gov.ipeds*.
(a) Significant at the 10% level. (b) Significant at the 5% level. (c) Significant at the 1% level.

## GLOSSARY OF VARIABLES IN APPENDIX G

DEPENDENT VARIABLES

| | |
|---|---|
| All Technology | Difference between mean total tech emp. in 1997–2001 and 1987–91 |
| Industrial Technology | Difference between mean industrial tech emp. in 1997–2001 and 1987–91 |
| Information Technology | Difference between mean information tech emp. in 1997–2001 and 1987–91 |
| Biotechnology | Difference between mean biotech emp. in 1997–2001 and 1987–91 |

INDEPENDENT VARIABLES

| | |
|---|---|
| tax91 | State and local property, sales, and income (both corporate and personal) taxes divided by state personal income in 1991 |
| chtax | Difference between the tax rate in 1999 and 1991 |
| vc95 | Sum of venture capital expenditures in the period 1995–98 |
| tottec87 | Mean value of total technology employment over the period 1987–91 |
| indtec87 | Mean value of industrial technology employment over the period 1987–91 |
| inftec87 | Mean value of information tech employment over the period 1987–91 |
| biotec87 | Mean value of biotechnology employment over the period 1987–91 |
| chtottot | Difference between total emp. 1997–2001 and 1987–91 excluding total tech |
| chtotind | Difference between total emp. 1997–2001 and 1987–91 excluding industrial tech |
| chtotinf | Difference between total emp. 1997–2001 and 1987–91 excluding information tech |
| chtotbio | Difference between total emp. 1997–2001 and 1987–91 excluding biotech |
| totbac90 | Mean number of bachelor's degrees awarded in all tech fields in 1990 and 1991 |
| chtotbac | Difference between the mean number of bachelor's degrees in all tech fields in 1997–98 and 1990–91 |
| indbac90 | Mean number of bachelor's degrees awarded in industrial tech fields in 1990 and 1991 |
| chindbac | Difference between the mean number of bachelor's degrees in industrial tech fields in 1997–98 and 1990–91 |
| infbac90 | Mean number of bachelor's degrees awarded in information tech fields in 1990 and 1991 |
| chinfbac | Difference between the mean number of bachelor's degrees in information tech fields in 1997–98 and 1990–91 |
| biophd90 | Mean number of doctoral degrees awarded in biotech fields in 1990 and 1991 |
| chbiophd | Difference between the mean number of doctoral degrees in biotech fields in 1997–98 and 1990–91 |

NOTE: All variables except for the two tax variables are divided by total employment in 1987–91.

**APPENDIX H**

## Total Venture Capital and Venture Capital Per Worker, by State, 1995–2001

| | Venture Capital Total 1995–2001 ($ millions) | Ranking of Venture Capital | Venture Capital Per Employee ($) | Ranking of Venture Capital Per Employee |
|---|---|---|---|---|
| United States | 260,871.2 | | 2,251 | |
| Alabama | 662.0 | 26 | 372 | 32 |
| Alaska | 3.5 | 50 | 15 | 49 |
| Arizona | 1,798.2 | 21 | 923 | 22 |
| Arkansas | 49.8 | 46 | 50 | 46 |
| California | 108,296.3 | 1 | 7,873 | 3 |
| Colorado | 10,336.5 | 5 | 5,368 | 4 |
| Connecticut | 4,209.1 | 15 | 2,845 | 6 |
| Delaware | 313.2 | 34 | 923 | 21 |
| D.C. | 1,921.3 | 19 | 10,278 | 1 |
| Florida | 6,014.9 | 10 | 965 | 19 |
| Georgia | 5,424.4 | 11 | 1,604 | 13 |
| Hawaii | 272.3 | 36 | 578 | 25 |
| Idaho | 60.0 | 45 | 111 | 44 |
| Illinois | 5,074.3 | 12 | 956 | 20 |
| Indiana | 488.7 | 30 | 182 | 41 |
| Iowa | 106.5 | 42 | 78 | 45 |
| Kansas | 469.2 | 31 | 403 | 29 |
| Kentucky | 459.1 | 32 | 283 | 34 |
| Louisiana | 616.1 | 27 | 374 | 31 |
| Maine | 301.7 | 35 | 533 | 26 |
| Maryland | 4,995.9 | 13 | 2,356 | 9 |
| Massachusetts | 26,227.6 | 2 | 9,360 | 2 |
| Michigan | 1,224.2 | 25 | 280 | 35 |
| Minnesota | 3,394.9 | 16 | 1,460 | 15 |
| Mississippi | 329.4 | 33 | 315 | 33 |
| Missouri | 2,179.0 | 18 | 892 | 23 |
| Montana | 85.1 | 43 | 226 | 36 |
| Nebraska | 174.2 | 39 | 224 | 37 |
| Nevada | 139.1 | 40 | 172 | 42 |
| New Hampshire | 1,459.6 | 23 | 2,531 | 7 |
| New Jersey | 7,527.6 | 7 | 2,164 | 11 |
| New Mexico | 131.3 | 41 | 208 | 39 |
| New York | 16,182.5 | 3 | 2,291 | 10 |
| North Carolina | 4,248.7 | 14 | 1,286 | 17 |
| North Dakota | 6.9 | 48 | 24 | 48 |
| Ohio | 2,300.9 | 17 | 470 | 27 |
| Oklahoma | 201.2 | 37 | 150 | 43 |
| Oregon | 1,868.3 | 20 | 1,269 | 18 |
| Pennsylvania | 6,934.7 | 9 | 1,365 | 16 |
| Rhode Island | 189.5 | 38 | 445 | 28 |
| South Carolina | 604.0 | 28 | 379 | 30 |
| South Dakota | 4.5 | 49 | 13 | 50 |
| Tennessee | 1,590.0 | 22 | 686 | 24 |
| Texas | 14,775.7 | 4 | 1,742 | 12 |
| Utah | 1,451.9 | 24 | 1,601 | 14 |
| Vermont | 62.6 | 44 | 219 | 38 |
| Virginia | 7,188.4 | 8 | 2,526 | 8 |
| Washington | 7,579.1 | 6 | 3,050 | 5 |
| West Virginia | 30.5 | 47 | 47 | 47 |
| Wisconsin | 525.6 | 29 | 208 | 40 |
| Wyoming | 0.0 | 51 | 0 | 51 |

SOURCE: Calculated by the authors using data from "Cyberstates 2002." Washington, D.C.: American Electronics Association, 2002.

## APPENDIX I

### Computer Use at School (Ages 6 to 15) by State, September 2001

| | % Use Computer | Rank | % Use Internet | Rank | | % Use Computer | Rank | % Use Internet | Rank | | % Use Computer | Rank | % Use Internet | Rank |
|---|---|---|---|---|---|---|---|---|---|---|---|---|---|---|
| U.S. | 88.5 | | 59.1 | | KY | 92.8 | 4 | 75.0 | 2 | OH | 90.2 | 22 | 68.4 | 11 |
| AL | 90.7 | 19 | 58.8 | 33 | LA | 83.2 | 47 | 48.8 | 49 | OK | 85.2 | 42 | 59.6 | 30 |
| AK | 91.1 | 14 | 68.3 | 12 | ME | 87.3 | 38 | 65.8 | 17 | OR | 80.6 | 50 | 53.1 | 44 |
| AZ | 82.4 | 48 | 56.9 | 37 | MD | 87.1 | 39 | 50.7 | 47 | PA | 89.9 | 23 | 53.9 | 42 |
| AR | 84.8 | 43 | 53.9 | 43 | MA | 88.1 | 35 | 51.9 | 45 | RI | 89.1 | 31 | 61.0 | 25 |
| CA | 82.3 | 49 | 49.2 | 48 | MI | 92.8 | 4 | 68.8 | 10 | SC | 83.6 | 46 | 54.9 | 40 |
| CO | 89.6 | 27 | 65.7 | 19 | MN | 91.0 | 15 | 69.2 | 9 | SD | 91.5 | 12 | 70.3 | 7 |
| CT | 89.3 | 29 | 59.9 | 27 | MS | 88.7 | 32 | 56.1 | 38 | TN | 93.6 | 2 | 55.6 | 39 |
| DC | 80.0 | 51 | 41.5 | 51 | MO | 89.7 | 25 | 59.6 | 29 | TX | 90.4 | 21 | 65.8 | 18 |
| DE | 84.5 | 45 | 60.7 | 26 | MT | 87.7 | 37 | 61.2 | 24 | UT | 93.0 | 3 | 70.7 | 4 |
| FL | 89.7 | 25 | 57.2 | 36 | NE | 92.0 | 10 | 65.2 | 20 | VT | 92.7 | 6 | 74.6 | 3 |
| GA | 89.8 | 24 | 51.5 | 46 | NV | 84.8 | 43 | 48.4 | 50 | VA | 92.1 | 9 | 58.5 | 34 |
| HI | 86.7 | 40 | 59.8 | 28 | NH | 89.4 | 28 | 59.3 | 32 | WA | 89.3 | 29 | 66.9 | 15 |
| ID | 88.6 | 33 | 67.2 | 14 | NJ | 88.5 | 34 | 58.3 | 35 | WV | 92.6 | 7 | 75.8 | 1 |
| IL | 91.0 | 15 | 59.4 | 31 | NM | 88.0 | 36 | 70.3 | 6 | WI | 91.4 | 13 | 68.1 | 13 |
| IN | 90.9 | 17 | 63.2 | 21 | NY | 86.1 | 41 | 54.7 | 41 | WY | 90.5 | 20 | 70.4 | 5 |
| IA | 90.8 | 18 | 61.2 | 23 | NC | 91.7 | 11 | 62.4 | 22 | | | | | |
| KS | 95.2 | 1 | 65.9 | 16 | ND | 92.2 | 8 | 69.8 | 8 | | | | | |

SOURCE: Special tabulation by David Macpherson, Florida State University, using unpublished data taken from the *Current Population Survey*, U.S. Bureau of the Census.

## APPENDIX J

### Computer Use at Work, Private Sector (Ages 25 to 60) by State, September 2001

| | % Use Computer | Rank | % Use Internet | Rank | | % Use Computer | Rank | % Use Internet | Rank | | % Use Computer | Rank | % Use Internet | Rank |
|---|---|---|---|---|---|---|---|---|---|---|---|---|---|---|
| U.S. | 55.9 | | 40.7 | | KY | 51.1 | 41 | 36.5 | 38 | OH | 56.1 | 27 | 36.0 | 41 |
| AL | 49.6 | 44 | 36.0 | 40 | LA | 48.9 | 48 | 32.0 | 46 | OK | 57.0 | 25 | 38.5 | 32 |
| AK | 61.0 | 8 | 46.9 | 6 | ME | 56.0 | 28 | 38.4 | 34 | OR | 61.5 | 6 | 47.9 | 5 |
| AZ | 60.9 | 9 | 45.0 | 14 | MD | 62.2 | 3 | 49.3 | 2 | PA | 57.2 | 24 | 42.2 | 20 |
| AR | 49.1 | 47 | 31.0 | 47 | MA | 58.3 | 18 | 46.8 | 7 | RI | 58.3 | 19 | 43.0 | 19 |
| CA | 55.3 | 32 | 41.9 | 24 | MI | 56.0 | 28 | 40.2 | 29 | SC | 49.4 | 45 | 33.9 | 44 |
| CO | 62.1 | 4 | 48.2 | 4 | MN | 64.5 | 1 | 48.9 | 3 | SD | 54.7 | 36 | 36.2 | 39 |
| CT | 58.0 | 21 | 45.1 | 13 | MS | 45.7 | 50 | 29.6 | 50 | TN | 56.5 | 26 | 38.4 | 33 |
| DC | 62.4 | 2 | 53.9 | 1 | MO | 59.2 | 16 | 43.1 | 17 | TX | 55.6 | 30 | 42.1 | 21 |
| DE | 59.7 | 14 | 45.5 | 10 | MT | 50.7 | 42 | 33.0 | 45 | UT | 61.5 | 5 | 45.5 | 11 |
| FL | 54.7 | 34 | 38.7 | 31 | NE | 60.6 | 12 | 43.9 | 16 | VT | 60.7 | 11 | 45.7 | 9 |
| GA | 53.8 | 37 | 41.8 | 25 | NV | 45.1 | 51 | 28.6 | 51 | VA | 54.7 | 35 | 42.1 | 22 |
| HI | 52.9 | 39 | 40.4 | 28 | NH | 60.7 | 10 | 45.3 | 12 | WA | 58.7 | 17 | 43.1 | 18 |
| ID | 51.5 | 40 | 34.6 | 43 | NJ | 61.5 | 7 | 45.9 | 8 | WV | 48.2 | 49 | 30.2 | 48 |
| IL | 57.3 | 23 | 41.3 | 26 | NM | 55.4 | 31 | 39.1 | 30 | WI | 60.0 | 13 | 41.0 | 27 |
| IN | 54.9 | 33 | 37.9 | 35 | NY | 50.7 | 43 | 37.7 | 36 | WY | 57.5 | 22 | 37.4 | 37 |
| IA | 59.3 | 15 | 42.0 | 23 | NC | 49.3 | 46 | 30.2 | 49 | | | | | |
| KS | 58.2 | 20 | 44.2 | 15 | ND | 53.7 | 38 | 35.3 | 42 | | | | | |

SOURCE: Special tabulation by David Macpherson, Florida State University, using unpublished data taken from the *Current Population Survey*, U.S. Bureau of the Census.

**APPENDIX K**

## Computer and Internet Availability among Households by State, September 2001

| | % with Computer | Rank | % with Internet | Rank | | % with Computer | Rank | % with Internet | Rank | | % with Computer | Rank | % with Internet | Rank |
|------|------|------|------|------|------|------|------|------|------|------|------|------|------|------|
| U.S. | 56.5 | | 50.6 | | KY | 49.8 | 45 | 44.2 | 43 | OH | 57.6 | 25 | 50.9 | 26 |
| AL | 43.7 | 50 | 37.6 | 49 | LA | 45.7 | 49 | 40.2 | 48 | OK | 49.9 | 44 | 43.8 | 44 |
| AK | 68.7 | 1 | 64.1 | 1 | ME | 62.8 | 10 | 53.3 | 16 | OR | 65.8 | 5 | 58.2 | 5 |
| AZ | 59.4 | 15 | 51.9 | 22 | MD | 64.1 | 8 | 57.8 | 6 | PA | 53.5 | 35 | 48.7 | 31 |
| AR | 46.8 | 48 | 36.9 | 50 | MA | 59.1 | 17 | 54.7 | 13 | RI | 58.6 | 20 | 53.1 | 17 |
| CA | 61.5 | 12 | 55.3 | 9 | MI | 58.3 | 22 | 51.2 | 23 | SC | 52.2 | 40 | 45.0 | 40 |
| CO | 64.7 | 6 | 58.5 | 4 | MN | 64.6 | 7 | 55.6 | 8 | SD | 55.3 | 31 | 47.6 | 33 |
| CT | 58.7 | 19 | 55.0 | 11 | MS | 41.9 | 51 | 36.1 | 51 | TN | 51.3 | 41 | 44.8 | 41 |
| DC | 49.3 | 46 | 41.4 | 46 | MO | 55.3 | 31 | 49.9 | 30 | TX | 53.7 | 34 | 47.7 | 32 |
| DE | 58.4 | 21 | 52.5 | 20 | MT | 56.0 | 28 | 47.5 | 34 | UT | 67.7 | 2 | 54.1 | 14 |
| FL | 55.9 | 29 | 52.8 | 18 | NE | 55.6 | 30 | 45.5 | 39 | VT | 60.4 | 14 | 53.4 | 15 |
| GA | 52.4 | 39 | 46.7 | 37 | NV | 58.2 | 23 | 52.5 | 20 | VA | 58.8 | 18 | 54.9 | 12 |
| HI | 63.1 | 9 | 55.2 | 10 | NH | 55.0 | 33 | 50.2 | 28 | WA | 66.5 | 4 | 60.4 | 3 |
| ID | 62.8 | 10 | 52.7 | 19 | NJ | 61.2 | 13 | 57.2 | 7 | WV | 48.0 | 47 | 40.7 | 47 |
| IL | 53.0 | 37 | 46.9 | 36 | NM | 67.7 | 2 | 61.6 | 2 | WI | 56.4 | 27 | 50.2 | 28 |
| IN | 53.2 | 36 | 47.3 | 35 | NY | 50.6 | 42 | 43.1 | 45 | WY | 58.1 | 24 | 51.0 | 24 |
| IA | 59.4 | 15 | 51.0 | 24 | NC | 50.1 | 43 | 44.5 | 42 | | | | | |
| KS | 57.5 | 26 | 50.9 | 26 | ND | 53.0 | 37 | 46.5 | 38 | | | | | |

Source: "A Nation Online: How Americans Are Expanding Their Use of the Internet," tables H1, H2. Washington, D.C.: National Telecommunications and Information Administration, U.S. Dept. of Commerce, 2002. *http://www.ntia.doc.gov/ntiahome/dn/hhs/HHSchartsindex.html.*

# 8

# Automotive and Other Manufacturing Industries in Michigan: Output, Employment, Earnings, and Collective Bargaining, 1980–2001

*Richard N. Block and Dale L. Belman*

## Introduction

As part of the complex of durable manufacturing arrayed around the southern rim of the Great Lakes, Michigan has been a preeminent manufacturing state for more than one hundred years. Dominated by the domestic automotive industry, the state has benefited from the success and consequent wealth of that industry, as well as from the success of manufacturing as a whole. The relative high pay and benefits of manufacturing workers have provided a strong economic foundation for residents and for generous public services. The last quarter century has, however, seen relative stagnation of the manufacturing sector in Michigan, with slower growth of output and declining employment. This trend reflects the slower growth in the manufacturing sector of the United States. It also reflects the concentration of Michigan manufacturing in mature sectors that have not experienced the rapid growth characteristic of new industries, and a shift in investment in new automotive plants to other states and countries, primarily Mexico. The poor performance of manufacturing over the last two decades has implications for the prosperity of citizens and the state of Michigan.

This chapter is divided between an overview of manufacturing in Michigan (Part 1) and a more detailed consideration of collective bargaining in the automotive industry (Part 2). Part 1 begins with a review of the current state of manufacturing in Michigan. It then considers trends in output, employment, and compensation since 1977 and compares these to trends in the broader Michigan economy, U.S. manufacturing, and other manufacturing states. Part 2 includes an overview of unionization in manufacturing with particular attention paid to the automotive industry. The shift in bargaining from wage and benefit increases to increased job security is explored, as are the declining fortunes of Flint. Part 3 provides a summary and conclusions.

## Part 1: Manufacturing in Michigan, 1980–2000

*Manufacturing in Michigan.* Manufacturing remains an important, if declining, sector of the Michigan economy. In 1999, manufacturing accounted for $80.7 billion of the $308.3 billion gross state product of Michigan, or 26.2% of total Gross State Product (see table 8.1). It provided employment to 979,800 of Michigan's 4,679,300 employees, 20.9% of Michigan's workforce (see table 8.4).

Manufacturing is well compensated relative to other sectors. The average annual earnings of

## TABLE 8.1

**Manufacturing Output: Michigan and the United States, 1977–1999**

| Year | Michigan Gross Product (in billions of current dollars) | | | U.S. Gross Product (in billions of current dollars) | | | Ratio MI to U.S. Gross Mfg. |
|------|------|------------|----------------|------|------|------|------|
|      | Mfg. | All Sectors | Ratio Mfg. GP/GSP | Mfg. | GDP | Ratio | |
| 1977 | $34.4 | $98.1 | 35.0% | $463 | $2,031 | 22.8% | 7.4% |
| 1980 | $32.0 | $113.3 | 28.3% | $588 | $2,796 | 21.0% | 5.4% |
| 1985 | $51.6 | $161.1 | 32.0% | $804 | $4,213 | 19.1% | 6.4% |
| 1990 | $53.1 | $194.2 | 27.4% | $1,041 | $5,803 | 17.9% | 5.1% |
| 1995 | $74.5 | $265.1 | 28.1% | $1,289 | $7,401 | 17.4% | 5.8% |
| 1997 | $75.1 | $291.6 | 25.8% | $1,380 | $8,318 | 16.6% | 5.4% |
| 1999 | $80.7 | $308.3 | 26.2% | $1,497 | $9,269 | 16.1% | 5.4% |

SOURCES: Data on United States gross product from *The Economic Report of the President.* Washington, D.C.: U.S. Government Printing Office, 2002, table B-12. Michigan state product data from Bureau of Economic Analysis, Gross State Product, Regional Accounts Data, Gross State Product for State and for Manufacturing (in millions of current dollars), *http://www.bea.gov/bea/regional.*

manufacturing workers were 56% higher than those of the typical Michigan employee, at $63,404 for manufacturing as compared to $40,731 for all employees (see table 8.5). Manufacturing is, however, not homogeneous, and averages conceal large variation in employment and wages. In 1999, hourly earnings ranged from $11.36 in textile mills (with 3,061 employees in 1997) and $12.60 in petroleum and coal products manufacturing (with 1,785 employees in 1997) to $24.62 in transportation equipment (with 268,015 employees). Although Michigan is less dependent on durable goods and automotive manufacturing now than in the past, durables accounted for 74.1%, and automotive for 33.5%, of Michigan's gross manufacturing sales in 1999.

*A Look Back.* The double dip recession of 1980–82 had a profound effect on manufacturing, and particularly on durable goods. During this recession, which bottomed out in July 1980 and again in November 1982, national unemployment rose from 5.8% in 1979 to 9.7% in 1982.[1] Nationally, manufacturing suffered a 12.5% decline in employment between 1979 and 1983. The decline in employment was accompanied by permanent closure of older manufacturing facilities and restructuring of the employment relationship within the manufacturing sector. Although job loss was less severe in Michigan than in some states, the recession permanently affected Michigan manufacturing. We begin our analysis in 1977, the Census of Manufactures prior to the recessions.

### Manufacturing Output

*Levels and Trends.* Manufacturing grew more slowly than the balance of both the national and the Michigan economy between 1977 and 1999 (see table 8.1). Slower growth in national manufacturing caused gross product originating in manufacturing to decline from 22.8 to 16.1% of GDP. Trends in Michigan closely paralleled national trends. Manufacturing's share of state output declined from 35.0% to 26.2% of gross state product. Michigan's share of national manufacturing also declined, falling from 7.4% to 5.4% of the gross national manufacturing product between 1977 and 1999.

Despite these trends, Michigan remains a leading manufacturing state. While manufacturing accounted for 16.1% of national GDP in 1999, 26.2% of Michigan's gross state product originated in manufacturing. Further, Michigan's third-ranked position among the states in value of manufacturing shipments remained unchanged from 1977 to 1997.

*Trends in Real Manufacturing Output.* Between 1977 and 1999, manufacturing prices rose by 202.4%.[2] Using 1999 dollars, Michigan's real manufacturing gross output increased by 16%, or by 0.7% per year, between 1977 and 1999 (see table 8.2). In contrast, the real state economy grew at an annualized rate of 1.2%, to 135.3% of its 1977 level.[3]

The severity of the recession of the 1980s is illustrated by trends in real output. Measured in 1999 dollars, real gross manufacturing product fell from $62.3 to $48.9 billion between 1979 and 1981. It did not return to its 1979 level until 1994, and has increased only slowly since. This pattern is more pronounced in motor vehicles, in which gross output has declined "permanently" from its 1977 peak of $34.4 billion. Gross product in the Michigan motor vehicle industry bottomed out at $18.9 billion in 1980. It recovered to nearly 90% of the 1977 value in 1984–85, but declined to $16.6 billion by 1991, further than in the recession of the early 1980s. Despite sustained growth in the late 1990s, 1999 motor vehicle gross product was $27.0 billion, or 78.5% of 1977 production.[4]

*A Closer Look at Output: Disaggregating the Manufacturing Sector.* Manufacturing is not homogeneous but is composed of differentiated industries. Some are closely linked (such as primary and fabricated metals and transportation equipment), while others are largely independent of other manufacturing industries (such as food and beverage products). Attention to manufacturing as a whole conceals considerable differences in industry performance within manufacturing.

At the broadest level, manufacturing can be divided into durable goods and nondurable goods. Michigan manufacturing has been dominated by durable goods manufacturing, and, within the durable goods sector, by motor vehicle production. In 1977, durable manufactures accounted for 83.1%, and transportation equipment for 45.6%, of gross manufacturing product. By 1999, durables and transportation equipment accounted for 74.1 and 33.5% of manufacturing gross product, respectively (see table 8.3). Despite this decline, durable goods and transportation equipment remain central to Michigan manufacturing.

## TABLE 8.2

**Nominal and Real Gross Product in Michigan Manufacturing (in millions of dollars)**

| Year | Manufacturing | | | Motor Vehicle | | |
|------|---------|------|---------|---------|------|---------|
| | Nominal | PPI | Real | Nominal | PPI | Real |
| 1977 | $34,355 | 62.5 | $69,535 | $15,675 | 64.6 | $34,407 |
| 1979 | $37,258 | 75.7 | $62,261 | $15,239 | 75.3 | $28,697 |
| 1980 | $31,999 | 88.0 | $45,999 | $11,051 | 82.9 | $18,903 |
| 1981 | $37,631 | 97.4 | $48,874 | $15,097 | 94.3 | $22,702 |
| 1982 | $35,854 | 100.0 | $45,355 | $15,203 | 100.0 | $21,558 |
| 1983 | $42,180 | 101.1 | $52,777 | $19,847 | 102.8 | $27,377 |
| 1984 | $49,823 | 103.3 | $61,013 | $23,044 | 105.2 | $31,061 |
| 1985 | $51,610 | 103.7 | $62,957 | $22,570 | 107.9 | $29,661 |
| 1990 | $53,145 | 115.8 | $58,056 | $16,881 | 121.5 | $19,701 |
| 1995 | $74,541 | 125.5 | $75,135 | $27,110 | 139.7 | $27,518 |
| 1997 | $75,100 | 127.7 | $74,394 | $24,212 | 141.6 | $24,246 |
| 1999 | $80,740 | 126.5 | $80,740 | $27,028 | 141.8 | $27,028 |

SOURCES: Nominal Product Data from Bureau of Economic Analysis, Gross State Product, Regional Accounts Data, Gross State Product for Manufacturing and Motor Vehicles (in millions of current dollars), *http://www.bea.gov/bea/regional*. Data on Producer Price Indicies (PPI) from *The Economic Report of the President*. Washington, D.C.: U.S. Government Printing Office, 2002, table B-67. Producer Price Index Data from the Bureau of Labor Statistics, U.S. Department of Labor, *http://www.bls.gov/ppi/*. NOTE: PPI is Producer Price Index; 1982 = 100.

A next step in disaggregation breaks the durable and nondurable goods sectors into their twenty component major Standard Industrial Classification (SIC) industries (see appendix A).[5] This table includes information on the number of establishments, value of shipments, and value added by SIC industry in Michigan, for industries that reported employment in the 1977, 1982, 1987, or 1997 Census of Manufactures (CM). The first three columns on the left side of the table provide, from left to right, the SIC code, the North American Industrial Classification System (NAICS)

## TABLE 8.3

**Michigan Gross Product: Total, Manufacturing, and Subsectors (in millions of current dollars)**

| | Manufacturing Gross Product | Durable | Nondurable | Durable as a % of Mfg. | Motor Vehicle Gross Product | Motor Vehicle as a % of Mfg. |
|------|---------|---------|---------|------|---------|------|
| 1977 | $34,355 | $28,551 | $5,804 | 83.1% | $15,675 | 45.6% |
| 1980 | $31,999 | $25,327 | $6,673 | 79.1% | $11,051 | 34.5% |
| 1985 | $51,610 | $41,481 | $10,129 | 80.4% | $22,570 | 43.7% |
| 1990 | $53,145 | $38,684 | $14,461 | 72.8% | $16,881 | 31.8% |
| 1995 | $74,541 | $55,479 | $19,062 | 74.4% | $27,110 | 36.4% |
| 1997 | $75,100 | $55,463 | $19,637 | 73.9% | $24,212 | 32.2% |
| 1999 | $80,740 | $59,832 | $20,908 | 74.1% | $27,028 | 33.5% |

SOURCES: Nominal Product Data from Bureau of Economic Analysis, Gross State Product, Regional Accounts Data, Gross State Product for Manufacturing, Durable Goods, Non-Durable Goods and Motor Vehicles (in millions of current dollars), *http://www.bea.gov/bea/regional*.

code, and a descriptive title for the industry. There are nineteen two-digit SIC industries with employment in Michigan, and between 5,380 (1977) and 5,753 (1997) manufacturing establishments (locations at which manufacturing takes place) in Michigan.

Industries vary considerably in size and economic importance. Measured by the number of establishments, the leading industries are printing, with 812 establishments; fabricated metals, with 1,272 establishments; and industrial machinery, with 1,141 establishments. At the other end of the scale are textiles, apparel, petroleum and coal products, and leather and allied products, with between 13 and 34 establishments in 1997. Transportation equipment falls between these extremes, with 689 establishments.

A better measure of the economic importance of an industry is value added, the difference between industry revenue and the costs of production, exclusive of capital costs. Ranked by 1997 value added, transportation equipment remains the largest industry in Michigan ($39.0 billion in value added). Industrial machinery is second ($9.6 billion) and fabricated metal products ranks third ($7.8 billion). Food products (including beverages and tobacco) and chemical manufacturing are tied for fourth, with $6.0 billion each. The next-largest industries are plastics and rubber products ($4.9 billion) and primary metal products ($4.0 billion). At the other end of the scale are apparel manufacturing ($90 million), textile manufacturing ($139 million), and leather and allied products ($213 million). Transportation equipment is Michigan's dominant manufacturing industry, accounting for 41.6% of total manufacturing value added.

Measured by value added, transportation equipment's share of manufacturing output has increased from 37.1% to 41.6% from 1977 to 1997. This is due primarily to the large decline in value added in metal products and industrial machinery. Primary metal products declined from 7.8% to 4.3% of Michigan value added; fabricated metal products declined from 12.1% to 8.3%; and industrial machinery declined from 13.2% to 10.2% in this period. In addition to transportation equipment, plastic and rubber products and furniture increased their share of Michigan value added by 3% and 2%, respectively.

*Output by Major Industry: Michigan and the United States.* Changes in value added are an imperfect metric of industry performance, as this measure combines changes in output with changes in the price of output. An alternative is to compare the performance of Michigan manufacturing industries with that of their national counterparts. This approach differentiates between issues specific to Michigan and those associated with the national industry. Appendix A (three furthest right columns) compares 1977 and 1997 value added by SIC major industries in Michigan and the United States. Michigan manufacturing has generally underperformed its national counterparts. Nominal value added in transportation equipment increased by 180% in Michigan against a 254% increase for the nation; fabricated metal products grew by 72% in Michigan against 193% for the nation. Even the Michigan industries that performed well over the last two decades grew more slowly than their national counterparts. Printing grew by 235% in Michigan but by 366% nationally; electric and electronic equipment grew by 190% in Michigan against 400% nationally. The exceptions to this among larger industries are furniture and plastic and rubber products: value added rose by 434% in the furniture industry in Michigan against a 291% increase nationally, while the Michigan plastic and rubber products industry grew by 446% against 312% growth for the United States.

Judged by output, Michigan remains an important manufacturing state. Although manufacturing plays a declining role in the Michigan economy, the relative economic impact of manufacturing remains substantially greater in Michigan than for the United States as a whole. Disaggregation of the manufacturing sector into its component major industries indicates that the motor vehicle industry has retained its dominant position in Michigan manufacturing. Along with many other manufacturing industries, however, value added in transportation equipment is growing more slowly within Michigan than in the country as a whole.

**Manufacturing Employment in Michigan**

*Levels and Trends in Employment.* The decline in the importance of manufacturing as an employer parallels its decline as a source of gross state product. Although employment in Michigan rose by 36%, from 3.4 million to 4.7 million, between 1977 and 2000, employment in manufacturing in the state declined by 13% in this time period, from 1.1 million to just under 1 million.

**TABLE 8.4**

**Employment (in millions): Michigan and the United States, 1977–2000**

| Year | Michigan | | | U.S. | | |
| | Mfg. | All Sectors | Mfg. as % of Total | Mfg. | All Sectors | Mfg. as % of Total |
|---|---|---|---|---|---|---|
| 1977 | 1,128.4 | 3,442.3 | 32.8% | 19,682 | 92,017 | 21.4% |
| 1980 | 998.9 | 3,442.8 | 29.0% | 20,285 | 99,303 | 20.4% |
| 1985 | 1,002.4 | 3,561.5 | 28.1% | 19,248 | 107,150 | 18.0% |
| 1990 | 943.6 | 3,969.6 | 23.8% | 19,076 | 118,793 | 16.1% |
| 1995 | 979.7 | 4,273.9 | 22.9% | 18,524 | 124,900 | 14.8% |
| 1997 | 966.3 | 4,448.2 | 21.7% | 18,675 | 129,558 | 14.4% |
| 2000 | 979.8 | 4,679.3 | 20.9% | 18,469 | 135,208 | 13.7% |

SOURCES: U.S. Employment Data from *Handbook of Labor Statistics: Employment, Earnings, Prices, Productivity and Other Labor Data,* edited by Eva E. Jacobs. Washington, D.C.: Bernan Associates, 2001, table 1–1 and 2–1. Michigan Employment Data from Bureau of Labor Statistics, U.S. Department of Labor, Employment, Hours, and Earnings from the Current Employment Statistics survey, series SAS2600000000001 (n), SAS2600000000001, *http://www.bls.gov/ces.*

This mirrors national trends; while national employment rose by 47%, employment in manufacturing fell by 6.2% (table 8.4). Despite the decline in manufacturing employment in Michigan, however the industry continues to provide employment for 20.9% of the state workforce, well above the 13.7% of the national workforce employed in manufacturing. Michigan currently employs 5.3% of the U.S. manufacturing workforce, close to the 5.7% it accounted for in 1977.

Michigan has been more successful in maintaining manufacturing employment than have some other prominent manufacturing states. While Michigan lost 287,000 total jobs and 160,000 production jobs in manufacturing between 1977 and 1997, New York lost 739,000 total jobs and 425,000 production jobs, and Pennsylvania lost 509,000 jobs total and 341,000 production jobs in manufacturing. As a result, Michigan has moved from sixth to fifth position nationally in total employment in manufacturing, from sixth to fourth in the number of production workers, and from seventh to fourth in total production worker hours. Among the eleven leading manufacturing states, only California, Georgia, and Wisconsin gained production employment since 1977, and only the first two realized increases in total manufacturing employment.

*Disaggregating Employment by Industry.* There is considerable variation in the level and trends of employment among major SIC industries in Michigan. Transportation equipment is the largest major industry in Michigan, with 268,000 employees and 32.3% of manufacturing employ-

ment in 1997 (appendix B). The next-largest industries are industrial machinery, with 106,400 employees and 12.8% of manufacturing employment, and the similarly sized fabricated metal, with 104,300 employees and 12.7% of employment. Although both are smaller than the transportation equipment industry, the difference in scale is far smaller when measured by employment than by value added. Plastic and rubber products employs 67,700 (8.1% of manufacturing employment) and printing, which was not among the seven largest industries measured by value added, employs 46,700 (5.6% of employment). Taken together, the five largest industries account for 71% of employment in manufacturing, the largest three for 58% of employment.

The broad trend in manufacturing employment has been downward, declining from 1.1 million in 1977 to 966,000 in 1997, a decline of 12.2%.[6] The largest losses were in transportation equipment, where employment fell by 16.5%, from 321,200 to 268,000; primary metals, where employment fell by 54.6%, from 83,000 to 37,700; fabricated metals, where total employment declined by 26.8%, from 142,600 to 104,400; and industrial machinery, with a decline of 26.9%, from 145,900 to 106,400. Large declines in employment were not confined to large industries. Employment in apparel fell from 25,500 to 1,600, signaling the industry's effective exit from Michigan. Not all Michigan industries lost employment. Reflecting a shift from metal to plastic parts in the automotive industry, employment in plastics and rubber manufacturing increased by 90%, from 35,600 to 67,700. Printing and publishing and furniture both experienced growth: the former

**TABLE 8.5**

**Wage and Salary Disbursements, Number of Jobs, and Annual Earnings for Manufacturing and All Michigan Employees, 1977–1999**

| | Wage & Salary Disbursements (in millions) | | Number of Jobs (in thousands) | | Employment (in thousands) | | Nominal Earnings | | | | Real Earnings in 1999 Dollars | | | |
| | | | | | | | Annual Earnings Per Job | | Annual Earnings Per Employee | | Annual Earnings Per Job | | Annual Earnings Per Employee | |
| Year | All | Mfg. | All | Mfg. | All | Mfg. | All | Mfg. | All | Mfg. | All | Mfg. | All | Mfg. |
|---|---|---|---|---|---|---|---|---|---|---|---|---|---|---|
| 1977 | $56,208 | $25,500 | 3544.2 | 1122.2 | 3442.3 | 1128.4 | $15,859 | $22,723 | $16,329 | $22,598 | $43,285 | $62,020 | $44,568 | $61,678 |
| 1980 | $69,892 | $29,082 | 3550.1 | 986.3 | 3442.8 | 998.9 | $19,688 | $29,487 | $20,301 | $29,114 | $39,519 | $59,189 | $40,750 | $58,440 |
| 1985 | $87,192 | $39,752 | 3696.4 | 993.8 | 3561.5 | 1002.4 | $23,588 | $40,000 | $24,482 | $39,657 | $36,259 | $61,487 | $37,633 | $60,960 |
| 1990 | $120,305 | $42,931 | 4150.8 | 945.7 | 3969.6 | 943.6 | $28,984 | $45,396 | $30,307 | $45,497 | $36,679 | $57,448 | $38,353 | $57,576 |
| 1995 | $159,086 | $59,579 | 4449.7 | 985.4 | 4273.9 | 979.7 | $35,752 | $60,462 | $37,223 | $60,814 | $38,802 | $65,620 | $40,398 | $66,002 |
| 1997 | $170,494 | $56,793 | 4609.7 | 975.9 | 4448.2 | 966.3 | $36,986 | $58,194 | $38,329 | $58,774 | $38,115 | $59,971 | $39,499 | $60,568 |
| 1999 | $186,629 | $62,250 | 4761.5 | 986.3 | 4582.0 | 981.8 | $39,195 | $63,115 | $40,731 | $63,404 | $39,195 | $63,115 | $40,731 | $63,404 |

SOURCES: Nominal Product Data from Bureau of Economic Analysis, Gross State Product, Regional Accounts Data. Compensation of Michigan Employees (in millions of current dollars), http://www.bea.gov/bea/regional. Employment Data from Bureau of Labor Statistics, U.S. Department of Labor, Employment, Hours, and Earnings from the Current Employment Statistics survey, http://www.bls.gov/ces/home.htm, Statewide Non-farm Employment for Michigan, series SAS2600000000001 (n).

added 13,300 jobs and increased employment by 40%, while the latter added 11,800 jobs, and increased employment by 54.4%.

How did the change in Michigan employment compare with that in the United States as a whole? Two of Michigan's larger industries, furniture and plastics, outperformed their national industries. Total employment in furniture grew by 54% in Michigan, but by only 30% nationally. Employment grew by 90% in plastics in Michigan against an increase of 42% nationally. Lumber and wood products; petroleum and coal products; stone, clay and glass products; and instruments also grew more rapidly in Michigan than nationally. More typically, employment growth as a whole was less robust in Michigan than in the United States. Transportation equipment, which lost 16.6% of its Michigan employment between 1977 and 1997, grew by 4.2% nationally. Similarly, employment in food products shrank to 84% of 1977 employment in Michigan, while increasing by 3.9% nationally. Paper products, primary metals, fabricated metals, and electronic and electric Machinery experienced slower employment growth, or more rapid decline, in Michigan than nationally.

### Employee Earnings

Manufacturing pays well relative to the balance of Michigan industries and remains a disproportionately important source of labor income for Michigan residents. In 1977, manufacturing accounted for 32.8% of Michigan employment but 45.4% of Michigan wages and salaries (table 8.5). In 1999, manufacturing provided 21.4% of employment and 33.4% of wages and salaries. As suggested by these data, manufacturing jobs pay considerably better than do jobs in other sectors. Annual earnings for manufacturing and for the full state labor force can be constructed as the ratio of wage and salary disbursements to the number of jobs or employees in the sector. The number of jobs is the number of positions reported by employers and, since some employees hold multiple jobs, is somewhat larger than the number of employees (table 8.5 columns three through five).[7] Measured in 1999 inflation adjusted dollars, average annual earnings per job in manufacturing rose from $62,020 to $63,115 or by 1.8% from 1977 to 1999 while average annual earnings per job for the Michigan labor force declined from $43,285 to $39,195, or 9.4%. Real earnings per employee followed a similar track, with earnings in manufacturing rising by 2.8%, from $61,678 to $63,404, and average employee earnings declining by 8.6%, from $44,568 to $40,731. In combination with the large decline in overall state earnings, the relative stability of manufacturing earnings acted to widen the earnings gap between manufacturing and other sectors. While manufacturing jobs paid 43% more than the average job in Michigan, and manufacturing employees earned 38% more than the average Michigan employee in 1977, by 1999 the advantage for manufacturing had risen to 61% per job and 56% per employee.[8]

*Earnings by Major Industries.* In 1999, the average Michigan production worker earned $18.38 per hour and $812.40 per week. The magnitude of wage increases varies considerably by industry within Michigan manufacturing (appendix C). The largest increases were in transportation equipment, where hourly earnings rose by 188%, from $8.44 to $24.32, and weekly earnings rose by 199%, from $378.11 to $1,130.88. Hourly wages in paper and allied products, the median industry when ranked by hourly earnings in 1999, rose 163%, from $6.25 to $16.44. Weekly earnings rose 159%, from $282.90 to $733.22. Hourly wages in printing, an industry near the bottom of the 1999 wage distribution, rose by 109%, from $6.56 to $13.73, while weekly earnings rose by 115%, from $248.78 to $535.47. Only in transportation equipment did the increase in hourly wages exceed the rate of inflation. In most industries hourly earnings fell behind inflation, and the decline was particularly large in printing, food manufacturing, primary and fabricated metals, electronic equipment, and furniture, where hourly wages lagged inflation by at least 30 percentage points.[9]

Average weekly hours in Michigan manufacturing increased from 43.3 in 1977 to 44.2 in 1999. The increase in weekly hours was particularly large in food products, where hours rose from 41.9 to 44.4 per week, furniture (increasing by 1.4 hours to 42.2 hours), printing (increasing by 1.1 hours to 39 hours), primary and fabricated metals (rising by 1.4 hours to 45.2 hours), industrial machinery (rising by 1.4 hours to 44.5 hours), and transportation equipment (rising by 1.7 hours to 46.5 hours). An important incentive to employers to use increased hours may be the relatively high level of fixed cost fringe benefits, which make new hiring more expensive than paying overtime rates.

## Summary: Manufacturing in Michigan over the Last Two Decades

Despite a decline in the relative size of the manufacturing sector in Michigan between 1977 and the present, Michigan remains an important manufacturing state, and manufacturing remains an important sector within the state. Between 1977 and 2000, the manufacturing share of gross state product declined from 35.0 to 26.2%, while its share of employment fell from 32.8 to 20.9%.

Much of this decline can be attributed to the absolute decline in the transportation equipment industry, the dominant industry within manufacturing, in the state. Despite this decline, manufacturing continues to provide a fifth of Michigan's employment and a disproportionate share, 33.4%, of state wage and salary income. Historically, annual earnings in manufacturing have been above those of the average Michigan wage and salary earner, and this differential has widened from a 38% advantage in 1977 to a 56% advantage in 1999. Particularly because manufacturing has been a source of well-paid employment for Michigan citizens, its decline poses long-term economic challenges for the state.

## Part 2: Unionization and Collective Bargaining in Michigan Manufacturing and the Michigan Automobile Industry, 1981–2000

Michigan continues to be a highly unionized state, especially in manufacturing. To a substantial extent, this is due to the high levels of unionization in auto assembly. These two institutional facts provide the basis for part 2. The first section of part 2 will provide basic data on unionization in manufacturing in Michigan. The second section of part 2 will focus on collective bargaining and labor relations in the automobile industry during the past twenty years.

### Overall Levels of Manufacturing Unionization

Michigan manufacturing is highly unionized relative to manufacturing nationally. Table 8.6 presents data on unionization and employment in manufacturing for Michigan and the United States for selected years. For the period 1986–2000, the manufacturing unionization rate in Michigan (union members as a percentage of manufacturing employment) was approximately 1.8 times greater than the manufacturing unionization rate nationwide. The average manufacturing union membership rate in Michigan declined from 42.5% to 28.8% from 1986 to 2000; nationally it declined from 24% to 14.8%. The ratio of Michigan manufacturing unionization to national manufacturing unionization was generally stable from the mid-1980s through the early 1990s, and grew in the mid-1990s, before starting a slight decline in the late 1990s. It was higher in 2000 than in 1986.

**TABLE 8.6**

**Union Membership Rates, Union Membership (in thousands), and Employment (in thousands), Manufacturing, United States, and Michigan, Selected Years, 1986–2000**

|                                          | 1986   | 1989   | 1992   | 1995   | 1998    | 1999    | 2000    |
|------------------------------------------|--------|--------|--------|--------|---------|---------|---------|
| U.S. manufacturing membership rate       | 24.0%  | 21.6%  | 19.7%  | 17.6%  | 15.8%   | 15.6%   | 14.8%   |
| Michigan manufacturing membership rate   | 42.5%  | 38.5%  | 36.0%  | 33.9%  | 32.2%   | 30.2%   | 28.8%   |
| Ratio, Michigan/U.S. mfg. membership rate| 1.77   | 1.78   | 1.83   | 1.93   | 2.04    | 1.94    | 1.95    |
|                                          |        |        |        |        |         |         |         |
| U.S. manufacturing union membership      | 4869   | 4467   | 3749   | 3440   | 3127    | 3024    | 2832    |
| Michigan manufacturing union membership  | 453.9  | 415.5  | 353.2  | 361.4  | 368.8   | 338.9   | 311.2   |
| Pct. of mfg. union members in Michigan   | 9.32%  | 9.30%  | 9.42%  | 10.51% | 11.79%  | 11.21%  | 10.99%  |
|                                          |        |        |        |        |         |         |         |
| U.S. manufacturing employment            | 20,296 | 20,690 | 19,076 | 19,520 | 19,763  | 19,323  | 19,167  |
| Michigan manufacturing employment        | 1,068.2| 1,079  | 980.3  | 1,067  | 1,147.1 | 1,122.7 | 1,079.5 |
| Pct. of mfg. employment in Michigan      | 5.26%  | 5.22%  | 5.14%  | 5.47%  | 5.80%   | 5.81%   | 5.63%   |

Table 8.6 also presents data on actual union membership in manufacturing, nationally and in Michigan, as well as employment in manufacturing. During the period 1986–2000, from 9% to 12% of manufacturing union members worked in Michigan. During this same period, Michigan never accounted for more than 6% of manufacturing employment nationally.

### Collective Bargaining in the Automobile Industry

*Introduction.* As shown in part 1 of the chapter, Michigan is highly dependent on manufacturing, and that manufacturing is heavily auto-related.

For the period 1980–2001, the percentage of Michigan manufacturing employment in the (three-digit) motor vehicle and equipment (MVE) industry averaged 30.9%. The highest annual percentage was 34%, in 1983 and 1985; the lowest annual percentage was 28.5% in 1998. The percentage exhibited a downward trend during the period from 1980 to 2001. The mean annual percentage from 1980–90 was 32.4%, while the mean annual percentage from 1991–2001 was 29.4% (Bureau of Labor Statistics, undated-a; Bureau of Labor Statistics, undated-b).

The downward trend, however, was not due to declining employment in the (two-digit) transportation equipment (TE) industry in Michigan

**FIGURE 8.1**

**Employment in Motor Vehicles and Equipment, U.S. and Michigan (in thousands); Percentage of U.S. Motor Vehicle Equipment and Employment in Michigan, 1980–2001**

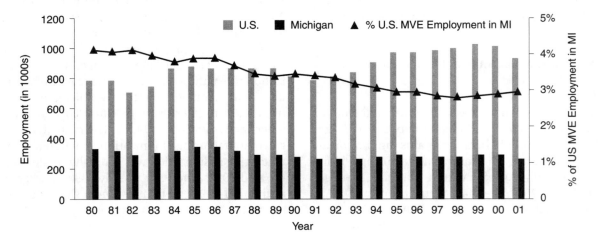

during the 1990s. Between 1991 and 2001, TE employment in Michigan increased from 266,000 to 275,000, with a high of 293,000 in 2000. Rather, over the period, overall manufacturing employment in Michigan increased faster than did TE employment (Bureau of Labor Statistics, undated-b).

The auto industry in Michigan is highly unionized, and since compensation and working conditions in the auto industry affect compensation and working conditions throughout the state, collective bargaining trends in that industry are extremely important to Michigan.[10] Some sense of the importance of auto industry collective bargaining to Michigan can be obtained by examining figure 8.1, which presents data on U.S. and Michigan employment in MVE. As can be seen, although Michigan's percentage of national employment in motor vehicle equipment has declined by almost a third since 1980, Michigan still remains a "center" of employment in the industry nationally. In 2001, 29.4% of all employees in the industry were employed in Michigan.

*Collective Bargaining and Earnings in the Auto Industry.* At least partially as a result of collective bargaining and unionization, Michigan autoworkers are well paid. Some sense of how well paid can be obtained by examining table 8.7. This table exploits the fact that during the last twenty years, foreign auto manufacturers have established nonunion plants in the United States: Toyota in Kentucky, Nissan in Tennessee, Mercedes in Alabama, and Honda in Ohio.[11] Thus, one can compare MVE and TE average hourly employee earnings (AHE) in Michigan with AHE in those same industries in other auto-producing states to obtain a very rough estimate of the impact of collective bargaining on the wages of Michigan workers in the auto industry.

Data are also included for Ohio, which is characterized by four distinct pockets of auto manufacturing. Three, Cincinnati, Cleveland, and Toledo, are unionized, but Columbus, where Honda is located, is not unionized. Thus, Ohio provides an opportunity to obtain a sense of the impact of collective bargaining on wages while controlling for geographic distance, which is one factor that may impact the union effect on a wage differential between Michigan and other states.

Finally, it should be noted that this table does not claim to be an accurate estimate of the union wage differentials within the industry, because it does not control for such factors as employee human capital (e.g., education, experience, skills) and firm differences in such factors as production processes, product mix, and capital stock. Although the data are presented for selected years, the means are for all years during the twenty-two-year period for which data were available.

As can be seen from table 8.7, (unionized) Michigan autoworkers earn substantially more than their counterparts in other states and cities in which a substantial percentage of autoworkers are not represented by a union. First, examining the data for MVE, for the full twenty-two-year period, the average hourly earnings of Michigan workers were roughly 4.7% higher than those of their Ohio counterparts. Yet the data for largely nonunion Columbus, which began to be published at the three-digit level in 1989, demonstrate that this differential in favor of Michigan was due primarily to the nonunion pocket in Columbus. For the period 1989–2001, Michigan (unionized) MVE employees earned on average, on an hourly basis, 36.9% more than MVE employees in nonunion Columbus.

Use of two-digit industry data for TE permits a comparison between Michigan and a broader range of states than could be done at the three-digit MVE level, although the two-digit level includes non-auto firms. For the period 1992–2001, which coincides most closely with the establishment of nonunion auto assembly plants by foreign firms, Michigan workers in TE earned 26.8%, on an annual basis, more than their counterparts in Alabama, and 16.2% more than their counterparts in Kentucky. Both Alabama and Kentucky have nonunion auto plants. For the period 1992–2001, Michigan workers had hourly earnings that were 40.1% higher than their counterparts in Tennessee, also with a large nonunion auto workforce. The Ohio data for TE are similar to the data for MVE, with a large differential for Columbus, and much smaller differentials for the unionized areas of Cincinnati, Cleveland, and Toledo.

An inspection of the data indicate that the percentage differential in favor of Michigan in AHE in TE increased vis-à-vis Kentucky and Columbus during the twenty-year period, and stayed stable vis-à-vis Alabama. It increased vis-à-vis Tennessee during the 1990s. This suggests that, over the last twenty years of the twentieth century, any increased production among nonunion foreign producers or declining market share among the domestic (Michigan) producers did not close the differential in wages.

## TABLE 8.7

### Average Hourly Earnings in Motor Vehicle and Transportation Equipment, Michigan and Other Automotive States

| | 1980 | 1985 | 1990 | 1991 | 1992 | 1993 | 1994 | 1995 | 1996 | 1997 | 1998 | 1999 | 2000 | 2001 | Mean 80–01 | Mean 89–01 |
|---|---|---|---|---|---|---|---|---|---|---|---|---|---|---|---|---|
| **Motor Vehicle Equipment** | | | | | | | | | | | | | | | | |
| Michigan | $11.01 | $15.01 | $17.39 | $18.43 | $18.54 | $19.81 | $21.15 | $21.03 | $21.34 | $22.31 | $23.67 | $24.62 | $26.07 | $26.61 | | |
| Ohio | $10.39 | $14.74 | $16.86 | $17.83 | $18.35 | $19.39 | $20.20 | $20.36 | $20.33 | $20.84 | $21.14 | $22.05 | $23.04 | $23.89 | | |
| Cincinnati | $10.80 | $15.17 | $18.26 | $19.14 | $20.90 | $21.70 | $22.70 | $22.81 | $22.52 | $22.60 | $24.02 | $25.13 | $25.42 | $26.19 | | |
| Cleveland | $10.98 | $15.36 | $18.41 | $19.20 | $19.19 | $20.31 | $21.25 | $21.28 | $21.22 | $21.81 | $22.92 | $24.18 | $24.85 | $25.30 | | |
| Columbus | | | $14.81 | $15.29 | $11.67 | $11.95 | $13.03 | $12.68 | $11.70 | $12.38 | $12.90 | $13.38 | $13.35 | $13.43 | | |
| **Percentage Difference, Michigan and . . .** | | | | | | | | | | | | | | | | |
| Ohio | 5.6% | 1.8% | 3.0% | 3.3% | 1.0% | 2.1% | 4.5% | 3.2% | 4.7% | 6.6% | 10.7% | 10.4% | 11.6% | 10.2% | 4.7% | 5.7% |
| Cincinnati | 1.9% | -1.1% | -5.0% | -3.9% | -12.7% | -9.5% | -7.3% | -8.5% | -5.5% | -1.3% | -1.5% | -2.1% | 2.5% | 1.6% | -4.2% | -4.6% |
| Cleveland | 0.3% | -2.3% | -5.9% | -4.2% | -3.5% | -2.5% | -0.5% | -1.2% | 0.6% | 2.2% | 3.2% | 1.8% | 4.7% | 4.9% | -1.1% | -0.5% |
| Columbus | | | 14.8% | 17.0% | 37.1% | 39.7% | 38.4% | 39.7% | 45.2% | 44.5% | 45.5% | 45.7% | 48.8% | 49.5% | | 36.9% |
| **Transportation Equipment** | | | | | | | | | | | | | | | | |
| Michigan | $10.93 | $14.81 | $17.11 | $18.19 | $18.33 | $19.61 | $20.94 | $20.85 | $21.13 | $22.08 | $23.40 | $24.32 | $25.73 | $26.24 | | |
| Alabama | $7.64 | $12.63 | $12.90 | $13.82 | $13.29 | $14.20 | $15.34 | $15.95 | $16.31 | $16.62 | $16.62 | $17.05 | $18.12 | $19.24 | | |
| Kentucky | $9.35 | $13.74 | $13.61 | $14.37 | $15.03 | $15.58 | $15.98 | $16.19 | $16.87 | $17.42 | $18.54 | $19.19 | $20.59 | $21.91 | | |
| Ohio | $10.02 | $14.18 | $16.37 | $17.33 | $17.80 | $18.77 | $19.67 | $19.89 | $19.95 | $20.45 | $20.81 | $21.71 | $22.69 | $23.59 | | |
| Cincinnati | $9.97 | $14.24 | $16.90 | $17.58 | $18.91 | $19.53 | $20.76 | $21.01 | $21.05 | $21.55 | $22.49 | $23.63 | $24.30 | $25.25 | | |
| Cleveland | $10.56 | $14.54 | $16.79 | $17.57 | $18.94 | $19.18 | $20.11 | $20.27 | $20.28 | $20.74 | $21.77 | $23.15 | $23.74 | $24.11 | | |
| Columbus | $9.02 | $12.32 | $14.73 | $15.11 | $11.91 | $12.16 | $13.06 | $12.71 | $11.72 | $12.40 | $12.93 | $13.40 | $13.37 | $13.46 | | |
| Toledo | $10.38 | $14.99 | $17.62 | $18.02 | $18.93 | $20.16 | $21.13 | $21.29 | $20.96 | $21.04 | $22.28 | $24.02 | $24.36 | $25.11 | | |
| Tennessee | | | | | $12.60 | $12.51 | $12.51 | $12.64 | $12.79 | $13.24 | $13.37 | $14.03 | $14.07 | $14.61 | | |

| | 1980 | 1985 | 1990 | 1991 | 1992 | 1993 | 1994 | 1995 | 1996 | 1997 | 1998 | 1999 | 2000 | 2001 | Mean 80–01 | Mean 92–01 |
|---|---|---|---|---|---|---|---|---|---|---|---|---|---|---|---|---|
| **Percentage Difference, Michigan and . . .** | | | | | | | | | | | | | | | | |
| Alabama | 30.1% | 14.7% | 24.6% | 24.0% | 27.5% | 27.6% | 26.7% | 23.5% | 22.8% | 24.7% | 29.0% | 29.9% | 29.6% | 26.7% | 25.2% | 26.8% |
| Kentucky | 14.5% | 7.2% | 20.5% | 21.0% | 18.0% | 20.6% | 23.7% | 22.4% | 20.2% | 21.1% | 20.8% | 21.1% | 20.0% | 16.5% | 16.2% | 20.4% |
| Ohio | 8.3% | 4.3% | 4.3% | 4.7% | 2.9% | 4.3% | 6.1% | 4.6% | 5.6% | 7.4% | 11.1% | 10.7% | 11.8% | 10.1% | 6.2% | 7.5% |
| Cincinnati | 8.8% | 3.8% | 1.2% | 3.4% | -3.2% | 0.4% | 0.9% | -0.8% | 0.4% | 2.4% | 3.9% | 2.8% | 5.6% | 3.8% | 2.4% | 1.6% |
| Cleveland | 3.4% | 1.8% | 1.9% | 3.4% | -3.3% | 2.2% | 4.0% | 2.8% | 4.0% | 6.1% | 7.0% | 4.8% | 7.7% | 8.1% | 3.2% | 4.3% |
| Columbus | 17.5% | 16.8% | 13.9% | 16.9% | 35.0% | 38.0% | 37.6% | 39.0% | 44.5% | 43.8% | 44.7% | 44.9% | 48.0% | 48.7% | 27.3% | 42.4% |
| Toledo | 5.0% | -1.2% | -3.0% | 0.9% | -3.3% | -2.8% | -0.9% | -2.1% | 0.8% | 4.7% | 4.8% | 1.2% | 5.3% | 4.3% | 0.2% | 1.2% |
| Tennessee | | | | | 31.3% | 36.2% | 40.3% | 39.4% | 39.5% | 40.0% | 42.9% | 42.3% | 45.3% | 44.3% | | 40.1% |

SOURCE: U.S. Department of Labor, Bureau of Labor Statistics.

*Collective Bargaining Outcomes in Autos, 1980–2000.* Through the 1970s, auto industry pattern bargaining generally focused on wage and benefit increases.[12] Buffeted by employment declines in the industry in the early 1980s, however, the focus of bargaining and the content of the pattern shifted from wage increases to long-term job security. This shift of the focus of bargaining from increasing wages to enhanced job security is the salient feature of collective bargaining in the auto industry during the last two decades.[13]

The 1979 UAW-GM and UAW Ford agreements had no provision on job security. This is to be expected, as production worker employment in the industry had been generally increasing over the previous two decades. From a recession-trough low of 452,500 in 1958, production worker employment in MVE climbed to 708,000 in 1969, and to a historical high of 782,000 in 1978 (Bureau of Labor Statistics, undated-b). While there were short-term fluctuations during this period, these were covered by the Supplemental Unemployment Benefit Plans that had been negotiated in 1955 (Katz 1987, 24–26).

There was a drop in employment in 1979 to 764,000, but the bottom fell out in 1980. In that year, production worker employment was only 575,000, a 25% decline from the previous year. Believing that this decline was not a familiar cyclical fluctuation in employment, but rather a structural decline in the number of production employees in the industry, the UAW sent a message to the automakers that job security was high on its agenda ("Job Security . . ." 1981).

The economic crisis in the auto industry spurred the parties to early negotiations. The UAW and Ford signed a thirty-one-month agreement in February 1982, seven months prior to the scheduled expiration date of the existing contract. The agreement included a twenty-four-month moratorium on plant closings. As a disincentive for Ford to reduce employment, the parties also agreed on a Guaranteed Income Stream, which provided workers with greater than fifteen years' seniority up to 95% of forty-hour take-home pay, with the percentage increasing with the employee's length of service ("Pay Concessions . . ." 1982; "Joint UAW-Ford Summary . . ." 1982; "Auto Workers Ratify . . ." 1982).

Significantly, Ford obtained relief on monetary employee compensation. Although there would be no reductions in wage rates paid on the date of the agreement, the Annual Improvement Factor (AIF) was eliminated. (In principle, the AIF was designed to provide workers with real wage increases as national productivity increased.) In addition, cost-of-living adjustments were deferred, employees would not receive their twenty-six paid personal holidays during the agreement, and a special December holiday would not be paid. The UAW also broke with tradition and modified its long-time opposition to profit sharing, opposition that had been based on the principle that employee compensation should be certain (Joint UAW-Ford Summary . . ." 1982).

The February 1982 agreement with Ford established the industry model that would eventually apply to GM, Ford, and, in 1996, Chrysler. Employees would obtain enhanced levels of job security and the company would receive relief on monetary compensation to employees. Although it would evolve over the next decade through the principle of incrementalism, the basic bargain had been struck.

A month later, consistent with pattern bargaining, a similar but not identical agreement was struck with General Motors. The major difference between the two agreements was that GM agreed to rescind four plant closings that had been announced and agreed to an experimental "Lifetime Job Security Program" at four plants. The plan used attrition and alternative assignments both within and outside GM to provide job security to 80% of the facilities' workforce ("General Motors and Auto Workers . . ." 1982; "UAW Council . . ." 1982; "UAW Summary . . ." 1982).

The pattern was not extended to Chrysler. In order for Chrysler to obtain loan guarantees from the U.S. government in 1979, the UAW was required to make wage concessions (Pine 1979; Pine and Brown 1979; Block 2001). In 1983, the UAW and Chrysler agreed on a contract that restored wage parity with Ford and GM. Reflecting the continuing precariousness of Chrysler's financial condition, no job security provisions were incorporated in the Chrysler agreement, and the agreement expired in 1985, one year after the Ford and GM agreements, thereby giving Chrysler a twelve-month advantage vis-à-vis the pattern applied to Ford and GM ("New Agreements . . ." 1983).

In the 1984 negotiations, the UAW, Ford, and GM agreed on enhanced job security with identical programs at the two companies: the Protected Employee Program (PEP) at Ford and the Job Opportunity Bank-Security Program (JOBS) at GM. PEP and JOBS provided job security for employees with at least one year of seniority in the event of technological change, outsourcing, productivity improvements, transfer of operations, and production consolidations. A decline in employment due to volume declines would be addressed through Supplemental Unemployment Benefits (SUB) (*Agreement between General Motors Corporation and the UAW* 1984 [hereafter cited as *Agreement-GM*]; *Agreements between Ford Motor Company and the UAW* 1984 [hereafter cited as *Agreements-Ford*]).

In addition, the parties for the first time agreed upon a dedicated maximum financial commitment. Ford promised $280 million over the life of the agreement and GM promised $1 billion (*Agreement-GM* 1984; *Agreements-Ford* 1984). This had the effect of institutionalizing the program while minimizing financial uncertainty for the companies and converting a component of

**TABLE 8.8**

### Estimated Cost of Job Security Provisions Negotiated in Collective Agreements between UAW and GM, UAW and Ford, and UAW and Chrysler, 1984–96

|  | 1984 | 1987 | 1990 | 1993 | 1996 |
|---|---|---|---|---|---|
| **Estimated Covered Employment** | | | | | |
| GM | 347,500 | 312,500 | 295,000 | 260,000 | 243,000 |
| Ford | 107,000 | 100,000 | 100,000 | 97,667 | 105,025 |
| Chrysler | | | | | 66,000 |
| **Maximum Job Security Commitment (in millions)** | | | | | |
| GM | $1,000 | $1,300 | $1,700 | $1,700 | $1,700 |
| Ford | $280 | $500 | $586 | $586 | $586 |
| Chrysler | | | | | $280 |
| **Estimated Hourly Job Security Cost** | | | | | |
| GM | $0.461 | $0.667 | $0.924 | $1.048 | $1.121 |
| Ford | $0.419 | $0.801 | $0.939 | $0.962 | $0.894 |
| DCX/Chrysler | | | | | $0.680 |
| **Median Negotiated Base Wage, Ford-UAW Agreement** | | | | | |
| | $11.94 | $14.33 | $15.97 | $18.20 | $21.50 |
| **Estimated Hourly Job Security Cost as a Percentage of Median Negotiated Base Wage** | | | | | |
| GM | 3.86% | 4.65% | 5.78% | 5.76% | 5.21% |
| Ford | 3.51% | 5.59% | 5.88% | 5.28% | 4.16% |
| Chrysler | | | | | 3.16% |

SOURCES: News Reports; Agreements between UAW and Ford Motor Company, 1984–96.

**TABLE 8.9**

### Percentage Change in Average Hourly and Average Weekly Earnings in Motor Vehicles and Equipment, Michigan, Selected Years, 1977–2000

|  | Mean % Change Average Hourly Earnings | Mean % Change Average Weekly Earnings |
|---|---|---|
| 1977–84 | 8.3% | 8.8% |
| 1977–79 | 9.4% | 7.8% |
| 1980–84 | 7.7% | 9.4% |
| 1985–2000 | 3.8% | 4.0% |
| 1985–92 | 3.3% | 2.4% |
| 1993–2000 | 4.4% | 5.7% |

SOURCE: U.S. Department of Labor, Bureau of Labor Statistics.

discussions regarding the program into traditional negotiations over labor costs.

The 1987 agreements converted these security promises into numbers. These agreements established Guaranteed Employment Numbers (GEN) at Ford and Secured Employment Levels (SEL) at GM. The initial GEN/SEL for a unit (generally a plant) was the number of active employees with at least one year of seniority in the unit on the date the agreement was signed. The GEN/SEL was to be reduced by one position for every two employees who left the company because of normal attrition (resignation, death, or retirement). This permitted employees to be shifted to jobs from the PEP and JOBS programs. The agreements also prohibited plant closings. The financial commitment was increased to $500 million for Ford and $1.3 billion for GM (*Agreements-Ford* 1987; *1987 National Agreement-General Motors* 1987; *UAW-Ford Report* 1987; "UAW-GM Pact . . ." 1987; "Excerpts . . ." 1987).

The sales volume exception in the agreements was addressed in 1990. The agreement limited layoffs for volume reasons to thirty-six weeks over the life of the agreement, with the employee either being recalled or shifted to the JOBS Bank/PEP, and off the SUB fund, if no job was available. Maximum funding was increased to $586 million at Ford and $1.7 billion at GM (*National Agreement-General Motors* 1990; *Agreements-Ford* 1990; "General Motors, UAW . . ." 1990; "UAW-Provided . . ." 1990; "UAW, Ford . . ." 1990).

By 1993, the system architecture for GM and Ford was basically complete and no major changes were made from 1990. The funding maximum remained at $586 million in the Ford-UAW agreement and $1.7 billion in the GM-UAW agreement (*Agreements-Ford* 1993; *UAW-GM Report* 1993).

The UAW then turned its attention to Chrysler, the smallest of the Big Three. After discussing the issue in 1993, the 1996 UAW-Chrysler agreement included a Memorandum of Understanding on the Employment Security System (ESS) program, which essentially mirrored the programs in the Ford-UAW and GM-UAW agreements. Base Employment Levels (BEL), determined by a "snapshot" of employment on the effective date of the agreement, would generally be guaranteed, with attrition replacement at one for two if employment in the unit was between 95% and 105% of BEL, no replacement if unit employment was 105% or more of BEL, and one-for-one replacement at 95% of BEL. The program was funded at a maximum of $280 million for 1996 ("Letters, Memoranda . . ." 1996 . . . ; *Agreements-GM* 1996).

Outside of the 95% "floor," there were no major changes negotiated in the programs at GM and Ford in 1996. Funding levels over the life of the agreements remained stable; $1.7 billion at GM and $586 million at Ford (*Agreement-GM* 1996).

Further adjustments were made in the 1999 agreements.[14] The major change was the creation of benchmark employment (SEL at GM, GEN at Ford, BEL at DaimlerChrysler[15]) minimums that would be reduced by .333% each quarter so that at the end of the agreement, benchmark levels in the agreements would be at 95% of benchmark levels at the commencement of the agreements. Funding levels over the life of the agreement were increased to $2.107 billion at GM, $944 million at Ford, and $451 million at DaimlerChrysler (*Agreement-GM* 1999; *Agreements-Ford* 1999; "Letters, Memoranda . . ." 1999).

What was the cost of these provisions? An upper-bound estimate of these costs (on the dates that the 1984–96 contracts were signed) can be obtained by examining table 8.8. These estimates assume a workweek of 2,080 hours; inclusion of overtime would reduce the hourly job security cost. They also assume that the company will spend to the maximum. To the extent employees would have otherwise remained employed, actual expenditures are likely to be less than maximum expenditures. In that sense, the estimated hourly cost is truly an upper bound, and is likely to be lower than that in the table.[16]

Examining the table, the estimates suggest that, at an absolute maximum, the job security provisions added 5.88% annually to the hourly wages actually paid by the companies. When one realizes that this is truly an upper bound, and that the actual percentage on the true hourly wage received by the employee is likely to be less, it appears that the job security system created by the parties was able to provide job security at a fairly reasonable cost to the companies.

Wage moderation appears to have been associated with job security. As can be seen in table 8.9, nominal wage increases in the pre-job security period, 1977–84, were roughly twice those of the post-job security period, 1985–2000.[17]

*The Case of Flint.* While Michigan has managed to weather the auto industry changes, this has not been the case for the Flint metropolitan area. Table 8.10 presents a picture of the disproportionate share of the employment adjustment that Flint has borne. In the early 1980s, approximately 15% of Michigan's transportation equipment employ-

**TABLE 8.10**

**Transportation Equipment Employment in Michigan, Michigan Excluding Flint MSA, and Flint MSA, 1980–2001 (in thousands)**

|  | Michigan Statewide | Flint MSA | MI, Outside Flint MSA | % in Flint MSA |
|---|---|---|---|---|
| 1980 | 340.2 | 49.8 | 290.4 | 14.6% |
| 1981 | 334.9 | 52.4 | 282.5 | 15.6% |
| 1982 | 302.7 | 45.3 | 257.4 | 15.0% |
| 1983 | 317.5 | 47.6 | 269.9 | 15.0% |
| 1984 | 343.7 | 50.8 | 292.9 | 14.8% |
| 1985 | 361.3 | 49.4 | 311.9 | 13.7% |
| 1986 | 359.7 | 49.8 | 309.9 | 13.8% |
| 1987 | 337.6 | 41.5 | 296.1 | 12.3% |
| 1988 | 314.4 | 34.1 | 280.3 | 10.8% |
| 1989 | 307.1 | 35.9 | 271.2 | 11.7% |
| 1990 | 295.0 | 34.9 | 260.1 | 11.8% |
| 1991 | 281.6 | 32.6 | 249.0 | 11.6% |
| 1992 | 286.0 | 31.6 | 254.4 | 11.0% |
| 1993 | 278.4 | 30.3 | 248.1 | 10.9% |
| 1994 | 289.0 | 32.1 | 256.9 | 11.1% |
| 1995 | 298.6 | 32.7 | 265.9 | 11.0% |
| 1996 | 294.9 | 29.8 | 265.1 | 10.1% |
| 1997 | 289.2 | 26.8 | 262.4 | 9.3% |
| 1998 | 287.7 | 23.7 | 264.0 | 8.2% |
| 1999 | 299.7 | 21.3 | 278.4 | 7.1% |
| 2000 | 304.8 | 17.1 | 287.7 | 5.6% |
| 2001 | 285.4 | 15.9 | 269.5 | 5.6% |

**Absolute Change, 1980–2001**

|  | −54.8 | −33.9 | −20.9 |  |
|---|---|---|---|---|

**Percent Change, 1980–2001**

|  | −16.1% | −68.1% | −7.2% |  |
|---|---|---|---|---|

SOURCE: U.S. Department of Labor, Bureau of Labor Statistics.

ment was in the Flint area. By 2001, that percentage had dropped by almost two-thirds, to only 5.6% of Michigan's transportation equipment employment. Between 1980 and 2001, TE employment in Michigan declined by approximately 54,800, from 340,200 to 285,400. Of these 54,800 employees, 33,900 were in the Flint area. While during this twenty-year period Flint never accounted for more than 15.6% of TE employment in Michigan, Flint accounted for 61.9% of the decline in Transportation Equipment employment during this period.[18] During this period, auto employment declined by 16.1% statewide, by 68.1% in the Flint area, but by only 7.2% in Michigan outside the Flint area.[19]

FIGURE 8.2

**Transportation Equipment Employment, Michigan Statewide and Michigan Excluding Flint MSA, 1958–2001 (in thousands)**

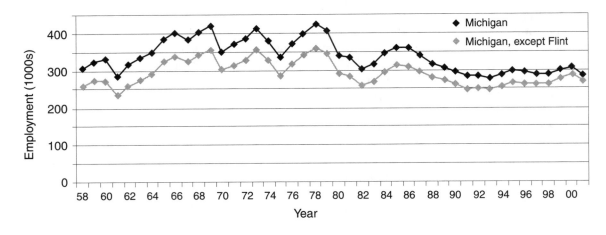

The change in Flint's situation during the last two decades is supported by a trend analysis, taking into account the preceding forty-four year period. This is depicted graphically in figures 8.2 and 8.3. Figure 8.2 graphs the level of TE employment in Michigan, statewide, and Michigan, excluding Flint, for the period 1958 to 2001. Figure 8.3 graphs the level of TE employment in the Flint MSA from 1958 to 2001. Observation of the data that underlay the figures indicates a break point in the early 1980s. The slope coefficients of the 1958–79 trend lines for Michigan statewide, Michigan excluding Flint, and Flint are .112, .129, and .356, respectively, suggesting that, for this period, TE employment in Flint increased roughly three times faster than overall TE employment in Michigan.

For the period 1980–2001, the slope coefficients for Michigan statewide, Michigan excluding Flint, and Flint are –0.175, –0.129, and –0.554, respectively. In contrast to the earlier period, TE employment in Flint declined approximately 3.5 to 4 times faster than overall state TE employment.

What contributed to this disproportionate decline in Flint TE employment? Two factors seem to be important. The first is the major reorganization that took place in GM in the early 1980s. The second is the history of conflictual labor relations in Flint.

FIGURE 8.3

**Transportation Equipment Employment, Flint MSA, 1958–2001 (in thousands)**

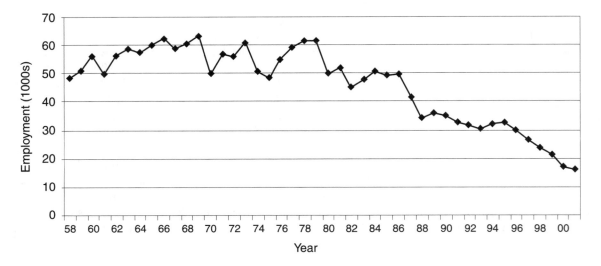

The GM reorganization in the early 1980s shifted design and production decisions from the divisions to the corporate central office. Under the pre-reorganization system, each of the divisions controlled its design and manufacturing facilities, in effect acting as an independent company, with overall corporate oversight. Each division, with corporate oversight, designed its own cars and assigned them to its plants for manufacture. Divisions and plants were linked (Block and Berg, forthcoming).

The reorganization separated the design and plants from the divisions. Design and production would be determined at the corporate level, with the old divisions becoming primarily marketing nameplates, with products assigned by the corporation. Thus, each of the plants was in a type of internal "competition" with all other corporate plants for product allocation from the corporation. Corporate product allocation would, in turn, determine plant survival.

A second major factor in Flint's decline appears to be the history of conflictual labor relations in the city. Some sense of this conflict can be obtained by examining table 8.11. This table is based on GM data on "crisis situations" provided to the author. A crisis situation under the collective agreement occurs when a dispute arises between GM and the union in the relevant unit over an issue in the collective agreement not subject to the grievance and arbitration procedure, for example, production and health and safety issues. At the first level of the dispute, the parties enter the stage of "concerted negotiations." If the concerted negotiations are unable to resolve the dispute, the union issues a "five-day strike letter" informing GM management that it reserves the right to strike within five days if the matter is not resolved.

Table 8.11 presents a summary of the data, comparing Flint and all other GM plants. First, looking at concerted negotiations, the less serious of the two crisis situations, 14.8% of the units in which at least one crisis situation occurred, and 14.8% of the crisis negotiations, occurred in Flint. These negotiations, however, lasted longer in Flint than in other units. While Flint accounted for only 14.8% of the incidents, Flint accounted for 23.7% of the days of concerted negotiations, suggesting that it took more time to resolve the matter in Flint than at other locations. The average Flint concerted negotiation took 42.25 days to resolve, while the average concerted negotiation outside of Flint took 23.7 days to resolve.

**TABLE 8.11**

**General Motors and UAW Crisis Situations, Flint, Outside Flint, and Total, 1984–2000**

|  | GM, Flint | GM, Except Flint | Total | % in Flint |
|---|---|---|---|---|
| **Concerted Negotiations, 1984–2000** | | | | |
| No. of units | 4 | 23 | 27 | 14.8% |
| No. of negotiations | 4 | 23 | 27 | 14.8% |
| No. of days | 169 | 544 | 713 | 23.7% |
| **5-Day Strike Letters, 1984–2000** | | | | |
| No. of units | 11 | 94 | 105 | 10.5% |
| No. of strike letters | 11 | 114 | 125 | 8.8% |
| No. of strike days[a] | 112 | 356 | 468 | 23.9% |

SOURCE: Data provided by General Motors and UAW.
(a) Estimated for "GM, Except Flint"

The situation in Flint is more dramatically demonstrated by the data on the five-day strike letters. The data indicate that while Flint units accounted for only 10.5% of the occurrences and 8.8% of the letters, it is estimated that Flint accounted for almost 24% of the strike days. Flint averaged over 10 strike days per strike letter, while the non-Flint estimate is only 3.1 days per strike letter.

Taking these data together, it is clear that for GM and the UAW, labor disputes were not uncommon occurrences. It is also clear, however, that the disputes in Flint facilities generally lasted longer than those at other GM facilities, and were generally more difficult to resolve in Flint facilities than in other GM facilities. Given the strong GM presence in Flint, and the reorganization of GM, it is necessarily true that employment declines in Flint were the result of GM decisions to allocate product to plants other than those in Flint. It is also reasonable to believe that the labor relations situation in Flint contributed to these GM product allocation decisions.

It is important to realize, however, that the drop in employment in Flint through GM product allocation decisions resulted in retirements or the exercise by Flint GM workers of interplant transfer rights. Flint GM workers have likely experienced disruptions to their family lives as a result of these decisions. New labor force entrants in the Flint area will not have the option of working for GM, as did their parents and grandparents. Other firms and businesses in Flint that depended on Flint GM employees have also been harmed.

## Part 3: Summary and Conclusions

The focus of this chapter was twofold. First, it provided an analysis of manufacturing in Michigan during the last twenty years. Second, because of the importance of the auto industry in Michigan manufacturing, and because the Michigan auto industry is highly unionized, the chapter also provided an overview of collective bargaining and labor relations in Michigan manufacturing in general, and autos in particular. Special attention was paid to the unique situation in Flint.

Manufacturing output in the United States grew more slowly than GDP during the period from 1977 to 2000. Michigan manufacturing, with its concentration of mature manufacturing industries, grew even more slowly than manufacturing nationally. Michigan, however, continues to be a leading manufacturing state. While manufacturing accounted for 16.1% of national GDP in 1999, it accounted for 26.2% of Michigan's gross state product. Measured by the value of shipments, Michigan manufacturing continues to be dominated by durable goods in general, and transportation equipment in particular. Industrial machinery and fabricated metals are the next-largest industries. Food manufacturing is the largest nondurable goods industry.

Manufacturing continues to be an important employer in Michigan. Although absolute and relative employment in manufacturing in Michigan has declined, as has manufacturing employment throughout the United States, at the new millennium manufacturing employed one in five Michigan workers, more than the 13.7% employed in manufacturing nationally. Michigan has done better than other traditional manufacturing states, such as New York and Pennsylvania, in retaining manufacturing jobs. During the last twenty years, the state has moved from sixth to fifth in total employment in manufacturing. As expected, transportation equipment is by far the largest employing industry.

The decline in manufacturing employment has not resulted in reduced earnings in manufacturing. In 1999, manufacturing in Michigan accounted for 33.4% of Michigan wages and salaries but only 20.9% of Michigan employment. As suggested by these percentages, manufacturing jobs in Michigan pay better than do nonmanufacturing jobs. Annual earnings per employee in Michigan manufacturing in 1999 were $63,404, while average annual employee earnings in Michigan overall were $40,731. The bulk of the advantage to manufacturing employees resulted from relatively high hourly pay, although a part of the advantage resulted from manufacturing employees working more hours than other Michigan employees.

Regarding collective bargaining and unionization, Michigan manufacturing continues to be highly unionized relative to manufacturing in the rest of the country. During the period from 1986 to 2000, levels of manufacturing unionization in Michigan were a little less than twice those of the country as a whole.

What has been the effect of collective bargaining in Michigan? This is most easily addressed for the auto industry. Earnings data suggest that Michigan autoworkers covered by collective bargaining agreements are paid more for similar work than their nonunion counterparts in other states.

Collective bargaining in the auto industry during the last two decades has focused on employment security, with the evidence suggesting that the parties have provided employees job security in return for wage moderation. In essence, it appears that the UAW has purchased a type of employment security insurance policy for its members through reduced wage increases. This has likely eased the transition of these workers out of the industry, as this transition has occurred in association with retirement. As such, the cost of industry structural changes has been internalized, and has not been borne by the public. Much of the human burden of transition has been borne by new labor force entrants, who have not had the job opportunities in the industry that were available to earlier generations. On the other hand, because they had not invested their lives in the auto industry-specific human capital, it is likely that new labor force entrants could more easily obtain non-auto jobs than could their older counterparts.

This chapter also has shown that the Flint area has borne a disproportionate share of the burden of employment adjustment in Transportation Equipment relative to the rest of Michigan. The evidence suggests that the early 1980s GM reorganization which centralized production allocation decisions, in combination with higher-than-average labor relations conflict in Flint GM facilities, encouraged GM to allocate production to locations other than Flint.

The job security provisions as well as the necessity of considering the interests of the UAW in production allocation decisions will likely result in Michigan continuing to account for a substantial share of domestic auto industry employment. The job security provisions have made labor costs fixed to a far greater extent in the auto assembly industry than in other industries, and, therefore in Michigan, relative to other states. These fixed costs are likely to encourage the domestic auto companies to produce in areas where they are paying employees in any event, that is, in or near their current facilities, many of which are in Michigan. Thus, we would predict that Michigan plants and Michigan UAW locals will be allocated a substantial share of future production by the domestic automakers.[20] Suppliers will continue to serve this production. Thus, we would not expect to see a substantial decline in auto employment in Michigan over the next decade. We would expect the trend from the 1990s, a very gradual decline with small cyclical variations, to continue.

In conclusion, it is clear that manufacturing continues to be the single most important contributor to the wealth and economic well-being in Michigan. Although the importance of manufacturing has declined over the past twenty years, this sector still dominates the employment and income landscape in Michigan.

■

## BIBLIOGRAPHY

*Agreement between General Motors Corporation and the UAW.* 1984, 1987, 1990, 1993, 1996, 1999. Labor and Industrial Relations Library, Michigan State University, East Lansing, Michigan.

*Agreements between Ford Motor Company and the UAW.* 1984, 1987, 1990, 1993, 1996, 1999. Labor and Industrial Relations Library, Michigan State University, East Lansing, Michigan.

Auto workers agree to divert pay increases at American Motors into investment plan. 1982. *BNA Daily Labor Report* 75 (19 April): A-4.

Auto workers ratify new agreement with Ford; attention shifts to American Motors and GM. 1982. *BNA Daily Labor Report* 40 (1 March): A-5 to A-6.

Block, Richard N. 2001. Collective bargaining, competitiveness, and employment in the United States. *Transfer: European Review of Labour and Research* 4:697–715.

Block, Richard N., and Peter Berg. Forthcoming. Auto assembly: The case of General Motors—Lansing, Michigan, and United Automobile Workers Local 652. In *Collective Bargaining, Competitiveness, and Employment in the United States,* edited by Richard N. Block. Kalamazoo, Mich.: W. E. Upjohn Institute for Employment Research.

Brazer, Harvey E., and Deborah S. Laren, eds. 1982. *Michigan's fiscal and economic structure.* Ann Arbor: University of Michigan Press.

Bureau of the Census, Statistical Research Division. 1980. *1977 Economic Census: Manufacturing: General summary.* Washington, D.C.: GPO.

———. 1986. *1982 Economic Census: Manufacturing: General summary.* Washington, D.C.: GPO.

———. 1991. *1987 Economic Census: Manufacturing: General summary.* Washington, D.C.: GPO.

———. 2001. *1997 Economic Census: Manufacturing: General summary.* Washington, D.C.: GPO. June.

Bureau of the Census, U.S. Department of Commerce. 1981–2000. *1977–1997 Economic Census: Manufacturing, Geographic Area Series, Michigan.* Washington, D.C.: GPO.

Bureau of Labor Statistics, U.S. Department of Labor. undated-a. *Employment hours and earnings from the current employment statistics (national)* at *http://www.bls.gov/ces/home.htm.*

———. undated-b. *Employment hours and earnings from the current employment statistics (state and metro area)* at *http://www.bls.gov/sae/home.htm.*

———. 1988. Union membership in 1987. News Release 88–27. 22 January.

———. 1990. Union membership in 1989. News Release 90–59. 7 February.

———. 1994. Union members in 1993. News Release 94–58. 9 February, at *http://www.bls.gov/schedule/archives/all_nr.htm#UNION2.*

———. 1996. Union members in 1995. News Release 96–41. 9 February, at *http://www.bls.gov/schedule/archives/all_nr.htm#UNION2.*

———. 1998. Union members in 1997. News Release 98–26. 30 January, at *http://www.bls.gov/schedule/archives/all_nr.htm#UNION2.*

———. 2000. Union members in 1999. News Release 00–16. 19 January, at *http://www.bls.gov/schedule/archives/all_nr.htm#UNION2.*

———. 2002. Economic news release: Union members summary. USDL 02–28 (17 January) at *http://www.bls.gov/news.release/union2.nr0.htm.*

Economic Advisers. *Economic Report of the President.* 2002, Washington, D.C.: GPO.

Excerpts from auto workers' summary of proposed settlement with General Motors Corporation. 1987. *BNA's Daily Reporter System* 197 (14 October): D-1 to D-7.

General Motors and auto workers select three plants for lifetime jobs experiment. 1982. *BNA Daily Labor*

*Report* 216 (8 November): A-5 to A-6.

General Motors and auto workers settle on early contract following Ford pattern. 1982. *BNA Daily Labor Report* 55 (23 March): AA-1 to AA2.

General Motors, UAW reach tentative pact that includes job security provisions. 1990. *BNA Daily Labor Report* 181 (18 September): A-3 to A-4.

Hirsch, Barry T., and David A. McPherson. 1993–2000. *Union membership and earnings data book: Compilations from the current population survey,* annual editions, Washington, D.C.: Bureau of National Affairs.

Job security and moderation in wages cited as key topics in 1982 auto talks. 1981. *BNA Daily Labor Report* 181 (18 September): A-1.

Joint UAW-Ford summary of terms of tentative national agreement. 1982. *BNA Daily Labor Report* 31 (16 February): E-1 to E-4.

Katz, Harry C. 1987. *Shifting gears: Changing labor relations in the U.S. automobile industry.* London, U.K., and Cambridge, Mass.: MIT Press.

Katz, Harry C., and John Paul McDuffie. 1994. Collective bargaining in the U.S. auto industry. In *Contemporary collective bargaining in the private sector,* edited by Paula B. Voos, 181–224. Madison, Wis.: Industrial Relations Research Association.

Letters, memoranda and agreements. 1996, 1999. Production, Maintenance and Parts Agreement between Chrysler Corporation and the UAW. Labor and Industrial Relations Library, Michigan State University, East Lansing, Michigan.

New agreements at Chrysler win approval of UAW members.1983. *BNA Daily Labor Report* 179 (14 September): A-8 to A-9.

New BLS survey confirms union membership decline since 1980; union salaries higher. 1985. *BNA Daily Labor Report* 31 (14 February): B-1 to B-5.

Pay concessions, job security breakthroughs highlight historic pact between Ford and UAW. 1982. *BNA Daily Labor Report* 31 (16 February): AA-1 to AA-3.

Pine, Art. 1979. Congress passes compromise bill to aid Chrysler; Congress sends president compromise Chrysler bill; union has to forgo $462 million of raise. *Washington Post,* 21 December, A1.

Pine, Art, and Warren Brown. 1979. Parties move to comply on Chrysler plan. *Washington Post,* 22 December, A9.

UAW Council overwhelmingly clears GM pact; rank and file vote results in two weeks. 1982. *BNA Daily Labor Report* 58 (25 March): AA-1.

UAW, Ford reach agreement on new three-year labor pact. 1990. *BNA Daily Labor Report* 196 (10 October): A-8 to A-9.

UAW-Ford report. 1987. *BNA Daily Labor Report* 183 (23 September): D-1 to D-7.

UAW, GM pact includes wage hike, job security patterned after Ford. 1987. *BNA Daily Labor Report* 196 (13 October): A-8 to A-9.

UAW-GM report. 1993. *BNA Daily Labor Report* 218 (15 November): D-1 to D-6.

UAW members at General Motors approve contract by 80 percent vote. 1990. *BNA Daily Labor Report* 191 (2 October): A-8 to A-10.

UAW members ratify Ford agreement; attention turns to Chrysler bargaining. 1990. *BNA Daily Labor Report* 205 (23 October): A-7 to A-8.

UAW-provided description of tentative accord with General Motors Corporation. 1990. *BNA Daily Labor Report* 182 (19 September): D-1 to D-3.

UAW summary of tentative accord with Chrysler Corporation. 1996. *BNA Daily Labor Report* 195 (8 October): E-12.

UAW summary of tentative accord with Ford Motor Company. 1996. *BNA Daily Labor Report* 184 (23 September): E-1 to E-4.

UAW summary of tentative agreement with General Motors Corporation. 1982. *BNA Daily Labor Report* 58 (25 March): E-1 to E-4.

Union membership decline eases somewhat in 1986 as proportion reaches 17.5 percent. 1987. *BNA Daily Labor Report* 34 (23 February): B-6 to B-10.

Union membership unchanged at 16.1 percent of employment in 1991. 1991. *BNA Daily Labor Report* 28 (11 February): B-1 to B-5.

## NOTES

The authors would like to thank Joanna Catalfio, Jean Gasper, Megan McRill, and Christopher Rice for their invaluable research assistance. They would also like to thank Susanne Ballard for her technical assistance; representatives of General Motors and the United Auto Workers for providing data; and representatives of DaimlerChrysler, Ford Motor Company, and General Motors for providing collective agreements. The views and conclusions expressed in this paper are those of the authors.

1. Dating of recessions may be found at *www.nber .org/cycles.htm.* Information on national unemployment and employment by sector may be found at *www.bls.gov.* Manufacturing employment is from series EEU30000001; data on employment status can be found at *www.bls.gov/cps/cpsaat1.pdf.*
2. Prices are adjusted with the producer price index.
3. State gross product was deflated using the GDP chain type price index, table B-3, Council of

Economic Advisers (2002).

4. For discussion of the automobile industry from the perspective of an earlier time period, see the articles by Mordechai E. Kreinin and Frank P. Stafford in Brazer and Laren (1982).

5. The recent conversion of the SIC system to the North American Industrial Classification System (NAICS) has entailed the redistribution of subindustries within manufacturing and the movement of some industries out of manufacturing. The data on major industries in this chapter are based on the SIC system, and where possible, 1997 data has been reallocated to be consistent with the SIC system.

6. We use the Census of Manufactures data on employment for Major Industries to assure consistency with major industry data in other sections. As the most recent Census is 1997, this may not include all of the robust growth of the late 1990s.

7. The number of jobs and employees track very closely over the period under study; there were relatively few dual job holds in Michigan and particularly in manufacturing. Only 180,000 Michigan employees held more than one job in 1999, and there were only 5,000 dual job holders in manufacturing.

8. A small part of this gain is attributable to a modest increase in weekly hours of work in Michigan manufacturing, from 43.3 to 44.2 hours per week. Data on weekly hours for the Michigan labor force are not available. However, national average weekly hours of work declined from 36.0 to 34.5 between 1977 and 2000 (AVERAGE Weekly Hours Of Production Workers: series EEU00500005).

9. Series Id:____CUUR0000SA0; Not Seasonally Adjusted; Area: U.S. city average Item: All items: Base Period: 1982–84 = 100.

10. For further discussion of unions and the Michigan labor force, see chapter 4 of this volume.

11. The unionized GM Saturn plant is also located in Tennessee, and Ford has a plant in Louisville. Thus, statewide earnings data in MVE and TE in these states are a blend of unionized and nonunion employees.

12. Under pattern bargaining, the UAW would negotiate a pattern-setting collective agreement with a (target) firm and then attempt to apply that same agreement to the other firms. Although there were occasional deviations from the pattern, such as a profit-sharing agreement with AMC in 1961 and wage concessions at Chrysler in 1993, as a rule, terms and conditions of employment were virtually identical for all UAW-represented employees of the auto companies in Michigan (Katz 1987).

13. Another important trend in the industry was the development of new flexible work practices at the plant level, often in negotiations with the local union. See Katz and McDuffie (1994).

14. The 1999 agreements have a four-year duration, expiring in 2003.

15. Chrysler Corporation and Daimler Benz Corporation merged in 1998 to form DaimlerChrysler.

16. Details of the calculation are available from the authors upon request.

17. Increases are presented as changes in nominal wage rates rather than changes in real wage rates because negotiations were carried out in nominal dollars rather than real dollars.

18. The employment decline in the Michigan auto industry over the last two decades, when viewed in the light of the relatively high wage rates in the Michigan auto industry, raises the question of whether the relatively high wage rates in the auto industry, wage rates that could be attributed at least in part to unionization and collective bargaining, were a cause of the employment decline, as would be predicted by conventional economic theory. While the high wage rates may have been a factor encouraging the domestic producers to produce in Mexico, it is not likely that new market entrants, primarily nonunion foreign auto manufacturers, would have located in Michigan in any event. Observations of their location decisions suggest that they generally prefer to locate in rural, less-developed areas where they can be the largest employer and act as monopsonists or, at least, oligopsonists in the labor market. As a result, they are wage setters rather than wage takers in the local labor market.

19. The employment decline in Flint, on a percentage basis, was much greater than the employment decline in cities that are geographically proximate to Flint and contain concentrations of GM facilities. Saginaw-Midland-Bay City, comparable to Flint in terms of concentration of blue-collar workers, experienced only a 29.9% decline in employment from 1980 to 2001 (Bureau of Labor Statistics, undated-b). Lansing experienced a 45.4% decline during the period 1980–2001 (Bureau of Labor Statistics, undated-b). Lansing, however, is not as comparable to Flint as is Saginaw because of a concentration in Lansing of white-collar and engineering employees associated with Oldsmobile. GM transferred these employees to the Detroit area in the mid-1990s.

20. GM's newest auto plant is in Lansing, Michigan. See Block and Berg (forthcoming).

## APPENDIX A

### Major Manufacturing Industries in Michigan, 1977–1997, Number of Manufacturing Establishments, Value of Shipments and Value Added

| SIC | NAICS | Industries[a] | Michigan | | | | | | | United States | | |
|---|---|---|---|---|---|---|---|---|---|---|---|---|
| | | | No. with > 20 Employees | | Value of Shipments[b] | | Value Added[b] | | Change in Value Added | Value Added[b] | | Change in Value Added |
| | | | 1977 | 1997 | 1977 | 1997 | 1977 | 1997 | | 1977 | 1997 | |
| | | Total | 5,380 | 5,753 | $93,757 | $241,901 | $37,566 | $93,810 | 250% | $585 | $1,826 | 312% |
| 20 | 311, 312 | Food mfg. (1997 including beverage and tobacco–NAICS 312) | | | | | | | | | | |
| | | | 337 | 258 | $5,587 | $12,158 | $2,114 | $5,960 | 182% | $60,396 | $220,109 | 264% |
| 22 | 313, 314 | Textile mills (includes 1997 category textile product mills [314]) | | | | | | | | | | |
| | | | 15 | 34 | $196 | $336 | $98 | $139 | 42% | $16,105 | $37,310 | 132% |
| 23 | 315 | Apparel mfg. | 81 | 17 | $1,757 | $220 | $821 | $90 | 11% | $19,671 | $33,780 | 72% |
| 24 | 321 | Lumber & wood products (wood product mfg.–NAICS 321and logging) | | | | | | | | | | |
| | | | 182 | 189 | $684 | $2,215 | $304 | $938 | 209% | $16,223 | $39,659 | 144% |
| 25 | 337 | Furniture and related product mfg. | | | | | | | | | | |
| | | | 132 | 161 | $1,099 | $5,811 | $670 | $3,582 | 434% | $8,922 | $34,839 | 291% |
| 26 | 322 | Paper mfg. | 170 | 143 | $2,026 | $4,878 | $816 | $2,263 | 177% | $22,171 | $70,300 | 217% |
| 27 | 323 | Printing & publishing–1997: Printing and related support activities | | | | | | | | | | |
| | | | 294 | 812 | $1,477 | $6,739 | $960 | $3,215 | 235% | $31,980 | $149,149 | 366% |
| 28 | 325 | Chemical mfg. | 146 | 179 | $3,761 | $11,477 | $1,876 | $5,971 | 218% | $56,721 | $224,685 | 296% |
| 29 | 324 | Petroleum & coal products | 24 | 19 | $1,081 | $1,235 | $185 | $318 | 72% | $16,378 | $37,611 | 130% |
| 30 | 326 | Plastics & rubber products | 317 | 537 | $1,795 | $9,547 | $892 | $4,868 | 446% | $19,740 | $81,349 | 312% |
| 31 | 316 | Leather & allied product mfg. | 14 | 13 | $143 | $656 | $73 | $213 | 191% | $3,719 | $5,408 | 45% |
| 32 | 327 | Stone, clay, and glass products, 1997: Nonmetallic mineral product mfg. | | | | | | | | | | |
| | | | 158 | 177 | $1,443 | $3,821 | $745 | $2,119 | 185% | $19,130 | $49,426 | 158% |
| 33 | 331 | Primary metal mfg. | 329 | 214 | $7,050 | $8,984 | $2,924 | $4,016 | 37% | $37,568 | $68,750 | 83% |
| 34 | 332 | Fabricated metal product mfg. | 1060 | 1272 | $9,373 | $13,725 | $4,557 | $7,817 | 72% | $45,512 | $133,493 | 193% |
| 35 | 333 | Industrial machinery & equipment; 1997: Machinery mfg. (for 1982, category entitled "Machinery except electrical") | | | | | | | | | | |
| | | | 1206 | 1141 | $9,117 | $18,048 | $4,962 | $9,581 | 93% | $67,223 | $137,935 | 105% |
| 36 | 334, 335 | Electronic & other electronic equipment (incl. 1997 computer and electronic product mfg. [334] and electric lighting equipment mfg. [335]) | | | | | | | | | | |
| | | | 201 | 203 | $2,071 | $6,425 | $1,059 | $3,068 | 190% | $50,366 | $251,561 | 400% |
| 37 | 336 | Transportation equipment mfg. | 304 | 689 | $44,094 | $108,942 | $13,924 | $39,045 | 180% | $64,291 | $227,511 | 254% |
| 38 | Misc. Combo | Instruments & related products | 96 | 152 | $542 | $2,106 | $333 | $1,249 | 276% | $18,762 | $88,898 | 374% |
| 39 | 339 | Miscellaneous mfg. | 89 | 111 | $463 | $1,495 | $255 | $863 | 239% | $10,291 | $30,839 | 200% |

SOURCE: Census of Manufactures: 1977 and 1997.
(a) All 3-digit mfg. less those with fewer than 10,000 employees.
(b) In millions.

## Employment in Michigan Manufacturing, 1977–1997 (in thousands)

| | | | | | | Production Employment | | | |
| | | Michigan | | United States | | Michigan | | United States | |
| SIC | Industries | 1977 | 1997 | 1977 | 1997 | 1977 | 1997 | 1977 | 1997 |
|---|---|---|---|---|---|---|---|---|---|
| 20 | Food mfg. | 46.2 | 38.6 | 1,580.6 | 1,642.7 | 32.5 | 28.2 | 1,122.4 | 1,210.6 |
| 22 | Textile Mills | 2.6 | 3.1 | 875.7 | 627.3 | 2.0 | 2.5 | 764.6 | 627.3 |
| 23 | Apparel and other textile products | 25.5 | 1.6 | 1,334.3 | 711.0 | 21.9 | 1.3 | 1,156.6 | 710.8 |
| 24 | Lumber and wood products | 15.0 | 15.7 | 692.4 | 653.2 | 12.4 | 11.1[a] | 594.8 | 592.3 |
| 25 | Furniture and fixtures | 21.7 | 33.5 | 463.8 | 603.7 | 16.4 | 24.4 | 383.6 | 484.6 |
| 26 | Paper and allied products | 23.1 | 19.7 | 628.7 | 574.3 | 17.5 | 14.8 | 486.3 | 440.1 |
| 27 | Printing and publishing | 33.4 | 46.7 | 1,092.2 | 1,573.1 | 19.6 | NA | 625.8 | 607.6 |
| 28 | Chemical and allied products | 33.9 | 33.2 | 880.2 | 882.6 | 20.8 | 17.9 | 543.8 | 512.2 |
| 29 | Petroleum and coal products | 2.2 | 1.8 | 146.8 | 107.6 | 1.4 | 1.0 | 101.1 | 71.6 |
| 30 | Rubber and misc. plastics products | 35.6 | 67.7 | 721.3 | 1,023.1 | 27.8 | 52.3 | 563.7 | 805.7 |
| 31 | Leather and leather products | 2.9 | 3.1 | 242.5 | 85.1 | 2.6 | 2.7 | 211.5 | 68.7 |
| 32 | Stone, clay, and glass products | 20.1 | 18.0 | 613.7 | 501.5 | 15.2 | 13.2 | 484.4 | 388.9 |
| 33 | Primary metal industries | 83.0 | 37.7 | 1,113.6 | 605.1 | 67.5 | 29.7 | 885.3 | 479.6 |
| 34 | Fabricated metal products | 142.6 | 104.4 | 1,555.7 | 1,763.8 | 116.1 | 79.7 | 1,191.6 | 1,327.1 |
| 35 | Machinery, except electrical | 145.9 | 106.4 | 2,083.3 | 1,420.5 | 105.0 | 71.6 | 1,413.8 | 936.0 |
| 36 | Electric and electronic equipment | 33.9 | 39.7 | 1,723.1 | 2,284.9 | 26.4 | 22.8 | 1,191.4 | 1,309.3 |
| 37 | Transportation equipment | 321.2 | 268.0 | 1,768.2 | 1,842.3 | 268.2 | 223.5 | 1,284.4 | 1,340.7 |
| 38 | Instruments and related products | 11.6 | 13.6 | 559.1 | 250.4 | 7.9 | 7.3 | 347.2 | 185.3 |
| 39 | Miscellaneous mfg. industries | 10.8 | 10.8 | 440.7 | 475.0 | 8.1 | 8.4 | 338.7 | 307.3 |

SOURCE: Census of Manufactures: 1977 and 1997.
(a) Plus logging.

## APPENDIX C

### Earnings and Hours of Work for Major Michigan Manufacturing Industries, 1977–1999, Using NAICS Classification Titles with [NAICS] SIC Groupings

| Year | Mfg. Average Hourly Wages | Food Mfg. + Beverage & Tobacco Products [311, 312] 20 | Furniture & Fixtures [337] 25 | Paper & Allied Products [322] 26 | Printing & Related Activities [323] 27 | Chemical Mfg. [325] 28 | Plastics & Rubber Products Mfg. [326] 30 | Nonmetallic Mineral Prod. Mfg. [327] 32 | Primary Metal Mfg. [331] 33 | Fabricated Metal Product Mfg. [332] 34 | Machinery Mfg. [333] 35 | Computer & Electronic Products + Electrical Equipment, Appliance | Transportation Equipment [336] 37 | Misc. [Instruments & Related Products+ Others] [MISC] Misc. |
|---|---|---|---|---|---|---|---|---|---|---|---|---|---|---|
| **Average Hourly Earnings** | | | | | | | | | | | | | | |
| 1977 | $7.54 | $6.29 | $5.45 | $6.25 | $6.56 | $7.29 | | | $8.15 | $7.58 | $7.41 | $6.63 | $8.44 | |
| 1987 | $12.97 | $10.77 | $10.14 | $12.45 | $10.42 | $12.91 | | 12.08 | $12.95 | $12.83 | $13.10 | $11.29 | $15.17 | $9.22 |
| 1997 | $17.18 | $13.79 | $12.78 | $15.55 | $13.26 | $17.69 | $11.03 | $15.00 | $16.47 | $16.70 | $16.60 | $14.15 | $22.08 | $12.68 |
| 1999 | $18.38 | $14.55 | $13.31 | $16.44 | $13.73 | $19.39 | $11.52 | $15.88 | $17.46 | $17.36 | $17.57 | $15.01 | $24.32 | $13.65 |
| **Average Weekly Earnings** | | | | | | | | | | | | | | |
| 1977 | $326.27 | $263.38 | $222.20 | $282.90 | $248.78 | $309.61 | | | $357.01 | $324.34 | $319.50 | $284.96 | $378.11 | |
| 1987 | $547.33 | $436.18 | $394.45 | $556.51 | $397.00 | $539.64 | | $540.29 | $556.85 | $536.29 | $565.92 | $468.53 | $650.79 | $380.79 |
| 1997 | $757.64 | $525.40 | $545.71 | $693.53 | $503.88 | $765.98 | $446.72 | $673.74 | $757.62 | $736.47 | $751.98 | $628.26 | $1,031.14 | $526.22 |
| 1999 | $812.40 | $646.02 | $561.68 | $733.22 | $535.47 | $814.38 | $470.02 | $741.60 | $789.19 | $755.16 | $781.87 | $654.44 | $1,130.88 | $569.21 |
| **Average Hours Per Week** | | | | | | | | | | | | | | |
| 1977 | 43.3 | 41.90 | 40.80 | 45.30 | 37.90 | 42.50 | | | 43.80 | 43.80 | 43.10 | 43.00 | 44.80 | |
| 1987 | 42.2 | 40.50 | 38.90 | 44.70 | 38.10 | 41.80 | | 44.80 | 43.00 | 43.00 | 43.20 | 41.50 | 42.90 | 41.30 |
| 1997 | 44.1 | 38.10 | 42.70 | 44.60 | 38.00 | 43.30 | 40.50 | 45.40 | 46.00 | 46.00 | 45.30 | 44.40 | 46.70 | 41.50 |
| 1999 | 44.2 | 44.40 | 42.20 | 44.60 | 39.00 | 42.00 | 40.80 | 46.70 | 45.20 | 45.20 | 44.50 | 43.60 | 46.50 | 41.70 |

SOURCE: Data on Earnings and Hours from U.S. Department of Labor, Bureau of Labor Statistics, State and Area Employment, Hours and Earnings: *www.bls.gov*

**APPENDIX D**

## Motor Vehicle and Equipment (MVE) Employment, 1980–2001, Michigan and the United States (in thousands)

| Year | United States | Michigan | Percentage of U.S. MVE Employment in Michigan |
|---|---|---|---|
| 1980 | 788.8 | 326.3 | 41.4% |
| 1981 | 788.7 | 319.4 | 40.5% |
| 1982 | 699.3 | 286.5 | 41.0% |
| 1983 | 753.6 | 299.7 | 39.8% |
| 1984 | 861.5 | 324.7 | 37.7% |
| 1985 | 883.1 | 341.1 | 38.6% |
| 1986 | 871.8 | 338.5 | 38.8% |
| 1987 | 865.9 | 316.5 | 36.6% |
| 1988 | 856.4 | 294.7 | 34.4% |
| 1989 | 858.5 | 289.5 | 33.7% |
| 1990 | 812.1 | 278.7 | 34.3% |
| 1991 | 788.8 | 266.7 | 33.8% |
| 1992 | 812.5 | 272.4 | 33.5% |
| 1993 | 836.6 | 266.1 | 31.8% |
| 1994 | 909.3 | 278.3 | 30.6% |
| 1995 | 970.9 | 287.8 | 29.6% |
| 1996 | 966.8 | 284.2 | 29.4% |
| 1997 | 985.6 | 278.7 | 28.3% |
| 1998 | 995.3 | 276.3 | 27.8% |
| 1999 | 1018.3 | 287.9 | 28.3% |
| 2000 | 1013.0 | 293.0 | 28.9% |
| 2001 | 932.5 | 274.3 | 29.4% |

SOURCE: U.S. Department of Labor, Bureau of Labor Statistics.

# 9

# Health Care
# in Michigan

*John H. Goddeeris*

Health is a critical element of well-being, and the provision of health care is a major activity in any economy. At a national level, health expenditures accounted for about 13% of gross domestic product in 2000 (Levit et al. 2002). In other words, more than one in every eight dollars spent on final goods and services produced in the United States was devoted to health care and related activities. Health and health care are thus very important to Michigan's—or, indeed, any state's—future, both because of the direct impact of health on quality of life and because our ability to deliver high-quality health care at an affordable cost has a significant effect on the attractiveness of the state as a place to live, work, and do business.

Health care looms even larger in the state government budget than it does in the economy as a whole. Spending by the Department of Community Health represented about 23% of total state government spending in Michigan in fiscal year 2002. At $8.5 billion in adjusted gross appropriations, the department represents the state's second-largest major budget area, exceeded only by the School Aid Fund, and larger than the next three—the Family Independence Agency, Higher Education, and Corrections—combined.[1] The large majority of this spending is associated with Medicaid, the state-federal pro-

gram that pays for health care for eligible low-income people.

For the most part, the policy issues surrounding health care in Michigan are the same issues faced by the national government and by all states. While space does not permit an extended discussion of national health policy, it is nonetheless important to place the issues in context, the subject of section 1. Section 2 compares Michigan with the nation and with neighboring states, on a variety of measures of health and health care. In section 3, I discuss in more detail several health policy issues of current and longer-term interest. Section 4 adds some concluding remarks.

To anticipate some of the main themes of this chapter, Michigan is not remarkably different from the typical state in spending on health care, or in broad indicators of population health. Its level of employer-provided health insurance coverage is high, leading to a relatively low uninsured rate. Following an unusual period of moderate increases, however, the last several years have seen quite rapid increases in health care spending nationally and in Michigan, affecting both private and public purchasers. Rising health insurance premiums create concern that employer-provided coverage may erode, particularly if the high economic growth of the late 1990s does not continue. The growth of spending in Medicaid at rates faster than in the economy as a whole is now creating serious budgetary difficulties for Michigan and most other states. These problems will continue for the foreseeable future, barring major changes in federal health policy. The aging of the population will also contribute to rising health spending, though improving health in the older population may mitigate this effect to some degree. Because we place great value on good health, and because growing health spending brings with it real improvements in longevity and quality of life, we should expect to see the share of our resources devoted to health care continue to rise. Finding ways to assure access to appropriate care for its less-fortunate citizens will continue to be a challenge in Michigan and the nation.

## 1. Background: The National Setting

In chapter 1 of his influential 1974 book, *Who Shall Live?*, Victor Fuchs identified three major areas of concern with the nation's health care system: cost, access, and health levels. Nearly three decades later, this succinct list remains remarkably apt. I will use Fuchs's list to organize the discussion of current health care issues, but will broaden and refocus the last concern to include health care delivery and quality.

### A. Cost

Spending on health care has grown much faster than incomes for decades. For example, between 1960 and 1993, real national health expenditures per capita grew from $700 to $3,876 in year 2000 dollars, a total increase of 454%, or an average increase of about 5.3% per year.[2] In contrast, real GDP per capita grew 111% over the same period, about 2.3% per year.

Concern about rising expenditures then subsided for a time, as the economy grew strongly and the growth of health spending slowed. Overall from 1993 to 2000, health expenditures increased a bit more slowly than GDP (2.6% versus 2.9% on an inflation-adjusted, per capita basis), and as a result the share of health care spending in GDP fell slightly. Beginning in about 1998, however, rising health care spending again became a serious concern. After a period of quite modest health insurance premium increases in the mid-1990s, premiums began to increase at a rate faster than general inflation in 1998, and the gap has widened

in the succeeding years (Gabel et al. 2001). Centers for Medicare and Medicaid Services (CMS) researchers estimate that national health expenditures reached 14% of GDP in 2001, and project that they will grow to 16% of GDP by 2007 (Heffler et al. 2002).

Increases in spending on prescription drugs have drawn particular attention. Drug spending accelerated sooner than did the rest of health care and is growing much faster. Adjusting for general inflation, it rose over 9% per year between 1994 and 1997 and more than 15% per year between 1997 and 2000. CMS researchers project that drug spending will continue to grow at double-digit (nominal) rates through 2011. Prescriptions still account for a modest fraction of total health care spending (less than 11% in 2000), and for that reason cannot account for the bulk of the recent growth in total expenditures or insurance premiums. Nonetheless, rising prescription drug costs have been very noticeable to employers and to state governments, and particularly to those citizens who lack drug coverage.

Trends in total spending and in costs of private insurance are mirrored, and to some extent magnified, in Medicaid spending. After rising extremely rapidly in the late 1980s and early 1990s, Medicaid spending plateaued for a time, but then reaccelerated. Medicaid spending is now projected to grow somewhat faster than national health expenditures over the next ten years (Heffler et al. 2002). Most states are increasingly concerned about their ability to support such growth (Kaiser Commission on Medicaid and the Uninsured 2001; Smith 2002).

### B. Access

The significant share of our population without an identified source of insurance coverage (almost 16% of those under age sixty-five in 2000) makes the United States unique among industrialized countries. Although lack of insurance coverage does not imply complete lack of access to care, having public or private insurance coverage generally facilitates access, and the uninsured rate is the most recognized indicator of access difficulties.

Nearly all of those aged sixty-five and over have at least basic health insurance coverage through the federally funded Medicare program. Medicare coverage has significant gaps, most notably the lack of coverage for outpatient prescription drugs and for long-term nursing home care. Health insurance for the under-sixty-five population is largely privately funded. According to U.S. Census Bureau estimates, about 72% of the under-sixty-five population had private health insurance in 2001 (Mills 2002). Of that group, about 92% had coverage linked to their own job or the job of a family member. At the same time, over 11% of the under-sixty-five population had public coverage through Medicaid. Medicaid also plays important roles in supplementing Medicare for low-income elderly, and in paying for long-term care.

The share of the under-sixty-five population without health insurance grew through the late 1980s and most of the 1990s, first through a reduction in employment-based coverage, and then through a decline in the proportion covered by Medicaid. In 1999 and 2000, growth in private coverage was strong enough to reverse the overall trend, not surprisingly in light of the strong performance of the economy and the tightness of labor markets at the time. However, as the economy weakened somewhat and the cost of health insurance increased sharply, the number of uninsured increased again in 2001.

## C. Health Care Delivery and Quality

Another major development in U.S. health care in the late 1980s and 1990s was the dramatic swing toward managed care as the dominant form of health insurance, followed by a degree of backlash beginning in the late 1990s.

Prior to 1985, private health insurers were largely passive with respect to health care delivery. Enrollees were free to see doctors and use hospitals of their choice. Decisions about services were left to enrollees and their doctors. Similarly, Medicare and Medicaid began in the 1960s with the idea of reimbursing providers for the reasonable costs of covered services, avoiding interference with the practice of medicine. As time went on and expenditures grew, however, these programs increasingly regulated the prices that providers received.

Concern with the continued rapid increases in the costs of health insurance eventually led payers to seek a more active role in managing care. By one measure, only about 20% of the privately insured were in managed care in 1985, but over 70% were by 1993 (Glied 2000). Medicare and Medicaid also moved strongly into managed care at about the same time. Among the tools used by

managed-care insurers are networks of "preferred providers" and incentives for enrollees to use them; negotiation of discounted rates from providers; financial incentives for providers to limit prescribed services; and limits on the use of expensive procedures.

In light of these tactics, the growth of managed care generated some predictable responses. Some enrollees began to bristle at restrictions on choice of providers, and at perceived difficulties in gaining access to desired services, fearing that the quality of health care was suffering. Doctors resented interference with their autonomy in practicing medicine—raising concerns about quality—and with the ability of insurers to limit their incomes. Hospitals likewise resented being placed in a take-it-or-leave it position with respect to insurers' offers of payment. Results have included political action at the state and national levels for "patient's bills of rights" and consolidation of hospitals and physician groups into larger entities in order to gain bargaining power. In the marketplace, less restrictive forms of managed care have gained enrollment relative to more restrictive forms.

## D. Looking Ahead

The forces influencing costs, access, and quality are closely intertwined. The movement to managed care in the 1990s probably contributed to the slowing of health spending growth during that period. If so, the pendulum swing back toward less-restrictive insurance is partly responsible for renewed upward pressure on costs. Increases in the cost of health care coverage, like those experienced in the last several years, are already reducing the willingness of employers to offer coverage, and will surely put a strain on the ability of government to provide coverage through public programs and to subsidize care for the uninsured.

In thinking about the longer horizon, it is important to ask what underlies the decades-old trend toward devoting a growing share of our resources to health care. Numerous factors are surely involved, but most experts believe that the most important has been the nature of progress in medicine, which has made it possible to extend and improve the quality of lives in ways not previously possible, but often at very high cost (Newhouse 1993; Aaron 1991). At the same time, health care is a unique sector of the economy in

**TABLE 9.1**

**Mortality Rates, 1997–99**

| | Age-Adjusted Annual Mortality per 100,000 Residents | | Infant Mortality per 1,000 Live Births | |
|---|---|---|---|---|
| | White | Black | White | Black |
| Michigan | 865 | 1,146 | 6.4 | 16.2 |
| U.S. | 858 | 1,142 | 5.9 | 13.8 |
| Illinois | 848 | 1,242 | 6.4 | 17.1 |
| Indiana | 914 | 1,232 | 7.1 | 15.2 |
| Ohio | 909 | 1,160 | 6.9 | 14.4 |
| Wisconsin | 819 | 1,162 | 5.8 | 15.7 |

SOURCES: T. J. Mathews, M. F. MacDorman, and F. Menacker. "Infant Mortality Statistics from the 1999 Period Linked Birth/Infant Death Data Set." *National Vital Statistics Reports* 50(4) Hyattsville, Md.: National Center for Health Statistics, 2002.

the degree to which most consumers are insulated from costs at the point of service use. In light of this, it is reasonable to ask whether the benefits of medical "advances" always justify their costs. In fact, a growing body of research suggests that on balance the benefits of medical progress have exceeded its considerable costs, perhaps by a wide margin (Cutler and McClellan 2001; Murphy and Topel 1999).

This is not to say that resource allocation cannot be improved. We should continue to look for ways to reduce waste, increase productivity, and improve quality in health care, and seek to harness market forces and design public institutions to promote these ends. Yet even if we are very successful, the share of health care in GDP may continue to rise.

Another long-term trend relevant to health care is the aging of the population. Individuals are living longer, and the baby boom generation is now well into middle age. Both factors mean that the share of the population in older age groups is increasing. Because health care spending increases strongly at older ages, one might expect that demographic change would also contribute to higher per capita health care expenditures. Yet the elderly are also getting healthier, so the relationship is not so simple. We will consider this issue in section 3.D.

## 2. Michigan Data in Context

Before moving to a discussion of major health policy issues in Michigan, we review some data on how Michigan compares with other states. Our

comparisons for the most part will be with national averages, and with the other Great Lakes states (Illinois, Indiana, Ohio, and Wisconsin).[3]

## A. Health

While most of the focus of this chapter is on *health care,* we should keep in mind that the primary objective of health care is good *health.* Health is multifaceted, and differences in health across populations and over time are not easily measured or summarized. However, one important indicator of health that is well measured and available at the state level is mortality. Death rates vary a good deal by racial and ethnic groups, so we will look at them separately for the white and black populations. Table 9.1 shows age-adjusted death rates among whites and blacks over the 1997–99 period. Michigan's white and black death rates are quite close to national averages, but its infant mortality rates, also shown in table 9.1, are somewhat high, particularly for blacks. Michigan ranks with three other states as twenty-eighth-lowest in infant mortality among whites, and is ninth-highest in black infant mortality among the forty states with large enough black populations to calculate meaningful rates. Infant mortality rates are generally high, compared with national rates, in the other Great Lakes states as well.

Mortality statistics have been improving for both blacks and whites. Nationally, age-adjusted death rates fell about 15% for whites and 13% for blacks between 1980–82 and 1997–99 (the earlier numbers are not published by state). Infant mortality rates fell about 43% for whites and 35% for blacks nationally, and about 38% and 36% in Michigan.

Differences in health across groups are by no means entirely due to differences in access to and use of health care, as such factors as income and education have important independent effects. In addition, some important influences—for example, smoking, alcohol consumption, physical activity, and nutrition—are at least partly subject to individual control. The best available data for comparisons of such risk factors across states come from the U.S. Centers for Disease Control and Prevention (CDC) Behavioral Risk Factor Surveillance System and Youth Risk Behavior Surveillance System.[4] While these data are based on self-reported information, and sample sizes are not always large enough to make precise estimates, the CDC estimates for 2000 show Michigan at above the national median in percentage of the adult population who smoke cigarettes (24.1% as compared with 23.2%) and in percentage of adults judged to be at risk of health problems due to excess weight (38.7% as compared with 36.7%). The percentage of Michigan high school students who had smoked at least one cigarette in the last month was estimated to be slightly below the national median (34.1% as compared with 34.8%), though still alarmingly high.

## B. Health Care Spending

Centers for Medicare and Medicaid Services (CMS) researchers also track health care spending at the state level (Martin et al. 2002). Table 9.2 summarizes the evidence on health care spending in Michigan as compared with other states. It shows that per capita personal health care spending was $3,759 nationally in 1998, the latest year for which state data are available. Spending in Michigan was estimated to be about 2% lower, probably not a meaningful difference, given the potential sources of error involved in creating these estimates. Spending grew somewhat more slowly in Michigan than nationally in the 1980s, but at about the national rate in the 1990s. For the most part, the level and rate of growth of spending in other Great Lakes states is similar to that of the rest of the country.

Health insurance premiums are another interesting point of comparison. The U.S. Medical Expenditure Panel Survey (MEPS) estimates average premiums for single and family health insurance coverage for employer-provided policies, by state.[5] In 1999 average total premiums (employer plus employee share) were $2,325 for single coverage and $6,058 for families nationally. The Michigan estimates are slightly higher, though not statistically different, at $2,435 and $6,268.[6] Averages for the other Great Lakes states fall between the Michigan and national numbers.

Table 9.3 gives a breakdown of spending into components, using the same CMS data, for 1998 and 1991. It shows some minor differences in the components of spending between Michigan, national averages, and averages of the other Great Lakes states. Perhaps the most striking numbers relate to nursing home care, where Michigan spends relatively little per capita, especially as compared with the other Great Lakes states.

## C. Facilities and Human Resources

Table 9.4 summarizes information about the availability of major health care facilities and the

### TABLE 9.2

**Per Capita Health Spending**

| | Per Capita Spending 1998 | Average Annual Real Growth 1980–90 | Average Annual Real Growth 1991–98 |
|---|---|---|---|
| Michigan | $3,676 | 4.3% | 2.2% |
| U.S. | $3,759 | 5.2% | 2.3% |
| Illinois | $3,801 | 4.4% | 2.1% |
| Indiana | $3,566 | 5.9% | 2.5% |
| Ohio | $3,747 | 5.5% | 2.1% |
| Wisconsin | $3,845 | 4.9% | 3.0% |

SOURCES: 1991 and 1998: Martin et al. (2002). 1980: Martin, Whittle, and Levit. (2001) adjusted for "border-crossing" using Basu (1996).
NOTE: Real growth rates are calculated using the personal consumption expenditure deflator.

### TABLE 9.3

**Per Capita Spending on Health Care and Components**

| | 1998 Michigan | 1998 U.S. | 1998 Other Great Lakes States | 1991 Michigan | 1991 U.S. | 1991 Other Great Lakes States |
|---|---|---|---|---|---|---|
| Total personal health care | $3,676 | $3,759 | $3,750 | $2,643 | $2,685 | $2,672 |
| Hospital care | $1,489 | $1,405 | $1,466 | $1,128 | $1,110 | $1,135 |
| Physicians' services | $973 | $1,095 | $1,027 | $745 | $795 | $749 |
| Home health care | $87 | $108 | $88 | $60 | $64 | $47 |
| Nursing home care | $255 | $325 | $387 | $186 | $227 | $276 |
| Drugs and other nondurables | $498 | $451 | $440 | $278 | $260 | $256 |
| Other | $375 | $374 | $342 | $245 | $230 | $210 |

SOURCES: Martin et al. (2002); Martin, Whittle, and Levit (2001); Basu (1996).

## TABLE 9.4

**Health Care Facilities and Workforce, Relative to Population, 2000**

| | (A) Hospital Beds per 1,000 | (B) Nursing Home per 1,000 65 yrs.+ | (C) Physicians per 1,000 | (D) Registered Nurses per 1,000 |
|---|---|---|---|---|
| Michigan | 2.6 | 42 | 2.6 | 7.9 |
| U.S. | 2.9 | 51 | 2.6 | 7.8 |
| Illinois | 3.0 | 74 | 2.6 | 8.3 |
| Indiana | 3.2 | 75 | 2.0 | 7.9 |
| Ohio | 3.0 | 70 | 2.5 | 8.9 |
| Wisconsin | 2.9 | 66 | 2.3 | 8.9 |

SOURCES AND DEFINITIONS: Table references are to National Center for Health Statistics (2002).
(A) Table 109. Community hospital beds per 1,000 resident population. "Community hospitals" is a broad classification used by the American Hospital Association. It excludes only federal hospitals and long-term hospitals.
(B) Table 111, and U.S. Census Bureau (for resident population).
(C) Table 100. Active nonfederal doctors of medicine or osteopathy per 1,000 civilian population.
(D) U.S. Bureau of Labor Statistics, Occupational Employment Statistics, 2000, *http://www.bls.gov/oes/2000/oessrcst.htm*. Employed registered nurses per 1,000 resident population.

## TABLE 9.5

**Health Insurance among Those under Age 18**

| | | Any Private Insurance | Employment-Based | Medicaid | Uninsured |
|---|---|---|---|---|---|
| **Michigan** | | | | | |
| | 2001 | 77.3% | 74.5% | 20.3% | 8.1% |
| | 2000 | 81.0% | 77.1% | 20.2% | 5.6% |
| | 1998 | 71.5% | 69.4% | 21.9% | 10.7% |
| | 1994 | 72.0% | 67.9% | 26.1% | 8.2% |
| | 1990 | 73.8% | 66.9% | 23.3% | 6.6% |
| **U.S.** | | | | | |
| | 2001 | 68.4% | 63.9% | 22.7% | 11.7% |
| | 2000 | 69.8% | 65.6% | 20.9% | 11.9% |
| | 1998 | 67.5% | 63.3% | 19.8% | 15.4% |
| | 1994 | 65.6% | 60.9% | 22.9% | 14.2% |
| | 1990 | 71.1% | 61.2% | 18.5% | 13.0% |
| **Other Great Lakes States** | | | | | |
| IL | 2001 | 72.8% | 68.6% | 19.3% | 10.3% |
| | 1990 | 72.5% | 63.3% | 20.6% | 9.8% |
| IN | 2001 | 78.3% | 73.3% | 15.3% | 11.2% |
| | 1990 | 73.8% | 65.4% | 15.8% | 12.1% |
| OH | 2001 | 75.1% | 72.1% | 21.2% | 7.5% |
| | 1990 | 77.4% | 70.6% | 16.7% | 9.0% |
| WI | 2001 | 82.8% | 78.3% | 18.5% | 4.2% |
| | 1990 | 83.8% | 77.5% | 12.9% | 5.7% |

SOURCE: U.S. Bureau of Labor Statistics, Health Insurance Coverage, 2001; *http://www.census.gov/hhes/hlthins/historic/* (21 October 2002).
NOTE: Private Insurance, Medicaid, and Uninsured do not sum to 100% because of other government sources of insurance, and because private insurance and Medicaid may both provide coverage at times during the year. Uninsured is an estimate of the percentage without insurance for the entire year.

health care labor force in Michigan. Column (A) shows the number of beds in community hospitals per thousand residents. Michigan is somewhat below average in hospital bed capacity. Bed capacity has been falling nationally for two decades, as health care has shifted increasingly from inpatient to outpatient settings and lengths of inpatient stays have fallen. The beds-to-population ratio fell somewhat faster in Michigan than nationally from 1990 to 2000, 3.5% per year as compared with 2.4% (National Center for Health Statistics 2002, table 109).

Column (B) gives a further indication of relatively low use of nursing home care in Michigan. The number of nursing home beds per thousand residents aged sixty-five and over is well below the national average and especially the average in other Great Lakes states. Use of nursing home care varies a great deal across the country. For example, while Michigan's "resident rate" (total number of nursing home residents per thousand state residents aged eighty-five and older) was 299 in 2000, compared with a national rate of 349, the average rate in the Pacific states was only 241. Nursing home resident rates have also been falling, about 13.7% nationally and 13.3% in Michigan between 1995 and 2000 (National Center for Health Statistics 2002, table 111).

Columns (C) and (D) give information about numbers of doctors and nurses. Michigan's number of active nonfederal physicians (including doctors of osteopathy) per thousand residents is at the national average, while the per capita number of registered nurses employed in nursing is a bit above the national average. On average, the other Great Lakes states are lower in number of doctors and higher in number of nurses.

## D. Insurance Coverage

The most widely used estimates of the number of uninsured come from the U.S. Census Bureau Current Population Survey (CPS). Tables 9.5 and 9.6 summarize recent findings from the CPS concerning health insurance status in the under-sixty-five population in Michigan, the United States as a whole, and the other Great Lakes states.

Prior to 1999, the uninsured share of the under-sixty-five population had risen nationally since at least 1987. Tables 9.5 and 9.6 show the trend from 1990 to 2001, separating the under-eighteen and aged–eighteen-to-sixty-four segments of the population. The tables show a substantial fall nationally in uninsured rates between 1998 and 2000, primarily through increases in employer-provided coverage. While some of this fall is real, perhaps half is an artifact of a change in CPS procedures (Nelson and Mills 2001). Private insurance rates then declined in 2001, leading to a higher uninsured rate for the aged–eighteen-to-sixty-four group nationally and for both groups in Michigan. Uninsured rates are lower for the under-eighteen than for the aged–eighteen-to-sixty-four groups, owing to much higher rates of Medicaid coverage among children.

The CPS estimates show a rather sharp rise in the Michigan uninsured rate in 2001, particularly for the under-eighteen group. While one should not read too much into such year-to-year variations (which could be largely due to sampling error), the trend bears watching. Generally, Michigan's uninsured rates have compared favorably with those of other states. They have usually been five to six percentage points below national rates for the under-eighteen population, and about four to five percentage points below national rates for those aged eighteen to sixty-four. Most of the difference can be accounted for by high rates of employer-based coverage in Michigan.[7] Levels of coverage are more similar between Michigan and the other Great Lakes states, all of which have relatively high rates of employer-provided coverage. Among these states, uninsured rates have been lowest in Wisconsin, followed by Michigan. Movements over time in coverage in Michigan and the other Great Lakes states broadly mirror those of the nation as a whole.

As table 9.5 suggests, coverage of low-income children (a particular focus of recent national health policy) is relatively high in Michigan. Other CPS data not shown indicate that the uninsured rate for those eighteen and under in families in Michigan with incomes below 200% of the poverty level averaged 13.8% from 1998 to 2000. The national figure was 21.8%, and the average among the other Great Lakes states was 18.9%.

Data on the structure of the health insurance market are limited, especially data that enable comparisons to be made across states. One difficulty for data collection is that many large firms choose to "self-insure." Rather than paying premiums to an insurance company or health maintenance organization (HMO) to bear the risks of uncertain medical expenses, a self-insured firm bears the risks itself, and typically relies on an insurer only for administrative services. Firms with a large enough employee base

**TABLE 9.6**

### Health Insurance among Those Aged 18–64

| | Any Private Insurance | Employment-Based | Medicaid | Uninsured |
|---|---|---|---|---|
| **Michigan** | | | | |
| 2001 | 79.7% | 75.7% | 6.8% | 13.2% |
| 2000 | 81.4% | 75.4% | 6.5% | 12.2% |
| 1998 | 76.3% | 72.5% | 7.2% | 17.0% |
| 1994 | 77.4% | 71.8% | 9.7% | 14.1% |
| 1990 | 79.8% | 69.7% | 9.9% | 12.0% |
| | | | | |
| **U.S.** | | | | |
| 2001 | 73.7% | 67.4% | 6.7% | 18.5% |
| 2000 | 74.8% | 68.6% | 6.4% | 17.8% |
| 1998 | 72.9% | 66.8% | 6.3% | 19.6% |
| 1994 | 72.8% | 65.9% | 7.9% | 18.4% |
| 1990 | 75.0% | 65.3% | 6.2% | 16.9% |
| | | | | |
| **Other Great Lakes States** | | | | |
| IL 2001 | 77.9% | 71.8% | 4.5% | 16.9% |
| 1990 | 78.5% | 69.6% | 6.7% | 13.2% |
| IN 2001 | 80.8% | 74.8% | 3.0% | 14.6% |
| 1990 | 82.0% | 73.1% | 4.1% | 12.3% |
| OH 2001 | 78.8% | 73.3% | 5.6% | 14.8% |
| 1990 | 80.4% | 71.2% | 5.8% | 12.9% |
| WI 2001 | 83.1% | 75.6% | 6.2% | 10.5% |
| 1990 | 85.4% | 76.0% | 5.6% | 8.8% |

SOURCE: U.S. Bureau of Labor Statistics, Health Insurance Coverage, 2001; *http://www.census.gov/hhes/ hlthins/historic/* (21 October 2002).
NOTE: Private Insurance, Medicaid, and Uninsured do not sum to 100 percent because of other government sources of insurance, and because private insurance and Medicaid may both provide coverage at times during the year. Uninsured is an estimate of the percentage without insurance for the entire year.

can pool risks nearly as well as an insurer, and self-insuring provides some advantages of flexibility and freedom from most state insurance regulation. States have little ability to collect data about self-insured health plans.

A study based on 1993 data from the National Employer Health Insurance Survey (Park 2000) found that 54.4% of employees in Michigan worked for firms that offered at least one fully or partially self-insured health plan. This percentage was higher than the U.S. average of 49.1%, and a little below the unweighted average for the other Great Lakes states, 56.2%. Although no definitive data exist, it is believed that self-insured firms in Michigan rely very heavily on Blue Cross Blue Shield of Michigan for administering their health plans.

Table 9.7 provides some information about the rest of the group health insurance market. Chollet, Kirk, and Chow (2000) gathered data collected by

**TABLE 9.7**

**Commercial, HMO, and Blue Cross Blue Shield Shares of Group Health Insurance Market**

|      |             | Commercial | HMO | BCBS |
|------|-------------|------------|-----|------|
| 1997 | Michigan    | 8%         | 30% | 61%  |
|      | U.S. median | 21%        | 40% | 36%  |
| 2001 | Michigan    | 8%         | 33% | 59%  |

SOURCES: 1997: Chollet, Kirk, and Chow (2000); 2001: Michigan Office of Financial and Insurance Services, from FIS 0322 form, lines 15–18 and HMOs reporting on line 21.
NOTE: Market shares are measured by premium volume.

state insurance commissioners to compare health insurance markets in 1997. They divided health insurers into three types: commercial insurers, (non–Blue Cross) HMOs, and Blue Cross Blue Shield plans (including HMOs). Chollet, Kirk, and Chow found Michigan's Blue Cross Blue Shield market share to be relatively high, and the shares of the other types, especially commercial insurers, to be relatively low. Blue Cross Blue Shield of Michigan (BCBSM), including its HMO Blue Care Network, had a market share of 61% in the group market, eighth-highest among the states. Updating the Michigan numbers to 2001 using data collected by the Office of Financial and Insurance Services (OFIS) provides a very similar picture.

In the segment of the market where insurance is purchased individually (not shown in the table), market shares in Michigan were found to be very close to national medians in 1997, and 2001 data show little change. BCBSM's share was about 53%, the commercial insurers' share was about 35%, and that of the HMOs was about 11%.

Much attention has recently been focused on the small-group health insurance market, usually defined as groups of fifty or less. Groups of this size are too small for self-insurance to be an attractive option, and they have recently experienced larger increases in insurance premiums than have larger groups (Gabel et al. 2001). BCBSM's share of the small-group market is particularly high. An analysis by the U.S. General Accounting Office (2002) reported BCBSM's share (including Blue Care Network's) as 79.1% in 2000, fourth-highest in the nation. Michigan was one of only five states with BCBS shares above 62%. The Michigan share may be overstated in 2000 due to data problems. However, revised OFIS data for 2001 still shows BCBSM's share in the small-group market to be 72.2%.

While the available data are somewhat sketchy, it appears that Blue Cross Blue Shield plays an unusually large role in Michigan health insurance markets. BCBSM is especially dominant in the small-group market, and in view of its prominent role as a third-party administrator for self-insured plans, it has a very large presence in the large-group market as well.

## E. Medicaid

Medicaid deserves special attention because of its importance in state budgets and in supporting health care for low-income populations.[8] The federal government pays a share of each state's Medicaid costs, varying with per capita income. Michigan's federal match rate was 56.4% in 2002, and the national average was about 57%. The federal government also imposes a variety of restrictions on the structure of state programs. Medicaid eligibility was originally limited mainly to groups that qualified for cash welfare—mostly in the categories of single-parent families, aged, blind, or disabled—but has expanded over the years. Expansions have been targeted especially to pregnant women and children. States are now required to provide Medicaid coverage to all pregnant woman and children under age six in families with incomes up to 133% of the poverty level, and children up to age nineteen with family incomes up to 100% of the poverty level. Like most states, Michigan has expanded eligibility for these groups beyond the required minimums. Current eligibility limits in Michigan are 185% of the poverty level for pregnant women and children under age one, and 150% of the poverty level for other children. In each case, Michigan is grouped with a number of other states at the national median level of eligibility.[9]

Although the link between Medicaid and cash welfare has to some degree been severed, states are still required to provide Medicaid to those who meet the criteria for eligibility for Aid to Families with Dependent Children that were in place in July 1996. In addition, states must extend Medicaid coverage for twelve months to beneficiaries of the current Temporary Assistance for Needy Families (TANF) program whose incomes rise above TANF eligibility levels.

A large majority of Medicaid beneficiaries are children and adults in low-income families. However, because these groups are for the most part relatively healthy, the majority of program expenditures—roughly three-quarters in recent data—go toward other, more costly, beneficiaries. These others may be broadly grouped into three types: low-income disabled individuals, low-income elderly who receive coverage supplemental to Medicare, and institutionalized elderly who have exhausted their own ability to pay for their long-term care. Table 9.8 shows 1998 national numbers for average Medicaid expenditures per enrollee by type. It clearly indicates that blind/disabled and elderly enrollees are much more expensive than children and nondisabled adults.

Some comparative information about Medicaid is provided in table 9.9. The table first shows total Medicaid spending per capita, including administrative spending, for fiscal years 1999 and 2001.[10] Michigan was quite close to the national average in both years. The average of the other Great Lakes states was lower, though their spending also grew more rapidly over the two-year period. Table 9.9 also shows expenditures on a per eligible basis for 1999 (the latest year for which comparative data on enrollments are available), indicating that Michigan's spending per eligible was relatively high.[11] The ratio of the number of Medicaid eligibles to the population in poverty also appears to be relatively high in Michigan. Finally, table 9.9 gives the shares of Medicaid eligibles of different types. The distribution across types looks somewhat different in Michigan from national averages, but the combined share of the two more expensive types is similar, so the medical needs of the "average" Medicaid beneficiary are probably not very different in Michigan and the nation as a whole.

## 3. Selected Policy Issues

### A. The Challenge of Rising Medicaid Costs

Nationally, Medicaid spending grew extremely rapidly in the early 1990s, more than doubling in nominal terms between 1990 and 1995.[12] Some of this extraordinary increase reflected states' use of "special financing" (discussed in the following) to increase federal funding at little cost in terms of their own resources, but much of the growth constituted a real cost to the states. Spending increased because of substantial growth in enrollment through expansions of eligibility for pregnant women and children, but also through significant increases in numbers of costly disabled enrollees. Spending per enrollee also

---

**TABLE 9.8**

**Annual Medicaid Expenditures per Enrollee, by Category, U.S. Average, 1998**

| Children | Adults | Elderly | Blind/Disabled |
|----------|--------|---------|----------------|
| $1,225 | $1,892 | $11,235 | $9,558 |

SOURCE: Urban Institute calculations reported in Bruen and Holahan (2001).
NOTE: Enrollee numbers based on average monthly enrollment.

---

**TABLE 9.9**

**Summary Information about Medicaid**

| | Michigan | U.S. | Other Great Lakes States |
|---|---|---|---|
| Total Spending/Capita, 2001 | $790 | $801 | $725 |
| Total Spending/Capita, 1999 | $688 | $696 | $585 |
| Annual Percent Change in Spending/Capita, 1999–2001 | 7.2% | 7.2% | 11.3% |
| Total Spending/Eligible, 1999 | $5,083 | $4,514 | $4,683 |
| Eligibles/Poverty Pop., 1999 | 1.37 | 1.27 | 1.27 |
| **Shares of Eligibles by Category, 1998** | | | |
| Aged | 7.3% | 10.8% | 9.4% |
| Blind/Disabled | 20.6% | 18.1% | 17.1% |
| Children | 53.4% | 52.6% | 51.8% |
| Nondisabled Adults | 17.2% | 21.5% | 21.7% |

SOURCES: Spending data from information reported on CMS-64 reports. Eligibles data from information reported on HCFA-2082 reports (now replaced by MSIS reports); see *http://www.hcfa.gov/medicaid/mcaidsad.htm*. Poverty population from U.S. Census Bureau, Historical Poverty Statistics.
NOTE: Spending includes administrative expenditures and disproportionate share payments to hospitals. Eligibles are individuals enrolled in Medicaid at least one month of the year. Population is total resident population.

---

increased faster than general inflation, as was generally true in private health insurance plans during this period. As a result, general fund Medicaid spending rose rapidly as a share of total general fund spending in the typical state, growing from 8.1% on average in 1987 to 14.4% in 1995.[13]

In contrast, 1996–99 was a period of relative calm for Medicaid spending. In 1999 Medicaid stood at 14.4% of general fund spending in the average state, as it had in 1995. Several factors contributed to this respite from rapid growth. Health care spending in general was growing only moderately, at rates well below long-term trends. States moved strongly to shift Medicaid beneficiaries to managed care plans paid at fixed rates per enrollee, and believed that they were achieving savings as a result. Enrollment also declined in most states, due to strong economic growth and declining welfare rolls. Nationally, enrollment of disabled beneficiaries continued to grow, but at much slower rates than in the early 1990s.

Michigan's Medicaid enrollment trends have been similar to national ones. According to Department of Community Health data, average monthly enrollment among children and non-aged, nondisabled adults increased 5.4% per year between 1990 and 1993, but then fell by 2.5% per year between 1993 and 2000. Blind or disabled enrollment grew by an average of 10.6% per year between 1990 and 1996, and at the much more modest rate of 1.3% from 1996 to 2000.

More recently, pressures are again building for Medicaid spending to grow at rates faster than the economy—creating budgetary difficulties for nearly all states, with Michigan being no exception. In Michigan, total monthly Medicaid enrollments began to increase in 2001 after six years of decline, probably mostly due to a weakening economy, and continued to increase sharply in 2002. Most of the recent increase in enrollment is among children and nondisabled adults, who will add to expenditure less than proportionately to their numbers. More importantly, however, Medicaid is subject to the same pressures as private-sector health care toward rising health care expenditures per person.

In light of the pressures for higher spending, the U.S. Congressional Budget Office (2002) projects federal Medicaid spending to grow at 8.5% per year on average between 2002 and 2012 (implying Medicaid spending for states will grow at a similar rate). This annual growth rate is more than three percentage points higher than the GDP growth CBO projects over the same period.

*A.1. Changes in special financing.*[14] As mentioned previously, most states have made use of special Medicaid financing arrangements enabling them to receive more federal funds at little cost in their own resources. Michigan is no exception. In simple terms, these arrangements involve payments by the state to medical providers in addition to regular Medicaid payments for services. These payments generate a federal match. In most cases, the providers then return nearly all of the payments to the state through intergovernmental transfers (hence participating providers must be government-owned), so that there is little net impact on the providers' financial situation. The state, however, generates in the process an increase in available revenues by the amount of the federal match.

The primary forms of special financing are Disproportionate Share Payments to Hospitals (DSH), which are payments to hospitals that serve disproportionate numbers of low-income patients, and Upper Payment Limit (UPL) arrangements, which take advantage of the fact that federal Medicaid rules allow for payments for services at rates up to those paid by Medicare, rates that are generally higher than Medicaid normally pays. Altogether, additional federal matching funds generated by special financing arrangements amounted to $785 million in Michigan in 2001.

In recent years the federal government has made changes that limit states' abilities to use DSH and UPL special financing. Anticipating that opportunities for UPL arrangements would diminish in the future, Michigan increased its use of them beginning in 2000, and created a "Medicaid Benefits Trust Fund" for deposit of the funds generated in excess of those committed to other uses. Net deposits were made to the trust fund in 2000 and 2001, bringing the balance to $421 million, but withdrawals exceeding deposits are expected to reduce the balance by $119 million in 2002, according to the State Budget Office.

Under current federal policy, annual federal matching funds generated by special financing arrangements are expected to decline gradually in Michigan from the peak of $785 million in 2001 to about $185 million in 2006. A loss of $600 million in annual revenue is clearly very substantial. In magnitude it represents more than 6% of total state general fund spending and nearly 24% of Department of Community Health general fund spending in 2002. While reductions in special financing are cushioned in the short term by the existence of the Medicaid Benefits Trust Fund, the trust fund is likely to be almost entirely depleted by the end of 2003 (current projections are for a balance of $60 million).

One form of special financing not previously used in Michigan, but used in a number of other states, is commonly referred to as a provider tax. Under such a mechanism, health care providers pay a share of their total revenues to the state. Some or all of these funds can then be used for Medicaid, generating a net increase in federal matching funds flowing into the state. The tax must apply to all of the provider's revenues, not only those derived from Medicaid, so a particular provider deriving a small share of revenue from Medicaid may find that it pays more in tax than it receives in additional funds. Economic theory predicts that a provider tax will act like a sales tax as it applies to non-Medicaid purchasers, and will be borne in part by them.

Provider taxes remain a viable option, within limits. Governor Engler proposed and the legislature enacted provider taxes for nursing homes and HMOs, referred to as Medicaid Quality Assurance Assessments, to begin in 2003.[15] Nursing homes will be required to contribute $2.76 per bed per day, and HMOs must contribute 1.87% of their premium revenue. The funds raised are to go entirely into Medicaid, and are expected to yield in total an additional $123.6 million in federal matching funds in the first year.

*A.2. Responding to the challenge.* Table 9.10 summarizes information about Michigan Medicaid spending over the last decade. Total program spending is reported in CMS-64 reports (formerly HCFA-64), but a better measure of spending on services and administration deducts special financing payments, as in table 9.10. The table also shows the amount of spending in each year that is federally financed, and the remainder that comes from state sources. State Medicaid spending is also shown as a share of general fund-general purpose revenues.

The long-term trend of Medicaid as a share of general fund revenues, in Michigan as in other states, has been decidedly upward. That share was about 8% in 1980, but had risen to about 17% by the early 1990s. Table 9.10 shows that due to a combination of factors, the share was somewhat lower in 1996 than it had been in 1992, but that thereafter it began to rise again. It matched the previous high of over 21% in 2001, when a modest increase in Medicaid spending from state sources was coupled with a decline in general revenue. The share will be even higher in 2002, possibly exceeding 25%, as revenues fall further and spending continues to rise.

In the absence of policy changes at the federal level to ease their plight, Michigan and most other states will find that Medicaid poses difficult choices over the next several years and probably much further into the future. Briefly put, it will not be possible to maintain current Medicaid coverage, with growth in per enrollee expenditures that approximates that in private-sector health care, without seeing Medicaid continue to grow substantially as a share of the general fund budget. State Budget Office revenue projections suggest that general fund revenues will not return to year 2000 levels before 2005 (see also chapter 25), even without adjusting for inflation. Furthermore, as argued previously, medical spending in the private sector will likely continue to increase faster than the economy grows, and Medicaid will see similar pressures. The impending decline in special financing revenues, not yet of significance in 2002, will further compound budgetary difficulties in succeeding years.

There are no magic bullets or politically easy answers. Responses must be some combination

**TABLE 9.10**

**Michigan Medicaid Spending and General Fund Revenue**

| Fiscal Year: | 1992 | 1994 | 1995 | 1996 | 1997 | 1998 | 1999 | 2000 | 2001 | 2002[h] |
|---|---|---|---|---|---|---|---|---|---|---|
| 1. Total spending[a] | $4,001 | $5,232 | $5,378 | $5,479 | $6,138 | $6,218 | $6,799 | $7,486 | $7,922 | $8,273 |
| 2. Special financing payments[b] | 489 | 888 | 898 | 999 | 1,080 | 1,032 | 1,073 | 1,436 | 1,439 | 1,369 |
| 3. Total spending on services and administration[c] | 3,512 | 4,344 | 4,480 | 4,480 | 5,057 | 5,186 | 5,726 | 6,051 | 6,483 | 6,904 |
| 4. Federal[d] | 2,226 | 2,951 | 3,061 | 3,110 | 3,397 | 3,344 | 3,610 | 4,131 | 4,450 | 4,658 |
| 5. State[e] | 1,286 | 1,394 | 1,419 | 1,371 | 1,660 | 1,841 | 2,116 | 1,919 | 2,033 | 2,246 |
| 6. General fund–general purpose revenue[f] | 7,604 | 8,296 | 8,221 | 8,745 | 8,573 | 8,910 | 9,813 | 9,853 | 9,414 | 9,061 |
| 7. State Medicaid as share of GFGP revenue[g] | 16.9% | 16.8% | 17.3% | 15.7% | 19.4% | 20.7% | 21.6% | 19.5% | 21.6% | 24.8% |

(a) SOURCE: Medicaid CMS-64 reports (formerly HCFA-64).
(b) SOURCE: State Budget Office. Includes federal matching funds as well as state payments that generate match.
(c) Line 1 – Line 2.
(d) Total federal payments from Medicaid CMS-64 reports. 1999–2001 subtract deposits to Medicaid Benefits Trust Fund.
(e) Line 3 – Line 4.
(f) Source: State Budget Office, 1992–2001. 2002 is estimated from May 2002 consensus estimate plus expected adjustments.
(g) Line 5 ÷ Line 6.
(h) Estimated. Total and federal spending estimates based on first two quarters; assume last two quarters the same as 2001.

of the following: (1) Increasing state revenues, which probably implies raising taxes as a share of income in the state; (2) Reallocating revenues from other state priorities to Medicaid; (3) Reducing the number of Medicaid beneficiaries; or (4) Reducing the growth of Medicaid expenditures per beneficiary. Response (1) will not be discussed further in this chapter, and response (2) will be discussed (in section 3.B.) only to the extent that reallocations might occur between Medicaid and other health programs. Responses (3) and (4) are constrained somewhat by federal rules for Medicaid participation—certain groups and certain types of services must be covered; optionally covered services, if offered, must for the most part be offered to all covered groups— but the state retains a good deal of discretion.

An important point about limiting eligibility or restraining expenditure per eligible is that it is costly to lose the federal match for any services that will be provided in any case and that can be covered through Medicaid. Because each dollar of Medicaid spending costs less than fifty cents of general fund revenue, it makes little sense to reduce Medicaid coverage of medically needy groups if the same or similar services will be provided in any case, funded largely by state-funded programs or safety net providers, or by the shifting of costs to private-sector health care. Reducing the number of Medicaid beneficiaries through legislative actions (response [3]) is, therefore, for the most part a very unattractive option. Income limits for Michigan Medicaid enrollees are generally above federal minimum requirements, but they are not unusually generous compared with other states.[16] Reducing coverage for certain optionally covered services and increasing enrollee cost-sharing in cases where it is permitted—forms of response (4)—share the drawback of sacrificing federal support for services that may be provided in any case. These strategies also reduce access to care for generally needy individuals and families.

Another strategy for limiting the growth of Medicaid expenditure per enrollee is to limit payment increases to Medicaid providers. The 2002 state budgets included no increases in payment rates, and the 2003 budget includes them only for nursing homes and HMOs, to the extent that they can be funded by the Quality Assurance Assessment.[17] Over the long run, rates need to reflect increases in the costs of efficiently provided services, if Medicaid enrollees are to have access to quality health care.[18] Rates must rise to reflect at least increases in market prices of inputs used in producing services. Productivity increases may sometimes make it possible to maintain quality while rates increase more slowly than input prices, but, as discussed earlier, the more common situation in health care seems to be that technological change alters the nature of services in a way that makes them more costly to provide but also more beneficial.

We should, of course, continue to look for ways to deliver services more efficiently, so that care of equivalent or superior quality can be provided while lessening pressure on costs. This was a major motivation behind Michigan's shift to managed care for most of the Medicaid population, which will be discussed in section 3.C.

## B. Assisting the Low-Income Uninsured

*B.1 MIChild.* Medicaid is the primary channel through which the state helps low-income people get medical care. Federal matching funds are a powerful incentive to rely on Medicaid to the extent possible rather than using state funds only. The Balanced Budget Act of 1997 created another way for the states to leverage federal funds on very favorable terms through the creation of State Children's Health Insurance Programs (SCHIP), which subsidize insurance coverage to uninsured children in families with incomes too high for Medicaid. A state's share of the cost of SCHIP programs is only 70% of its share for Medicaid, so in Michigan it is about 31%. All states have taken advantage of the opportunity to set up such programs.

Michigan's SCHIP program is called MIChild. It was initiated in 1998, and provides insurance coverage to children ineligible for Medicaid but with family incomes less than 200% of the poverty line. The benefit package is based on the health plans of state employees, with some additional benefits. Coverage is provided through the Blue Cross Blue Shield preferred provider network, and through various health maintenance organizations. Eligible families pay a premium of $5 per month, and there are no co-payments or deductibles.

Because of the relatively low cost of covering children and the high federal match rate, MIChild is an attractive program. Enrollment was about twenty-seven thousand in 2002. Potential enrollees found to be eligible for Medicaid must be enrolled in that program, a factor that probably accounts for some of the recent increase in

Medicaid enrollments. Although Michigan compares favorably with national averages in this respect, a significant share of children in families with incomes less than 200% of the poverty line remain uninsured (about 14% on average from 1998 to 2000, and 17% in 2001, by CPS estimates), even though all or nearly all should be eligible for Medicaid or MIChild.

*B.2 County-based programs and the MIFamily proposal.* An important weakness of Medicaid as a source of insurance coverage for the poor is that it does not cover nondisabled adults below age sixty-five without children, regardless of how low their incomes are. The state has encouraged counties to provide assistance to these individuals through county-based programs, and allocated about $80 million of funds generated through Medicaid special financing for this purpose in 2000.[19] The longest-established programs are in Wayne County. The Wayne County PlusCare program offers rather comprehensive benefits to residents aged twenty-one to sixty-four with very low incomes, below $250 per month. Enrollment was about twenty thousand in 2002. Wayne County also runs the Health Choice program, which assists employers of low-wage workers to offer insurance coverage. The program covers one-third of the cost of coverage, and the employer and employee share the other two-thirds. Health Choice covered about twenty thousand enrollees in 2000. The State Medical Program (SMP) provides limited coverage to individuals with incomes below 35% of the poverty line (currently about $260 per month for a single individual) in other parts of the state, serving about fifty-two thousand enrollees in 2002 (including those in PlusCare). A few other counties have, in cooperation with the state, recently developed their own versions of the SMP, sometimes providing coverage to individuals with somewhat higher incomes.

The expansion of county initiatives has slowed as the state's worsening budget situation has reduced the availability of funds (Access to Health Care Coalition 2002). A proposal in early 2002 by Governor Engler to use federal matching funds to expand health coverage to low-income populations was later pulled back due to concerns about potential costs. The proposal, referred to as MIFamily, was a response to a federal demonstration initiative called Health Insurance Flexibility and Accountability (HIFA) (Rosenbaum 2002).

The MIFamily proposal sought to expand coverage primarily to parents of Medicaid-eligible children, and to low-income childless adults. Parents of Medicaid-eligible children with incomes between 50 and 100% of the poverty level would receive what the state described as an "HMO-like benefit," more limited than standard Medicaid. Current Medicaid coverage for these adults extends only to incomes up to 50% of the poverty level. Childless adults with incomes up to 35% of the poverty level would have gotten limited coverage (not including inpatient hospital services). Similar coverage is currently available to this group through county programs or the SMP. The MIFamily proposal anticipated expansion of such coverage to individuals with incomes up to the poverty level, through the expansion of county medical programs.

As discussed previously, cost pressures are likely to be such that maintaining and adequately funding coverage for the current Medicaid population will be very challenging for the foreseeable future. Finding additional state funds to expand coverage for the low-income uninsured seems a very doubtful prospect. The appeal of MIFamily, from the state's perspective, was that it would reallocate state and local funds already being spent, some of which were not being matched with federal dollars, to capture additional federal funds at the enhanced SCHIP matching rate.[20]

*B.3. The safety net.* The low-income uninsured have other sources of access to free or low-cost health care through the health care "safety net" (Lewin and Altman 2000). The safety net has many aspects, including but not limited to federally qualified health centers, federal- and state-funded rural health clinics, school-based health centers, city or county public health departments, public hospitals, and private hospitals and physicians providing uncompensated care (Access to Health Care Coalition 2002). Advocates argue that safety net providers are generally overburdened, and that the highly fragmented nature of the system limits its effectiveness and makes it difficult for intended beneficiaries to understand and use. To the extent that safety net providers rely on state funding, prospects for increases in funding are strongly limited by current budget realities, particularly in competition with programs that generate federal matching funds. One element of the safety net that may receive more support is the set of federally qualified health centers (twenty-six of which were operating at ninety locations in Michigan in 2002), the expansion of which has been a priority of the Bush administration.

## C. Value for Money in Public Health Care

*C.1 Medicaid managed care.* Prior to the 1990s, Medicaid programs were typically a prime example of unmanaged health care. Medicaid coverage nominally brought access to a very broad set of services, with free choice of providers paid on a fee-for-service basis. However, enrollees sometimes had difficulty finding providers willing to serve them at rates that Medicaid would pay, and no entity had a financial incentive to manage an enrollee's care with an eye on both quality and cost. As private-sector health care moved toward managed care in the late 1980s and the 1990s, many states also looked to adapt managed-care principles into their Medicaid programs. Federal government data show the share of Medicaid enrollees in managed care rising from 10% in 1991 to 56% in 1999.

Michigan's initial involvement with Medicaid managed care was primarily with primary care case management. In that model, physicians are paid a small monthly fee per enrollee to serve as primary care doctors and manage referrals to specialty care. They are still paid for services provided, and bear no risk for the costs of an enrollee's total care, hence there are no strong financial incentives to contain costs. In the mid-1990s Michigan began to move strongly toward capitated managed care, under which the insurer accepts full risk for the costs of covered services, in return for a fixed monthly payment per enrollee. In 1997, the state received a waiver allowing it to require that most Medicaid enrollees sign up with managed-care plans. It began this process in five counties of southeastern Michigan in 1997, expanding it to the rest of the state in 1998 and 1999.

Because managed care adds an additional layer of administration not present when the state paid Medicaid providers directly, a key question is whether the incentives it creates add value that more than offsets the additional administrative cost. Ideally, capitation payment creates incentives for participating health plans to reduce waste of resources by, for example, promoting preventive care to eliminate unnecessary hospitalizations. A great deal of research has addressed the issue of resource use, and much of it supports the idea that managed-care plans use fewer resources than fee-for-service insurers to care for comparable populations (Glied 2000). Not enough is known, however, to generalize confidently about the effects of particular forms of managed care in particular settings.

Moreover, a primary concern about capitation, particularly when applied to Medicaid populations, is whether there are adequate incentives to promote quality. Incentives to skimp on quality are stronger when capitation rates are lower. General strategies for promoting quality include (1) incorporating direct rewards for quality in the methods of paying health plans, (2) promoting enrollee choice among plans, and making quality information available to help inform choices, and (3) requiring accreditation by external review organizations. All three approaches are of interest to managed-care purchasers, including state governments and employers, though knowledge of what works best is still rather limited.[21] Michigan is requiring that all Medicaid health plans be accredited or in the process of accreditation by October 2002.

Payment rates to Medicaid managed-care plans have been a subject of some controversy. The initial bidding process in southeast Michigan was designed to keep rates below Medicaid fee-for-service costs for the same populations, and in most cases rates were set at less than 80% of fee-for-service costs (Weissert and Goggin 2002). The situation provoked complaints from the health plans, and from the doctors and hospitals contracting with them. When capitation was extended to the rest of the state, there was no similar attempt to capture immediate savings, given the state's interest in promoting the development of managed-care capacity in some places where little existed. Capitation rates were also increased by 4% in 2000 and 11.7% in 2001.

*C.2. Public mental health care.* In implementing its capitated managed-care plan for most of the Medicaid population, the state "carved out" mental health services separately from the rest of health care, as is frequently done in private managed-care programs and in Medicaid in other states. The state contracts with forty-nine community mental health services programs (CMHSPs) representing counties and groups of counties. Since October 1998 the state has contracted with the CMHSPs on an at-risk basis for mental health, substance abuse, and developmental disability services to the Medicaid population, paying capitated rates based on the number of Medicaid enrollees served. Contracting in this way requires a federal waiver, and the state originally announced a plan that provided for opening the process to competitive bids, as required under federal policy (Tilly, Ullman, and Chesky 2002). In response to objections from CMHSPs and other interested groups, the plan has been amended to give CMHSPs first opportunity to meet contractual requirements. Contract conditions are intended to promote competition and consumer choice in the procurement of services, and quality assurance. Programs must serve areas with at least twenty thousand Medicaid beneficiaries, which will require some consolidation among smaller CMHSPs. If contract conditions cannot be met by an area's existing CMHSP, the process is to be opened to competitive bidding. The federal government has approved the revised process, which is to be implemented in October 2002.

*C.3. Medicaid Pharmaceutical Best Practices Initiative.* Pharmaceutical drug spending has grown especially rapidly over the last several years, and is increasing as a share of national health spending. Medicaid programs have felt the impact of rising drug expenditures quite strongly. One national estimate shows Medicaid drug spending growing at 18.1% per year over the period 1997 to 2000, while Medicaid spending for all medical services was growing at only 7.7% per year (Bruen 2002). While a significant share of the growth of drug spending in Medicaid (and in other insured populations) has been in the number of prescriptions per enrollee, price per prescription has also grown rapidly, particularly as newer, higher-priced drugs are substituted for older ones.

Michigan's Medicaid program has received some national attention for a plan that aims to put pressure on pharmaceutical manufacturers for lower prices, while also increasing prescribing doctors' consciousness of the cost of drugs (Bruen 2002; Caffrey 2001). Under the plan, a committee of physicians and pharmacists selects in each of forty therapeutic classes at least two drugs designated as "best in class," based on "clinical effectiveness, safety, outcomes and cost."[22] Drugs not classified as best in class require prior authorization, but manufacturers of such drugs may offer supplemental rebates to attain best-in-class status. The plan was challenged in court by the Pharmaceutical Research and Manufacturers Association, but in January 2002 the Michigan Court of Appeals overturned a lower court injunction to block implementation. Implementation began in February 2002.

Private health insurance now frequently requires higher consumer cost sharing for high-cost drugs viewed as offering little benefit relative to lower-cost alternatives, as a way of instilling some consciousness of cost. Such an approach is not practical for Medicaid programs, given the low incomes of the populations they serve (and federal regulations). Where consumer incentives are not feasible, the idea of selecting best-in-class drugs by therapeutic class—allowing for exceptions through prior authorization—is particularly appealing in principle. The approach has some similarities to "reference price" systems used in some European countries (Reinhardt 2001). As always, the details of implementation are important. At the margins, potential cost savings must be balanced against the access of enrollees to appropriate care.

## D. Demographic Change and the Elderly

*D.1. Population aging.* Significant population aging—movement of larger shares of residents into older age groups—is expected to occur over the next several decades in the United States, for two primary reasons. One is the aging of the baby boom generation, the product of unusually high birth rates from 1946 to 1964. The other is increasing longevity. Current Census Bureau "middle series" projections see the national population aged sixty-five and over growing by 13% between 2000 and 2010, and then by an additional 58% by 2025 as the baby boomers reach the traditional retirement age.[23] Numbers of those aged eighty-five and over are projected to increase by 33% between 2000 and 2010, and an additional 29% by 2025. Future increases in longevity are difficult to predict, and some believe that Census Bureau projections of such increases are too conservative (Lee and Skinner 1999). Projecting the state population, both in total and by age group, is even more difficult than projecting the national population, because of easier migration in and out of states. Still, it is highly likely that Michigan will experience substantial growth in the sixty-five-and-over and eighty-five-and-over segments of its population, both in absolute numbers and relative to the size of the population at traditional working age (Menchik 2002).

Use of health care increases with age, especially beyond about age fifty.[24] Population aging might therefore be expected to increase health care spending on a per capita basis. Aging may create further difficulties for funding the Medicaid program, in light of the fact that elderly enrollees are so much more expensive than the more numerous children and nonelderly adults.

*D.2. Nursing home care and alternatives.* Individuals aged eighty-five and over are much more likely to reside in nursing homes than are younger individuals. Nationally in 1999, about 18% of individuals aged eighty-five and over were in nursing homes, compared with about 1% of those aged sixty-five to seventy-four, and less than 0.1% of those under sixty-five.[25] In Michigan, Medicaid pays for about 67% of nursing home days, slightly less than the national average of 68% (American Health Care Association 2001).

The effect of population aging and increased longevity on use of nursing home care is not as straightforward as it may appear, however. Within age groups, the rate of nursing home residency has been falling over time nationally since at least 1985.[26] In Michigan, total days of nursing home care and Medicaid-funded days both fell slightly from 1990 to 2000, despite the fact that the population aged eighty-five and over grew by one-third. Nursing home use was not limited solely by the availability of beds, as occupancy rates fell through the 1990s, from 90.5% in 1992 to 86.3% in 2000.[27] One reason that the nursing home population has not grown while the number of elderly has is that health among the elderly has been improving (Lee and Skinner 1999; Cutler 2001). If such improvements continue, this factor will continue to mitigate the effects of rising numbers of the very old on demand for nursing home care.

In order for Medicaid to pay for nursing home care, an individual must meet an asset test, and must "spend down" income toward the cost of the care.[28] Thus future demands for nursing home care financed by Medicaid will depend on the financial status of seniors as well as their health. They will also depend on the availability and costs of alternatives to nursing home care, such as assisted living. Public programs that subsidize community-based services for those who need assistance with daily living may provide another alternative to nursing home care. Michigan currently has two such programs supported by Medicaid funds, the MI Choice Waiver for the Elderly and Disabled, and the Medicaid Home Health Program (Tilly and Kasten 2001; Mickus, Hogan, and Luz 2002). Total spending on these two programs exceeded $250 million in 2000, about one-quarter of the amount Medicaid spent on nursing homes. To be eligible, individuals must meet Medicaid asset and income tests.

Nursing home care is expensive—more than $40,000 per resident per year at Medicaid reimbursement rates. The community-based programs, while also expensive (about $7,000 per enrollee per year in the MI Choice Waiver Program and about $4,000 per enrollee per year in the Home Health Program in 2000), cost much less. It is therefore sensible to support alternatives to nursing home care that are less expensive and may also provide the frail elderly and disabled adults with more choice and a higher quality of life. An important issue with implications for total state spending, however, is the extent to which the availability of home and community-based services draws in additional enrollees, rather than substituting for nursing home care. The state has begun a process of considering long-term care programs in Michigan in a comprehensive and integrated way through the appointment of a Long Term Care Work Group, which issued a report in June 2000.[29]

Even with improvements in the health of the elderly, increases in their numbers (particularly at quite advanced ages), the high costs of long-term care, and the extent to which such care is financed with state tax dollars will all make long-term care an increasingly important area of concern for state health policy.

*D.3. Prescription drugs and the elderly.* Another area of concern for the elderly is the cost of prescription drugs. A number of states have implemented programs to assist the elderly with purchases of prescriptions (National Conference of State Legislatures 2002). In October 2001, Michigan introduced the Elder Prescription Coverage Program (EPIC) to provide pharmaceutical assistance to elderly with incomes below 200% of the poverty line (Tilly, Ullman, and Chesky 2002). The program replaced two previous and (in principle) less generous programs. However, at this writing enrollment in EPIC is closed, except for "emergency" enrollment limited to households with incomes less than 150% of the poverty line. Given current budget realities, full funding of EPIC may depend on additional federal support, or the program's purpose may be served if Congress adds a prescription drug benefit to Medicare.

## E. Blue Cross Blue Shield and Small-Group Insurance Reform

Michigan's Office of Financial and Insurance Services (OFIS) conducted an audit of BCBSM, the results of which were announced in September

2001.[30] The audit highlighted the need to address the possibility of a conversion of the nonprofit BCBSM to for-profit status, a point reiterated by Governor Engler in his 2002 *State of the State* address. Since the national Blue Cross Blue Shield Association agreed to permit such conversions in 1994, sixteen Blue plans around the country have converted to for-profits, and an additional seven conversions are pending. In light of the Blues' very large role in Michigan insurance markets and status as "insurer of last resort" (required to make coverage available to all firms and individuals), the subject of conversion raised a good deal of public concern. This issue appears to have been settled for the time being with the passage of Senate Bill 749 (now Public Act 559 of 2002), which prohibits BCBSM from converting to a for-profit.

The OFIS audit also highlighted problems experienced by the Blues in the small-group market, citing losses in this market of nearly $500 million between 1995 and 2001. The small-business community has also been very concerned about the growth of insurance premiums. Over the past several years, premium increases have been even larger for small firms than for large ones, and have fallen unevenly across firms. These developments have heightened interest in reform in the small-group insurance market.

Health insurance markets are complex entities, with the small-group market a middle ground that interacts with larger groups on one side and individuals on the other (Hall 1999). If premiums are largely unregulated, markets will tend to segregate by level of risk, with the less risky (i.e., the young and healthy) pooling among themselves to obtain the lowest rates possible, leaving the more risky to pay more. Public policy usually seeks to resist this tendency, so that the risks of medical expenses may be pooled broadly, and the sick are not required to pay far more than the healthy.

Michigan is one of only three states that did not engage in small-group insurance market reform in the 1990s. A primary thrust of the reforms adopted by other states was to assure the availability of health insurance to all firms, and to limit the extent to which firms with older and less healthy employees would face higher premiums than others. Such reforms seemed less urgent in Michigan than in many other states, because the dominant insurer, BCBSM, was already required to sell to all businesses, and was not permitted to differentiate rates by the age or health status. The federal Health Insurance Portability and Accountability Act (HIPAA), passed in 1996, requires that any insurer selling to small firms (defined as two to fifty workers) make available any plans that it offers to all potential purchasers. It does not, however, regulate premium increases, or restrict insurers from charging different premiums for the same coverage to different firms.

BCBSM has argued that much of its difficulty in the small-group market stems from the fact that it operates under different rules than its competitors. While it may not take into account age or health status in setting premiums for small groups, other insurers face no such restriction. BCBSM argues that other insurers can attract younger and healthier groups by offering them better rates, leaving it with an increasingly expensive population of enrollees.

While BCBSM's argument is not implausible, I know of no evidence that increased "cherry-picking" by other insurers has had a significant impact on its recent experience in the small-group market. The Blues retain a very substantial market share (72%, as reported in section 2.D.) that is not obviously declining. Furthermore, OFIS data for 2001 indicate that claims paid per member month for major medical insurance in the small-group market were lower for BCBSM than the average for its competitors ($136 vs. $158). While these numbers are unaudited and are not adjusted for any differences in the scope of coverage that may exist, they do not support the claim that other insurers are differentially siphoning off the healthiest groups.

Nonetheless, Michigan may wish to follow most other states in adopting some form of the National Association of Insurance Commissioners (NAIC) small-group rating model (Bluhm 2002). This model would require insurers to adhere to "rate bands," whereby differentials in rates charged by the same insurer to different groups for the same coverage would be limited, as would differentials across groups in annual rate increases. Insurers other than BCBSM would thus have less discretion than they now have to vary premiums across groups; if the same rules were applied to the Blues, they would have more ability to differentiate rates than they now do.

The effects of such a reform on the small-group market are difficult to predict precisely, and surely would depend on the details. If the Blues' rate-setting practices are unchanged but other insurers are required to adhere to rate bands, we should expect some leveling of rates across firms, with older and less healthy groups paying less while the younger and healthier pay more. Given BCBSM's large market share, however, any change that increases its ability to differentiate rates may well increase premium differences across firms, regardless of the reform's effect on other insurers.

What we should *not* expect from reform of the NAIC type is any substantial retarding effect on the growth of average insurance premiums, or any substantial effect on the number of workers covered in the small-group market. If reform does reduce disparities in premiums across firms, it will increase them for some while decreasing them for others. While the less healthy may find that opportunities for coverage are somewhat better, opportunities may be worse for the young and healthy (Hall 1999; Simon 2000a, 2000b).

## 4. Concluding Remarks

A decade ago, the newly elected Clinton administration put health care reform at the top of its domestic policy agenda, vowing to assure coverage for all while reining in soaring health expenditures. The ensuing national debate was sometimes acrimonious, reached no consensus, and sputtered out as the rate of spending growth ebbed. The number of uninsured continued to creep upward through most of the 1990s, but for a time attracted relatively little attention.

Early in the new millennium, however, health care issues are returning to the spotlight. Rapid spending growth has returned, and after a small improvement at the peak of the economic boom, uninsured rates have again risen. With difficult budgetary times upon them, most states are finding that maintaining adequate Medicaid coverage for vulnerable populations is among their most daunting challenges. Soaring insurance premiums also put increasing stress on our employment-based system of coverage for most of the population.

Michigan may take some comfort in the fact that the health policy issues it faces are by no means unique. On most measures its health care system is roughly at national averages, with uninsured rates considerably lower. Furthermore, despite troubling disparities across racial, economic, and geographic lines, population health continues to improve. Still, trends in health care will force difficult policy choices in Michigan, as in other states, both immediately and in the years ahead. In some areas—such as maintaining Medicaid coverage and expanding it to assist

more of the currently uninsured, and helping seniors with the cost of prescription drugs—changes in federal policy may help, but this is by no means assured.

While health care is expensive and becoming more so, we place great value on good health. As we strive to promote individual responsibility for healthy living and to get the most we can get from each health dollar spent—publicly or privately—we should nonetheless recognize that the share of our resources devoted to health may continue to grow. For the most vulnerable and disadvantaged, adequate state support will continue to be needed.

■

## REFERENCES

Aaron, Henry J. 1991. *Serious and unstable condition.* Washington, D.C.: Brookings Institution.

Access to Health Care Coalition. 2002. *Closing the gap: Improving access to health care in Michigan*, April. *http://www.bcbsm.com/blues/sm/pdf/access_rpt_full.pdf.* 30 August 2002.

American Health Care Association. 2001. *Facts and trends, 2001: The nursing facility sourcebook.* Washington D.C.: American Health Care Association.

Basu, Joy. 1996. Border-crossing adjustment and personal health care spending by state. *Health Care Financing Review* 18(fall): 215–36.

Bluhm, William F. 2002. The NAIC Small Group Model and Michigan. Prepared for the Coalition for Health Insurance Market Reform. March. *http://www.chimr.org/pdf/BMIwhitepaper.pdf.* 17 September 2002.

Bruen, Brian K. 2002. States strive to limit Medicaid expenditures for prescribed drugs. Kaiser Commission on Medicaid and the Uninsured. February. *http://www.kff.org/content/2002/20020213/4030.pdf.* 17 September 2002.

Bruen, Brian K., and John Holahan. 2001. Medicaid spending growth remained modest in 1998 but likely headed upward. Issue paper, Kaiser Commission on Medicaid and the Uninsured, publication no. 2230, February.

Caffrey, Andrew. 2001. Michigan is poised to reduce drug costs by setting restrictions on medications list. *Wall Street Journal*, 12 November, B8.

Chollet, Deborah J., Adele M. Kirk, and Marc E. Chow. 2000. *Mapping state health insurance markets: Structure and change in the states' group and indi-*

*vidual health insurance markets, 1995–1997.* Academy for Health Services Research and Health Policy. *http://www.statecoverage.net/mapping.pdf.* 17 September 2002.

Citizens Research Council of Michigan. 2001. State health expenditures in Michigan. CRC Note 2001–04, August. *http://crcmich.org//PUBLICAT/2000s/2001/note0104.pdf.* 17 September 2002.

Cutler, David M. 2001. Declining disability among the elderly. *Health Affairs* 20(6): 11–27.

Cutler, David M., and Mark McClellan. 2001. Is technological change in medicine worth it? *Health Affairs* 20(5): 11–29.

Fairgrieve, Bill. 2000. Medicaid special financing payments and intergovernmental transfers. Michigan House Fiscal Agency, *Fiscal Forum* 6(1).

Gabel, Jon, Larry Levitt, Jeremy Pickreign, Heidi Whitmore, Eric Holve, Diane Rowland, Kelley Dhont, and Samantha Hawkins. 2001. Job-based health insurance in 2001: Inflation hits double digits, managed care retreats. *Health Affairs* 20(5): 180–86.

Glied, Sherry. 2000. Managed care. In *Handbook of health economics, volume 1A,* edited by A. J. Culyer and J. P. Newhouse. Amsterdam: Elsevier.

Gruber, Jonathan. 2000. Medicaid. National Bureau of Economic Research Working Paper 7829.

Hall, Mark A. 1999. An evaluation of health insurance market reforms. February. *http://www.phs.wfubmc.edu/insure/summary.html.* 17 September 2002.

———. 2000. The geography of health insurance regulation. *Health Affairs* 19(2): 173–84.

Heffler, Stephen, Sheila Smith, Greg Won, M. Kent Clemens, Sean Keehan, and Mark Zezza. 2002. Health spending projections for 2001–2011: The latest outlook. *Health Affairs* 21(2): 207–18.

Kaiser Commission on Medicaid and the Uninsured. 2001. The role of Medicaid in state budgets. Policy Brief, October. *http://www.kff.org/content/2001/4024/4024.pdf.* 17 September 2002.

Lee, Ronald, and Jonathan Skinner. 1999. Will aging baby boomers bust the federal budget? Longevity, health status, and medical costs in the next century. *Journal of Economic Perspectives* 13(1): 117–40.

Levit, Katharine, Cynthia Smith, Cathy Cowan, Helen Lazenby, and Anne Martin. 2002. Inflation spurs health spending in 2000. *Health Affairs* 21(1): 172–81.

Lewin, Marion E., and Stuart Altman. 2000. *America's health care safety net: Intact but endangered.* Washington, D.C.: National Academy Press.

Martin, Anne B., Lekha S. Whittle, and Katharine R. Levit. 2001. Trends in state health care expenditures and funding: 1980–1998. *Health Care Financing Review* 22(summer): 111–40.

Martin, Anne, Lekha Whittle, Katharine Levit, Greg Won, and Lindy Hinman. 2002. Health care spending during 1991–1998: A fifty-state review. *Health Affairs* 21(4): 112–26.

Medicare Payment Advisory Commission (MedPAC). 2002. *Report to the Congress: Medicare payment policy,* March. *http://www.medpac.gov/.* 17 September 2002.

Menchik, Paul L. 2002. Demographic change and fiscal stress on states—The case of Michigan. Presented at the 94th Annual Conference of the National Tax Association, March.

Mickus, Maureen A., Andrew J. Hogan, and Clare C. Luz. 2002. Rationing long-term care: Michigan's home- and community-based waiver program. IPPSR White Paper, Michigan State University.

Miller, Robert H., and Harold S. Luft. 1997. Does managed care lead to better or worse quality of care? *Health Affairs* 16(5): 7–25.

Mills, Robert J. 2002. Health insurance coverage: 2001. *Current population reports* (P60–220), September. *http://www.census.gov/prod/2002pubs/p60–220.pdf.* 21 October 2002.

Murphy, Kevin M., and Robert Topel. 1999. The economic value of medical research. Graduate School of Business Administration, University of Chicago.

National Association of State Budget Officers. *State Expenditure Reports,* various years *http://www.nasbo.org/Publications.html* (29 August 2002).

National Center for Health Statistics (NCHS). 2002. *Health, United States, 2002.* Hyattsville, Md. *http://www.cdc.gov/nchs/hus.htm.* 17 September 2002.

National Conference of State Legislatures (NCSL). 2002. State pharmaceutical assistance programs. Updated September. *http://www.ncsl.org/programs/health/drugaid.htm.* 17 September 2002.

National Vital Statistics Reports, 50, no. 4 (30 January 2002).

Nelson, Charles T., and Robert J. Mills. 2001. The March CPS health insurance verification question and its effect on estimates of the uninsured. U.S. Census Bureau, August. *http://www.census.gov/hhes/hlthins/verif.html.* 17 September 2002.

Newhouse, Joseph P. 1993. An iconoclastic view of cost containment. *Health Affairs* 12 (supl.): 152–71.

Park, Christina H. 2000. Prevalence of employer self-insured health benefits: National and state variation. *Medical Care Research and Review* 57(3): 340–60.

Reinhardt, Uwe E. 2001. Perspectives on the pharmaceutical industry. *Health Affairs* 20(3): 136–49.

Rosenbaum, Sara. 2002. Medicaid. *New England Journal*

*of Medicine* 346 (21 February): 635–40.

Schneider, Andy, and David Rousseau. 2002. Upper payment limits: Reality and illusion in Medicaid financing. Kaiser Commission on Medicaid and the Uninsured, February. *http://www.kff.org/content/2002/4043/4043.pdf.* 17 September 2002.

Simon, Kosali I. 2000a. Adverse selection in health insurance markets: Evidence from state small-group health insurance reforms. Working Paper.

———. 2000b. The effect of state insurance regulations on price and availability of health benefits in small firms. Michigan State University Econometrics and Economic Theory Working Paper No. 2001.

Smith, Vernon K. 2002. Making Medicaid better. Prepared for the National Governors Association. *http://www.nga.org/cda/files/MAKINGMEDICAID-BETTER.pdf.* 17 September 2002.

Tilly, Jane, and Jessica Kasten. 2001. Home- and community-based services for older people and younger adults with physical disabilities in Michigan. The Lewin Group, February.

Tilly, Jane, Frank C. Ullman, and Julie Chesky. 2002. Recent changes in health policy for low-income people in Michigan. Urban Institute, March. *http://www.urban.org/UploadedPDF/310442.pdf.* 17 September 2002.

U.S. Congressional Budget Office. 2002. The budget and economic outlook: Fiscal years 2003–2012. January. *http://www.cbo.gov/showdoc.cfm?index=3277&sequence=0.* 17 September 2002.

U.S. General Accounting Office. 2002a. Private health insurance: Number and market share of carriers in the small group health insurance market. Letter to Senator Christopher Bond, 25 March. *http://www.gao.gov/new.items/d02536r.pdf.* 30 August 2002.

———. 2002b. Medicaid and SCHIP recent HHS approvals of demonstration waiver projects raise concerns. GAO-02–817, July. *http://www.health-law.org/pubs/waivers/GAOreport.pdf.* 30 August 2002.

Weissert, Carol S., and Malcolm C. Goggin. 2002. Nonincremental policy change: Lessons from Michigan's Medicaid managed care initiative. *Public Administration Review* 62(2): 206–16.

## NOTES

I am grateful to Bill Fairgrieve, Paul Reinhart, Farah Hanley, John Walker, and Fran Wallace for helpful discussions and assistance with data.

1. The Citizens Research Council of Michigan (2001) compiled data on fiscal year 2001 appropriations for health across the state budget, arriving at a total of $10.3 billion. The largest part outside the Department of Community Health was $1.25 billion for health insurance for current and retired state employees, including retired public school employees.

2. Author's calculations from U.S. Centers for Medicare & Medicaid Services data, found at *http://www.cms.hhs.gov/statistics/nhe/* (28 August 2002). The personal consumption expenditure deflator is used to convert to 2000 dollars.

3. The District of Columbia is treated as a state in all comparative data in this chapter.

4. See *http://apps.nccd.cdc.gov/brfss/* and *http://apps.nccd.cdc.gov/YRBSS/.*

5. See *http://www.meps.ahrq.gov/MEPSDATA/ic/1999/Index299.htm* (29 August 2002).

6. The trend, however, bears watching as additional data become available. In the MEPS data, Michigan's premiums for both single and family coverage are lower than national averages in 1996 and 1997, but higher in 1999.

7. The National Survey of American Families shows similarly higher rates of insurance, especially employer-provided insurance, in Michigan as compared with the United States generally. See *http://www.urban.org/UploadedPDF/310393_MI_Health Profile.pdf* (30 August 2002).

8. Good general references include Gruber (2000) and Rosenbaum (2002).

9. In addition, Michigan and other states have responded to federal incentives to enact Children's Health Insurance Programs, extending insurance eligibility to children in families with incomes previously too high for Medicaid. See section 3.B.1.

10. All Medicaid data referenced in this chapter are for fiscal years.

11. In contrast, Martin et al. (2002) use a slightly different definition of total Medicaid spending and divide by the average number of enrollees per month, and find that in 1998 Medicaid spending per enrollee was $5,032 nationally and $4,940 in Michigan.

12. This paragraph and the next draw on Bruen and Holahan (2001).

13. From National Association of State Budget Officers, *State Expenditure Reports,* various years *http://www.nasbo.org/Publications.html* (29 August 2002).

14. This section draws heavily on Fairgrieve (2000), which provides further detail. See also Schneider and Rousseau (2002).

15. A similar tax on hospitals remains under consideration by the legislature at this writing.

16. See Kaiser Family Foundation State Health Facts Online at *http://www.statehealthfacts.kff.org/*

17. Most types of providers received rather substantial rate increases during 2000 and 2001. For example, rates paid for hospital outpatient services increased about 14%, physician fees about 15%, and capitation rates paid to health maintenance organizations about 16% over the two-year period.

18. Medicare Payment Advisory Commission (2002) provides a good discussion in the context of Medicare payment policies.

19. This paragraph draws on Tilly, Ullman, and Chesky (2002).

20. HIFA opens the possibility of using unspent funds authorized for SCHIP to serve groups other than children. However, the U.S. General Accounting Office (2002b) has questioned the legality of using SCHIP funds in this way.

21. Studies comparing managed care and fee-for-service insurance in a variety of settings have found mixed results on quality, with neither form consistently superior (Miller and Luft 1997).

22. See press release at *http://www.michigan.gov/mdch/ 1,1607,7-132-8347-17866-M_2001_11,00 .html*

23. Author's calculations from data at *http://www.census.gov/population/www/projections/natsum.html* (30 August 2002).

24. In the Medical Expenditure Panel Survey for 1998, average total medical expenditure for those sixty-five and over (excluding the institutionalized, whose average expenditures are even higher) was $5,964. For those aged forty-five to sixty-four it was $2,673, and for those under forty-five it was $1,108.

25. See National Nursing Home Survey, *http://www .cdc.gov/nchs/about/major/nnhsd/nnhsd.htm* (30 August 2002).

26. See *http://www.agingstats.gov/chartbook2000/ listoftables.html* (30 August 2002), table 30A.

27. Data on Michigan nursing home days and occupancy were provided by the Health Care Association of Michigan.

28. Rules of eligibility in Michigan are described in more detail at *http://www.michigan.gov/ documents/NursingHome5_10358_7.5x8.pdf* (30 August 2002).

29. Available at *http://www.michigan.gov/documents/ ltcrpt_6955_7.pdf* (30 August 2002).

30. Information may be found at the OFIS website, at *http://www.michigan.gov/cis/1,1607,7–154–10555_ 13251_13255—,00.html* (30 August 2002).

# 10

# Michigan's Agricultural, Forestry, and Mining Industries

*Arlen Leholm, Raymond Vlasin, and John Ferris*

Michigan is blessed with a rich natural resource base. Its agriculture, forestry, and mining industries depend absolutely on that natural resource base to produce commodities and goods that contribute substantially to Michigan's economy. Those same natural resources are essential for defining our quality of life and shaping the character and image of our state. The health of these industries plays a major role in sustaining the quality of life in Michigan, while the state's beautiful forests, mining heritage, and scenic farmland help propel Michigan's tourism industry.

Michigan's location, geography, and geology combine to form an ecologically unique landscape. A combination of climate, topography, soils, geological formations, and the moderating influences of the Great Lakes have created a very favorable environment for its agricultural, forestry, and mining industries.

This chapter addresses three important industries that depend on Michigan's natural resource base: (1) agricultural production and food processing, (2) forest and forest products, and (3) the mineral industry. The chapter also addresses land use issues and provides forecasts of land use changes associated with these industries, along with a discussion of some of the policy consider-ations involved in keeping these industries viable in the face of urban development pressures.

## Agricultural Production and Food Processing

Agriculture and food processing is a major industry in Michigan. A trademark of Michigan's agriculture has been its diversity and close interface with urban areas. The major farm enterprise is dairying, followed by ornamentals, corn, soybeans, and hay. Other important crops include fruit, vegetables, sugar beets, dry beans, wheat, and potatoes. The major livestock enterprises, in addition to dairy, include cattle, hogs, and equine. The diversity of Michigan's agriculture, based on the number of commodities grown, is greater than that of all states except California and possibly Florida. The range of commodities that can be grown in Michigan gives the state a significant advantage over states that are highly dependent on only three or four farm enterprises (Ferris 2001).

The link is quite strong between agricultural production and food processing for a number of commodities, particularly sugar beets, fruit, and vegetables. For that reason, production and food processing are often viewed as a tandem.

**FIGURE 10.1**

**Number of Farms in Michigan, 1860–2000**

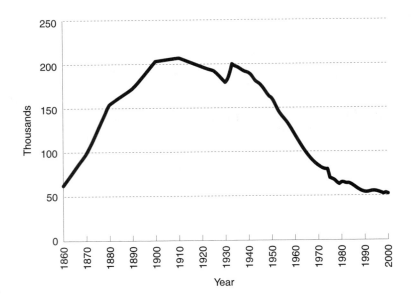

SOURCES: Ferris (2001); Kleweno (2001).

**FIGURE 10.2**

**Land in Farms in Michigan, 1860–2000**

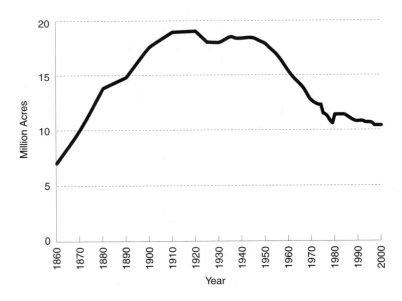

SOURCES: Ferris (2001); Kleweno (2001).

There are many positive aspects to the close agriculture-urban interface, both for agriculture and for the urban sector. The availability of non-farm employment enhances and stabilizes farm family incomes. The open spaces associated with agriculture can provide aesthetic benefits that can be enjoyed by all. Michigan's farmers produce a wide range of fresh commodities that can be purchased at farmers' markets and roadside stands as well as other retail establishments. The large ornamental and landscape industry is a major benefit to urban dwellers.

However, proximity to farms by an increasing nonfarm population poses challenges to farmers to minimize annoyances that may result from their operations. This can be a major problem for confined livestock operations, with conflict arising from other farmers as well. As Michigan's population expands to rural areas, the potential for land use conflicts will rise.

### History of Michigan Agriculture

Some of the earliest assessments of Michigan's agricultural potential were not very optimistic. One survey, made in 1815 in an effort to locate two million acres of land in Michigan as bounty for soldiers in the War of 1812, cited extensive swamps and marshland, and concluded, "not more than one acre in one hundred would admit of cultivation" (Chase 1992). Others considered the dense forests a sign of superior soil qualities. Forest clearing and settlement proceeded rapidly in the 1830s and 1840s. Settlers found many wild fruits, including cherries, plums, apples, grapes, raspberries, strawberries, huckleberries, and cranberries.

The first white farmers were French, and located in the southeastern part of what is now Michigan. The opening of the Erie Canal in 1825 provided passage to the area for New Englanders. Not long after, immigrants from the Old World began arriving, including French, Germans, Dutch, and Finns, among others.

A number of institutions played a role in early development of the agricultural industry, including the establishment of the Michigan Agricultural College, the pioneer land-grant college (now Michigan State University), in 1855. Improvements in transportation facilities and the creation of drainage laws made a significant impact on Michigan's early agricultural development.

At the turn of the twentieth century, agriculture was the backbone of Michigan's economy. At that time, nearly 300,000 people were engaged in agriculture, equal to the total number employed in manufacturing, trade, and transportation. The number of farms in Michigan in 1900 was about 200,000, close to the peak of 207,000 farms reached in 1910, as shown in figure 10.1 (Ferris 2001). In the fifty-year period from 1860 to 1910, farm numbers increased over threefold from the 1860 total of 62,000. After 1910, farm numbers declined to 52,000 by the end of the twentieth century.

Land in farms reached a peak of 19 million acres in 1920. Land in farms declined by a smaller percentage over the following years than did farm numbers, because of consolidation into larger farm units (figure 10.2). However, the decrease in land in farms over the course of the remainder of the century was still significant, dropping to 10.4 million acres by 2000 (Ferris 2001; Kleweno 2001). The average farm size had doubled in that time, from about one hundred acres in 1920 to about two hundred acres in 2000. However, the census definition of a farm includes any unit selling $1,000 or more of agricultural commodities annually.

With the rapid growth of manufacturing in Michigan, opportunities for off-farm employment have resulted in many part-time farms in the state. In 1997, 84% of farmers grossed less than $100,000 annually, and produced only 17% of the total product. The largest 16% of the farms grossed over $100,000 annually and were responsible for 83% of the product (U.S. Department of Agriculture 1999). A gross of $100,000 is about the lower limit to be considered a full-time farmer. In 2000, of the 52,000 farms in Michigan, 8,000 had gross incomes greater than $100,000; 16,500 had gross incomes between $10,000 and $99,999; and 27,500 had gross incomes between $1,000 and $9,999 (Kleweno 2001). The large number of part-time farmers occurs in part because of off-farm employment opportunities, which provide supplemental family income, plus, for many, fringe benefits, including health insurance.

### Trends in Cash Receipts from Farming

Gross cash receipts from farming come from crop and livestock sales and from federal program payments. Federal payments have come from a variety of programs over the years, with most payments going to producers of corn, wheat, and most recently soybeans.

**FIGURE 10.3**

**Real Gross Cash Receipts of Michigan Farmers in 1996 Dollars**

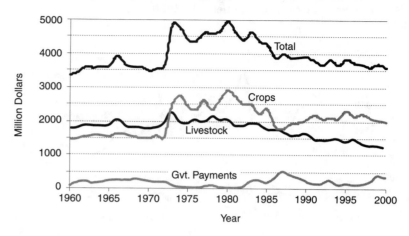

SOURCE: Ferris (2001).

In terms of 1996 dollars, gross cash receipts of Michigan farmers reached peaks near $5 billion during the 1970s, mostly due to shortfalls in global grain supplies, which boosted crop prices (figure 10.3; Ferris 2001). The high commodity prices of the 1970s generated overproduction in the following decade, coupled with a strong dollar, which trimmed exports. After the mid-1980s, real receipts from crops were reasonably well maintained, while real receipts from livestock sales trended lower. Fluctuations in crop receipts were somewhat offset by federal government program payments.

Real net cash income of Michigan farmers declined after the mid-1970s, but, of course, these amounts were shared among fewer farmers (figure 10.4; Ferris 2001). Furthermore, with rising farmland prices, equities on Michigan farms increased. During the 1990s, the real net cash farm income averaged about $1 billion. The average annual increase in the value of farm real estate was about 750 million dollars. Toward the end of the 1990s, the importance of government payments relative to net cash farm income increased to about 35 to 40%, and even more in terms of net farm income. In essence, net farm income is net cash income less depreciation.

Michigan farmers maintained their share of U.S. gross cash farm income after the mid-1970s—at about 1.8 to 1.9%. Michigan's shares of the national crops of corn, soybeans, sugar beets, and potatoes were maintained or increased. Shares of wheat and dry beans declined in a long-term perspective but leveled off in the 1990s. Consistent

**FIGURE 10.4**

**Real Net Cash Income of Michigan Farmers Compared with Cash Receipts from Government Payments in 1996 Dollars**

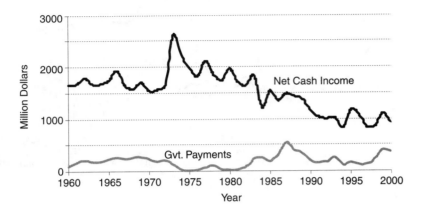

SOURCE: Ferris (2001).

have maintained their shares in recent years. The beef cow enterprise, however, has lost ground to that of other states due to the bovine tuberculosis problem in the northern part of the state.

**Trends in Food Processing**

The strength of agricultural enterprises depends increasingly on the linkages with food processing. With bulky commodities like sugar beets, local processing facilities are essential for production of that crop. One exception to this close linkage has been the breakfast cereal processors that have purchased only a relatively small proportion of their grains from Michigan. This is partly attributed to the nominal costs of transporting the raw material, compared to the value of the finished product. The presence of major breakfast cereal processors in Michigan is an example of the role of entrepreneurship in determining the location of an industry.

losses in shares were observed in fruit and vegetables, but gains were registered in ornamentals.

Relative to U.S. totals, Michigan's share of livestock production has declined over the past twenty-five years. However, if comparisons are made with the surrounding North Central states of Wisconsin, Minnesota, Ohio, Indiana, Illinois, and Iowa, Michigan dairy farmers have gained significantly in recent years—and milk is the state's most important agricultural product. In comparison with the North Central states, Michigan's hog and cattle feeding enterprises

**Value Added in Michigan after the Farm Gate**

The food-processing industry has expanded its value added contribution to the Michigan economy over time. Value added refers to the value of shipments less the cost of materials used by the industry. In food processing, this includes packaging materials as well as the farm product. Also, the inputs may include prepared items—that is, farm products that have been subjected to some initial processing prior to their acquisition by a food-processing firm. The value added represents compensation to labor, capital, and management.

In "real dollar" terms, value added by Michigan food processors increased over time until the 1992–97 time period, when several contributing sectors declined (figure 10.5, Ferris 2001). Real dollar value added is calculated by dividing the "actual dollar" value added (expressed in then current prices) by the Chain-type Price Index for Personal Consumption Expenditures (1996 = 100%). Between 1958 and 1997, the annual real dollar growth in value added was about 1.65%.

Trends in real dollar value added by seven food-processing sectors are presented in table 10.1. Value added has increased over the 1958–97 period, except for major reversals in real value added on beverages after 1977, and for grain mill products, dairy, meat processing, fruit and vegetables, and "other" between 1992 and 1997. Loss

**FIGURE 10.5**

**Value Added in Food Processing in Michigan in 1996 Real Dollars, 1958–1997**

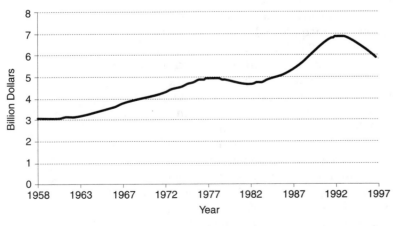

SOURCE: Ferris (2001).

**TABLE 10.1**

**Real Value Added by Michigan Food Processors (in millions of 1996 dollars)**

| Industry | 1958 | 1963 | 1967 | 1972 | 1977 | 1982 | 1987 | 1992 | 1997 |
|---|---|---|---|---|---|---|---|---|---|
| Meat | 338 | 325 | 333 | 447 | 505 | 569 | 510 | 689 | 865 |
| Dairy | 672 | 585 | 585 | 506 | 608 | 646 | 865 | 1278 | 1028 |
| Fruit and Vegetables | 282 | 404 | 536 | 576 | 639 | 710 | 677 | 764 | 674 |
| Grain Mill | 737 | 800 | 1,015 | 1,138 | 1,308 | 1,216 | 1,588 | 2,037 | 1,223 |
| Bakery | 418 | 440 | 512 | 579 | 541 | 468 | 630 | 742 | 841[b] |
| Beverage | 380 | 413 | 552 | 751 | 857 | 597 | 533 | 640 | 598 |
| Other | 263 | 237 | 232 | 328 | 487 | 479 | 597 | 719 | 616 |
| Total | 3,091 | 3,204 | 3,765 | 4,325 | 4,945 | 4,685 | 5,401 | 6,869 | 5,846 |

SOURCE: U.S. Department of Commerce, Bureau of the Census, Census of Manufactures, various issues.
(a) Deflated by the Chain-Type Price Index for Personal Consumption expenditures, 1996 = 100%.
(b) Not consistent with previous censuses.

of the hog slaughter facilities after 1997 has weakened the meat sector. A major Michigan firm ceased slaughtering hogs but continued to process carcasses.

Meat slaughtering and processing was Michigan's most rapidly growing food sector in percentage of value added, before the loss of slaughtering facilities. Following meat in growth rate were fruit and vegetables, bakeries, grain mill products, beverages, and dairy products in that order. Of particular note is the $814 million drop in real dollar value added in the grain mill sector from 1992 to 1997. Since the early 1990s, cereal manufacturers in Michigan and nationwide have experienced

**TABLE 10.2**

**Employment in the Michigan Food Processing Industry (in thousands)**

| Industry | 1958 | 1963 | 1967 | 1972 | 1977 | 1982 | 1987 | 1992 | 1997 | 2001 |
|---|---|---|---|---|---|---|---|---|---|---|
| **Census** | | | | | | | | | | |
| Meat | 6.8 | 6.2 | 6.1 | 7.0 | 6.6 | 7.7 | 7.5 | 8.2 | 7.7 | |
| Dairy | 12.6 | 9.6 | 8.2 | 6.2 | 5.8 | 4.8 | 4.2 | 4.7 | 4.7 | |
| Fruit and Vegetables | 7.1 | 7.4 | 8.0 | 8.3 | 8.4 | 7.3 | 6.6 | 6.7 | 5.7 | |
| Grain Mill | 7.6 | 6.9 | 7.5 | 6.8 | 6.7 | 5.7 | 5.1 | 5.5 | 3.7 | |
| Bakery | 10.9 | 11.0 | 10.3 | 8.7 | 7.3 | 6.5 | 7.3 | 7.4 | 8.6[a] | |
| Beverage | 6.6 | 6.5 | 7.3 | 6.8 | 6.4 | 5.2 | 3.5 | 2.4 | 3.1 | |
| Other | 6.1 | 4.9 | 4.2 | 4.3 | 5.0 | 5.8 | 5.0 | 5.1 | 5.1 | |
| TOTAL | 57.7 | 52.5 | 51.6 | 48.1 | 46.2 | 43.0 | 39.2 | 40.0 | 38.6 | |
| **Bureau of Labor Statistics** | | | | | | | | | | |
| Meat | | | | 7.2 | 7.1 | 7.9 | 8.2 | 8.2 | 9.3 | 5.8 |
| Dairy | | | | 6.3 | 5.7 | 3.8 | 3.5 | 4.7 | 4.3 | 4.7 |
| Fruit and Vegetables | | | | | | | | 7.9 | 7.1 | 6.6 |
| Grain Mill | | | | 8.7 | 8.7 | 7.3 | 7.1 | 6.5 | 5.4 | 5.3 |
| Bakery | | | | 9.4 | 8.7 | 7.5 | 6.5 | 6.7 | 5.9 | 5.7 |
| Other | | | | | | | | 9.9 | 9.3 | 9.3 |
| TOTAL | 61.6 | 57.3 | 57.6 | 52.3 | 51.9 | 46.1 | 45.2 | 43.9 | 41.3 | 37.4 |

SOURCES: U.S. Department of Commerce, Bureaus of the Census, *Census of Manufactures*, various issues; Ferris (2001).
(a) Not consistent with previous censuses.

**TABLE 10.3**

**Food-Processing Establishments in Michigan**

| Industry | Year | | | | | | | | |
|---|---|---|---|---|---|---|---|---|---|
| | 1958 | 1962 | 1967 | 1972 | 1977 | 1982 | 1987 | 1992 | 1997 |
| Meat | 245 | 246 | 215 | 191 | 170 | 119 | 94 | 96 | 88 |
| Dairy | 449 | 346 | 235 | 153 | 113 | 79 | 73 | 56 | 57 |
| Fruit and Vegetables | 159 | 162 | 142 | 126 | 128 | 105 | 90 | 89 | 68 |
| Grain Mill | 83 | 78 | 59 | 56 | 60 | 50 | 45 | 55 | 44 |
| Bakery | 260 | 224 | 168 | 149 | 128 | 85 | 85 | 92 | 451[a] |
| Beverages | 152 | 134 | 120 | 103 | 89 | 63 | 53 | 42 | 62 |
| Sugar | | | 5 | 5 | 5 | 5 | 5 | 5 | 5 |
| Candy | 37 | | 24 | 21 | 31 | 21 | 28 | 29 | 63 |
| Fats and Oil | | | | 14 | 19 | 12 | 10 | 7 | |
| Other | 163 | 154 | 105 | 87 | 86 | 87 | 96 | 98 | 87 |
| Grand Total | 1,548 | 1,344 | 1,073 | 905 | 829 | 626 | 579 | 569 | 925 |

SOURCE: U.S. Department of Commerce, Bureau of the Census, *Census of Manufactures*, Michigan, various issues.
(a) Not consistent with previous censuses.

substantial competitive pressure as consumers have shifted from breakfast cereals to other food products.

Employment in the food-processing sector in the state has been declining (table 10.2). It has declined in nearly all sectors from 1958 to 1997, as shown in the census data, the top half of table 10.2. Employment declined from 52,000 in 1972 to around 41,000 in 1997, and continued to decline into 2001, as shown in the Bureau of Labor Statistics (BLS) data on the bottom half of table 10.2 (Ferris 2001). Employment tended downward in all sectors except for meat from 1972 to 1997. However, employment in meat slaughtering and processing dropped sharply from 9,300 in 1997 to 5,800 in 2001, a loss of 38% of the jobs.

Based on BLS data, employment in food processing in Michigan dropped steadily from 3.0% of the national total in 1972 to 2.2% in 2001. Declines in the national share were noted in all of the major categories except dairy, in which the share increased between 1987 and 2001.

Just as farm numbers have declined over time, so, too, have the numbers of food processors in Michigan. The total number of food-processing establishments in 1992 was 569, just over a third of the 1548 in operation in 1958. The total of 925 establishments in 1997 is distorted because of elevated counts of bakeries and candy establishments resulting from a change in definition from previous years (table 10.3). The scale of individual food-processing operations has increased substantially over time, as has the productivity per employee, resulting in fewer but much larger operations.

## Distribution of Value by Farm Production and Food Processing

A review of the value of production by crop and livestock enterprises provides useful insights about their relative economic importance. The distribution of the value of production from all crop categories for 1997–99 is presented in figure 10.6 (Ferris 2001). Corn remained the most important crop, representing nearly 21% of the total value, with ornamentals close behind at 20%, followed by soybeans at 15%, hay at 13%, fruit at 9%, and vegetables at 7%, with sugar beets, dry beans, and potatoes representing about 4% each.

The distribution of livestock sales is shown in figure 10.7 (Ferris 2001). Sales of milk continue to dominate, accounting for 58% of all livestock receipts. This is followed by cattle at over 16%, hogs at 12%, and poultry at 9%.

Michigan's agriculture is very diverse. This diversity is apparent from the state rankings of enterprises for the fifty states. In 2000, Michigan ranked first in the United States in the production of blueberries, tart cherries, cucumbers (for processing), black beans, cranberry beans, light red kidney beans, navy beans, Niagara grapes, geraniums, hosta, impatiens, marigolds, petunias, other potted perennials, and flowering hanging baskets (Kleweno 2001). Among the state's numerous other products, Michigan was second nationally in the production of dry beans and celery; third in apples, fresh market carrots, and asparagus; and fourth in cucumbers for fresh market, sweet cherries, grapes, and processing tomatoes. Among the states, Michigan ranked eighth in milk production, tenth in potatoes and soybeans, and eleventh in corn.

Total shipments by food processors in Michigan in 1997 amounted to $12.2 billion, with about half of that—just under $6 billion—being value added. The distribution of this $6 billion of value added by type of food processor is illustrated in figure 10.8 (Ferris 2001). The most prominent category was grain mill, representing 21% of the total. Within the grain mill category, some 92% was value added by breakfast cereal manufacturers, totaling $1,147 million. Dairy processing was the second most important category at 17.6%, followed by meat, bakeries, fruit and vegetables, and beverages.

## Direct and Indirect Impacts of Agriculture and Food Processing

Agriculture and food processing contribute some $15 billion directly to the Michigan economy, of which about 25% is represented by agriculture. If the "backward linked" effects of the impacts of agriculture and food processing on input industries such as fertilizers, fuels, and farm chemicals are considered, another $12 billion is added to the economy, for a total of $27 billion. This does not include the "forward linked" effects from transportation and wholesaling of farm products that leave the state and transportation and wholesaling of products of food processors that are consumed in the state or shipped out. Though difficult to measure, these effects contribute another $2–3 billion to the state's economy, for a total impact approaching $30 billion. If one includes landscape and horticultural services, another $1 billion could be added to the total. These data are relevant for the period from1999 to 2000.

Viewed in terms of employment, the direct and indirect magnitude of this industry exceeds 240,000, about 5% of the total employment in the state. A more relevant comparison of basic industries, such as agriculture and food processing, would be to relate the direct employment to other basic industries. Direct employment in agriculture and food processing has been about 100 thousand in full time equivalents of which agri-

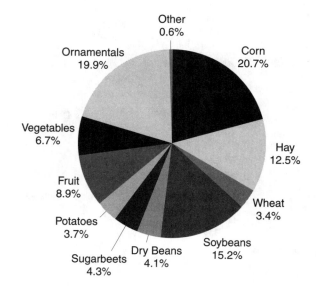

**FIGURE 10.6**

**Distribution of Value of Crop Production in Michigan, 1997–1999**

SOURCE: Ferris (2001).

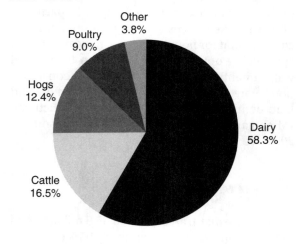

**FIGURE 10.7**

**Distribution of Livestock Sales in Michigan, 1997–1999**

SOURCE: Ferris (2001).

culture represents two-thirds. Employment in other basic industries in manufacturing, forestry and mining has been about 900 thousand. That means that agriculture and food processing employment represents about 11 percent of these other basic industries. Direct employment in agriculture and food processing is about one-third

**FIGURE 10.8**

**Distribution of Value Added by Food Processors in Michigan in 1997**

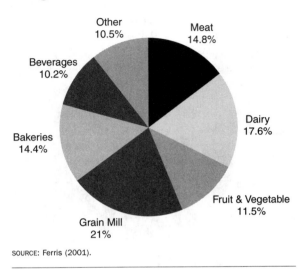

SOURCE: Ferris (2001).

the employment of Michigan's motor vehicles and parts sector (Ferris 2000).

## Forest and Forest Products

Michigan's forests provide a wide range of benefits to the state's citizens. The Michigan Department of Natural Resources notes, "these benefits include habitat for flora and fauna, recreational and sightseeing opportunities, filtration for air and water quality, and timber for societal consumption." Forests contribute to our quality of life and help define what it means to be from Michigan (Michigan Department of Natural Resources 2002).

## History of Michigan's Forests

Before settlement, an estimated 35.5 million acres of forestland extended over nearly 95% of what is now Michigan. This original forest was estimated to contain about 10 million acres of prime pine and 9 million acres of high-quality northern hardwoods (Michigan Department of Natural Resources 1996).

By the middle of the 1800s, the forests of Michigan had begun to undergo rapid change, and by the start of the twentieth century only a remnant of the pine forests was left. White pine and timber products from Michigan's forests provided the

wood products for building the urban centers of the Midwest. After a century of extensive logging and clearing of land for agricultural production, the forests were reduced to conditions that hardly resembled the original forests.

The first statewide forest inventory was conducted in 1935 by the USDA Forest Service. Four other forest inventories were conducted in Michigan, in 1955, 1966, 1980, and 1993. New summary information is expected from the Forest Service by early 2003. The inventories provide essential data for assessing statewide forest conditions (Leatherberry and Spencer 1996).

Michigan's forestland has made a significant recovery from the period of exploitation, and the quality of the timber continues to improve. Modern forest management practices have played a major role in improving the conditions of the present forest. These forest management practices have enabled Michigan to have both an expanding forest industry and a vibrant tourist industry that depends heavily on the health and beauty of Michigan's forestland.

## Michigan Forestland

The 1993 forest inventory revealed 19.3 million acres of forestland in Michigan. Forestland accounts for 53% of the state's total of 36.4 million acres. For inventory purposes, Michigan is divided into four survey units. In the Eastern Upper Peninsula and the Western Upper Peninsula Survey Units, about 80% of the land is forested. In the Northern Lower Peninsula Survey Unit, about 60% of the land is forested, and in the Southern Lower Peninsula Survey Unit, about 20% of the land is forested (Leatherberry and Spencer 1996). Forestland percentages by county are shown in figure 10.9, which clearly shows the increases in the percentage of forest acreage from south to north.

## Michigan Timberland

Forestland that is classified as timberland must meet minimum timber productivity standards. Timberland totaled 18.6 million acres in the 1993 inventory, and amounts to 97% of the forestland in Michigan. Michigan's timberland is the fifth-largest in the United States, exceeded only by that of Georgia, Oregon, Alabama, and Montana (Smith et al. 2001).

To provide state comparisons, the timberland acreages for eight North Central states are shown in table 10.4, along with the percentage of the total North Central timberland acreage held by each state. Michigan has over 23% of the timberland acreage in the North Central region of the United States. It is followed by Wisconsin, Minnesota, Missouri, and Ohio, in that order.

Timberland area in Michigan increased from 15.5 million acres in 1935 to 19.1 million acres in 1955, but diminished from 1955 to 1980. That trend turned around after 1980. The area of timberland is reported to have increased in Michigan by almost 1.2 million acres between 1980 and 1993 (table 10.5). More than 90% of this increase occurred in the Lower Peninsula. This increase largely came from abandoned cropland and pasture on which trees became established, so that the land could be reclassified as forestland, and from marginal forestland that became productive forestland (Smith et al. 2001).

Michigan's forest composition has shifted over time. In 1993, there were about 13.9 million acres of hardwood forests, an increase of 830,000 acres since 1980. Hardwoods (broadleaf deciduous tree species like oak, aspen, and maple) make up 75% of the timberland area in Michigan, while softwoods (tree species like pine, spruce, and cedar) account for 25% of the timberland area.

Michigan's forests matured between 1980 and 1993, with large-diameter trees (roughly greater than ten inches in diameter) increasing in acreage by 55%. The trend toward maturity of Michigan's forests provides added alternatives for managing and harvesting the forest resource. Choices include managing for old-growth attributes and harvesting the mature trees to improve structural diversity or to regenerate the forests. The volume of growing stock (trees five inches and larger in diameter) increased from 19.7 billion cubic feet in 1980 to 26.6 billion cubic feet in 1993, a 35% gain (Leatherberry and Spencer 1996).

## Sustainability of Timberland Harvest Rates

One important resource question is sustainability of harvest in relationship to growth. Comparing the net annual growth in growing stock to removals (harvests) over time helps reveal how a state is managing its timberland resources, and whether harvest levels are sustainable. If net growth is substantially higher than removals, there may be opportunity for both increases in

**FIGURE 10.9**

**Percent Forest Land in Michigan**

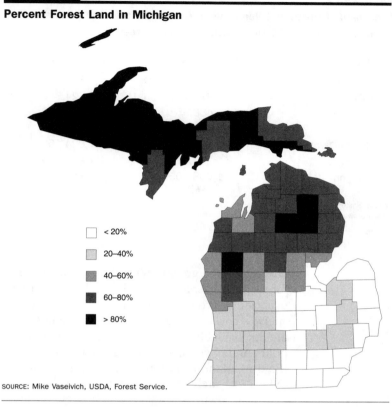

< 20%

20–40%

40–60%

60–80%

> 80%

SOURCE: Mike Vaseivich, USDA, Forest Service.

**TABLE 10.4**

**Timberland Acreage in the North Central Region of the United States, 1997**

| State | Timberland (thousands of acres) | Percentage of Total Timberland Acres |
|---|---|---|
| Michigan | 18,667 | 23.2 |
| Illinois | 4,058 | 5.0 |
| Indiana | 4,342 | 5.4 |
| Iowa | 1,944 | 2.4 |
| Minnesota | 14,819 | 18.4 |
| Missouri | 13,411 | 16.7 |
| Ohio | 7,568 | 9.4 |
| Wisconsin | 15,701 | 19.5 |
| Total North Central Region | 80,510 | 100.0 |

SOURCE: Smith et al. (2001).

**TABLE 10.5**

**Timberland Acreage in Michigan, 1935–1993 (thousands of acres)**

|  | 1935 | 1955 | 1966 | 1980 | 1993 |
|---|---|---|---|---|---|
| Michigan | 15,491 | 19,121 | 18,900 | 17,468 | 18,667 |

SOURCE: Data are from the Forest Inventories of Michigan, including the most recent in 1993, conducted by the USDA Forest Service.

**TABLE 10.6**

**Net Annual Growth and Removals of Growing Stock on Timberland in Selected States, 1996 (in thousands of cubic feet)**

| State | Net Growth[a] | Removals |
|---|---|---|
| Michigan | 756,404 | 352,729 |
| Minnesota | 370,112 | 324,388 |
| Wisconsin | 488,957 | 359,789 |
| Georgia | 1,518,637 | 1,506,459 |
| North Carolina | 1,159,584 | 1,024,150 |
| Alabama | 1,223,677 | 1,441,144 |
| Oregon | 1,738,705 | 855,969 |

SOURCE: Smith et al. (2001).
(a) Net Growth is net after mortality.

harvesting and growth in the consumptive use of forest products. Some caution is in order, however, since growth and removal ratios vary by species, cover type, and region. Also, many acres are not available for harvest due to administrative policy and physical features. Further, some 50% of the timberland is in nonindustrial private forests (NIPF) (privately owned) and only about one half of these owners engage in timber harvest. Furthermore, 47% of the NIPF land is in parcels of fewer than nineteen acres. Small acreages are more costly to harvest.

Table 10.6 illustrates how Michigan compares to its neighboring Great Lake states Minnesota

and Wisconsin and to four other of the largest timberland states, using 1996 estimates. Michigan had a net growth (gross growth minus mortality) of over 756 million cubic feet of growing stock, compared to a harvest (removals) of more than 352 million cubic feet of growing stock. Overall, the ratio of current net growing stocks to harvest exceeds 2 to 1. It is difficult to say how much of this net growth is available for harvest, however, given the constraints on harvest identified previously.

By comparison, it appears that the harvest practices for Alabama are not sustainable over the long term at the 1996 level. Those for North Carolina and Georgia appear possibly sustainable, with a balance between net growth and removal in 1996. Michigan shows potential for increased timberland harvest that is biologically sustainable.

### Ownership of Michigan's Forests

Michigan's private timberland is held by a wide range of owners, who possess a variety of ownership objectives. Private owners control 65% of the state's timberland, with the remainder in public ownership (figure 10.10). Nonindustrial private owners (individuals, hunt clubs, farmers, and others) account for 57% of the total. This 57% represents some 312,000 individuals with an average of 27.6 acres (Michigan Department of Natural Resources 1996).

Eight percent of the state's total timberland acreage is under private forest industry ownership. The collective private ownership objectives range from economic, to recreational, to aesthetic.

Public ownership, accounting for 35% of the timberland acreage, is comprised of federal, state, and local governmental entities (figure 10.10). National forests in Michigan, under federal management, include the Ottawa, the Hiawatha, and the Huron-Manistee, which collectively account for 14% of the total. State ownership represents 20% of the total, with management by Michigan's Department of Natural Resources. Both federal and state management plans include harvesting as one of their multiple objectives. Principal ownership objectives of public lands also include protecting naturalistic values associated with the wilderness, wildlife habitat, and ecological communities, and fostering community stability through the timber and recreational industries.

**FIGURE 10.10**

**Area of Timberland by Owner in Michigan in 1993**

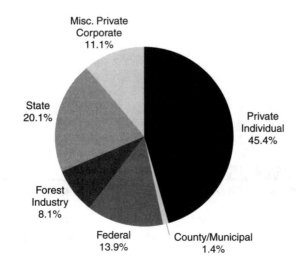

- Misc. Private Corporate 11.1%
- State 20.1%
- Forest Industry 8.1%
- Federal 13.9%
- County/Municipal 1.4%
- Private Individual 45.4%

SOURCE: Michigan DNR (1996).

## Direct and Indirect Impacts of Michigan's Forest Products

Michigan's timber resources have made the timber industry an important part of the Michigan economy. They have enabled logging and primary processing in the northern Lower Peninsula and in the Upper Peninsula, and secondary processing in the southern Lower Peninsula (Potter-Witter 2002).

In 1994, Michigan's forestry and timber products industry contributed $536 million to the state's economy at the raw usable level of production, in the form of pulpwood, sawtimber, veneer, posts, poles, Christmas trees, and fuel (table 10.7). Pulpwood and sawtimber each contributed about one-third of this total, followed by Christmas trees, which contributed 11% of the total. The $536 million represents "Michigan forest products delivered values," the crucial first stage in the value added process involving Michigan's timber-dependent industries (Potter-Witter et al. 2000). This is a roughly equivalent measure to the farm gate value for agriculture or the mine mouth value for the mining industry.

Using USDA Forest Service data, research by Potter-Witter shows that in 1996 delivered values for pulpwood, sawtimber, and veneer had decreased from their 1994 levels, while delivered values for industrial fuel had increased from 1994 levels (see Potter-Witter 2002).

The industry contribution to employment is also quite significant. A 2000 study of Michigan's forest product industry estimated that in 1997 Michigan's timber industry directly employed 4,270 people, with a payroll of $92 million in logging and forestry management. Michigan's forest products–dependent industries in 1997 employed about 70,000 people in 1,835 firms. These employ-

### TABLE 10.7

**Michigan's Forest Products Delivered Values, 1994**

| Source of Revenues | Value (millions of dollars) | Percentage |
|---|---|---|
| Pulpwood | $181.6 | 34.0 |
| Sawtimber | 180.6 | 33.5 |
| Industrial fuel | 20.1 | 4.0 |
| Domestic fuel[a] | 43.4 | 8.0 |
| Veneer | 46.9 | 9.0 |
| Posts/poles | 3.4 | 0.5 |
| Christmas Trees | 60.0 | 11.0 |
| Total Delivered Value | $536.0 | 100.0 |

SOURCE: Potter-Witter et al. (2000).
(a) Figures given here are for 1992.

ment figures reflect the total of all primary, intermediate, and final forest product–dependent industries. The study estimated total wages for the forest industry as a whole in 1997 to be $2.6 billion (Potter-Witter et al. 2000). Also, forests contribute substantially to Michigan's tourist and recreation industry (see chapter 22 for further discussion of the tourism industry). Michigan forests provided the genesis of the state's office furniture industry and contributed to Michigan's status as the leading producer of office furniture in the nation.

Within the overall Michigan forestry and forest products industry is a substantial forest product manufacturing sector. The value added to the first stage of raw lumber is shown in table 10.8. The lumber and wood products sector employed 16,300 people in 1996, with over $900 million of value added by manufacturing. In 1996, the paper and allied products sector contributed over $2.3 billion of value added by manufacturing, employing 21,500 people, and the logging sector provided

### TABLE 10.8

**Michigan Forest Products Industry Value Added by Manufacturing and Employment**

| SIC Group[a] | All Employee | | Value Added by Manufacturing (thousands of dollars) | |
|---|---|---|---|---|
| | 1987 | 1996 | 1987 | 1996 |
| Lumber and wood products (SIC 24) | 14,900 | 16,300 | 601,500 | 909,808 |
| Paper and allied products (SIC 26) | 20,600 | 21,500 | 1,684,500 | 2,336,100 |
| Logging (SIC 241) | 1,700 | 1,200 | 50,600 | 48,800 |

SOURCE: U.S. Department of Commerce, Bureau of the Census, *Census of Manufacturers*, 1997.
(a) Not included is the wood component of the furniture manufacturing industry.

**TABLE 10.9**

**Michigan's Major Mineral and Fuel Resources, 2000**

| Commodity | Michigan's Production for 2000 Quantity | Units (in millions) | Value (in millions) at Well Head or Mine Mouth | Michigan's Rank Among the States |
|---|---|---|---|---|
| Iron ore | 15.9 | metric tons | $556.5 | 2 |
| Natural gas | 289.0 | mcf | $1,029.0 | 10 |
| Oil, crude | 8.3 | barrels | $211.3 | 17 |
| Cement | 6.6 | metric tons | $500.7 | 4 |
| Sand and gravel | 78.1 | metric tons | $299.3 | 3 |
| Stone (crushed) | 44.0 | metric tons | $155.0 | 13 |
| Lime | 0.8 | metric tons | $43.9 | 10 |
| Gypsum | 2.3 | metric tons | $16.5 | 3 |
| Clay | 0.6 | metric tons | $3.6 | 4 |
| Peat | 0.2 | metric tons | $4.5 | 2 |
| Combined bromide, iron oxide pigments, magnesium compounds, potash, salt, silver, plus others | | | $ 103.6 | 1 to 11 |
| TOTAL VALUE | | | $ 2,923.9 | |

SOURCE: Kakela (2002).

$48.8 million in value added by manufacturing, employing 1,200 people.

## Michigan's Mineral Industry

Michigan is well known as a major industrial state, and its largest city, Detroit, is known as the home of the largest automobile makers. Not so well known is the historical role that Michigan's mineral industry played in turning the United States from an agrarian nation to a manufacturing powerhouse. Even less well known is the fact that Michigan's mineral industry continues today as a significant contributor to its economy and as a source of raw materials for the state's automotive and agricultural industries and its construction sectors. Despite over 150 years of consistent mining, Michigan's mineral wealth continues to make an important contribution to the Michigan economy. In 2000, the total value of minerals produced in Michigan was over $2.9 billion. Of this total, $1.68 billion was from nonfuel minerals, and $1.24 billion was from oil and natural gas (table 10.9).

## History of Michigan's Mineral Industry

The discovery of the rich iron ore deposits of the Marquette Range in 1844 played a key role in launching the industrialization of America. Subsequent discoveries of iron ore in the Menominee and Gogebic Ranges in Michigan and the Mesabi Range in Minnesota, all in the latter part of the 1800s, enhanced industrialization of the United States. These rich ores were located near the Great Lakes, allowing easy access to the "Lower Lakes," where they met coal coming north by train from West Virginia, southern Ohio, Kentucky, Indiana, and Illinois. This convergence of key natural resources spurred the construction of the great steel mills in the port cities of Michigan, Illinois, Indiana, and Ohio (Kakela and Hass 2000).

## Michigan's Minerals

The mineral industry of Michigan has two outstanding characteristics. The first is its contribution to Michigan's economy. Second is its diversity in type and location—that is, the wide variety of minerals produced and the many parts of the state that produce them. In 2000, Michigan ranked sixth nationally in total nonfuel mineral production, and accounted for more than 4% of the U.S. total (Gere 2001). Michigan continues to be the nation's second-largest iron ore producing state. Michigan mines still provide approximately a quarter of all the iron ore produced in the United States.

Michigan's $2.9 billion mineral industry, high-lighted in table 10.9, reflects the first stage in the value added process. This first stage, the raw mineral stage, is equivalent to the farm gate value in agriculture or the delivered value for Michigan's raw forest products. Iron ore and cement are the two leading nonfuel minerals in Michigan, contributing $557 and $501 million respectively, to Michigan's economy. Michigan's oil and gas industry is also significant, with its natural gas production of over one billion dollars ranking tenth nationally, and its crude oil production of $211 million ranking seventeenth nationally in 2000. Compared to other states, Michigan ranks first as a producer of magnesium compounds, second in the production of peat and iron ore, and third in gypsum and sand and gravel production.

## Employment in the Mineral Industry and Its Indirect Economic Impacts

Michigan's mineral industry directly employed nearly 9,400 people in 1997, with some 7,000 employed in the Lower Peninsula and 2,400 employed in the Upper Peninsula (U.S. Department of Commerce 2000). The oil and gas industry directly employed 2,703 people, and the nonfuel mineral industry 6,693 people in 1997 (table 10.10).

Minerals are a basic input to Michigan's manufacturing-based industry. According to Kakela and Hass (2000), the intermediate-level value added to Michigan's economy by the mineral industry was at least $12 billion in 2000. Intermediate value for minerals includes, for example, turning iron ore into steel and crude oil into petroleum products. Minerals obviously contribute an even larger multiple to the final manufacturing process and products in Michigan.

## Framing Michigan Land Use Challenges

It is useful to distinguish between two major land use challenges that confront Michigan policymakers and citizens. One is deciding whether and how to help preserve the basic industries of agriculture, forestry, and mining for the employment, income, and other benefits they can provide to Michigan citizens and their communities. The other is determining the patterns of land use that are desired by Michigan citizens now and in the years ahead, and the actions to be taken to

**TABLE 10.10**

**Mining Jobs in Michigan, 1997**

| Commodity | Upper Peninsula | Lower Peninsula | Statewide |
|---|---|---|---|
| Oil and gas | 0 | 2,703 | 2,703 |
| Nonfuel | 2,400 | 4,293 | 6,693 |
| TOTAL | 2,400 | 6,996 | 9,396 |
| % OF TOTAL | 26% | 74% | 100% |

SOURCE: Kakela (2002).

achieve them. State public policy makers can have a significant influence on the outcome of these two challenges.

It is important to distinguish between federal laws and policies and state laws and policies pertaining to land use. Federal policies toward an industry, such as subsidies associated with farm commodities, are important but largely beyond the bounds of this chapter. The focus here is on state public policy considerations toward future land use and the role agriculture, forestry, and mining can serve in Michigan's land use objectives.

It is also important to recognize that land uses and land transactions can convey both "public good" and "private benefit." From a strictly private-benefit perspective, with no public guidance, individual owners of land could use their property for any use and sell it for any purpose. This perspective does not take into account the external effects of these actions on other private individuals, and more broadly on their communities and the general citizenry. While these external effects, called "externalities," can be both positive and negative, unguided market action on the urban fringe frequently has negative repercussions regarding the "public good." The public good in these instances may include maintenance of an aesthetic environment, minimization of public service costs, and avoidance of unnecessary irreversible changes. Both perspectives, "public good" and "private benefit," are important, and public policy makers play a role in determining the balance.

## Land Use Issues for the Agriculture, Forestry, and Mining Industries

Agriculture, forestry, and mining are essential for our economic well-being and our quality of life. Agricultural enterprises are necessary for food;

forests are needed to build our homes and businesses and as a place for recreation; and minerals are required for energy and materials for building cars, roads, and much more. These vital industries may be seriously threatened if the land use patterns that existed in Michigan at the turn of the twenty-first century continue in the decades ahead. To better address land use impacts, a comprehensive study was undertaken by Public Sector Consultants in 2001, with contributions from many university and private-sector authors. Their report, entitled *Michigan Land Resource Project,* presents a careful assessment of the potential impacts future land use patterns may have on the agriculture, forestry, and mining industries. The study assessed future impacts out twenty and forty years.

The authors used a spatialized trend model, developed at Michigan State University, called the Land Transformation Model (LTM). They simulated future changes in land use and land cover, based on the inputs of historical and recent land cover and land use change data. An important insight from the study was the revelation that, between 1980 and 1995, the seventeen counties that had updated their Michigan Resource Information System databases showed a population increase of 3%, from 6.13 million to 6.3 million. However, for the same time period, their urban land usage had increased 25% (Public Sector Consultants 2001). This 25 to 3 ratio for the seventeen counties represents more than an eightfold increase in percentage of urban land usage in relation to the population increase. Based on the USDA's Natural Resources Inventory and U.S. Census data, the statewide ratio of urban land usage to population increase is estimated to be 4 to 1. If Michigan continues its current trend in urban land usage to the year 2040, the built-up areas of Michigan are expected to increase substantially.

One major finding from the study that cuts across agriculture, forestry, and mining, is that fragmentation of the landscape makes resource access, production, harvesting, and extraction much more difficult. The fragmentation is caused by both physical separation into smaller parcels and ownership separation into many holdings (see Norgaard 1994). If we want to preserve and continue the land-based industries of agriculture, forestry, and mining as vibrant industries with a future in Michigan, our public decision makers will need to consider in their policies fragmentation impacts on the ecological and economic integrity of the land.

Based on the comprehensive and thorough land resource analysis of the 2001 Public Sector Consultants study, we list the major findings for land use on agriculture, forestry, and mining to the year 2040. These key findings are based on the use of the LTM model and its most likely economic forecasts into the future for each sector. No one has a crystal ball. The *magnitude of the forecasts* made by these authors may not be accurate, being more or less than what actually occurs. Yet it is highly likely that the *directional changes* that occur will be fully consistent with the study's forecasts. Therefore, policy implications associated with key findings of the study should be most useful to Michigan's policy makers.

### Agriculture Conditions and Projections

- The state's agriculture (including food processing) provides needed stability to the state's economy, since agricultural cyclical conditions differ from those in the automotive industry. A trademark of Michigan agriculture has been its diversity, with substantial sectors in livestock, field crops, specialty food crops, and ornamentals. In addition, the industry enhances the state's aesthetics associated with open spaces.
- The close interface between agriculture and urban areas has a positive influence on farm households, but presents challenges for farmers to control nuisance factors, especially odor from livestock operations. This problem is intensified with urban sprawl.
- Using the LTM projections to 2040, Michigan will lose about 15% of its farmland overall, with about a 25% loss of farmland in metropolitan counties.
- Michigan agriculture is in danger of losing some of its diversity, as the fruit acreage is projected to decline by about 25%, dry bean acreage by 36%, potato acreage by 16%, and vegetable acreage by 13% by 2040. These projected declines are due in part to locations near urban areas and in part to likely market conditions. Acres in corn, soybeans, wheat, and sugar beets are not expected to change appreciably. Acres in ornamentals will continue to expand.
- Over 40% of the land in farms is in hay, pasture, woodland, and other less intensive uses that have environmental benefits. Losses of these areas will approach one-third by the year 2040.
- In spite of the projected declines in crop acreages, increased productivity per acre will

more than offset reduction in areas harvested, with few exceptions.

- Dairying will shift out of metropolitan counties, and cow numbers will drop by at least 25% statewide. Total milk production, however, will continue to increase.

- For the livestock industries to remain viable in Michigan, major adjustments will be needed to comply with environmental and nuisance restrictions. With rapid structural change, conversion to larger units, and new technology, remaining producers will be more capable of making this adjustment. If not, production will shift to less populated areas in other states.

- The number of farms in Michigan is projected to decline from 52,000 in 2000 to about 24,000 by 2040. The number of very small farms will not change much, but dramatic reductions will be noted in farms of fifty to five hundred acres. Farms over one thousand acres will increase in number significantly. The output of Michigan agriculture will continue to increase as farmers produce more from less land and with less labor.

- The main rationale for Michigan public policy dealing with the impact of urban sprawl on agriculture is to preserve open space and the character of Michigan's landscape, rather than to ensure world food supplies.

- A major dilemma is how to prevent conversion of farmland without diminishing farm family equities. In the 1990s, the annual gain in farm real estate values was 65% greater than the average annual gain in net farm income.

- Pressure for farmers to sell to nonfarm buyers is illustrated by appraisers' evaluation of farmland in the Southern Lower Peninsula in 2000: $1,839 per acre for farming, $7,423 per acre for residential, $19,495 per acre for commercial/industrial use, and $2,739 per acre for recreation. Programs such as the Purchase of Development Rights (PDR) and Transfer of Development Rights (TDR), plus other land use, planning, and guidance tools can be employed to slow the exodus of farmland.

## Forestry Conditions and Projections

- Due to abandonment of farmland and its conversion to forest, forestland acreage will appear to increase in the future. However, the LTM data show a state-wide decrease in forestland acreage of 1–3% through 2020 and a decrease of 2–7% through 2040.

- Forestland loss will be greatest in Southern Lower Michigan, up to 13% by 2020 and up to 25% by 2040.

- Encroaching urbanization may force forest managers to alter practices (for example, discontinuing pesticide use or prohibiting scheduled, regenerative burns). This will most certainly delay timber harvesting or restrict the frequency of harvests. It may also add costs if restrictions are imposed on harvesting methods to accommodate urban sprawl or planned new urban expansion.

- A primary effect of development on forestland in the future will be fragmentation. As land is divided and sold, contiguous large tracts of land become small parcels with many owners who are not likely to manage a forest for harvesting or to be willing to harvest. In order to keep harvesting costs down, access to large parcels is necessary. As the land becomes more fragmented, the price of harvesting Michigan's timber will increase.

## Mining Conditions and Projections

- Pressure on the ability to produce local minerals will certainly affect the state's economy. These minerals will become more expensive if they must be shipped from farther away. This expense will raise the cost of building and construction activities as well as other industrial production, making for less profit and less competitive industries.

- Accessibility to land for mineral exploration, development, and production is a principal factor that is directly and negatively impacted by land fragmentation, sprawl, and urbanization. There is an even stronger impact on siting new mineral extraction operations near urban areas for construction materials, than on existing operations. Potential mineral producers must compete against other land uses that are often perceived as having higher direct value to the local community and, accordingly, higher political value.

- Existing extraction sites will come under pressure as urbanization occurs around them and new neighbors object to the extraction operations.

- There is a clear link between urbanization and the production of sand, gravel, and crushed stone that urban areas require. Their production is dependent on local economic patterns, and therefore should be highly influenced by urbanization and local land use patterns. Usually, construction materials cannot be economically transported more than about forty miles. Increased urbanization and development will clearly create additional need for these building materials, but these industries are not welcome in urban, suburban, or resort areas. Price increases permitting longer hauls for building materials and substitution by users of alternative building materials would serve to mitigate some of the impact on developing areas.

- The drilling of oil and gas wells is another segment of the minerals industry likely to be affected by land fragmentation. The most relevant land-based constraint is ownership of mineral rights. Conflicts with surface owners add to the costs and difficulty of exploring for, developing, and producing oil and gas. Increased urbanization and land fragmentation will make it more difficult and costly for the industry to continue.

- The counties that have recently lost clay and salt production show signs of an increase in population density, built-up areas, and urban sprawl, hence there may be some effect of increased land fragmentation on production of these minerals. Increased land values and increased difficulty in gaining access to the minerals can drive up the costs of production, and may already have contributed to the decrease in production in these counties.

- Peat production is likely to be sensitive to land fragmentation and especially to perceptions about the environmental effects of its production. This is a problem, since peat-producing counties are forecasted to have more urban land-use growth than the state average.

## General

- As rural areas become more populated, we can reasonably expect further confrontations with residents who are unfamiliar with the individuals and companies that gain their livelihood from the land. We can expect conflict over industry practices and procedures, such as cutting of forestland, spreading of manure on agricultural fields, excavation of minerals, and trucking associated with these industries.

- For all of the land-based industries, growing distances between them and supporting indus-

tries and businesses make it more difficult to conduct business efficiently. Transportation and production costs are a major economic factor for these industries. If those costs increase, the profitability of the industries declines.

- Most of the assets of the land-based industries are not in products or facilities, but in the land itself. While the value of products may fluctuate, the value of the land for its development potential is increasing in both absolute and real terms. Some of that development potential relates to opportunities to live in or near natural resources. We are experiencing a phenomenon where agriculture, forestry, and mining are unable to compete with the development values of the land, and therefore are being priced out of some areas at the same time that development is fragmenting land once dedicated to those land-based industries.

The reader is encouraged to see chapter 5 of this book for a broader coverage of land use conditions and issues.

## Public Policy Toward Land Preservation in Michigan

The logic for public policy makers to use in considering preservation of farmland, forestland, and mineral land is couched in terms of balancing the "public good" and "private benefit" concepts. Even if land values are substantially higher in alternative uses, public policy makers may want to consider preserving certain lands in current uses, with appropriate compensations, because of the "public good" that those lands convey. The lands most likely to be considered for preservation in current uses are those closest to urbanizing areas and those elsewhere having special importance to their communities.

## Public Policy Toward Farmland Preservation in Michigan

Michigan has two state-level farm preservation programs. These are the P.A. 116 program and the Purchase of Development Rights (PDR) program. Both programs are administered by the Michigan Department of Agriculture (MDA) and both were authorized by the Farmland and Open Space Preservation Act, passed in 1974 and amended in 2000 (codified as parts 361 and 362 of the Natural

Resources and Environmental Protection Act, Act 451) (Norris and Deaton 2001).

Farmland owners participating in the P.A. 116 program enter into development rights agreements with the state. A farmland owner transfers development rights to the state for a period of no fewer than ten years under this agreement. In return, the owner claims a credit against state income tax liability for the amount by which property taxes exceed 3.5% of household or business income. When the P.A. 116 development rights agreement ends, an amount equal to the tax credits from the last seven years is placed as a lien against the property. The lien is due when the land is sold or converted to a nonagricultural use. (Norris and Deaton 2001).

The current eligibility requirements for P.A. 116 are that farmland be one or more of the following:

- Forty acres or more under one ownership, with 51% or more of the land area devoted to agriculture.
- Five acres or more under one ownership, but fewer than forty acres, with 51% or more of the land area devoted to agriculture, and producing a gross annual income from agriculture of $200 or more per acre.
- A farm designated by the MDA as a specialty farm under one ownership that has produced a gross annual income of $2,000 or more from an agricultural use.
- Parcels of land under one ownership that are not contiguous but that constitute an integral part of a farming operation.

Any income collected from P.A. 116 liens helps fund the state's PDR program (Michigan's Purchase of Development Rights). The PDR program purchases the development rights from farmland owners. Landowners retain all other rights in the land, but its development for nonagricultural purposes is precluded. With the 2000 amendment, the state PDR program also can make grants to township-administered or county-administered PDR programs whose local farmland preservation efforts satisfy certain requirements (Norris and Deaton 2001).

Both the P.A. 116 program and the PDR program were designed to protect land in agricultural use and to support farmers. The PDR program is both more general and more targeted than the P.A. 116 program. The PDR program is more general in that it focuses on characteristics of the land resource, rather than on an economic definition of the farm. The PDR program is more targeted because it focuses on the agricultural capacity of the farm. It also emphasizes (1) location relative to development pressures and other preserved areas, and (2) the importance of community planning and participation as important criteria in allocating state funds. The structure of the PDR program provides an opportunity for communities to examine their farmland preservation objectives and assess where preservation objectives are best targeted (Norris and Deaton 2001).

Should Michigan policymakers try to preserve farmland? Arguments for preserving farmland are most commonly voiced in four ways (see Norris and Deaton 2001 for a more complete treatment of this issue):

- Maintain the food supply;
- Achieve local economic benefits;
- Enable growth management;
- Preserve environmental amenities.

Each of these arguments has merit. Most economists moderate the importance of maintaining the food supply by concluding that despite the loss of farmland in any given county or state, the loss of productivity from that farmland likely will be made up by increases in agricultural productivity on the remaining acres, at least for the foreseeable future. However, in Michigan the loss of specialty agriculture is of major concern. In a 1997 report on farmland loss, the American Farmland Trust included two areas in western Michigan (the southwestern Michigan fruit and truck belt, comprised of land in Allegan, Berrien, and Van Buren Counties, and the western Michigan fruit and truck belt, including Antrim, Benzie, Charlevoix, Emmet, Grand Traverse, Kalkaska, Leelanau, Manistee, Mason, and Oceana Counties) among a list of the twenty most threatened farmland areas in the United States (Sorensen, Greene, and Russ 1997).

The local economic benefits argument is a concern in areas where local economies are highly dependent on agriculture. This argument has the most merit in counties where food processing and other forward and backward business linkages to production agriculture constitute a significant portion of the economy and the communities involved wish to preserve this economic base and the multiplier effects it provides as a primary industry.

The growth management argument for preserving farmland appears to have significant merit in Michigan. Metropolitan counties (those that include cities or contiguous groups of cities with a total population over fifty thousand) have an average of 42% of their land base in farmland. This compares to an average for all Michigan counties of 28% of the total land base in farmland. As metropolitan areas continue to grow, a high percentage of the farmland in these counties will be subject to development pressures. Growth management minimizes sprawl and the increased local public service inefficiencies and costs that sprawl entails. These public service inefficiencies include higher per capita cost of roads, water, sewer, and other infrastructure and inefficient use of developable lands. A study of eighteen Michigan communities comparing current development versus compact growth describes these costs (Burchell and Neuman 1997).

Perhaps the strongest argument for preserving farmland in Michigan is from a broad "public good" perspective. Farmland and other open spaces can help preserve the aesthetic and environmental amenities that Michigan citizens desire. The perceived loss of open landscapes associated with the loss of farmland or forestland is a widely cited problem of urbanizing land use patterns. Residents in a number of states have ranked the loss of environmental amenities equal to or higher than the loss of agricultural production capacity as a basis for concern about farmland loss (Norris and Deaton 2001). Preserving farmland in urbanizing areas does not reduce the need for attention to the environmental challenges highlighted in chapter 21. For a detailed treatment of the roles of farms in providing environmental amenities, see Jackson and Jackson 2002.

One might argue that the aesthetic environmental amenities could be met by alternative uses of the land resources, other than for agriculture. Possibilities include private holdings such as for resale into small parcels or for large tract developments at some future time, or public holdings for uses such as public parks or forest preserves. The resale into small private holdings makes productive management of these lands very difficult because of physical and ownership fragmentation. The holding of land for future large-tract development most often results in the land becoming idle and unmanaged for extended periods. The extensive use of farmland for public parks or public forest preserves necessitates substantial capital outlays that local or state governments likely would find difficult to achieve.

The four arguments advanced for farmland preservation encompass most of the reasons given for why public policy makers may want to address farmland conversion. The working definition of a farm or farmland, coupled with the objectives of a farmland preservation program, will influence which approaches to farmland preservation are most important. As Michigan citizens and state and local government units explore ways to preserve farmland, an understanding of the actual status of farmland conversion, along with an understanding of the public's objectives in preserving the services supplied by farmland, will be essential. This increased understanding will enable the most appropriate land use policy choices to be made for the long-term benefit of Michigan citizens and their communities (Norris and Deaton 2001).

In preserving farmland, as in any public policy decision, it is difficult to achieve a solution where everybody is better off because of the policy. Obviously, some restrictions on individual freedom result from an effort to achieve a public good. We live in a mixed economy where we are free to exercise many choices but have rules to follow. A program to manage urban sprawl would add rules and would involve costs in administration.

Strict zoning regulations would be the most intrusive on private owners' freedom to decide land use, with the least government/taxpayer cost. We are all subject to such regulations in urban areas and accept them, most of the time, as best for the community. Transfer of Development Rights would involve minimal costs to the taxpayer. The Purchase of Development Rights would be essentially a direct transfer from taxpayers to farmers.

## Commercial Forest Program and Private Forest Reserve Program

The Commercial Forestry Program (originally Act 94, P.A. 1925, and recodified in 1994 as Part 511 of P.A. 451), administered by the Michigan Department of Natural Resources (MDNR), provides a property tax reduction to private landowners as an incentive to retain and manage forestland for long-term timber production. Landowners in this Commercial Forest program agree to develop, maintain, and manage their land as a commercial forest, through planting, natural reproduction, or other silvicultural practices.

Landowners in the program pay a reduced

property tax rate of $1.10 per acre, and the State of Michigan pays $1.20 per acre annually to each county where land is enrolled in this program. Lands in this program are open to the public for fishing and hunting. According to the MDNR, in 2001, approximately 2.2 million acres were enrolled in the Commercial Forest Land program, representing 1,300 private forestland owners (Michigan Department of Natural Resources 2002). Another program with potential for expansion is the Private Forest Reserve Act (Part 513, P.A. 451 of 1994), which currently involves only approximately 5,000 acres, much of it in Newaygo County. It is designed for farms of 160 acres or less and provides a tax incentive for private owners on up to 40 acres of forest.

Conflicts over competing land uses for forestland will require policy makers to look at a range of options to achieve the objectives of the diverse set of interests held by Michigan citizens. (See chapter 5 for a broader treatment of land use issues.)

## Concluding Comments

In framing our concluding comments, we draw again upon excellent forward-looking sources made available to us by a number of contributors. The future of all three sets of industries, agriculture, forestry, and mining, necessitates profitability for them at the raw materials level; namely, the first stage of the value added process. At the enterprise level, it means that the units must have efficient production. Beyond the unit, they must have both inputs that are accessible and economical, and viable processing and manufacturing opportunities. The greater the units' involvement in the processing/manufacturing opportunities and the more value they can add to their raw materials, the greater the likelihood they can compete and remain viable.

To compete in the raw commodity stage of each industry, the units must be low-cost producers to survive in the longer run. To help them prosper in Michigan, policies that encourage them to differentiate their products, create market niches from which they can benefit, and otherwise become more consumer responsive will be beneficial. Further, policies that help these units and their industry capture added value through processing or manufacturing will further enhance their viability, and contribute more employment and income to the Michigan economy.

These industries are important in their own right, because of the necessary products they provide and the employment and income they represent. Through their multiplier effects as primary industries, they add substantially to the employment and income of Michigan. Further, they provide diversification to an economy heavily dependent on durable goods industries, principally motor vehicles and parts. Cycles in agriculture, in particular, are not highly correlated with the business cycle that swings Michigan's economy. While cycles today may not be as intense as in prior times, they do exist and have an influence. Further, these industries enhance the recreation and aesthetic values and heritage that define Michigan's character.

It is important from a policy perspective that we increase the public and governmental knowledge about these industries. As possible and appropriate, Michigan policy makers may want to consider economic policies and economic development incentives that help these primary industries to survive and flourish. Further, through public education and participatory action, Michigan could enhance the natural resource base on which the state so directly depends. This will require possible assistance to local and state agencies and industry and other interest groups, to plan for and protect those resources and help preserve their industries.

The future of the agricultural industry depends on a variety of considerations, and differs by geographic areas and enterprise groups. There is much consensus that farm numbers overall will decline but the number of large farms will increase because of expansion and consolidation to create more economically viable farm units. The strength of agricultural enterprises depends in major ways on the linkages with agricultural suppliers and with food processors. The agricultural input suppliers have consolidated rapidly in the recent decade, and are expected to go through additional major changes in the decade ahead. The food-processing sector has expanded its contribution to the Michigan economy over time, but in the last decade has shown some signs of weakening. Over the next decade, the impact of biotechnology; the ownership of intellectual property rights; the extensive concentration and vertical integration of production, processing, and marketing; and the influence of trade agreements, multinational economic blocks, and globalization will likely accentuate changes in agriculture that are difficult to predict.

Growth in large-scale animal agriculture, particularly as it pertains to large confined animal enterprises, has brought with it conflicts over siting, concern about environmental issues, and complaints about odors and aesthetic problems experienced by adjacent or nearby farm and residential home owners (see chapter 21 for a broader discussion). From 1998 to 2001, the percentage of Michigan's total dairy cow numbers in herds of five hundred or more increased from 10% to 22%. Likewise, between 1993 and 2001, the percentage of Michigan's total hog numbers in operations of five thousand or more hogs increased from 27% to 35%. This is significant because in a recent study of the North Central states that included Michigan, while nonfarmers in rural and urban areas had a positive attitude toward farmers, even with an occasional nuisance, there was a general negative attitude toward large livestock operations (Wachenheim and Rathge 2002).

The Michigan Right to Farm Act (RTFA) was passed to protect agricultural uses of land if the farm in question is operating in conformance with generally accepted agricultural and management practices as determined by the Michigan Department of Agriculture. Local governments, in cooperation with agricultural and other interests, must find a balance between viable farm enterprises and other community interests, and plan land use accordingly (Norris et al. 1999). Achieving this balance for large-scale animal agriculture likely will be a difficult public policy issue in the decade ahead.

There is also consensus that Michigan is losing land to nonfarm uses. However, the losses of farmland are not occurring evenly across the state. Much of Michigan's farmland is located in or near metropolitan counties. Urban growth in those areas has taken farmland and will significantly impact farmland in the future. Agriculture cannot compete at the margin of development through market forces alone, and will obviously lose to housing and other commercial developments. The relevant question is how to manage that transfer.

Land-owner compensation for development values is one means of holding back farm tract fragmentation and sprawl on the urban fringe. Research and extension education are important in achieving innovations in consumer-responsive agriculture, increasing crop yields and livestock performance, and enhancing farm income. Yet, in the absence of viable financial incentives for farm owners not exercising their development oppor-

tunities, it is likely that incentives for farmers to sell to developers on the urban fringe will remain very strong.

Michigan's two programs, the P. A. 116 program and the Purchase of Development Rights program, both contribute directly to farmland and open space preservation and can serve as direct inhibitors to tract fragmentation and sprawl development. Their continuation and augmentation with assistance to local governmental units would appear to be important policy considerations.

Not to be overlooked is the importance of the reuse of land that has suspected contamination from industrial sources, often called brownfield redevelopment of land, and the state and local programs that help advance it. Greater reuse of the many brownfield sites in Michigan will help alleviate the pressures of commercial and industrial developments on open spaces, including open farmland. A phrase that is growing in popularity is, "to save our farmland, we must save our cities."

Also important for viable agriculture would be added emphasis on business retention and expansion in the food-processing and farm input supply industries. Such retention and expansion efforts could cover not only large establishments but also small and potentially growing ones, as well as those farms that undertake some processing, and niche marketing and farm tourism.

Probably there is no more important public policy consideration than increasing the understanding of the impacts of urbanization, sprawl, and tract fragmentation on agriculture. While farms provide food, employment, and local income, they also provide significant "public goods"—protection of open space, watersheds for conservation of soil and water, habitat for wildlife, and aesthetic and amenity values for urban inhabitants and others. Increasingly, these combined values are motivating support for farmland preservation. Education about farmland benefits to urban environments and the broader Michigan economy will go far in augmenting the efforts of communities and the state to address protection of farmland.

The future of the forest industry in Michigan depends on the demand for its products as well as the forest industry's capacity to respond to that demand efficiently. The demand for forest products of all types continues to increase, both in Michigan and worldwide. However, land development, land use, and tract fragmentation occurring across Michigan are impacting the forest industry's ability to efficiently provide forest products. Federal, state, and local governmental units, industry, and the public must work together to ensure future availability of the supply of raw materials from both private and public lands.

Of major importance is raising the understanding of how fragmentation of forestlands has affected and will continue to affect the forest industry. The relocation of former urban dwellers to forested landscapes, the division of larger land tracts into smaller parcels for resale, and other fragmentation actions adversely affect the ability of the forest industry to continue to provide the products our state and society need. Additional education focused on private owners of forest tracts, over 300,000 in number, could bring greater understanding of multiple use possibilities and potential benefits of forestland to Michigan. Better coordination of existing information and technical assistance programs, including cost sharing across federal, state, and local agencies and the private and nonprofit entities, would enhance forest resources for the future.

For policymakers, it may be appropriate to revisit such matters as whether the incentives for private forest harvesting can be enhanced. Further, policymakers may wish to revisit management policies that would enhance forest production as well as permit harvesting on public lands to bring net timber growth and harvesting into greater balance for the benefit of Michigan, while preserving its landscape and aesthetic heritage. For example, Michigan had an abundance of tree planting programs in the 1930s, 1940s, and 1950s. The resulting forest stands are approaching maturity. The question of their harvest and regeneration is a current matter to be addressed. Public policy education for the citizenry, industry, and government, plus participatory approaches to planning, organization, and action can be used as key tools to help address these matters and achieve continued viability for the industry, while meeting objectives of the other interest groups, including governmental units.

The future of the minerals industries is better understood if distinctions are made concerning the different mineral components. The economic viability of the different minerals varies over time as market and industry conditions change. Michigan has seen a decline over the years in mineral industries for copper, iron ore, coal, and salt. By contrast, mineral industries for construc-

tion materials and natural gas have risen as market conditions and consumption needs have changed.

Also, the various mineral deposits in Michigan are subject to different degrees of risk from urbanization, sprawl, and land fragmentation. For example, sand, gravel, and crushed stone for construction must be available close to urbanizing areas, but in turn are impacted by urban development and incompatible adjacent land uses, as well as by sprawl and tract fragmentation. Peat and clay production, given their locations, are expected to be impacted because of urbanization in their areas. Industrial sand production is impacted by recreational, habitat, and aesthetic interests, as well as by recreational and second home development. By contrast, current production of gypsum, lime, and cement appear less likely to be impacted by Michigan's land use changes.

While Michigan has favorable geological conditions for a variety of minerals, finding new mineral extraction sites can be an expensive process. The economics of the industry must justify both the cost of exploration and the cost of actual production at the new site. Needed at a new site is an economic resource, both in terms of production and transportation and an efficient operation while minimizing potential conflict from adjacent land users. For minerals, extraction must occur at the sites where the resources are available and accessible, or extraction does not occur at all. Thus, in general, the mineral industries cannot remain strong over time unless sites are identified and protected for current and future use. Also highly desirable are plans for how the sites will look after the mineral extraction is completed. Predevelopment planning is essential for future spatial use of the land involved.

Governmental units, in cooperation with the industry and the various public interests, must address identification and protection of mineral sites and the compatibility of adjacent land uses. From a policy perspective, of major importance is raising the understanding of how urbanization, sprawl, and tract fragmentation have already affected and will continue to affect the various mineral industries. Also of major importance is identification and protection of possible mineral production sites, while recognizing both industry and other interests. Wise planning of adjacent land uses also is an important consideration in this process. As in the case of timberland harvest, public policy education for citizenry, industry, and governmental units, plus participatory approaches to planning and action can be used as key tools to help achieve continued viability for mineral industries while also meeting the objectives of other interest groups.

## Summary Policy Observations

The agriculture, forestry, and mining industries of Michigan are described in the first half of this chapter, and conditions affecting the status of those three industries are presented. In the second half of this chapter, land use challenges confronting the three industries are described. An important distinction is made between "public goods" and "private benefits." It is useful to highlight what appear to be the key public policy considerations influencing these primary industries.

Key policy considerations for the three industries to remain viable:

- Policies that encourage product differentiation, creation of market niches, and consumer responsiveness.
- Approaches that balance viable farm interests and community interests, particularly for large-scale animal agriculture.
- Policies that balance sustainable commercial timber harvest with other competing uses of Michigan public forestlands.
- Policies that protect crucial mineral sites from irreversible change, particularly on the urban fringe.

Key policy considerations for land use in Michigan's future:

- Approaches that foster increased understanding of the impacts of urbanization and sprawl, plus tract and ownership fragmentation on Michigan's agricultural, forestry, and mining lands.
- Policies that clarify the future land use patterns that are desired by Michigan citizens.
- Policies that coordinate land use guidance approaches that achieve the desired future land use patterns and industry viability.

The authors are indebted to the following persons for the time and source materials they so generously provided: Peter Kakela, Department of Resource Development, Michigan State University; Patricia Norris, Department of Agricultural Economics and Resource Development, Michigan State University; and Karen Potter-Witter, Department of Forestry, Michigan State University. We are also grateful to Larry Pederson, Forest Resources Management, Michigan Department of Natural Resources; and William Rustem and Holly Madill of Public Sector Consultants, Inc., Lansing, Michigan, as well as the Michigan Agricultural Statistics Service of the Michigan Department of Agriculture. Because of the high quality of their inputs, we have used them in whole or in part with little or no elaboration. We acknowledge their excellent work and thank them for it.

■

## REFERENCES

Burchell, Robert, and Nancy Neuman. 1997. The costs of current development versus compact growth. *Planning & Zoning News*, August.

Chase, Lew Allen. 1992. *Rural Michigan*. New York: Macmillan.

Ferris, John N. 2000. An analysis of the importance of agriculture and the food sector to the Michigan economy. Staff paper No. 00–11. East Lansing: Department of Agricultural Economics, Michigan State University.

———. 2001. Status and potential of Michigan natural resources. *Agricultural production in Michigan*. Special Report 115, Michigan Agricultural Experiment Station, Michigan State University.

Gere, Milton A. 2001. *The mineral industry of Michigan*. U.S. Geological Survey, 2000 Minerals Yearbook. Washington, D.C.: U.S. Government Printing Office.

Jackson, Dana L., and Laura L. Jackson. 2002. *The farm as natural habitat.* Washington, D.C.: Island Press.

Kakela, Peter. 2002. Michigan's major mineral and fuel resources, 2000. Working paper in process updating Status and Potential of Michigan's Natural Resources. *Nonrenewable Resources.* Special Report 81. 1995. Michigan Agricultural Experiment Station, Michigan State University.

Kakela, Peter, and Howard Haas. 2000. Status and potential of Michigan natural resources. *Michigan's Mineral Wealth.* Special Report 111, Michigan Agricultural Experiment Station, Michigan State University.

Kleweno, David D. 2001. *Michigan agricultural statistics 2000–2001.* Michigan Department of Agriculture 2000 Annual Report, Michigan Agricultural Statistics Service, USDA.

Leatherberry, Earl C., and J. S. Spencer Jr. 1996. *Michigan forest statistics, 1993.* Resource Bulletin NC-170, USDA, Forest Service, St. Paul, Minnesota.

Michigan Department of Natural Resources (DNR). 1996. *Michigan's forests.* Forest Management Division, DNR. Lansing, Michigan.

———. 2002. Michigan's growing and expanding forest resource. *http://www.dnr.state.mi.us.*

Norgaard, Kurt J. 1994. Subdivision Control Act causes 10+ acre land divisions. *Planning & Zoning News.* March.

Norris, Patricia E., and B. James Deaton. 2001. Understanding the demand for farmland preservation: Implications for Michigan policies. Staff Paper 2001–18, Department of Agricultural Economics, Michigan State University.

Norris, Patricia E., Michael Kaplowitz, Kurt Schindler, Laura Cheney, and Roger Bairstow. 1999. *Planning and zoning for animal agriculture in Michigan: A handbook for local governments.* Extension Bulletin E-2699, Michigan State University Extension.

Potter-Witter, Karen, 2002. Michigan forest products industry update. Working paper, Dept. of Forestry, Michigan State University.

Potter-Witter, Karen, Mel Koelling, Peter Kakela, and Howard Haas. 2000. Status and potential of Michigan natural resources. *Michigan's forest products industry.* Special Report 114, Michigan Agricultural Experiment Station, Michigan State University.

Public Sector Consultants, Inc. 2001. *Michigan land resource project.* Project Managers William Rustem and Holly Madill, Lansing, Michigan.

Smith, W. Brad, John S. Vissage, David R. Darr, and Raymond M. Sheffield. 2001. Forest resources of the United States, 1997. General Technical Report NC-219, USDA-Forest Service, St. Paul, Minnesota.

Sorensen, A. A., R. P. Greene, and K. Russ. 1997. Farming on the edge. American Farmland Trust. Northern Illinois University.

U.S. Department of Agriculture. 1999. *1997 Census of agriculture, Michigan, state and county data, volume 1, geographic area services.* Part 22. National Agricultural Statistics Service.

U.S. Department of Commerce. 2000. *1997 economic census, manufacturing, Michigan.* Economic and Statistics Administration, Census Bureau.

———. Bureau of the Census. *Census of manufactures* (various issues).

Wachenheim, Cheryl J., and Richard Rathge. 2002. Residence and farm experience influence perception of agriculture: A survey of north central residents. *Rural America* 16(4): 18–29.

# 11

# Economic Performance of Michigan Cities and Metropolitan Areas

*David Crary, George Erickcek, and Allen C. Goodman*

Acity provides local government services such as police and fire protection, water and sewer utilities, roads and streets, public transportation, and zoning establishment and enforcement. Geographic boundaries of cities once coincided with areas of regional economic interaction, but long ago urban population and economic activity grew beyond the political boundaries of most cities. Our analysis focuses on both cities and the larger metropolitan areas of which they are a declining part.[1] As economic activity has pushed beyond city boundaries, many central cities have suffered declines in population and economic activity, with fiscal problems exacerbated by the departure of high-income families who are better able and more likely to move to suburbs.

This chapter examines Michigan's cities and metropolitan areas with respect to employment and population growth, per capita income relative to the U.S. average, racial composition, central city population and housing, and public policy related to cities. In evaluating the economic performance of Michigan cities and their surrounding metropolitan areas, we focus on the following topics and find the following results:

*1. Industrial Mix and Metropolitan Area Employment Growth.* During the 1990s, Michigan MSA employment changes ranged from a decline of 0.5% for Flint to a growth of 31.4% for the Grand Rapids–Muskegon–Holland MSA. These differences in performance relate closely to the industrial specializations of different regions, but are also influenced by changing industrial competitiveness. Michigan and all of its MSAs except Benton Harbor specialize heavily in the motor vehicle industry. During the 1990s, motor vehicle jobs grew by nearly 25% for the United States, but by only 5% for Michigan. Michigan's loss of competitiveness in motor vehicles was shared across most of its MSAs, with Ann Arbor, Lansing–East Lansing, and particularly Flint suffering large percentage declines in motor vehicle employment.[2] All Michigan MSAs except the Grand Rapids–Muskegon–Holland area experienced job losses over the past decade compared to expectations based upon their industrial composition alone. Grand Rapids performed well by maintaining its competitiveness in the growing office furniture industry while improving its competitiveness in a number of other manufacturing industries, including suppliers to the furniture industry.

*2. Population and Income Growth.* Except for Ann Arbor and Grand Rapids–Muskegon–Holland area, population and income growth in the state's metropolitan areas lagged behind the U.S. average from 1969 to 2000. Population growth for the Greater Detroit area (Combined Metropolitan Statistical Area or CMSA of Detroit, Ann Arbor, and Flint) ranked third from the bottom of the nation's thirty-two largest MSAs, with growth of 3.4% versus 40.2% for the United States as a whole. The Detroit CMSA saw its relative per capita income fall from 117% of the U.S. average in 1969 to 110.9% in 2000. Within Michigan, population growth between 1969 and 2000 ranged from slight declines for the Detroit, Flint, and Benton Harbor MSAs to growth of 44.8% for Grand Rapids–Muskegon–Holland area and 62.1% for Ann Arbor. Between 1969 and 2000, per capita income relative to that of the United States as a whole declined for all nine of Michigan's MSAs, with declines ranging from only 0.8% for Ann Arbor to 21% for Flint and Jackson. Population growth and changes in relative per capita income also differed substantially across counties in multicounty MSAs. In the Detroit MSA, for example, population declined by 23.3% in Wayne County but grew by 35.1% in Oakland County; Wayne's relative per capita income fell by 17%, while Oakland's grew by 11%.

3. *Regional Migration Patterns and Problems of Central Cities.* In Michigan's MSAs, outward movement from central cities and counties to suburban areas continued during the 1990s, and has been a pattern common to MSAs throughout the country and world for several decades. Between 1995 and 2001, the core county in six of Michigan's nine MSAs lost several thousand households, and seven suffered total income declines. With only two exceptions (Benton Harbor and Jackson), people moving out of core counties had higher average incomes than those moving into these counties. Analysis of major Midwest MSAs and their central cities reveals a general pattern of rapidly declining central city population between 1970 and 2000 combined with population growth in outlying areas of the MSAs. Grand Rapids was the key exception to this pattern, with no net change in the central city population as total MSA population increased by 43%.

Between 1980 and 2000, declining central city population was partly due to declining household size, which was the general pattern for both central cities and suburban areas. However, while housing units were being added in the suburban areas, central cities were often losing households, with a 24% decline for Detroit and declines in excess of 15% for Flint and Saginaw. In the Detroit MSA, inner suburban areas of Wayne, Macomb,

and Oakland Counties also experienced declining populations, as small increases in number of households have not offset declines in household size.

4. *Policy Options for Michigan and Its Cities and Suburbs.* Suburban growth creates severe challenges for older core cities and counties in providing and financing local government services. This is exacerbated by the fact that the state's core cities house high percentages of persons living in poverty, while serving as workplaces for many suburban commuters. The long search for policy changes or new policies to promote central city revival has not revealed any clear and politically feasible options. Michigan's school finance reform, to the extent that it improves school quality while reducing tax burdens in urban areas, could mitigate urban decline. Similar finance reform could be explored for other local government services, through expanded state or regional revenue sharing. Urban enterprise zones with tax abatements and business subsidies have been tested on a limited basis, and could perhaps be expanded. Greater planning coordination among city, township, and county governments within MSAs might also play an important role, but this option is limited by strong "home rule" policies in Michigan that make such coordination voluntary. These policies will be politically acceptable only if suburban residents can be convinced that helping to fund urban revitalization is in their best interest.

### Industrial Mix and Metropolitan Area Employment Growth

A city's location is typically determined by historical availability of transportation and productive resources, and each city or metropolitan area usually has an identifiable specialization in one or more industries. These nodes of concentrated economic activity typically expand over time as population and economic activity of the nation and world grow. The bulk of the state's economic activity takes place in its densely populated cities and adjacent urban and suburban areas. In 2000, the state's nine metropolitan areas covered only twenty-four of the state's eighty-three counties but accounted for 82.2% of the state's population, 89.3% of its earnings, and 84.9% of the state's total employment. While these shares have declined some since 1969, metropolitan areas still maintain a larger than average share of the state's economic activity relative to the nation.[3]

Historically, cities have provided innovative environments that have generated business growth through agglomerative economics. Hoover and Giarratani (1985, 339) note, "[Cities] have been the main seedbeds of innovations; in economic terms, this involves the genesis of new techniques, new products and new firms. Such places provide the exposure to a wide range of ideas and problems from which solutions emerge."

Over time, cities or metropolitan areas grow at different rates, depending on their industrial specialization and competitiveness. Thompson (1982) and Hoover and Giarratani (1985) provide good explanations of the typical structure of a region's economy. Every region in a modern economy tends to specialize in production of one or more *export* products or services that are sold to people outside of that region. In Michigan, for example, Detroit and Flint specialize in motor vehicles, Grand Rapids–Muskegon–Holland in office furniture, Lansing–East Lansing in state government, and Ann Arbor in higher education. Regional *export* activities provide the basis for other employment in a region. Other firms in the region may provide parts or services that are used in producing goods or services exported from a region; metal products used in motor vehicles in Detroit, and plastics used in office furniture in the Grand Rapids–Muskegon–Holland area, for example. These are referred to as *indirect export* activities. These inputs can either be imported or produced locally. One way for a region to expand is through *import substitution,* in which a parts supplier locates in the area in order to produce parts that were previously being imported.

The auto industry, with its strong focus on just-in-time production, encourages, if not demands, suppliers to locate in close proximity to their assembly plants in order to insure timely delivery. General Motors, for example, has requested that state economic development efforts to attract major suppliers to its new Lansing production facility be limited to a thirty-mile radius around the plant. A local parts supplier to a local finished goods export industry might also export some of its parts to finished goods producers in other regions, thus representing both *indirect export* and *export* activity, respectively. Finally, a large percentage of employment in a region generally provides basic services to the people living in the area: schoolteachers, retail workers, construction workers, bank tellers, and so on. These are referred to as *local service* activities. In the Grand Rapids–Muskegon–Holland MSA, for example, export employment accounts for an estimated 47.6% of the four-county total employment, indirect exports employment accounts for 7.8%, and private and public local service producers make up the remaining 44.6%.[4]

Regional specialization is most often measured by a location quotient (LQ) for an industry, which equals the industry's share of regional employment divided by the industry's share of U.S. employment. In 2000 for example, 20.9% of Michigan's employment was in manufacturing and 14% of U.S. employment was in manufacturing. Dividing 20.9% by 14% gives Michigan's location quotient for manufacturing as 1.49. Typically, location quotients are calculated at more detailed levels than for total manufacturing, but a manufacturing LQ gives a quick indication of employment composition in a region. Industrial location quotients somewhat greater than 1.0 are generally used to identify an *export* or *indirect export* industry for a region. In the analysis below we focus on those greater than 1.5.[5] Table 11.1 provides manufacturing LQs for Michigan and each of its nine metropolitan areas, and identifies leading industries of specialization for each region for 1990 and 2000.

Except for the Lansing–East Lansing MSA, which houses the State's capitol and Michigan State University, LQs for manufacturing are considerably greater than one in each of the metropolitan areas. Moreover, except for Flint, which suffered a nearly 40% decline in manufacturing employment, the location quotient for manufacturing either held its own or grew in the 1990s in each region. The Grand Rapids–Muskegon–Holland MSA, for example, ended the decade with a manufacturing concentration that was nearly twice that for the nation as a whole, making it the most specialized in manufacturing of Michigan's MSAs.

A more detailed examination of metropolitan area LQs reveals that their heavy concentration in manufacturing activity is focused mostly in one or two industrial sectors (table 11.1). To no one's surprise, the motor vehicle industry tops the industrial specialization for the state and for six of its nine metro areas. For example, the Detroit area started the 1990s with a concentration in motor vehicles employment that was over 12 times greater than the national average. At the end of the ten years, its concentration dipped only slightly, to 11.8 times as great. Flint, the MSA most heavily specialized in motor vehicles, fared far

**TABLE 11.1**

**Regional Location Quotients for Manufacturing and for Industries with LQs Greater than 1.50 in 2000**

| | 1990 | 2000 | | 1990 | 2000 |
|---|---|---|---|---|---|
| **Ann Arbor** | | | **Benton Harbor** | | |
| Manufacturing | 1.34 | 1.36 | Manufacturing | 1.84 | 1.89 |
| State Education | 7.56 | 7.24 | Primary Metal Products | 5.12 | 5.91 |
| Motor Vehicles & Equipment | 11.45 | 7.16 | Industrial Mach. & Computers | 4.78 | 3.47 |
| Federal Medical | 2.98 | 3.58 | Rubber and Plastics Products | 4.00 | 3.20 |
| Fabricated Metal Products | 1.46 | 1.82 | Fabricated Metal Products | 1.48 | 1.75 |
| Industrial Mach. & Computers | 1.58 | 1.71 | Printing and Publishing | 1.85 | 1.74 |
| Chemicals and Allied Products | 1.02 | 1.60 | | | |
| | | | **Flint** | | |
| **Detroit** | | | Manufacturing | 1.72 | 1.29 |
| Manufacturing | 1.32 | 1.49 | Motor Vehicles & Equipment | 27.62 | 13.09 |
| Motor Vehicles & Equipment | 12.30 | 11.82 | Local Gov't Medical | 2.98 | 3.38 |
| Fabricated Metal Products | 2.35 | 2.49 | General Merchandise Stores | 1.70 | 1.65 |
| Industrial Mach. & Computers | 1.76 | 1.75 | | | |
| | | | **Jackson** | | |
| **Grand Rapids–Muskegon–Holland** | | | Manufacturing | 1.35 | 1.40 |
| Manufacturing | 1.72 | 1.96 | Motor Vehicles & Equipment | 3.89 | 3.62 |
| Furniture and Fixtures | 11.34 | 10.44 | Industrial Mach. & Computers | 2.26 | 3.57 |
| Fabricated Metal Products | 3.30 | 3.30 | Fabricated Metal Products | 5.71 | 3.19 |
| Rubber and Plastics Products | 2.03 | 2.53 | | | |
| Industrial Mach. & Computers | 2.17 | 2.51 | **Kalamazoo–Battle Creek** | | |
| Motor Vehicles & Equipment | 2.51 | 2.49 | Manufacturing | 1.49 | 1.62 |
| Stone, Clay, Glass, Concrete | 1.44 | 2.15 | Motor Vehicles & Equipment | 2.59 | 5.59 |
| Chemicals and Allied Products | 1.79 | 2.05 | Paper and Allied Products | 4.07 | 3.63 |
| Primary Metal Products | 1.61 | 1.91 | Fabricated Metal Products | 2.88 | 2.06 |
| General Merchandise Stores | 1.53 | 1.57 | Food and Kindred Products | 2.80 | 2.03 |
| | | | State Education | 1.90 | 1.83 |
| **Lansing-East Lansing** | | | Primary Metal Products | 1.50 | 1.75 |
| Manufacturing | 0.83 | 0.84 | | | |
| Motor Vehicles & Equipment | 11.95 | 7.14 | **Michigan** | | |
| State Education | 5.99 | 5.85 | Manufacturing | 1.37 | 1.50 |
| Other State Government | 4.42 | 4.04 | Motor Vehicles & Equipment | 9.47 | 8.12 |
| Insurance Carriers | 1.52 | 2.16 | Fabricated Metal Products | 2.35 | 2.38 |
| | | | Furniture and Fixtures | 1.96 | 2.23 |
| **Saginaw–Bay City–Midland** | | | Rubber and Plastic Products | 1.65 | 1.81 |
| Manufacturing | 1.52 | 1.52 | Industrial Mach. & Computers | 1.67 | 1.77 |
| Motor Vehicles & Equipment | 10.88 | 8.61 | | | |
| General Merchandise Stores | 1.45 | 1.79 | | | |

SOURCE: U.S. Department of Labor, Michigan Department of Career Development, and authors' calculations.

worse, with its LQ in vehicles falling from nearly 28 in 1990 to about 13 in 2000, as it lost over one-half of the motor vehicle jobs it had in 1990. Even the Grand Rapids–Muskegon–Holland MSA had LQs in motor vehicles of about 2.5, despite its primary specialization in furniture, where its LQs were over 10 for the two years.

Table 11.1 also reveals a few *direct export* industries besides motor vehicles and furniture for certain regions: chemicals in Grand Rapids–Muskegon–Holland and Ann Arbor, food (cereal) in Kalamazoo–Battle Creek, and industrial machinery and computers for Benton Harbor, for example.[6] Most of the remaining manufacturing industries with high LQs—metals, and rubber and plastic products in various regions—probably represent *indirect export* activity by providing supplies to the motor vehicle or furniture industries. For example, many of the manufacturing industries with high LQs in Grand Rapids–Muskegon–Holland are likely to supply parts to both the furniture and/or auto industries.

Finally, table 11.1 shows that many of the state's metropolitan areas hold strong concentrations in activities in addition to manufacturing. Saginaw–Bay City–Midland, Flint, and Grand Rapids–Muskegon–Holland all have above average concentrations in general merchandise stores, reflecting their role as regional retail centers. Of course, Ann Arbor has heavy specialization in state education (University of Michigan), as well as federal medical (VA) and other state employment (U of M hospital). In addition, the Lansing–East Lansing MSA has a strong concentration in insurance in addition to its obvious concentration in state government and state education (Michigan State University).

Areas with high concentrations in any manufacturing or nonmanufacturing industry may be extremely vulnerable to industry-specific downturns. However, a region is typically pleased with its high specialization in an industry, as long as that industry is doing well and the region is maintaining or increasing its share in the industry. This was the case with the furniture industry in Grand Rapids–Muskegon–Holland during the 1990s before the industry took a major stumble in 2000 and 2001. If industry employment or the regional share of the industry's employment declines significantly, then concern with overspecialization can become intense. This has occurred for the motor vehicle industry in most regions of Michigan since 1980, and it has become a concern in Grand Rapids–Muskegon–Holland with the recent decline in demand for office furniture.

Total wage and salary employment in all metropolitan areas of Michigan except for Flint increased during the 1990s (table 11.2) as the nation enjoyed its longest expansion on record during the decade, and U.S. employment rose by 20.4%. Only the Grand Rapids–Muskegon–Holland and Ann Arbor MSAs outpaced the nation in job growth during the 1990s. Employment in Grand Rapids–Muskegon–Holland rose by 31.4%, while Ann Arbor surpassed the national average by less than a half percent. Employment in the other areas increased more slowly than the national rate. Flint posted a slight (0.5%) decline.

There are two reasons for a region to lag the national average in job growth. One is that the region's industrial composition of industries grew more slowly than the national growth rate. The other is that many of the region's firms grew below their industries' average, which suggests that the region's firms in those industries lost their competitive edge. This concept is illustrated first by analyzing the panel for Michigan in table 11.2. In the "Actual Job Growth" columns, total jobs in Michigan grew by 17.7% compared to 20.4% for the United States. Manufacturing employment in Michigan increased by 3.8%, while nationwide manufacturing employment fell by 3.2% during the 1990s. Michigan lagged behind the United States considerably in motor vehicles with a 5.0% growth rate versus 25.2% for the United States as a whole. In other words, manufacturing employment grew more in Michigan than it did nationwide, despite employment growth in its flagship industry, motor vehicles, being well below national employment growth in the industry.

The columns labeled "Predicted Job Growth" calculate Michigan's job growth if each Michigan industry had grown at the same rate as job growth in that industry for the United States. This analysis was carried out for between twenty and fifty industries, depending on data availability by industry for each region. The application of this analysis for a particular industry is demonstrated using the motor vehicle industry. Since national job growth in motor vehicles was 25.2% for the decade, Michigan would have gained seventy thousand motor vehicle jobs *if it had maintained its 1990 share of motor vehicle employment through 2000*. The difference between Michigan's actual job growth in motor vehicles of fourteen thousand and the predicted growth of seventy thousand is the loss of fifty-six thousand jobs due to loss in state competitiveness or market share in motor vehicle jobs. Michigan's share of U.S. motor vehicle jobs declined from about 42% in 1980 to about 35% in 1990, and to about 28% in 2000. The declining share in the 1990s was related to extensive GM plant closings announced early in the 1990s (Crary and Hogan 1992) and expansion of non-Michigan plants, particularly the Japanese-owned "transplants" located in other parts of the United States.

To calculate "Predicted Job Growth" for the manufacturing rows of table 11.2, each manufacturing industry in a region is increased (or decreased) by the growth rate for that industry for the United States, with results summed to yield the predicted job growth for manufacturing. Here we find some good news for Michigan; while the

**TABLE 11.2**

**Wage and Salary Employment Growth for Michigan MSAs, 1990–2000, Actual and Predicted Based on Shift-Share Analysis**

| Region | Actual Job Growth Number | Actual Job Growth Percentage | Predicted Job Growth[a] Number | Predicted Job Growth[a] Percentage | Local Competitiveness[b] Number | Local Competitiveness[b] Percentage |
|---|---|---|---|---|---|---|
| **United States** | | | | | | |
| Total jobs | 22,356,000 | 20.4% | | | | |
| Manufacturing | −609,000 | −3.2% | | | | |
| Motor vehicle | 200,900 | 25.2% | | | | |
| **Michigan** | | | | | | |
| Total jobs | 701,000 | 17.7% | 1,105,000 | 27.8% | −404,000 | −10.1% |
| Manufacturing | 36,000 | 3.8% | 69,000 | 6.9% | −33,000 | −3.1% |
| Motor vehicle | 14,000 | 5.0% | 70,000 | 25.2% | −56,000 | −20.2% |
| **Ann Arbor** | | | | | | |
| Total jobs | 49,300 | 20.7% | 56,600 | 23.8% | −7,300 | −3.1% |
| Manufacturing | −1,000 | −1.8% | 5,000 | 9.0% | −6,000 | −10.8% |
| Motor vehicle[c] | −4,400 | −21.8% | 5,000 | 25.2% | −9,400 | −47.0% |
| **Benton Harbor** | | | | | | |
| Total jobs | 6,000 | 8.8% | 16,500 | 24.3% | −10,500 | −15.5% |
| Manufacturing | −2,400 | −11.0% | 200 | 0.9% | −2,600 | −11.9% |
| Motor vehicle | n.a. | n.a. | n.a. | n.a. | n.a. | n.a. |
| **Detroit** | | | | | | |
| Total jobs | 302,000 | 15.9% | 576,500 | 30.3% | −274,500 | −14.4% |
| Manufacturing | 21,000 | 4.8% | 41,200 | 9.4% | −20,200 | −4.6% |
| Motor vehicle | 28,000 | 16.2% | 43,500 | 25.2% | −15,500 | −9.0% |
| **Flint** | | | | | | |
| Total jobs | −900 | −0.5% | 38,900 | 22.9% | −39,800 | −23.4% |
| Manufacturing | −20,500 | −40.2% | 8,100 | 15.9% | −28,600 | −56.1% |
| Motor vehicle[c] | −17,800 | −51.0% | 8,700 | 25.2% | −26,500 | −76.2% |
| **Grand Rapids–Muskegon–Holland** | | | | | | |
| Total jobs | 141,400 | 31.4% | 85,700 | 19.0% | 55,700 | 12.4% |
| Manufacturing | 27,900 | 20.7% | 3,200 | 2.4% | 24,700 | 18.3% |
| Furniture | 2,500 | 10.6% | 2,400 | 10.2% | 100 | 0.4% |
| Motor vehicle[c] | 3,000 | 35.7% | 2,100 | 25.2% | 900 | 10.5% |
| **Jackson** | | | | | | |
| Total jobs | 9,000 | 16.2% | 11,000 | 19.9% | −2,000 | −3.7% |
| Manufacturing | −400 | −3.1% | 500 | 3.8% | −900 | −6.9% |
| Motor vehicle[c] | 200 | 12.5% | 400 | 25.2% | −200 | −12.7% |
| **Kalamazoo–Battle Creek** | | | | | | |
| Total jobs | 23,000 | 11.9% | 34,500 | 17.9% | −11,500 | −6.0% |
| Manufacturing | −1,000 | −2.0% | −700 | −1.4% | −300 | −0.6% |
| Motor vehicle[c] | 5,600 | 151.4% | 900 | 25.2% | 4,700 | 126.2% |
| **Lansing–East Lansing** | | | | | | |
| Total jobs | 21,500 | 10.0% | 46,500 | 21.5% | −25,000 | −11.5% |
| Manufacturing | −3,200 | −10.2% | 4,700 | 15.0% | −7,900 | −25.2% |
| Motor vehicle[c] | −6,100 | −31.8% | 4,800 | 25.2% | −10,900 | −57.0% |
| **Saginaw–Bay City–Midland** | | | | | | |
| Total jobs | 18,800 | 11.5% | 33,200 | 20.3% | −14,400 | −8.8% |
| Manufacturing | −4,500 | −10.4% | 1,400 | 3.2% | −5,900 | −13.6% |
| Motor vehicle[c] | −1,100 | −8.3% | 3,300 | 25.2% | −4,400 | −33.5% |

SOURCE: U.S. Department of Labor, Michigan Department of Career Development, and authors' calculations.
(a) Uses U.S. growth rate for detailed industries to predict industrial job growth for each region.
(b) Difference between actual growth for region and prediction using U.S. growth by industry.
(c) Except for U.S., Michigan, and Detroit, regional employment data are published for transportation equipment and not for motor vehicles separately. Since 95% of Michigan transportation equipment employment is in motor vehicles, we have treated transportation equipment employment in other regions as motor vehicle employment.

competitive job loss in motor vehicles was fifty-six thousand, the loss for manufacturing *including* motor vehicles was only thirty thousand. Thus, other manufacturing jobs increased by twenty-three thousand jobs more than predicted. Michigan gained market share in some manufacturing industries that partially offset its declining share in motor vehicles. Had every Michigan industry grown at the national rate for that industry, job growth would have been the predicted rate of 27.8% rather than the actual 17.7% growth rate, so there was a competitive loss of 10.1% in total jobs. Part of the competitive loss for total jobs represents multiplier effects in the local service industries based on the competitive job losses in the state's export sectors.

Returning to the MSAs, manufacturing employment grew by 20.7% for Grand Rapids–Muskegon–Holland and 4.8% for Detroit, but declined for each of the other seven regions. Declines ranged from less than 4% for Ann Arbor, Jackson, and Kalamazoo–Battle Creek to between 10 and 11% for Benton Harbor, Lansing–East Lansing, and Saginaw–Bay City–Midland, and a staggering 40% for Flint. There was a significant reallocation of motor vehicle jobs by region, with losses of 4,400 in Ann Arbor, 17,800 in Flint, 6,100 in Lansing–East Lansing, and 1,100 in Saginaw–Bay City–Midland offset by gains of 28,000 in Detroit, 5,600 in Kalamazoo–Battle Creek,[7] 3,000 in Grand Rapids–Muskegon–Holland, and 200 in Jackson. Only in Grand Rapids–Muskegon–Holland and Kalamazoo–Battle Creek did motor vehicle employment grow at a faster rate than the national rate, but these two areas were starting from very small bases.

As mentioned previously, the state's manufacturers, outside of the automotive industry, remained competitive. In Ann Arbor, Grand Rapids–Muskegon–Holland, and Lansing–East Lansing, non-auto manufacturers generally took market share from their national rivals. However, in Detroit, Flint, Jackson, and Saginaw–Bay City–Midland non-auto manufacturers did not successfully retain market shares. For Kalamazoo-Battle Creek, a large competitive job gain in motor vehicles, due to the strong performance of Japanese-controlled transplants, was more than offset by competitive job losses in other industries, such as food (cereal), fabricated metals, and chemicals (not shown separately in the table). The competitive job loss in manufacturing across regions ranged from a low of –0.6% for the Kalamazoo–Battle Creek area to a high of –56.1%

for Flint. The Grand Rapids–Muskegon–Holland MSA was the only region to enjoy a competitive increase in manufacturing jobs, with 18.3% of its 20.7% growth in this sector coming from competitive increases. Interestingly, job growth in the area's world-renowned furniture industry was only slightly above the predicted level, with all of the competitive gains coming in other manufacturing industries.

If an area's economic base is competitive, and thus gains market share from its national rivals, then its nonbase industries (retail trade, for example) are also likely to show a competitive gain as these industries expand to serve the larger number of employees in the economic base industries. This endogenous relationship magnifies the area's true competitiveness or lack thereof. For example, total competitive job gains of 55,700 in the Grand Rapids–Muskegon–Holland area were slightly more than double its competitive job gains of 24,700 in manufacturing, for an addition of 12.4% to its total job growth over the decade. For the other eight regions, competitive manufacturing job losses produced competitive losses in total jobs as a multiple of the competitive losses in manufacturing. The multipliers ranged from a low of about 1.2 (7,300 ÷ 6,000) relative to Ann Arbor's manufacturing losses, to 13 for Detroit. Although Ann Arbor nonmanufacturer's lost ground as well, their losses were slight. In fact, Ann Arbor's trade and finance sectors gained share, probably as a result of rapid population growth in this region with many residents commuting to jobs in the Detroit metropolitan area but shopping and banking locally. Many of these new residents may have moved out of the Detroit metropolitan area, thereby reducing nonmanufacturing employment in the Detroit PMSA. Similarly, competitive job losses in nonmanufacturing for Flint might have been considerably greater if Flint were not a fairly easy commute to alternate jobs in neighboring metropolitan areas (including Ann Arbor, Detroit, and Saginaw–Bay City–Midland) so that residents could continue to live in Flint even if they had lost a prior job in Flint.

As the market for a product or service matures and production becomes more standardized, new producers from other areas might expand. Also, local producers will seek less expensive and, typically, more rural environments in which to locate, either at the edge of their cities of origin or in a new region, as indicated by Mills and Lubuele (1997, 731). This suggests that cities must continually provide an environment for the cultivation of new ideas and products in order to grow and prosper (Markusen 1985). Therefore, it is probably a mistake to blame the state and its cities for not providing a competitive environment for their long-time motor vehicle industry. Motor vehicles are a mature industry, and the tremendous market gains made by foreign nameplates during the 1990s repeat a pattern seen earlier in other industries, such as steel and consumer electronics, where U.S. producers were once dominant. Unfortunately, in six of the state's metropolitan areas, non-auto industries also lost ground. Still, the fact that in three of the metropolitan areas the other manufacturers gained share suggests that the state's cities are still contenders. This is especially true for the Grand Rapids–Muskegon–Holland area, which proved itself as a very productive location for the rapidly innovating office furniture industry and for suppliers wanting to locate close to this expanding industry.

## Population and Per Capita Income in Metropolitan Areas

Given the relationship between an area's export-focused manufacturing base and its nonexport services sectors, the loss of competitiveness in most of Michigan's cities and metropolitan areas clearly has had a negative impact on all sectors of their economies. Over the past three decades, Michigan's metropolitan areas as a group lost ground to the nation in terms of population and per capita income. Despite strong population gains in the Ann Arbor PMSA, the greater Detroit CMSA experienced sluggish population growth and witnessed a relative decline to the nation in per capita income.

Among the top thirty-two metropolitan areas in the country, ranked in order of their 2000 population, the Detroit CMSA was ranked sixth in 1969 and eighth in 2000, with San Francisco and Boston moving ahead of Detroit in population over this period.[8] While total U.S. population grew by 40.2% over this thirty-one-year period, Detroit's population grew by only 3.4%, so Detroit's share of U.S. population fell from 2.6% in 1969 to 1.9% in 2000. Cleveland and Pittsburgh were the only two MSAs that performed worse than Detroit in terms of population growth over the thirty-one-year period, with population falling by 4.3% and 12.2% in these two areas, respectively. Other major metropolitan areas from the Great Lakes and Northeast sections of the country, such

as New York, Chicago, Philadelphia, and Boston, all grew considerably faster over this period than did the Detroit area.

Virtually all of the areas located in the Great Lakes and Northeast sections of the country experienced growth rates less than half of that for the United States, while areas in the South and West grew by considerably more than the United States as a whole, with many doubling or tripling in size over this period. Glaeser, Scheinkman, and Shleifer (1995) found that a high initial concentration of jobs in manufacturing for an area, which was the case for most Great Lakes and Northeastern urban areas, led to slower population growth over the period from 1960 to 1990. This relationship is explained partly by the fact that jobs in manufacturing declined by 8% between 1969 and 2000, while total jobs increased by 87%. Also, the Great Lakes and Northeastern areas suffered further erosion of jobs in their manufacturing bases, as manufacturing jobs shifted increasingly to areas in the South and West, as documented by Bram and Anderson (2001).

While population growth is an important measure of performance for a region, per capita income is a better measure of a region's economic health. For 1969, per capita income for San Antonio was 82.3% of that of the United States as a whole, and per capita income for San Francisco was 128.8%; for 2000, their incomes were 87.3% and 158.1% of the national rate, respectively. Glaeser (1998) and other researchers have found a positive correlation between the size of a metropolitan area and its per capita income. For 1969, we find a positive correlation of 0.62 between regional per capita income and a region's population, but this correlation falls to 0.47 for 2000. Over the same period, New York increased its relative income level from 128% to 134.3% of that of the United States, despite its relatively slow population growth. Similarly, Boston increased its relative income position by 21.3% despite slow population growth. In contrast, relative income for the Detroit CMSA fell from 117% to 110.9% of the U.S. average between 1969 and 2000 as its manufacturing base eroded and population growth stagnated. Similarly, Cleveland's declining population and manufacturing base was accompanied by a 9.5% decline in its relative income.

Industrial specialization is also important. The relative income in the high-tech region of San Francisco (Silicon Valley) increased significantly even as relative income was declining significantly for Los Angeles. Growth in the high-tech sector also helps explain increasing relative incomes in Boston and Seattle (Microsoft). Returning to Detroit, loss of high-wage manufacturing jobs in the vehicle industry during the 1980s was the primary cause for the decline in the area's relative income. Michigan has increased per student spending relative to the national average, but new high-wage jobs have still not been found to fully replace high-paying manufacturing jobs that were lost. This pattern is best explored by looking at economic performance and industrial specialization of the different metropolitan areas of Michigan.

Finally, a metropolitan area's perceived quality of life, especially for younger professionals, has grown as an important determinant of its economic health. Richard Florida (2002) has developed a "Creativity Index" for all metropolitan areas in the nation based on: (1) percentage of workers in "creative class" occupations, including information technology, computer programming, engineering, education, health, and entertainment; (2) the Milken Institute's High Tech Index; (3) patents per capita; and (4) population and cultural diversity. Of the forty-nine metropolitan areas of greater than one million, Detroit is ranked thirty-ninth and Grand Rapids–Muskegon–Holland forty-fourth.

Quality-of-life indexes are plagued with problems, and Florida's study has its critics. Nevertheless, quality of life matters, regardless of how it is measured, and it is rare for any of Michigan's metropolitan areas to make the top ten of one of these lists. It cannot be denied that the Detroit metropolitan area faces serious economic challenges that may hinder its ability to hold its own against the nation's better-performing areas.

Data on population and per capita income for Metropolitan areas in Michigan and the counties they include appear in table 11.3. There are currently nine MSAs in Michigan, with three of these combined into the Detroit–Ann Arbor–Flint CMSA. Population in these metropolitan areas as a whole has grown more slowly than for the state, but still accounted for 82.2% of Michigan's population in 2000, compared to 85.5% in 1969. In 2000, the six-county Detroit PMSA accounted for 44.7% of Michigan's (eighty-three counties) population, down from about 51.0% in 1969. There is no question that Detroit remains the dominant MSA in terms of population in spite of its declining share. In 2000, the Grand Rapid–Muskegon–Holland area's population was about one-fourth of Detroit's, Ann Arbor's about one-eighth, Flint's, Lansing–East Lansing's, Kalamazoo–Battle Creek's, and Saginaw–Bay City–Midland's each about one-tenth, and Benton Harbor's and Jackson's each about one-thirtieth of Detroit's.

Four of Michigan's MSAs, Detroit, Flint, Saginaw–Bay City–Midland, and Benton Harbor, showed virtually no net growth or slight declines in population between 1969 and 2000, with the Detroit PMSA showing a loss of about 5% by 1989 but reversing this loss by 2000. Each of these four regions suffered significant manufacturing job losses in the 1980s and/or the 1990s. Only Grand Rapids–Muskegon–Holland and Ann Arbor exceeded the U.S. population growth of 40.2% over this period.

As is the case for MSAs throughout the United States, wide variation exists in relative per capita income levels for Michigan MSAs. For 1969, relative income levels ranged from 18.1% above the U.S. level for Detroit to 1.3% below for Grand Rapids–Muskegon–Holland. By 2000, this range had widened substantially to 15.3% above the U.S. level for Ann Arbor and 17.3% below for Jackson. Between 1969 and 2000, per capita income relative to the U.S. declined for all nine of Michigan's MSAs, with declines ranging from only 0.8% for Ann Arbor to over 20% for Flint and Jackson. While seven of Michigan's nine MSAs had per capita income above the national average in 1969, only the Ann Arbor and Detroit PMSAs exceeded the national average in 2000.

If the Michigan MSAs are ranked from highest relative income level 1 to lowest level 9, dramatic shifts occurred in rankings between 1969 and 2000. Grand Rapids–Muskegon–Holland increased its ranking from 9 to 3, while Flint's ranking declined from 3 to 8 and Jackson's fell from 4 to 9. As expected, these changes in relative income position are partly related to changing industrial composition for Michigan's MSAs, as discussed in the previous section. The competitiveness of the Grand Rapids–Muskegon–Holland MSA's manufacturing base helped it significantly improve its relative income ranking in Michigan. Ann Arbor saw strong population growth of 62.1% and fairly stable per capita income despite below predicted employment growth during the 1990s. For all of the state's other MSAs, weak employment growth contributed to their lackluster population growth and falling relative per capita income trends.

Population growth and relative income levels often show greater variation across counties

**TABLE 11.3**

**Population, Per Capita Income, and Unemployment for Michigan MSAs and Counties**

| Region | 1969 Population Thousands | 1969 Population % of MI | 2000 Population Thousands | 2000 Population % of MI | % Change from 1969 | Regional Per Capita Income as % of US 1969 | Regional Per Capita Income as % of US 2000 | Unemployment Rate 2001 |
|---|---|---|---|---|---|---|---|---|
| **Michigan** | **8,781** | **100.00%** | **9,952** | **100.00%** | **13.3%** | **107.8** | **98.8** | **5.0%** |
| Metropolitan portion | 7,505 | 85.47% | 8,180 | 82.20% | 9.0% | 112.0 | 104.4 | n.a. |
| Nonmetropolitan portion | 1,276 | 14.53% | 1,772 | 17.80% | 38.9% | 82.7 | 73.0 | n.a. |
| **Detroit–Ann Arbor–Flint (CMSA)** | **5,282** | **60.15%** | **5,464** | **54.90%** | **3.4%** | **117.0** | **110.9** | **n.a.** |
| **Detroit (PMSA)** | **4,477** | **50.98%** | **4,445** | **44.66%** | **–0.7%** | **118.1** | **112.9** | **4.8%** |
| Wayne | 2,685 | 30.58% | 2,059 | 20.68% | –23.3% | 112.2 | 95.1 | 5.5% |
| Oakland | 885 | 10.08% | 1,196 | 12.02% | 35.1% | 144.6 | 155.7 | 3.6% |
| Macomb | 621 | 7.07% | 791 | 7.94% | 27.4% | 114.6 | 105.8 | 4.7% |
| St. Clair | 118 | 1.35% | 165 | 1.65% | 39.8% | 100.8 | 86.9 | 6.5% |
| Monroe | 116 | 1.32% | 146 | 1.47% | 25.9% | 98.3 | 95.2 | 4.1% |
| Lapeer | 51 | 0.58% | 88 | 0.89% | 72.5% | 92.2 | 87.8 | 6.3% |
| **Grand Rapids–Muskegon– Holland (MSA)** | **754** | **8.59%** | **1,092** | **10.97%** | **44.8%** | **98.7** | **94.9** | **4.7%** |
| Kent | 411 | 4.68% | 576 | 5.79% | 40.1% | 101.6 | 101.0 | 4.7% |
| Ottawa | 123 | 1.40% | 239 | 2.41% | 94.3% | 100.3 | 95.1 | 4.0% |
| Muskegon | 157 | 1.78% | 171 | 1.71% | 8.9% | 93.1 | 77.5 | 6.5% |
| Allegan | 64 | 0.72% | 106 | 1.07% | 65.6% | 90.5 | 89.7 | 4.3% |
| **Ann Arbor (PMSA)** | **359** | **4.09%** | **582** | **5.84%** | **62.1%** | **116.1** | **115.3** | **2.9%** |
| Washtenaw | 224 | 2.55% | 324 | 3.26% | 44.6% | 123.9 | 124.5 | 2.2% |
| Livingston | 54 | 0.62% | 158 | 1.59% | 192.6% | 112.2 | 115.3 | 3.0% |
| Lenawee | 81 | 0.92% | 99 | 1.00% | 22.2% | 97.5 | 85.5 | 5.3% |
| **Kalamazoo–Battle Creek (MSA)** | **393** | **4.48%** | **453** | **4.55%** | **15.3%** | **101.6** | **88.1** | **4.5%** |
| Kalamazoo | 196 | 2.23% | 239 | 2.40% | 21.9% | 104.6 | 94.3 | 3.9% |
| Calhoun | 142 | 1.62% | 138 | 1.39% | –2.8% | 102.1 | 86.9 | 5.1% |
| Van Buren | 56 | 0.63% | 76 | 0.77% | 35.7% | 89.9 | 70.6 | 5.7% |
| **Lansing–East Lansing (MSA)** | **371** | **4.23%** | **448** | **4.50%** | **20.8%** | **101.7** | **91.3** | **3.3%** |
| Ingham | 258 | 2.94% | 279 | 2.81% | 8.1% | 102.6 | 93.6 | 3.5% |
| Eaton | 66 | 0.75% | 104 | 1.04% | 57.6% | 102.8 | 85.2 | 3.1% |
| Clinton | 47 | 0.54% | 65 | 0.65% | 38.3% | 95.1 | 90.9 | 2.7% |
| **Flint (PMSA)** | **446** | **5.08%** | **437** | **4.39%** | **–2.0%** | **106.6** | **85.6** | **7.1%** |
| **Saginaw–Bay City–Midland (MSA)** | **398** | **4.53%** | **403** | **4.05%** | **1.3%** | **99.1** | **90.7** | **5.1%** |
| Saginaw | 219 | 2.50% | 210 | 2.11% | –4.1% | 97.6 | 84.6 | 5.6% |
| Bay | 116 | 1.32% | 110 | 1.11% | –5.2% | 93.7 | 88.4 | 5.3% |
| Midland | 62 | 0.71% | 83 | 0.83% | 33.9% | 114.3 | 109.2 | 3.8% |
| **Benton Harbor (MSA)** | **164** | **1.86%** | **163** | **1.63%** | **–0.6%** | **102.3** | **87.1** | **5.3%** |
| **Jackson (MSA)** | **143** | **1.63%** | **159** | **1.59%** | **11.2%** | **103.8** | **82.7** | **5.0%** |

SOURCE: U.S. Department of Commerce, Bureau of Economic Analysis, Regional Economic Information System.
NOTES: MSAs in this table have been ranked in descending order based upon their 2000 population. MSA = Metropolitan Statistical Area of one or more counties. The Detroit, Ann Arbor, and Flint Primary MSAs are also shown as the Detroit–Ann Arbor–Flint Combined MSA in this table.

within a given MSA than across different MSAs. The Detroit six-county PMSA, for example, experienced a 22,000 or 0.7% population decline from 1969 to 2000, as population in Wayne County (the center) declined by 636,000 or 23% while the five outlying counties each experienced population growth of 25% or more. Nearly half of the popula-tion loss for Wayne County was made up for by gains in Oakland County, with most of the rest of the loss made for up by gains in the other four counties. Of counties in the Detroit PMSA, the highest percentage increase in population was 72.5% for sparsely settled Lapeer County. Of all the counties listed in table 11.3, Livingston's population grew at the fastest rate, with an increase of 192.6% between 1969 and 2000. This rapid growth is related to the county's location at the intersection of US-23 and I-96, which gives its residents convenient access to jobs in Ann Arbor, Oakland County, Lansing–East Lansing, and Flint. In terms of per capita income relative to the United States, there is huge variation across counties in the Detroit PMSA as well, from a low of 86.9% for St. Clair County to 155.7% for Oakland County in 2000. This illustrates a national trend toward increasing geographic segregation for residents of large MSAs based on income levels, as discussed by Anas, Arnott, and Small (1998) and Mills and Lubuele (1997). In contrast to the wide range of income levels for the Detroit, Grand Rapids–Muskegon–Holland, Ann Arbor, and Saginaw–Bay City–Midland multicounty MSAs, income levels were fairly homogeneous across the three counties in the Lansing–East Lansing MSA.

The final column of table 11.3 gives unemployment rates for 2001. Unemployment rates ranged from a low of 2.9% for Ann Arbor to a high of 7.1% for Flint. There is a fairly strong pattern of a negative correlation between an area's unemployment rate and its relative income position, but this is most often related to both variables being influenced by average education levels in a region. For example, relatively high incomes and low unemployment rates occur in Washtenaw County (Ann Arbor) and Oakland County due to relatively high education levels in these counties. Twenty years ago, Thompson (1982, 240) identified Flint as an exception to this pattern, as Flint had a high relative income but high relative unemployment, despite having a low relative education level. Since then, Flint has lost its relative income advantage.

## Regional Migration and Problems of Central Cities

In the previous section, we identified a general pattern of rapid population growth for MSAs in the South and West of the United States, while Detroit and other MSAs in the Great Lakes and Northeast regions have shown little growth or even declines in populations in recent decades. In this section, we analyze population movements within U.S. and Michigan MSAs, and find a pronounced pattern for declining central city and central county populations and relative incomes as population migrates to more and more distant suburbs over time. We also find that African Americans have accounted for increasing shares of central city population in Michigan's MSAs over the past twenty years.

In table 11.4, tax return data from IRS are analyzed to reveal patterns of migration of households into and out of core counties of each of these MSAs. These data span the period from 1995 to 2001, so they do not correspond specifically to the time period (1969–2000) covered in table 11.3, but they demonstrate important patterns in the flow of households and accompanying incomes among regions. These patterns in migration aid in understanding some of the differences in population growth and income levels revealed in table 11.3, and demonstrate a general pattern of urban decentralization.

In table 11.4, the MSA and its core county are shown in the center column, together with net inflows (+) or outflows (–) of households and income in millions of dollars for that core county with respect to all outside areas. The left-hand set of columns identifies migration between each core county and its neighboring counties (see list at bottom of table), with the first row showing migration from the neighboring counties to the core county and the second row showing migration to the neighboring counties from the core county. For Washtenaw County, for example, 8,695 households moved from neighboring counties *to* Washtenaw, representing earnings of $348 million, while 9,848 households moved *from* Washtenaw to neighboring counties, representing earnings of $449 million. This produced a net outflow of 1,153 households (8,695 less 9,848) and $101 ($348 less $449) million from Washtenaw to neighboring counties. The right-hand set of columns provides similar information, but with respect to all migration to or from Washtenaw County from areas beyond the neighboring counties. For these "More Distant Areas," the net inflow is 12,063 households and $499 million in income. Combining the migration for the two outside areas produces combined net inflows of 10,910 households and $398 million for Washtenaw County, as shown in the central column.

The intercounty migration data in table 11.4 show that we are a nation of movers and that the gross flows of households and income to and from the core counties of Michigan's MSAs are large. For example, as shown in table 11.4, although Wayne County lost 60,000 households, on net, during the six-year period, 174,000 households moved into the county and nearly 90,000 of these

**TABLE 11.4**

## Household Migration to and from Core Counties of MSAs, 1995–2001

| Household Migration From & To Neighboring Counties | | | | MSA Core County | | | Household Migration From & To More Distant Areas | | |
|---|---|---|---|---|---|---|---|---|---|
| # of HH Moving | Average $ per HH | Million $ Moving | | COMBINED NET CHANGE IN: # of HH / Income $Mil. | | | # of HH Moving | Average $ per HH | Million $ Moving |
| 8,695 @ $40,036 = | | $348 | ⇒ | Ann Arbor | | ⇐ | 53,798 @ $44,992 = | | $2,421 |
| 9,848 @ $45,636 = | | $449 | ⇐ | Washtenaw County | | ⇒ | 41,735 @ $46,032 = | | $1,921 |
| –1,153 | | –$101 | NET | 10,910 | $398 | NET | 12,063 | | $499 |
| | | | | | | | | | |
| 5,431 @ $29,357 = | | $159 | ⇒ | Benton Harbor | | ⇐ | 15,595 @ $37,444 = | | $584 |
| 6,171 @ $27,967 = | | $173 | ⇐ | Berrien County | | ⇒ | 18,330 @ $36,956 = | | $677 |
| –740 | | –$13 | NET | –3,475 | –$107 | NET | –2,735 | | –$93 |
| | | | | | | | | | |
| 89,866 @ $39,488 = | | $3,549 | ⇒ | Detroit | | ⇐ | 83,926 @ $33,405 = | | $2,804 |
| 131,954 @ $44,109 = | | $5,820 | ⇐ | Wayne County | | ⇒ | 101,789 @ $40,303 = | | $4,102 |
| –42,088 | | –$2,272 | NET | –59,951 | –$3,571 | NET | –17,863 | | –$1,299 |
| | | | | | | | | | |
| 7,337 @ $34,431 = | | $253 | ⇒ | Flint | | ⇐ | 40,457 @ $35,324 = | | $1,429 |
| 6,724 @ $37,229 = | | $250 | ⇐ | Genesee County | | ⇒ | 47,863 @ $35,841 = | | $1,715 |
| 613 | | $2 | NET | –6,793 | –$284 | NET | –7,406 | | –$286 |
| | | | | | | | | | |
| 27,318 @ $32,481 = | | $887 | ⇒ | Grand Rapids | | ⇐ | 53,752 @ $35,515 = | | $1,909 |
| 31,474 @ $39,015 = | | $1,228 | ⇐ | Kent County | | ⇒ | 48,966 @ $37,135 = | | $1,818 |
| –4,156 | | –$341 | NET | 630 | –$250 | NET | 4,786 | | $91 |
| | | | | | | | | | |
| 6,306 @ $33,062 = | | $208 | ⇒ | Jackson | | ⇐ | 13,396 @ $34,179 = | | $458 |
| 5,786 @ $32,224 = | | $186 | ⇐ | Jackson County | | ⇒ | 13,731 @ $32,902 = | | $452 |
| 520 | | $22 | NET | 185 | $28 | NET | –335 | | $6 |
| | | | | | | | | | |
| 11,166 @ $29,534 = | | $330 | ⇒ | Kalamazoo | | ⇐ | 30,372 @ $33,726 = | | $1,024 |
| 10,852 @ $33,386 = | | $362 | ⇐ | Kalamazoo County | | ⇒ | 33,878 @ $40,771 = | | $1,381 |
| 314 | | –$33 | NET | –3,192 | –$389 | NET | –3,506 | | –$357 |
| | | | | | | | | | |
| 19,306 @ $29,311 = | | $566 | ⇒ | Lansing | | ⇐ | 39,554 @ $27,568 = | | $1,090 |
| 21,800 @ $34,475 = | | $752 | ⇐ | Ingham County | | ⇒ | 43,129 @ $32,359 = | | $1,396 |
| –2,494 | | –$186 | NET | –6,069 | –$491 | NET | –3,575 | | –$305 |
| | | | | | | | | | |
| 4,896 @ $30,466 = | | $149 | ⇒ | Saginaw | | ⇐ | 18,255 @ $31,616 = | | $577 |
| 5,047 @ $34,322 = | | $173 | ⇐ | Saginaw County | | ⇒ | 23,653 @ $32,558 = | | $770 |
| –151 | | –$24 | NET | –5,549 | –$217 | NET | –5,398 | | –$193 |

SOURCE: Internal Revenue Service.

NEIGHBORING COUNTIES FOR EACH CORE COUNTY (COUNTIES IN EACH MSA ARE SHOWN IN BOLD):

**Washtenaw** (Ann Arbor): Lenewee, **Livingston**, and Monroe
**Berrien** (Benton Harbor): Cass, LaPorte (IN), St. Joseph (IN), Van Buren
**Wayne** (Detroit): Genesee, **Lapeer**, **Livingston**, **Macomb**, **Monroe**, **Oakland**, **St. Clair**, Washtenaw
**Genesee** (Flint): Lapeer, Livingston, Shiawassee
**Kent** (Grand Rapids): **Allegan**, Barry, Ionia, Montcalm, **Muskegon**, Newaygo, **Ottawa**
**Jackson** (Jackson): Calhoun, Hillsdale, Ingham, Washtenaw
**Kalamazoo** (Kalamazoo): Allegan, **Calhoun**, St. Joeseph, **Van Buren**
**Ingham** (Lansing): **Clinton**, **Eaton**, Ionia, Livingston, Shiawassee
**Saginaw** (Saginaw): **Bay**, **Midland**, Tuscola.

households moved into Wayne County from its surrounding counties. Of the 234,000 households that moved out of Wayne County, more than half moved to its neighborhood suburban counties. On net, Wayne lost 42,000 households to neighboring counties and 18,000 to more distant areas. The loss of households was accompanied by a net loss of about $3.6 billion in income, and the loss in income from lost households was compounded because the incomes of out-migrants from the county were considerably higher than the incomes of in-migrants.

Washtenaw (Ann Arbor), Kent (Grand Rapids), and Jackson (Jackson) Counties gained population through net household migration, with the other six MSAs all losing population in their core counties. Washtenaw is clearly the big gainer, attracting on net nearly 11,000 households during the period. The net gains in households for Washtenaw and Kent counties occurred in the two MSAs in Michigan with the fastest population growth, as shown in table 11.3. The net inflow of households for Kent County was too small to offset lower incomes for in-migrants than for out-migrants, so there was a net loss of income as a result of migrating households. The other six MSAs all suffered fairly large net out-migrations of both households and income from their core counties.

For most of the core counties, migration to and from neighboring counties was only a fraction of that to and from more distant areas. The exception to this was Wayne County in the Detroit PMSA, where migration to neighboring counties exceeded that to more distant areas. This may be due partly to the extensive list of neighboring counties in this case. It was also the case that incomes of out-migrants from core counties were typically 10% to 20% higher than those of in-migrants. This may reflect a tendency for younger generations with lower incomes to move into core counties to be closer to jobs, while older generations with higher incomes move to the suburbs for a more peaceful family life. The only two areas with higher average incomes for in-migrants than out-migrants were Berrien County (Benton Harbor MSA), which is likely due to the "lake effect," as wealthier households seek shoreline residences, and, surprisingly, Jackson, which could be spillover growth from fast-growing and higher-income Washtenaw County.

The nation's cities have always played important roles in the lifecycle of households. Young households with low initial incomes often find cities attractive for greater opportunities for entertainment, employment, and reasonable housing costs. However, as households mature and gain income they tend to move to the suburbs. In addition, professional households tend to be the most mobile and, thus, the most likely to leave the core counties of slow-growing metropolitan areas for other urban areas or for more rural settings. Finally, wealthy retirees are known to flock southward to enjoy warmer weather. Due to all these factors, it is not surprising that most of the state's core counties lost millions of dollars in income due to net out-migration from 1995 to 2001, as shown in table 11.4. Again, Washtenaw County is a strong exception, as well as Jackson County, which, again, may be capturing some of the spillover growth from Washtenaw County. These overall trends reveal an on-going challenge to the state's core counties. If the outflows continue and grow, core counties will find themselves in more severe fiscal and economic situations in the future, and as we are about to see, the plight of central cities may be even worse.

Table 11.5 displays population patterns over the past three decades for central cities and suburbs in Detroit and Flint PMSAs and Grand Rapids–Muskegon–Holland MSAs, in the context of other MSAs in the Midwest and the Great Lakes area. With the exception of Grand Rapids and Chicago, central city population has declined for each of the past three decades for the MSAs shown in table 11.5. By 2000, Detroit's central city population had declined to 63% of its 1970 level, and central city population had declined by similar amounts for Flint, Buffalo, Cleveland, and Pittsburgh, and by even more for St. Louis. Smaller net declines of 14 to 18% occurred for central cities of Chicago, Milwaukee, and Toledo. Only Grand Rapids has successfully reversed earlier population central city declines, with gains in the 1980s and 1990s fully offsetting population losses of the 1970s. Chicago's recovery has been confined to the 1990s, and is far less complete than that for Grand Rapids.

For Detroit and Flint, suburban population increases roughly offset central city population losses, and Toledo demonstrated a similar pattern.[9] Interestingly, the examples of Grand Rapids and Chicago suggest that rapid population growth for an MSA may be needed to provide adequate housing demand for population to increase in central cities. In other words, core cities may depend on strong suburbs to support the public and civic functions, as well as employment oppor-

## TABLE 11.5

### Population Change for Selected PMSAs, MSAs, and Central Cities in the Midwest

| MSA | Area | Population Based on Census for | | | | Population Index: 1970 = 100 | | |
|---|---|---|---|---|---|---|---|---|
| | | 1970 | 1980 | 1990 | 2000 | 1980 | 1990 | 2000 |
| **Michigan Cities** | | | | | | | | |
| Detroit PMSA | Metro area | 4,490,902 | 4,387,783 | 4,266,654 | 4,441,551 | 98 | 95 | 99 |
| | Central city | 1,511,336 | 1,203,339 | 1,027,974 | 951,270 | 80 | 68 | 63 |
| | Outer area | 2,979,566 | 3,184,444 | 3,238,680 | 3,490,281 | 107 | 109 | 117 |
| | City share | 33.7% | 27.4% | 24.1% | 21.4% | | | |
| Flint PMSA | Metro area | 441,341 | 450,449 | 430,459 | 436,141 | 102 | 98 | 99 |
| | Central city | 193,380 | 159,611 | 140,761 | 124,973 | 83 | 73 | 65 |
| | Outer area | 247,961 | 290,838 | 289,698 | 311,168 | 117 | 117 | 126 |
| | City share | 43.8% | 35.4% | 32.7% | 28.7% | | | |
| Grand Rapids–Muskegon–Holland MSA | | | | | | | | |
| | Metro area | 763,226 | 840,824 | 937,891 | 1,088,514 | 110 | 123 | 143 |
| | Central city | 197,534 | 181,843 | 189,126 | 197,800 | 92 | 96 | 100 |
| | Outer area | 565,692 | 658,981 | 748,765 | 890,714 | 117 | 132 | 158 |
| | City share | 25.9% | 21.6% | 20.2% | 18.2% | | | |
| **Other Midwest/Great Lakes Cities** | | | | | | | | |
| Buffalo | Metro area | 1,349,211 | 1,242,826 | 1,189,288 | 1,170,111 | 92 | 88 | 87 |
| | Central city | 462,783 | 357,870 | 328,123 | 292,648 | 77 | 71 | 63 |
| | Outer area | 886,428 | 884,956 | 861,165 | 877,463 | 100 | 97 | 99 |
| | City share | 34.3% | 28.8% | 27.6% | 25.0% | | | |
| Chicago | Metro area | 7,099,469 | 7,246,032 | 7,410,858 | 8,272,768 | 102 | 104 | 117 |
| | Central city | 3,362,825 | 3,005,072 | 2,783,726 | 2,896,016 | 89 | 83 | 86 |
| | Outer area | 3,736,644 | 4,240,960 | 4,627,132 | 5,376,752 | 114 | 124 | 144 |
| | City share | 47.4% | 41.5% | 37.6% | 35.0% | | | |
| Cleveland | Metro area | 2,419,274 | 2,277,949 | 2,202,069 | 2,250,871 | 94 | 91 | 93 |
| | Central city | 751,046 | 573,822 | 505,616 | 478,403 | 76 | 67 | 64 |
| | Outer area | 1,668,228 | 1,704,127 | 1,696,453 | 1,772,468 | 102 | 102 | 106 |
| | City share | 31.0% | 25.2% | 23.0% | 21.3% | | | |
| Milwaukee | Metro area | 1,403,688 | 1,397,143 | 1,432,149 | 1,500,741 | 100 | 102 | 107 |
| | Central city | 717,124 | 636,212 | 628,088 | 596,974 | 89 | 88 | 83 |
| | Outer area | 686,564 | 760,931 | 804,061 | 903,767 | 111 | 117 | 132 |
| | City share | 51.1% | 45.5% | 43.9% | 39.8% | | | |
| Pittsburgh | Metro area | 2,683,853 | 2,571,223 | 2,394,223 | 2,358,695 | 96 | 89 | 88 |
| | Central city | 520,167 | 423,938 | 369,879 | 334,563 | 82 | 71 | 64 |
| | Outer area | 2,163,686 | 2,147,285 | 2,024,344 | 2,024,132 | 99 | 94 | 94 |
| | City share | 19.4% | 16.5% | 15.4% | 14.2% | | | |
| St. Louis | Metro area | 2,461,367 | 2,419,552 | 2,498,186 | 2,603,607 | 98 | 102 | 106 |
| | Central city | 622,236 | 453,085 | 396,685 | 348,189 | 73 | 64 | 56 |
| | Outer area | 1,839,131 | 1,966,467 | 2,101,501 | 2,255,418 | 107 | 114 | 123 |
| | City share | 25.3% | 18.7% | 15.9% | 13.4% | | | |
| Toledo | Metro area | 607,163 | 616,864 | 614,128 | 618,203 | 102 | 101 | 102 |
| | Central city | 384,015 | 354,635 | 332,943 | 313,619 | 92 | 87 | 82 |
| | Outer area | 223,148 | 262,229 | 281,185 | 304,584 | 118 | 126 | 137 |
| | City share | 63.2% | 57.5% | 54.2% | 50.7% | | | |

SOURCE: U.S. Bureau of Census and authors' calculations.

tunities of the core cities, which highly affect their attractiveness to potential residents. However, a more traditional argument would be that Grand Rapids and Chicago succeed because of the strength of their private sectors in generating jobs that support the suburban population growth.

Table 11.6 focuses more closely on a range of Michigan cities and their population patterns relative to their surrounding counties. The MSAs comprise from one to six counties, and the numbers in parentheses after each MSA indicate the number of counties in the area. Data for 1980, 1990, and 2000 indicate a continuing decentralization within urban counties in Michigan. Eight of the twelve major central cities lost population in both the 1980s and 1990s, as indicated by the "Total" percentage change columns, and Kalamazoo City gained population during the 1980s but lost population during the 1990s. For these cities, percentage declines over the two decades summed to lows of approximately 3% and 5% for Kalamazoo and Battle Creek, respectively, and more severe decreases exceeding 20% for Detroit, Flint, and Saginaw. Ann Arbor, Grand Rapids, and Midland were exceptions, with their central city populations growing over the two decades by about 6%, 9% and 12%, respectively.

Outside the central cities, central county population increased for every county during the 1990s and in all but five counties in the 1980s. Four counties suffered net declines in their suburban population over the two decades, but declines were only about 1% for suburban Wayne (Detroit), Calhoun (Battle Creek), and Saginaw Counties, with a more substantial 6% decline for suburban areas of Bay County. For the more common pattern of expanding population, suburban population increased by a low of 7% for Genesee County (Flint) and a high of 40% for Kent County (Grand Rapids) over the two decades. Given patterns of declining or slow-growing city populations and generally increasing suburban population, the city share of each county usually declined significantly between 1980 and 2000. Flint's share of Genesee County population fell from 35% to 29%, and even the 9% growth in city population for Grand Rapids failed to prevent a decline in its share of county population from 41% in 1980 to 34% in 2000. Three cities nearly maintained their shares of county population, however. These were Midland, where city and suburban population both grew by about 12% over the two decades, and Battle Creek and Bay City, where city population declines were nearly

matched by suburban population declines.[10]

Table 11.6 also decomposes population changes in some very useful ways. Fundamentally it starts with the population in households (excluding, primarily, college dormitories and prisons). There are two reasons that total household population may change. First, the number of households may change, usually through changes in numbers of dwelling units (vacancy rates can also change), and this represents an important measure of net housing stock. Second, household size may change. If a child moves out of a house in Detroit to live in an apartment in suburban Warren, for example, the population of Detroit has fallen even though the family still lives in Detroit; the child now represents a new household in Warren. Beginning in the 1970s, the end of the "baby boom" reduced household size in most U.S. cities from well over 3 people per household to 2.5 people per household or less. A drop of 0.5 members per household would reduce population over 16%, even with *no change* in the number of households.

To understand this, consider Flint, where population within households fell by about 12.5% between 1980 and 1990. Assuming that the number of households had stayed constant, Flint's population would have still fallen by 6.3%, because households became smaller. However, almost half of the change, 6.2%, occurred because of a decrease in the number of occupied housing units. Housing units typically leave the market either through vacancy or abandonment (and ultimately being torn down). We see in table 11.6 that about 6% of the Flint housing supply left the market from 1980 to 1990, and an even larger 9% left from 1990 to 2000.

From 1980 to 1990, household size declined in all of the cities and suburban areas of their counties listed in table 11.6. Number of households (occupied housing units) increased in the suburban portion of every county, but number of city households declined by 13.6% in Detroit, and by smaller amounts in Pontiac, Flint, Jackson, Battle Creek, and Saginaw. This suggests substantial deterioration of central city housing stock in these cities relative to the surrounding counties. During the 1980s, the number of housing units (housing supply) in the remaining six central cities increased, and by enough to more than offset declines in household size in Ann Arbor, Grand Rapids, Kalamazoo, and Midland. Change in supply varied dramatically for different central cities, from a decline of 13.6% for Detroit/Highland Park to an

## TABLE 11.6

### Impact of Changes in Number of Housing Units and Household Size on Central City and County Population

| MSA Central City/County | Population 1980 | % Population Change Due to # HHs | HH Size | Total | Population 1990 | % Population Change Due to # HHs | HH Size | Total | Population 2000 |
|---|---|---|---|---|---|---|---|---|---|
| **Ann Arbor PMSA (3)** | | | | | | | | | |
| Ann Arbor city | 107,966 | 6.0% | −3.7% | 1.5% | 109,592 | 8.4% | −4.0% | 4.0% | 114,024 |
| Rest of Washtenaw County | 156,782 | 15.2% | −5.6% | 10.6% | 173,345 | 24.8% | −4.3% | 20.5% | 208,871 |
| City as % of county | 40.8% | | | | 38.7% | | | | 35.3% |
| **Detroit PMSA (6)** | | | | | | | | | |
| Detroit and Highland Park | 1,231,248 | −13.6% | −1.0% | −14.9% | 1,048,095 | −10.3% | 2.2% | −7.6% | 968,016 |
| Rest of Wayne County | 1,106,643 | 4.5% | −8.4% | −3.9% | 1,063,592 | 6.7% | −4.0% | 2.8% | 1,093,146 |
| City as % of county | 52.7% | | | | 49.6% | | | | 47.0% |
| Pontiac city | 76,715 | −3.4% | −3.9% | −7.2% | 71,166 | −2.1% | −2.8% | −6.8% | 66,337 |
| Rest of Oakland County | 935,078 | 16.3% | −8.1% | 8.3% | 1,012,426 | 15.4% | −4.4% | 11.4% | 1,127,819 |
| City as % of county | 7.6% | | | | 6.6% | | | | 5.6% |
| **Flint PMSA (1)** | | | | | | | | | |
| Flint city | 159,611 | −6.2% | −6.3% | −11.8% | 140,761 | −9.3% | −1.8% | −11.2% | 124,943 |
| Rest of Genesee County | 290,838 | 10.1% | −10.5% | −0.4% | 289,698 | 12.3% | −5.3% | 7.4% | 311,198 |
| City as % of county | 35.4% | | | | 32.7% | | | | 28.6% |
| **Grand Rapids–Muskegon–Holland MSA (4)** | | | | | | | | | |
| Grand Rapids city | 181,843 | 5.0% | −1.1% | 4.0% | 189,126 | 5.7% | −1.1% | 4.6% | 197,800 |
| Rest of Kent County | 262,663 | 24.3% | −5.8% | 18.6% | 311,505 | 23.4% | −2.7% | 20.9% | 376,535 |
| City as % of county | 40.9% | | | | 37.8% | | | | 34.4% |
| **Jackson MSA (1)** | | | | | | | | | |
| Jackson city | 39,739 | −1.8% | −4.5% | −5.8% | 37,446 | −3.4% | 0.4% | −3.0% | 36,316 |
| Rest of Jackson County | 111,756 | 7.4% | −7.7% | 0.5% | 112,310 | 11.7% | −3.7% | 8.7% | 122,106 |
| City as % of county | 26.2% | | | | 25.0% | | | | 22.9% |
| **Kalamazoo–Battle Creek MSA (3)** | | | | | | | | | |
| Kalamazoo city | 79,722 | 3.2% | −2.2% | 0.7% | 80,277 | 0.0% | −4.0% | −3.9% | 77,145 |
| Rest of Kalamazoo County | 132,656 | 14.8% | −6.8% | 7.9% | 143,134 | 17.4% | −5.0% | 12.8% | 161,458 |
| City as % of county | 37.5% | | | | 35.9% | | | | 32.3% |
| Battle Creek city | 56,339 | −1.1% | −4.3% | −5.0% | 53,540 | −0.5% | −0.8% | −0.3% | 53,364 |
| Rest of Calhoun County | 85,218 | 3.0% | −6.0% | −3.3% | 82,442 | 7.4% | −3.9% | 2.6% | 84,621 |
| City as % of county | 39.8% | | | | 39.4% | | | | 38.7% |
| **Lansing–East Lansing MSA(3)** | | | | | | | | | |
| Lansing and East Lansing | 177,366 | 2.7% | −4.4% | −2.2% | 173,377 | −0.5% | −4.8% | −7.2% | 160,812 |
| Rest of Ingham County | 98,154 | 15.5% | −5.2% | 10.6% | 108,535 | 15.1% | −5.7% | 9.2% | 118,508 |
| City as % of county | 64.4% | | | | 61.5% | | | | 57.6% |
| **Saginaw–Bay City–Midland MSA (3)** | | | | | | | | | |
| Bay City | 41,593 | 0.2% | −6.4% | −6.4% | 38,936 | −2.3% | −4.0% | −5.4% | 36,817 |
| Rest of Bay County | 78,288 | 3.0% | −10.0% | −7.0% | 72,787 | 7.5% | −7.4% | 0.8% | 73,340 |
| City as % of county | 34.7% | | | | 34.9% | | | | 33.4% |
| Midland city | 37,016 | 12.4% | −9.7% | 2.2% | 37,819 | 12.6% | −2.9% | 9.6% | 41,463 |
| Rest of Midland County | 36,562 | 12.7% | −9.1% | 3.5% | 37,832 | 15.1% | −5.9% | 9.5% | 41,411 |
| City as % of county | 50.3% | | | | 50.0% | | | | 50.0% |
| Saginaw city | 77,508 | −4.1% | −5.9% | −10.3% | 69,512 | −11.2% | −0.4% | −11.1% | 61,799 |
| Rest of Saginaw County | 150,551 | 6.4% | −11.7% | −5.4% | 142,434 | 9.5% | −7.1% | 4.1% | 148,240 |
| City as % of county | 34.0% | | | | 32.8% | | | | 29.4% |

SOURCE: U.S. Bureau of Census and authors' calculations.

NOTES: Total % change for population includes changes in institutional population (mostly dormitories and prisons) in addition to changes in number of households and household size. Number in parentheses after MSA indicates number of counties in the MSA.

increase of 12.4% for Midland.

From 1990 to 2000, the trends of the 1980s continued, with a few exceptions. The general pattern of declining household size was repeated, except for Detroit/Highland Park and Jackson, where household size increased by 2.2% and 0.4%, respectively. These increases in household size might be caused by an increasing concentration of low-income families that often have larger families. Another possibility might be an increase in immigrant families that also may have larger families. In another change, the number of cities with an increased number of households fell from six in the 1980s to three in the 1990s, with Ann Arbor, Grand Rapids, and Midland still benefiting from between 5% and 13% increases in their housing supply. At the other extreme, Detroit/Highland Park, Flint, and Saginaw experienced declines of about 10% in their housing supply in the 1990s, and total declines in housing supply of about 15% to 25% over the two decades.

Another important aspect of metropolitan area dynamics is the high and increasing concentration of African Americans in central city areas of Michigan MSAs. African Americans comprise a higher percentage of the population in Michigan's core cities today than they did twenty years ago.[11] The many strong inner-city neighborhoods retain or attract African Americans into the cities, while the lack of low- to medium-cost housing opportunities and, unfortunately, housing discrimination continue to keep many African American households from moving into the suburbs. What is surprising is the variation in racial composition among the state's major core cities. For example, in 2000 Detroit's population was 82.6% African American, while African Americans represented only 2.1% of Midland's population (table 11.7a). In 2000, African Americans represented 93.7% of Benton Harbor's population, having increased from 86.3% in 1980, while Detroit's black population had increased nearly 20 percentage points to 82.6% in 2000 from 63.1% in 1980. At the other end of the spectrum, African Americans represented less than 10% of the population in Ann Arbor and less than 4% in the cities of Midland and Bay City in 2000. The largest share of the African American population living in the Saginaw–Bay City–Midland MSA resides in Saginaw.

While African Americans continue to account for a larger share of the core cities' population, the cities themselves house a smaller share of their metropolitan areas' African American population. For example, in 1990, 80% of all African Americans

**TABLE 11.7**

**Minority Percentages of Cities and Segregation**

**a. African Americans as a % of total City Population**

|  | 1980 | 1990 | 2000 |
|---|---|---|---|
| Ann Arbor | 9.3% | 9.0% | 9.8% |
| Battle Creek | 22.8% | 16.5% | 19.2% |
| Bay City | 1.8% | 2.4% | 3.4% |
| Benton Harbor | 86.3% | 92.2% | 93.7% |
| Detroit | 63.1% | 75.7% | 82.6% |
| Flint | 41.4% | 47.9% | 55.0% |
| Grand Rapids | 15.7% | 18.5% | 21.8% |
| Jackson | 15.4% | 17.7% | 21.8% |
| Kalamazoo | 15.6% | 18.8% | 22.0% |
| Lansing | 13.9% | 18.6% | 24.1% |
| Midland | 1.4% | 1.7% | 2.1% |
| Muskegon | 21.4% | 27.1% | 33.2% |
| Saginaw | 35.6% | 40.3% | 44.7% |

NOTE: Battle Creek city annexed Battle Creek Township in 1982.

**b. Index of Segregation: Core Counties**

|  | 1980 | 1990 | 2000 |
|---|---|---|---|
| Ann Arbor |  |  |  |
| Washtenaw County | 0.48 | 0.49 | 0.51 |
| Benton Harbor |  |  |  |
| Berrien County | 0.73 | 0.74 | 0.75 |
| Flint |  |  |  |
| Genesee County | 0.84 | 0.81 | 0.75 |
| Grand Rapids–Muskegon |  |  |  |
| Kent County | 0.73 | 0.69 | 0.62 |
| Muskegon County | 0.73 | 0.77 | 0.78 |
| Jackson |  |  |  |
| Jackson County | 0.74 | 0.70 | 0.53 |
| Kalamazoo–Battle Creek |  |  |  |
| Kalamazoo County | 0.57 | 0.53 | 0.48 |
| Calhoun County | 0.55 | 0.63 | 0.61 |
| Lansing |  |  |  |
| Ingham County | 0.47 | 0.49 | 0.51 |
| Saginaw–Midland–Bay City |  |  |  |
| Saginaw County | 0.81 | 0.82 | 0.73 |
| Bay County | 0.50 | 0.49 | 0.46 |
| Midland County | 0.44 | 0.43 | 0.38 |
| Detroit |  |  |  |
| Wayne County | 0.82 | 0.85 | 0.86 |

SOURCE: U.S. Bureau of the Census and authors' calculations.

living in Genesee County resided in Flint, compared to 75% in 2000. Although many African American households moved to more suburban locations, their numbers are still small relative to the movement of white families. Most of the

African American households moving to suburban locations are taking away higher-than-average purchasing power from inner-city markets, leaving their former inner-city neighborhoods even more economically depressed.

Statistics on the overall percentage composition of the cities' African American population reveal little about neighborhood segregation. African Americans and whites could be residing in strongly segregated or highly integrated neighborhoods regardless of the overall African American percentage composition of an area's population. The most common racial segregation descriptor, the *index of dissimilarity*, compares the racial make-up of neighborhoods (typically measured at the census tract level) with the racial make-up of the reference area, in this case the county.[12] If, for example, the metropolitan county was 30% minority, then if each census tract was 30% minority, there would be no dissimilarity of neighborhoods, and the index of dissimilarity would take on a value of 0, indicating that (in theory) no residents would have to be "moved" to achieve full integration. If all census tracts were either entirely white or entirely minority, the index of dissimilarity would have a value of 1.0 (sometimes multiplied by 100 for a percentage factor). This would mean that all (100%) of either the minority or the white populations would (again, in theory) have to be moved to achieve full integration.

Segregation is a measure of separation, and may relate variously to preferences to live with one's own kind, separation by income, or racial discrimination. Racial segregation may impact families' abilities to purchase housing of the types they might wish, or to live close to jobs that they might wish to have. As noted in table 11.7b, all of the counties containing the state's major core cities have remained relatively unchanged in terms of neighborhood (census tracts) segregation. Neighborhoods in Wayne, Berrien, Muskegon, Calhoun, Washtenaw, and Ingham Counties have become more segregated during the past twenty years, but racial segregation has declined in the state's other core counties.

In summary, African American residents account for a larger share of the state's core cities' population, however the cities themselves are housing a declining share of the overall metropolitan areas' African American population. On the neighborhood level (Census Tracts), racial segregation between African Americans and whites remained fairly constant in the past twenty years, with perhaps a slight overall decrease in segregation.

Table 11.8 examines changes in the Detroit metropolitan area, which represented about 45% of Michigan's 2000 population. The analysis looks at the central-city-core of Detroit/Highland Park/Hamtramck, and compares it to the inner ("inner suburbs") and outer ("outer suburbs") rings of Wayne, Oakland, and Macomb Counties, and to the outlying counties of Lapeer, Monroe, and St. Clair ("outer 3 counties"). Detroit MSA population grew by only 1.3% between 1980 and 2000. Growth in the outer suburbs of Wayne, Oakland, and Macomb, and the three outer counties slightly more than offset population losses in the central city core and the inner ring suburbs in Wayne, Oakland and Macomb Counties. During the 1980s, MSA population declined by 2.8% as a 4% housing increase was more than offset by a 6.8% decrease in family size. In the 1990s, population increased by 4.1%; with a 7.1% housing supply increase more than offsetting a 3.3% decrease in family size.

From 1980 to 1990 the Detroit/Highland Park/Hamtramck central city lost nearly 15% of its population, due to a 13.6% decline in housing supply and a 1% decrease in household size. During the 1980s, the inner ring suburbs for each of the three inner counties lost population also, but the population loss was due to reduced household size, rather than reduced housing supply. Housing supply increased by about 3% in the inner suburbs of Wayne and Oakland Counties and over 6% in the inner suburbs of Macomb County, but declining family size produced population declines of about 4 to 6% in these areas. Except for Monroe County, the outer ring suburbs of the three inner counties and the three outer counties each had double-digit housing supply increases that more than offset declining household size. Population growth ranged from about 4% for the outer suburbs of Wayne County to 22% for the outer suburbs of Macomb County. Monroe County's 7.5% housing supply increase was more than offset by declining family size for a net population decline of 0.8%.

From 1990 to 2000, an improved local economy slowed the population losses in the central city and inner suburbs to about 7% and 2%, respectively, or to less than half the declines for the 1980s. Nonetheless, the population patterns of the 1980s continued, with continued losses in the central city and in the inner suburban ring, and with even larger population gains in the outer suburban ring and in the outer counties than in the 1980s. For the MSA as a whole, population increased by 4.1% in the 1990s, as a 7.1% increase

**TABLE 11.8**

**Impact of Changes in Number of Housing Units and Household Size on Population of Inner City, Inner Suburb, Outer Suburb, and Outer County Regions of the Detroit PMSA**

| County | Area | Population 1980 | % Population Change Due to | | | Population 1990 | % Population Change Due to | | | Population 2000 | Shares of MSA Population | | |
|---|---|---|---|---|---|---|---|---|---|---|---|---|---|
| | | | # HHs | HH Size | Total* | | # HHs | HH Size | Total* | | 1980 | 1990 | 2000 |
| **Total Detroit PMSA** | | 4,387,783 | 4.0% | -6.8% | -2.8% | 4,266,326 | 7.1% | -3.3% | 4.1% | 4,441,225 | 100% | 100% | 100% |
| **Analysis by Regions of Counties** | | | | | | | | | | | | | |
| Wayne | Detroit/Ham./HP | 1,252,548 | -13.6% | -1.0% | -14.9% | 1,066,467 | -10.1% | 2.5% | -7.1% | 990,992 | 28.5% | 25.0% | 22.3% |
| | Inner Suburbs | 820,115 | 2.8% | -8.9% | -6.1% | 769,938 | 2.2% | -4.2% | -2.0% | 754,716 | 18.7% | 18.0% | 17.0% |
| | Outer Suburbs | 265,228 | 11.8% | -7.9% | 3.8% | 275,282 | 20.2% | -5.8% | 14.6% | 315,454 | 6.0% | 6.5% | 7.1% |
| Macomb | Inner Suburbs | 486,875 | 6.3% | -11.3% | -4.7% | 463,887 | 2.7% | -4.7% | -1.7% | 455,800 | 11.1% | 10.9% | 10.3% |
| | Outer Suburbs | 207,725 | 34.2% | -12.1% | 22.0% | 253,513 | 41.0% | -10.7% | 31.1% | 332,349 | 4.7% | 5.9% | 7.5% |
| Oakland | Inner Suburbs | 499,353 | 2.7% | -6.3% | -3.7% | 480,889 | 3.5% | -5.3% | -1.9% | 471,967 | 11.4% | 11.3% | 10.6% |
| | Outer Suburbs | 512,440 | 27.5% | -10.2% | 17.6% | 602,375 | 23.5% | -4.1% | 19.8% | 721,863 | 11.7% | 14.1% | 16.3% |
| Lapeer County Total | | 70,038 | 15.3% | -8.4% | 6.8% | 74,768 | 23.4% | -6.4% | 17.6% | 87,904 | 1.6% | 1.8% | 2.0% |
| Monroe County Total | | 134,659 | 7.5% | -8.3% | -0.8% | 133,600 | 15.0% | -5.9% | 9.2% | 145,945 | 3.1% | 3.1% | 3.3% |
| St. Clair County Total | | 138,802 | 11.3% | -6.7% | 4.9% | 145,607 | 16.9% | -4.4% | 12.8% | 164,235 | 3.2% | 3.4% | 3.7% |
| **Analysis by Regions of PMSA** | | | | | | | | | | | | | |
| Wayne | Detroit/Ham./HP | 1,252,548 | -13.6% | -1.0% | -14.9% | 1,066,467 | -10.1% | 2.5% | -7.1% | 990,992 | 28.5% | 25.0% | 22.3% |
| | Inner Suburbs | 1,806,343 | 3.7% | -8.8% | -5.1% | 1,714,714 | 2.7% | -4.6% | -1.9% | 1,682,483 | 41.2% | 40.2% | 37.9% |
| | Outer Suburbs | 985,393 | 24.7% | -10.0% | 14.8% | 1,131,170 | 26.6% | -6.0% | 21.1% | 1,369,666 | 22.5% | 26.5% | 30.8% |
| | 3 Outer Counties | 343,499 | 10.6% | -7.7% | 3.0% | 353,975 | 17.6% | -5.4% | 12.5% | 398,084 | 7.8% | 8.3% | 9.0% |

SOURCE: U.S. Bureau of Census and authors' calculations.

NOTE: Total percentage change for population includes changes in institutional population (mostly dormitories and prisons) in addition to changes in number of households and household size.

in housing supply more than offset a 3.3% decrease in household size.

The decline in household size in the 1990s was only about half of that in the 1980s, and as in table 11.6, the central city area even had a 2.5% increase in family size. The increase in household size for the central city area was more than offset by a 10% decline in housing supply, however, for a net population loss of 7%. The combined inner ring suburbs increased their housing supply by about 3% in the 1990s as undeveloped land remained scarce, and declining family size produced a net population decline in these areas of about 2%. Numbers of households in the outer suburban ring and in the outer counties increased by double-digit percentages, and ranged as high as 41% for Macomb County during the 1990s. In both decades, housing supply and population have increased faster for the outer suburbs of Macomb County than for the outer suburbs of Oakland County, which suggests that Oakland County had less and therefore more expensive undeveloped land available than did Macomb.

The final three columns of table 11.8 look at the impact of declining population in the inner areas and increasing population in the outer areas in terms of regional shares of total Detroit MSA population. Between 1980 and 2000, the central city's share of MSA population fell from 28.5% to 22.3%, with a smaller decline from 41.2 to 37.9% for the inner suburbs. The combined share for these two groups fell from about 70% to 60%, with a corresponding increase for the outer areas. There was about an eight-percentage point increase in the population share for the outer suburbs and about a one-percentage point increase for the three outer counties combined.

The data for table 11.8 represent measures of the occupied housing stock. Small increases in number of households can result from reduced vacancy rates for existing housing stock, but sustained increases come primarily from new construction. Table 11.9 examines housing permit data for the Detroit MSA. Housing permits constitute a set of key "leading" indicators of development. Although not all permitted housing is constructed in the permit year, permits indicate planned activities. In 1990, 66% more permits were issued for the

**TABLE 11.9**

**Distribution of Housing Permits within the Detroit MSA**

| Region within MSA | Number of Permits | | | Percentage Distribution | | |
|---|---|---|---|---|---|---|
| | 1980 | 1990 | 2000 | 1980 | 1990 | 2000 |
| Central cities (Detroit/Ham./HP) | 928 | 633 | 371 | 10.4% | 4.3% | 2.0% |
| % change | | −32% | −41% | | | |
| Inner suburbs, inner 3 counties | 2,601 | 2,919 | 3,067 | 29.3% | 19.8% | 16.6% |
| % change | | 12% | 5% | | | |
| Outer suburbs, inner 3 counties | 4,140 | 9,105 | 12,146 | 46.6% | 61.9% | 65.9% |
| % change | | 120% | 33% | | | |
| Outer 3 Counties | 1,214 | 2,063 | 2,846 | 13.7% | 14.0% | 15.4% |
| % change | | 70% | 38% | | | |
| Total | 8,883 | 14,720 | 18,430 | 100.0% | 100.0% | 100.0% |
| % change | | 66% | 25% | | | |

SOURCE: U.S. Bureau of the Census and authors' calculations.

Detroit MSA than had been issued in 1980, and in 2000, 25% more permits were issued than in 1990. Part of this increase was probably related to the timing of these years in terms of cyclical activity in the national economy. The economy was in recession in 1980, in a less severe recession in 1990, and in the latter part of an expansion in 2000. The increase is also consistent with the shift from population losses in the 1980s and population growth in the 1990s, however.

The growth rates in permit activity differed considerably across the four different parts of the Detroit PMSA. The Central City area showed sharp declines from the prior period in both 1990 and 2000, while the Inner Suburb area showed weak growth of 12% and 5%, or about one-fifth the growth rates for the total PMSA. Permit activity more than doubled between 1980 and 1990 for the Outer Suburb area, and increased by 70% for the Outer three county area in these years, while it increased by about one-third between 1990 and 2000 for the two outer areas.

Given these differences in growth rates, there were dramatic changes in the distribution of total permit activity among the four areas between 1980 and 2000. The share of total permits issued by the Central City area fell from over 10% in 1980 to 2% in 2000, while that for the Inner Suburb area fell from about 29% to about 17%. Together these two areas saw their share of regional building permits fall by over one-half from about 40% to 19%. The Outer Suburb area picked up most of the share lost by the inner areas, with its share rising from about 47% to 66%, and the three outer coun-

ties saw their share increase from 13.7% to 15.4%. Although housing permits can vary significantly from year to year, and while using different reference years would provide slightly different results, it is apparent that housing construction and development has shifted dramatically from the inner areas into the outer suburbs of Wayne, Oakland, and Macomb Counties, and to a lesser extent, to the outer three counties of the Detroit PMSA.

In short, the housing stock deteriorated steadily in the central cities, held its own in the inner suburbs, and exploded in the outer ring in all three central counties and to a lesser extent in the outlying counties. The massive deterioration in housing stock in the central city apparently represents a continuation from the previous twenty years, based on Fisher and Kohlhase (1982). What has become more apparent in the last twenty years is that the population decline does not stop at the city line. This detailed analysis of the Detroit metropolitan area indicates that the inner suburbs have *also* lost population, but at a slower rate. The distinction is that central city population losses are largely, although not entirely, due to reduction in housing stock (supply), while inner suburban population losses are thus far due to reduction in household size. In the outer suburbs of the cities, new stock and new households are increasing the population.[13]

One can point to a combination of economic factors in this continuing decentralization. Large amounts of undeveloped land surround all of Michigan's cities, within easy commuting range. It is easier to build where nothing else has been built than to tear down existing housing, and greater availability of undeveloped land, in proximity to decentralizing jobs, explains decentralization into the outer reaches of Wayne, Oakland, and Macomb Counties and beyond. Counteracting the trend toward decentralization, one also sees selected "tear downs" in suburbs such as Huntington Woods and Birmingham, where economically viable residences are purchased and razed so that owners can build newer and larger homes on the land, presumably to take advantage of the surrounding community. One also sees structural "add-ons" in many suburban neighborhoods that essentially replace an older house with a functionally newer one, sometimes with double the inside space on the same lot. Simply speaking, attractive neighborhood attributes and high-quality public services such as quality schools, effective crime control, and concerts in the park are essential features in the development of viable neighborhoods, whether located in central cities or in the suburbs.

## Policy Options for Michigan and Its Cities and Suburbs

As far back as data are available, analysts have noted a general decentralization of urban areas. Urban sprawl is often blamed for (1) increased traffic congestion, (2) high costs of providing public services, and (3) increased concentration of poverty in central cities of metropolitan areas. The push toward decentralization comes from growing population and the need for more housing, declining family size, rising incomes, and declines in intra-urban transportation costs related to improved road and highway systems. This so-called traditional model of decentralization has been supplemented in the past thirty years by a variant called "flight from blight." A third explanation relates to political boundaries, where a move to the suburbs may only slightly reduce access to positive aspects of cities while avoiding the generally higher taxes paid by city residents for public services. Combining these factors, Glaeser (1998); Mills and Lubuele (1997); Mieszkowski and Mills (1993); and Staley (1998) all suggest that out-migrants are (a) seeking more land and open space; (b) fleeing perceived or real problems in central cities related to crime, poverty, race-related issues, or poor public services; and (c) avoiding higher taxes.

In analyzing urban dynamics and the problems of central cities, the optimal level of local government boundaries becomes a major issue. Mills and Lubuele (1997, 727) note, "What we now call inner cities once constituted entire MSAs, and city boundaries tended to move outward as MSAs grew and decentralize." However, outward expansion of city boundaries stopped quite a while ago, yet outward expansion of economic activity and MSAs has proceeded rapidly. As documented previously, central cities have been plagued in recent decades by declining population and housing stock, and have increasingly become concentrated centers of poverty, as higher-income individuals have increasingly moved to the suburbs. A Public Sector Consultants (2002) report, "Status of Michigan Cities," documents many of the challenges for cities in Michigan. The fiscal difficulties created by these challenges have culminated in the state government taking over temporary financial management of the cities of Hamtramck, Highland Park, and Flint.

Olson (1969) and Oates (1972) argued for fiscal federalism, in which several levels of government, including cities, townships, counties, and school districts, offer different bundles of public goods. In this model, having city political boundaries overlap with economic or MSA boundaries offers no advantages and may be a disadvantage. More recently, however, Hochman, Pines, and Thisse (1995) argued that, when space and transportation costs are considered, the optimal level of local government should occur at the MSA level. They indicate that such consolidations have occurred to some extent in the United States and more extensively in Belgium and France. Recent voter initiatives from areas wanting to separate from the City of Los Angeles represent movement in the opposite direction, however. Part of the problem is that local government spending and taxes tend to be much higher in cities than in townships. For example, cities and townships each account for about half of Michigan's population, but city governments account for nearly 85% of the combined spending of these two classes of municipalities, as noted by Fisher and Guilfoyle in chapter 31 of this volume.

The argument for more unified regional government builds on the assumption of economies-of-scale in providing local government services. For example, a regional public transit system will more likely provide effective service than several disconnected local systems. There has been extensive political struggle on the public transit issue in the Detroit MSA, with the city and the suburbs often finding cooperation difficult. A similar argument can be made for more unified regional planning. Townships and cities are granted substantial land use and public service authority ("home rule") in Michigan. The Citizens Research Council of Michigan (1999, 22) reported, "[Townships] have full planning and zoning powers, they can provide police and fire protection, and they can construct, maintain and operate libraries, parks and water and sewage systems." Hence, coordination of land use planning between neighboring townships and cities is strictly voluntary. Since increased development is associated with increased property tax revenues, many outlying townships have incentives to promote and encourage residential growth at the expense of the core city and older neighborhoods, even when this might not produce the most efficient allocation of resources from a county or MSA perspective. Rusk (1999) indicates that while vertical intergovernmental revenue agreements (revenue sharing) are commonplace, horizontal revenue agreements are very rare. This leaves the fate of metropolitan growth in the hands of competing local governments, an arena where the central city is apt to be at a strong disadvantage. Braid (1996) discusses this type of tax competition between jurisdictions within metropolitan areas.

Local governments should more carefully examine possible benefits of greater regional cooperation in development planning, revenue sharing, and the joint provision of government services. For example, Oakland County's ability to attract high-tech businesses and highly skilled workers from outside of Michigan is probably hindered by its proximity to Detroit, if Detroit is viewed as a city in decline. Also, the ability of suburban residents to enjoy cultural and sporting events in Detroit or another central city is reduced if the crime rate is high in the city. A Citizens Research Council of Michigan (2001a) publication, "Regional Issues from a Statewide Perspective," provides an excellent discussion of problems and successes in regional cooperation within Michigan as viewed by four city and county executives.

State government can help provide greater balance between the fiscal position of cities and suburbs through revenue sharing. Michigan has a general revenue sharing program for its local governments. Expansion of this program could be considered, and policy makers may wish to reevaluate whether it is better to allocate these funds on a needs-based versus a per capita formula. A variant on the revenue sharing approach was Michigan's school finance reform of the 1990s, in which a state property tax largely replaced local property taxes for funding public schools. Murray, Evans, and Schwab (1998) evaluated similar programs in other states and found they typically increased per-pupil funding in the poorest districts while largely maintaining per-pupil funding in richer districts. By improving educational funding in the fiscally pressed cities, this finance reform may help mitigate flight from cities in pursuit of better schools in the suburbs. Along these lines, Glaeser (1998) and Mieszkowski and Mills (1993), among others, suggest that income support programs such as welfare and Medicaid are most appropriately funded at the state or federal level, rather than the local level.

Another way that the state and federal governments have attempted to revitalize cities is through enterprise zones, in which business formation and employment are subsidized, taxes are reduced, and public infrastructure is provided. Another Citizens Research Council of Michigan report, "Survey of Economic Development Programs in Michigan" (2001b), provides extensive information on these programs in Michigan. The performance of these programs must be reevaluated to see if they should be expanded or abandoned. Related to this type of redevelopment activity, problems of past industrial pollution deter reinvestment in many central cities. State-funded cleanup of these "brown field" areas could help promote central city redevelopment, but of course the state must evaluate whether the benefits of doing so justify the costs.

A final question, of course, is what cities can do to help themselves. Many analysts have suggested that cities should focus their limited resources on providing quality public services and deemphasize attempts to redistribute income at the local level. Glaeser (1998) specifically identified 1960s and 1970s attempts to achieve income redistribution at the city level, under Lindsay in New York and Young in Detroit, as contributing to economic decline in those cities, and identified a focus on providing quality public services for the relative success of New York and Chicago in the 1990s. Staley (1998) identified reducing city taxes and improving public service delivery as the most promising means to make cities in Michigan more attractive as places to live and work.

Different political philosophies come into play

in seeking public policy to provide efficient and balanced growth for cities and their suburbs. For example, the Southeast Michigan Council of Governments (SEMCOG, 1999) called for a fairly wide-ranging set of state policies to promote more balanced growth between cities and suburbs. On the other hand, Staley (1998), in a study published by the Mackinac Center for Public Policy, called for less intrusive government policies and a greater reliance on private markets and property rights as the best way to provide efficient regional development.

## Conclusion

Cities have historically been concentrated centers of commerce, transportation, industry, finance, and technology that provided above-average per capita income for their residents. Boundaries of cities and metropolitan areas originally expanded together, but this stopped several decades ago. Since then, central cities have typically declined in population, housing stock, and relative income levels, as population, housing, jobs, and higher-income residents have pushed into the suburbs of the metropolitan areas.

Economic success of a metropolitan area and its component cities and counties depends heavily upon the industrial specialization of the region, such as motor vehicles in most of Michigan, and furniture in Grand Rapids, for example, and upon the competitiveness of the region's businesses in these industries. Manufacturing has not generally been a favorable area for specialization in recent decades, and this has retarded the ability of Michigan and its MSAs to grow. Nevertheless, the 1990s was a good decade in which to specialize in motor vehicles, since employment grew rapidly in this industry in the United States. However, Michigan vehicle producers lost share to competitors and therefore the state saw relatively little job growth in its vehicle industry, and most Michigan MSAs specializing in vehicles saw jobs and population grow more slowly and incomes fall relative to those of the rest of the United States.

The relatively poor job and income performance for most Michigan MSAs was particularly devastating for Michigan's cities, for it reinforced a national trend of economic activity and population moving out of the cities and into the surrounding suburbs. In the case of Grand Rapids–Muskegon–Holland, for example, it took strong employment growth in the furniture industry and expansion into industries supplying the furniture industry in the MSA to keep population from declining in Grand Rapids city over the past twenty years. All other central cities in Michigan lost population through a general decline in family size, and in the more serious cases, through abandonment of existing housing stock.

As a result of these trends, cities in Michigan and to a lesser extent throughout the country have become concentrated centers of poverty surrounded by a suburban population of considerably higher income levels. This growing economic and social imbalance between cities and suburbs could curtail future growth in the MSAs where the imbalance is most severe. An MSA is more likely to be successful over time if it has both a healthy central city and a healthy suburban ring. The distress of a central city is likely to tarnish the image of its suburbs, at least in the eyes of the outside world. Also, quality-of-life in an MSA is better if suburban residents can benefit from quality entertainment and cultural events that a thriving central city can provide, and better conditions in the city mean fewer negative spillover effects, such as crime, from the central city.

We have discussed public policy options with respect to cities and their suburban neighbors. These include possible cooperation on planning, provision of government services, and revenue sharing across various levels of local government in a metropolitan area. Enhanced revenue sharing by the state is also a possibility, with Michigan's education finance reform being an example of a policy that helped equalize government spending across districts within MSAs and throughout the state. The difficult economic and fiscal situation of Michigan's cities also demands that they focus heavily on efficient provision of local government services, and perhaps less on local attempts to redistribute income within their jurisdictions. All of these policies involve choices, however, and while economists can provide guidance on how to achieve a particular goal efficiently, setting the goals is a political and moral decision that must be made by citizens and their elected representatives. Selecting appropriate goals and efficient urban development and fiscal policies to achieve these are major challenges for Michigan at the millennium.

■

## REFERENCES

Anas, Alex, Richard Arnott, and Kenneth A. Small. 1998. Urban spatial structure. *Journal of Economic Literature* 36 (3): 727–56.

Braid, Ralph M. 1996. Symmetric tax competition with multiple jurisdictions in each metropolitan area. *American Economic Review* 86 (5): 1279–90.

Bram, Jason, and Michael Anderson. 2001. Declining manufacturing employment in the New York–New Jersey region: 1969–99. *Current Issues in Economics and Finance.* Federal Reserve Bank of New York 7(1).

Citizens Research Council of Michigan (CRC). 1999. *A bird's eye view of Michigan local government at the end of the twentieth century.* Report no. 326, August.

———. 2001a. Regional issues from a statewide perspective. November.

———. 2001b. *Survey of economic development programs in Michigan.* Report no. 334, May.

Crary, David, and Carol Hogan. 1992. *Willow Run and related plant closings: Causes and impacts.* Ypsilanti: Eastern Michigan University-ICARD.

Fisher, Ronald C., and Janet E. Kohlhase. 1982. Fiscal problems and policies of the cities. In *Michigan's Fiscal and Economic Structure,* edited by Harvey E. Brazer. Ann Arbor: University of Michigan Press.

Florida, Richard. 2002. *The rise of the creative class.* New York: Basic Books.

Glaeser, Edward L. 1998. Are cities dying? *Journal of Economic Perspectives* 12 (2): 127–38.

Glaeser, Edward L., J. Scheinkman, and A. Shleifer. 1995. Economic growth in a cross-section of cities. *Journal of Monetary Economics* 36 (5): 117–43.

Goodman, Allen C. 1982. Household size and population size: A tract level analysis. Johns Hopkins University, Center for Metropolitan Planning and Research.

Goodman, Allen C., and Rachel T. Talalay. 1981. Ten years of population change in the Baltimore urbanized area. Johns Hopkins University, Center for Metropolitan Planning and Research.

Hochman, Oded, David Pines, and Jacques-Francois Thisse. 1995. On the optimal structure of local governments. *American Economic Review* 85 (5): 1124–240.

Hoover, Edgar M., and Frank Giarratani. 1985. *An introduction to regional economics.* 3d ed. New York: Alfred A. Knopf.

Markusen, Ann. 1985. *Profit cycles, oligopoly and regional development.* Cambridge, Mass.: MIT Press.

Mieszkowski, Peter, and Edwin S. Mills. 1993. The causes of metropolitan suburbanization. *Journal of Economic Perspectives* 7 (3): 135–47.

Mills, Edwin S., and Luan Sende Lubuele. 1997. Inner cities. *Journal of Economic Literature* 35 (2): 727–56.

Murray, Sheila E., William N. Evans, and Robert M. Schwab. 1998. Education-finance reform and the distribution of educational resources. *American Economic Review* 88 (4): 789–812.

Oates, Wallace E. 1972. *Fiscal federalism.* New York: Harcourt, Brace, and Jovanovich.

Olson, Mancur, Jr. 1969. The principle of "fiscal equivalence": The divisions of responsibilities among different levels of local government. *American Economic Review* (Papers and Proceedings) 59 (2): 479–87.

Public Sector Consultants. 2002. *Status of Michigan cities: An index of urban well-being.* April.

Rusk, David. 1999. *Inside game outside game.* Washington, D.C.: Brookings Institution Press.

Southeast Michigan Council of Governments (SEMCOG). 1999. *Promoting redevelopment: Recommendations for state policies.* September.

Staley, Samuel R. 1998. *"Urban sprawl" and the Michigan landscape: A market-oriented approach.* Midland, Mich.: Mackinac Center for Public Policy, October.

Thompson, Wilbur R. 1982. Industrial location: Causes and consequences. In *Michigan's Fiscal and Economic Structure,* edited by Harvey E. Brazer. Ann Arbor: University of Michigan Press.

## NOTES

1. The U.S. Department of Commerce generally defines a metropolitan statistical area (MSA) as a group of one or more counties within which economic activity is highly integrated around a central city. An MSA includes at least the county that contains the central city, and in many cases multiple counties. Very large metropolitan areas are called Consolidated Metropolitan Statistical Areas (CMSA) and contain two or more Primary Metropolitan Statistical Areas(PMSA). The Detroit CMSA contains the Ann Arbor, Detroit, and Flint PMSAs.

2. This probably occurred because much of the auto industry employment growth came from companies outside the Big Three (General Motors, Ford, and Daimler/Chrysler). Except for the Mazda plant (joint with Ford) in Flat Rock, no European or Far Eastern producers have assembly plants in Michigan.

3. In 1969, the state's nine metropolitan areas held 85.5% of the state's population, 90.8% of its earned

income, and 87.2% of its employment. Nationwide, metropolitan areas accounted for 80.4% of the nation's population, 88.0% of its earned income, and 82.7% of its employment in 2000.

4. Estimates prepared by the W. E. Upjohn Institute using its Regional Economic Models, Incorporated (REMI) model for the Grand Rapids-Muskegon-Holland Area.

5. If all areas had LQs of 1.0, then they would all be the "same." Since the LQ is expressed relative to the U.S. average, if some areas have LQs that exceed 1.0, others must fall short. Focusing on LQs that exceed 1.5 concentrates on those areas with considerable specialization.

6. Pharmaceuticals have a very strong presence in the Kalamazoo–Battle Creek area, as well, however, confidentiality constraints on published employment data did not allow us to include it in the table.

7. General Motors closed its metal stamping plant in Kalamazoo in 1997, however, eliminating approximately three thousand jobs.

8. Data for 1969 are used in this analysis, since it is the first year for which data are available for MSAs on a consistent basis, and because 1969 was a cyclical peak, as was the year 2000. The Detroit–Ann Arbor–Flint Consolidated MSA consists of a contiguous ten-county area in southeast Michigan that includes the six-county Primary Metropolitan Statistical Area (PMSA) of Detroit, the three-county PMSA of Ann Arbor, and the one-county Genesee County PMSA of Flint. The Detroit PMSA includes Lapeer, Macomb, Monroe, Oakland, St. Clair, and Wayne Counties. The Ann Arbor PMSA includes Lenawee, Livingston, and Washtenaw Counties. A table with all thirty-two areas is available from the authors on request.

9. For Detroit PMSA the previously presented IRS data on intercounty moves (table 11.4) support the finding here regarding out-migration in the Detroit MSA. However, since Flint is a one-county PMSA, the population shifts were intracounty in scope and, thus, not detected by the IRS data.

10. The 1980 population for Battle Creek included Battle Creek Township, which was actually annexed into the city in the early 1980s, to allow for later comparisons.

11. The decline in the percentage of African American residents in the City of Battle Creek from 1980 to 1990 was due to the city's annexation of neighboring Battle Creek Township in 1982.

12. The formula for the index of dissimilarity $D$ is:

$$D = \left[\sum_i t_i \left| p_i - p^* \right|\right] \div [2Tp^*(1 - p^*)],$$

where: $p_i$ is the mean percentage minority in neighborhood $i$, $p^*$ is the mean percentage minority in the metropolitan area, $t_i$ is the population of neighborhood $i$, $T$ is the population of the metropolitan area, and $|p_i - p^*|$ is the absolute value of the percentage minority in neighborhood $i$ less the mean percentage minority in the metropolitan area.

If all $p_i = p^*$, there is no segregation, the numerator equals 0, and $D = 0$.

If there is total segregation, then $p_i$ equals 0 in some neighborhoods and 1 in the others, Recognizing that the sum of all of the minority population equals $p^*T$, mathematical substitution establishes that the maximum value for the numerator is $2Tp^*(1 - p^*)$. If this occurs (full segregation) then $D = 1$.

13. These features are not unique to Michigan. Goodman and Talalay (1981) and Goodman (1982) found this to be the case in Baltimore, and Goodman's ongoing work suggests similar trends in cities such as Cleveland and Milwaukee.

# 12

# Overview of State Government Expenditures in Michigan

*Gary S. Olson*

The State of Michigan will spend approximately $37.5 billion during fiscal year (FY) 2001–02 to provide a wide range of services to the people of the state. The distribution of these expenditures among the major programs financed by the state is consistently changing over time. This chapter provides a detailed overview of the state budget process and reviews the trends in state-financed spending over the past twenty fiscal years. Finally, the chapter includes a discussion of the issues that the state budget will likely face in the years ahead.

## Michigan State Budget Process

### Constitutional Budgetary Provisions

The parameters of the Michigan state budget are jointly determined by the governor and the 148 members of the Michigan legislature. The governor provides a detailed set of recommendations for the expenditure of state funds to the legislature in February of each year, and the legislature then is responsible for implementing the state budget through a series of annual appropriation bills that provide the detailed guidelines for all state expenditures. The budget process is controlled by numerous constitutional and statutory provisions that establish procedures and set controls on both the recommendations of the governor and the budget enacted into law by the legislature.

The general framework of the state budget is established in the State Constitution of 1963. These constitutional provisions provide high-level controls and limitations on the expenditure of state funds and are the first factor that must be understood in reviewing the state budget. The major constitutional provisions relating to the state budget can be grouped into three major categories. These categories are: Delegation of Powers between the Executive and Legislative Branches, Requirements of a Balanced State Budget, and Expenditure Mandates.

### Delegation of Powers between the Executive and Legislative Branches

*Article IV, Sec. 33:* Provides that the legislature, with a two-thirds vote of the House of Representatives and the Senate, can restore any line item appropriation vetoed by the governor.

*Article V, Sec. 19:* Provides that the governor has the ability to veto individual line items in the appropriation bills approved by the legislature. This ability is different from the authority of the governor over nonappropriation bills approved by the legislature, in that the governor can veto only an entire nonappropriation bill.

### Requirements of a Balanced State Budget

*Article IV, Sec. 31:* Provides that the appropriation bills approved by the legislature for a fiscal year period shall not in total exceed the estimated amount of revenues available for expenditure. This section assures that the legislature approves a balanced budget.

*Article V, Sec. 18:* Provides that the governor must submit to the legislature, at a time established in state law, a budget for the ensuing fiscal year period, setting forth in detail, for all operating funds, the proposed revenues and expenditures of the state. This constitutional section also establishes that the governor must submit to the legislature a budget in which estimated expenditures do not exceed estimated revenues. The governor also is required to submit detailed appropriation bill recommendations along with the overall budget recommendations.

*Article V, Sec. 20:* Provides a mechanism to ensure that the enacted state budget continues to be in balance between projected expenditures and revenues when the revenue estimate upon which the original appropriation bills were based is reduced. In this instance the governor can recommend to the legislature specific reductions in enacted appropriations. These appropriation reductions, referred to as executive order reductions, cannot apply to the appropriations for the legislative and judicial branches. State statute provides that these executive order budget reductions will take effect only if approved by a majority of the members of the appropriations committees of the House of Representatives and the Senate.

*Article IX, Sec. 26:* Provides a limit on the amount of state revenues that may be collected in any specific state fiscal year. This limit is equal to 9.49% of the level of Michigan personal income reported during the prior calendar year. This revenue limit effectively limits the overall size of the state budget.

*Article IX, Sec. 28:* Provides that no expenditures of the state shall exceed estimated revenues plus any balances carried forward from the prior fiscal year.

### Expenditure Mandates

*Article IV, Sec. 30:* Provides that any state appropriation for a private or local purpose must be approved by a two-thirds vote of both bodies of the legislature. This section attempts to keep the public purpose of the state budget as the primary purpose and use of state expenditures.

*Article VIII, Sec. 2:* Provides that the legislature shall be responsible for the support of a system of free public elementary and secondary education in the state.

*Article IX, Sec. 17:* Provides that no payment shall be made from the state treasury except by an appropriation approved pursuant to law. This section provides the legislature with the ultimate decision-making authority on the state budget.

*Article IX, Sec. 30:* Provides that the proportion of total state appropriations paid to units of local government shall not be reduced below the proportion in effect for FY 1978–79.[1] This provision ensures that at a minimum 48.97% of state appropriations are paid to units of local government. During FY 2001–02 actual state appropriations paid to units of local government will exceed this constitutional requirement by $2.9 billion.

These are the major constitutional provisions that control the expenditure of state funds. The implementation of these constitutional provisions is provided for in state statute.

### Statutory Budgetary Provisions

While the State Constitution of 1963 establishes the general framework for the enactment and implementation of the state budget, the details of the budget process are established in state statutes. The Management and Budget Act (Public Act 431 of 1984, Michigan Compiled Laws Sections 18.1101 to 18.1594) is the comprehensive state statute that establishes the procedures and controls dealing with the implementation and the execution of the state budget. The following are some of the major statutory provisions contained in the Management and Budget Act that are important controls on the overall state budget process.

*Fiscal Year Period.* The act establishes the state fiscal year as the period from 1 October through 30 September (MCL 18.1491). For future reference the state fiscal year between 1 October 2002 and 30 September 2003 is referred to as fiscal year (FY)

2002–03. Prior to FY 1975–76, Michigan's fiscal year ran from 1 July to 30 June. Most state fiscal years run from 1 July to 30 June. Michigan and Alabama's fiscal years begin 1 October, while New York's fiscal year begins 1 April and Texas's begins 1 September.

*Transmittal of Governor's Budget Recommendations to the Legislature.* The act provides that the governor must submit detailed budget recommendations to the legislature for the ensuing fiscal year no later than thirty days after the legislature convenes in regular session each year (MCL 18.1363). This means that the governor's budget recommendations are usually received in the legislature by the end of the first week in February. The act does provide for an extra thirty days to submit the budget recommendations to the legislature during the first year in which a newly elected governor is in office. Historically, governors have always met this budget submission deadline, and several times the budget submission has occurred well before the deadline.

*Consensus Revenue Estimating Conference.* Since 1991, the act has provided for a statutory procedure to be followed in determining the revenue estimates that will be used in the state budget (MCL 18.1367a to 18.1367f). In January and May of each year, the Consensus Revenue Estimating Conference meets to establish official state revenue estimates. The participants in the Consensus Revenue Estimating Conference include the state treasurer, the director of the Senate Fiscal Agency, and the director of the House Fiscal Agency. Each participant brings an independent economic and revenue forecast to the conference. In order to reach a consensus revenue estimate, all three participants in the conference must concur in the estimate. This means the participants must compromise in order to reach an agreement. Once a consensus revenue estimate is reached, the governor and the legislature must abide by this estimate as the state budget is developed and enacted into law.

*Powers and Duties of the State Budget Director.* The act outlines the powers and duties of the state budget director (MCL 18.1323). The state budget director is the principal advisor to the governor on the state budget and is responsible for assembling the governor's budget recommendations to the legislature and for monitoring the execution of the enacted budget. In addition, the state budget director is mandated by the act to provide numerous reports on all aspects of the state budget to the legislature.

*Capital Outlay Process.* The act provides the procedures to be followed by the governor and the legislature for the construction of state-financed buildings (MCL 18.1237 to 18.1249). The responsibilities of the governor and the legislature in terms of the planning, the appropriation of funds, and the construction of state-financed buildings are outlined in considerable detail. The capital outlay process applies to the construction of buildings at Michigan's public universities and community colleges as well as buildings for state departments and agencies. The state budget process does provide considerable flexibility in the capital outlay process, as state departments and agencies are free to spend portions of their operating appropriations on renovations of existing facilities that fall outside the direct capital outlay budget process. Currently, the State of Michigan has no comprehensive planning or allocation process for the distribution of capital outlay funds among the state departments and agencies and the public universities and community colleges. The process often takes the form of a political process based on priorities of the governor or members of the legislature.

*State Purchasing.* The act sets the procedures that must be followed by the executive branch of state government in purchasing goods or services that are necessary for the operation of state government (MCL 18.1261 to 18.1269). The purchase of state goods and services requires a competitive bidding process unless emergency conditions exist that would force a noncompetitive bidding process. Included in these procedures are detailed requirements for reporting to the legislature.

*Internal Auditing.* The act mandates that executive branch state departments employ internal auditors to ensure that the financial management of the departments is following all state laws and rules. These internal auditors are designed to supplement the general audit oversight functions of the legislative auditor general.

*Transfers of Enacted Appropriations.* The act provides for two separate mechanisms that can be used by the governor and the legislature to move enacted appropriations within a state department (MCL 18.1393). These appropriation adjustments are referred to as legislative and administrative transfers. Legislative transfers involve the transfer of funds within a department for any purpose. These transfers become effective if they are approved in an identical amount by a majority of the members of the House and Senate appropriations committees. Administrative transfers involve the transfer of funds within a department to reflect price variances and lawsuit settlements. These transfers become effective thirty days after they are recommended to the House and Senate appropriations committees unless disapproved by either committee. The transfer process is utilized extensively in the state budget process and is designed to provide a mechanism to adjust the enacted budget to reflect current expenditure patterns in a more timely fashion than enacting a supplemental appropriation bill.

*Work Project Accounts.* The act prescribes the procedures to be followed in establishing work project accounts at the close of the fiscal year (MCL 18.1451a). These work project accounts supply the authorization to continue to spend annual appropriations even after the fiscal year is completed. In most instances the act provides that annual appropriations not spent at the close of the fiscal year shall return or lapse back to the fund from which the appropriations originated. Work project accounts authorize the continuation of these expenditures for a maximum of three additional fiscal years.

## State Budget Expenditure Controls

The approval of the annual state appropriation bills by the legislature and the signing into law of the appropriation bills by the governor mark the end of the first major phase of the state budget. Following the original enactment of the state budget, the budget process moves into the execution and oversight phases. There are four major groups that provide for the execution and oversight of the enacted state budget.

The Office of Financial Management (OFM), under the direction of the Office of the State Budget, is the executive branch agency responsible for the execution of the enacted budget. The OFM is the lead accounting agency for the State of Michigan. Following the enactment of the budget, the OFM provides for the allotments of the appropriations to state departments and then ensures,

through a variety of financial accounting controls, that state expenditures are conforming with the requirements of the appropriation bills. In addition, the OFM maintains the state's central accounting system, which provides for real-time data on state revenue collections and state expenditures.

At the close of the fiscal year, the OFM is responsible for the final accounting of state revenues and expenditures. This final accounting involves two significant steps. The first step is the preliminary closing of the state's accounts, which must be completed within 120 days of the close of the fiscal year. The second step is the final closing of the state's accounts for the prior fiscal year. This final closing is accomplished with the publication of the state's Comprehensive Annual Financial Report. This report must be completed within six months of the close of the fiscal year. Michigan reports all of its financial data in accordance with Generally Accepted Governmental Accounting Principals (GAAP).

The Office of the Auditor General, a legislative agency, conducts oversight of the state budget. The Office of the Auditor General conducts postfinancial and performance audits of all state government operations. During FY 2002–03 the Office of the Auditor General has an appropriation of $15.7 million and will conduct approximately one hundred audits. Financial audits have two principal purposes: (1) to ensure that state expenditures are conforming with the appropriations approved by the legislature, and (2) to ensure that all expenditures are following all of the financial controls outlined in state laws and regulations. The Office of the Auditor General establishes regular schedules for the timing of these financial audits. Performance audits are conducted in an effort to evaluate the effectiveness of state programs. The results of these performance audits are reviewed by the executive and legislative branches and are used to change current programs in an effort to improve program performance.

The Senate Fiscal Agency and the House Fiscal Agency are nonpartisan legislative agencies that have oversight responsibilities for the state budget. During FY 2002–03 the Senate and House Fiscal Agencies each had an appropriation of approximately $3 million. The agencies monitor state revenues and expenditures to ensure that the execution of the enacted state budget is conforming with the requirements outlined by the legislature in the enacted appropriation bills. This

**TABLE 12.1**

### FY 2003–04 Budget Development Timeframe

| Month/Year | Action Taken |
| --- | --- |
| May 2002 | Department of Management and Budget (DMB–Executive Branch) develop program policy guidelines |
| June 2002 | Guidelines sent to departments to draft their budgetary requests |
| September 2002 | Departments return budget requests to DMB |
| October/November 2002 | Departments meet with governor's budget officials |
| December 2002 | Governor's decisions made |
| January 2003 | Governor's recommendation prepared for submission to legislature; governor's State-of-the-State and budget message prepared; consensus revenue estimating conference meets |
| February 2003 | Budget documents delivered to legislature; legislative action begins |
| March–May 2003 | Legislative action: subcommittee and committee hearings, floor votes |
| June 2003 | Consensus revenue estimating conference meets; budget targets are set; conference committees meet |
| July–August 2003 | Governor signs (or vetoes) bills; may include line-item vetoes |
| October 1, 2003 | Fiscal Year 2003–04 begins |
| Oct. 1, 2003–Sept. 30, 2004 | Possible supplementals and transfers |
| Sept. 30, 2004 | Fiscal Year 2003–04 ends |
| January 2005 | Preliminary book closings, FY 2003–04 |
| March 2005 | Final book closings, FY 2003–04 |

oversight includes the monitoring of state revenue collections and the analysis of these collections versus the revenue estimates upon which the state budget was based. The agencies also provide oversight of state expenditures by monitoring actual expenditures versus the amounts approved in the enacted budget. In addition, the agencies prepare unbiased reports on a variety of state programs. These reports are designed to provide members of the legislature with information that can be used to make policy changes to state programs. Finally, the agencies review reports submitted to the legislature from state agencies in regard to numerous aspects of the state budget.

The final major group that provides for oversight of the enacted state budget consists of outside interest groups. These groups include associations that represent a variety of special interests, the news media, and the general public. These groups provide oversight in a variety of ways, including testimony in front of legislative committees, investigative reporting by the news media, and interaction by the public with the legislature to influence future public policy decisions.

### Legislative Budget Process and Time Frame

The actual process for the enactment of the annual state budget is quite complex. While the state fiscal year begins on 1 October and ends on 30 September, the work on the budget for that fiscal year begins approximately sixteen months before the start of the fiscal year, and the final closing of the books for the fiscal year does not occur until six months after the close of the fiscal year. In total the fiscal year budget process, from start to finish, takes almost three full years to complete. In addition, the auditor general often reviews state expenditures made several fiscal years earlier. The following information provides an overview of the major steps involved in the state budget process. To help explain this process, the dates used in this section refer to the development, execution, and final actions on the fiscal year (FY) 2003–04 state budget.[2] This fiscal year will begin on 1 October 2003 and end on 30 September 2004. Table 12.1 provides a graphical summary of the FY 2003–04 state budget process time frame.

The FY 2003–04 state budget process actually commenced in May 2002, when the Office of the State Budget began the process of developing the budget by preparing program guidelines and directions for the state departments. The guidelines and directions include broad general assumptions regarding revenue changes, federal funds, and economic adjustments. These guidelines also include instructions for the preparation of different expenditure alternatives based on several different assumed levels of appropriations for each department. During June 2002 the Office of the State Budget transmitted the program guidelines and directions to each state department with detailed directions as to how to complete the documents.

By September 2002, the state departments had completed their budget requests and returned them to the Office of the State Budget for review. During October and November 2002, the state departments met with the Office of the State Budget and the governor to discuss the departmental budget requests in detail. At this stage of the budget preparation process, the first rough parameters of the governor's budget recommendation have begun to take shape. During December 2002 the governor and the Office of the State Budget will begin to prepare the FY 2003–04 state budget recommendations. At this point in the process, the governor will use a working estimate of projected state revenues prepared by the state treasurer to set the approximate amount of revenue available to fund appropriations.

In January 2003, the Consensus Revenue Estimating Conference will meet to establish the state's official FY 2003–04 revenue estimate. The Consensus Revenue Estimating Conference is conducted by the directors of the Senate and House Fiscal Agencies and the state treasurer. Assuming an agreement is reached, the consensus revenue estimate reached at this conference then must be incorporated into the governor's budget recommendations.

Normally, during the first week of February 2003, the governor formally transmits her FY 2003–04 state budget recommendation to the legislature. This spells out the governor's recommendations for appropriations, tax policy changes, or any statutory changes that need to be enacted to implement the budget recommendation. The governor's budget recommendation traditionally is delivered to the legislature at a joint meeting of the Senate and House of Representatives appropriations committees. This presentation is delivered to the joint committee meeting by the state budget director. For FY 2003–04 this deadline is extended by thirty days to allow the new governor additional time to prepare her first budget recommendation.

The governor's budget recommendation to the Legislature includes a series of appropriation bills to implement the spending recommendations. These appropriation bills then are introduced in the legislature by a member of the governor's political party in both the Senate and the House of Representatives. Upon introduction, the governor's recommended appropriation bills are referred to the appropriations committees and then referred to the proper appropriations subcommittees by the chairperson of each appropriations committee. Based on tradition, approximately one-half of the appropriation bills initiate in the Senate and the other half of the appropriation bills initiate in the House of Representatives.

Once the governor's recommended FY 2003–04 appropriation bills are introduced in the legislature during February 2003, the legislative debate on the state budget begins. The appropriations subcommittees take extensive testimony on the budget recommendations and develop alternatives or amendments to the governor's budget recommendations. Normally, by mid-March 2003 these formal subcommittee recommendations would be expected to be reported out to the full Senate or House appropriations committees. The subcommittee recommendations then are debated in the full appropriations committees and passed on to the full membership of the Senate or the House of Representatives. By the end of March 2003, the appropriation bills would normally be expected to pass the Senate or House of Representatives and the bills would go through a similar hearing and debating process in the opposite chamber. The appropriation bills are generally different in each house, as members offer amendments to formulate the final bill in each house. At the same time that the appropriation bills are being considered by the legislature, other revenue or statutory bills that are part of the overall budget also are being debated and approved by the legislature. Due to the gubernatorial transition, most of these normal deadlines may be delayed about one month.

During the middle part of May 2003 the Consensus Revenue Estimating Conference meets again to debate and agree upon updated estimates of FY 2003–04 revenues. This revised consensus revenue estimate then is used to make final legislative adjustments on the appropriation bills pending before the legislature. At the same time the Consensus Revenue Estimating Conference is meeting, the legislature is completing action through the second house on the appropriation bills. By the end of May 2003, this process should be completed.

In late May to June 2003, legislative leaders should meet with the state budget director in an effort to establish the final appropriation levels for each appropriation bill. This process is commonly referred to as the target-setting process and is necessary to ensure that the total of the appropriation bills does not exceed the consensus revenue estimate. These appropriation targets then are transmitted to the members of the legislature and the final action on the FY 2003–04 appropriation bills begins. By mid-June 2003 the appropriation bills should be before joint Senate and House of Representatives conference committees, where the final versions of the appropriation bills will be agreed to. The conference committees are expected to ensure that the final level of appropriations in the bills does not exceed the targets established by legislative leadership.

By late June 2003 the conference committees should complete action on the appropriation bills and the Senate and the House of Representatives should vote on and approve the conference committees' recommendations. The appropriation bills approved by the legislature then are transmitted to the governor. Upon receiving the appropriation bills from the legislature, the governor has fourteen days to review the bills and sign the bills into law or to approve the bills with specific items vetoed. This line-item veto power of the governor does have a significant impact on the state budget process. Governors often utilize this power to remove from the appropriation bills items approved by the legislature and not recommended by the governor. This tends to create another method to balance power between the executive and legislative branches in the state budget process.

On 1 October 2003, the FY 2003–04 budget year begins. Throughout the fiscal year period, 1 October 2003 through 30 September 2004, the governor can propose to the legislature adjustments to the enacted FY 2003–04 budget. These adjustments can take the form of supplemental appropriation requests or appropriation transfer requests. Supplemental appropriations add additional appropriations to the level of appropriations contained in the initial budget. Appropriation transfers move existing appropriations from one appropriation line item within a state department to another without increasing the overall level of appropriations. Supplemental appropriations require the approval of both houses of the legislature and the governor's signature to be effective. Appropriation transfers require approval by both the Senate and House of Representatives appropriations committees to be effective.

On 30 September 2004, the FY 2003–04 budget period ends. Pursuant to statutory requirements, no later than 120 days after the close of the fiscal year, the Office of the State Budget releases its initial estimates of actual year-end balances in the General Fund and School Aid Fund budgets. These estimates are contained in a report referred to as the preliminary closing report. Within six months after the close of the fiscal year, or by 1 April 2005, the Office of the State Budget releases the final accounting of FY 2003–04 revenues and expenditures. These data are contained in the State of Michigan Comprehensive Annual Financial Report.

Therefore, a budget process for FY 2003–04, which began during May 2002, is completed by 1 April 2005. Even after this date, the Office of the Legislative Auditor General may conduct random or selective past audits of program performance during a previous year. Throughout this period the Office of the State Budget and the legislature are also working on other state fiscal year budgets.

## Growth in the State Budget

State appropriations over the past twenty years have changed dramatically. Nominal Gross State appropriations, which totaled $10.9 billion in FY 1982–83, have grown to $37.5 billion in FY 2001–02. This represents an annual rate of growth of 6.7%. However, if we correct for inflation, the annual growth rate is reduced to 4.4%. With the growth in overall state appropriations, a number of significant changes have had an impact on the state budget and will likely have an impact on future budgets. These changes include the reform of state funding for public K–12 education, the growth of state appropriations for the state prison system, and the increasing importance of health-related expenditures.

A review of state appropriations from FY 1982–83 through FY 2001–02 shows that the past twenty years have been characterized by major changes in the structure, overall level, and priorities of the state budget. This section provides an overview of the structural changes that have occurred in the state budget over the past twenty years, a discussion of the overall growth in the state budget as measured by growth in state appropriations, and a discussion of how the priorities in the state budget have changed, by reviewing the growth in appropriations by major program areas.

The power to restructure the delivery of state programs through the reorganization of state government rests with the governor. Section 2 of Article V of the State Constitution of 1963 provides the governor with the power to reorganize the executive branch of state government. The governor's reorganization proposals are delivered to the legislature in the form of an executive order. Executive orders spell out the changes recommended by the governor in the structure of state government. Executive reorganization orders take effect in sixty days unless majority votes of both the Senate and the House of Representatives reject the proposed restructuring.

Governors use the executive order reorganization process as a tool to streamline the delivery of state services to the public. Each governor has different desires and goals as to how essential services should be delivered. The executive order reorganization process provides the current governor with the opportunity to structure state government in the manner she believes is most efficient. Adding to the complexity of this government reorganization process is the fact that the next governor may have a different approach for the delivery of services and the reorganization changes brought by the current governor could be adjusted significantly.

The reorganization of the executive branch of state government accomplished by this executive order process over the past twenty years is very extensive. Six state departments that existed in the FY 1982–83 state budget no longer exist in FY 2001–02. These are the Department of Commerce, the Department of Labor, the Department of Licensing and Regulation, the Department of Mental Health, the Department of Public Health, and the Department of Social Services. Six state departments that currently exist in FY 2001–02 were not in existence in FY 1982–83. These are the Department of Career Development, the Department of Community Health, the Department of Consumer and Industry Services, the Department of Environmental Quality, the Family Independence Agency, and the Strategic Fund Agency. The extent of this reorganization makes it very difficult to analyze how state appropriation priorities have changed over the past twenty years. Therefore, for purposes of this analysis, government programs will be grouped in broad program categories in order to analyze the changes in state appropriations over the past twenty years.

In addition to the problems that the reorganization of state government departments causes in looking at state appropriation patterns over the past twenty years, the restructuring of the funding of public K–12 education also causes problems when reviewing overall state budget trends. On 15 March 1994, the state's voters approved a consti-

tutional amendment (Proposal A) that provided for major changes in the funding of K–12 education across the state. This constitutional amendment shifted the funding of K–12 education from approximately two-thirds local funding to a new system under which four-fifths of the total funding comes from the state budget. This change led to a major increase in state appropriations for K–12 education beginning in FY 1993–94 and tends to distort the overall growth in the state budget beginning with partial implementation in FY 1993–94.

This analysis of the growth in state appropriations over the past twenty years will focus on one measure of state appropriations. This measure is referred to as Adjusted Gross appropriations. Adjusted Gross appropriations are defined as appropriations financed by all sources of funds, including all state taxes, fees, licenses, permits, and fines, as well as federal funds allocated to Michigan for appropriation in the state budget. In addition, Adjusted Gross appropriations include a small amount of local and private funds appropriated in the state budget.

While other measures are possible and in some cases more appropriate for specific comparisons, Adjusted Gross appropriations has the advantage of showing the "big picture" of major state spending trends. It is important for the reader to realize that underneath the "big picture" level are a number of important specifics that play major roles in the actual appropriation of funds for the delivery of state services. We will briefly cover a few key points that readers should keep in mind as they look at specific areas of the state budget. We will then begin our overall analysis of the budgetary "big picture" of Adjusted Gross appropriations.

Like most governmental entities, Michigan's finance system is structured on a funds accounting and budgeting system. Also, like most governments, Michigan revenues are often earmarked or restricted for a specific purpose by either the state constitution, state laws, or providers of other funds such as the federal government. Federal funds received appropriated in the state budget are restricted for specific uses such as highways, the Medicaid program, education programs, or other human service programs. These federal funds must be used by the states for the purpose designated by federal government.

Key funds in the Michigan budget and accounting system include the following.

## General Fund

The state's General Fund has two component pieces, general fund/general purpose and general fund/special purpose. General fund/general purpose funds can be used by the governor and the legislature in the state appropriation process for any purpose. These funds are the completely unrestricted portion of the state budget. General fund/special purpose funds include the majority of federal funds received by the state and other restricted state funds. With the gross budget of approximately $37.5 billion during FY 2001–02, general fund/general purpose appropriations amounted to $9.2 billion while general fund/special purpose appropriations amounted to $12.0 billion.

## School Aid Fund

The State School Aid Fund was constitutionally created for the purpose of funding public K–12 education programs. It is funded by revenues earmarked to the fund by the state constitution or state law. The School Aid Fund is also supplemented by federal funds received by the state and an appropriation from the general fund/general purpose fund. For FY 2001–02, appropriations from the School Aid Fund will total approximately $11.4 billion.

## Transportation Funds

The state has several distinct funds that in total make up the transportation-related funds in the budget. These funds include the following: State Aeronautics Fund, State Trunkline Fund, Michigan Transportation Fund, Comprehensive Transportation Fund, and other small transportation-related funds. Revenues from these funds are restricted for the appropriation of transportation-related projects. For FY 2001–02, appropriations from these transportation-related funds will total approximately $3.3 billion.

## Other State Funds

The state budget contains many other funds outside of the major funds mentioned previously. Some of these other funds include the Budget Stabilization Fund, natural resource-related funds, environmental-related funds, and regulatory and administrative funds. The combination of all of these funds makes up the state budget.

During FY 1982–83, Adjusted Gross appropriations totaled $10.9 billion. Adjusted Gross appropriations in FY 2001–02 totaled $37.5 billion, representing an increase of $26.5 billion or 242.6% growth over the past twenty years. However, if these appropriation data are adjusted to remove the impact of the 1993 school finance reform initiative from the state budget, a different picture of overall state budget growth emerges. Excluding any funding of K–12 education, the overall growth in the state budget over the past twenty years is $16.3 billion or 185.2%.

This growth in the state budget can be put into context if it is compared with several other economic and demographic factors. It is commonly thought that the growth of the state budget is influenced by growth in the population of the state, along with inflation and the overall level of income in the state. State income levels are measured by personal income. The growth in personal income is likely to correspond to growth in the state budget, as state tax systems tend to generate revenues that roughly correspond to income growth.

Figure 12.1 provides a graphic summary of the growth in state Adjusted Gross appropriations, versus Michigan personal income, inflation as measured by the Government Consumption Deflator, and Michigan population growth from the period FY 1982–83 through FY 2001–02. The graph establishes each indicator's value equal to 100.0 in FY 1982–83 and provides comparable growth through FY 2001–02. As shown in figure 12.1, the rate of growth in state Adjusted Gross appropriations adjusted to exclude K–12 School Aid appropriations closely follows the growth in Michigan personal income. By either measure, Gross appropriations have grown considerably faster than inflation or the state's population over this time frame.

While the growth in overall state appropriations over the past twenty years, adjusted for changes in the financing of K–12 education, has been equal to the growth in Michigan personal income, the distribution of the overall appropriations among the programs funded in the state budget has changed considerably during that period. Table 12.1 provides a summary of the level of Adjusted Gross appropriations in FY 1982–83 versus the appropriations in FY 2001–02. The Adjusted Gross appropriation data are presented

**FIGURE 12.1**

**State Appropriation Growth versus Other Economic Indicators**

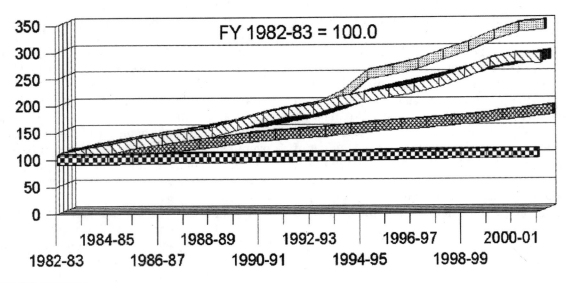

SOURCE: State Fiscal Agency.

in the form of a summary of major programs in the state budget and not by state departments, in order to portray accurately the broad spending priorities that have been greatly influenced by the reorganization of state government over this time period. Appendix A provides the annual summary of this appropriation data for the period FY 1982–83 through FY 2001–02.

As illustrated in table 12.1, while overall Adjusted Gross appropriations have increased by 242.6%, the increases for specific major programs

funded by state appropriations range from 67.6% growth for general governmental programs to 627.2% for corrections. The appropriations for K–12 education have increased by 475.2%, but a significant share of this growth is a direct result of the school financing reform proposal approved by the voters in 1994. The growth in appropriations for corrections programs can be explained by a combination of increases in the number of inmates in the state corrections system and inflation. During FY 1982–83, approximately

**TABLE 12.2**

**Growth in Adjusted Gross Appropriations by Major Program Area (thousands of dollars)**

| Program Area | FY 1982–83 | FY 2001–02 | Dollar Difference | % Change |
|---|---|---|---|---|
| Higher education | $ 918,604.8 | $ 2,262,438.7 | $ 1,343,833.9 | 146.3% |
| K–12 education | 2,163,579.2 | 12,445,720.3 | 10,282,141.1 | 475.2% |
| Human services support | 4,504,004.2 | 12,309,036.4 | 7,805,032.2 | 173.3% |
| Public safety | 258,550.1 | 779,289.3 | 520,739.2 | 201.4% |
| Corrections | 230,660.3 | 1,677,301.4 | 1,446,641.1 | 627.2% |
| Agriculture and natural resources | 219,927.9 | 814,014.8 | 594,086.9 | 270.1% |
| General government operations | 512,108.3 | 858,149.6 | 346,041.3 | 67.6% |
| Economic development and regulatory | 396,894.0 | 1,251,480.8 | 854,586.8 | 215.3% |
| Capital outlay | 133,503.6 | 479,161.2 | 345,657.6 | 258.9% |
| Transportation | 1,007,799.4 | 3,064,612.9 | 2,056,813.5 | 204.1% |
| Revenue sharing | 595,092.3 | 1,540,600.0 | 945,507.7 | 158.9% |
| Total appropriations | $10,940,724.1 | $37,481,805.4 | $26,541,081.3 | 242.6% |

SOURCE: State Fiscal Agency.

fifteen thousand inmates were incarcerated in the state corrections system. By FY 2001–02, the number of inmates incarcerated had jumped to almost forty-nine thousand or an increase of thirty-five thousand inmates over the twenty-year period. This emphasis on corrections programs has come at the expense of programs such as state spending on higher education, which increased by 146.3% over the same time period. While this increase is significantly less than the overall average growth in state appropriations, it is still important to remember that inflation, as measured by the Detroit Consumer Price Index, increased by only 79.3% over the same period.

In order to illustrate the changes in state appropriation priorities over this time period, figure 12.2 provides a graphic summary of the percentage shares of Adjusted Gross appropriations for major state programs in FY 1982–83 as compared with FY 2001–02. Appropriations for corrections programs, which accounted for only 2.1% of total appropriations in FY 1982–83, grew to 4.5% of appropriations in FY 2001–02. Most other areas of the budget, with the exception of appropriations for K–12 education, saw their share of the total level of appropriations decline over this period.

While many factors, most notably the changes in the financing of K–12 education, have influenced the growth of the state budget over this twenty-year period, another factor that has influenced the growth in the state budget is the level of federal funds appropriated in the state budget. Federal funds received through the federal budget process and earmarked specifically for programs in the State of Michigan are appropriated as a component of Adjusted Gross appropriations. The level of federal funds appropriated in the state budget has seen considerable growth over the past twenty years. During FY 1982–83, federal funds appropriated in the state budget amounted to $2.9 billion and accounted for 26.4% of Adjusted Gross appropriations. During FY 2001–02, federal funds appropriated in the state budget amounted to $10.2 billion, or 27.3% of Adjusted Gross appropriations. While federal funds are an important component of the overall state budget, the ability of the state to use these funds is strictly regulated by federal guidelines. The state has little or no flexibility to spend these funds on programs not spelled out by the federal government. Federal transportation funds received by the state offer the greatest flexibility but they still must be strictly spent on transportation programs and not shifted to other programs.

In many respects, state government is a check-writing machine. It collects funds from its own taxes and fees and receives significant resources directly from the federal government. It then appropriates most of these funds to individuals or

**FIGURE 12.2**

**State Appropriations by Major Program, Percentage of Total Appropriations**

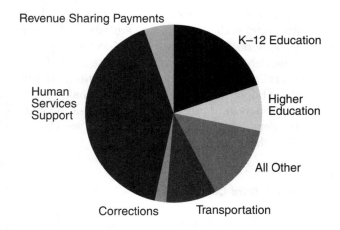

FY 1982–83 YTD

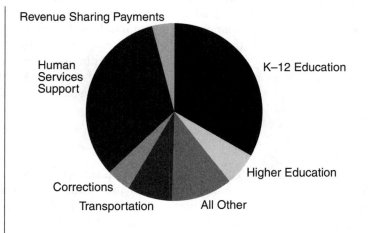

FY 2001–02 YTD

SOURCE: State Fiscal Agency.

other government or nonprofit groups that actually provide a large amount of the basic services to the citizens. For example, nearly all of the $12.4 billion appropriated for K–12 education in FY 2001–02 goes to local and intermediate school districts and public school academies, where locally elected school boards determine the exact expenditure of these appropriations. Similarly, the $1.5 billion appropriated in FY 2001–02 for revenue sharing payments is spent at the discretion of the elected boards of cities, villages, townships, and counties.

## Major State Budget Issues over the Past Twenty Years

While state spending increases or decisions are always controversial, five major issues have driven budget policy over the past twenty years. While this list is subjective, it will provide a summary of major policy decisions that have been debated in the state budget in recent times. The five major state budget expenditure issues are as follows.

### School Finance Reform

As previously noted, the state's voters and the Michigan legislature completely reformed the funding of public K–12 schools in this state in 1993 and 1994. This shift from a funding system relying heavily on local revenue generated from property taxes to a funding system more heavily reliant on a combination of state-generated revenues has been the fundamental fiscal change in the past twenty years in Michigan. This school financing change not only had a major impact on the state's revenue system, but also was designed to reduce the overall funding differences among similar school districts. See chapter 15 in this volume for a more thorough discussion of this issue.

### Welfare Reform

The delivery of welfare services to eligible low-income citizens of the state has seen a major transformation in recent years. Beginning in the early 1990s, the State of Michigan began to institute a series of reforms in the delivery of welfare programs. These reforms centered on new efforts to move welfare recipients into the workforce. These welfare reform efforts were further moved

along in 1996 when the U.S. Congress enacted the Personal Responsibility and Work Opportunity Reconciliation Act. This federal welfare reform legislation provided states with increased flexibility to redesign existing welfare programs. Over the past ten years, and especially since 1996, numerous changes to the state welfare delivery system have resulted in a complete change in Michigan's welfare programs. See chapter 17 in this volume for a more in-depth discussion of this issue.

### Corrections Spending

The growth in the spending for the Department of Corrections has been a significant issue in the state budget in recent times. The additional state resources necessary to house the increased prison population have consistently been a major topic of discussion in the state budget. See chapter 25 in this volume for a more in-depth discussion of this issue.

### Growth in State-Financed Capital Construction Projects

Over the past twenty years, the State of Michigan has undertaken a major effort to use long-term borrowing to finance the construction of new state buildings, as well as construction at the state's public universities and community colleges. This debt financing has occurred with bonds issued by the State Building Authority. At the close of FY 1982–83, the State Building Authority had outstanding bonds that totaled approximately $444 million. At the close of FY 2001–02, State Building Authority bonds outstanding are expected to total $2.6 billion. This increase in the level of long-term state debt has had an impact on the level of state spending for the debt service requirements on these bonds and also has resulted in major capital construction of public buildings across the state. For detailed discussion of public debt, see chapter 30 in this volume.

### Health Care Cost Increases

A fiscal issue that is not unique to the State of Michigan's budget but is still a major state budget issue is the rising cost of health care services provided in the state budget. These health care cost increases have led to significant state budget pressures in areas such as the State Medicaid program, health care costs for active state employees, health care costs for retired state employees, and the provision of health care to a rapidly expanding prison population. Health care cost increases have also affected other budgets, such as K–12 education and higher education. See chapter 9 of this volume for a more in-depth discussion of this issue.

## Future State Budget Issues

Michigan's recent budget history has largely paralleled that of other states in the region and the nation. Some issues have been more or less critical and some problems have been of greater or lesser duration, but Michigan's experience has generally followed the trends in other states. There will always be issues of great pressure that have an impact on the delivery of public services. The continuing challenge of providing for and funding a high-quality system of public education may be the greatest of these future challenges. There will be others that will have less routine impacts. They will certainly include, but not be limited to the following.

## Controlling Health Care Costs

While the rapidly rising cost of providing health care to Michigan citizens has been a major budget issue over the past twenty years, it will expand dramatically in the future. The state's Medicaid program is expected to undergo considerable fiscal stress in the future as rising health costs coupled with an aging state population continue to provide major state budget challenges.

## Prison Expenditures

The issue of the rising costs of the state's corrections budget will continue to confront state budget policy makers in the coming years. The legislature continues to enact legislation to increase minimum sentences for crimes and to require convicted felons to serve longer terms in prison. These policies will result in the need to continue to build new prison facilities and to increase the operational budgets for the Department of Corrections. In addition, an aging prison population will result in higher prison health care costs.

## State Infrastructure Needs

The future is likely to present numerous budget challenges concerning many forms of infrastructure needs across the state. These diverse infrastructure needs include renovation of crowded and aging highway systems, renovation of aging sewage and water treatment systems, renovation of state office buildings, renovation of aging state facilities at public universities and community colleges, and infrastructure needs at public K–12 schools across the state. Much of this infrastructure was constructed in the two decades following World War II and is nearing the end of its useful life. Further growth pressures created by geographical shifts in Michigan population have created and will continue to create infrastructure demands in previously undeveloped areas of the state.

## Revenue Adequacy

As the State of Michigan has recently struggled with the combined impacts of a slowing economy and the phase-in of reductions in the rate of the state income and single business tax, questions have been raised regarding the adequacy of the state revenue base versus the spending desires of the state. During FY 2002–03, ongoing state appropriations significantly exceeded on-going state revenues. In order to meet the constitutional balanced budget requirements, a variety of non-ongoing revenue sources have been used to supplement revenues; these include the utilization of a variety of state reserve funds. To the extent that these reserve funds have been depleted, decisions will have to be made by the governor and the legislature to either decrease state appropriations or increase state revenues. This debate is likely to be intense over the next several years.

■

## NOTES

1. This is part of the constitutional language added by the 1978 initiative petition often referred to as the "Headless Amendment." See chapter 33 of this volume.
2. This chapter was written in the fall of 2002.

## APPENDIX A

### Adjusted Gross Appropriations by Major Program Area

|  | FY 1982–93 | FY 1983–84 | FY 1984–85 | FY 1985–86 | FY 1986–87 |
|---|---|---|---|---|---|
| Higher education | $918,604,801 | $908,448,200 | $1,008,904,900 | $1,157,045,200 | $1,242,280,317 |
| K–12 education | 2,163,579,163 | 2,446,645,500 | 2,679,671,600 | 2,929,728,500 | 3,064,199,090 |
| Human services support | 4,504,004,182 | 4,963,113,600 | 5,091,453,000 | 5,385,381,700 | 5,670,856,500 |
| Public safety | 258,550,100 | 285,019,000 | 310,086,600 | 328,268,100 | 345,986,200 |
| Corrections | 230,660,300 | 268,085,900 | 316,552,000 | 394,052,300 | 490,941,100 |
| Agriculture and natural resources | 219,927,900 | 263,156,300 | 296,567,300 | 338,865,700 | 369,349,200 |
| General government (op) | 512,108,343 | 500,930,900 | 508,462,100 | 619,290,300 | 614,805,800 |
| Economic Development and Regulatory | 396,894,000 | 614,769,700 | 508,678,000 | 522,785,500 | 621,841,500 |
| Capital outlay | 133,503,600 | 0 | 198,702,900 | 336,274,200 | 228,694,900 |
| Transportation | 1,007,799,400 | 1,158,672,000 | 1,289,267,900 | 1,320,577,500 | 1,373,381,100 |
| Revenue sharing | 595,092,300 | 673,430,100 | 755,700,000 | 814,835,000 | 863,000,000 |
| Total appropriations | 10,940,724,089 | 12,082,271,200 | 12,964,046,300 | 14,147,104,000 | 14,885,335,707 |

|  | FY 1987–88 | FY 1988–89 | FY 1989–90 | FY 1990–91 | FY 1991–92 |
|---|---|---|---|---|---|
| Higher education | 1,311,677,886 | 1,353,332,700 | 1,412,459,320 | 1,361,339,478 | 1,540,984,262 |
| K–12 education | 3,239,153,430 | 3,241,754,780 | 3,586,122,500 | 3,805,995,100 | 3,915,771,100 |
| Human services support | 5,941,434,600 | 6,207,502,600 | 6,595,134,600 | 7,587,028,900 | 7,751,895,900 |
| Public safety | 369,610,500 | 408,428,100 | 459,147,302 | 465,944,800 | 535,134,200 |
| Corrections | 567,887,900 | 645,975,800 | 760,675,900 | 839,529,300 | 905,196,300 |
| Agriculture and natural resources | 366,396,014 | 349,094,959 | 537,458,885 | 630,130,482 | 610,646,935 |
| General government (op) | 637,459,800 | 600,225,900 | 593,093,600 | 674,964,250 | 1,189,868,100 |
| Economic Development and Regulatory | 705,831,950 | 744,852,800 | 815,973,100 | 774,472,100 | 766,834,310 |
| Capital outlay | 102,678,700 | 289,693,400 | 388,840,900 | 299,755,310 | 333,042,210 |
| Transportation | 1,504,573,500 | 1,495,688,100 | 1,585,000,400 | 1,630,723,200 | 1,642,700,200 |
| Revenue sharing | 932,800,000 | 946,600,000 | 1,025,500,000 | 1,075,500,000 | 963,100,000 |
| Total appropriations | 15,679,504,280 | 16,283,149,139 | 17,759,406,507 | 19,145,382,920 | 20,155,173,517 |

|  | FY 1992–93 | FY 1993–94 | FY 1994–95 | FY 1995–96 | FY 1996–97 |
|---|---|---|---|---|---|
| Higher education | 1,556,524,600 | 1,563,963,600 | 1,634,630,035 | 1,682,046,887 | 1,762,123,916 |
| K–12 education | 4,297,502,600 | 5,391,252,400 | 8,773,101,900 | 9,100,511,200 | 9,431,402,000 |
| Human services support | 8,304,797,800 | 9,066,145,300 | 9,433,321,500 | 9,498,989,600 | 9,986,827,787 |
| Public Safety | 573,246,700 | 625,891,800 | 658,951,900 | 702,968,600 | 685,257,615 |
| Corrections | 1,030,413,700 | 1,147,306,700 | 1,214,430,900 | 1,308,462,100 | 1,343,983,333 |
| Agriculture and natural resources | 616,350,290 | 612,040,200 | 860,859,600 | 821,851,421 | 773,691,496 |
| General government (op) | 687,839,600 | 688,256,300 | 659,413,000 | 866,461,700 | 789,952,400 |
| Economic development and regulatory | 813,103,400 | 884,494,400 | 965,126,400 | 1,081,311,900 | 1,012,191,025 |
| Capital outlay | 265,435,400 | 410,443,100 | 330,257,000 | 315,222,300 | 368,397,900 |
| Transportation | 1,755,862,800 | 1,808,058,200 | 1,823,443,100 | 1,872,577,100 | 2,186,852,900 |
| Revenue sharing | 1,032,200,000 | 1,105,800,000 | 1,170,000,000 | 1,243,451,000 | 1,315,784,700 |
| Total appropriations | 20,933,276,890 | 23,303,652,000 | 27,523,535,335 | 28,493,853,808 | 29,656,465,072 |

|  | FY 1997–98 | FY 1998–99 | FY 1999–2000 | FY 2000–01 | FY 2001–02 |
|---|---|---|---|---|---|
| Higher education | 1,836,509,391 | 1,886,252,000 | 2,083,187,327 | 2,235,562,627 | 2,262,438,685 |
| K–12 education | 10,237,797,200 | 10,498,969,600 | 11,081,895,000 | 11,821,761,900 | 12,445,720,300 |
| Human services support | 10,367,897,740 | 10,943,722,300 | 12,015,982,900 | 12,238,271,100 | 12,309,036,400 |
| Public safety | 663,968,900 | 698,569,900 | 734,011,000 | 798,950,814 | 779,289,275 |
| Corrections | 1,383,227,600 | 1,443,603,200 | 1,558,085,200 | 1,699,566,400 | 1,677,301,400 |
| Agriculture and natural resources | 709,403,350 | 888,051,908 | 898,299,299 | 979,583,900 | 814,014,800 |
| General government (op) | 730,947,678 | 796,249,090 | 860,638,500 | 890,476,600 | 858,149,640 |
| Economic development and regulatory | 1,012,438,800 | 1,068,557,400 | 1,262,612,400 | 1,244,522,000 | 1,251,480,800 |
| Capital outlay | 545,400,200 | 778,789,500 | 574,694,200 | 455,771,100 | 479,161,200 |
| Transportation | 2,629,196,000 | 2,770,965,300 | 2,861,447,200 | 3,026,013,725 | 3,064,612,900 |
| Revenue sharing | 1,356,000,000 | 1,386,600,000 | 1,470,522,000 | 1,655,000,200 | 1,540,600,000 |
| Total appropriations | 31,472,786,859 | 33,160,330,198 | 35,401,375,026 | 37,045,480,366 | 37,481,805,400 |

SOURCE: State Fiscal Agency.

# 13

# An Overview of Local Government Expenditures in Michigan: Patterns and Trends

*Earl M. Ryan and Eric W. Lupher*

## Types of Local Units

Local government in Michigan, as elsewhere, is composed of general-purpose and special-purpose units. General-purpose units—counties, townships, cities, and villages—perform certain state-mandated services, but most of their expenditures are for a wide range of services configured in ways chosen by their residents. Special-purpose units normally perform only one function, often serving the residents of more than one general-purpose unit. (The predominant form of special-purpose unit, the school district, is discussed in chapter 15 and will not be covered here.)

### Counties

The eighty-three Michigan counties encompass the entire state. Originally conceived as administrative arms of the state, counties have evolved to provide an array of local services as well. More so than for other local units, the structure and powers of counties are prescribed in the Michigan constitution. The constitution and state statutes permit three basic forms of county government:

1. General law counties (eighty counties), meaning they operate under a structure dictated by

state law that has the county board of commissioners perform both executive and legislative roles, although state statutes provide several options for centralizing administrative responsibilities;
2. Optional unified counties, which may adopt one of two forms of government prescribed in Public Act 139 of 1973:
   a. Elected county executive (two counties—Oakland and Bay)
   b. Appointed county manager (zero counties)
3. Charter counties governed by a locally drafted and approved charter (one county—Wayne)

### Townships

Townships were laid out in a grid of thirty-six-square-mile units covering the state while Michigan was part of the Northwest Territory. The purpose was to provide basic governmental services to an essentially rural population. Today townships cover all unincorporated portions of the state. State law provides for two forms of government for Michigan's 1,242 townships:

1. General law townships (1,114 townships)
2. Charter townships, which may adopt provisions of state law in order to acquire enhanced

authority for taxation and service provision (128 townships)

### Cities

In order to provide local services to residents in urbanized areas, Michigan law provides for home rule cities, governed by locally drafted and approved charters, which can be tailored to meet a wide range of local preferences as to structure and powers. There are currently 273 Michigan cities. When a jurisdiction incorporates and becomes a city, the township no longer collects revenue or provides services within the boundaries of the new city. This has led to situations in which certain townships have been reduced to very small and sometimes discontiguous remnants.

### Villages

Units intended to provide enhanced levels of service to certain residents of a township, villages do not supplant the portions of the townships they serve, but are layered on top of the townships. Michigan's 262 villages are either general law (213) or home rule villages with charters (49). Because the General Law Village Act provisions for new incorporations were superseded by the Home Rule Village Act, all new villages must be home rule villages. (This chapter groups villages with cities under the heading "Municipalities.")

### Special Authorities

Certain functions do not fit conveniently within the jurisdictions of general-purpose governmental units in that the service area of the function will extend beyond the borders of any single unit. In these cases it often makes sense to spread the responsibility for funding the service over more than one unit. State laws provide for the establishment of authorities for regional parks, soil conservation, water and sewer, solid waste disposal, and transit, to name a few. Special authorities are created to provide multijurisdictional services in these and other functional areas. The *1997 Census of Governments* counted 277 noneducational special authorities in Michigan.

### About the Data

The data used in this chapter are ultimately derived from financial reports filed annually by local units with the Michigan Department of Treasury. Those reports are used to create databases maintained by both the U.S. Bureau of Census and the Michigan Municipal League.

In addition, the Bureau of the Census conducts a *Census of Governments* every five years. Data from the 1977, 1987, and 1997 *Census of Governments* are used in this chapter to augment the comparisons possible with state data. Adjustments were made to the census data to facilitate comparisons across years. First, adjustments were made to eliminate education expenditures from the data, leaving only general-purpose governments—counties, cities, villages, and townships—and special authorities. Second, the data were adjusted for inflation using the chain-type price index for the state and local government consumption expenditures.[1] To correlate with the *Census of Governments,* the index figures were used for 1977, 1987, and 1997.

Finally, the data were adjusted to convert expenditure values into per capita amounts. Population figures from the 1980, 1990, and 2000 decennial censuses were used for these calculations. Total statewide population and the sum of the county populations are equal, since the eighty-three counties encompass the state, and no one is a resident of more than one county. Municipal expenditures were adjusted using the total city and village populations. Township expenditures were adjusted using the balance of statewide population (those not living in a city or village reside in a township). The use of per capita amounts provides comparability in analyzing expenditure amounts across years, as expenditure levels for any unit or type of government could be expected to increase or decrease with changes in the number of constituents being served. Per capita amounts also provide comparability in analyzing expenditure amounts across types of units. Interstate comparisons are made using data from *Government Finances: 1998–99* compiled by the Bureau of the Census. Expenditure data for Washington, D.C., are not included in these comparisons due to the dual state/local nature of the district government. Data for the U.S. median are included to avoid biases that result from larger states spending very high or very low amounts on any function. Because the median value represents the midpoint between the spending of the twenty-fifth state and that of the twenty-sixth state, the values do not represent any given state. Also, each median is calculated individually, so that the values reported for per capita spending and for local expenditures as a percentage of state and local expenditures are not related. Interstate comparisons to the Great Lakes states averages include spending in Illinois, Indiana, Michigan, Ohio, and Wisconsin.

## Patterns of Local Expenditure

Local governments in Michigan provide health and welfare services; transportation services in the form of highways, airports, and mass transit; public safety services; and services to protect the environment and provide housing. Other local spending goes to administrative services, operating courts and providing legal services, maintaining and operating government buildings, and for interest on outstanding debt. See figure 13.1.

County expenditures are heavily dominated by three broad functions: Health and welfare, highway construction and maintenance, and public safety and judicial. Activities included under those general headings constituted over 70% of county spending in 1997. Health services alone, primarily community mental health services, absorbed fully one-quarter of county expenditures. See figure 13.2.

Municipal (city and village) and township spending is spread over a wider range of functions, with public safety (police and fire), waste disposal (both sewerage and solid waste), and roads accounting for about half of total municipal expenditures. See figures 13.3 and 13.4.

## Trends in Local Expenditure

In addition to the evolving preferences of residents, changes in local government expenditures are the result of (1) population movement; (2) changing state policy, especially policy regarding intergovernmental finance; and (3) changes in local taxing capacity. These factors become evident in reviewing the expenditure trends for Michigan local government from 1977 to 1997. For example,

1. As population has moved outward from central cities, rapid growth has occurred in townships, and township expenditure growth has indeed exceeded that of other local units.

**FIGURE 13.1**

**Total Local Government Expenditures by Function, 1997**

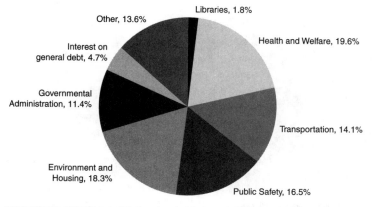

SOURCE: Bureau of the Census, U.S. Department of Commerce, *1997 Census of Governments.*

**FIGURE 13.2**

**County Expenditures by Function, 1997**

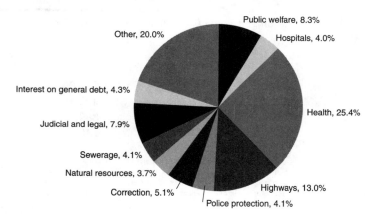

SOURCE: Bureau of the Census, U.S. Department of Commerce, *1997 Census of Governments.*

**FIGURE 13.3**

**City and Village Expenditures by Function, 1997**

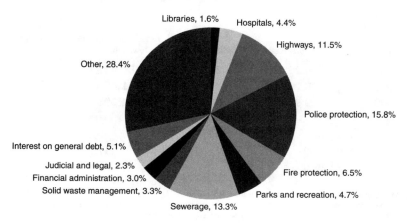

SOURCE: Bureau of the Census, U.S. Department of Commerce, *1997 Census of Governments.*

**FIGURE 13.4**

**Township Expenditures by Function, 1997**

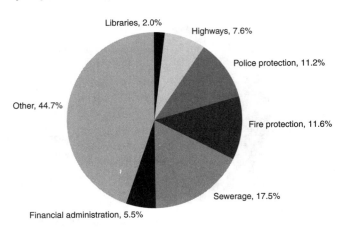

SOURCE: Bureau of the Census, U.S. Department of Commerce, *1997 Census of Governments.*

2. Changing state policy regarding the treatment of mental illness has resulted in the closing of most state psychiatric hospital beds and consequent reliance on county community mental health programs for delivery of services, with some state funding following the service delivery shift.

3. Part of the growth of township expenditures can be explained by the change by many townships to charter status, providing them with significantly enhanced property tax authority.

*Total Direct General Expenditure.* The most notable trend in total local government expenditure in Michigan from 1977 to 1997 was the growth in spending by townships (an 83.5% increase), which grew at a rate double that of spending by counties (39.7%) and more than three times as fast

**TABLE 13.1**

**Michigan Local Government Per Capita Direct General Expenditures, 1977–97 (constant 1997 dollars)**

|  | 1977 Amount | 1987 Amount | % Change 1977–87 | 1997 Amount | % Change 1987–97 | % Change 1977–97 |
|---|---|---|---|---|---|---|
| Total | $ 1,060.06 | $ 1,144.90 | 8.0% | $ 1,384.50 | 20.9% | 30.6% |
| Counties | 422.15 | 443.48 | 5.1% | 589.81 | 33.0% | 39.7% |
| Municipalities | 889.03 | 964.57 | 8.5% | 1,125.77 | 16.7% | 26.6% |
| Townships | 140.70 | 164.88 | 17.2% | 258.25 | 56.6% | 83.5% |

SOURCE: Bureau of the Census, U.S. Department of Commerce, *1977, 1987,* and *1997 Census of Governments.*
NOTE: General Expenditures are defined by the Bureau of the Census as "all expenditures of a government other than utility expenditures, liquor stores expenditures, and insurance-trust expenditures." Direct expenditures reflect the spending as something other than intergovernmental transfers. They are "payments to employees, suppliers, contractors, beneficiaries, and other final recipients of governmental payments." For purposes of this chapter, education expenditures have been excluded.

**TABLE 13.2**

**Population Change by Type of Local Government, Michigan, 1980–2000**

| Year | Population Total State | Cities/Villages | Townships[a] | Townships as a Percentage of Total |
|---|---|---|---|---|
| 1980 | 9,262,044 | 5,601,617 | 3,660,427 | 39.5 |
| 1990 | 9,295,297 | 5,453,808 | 3,841,489 | 41.3 |
| 2000 | 9,938,494 | 5,436,801 | 4,501,693 | 45.3 |
| % change, 1980–90 | 0.4 | −2.6 | | 5.0 |
| % change, 1990–2000 | 6.9 | −0.3 | | 17.2 |
| % change, 1980–2000 | 7.3 | −2.9 | | 23.0 |

SOURCE: Bureau of the Census, U.S. Department of Commerce.
(a) This table separates villages from townships in keeping with Census Bureau definitions used elsewhere in this chapter. In Michigan, a village actually remains part of the township after incorporation.

as spending by municipalities (26.6%). These figures are summarized in table 13.1.

Two factors may be responsible for the growth of township spending. First, townships in Southeast Michigan and in other metropolitan areas are in the path of urban expansion and their populations are growing accordingly. See table 13.2 for a summary of recent population changes in Michigan.

Second, in the decades of the 1970s, 1980s, and 1990s, general law townships have been converting to charter status, which provides them with enhanced property tax authority (up to ten mills for operations) and service powers. Townships that might have become cities in prior years are now becoming charter townships, and very few new city or village incorporations have occurred since 1970. See table 13.3.

A second major point shown in table 13.1 is that growth in local government expenditures was far stronger in the period 1987–97 than in the previous ten years. In the period from 1977 to 1987, total Michigan local government spending increased by only 8.0%, with townships experiencing the fastest rate of growth. In contrast, local government spending increased at a rate two and one-half times greater from 1987 to 1997. It is likely that slow population growth and weak economic performance in the early 1980s accounts for much of the difference.

## Interstate Comparisons

In 1999, total per capita, noneducational, local government direct general expenditures in Michigan were just below the national average. The national average for total local government expenditures, like several of the averages for individual expenditure categories, is largely driven by the per capita expenditures of some of the larger states. In particular, California ($2,282 per capita) and New York ($2,944 per capita) provide an upward bias in the average for total local government expenditures.[2] Because these few large states skew the average upward, thirty-eight states had total per capita expenditures below the national average.

To compensate for this effect, Michigan's per capita expenditures are also compared to the median local government expenditures per capita for the fifty states.[3] See table 13.4. Michigan per capita expenditures were the twelfth-highest among the states. The 1999 median level of local government direct general expenditures was $1,372 per capita, meaning that Michigan and twenty-four other states spent more than this amount, and twenty-five states spent less.

Some variation in expenditure levels between states can be explained by differences in service responsibilities at the state or local level. The average state relies on its local governments for 49.7% of its total direct state and local government expenditures, and the U.S. median relies on local governments for 44.7%. Differences in levels of expenditure responsibility range from Nevada, where local governments are responsible for 61.5% of total state and local government direct general expenditures, to Delaware, where local governments are responsible for only 21.0%. Michigan local governments are responsible for 54.2%, the twelfth-highest percentage among the states.

**TABLE 13.3**

**Changes in Status of Local Government Units, Michigan, 1950–2001**

| Decade | Unit Became: | | |
|---|---|---|---|
| | Charter Township | Village | City |
| 1950–59 | 3 | 9 | 13 |
| 1960–69 | 10 | 8 | 13 |
| 1970–79 | 42 | 3 | 3 |
| 1980–89 | 53 | 2 | 2 |
| 1990–99 | 16 | 1 | 1 |
| 2000–01 | 4 | 0 | 0 |

SOURCES: Legislative Service Bureau, *Michigan Manual;* Michigan Townships Association.
NOTE: The last unit to change from township to city was Rochester Hills (1984). Clarkston was the last village to change to a city (1992).

**TABLE 13.4**

**Interstate Comparison of Local Government Direct General Expenditures, 1999**

| | Per Capita Spending | Local Expenditures as a % of State and Local Expenditures |
|---|---|---|
| U.S. average | $ 1,664.62 | 49.7% |
| Median state | 1,372.20 | 44.7 |
| Great Lakes states average | 1,593.49 | 52.5 |
| Michigan | 1,611.34 | 54.2 |

SOURCE: Bureau of the Census, U.S. Department of Commerce, *Government Finances: 1998–99.*

While Michigan ranks high in the percentage of governmental functions delivered by local governments (excluding education services), it is interesting to note that Michigan ranks low in the percentage of local expenditures funded with own-source revenues. While the percentage of local expenditures funded with revenues from taxes and fees imposed by local governments ranges as high as 84.3% (New Hampshire), the percentage of local government revenues in Michigan funded through these sources is 48.6%, which is lower than that for all other states except Vermont (40.7%) and New Mexico (44.3%). See table 13.5. In the discussion that follows, interstate comparisons show that local government spending in Michigan ranks relatively high for functions such as health, highways, judicial and legal, and sewers, reflecting intergovernmental

**TABLE 13.5**

**Interstate Comparison of Local Government Expenditures Funded with Own-Source Revenues, 1999**

| | Own-Source Revenue as a Percentage of Total General Revenues |
|---|---|
| U.S. average | 60.9% |
| Median state | 61.6 |
| Great Lakes states average | 58.9 |
| Michigan | 48.6 |

SOURCE: Bureau of the Census, U.S. Department of Commerce, *Government Finances: 1998–99.*

transfer programs that benefit local governments. (See chapter 30 for more discussion of state aid programs to local governments.)

The high level of local government expenditures funded from intergovernmental transfers also helps to explain the growth in township expenditures over the past twenty years. Un-

restricted state revenue sharing programs like Michigan's are not found in every state, and the level of funding distributed through Michigan's program is relatively high compared to that of those states that do have such a program. Michigan's revenue sharing program distributes aid to all cities, villages, and townships in the state, and is sufficient to permit a number of villages and townships to fully fund services without need for a local tax.

## Expenditures by Category

Inflation-adjusted per capita expenditures have increased over the past twenty-five years in most categories, with health, sewerage, and corrections experiencing the largest increases. The only major expenditure categories to experience declines from 1977 to 1997 were hospitals, welfare, and housing and community development. These changes are summarized in table 13.6. While counties were the primary provider of services that experienced the largest increases, they were

**TABLE 13.6**

**Summary of Michigan Local Government Expenditure Trends, 1977–97**

| Function | Level of Government with Primary Service Delivery Responsibility | Percentage of Total Local Government Expenditures in 1997 | Average Annual Rate of Change |
|---|---|---|---|
| Health and welfare | | | |
|     Health | Counties | 11.7% | +12.2% |
|     Hospitals | Counties/Municipalities | 4.3% | −2.3% |
|     Welfare | Counties | 3.6% | −0.8% |
| Transportation | | | |
|     Highways | Counties/Municipalities | 11.3% | +0.8% |
|     Airports | Counties/Municipalities | 1.4% | +2.5% |
| Public safety | | | |
|     Police protection | Municipalities | 9.7% | +1.0% |
|     Fire prevention | Municipalities/Townships | 3.9% | +0.5% |
|     Corrections | Counties | 2.2% | +3.6% |
|     Protective inspection and regulation | Municipalities/Townships | 0.7% | +3.2% |
|     Judicial and legal | Counties/Municipalities | 4.5% | +3.6% |
| Environment and Housing | | | |
|     Housing and commercial development | Municipalities | 1.3% | −1.0% |
|     Natural resources | Counties | 1.7% | +1.0% |
|     Parks and recreation | Municipalities | 3.1% | +0.3% |
|     Sewerage | Municipalities/Townships | 9.7% | +3.7% |
|     Solid waste management | Municipalities/Townships | 2.5% | +2.1% |
| Libraries | Municipalities | 1.8% | +6.2% |

SOURCE: Bureau of the Census, U.S. Department of Commerce, *1977* and *1997 Census of Governments.*

**TABLE 13.7**

### Michigan Local Government Per Capita Health Expenditures, 1977–97 (constant 1997 dollars)

|  | 1977 Amount | 1987 Amount | % Change 1977–87 | 1997 Amount | % Change 1987–97 | % Change 1977–97 |
|---|---|---|---|---|---|---|
| Total | $ 46.90 | $ 87.92 | 87.5% | $ 161.33 | 83.5% | 244.0% |
| Counties | 35.95 | 76.54 | 112.9% | 150.10 | 96.1% | 317.6% |
| Municipalities | 18.04 | 19.00 | 5.3% | 19.42 | 2.2% | 7.6% |
| Townships | 0.11 | 0.55 | NA | 1.34 | NA | NA |

SOURCE: Bureau of the Census, U.S. Department of Commerce, *1977, 1987,* and *1997 Census of Governments.*
NOTE: Health Expenditures are defined by the Bureau of the Census as "Health services, other than hospital care, including health research, clinics, nursing, immunization, and other categorical, environmental, and general public health activities. School health services provided by health agencies are included here."

also the level of government with primary responsibility for the categories that experienced decline.

## Health and Welfare Expenditures

Local spending on health and welfare has long been the domain of the counties and has been subject to changes in state policy. Along with county road commissions and county law enforcement, county public health and county welfare departments make up the historical core of county services. County community mental health boards are a more recent addition to this core. A more in-depth discussion of welfare and human-services policies is found in chapter 17.

*Health.* State policy changes are reflected in the dramatic increase in local health expenditures from 1977 to 1997, nearly all of which occurred at the county level. County per capita health spending went from 76.7% of total local government per capita health spending in 1977 to 93.0% in 1997. The principal reason for the increase was the phasing down of state psychiatric hospitals and the concurrent rise of community mental health services, which are delivered at the county (or multicounty) level and funded in large part through a state aid program. See table 13.7.

While Michigan ranked seventh in the nation on total health expenditures by state and local governments, Michigan local governments had the highest level of spending on this function of any state. With 1999 health expenditures of $177 per capita, Michigan was well above the national average, the Great Lakes states average, and the U.S. median. Also, in making 74% of all health expenditures at the local level, Michigan was one of eight states with at least two-thirds of all health

**TABLE 13.8**

### Interstate Comparison of Local Government Health Expenditures, 1999

|  | Per Capita Spending | Local Expenditures as a % of State and Local Expenditures |
|---|---|---|
| U.S. average | $ 82.76 | 47.5% |
| Median state | 38.11 | 30.5 |
| Great Lakes states average | 108.44 | 55.6 |
| Michigan | 176.90 | 74.0 |

SOURCE: Bureau of the Census, U.S. Department of Commerce, *Government Finances: 1998–99.*

expenditures made by local government, and was above the national average, the Great Lakes states average, and the U.S. median. See table 13.8.

*Hospitals.* At the same time that total local per capita health expenditures have been increasing, local expenditures for hospitals, both county and municipal, have been declining. See table 13.9. The rise of Medicaid in the late 1960s reduced the need for governmentally funded hospitals at the local level, and many of these facilities, such as Detroit Receiving and Ingham Medical (Lansing), have been closed or transferred to private ownership. In just a ten-year period, the number of hospitals operated by local governments declined from forty-five in 1987 to twenty in 1997 (see appendix A).

*Special Authorities.* As is the case for hospital expenditures by general-purpose local governments, expenditures by hospital districts have also experienced major declines in the last decade. From 1977 to 1987, the expenditures of

**TABLE 13.9**

**Michigan Local Government Per Capita Hospital Expenditures, 1977–97 (constant 1997 dollars)**

|  | 1977 Amount | 1987 Amount | % Change 1977–87 | 1997 Amount | % Change 1987–97 | % Change 1977–97 |
|---|---|---|---|---|---|---|
| Total | $ 110.84 | $ 109.75 | −1.0% | $ 59.57 | −45.7% | −46.3% |
| Counties | 44.23 | 36.24 | −18.1% | 23.71 | −34.6% | −46.4% |
| Municipalities | 72.68 | 72.85 | +0.2% | 50.08 | −31.3% | −31.1% |
| Townships | — | — |  | — |  |  |

SOURCE: Bureau of the Census, U.S. Department of Commerce, *1977, 1987, and 1997 Census of Governments.*
NOTE: Hospital Expenditures are defined by the Bureau of the Census as expenditures for the "establishment and operation of hospital facilities, provision of hospital care, and support of other public or of private hospitals."

**TABLE 13.10**

**Interstate Comparison of Local Government Hospital Expenditures, 1999**

|  | Per Capita Spending | Local Expenditures as a % of State and Local Expenditures |
|---|---|---|
| U.S. average | $ 154.08 | 58.7% |
| Median state | 116.97 | 56.5 |
| Great Lakes states average | 103.71 | 55.5 |
| Michigan | 83.61 | 43.9 |

SOURCE: Bureau of the Census, U.S. Department of Commerce, *Government Finances: 1998–99.*

hospital districts almost doubled. Then, from 1987 to 1997, the expenditures of hospital districts declined by 72%, to just over $84 million.

Michigan local hospital expenditures per capita of $84 (twenty-ninth in the United States) were well below the national average, the Great Lakes states average, and the U.S. median. See table 13.10.

*Public Welfare.* Although per capita county expenditures for public welfare increased from 1987 to 1997, the overall level is down from earlier years. Counties have historically had responsibility for the delivery of welfare and social services at the local level, but economic strength during the 1990s and changing public policy have combined to reduce the impact of these programs on state and county budgets. In Michigan, the change from Aid to Families with Dependent Children to the much more limited Temporary Assistance to Needy Families, together with the discontinuation of the state-funded General Assistance program, has resulted in a large decline in public assistance caseloads and a corresponding reduction in county public welfare expenditures. See table 13.11.

Local governments play a major role in providing public welfare in only about a quarter of the states, including several of the larger states, such as California (where local government expenditures account for 37.2% of state and local expenditures), New York (29.8%), New Jersey (21.1%), Ohio (19.5%), and Pennsylvania (15.3%). Even

**TABLE 13.11**

**Michigan Local Government Per Capita Public Welfare Expenditures, 1977–97 (constant 1997 dollars)**

|  | 1977 Amount | 1987 Amount | % Change 1977–87 | 1997 Amount | % Change 1987–97 | % Change 1977–97 |
|---|---|---|---|---|---|---|
| Total | $ 60.53 | $ 39.03 | −35.5% | $ 50.28 | +28.8% | −16.9% |
| Counties | 60.00 | 38.45 | −35.9% | 49.24 | +28.1% | −17.9% |
| Municipalities | 0.81 | 0.96 | +18.1% | 1.58 | +64.5% | +94.3% |
| Townships | 0.10 | 0.04 | −62.1% | 0.40 | +956.9% | +300.4% |

SOURCE: Bureau of the Census, U.S. Department of Commerce, *1977, 1987, and 1997 Census of Governments.*
NOTE: Public Welfare Expenditures are defined by the Bureau of the Census as "support of and assistance to needy persons contingent upon their need. Such expenditures exclude pensions to former employees and other benefits not contingent on need. Expenditures under this heading include: Cash assistance payments directly to needy persons under categorical and other welfare programs; vendor payments made directly to private purveyors for medical care, burials, and other services provided under welfare programs; welfare institutions; and any intergovernmental or other direct expenditures for welfare purposes."

though local government public welfare expenditures in Michigan (fourteenth in the United States) are higher than the U.S. median, they are significantly less than Great Lakes state average or the U.S. average, which is skewed upward by the practices of these large states. See table 13.12.

## Transportation Expenditures

Transportation expenditures consist primarily of highway spending, but public transit and airports involve significant amounts as well. See table 13.13. More discussion of transportation issues follows in chapter 16.

*Highways.* Local expenditures for transportation are dominated by spending for roads. Counties and cities account for the bulk of local highway expenditures. While population growth is occurring in townships, their share of highway expenditures has remained stable over the 1977–97 period primarily because townships do not participate in state road funding formulas and are dependent on the counties for their local street construction and maintenance.

Michigan is fairly unusual in that it vests responsibility for a very large share of its overall highway system with local government. Local governments accounted for 57.8% of all state and local government highway expenditures in 1999, while local governments in the average state accounted for 39.5% of the total, and local governments in the U.S. median accounted for only 35.1%. Michigan local governments spent $178 per capita on highways (fourteenth in U.S.), 32.4% greater than the national average, 8.4% greater than the Great Lakes states average, and 41.7% greater than the U.S. median.

### TABLE 13.12

**Interstate Comparison of Local Government Public Welfare Expenditures, 1999**

|  | Per Capita Spending | Local Expenditures as a % of State and Local Expenditures |
|---|---|---|
| U.S. average | $ 116.49 | 14.8% |
| Median state | 22.66 | 3.2 |
| Great Lakes states average | 97.18 | 13.5 |
| Michigan | 54.97 | 8.4 |

SOURCE: Bureau of the Census, U.S. Department of Commerce, *Government Finances: 1998–99*

Michigan local governments rely on state funding to maintain regional and local roads to a much greater extent than do local units in most other states, where local tax sources supplement state revenues. According to the Federal Highway Administration, the average state government contributed 22.8% of the local government revenues for highway construction and maintenance in 1999, compared to 58.1% in Michigan.[4]

*Air Transportation.* Michigan has sixty cities, villages, and townships that operate airports individually, twenty-two airports are operated by special authorities created by one or more municipalities, and thirty-six counties operate airports, but 94% of the 1997 expenditures for air transportation occurred in Wayne, Oakland, and Kent counties—primarily operation of the Detroit Metropolitan Wayne County Airport. Table 13.14 summarizes the per capita expenditures of Michigan relative to the United States and Great Lakes state averages and the median state for all

### TABLE 13.13

**Michigan Local Government Per Capita Transportation Expenditures, 1977–97 (constant 1997 dollars)**

|  | 1977 Amount | 1987 Amount | % Change 1977–87 | 1997 Amount | % Change 1987–97 | % Change 1977–97 |
|---|---|---|---|---|---|---|
| Total | $ 165.42 | $ 182.51 | 10.3% | $ 194.93 | 6.8% | 17.8% |
| Counties | 84.32 | 90.67 | 7.5% | 93.84 | 3.5% | 11.3% |
| Municipalities | 98.22 | 118.12 | 20.3% | 137.21 | 16.2% | 39.7% |
| Townships | 17.21 | 12.75 | −25.9% | 19.78 | 55.1% | 15.0% |

SOURCE: Bureau of the Census, U.S. Department of Commerce, *1977, 1987, and 1997 Census of Governments.*
NOTE: Highway Expenditures are defined by the Bureau of the Census as expenditures for "streets, highways, and structures necessary for their use, street lighting, snow and ice removal, toll highway and bridge facilities, and ferries." Air Transportation Expenditures are defined by the Bureau of the Census as expenditures for "construction, maintenance, operation, and support of airport facilities." Other transportation expenditures are made for parking facilities, water transportation and terminals, and transit subsidies.

**TABLE 13.14**

**Interstate Comparison of Local Government Transportation Expenditures, 1999**

|  | Per Capita Spending | Local Expenditures as a % of State and Local Expenditures |
|---|---|---|
| U.S. average | $ 190.44 | 47.1% |
| Median state | 171.35 | 40.9 |
| Great Lakes states average | 203.36 | 54.6 |
| Michigan | 210.99 | 61.6 |

SOURCE: Bureau of the Census, U.S. Department of Commerce, *Government Finances: 1998–99.*

transportation spending, which includes highway spending, in addition to air, water, and mass transit transportation spending and capital spending on parking facilities.

## Public Safety and Judicial Expenditures

Public safety and lower courts are generally considered basic functions of local government and claim an accordingly large share of local resources.

*Police Protection.* The largest single item of general-purpose local expenditure, police protection, is growing slowly relative to other functions. Interestingly, police protection expenditures grew more rapidly in the counties than in the townships from 1977 to 1997, in part the result of contractual arrangements between the counties and the townships in which township police protec-

**TABLE 13.15**

**Michigan Local Government Per Capita Police Protection Expenditures, 1977–97 (constant 1997 dollars)**

|  | 1977 Amount | 1987 Amount | % Change 1977–87 | 1997 Amount | % Change 1987–97 | % Change 1977–97 |
|---|---|---|---|---|---|---|
| Total | $ 112.34 | $ 118.92 | 5.9% | $ 134.68 | 13.2% | 19.9% |
| Counties | 17.68 | 19.60 | 10.9% | 24.32 | 24.1% | 37.6% |
| Municipalities | 142.33 | 156.27 | 9.8% | 177.79 | 13.8% | 24.9% |
| Townships | 21.73 | 18.48 | –15.0% | 28.92 | 56.5% | 33.1% |

SOURCE: Bureau of the Census, U.S. Department of Commerce, *1977, 1987, and 1997 Census of Governments.*
NOTE: Police Protection Expenditures are defined by the Bureau of the Census as expenditures for the "preservation of law and order and traffic safety. Includes highway police patrols, crime prevention activities, police communications, detention and custody of persons awaiting trial, traffic safety, vehicular inspection, and the like."

**TABLE 13.16**

**Interstate Comparison of Local Government Police Protection Expenditures, 1999**

|  | Per Capita Spending | Local Expenditures as a % of State and Local Expenditures |
|---|---|---|
| U.S. average | $ 166.23 | 85.3% |
| Median state | 136.36 | 81.6 |
| Great Lakes states average | 164.00 | 87.3 |
| Michigan | 146.92 | 84.6 |

SOURCE: Bureau of the Census, U.S. Department of Commerce, *Government Finances: 1998–99.*

tion often is provided by county sheriffs. From 1987 to 1997, however, township expenditures grew more rapidly, indicating that more townships are beginning to provide their own police forces. See table 13.15.

While police protection expenditures by Michigan local governments (twentieth in the United States) were higher than the U.S. median, they were less than the national average. As is true for other functions, the national average of local government expenditures for police protection was skewed upward by a few states, several of which are also populous, coastal states (Alaska, California, Florida, Illinois, Nevada, New Jersey, and New York). See table 13.16 for a summary of these figures.

*Fire Protection.* Expenditures for fire protection have been growing very slowly, and nearly all of

**TABLE 13.17**

**Michigan Local Government Per Capita Fire Protection Expenditures, 1977–97 (constant 1997 dollars)**

|  | 1977 Amount | 1987 Amount | % Change 1977–87 | 1997 Amount | % Change 1987–97 | % Change 1977–97 |
|---|---|---|---|---|---|---|
| Total | $ 48.60 | $ 48.07 | –1.1% | $ 53.93 | 12.2% | 11.0% |
| Counties | 0.16 | 0.24 | 55.7% | 0.14 | –43.9% | –12.7% |
| Municipalities | 67.01 | 65.74 | –1.9% | 73.41 | 11.7% | 9.6% |
| Townships | 20.03 | 22.25 | 11.1% | 29.97 | 34.7% | 49.6% |

SOURCE: Bureau of the Census, U.S. Department of Commerce, *1977, 1987, and 1997 Census of Governments.*

NOTES: Fire Protection Expenditures are defined by the Bureau of the Census as expenditures for "Fire fighting organization and auxiliary service thereof, inspection for fire hazards, and other fire prevention activities. Includes cost of fire fighting facilities such as fire hydrants and water."

the growth has been occurring in townships, which actually spend more per capita on fire protection than on police protection. Cities, on the other hand, spend nearly two-and-a-half times as much on police protection. The fact that counties do not provide fire services, and thus townships may not contract with counties for their provision, as is the case for police protection, may explain the relative emphasis placed by townships on fire protection. Table 13.17 provides per capita spending data for counties, cities, and townships in Michigan.

Fire protection is the most local of all government expenditures. Local governments in Michigan, like local governments throughout the nation, are responsible for 100% of the state and local government expenditures for fire protection. Per capita spending for fire protection by Michigan local governments (thirty-second in the United States) was below the U.S. average and the U.S. median. See table 13.18.

*Corrections.* One of the most rapidly rising expenditures at the state level during the period was corrections spending. Local spending growth

**TABLE 13.18**

**Interstate Comparison of Local Government Fire Protection Expenditures, 1999**

|  | Per Capita Spending | Local Expenditures as a % of State and Local Expenditures |
|---|---|---|
| U.S. average | $ 77.74 | 100.0% |
| Median state | 66.60 | 100.0 |
| Great Lakes states average | 76.34 | 100.0 |
| Michigan | 59.20 | 100.0 |

SOURCE: Bureau of the Census, U.S. Department of Commerce, *Government Finances: 1998–99.*

in this function did not, however, match the state increase. Real per capita state spending on corrections rose 219% from 1977 to 1997, whereas the increase in local corrections was 71%, nearly all of it in the counties. This is summarized in table 13.19.

Michigan's relatively low level of local government expenditures for corrections (twentieth in

**TABLE 13.19**

**Michigan Local Government Per Capita Corrections Expenditures, 1977–97 (constant 1997 dollars)**

|  | 1977 Amount | 1987 Amount | % Change 1977–87 | 1997 Amount | % Change 1987–97 | % Change 1977–97 |
|---|---|---|---|---|---|---|
| Total | $ 17.89 | $ 21.36 | 19.4% | $ 30.66 | 43.5% | 71.4% |
| Counties | 16.23 | 21.13 | 30.2% | 30.12 | 42.6% | 85.6% |
| Municipalities | 2.74 | 0.39 | –85.7% | 0.83 | 111.1% | –69.8% |
| Townships | — | 0.02 | NA | 0.17 | 632.1% | NA |

SOURCE: Bureau of the Census, U.S. Department of Commerce, *1977, 1987, and 1997 Census of Governments.*

NOTE: Corrections expenditures are defined by the Bureau of the Census as expenditures for "Confinement and correction of adults and minors convicted of offenses against the law, and pardon, probation, and parole activities. Detention pending trial, as in municipal jails, is classed under Police Protection."

**TABLE 13.20**

**Interstate Comparison of Local Government Corrections Expenditures, 1999**

|  | Per Capita Spending | Local Expenditures as a % of State and Local Expenditures |
|---|---|---|
| U.S. average | $ 53.41 | 32.1% |
| Median state | 33.09 | 26.8 |
| Great Lakes states average | 36.82 | 24.6 |
| Michigan | 36.59 | 19.8 |

SOURCE: Bureau of the Census, U.S. Department of Commerce, *Government Finances: 1998–99.*

the United States) is affected by the low level of responsibility Michigan local governments have for corrections provision. With its division of state and local corrections responsibilities heavily weighted on the state side, Michigan is closer to many of the states with small populations, such as Arkansas, Idaho, West Virginia, and Wyoming. Connecticut, Delaware, Hawaii, and Rhode Island, all small in area, rely on their state governments for 100% of the cost of providing corrections. Issues related to criminal justice and corrections systems and policies in Michigan are discussed in chapter 24. See table 13.20 for comparative per capita spending figures for Michigan, the United States, and the Great Lakes states.

*Judicial and Legal.* Although most expenditures in this category are focused at the county level, the fastest growth is occurring in municipalities.

**TABLE 13.21**

**Michigan Local Government Per Capita Judicial and Legal Expenditures, 1977–97 (constant 1997 dollars)**

|  | 1977 Amount | 1987 Amount | % Change 1977–87 | 1997 Amount | % Change 1987–97 | % Change 1977–97 |
|---|---|---|---|---|---|---|
| Total | $ — | $ 45.66 | NA | $ 62.03 | 35.9% | NA |
| Counties | — | 35.31 | NA | 46.32 | 31.2% | NA |
| Municipalities | — | 16.01 | NA | 26.22 | 63.8% | NA |
| Townships | — | 2.33 | NA | 3.01 | 29.3% | NA |

SOURCE: Bureau of the Census, U.S. Department of Commerce, *1977, 1987, and 1997 Census of Governments.*
NOTE: The 1977 Census of Governments did not report Judicial and Legal Expenditures. Judicial and Legal Expenditures are defined by the Bureau of the Census as expenditures for "courts and activities associated with courts including law libraries, prosecutorial and defendant programs, probate functions, and juries."

**TABLE 13.22**

**Interstate Comparison of Local Government Judicial and Legal Expenditures, 1999**

|  | Per Capita Spending | Local Expenditures as a % of State and Local Expenditures |
|---|---|---|
| U.S. average | $ 51.05 | 55.0% |
| Median state | 31.00 | 47.2 |
| Great Lakes states average | 60.08 | 75.9 |
| Michigan | 70.92 | 84.6 |

SOURCE: Bureau of the Census, U.S. Department of Commerce, *Government Finances: 1998–99.*

Township spending on the judicial and legal functions is both low and slowly growing. See table 13.21.

The average and the median levels of judicial and legal expenditures by local governments do not reflect the wide range of variation in state/local responsibilities across the country. With 84.6% of all expenditures made at the local level, Michigan is second to only Washington (85.3%) in the level of local responsibility. On the low end, Delaware (8.8%) and Massachusetts (8.2%) rely very little on their local governments for provision of this service. In terms of the level of per capita judicial and legal expenditures by local governments, Michigan is sixth-highest in the United States. Michigan's high ranking reflects the high level of local responsibility more than an overall high level of spending. Total state and local government spending on this function in Michigan

**TABLE 13.23**

**Michigan Local Government Per Capita Housing and Community Development Expenditures, 1977–97 (constant 1997 dollars)**

|  | 1977 Amount | 1987 Amount | % Change 1977–87 | 1997 Amount | % Change 1987–97 | % Change 1977–97 |
|---|---|---|---|---|---|---|
| Total | $ 23.50 | $ 29.76 | 26.6% | $ 18.60 | –37.5% | –20.8% |
| Counties | 0.08 | 2.05 | NA | 1.42 | –30.8% | NA |
| Municipalities | 38.73 | 46.61 | 20.4% | 30.85 | –33.8% | –20.3% |
| Townships | 0.00 | 0.88 | NA | 0.68 | –22.0% | NA |

SOURCE: Bureau of the Census, U.S. Department of Commerce, *1977, 1987, and 1997 Census of Governments.*
NOTE: Housing and Community Development Expenditures are defined by the Bureau of the Census as expenditures for "Construction and operation of housing and redevelopment projects, and other activities to promote or aid housing and community development."

($83.85) is less than the average ($92.89), but higher than the U.S. median ($78.54). See table 13.22.

### Environment and Housing Expenditures

This category comprises a number of functions whose common thread is a heavy emphasis on capital outlay. Township spending growth in this area is far outpacing growth in counties and municipalities.

*Housing and Community Development.* This function, heavily dominated by the cities, is the only one to show a decline in per capita expenditures over the period 1977–1997, with all of the decline occurring in the second decade, a period of strong growth in most other functions. Declines in federal aid for housing for the elderly, Section 108 loan guarantees, and other federal programs, together with flat spending on Community Development Block Grants, may have accounted for much of this decline. See table 13.23.

**TABLE 13.24**

**Interstate Comparison of Local Government Housing and Community Development Expenditures, 1999**

|  | Per Capita Spending | Local Expenditures as a % of State and Local Expenditures |
|---|---|---|
| U.S. average | $ 83.73 | 90.5% |
| Median state | 59.29 | 87.6 |
| Great Lakes states average | 71.35 | 91.4 |
| Michigan | 26.70 | 88.3 |

SOURCE: Bureau of the Census, U.S. Department of Commerce, *Government Finances: 1998–99.*

Michigan local government spending on housing and community development is significantly below both the national average and the U.S. median. Nationally, most of these expenditures are at the local level, and Michigan's share as shown in table 13.24 is only slightly below the U.S.

**TABLE 13.25**

**Michigan Local Government Per Capita Natural Resources Expenditures, 1977–97 (constant 1997 dollars)**

|  | 1977 Amount | 1987 Amount | % Change 1977–87 | 1997 Amount | % Change 1987–97 | % Change 1977–97 |
|---|---|---|---|---|---|---|
| Total | $ 19.41 | $ 8.08 | –58.4% | $ 23.12 | 186.1% | 19.1% |
| Counties | 19.00 | 6.38 | –66.4% | 21.63 | 239.1% | 13.9% |
| Municipalities | — | 1.01 | NA | 0.55 | –45.5% | NA |
| Townships | 0.01 | 1.21 | NA | 0.61 | –49.1% | NA |

SOURCE: Bureau of the Census, U.S. Department of Commerce, *1977, 1987, and 1997 Census of Governments.*
NOTE: Natural Resources Expenditures are defined by the Bureau of the Census as expenditures for "Conservation and development of agriculture, fish and game, forestry, and other soil and water resources, including irrigation, drainage, flood control, and the like. Includes agricultural experiment stations and extension services, and Federal programs relating to farm price stabilization, farm insurance and credit activities, and multi-purpose power and reclamation projects."

### TABLE 13.26

**Interstate Comparison of Local Government Natural Resources Expenditures, 1999**

|  | Per Capita Spending | Local Expenditures as a % of State and Local Expenditures |
|---|---|---|
| U.S. average | $ 17.01 | 25.4% |
| Median state | 8.51 | 16.2 |
| Great Lakes states average | 10.49 | 24.2 |
| Michigan | 11.15 | 23.5 |

SOURCE: Bureau of the Census, U.S. Department of Commerce, *Government Finances: 1998–99.*

average and above the U.S. median. The overall Michigan level, however, is near to the bottom nationally, ranking forty-ninth. See table 13.24.

*Natural Resources.* Per capita natural resources spending, which occurs primarily at the county level, has increased over the period. However, the growth has been erratic in both pattern and magnitude. See table 13.25. Environmental and natural resources issues are discussed in chapter 21.

One of the most commonly used special district laws in Michigan allows for the creation of soil conservation districts. The growth in expenditures by these districts reflects the growing role of these districts. Expenditures by soil conservation districts increased by 140%, in real dollars, from 1977 to 1997. Soil conservation districts spent $9 million in 1997, almost 90% of which was for current operations.

Michigan had below average combined state and local government per capita spending for natural resources, with a rank of thirty-fifth out of

fifty states, but was close to the national average (twenty-fourth) in just local government per capita spending for this function. Again, rankings in this category are biased by the spending patterns of local governments in just a few of the heavily populated states. Only seventeen states ranked above average in per capita local government spending for this function. See table 13.26.

*Parks and Recreation.* Total local government per capita spending on parks and recreation declined from 1987 to 1997, although it was still higher in 1997 than it had been in 1977. The entire decline occurred at the municipal level, with increases being recorded at the county and township levels. See table 13.27. The provision of parks, recreation, travel, and tourism in Michigan is discussed in chapter 22.

Expenditures by special districts established to provide parks and recreation services experienced growth throughout both decades going back to 1977. Expenditures by these districts were 58% greater in 1987 than they were in 1977, and 45% greater in 1997 than in 1987. With total 1997 expenditures of $37 million, parks and recreation spending by special districts was almost 130% greater in 1997 than in 1977.

The national average does not reflect the wide range of local government spending on this function, from $187 per capita in Nevada, where local governments are responsible for 95.7% of the total, to $22 per capita in Delaware, where local governments are responsible for 24.7% of the total. See table 13.28.

*Sewerage and Solid Waste Management.* Now rivaling police protection for the function with the highest per capita state and local expenditure in Michigan, sewerage is the fastest growing of the

### TABLE 13.27

**Michigan Local Government Per Capita Parks and Recreation Expenditures, 1977–97 (constant 1997 dollars)**

|  | 1977 Amount | 1987 Amount | % Change 1977–87 | 1997 Amount | % Change 1987–97 | % Change 1977–97 |
|---|---|---|---|---|---|---|
| Total | $ 40.48 | $ 45.53 | 12.5% | $ 42.68 | –6.3% | 5.4% |
| Counties | 5.17 | 4.19 | –19.0% | 6.61 | 58.0% | 28.0% |
| Municipalities | 54.70 | 62.56 | 14.4% | 53.44 | –14.6% | –2.3% |
| Townships | 1.26 | 4.62 | NA | 6.92 | 49.8% | NA |

SOURCE: Bureau of the Census, U.S. Department of Commerce, *1977, 1987, and 1997 Census of Governments.*
NOTE: Parks and Recreation Expenditures are defined by the Bureau of the Census as expenditures for "Cultural-scientific activities, such as museums and art galleries; organized recreation, including playgrounds and play fields, swimming pools and bathing beaches; municipal parks; and special facilities for recreation, such as auditoriums, stadiums, auto camps, recreation piers, and boat harbors."

major local government functions. Real per capita spending on sewerage rose by approximately half in the counties and municipalities from 1977 to 1997, but rose nearly thirteenfold in townships, testament to the position of many townships in the path of urban expansion.

Although not growing as rapidly as sewerage expenditures, spending on solid waste management also is growing faster than the average of local expenditures. Once again, townships are experiencing the most rapid growth. See table 13.29.

*Special Authorities.* Expenditures by sewerage districts have grown faster in the last two decades than those of any other function served by special districts. The 1997 expenditures by sewerage districts of $80 million were more than 550% greater than they were in 1977. Only about 2.5% of the 1997 expenditures by these districts were for capital outlay, with almost 90% going for current operations.

Expenditures by solid waste management districts also have experienced strong growth. While the expenditures of these districts experienced some decline from 1977 to 1987, the expenditures of solid waste districts in 1997 of $82 million, were almost 250% greater than in 1987.

Michigan ranks low on interstate comparisons of government spending for solid waste management, thirty-fifth in local government spending per capita and thirty-seventh in state and local government spending per capita.

Overall, Michigan's rank for local government combined sewerage and solid waste per capita expenditures ranks sixth in the nation. See table 13.30. This is greatly influenced by Michigan's local government sewerage expenditures, which

---

**TABLE 13.28**

**Interstate Comparison of Local Government Parks and Recreation Expenditures, 1999**

| | Per Capita Spending | Local Expenditures as a % of State and Local Expenditures |
|---|---|---|
| U.S. average | $ 71.35 | 83.5% |
| Median state | 59.38 | 81.5 |
| Great Lakes states average | 90.80 | 89.5 |
| Michigan | 55.93 | 83.9 |

SOURCE: Bureau of the Census, U.S. Department of Commerce, *Government Finances: 1998–99.*

---

are the highest in the nation. While state government is responsible for some level of sewerage expenditures in some other states, Michigan is like twenty-seven other states in that local governments account for 100% of the state's sewerage expenditures. Michigan, like many surrounding states, ranks high on sewerage expenditures due to the large number of older sewerage systems and the costs associated with making capital improvements to bring them to the standards of today, as well as the high costs associated with the advanced levels of treatment required of many communities in Michigan.

*Libraries.* Despite an uncertain revenue base, which rests largely on penal fines and property taxes, library expenditures in the 1977–97 period showed relatively strong growth. Two-thirds of library expenditures by general-purpose units of government are by municipalities, but townships, which had insignificant library spending in 1977,

---

**TABLE 13.29**

**Michigan Local Government Per Capita Sewerage and Solid Waste Management Expenditures, 1977–97 (constant 1997 dollars)**

| | 1977 Amount | 1987 Amount | % Change 1977–87 | 1997 Amount | % Change 1987–97 | % Change 1977–97 |
|---|---|---|---|---|---|---|
| Total | $ 101.45 | $ 105.61 | 4.1% | $ 169.04 | 60.1% | 66.6% |
| Counties | 16.60 | 13.52 | –18.6% | 26.76 | 97.9% | 61.2% |
| Municipalities | 129.41 | 129.10 | –0.2% | 186.19 | 44.2% | 43.9% |
| Townships | 4.45 | 23.72 | 433.0% | 53.25 | 124.5% | 1096.6% |

SOURCE: Bureau of the Census, U.S. Department of Commerce, *1977, 1987, and 1997 Census of Governments.*

NOTE: Sewerage Expenditures are defined by the Bureau of the Census as expenditures for the "Provision of sanitary and storm sewers and sewage disposal facilities and services, and payments to other governments for such purposes." Solid Waste Management Expenditures are defined by the Bureau of the Census as expenditures for "street cleaning, solid waste collection and disposal, and provision of sanitary landfills and resource recovery facilities."

**TABLE 13.30**

**Interstate Comparison of Local Government Combined Sewerage and Solid Waste Management Expenditures, 1999**

|  | Per Capita Spending | Local Expenditures as a % of State and Local Expenditures |
|---|---|---|
| U.S. average | $146.21 | 92.8% |
| Median state | 126.51 | 96.2 |
| Great Lakes states average | 143.18 | 93.4 |
| Michigan | 184.49 | 97.4 |

SOURCE: Bureau of the Census, U.S. Department of Commerce, *Government Finances: 1998–99.*

provided one dollar in five by 1997. See table 13.31.

One of the consequences of Proposal A, the school finance reform approved by the voters in 1994, was that school districts had to get out of the business of operating community-wide public library systems (but not the school libraries available for students). Municipal governments assumed responsibility for some of these libraries, but library districts were established to support others. No data on library districts were available in the 1977 *Census of Governments*, but the data in the 1987 and 1997 *Census of Governments* show that expenditures of library districts grew by more than 750% in that ten-year interval, to over $94 million in 1997. Current operations accounted for more than three-quarters of the total expenditures.

Michigan library expenditures (twentieth in the United States) are like those of most other

**TABLE 13.31**

**Michigan Local Government Per Capita Library Expenditures, 1977–97**

|  | 1977 Amount | 1987 Amount | % Change 1977–87 | 1997 Amount | % Change 1987–97 | % Change 1977–97 |
|---|---|---|---|---|---|---|
| Total | $ 11.06 | $ 13.78 | 24.5% | $ 24.79 | 79.9% | 124.1% |
| Counties | 3.28 | 2.86 | −12.9% | 3.26 | 14.2% | −0.5% |
| Municipalities | 12.64 | 14.23 | 12.6% | 17.71 | 24.5% | 40.2% |
| Townships | 0.35 | 3.38 | NA | 5.19 | 53.8% | NA |

SOURCE: Bureau of the Census, U.S. Department of Commerce, *1977, 1987, and 1997 Census of Governments.*
NOTE: Library Expenditures are defined by the Bureau of the Census as expenditures for the "Establishment and operation of public libraries and support of privately operated libraries."

**TABLE 13.32**

**Interstate Comparison of Local Government Library Expenditures, 1999**

|  | Per Capita Spending | Local Expenditures as a % of State and Local Expenditures |
|---|---|---|
| U.S. average | $23.89 | 95.4% |
| Median state | 21.20 | 93.4 |
| Great Lakes states average | 30.78 | 96.5 |
| Michigan | 24.99 | 95.4 |

SOURCE: Bureau of the Census, U.S. Department of Commerce, *Government Finances: 1998–99.*

states both in the amount spent per capita and in the level of local government responsibility to make these direct expenditures. Some comparative figures are given in table 13.32.

## Discussion

### The Rise of Townships

Based on the data examined here, the most striking trend must be the growth of township expenditures relative to those of other local governments. In particular, growth in township spending on sewerage and other capital projects is significant. Township population growth is clearly part of the reason for the rapid growth in spending. As urban areas in Michigan expand outward, townships, as in prior years, are the units of government that lie in the path of that expansion. In contrast to the experience in prior years, however, townships that achieve high population densities are no longer incorporating and becoming cities. Instead, they are becoming charter townships. If it were a city, Clinton Township in Macomb County, with a 2000 population of 95,648, would be the tenth-largest in Michigan, just behind Dearborn at 97,775. Twenty-five townships had 2000 populations over 25,000, and all but two of those large townships were charter townships.

Charter township status confers certain advantages unavailable to general law townships. First, the charter township may appoint a superintendent to handle administrative affairs of the township. Second, the charter township may levy a property tax of up to ten mills for general purposes and, importantly, these mills are outside of the fifteen to eighteen mill constitutional limit that restricts general law townships. Finally, charter townships that meet certain standards of property value, population density, and service provision may be exempted from annexation by a contiguous city. For residents who are concerned that a city could levy twenty or more mills for operations, the charter township can constitute an attractive and more limited form of local government.

It may be relevant that among the standards required by state law to exempt a charter township from annexation are:

- governance by a zoning ordinance or master plan
- provision of solid waste disposal services
- provision of water and sewer services
- provision of fire protection
- provision of police protection through contract with the sheriff or another local unit, or through its own police department

Expenditures for these functions at the township level are growing very rapidly, suggesting strongly that not only expanded service provision but also protection against annexation may be a motivation. (In addition, the state unrestricted revenue sharing formula provides that a township that has a population of more than 20,000, *or* that is between 10,000 and 20,000, and which provides police and fire protection and water and sewer services to at least half its population, is treated as if it were a city under the formula, meaning a higher level of state funding.)

*Disposal of waste,* both solid waste and sewerage, reflects the growth of townships in urban areas and the role township spending has played in growth of total local government spending. As a growing part of township budgets, real per capita township sewerage expenditures grew by nearly 1,200% from 1977 to 1997, reflecting the urbanization of many townships, the shift to charter status, and tightened water pollution standards.

The trend toward the provision of local services by townships in urban areas is already having certain consequences and may have others if it continues, as seems likely.

*State-local fiscal relations* are evolving in the direction of greater state support of townships. The principal example of this trend is the 1998 restructuring of state general revenue sharing, which not only provides for a shift of funding away from the City of Detroit, but also away from cities, in general, to townships. Under the old statutory revenue sharing formula, cities received 78% of the distribution, with townships receiving 18%. The new formula changed those figures to 70% and 27%, respectively.

In November 2002, voters gave the state authority to issue $1 billion in general obligation debt to fund local sewer construction and containment of nonpoint source pollution. Significantly, the proposal makes private septic systems, largely found in townships, eligible for funding under the program.

*Counties* may find an expanded role as a result of the shift toward townships. First, when a jurisdiction incorporates and becomes a city, it does so, at least in part, to gain the legal and fiscal ability to provide a higher level of services to its residents. County sheriffs, for example, who are responsible for enforcing state laws in the county and for patrolling county roads, will leave police protection and law enforcement to the city police department when the unit becomes a city. The situation respecting townships is somewhat different. Townships received the legal authority to have their own police departments only in the 1960s, and since then a number have created them. They may be police departments as in cities, but they may also be local extensions of the sheriff's department, deriving their law enforcement powers from the sheriff. Other townships contract with the sheriff for police protection. Still others simply rely on the sheriff to patrol the county roads in the township. To the extent that the relationship between counties and townships

## TABLE 13.33

### Examining the Finances of Large Townships

| | Estimated 1999 Population |
|---|---|
| **Ten Townships with Largest Populations** | |
| Clinton Charter Township, Macomb County | 94,670 |
| Canton Charter Township, Wayne County | 74,433 |
| Waterford Charter Township, Oakland County | 70,752 |
| West Bloomfield Charter Township, Oakland County | 59,437 |
| Shelby Charter Township, Macomb County | 55,390 |
| Redford Charter Township, Wayne County | 51,899 |
| Ypsilanti Charter Township, Washtenaw County | 47,823 |
| Macomb Township, Macomb County | 47,702 |
| Bloomfield Charter Township, Oakland County | 42,968 |
| Georgetown Charter Township, Ottawa County | 40,759 |
| | |
| **Ten Cities with Populations Comparable to Ten Largest Townships** | |
| Dearborn | 96,926 |
| Kalamazoo | 77,458 |
| Wyoming | 68,820 |
| Rochester Hills | 68,359 |
| Taylor | 66,362 |
| Battle Creek | 53,382 |
| Novi | 45,947 |
| Kentwood | 44,512 |
| Portage | 44,512 |
| Muskegon | 40,123 |
| | |
| **Ten Townships with Average Populations** | |
| Sands Township, Marquette County | 2,184 |
| Seville Township, Gratiot County | 2,277 |
| Olive Township, Clinton County | 2,302 |
| Leslie Township, Ingham County | 2,307 |
| Hillman Township, Montmorency County | 2,357 |
| Porter Township, Van Buren County | 2,374 |
| Adams Township, Hillsdale County | 2,431 |
| Sanilac Township, Sanilac County | 2,463 |
| St. Charles Township, Saginaw County | 2,468 |
| Caseville Township, Huron County | 2,579 |

continues as townships grow, counties will find their roles expanding as well.

Expansion of the role of the county may occur in another significant way as well. Presently, townships do not receive road funding from the state. The decisions on township roads occur at the county level and, while townships levy millages to support road building in their jurisdictions, as townships grow, the county road function will increase relative to that of cities.

It is clear that a widespread preference for low taxes has fostered much of the growth of townships in urban areas. Whether low tax rates can be sustained into the future remains to be seen. Expenditures for various municipal functions, particularly sewers and sewage treatment, are certain to rise as population grows, placing strain on township budgets. Furthermore, state subsidization of local revenues through revenue sharing may be at risk. Historically, the statutorily authorized portion of revenue sharing has figured in most plans to reduce state expenditures to maintain a balanced state budget. Revenue sharing was reduced in Fiscal Year 2001–02 by $122 million, and as Fiscal Year 2002–3 began, it appeared that further reductions would be difficult to avoid. For many townships, further reductions could result in a demand for replacement revenue in the form of property taxes.

Since the adoption of the 1908 Constitution, Michigan has been considered a strong home rule state, as indicated by the constitutional provisions providing for adoption of charters by cities and villages as well as the limitations on the passage of local laws. Charters were viewed as effective instruments of local determination, freeing the legislature from the necessity of passing local laws, frequently numbering in the hundreds per session, to shape local organization, service, and finance powers. Nearly all of the existing Michigan cities were incorporated over the seventy years following 1908. By contrast, nearly all of the existing charter townships, whose powers and structures are found in state law rather than in local charters, have come into being since 1970. Whether this indicates an erosion in the role of home rule in local government or whether it is a temporary phenomenon should become evident as the demands on service levels and financial resources of townships increase in the years ahead.

### Large Townships and Cities

An examination of the finances of the ten largest townships, nine of which are charter townships, ten cities of comparable population, and ten general law townships of average population suggests that expenditure patterns of large townships are closer to those of cities than to those of smaller townships. These comparisons are drawn from the 1999 Michigan Municipal League database of finances for individual units (see tables 13.33 and 13.34).

**TABLE 13.34**

## Finances of Select Cities and Townships

| | 10 Largest Townships | | 10 Cities of Comparable Size | | 10 General Law Townships Roughly Average in Population | |
|---|---|---|---|---|---|---|
| | Total | % of Total | Total | % of Total | Total | % of Total |
| LAND AREA (SQ. MILES) | 293.7 | | 270.6 | | 375.6 | |
| TOTAL POPULAITON | 569,053 | | 503,998 | | 20,533 | |
| Property tax revenue | $ 52,198,416 | 32.8% | $133,135,805 | 45.7% | $ 521,215 | 24.3% |
| Total tax revenue | 53,599,762 | 33.7% | 148,110,986 | 50.8% | 690,791 | 32.3% |
| License revenue | 14,134,348 | 8.9% | 12,753,651 | 4.4% | 93,172 | 4.4% |
| State shared revenue | 47,695,787 | 30.0% | 59,289,886 | 20.3% | — | 0.0% |
| Intergovernmental revenue | 49,144,328 | 30.9% | 68,035,389 | 23.3% | 1,191,542 | 55.6% |
| Charges for services | 19,385,792 | 12.2% | 25,742,996 | 8.8% | 33,890 | 1.6% |
| Interest and dividend revenue | 7,855,179 | 4.9% | 7,354,461 | 2.5% | 55,421 | 2.6% |
| Other revenue | 22,911,790 | 14.4% | 36,926,760 | 12.7% | 131,852 | 6.2% |
| TOTAL REVENUE | $159,176,020 | | $291,569,782 | | $2,141,246 | |
| Legislative expenses | $ 900,205 | 0.6% | $ 1,941,585 | 0.7% | $ 97,233 | 4.8% |
| Judicial expenses | 9,541,759 | 6.2% | 7,412,284 | 2.6% | — | 0.0% |
| General expenses | 37,337,142 | 24.2% | 48,137,068 | 16.9% | 798,120 | 39.5% |
| Police protection expenses | 28,222,498 | 18.3% | 85,909,536 | 30.1% | — | 0.0% |
| Fire protection expenses | 20,150,528 | 13.0% | 27,486,608 | 9.6% | 184,588 | 9.1% |
| Public safety expenses | 11,248,870 | 7.3% | 18,078,351 | 6.3% | 100,572 | 5.0% |
| Public works expenses | 10,676,767 | 6.9% | 24,315,626 | 8.5% | 580,681 | 28.8% |
| Health and welfare expenditures | 958,083 | 0.6% | 4,132,625 | 1.4% | — | 0.0% |
| Recreation and culture | 9,772,972 | 6.3% | 19,852,516 | 7.0% | 33,092 | 1.6% |
| Debt expenses | 597,322 | 0.4% | 6,123,710 | 2.1% | — | 0.0% |
| Other expenses | 4,175,327 | 2.7% | 10,652,877 | 3.7% | 135,217 | 6.7% |
| Transfers | 20,845,078 | 13.5% | 31,396,091 | 11.0% | 89,678 | 4.4% |
| TOTAL GENERAL FUND EXPENSES | $154,426,551 | | $285,438,877 | | $2,019,181 | |
| Total restricted fund balance | $ 4,954,514 | | $ 18,241,520 | | — | |
| Total unrestricted fund balance | 77,698,124 | | 57,536,568 | | — | |
| TOTAL FUND BALANCE | $ 82,652,638 | | $ 75,778,088 | | $1,598,678 | |
| Long-term debt outstanding | $127,125,361 | | $379,100,164 | | $ 10,826 | |

SOURCE: Michigan Municipal League database of local government finances.

For example, police expenditures represented 18% of total spending in large townships, which is less than the 30% devoted to police expenditures in cities. However, the ten general law townships sampled spent nothing on this function. Large townships spent 6% and cities spent 7% of their budgets on recreation and culture, compared to less than 2% for general law townships. Furthermore, while cities, large townships, and general law townships spend roughly comparable proportions of their budgets on fire protection (large townships 13%, cities 10%, general law townships 9%), per capita spending on this function in general law townships is only about one-third the amount in either cities or charter townships.

The traditional reason for incorporation has been that cities have been given the fiscal and organizational latitude to provide the services demanded by residents in an urban setting. Increasing urbanization of townships will determine whether residents of those units will remain content with the forms of government and fiscal powers available to townships or will begin to look for the options currently available only in cities.

## County Health and Hospital Expenditures

The most obvious trend at the county level is the dramatic rise in health expenditures associated with the growth of community mental health (CMH). In 1977, health expenditures represented 8.5% of county expenditures. Twenty years later this had risen to 25.4%. This has not meant a dramatic increase in county taxes, however, since all but a small portion of CMH expenditures are paid for by the state, in part accounting for the difference between relatively high local expenditures and relatively low own-source revenues.

On the other hand, expenditures for county and municipal hospitals have declined. Many of these hospitals were established to care for low-income individuals or for those with tuberculosis. With the rise of Medicaid, a state-federal program of health care services for those with low incomes, and with the reduction in the incidence of tuberculosis, the justification for these hospitals has eroded and many have been closed or transferred to private ownership.

■

## NOTES

1. Economic and Statistics Administration, Bureau of Economic Analysis, U.S. Department of Commerce (*http://www.bea.gov/bea/dn/nipaweb/TableViewFixed.asp?SelectedTable=154&FirstYear=1977&LastYear=2002&Freq=Qtr*).

2. While local government spending in California and New York ranks high among the states in a number of functions, much of the high level of per capita local government expenditures in these states is accounted for by the roles local governments play in the provision of public welfare.

3. Because the government of the District of Columbia is responsible for carrying out tasks for which a state government would normally be responsible, as well as those typically associated with local government, expenditure data for the District are not included in these comparisons, either in the national averages or in figuring the median.

4. Highway Statistics 2000, Office of Highway Policy Information, Federal Highway Administration, U.S. Department of Transportation, *http://www.fhwa.dot.gov/ohim/hs00/index.htm*.

## APPENDIX A

### Hospitals Operated by Local Governments, 1987 and 1997

| | 1987 | | 1997 |
|---|---|---|---|
| 1 | Addison Community Hospital* | | |
| 2 | Albion Community Hospital | | |
| 3 | Alpena General Hospital | | |
| 4 | Anderson Memorial | | |
| 5 | Annapolis Hospital* | | |
| 6 | Baraga County Memorial Hospital | 1 | Baraga County Memorial Hospital |
| 7 | Berrien General Hospital | | |
| 8 | Beuer Hospital* | | |
| 9 | Caro Community Hospital | | |
| 10 | Community Health Center of Branch County | | |
| 11 | Crystal Falls Community Hospital | | |
| 12 | Dickinson County Memorial Hospital | 2 | Dickinson County Memorial Hospital |
| 13 | Grand View Hospital–Ironwood | | |
| 14 | Helen Newberry Joy Hospital | 3 | Helen Newberry Joy Hospital |
| 15 | Heritage Hospital* | | |
| 16 | Herrick Memorial Hospital | 4 | Herrick Memorial Hospital |
| 17 | Hillsdale Community Health Center | | |
| 18 | Holland Community Hospital* | | |
| 19 | Hurley Medical Center–Flint | 5 | Hurley Medical Center–Flint |
| 20 | Ingham Medical Center–Ingham County | | |
| 21 | Ionia County Memorial Hospital | 6 | Ionia County Memorial Hospital |
| 22 | Iron County General Hospital | | |
| 23 | Kalkaska Memorial Health Center* | 7 | Kalkaska Memorial Health Center* |
| 24 | Kent Community Hospital–LTU | 8 | Spectrum–Kent Community Campus |
| 25 | Lake View Community Hospital* | 9 | Lake View Community Hospital* |
| 26 | Mackinac Straits Hospital* | 10 | Mackinac Straits Hospital* |
| 27 | Mecosta County General Hospital | 11 | Mecosta County General Hospital |
| 28 | Morenci Area Hospital | | |
| 29 | North Ottawa Community Hospital* | | |
| 30 | Ontonagon Memorial Hospital | 12 | Ontonagon Memorial Hospital |
| 31 | Outer Drive Hospital* | | |
| 32 | Pontiac General Hospital | | |
| 33 | Reed City Hospital | 13 | Spectrum–Reed City |
| 34 | River District Hospital* | | |
| 35 | Rogers City Rehabilitation Hospital | | |
| 36 | Saginaw Community Hospital | 14 | Health Source–Saginaw |
| 37 | Schoolcraft Memorial Hospital | 15 | Schoolcraft Memorial Hospital |
| 38 | Seaway Hospital* | | |
| 39 | South Haven Community Hospital* | 16 | South Haven Community Hospital* |
| 40 | Sturgis Memorial Hospital | 17 | Sturgis Memorial Hospital |
| 41 | Thorn Hospital | | |
| 42 | Three Rivers Hospital* | 18 | Three Rivers Hospital* |
| 43 | West Branch Medical Center | 19 | West Branch Medical Center |
| 44 | West Shore Medical Center* | 20 | West Shore Medical Center* |
| 45 | Wyandotte General Hospital | | |

SOURCE: Michigan Department of Community Health.
* Hospital Authority

# Economic Development Policy in Michigan

*Timothy J. Bartik, Peter Eisinger, and George Erickcek*

What is meant by "economic development"? Economic development is using local resources, such as labor and land, more productively. Economic development can occur through local job growth, which causes unemployed local labor and land to be used. Yet economic development also occurs by shifting employed labor and land to more productive uses, for example, by upgrading the job mix to better jobs.

What is meant by "economic development policy"? Economic development is affected by all state and local government activities. However, economic development policy is usually defined as a special set of activities, undertaken by state and local public, quasi-public, and private organizations, to promote economic development. The characteristic activities of these economic development organizations fall into two categories:

• Providing "customized" assistance targeted at individual businesses that provide greater economic development benefits. This customized business assistance includes: firm-specific tax reductions to new and expanding businesses such as property tax abatements or Michigan's MEGA program; customized job training grants to businesses for job expansion or job retention; extra infrastructure services pro-

vided to businesses located in tax increment financing (TIF) areas; research grants to promote high-tech businesses; "ombudsman" assistance to help individual businesses resolve problems with government regulations; and site information for businesses considering new locations.

• Advocating strategic initiatives to promote economic development. Examples of such initiatives include the advocacy of Michigan's economic development agency, the Michigan Economic Development Corporation, for improved broadband infrastructure and better credentialing in Michigan's technical training system (Michigan Economic Development Corporation 2001b, 2002b).

The rationale for targeting some businesses for assistance and not others is that the growth of the assisted businesses may provide above-average benefits to the communities in which they are located. Export-based businesses that sell their goods or services to buyers outside the local economy will have multiplier effects on the local economy that are greater than for businesses selling to local buyers. Moreover, the employment benefits and fiscal benefits from growth of an individual business will be greater if the business hires more local residents versus in-migrants, and more of those out of work versus the employed.

This chapter reviews Michigan's economic development efforts, including their history and current status, and discusses how to best evaluate their success. Among the questions to be addressed are:

- Have Michigan's economic development programs and organizations been stable enough to maximize their effectiveness?
- What are the appropriate goals by which economic development programs should be evaluated? What techniques can be used for evaluation? What does the evidence suggest about the effectiveness of Michigan's economic development programs?

## History

As economic development was becoming a nearly universal state function in the early 1980s, Michigan emerged as a leader.[1] With the release in 1984 of *The Path to Prosperity,* the report of Governor James Blanchard's Task Force for a Long-Term Economic Strategy, Michigan became one of the first states to embrace strategic planning as the foundation for a more active government role in fostering economic prosperity. By the end of the 1980s, initiatives in export promotion, high-tech development, capital market interventions, customized job training, mature industry modernization, and support for local community growth groups had given Michigan a national reputation as one of the most innovative states in economic development (Eisinger 1988, 1990; Corporation for Enterprise Development 1992; Osborne 1988; Jackson 1988). As the Michigan Economic Development Corporation's official history of economic development in Michigan put it, "The 1980s can certainly be defined as a time of innovation." (Michigan Economic Development Corporation 2001a, 9).

After a hiatus, the state of Michigan again became a leader in economic development in the 1990s, but with more focus on improving the state's business climate and making the delivery of economic development assistance more effective. The state had actually ceased economic development activity for a brief period at the beginning of John Engler's governorship in 1991, to deal with a $1.8 billion deficit and because of the governor's belief that the key economic devel-

opment priority was to lower overall taxes and change government regulations, rather than offer firm-specific tax reductions. However, the political reality of modern American states is that governors are expected by opinion leaders and the public to take specific actions to attract and retain business. This expectation led to criticism of the Engler administration when General Motors in 1992 announced the closing of the Willow Run Plant in Ypsilanti after a publicized contest with a Texas GM plant to see which would be downsized (Buchholz n.d.). In the second half of his first term, Governor Engler moved to emphasize a "back-to-basics" economic development policy of marketing and job retention by trying to make such programs more aggressive and customer-focused. These traditional economic development activities were accompanied by new programs in brownfield redevelopment (brownfields are older, industrial sites that typically have pollution problems), renaissance zones, high-technology promotion, business-specific tax reductions, and customized job-training programs. These programs and the organizational framework delivering them received national recognition when Michigan was ranked first among the states in the number of new plants and expansions for five years in a row (1997–2001), and its economic development organization was ranked among the top ten economic development groups for four years in a row (1998–2001) (*Site Selection* magazine, various issues). Thus, the first thing to know about Michigan and economic development is that the state for many years has been a national leader.

### A Thematic Perspective on Michigan Economic Development

Certain themes stand out in Michigan's economic development activity over the past quarter century.

*Rapid Program Changes.* Economic development programs and initiatives come and go in Michigan at a rapid rate. The pace of program implementation and termination has often been driven by shifts in political climate. According to the MEDC's official history, programs "have been continually restructured, subjected to political attacks. . . . [M]ajor strategic economic development initiatives were initiated, then canceled, redirected or put on hold for significant periods when new administrations took office" (Michigan Economic Development Corporation 2001a, 3).

During the Milliken administration (1969–83), Michigan was a major innovator in economic development policy. It established the first state minority business program, and was among the first states to allow its public employee pension fund to invest in venture capital. The state set up one of the early small business offices, and created a small business lending corporation. These innovations have not survived in their original form, although some state activities persist in venture capital and small business.

The state was also quick to copy economic development initiatives pioneered by other states. In 1986, for example, the legislature passed an enterprise zone program, a movement sweeping the states at the time. Since the Michigan law provided for a zone only in the city of Benton Harbor, it appears in retrospect that the intent was to do something dramatic for one of the poorest, but often overlooked, cities in the state. The enterprise zone legislation expired in 1996, and was replaced by the novel Engler-era Renaissance Zones.

Innovations during Governor James Blanchard's administration (1983–90) brought the state more solidly into the competition for high-tech industry. The establishment of the Michigan Strategic Fund (MSF), a new state funding mechanism for economic development that combined the earlier Michigan Job Development Authority and Michigan Economic Development Authority, was an attempt by the state to foster technology transfer and encourage business start-ups through high-risk venture investment and other financing strategies. These capital market interventions superceded the financing programs created under the Milliken administration.

The Michigan approach was unique among the states at the time. The MSF created a package of financing programs that addressed different stages of the business cycle, from early research and development and prototype development to emerging stage businesses to middle-risk growth companies involved in product and market development. The MSF strategy was in part to use small amounts of money derived from the Michigan Natural Resources Trust Fund (revenues from the sale of oil, gas, and mineral leases on state lands) to seed private venture capital funds (the Seed Capital Program) or to provide insurance to banks that made moderate-risk loans (the Capital Access Program).[2] Other financing initiatives by the MSF included direct investment of state funds in business product development, and grants to three established nonprofit centers involved in R&D and technology transfer (the Michigan Biotechnology Institute, the Industrial Technology Institute, and the Metropolitan Center for High Technology).

Several programs of the Michigan Strategic Fund were the subject of a performance audit by the Office of the Auditor General (Michigan Office of the Auditor General 1993). The audit criticized the MSF for poor monitoring procedures (MSF relied on company job creation projections, for example, rather than figures for actual jobs created) and for inadequate benchmarks for assessing the effectiveness of certain of its programs. Perhaps most troubling to the auditor general was the finding that the MSF did not independently verify the impact of the centers for research and technology transfer. Nevertheless, the audit determined that at least one program—Capital Access—had been effective in accomplishing its stated purpose.

The administration of John Engler moved to shift the focus of economic development programs in Michigan to making basic economic development activities more effective. Much of this effort occurred through changes in organizational structure, to be discussed in the next section, as well as increased emphasis on customer feedback, to be discussed in the section on evaluation methodology. However, the state also terminated some programs and implemented some new ones. Most of the small business financing programs from previous administrations were phased out. New programs included the Renaissance Zones, brownfield redevelopment, biomedical research in the Life Sciences Corridor, and the MEGA tax credit program, all to be discussed further in the following.

Like many states, Michigan created a large number of economic development programs in a short space of time. Most had a brief lifespan. Although some changes were influenced by assessments of program effectiveness, much of this cycle of innovation or replication, termination, and replacement was driven more by changes in political administrations. Shifts in focus and the choice of programs terminated were dictated by the desire of each successive gubernatorial administration to put its own stamp on economic development. This is evident not only from an examination of the program history, but also from observing the changes in the nature of the state economic development agencies, which we explore in the next section.

*The Search for Organizational Flexibility.* Michigan's first state economic development agency was the Department of Economic Development, created in 1947. This was superceded in 1963 by the Department of Economic Expansion. Since then, the state has changed the name and character of the state development organ at least five times, moving from a purely public department of state government to the current Michigan Economic Development Corporation, a public corporation outside the state bureaucracy.

In part, these changes attempt to deal with a recurring challenge in state economic development, namely, to create vehicles that can operate effectively in the flexible world of business and avoid bureaucratic or state constitutional limits. The first steps toward this flexibility occurred in 1975, when Governor Milliken established the Michigan Job Development Authority to sell industrial revenue bonds to raise capital for business firms. Then in 1982 he established the Michigan Economic Development Authority to fund state economic development programs. It was governed by an independent board and relied on off-budget revenues (gas and oil lease royalties) to finance business loans and grants (Michigan Economic Development Corporation 2001a, 7). Recipients of this financial support included expanding Michigan businesses and centers of excellence in biotechnology and advanced manufacturing. For both the Michigan Job Development Authority and the Michigan Economic Development Authority, program operations were managed and staffed by employees of the state Department of Commerce. The independent authorities were created as financing vehicles in part because of the argument that the state constitution prohibited the state from providing businesses with direct financial assistance.

Neither of these Milliken-era authorities lasted long. Shortly after James Blanchard became governor, a new financing mechanism for economic development, the Michigan Strategic Fund, was created by combining the Michigan Job Development Authority and the Michigan Economic Development Authority. The MSF, created in 1984, was governed by a nine-member board, consisting of the state budget director and treasurer, and seven private-sector members appointed by the governor with the advice and consent of the Senate. The governance structure of the MSF represented an institutional transition toward an increasingly independent public corporation. The MSF was financed in part by off-budget revenues, as noted previously. As with the Michigan Economic Development Authority, program operations were staffed and managed by state Department of Commerce employees.

The Engler years saw a series of complex institutional reforms, beginning with the 1993 creation of the Michigan Jobs Commission (MJC), a temporary autonomous agency governed by a twenty-member commission. The MJC was given departmental status in 1995 by executive order. The Jobs Commission took over the staffing and management of economic development and related programs from the Department of Commerce and other state agencies, including the various customized business assistance programs and workforce training programs. The private sector was given a major role in state economic development through the creation of Michigan First, a private nonprofit corporation whose task was to market the state as an industrial location.

Michigan First was soon terminated, and the economic development functions of the MJC were absorbed in 1999 into the new Michigan Economic Development Corporation (MEDC), with workforce training programs (except for "customized" job training) transferred to the new state Department of Career Development. The MEDC is described as a corporation, not a traditional government agency. It was created through interlocal agreements between the Michigan Strategic Fund (which continues as the vehicle by which state appropriations are made for economic development) and local economic development agencies. The MEDC is funded (via the MSF) by legislative appropriations, an 8% tax paid by some tribal casinos, and repayments of economic development loans. The MEDC administers the portion of tobacco settlement funds used for the Life Sciences Corridor, and the federal Community Development Block Grant (CDBG) funds allocated to state governments for use in smaller communities that do not receive CDBG funds directly from the federal government. The MEDC is governed by an executive committee of seventeen members from the private sector—businesspeople, college presidents, local economic development professionals—appointed by the governor for staggered eight-year terms.

The point of this institutional history is to show that successive gubernatorial administrations have sought to free economic development from the confines of the state civil service, state salary limitations, legislative appropriations, and the rules of government bureaucracy. Economic development is more privatized in Michigan than it was two decades ago, under the theory that this will result in greater flexibility, speed, responsiveness, and understanding of business needs. In 2001 and 2002, *Site Selection* magazine named the MEDC as one of the top ten economic development organizations in the nation.

*Continuity of Core Economic Development Services.* Despite the many changes in programs and organizations, many core economic development services have persisted. Business recruitment has been pursued by Michigan since the 1950s. An emphasis on business retention goes back to Governor Romney in the 1960s. Business-specific tax reductions have been used in Michigan since the authorization of property tax abatements in the 1970s. "Ombudsman" services to businesses—in which individual businesses are helped to deal with state regulations and agencies—date back to the creation of a "Pro Business Office" in Michigan in the 1970s. Economic development infrastructure has been supported by Michigan's use of federal Community Development Block Grant dollars since the 1970s. High-technology development efforts have been pursued since the 1980s.

In some cases, these economic development services have been delivered by the same personnel, under a variety of program and organizational names. For example, many MEDC staff members have worked on economic development for two or three governors.

Despite this continuity, the numerous changes in programs and organization have probably interfered with program effectiveness. Particularly during a changeover in administrations, changes in organizations and programs distract attention from improving services. As acknowledged by the MEDC's official history, "the impact of continuous change also contributed in part to mixed results" (Michigan Economic Development Corporation 2001a, 3).

*Repairing the Business Climate.* Michigan has persistently been concerned about how the nation's businesses perceive the state's "business climate," that is, the state's tax, regulatory, and labor environment. In common with other Upper Midwestern states in the late 1970s, Michigan began to explore a more active role in economic development, largely in response to evidence that the state was perceived as a costly and unfriendly place to do business. For example, a ranking of state business climates by the Alexander Grant Company placed Michigan forty-eighth—the least hospitable—out of forty-eight states in both 1979 and 1980 (Southeast Michigan Council of Governments 1982, 215).

With its heavily unionized workforce, high wages, and high taxes, Michigan was concerned that it was losing industry to neighboring states and the South. In response to these concerns, Governor William Milliken (1969–83) sought to reduce business costs by reforming workers' compensation and unemployment insurance. The cost of workers' compensation still remained high in the 1980s, however, as did property taxes, prompting Governor Blanchard's Task Force to recommend bringing these costs in line with those in neighboring states, "to let the rest of the nation know that Michigan is a good place to do business" (Task Force for a Long-Term Economic Strategy for Michigan 1984, 96).

It appeared that Michigan could no longer even retain the automobile industry. As foreign automakers and GM's Saturn division chose locations for new plants outside of Michigan, the Hudson Institute concluded, in a 1985 report done for the Michigan Senate, that "the state has lost its competitive edge as an auto producer" (Hudson Institute 1985, xiii). In the 1990s the Engler administration embarked on a campaign of major tax cuts. These included huge reductions in local property taxes, the gradual phase-out of the Single Business Tax, reductions in the rate and base of the Individual Income Tax, the complete repeal of the Intangibles Tax, and shifting from a state Inheritance Tax to a federal "pick-up" Estate Tax. In addition, a host of tax exemptions and tax credits, such as the elimination of virtually all taxation in the state's Renaissance Zones, brownfield development tax credits, and a high-tech investment credit, targeted economic development specifically. The result was that the state was able to claim that it had gone from having the nation's sixth-highest tax burden in the 1980s to the eighteenth-lowest at the end of the 1990s (Michigan Economic Development Corporation 1999a).

Nevertheless, Michigan continues to be uncertain about its business climate reputation. In a recent version of the state's economic development strategic plan, the MEDC is concerned that Michigan still is not a state to which business

**FIGURE 14.1**

**Real Tax Expenditure on Property Tax Abatement**

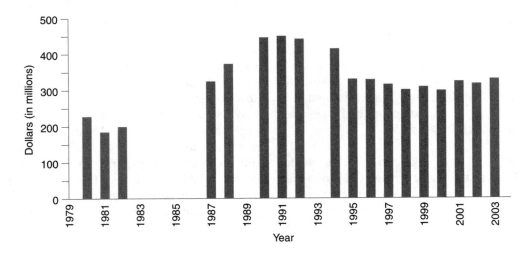

NOTES: Years without bars do not have available data. Derived from various editions of tax expenditure appendix to Governor's Executive Budget. All data are for fiscal years. All tax expenditures are adjusted to FY 2003 dollars using the personal consumption deflator of the GDP, available in table 7.4 at *http://www.bea.doc.gov/ bea/dn/nipaweb/SelectTable.asp?Selected=N#S7*, and forecasts of inflation for 2002 and 2003 are from Congressional Budget office in January 2002 budget outlook, at *http://www.cbo.gov/showdoc.cfm?index=3277&sequence=3*.

leaders across the nation think about relocating (Michigan Economic Development Corporation 1999b, 21). Indeed, even though Michigan has been a leader in attracting new plants and expansions, it placed only seventeenth as a desirable location in a national survey of corporate real estate executives who work for companies considering branch sites (Starner 2001).

Concerns about the state's competitive position on business costs have kept the state focused on maintaining business climate policies as the core of its economic development efforts, a commitment designed to demonstrate the state's receptiveness to business and to reducing business costs. Although both Democratic and Republican gubernatorial administrations have maintained a commitment to traditional business incentives and customer-first business advocacy, this approach was particularly emphasized in the Engler years (1991–2003 ), when economic development policy was characterized as moving "back to the basics" (Michigan Economic Development Corporation 2001a). In addition to tax cuts, the administration froze the maximum weekly unemployment benefit in 1996, developed one of the nation's largest job-training programs, funded basic business and community infrastructure, and completed a business climate benchmarking study that led to workers' compensation reforms. The state also instituted a one-stop business serv-

ice program: the MEDC now designates an "account manager" for new firms choosing Michigan, as well as for resident urban firms with more than one hundred employees and rural firms with twenty or more employees. The account managers serve as the single point of contact for help with site development, regulatory issues, infrastructure financing, and other problems. Michigan is clearly active in using the state's resources to create a low-cost business climate.

*The Importance of Property Taxes.* Historically, a big concern about Michigan's business climate was high property taxes. Concern over property taxes led to a large economic development program, property tax abatements for industrial property. Tax abatements were originally authorized by the legislature in 1974 and have continued with modest modifications ever since. Tax abatements reduce property taxes to half their normal level for new industrial projects, and eliminate additional property taxes on industrial expansions. Tax abatements are approved by local governments, but the state government provides local schools and other local governments that might be adversely affected by abatements with some additional state aid.

Although not every new or expanded industrial project in Michigan receives an abatement, most major projects do.[3] The result has been a consistently large abatement program. For most of the last quarter century, property tax abatements in Michigan represent the largest single use of state and local resources in supporting economic development. As shown in figure 14.1, property tax abatements are associated with a "tax expenditure" of over $200 million per year.[4] These official "tax expenditure" figures calculate how much extra property tax revenue would have been collected if the full property tax rate had been applied and the new industrial projects had been undertaken anyway, without the abatements. As will be discussed later, a full fiscal analysis would have to also reflect the extra revenue associated with investment induced by the abatements, minus public spending needed because of induced investment.

*The Continuing Attraction of High-Tech Business.* In late 2001 the MEDC launched a national media campaign to boost Michigan's image as a place to do high-tech business (Bennett 2001). The state has long pursued a high-tech strategy, initially to reinforce the state's traditional manufacturing and then also to develop new industries. In 1984 the authors of *The Path to Prosperity* argued that the state should "get smart" by transforming its auto and parts plants into "factories of the future." Introducing robotics, machine vision, and computer-assisted manufacturing into heavy industries was the smart high-tech route Michigan should follow, rather than competing with Silicon Valley for electronic components firms.

Such a strategy made sense when Michigan's domestic competitors were its neighbors, but by 1999 the state had shifted its reference points. In MEDC's report, *Strategic Directions for Michigan's Future* (1999b), planners used states that had transitioned to a high-tech economy as the benchmark competitors, rather than the traditional manufacturing states around the Great Lakes. The new group included Arizona, California, Virginia, Massachusetts, and Washington. "State-of-the-art high technology is generally more fundamental to these new competitors than to Michigan's previous competitors," the report declared (4).

The MEDC laid out the state's new high-tech strategy in a report entitled *State Smart: Michigan* (1999a), pointing out that "While manufacturing will always be important to the state of Michigan, [the] new brain power industries will continue to create more 'Gold Collar Jobs,' whether they be in

support of our manufacturing structure or whether they take Michigan off in an exciting new direction" (4). New industry development, according to this plan, was to be focused on advanced manufacturing in the traditional industries, information technologies (Michigan ranks fourth nationally in employment in this sector), and life sciences. The report proposed measures to encourage high-tech growth, including marketing the state as a high-tech location, targeting job training programs to high-tech needs, and offering tax exemptions and credits, partly through the SmartZone program, to attract existing firms and build new ones.

What is finally striking about these recommendations is that they echo themes from past administrations. The Michigan Strategic Fund, established in 1984, funneled millions of dollars in grants to three established "centers of excellence," including the Michigan Biotechnology Institute, the Industrial Technology Institute, and the Metropolitan Center for High Technology. Technology transfer, product development, and venture capital were the central ideas of state high-tech policy then, as now.

The various themes in Michigan's economic development history—the changes in programs and organizations, the continuing concern for the nature of the business climate, the importance of property tax relief, and the persistent attraction of high-tech industry—paint a portrait of an often innovative, active state. Yet the state's economic development efforts could also be said to lack stability. Although some of these changes are due to informal feedback on program effectiveness, very little of the changes in programs and approaches can be attributed to formal evaluations of the effectiveness of economic development initiatives. We turn now to a description of the state's current array of economic development programs, followed by a consideration of various approaches to evaluating their effectiveness.

## Current Programs

Table 14.1 provides a summary of the resources devoted to various economic development programs in Michigan. The table includes "tax expenditures" as well as regular government expenditures, and local and federal activities as well as state activities. We will discuss some issues with measuring the costs of economic development before discussing the programs.

| TABLE 14.1 |
|---|

## Annual Resources Devoted to Economic Development Activities in Michigan

| Program | Brief Description | Level of Goverment Financing Program | Tax Credit or Expenditure? | Annual Dollars Devoted to Program[a] |
|---|---|---|---|---|
| **Location Subsidies** | | | | |
| Industrial facilities property tax abatements | 50% tax break on new projects, 100% on expansion portion of old projects | Local; state indirectly via funding formulas | Tax credit | 330 |
| Tax increment financing | Property taxes devoted to infrastructure and other services to designated areas | Local; state indirectly via funding formulas | Tax credit | 90 |
| MEGA tax credits | Refundable tax credits for selected projects | State | Tax credit | 46 |
| Brownfield tax credits | Tax credits for redevelopment of brownfield areas | State | Tax credit | 28 |
| Renaissance zones | Designated areas with complete tax exemption from property and income taxes | Local and state | Tax credit | 26 |
| Federal Empowerment Zone and Enterprise Community program | Tax credits plus targeted expenditures in selected areas | Federal | Tax credit and expenditure | 11 |
| SBA loans | Guaranteed loans to small businesses | Federal | Implicit expenditure | ? |
| SUBTOTAL | | | | 531 |
| | | | | |
| **Subsidies for Specific Activities** | | | | |
| Economic development job training grants | Grants from state to support job training for specific firm, including new location, expansion, retention | State | Expenditure | 13 |
| Life Sciences Corridor Grants | Funds for biotech research at universities that will lead to job-creating projects | State | Expenditure | 42 |
| Michigan Manufacturing Technology Center | Technical assistance to improve productivity of small- and medium-sized manufactureres (< 1,000 employees) | 30% federal, 20% state 50% fees | Expenditure | 7 |
| SUBTOTAL | | | | 62 |
| | | | | |
| **Infrastructure** | | | | |
| Community development block grants | Federal program that provides funds to state to fund community development projects in local nonurban communities, typically for infrastructure projects supporting economic development | Federal | Expenditure | 60 |
| SUBTOTAL | | | | 60 |
| | | | | |
| **Business Retention & Recruitment** | | | | |
| State activities | State efforts to retain and recruit business, including heavy reliance on personal contacts by staff, and providing assistance to business to overcome various location problems, such as regulation | State | Expenditure | 33 |
| Local activities | Similar to state efforts, but by local organizations | Local, sometimes with federal funding supports | Expenditure | 15 |
| Federal activities | Federal support for local small business development centers, designed to encourage start-up and growth of successful small businesses | Federal/local (55%/45%) | Expenditure | 5 |
| SUBTOTAL | | | | 53 |
| TOTAL | | | | 706 |

SOURCE: Tax credit figures are from tax expenditure appendix to state budget for FY 2003. It is assumed that approximately one-third of tax increment financing (TIF) supports economic development; the rest is assumed to support downtown development. State expenditure figures come from executive budget for 2003, and data provided by the MEDC. Local efforts in economic development are estimated by examining data from surveys conducted by Michigan Economic Developers' Association of spending per capita of their members. Data on Michigan Manufacturing Technology Center (MMTC) spending is from personal communication with Dan Luria at MMTC. Data on Small Business Development Center (SBDC) spending is from personal communication with Carol Lopucki at Michigan SBDC.

(a) in millions.

*Cost Accounting Issues.* The costs reported in table 14.1 are "gross costs," in that these calculations ignore effects of economic development programs on revenues and expenditures due to any new business activity induced by the program, and resulting effects on population migration. For example, the tax expenditure numbers calculate how much tax revenue is lost due to the tax break, compared to what would have been collected if the tax break did not exist but the investment still occurred. These gross costs represent the true fiscal costs of economic development programs under either of two assumptions: (1) economic development programs have zero effect in inducing new investment and jobs; or (2) the induced business activity and population have effects on government revenues and expenditures that are exactly offsetting.

Ignoring effects of government on economic activity is conventional practice in government budgetary accounting, because it avoids controversy over the economic effects of government. This conventional practice seems strange in the case of economic development policy. The rationale of these programs is the hope that they will induce additional economic activity. Many government officials back economic development programs in the belief that new economic activity will augment revenue more than required expenditures.

The economics literature suggests that economic development programs have some effect in inducing additional business activity in a state (Bartik 1991), but with some uncertainty over the size of this effect. Most studies suggest that usually businesses pay more in tax revenue than they directly require in expenditure. However, increased business activity in a state induces significant population growth: for every 1% increase in jobs in a state, a state's population will be 0.8% greater than it otherwise would be, due to induced in-migration and reduced out-migration (Bartik 1993). If the same quality of public services is to be maintained, this increased population will need to be accompanied by increased public expenditures.[5]

Under reasonable assumptions, based on previous research and Michigan data, the induced economic activity due to Michigan's economic development activities, and the resulting effects on state and local revenue and expenditure, might offset about half the gross costs of Michigan's economic development programs, resulting in net costs for the programs of about half the gross costs given in table 14.1.[6]

*Summary Description of Michigan's Economic Development Programs.* In many respects, Michigan's economic development activities are similar to those of other states. Most resources go to firm-specific assistance, providing an incentive for firms to locate or expand in the state, and most of this assistance is in the form of tax breaks. Some economic development funds go for public infrastructure improvements to support economic development. An important economic development function is providing existing or prospective businesses with help to overcome problems impeding profitability at a location, such as problems with government regulations. Even though government spending on this function is modest, such efforts can have significant effects on the attractiveness of an area to business. Uncertainties about delays in obtaining regulatory permits for business locations or expansions can cause significant problems in competitiveness and profitability for a business. As one of Michigan's economic developers put it, "Frankly, the whole area of business services is more utilized than just the incentives which get all of the publicity" (interview with authors). These services are important, according to another economic developer, because a company will say, "we have to be in production by $x$ and we just found out about it and isn't there a way to . . . speed [the process] up a little bit?"

There are several important points to recognize about state economic development efforts. First, these programs can have large effects on business profitability. As shown in table 14.2, state and local taxes have significant effects on profits, and economic development incentives often are equivalent to eliminating 20% to 90% of normal state and local business taxes. Michigan is more aggressive than its competitors in using incentives to reduce business taxes.

Second, economic development includes a key role for local organizations, which do a sizable share of the retention and business recruitment, as well as providing the bulk of the economic development incentives in the form of forgone property tax revenue. As in most states, the state government plays a more prominent role in economic development in rural areas, which have less sophisticated development efforts. For example, the State of Michigan currently has a Community Assistance Team (CAT) that provides technical assistance to boost local capacity to act strategically about economic and community development, and CAT, according to one informed

**TABLE 14.2**

**Effects of Economic Development Incentives on Effective State and Local Business Tax Rates, Michigan and Nearby States**

| State | Effective State and Local Business Tax Rate without Incentives (% Reduction in Rate of Return) | % Reduction in State and Local Taxes Due to Normal Incentives | % Reduction after Discretionary Incentives Such as MEGA | % Reduction after State and Local Enterprise Zone Incentives |
|---|---|---|---|---|
| Michigan | 11.3 | 27.7 | 63.6 | 85.0 |
| Indiana | 20.5 | 20.0 | | 57.1 |
| Ohio | 15.0 | 22.6 | 28.1 | 48.8 |
| Illinois | 8.6 | 6.8 | | 25.6 |
| Wisconsin | 9.3 | 0 | | 31.7 |

NOTES: These tables are derived by simulations of the Tax and Incentive Model (TAIM) developed and maintained by Peter Fisher and Alan Peters of the University of Iowa. Fisher and Peters (1998) describe the model in detail. The model is a hypothetical firm model. State and local taxes and incentives are defined as of 1998 in the current version of the model. The results here are based on results for sixteen manufacturing industries at the two-digit level (SICs 20, 23–28, 30–38). The average results reported here are aggregated using GDP shares of each industry in Michigan in 1999. The effective state and local business tax rate is defined as the percentage reduction in the internal rate of return in a project located in the state, compared to locating the same project in a hypothetical state that has no state or local taxes. For example, a reduction from a 10% return to an 8% return is a 20% effective tax rate. The percentage reduction in state and local taxes is simply the reduction in taxes with the incentive in question, compared to if there were no incentives, divided by the taxes if there were no incentives, and multiplied by 100. Both the discretionary calculations and the enterprise zone calculations also assume all the normal incentives are applied, but the enterprise zone calculations assume that discretionary incentives such as MEGA are also not applied. Michigan and Ohio are the only ones of these states that have truly discretionary incentives.

observer, is "more rural, but it's within downtown areas of rural, what we would consider . . . core communities or traditional centers of commerce, [such as] county seats" (interview with authors). In urban areas, better-funded and more expert local economic developers take more of the lead in development projects, albeit with significant state support.

A final observation is that state and local economic development receives significant federal support. Federal funds support rural community development projects that in Michigan, as well as many other states, support economic development.[7] Federal funds provide a network of support for small business development and for industrial extension activities.

*Distinctive Michigan Economic Development Programs.* There are several distinctive Michigan economic development programs: Renaissance Zones; brownfield development; the Life Sciences Corridor; state account managers; and, the MEGA program.

Michigan's Renaissance Zones are an Engler-era (1996) version of enterprise zones, which offer tax breaks for investment in distressed city neighborhoods or distressed rural areas. However, compared to the average state enterprise zone program, Renaissance Zones offer much larger tax breaks: within the designated zone (an area within a city or a rural area), the Renaissance Zones waive all business and resident state and local taxes for up to fifteen years. Taxes from

which business owners and residents are exempt include city and state income taxes, the general property tax, and the Single Business Tax. The program has so far designated twenty zones, including zones within the cities of Detroit and Grand Rapids; in Oscoda, where the Pentagon closed Wurtsmith Air Force base; and in a rural area in Manistee County.

A second notable initiative in Michigan is brownfield reclamation, which seeks to redevelop older industrial sites that typically have pollution problems. Michigan, which ranks ninth in the nation with thirteen thousand brownfield sites, is regarded as a leader in brownfield redevelopment (Simons 1998, 100). The state uses grants, loans, brownfield tax increment financing (TIF) authorities, and tax credits to underwrite site assessment and cleanup costs. The state sets different cleanup standards depending on whether the site is to be used for residential, commercial, or industrial development, and establishes liability exemptions for lenders. In 2000 the Michigan Department of Environmental Quality reported that investment in brownfields amounted to $1.75 billion, an increase of 75% over the prior year (Citizens Research Council of Michigan 2001, 11).

A third pioneering Michigan program is its 1999 decision, since imitated by other states, to allocate a significant portion of the Tobacco Settlement Trust Fund for biotechnology research, about $1 billion over the next twenty-five years ($45 to $50 million per year, about 12% of the state's tobacco settlement) (Bole 2002).

**TABLE 14.3**

**Types of Business Services Provided by State of Michigan to Encourage Business Retention**

| Type of Service | % of This Service Out of All Services Provided |
|---|---|
| Information on general business planning, technology, exports, procurement | 29 |
| Information related to worker training | 22 |
| Information related to new site or site expansion | 14 |
| Workers' compensation cost management | 13 |
| Ombudsmen help with regulatory agencies | 11 |
| Other services | 11 |
| TOTAL | 100%, corresponding to 4,307 services provided to businesses in FY 2001 |

SOURCE: Authors' classification, based on data provided by Michigan Economic Development Corporation for FY 2001.

Major universities, nonprofit laboratories, and businesses located in the "Life Sciences Corridor" stretching from Detroit through Ann Arbor and Lansing and on to Grand Rapids are eligible to compete for research grants. Some funding will go for basic university research, but more than half is to go to joint university-business partnerships and nonprofit or for-profit entities that pursue projects that lead to commercialization.

A fourth distinctive Michigan effort is providing business retention services via account managers. These twenty-three account managers meet with five thousand Michigan businesses per year, two-fifths of which have over one hundred employees. Account managers try to call annually on every export-base company with over one hundred employees, as well as on export-base "gazelles" (companies with over 20% growth for three years in a row). As table 14.3 shows, businesses are provided with services such as information related to job training, site expansion, technology, exports, and government procurement; help with workers' compensation; and assistance with regulatory agencies.

Michigan is more active than most states in using field staff to provide job retention services. The state's twenty-three account managers working on retention compare with only eight staff persons who work on attracting new companies. According to state officials, this ratio of "amount of effort we put into retention versus attraction . . . is usually reversed in many other states where they don't have the same amount of retention activity." According to one outside observer, Michigan "has been a trend setter [in industrial retention]. I do not think they were the first ones to do it—I think Pennsylvania was, but they are pretty close to trend setters. They are one of the

first states [to be active in job retention]. And I think that . . . industrial retention . . . is one of the best things they have done" (interview with authors).

A fifth distinctive Michigan effort is the MEGA tax credit program, which provides tax credits to business projects that create new jobs and investment. Although other states (i.e., Kentucky, Ohio) have similar programs, Michigan's program appears to provide larger credits per firm and use data more extensively in project selection. Begun in 1995, the MEGA program can provide tax credits to twenty-five non-high-tech projects and fifty high-tech projects per year, although the state has averaged twenty-one regular MEGA projects and ten high-tech MEGA projects per year. MEGA can reimburse a business for up to twenty years of its normal Single Business Tax, plus provide a refundable credit tied to personal income taxes paid by the additional employees hired because of the project, but the awarded credits are negotiated with applicant businesses, and are paid only if the associated SBT liabilities and payroll are actually created. The average annual subsidy per job creation associated with MEGA is about $2,000, and the average term of the subsidy is thirteen years. Eligible projects must be in manufacturing, high tech, mining, wholesale/trade, and office operations. MEGA credits must be shown to overcome disadvantages compared to non-Michigan sites that would have caused the project to be located outside of Michigan but for the MEGA credit, and the project should result in a net fiscal gain for the state treasury. According to state officials, MEDC staff screen out over 90% of the companies interested in MEGA, and fill only 30–50% of the gap between the company's costs in Michigan versus its best alternative state,

**FIGURE 14.2**

## Time Trends in Real Tax Expenditures for MEGA

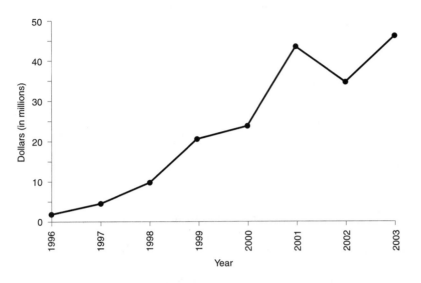

NOTES: Derived from various editions of tax expenditure appendix to Governor's Executive Budget. All data are for fiscal years. All tax expenditures are adjusted to FY 2003 dollars using the personal consumption deflator of the GDP, available in table 7.4 at *http://www.bea.doc.gov/bea/dn/nipaweb/SelectTable.asp? Selected=N#S7* and forecasts of inflation for 2002 and 2003 are from Congressional Budget office in January 2002 budget outlook, at *http://www.cbo.gov/showdoc.cfm?index=3277&sequence=3.*

because "we think there's an intrinsic reason that . . . [these] companies want to be here" (interview with authors).

As shown in figure 14.2, MEGA has grown greatly since beginning in 1995, with its gross costs (the tax credit actually paid) now close to $50 million annually. As mentioned previously, for an average economic development program, the induced business activity and the resulting increases in revenues and spending might offset about half of these gross costs. However, because MEGA is so selective, it may do better than average in targeting projects in which it tips the location decision. By statute, MEGA is supposed to be decisive in 100% of its projects, an unrealistic standard. Under reasonable assumptions, the MEGA program will break even from a state budget perspective if MEGA is decisive in 28% of its projects , which we think is quite possible.[8] However, the gross costs of MEGA that are reported in the state budget are high, and will continue to grow because the program awards long-term credits and is still relatively young.[9] The growing gross costs may create political problems for MEGA.

## Rationale and Goals for Economic Development Policies

Economic development policies should ultimately be evaluated on whether they achieve the benefits implied by these programs' goals.[10] Why should government promote economic development? Government promotion of economic development is justified because private markets do not fully consider job growth's social benefits. These social benefits include "employment benefits": the wages provided by new jobs are often likely to exceed the value of time of the new workers. Social benefits of growth also include "fiscal benefits": the job growth and accompanying population growth may increase tax revenue more than required public spending.

Economic developers should select policies or projects that maximize fiscal and employment benefits. Fiscal benefits will be greater in local economies with underutilized infrastructure, possibly because of recent population decreases. Both fiscal benefits and employment benefits are greater if the new jobs are filled by nonemployed local residents, reducing in-migration. In-migration results in greater public spending needs. Nonemployed local residents are likely to benefit more from obtaining jobs than will in-migrants, because they have fewer good alternatives. Employment benefits will also be higher if the new jobs pay higher wages, or are filled by local residents with fewer good alternatives, such as the disadvantaged. Employment benefits will be greater in local economies with high unemployment, as the unemployed in these economies will have fewer good alternatives.

Government promotion of economic development may need to be customized for individual firms because job creation in some firms may generate greater employment and fiscal benefits than job creation in other firms, for example a firm's job creation will have greater benefits if the firm pays greater wages and hires more disadvantaged local residents. In addition, government promotion of growth in export-base firms that sell their goods and services outside the local economy will have greater effects on local job growth than promotion of growth in non-export-base firms. Export-base firms bring new dollars into the local economy, resulting in multiplier effects and creating jobs in local suppliers and retailers. In contrast, government promotion of growth in a local retail firm may reduce sales and employment in other local retailers, with little effect on local job growth. Finally, economic development can be promoted in some cases by providing government services to firms, and these services will be of higher quality if customized to the needs of the individual firm. Such services are sensible for government to provide if private markets fail to fully provide the service and there is some gap that can be effectively filled by government. Examples of services that may be inadequately provided without government intervention include: roads and other public infrastructure; training and education; information on new business sites, modernization options, or government regulation; and some types of high-risk financing.

## Approaches to Evaluation

We describe here a variety of approaches to evaluation, listing how they have been used in Michigan to evaluate programs, and the results of such evaluation. If no Michigan-specific evaluations are available, we mention evaluations of similar programs in other states.

*Benchmarking.* An informal method of evaluating economic development is to "benchmark" the state or local area's performance on "indicators" of economic development versus other states or local areas. The state of Michigan has gone through such benchmarking, most recently in a study done for the MEDC by SRI (Michigan Economic Development Corporation 2002a). Benchmarking may suggest useful hypotheses about the state's strengths and weaknesses that may lead to useful policies. However, without further investigation, benchmarking cannot measure the effects of economic development policy. For example, in the recent SRI study, Michigan is ranked number one in new corporate facilities and expansions, and number fifteen (among eighteen competitor states) in new business start-ups. Without further analysis, it is unclear whether Michigan's rankings are due to the industries in which Michigan specializes, or to public policies.

*Estimating the Overall Impact of Economic Development Policies on the Michigan Economy.* Ideally, we would like to evaluate Michigan's economic development programs by comparing the

---

**FIGURE 14.3**

**Changes over Time in Michigan's "Competitive Shift" in Manufacturing**

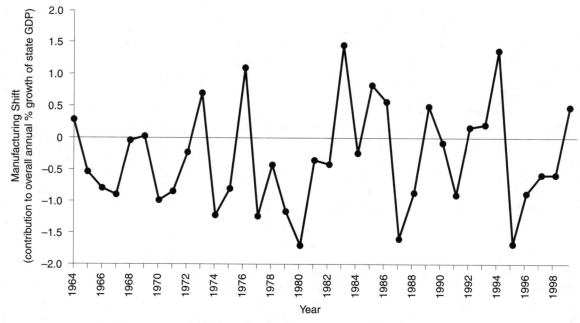

SOURCE: Authors' calculations. Underlying data is real GDP data by two-digit manufacturing industry, available from 1969 to 1999 from Regional Economic Models, Inc., and prior to 1969, was obtained for a previous project from the U.S. Bureau of Economic Analysis. Number calculated is contribution to overall state growth rate of GDP (in % terms) of differential growth of GDP in individual manufacturing industries in Michigan vs. United States. Formally, the calculation is sum over all manufacturing industries *i* of (*Grimt* − *Griust*)[(*GSPimt* − 1)/(*GSPmt* − 1)], where *Grimt* is real growth rate between year *t* − 1 and *t* of industry *i* in Michigan, *Griust* is analogous growth rate for U.S. (growth rates are calculated in percentage terms) *GSPimt* − 1 is GSP in industry *i* in Michigan in year *t* − 1, and *GSPmt* − 1 is total GSP in Michigan in year *t* − 1. The final resulting number is interpreted as the annual percentage growth rate of GSP due to differential growth in Michigan vs. United States of individual manufacturing industries.

state's economy with the policies to what would have happened without the policies. Yet it is difficult to determine how Michigan would have done in a hypothetical world. Because Michigan has long had active economic development policies, it is difficult to compare Michigan's performance "before" and "after" a dramatic change in policy. Because other states have become more active in economic development, comparing Michigan's performance to that of other states is comparing to a moving target.

For this chapter, we performed a shift-share analysis of manufacturing production growth in Michigan for each year from 1964 to 1999. This analysis shows how much of Michigan's production growth each year is due to individual Michigan manufacturing industries simply keeping market share and matching the growth of their national counterparts, and how much is due to Michigan manufacturing industries gaining market share. Controlling for industrial mix is especially important in analyzing Michigan's economy because of the state's extraordinary dependence on the auto industry, which means that many Michigan trends have more to do with the fortunes of the U.S. auto industry than the state's actions. It is the gain or losses of market share that state economic development policy can plausibly affect.

As figure 14.3 shows, there are no clear trends in Michigan's industries growing faster or slower than their national counterparts. For example, there is no obvious effect of the adoption of manufacturing property tax abatements in 1974. Does this mean that state economic development policy has had zero effect on Michigan's manufacturing growth? Not necessarily, for two reasons. First, this analysis controls only for national trends in demand for Michigan's industries. A fuller model would control for other factors affecting the growth of Michigan industries before determining a residual that might be due to policy. Second, other states have also been expanding and modifying their economic development programs.

*Estimating the overall impact of geographically targeted economic development policies, such as enterprise zones or Renaissance Zones.* These policies should be evaluated by comparing these areas' performance to how they would have performed without such assistance. No study has yet been released or published that compares the performance of Renaissance Zones, before and after zone designation, with the performance of

well-chosen comparison areas. Some studies have been done for other states' enterprise zones. Most of these studies find little effect of enterprise zones on the overall level of business activity (Greenbaum 1998; Peters and Fisher 2002), but some studies do find some effects of enterprise zones (Papke 1993, 1994). However, Renaissance Zones provide far larger tax reductions than most state enterprise zone programs.

*Estimating the effects of economic development programs on assisted businesses versus a control group of businesses.* For economic development programs that target some firms for assistance, it is possible to evaluate the programs by comparing the performance of assisted firms with that of similar firms that did not receive assistance. The difficulty is in finding comparison firms, as firms receiving economic development assistance usually apply for and receive such assistance for reasons that make them different from other firms; for example, such firms may apply for assistance to expand.

The only Michigan economic development program that has been evaluated in this way is the economic development job training programs of the 1980s. An evaluation by Holzer et al. (1993) compared the performance of firms receiving training grants with firms that applied for such grants too late in the fiscal year to receive them. Firms that received grants engaged in more training, and their product scrappage rate declined relative to the comparison firms.

Entrepreneurial training programs, similar to the training provided at Small Business Development Centers in Michigan, have been evaluated using random assignment, in which unemployment insurance recipients interested in starting their own business were randomly assigned to a "treatment" group that received entrepreneurship training and a "control" group that did not receive training. This evaluation suggests that entrepreneurship training increases the number of successful small business start-ups by 60 to 100% (Benus, Wood, and Grover 1994).

The services provided by the federal Manufacturing Extension Partnership (MEP), which helps fund the Michigan Manufacturing Technology Center (along with MEDC and client fees) have been evaluated by matching firms receiving consulting advice on manufacturing productivity from MEP-funded centers with similar firms not receiving such consulting services. This evaluation suggests that MEP-funded services have significant effects in increasing the productivity of assisted firms (Jarmin 1999).

*Simulation of effects of financial assistance based on previous studies of how tax cuts affect business location decisions.* Previous research suggests that an $x$% cut in the overall state and local tax burden on business, with public services to business kept constant, will increase business activity—the number of new plant openings, or, in the long run, private employment—by about ¼th of $x$ percent.[11] This previous literature would be applicable to economic development programs that provide tax breaks or other financial assistance without a strong effort to select firms for which the assistance would tip the location decisions. For example, property tax abatements are generally not particularly selective in targeting firms. Based on table 14.2, Michigan's normal assistance provided to a firm opening a new plant reduces state and local business taxes by 28%, which would imply that the number of new plants choosing the state would increase by 7%, and total manufacturing activity would increase in the long run by 7%.[12] This assumes that Michigan's economic development programs have not led to cuts in public services valued by businesses, such as roads; cuts in such services have been estimated to reduce state business activity (Bartik 1991; Fisher 1997).

*Simulated economic impact analysis for business location decisions.* Even without determining how much a particular business location decision is affected by a program, useful information can be obtained by simulations that analyze the impact of that business location decision on the state's economy. Michigan's MEGA tax credit program does a sophisticated economic and fiscal analysis of the impact of each MEGA project. This analysis uses a regional econometric model (the REMI model of Treyz 1993) to estimate the effects of each project on state income and state revenues.

Despite its sophistication, the MEGA analysis omits a full fiscal analysis that would consider impacts of MEGA projects on local revenues. Neither does it estimate required spending on state and local public services to keep service quality constant as population increases in response to the project. The MEGA analysis also omits estimates of how the employment benefits of the project—the income generated minus the value of time of the additional workers—will vary with whether the project is located in a high-unemployment area or with whether the project

hires disadvantaged Michigan residents, other Michigan residents, or in-migrants. More complete impact models, such as those used by the states of New York and Maryland, are discussed in the study by Poole et al. (1999).

These omissions from the MEGA impact model are implicit in the MEGA authorizing legislation, which focuses on fiscal benefits to the exclusion of employment benefits, and on state fiscal benefits to the exclusion of local fiscal effects.

*Program-specific measures to see if the program deals with its targeted "gap" in private markets.* Some economic development services aim at filling a particular gap in services provided by private markets to business. Monitoring data may provide evidence on whether the program is helping fill that gap. For example, Michigan's Capital Access Program (terminated as of September 2002) provided a subsidy for private banks to provide loans to small businesses that were higher risk than normally would be bankable. Internal monitoring reports led program managers to a reasonable conclusion that the program was hitting its intended target:

> There is strong evidence from a variety of sources that the Capital Access Program is causing banks to make loans that they otherwise would not make. The most compelling evidence comes from the . . . loss rate under the program. The loss rate under the program has been running probably at least 7 times . . . a normal bank loss rate. If banks, on average, when using the program take 7 or more times the risk they normally take without the program, it is a reasonable conclusion that the program is making a difference in causing them to take this added risk. (Rohde, Cash, and Ammarman 1990)

A sure sign of failure in a program that is seeking to encourage higher-risk investments than are normally made in the market is if the program runs a zero loss rate, which makes it likely that the program is substituting for private financing.

This evidence by itself does not show that a program such as the Capital Access Program has benefits that exceed costs. This analysis suggests that the program increases certain types of lending. A fuller analysis would have to look at the employment and fiscal benefits of that additional lending, and see if these benefits justify the program's costs.

*Surveys.* Another method for evaluating economic development programs is customer satisfaction surveys. Such surveys are not useful for economic development incentives. It is difficult to imagine why anyone would not be "satisfied" with being provided a cash incentive, and the relevant question, whether the incentive was decisive, invites less than candid answers. However, surveys of customer satisfaction with business retention services are more useful. For services to businesses, the business respondents have a greater incentive to be candid, as there is no real reason to claim that a service was useful if the business found it useless.

The MEDC already regularly arranges for customer satisfaction surveys for businesses receiving various types of business retention services. Such surveys suggest very high satisfaction with MEDC's services, typically over 97%. The MEDC also does customer satisfaction surveys with a broader array of stakeholders, including local development organizations, educators, the media, state agencies, and so on. These surveys also suggest very high satisfaction rates with the MEDC. For example, in a survey done in November 2001 by Public Sector Consultants, 77% of surveyed stakeholders having experience with MEDC reported that they were very satisfied, and 16% reported that they were somewhat satisfied. As the report comments, these satisfaction ratings are extremely high: "In general, customer satisfaction surveys of government and member organizations yield 50–60% satisfaction ratings. Just once in PSC's experience of administering customer satisfaction surveys have we encountered satisfaction numbers in the high nineties." However, as PSC's report noted, these survey results reflect a population of stakeholders that MEDC selected, some of whom may have received funding from MEDC.

For accountability purposes, it would be useful to periodically have such customer satisfaction measures independently done by an outside agency that would use some of the same questions over time and independently select the surveyed sample. Although the current surveys are adequate for internal purposes, outside replication of these results every few years would be more useful for holding MEDC accountable.

## Conclusion

Based on these observations on Michigan's economic development efforts, are there policy changes that ought to be considered in seeking future program improvements?

- Michigan needs more continuity in its economic development efforts. It is hard to see much substantive purpose in the repeated changes of program and organizational forms with each new gubernatorial administration. Obviously there is a political purpose to be served in relabeling the economic development programs so that the new governor can claim credit, but this process has been unduly disruptive in the past to Michigan's economic development programs. Governors should be able to assert their legitimate interest in refocusing the state's economic development programs on the new administration's priorities by the mix of appointments they make to the board of the MEDC and to key staff positions, and by the appropriations that the state provides to the MEDC. Under any governor, most of the economic development programs of the state will continue, providing the same services, and it does not make sense to frequently reorganize such programs in different agencies and under different names. The MEDC must meet both a substantive challenge and a political challenge. The substantive challenge for the MEDC is how to be appropriately responsive to the policy directions of whatever governor is in power, while continuing to deliver core economic development services. The political challenge is to make sure that any governor can take political credit for the economic development successes of the state without having to create a new economic development agency.

- The state's analysis of project impacts, already more sophisticated than that of most states, should be made even more sophisticated to include an analysis of the public expenditure effects of projects and the employment benefits resulting from the labor market effects of projects. These project impacts should help to guide project selection and to modify program design, with the goal of better targeting assistance to maximize its impact.

- The state's economic development efforts should be subjected to periodic outside reviews to increase accountability. These outside reviews should include surveys and focus groups with the various stakeholders of the MEDC, including client businesses as well as local economic development organizations.

Outside reviewers should be free to randomly select respondents from categories agreed upon with the MEDC. Some survey questions should remain the same over time to allow these outside reviews to better track trends in MEDC performance.

Fundamentally, we are suggesting that the state's efforts in economic development need to become more stable and sophisticated. With a more stable structure, more sophisticated analysis of projects, and outside reviews, we are confident that the state's economic development efforts will continue to improve relative to those of other states, and will result in more effective economic development to benefit state residents.

■

## REFERENCES

Bartik, Timothy J. 1990. The market failure approach to regional economic development policy. *Economic Development Quarterly* 4(4): 361–70.

———. 1991. *Who benefits from state and local economic development policies?* Kalamazoo, Mich.: W. E. Upjohn Institute for Employment Research.

———. 1992. The effects of state and local taxes on economic development: A review of recent research. *Economic Development Quarterly* 6(1): 102–10.

———. 1993. Who benefits from local job growth, migrants or the original residents? *Regional Studies* 27: 297–311.

———. 1994. Jobs, productivity, and local economic development: What implications does economic research have for the role of government? *National Tax Journal* 47(4): 847–61.

Bennett, Jeff. 2001. Michigan to polish a high-tech image: Ads aim to dispel rust belt association. *Detroit Free Press,* 1 November, C2.

Benus, J. M., M. Wood, and N. Grover. 1994. A comparative analysis of the Washington and Massachusetts UI self-employment demonstrations. Unpublished report prepared for the U.S. Department of Labor, Employment and Training Administration, Unemployment Insurance Service under Contract No. 99-8-0803-98-047-01.

Bole, Kristen. 2002. Smokin': Tobacco windfall spurs biotech investment. Retrieved from Bio-itworld .com website; available at *http://www.bio-itworld .com/archive/030702/ smoking.html.*

Buchholz, David E. n.d. General Motors. Case study downloaded from the Business Incentive Reform Clearinghouse website at *http://www.cfed.org.*

Citizens Research Council of Michigan. 2001. *Survey of economic development programs in Michigan.* Report 334, Citizens Research Council of Michigan, Livonia, Michigan.

Corporation for Enterprise Development. 1992. *The 1992 Third Wave Development awards.* Washington, D.C.: Corporation for Enterprise Development.

Courant, Paul S. 1994. How would you know a good economic development policy if you tripped over one? Hint: don't just count jobs. National Tax Journal 47(4): 863–81.

Eisinger, Peter. 1988. *The rise of the entrepreneurial state: State and local economic development policy in the United States.* Madison: University of Wisconsin Press.

———. 1990. Do the American states do industrial policy? *British Journal of Political Science* 20: 509–35.

Fisher, Ronald C. 1997. The effects of state and local public services on economic development. *New England Economic Review* (March/April): 53–67.

Fisher, Peter S., and Alan H. Peters. 1998. *Industrial incentives: Competition among American states and cities.* Kalamazoo, Mich.: W. E. Upjohn Institute for Employment Research.

Greenbaum, Robert. 1998. An evaluation of state enterprise zone policies: Measuring the impact on business decisions and housing market outcomes. Ph.D. diss., Carnegie Mellon University.

Holzer, H. J., R. N. Block, M. Cheatham, and J. H. Knott. 1993. Are training subsidies for firms effective? The Michigan experience. *Industrial and Labor Relations Review* 46: 625–36.

Hudson Institute. 1985. *Michigan beyond 2000.* Indianapolis, Ind.: Hudson Institute.

Jackson, John E. 1988. Michigan. In *The new economic role of American states; strategies in a competitive world economy,* edited by R. Scott Fosler. New York: Oxford University Press.

Jarmin, Ronald S. 1999. Evaluating the impact of manufacturing extension on productivity growth. *Journal of Policy Analysis and* Management 18(1): 99–119.

Michigan Economic Development Corporation. 1999a. *State smart: Michigan.* Lansing, Mich.: Michigan Economic Development Corp.

———. 1999b. *Strategic directions for Michigan's future: The next decade.* Lansing, Mich.: Michigan Economic Development Corp.

———. 2001a. *The evolution of economic development in Michigan.* Lansing, Mich.: Michigan Economic Development Corp.

———. 2001b. *LinkMichigan initiative: Plan offers recommendations on developing Michigan into a national telecommunications infrastructure leader.* Lansing, Mich.: Michigan Economic Development Corp.

———. 2002a. *Benchmarks for the next Michigan: Measuring our competitiveness.* Lansing, Mich.: Michigan Economic Development Corp.

———. 2002b. *Workforce and career development: Building upon key Michigan strengths.* Lansing, Mich.: Michigan Economic Development Corp.

Michigan Office of the Auditor General. 1993. *Performance audit of the Michigan strategic fund. October 1, 1988 through October 31, 1992.* Lansing, Mich.: Michigan Office of the Auditor General.

Osborne, David. 1988. *Laboratories of democracy.* Boston, Mass.: Harvard Business School Press.

Papke, Leslie. 1993. What do we know about enterprise zones? In *Tax Policy and the Economy,* edited by James Poterba. Cambridge, Mass.: National Bureau of Economic Research and MIT Press.

———. 1994. Tax policy and urban development: Evidence from the Indiana enterprise zone program. *Journal of Public Economics* 54(1): 37–49.

Peters, Alan H., and Peter S. Fisher. 2002. *State enterprise zone programs: Have they worked?* Kalamazoo, Mich.: W. E. Upjohn Institute for Employment Research.

Poole, Kenneth E., George A. Erickcek, Donald T. Iannone, Nancy McCrea, and Pofen Salem. 1999. *Evaluating business development incentives.* National Association of State Development Agencies; the W. E. Upjohn Institute for Employment Research; and the Urban Center, Cleveland State University: U.S. Department of Commerce, Economic Development Administration.

Public Sector Consultants, Inc. 2001. *Perceptions of the Michigan economic development corporation: Results from the 2001 stakeholder study.* Lansing, Mich.: Public Sector Consultants, Inc.

Rohde, S., J. Cash, and K. Ammarman. 1990. Study of the Capital Access program. Unpublished working paper, Michigan Strategic Fund, Lansing, Michigan.

Sands, Gary, and Paul Zalmezak. 2000. *Michigan industrial property tax abatements: A summary of activity under Public Act 198 of 1974, 1985–98.* Urban Planning Program, College of Urban, Labor and Metropolitan Affairs, Wayne State University, Detroit.

Simons, Robert. 1998. *Turning brownfields into greenbacks.* Washington, D.C.: Urban Land Institute.

Southeast Michigan Council of Governments. 1982. *Base report on economic development.* Detroit, Mich.: Southeast Michigan Council of Governments.

Starner, Ron. 2001. North Carolina claims no. 1 business climate ranking. *Site Selection Magazine* (November): 7–14.

Task Force for a Long-Term Economic Strategy for Michigan. 1984. *The path to prosperity.* Lansing, Mich.: Task Force.

Thompson, Wilbur R. 1982. Industrial location: Causes and consequences. In *Michigan's fiscal and economic structure,* edited by Harvey E. Brazer and Deborah S. Laren. Ann Arbor: University of Michigan Press.

Treyz, George. 1993. *Regional economic modeling: A systematic approach to economic forecasting and policy analysis.* Boston: Kluwer Academic.

U.S. Bureau of the Census. 2000. *1997 economic census.* Washington, D.C.: U.S. Census Bureau.

Wasylenko, Michael. 1997. Taxation and economic development: The state of the economic literature. *New England Economic Review* (March/April): 37–52.

Wolkoff, Michael. 1982. Tax abatement as an incentive to industrial location. In *Michigan's fiscal and economic structure,* edited by Harvey E. Grazer and Deborah S. Laren. Ann Arbor: University of Michigan Press.

## NOTES

The authors would like to thank Doug Rothwell, Sabrina Keeley, Dana Lee Cole, Mark Morante, John Czarnecki, Doug Harris, Jeff Horner, and the editors for their helpful comments and suggestions. We also appreciate information from interviews with Kathy Black, Jim Donaldson, Harry Whalen, Michael Finney, Cindy Douglas, Robert Filka, Jeffrey Kaczmarek, Mark Morante, Penny Stump, Birgit Klohs, James Hettinger, Mike Brady, and other state and local officials who wished to remain anonymous. We appreciate the assistance of Mike Brady, Heather Lockhart, Leah Ballenger, Sabrina Keeley, and Doug Rothwell in helping facilitate this study. None of these individuals is responsible for the conclusions of this study or for any errors.

1. This history relies in part on Michigan Economic Development Corporation (2001a).

2. In 1994 the funding source was switched from resource leases to gaming revenues from tribal casinos, via 8% of revenues from electronic slot machines. The original compacts between the tribes and the state required this 8% payment only if the Indian tribes had exclusive rights to have casinos in Michigan, which meant that the tribes were not required to make payments after Detroit

casinos were approved by Michigan voters in 1996. However, new compacts including an 8% payment were agreed upon by the state with some tribes. Today, Michigan's economic development programs are funded by a combination of state general funds, the tobacco settlement, federal community development block grants, tribal casinos, and repayments on previous loans and investments.

3. Aggregate figures suggest that the percentage of major plant openings or expansions receiving an abatement must be high. In 1997, according to U.S. Census of Manufacturers data, manufacturing firms in Michigan made capital investments of $9.2 billion. According to a Wayne State University study, total investment receiving abatements was slightly over $5 billion in that year. Capital investment includes many small projects that would be unlikely to apply for an abatement. It seems likely that most plant openings and expansions that create more than, say, fifty jobs probably receive an abatement (U.S. Bureau of the Census 2000; Sands and Zalmezak 2000).

4. As the figure shows, the tax expenditure on property tax abatements dipped in the early 1990s. This is due to the 1994 adoption of the Proposal A property tax reform pushed by Governor Engler.

5. One could argue that this increased expenditure is "voluntary," in that state or local governments could choose to maintain the same real expenditure and accept a deterioration in public services as real expenditure per capita declines. However, this deterioration in services is also a social cost that should be considered.

6. An appendix A to this chapter, available from the authors or at *www.upjohn.org*, presents the basis for this calculation.

7. The exact usage of these funds for economic development versus housing-related community development is left to state discretion, and Michigan has chosen to focus these funds on infrastructure related to economic development.

8. An appendix B to this chapter, available from the authors or at *www.upjohn.org*, presents the basis for this calculation.

9. If the state awards $x in credits each year, payable over t years, and all promised credits are paid, after t years the gross costs will be $x annually. In 2001, MEGA promised credits with a cumulative value over the life of the credits of $256 million. Long-run annual gross costs will be less than this amount because some promised credits will not be paid, or if 2001 proves to be an unusually high year for MEGA.

10. For more discussion along these lines, see Bartik (1990, 1994), and Courant (1994).

11. This figure splits the difference between Bartik's (1991, 1992) summary of the literature that the elasticity of business activity with respect to state and local taxes is −0.3, and Wasylenko's (1997) summary that concludes the elasticity is −0.2. The significant effect of state and local taxes does not contradict the previous conventional wisdom (e.g., Thompson 1982 and Wolkoff 1982) that taxes are not as important as other location factors.

12. A similar analysis applied to the 36% tax cut provided by MEGA suggests that MEGA will increase new plant locations by 9%. However, MEGA is highly selective in targeting firms, so we would expect MEGA to affect more than 9% of the assisted firms.

# 15

# K–12 Education in Michigan

*Julie Berry Cullen and Susanna Loeb*

## 1. Introduction

Nationally, K–12 education has been undergoing dramatic changes aimed to improve equity, adequacy, and efficiency. The school finance equalization movement has increased the centralization of school finance and reduced variation in revenues across local school districts. Michigan's Proposal A stemmed from concerns about inequities in property tax burdens and school spending across districts, and fits within the latter part of this broad movement. Two other leading movements have increased school choice and increased reliance on accountability systems. Michigan has been one of the innovators in fostering more flexible school choice, and has recently adopted reward systems based on student academic performance. This chapter describes recent reforms in the nation and in Michigan, as well as future challenges.

We begin by presenting a broad view of the structure and state of K–12 education in Michigan. There are 524 K–12 and 31 less-comprehensive school districts in Michigan. The charter school movement has added another 210 districts as of fall 2002. As in other states, in Michigan there are two more aggregate layers of government institutions that shape the provision of education. At the state level, the Michigan Department of Education (DOE) and State Board of Education provide leadership and supervision. These offices inform the legislature about schools' financial needs, approve the certification of teachers, and formulate policies to guide as well as to respond to legislative mandates. In addition, 57 intermediate school districts (ISDs) serve as a liaison between the DOE and their constituent school districts. These regional education centers are established as separate taxing units and are financed from a combination of federal, state, and local sources. They provide a range of services according to local needs, including administrative and technology support, community outreach, and instructional services such as special and vocational education.

Michigan is currently the state with the eighth-largest school enrollment. In keeping with the national trend, enrollment in Michigan decreased through the 1970s and 1980s and increased in the 1990s.[1] Between 1990 and 1999, Michigan's average daily attendance increased by 8.5%. This places it in the middle nationally (thirty-fourth) in terms of the rate of growth.[2] Despite the sizeable shifts in aggregate numbers of students, the race/ethnicity composition of Michigan's K–12 students has been relatively stable over the last fifteen years. In 1986, 76.4% of students were white, 19.8% black, 1.8% Hispanic, and 1.2% Asian

FIGURE 15.1

## Current Expenditures Per Pupil

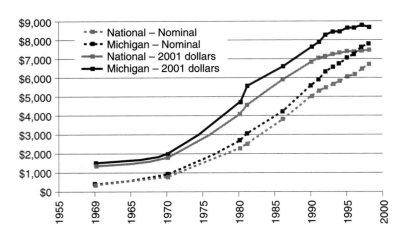

SOURCE: *Digest of Education Statistics 2000*, Table 168. Price Index from the Bureau of Economic Analysis, National Income and Product Accounts Table for local and state governments.

TABLE 15.1

## Rankings of Michigan K–12 Expenditures Relative to Other States, 1999

|  | Rank (per Pupil) | % of Total Expenditures (Operating + Capital) |
|---|---|---|
| Instructional expenditures | | |
| Salaries | 8 | 33.3 |
| Benefits | 12 | 10.7 |
| Purchased services | 10 | 1.2 |
| Supplies | 16 | 2.1 |
| Tuition and other | 21 | 0.3 |
| TOTAL INSTRUCTIONAL EXPENDITURES | 14 | 47.6 |
| Support services expenditures | | |
| Student support[a] | 4 | 5.3 |
| Instructional staff[b] | 9 | 3.7 |
| General administration | 15 | 2.0 |
| School administration | 7 | 5.2 |
| Operations and maintenance | 6 | 8.7 |
| Transportation | 16 | 3.3 |
| Other support services | 6 | 3.8 |
| TOTAL SUPPORT SERVICES EXPENDITURES | 4 | 31.9 |
| Food service | 43 | 2.4 |
| TOTAL K–12 OPERATIONS | 9 | 81.9 |
| Current expenditures—other[c] | 6 | 2.1 |
| Non-current expenditures | | |
| Capital outlay[d] | 3 | 13.0 |
| Interest on debt | 7 | 3.0 |
| TOTAL NON-CURRENT EXPENDITURES | — | 16.0 |

SOURCE: Data are from Tables 67, 162 & 166 of the *Digest of Education Statistics, 2001*.
(a) Student support services include expenditures for health, attendance, and speech pathology services.
(b) Instructional staff includes expenditures for curriculum development, staff training, libraries, and media and computer centers.
(c) Other current expenditures include expenditures for adult education, community colleges, private school programs funded by local and state education agencies, and community services.
(d) Capital outlay includes expenditures for property and for building and alterations.

or Pacific Islander. In 1999, these percentages were 74.4%, 19.6%, 3.2% and 1.7%, respectively.[3]

In 1999, Michigan's current expenditures per pupil were $8,142, 16.1% more than the national average.[4] Figure 15.1 plots these expenditures over time, along with average national expenditures. Since the 1960s, Michigan has spent more on average than has the nation as a whole, and this gap has increased over the past decade. While Michigan ranked twenty-sixth in expenditures per pupil in 1990, the state ranked ninth by 1999.

Table 15.1 gives Michigan's 1999 ranking for expenditures by area. Note that the state's rank in instructional expenditures was somewhat lower than its overall rank (fourteenth vs. ninth), though still high relative to other states ($4,733 compared to a national average of $4,324). Michigan has consistently dedicated a smaller proportion of current expenditures to instruction than most other states. Figure 15.2 shows that while expenditures on instruction rose during the past decade, the proportion of expenditures going to instruction did not. The 48% share in 1999 places Michigan forty-eighth among states. Conversely, expenditures on support services have been particularly high in Michigan (ranking fourth in 1999).

Michigan does not hire as many teachers per pupil as many other states do. The pupil-teacher ratio in Michigan declined from 19.7 in 1990 to 18 in 1999 (compared to a fall in the national average from 17.2 to 16.1), but was still the ninth-highest in the nation.[5] However, teacher salaries have historically been high, potentially compensating for large class sizes. Average salaries have ranged from between 13 to 23% above the national average since 1970.[6] According to our estimates from the 1999–2000 Schools and Staffing Surveys, the average starting salary for teachers with a Bachelor's degree across all states was $25,888 (median of $25,321). In Michigan the average base salary was $28,999 (median of $28,900). Michigan also has particularly high returns to experience, with an average premium to ten years of experience of 52.8%, compared to a national average of 31.1%. The return to additional education (a 9.4% premium for a Master's degree and no experience) is more similar to that of the nation as a whole. Starting salaries vary more across districts in Michigan than in other states, with a coefficient of variation of 0.092, compared to 0.079 nationally.[7]

A possible explanation for the high base salaries and returns to experience is the strength of the teacher labor union. Nearly all school districts in Michigan are unionized. The Michigan

Education Association (MEA) is the largest employee union in Michigan, and the third-largest education association in the United States.[8] The high variability in starting salaries is likely partly due to the traditional reliance on local funding and to disparities in the cost of living across rural and urban areas (rural districts pay starting salaries that average 10% below those of other districts in the state).

Relative academic achievement for Michigan students appears to have improved (though unsteadily) in recent years. Across the nation, thirty-seven states participated in the National Assessment of Educational Progress (NAEP) for eighth-grade mathematics in 1992, 1996, and 2000. Michigan ranked eighteenth in 1992, ninth in 1996, and thirteenth in 2000.[9] Between 1992 and 2000, Michigan made the sixth-largest gain among states in points on this exam. Figure 15.3 shows the percentage of fourth- and eighth-graders scoring at the basic level or above in math in 2000 for each of the participating states. Michigan is at about the same place in the distribution at both grade levels.

Figure 15.4 illustrates the performance of Michigan students on the fourth-grade mathematics NAEP separately by race/ethnicity. Eighth-grade scores show a very similar distribution. The numbers are expressed in standard deviations from the overall national mean. White students in Michigan scored higher on average than white students nationally, while black and Hispanic students in Michigan scored slightly below students of the same race and ethnicity nationally. Figures 15.5A and 15.5B plot the fourth- and eighth-grade gains in the math NAEP relative to the national average gains. The NAEP gains were slightly higher in Michigan than nationally for black students in both grades, and, for Hispanic students, in eighth grade.[10] White students in Michigan gained less than the average student nationally, but more than the average white student nationally. Overall gains were not as high in Michigan as in two surrounding states, Indiana and Ohio.[11]

In the next sections, we will describe the policy changes that have played a role in the recent evolution of K–12 education in Michigan and consider to what extent these reforms have had both desired and undesired effects. We address each of the key areas of reform in turn, starting with school finance in the next section. School choice and accountability systems are addressed in sections 3 and 4. Section 5 provides a brief concluding discussion.

**FIGURE 15.2**

**Total Expenditures and Instructional Expenditures Per Pupil in Michigan 1990–98 (2001 dollars)**

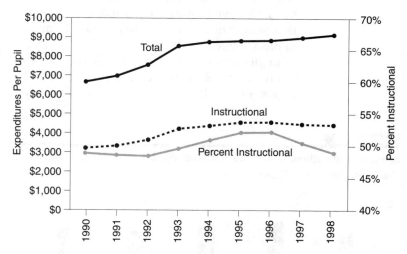

SOURCE: *Digest of Education Statistics 2000,* Table 168. Price Index from the Bureau of Economic Analysis, National Income and Product Accounts Table for local and state governments.

**FIGURE 15.3**

**Percentage of Students Scoring at the Basic Level or Above on the NAEP Mathematics Exam, 2000**

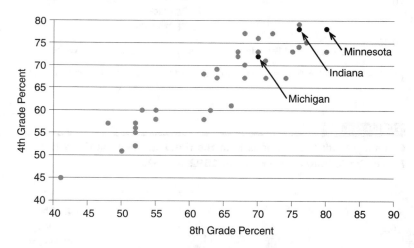

SOURCE: National Center For Education Statistics (*http://nces.ed.gov/nationsreportcard/naepdata*).

## 2. School Finance Reform

Following the elimination of local property taxes in August 1993, Governor Engler proposed two key school reforms in a message to a joint session of the Michigan legislature in October 1993 (Knittel and Haas 1998). He called for improving funding equity, as well as expanding schooling options. Legislation passed on 24 December 1993 enacted a new foundation system for distributing revenues to schools. In March 1994, voters chose to finance this new program with an increase in sales taxes (rather than an increase in income taxes) through Proposal A. For more detail on the tax changes of this reform see chapters 25 and 27 in this volume.

In this section, we describe the finance systems in Michigan before and after the reform and the impact of the change on the pattern of expendi-

tures across districts. To set the stage for this, we first review school funding mechanisms in general and the changes that have occurred in the finance of schools across the nation.

## 2.1 Background on School Finance Equalization

In the United States, the financing of public schools has traditionally been the responsibility of local jurisdictions. Under a system of pure local provision, parents are, in theory, free to "shop" across localities, choosing both the quality of public schooling and the amount paid for it through property taxes. The great advantage to this shopping model is the possibility for parents to find a community that closely matches their tastes for education (Tiebout 1956). Families that value education more will cluster in communities that spend more on schools, while families that value parks or private spending more will cluster in communities with those priorities. The argument for local funding for schools is very much like the argument for free markets in general. Families will purchase what they value and thus only goods that are valued will be produced. In addition, since families are choosing expenditure levels, they may be more likely to monitor how those dollars are spent.

However, a system of pure local funding of schools has disadvantages as well. Such a system inevitably leads to self-segregation by income and large inequities in the level of service provision across communities (Ladd and Yinger 1994). In many states, the resulting system has been deemed unconstitutional, for violating state constitutional equal protection clauses.[12] Starting in 1971 with the *Serrano v. Priest* decision in California, state courts have called for greater state involvement to provide more equal access to education across communities.

Determining whether an educational system is equal or equitable is not straightforward. Generally the goal is to treat similar people in a similar way (horizontal equity) and to treat different people in a different but equitable way (vertical equity). All those with a similar ability to pay should pay the same amount for the same level of services, while it may be argued that those with a lesser ability to pay should pay less for that same level of service.

Since most local school districts finance education expenditures through property taxes, property wealth is the most commonly used measure

---

**FIGURE 15.4**

**Standard Deviations above the National Mean for the NAEP Fourth-Grade Mathematics Exam, 2000**

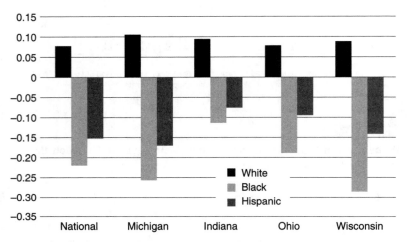

SOURCE: National Center For Education Statistics (*http://nces.ed.gov/nationsreportcard/naepdata*).

---

**FIGURE 15.5A**

**Gains in Standard Deviations from the National Mean on the NAEP Fourth-Grade Mathematics Exam, 1992 to 2000**

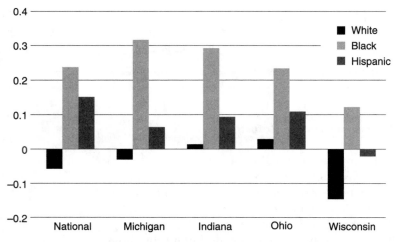

SOURCE: National Center For Education Statistics (*http://nces.ed.gov/nationsreportcard/naepdata*).

of ability to pay. One problem with this measure is that home value is not always highly correlated with income. The elderly, for example, tend to have a disproportionate share of wealth in housing. The link between residents' means and tax base wealth can also be weak at the district level due to nonresidential property. A revealing fact that has only recently come to light is that the strong negative relationship between property wealth and per pupil spending that led to California's reform coexisted with a much more even distribution with respect to income (Sonstelie, Brunner, and Ardon 2000).

A separate problem arises due to capitalization, which means that property values reflect community characteristics. Consider the case of two identical homes in neighborhoods that are identical, except that one is in a district with a greater per pupil tax base. Families will be willing to pay less for the house in the low-wealth district, anticipating that property taxes will be higher. The natural result is that the lower-cost house has a higher tax rate, though this is not a sign of inequitable treatment, since the homeowner has already been compensated through a lower purchase price. Few states have addressed these problems by incorporating alternative measures of ability to pay, such as per capita income, when making inferences about equity.[13]

A twin issue to fiscal capacity is resource need. School districts may serve student populations with very different characteristics, which implies that different levels of resources are needed in order to achieve the same outcomes. In addition, resource costs may differ. For example, districts in labor markets that provide high wages to college graduates may need to pay more to attract teachers of any given quality. One way to assess the impact of school characteristics is to attempt to measure how much it costs to achieve any given level of achievement in varying schooling environments. While there is an extensive literature that attempts to do just this, there is little consensus (Duncombe and Yinger 1999). The difficulty arises because it is unclear whether differences in outcomes between districts with the same level of expenditures result from differences in costs, in goals, or in efficiency. Any reliable measure of underlying need should be based on characteristics that are not directly within the control of the school district.

There are two broad mechanisms that states use to target resources to communities with lower fiscal capacity and higher need: foundation plans

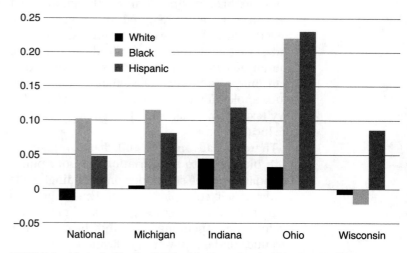

**FIGURE 15.5B**

**Gains in Standard Deviations from the National Mean on the NAEP Eighth-Grade Mathematics Exam, 1992 to 2000**

SOURCE: National Center For Education Statistics (*http://nces.ed.gov/nationsreportcard/naepdata*).

and power-equalization (or guaranteed-tax-base or percentage-equalization) plans.[14] States that implement a foundation plan choose a foundation level per pupil and a required local property tax rate. Local districts receive the difference between what is raised with the required levy and the total foundation amount.

Foundation plans differ in two important aspects. First, districts may or may not be allowed to levy additional local taxes to supplement the foundation level. Second, districts that raise more than the foundation level with the required local property tax rate may or may not be required to return the excess revenue to the state, though recapture is not common. Need is addressed either through district-specific adjustments to the basic foundation amount or through categorical aid programs. In practice, these adjustments take into account a variety of district characteristics, including the share of students served in more costly programs such as special education (most often through pupil weighting), the concentration of low-income students, district size, and relative teacher salaries.

Power-equalization plans do not set a floor on district expenditures. Instead, they set a guaranteed tax base per pupil (which may vary with district characteristics) and allow districts to choose the local tax rate. For districts with tax bases below the guaranteed level, the state supplements local revenues so that the district receives what it would have raised with the same tax rate applied to the guaranteed level. Recapture is an issue with power-equalization plans, as it was with foundation plans, though also uncommon. If a district has a tax base per pupil above the guaranteed base, then it may be required to give back to the state the difference between the revenues it raises and those that it would have raised had it had the guaranteed tax base level. Power-equalization plans may also be capped, so that the state guarantee applies up to a given tax rate. If permitted to levy taxes above that rate, districts rely solely on the local tax base.

There are advantages and disadvantages to both plans and to the variations of both plans. Foundation plans set a floor on spending, while power-equalization plans do not. Thus, schools in districts in which the average demand of the voters for school spending is low may have very low revenues under a power-equalization plan. Since local revenue is matched by state revenue for low-wealth districts under power equalization, the implicit price of an additional dollar of per pupil spending is less than one. Though in theory this price effect could lead low-wealth districts to spend as much as higher-wealth districts, in practice the response of education demand to price is not great enough to break the link between wealth and expenditures (Reschovsky 1994).

Foundation plans that do not allow districts to supplement are more equalizing (and, if they require recapture, perfectly equalizing). However, they may force high-demand districts far from their preferred level of spending. As a result, residents may search for ways around the constraints, such as by attending private schools (Downes and Schoeman 1998) or making private donations to public schools (Brunner and Sonstelie 1997). Foundation plans that allow local supplementation do not constrain the high-demand districts. However, because these districts often find it less costly to raise funds independently than through state revenue sharing, residents have little reason to support a high foundation grant level if they can raise unlimited amounts over this level locally. Their lack of support may depress the foundation level and reduce the amount of equalization (Loeb 2001).

The appropriate design of the funding system depends upon the goals of the policy. The early legislative focus around the country was on equalizing spending across districts and eliminating the relationship between spending and district property wealth. However, due to cost differences across districts, equalizing spending does not necessarily equalize effective resources. In addition, the high burden imposed on high-wealth districts can have negative general equilibrium effects. In a case like California's, where property taxes and spending were equalized across localities through Proposition 13, the unexpected consequence was an overall decline in the level of resources dedicated to schools. Partially as a result, the focus of more recent reforms has shifted from equity to adequacy.[15] The finance system that meets the goals of equity may not meet the goals of providing sufficient funding to attain minimum academic standards.

Evans, Murray, and Schwab (2001) summarize a number of studies assessing the impact of court-mandated school finance reform. They find that these reforms have reduced disparities in per-student expenditures within states by 16% to 38%. Most states used foundation plans to raise revenues of previously low-spending districts without leveling down expenditures in high-spending districts, though California is a notable exception. Evans, Murray, and Schwab (2001) also find that although 40% of the increase in state aid to poor districts went to local tax relief, per pupil expenditures in these districts did increase.[16] There is little evidence that links these changes to improved achievement.

## 2.2. Description of the Policy Change in Michigan

The implementation of Proposal A for the 1994–95 school year marked a radical change in the financing of public schools in Michigan. The system, previously relying largely on local revenue, became highly centralized at the state level. Local property taxes were sharply reduced and spending per pupil was sharply increased in previously low-spending districts, while these items remained approximately the same in other districts.

Prior to the reform, Michigan relied on a power-equalization program.[17] The state permitted full local discretion in assessing property tax millage rates, and then supplemented the revenue raised by low-wealth districts. In 1994, the year prior to reform, the guaranteed tax base was $102,500 in state equalized valuation (SEV) per pupil. Districts with SEV of less than $102,500 were subsidized such that each mill levied would raise $102.50 per pupil. In addition, these districts received a foundation grant of $400 per pupil. Districts with greater SEV per pupil had this foundation grant and categorical aid phased out, but there was no recapture beyond this. The number of districts receiving state aid under this system fell throughout the 1980s and into the 1990s (Fisher and Wassmer 1995). In 1993–94, over 39% of districts (with nearly 42% of all students) were above the minimum tax base. As a result of the weakness of the power-equalization program, district revenues varied greatly. The Onaway Area Community School District (with a millage rate of 22.66) received $3,404 per pupil from state and local sources for general expenditures, while the Bloomfield Hills District (with a millage rate of 24.41) received $10,295.

While there was dissatisfaction with the power-equalization plan, the driving force behind school finance reform was not the finance of schools but the property tax (see chapters 25 and 27 in this volume for more detail). After the surprising elimination of the property tax as a source of local revenue, voters were presented with two alternatives. Though the mix of revenues used to replace the local property tax differed between the two proposals, both plans utilized the same distribution scheme and would have centralized school finance decisions and increased spending per pupil in previously low-spending districts. Proposal A passed by a two-to-one margin, carrying all eighty-three counties in the state (Courant and Loeb 1997). As a result, the sales and use tax increased from 4% to 6%, while the property tax on homestead property dropped from an average of thirty-four mills to six mills (Addonizio, Kearney, and Prince 1995).[18] Local jurisdictions are also required to levy eighteen mills on nonhomestead property in order to participate in the school finance program.[19] Had the alternative plan been implemented, the sales and use tax would have remained at 4%, but the income tax would have increased to 6% instead of dropping to 4.4%. Local homestead property would have been taxed at twelve mills.[20]

The new Proposal A revenues are deposited to the state School Aid Fund (SAF) to finance district foundation programs. The two-percentage-point increase in the sales and use tax (residential energy utility is exempt), the fifty cent per pack increase in the cigarette tax, the new six-mill state education tax (on both homestead and nonhomestead property), the 0.75% real estate transfer tax, and 14.4% of individual income tax revenues (increased to 23.0% in 1995 and currently at 24.5%) are all directly deposited to this fund. The rapid growth in the SAF shows up in a dramatic increase in the state share of K–12 education

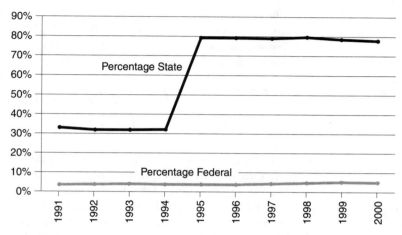

**FIGURE 15.6**

**Percentage of Total School Revenues from State and Federal Sources, Michigan, 1991–2000**

SOURCE: Michigan Department of Education Bulletin 1014 data files (*http://www.michigan.gov/mde/1,1607, 7-140-6525_6530_6605-21514-,00.html*).

spending (see figure 15.6). The state share of general funds was 32.1% in 1994 and jumped to 78.8% by 1995.

Proposal A improves equity primarily by creating a spending floor. It also limits district revenues based on 1994 spending levels. The "basic" foundation grant for 1995 was set at $5,000. The maximum or "hold-harmless" level of state-guaranteed foundation was set at $6,500. Funding for the lowest-spending districts, those spending less than $3,950 per pupil in 1994, increased to $4,200 (the minimum) for 1995.[21] Those districts spending between $3,950 and $6,500 in 1994 received foundation grants of $160 to $250 more than their prior year spending, with the increase based on a sliding scale and inversely related to prior spending. The fifty-two districts that spend more than $6,500 were allowed to levy additional local taxes called "hold-harmless" mills, to reach $160 above their actual 1994 level. The state appropriated additional funds for districts with only small fractional mills authorized, so that these did not actually have to be levied.

The basic foundation grant increases each year according to an index that equals the total statewide revenues per pupil for all taxes that are earmarked for the SAF, divided by the 1995 level. Until 2001, the minimum grant increased by twice the calculated amount. Districts above the minimum but below the basic grant level received an amount between the calculated amount and twice that amount, while those above the basic

**TABLE 15.2**

**Per Pupil Foundation Levels**

|  | 1995 | 1996 | 1997 | 1998 | 1999 | 2000 | 2001 | 2002 | 2003 |
|---|---|---|---|---|---|---|---|---|---|
| Minimum foundation | $4,200 | $4,506 | $4,816 | $5,124 | $5,170 | $5,700 | $6,000 | $6,300 | $6,700 |
| Basic foundation | $5,000 | $5,153 | $5,308 | $5,462 | $5,462 | $5,700 | $6,000 | $6,300 | $6,700 |
| Academies (maximum) | $5,500 | $5,653 | $5,808 | $5,962 | $5,962 | $6,200 | $6,500 | $6,800 | $7,000 |
| Hold harmless (maximum) | $6,500 | $6,653 | $6,808 | $6,962 | $6,962 | $7,200 | $7,500 | $7,800 | $8,000 |

SOURCE: Michigan Department of Education (*http://www.michigan.gov/documents/sw_fndamts_11719_7.pdf*).
NOTE: Hold harmless maximum is $1,500 above the basic foundation through fiscal year 2002, after which the difference becomes $1,300.

foundation received just the calculated increase. Since 2000, when the minimum passed $5,800, foundation amounts for all districts have increased by the same calculated amount. Now that the system is fully phased in, the nominal disparities in revenues between districts are built into the system, unless the legislature chooses to make additional ad hoc increases, as it did in 2002.[22] Over time, continued equalization will occur as the value of the nominal differences between districts decreases.

Table 15.2 gives the foundation levels for each year since the implementation of Proposal A. Note that charter schools have an alternative foundation level, discussed in more detail in the following. In 2002, the maximum foundation grant exceeded the minimum by 24%. In that year, there were fifty-two districts with foundation allowances over the maximum (ranging from $7,810 to $15,187), so that the spending in the top district was permitted to exceed spending in the bottom district by 2.5 times. In spite of the remaining disparity, annual funding increases have been below the inflation rate for the hold-harmless districts. Many of these districts, two-thirds of which are in Southeast Michigan, are being forced to cut back on services.[23] The equal dollar increases of this foundation system at the source of these spending pressures are also the source of the moderate ongoing equalization noted in the previous paragraph.

The system as a whole allows for very little local leeway. For the three years immediately following the policy change (1995–97), districts had the option of levying up to three additional mills for operating expenditure.[24] Starting in 1998, intermediate school districts (ISDs) could levy up to three enhancement mills that would be distributed on a per pupil basis across the member districts. An enhancement question may reach the ballot if requested by districts representing a majority of the pupils in the ISD and can be approved by a majority vote of the entire ISD. Only one ISD (Monroe) has approved additional mills through this revenue-sharing program. This policy has not successfully alleviated the constraints on districts that wish to spend more on education.[25]

In addition to providing general operating revenues to districts on a per pupil basis, Michigan uses categorical grants to adjust for cost differences across districts. Proposal A folded dozens of categorical programs into the foundation grant, including state contributions to teacher retirement. Categorical grants now constitute about 15% of state support for K–12 education, down from 44%. By far the largest of these programs is targeted for special education, with funding equivalent to nearly 10% of total foundation aid in 2000 ($777.6 million; Act No. 297, Public Acts of 2000).[26] The second-largest categorical grant ($269.1 million in 2000) was for "at risk" students, defined by income.[27] Other smaller categorical grants target adult education, bilingual education, gifted and talented education, vocational education, career preparation, technical assistance for school accreditation, and so on. There were no categorical programs to help districts with capital improvements.[28]

### 2.3 A Look at the Impact and Legacy of Proposal A

Revenues and expenditures across districts have equalized in the 1990s. The range in spending fell from $10,207 in the year preceding reform to $8,013 in the first year of reform, and to $6,685 by 2000, in 2001 constant dollars.[29] The coefficient of variation between districts dropped from 0.22 to 0.14 between 1991 and 2000 (figure 15.7).[30] In 1991, total revenue per pupil ranged from $4,680 at the fifth percentile to $8,620 at the ninety-fifth percentile (again in 2001 dollars). By 2000, the values for these same districts were $6,355 and $9,285, implying a fall in the ratio from 1.84 to 1.46. This is in keeping with Prince (1996), who finds that the reform increased equity, though disparities still remain.

On average per pupil revenues rose by 26% between 1991 and 2000 in real terms, though the gains varied across districts. The districts that experienced the least growth during the 1990s were those with the highest total revenues at the beginning of the decade, reflective of the structural growth limits of Proposal A on high-spending districts. The average real growth rate for districts in the top decile in 1991 was only 3.1%, versus 42.8% for districts in the bottom decile.[31] Table 15.3 shows the correlations between percentage gains and demographic characteristics of districts from the 1990 Census. Many of the expected relationships are evident. Districts with lower income per capita, higher poverty rates, and lower state equalized property values witnessed greater gains in total revenues. However, schools with high proportions of black and Hispanic students and urban schools did not see greater gains.

The average gains per pupil in urban districts were lower (18%, 20% weighted by pupils) relative to those of other districts (28%, 27% weighted by pupils), defining urban districts as those with at least half of the population "inside" urban areas. The fifteen urban districts that saw the least gains were Lamphere, Warren Woods, Waterford, Oak Park, Bloomfield Hills, Garden City, Livonia, Farmington, Center Line, South-

**FIGURE 15.7**

**Average Total Revenues Per Pupil and Coefficients of Variation (Standard Deviation/Mean) by Year, 1991–98 (2001 dollars)**

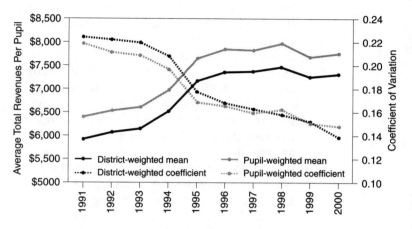

SOURCE: Michigan Department of Education Bulletin 1014 data files (*http://www.michigan.gov/mde/1,1607, 7-140-6525_6530_6605-21514-,00.html*).

field, Walled Lake, Pontiac, Melvindale Allen, Avondale, and Wyandotte, many of which are in the Detroit area and were among the higher-spending districts before Proposal A. However, most of the large inner-city districts did see substantial gains. Detroit's revenues rose by 31.8%; Flint's by 37.7%; and Lansing's by 31.9%. Grand Rapids saw an increase of only 16.6%. The large increases in total revenues for the first three inner-city districts led to an increase in their statewide percentile revenue ranks between 1991 and 2000: from top 19% to top 9% for Detroit; from top 18% to top 6% for Flint; from top 15% to

**TABLE 15.3**

**Correlations Between Revenue Gains in the 1990s and District Demographics**

| | Revenue Gain | % Revenue Increase | Income per Capita | Hmstd. SEV | Non-Hmstd. SEV | % Urban | % Poor | % Black or Hispanic |
|---|---|---|---|---|---|---|---|---|
| Revenue gain | 1.00 | | | | | | | |
| % revenue increase | 0.95* | 1.00 | | | | | | |
| Income per capita | −0.47* | −0.51* | 1.00 | | | | | |
| Homestead SEV | −0.44* | −0.48* | 0.75* | 1.00 | | | | |
| Non–Homestead SEV | −0.27* | −0.29* | 0.027 | 0.29* | 1.00 | | | |
| % urban | −0.24* | −0.34* | 0.46* | 0.17 | −0.014 | 1.00 | | |
| % poor | 0.49* | 0.47* | −0.66* | −0.53* | −0.016 | −0.14* | 1.00 | |
| % black or Hispanic | 0.12* | 0.013 | −0.11* | −0.25* | −0.009 | 0.39* | 0.50* | 1.00 |

SOURCE: Authors calculations based on National Center for Education Statistics 1990, School District Data Book data, and Michigan Department of Education Bulletin 1014 data files (*http://www.michigan.gov/mde/1,1607,7-140-6525_6530_6605-21514-,00.html*).

NOTE: * indicates correlation is significant at the 1% level.

top 5% for Lansing. Grand Rapids fell slightly in ranking, from the top 16% to the top 17%.

The shifts in revenues and tax burdens across districts may have affected property values. Using Proposal A as a natural experiment, Guilfoyle (1998) measures the extent to which differences in spending and tax burdens are reflected in higher home sale prices. He finds that a $1 tax differential leads to a $5.20 home value differential, and that a $100 increase in per pupil spending raises home values 0.4 to 0.6%. If a community were to raise spending through property taxation, the magnitudes of these effects would come close to canceling one another. This implies that districts with low spending and high property tax rates before the reform would have benefited from increased property values due to the combination of tax cuts and increased spending from Proposal A. Given that localities rely on local property taxes to finance nonoperating expenditures, this form of capitalization provides an additional equalizing mechanism.

In equalizing revenues across districts and increasing the revenues of the lowest-spending districts, school finance reform may also have translated into higher and more equal student achievement outcomes. Papke (2001) finds that student pass rates improved the most in those districts that had the greatest influx of new revenues. However, it is also true that high-performing districts did not have much room to improve under this crude measure of achievement (Cullen and Loeb 2002b).

Despite its apparent successes, Proposal A also created a number of tensions, most the result of the reduced flexibility at the local level. Prior to the reform, local districts had substantial control over the level of funding in their schools. Proposal A changed this, increasing funding in previously low-spending districts and constraining revenues in previously high-spending districts. Districts subject to spending ceilings are actively seeking to change the policy to allow for local supplementation. Legislation proposed in the summer of 2001 called for a revision to the law that would allow districts to raise up to one mill for school operating costs with voter approval. However, that bill did not pass, due to fears that it would undermine the initial reform and be a gateway to rising property taxes and inequities.[32] Voters do currently have access to equalized ISD millage, and it is likely that any further expansion of local leeway will also involve revenue sharing.

Constrained districts may find other ways

around the restrictions without policy change. One way would be to expand special programs to garner more categorical aid. There is evidence from California's Proposition 13, which imposed strict limits on noncategorical program expenditures while exempting programs such as vocational and special education, that increased disparity in spending on these programs partly offset the reduced dispersion in general education spending per pupil (Sonstelie, Brunner, and Ardon 2000). Private contributions to schools may also partially offset the equalization. In California, prior to school finance reform there were 6 local education foundations designed to channel voluntary contributions to local schools; by 1992, there were 537 of these foundations, raising nearly $100 million in private money. Most of these contributions came to districts whose revenues fell as a result of school finance reform (Evans, Murray, and Schwab 2001). Fisher and Gade (1991) note that Arizona school districts have an incentive to mask expenditures normally considered to be operating expenditures as capital expenditures to avoid constraints imposed only on operating expenditures. This same incentive exists for the high-spending districts in Michigan (although the state does have some specific statutory definitions of eligible capital expenditures), while the reverse incentive may hold for low-spending districts. Preliminary analysis of Michigan data suggests that low-demand districts that saw their operating revenues expand dramatically following Proposal A were less likely to raise additional revenues for capital (Cullen and Loeb 2002a).

Three other tensions are worth noting. First, the current school finance program does nothing to equalize capital expenditures. Given this, districts with higher ability to pay will have better facilities. There are clear signs that many districts do not have access to sufficient funds to maintain current buildings or build for growing student populations. Options for expanding the state role range from providing subsidized loans to establishing a parallel foundation system for capital to full state takeover of responsibility (Theobald 2002). The difficulty with involving the state comes in designing an equitable system that does not penalize districts for investments already made.

Second, the system may impair districts with falling enrollment (Theobald 2002). When school finance was controlled locally, revenues were not tied to per pupil enrollment, as they are now. If a district loses a student, revenues fall by the foundation amount while costs do not necessarily follow suit, since many are fixed, at least in the short run. Existing facilities need to be maintained and programs need to run while they are reorganized to fit a shrinking population.[33] Even year-to-year fluctuations can be difficult if fewer students than expected enroll, since teachers are hired on the basis of projected enrollment. The current program partially addresses these concerns by determining funding enrollment counts based partly on February of the prior year (20%) and partly on September of the current year (80%). Some districts have been pushing the legislature to use a wider window for averaging.

Finally, the shift from local to state control means that K–12 education has to compete with other state priorities for funding. The vast majority of state funding for education is earmarked for education and does not come out of the general fund; thus, there is little competition in the short run. However, in the long run legislation can alter allocations to education. The state's revenue surpluses, substantial at the time of reform, have been used up, and there have been concerns about reductions in other state budget areas because of the guaranteed funding commitments for K–12 (Harvey 1995). The concern could easily go the other way. While the sales tax allocation is fixed in the constitution, the other earmarked revenues have a statutory basis. The 1994 legislation automated the yearly change in the funding level based on the statewide revenues per pupil for taxes earmarked for the School Aid Fund. To date, the legislature has used this level as a floor, going above it several times. In the future, fiscal pressure may lead the legislature to adjust the funding structure. Also, categorical aid is not protected in the same way that foundation aid is, so that high-cost districts with disadvantaged populations that rely on categorical grants may be at risk.

As these pressures grow over time, the state may have to respond by revising Proposal A. The challenge will be to correct weaknesses without undermining the progress that has been made.

## 3. The Choice Movement

While funding is a critical input to the education process, many feel that the K–12 system is not designed in a way that ensures the efficient use of resources. In the absence of direct mechanisms for holding administrators and educators accountable, parents' primary recourse when dissatisfied with a school system is to move or to attend a private school. Since both of these options can be costly, the traditional system under which students are assigned to schools based on where they live can lead to what are effectively local monopolies.

Proponents of school choice claim that providing parents with flexible nontraditional alternatives will give them more power to discipline schools that are not performing well, by exercising their choice to attend another school. The hope is that this market mechanism will benefit not only the students who actively participate but also the students who remain behind in public schools that are forced to improve by competitive pressures. Critics worry that only the most advantaged students will opt out, hurting the students who remain behind in the public schools that may not be able to improve in the face of declining resources.

School choice encompasses a wide variety of alternatives, both public and nonpublic. There has been a dramatic expansion of nontraditional schooling options over the past decade through both sectors. Currently, one in seven school districts nationally allows students to transfer schools within the same district (National Center for Education Statistics 1996), and nearly every major urban district has at least one magnet school that attracts students districtwide (Blank 1990). Since the first authorizing law was passed in Minnesota in 1991, the number of charter schools has increased to over 2,300 across thirty-four states (Center for Education Reform 2000). In addition, more than thirty cities have newly established privately funded voucher programs, and programs in Milwaukee, Cleveland, and Florida provide public funding for religious and nonsectarian schools.[34] Finally, while the rate of home schooling is low, it may have as much as tripled between 1991 and 1996 (Lines 1999) and was estimated to be 1.7% in 1999 (National Center for Education Statistics 2001c). Though all of these options break the link between where the family chooses to live and where the children attend school, each is subject to a distinct legal and regulatory environment. As such, the impact of expanding school choice will vary depending on the form the expansion takes.

Michigan legislators have supported aggressive expansion of choice through the public sector, authorizing both public school academies and schools of choice. The regulations regarding home schools have also been relaxed so that home school families are subject to fewer restrictions and are no longer necessarily categorized as non-public. However, the MEA has not supported increased choice, especially in the form of vouchers. In 2000, after a vigorous campaign by the MEA, Michigan voters rejected a private school voucher proposal by a margin of more than two to one. Before discussing these specific state reforms, we first provide some background on the forms of choice and the evidence in favor of and against school choice.

### 3.1 Background on School Choice

The form of school choice that represents the most modest departure from the traditional system is open enrollment. These programs simply enlarge geographic attendance boundaries, so students may attend schools other than their neighborhood schools. The sending and receiving schools are typically on the same legal footing, though some magnet schools can selectively admit students. For transfers across district boundaries, sending districts typically lose the amount of per pupil state aid for each child who opts to leave; the resources are transferred to receiving districts. It is this explicit tie between funding and enrollment that is expected to discipline low-quality schools.

Charter schools represent an intermediate step toward private schools. They are public schools, but are often released from many state and local regulations. For example, in some states charter schools are not required to hire certified teachers. However, charter schools are held accountable through the oversight of the chartering authority. Further, most states do not allow charter schools to select students in any manner other than through a lottery. The hope is that the flexibility will foster innovation, while the constraints will maintain equal access.

Voucher programs integrate private schools into the finance of public education. Unlike neighborhood schools, private schools charge tuition, can be selective in admissions, and are not subject to the same comprehensive state regulations. They are also not subject to the same degree of public oversight, since curriculum and testing are generally not monitored. Home schools in most states are often subject to the same legal requirements as private schools. Voucher programs typically impose constraints on participating private schools, such as disallowing tuition charges in excess of the level of the voucher.

The first-order question about any of these forms of school choice is whether benefits accrue to students who take advantage of alternatives to traditional public schools. The bulk of the evidence is based on comparisons between students who attend public and private schools. The difficulty with attributing differences in outcomes between these students to choice alone is that they have actively chosen different paths, and are likely to differ according to other unobserved characteristics, such as motivation or parental effort. Though private school students outperform public school students on average, studies that account for this type of self-selection do not necessarily find the same positive effects.[35]

More recent studies are based on experimental designs. Studies of Milwaukee's private school voucher program that randomly selects recipients from among low-income students use a variety of methods to establish valid control groups and find anywhere from no achievement gains to large advantages.[36] While in theory randomization provides an ideal context for the evaluation of school choice, in this case over half of the unsuccessful applicants never returned to the public schools, and those who did return were from less-educated, lower-income families (Witte 1998). However, subsequent voucher experiments that have been more carefully designed from the outset also present a wide range of estimated program effects (see *www.ksg.harvard.edu/pepg/papers.htm*). Paralleling the research findings for private-sector options, studies of public-sector options such as charter schools and open enrollment also find mixed evidence for whether participants benefit (Cullen, Jacob, and Levitt 2000; Bettinger 2002).

The recent school choice experiments through voucher and charter school programs in the United States have generally not been large enough to estimate the effects on stratification, public school performance, and spillovers to students who remain behind.[37] There is evidence, though, that competition between neighborhood schools and between public and private schools under the traditional system of neighborhood assignment improves school efficiency by both reducing costs and improving student achievement (Hoxby 2000). Also, the high school open enrollment system in Chicago, in which nearly half of the students participate, appears to have benefited the students that did not participate despite substantial sorting by ability, perhaps through competitive effects (Cullen, Jacob, and Levitt

2000). Though it may simply be too early to expect systemic effects, Michigan's charter schools have apparently not improved achievement at neighboring public schools (Bettinger 2002).

A caveat to applying lessons from the existing literature to predicting the impact of expansive school choice programs is that the general equilibrium effects may be very different from the partial equilibrium effects that have been measured. For example, even if current private school students outperform public school students, this does not mean attending private schools under a universal voucher program would have the same effect. For one, these benefits could arise from peer quality, which would then be significantly diluted. Also, schools that enter the system in response to choice to satisfy new demand may be very different from those that currently exist. Our state of knowledge is simply not complete enough to predict conclusively how the distribution of opportunity across students will ultimately be affected by school choice.

We focus below on recent innovations in public schooling options in Michigan. Neither institutional private schools nor home schools are currently eligible for public funds. The rate at which elementary and secondary education students enroll in private schools in Michigan has been declining slightly over recent years and is approximately at the national average.[38] Though the rate of reported home schooling has grown dramatically, from 887 students in 1990 to 1,914 in 2001, this represents an insignificant share of the student population.[39]

## 3.2 Public Schooling Options in Michigan

Michigan introduced a choice plan in 1994 as part of the implementing legislation for Proposal A. Under the choice plan, students can opt to attend public academies, known more widely as charter schools. Options were expanded in 1997 through "schools of choice" legislation that allows students to attend schools outside their home district. In both cases, state per pupil foundation aid follows the student. The idea is that schools will compete to attract students, since funding is directly tied to enrollment.

*Open enrollment.* Within Michigan districts, whether or not students can transfer across schools historically has been under the discretion of the local district. When intradistrict school choice was first introduced in 1997 (PA 300), students could choose to attend a traditional public school in a district outside of their home district but within the same ISD. The open enrollment program was expanded in 2000 (PA 297) to include contiguous districts outside the ISD, and to include districts in any contiguous ISD in the following year. School districts can refuse to provide slots for transfer students, but if they do and are oversubscribed, admission is based on a lottery. The receiving school district receives the minimum of its own and the sending district's per pupil state foundation aid. Students must pay for their own transportation.

The initial reaction on the part of districts was mixed. Some districts were hesitant to participate, while others saw this as an opportunity to expand their budgets. By the second year of operation, 45% of districts were accepting students. By 2001, four out of every five school districts had signed on to participate. Between 1997 and 2001, the number of students participating grew from 7,836 to 33,506, approximately 2% of total enrollment.

Schools of choice have largely been a Detroit phenomena, with more than one-third of all transfers taking place within the metro area. However, figure 15.8 shows that there are pockets with greater activity in terms of transfers as a share of local enrollment. In terms of absolute numbers, the Detroit Public Schools have lost more students than any other in the state. In 2001, 3,082 left the city for schools in the suburbs. Early on, several neighboring districts hoping to expand their budgets took aggressive approaches to attract city students.[40] Metro districts that are losing students have been forced to respond. In the summer of 2001, the Detroit Public School system spent over $145,000 on its own marketing campaign.[41] The system is responding by offering free full-day kindergarten in several schools.

The general view is that open enrollment is having a positive impact in places with active student participation. However, schools that are losing students at rapid rates are experiencing budgetary problems.[42] The schools are finding that they cannot cut back on staff in equal proportions to the number of students that leave, particularly since students are drawn from different classes. Furthermore, once they cut services, the problem of student outflow is exacerbated. Proposals to help these schools maintain quality and respond have been put forward that would base state funding on the average of several years of student enrollment.

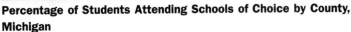

**FIGURE 15.8**

**Percentage of Students Attending Schools of Choice by County, Michigan**

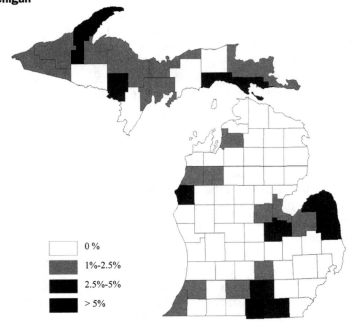

0 %

1%–2.5%

2.5%–5%

> 5%

SOURCE: Michigan School Report 1999 data files (*http://www.state.mi.us/mde/reports/msr99*).

**FIGURE 15.9**

**Percentage of Students Attending Charter Schools by County, Michigan**

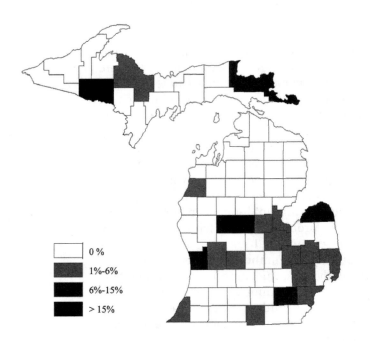

0 %

1%–6%

6%–15%

> 15%

SOURCE: Michigan School Report 1999 data files (*http://www.state.mi.us/mde/reports/msr99*).

*Charter schools.* Michigan first passed charter school legislation in December 1993 as part of the school finance reform (PA 362). In Michigan, charter schools are known as public school academies (PSAs). The first PSA opened in the 1993–94 school year. In the next two years of operation there were 14 and 44 PSAs, respectively. The numbers since then have steadily increased: 78 in 1996–97, 108 in 1997–98, 138 in 1998–99, 171 in 1999–2000, and 184 in 2000–2001. Despite the rapid growth in numbers of schools, only a small minority (1%) of students statewide attends PSAs. Figure 15.9 shows that the location of these schools is concentrated, so that participation rates in some counties are quite high.

Michigan's charter school law is one of the most permissive in the nation, Since the passage of the initial law, the state's control over charter schools has increased. A 1994 lawsuit charged that the law violated the state's constitution by allocating public funds to essentially private schools, since these schools had such a great degree of autonomy. Amendments to the law, including a requirement that PSAs hire certified teachers, were ruled sufficient for these schools to be classified as public by the Michigan Supreme Court in 1997. PSAs still do not necessarily have to participate in collective bargaining (collective bargaining requirements vary by authorizer), but unlike private schools they cannot discriminate in admissions (acceptance is by lottery) and cannot teach a religious-based curriculum.

In Michigan, several entities are eligible to grant charters. These include local and regional school districts, community colleges, and state universities. The cap on the number of university-sponsored charter schools will grow from 150 to 230 by 2017 (the cap was 100 in 1997, 125 in 1998). The entity that authorizes a charter, by accepting an application from an individual or nonprofit group, is responsible for monitoring its performance, and can revoke the charter. As of 2000, only six schools had been closed (Center for Education Reform 2000).

PSAs are financed by state allocations, which are based on the same per pupil foundation formula that applies to other public schools. A charter school receives either the per pupil foundation allowance for the district in which it is located or the state basic allowance plus $500, whichever is less (see table 15.2). There are no provisions for sources of capital funds or any access to local revenue bases, which is a problem since PSAs normally have large start-up costs.

Because charter schools are reimbursed the same amount regardless of grade level, and elementary per pupil costs tend to be lower, charter schools are concentrated in the lower grades. To address this, Horn and Miron (2000) recommend differentiated foundation grants based on average costs by grade level.

Early charter schools entered to serve minority and disadvantaged students. Along with the rise in the rate of charter schools operating for-profit from 16.7% to 71.4% between 1996 and 2000 (Horn and Miron 2000), the composition of students has shifted toward more advantaged majority students. Also, charter schools are serving special education students at less than one-third the rate of traditional schools. There are concerns that these patterns are, at least in part, due to selectivity on the part of charter schools through a variety of indirect means (Horn and Miron 2000).

There have been initial concerns about the performance of charter schools. Michigan's charter schools have performed below the state average in terms of the fraction of students achieving proficiency. However, it is important to remember that these schools serve disproportionate numbers of economically disadvantaged students, not including special education students. Still, recent studies that correct for the selection of less-advantaged students to PSAs continue to find no evidence of a positive impact on test outcomes (Bettinger 2002). The impact is likely to change, however, as the teaching force becomes more experienced and the schools have had more time to get established. Most PSAs have been in existence for a very short period of time and may have had large numbers of their students for even less time.

## 4. Accountability

In addition to implementing school choice programs with the hopes that market pressure will impose accountability, many states have turned to systems that hold students, teachers, and schools directly accountable for performance. Such systems can be valuable complements to school choice programs, ensuring that increased flexibility in schooling options does not compromise shared educational goals. However, those who are concerned that choice undermines support for the public sector often view accountability systems as preferred alternatives that focus energy on improving traditional public schools. Following the emphasis on the equalization of school resources and the growth in the state role in financing K–12 education over recent decades, it is also natural that states are turning their attention to monitoring the impact on outcomes and on efficiency.

On 8 January 2002, President Bush signed the "No Child Left Behind" Education Bill into law, requiring states to adopt standardized testing for students in grades three to eight, and to use the test scores in order to grade schools. Before this bill, "high stakes" standardized testing had been playing an increasing role in states' public education systems. Some states hold students directly accountable for their test performances. By 2000, twenty-eight states had passed legislation to establish minimum test standards required for a student to graduate from high school.[43] Some states also use test scores to determine grade promotions and summer school enrollments. Most states publish student test score information by school or district, and some use these scores as a basis for rewards or interventions. Currently, at least thirty-five states use student test scores to determine school ratings or school accreditation status. Of these states, fourteen use student performance measures to assign discrete grades or ratings to all schools or school districts.

Michigan recently implemented a reward system at the student level, and has continually revamped its school-level accreditation system since it was first established in 1990. Before we focus on Michigan's policies, however, we describe the general considerations associated with designing accountability systems and present evidence on the impact of these systems on both intended and unintended behaviors.

## 4.1 Issues in the Design of Accountability Systems

Performance-based incentive systems are common to public-sector bureaucracies where it is difficult to evaluate the production process. In the context of K–12 education, the lack of understanding, or at least of consensus, about what works makes measuring outputs particularly attractive relative to monitoring inputs and processes. Accountability systems are intended to improve school efficiency and student outcomes by focusing on the end product, however, these types of systems are inevitably imperfect.

The potential pitfalls fall into three broad classes. First, schools typically pursue multiple goals, some of which are not easily measurable. Since schools are evaluated on only some subset of activities, administrators and teachers may divert resources toward the measured outcomes and away from other valuable unmeasured outcomes. As an example, consider the testing of basic skills and area content. While this may encourage teachers to teach the standard curriculum and allow a way of quantifying quality, such testing may reduce opportunities for students to learn higher-order skills (McNeil and Valenzuela 2001).

A second class of problems arises because the specific instrument chosen to measure performance is typically only indirectly related to the outcomes that we care about. For example, consider that the goal is increasing math skills. If a specific test is used to evaluate those skills, teachers have an incentive to teach the content of that exam, which may not translate into an increase in student skills that would generalize to other test instruments. A second example is a policy that is based on pass rate thresholds. Though the goal may be to enhance learning for all students, evaluating schools based only on the number above or below that threshold may lead schools to neglect the highest- and lowest-achieving students. Different measures will have different distributional consequences, depending on how changes in students' performance at different points in the ability distribution translate into increased aggregate performance.

A third example of the disconnect between goals and implementation are systems that reward schools for average student achievement *levels*, when the goal is a move toward increased learning or value added to students. Achievement levels may largely be a measure of students' background when entering their schools. Schools with more advantaged student populations will appear to outperform other schools, whether or not they are equally effective at fostering student learning. More recent systems focus explicitly on value added by looking at changes in test scores.[44]

The final class of problems arises from the difficulty in designing systems that are "manipulation proof." For example, one method that has been used to account for students' preexisting academic abilities is to exclude some students from the exams. While this may enhance equity, it also provides schools with the opportunity to improve measured performance outcomes by controlling the composition of students taking the exam. States can safeguard against this and most of the other pitfalls by designing comprehensive and universal accountability systems (Ladd 1999).

A consideration that interacts with design issues is the level at which accountability is assigned. If an important reason for underachievement is the lack of student effort, then providing incentives to individual students can be efficacious. However, if it is schools and not students who are responsible for underperformance, then it is not necessarily fair to punish students for their misfortune. To the extent that teacher effort is the problem, policies that reward and punish teachers based on classroom performance are more relevant. Proponents of systems like merit pay also contend that tying pay more closely to performance will attract more able teachers to the profession. The dangers are that there are myriad opportunities for teachers to attempt to manipulate the system, such as by controlling class composition, and such policies may stand in the way of teacher cooperation. Providing incentives at the school level can encourage the kind of teamwork that is necessary for concerted improvement and systemic change.

### 4.2 Evidence on the Impact of Accountability Systems

Since testing has been the central element of most recently implemented accountability systems, the natural first-order question is whether state-imposed reforms have had an impact on learning, as measured by test scores. The evidence on this is mixed, and much of the controversy has centered on Texas. There is no question that Texas students have made dramatic improvements, according to the state-administered exams. However, researchers disagree about whether these gains are matched by gains on the NAEP (Grissmer and Flanagan 1998; Klein et al. 2000). Studies of a wider set of state reforms also find contradictory results (Rothstein 1998; Carnoy and Loeb 2002).

There is also an active debate about whether focusing on test scores has worsened other student outcomes. There is some evidence that minimum competency testing has increased disadvantaged students' probability of dropping out (Haney 2000; Lillard and De Cicca 2001). Reardon (1996) finds that high-stakes tests in the eighth grade are associated with 6–8% higher dropout rates by the tenth grade. In contrast, Carnoy, Loeb, and Smith (2001) find that while higher scores on Texas's exams are associated with reduced dropout behavior in Texas, graduation and college enrollment rates have not improved in Texas since the implementation of high-stakes testing. It seems clear that performance gains do not spill over to other important indicators of educational improvement, though it is less clear whether these other areas are actually harmed.

The evidence on undesirable responses to accountability systems clearly demonstrates that the design problems mentioned in the prior section are of practical importance. Several studies support the fact that teachers are teaching to the specific tests, such as those studies listed previously that document that improvements on test instruments are not matched by parallel gains on other exams (Jacob 2002; Klein et al. 2000). Other researchers have uncovered evidence of a more pernicious form of manipulation through cheating by both students and teachers (Jacob and Levitt 2002). Schools also appear to be strategically manipulating which students are in the test-taking pool (Cullen and Reback 2002; Figlio and Getzler 2002), in some cases by classifying marginal students as disabled.

All of these undesirable behaviors involve real costs in terms of resources and diverted effort. There are also costs due to decisions that are made based on distorted measures of performance. To the extent that the accountability ratings reflect arbitrary differences in classification practices, these misleading ratings can lead to inefficiencies such as misguided educational policy decisions, misguided enrollment decisions, and unwarranted changes in property values.[45]

## 4.3 Accountability in Michigan

Michigan emphasizes accountability at the school level and has limited accountability at the student level. The basis for assessment is the Michigan Education Assessment Program (MEAP). The current version is designed to test specific criteria in each subject area, but a new version that is more closely aligned with state standards will be first implemented in 2003. Students are tested in math and reading in grades four and seven; in writing, social studies, and science in grades five and eight; and in all areas in grade eleven. While students need not score above a certain level on the high school proficiency tests in order to graduate,

they do in order to graduate with state endorsement (CPRE 2000).

Though there are no student-level sanctions, a reward program was established through the Michigan Merit Award Scholarship Program in 1999 (PA 94). The goals were to increase access to postsecondary education and to reward high-achieving high school graduates. Under the program, eligible students receive a $2,500 scholarship to attend an in-state college and $1,000 to attend out-of-state colleges. To be eligible, students must take the MEAP high school tests for math, reading, science, and writing and meet the standards (score at Level 1 or 2) on all four.[46]

Very little is known about whether this program affects student effort while in school or influences student decisions about whether to pursue postsecondary education. If there are these types of benefits, they appear to be very unevenly distributed. While 34% of eligible white students qualified in the first year, only 20% of Hispanics and 7% of black students did.[47] The gap was also large between poor and more affluent school districts.[48] The concern is that the program ends up subsidizing students from more advantaged families because of the strong tie between family background and academic achievement.

The system of accountability through accreditation at the school level has been recently revamped. The system in place since 1993 had three levels of accreditation: summary, interim, and unaccredited. Though the top category had ambitious test performance thresholds and required full compliance with nonperformance provisions, the threat of losing accreditation was not real. A school could land in the middle category if more than half of the students passed only one MEAP test in any of the last three consecutive years. In 2000, only eight out of the more than three thousand schools were not accredited, even though many students were scoring poorly on the MEAP.

Fears that the interim category housed many failing schools and that Title I funds might be withdrawn without better monitoring of yearly progress led the State Board to develop a new performance-based accreditation system in May 1999. When the board moved to implement the plan in the spring of 2001, more than six hundred schools (one in five) were expected to lose accreditation, including nearly 40% of metro Detroit high schools.[49] Due to public backlash, the system was never implemented. Though the system included measures to capture improvement, critics argued that the simultaneous inclusion of level thresholds unfairly penalized schools in low-income areas that could have low scores even if students were learning effectively.

With additional impetus from Bush's "No Child Left Behind" bill, the State Board has just approved the Education Yes! Accreditation System (14 March 2002). Under this system, schools receive letter grades of A, B, C, D-Alert, or Unaccredited. Schools not only receive an overall composite grade, but are also individually graded in six separate subareas: MEAP achievement level, change, and growth, as well as indicators of community engagement, instructional quality, and learning opportunities. Not only will reading, math, and science scores count, but so will social studies scores. Attendance and dropout rates are included among the student performance indicators to allay concerns about an overemphasis on test scores. The comprehensiveness of this new program promises to better measure what schools actually do.

There have been no specific negative consequences of losing accreditation in the short-run, since this status has been interpreted by the state as a signal of need for increased resources and support. In 2000, the State Board adopted a new policy entitled "Partnership for Success." Skilled educators are recruited to provide assistance and leadership to failing schools.[50] That same year the legislature introduced the Golden Apple Award to reward elementary schools that demonstrate sustained improvement.[51] Schools that have a minimum participation rate and significant test score gains over a three-year period are eligible for a minimum of $50,000 ($10,000 for use by the principal, plus $1000 for each full-time employee).

## 5. Prospect for the Future

The state of Michigan is simultaneously pursuing reform on a series of fronts in K–12 education. The school finance formula has been redesigned with an emphasis on equity. At the same time, school choice and accountability have been revamped to address the goals of flexibility and efficiency. Though these programs can complement one another, they can also be in conflict. For example, school choice has brought new complications for the design of school finance. Furthermore, as state-centered school finance and strong accountability increase state control, charter school reform strives to decentralize educational

decision making. In order to continue to iterate toward a sustainable balance between this diverse set of goals, complicated interactions between the set of policies cannot be ignored.

It is also clear at this point that Michigan will face ongoing pressure regarding the overall adequacy of Proposal A funding levels to keep pace with school costs. There will also be a continuing debate over the proper balance of funding equity and local options for additional revenue for operations. There is growing pressure to consider how to address the inequity in the ability to finance capital that was explicitly ignored under Proposal A. The design of a new system for financing capital will create a second set of adequacy and equity questions for debate. Accountability will be a perennial issue, and Michigan may be destined to repeat its performance on accreditation, designing system after system with no true willingness to penalize failure or to intervene. Reaching broad social consensus on just exactly what we want our schools to do is counter to the very strong Michigan tradition of local control over educational programming—even when these local decisions are not wisely made or well implemented.

■

## REFERENCES

Addonizio, Michael F., C. Philip Kearney, and Henry J. Prince. 1995. Michigan's high wire act. *Journal of Education Finance* 200 (winter): 235–69.

Altonji, Joseph, Todd Elder, and Christopher Taber. 2000. Selection on observed and unobserved variables: Assessing the effectiveness of Catholic schools. National Bureau of Economic Research Working Paper No. 7831. Cambridge, Mass..

Arasim, Liz. 2000. *School accreditation: An overview.* Michigan Senate Fiscal Agency Issue Paper, September.

Bettinger, Eric. 2002. The effect of charter schools on charter students and public schools. Mimeograph, Case Western Reserve University.

Blank, Rolf K. 1990. Educational effects of magnet high schools. In *Choice and control in American education,* vol. 2., edited by W. Clune and J. Witte. Bristol, Penn.: Falmer Press.

Brazer, Harvey E., Deborah S. Laren, and Frank Yu-Hsieh Sung. 1982. Elementary and secondary school financing. In *Michigan's fiscal and economic structure,* edited by Harvey E. Brazer. Ann Arbor: University of Michigan Press.

Brunner, Eric, and Jon Sonstelie. 1997. Coping with Serrano: Private contributions to California's public schools. *Proceedings of the 89th Annual Conference on Taxation.* National Tax Association.

Carnoy, Martin, and Susanna Loeb. 2002. Does external accountability affect students outcomes? A cross-state analysis. Stanford University School of Education mimeo.

Carnoy, Martin, Susanna Loeb, and Tiffany L. Smith. 2001. Do higher state test scores in Texas make for better high school outcomes? Paper presented at the American Educational Research Association Annual Meeting, New Orleans, 24–28 April.

Center for Education Reform. 2000. Charter school highlights and statistics. *www.edreform.com/pubs/ chglance.htm.*

Cleary, Mary Ann, and Kathryn Summers-Coty. 1999. Durant: What happened and implications for the future. *Fiscal Forum* 5(2), Michigan House Fiscal Agency.

Consortium for Policy Research in Education (CPRE). 2000. Assessment and accountability in the fifty states: 1999-2000. Available at *http://www.cpre.org/ Publications/Publications_Accountability.htm.*

Courant, Paul N., and Susanna Loeb. 1997. Centralization of school finance in Michigan. *Journal of Policy Analysis and Management* 16 (1): 114–36.

Cronin, Thomas E. 1989. *Direct democracy.* Cambridge, Mass.: Harvard University Press.

Cullen, Julie Berry, and Susanna Loeb. 2002a. Fiscal substitution in the context of school finance equalization. Working Paper. Mimeograph, University of Michigan and Stanford University.

———. 2002b. School finance reform in Michigan: Evaluating Proposal A. Prepared for the Education finance and Accountability Program Conference on state aid to education, Syracuse University, 5–6 April 2002.

Cullen, Julie Berry, and Randall Reback. 2002. Tinkering towards accolades: School gaming under a performance accountability system. Mimeograph, University of Michigan.

Cullen, Julie Berry, Brian Jacob, and Steven Levitt. 2000. The impact of school choice on student outcomes: An analysis of the Chicago public schools. National Bureau of Economic Research Working Paper No. 7888. Cambridge, Massachusetts.

Downes, Thomas, and David Schoeman. 1998. School finance reform and private school enrollment evidence from California. *Journal of Urban Economics* 43(3): 418–43.

Drake, Douglas C. 2002. *A review and analysis of Michigan tax policies impacting K–12 finances.* A report commissioned by the Michigan Association of School Administrators, School Business Officials, and School Boards. *www.gomasa.org/full _report.pdf.*

Duncombe, William, and John Yinger. 1999. Performance standards and educational cost indexes: You can't have one without the other. In *Equity and adequacy in education finance: Issues and perspectives,* edited by Helen F. Ladd, Rosemary Chalk, and Janet S. Hansen. Washington, D.C.: National Academy Press.

Education Commission of the States. 2000. ECS State Notes: School Finance Litigation (March) (*www.ecs .org/clearinghouse/18/23/1823.pdf*).

Evaluation of Michigan Charter Schools: Final Report. 2000 (July). Western Michigan University.

Evans, William N., Sheila E. Murray, and Robert M. Schwab. 2001. The property tax and education finance, uneasy compromises. In *Property taxation and local government finance,* edited by Wallace E. Oates. Cambridge, Mass.: Lincoln Institute of Land Policy.

Figlio, David N., and Lawrence S. Getzler. 2002. Accountability, ability, and disability: Gaming the system. National Bureau of Economic Research working paper, No. 9307. Cambridge, Massachusetts.

Figlio, David N., and Mel Lucas. 2000. What's in a grade? School report cards and house prices. National Bureau of Economic Research. Working Paper no. 8019. Cambridge, Massachusetts.

Fisher Ronald C., and Robert W. Wassmer. 1995. Centralizing educational responsibility in Michigan and other states: New constraints on states and localities. *National Tax Journal* 48(3): 417–28.

Fisher, Ronald C., and Mary N. Gade. 1991. Local property tax and expenditure limits. In *State and local finance for the 1990s: A case study of Arizona,* edited by Therese J. McGuire and Dana Wolfe Naimark. Tempe, Az.: Arizona State University.

Grissmer, David, and Ann Flanagan. 1998. Exploring rapid achievement gains in North Carolina and Texas. Washington, D.C.: National Education Goals Panel.

Guilfoyle, Jeffrey R. 1998. The effect of property taxes and school spending on house prices: Evidence from Michigan's Proposal A. Mimeograph, Michigan Department of Treasury, February.

Haney, Walter. 2000. Report for testimony in *G.I. Forum v. Texas Education Agency.* Mimeograph, Boston College, School of Education.

Harvey, Lynn. R. 1995. 1994 Michigan school finance and property tax reform. In *Increasing understanding of public problems and policy,* Proceedings of the National Public Policy Education Conference. Oak Brook, Ill.: Farm Foundation.

Horn, Jerry, and Gary Miron. 2000. An evaluation of the Michigan charter school initiative: Performance, accountability, and impact. Western Michigan University, Evaluation Center.

Hoxby, Caroline M. 2000. Does competition among public schools benefit students and taxpayers? *American Economic Review* 90(5): 1209–38.

———. 1998. All school finance systems are not created equal. National Bureau of Economic Research. Working Paper No. 6792. Cambridge, Massachusetts.

Hsieh, Chang-Tai, and Miguel Urquiola. 2002. When schools compete, how do they compete? Assessing Chile's nationwide school voucher program. Princeton University Working Paper.

Jacob, Brian. 2002. Accountability, incentives, and behavior: The impact of high-stakes testing in the Chicago Public Schools. National Bureau of Economic Research. Working Paper No. 8968. Cambridge, Massachusetts.

Jacob, Brian, and Steven Levitt. 2002. Rotten apples: An investigation of the prevalence and predictors of teacher cheating. Mimeograph, Harvard University and University of Chicago.

Klein, Stephen P., Laura S. Hamilton, Daniel F. McCaffrey, and Brian M. Stecher. 2000. What do test scores in Texas tell us? Santa Monica, Calif.: RAND.

Knittel, Matthew J., and Mark P. Haas. 1998. *Proposal A: A retrospective.* Michigan Department of Treasury Report, August.

Ladd, Helen F., and Edward B. Fiske. 2000. *When schools compete: A cautionary tale.* Washington, D.C.: Brookings Institution Press.

Ladd, Helen F. 1999. The Dallas school accountability and incentive program: an evaluation of its impacts on student outcomes. *Economics of Education Review* 18(1): 1–16.

Ladd, Helen F., and John Yinger. 1994. The case for equalizing aid. *National Tax Journal* 47(1): 211–24.

Lillard, Dean R., and Philip DeCicca. 2001. Higher standards, more dropouts? Evidence within and across time. *Economics of Education Review* 20: 459–73.

Lines, Patricia M. 1999. Homeschoolers: Estimating numbers and growth. U.S. Department of Education, web version (*http://www.ed.gov/offices/OERI /SAI/homeschool/*).

Loeb, Susanna. 2001. Estimating the effects of school finance reform: A framework for a federalist system. *Journal of Public Economics* 80(2): 225–47.

McNeil, Linda, and Angela Valenzuela. 2001. The harmful impact of the TAAS system of testing in Texas: Beneath the accountability rhetoric. In *Raising Standards or Raising Barriers? Inequality and High Stakes Testing in Public Education,* edited by Gary Orfield and Mindy Kornhaber. Cambridge, Mass.:

Harvard Civil Rights Project.

National Center for Education Statistics. 2002. Digest of Education Statistics, 2001. NCES 2002-130.

———. 2001a. Digest of Education Statistics, 2000. NCES 2001-034.

———. 2001b. Public school finance programs of the United States and Canada: 1998-99. NCES 2001-309.

———. 2001c. *Homeschooling in the United States: 1999.* NCES 2001–033.

———. 1998. Digest of Education Statistics, 1997. NCES 98-015.

———. 1996. *Public school choice programs 1993–94: Availability and student participation.* NCES 97–909.

Papke, Leslie E. 2001. The effects of spending on school inputs and outputs: Evidence from Michigan. Mimeograph, Michigan State University, East Lansing, Michigan.

Peterson, Paul E., David Myers, and William G. Howell. 1998. An evaluation of the New York City school choice scholarships program: The first year. Program on Education Policy and Governance, Working Paper 98–12. John F. Kennedy School of Government, Harvard University.

Prince, Hank. 1996. *Proposal A and pupil equity.* Michigan House Fiscal Agency Report. *http://www .house.state.mi.us/hfa/prop_a.htm.*

Reardon, Sean F. 1996. Eighth grade minimum competency testing and early high school dropout patterns. Paper presented at the Annual Convention of the American Education Research Association, New York, April.

Reschovsky, Andrew. 1994. Fiscal equalization and school finance. *National Tax Journal* (March): 185–97.

Rothstein, Richard. 1998. *The way we were?* New York: The Century Foundation Press.

Rouse, Cecilia E. 1998. Private school vouchers and student achievement: An evaluation of the Milwaukee parental choice program. *Quarterly Journal of Economics* 113(2): 553–602.

School Equity Caucus. 2001. Does the State of Michigan distribute its financial resources to public schools in a manner that promotes equal educational opportunity for its children and youth? Lansing, Michigan, August. *http://www.schoolequitycaucus .org.*

Sonstelie, Jon, Eric Brunner, and Kenneth Ardon. 2000. *For better or for worse? School finance reform in California.* San Francisco, Calif.: Public Policy Institute of California.

Theobald, Neil. 2002. From Proposal A to Proposal A+. Report commissioned by the Michigan State Board of Education, March. Available at *www.michigan .gov/documents/proposalareport_24409_7.pdf.*

Tiebout, Charles, 1956. A pure theory of local expenditures. *Journal of Political Economy* 64: 416–24.

Witte, John F. 1993. The Milwaukee private-school parental choice program. In *School choice: Examining the evidence*, edited by E. Rasell and R. Rothstein. Washington, D.C.: Economic Policy Institute.

———. 1998. The Milwaukee voucher experiment. *Education Evaluation and Policy Analysis* 20(4): 229–51.

Witte, John F., Troy D. Sterr, and Christopher A. Thorn. 1995. Fifth-year report: Milwaukee parental choice program. Department of Political Science and the Robert M. La Follette Institute of Public Affairs, University of Wisconsin–Madison.

## NOTES

1. Average daily attendance in public elementary and secondary schools in Michigan was 1,991,235 in 1970; 1,758,425 in 1980; 1,446,996 in 1990; and 1,570,283 in 1999. In all four years, the state ranked either seventh or eighth in the nation (*Digest of Education Statistics, 2000*, table 43).

2. Here, and throughout the chapter, we refer to years by the fiscal year. For example, 1990 refers to the 1989–90 school year.

3. *Digest of Education Statistics, 2000*, table 44.

4. 1998–99 is the latest year available for the cross-state comparisons.

5. *Digest of Education Statistics, 1997*, table 66, and *Digest of Education Statistics, 2001*, table 67.

6. Average teachers salaries in Michigan were $9,826 in 1970; $19,663 in 1980; $37,072 in 1990; and $48,695 in 2000. The comparable national averages were $8,626; $15,970; $31,367; and $41,724 (*Digest of Education Statistics*, 2001, table 76).

7. The coefficient of variation is the standard deviation divided by the mean. It is a measure of the spread of the distribution.

8. The source for these facts is the MEA home page (*http://www.mea.org/Design.cfm?p=56*).

9. In keeping with its mathematics performance, Michigan scored slightly above the national average on all other NAEP tests, including fourth-grade reading in 1992 and 1998, fourth-grade science in 2000, and eighth-grade science in 1996 and 2000.

10. The SAT provides another potential achievement benchmark. However, only 11% of Michigan high school graduates took the SAT in 2000, placing it fifteenth from the bottom in terms of state-level participation. Though difficult to interpret because the pool of test-takers is particularly select, Michigan students scored above the national average on both the verbal (557 vs. 505) and math (569 vs. 514) sections.

11. Illinois data are not available for 1992, so we could not compare the gains in Michigan with the gains in Illinois.

12. The following education finance systems have been ruled unconstitutional by state courts: Alabama, 1993; Arizona, 1994; Arkansas, 1983; California, 1971, 1976; Connecticut, 1977; Kentucky, 1989; Massachusetts, 1993; Missouri, 1994; Montana, 1989; New Hampshire, 1997; New Jersey, 1973, 1990; North Carolina, 1997; North Dakota, 1993; Ohio, 1997; Tennessee, 1993; Texas, 1989; Vermont, 1997; Washington, 1978; West Virginia, 1979; Wyoming, 1980 (Education Commission of the States, 2000).

13. Connecticut is an example of a state that weights per capita income as well as property value in its formula.

14. Some states, such as Texas and Kentucky, use a combination of both types. Of the nearby states, Illinois and Ohio have modified foundation systems, and Indiana and Wisconsin have power-equalization systems.

15. For example, in Kentucky's *Rose v. Council for Better Education Inc. et al.* in 1989, the court held the state government responsible for providing an adequate education and went further to define adequate as providing students with the opportunity to develop seven specified capabilities (Evans, Murray, and Schwab 2001).

16. This picture of the average experience, however, masks variation in results across states that are at least in part due to differences in the types of equalization policies implemented (Hoxby 1998).

17. Prior to 1974, Michigan had a foundation plan with no local cap on mills (Brazer, Laren, and Sung 1982).

18. A small number of the highest-spending districts prior to reform are allowed to levy additional mills on homestead property.

19. A grandfather clause allowed 13 (of the 524) K–12 districts that levied less than eighteen mills prior to reform to levy their previous millage rate.

20. In addition, the personal exemption on income taxes would have increased from $2,100 to $3,000; the single business tax would have increased from 2.35% to 2.75%; the real estate transfer tax would have increased from 0.10 to 0.75%, as it did under Proposal A; and the cigarette tax per pack would have increased from $0.25 to $0.40, instead of to $0.75 as under Proposal A.

21. Revenue eligible to be counted in the base consisted of local school operating property tax revenue, state aid payments for formula aid, and categorical programs that were "rolled up" into the foundation allowance, including state payments for retirement and social security for district employees.

22. For 2002 the legislature made a special equity payment of $6,500 per pupil minus the foundation level for districts with foundations of less than $6,500.

23. "The Legacy of Proposal A: Tax Reform Shackles Many Metro Schools, Wealthy Districts Hit Hardest," *Detroit News*, 26 August 2001, *www.detnews.com /specialreports/2001/propa/sunlead/sunlead.htm*.

24. Sixty-two of the 524 K–12 districts approved these mills for 1996 (Prince 1996).

25. Martha A. Trafford, "Proposal A Needs to Be Repaired," *Ann Arbor News*, 24 March 2002.

26. Special education funds are allocated through three programs. The largest reimburses districts at a minimum of 28.6138% of local costs for special education in general and 70.4165% of special education transportation costs. These rates are a result of the Supreme Court decision in *Durant v. State of Michigan* that the state had violated the Headlee Amendment by not maintaining proportional funding levels for the mandated program.

27. The allocation was 11.5% of the foundation allowance multiplied by the number of free-lunch-eligible students. Prior to 2000, the fifty-two "hold-harmless" districts, those with a foundation level $1,500 or more above the basic foundation, were not eligible for this aid. These districts now receive aid, but at a lower rate of 5.75%.

28. Michigan is one of only fifteen states that do not provide direct state aid for capital outlay and debt service (Public School Finance Programs of the United States and Canada: 1998–99, table 3.5). See chapter 30 on borrowing for a description of the method the state uses to make finance through debt easier for localities.

29. Adjustments from nominal to real dollars used the local and state government price index from the Bureau of Economic Analysis, National Income and Product Accounts Tables (*www.bea.gov/bea/ dn/nipaweb/index.asp*), table 7.11: Chain-Type Quantity and Price Indexes for Government Consumption Expenditures and Gross Investment by Type. Revenue numbers are based on the 522 school districts in Bulletin 1014 data files in every year from 1991 through 2000. These data are available from the Michigan Department of Education at *www.michigan.gov/mde/1,1607,7-140-6525_ 6530_6605-21514--,00.html*.

30. The coefficient of variation is the standard deviation divided by the mean. It is a measure of the spread of the distribution.

31. Prince (1996) finds that revenues in the lowest-revenue districts increased by 30% between 1994 and 1997, while those in the highest-revenue districts declined by 4% in real terms.

32. "Fallout: Schools Face Budget Woes," *Detroit News*, Sunday, 26 August 2001, *www.detnews.com/special-reports/2001/propa/sunwoes/sunwoes.htm*.

33. The district that partly instigated the reform has gained 58% in revenues since then, but is having to cut special programs and eliminate staff because of shrinking enrollments ("Kalkaska Saved by Funding Law, but Small District Still Has Problems," *Detroit News*, 28 August 2001, *www .detnews.com/specialreports/2001/propa/tuckalk/tu ekalk.htm*).

34. In *Zelman, Superintendent of Public Instruction of Ohio, et. al. v. Simmons-Harris, et.al.* (2002) the Supreme Court upheld vouchers for religious schools.

35. See Altonji, Elder, and Taber (2000) for a recent example and a review of the literature.

36. See Rouse (1998) for a review and critique of this literature.

37. Other evidence comes from international policy experiments with more expansive systems of school choice, though the lessons are somewhat limited by the lack of individual-level data. For example, New Zealand introduced unrestricted choice among all public and religious schools in 1991. Ladd and Fiske (2000) find that the gap between successful and unsuccessful schools has widened since then. However, because researchers have access to only aggregate data, whether this is due to real effects of choice or to changes in school composition cannot be determined. Hsieh and Urquiola (2002) find no evidence that the introduction of universal vouchers for private schools improved average educational performance in Chile, but found a sizeable increase in sorting.

38. Between the fall of 1991 and 1997, Michigan private school enrollment rates decreased from 10.7% to 9.9% (*Digest of Education Statistics, 2000*, tables 39 and 64).

39. Since 1996, legal parents and guardians do not need to be certified. The reported rate understates the actual rate, since these "exempt" home schools are not required to report to the state.

40. The source for the information in this paragraph is "Schools of Choice: Crossovers Reach 26,000; 1996 State Law Forced Competition," *Detroit Free Press*,

23 January 2001, *www.freep.com/news/education /choice 23-20010123.htm.*

41. "Detroit Pulls Out Stops to Enroll Pupils," *Detroit News,* 23 August 2001, *www.detnews.com/2001/ schools/0108/23/901-276244.htm.*

42. "Choice Plan Shifts Funds for Schools," *Detroit News,* 2 December 2001, *www.detnews.com/2001/ schools/0112/02/d01-356898.htm.*

43. These statistics are based on the individual state summaries compiled by the Consortium for Policy Research in Education (2000).

44. Some states have approximated value added with changes over time in the average scores in particular grades. These can be very noisy measures due to student mobility and other sources of variability. Changes in the test scores of individual students over time are a more accurate measure.

45. Figlio and Lucas (2000) find that Florida's school report card ratings impact property values.

46. There are alternative routes to qualification based on combined MEAP and ACT or SAT performance.

47. "Merit Test Is Biased, ACLU Says," *Detroit News,* 28 June 2000, *www.detnews.com/2000/schools/0006 /28/d01-82686.htm.*

48. School Equity Caucus (2001).

49. "State Flunks 600 Schools," *Detroit News,* 11 April 2001, *www.detnews.com/2001/schools/0104/11/901- 210687.htm;* "No MEAP to Cost Schools Credit," *Detroit News,* 7 May 2001, *www.detnews.com/ schools/0105/07/901-221480.htm.*

50. The funds sets aside for educators to help in the accredited school systems were to reach $10 million in 2003.

51. Appropriations for the Golden Apple Award were scheduled to be $8 million from 2000 through 2003.

# 16

# Michigan's Transportation System and Transportation Policy

*Kenneth D. Boyer*

Michigan calls itself the automobile state, a reputation based on its role as the center of vehicle building. Yet does the transportation that we use favor the automobile? In this chapter, we will see that Michigan is in fact somewhat more oriented toward automotive transportation than the nation and our Great Lakes neighbors, but the difference is subtle, and by almost no measure does Michigan lead the nation or region in the use of automotive transport.

Michigan closely resembles its neighbors in the transportation decisions that are made. There are some notable differences, however, that are analyzed in the following. One of these is the poor quality of some classes of Michigan roads relative to those of other Great Lakes states and relative to the nation.[1] One possible cause is found in the unique truck weight laws in the state. Another is in the highly unusual funding formulas that favor county roads over through roads and rural counties over urban areas. A second major difference is that Michigan's metropolitan areas—notably the Detroit area—have extraordinarily little use of public transit, a factor that is attributable to the absence of standard forms of rail transit in southeast Michigan.

## Michigan Vehicle Stocks

Table 16.1 shows that there were about eight million automobiles, pickups, vans, sport utility vehicles, and other light trucks registered in Michigan in 2000. This is about 0.81 vehicles per resident. If only automobiles are considered, there is one car for every two Michigan residents. In this statistic, Michigan is very close to the average both among Great Lakes states as well as within the nation as a whole. Automobile and vehicle holdings are slightly lower in Michigan than the average in neighboring states, and slightly higher than the average for the nation as a whole.

The two main determinants of vehicle ownership in a state are the percentage of people living in urban areas and per capita income. The partial relationship between per capita income and automobile ownership is positive. Residents of a more rural state buy more trucks for personal transportation and fewer cars. Michigan residents own slightly more automobiles and vehicles in general than would be predicted by these two factors, but the difference is small. Based on the extent of urban population and per capita income, Michigan would be predicted to have passenger vehicle registrations equal to 0.78 per capita instead of the 0.81 observed in 2000.[2]

TABLE 16.1

**Vehicle Registrations in Great Lakes States, 2000**

| | Autos | Pickups | Vans | Sport Utilities | Other Light Trucks | Total |
|---|---|---|---|---|---|---|
| | | | **Total Units Registered** | | | |
| Illinois | 5,887,663 | 1,107,552 | 848,178 | 782,510 | 19,010 | 8,644,913 |
| Indiana | 3,221,972 | 1,090,378 | 520,011 | 454,862 | 11,348 | 5,298,571 |
| Michigan | 4,976,218 | 1,316,356 | 871,578 | 862,580 | 12,864 | 8,039,596 |
| Ohio | 6,662,157 | 1,588,069 | 995,034 | 837,443 | 18,703 | 10,101,406 |
| Wisconsin | 2,511,461 | 769,508 | 439,207 | 401,656 | 8,228 | 4,130,060 |
| G.L. states | 4,651,894 | 1,174,373 | 734,802 | 667,810 | 14,031 | 7,242,909 |
| U.S. total | 132,247,286 | 38,216,835 | 17,250,102 | 21,466,592 | 863,298 | 210,044,113 |
| | | | **Per Capita Registations** | | | |
| Illinois | 0.47 | 0.09 | 0.07 | 0.06 | 0.00 | 0.69 |
| Indiana | 0.58 | 0.20 | 0.09 | 0.08 | 0.00 | 0.96 |
| Michigan | 0.50 | 0.13 | 0.09 | 0.09 | 0.00 | 0.81 |
| Ohio | 0.59 | 0.14 | 0.09 | 0.07 | 0.00 | 0.89 |
| Wisconsin | 0.45 | 0.14 | 0.08 | 0.07 | 0.00 | 0.74 |
| G.L. states | 0.52 | 0.14 | 0.08 | 0.08 | 0.00 | 0.82 |
| U.S. total | 0.47 | 0.14 | 0.06 | 0.08 | 0.00 | 0.75 |

SOURCE: Calculations by author based on data in U.S. Federal Highway Administration, Highway Statistics, 2000, Tables MV-1, MV-9 and PS-1.

States are far less homogeneous with respect to truck registrations. In comparison to cars, freight-hauling trucks spend a much higher percentage of their time outside the borders of the state of registration, and to some extent, trucking firms can choose to register their equipment in the states with the lowest fees. Thus the state registration figures are not an accurate reflection of the number of freight vehicles available for service on the highways in any location. An added difficulty in the analysis of trucking policy is the astonishingly broad variety of vehicles that are counted in the stock of trucks. The great majority of trucks are pickups, as noted in table 16.1, and most of these are in fact used as primarily passenger vehicles. These vehicles blend in with panel vans, delivery trucks, and similar road vehicles that are not much heavier than cars and tend to have well-defined local territories within which they operate. There is, in fact, no clearly defined group of vehicles that one can identify as used solely for intercity transportation. Some of the heaviest trucks are dump trucks and garbage trucks, both of which serve primarily local areas. For all of these reasons, it is not possible to identify through counts of trucks the adequacy of the fleet for a particular state.

There is, however, one way in which Michigan trucking is quite distinctive. This is shown in table 16.2, which shows counts of heavy trucks registered in the Great Lakes states as well as the United States as a whole. Michigan registers slightly less than 3% of the heavy trucks in the United Sates. It is the average weight of Michigan heavy trucks that is striking. According to the 1997 Truck Inventory and Use Survey, Michigan truckers reported using 20,000 trucks with average weight between 60,000 and 80,000 pounds. This is about half the number registered to truckers in Ohio, Indiana, or Wisconsin, and only one fifth of the number registered in Illinois. However, Michigan truckers used 3,500 units at an average weight of 80,000 to 100,000 pounds, 2,700 between 100,000 and 130,000 pounds, and 4,700 with an average weight above 130,000 pounds. Truckers in Indiana, Illinois, and Ohio reported no trucks in this range. Only in Wisconsin were there a few hundred trucks weighing on average more than 80,000 pounds. As shown in table 16.2, there were only 5,900 trucks in the entire country that operated at average weights over 130,000 pounds, and of these, 80% were in Michigan. Furthermore, these ultraheavy so-called Michigan trains stay on Michigan roads, since the laws of other states prohibit them, with the exception of a small corridor from the Michigan border to the Indiana steel mills.

Michigan has the most permissive gross weight limits on trucks in the nation, as will be described later. Supporters of these liberal weight regulations argue that the fact that Michigan has fewer trucks than neighboring states is the result of these laws—if a truck can carry twice as much, it takes only half as many trucks to carry the same load (State of Michigan, Department of Transportation, Office of Communications 1998). There are in addition, several other possible explanations for the relatively small number of trucks registered in Michigan—there may be financial advantages to registering equipment in other states, or the commodities carried on Michigan highways may be such that fewer units are needed to carry the freight generated. The relative influence of these effects has not been determined.

## Michigan Roads

Highway transportation requires vehicles, roads, fuel, driver time, and other service labor. The state's role is most prominent in provision of roads. Using the most basic measure of roads, lane miles, Michigan appears to be quite normal both among the Great Lakes states and in comparison to the nation as a whole. This is shown in table 16.3, which divides road mileage into urban and rural components.

The two primary determinants of road mileage in any state are population and land area. There are two different relationships, one for urban areas, and one for rural regions. Looking first at rural areas, table 16.3 shows that Michigan has 1.5% of the nation's rural land area, slightly above the average for Great Lakes states. It has 3.9% of the nation's rural population, again slightly above

**TABLE 16.2**

**Number of Heavy Trucks by Average Weight (1000s)**

| State | 60,000–80,000 lbs. | 80,000–100,000 lbs. | 100,000–130,000 lbs. | > 130,000 lbs. | Total Heavy Trucks |
|---|---|---|---|---|---|
| Illinois | 104 | 0 | 0 | 0 | 104 |
| Indiana | 38.9 | 0 | 0 | 0 | 38.9 |
| Michigan | 20 | 3.5 | 2.7 | 4.7 | 30.9 |
| Ohio | 46 | 0 | 0 | 0 | 46 |
| Wisconsin | 35.3 | 0.7 | 0.2 | 0 | 36.2 |
| U.S. total | 1069.8 | 46.3 | 17.9 | 5.9 | 1139.9 |

SOURCE: U.S. Department of Census, 1997, table 3a for U.S., table 2 for states.

**TABLE 16.3**

**Rural and Urban Lane Miles and Selected Characteristics, 2000**

| | Rural Area (Sq. Miles) | Rural Area as % of U.S. Rural Area | Rural Population (1000s) | Rural Pop. as % of U.S. Rural Pop. | Rural Lane Miles | Rural Lane Miles as % of U.S. Rural Lane Miles |
|---|---|---|---|---|---|---|
| Illinois | 51,484 | 1.5% | 2,829 | 3.7% | 207,669 | 3.3% |
| Indiana | 34,004 | 1.0% | 2,096 | 2.7% | 150,927 | 2.4% |
| Michigan | 53,244 | 1.5% | 3,000 | 3.9% | 187,331 | 3.0% |
| Ohio | 36,474 | 1.0% | 3,339 | 4.3% | 171,409 | 2.7% |
| Wisconsin | 52,974 | 1.5% | 1,340 | 1.7% | 194,440 | 3.1% |
| G.L. average | 45,636 | 1.3% | 2,521 | 3.3% | 182,355 | 2.9% |
| U.S. total | 3,515,266 | 100.0% | 77,392 | 100.0% | 6,308,213 | 100.0% |

| | Urban Area (Sq. Miles) | Urban Area as % of U.S. Urban Area | Urban Population (1000s) | Urban Pop. as % of U.S. Urban Pop. | Urban Lane Miles | Urban Lane Miles as % of U.S. Urban Lane Miles |
|---|---|---|---|---|---|---|
| Illinois | 4,104 | 3.6% | 9,677 | 4.8% | 81,209 | 4.2% |
| Indiana | 2,093 | 1.8% | 3,449 | 1.7% | 42,708 | 2.2% |
| Michigan | 3,560 | 3.1% | 6,939 | 3.4% | 68,825 | 3.6% |
| Ohio | 4,479 | 3.9% | 8,014 | 4.0% | 77,313 | 4.0% |
| Wisconsin | 2,090 | 1.8% | 4,241 | 2.1% | 36,900 | 1.9% |
| G.L. average | 3,265 | 2.9% | 6,464 | 3.2% | 61,391 | 3.2% |
| U.S. total | 113,576 | 100.0% | 202,874 | 100.0% | 1,915,180 | 100.0% |

SOURCE: Author's calculations based on U.S. Federal Highway Administration, (2000), table PS-1.

## TABLE 16.4

**Ownership of Federal-Aid and Non-Federal-Aid Highways**

| | State Highway Agency | County | Town, Township, Municipal | Other Jurisdiction | Federal Agency | Total Miles |
|---|---|---|---|---|---|---|
| | | | Percentage of Federal-Aid Highway Miles | | | |
| Illinois | 45.4% | 36.1% | 17.6% | 0.9% | 0.0% | 34,272 |
| Indiana | 50.3% | 35.0% | 14.7% | 0.0% | 0.0% | 22,195 |
| Michigan | 29.2% | 60.3% | 10.5% | 0.0% | 0.0% | 33,241 |
| Ohio | 64.6% | 16.9% | 17.7% | 0.9% | 0.0% | 27,970 |
| Wisconsin | 42.3% | 43.6% | 14.0% | 0.1% | 0.0% | 27,739 |
| G.L. average | 45.5% | 39.2% | 14.9% | 0.4% | 0.0% | 29,083 |
| U.S. total | 57.6% | 27.5% | 13.5% | 0.7% | 0.7% | 956,679 |
| | | | Percentage of Non-Federal-Aid Highway Miles | | | Total Miles |
| Illinois | 0.5% | 3.0% | 71.3% | 0.3% | 0.2% | 104,098 |
| Indiana | 0.1% | 62.9% | 13.4% | 0.0% | 0.0% | 71,412 |
| Michigan | 0.0% | 56.9% | 14.1% | 0.0% | 1.7% | 88,738 |
| Ohio | 1.0% | 20.9% | 51.5% | 2.6% | 0.1% | 88,994 |
| Wisconsin | 0.0% | 7.6% | 66.9% | 0.1% | 0.7% | 84,623 |
| G.L. average | 0.4% | 28.3% | 45.2% | 0.6% | 0.6% | 87,573 |
| U.S. total | 5.6% | 38.4% | 27.3% | 1.6% | 2.8% | 2,979,568 |

SOURCE: U.S. Federal Highway Administration, Highway Statistics 2000, Table HM-14.

the average of neighboring states. Michigan has 3.0% of the nation's rural lane miles. Michigan has 3.1% of the nation's urban land, 3.4% of the U.S. urban population, and 3.6% of the nation's urban lane miles. All of these are fractionally more than the average for the Great Lakes states.

Multiplicative cross-state regressions of lane miles on area and population show that a state that is 1% larger in rural land area has on average 0.50% more rural lane miles, and one with a 1% larger rural population has 0.54% more lane miles. At the mean, this corresponds to 48,000 rural lane miles plus 0.17 extra lane miles for each square mile and 42 extra lane miles for each one thousand rural population. Using this standard, Michigan has 4,300 (about 4.3%) more rural lane miles than we would expect, based on the relationship developed across the fifty states. The difference is not statistically significant, however.[3]

Similarly, a state with 1% more urban land has 0.31% more urban lane miles (about 6.7 lane miles per square mile of urban area). A state with 1% higher urban population has on average 0.67% more urban lane miles (4.5 more lane miles per thousand urban population.) Using this measure, Michigan has about 8,800 more urban lane miles (4.8%) than would be predicted from a relationship based on the fifty states plus the District of

Columbia. As was the case for rural roads, this difference does not come close to standards of statistical significance.[4]

While Michigan is close to normal in terms of the number of lane miles, Michigan is unusual in the ownership patterns of those roads. Major highways that carry significant quantities of interstate traffic are designated federal aid highways, because funding for these roads, as noted later in this chapter, is a joint responsibility of state and federal authorities. Federal funds are not used for local streets and roads. Thus we can use the fact that a highway receives federal aid as an indication that it is a major road. In most states, the state highway authority owns most federal aid highways while counties and townships are responsible for the great majority of non-federal-aid highways.

Table 16.4 shows that Michigan is an outlier from this pattern. County road commissions own 60.3% of federal-aid highways in Michigan, far above the national average of 27.5% and the Great Lakes states average of 39.2%. The Michigan Department of Transportation owns only 29.2% of through roads, compared to Ohio's 64.6% and the national average of 57.6%. County road commissions also have a major ownership claim in local roads, claiming 56.9% of non-federal-aid highways

**TABLE 16.5**

## Miles of Highway with Different Characteristics

| | RURAL | | | | URBAN | | | |
|---|---|---|---|---|---|---|---|---|
| | ≥ 4-Lane Div. Hwy. w/ Full Access Control | ≥ 4-Lane Div. Hwy. w/out Full Access Control | 2-Lane Highway | Other Highways[a] | ≥ 4-Lane Div. Hwy. w/ Full Access Control | ≥ 4-Lane Div. Hwy. w/out Full Access Control | 2-Lane Highway | Other Highways[a] |
| Illinois | 7.3% | 2.0% | 90.7% | 0.1% | 6.2% | 12.4% | 57.9% | 23.5% |
| Indiana | 5.5% | 8.3% | 85.9% | 0.3% | 4.7% | 8.0% | 67.4% | 19.9% |
| Michigan | 4.5% | 0.9% | 94.0% | 0.5% | 6.9% | 6.9% | 47.9% | 38.3% |
| Ohio | 6.6% | 4.8% | 85.9% | 2.7% | 9.7% | 6.5% | 60.2% | 23.6% |
| Wisconsin | 5.2% | 1.7% | 92.6% | 0.4% | 4.2% | 10.8% | 45.7% | 39.3% |
| G.L. average | 5.8% | 3.5% | 89.8% | 0.8% | 6.4% | 8.9% | 55.8% | 28.9% |
| U.S. total | 5.3% | 3.4% | 89.5% | 1.7% | 6.2% | 10.4% | 49.8% | 33.5% |

SOURCE: Author's calculation based on U.S. Federal Highway Administration (2000), table HM-35.
(a) Includes undivided 3- and 4-lane highways.

in Michigan. The national average is 38.4% for county road commissions. Michigan is unique among its neighbors in having county road commissions owning a majority of both local and through roads.

One possible place where the unusual influence of country road commissions may be seen is in the decisions as to what sort of highways to invest in. The result of these decisions is shown in table 16.5. In rural areas, Michigan relies heavily on two-lane highways and has correspondingly fewer multilane highways in comparison to its neighbors and to the nation as a whole. Michigan has almost no reliance on the four-lane roads without full access ramps that are common in Ohio and Indiana and in other parts of the country. Michigan also has a smaller percentage of rural roads that are fully access-controlled divided roads with four or more lanes than do the other Great Lakes states or the nation as a whole. It is entirely possible, of course, that these decisions are appropriate for conditions in Michigan that are different from those found in other states.

Decisions made about investment in urban roads in Michigan are more similar to those made in neighboring states and in the country as a whole. Michigan relies somewhat more than average on urban freeways and somewhat less than average on divided highways without full access control.

Another area in which Michigan's unusual delegation of decision-making authority to county road commissions may be expressed is in road construction techniques. Road-building materials and methods vary widely from region to region and state to state, in large part due to highway engineers' attempts to adapt road building to local climate and soil conditions. However, these decisions may also reflect local biases and experiences of those decision makers in determining how roads should be built.

The huge variation in road-building techniques within the region is shown in table 16.6. Despite the fact that the Great Lakes states are reasonably similar in terms of weather and soil conditions, highway engineers in the different states have made vastly different decisions about road-building techniques. Ohio, Indiana, and Illinois favor composite materials, but Michigan road builders use less of them. Wisconsin does not use flexible (asphalt-based) materials for interstates, while Ohio uses them for both rural and urban freeways and Michigan and Indiana use them on some rural interstates.

Despite the fact that different states favor different road-building materials for different types of highways, a few generalizations about Michigan roads can be made. First, Michigan uses far more unpaved roads than its neighbors. Only 27% of rural Michigan roads and 88% of urban roads in Michigan are paved; at the opposite extreme, Wisconsin paves 71% of its rural roads and 98% of its urban roads. Michigan paving rates for local roads are below the national average and far below the average for its neighbors.

Michigan is also unusual for using rigid (concrete) pavements for some collector highways whereas most other states use only cheaper and less durable paving in this situation. Michigan's use of strong pavements in interstate and other freeways is above both the national average and the average of other states in the region. If a

**TABLE 16.6**

**Paving Techniques for Different Categories of Roads**

**Rural Highways**

| | Interstates | | | Arterials | | | Major Collectors | | | Minor Collectors | Local |
|---|---|---|---|---|---|---|---|---|---|---|---|
| | Flex. | Comp. | Rigid | Flex. | Comp. | Rigid | Flex. | Comp. | Rigid | Paved | Paved |
| Illinois | 4.0% | 61.5% | 34.5% | 4.4% | 89.9% | 5.7% | 53.3% | 21.6% | 1.9% | 81.2% | 55.6% |
| Indiana | 10.0% | 75.9% | 14.1% | 45.8% | 35.9% | 8.1% | 39.7% | 4.4% | 2.1% | 80.3% | 47.7% |
| Michigan | 17.5% | 24.8% | 57.6% | 50.9% | 42.4% | 6.6% | 54.2% | 14.6% | 4.7% | 73.5% | 26.6% |
| Ohio | 11.8% | 82.4% | 5.8% | 55.1% | 41.8% | 3.0% | 83.9% | 11.3% | 0.0% | 97.5% | 76.6% |
| Wisconsin | 0.0% | 48.7% | 51.3% | 57.0% | 23.7% | 12.6% | 28.8% | 6.3% | 0.4% | 92.3% | 71.4% |
| G.L. average | 8.7% | 58.7% | 32.7% | 42.6% | 46.7% | 7.2% | 52.0% | 11.6% | 1.8% | 85.0% | 55.6% |
| U.S. total | 49.5% | 21.3% | 29.2% | 69.2% | 15.2% | 6.7% | 44.6% | 4.5% | 2.2% | 66.6% | 39.8% |

**Urban Highways**

| | Interstates + Other Freeways | | | Arterials | | | Collectors | | | Local |
|---|---|---|---|---|---|---|---|---|---|---|
| | Flex. | Comp. | Rigid | Flex. | Comp. | Rigid | Flex. | Comp. | Rigid | Paved |
| Illinois | 1.8% | 75.6% | 22.6% | 18.0% | 61.8% | 14.8% | 39.3% | 31.4% | 6.4% | 98.4% |
| Indiana | 6.4% | 68.1% | 25.6% | 34.3% | 19.7% | 8.1% | 18.2% | 0.6% | 1.3% | 92.8% |
| Michigan | 2.3% | 48.5% | 49.2% | 38.8% | 26.6% | 18.3% | 51.4% | 12.8% | 11.1% | 88.1% |
| Ohio | 13.1% | 74.6% | 12.2% | 58.3% | 34.7% | 4.8% | 79.8% | 9.0% | 2.0% | 93.9% |
| Wisconsin | 0.6% | 48.2% | 51.2% | 17.2% | 25.0% | 35.0% | 18.3% | 9.1% | 11.5% | 98.1% |
| G.L. average | 4.9% | 63.0% | 32.1% | 33.3% | 33.6% | 16.2% | 41.4% | 12.6% | 6.5% | 94.3% |
| U.S. total | 37.2% | 28.3% | 34.0% | 59.2% | 19.1% | 8.5% | 53.3% | 7.9% | 4.8% | 93.7% |

SOURCE: Author's calculations from U.S. Federal Highway Administration (2000), table HM-51. The three paving materials listed are not the sole paving materials. Weaker paving methods are used particularly for collectors.

generalization is possible, it appears that Michigan saves paving dollars by using dirt roads in circumstances where other states would not and then uses these savings to provide unusually durable types of pavements for a variety of roads. As is typical of all states, Michigan tends to use cheaper flexible paving materials on collectors and arterials (major through roads that are not expressways) and to use stronger composite materials and rigid paving on interstates and other freeways. It is reasonable to presume that both Michigan's extraordinary truck weight rules and the unusually prominent role played by county road commissions have a role in road-building decisions made in the state.

A final aspect in which Michigan roads are different from those of neighboring states and the nation is illustrated in tables 16.7 and 16.8. The tables show the percentage of roads in the Great Lakes states that meet various roughness standards. Table 16.7 is for rural roads and table 16.8 is for urban roads. The percentage of a state's highways meeting the most stringent roughness standard is shown in the first column. The proportion meeting the weakest standard is listed in the last column. Thus, reading across the first row of the table, only 6.5% of Illinois's rural interstates meet the most stringent standard for roughness, while 99.9% of those roads are better than extremely rough. The sixth row of each panel shows the average among neighboring states (excluding Michigan) of the percentage of road miles meeting each roughness standard. The seventh row shows the average for the nation. The final two rows of each panel show how Michigan compares to its neighbors and to the nation.

Michigan stands out in table 16.7 as having rural interstates that are far rougher than those of our neighbors and the nation as a whole. Taking a medium standard of the percentage of roads with International Roughness Index (IRI) less than or equal to 120, 85.6% of the nation's interstates are satisfactory, and 91.8% of our neighbors' rural freeways are acceptable, while only 68.6% of Michigan rural freeway miles meet the standard. The same pattern is true across all standards, from weakest to most stringent. Michigan rural interstates are simply in much worse condition than those of other states.

The same pattern cannot be found for other

**TABLE 16.7**

## Percentage of State Rural Roads Meeting Various Roughness Standards

| Roughness Standard: | 60 (very smooth) | 95 (smooth) | 120 | 145 | 171 | 195 (rough) | 220 (very rough) |
|---|---|---|---|---|---|---|---|
| **Rural Interstates** | | | | | | | |
| Illinois | 6.5% | 59.2% | 81.0% | 96.4% | 99.5% | 99.9% | 99.9% |
| Indiana | 53.2% | 93.2% | 99.3% | 99.9% | 100.0% | 100.0% | 100.0% |
| Michigan | 9.0% | 43.7% | 68.6% | 86.1% | 93.5% | 96.6% | 98.5% |
| Ohio | 43.5% | 87.8% | 98.2% | 99.9% | 100.0% | 100.0% | 100.0% |
| Wisconsin | 10.5% | 66.0% | 88.6% | 95.7% | 100.0% | 100.0% | 100.0% |
| G.L. average | 28.4% | 76.6% | 91.8% | 98.0% | 99.9% | 100.0% | 100.0% |
| U.S. total | 23.9% | 68.7% | 85.6% | 94.0% | 97.9% | 99.0% | 99.6% |
| Michigan – U.S. | –14.9% | –25.0% | –17.0% | –7.9% | –4.3% | –2.4% | –1.1% |
| Michigan – G.L. | –19.4% | –32.9% | –23.2% | –11.8% | –6.3% | –3.3% | –1.4% |
| | | | | | | | |
| **Rural Principal Arterial Roads** | | | | | | | |
| Illinois | 3.6% | 38.5% | 61.5% | 80.8% | 91.6% | 97.2% | 98.8% |
| Indiana | 19.5% | 64.2% | 81.9% | 92.2% | 97.0% | 99.8% | 99.9% |
| Michigan | 17.1% | 57.7% | 78.0% | 88.8% | 94.9% | 97.3% | 98.8% |
| Ohio | 16.7% | 79.3% | 95.1% | 98.3% | 99.1% | 99.6% | 99.9% |
| Wisconsin | 16.7% | 54.9% | 76.4% | 89.9% | 95.3% | 97.7% | 99.1% |
| G.L. average | 14.1% | 59.2% | 78.7% | 90.3% | 95.8% | 98.6% | 99.4% |
| U.S. total | 14.4% | 57.3% | 78.4% | 90.1% | 96.0% | 98.2% | 99.2% |
| Michigan – U.S. | 2.7% | 0.4% | –0.3% | –1.3% | –1.1% | –0.9% | –0.4% |
| Michigan – G.L. | 3.0% | –1.5% | –0.7% | –1.5% | –0.8% | –1.3% | –0.6% |
| | | | | | | | |
| **Rural Minor Arterial Roads** | | | | | | | |
| Illinois | 8.4% | 32.6% | 61.1% | 70.8% | 91.1% | 92.4% | 95.6% |
| Indiana | 15.3% | 53.2% | 81.4% | 90.0% | 98.4% | 99.4% | 100.0% |
| Michigan | 21.3% | 61.9% | 78.0% | 88.1% | 96.0% | 97.5% | 98.4% |
| Ohio | 4.9% | 74.2% | 92.7% | 98.9% | 98.9% | 99.9% | 100.0% |
| Wisconsin | 21.1% | 53.2% | 72.7% | 86.8% | 91.4% | 93.6% | 99.3% |
| G.L. average | 12.4% | 53.3% | 77.0% | 86.6% | 95.0% | 96.3% | 98.7% |
| U.S. total | 11.2% | 46.8% | 71.9% | 85.3% | 93.0% | 96.3% | 98.3% |
| Michigan – U.S. | 10.2% | 15.1% | 6.1% | 2.8% | 3.0% | 1.2% | 0.0% |
| Michigan – G.L. | 8.9% | 8.6% | 1.0% | 1.4% | 1.1% | 1.2% | –0.3% |

SOURCE: Author's calculations from statistics presented in U.S. Federal Highway Administration, Highway Statistics 2000, Table HM-64.

rural highways. Michigan rural principal arterial highways are not substantially poorer than those of either the nation or our neighbors. The quality of Michigan's rural minor arterial highways in fact is slightly better than that of both the nation as a whole and our neighbors.

Table 16.8 shows the same data for urban highways. By any standard, Michigan urban roads are in bad condition. Using a roughness standard of 120 IRI, only 61.5% of Michigan urban interstate miles are considered satisfactory, compared to an average of 71.8% for the nation and 83.3% for neighboring states. Noninterstate urban freeways are even worse. Michigan is 19 percentage points

below both the national average and the average roughness other Great Lakes states. Worst of all are nonfreeway urban arterial highways. Only 13.6% of Michigan highways in this category meet this medium roughness standard. This is 27.8 percentage points below the nation as a whole and 30.8 percentage points behind our Great Lakes neighbors. Only 71% of Michigan urban nonfreeway arterial highways meet even the most forgiving standard for roughness.

In summary, Michigan rural interstate highways and all classes of major urban highways are of poor quality, as measured by the International Roughness Index. Among major highways only

**TABLE 16.8**

## Percentage of State Urban Roads Meeting Various Roughness Standards

| Roughness Standard: | 60 (very smooth) | 95 (smooth) | 120 | 145 | 171 | 195 (rough) | 220 (very rough) |
|---|---|---|---|---|---|---|---|
| **Urban Interstates** | | | | | | | |
| Illinois | 1.7% | 35.3% | 69.5% | 89.1% | 93.7% | 99.7% | 100.0% |
| Indiana | 22.6% | 74.5% | 91.2% | 95.0% | 98.1% | 99.4% | 100.0% |
| Michigan | 4.0% | 40.1% | 61.5% | 81.6% | 90.2% | 95.2% | 97.8% |
| Ohio | 23.7% | 78.0% | 93.5% | 97.0% | 98.7% | 99.5% | 99.9% |
| Wisconsin | 13.3% | 53.2% | 79.1% | 89.2% | 100.0% | 100.0% | 100.0% |
| G.L. average | 15.3% | 60.3% | 83.3% | 92.6% | 97.6% | 99.6% | 100.0% |
| U.S. total | 13.3% | 50.4% | 71.8% | 85.2% | 93.5% | 97.0% | 98.6% |
| Michigan – U.S. | –9.3% | –10.3% | –10.3% | –3.6% | –3.3% | –1.8% | –0.8% |
| Michigan – G.L. | –11.3% | –20.2% | –21.8% | –11.0% | –7.4% | –4.4% | –2.2% |
| **Non-Interstate Urban Freeways** | | | | | | | |
| Illinois | 0.0% | 4.7% | 61.2% | 85.9% | 90.6% | 92.9% | 95.3% |
| Indiana | 12.3% | 29.2% | 53.1% | 69.2% | 82.3% | 91.5% | 93.1% |
| Michigan | 3.6% | 19.1% | 42.7% | 65.3% | 81.8% | 92.0% | 96.4% |
| Ohio | 12.5% | 56.9% | 78.1% | 88.5% | 97.4% | 99.2% | 99.5% |
| Wisconsin | 4.5% | 35.8% | 54.7% | 74.9% | 88.3% | 93.9% | 97.2% |
| G.L. average | 7.3% | 31.6% | 61.8% | 79.6% | 89.7% | 94.4% | 96.3% |
| U.S. total | 6.8% | 38.4% | 61.2% | 78.6% | 89.1% | 94.7% | 97.2% |
| Michigan – U.S. | –3.3% | –19.3% | –18.5% | –13.2% | –7.3% | –2.7% | –0.7% |
| Michigan – G.L. | –3.8% | –12.5% | –19.1% | –14.3% | –7.9% | –2.4% | 0.2% |
| **Urban Other Arterial Highways** | | | | | | | |
| Illinois | 3.4% | 29.2% | 49.7% | 68.0% | 80.7% | 88.9% | 95.0% |
| Indiana | 4.6% | 27.4% | 47.5% | 66.5% | 79.6% | 88.8% | 92.1% |
| Michigan | 0.6% | 6.0% | 13.6% | 23.7% | 43.6% | 57.8% | 71.0% |
| Ohio | 3.5% | 29.9% | 51.6% | 70.8% | 82.9% | 89.5% | 94.3% |
| Wisconsin | 2.1% | 13.9% | 28.6% | 44.3% | 59.6% | 73.3% | 82.8% |
| G.L. average | 3.4% | 25.1% | 44.4% | 62.4% | 75.7% | 85.1% | 91.1% |
| U.S. total | 5.4% | 24.9% | 41.4% | 56.6% | 70.0% | 79.4% | 86.8% |
| Michigan – U.S. | –4.8% | –18.9% | –27.8% | –33.0% | –26.4% | –21.6% | –15.9% |
| Michigan – G.L. | –2.8% | –19.1% | –30.8% | –38.7% | –32.1% | –27.3% | –20.1% |

SOURCE: Author's calculations from statistics presented in U.S. Federal Highway Administration, Highway Statistics 2000, Table HM-64.

**TABLE 16.9**

## Vehicle Miles of Traffic, 2000

| | Rural | | Urban | | | | Truck VMT/ |
|---|---|---|---|---|---|---|---|
| | Annual Vehicle Miles of Travel (millions) | % Trucks | Annual Vehicle Miles of Travel (millions) | % Trucks | % Urban | VMT/Capita ($1000) | $1000 Gross State Product |
| Illinois | 31,302 | 14.1 | 71,564 | 9.1 | 69.6 | 8.2 | 27.7 |
| Indiana | 35,968 | 16.9 | 34,894 | 10.0 | 49.2 | 12.8 | 59.1 |
| Michigan | 37,525 | 11.0 | 60,267 | 7.0 | 61.6 | 9.8 | 30.6 |
| Ohio | 41,884 | 17.3 | 64,014 | 8.0 | 60.4 | 9.3 | 38.5 |
| Wisconsin | 31,346 | 9.5 | 25,920 | 6.9 | 45.3 | 10.3 | 32.4 |
| G.L. average | 35,605 | 13.8 | 51,332 | 8.2 | 59.0 | 10.1 | 38.0 |
| U.S. total | 1,084,961 | 14.8 | 1,664,842 | 7.0 | 60.5 | 9.8 | 34.2 |

SOURCE: Author's calculations based on information in U.S. Federal Highway Administration, Highway Statistics 2000, Table PS-1.

rural noninterstates are at the same level of smoothness in Michigan as highways in other parts of the country.

## Travel Volumes

Michigan's poor-quality roads are not the result of Michiganians driving more. This is illustrated in table 16.9, which shows that Michigan is quite average in terms of the number of vehicle miles traveled (VMT) within its borders. The 9,800 miles of vehicle traffic per capita in Michigan is right at the national average, as is the 7% proportion of truck VMT to total VMT. The rural/urban split is also close to both the national average and that of the Great Lakes states. Each $1000 of gross state product is associated with about 31 miles of truck traffic. This is somewhat below the national average, perhaps reflecting a commodity mix that calls for less truck traffic per dollar of output, or perhaps reflecting the fact that Michigan allows ultraheavy trucks on its roads and that fewer trips are needed by these trucks than by comparable lighter vehicles.

The distribution of traffic among different types of roads in the state is shown in table 16.10.

About half of rural traffic in Michigan is carried on the arterial roads, while the other half is on rural interstate highways. Michigan noninterstate rural arterials are somewhat more heavily traveled, compared with those of other states, but the difference is not large. A similar pattern is seen on urban roads. Michigan drivers use urban freeways somewhat less than drivers in the nation as a whole, but somewhat more than drivers in other Great Lakes states.

A slightly different view of the traffic distribution is reported in table 16.11, which measures the percentage of miles of different classes of highways that carry heavy traffic. The table presents two different definitions of what heavy traffic means. The first column under each road category has a looser definition, while the second has a tighter definition. Thus, for example, 86.6% of Michigan rural interstates carry heavy traffic volumes, if our definition of heavy traffic is that heavy means more than ten thousand vehicles per day, while only 56.4% will be classified as carrying heavy traffic if what we mean by "heavy traffic" is more than twenty thousand vehicles per day.

Table 16.11 shows that a smaller proportion of Michigan's rural interstates carry heavy traffic, in comparison with other Great Lakes states. Its

## TABLE 16.10

**Proportion of Rural and Urban Traffic on Different Classes of Highways**

| | Percent of Rural VMT | | | | |
|---|---|---|---|---|---|
| | Interstate | Arterial | Collector | Local | Total |
| Illinois | 73.9% | 26.1% | 0.0% | 0.0% | 100.0% |
| Indiana | 63.7% | 36.2% | 0.2% | 0.0% | 100.0% |
| Michigan | 48.8% | 51.2% | 0.0% | 0.0% | 100.0% |
| Ohio | 57.9% | 41.9% | 0.1% | 0.0% | 100.0% |
| Wisconsin | 44.7% | 55.3% | 0.0% | 0.0% | 100.0% |
| G.L. average | 57.5% | 42.4% | 0.1% | 0.0% | 100.0% |
| U.S. total | 54.5% | 45.2% | 0.2% | 0.0% | 100.0% |

| | Percent of Urban VMT | | | | | |
|---|---|---|---|---|---|---|
| | Interstate | Other Freeways | Arterial | Collector | Local | Total |
| Illinois | 54.6% | 3.1% | 41.7% | 0.6% | 0.0% | 100.0% |
| Indiana | 68.5% | 7.7% | 23.8% | 0.0% | 0.0% | 100.0% |
| Michigan | 50.7% | 15.5% | 33.8% | 0.0% | 0.0% | 100.0% |
| Ohio | 70.3% | 16.5% | 13.1% | 0.1% | 0.0% | 100.0% |
| Wisconsin | 37.1% | 25.8% | 37.0% | 0.1% | 0.0% | 100.0% |
| G.L. average | 57.3% | 12.2% | 30.3% | 0.2% | 0.0% | 100.0% |
| U.S. total | 54.3% | 22.5% | 23.1% | 0.1% | 0.0% | 100.0% |

SOURCE: Author's calculations based on information in U.S. Federal Highway Administration (2000), table HM-44.

**TABLE 16.11**

## Proportion of Highways Carrying Heavy Traffic

**Rural Highways**

| | Interstates | | Other Principal Arterials | | Minor Arterials | | Major Collectors | |
| --- | --- | --- | --- | --- | --- | --- | --- | --- |
| | | | PERCENT OF ROAD MILES WITH DAILY TRAFFIC LEVELS | | | | | |
| | >10,000 | >20,000 | >10,000 | >15,000 | >10,000 | >15,000 | >5,000 | >10,000 |
| Illinois | 86.1% | 41.8% | 8.5% | 2.4% | 1.5% | 0.2% | 1.9% | 0.0% |
| Indiana | 99.3% | 72.1% | 29.5% | 14.3% | 10.5% | 5.9% | 13.2% | 2.6% |
| Michigan | 86.6% | 56.4% | 24.3% | 13.6% | 6.1% | 1.8% | 4.5% | 0.4% |
| Ohio | 99.8% | 88.5% | 38.9% | 17.9% | 4.7% | 0.5% | 9.3% | 1.2% |
| Wisconsin | 100.0% | 74.7% | 22.3% | 9.0% | 2.5% | 0.6% | 1.1% | 0.1% |
| G.L. average | 93.0% | 62.7% | 23.8% | 10.9% | 4.3% | 1.4% | 5.5% | 0.8% |
| U.S. total | 77.3% | 47.8% | 20.3% | 9.9% | 4.9% | 1.7% | 4.2% | 0.7% |

**Urban Highways**

| | Interstates | | Other Expressways & Freeways | | Other Principal Arterials | | Minor Arterials | | Collectors | |
| --- | --- | --- | --- | --- | --- | --- | --- | --- | --- | --- |
| | | | | PERCENT OF ROAD MILES WITH DAILY TRAFFIC LEVELS | | | | | | |
| | >60,000 | >100,000 | >60,000 | >100,000 | >10,000 | >20,000 | >10,000 | >20,000 | >10,000 | >20,000 |
| Illinois | 45.8% | 34.8% | 15.7% | 7.2% | 78.9% | 44.6% | 46.5% | 13.4% | 20.4% | 1.9% |
| Indiana | 40.2% | 19.9% | 1.5% | 0.0% | 79.7% | 36.3% | 34.2% | 6.2% | 3.3% | 0.1% |
| Michigan | 52.1% | 27.5% | 31.1% | 13.3% | 88.0% | 50.0% | 44.8% | 11.1% | 9.5% | 0.2% |
| Ohio | 54.4% | 21.8% | 12.8% | 2.0% | 74.3% | 29.8% | 37.3% | 5.0% | 4.4% | 0.1% |
| Wisconsin | 41.7% | 25.2% | 21.7% | 6.1% | 66.8% | 20.8% | 20.4% | 2.5% | 0.5% | 0.0% |
| G.L. average | 48.8% | 26.5% | 17.1% | 5.4% | 78.3% | 37.9% | 38.6% | 8.4% | 9.3% | 0.6% |
| U.S. total | 52.4% | 29.8% | 28.9% | 12.9% | 78.2% | 41.9% | 38.8% | 10.5% | 8.8% | 1.0% |

SOURCE: Author's calculations based on information in U.S. Federal Highway Administration (2000), table HM-44.

other rural roads have about the same proportion of miles that can be classified as carrying heavy traffic as in the region and the nation as a whole.

The view of Michigan roads as carrying generally light traffic changes, however, when we move to urban highways. For most categories of urban highways, Michigan has a larger percentage of its roads carrying heavy traffic than its neighbors and the nation as a whole. The difference is most pronounced for noninterstate urban freeways and urban arterial highways. These latter highways are also those on which the quality difference between Michigan highways and those of the comparison groups is largest.

Urban roads have more lanes and more capacity than do rural highways. This is reflected in the different standards for what constitutes heavy traffic in table 16.11. Traffic engineers estimate maximum traffic volumes for different highways based on the number of lanes, speed limits, and access controls(Mannering and Kilareski 1998). The observed volume is then recorded and the Volume/Service Ratio (VSR) is computed. VSR measures the degree of congestion. A highway

that approaches VSR = 1 is likely to have more and longer episodes of traffic congestion than one that has a lower VSR. Table 16.12 uses two VSR thresholds, 0.70 and 0.95, to measure the extent to which roads are heavily enough used to have likely congestion problems. Table 16.12 shows that there are few capacity problems on rural highways in Michigan. The state's VSR figures look very much like those of other states in the region and the nation.

Traffic congestion is really an urban problem, and this shows up in the bottom panel of table 16.12. Michigan urban highways do not have significantly worse traffic congestion than in neighboring states or the nation. In fact, Michigan's urban expressway capacity is slightly better matched to volume than that of other states. The state's arterial and collector highways appear to have about the same level of congestion as peer states.

Urban traffic figures in Michigan are dominated by the Detroit region, the second-largest urban area in the Great Lakes states, half as large as Chicago and twice as large as Cleveland. Table 16.13 shows that Detroit has 63% of Michigan's

**TABLE 16.12**

## Proportion of Roads that Are Congested

### Rural Highways

| | Interstates | | Other Principal Arterials | | Minor Arterials | | Major Collectors | |
|---|---|---|---|---|---|---|---|---|
| | PERCENT OF ROAD MILES WITH CONGESTION LEVELS | | | | | | | |
| | VSR > .70 | VSR > .95 | VSR > .70 | VSR > .95 | VSR > .70 | VSR > .95 | VSR > .70 | VSR > .95 |
| Illinois | 2.4% | 0.5% | 0.2% | 0.0% | 0.0% | 0.0% | 0.0% | 0.0% |
| Indiana | 0.1% | 0.0% | 4.7% | 0.3% | 0.4% | 0.2% | 0.3% | 0.0% |
| Michigan | 4.6% | 0.0% | 6.2% | 0.8% | 1.9% | 1.2% | 0.1% | 0.1% |
| Ohio | 16.0% | 1.7% | 5.5% | 2.5% | 1.6% | 0.1% | 1.1% | 0.0% |
| Wisconsin | 10.7% | 1.0% | 1.3% | 0.1% | 0.2% | 0.0% | 0.0% | 0.0% |
| G.L. average | 5.9% | 0.6% | 3.3% | 0.7% | 0.8% | 0.3% | 0.3% | 0.0% |
| U.S. total | 7.0% | 1.2% | 4.1% | 1.3% | 1.7% | 0.5% | 0.3% | 0.1% |

### Urban Highways

| | Interstates | | Other Expressways & Freeways | | Other Principal Arterials | | Minor Arterials | | Collectors | |
|---|---|---|---|---|---|---|---|---|---|---|
| | PERCENT OF ROAD MILES WITH CONGESTION LEVELS | | | | | | | | | |
| | VSR > .70 | VSR > .95 | VSR > .70 | VSR > .95 | VSR > .70 | VSR > .95 | VSR > .70 | VSR > .95 | VSR > .70 | VSR > .95 |
| Illinois | 33.9% | 6.6% | 6.3% | 0.0% | 25.4% | 10.0% | 34.1% | 18.2% | 20.9% | 11.5% |
| Indiana | 15.8% | 8.2% | 9.5% | 2.9% | 29.9% | 10.1% | 32.4% | 17.5% | 12.2% | 5.7% |
| Michigan | 39.7% | 5.8% | 23.6% | 3.6% | 29.3% | 12.2% | 26.1% | 12.4% | 7.6% | 3.8% |
| Ohio | 55.8% | 15.6% | 13.1% | 5.0% | 18.8% | 5.7% | 14.8% | 4.0% | 6.9% | 1.5% |
| Wisconsin | 32.1% | 15.1% | 19.3% | 5.5% | 27.0% | 12.9% | 33.4% | 18.7% | 13.4% | 3.7% |
| G.L. average | 39.4% | 10.0% | 15.5% | 4.1% | 25.8% | 10.0% | 27.5% | 13.6% | 12.6% | 5.7% |
| U.S. total | 40.2% | 13.5% | 32.4% | 13.7% | 24.5% | 9.7% | 19.5% | 8.0% | 10.3% | 4.7% |

SOURCE: Author's calculations based on information in U.S. Federal Highway Administration (2000), table HM-61.

urban population, 56% of the state's urban road miles, 52% of the state's freeway lane miles, and 63% of the daily vehicle miles traveled. Detroit has a higher population density per square mile than do other Michigan cities. However, based on a multiplicative regression of all metropolitan areas in the Great Lakes region, Detroit appears to be completely normal. According to this regression, reported at the bottom of table 16.13, daily vehicle miles traveled increase 0.48% for every 1% increase in road miles, 0.30% for every 1% increase in population, 0.29% for every 1% increase in land area, and 0.06% for every 1% increase in freeway lane miles. These four factors account for more than 98% of the variation in total vehicle miles traveled in all metropolitan areas in the region. Detroit's traffic levels can be forecast almost precisely using these four factors. The last column of table 16.13 shows that Detroit's traffic is less than 1% more than what would be expected, given its characteristics. The areas with more traffic than would be expected from their characteristics are Ann Arbor (25% more traffic) and Benton Harbor (22% more). Muskegon's traffic is 15% less than

would be expected. On average, Michigan cities have about 5% more VMT than would be expected from the regression in table 16.13. This difference is not statistically significant, and thus we cannot reject the hypothesis that Michigan's cities generate traffic at the same rate as others in the Great Lakes region.

## Road Finance

The funds used by the State of Michigan and its local subgovernments to finance road construction and repair come from the same general sources as those in any other state. In the United States, roads are funded almost exclusively by user fees. These imposts are in the form of fuel taxes, registration fees, and tolls. Table 16.14 shows how Michigan funds its roads in comparison to other states.

Total funds earmarked for highways by the fifty states in the year 2000 were $91.5 million. Michigan's $2.8 billion funding level was 3.1% of this total, slightly less than Michigan's 3.5% of the

**TABLE 16.13**

**Daily Vehicle Miles Traveled in Michigan Metropolitan Areas with Selected Characteristics**

| | Estimated Population (1000s) | Net Land Area (sq. miles) | Persons per Square Mile | Total Roadway Miles | Total Est. Freeway Lane Miles | Total DVMT (1000s) | DVMT Unexplained by Pop., Roads, and Land |
|---|---|---|---|---|---|---|---|
| Detroit | 3,836 | 1,304 | 2,942 | 13,808 | 1,813 | 92,359 | 0.9% |
| Grand Rapids | 530 | 318 | 1,667 | 2,273 | 292 | 12,151 | −2.5% |
| Flint | 339 | 237 | 1,430 | 1,700 | 322 | 9,699 | 10.3% |
| Lansing–East Lansing | 285 | 157 | 1,815 | 1,236 | 206 | 6,376 | 3.7% |
| Ann Arbor | 277 | 159 | 1,742 | 991 | 244 | 7,131 | 24.6% |
| Kalamazoo | 184 | 123 | 1,496 | 881 | 113 | 4,635 | 12.5% |
| Saginaw | 135 | 78 | 1,731 | 749 | 97 | 3,113 | 4.2% |
| Muskegon | 119 | 87 | 1,368 | 685 | 62 | 2,357 | −15.7% |
| Jackson | 90 | 78 | 1,154 | 544 | 87 | 2,204 | −2.1% |
| Battle Creek | 81 | 79 | 1,025 | 557 | 57 | 2,082 | −3.1% |
| Port Huron | 78 | 62 | 1,258 | 452 | 60 | 1,829 | 1.6% |
| Bay City | 74 | 49 | 1,510 | 415 | 47 | 1,585 | 1.5% |
| Benton Harbor | 60 | 49 | 1,224 | 412 | 84 | 1,891 | 22.0% |
| Michigan Urban total | 6,088 | 2,780 | | 24,703 | 3,483 | 147,413 | |
| Detroit's proportion | 63.0% | 46.9% | | 55.9% | 52.1% | 62.7% | |
| AVERAGE | | | 1,566 | | | | 4.5% |

SOURCE: Author's calculations based on data in U.S. Federal Highway Administration (2000), table HM-72.

NOTE: The final column contains residuals for each Michigan city based on the following regression for all metropolitan areas in the great Lakes states: $\ln DVMT = 1.79 + 0.48(\ln roadmi) + 0.30(\ln pop) + 0.29(\ln area) + 0.06(\ln freelnmi)$, $R^2 = 0.98$; (0.15), (0.09), (0.10), (0.04); $N = 58$. This regression should be seen as a reduced form inasmuch as at least freeway miles and road miles are endogenous.

nation's population. Among the Great Lakes states, only in Indiana is the percentage of local road expenditures as a proportion of the nation's larger than the state's share of population.

Table 16.14 shows that state fuel taxes and registration fees fund on average 57% of highway spending in the Great Lakes region and 48% nationally. Michigan is right at the regional average. However, Michigan collects very little toll revenue, in comparison to the nation and to its neighbors. Michigan also relies on funding sources other than bonds and user fees to fund its roads. This is something that its neighbors do not do, but is more common nationally.

Michigan is also very close to average in the percentage of highway funds coming from transfers from the federal government. Federal transfers, in turn, are derived from the Highway Trust

**TABLE 16.14**

**Source of Highway Funds, 2000**

| | State Hwy. User Tax Revenues | Road & Crossing Tolls | Other Imposts & General Funds | Misc. Income | Bond Proceeds | Payments from Fed. Gov't. | Payments from Local Gov'ts. | Total Receipts (in millions of dollars) |
|---|---|---|---|---|---|---|---|---|
| Illinois | 55.4% | 8.9% | 6.7% | 1.6% | 4.6% | 22.1% | 0.7% | 3,860 |
| Indiana | 48.9% | 4.4% | 0.0% | 0.9% | 12.5% | 32.1% | 1.2% | 1,959 |
| Michigan | 57.2% | 1.1% | 11.4% | 2.6% | 0.0% | 26.5% | 1.2% | 2,815 |
| Ohio | 60.8% | 5.7% | 0.2% | 3.2% | 8.0% | 21.1% | 1.0% | 3,126 |
| Wisconsin | 62.0% | 0.0% | 0.1% | 2.2% | 0.0% | 31.4% | 4.2% | 1,612 |
| G.L. average | 56.9% | 4.8% | 4.4% | 2.2% | 5.0% | 25.4% | 1.4% | 2,675 |
| TOTAL | 48.4% | 5.2% | 7.2% | 3.0% | 8.9% | 25.7% | 1.6% | 91,476 |

SOURCE: Calculations by the author from data in U.S. Federal Highway Administration (2000), table SF-21.

Fund. By far the largest source of revenue for the trust fund is a national tax of 18.4 cents/gallon on gasoline. A further source of revenue for the trust fund is the national diesel tax, which is set at 24.4 cents/gallon. Despite the higher tax rate on diesel fuel, this tax raises substantially less revenue than the gasoline tax, due to the much smaller amount of diesel fuel sold. There are also some minor excise taxes on trucks, truck trailers, and tires that bring in a small fraction of the amount raised by the gasoline tax. Since the Highway Trust Fund is funded almost exclusively by a fuel tax, payments into the fund are determined primarily by the amount of urban and rural driving. Since urban driving is less fuel-efficient than rural vehicle miles, it is effectively taxed more heavily per mile. Disbursements from the trust fund to the states do not solely reflect fuel usage, and thus there is no presumption that states will receive from the fund an amount equal to what is raised from their citizens. Michigan has historically received a smaller share of payments from the trust fund than the state's share of payments into the fund.

Ninety-five percent of the variation among federal transfers to the states for highways is explainable by a simple regression on urban car miles, urban truck miles, urban lane miles, rural car miles, rural truck miles, and rural lane miles. In this regression, the level of Michigan's receipts from the federal government is almost precisely fitted, meaning that Michigan receives an appropriate share of federal funds, assuming that the six factors used to explain disbursements correctly reflect national priorities.[5]

User fees collected by the state fund the largest part of Michigan's highway expenditures. This is shown in table 16.15. Michigan is very close to

### TABLE 16.15

**State User Fees Collected for Highway Purposes**

|  | State Motor-Fuel Receipts | State Motor-Vehicle Receipts | State Toll Revenue | Total Collections for Hwy. Purposes[a] |
|---|---|---|---|---|
| Illinois | 47.6% | 38.5% | 13.9% | $ 2,482 |
| Indiana | 70.9% | 21.0% | 8.2% | $ 1,043 |
| Michigan | 55.8% | 42.2% | 1.9% | $ 1,643 |
| Ohio | 65.9% | 25.6% | 8.5% | $ 2,079 |
| Wisconsin | 69.9% | 30.1% | 0.0% | $ 1,000 |
| G.L. average | 59.5% | 32.7% | 7.8% | $ 1,650 |
| TOTAL | 58.6% | 31.7% | 9.7% | $ 48,986 |

SOURCE: Author's calculations based on U.S. Federal Highway Administration (2000), table SDF.
(a) In millions of dollars.

average in the proportion of state collections attributed to fuel taxes. The state has an unusually low reliance on toll revenue, as noted previously, and a slightly higher dependence on registration fees and other taxies levied on vehicles. While the total amount of fuel taxes collected by the state is quite normal, the distribution of revenues between gasoline and diesel taxes is quite unusual. This is shown in table 16.16.

There are only a few states in the nation that have a lower tax rate on a gallon of diesel fuel than on a gallon of gasoline. Michigan, in fact, has the lowest relative diesel tax rate of all states in the nation, in comparison to the tax rate on gasoline. Gasoline tax rates in Michigan are quite average, compared to the nation as a whole, but the state's diesel tax rates are extraordinarily low. Michigan also exempts more nondiesel fuels from motor fuel taxes than do other states. As a result, gasoline represents 84.3% of all gallons of motor fuel

### TABLE 16.16

**Motor Fuel Taxes, 2000**

|  | Gasoline Tax per Gallon | Diesel Fuel Tax per Gallon | Total Gallons of Motor Fuel Taxed | Gasoline Gallons Taxed as % of Total | Revenue from Gasoline Tax (millions) | Gas Tax Revenue as % of Motor Fuel Tax Collections |
|---|---|---|---|---|---|---|
| Illinois | 19 | 22 | 6,322,986 | 79.7% | $ 95.79 | 76% |
| Indiana | 15 | 16 | 4,393,014 | 70.9% | $ 46.74 | 62% |
| Michigan | 19 | 15 | 5,858,258 | 84.3% | $ 93.88 | 88% |
| Ohio | 22 | 22 | 6,435,199 | 77.4% | $ 109.63 | 71% |
| Wisconsin | 25.4 | 25.4 | 3,078,710 | 78.9% | $ 61.66 | 75% |
| G.L. average | 18.08 | 19.98 | 5,217,633 | 78.6% | $ 82.74 | 76% |
| TOTAL | 19.29 | 19.96 | 162,275,818 | 79.8% | $ 2,499.37 | 78% |

SOURCE: Author's calculations based on data in U.S. Federal Highway Administration (2000), tables MF-1, MF-2, and MF-121t.

**TABLE 16.17**

**State Taxes and Fees on Vehicles, Drivers, and Carriers**

| | Auto. Registr. Fee Incl. Taxicabs | Trucks, Tractors & Trailers Reg. Fee | Driver's Licenses | Title Fees | Carrier Gross Receipts Tax | Mileage, ton-Mileage, & Pass.-Mile Tax | Special Fees & Franchise Tax | Cert. or Permit Fees | Total Fees (millions of dollars) |
|---|---|---|---|---|---|---|---|---|---|
| Illinois | 38.2% | 28.4% | 0.7% | 9.7% | 0.0% | 0.0% | 0.5% | 0.0% | $ 1,087 |
| Indiana | 17.1% | 53.0% | 2.3% | 5.6% | 0.0% | 0.0% | 0.7% | 0.0% | $ 311 |
| Michigan | 53.9% | 29.5% | 1.0% | 4.5% | 0.0% | 0.0% | 0.0% | 0.9% | $ 845 |
| Ohio | 36.1% | 26.3% | 2.2% | 2.1% | 0.4% | 0.0% | 0.0% | 0.0% | $ 701 |
| Wisconsin | 34.1% | 41.0% | 1.1% | 2.3% | 0.0% | 0.0% | 0.0% | 0.8% | $ 397 |
| G.L. average | 39.3% | 32.0% | 1.3% | 5.7% | 0.2% | 0.0% | 0.5% | 0.6% | $ 668 |
| U.S. total | 30.4% | 23.8% | 3.0% | 18.0% | 0.1% | 2.1% | 0.2% | 0.3% | $ 24,985 |

SOURCE: Author's calculations based on U.S. Federal Highway Administration (2000), table MV-2. Rows do not sum to 100% due to the omission of minor vehicle classes and the collection of miscellaneous fees.

that are taxed in Michigan—much higher than the national and regional averages. Combined with the lower tax on diesel fuel, 88% of the Michigan motor fuel tax burden falls on drivers using gasoline engines, a much higher percentage than in the region and the nation.

Higher fees on trucking vehicles, their drivers, or trucking operations do not offset this very low fuel tax burden on trucks. This is shown in table 16.17, which compares Michigan's revenues raised from drivers and carriers from nonfuel sources. Michigan automobile drivers pay 53.9% of these fees in the form of registration fees, by far the highest percentage of any state in the region, and far higher than the national average. Truck registration fees are lower than the regional average. Michigan also forgoes the collection of taxes on the gross receipts of carriers, of taxes on ton-mileage or vehicle mileage of motor carriers, and of franchise fees, all of which would shift the bur-

den of highway finance to trucks, but forgoing these revenue sources used in other states is not unusual in the region.

Earlier in this chapter, it was noted that Michigan is unusual in giving a major responsibility for through roads in the state to country road commissions. Many roads that would be state-owned in other states are owned by counties in Michigan. This is reflected in table 16.18, which shows that in Michigan only 17.9% of funds raised by state fuel taxes and motor vehicle fees are spent on building and maintaining state-owned roads. This is a far smaller percentage than in the region and the nation. It is reasonable to infer that this low level of state funding of state highways is one reason for the poor condition of Michigan through highways, in comparison to those of other states. By contrast, 55.9% of these funds are spent on local roads and streets—again, far out of line with the region and the nation. Fuel taxes are paid into

**TABLE 16.18**

**State Revenues Spent on State and Local Highways and Mass Transit**

| | State Hwy. Capital Expend., Maint., Admin. | State Hwy. Law Enforcement | Debt Service on State Roads | Total Distrib. for State Roads | Total Distrib. for Local Roads & Streets | Mass Transit | Total Funds Distributed (millions of dollars) |
|---|---|---|---|---|---|---|---|
| Illinois | 57.5% | 5.5% | 0.3% | 63.3% | 33.5% | 1.8% | $2,208 |
| Indiana | 51.2% | 5.7% | 3.2% | 60.2% | 39.6% | 0.1% | $961 |
| Michigan | 17.9% | 11.4% | 2.4% | 31.7% | 55.9% | 12.3% | $1,839 |
| Ohio | 29.1% | 4.5% | 10.2% | 43.8% | 50.6% | 1.1% | $2,013 |
| Wisconsin | 29.0% | 5.0% | 7.7% | 41.7% | 46.3% | 8.5% | $1,137 |
| G.L. average | 36.8% | 6.6% | 4.6% | 48.0% | 45.3% | 4.7% | $1,631 |
| TOTAL | 42.3% | 7.9% | 7.7% | 58.0% | 24.6% | 3.8% | $53,593 |

SOURCE: Author's calculations, based on information in U.S. Federal Highway Administration (2000), table DF.

the Michigan Transportation Fund. Payments from the fund are divided, with 39.1% going to the Michigan Department of Transportation, 39.1% going to county road commissions, and 21.8% going to cities and villages, as mandated by Public Act 51 of 1951. This historical imbalance between spending on trunk routes and on local roads and streets is undoubtedly part of the explanation for the poor quality of Michigan through roads.

If the funds distributed to the county road commissions were further allocated among the counties based on population, the fact that county road commissions play an unusually large role in Michigan highway finance would be less important. However, there is a clear rural bias in the way that highway funds are distributed among the Michigan counties. The largest county in the state, Wayne County, gets only $32 per person for its roads, while Schoolcraft County, a very small county, gets more than $1,000 per person. Table 16.19 shows that there is a very strong negative relationship between the population of Michigan counties and per-capita state spending on county roads. This apparent overfunding of rural non-state roads is consistent with the patterns of road quality noted earlier: Rural minor arterial highways are in good condition, comparable to those of other states, while interstate highways and all urban arterial highways are in poor condition.

## Efficient Road Pricing

The discussion of payment for the use of road services has traditionally proceeded in terms of equity—for example, whether Michigan gets its fair share of the federal fuel tax, or whether truckers pay their fair share of road expenditures. From this perspective, the cost of using roads is identified as the total expenditure made by road authorities. Tax rates and fees serve simply to allocate the burden of these expenses, rather than to shape behavior of users or the road authority.[6] This perspective is slowly changing, however, and increasingly issues of pricing efficiency are entering into the road finance discussion.[7]

The efficiency criterion for road pricing sees the critical issue not as whether, for example, trucks pay a fair share, but whether the prices that trucks pay give them an incentive to operate the correct number of trucks, to use equipment that provides transportation at the lowest overall cost (where costs include not only operator cost but also the road repair and rebuilding expenses), and

**TABLE 16.19**

**Distributions Per Capita from Michigan Transportation Fund to Counties, Fiscal Year 1998–99**

| County Population | State Transfers Per Capita |
| --- | --- |
| greater than 100,000 | $ 44.59 |
| between 50,000 and 100,000 | $ 66.53 |
| between 20,000 and 50,000 | $105.04 |
| less than 20,000 | $199.74 |

SOURCE: Calculations by the author based on data in MDOT Facts and Figures produced by MDOT.

to make location and travel decisions that maximize community welfare. From this perspective, the fact that Michigan collects an unusually small amount of taxes and fees from the truckers who use its roads and allows trucks that are far heavier than those used in other states is of concern not because it is unfair, but because by underpricing trucking services, we give an incentive to use types of equipment that may not be optimal. This may also give firms an incentive to use trucks in places where other modes might be cheaper as well as encourage the placement of factories and warehouses in locations that require too much travel relative to the optimum. A principal concern is that by underpricing the use of heavy trucks, the state allows the more rapid consumption of its highway stock than a rational manager would permit. We throw away some of the state's resources without getting enough in return to recompense us for our losses, making the state effectively poorer than it otherwise could be if we had more rational road pricing.

An efficient road price is one that makes the user pay the full marginal cost of the decision that he or she makes.[8] What is done with the proceeds of these efficient prices is of secondary importance, since it is the pricing itself that induces efficient behavior on the part of the users—for example, restraining the weight of trucks if the operator decides that he or she is unwilling to pay for the road damage that would be caused by operating heavy vehicles. In most industrialized countries, road pricing returns to the government revenues far in excess of the costs borne by the road authorities, a practice that is entirely consistent with efficient pricing.

Driving decisions affect not only the speed of consumption of the road stock, but also (during congested periods) the time that it takes other drivers to complete their trips. Road pricing decisions also affect environmental quality and the rate of conversion of farmland to nonagricultural uses. Efficient prices would charge drivers for all of these effects. Each of these sources of inefficiency in the current road finance mechanism is discussed briefly in the following.

### Truck Weight Regulations

While the principles of road pricing are clear, the practical implementation of fees to induce transportation decisions that maximize the welfare of the community often depends on knowledge that is fragmentary at best. A prime example of this is given by the issue of how best to control truck weights. It should be emphasized that, despite the fact that Michigan both allows ultraheavy trucks on its roads and has unusually poor quality roads, the causal relationship between the presence of heavy trucks and deteriorating roads is not clear.[9] As noted previously, the poor quality of roads could be due to bad decisions about paving materials or to spending patterns that do not target the poorest roads for repair. In addition, the basic understanding of how roads deteriorate is surprisingly weak.

The basic data on the effect of highway traffic on road deterioration are from a series of tests done on specially designed test loops by the American Association of State Highway and Transportation Officials (AASHTO) between 1958 and 1960. In the tests, pavement design and axle loads were independently varied and the rate of depreciation measured. It should be noted that these were controlled experiments, and are subject to the same criticism as the fuel economy measures produced by the Environmental Protection Agency, namely that the actual conditions of road usage do not match the controlled conditions of the test.

The main conclusion of the AASHTO tests was that the damage done to highways increases with the fourth power of axle loading. Thus an axle loaded eight times heavier (a typical ratio of truck axle to car axle loading) will have the equivalent effect as $8^4$, or more than 4,000, of the lighter axles.[10] Michigan trucking regulations follow the AASHTO test results, putting limits on axle loadings that are the same as the limits in other states. What is unusual is that Michigan rules allow for an essentially unlimited number of axles, so long as each is below the maximum allowed weight (between 9,000 and 18,000 pounds, depending on axle spacing and number and type of tires) and so

long as the total truck weighs less than 164,000 pounds.[11] This gross limit is more than double the limit imposed by the federal government on federal aid highways in states without the grandfather provision that allows Michigan to retain the laws that were in place in the 1960s. To the extent that the AASHTO test results are to be believed, Michigan roads should have no more damage as a result of the use of Michigan's ultraheavy trucks than if the same load were carried in more trucks, each weighing less, but having the same axle loadings.

It is now known that highway damage is far more complex than was assumed in 1960, when the results of the AASHTO tests were analyzed, and the damage that a truck does to a road cannot simply be determined by dividing the total weight of a truck by the number of axles and using the fourth power rule. The AASHTO tests were done using conditions that exactly controlled truck weights, rather than depending on the very spotty weight checks that are used today. The standard defense of Michigan's laws allowing ultraheavy trucks—that they are justified by the AASHTO tests—thus seems to be vulnerable to the criticism that the tests were not based on actual road operating conditions. Since Michigan has both uniquely liberal road weight limits and roads that are in unusually bad condition, a plausible case could be made for rolling back the weight limits unless they can be proved to be as benign as the AASHTO tests make them appear to be. To date no research has been done to confirm the presumption that Michigan's ultraheavy trucks are not a source of the bad quality of state roads, nor is any research on the subject contemplated.

While it is debatable whether there is an effect of ultraheavy trucks on road deterioration beyond what would be indicated by the weight of truck axles under the frame of the vehicle, the total weight of a truck unquestionably does affect how bridges are designed, as well as their longevity. Required bridge strength depends on the product of weight and the distance from the center of a span. Bridges must be built stronger to support heavy trucks because they concentrate the load relative to two trucks carrying the same weight traveling in tandem. In addition, the fatigue placed on bridges depends on the frequency of heavy loading, a factor that clearly rises when 164,000-pound trucks are permitted on the roads. The general defense of the use of ultraheavy trucks in Michigan is based on the fact that Michigan has relatively few long-spanned bridges, since the state's rivers tend to be narrow. Thus the effect of heavy trucks on bridge design and fatigue, which would be important in other states with a larger number of longer spans, is assumed to be less of an issue in this state.

### Pricing Based on Costs Imposed on Other Drivers

A recent study of truck size and weight issues at the national level identified the cost of repairing and replacing bridges as the most important deterrent to nationwide liberalization of truck weight laws(U.S. Deparment of Transportation, Federal Highway Administration 2001). This study has been criticized for making unnecessarily pessimistic assumptions about the number of bridges that would need to be replaced if heavier trucks were allowed on the nation's highways. An interesting part of the calculation, however, has escaped criticism—the evaluation that the time costs of travel delay imposed on drivers who waited in traffic jams caused by the temporarily reduced road capacity during bridge replacement would be a considerably larger cost than the actual out-of-pocket expenditure made on the new bridges. According to the study, the time-delay costs imposed on other drivers during bridge replacement would be so large as to exceed the benefits that shippers would receive from using the larger vehicles accommodated by the stronger bridges.

Transport economists have long argued that time costs that vehicles impose on one another are real and should be part of the prices that drivers pay for roads. This is the logical basis for the congestion toll—a fee paid by drivers to use a highway during a congested period rather than find an alternate route or reschedule the trip to another, less congested, time of the day.[12] These fees have the promise of increasing effective road capacity and increasing average speeds on all types of roads. Price differences that are effectively congestion tolls are quite common both inside the transport sector and in the service sector as a whole. Their use in road finance, however, is quite recent.

An example of congestion tolls, or so-called value pricing of roadways, is provided by the privately funded expansion of I-15 in California, where prices vary by the half hour during both the morning and evening rush hours; the lowest toll is $0.75, while the highest is $4.00. Full implementation of efficient congestion tolls would neces-

sarily be much more complex, however, varying by road segment and traffic level. Until recently, the metering technology has not been available to implement congestion tolls. The price of metering has been dropping rapidly, however. Geographic Information Systems (GIS), in particular, show the promise of being able to efficiently implement full congestion tolls. Some European countries are using GIS to levy road user fees on trucks, and it is reasonable to assume that the technology will soon appear in the United States as well.

To date, sophisticated traffic metering has not been used for congestion pricing, but to increase road capacity through optimal signal light timing. This is the heart of the FasTrak system used by Oakland County to increase the effective capacity of roads in this suburban Detroit region by as much as 20%. Congestion tolls have the promise of increasing capacity by far more, by inducing optimal household and trucking firm decisions on the timing and destination of trips. Tolls could be raised at times when congestion is anticipated, to prevent roads from becoming gridlocked. By maintaining a smooth flow of traffic at all times, the capacity of the road system could be greatly increased by preventing more cars to access a road than the highway can efficiently handle. Congestion tolls would almost certainly not be implemented with the type of toll plazas traditionally used by toll roads. The levying of tolls would be done automatically, with the driver either pre-paying or being sent a bill at the end of the month.

Congestion tolls have the promise of revamping the system of road finance. Under ideal conditions, all fuel and vehicle taxes could be eliminated and replaced with per-vehicle-mile or per-ton-mile charges that vary with traffic levels. By eliminating fuel and registration fees and replacing them with time-, location-, and traffic-varying fees per vehicle or per ton-mile, traffic flow could be improved while solving all of the road finance problems that appear to have skewed Michigan's road investment and maintenance decisions. Of course, there are strong political interests in maintaining the current system, and the conversion of road finance from equity to efficiency principles will not be easy.

### Fuel Taxes and Environmental Externalities

Driving decisions affect not only the required maintenance levels by road authorities and the time that other drivers need to get to their des-

**TABLE 16.20**

**Journey-to-Work Statistics for Great Lakes States**

|  | % Drove Alone | % Carpool | % Public Transport | Total Workers | Average Journey to Work One-Way |
|---|---|---|---|---|---|
| Illinois | 73.2% | 10.6% | 9.3% | 5,713,973 | 27.1 |
| Indiana | 81.5% | 11.2% | 1.1% | 2,823,855 | 21.7 |
| Michigan | 83.7% | 9.2% | 1.1% | 4,458,323 | 22.7 |
| Ohio | 83.7% | 8.3% | 2.4% | 5,204,322 | 22.1 |
| Wisconsin | 79.7% | 10.4% | 1.7% | 2,606,775 | 20.1 |
| G.L. average | 80.4% | 9.9% | 3.1% | 4,161,450 | 22.7 |
| U.S. total | 76.3% | 11.2% | 5.2% | 127,448,586 | 24.3 |

SOURCE: Calculations by the author, based on data in U.S. Department of Commerce, Bureau of the Census (2000). Rows do not sum to 100% due to the omission of walking, working at home, and other modes of transportation.

tination, but also the broader environment. The size of these costs, however, is subject to considerable uncertainty. A recent estimate put pollution, congestion, and land-use costs of automotive transportation during periods of peak congestion in the range of $1.00/mile—far higher than the pennies per mile now paid to road authorities in the form of fuel taxes and vehicle registration fees.[13]

One estimate of the environmental cost of truck transportation found that whether trucks had a significant environmental cost depended on the carcinogenic properties of diesel particulates—a medical relationship that is not well understood (National Research Council, Transportation Research Board 1996). Perhaps the major uncertainty involved in the environmental cost of driving is the effect that automotive emissions have on global warming. If the climatological relationships between automotive pollution and global warming are correctly understood, the true costs of driving may be many times higher than what we are now paying.

## Other Forms of Passenger Transportation

Private automobiles are the backbone of passenger transportation in the United States. Public transportation is a small part of the passenger transportation mix, as shown in table 16.20. Michigan, the automobile state, relies even less heavily on public transportation than other states do. In Michigan 83.7% of the journeys to work are done alone. The average for the Great Lakes states is 80.4%, while in the nation as a whole, 76.3% of workers drive to work alone. Among the Great

Lakes states, Michigan and Indiana have the lowest levels of public transit usage for the journey to work, at 1.1 % of commuter trips.

## Transit

Michigan's very low level of transit usage is primarily the result of a single anomalous case—the Detroit Metropolitan Area's extremely low level of public transit ridership. This is illustrated in table 16.21, which shows the same information as table 16.20 for the twenty-two largest metropolitan areas in the Great Lakes region. On average, the smaller the city, the lower the usage of public transportation for the journey to work. This is evident from the generally declining numbers in the fourth column of table 16.21. A regression of the proportion of commutation trips that use public transportation on the total number of workers in the metropolitan area finds that city size by itself explains 70% of the variation in commuting decisions, with, on average, each additional 100,000 commuters increasing the public transport percentage by approximately 3 percentage points.

The final column in table 16.21 is the residual from this regression for each city. It shows that Detroit's 1.6% public transit usage falls below what would be expected on the basis of the city size by 4.6 percentage points—that is, given the number of commuters, Detroit would be expected to have 6.2% of its workers using public transportation rather than the 1.6% that is observed. Grand Rapids, Michigan's second-largest city, also has much lower public transit usage than would be predicted by city size. Among Great Lakes region cities outside of Michigan, only Indianapolis has as low levels of public transit usage relative to what would be expected on the basis of population.

Some hints about the reason for Detroit's very low transit usage are found in a comparison of Detroit with its peer cities, Chicago and Cleveland. Chicago residents take many more bus trips than residents of either Detroit or Cleveland, but they tend to be shorter trips. The overwhelming reason for the higher participation of transit in urban travel in Chicago and Cleveland, however, is the presence of their rail systems. The Chicago rail system carries nearly four times the number of passenger miles as the Chicago bus system. Even in Cleveland, with a far less extensive rail system, rail commutation carries 1.5 times more passenger miles than the bus system. Lacking

**TABLE 16.21**

**Journey-to-Work Statistics for the Twenty-Two Largest Metropolitan Areas in the Great Lakes States**

| Metropolitan Area | % Drive Alone | % Carpool | % Public Transport | Total Workers | Average Commute Minutes | Publ. Transit Use Unexpl. by Size |
|---|---|---|---|---|---|---|
| Chicago–northwestern Indiana | 69.3% | 10.4% | 13.3% | 3,841,682 | 30.5 | 1.9% |
| Detroit | 84.8% | 9.2% | 1.6% | 1,982,867 | 24.9 | –4.6% |
| Cleveland | 83.1% | 6.8% | 5.5% | 1,022,303 | 23.6 | 2.1% |
| Indianapolis | 83.9% | 9.6% | 1.3% | 796,908 | 22.8 | –1.5% |
| Milwaukee | 80.5% | 10.0% | 3.7% | 724,773 | 21.2 | 1.1% |
| Grand Rapids | 85.6% | 8.1% | 0.6% | 513,542 | 19.8 | –1.4% |
| Dayton | 83.9% | 9.5% | 1.5% | 443,659 | 20.6 | –0.3% |
| Akron | 86.0% | 8.3% | 1.2% | 323,638 | 21.3 | –0.2% |
| Toledo | 85.3% | 7.1% | 1.8% | 293,749 | 18.5 | 0.4% |
| Ann Arbor | 82.8% | 7.4% | 1.1% | 279,442 | 24.0 | –0.3% |
| Youngstown–Warren | 86.7% | 7.3% | 1.0% | 255,352 | 21.7 | –0.3% |
| Fort Wayne | 84.2% | 9.9% | 1.2% | 239,354 | 19.5 | 0.0% |
| Madison | 75.7% | 7.8% | 4.8% | 229,926 | 17.8 | 3.6% |
| Lansing–East Lansing | 84.1% | 7.8% | 2.2% | 216,985 | 19.8 | 1.1% |
| Flint | 82.5% | 8.5% | 1.3% | 184,540 | 25.1 | 0.2% |
| Appleton–Neenah | 85.7% | 9.6% | 0.2% | 181,833 | 17.7 | –0.9% |
| Canton | 86.5% | 7.3% | 0.6% | 180,323 | 20.2 | –0.5% |
| Davenport–Rock Island–Moline | 85.1% | 8.4% | 1.0% | 170,810 | 18.0 | 0.0% |
| Peoria | 84.3% | 7.8% | 0.6% | 154,462 | 20.4 | –0.4% |
| South Bend–Mishawaka | 81.3% | 13.9% | 0.7% | 117,405 | 19.2 | –0.2% |

SOURCE: Calculations by the author, based on data in U.S. Department of Commerce, Bureau of the Census (2000). Rows do not sum to 100% due to the omission of walking, working at home, and other modes of transportation. Cincinnati and Columbus, Ohio, are omitted due to lack of information on the metropolitan area.

these passenger-miles, Detroit's split between transit and road looks more like those of the generally smaller cities that lack rail commutation.

Successful rail transit operations have much lower operating costs per passenger mile than do bus systems. Subway, suburban rail, and light rail systems in Chicago and Cleveland have operating costs in the range of twenty-five to forty cents per mile. Bus systems in the three cities, by contrast, have operating costs in the range of sixty-five to eighty-five cents per passenger mile. The main advantage of bus systems over rail is that the capital expenditures are much lower. In order to get the total cost per passenger mile (including both operating and fixed costs) for rail systems lower than bus systems, the available traffic density in the corridor served by the line must be higher than the traffic density that is typical of Midwestern cities.

It should be recognized that automobile operating costs are typically measured in the range of ten to twenty cents per mile, though by adding in use-based depreciation, insurance, and other variable costs, the equivalent of operating costs

for automobiles can be raised into the range of twenty-five to thirty cents per vehicle mile. These costs are far lower than either bus or rail transit costs, even if automobile occupancy is only one driver per vehicle. However, passengers pay only a minor fraction of the operating costs for transit in the form of fares. In Detroit, passengers in both the city and suburban bus systems pay less than twenty cents for each dollar of operating expense. Capital expenses are covered by grants from the local, state, and federal governments. In the case of Detroit, between 80 and 90% of capital expenses are covered by the federal government.

Since transit operators have no hope of covering their expenses from sales of their services, it is not surprising that these operations are organized as government corporations. It should be recognized that the practice of fare box revenues covering a small fraction of operating costs and none of capital costs is not unique to the Midwest, or to the nation, but characterizes transit operations everywhere in the industrialized world. European transit operations, much admired for their contribution to the life of European capitals, suffer from

## TABLE 16.22

**Aircraft Traffic in Great Lakes Region**

|  | Aircraft Departures | Enplaned Passengers | Freight Tons | Mail Tons |
|---|---|---|---|---|
| Illinois | 517,833 | 38,865,020 | 521,823 | 122,007 |
| Indiana | 115,731 | 4,536,201 | 493,587 | 158,958 |
| Michigan | 311,078 | 19,300,152 | 155,235 | 46,525 |
| Ohio | 400,200 | 20,799,903 | 575,820 | 55,191 |
| Wisconsin | 103,204 | 4,326,083 | 49,677 | 12,645 |
| G.L. average | 289,609 | 17,565,472 | 359,228 | 79,065 |
| U.S. total | 8,851,395 | 631,994,748 | 12,535,631 | 2,291,666 |
| **Percent of U.S. Total** | | | | |
| Illinois | 5.9% | 6.1% | 4.2% | 5.3% |
| Indiana | 1.3% | 0.7% | 3.9% | 6.9% |
| Michigan | 3.5% | 3.1% | 1.2% | 2.0% |
| Ohio | 4.5% | 3.3% | 4.6% | 2.4% |
| Wisconsin | 1.2% | 0.7% | 0.4% | 0.6% |
| G.L. average | 3.3% | 2.8% | 2.9% | 3.5% |
| U.S. total | 100.0% | 100.0% | 100.0% | 100.0% |

SOURCE: U.S. Federal Aviation Administration (2000), table 4.6.

the same economics of transit deficits, though softened to some extent by the high fuel taxes paid by European drivers.

The economic rationale for the existence of public transit cannot be found in the cost-effectiveness of bus and rail systems, but, if there is a justification, it must be found in the external benefits for transit systems. The standard argument starts with the assumption that drivers do not pay the full costs of operating automobiles. This was acknowledged in the discussion of efficient pricing earlier in this chapter. If the true cost of driving a car in peak periods is, in fact, $1.00/vehicle mile, then economic rationality of transit becomes a question worth discussing. If driving is as seriously underpriced as is assumed by this argument, then public subsidies to the operation of transit systems may be justified by arguments of economic efficiency.

An important part of this argument is the presumed ability of rail transit to induce density of commercial and residential development, together with the desirability of such density. These benefits claimed for transit are for rail modes only. Subsidies for buses rely instead on the noneconomic goal of the right to mobility for all parts of the population, including those who cannot drive.[14] This is especially apparent in the case of demand-response bus systems, which are far more costly on a per-passenger-mile basis

than are line-haul buses.

### Intercity Rail

The same economics that prevent private transit operators from operating profitably extend to intercity rail passenger operations. Michigan has three rail passenger routes across Southern Lower Michigan, with a ridership of approximately 600,000 people annually. Amtrak gets a higher percentage of operating expenses from the fare box than most passenger railroads in the world, but would not survive without continued financial support from the federal government. Michigan is currently part of a group discussing introducing high-speed rail into the Midwest. Under this plan, both speeds and frequencies of trains on the southern Michigan passenger routes would be increased. However, the financial issues of finding funds for a likely money-losing service have prevented the plan from progressing.

### Intercity Air Traffic

The one passenger mode that has successfully drawn passengers away from their automobiles and simultaneously covered costs through ticket prices is the airline industry. Table 16.22 shows enplanements, passenger counts, and cargo liftings from airports in the region. Michigan's air

**TABLE 16.23**

**Passenger Enplanements at Michigan Airports with Scheduled Service, 2000**

| Community | Airport Name | Passenger Enplanements | Percent of State |
|---|---|---|---|
| Alpena | Alpena County Regional | 10,544 | 0.1% |
| Detroit | Metro Wayne County | 17,572,823 | 86.8% |
| Detroit | Detroit City | 124,291 | 0.6% |
| Escanaba | Delta County | 19,300 | 0.1% |
| Flint | Bishop International | 299,692 | 1.5% |
| Grand Rapids | Gerald Ford International | 968,265 | 4.8% |
| Gwinn | Sawyer International | 45,076 | 0.2% |
| Houghton/Hancock | Houghton County | 32,482 | 0.2% |
| Iron Mountain/Kingsford | Ford | 8,729 | 0.0% |
| Ironwood | Gogebic–Iron County | 2,075 | 0.0% |
| Kalamazoo/Battle Creek | Kalamazoo–Battle Creek International | 258,118 | 1.3% |
| Lansing | Capital City | 331,363 | 1.6% |
| Manistee | Manistee–Blacker | 1,196 | 0.0% |
| Muskegon | Muskegon County International | 47,141 | 0.2% |
| Pellston | Pellston Regional | 32,131 | 0.2% |
| Sault Ste. Marie | Chippewa County International | 15,504 | 0.1% |
| Saginaw/Bay City/Midland | MBS International | 281,305 | 1.4% |
| Traverse City | Cherry Capital | 202,832 | 1.0% |
| STATEWIDE TOTAL | | 20,252,867 | 100.0% |

SOURCE: Michigan Department of Transportation, Aeronautics Division, Transportation Management System.

traffic is approximately proportional to its population, slightly behind that of Ohio and considerably behind that of Illinois.

The relative positions of the Great Lakes states in passenger enplanements are primarily the result of the economics of hubbing, which give overwhelming cost advantages to operating flights out of large cities. In Michigan, 87% of passengers depart from Detroit Metropolitan Airport. The next largest airport, in Grand Rapids, has only 4.8% of enplanements. Detroit thus has eighteen times as many enplanements, with a metropolitan area population only five times as large as that of Grand Rapids. The same pattern is repeated for other airports in Michigan, as shown in table 16.23. Lansing, Flint, the Tri-Cities, Kalamazoo, and Traverse City each have between 200,000 and 350,000 enplanements per year, with no other metropolitan areas having more than 50,000.

Part, but not all, of Detroit's outsized passenger count comes from its role as a large hub airport. As shown in table 16.24, there are three large hubs in the region—Chicago, Detroit, and Cincinnati. In each case, the percentage of passenger enplanements is substantially above the population percentage of the airport's metropolitan area. The region has four medium hubs—Cleveland, Colum-bus, Indianapolis, and Milwaukee. For these cities, the passenger enplanement percentages approximately match the national population percentages of the corresponding metropolitan areas. The region has five small hubs—Dayton, Grand Rapids, Madison, Moline, and South Bend. In each case, the passenger enplanement percentages are less than national population percentage. All remaining airports are classified as nonhubs; at these airports, the gap between passenger counts and population is wider than at hub airports.

Small cities are at an inherent disadvantage in attracting passengers, since the per-seat operating costs of the small aircraft serving lightly used routes are higher and, with passenger counts less predictable, the average load factor is lower. Ticket prices from small cities reflect these higher costs, thus dampening demand for air service. Nonetheless, most states consider it important to maintain mobility of rural residents, and this has led them to promote the use of small airports. Michigan's program involves 90% matching funds for capital and equipment for airports with fewer than 150,000 passenger enplanements. The state also provides funds to small airports to provide incentives to carriers to start or continue service, and also provides small grants to increase public

**TABLE 16.24**

### Airline Activity at Hub Airports in Great Lakes Region

| Metropolitan Area | Enplaned Passengers | Passenger Percentage | Enplaned Revenue Freight Tons | Freight Percentage | Enplaned Revenue Mail Tons | Mail Percentage | Population Percentage |
|---|---|---|---|---|---|---|---|
| **Large Hubs** | | | | | | | |
| Chicago, IL | 37,860,677 | 5.93% | 368,197 | 2.90% | 121,548 | 5.28% | 3.25% |
| Cincinnati, OH | 9,962,935 | 1.56% | 243,677 | 1.92% | 26,261 | 1.14% | 0.70% |
| Detroit, MI | 17,055,589 | 2.67% | 122,781 | 0.97% | 42,786 | 1.86% | 1.94% |
| TOTAL, LARGE HUBS | 478,845,117 | 74.95% | 6,661,816 | 52.49% | 1,649,611 | 71.67% | |
| **Medium Hubs** | | | | | | | |
| Cleveland, OH | 6,154,384 | 0.96% | 49,562 | 0.39% | 13,912 | 0.60% | 1.05% |
| Columbus, OH | 3,105,364 | 0.49% | 38,111 | 0.30% | 8,517 | 0.37% | 0.55% |
| Indianapolis, IN | 3,629,716 | 0.57% | 399,497 | 3.15% | 158,715 | 6.90% | 0.57% |
| Milwaukee, WI | 2,837,795 | 0.44% | 38,994 | 0.31% | 11,505 | 0.50% | 0.60% |
| TOTAL, MEDIUM HUBS | 101,986,095 | 15.96% | 4,450,392 | 35.07% | 503,965 | 21.90% | |
| **Small Hubs** | | | | | | | |
| Dayton, OH | 1,033,145 | 0.16% | 149,838 | 1.18% | 6,488 | 0.28% | 0.34% |
| Grand Rapids, MI | 866,936 | 0.14% | 10,575 | 0.08% | 3,697 | 0.16% | 0.39% |
| Madison, WI | 650,270 | 0.10% | 5,123 | 0.04% | 674 | 0.03% | 0.15% |
| Moline, IL | 374,414 | 0.06% | 3,725 | 0.03% | 512 | 0.02% | 0.13% |
| South Bend, IN | 411,143 | 0.06% | 7,431 | 0.06% | 222 | 0.01% | 0.09% |
| TOTAL, SMALL HUBS | 40,116,465 | 6.28% | 930,518 | 7.33% | 108,581 | 4.72% | |
| TOTAL, ENTIRE NATION | 638,902,993 | 100.00% | 12,690,673 | 100.00% | 2,301,666 | 100.00% | 100.00% |

SOURCE: Author's calculations based on data in U.S. Department of Transportation, Bureau of Transportation Statistics (2000). Population percentage is for the metropolitan area containing the named city.

awareness of service at small airports.

The largest airports are effectively public/private partnerships in which the public airport authority raises funds by selling bonds backed by long-term contracts with individual airline companies. The federal government also provides matching funds for new runways, runway extensions, parallel taxiways, and similar large capital improvements.

### Freight Transportation: Trucks and Other Modes

Freight is bound to modes by distance and commodity, and states will vary in the use of different modes of transport based on location of their trading partners and the characteristics of the commodities that are shipped and received. Highways carry by far the largest amount of freight, measured by tons. This is due primarily to the fact that most freight moves only short distances; in Michigan, 57% of the tons move fewer than 50 miles and 83% move fewer than 250 miles. In this range, other modes cannot carry freight with the same efficiency as highways.

Table 16.25 shows the amount of traffic originating in Michigan and its neighboring states. Total traffic is also determined by terminating and transit traffic. Michigan's share of freight originations is above its population percentage, measured by both value and tons. Michigan is unusual in the region and the nation in having a high percentage of freight originating in intermodal shipments, a factor that closely tracks a state's dependence on transportation equipment shipments. As is true of its neighbors, however, the overwhelming percentage of freight, about 77% whether measured by value or tons, is shipped by truck.

Thirty-three percent of Michigan commodities shipped, measured by value, is transportation equipment. Other major commodities by this measure are food, fabricated metal products, and machinery. Measured by tonnage, however, nonmetallic minerals like limestone, petroleum, or coal products, and clay, concrete, glass, and stone products, along with food products, are the main commodities shipped. Michigan's major trading partners are its Great Lakes neighbors. The pattern of main destination states being the adjacent neighbors generally holds true throughout the

**TABLE 16.25**

### Freight Originations and Modal Shares in Great Lakes States

| | MEASURED BY VALUE | | | | MEASURED BY WEIGHT | | | | |
| | Billions ($) | Truck % | Rail % | Water % | Intermodal | Tons (millions) | Truck % | Rail % | Water % | Intermodal |
|---|---|---|---|---|---|---|---|---|---|---|
| Illinois | 346.6 | 74.5 | 5.0 | 1.1 | 1.6 | 525.2 | 59.2 | 18.6 | 7.3 | 0.4 |
| Indiana | 178.7 | 77.3 | 6.9 | 0.6 | 0.4 | 285.8 | 74.0 | 15.2 | 3.7 | 0.2 |
| Michigan | 256.3 | 77.0 | 6.6 | 0.1 | 5.5 | 323.8 | 77.3 | 9.4 | 6.8 | 0.5 |
| Ohio | 325.6 | 76.9 | 3.9 | 0.3 | 3.5 | 469.6 | 78.0 | 8.2 | 1.7 | 0.4 |
| Wisconsin | 143.3 | 83.8 | 2.5 | * * | 0.4 | 166.0 | 87.8 | 6.6 | * * | 0.3 |
| G.L. average | 250.1 | 77.9 | 5.0 | 0.5 | 2.3 | 354.1 | 75.26 | 11.60 | 4.88 | 0.36 |
| U.S. total | 6,132,832 | 71.9 | 4.0 | 1.0 | 1.4 | 12,157,105 | 52.5 | 12.7 | 4.3 | 0.3 |

SOURCE: U.S. Bureau of Transportation Statistics, Commodity Flow Survey, 1993, State detail tables. Intermodal refers to truck-rail combinations.

region. The major exception is that in Illinois, Louisiana is the third-largest recipient of tonnages—the result of grain exports from Illinois that are moved on the Mississippi River and transshipped in Louisiana. All of the Great Lakes states have transportation equipment and food among the four top commodities shipped, measured by value, though the percentages and rank of each commodity varies considerably. To the extent that Michigan's traffic division among modes and distances shipped varies from that of its neighbors, the different composition of originated traffic is likely the cause.

Michigan's unique truck weight regulations have been noted previously. These laws do not seem to have had an affect on the aggregate traffic split between highways and other modes. Wisconsin, without the extraordinary regulations, has a much higher percentage of truck traffic than Michigan. There may, of course, be more subtle location decisions that are affected by the lower out-of-pocket costs to shippers that are made possible by the truck weight laws. Since trucking deregulation, passed in two stages in 1980 and 1994, the trucking industry can be assumed to be competitive, with costs of the industry passed along to shippers. Thus the truck weight laws allow the industry to charge lower rates than they would be able to if they were forced to abide by weight limits imposed by neighboring states. It is reasonable to assume that the ultimate beneficiaries of the weight laws are shippers of heavy commodities and the consumers who use their products.

### Air Freight

Michigan trails neighboring states in the use of airfreight, as seen in table 16.22, with less than a third of the air freight and tonnage of Illinois, Ohio, and Indiana. Unlike with passenger enplanements, the size of the metropolitan area is not closely related to the quantity of airfreight passing through the airports. This is seen in table 16.24, which shows that the largest airfreight hub in the region is Indianapolis, with 3.15% of all cargo lifting in the country, despite the fact that it is only a medium hub in terms of passenger counts. Chicago is second, followed by Cincinnati, and Dayton. Most air cargo leaving from Michigan airports passes through Willow Run Airport, which together with Detroit Metropolitan, accounts for 0.97% of the nation's air cargo lifting, a percentage that is only half of the corresponding proportion of the nation's population. Unlike those in Dayton, Cincinnati, and Indianapolis, Michigan's airports have not been developed to permit the rapid unloading and reloading of freight for further dispatch across the nation. The airfreight arriving in Michigan generally has this state as its final destination, and most freight leaving Michigan originated here.

### Railroads

Michigan is unusual in having a relatively high level of inter-railroad competition. Though mergers have reduced the number of independent carriers with whom a shipper can bargain, and recent regulatory interpretations have limited the power of shippers to bargain for lower rates by threatening to divert traffic to carriers who have tracks nearby, but do not connect directly to the shipper or receiver, Michigan is served by both of the main Eastern rail carriers, CSX and Norfolk Southern. It

**TABLE 16.26**

**Waterborne Tonnages Shipped and Received in Great Lakes States, Calendar Year 2000 (thousands of tons)**

| State | Totals | SHIPPING | | RECEIVING | | |
| | | Domestic | Foreign | Domestic | Foreign | Intrastate |
| --- | --- | --- | --- | --- | --- | --- |
| Illinois | 118,382 | 84,753 | 557 | 20,296 | 3,340 | 9,436 |
| Indiana | 74,434 | 14,407 | 598 | 54,505 | 2,477 | 2,447 |
| Michigan | 79,284 | 27,651 | 5,867 | 21,797 | 8,513 | 15,456 |
| Ohio | 130,914 | 22,684 | 19,431 | 66,704 | 6,420 | 15,675 |
| Wisconsin | 39,300 | 21,790 | 8,658 | 7,222 | 962 | 668 |
| TOTAL | 2,461,631 | 757,025 | 415,042 | 757,025 | 976,784 | 312,780 |

SOURCE: U.S. Army Corps of Engineers (2000).

also is served by the Canadian National, a railroad with an extensive network in Canada and in the central part of the country. The other main Canadian carrier, CP Rail, also reaches Michigan shippers through trackage rights over CSX. It is unusual for a state to have such a high degree of inter-railroad competition, with most states having a single dominant carrier or at most two important railroads. However, most industry observers believe that there will be more railroad consolidation and that the current group of two major Western carriers, two major Eastern carriers, and two major Canadian-based railroads, will eventually be reduced to two transcontinental railroads. Michigan shippers could lose the bargaining advantage that they currently have if, for example, the Canadian National merges with one of the two Eastern Carriers, or if the railroads serving the region east of the Mississippi River merge with one another.

## Great Lakes Navigation

Michigan uses the Great Lakes for navigation, but unlike its neighbors has no ports serving shallow-draft inland navigation. Michigan has deposits of ore, limestone, and other sand and stone products, and is a producer and user of steel, but ships no coal and almost no grain. (Ninety-four percent of Michigan's waterborne commerce consists of sand and stone, coal, iron ore, and cement.) This limited range of commodities to be carried and the fact that Michigan has no direct access to the Mississippi/Ohio River system limits the state's use of waterborne commerce. This is seen in table 16.26, which shows that Michigan falls far behind Illinois and Ohio (which use rivers to ship primarily corn and coal, respectively) in terms of ton-

nage shipped by water. Michigan waterborne commerce is limited to Detroit, Marquette, Calcite, and a few other ports that handle the limited range of cargoes that are appropriate for shipping on the Lakes.

Michigan was expected to benefit from the completion of the St. Lawrence Seaway, providing the state direct access to ocean shipping. However, a combination of factors has prevented the state from receiving any substantial benefit from the project. Containerization and a worldwide shift to very large ocean-going vessels—much larger than the locks on the Seaway—have made it uneconomic for the vast majority of Atlantic Ocean ships to enter the Lakes. In addition, the Seaway, uniquely among American waterways, charges tolls.

Like those in other states using inland waterways, Michigan shippers who use the Seaway benefit from the subsidies provided to water transportation in the form of free navigation services provided by the U.S. Army Corps of Engineers. The federal government provides free dredging services for harbors and channels on the Great Lakes. Lake levels are currently quite low, requiring considerable dredging to maintain draft levels. If lake levels continue to drop, shippers will not be able to fully load their vessels unless there is more accelerated dredging of channels. The Corps of Engineers must balance the interests of navigation against those of other users of the lakes, notably fishermen and water users, and this often leads to limitations on the amount of dredging that is done. Another area where the interests of navigation conflict with those of other users of the Lakes is in the introduction of exotic species, like the zebra mussel. These species would not be in the Lakes, were it not for their use in navigation. Control of exotic species is already leading to limits on the discharge of bilge water and may lead to more serious limits on operations in the future.

## Conclusion

Highways dominate Michigan's transportation, both for passengers and for freight. Michigan is slightly more road-oriented than other states, but Michigan's transportation decisions are not greatly different from those of other states in the region or the nation as a whole. Road inventory levels and vehicle stocks are at levels comparable to those of other states in the region and nation.

Michigan's roads and road transportation differ from those of its neighbors in several important respects, however. Michigan's major urban roads and rural freeways are in much poorer condition than those of neighboring states or the nation, while rural nonlocal roads are, in general, in good condition. This pattern may be due to road finance constraints. Michigan spends roughly comparable amounts on its roads as do other states, but funding formulas are skewed toward rural county road commissions at the expense of the largest metropolitan areas and the state Department of Transportation.

A second factor that may explain Michigan's poor-quality roads is the unique truck weight law that allows trucks up to 164,000 pounds on roads that are limited to 80,000 pounds in other states. There is very little solid knowledge on the effect that trucks have on road deterioration, however, and trucking interests are convinced that road deterioration is affected by individual axle weights, where Michigan has relatively normal laws, rather than by overall truck weight.

Regardless of whether trucks impose excessive wear on the highways, trucks in Michigan have a much lighter user-cost burden than in other states, with both unusually low tax rates on diesel fuel and an unusually high volume of diesel motor fuel untaxed. Michigan uses quite traditional methods of highway finance and forgoes the use of tolls and other efficiency-based charges on its road users. Efficiency-based pricing systems, made possible by recent advances in metering technology, have the promise of decreasing the cost of transportation and increasing the capacity of roads without new investment.

Michigan's public transportation systems in its two largest cities, and especially in Detroit, are far less well developed than those in other cities of comparable size in the region and the nation. Detroit is unusual in the nation as a major city with no rail-based commuter transit, and this is the main reason for the very low usage levels of public transportation. All forms of public passenger transportation, with the exception of air travel, have the characteristic that it is impossible to cover the costs of operations from fares paid by users. The economic justification for public passenger transportation, to the extent that there is one, must be found in pricing distortions in the road sector or external benefits of public transport on the community.

Freight transportation in Michigan is dominated by highway freight, as it is in other states. Michigan benefits from having an unusually high level of inter-railroad competition, an advantage that may disappear with railroad mergers in the years ahead. Michigan also has the benefit of Great Lakes water transportation of bulk commodities. Like all states with water transport, Michigan is dependent on the U.S. Army Corps of Engineers for maintaining harbors and channels. While these services are offered without charge to the states, the use of waterways for commercial navigation does impose costs on other user groups and on the environment.

■

## REFERENCES

Boyer, Kenneth D. 1998. *Principles of transportation economics.* Reading, Mass.: Addison Wesley.

Dupuit, Jules. [1844]. 1968. On the measurement of the utility of public works. In *Transport: Selected readings,* edited by Dennis Munby. New York: Penguin Books.

Gomez-Ibanez, Jose A. 1999. Pricing. In *Essays in transportation economics and policy,* edited by Jose Gomez-Ibanez, William Tye, and Clifford Winston. Washington, D.C.: Brookings Institution Press.

Litman, Todd. 2002. *Transportation cost analysis.* Victoria, B.C.: Victoria Transport Policy Institute.

Mannering, Fred, and Walter Kilareski. 1998. *Principles of highway engineering and traffic analysis.* 2d ed. New York: John Wiley.

Michigan Department of Transportation, Aeronautics Division, Transportation Management System Database.

Michigan Department of Transportation, Bureau of Finance, Financial Operations Division. 2000. *Facts and figures.* Lansing, Mich.: State of Michigan.

Michigan Department of Transportation, Office of Communications. 1998. Trucks and transportation: A position paper from the Michigan Department of Transportation. Pamphlet. Lansing, Mich.: State of Michigan, February.

Mohring, Herbert. 1999. Congestion. In *Essays in transportation economics and policy,* edited by Jose Gomez-Ibanez, William Tye, and Clifford Winston. Washington, D.C.: Brookings Institution Press.

National Research Council, Transportation Research Board. 1996. *Paying our way: Estimating marginal social costs of freight transportation.* Special Report 246. Washington, D.C: National Academy Press.

———. 2002. *Regulation of weights, lengths, and widths of commercial motor vehicles.* Special Report 262. Washington, D.C: National Academy Press.

O'Regan, Katherine M., and John M. Quigley. 1999. Accessibility and economic opportunity. In *Essays in transportation economics and policy,* edited by Jose Gomez-Ibanez, William Tye, and Clifford Winston. Washington, D.C.: Brookings Institution Press.

Small, Kenneth A., Clifford Winston, and Carol A. Evans. 1989. *Road work: A new highway pricing and investment policy.* Washington, D.C.: Brookings Institution.

U.S. Army Corps of Engineers. 2000. *Waterborne commerce of the United States, calendar year 2000* (New Orleans: Waterborne Commerce Statistics Center Public Domain Datatbase).

U.S. Department of Commerce, Bureau of the Census. 1967. *Truck inventory and use survey.* Washington, D.C.: GPO.

———. 2000. *Decennial Census.* Washington, D.C.: GPO.

U.S. Department of Transportation, Bureau of Transportation Statistics. 1993. *Commodity flow survey.* Washington, D.C.: GPO.

———, Bureau of Transportation Statistics. 2000. *Airport activity statistics of certificated air carriers, summary tables, for twelve months ending December 31, 2000, tables 3, 4, and 5.* Washington, D.C.: GPO.

———, Federal Aviation Administration. 2000. *Statistical handbook of aviation.* Washington, D.C.: GPO.

———, Federal Highway Administration. 1997. *Federal highway cost allocation study.* Washington, D.C.: GPO.

———, Federal Highway Administration. 2000. *Highway statistics.* Washington, D.C.: GPO.

———, Federal Highway Administration. 2001. *Comprehensive truck size and weight study.* Washington, D.C.: GPO.

## NOTES

1. In this chapter, comparisons are made to national averages and to the average of the neighboring states, Illinois, Indiana, Ohio, and Wisconsin. These states, together with Michigan, are called the "Great Lakes states."

2. The regression of automobile registrations on per capita income and the percentage of the population living in urban areas is: PerCapAutoReg = $0.3598 + 0.0000073 \times$ Inc $- 0.0016 \times$ PctUrban; $R^2 = 0.12$; (0.00000030) (0.00081); $N = 51$.

3. For rural lane miles, the regression is: LnRuralMi = $2.36 + 0.50 \times$ lnRuralArea $+ 0.53 \times$ lnRuralPop; $R^2 = 0.78$; (0.058) (0.077); $N = 50$. Michigan's residual from this regression is +0.04, 0.08 standard deviations above the mean.

4. For urban lane miles, the regression is: $\ln UrbanMi = 2.80 + 0.31(\ln UrbanArea) + 0.65(\ln UrbanPop)$; $R^2 = 0.97$; (0.055), (0.065); $N = 51$. Michigan's residual from this regression is +0.05, 0.25 standard deviations above the mean.

5. The regression explaining federal disbursements to the states in 1980 is:

| | *Coefficients* | *Standard Error* |
|---|---|---|
| Intercept | 92047.67 | 23811.58 |
| Urban Car Miles | 1.08 | 2.35 |
| Urban Truck Miles | −10.77 | 19.39 |
| Rural Car Miles | 5.50 | 2.35 |
| Rural Truck Miles | 4.34 | 15.55 |
| Rural Lane Miles | 0.03 | 0.24 |
| Urban Lane Miles | 6.49 | 1.97 |

$R^2 = 0.95$; $N = 50$. Note that while as a group the variables explain 95% of the variation in federal payments to states, there is insufficient variation among the independent variables to precisely estimate the degree to which each characteristic independently tracks federal disbursements.

6. The traditional approach to roadway finance is illustrated by U.S. Department of Transportation, Federal Highway Administration 1997. This study has been done periodically, but in the most recent edition, the ratio of payments by a class of traffic to costs attributable to that class are called "equity ratios," to emphasize that this calculation does not conform to standard economic procedures.

7. The efficiency approach to road pricing is, in fact, as old as the study of transportation economics itself. See, for example, Dupuit [1844] 1968. A good modern summary of the efficiency approach to road pricing is found in Gomez-Ibanez 1999.

8. An accessible reference on efficient pricing is found in Boyer 1998.

9. The most comprehensive recent survey of truck size issues is found in National Research Council, Transportation Research Board 2002.

10. A recent reworking of the original data from the AASHTO tests argued that damage done to the highway is closer to the third power of axle loading. See Small, Winston, and Evans 1989.

11. Section 257.722 of the Michigan Vehicle Code describes the truck weight limits.

12. Congestion pricing is well summarized in Mohring 1999.

13. There is a voluminous literature on the external costs of driving. This literature is summarized in Litman 2002.

14. As representative of this argument, see O'Regan and Quigley 1999.

# 17

# Michigan's Welfare System

*Kristin S. Seefeldt, Sheldon Danziger, and Sandra K. Danziger*

Michigan's welfare system has undergone dramatic changes over the last twenty years, some of which have resulted from federal legislation, others from state initiatives. This chapter focuses on changes in cash assistance for the poor. We begin by briefly reviewing the recent history of welfare policy in the United States. Then, we turn to Michigan's response to the Family Support Act of 1988, the first significant piece of welfare reform legislation since the 1960s. Most of the remainder of the chapter focuses on Michigan's implementation of the Personal Responsibility and Work Opportunity Reconciliation Act of 1996, which dramatically restructured the cash welfare system into a work-based system. We then review the effects on recipients of the post-1996 welfare changes. We conclude with a discussion of unresolved issues facing the state, present some policy options the state might consider implementing in the future, and provide information on trends in poverty during the 1980s and 1990s.

## A Brief Overview of AFDC, 1960–80

In the United States, "welfare" is most often associated with cash assistance for low-income families, usually those headed by a single mother with children. Until 1996, this program was known as Aid to Families with Dependent Children (AFDC). The purpose of AFDC was to provide financial support to children who were "deprived of parental support or care because their father or mother is absent from the home continuously, is incapacitated, is deceased or is unemployed" (U.S. House of Representatives 1994). In certain instances, two-parent families were also eligible for cash assistance (this will be discussed later in the text). AFDC evolved out of the Aid to Dependent Children (ADC) program, created by the Social Security Act of 1935. ADC was not a large program, serving about 350,000 families in 1940, primarily widows and their children. By the 1960s, the program's name had changed (to AFDC), the number receiving assistance had grown (to about 4 million recipients in just over 1 million families in the mid-1960s), and the type of family served was different (primarily divorced or never-married mothers and their children).

Throughout the 1970s, the AFDC caseload continued to grow. By 1980, 10.6 million people in 3.6 million families were on the rolls, an increase of 3.2 million recipients and 1.7 million families from 1970. Caseloads in Michigan increased from 304,000 to 782,000 between 1970 and 1980. Increased caseloads led to rapid increases in spending. States shared responsibility with the

**TABLE 17.1**

**Trends in AFDC Caseloads: U.S. and Michigan**

|  | United States | | Michigan | |
|---|---|---|---|---|
|  | Cases | Recipients | Cases | Recipients |
| FY 1977 | 3,575,494 | 11,188,354 | 202,214 | 650,814 |
| FY 1980 | 3,642,404 | 10,596,045 | 225,095 | 683,799 |
| FY 1983 | 3,650,746 | 10,659,365 | 240,069 | 751,634 |
| FY 1987 | 3,784,014 | 11,065,027 | 214,410 | 652,076 |
| FY 1990 | 3,974,321 | 11,460,379 | 218,137 | 665,101 |
| FY 1994 | 5,046,326 | 14,225,651 | 223,950 | 665,785 |

SOURCE: U.S. Department of Health and Human Services (2001a).

federal government for financing AFDC. States with lower per-capita incomes received a greater proportion of their AFDC funds (close to 80% in a state like Mississippi) from the federal government than states with higher incomes, such as Michigan—which received approximately 50% of costs.

In the 1980s, the Reagan administration sought to cut welfare rolls and reduce spending on welfare. The 1981 Omnibus Budget Reconciliation Act (OBRA) tightened AFDC eligibility requirements and increased the rate at which AFDC benefits were reduced when a recipient went to work. These changes removed just under 500,000 families from the rolls, saving an estimated $93 million in state and federal funds (U.S. House of Representatives 1993) but also pushing many families into poverty (Levitan 1985). Additionally, OBRA allowed states to implement community work experience or "workfare" programs, whereby recipients had to earn their grants by working in unpaid positions for a certain number of hours (equal to their grant amount divided by the minimum wage). These programs were the precursors to the changes that would unfold a decade later.

### Welfare in the Late 1980s and Early 1990s

A great deal of welfare reform activity occurred in the late 1980s and early 1990s, at both the federal and the state levels. Changes in federal law sought to move more welfare recipients into work, and states, including Michigan, began experimenting with their own policies to encourage work and parental responsibility. This section describes changes in federal law, Michigan's implementation of those laws, and other policies enacted by the state prior to 1996.

### The Family Support Act

In 1988 Congress passed the Family Support Act (FSA). Its centerpiece was the Job Opportunities and Basic Skills (JOBS) program, which encouraged participation in education and training programs, with the ultimate goal of moving recipients from welfare to self-sufficiency. States could offer a variety of activities under JOBS, such as education and training programs—including high school completion and post-secondary education, job-search assistance, and placement in community-service jobs. Beginning in 1990, at least 7% of a state's caseload had to participate in these activities, with this rate rising to 15% in 1995. Some recipients were excluded from the participation requirements due to their age, health, or other factors. Recipients not meeting these criteria were mandatory JOBS participants.

Michigan's JOBS program was called "MOST"— the Michigan Opportunities and Skills Training program. The state chose to offer the full range of JOBS activities, although it did not use JOBS funds to support post-secondary education. Recipients could fulfill the JOBS participation requirement by attending college if they could access federal scholarships and loans. In the early 1990s the largest proportion of MOST/JOBS participants in an average month in Michigan were in high-school completion programs (about 20% of participants, or between 8,500 and 9,300 individuals, depending on the year) or in college (16% to 24%, or between 7,900 and 10,000 individuals) (U.S House of Representatives 1994, 1996).

At the same time that states had to start meeting JOBS participation requirements, a recession hit. As a result, AFDC caseloads increased from about 11 million recipients in the late 1980s to about 14 million in 1994. Caseloads in Michigan during this period ranged from 650,000 to 700,000 persons, and, unlike U.S. caseloads, peaked in the mid-1980s and then declined (see table 17.1). This is due in part to benefit reductions instituted in the early 1990s (discussed later in the text), which had the effect of making fewer families eligible for assistance.

### AFDC Benefits and Eligibility

While passage of FSA changed the education and training component of AFDC, it did not alter the basic eligibility and benefit structure of the program. Within certain limits, states could set financial eligibility criteria (including the amount of income and assets a family could have) and cash benefit levels. Due to this flexibility, there was a great deal of variation in AFDC benefit levels across states. In the late 1980s and early 1990s, the maximum monthly benefit for a family of three ranged from $120 in Mississippi to $924 in Alaska. This large difference is in part due to different costs of living between states, in part to differences in state per-capita income, and in part to political factors, such as states' willingness to raise revenues.

To some degree, AFDC benefit differences were offset by Food Stamps, a fully federally funded program providing food assistance to low-income families in the form of vouchers. Families in lower-benefit states were eligible for more assistance from food stamps than families living in higher-cash-benefit states. Nearly all AFDC recipients were eligible for and received food stamps, and payment levels were adjusted each year for inflation. Additionally, families receiving AFDC were automatically eligible for Medicaid, a federal-state-funded program providing health care benefits to low-income families.

Michigan's AFDC benefit levels varied by region of the state, with differences based on the cost of housing in the area. Maximum benefit levels in 1990 in Washtenaw County, for example, were $546 (for a family of three), compared to $516 in Wayne County. As shown in table 17.2, compared to other Midwestern states, Michigan's benefit levels were above the average, but the state reduced benefit amounts after 1990. In most of the nation, benefit levels were fairly constant during the 1990s, contributing to a decline in purchasing power, since benefits were not adjusted for inflation. This trend began in the 1970s, with the real spending power of AFDC in the median state eroding by 21% over the 1970–80 period, although by only 2% in Michigan.

### Funding for AFDC and JOBS

Like most states, Michigan faced fiscal challenges in implementing FSA. One challenge stemmed from the legislation that required a mix of federal and state funds for JOBS, as had been the case for AFDC funding. The proportion of state matching funds for both programs varied based on a state's income relative to that of other states. Michigan was responsible for about 55% of AFDC-related costs, with the federal government covering the

**TABLE 17.2**

**Maximum AFDC Benefits (for a Three-Person Family with No Income) in Nominal Dollars, Midwestern States, 1987–92**

|  | 1987 | 1990 | 1992 | 1996 |
|---|---|---|---|---|
| Illinois | $342 | $367 | $367 | $377 |
| Indiana | $256 | $288 | $288 | $288 |
| Iowa | $381 | $410 | $426 | $426 |
| Michigan (Wayne County) | $473 | $516 | $459 | $459 |
| Minnesota | $532 | $532 | $532 | $532 |
| Ohio | $302 | $334 | $334 | $341 |
| Wisconsin | $544 | $517 | $517 | $517 |

SOURCE: U.S. House of Representatives (1994, 1998).

rest. Including costs paid by the federal government, in the early 1990s this was approximately $1.2 billion per year (equivalent to $1.4 billion in 2001 dollars) (U.S. House of Representatives 1996). Total AFDC expenditures in Michigan were third-highest in the nation, behind California and New York.

Whereas states were mandated to pay their share of AFDC benefit costs, the same was not true for JOBS. In order to receive the full amount of federal funds available under JOBS, states had to contribute their full "match." However, they could receive some proportion of federal funds if they matched with state funds at a lower level. The economic downturn in the early 1990s meant that most states did not commit their full state obligation and were unable to obtain the maximum amount of federal JOBS funds available. Michigan spent just 42% of available federal funds in fiscal year 1990, rising to 64% and 71% by fiscal years 1993 and 1994 (U.S. House of Representatives 1996).

### To Strengthen Michigan Families

As did many states during the early 1990s, Michigan pursued changes to its welfare system, some by changes in state laws and regulations, and others through a federal "waiver" process. Beginning in 1992, Michigan obtained a number of waivers. Most of these changes were part of a vision for reform called *To Strengthen Michigan Families* (TSMF). TSMF articulated principles such as encouraging employment and increasing personal responsibility of welfare recipients.

Although many policy changes were enacted to achieve these goals, a core set focused on the

AFDC program (Werner and Kornfeld 1997). In 1992, the state received waivers to broaden eligibility for two-parent families, to allow families to keep more of their AFDC checks when they took a job (i.e., to reduce the marginal tax rate on earnings), and to extend participation in employment-related activities. Under AFDC, two-parent families were served by the AFDC-UP (Unemployed Parent) program, and eligibility criteria were strict (for example, parents had to meet a series of requirements including a previous work history, but benefits were easily lost if a parent went back to work). Because state policy makers believed that these rules created a disincentive for two-parent families to remain together or to seek employment, Michigan received waivers to eliminate these rules.

After OBRA, once a parent went to work, AFDC benefits were reduced by nearly a dollar for each dollar of earnings after four months of employment. In some cases, children's earnings were treated the same way. Because of expenses associated with going to work (e.g., child care and transportation), parents taking low-wage jobs often found themselves no better off, or even worse off, financially than when they received AFDC (Blank 1997). As a way to encourage employment, Michigan obtained a waiver allowing working recipients to keep the first $200 per month and 20% of the remaining earnings, without affecting the amount of AFDC received.

As another way to encourage and move recipients to employment, all adults receiving AFDC were required to enter into a "Social Contract" with the Michigan Department of Social Services (MDSS), the agency overseeing welfare programs. The Social Contract specified that the client would attempt to achieve self-sufficiency, and the state would provide services and other assistance to help the recipient leave the welfare rolls. Additionally, in 1994 the state received a waiver to eliminate nearly all exemption categories, meaning that many more AFDC recipients could be mandated to participate in JOBS/MOST.

JOBS/MOST participants could have their benefits reduced if they did not participate in assigned activities. Between 1992 and 1994, the federally specified penalty for noncompliance, called a sanction, was removal of the noncompliant person from the grant calculation, resulting in a reduced AFDC check. This reduction continued until the person was compliant or, in cases of repeated noncompliance, for a minimum of one to six months. Toward the end of fiscal year 1994,

roughly 3% of the state's AFDC caseload was in sanction status (computations based on data reported in Michigan Department of Social Services 1995a).

Waivers also let the state increase penalties for noncompliance: recipients faced a 25% reduction in their AFDC check and in their food stamp benefits for every month of noncompliance. After twelve months of noncompliance, the AFDC case could be closed and the family would receive no cash assistance, although food stamp benefits could continue. From April through June 1996, the first few months that cases could lose benefits under the new policy, 1,201 families had their cases closed due to sanctions, representing 4.5% of all closed AFDC cases during those months (Michigan Department of Social Services 1996).

### The General Assistance Program

Another major change in Michigan's income-support system was the elimination of the state's General Assistance (GA) program in 1991. General Assistance programs are state-funded cash or in-kind programs, primarily serving low-income persons ineligible for AFDC or federal disability programs. Because they are fully funded by states, there is variability between state programs (and sometimes within a state) in terms of eligibility and payments. Some states never operated a GA program.

In the late 1980s, thirty-eight states had General Assistance programs, including Michigan (Gallagher 1999). Until 1991, Michigan provided maximum benefits of $231 per month for nonelderly, impoverished adults without dependent children. To qualify in Michigan, recipients had to earn less than $160 per month, have less than $250 in assets, and if they owned a car, its value had to be less than $1,500. In addition to cash benefits, GA recipients received state medical coverage and were eligible for federal food stamp benefits.

Governor Engler proposed to end the program in Michigan, and GA benefits ceased in October 1991. More than 80,000 people lost benefits, although about 11% were automatically transferred to one of two new state-funded programs, State Disability Assistance (SDA) or State Family Assistance (SFA), a program for individuals formerly covered by GA family benefits. At the time of GA elimination, the MDSS director noted that the state expected to save about $240 million in fiscal year 1992 and "help break this cycle of dependence" on public assistance (Walsh 1991).

A number of analysts have characterized Michigan's GA termination as among the most drastic of state social welfare spending cuts that were implemented across the nation in the early 1990s (Center on Social Welfare Policy, and Law 1994; Nichols and Porter 1995). Research on the effects of the GA termination documented that the majority of former recipients did not find jobs after they lost benefits. A study found that slightly less than one-third of the 530 former recipients surveyed had found employment one year after GA ended; and much of this employment was unstable (Henly and Danziger 1996). While tremendous increases in homelessness, predicted by many advocates, did not occur, a survey of former recipients reported that more than one-fifth were living in shelters, on the streets, or in other unstable living arrangements, up from 11% the year before GA was eliminated (Kossoudji, Danziger, and Lovell 1993).

## Reforming Welfare at the State and Federal Level in the Mid-1990s

Michigan took on a leadership role in the welfare reform debate of the mid-1990s, in part because of the reforms the state was implementing, and in part due to the lobbying efforts in Washington of Governor Engler and his staff. This section discusses the evolution of state and national welfare policies, provides an overview of Michigan and federal welfare reform laws, and highlights important changes in funding for welfare programs.

### Michigan's Role in Welfare Reform

The waivers and other policy changes Michigan implemented during the early 1990s were relevant to the national welfare reform debate, and Michigan emerged as one of the leaders in welfare reform. For example, Michigan and several other states moved away from the education and training philosophy of JOBS and implemented "work first" programs that assume that finding a job quickly and developing work skills through direct experience—rather than participating in education and training—will be more effective in moving recipients off the rolls. The Engler administration implemented its "Work First" program in October 1994. The popularity of work first

programs was due in part to the success of a Riverside, California, welfare-to-work program that placed a strong emphasis on finding work.

During 1994 and 1995 a number of federal welfare reform plans were proposed to turn welfare into a work-based system. In June 1994, President Clinton unveiled his welfare reform plan, but no action was ever taken on it. In December 1995 and January 1996, President Clinton vetoed two Republican welfare reform plans. Although Clinton and congressional Republicans shared a similar vision, they differed on key issues: (*a*) funding levels (Republicans wanted federal funding cuts, Clinton's plan would have increased funding); (*b*) the entitlement to assistance (Republicans favored capped block grants to states, with states deciding how to fund particular welfare provisions, while Clinton wanted to maintain the entitlement to cash assistance); and (*c*) time limits (Republicans proposed putting an absolute limit on the amount of time that families could receive welfare benefits, whereas Clinton would have provided assistance in the form of community-service jobs to families who had not found employment after two years of receiving benefits).

Despite federal impasse during this time, welfare reform occurred in Michigan. Public Acts 223 and 224 were signed into law by Governor Engler on 6 December 1995, amending the Social Welfare Act of 1939 (P.A. 280) and the Administrative Procedures Act of 1980 (P.A. 122). Michigan's new laws were quite similar to legislative proposals being discussed in Washington, D.C. Michigan eliminated the AFDC program and replaced it with a new cash assistance program called the Family Independence Program (FIP), administered by the Family Independence Agency (FIA), the new name for the Department of Social Services. Unlike AFDC, FIP would not be an entitlement program, meaning that eligible families would not necessarily be assured of assistance. Adult recipients, unless exempted, would be required to participate in Work First or go to work at least part-time.

Additionally, Michigan's new law gave greater discretion to MDSS/FIA, by exempting it from the Administrative Procedures Act for twelve months after the law went into effect (Weissert 2000). This provision allowed the state to develop program rules and regulations for FIP without, for example, holding public hearings on them. However, unless the federal law changed, Michigan would need waivers to implement its reform plan.

## The Personal Responsibility and Work Opportunity Reconciliation Act of 1996

Nearly six months after Clinton's second veto, Congress passed the Personal Responsibility and Work Opportunity Reconciliation Act (PRWORA) of 1996. The body representing the nation's governors, the National Governors' Association (NGA), played a key role in this process by proposing its own welfare reform plan, which was viewed by many as a bipartisan compromise (Weaver 2000). Many of the provisions in Michigan's P.A. 223 are similar to those in PRWORA. This is not surprising, since Governor Engler helped formulate the NGA plan (Weaver 2000; Weissert 2000).

Clinton signed PRWORA in August 1996; states could begin implementing the Temporary Assistance to Needy Families (TANF) program, which replaced AFDC, as early as 1 October 1996. TANF was authorized and funded through 30 September 2002 and, like P.A. 223, ends the entitlement to cash assistance, gives increased discretion for states and localities in defining and operating their programs, imposes work requirements, and makes it more difficult for teen mothers to receive cash assistance on their own.

A major difference between TANF and AFDC is the former's lack of entitlement—each state decides which families to assist, subject only to a requirement that they receive "fair and equitable treatment." Additionally, states must meet "work participation rate" requirements. A certain proportion of the state's caseload must be working or participating in a work-related activity (e.g., looking for a job, receiving short-term training in how to find a job, and, on a limited basis, participating in a short-term training program that prepares the recipient for a specific job). In fiscal year 1997, states had to have 25% of the caseload in work activities for at least twenty hours a week. Each year that proportion rose by five percentage points, to 50% in 2002. Additionally, hours of participation required climbed, to twenty-five hours in 1999 and to thirty hours in 2000 and thereafter, although parents with a child under age six are required to participate only twenty hours per week. Two-parent cases are held to a different participation standard. In 1997 and 1998, states had to have 75% of these cases engaged in work activities for thirty-five hours per week, and the rate rose to 90% in 1999 and thereafter.

Having already passed its own welfare reform law, Michigan quickly implemented PRWORA, since the new law eliminated the need for waivers.

The newly renamed Michigan Family Independence Agency (FIA) administered FIP, the state's TANF program. Individuals could meet TANF's work requirements through participation in Work First. Unlike P.A. 223, though, PRWORA includes time limits on receipt of cash assistance funded by federal dollars, to ensure that assistance is "temporary." First, recipients who are not employed or in a work activity after receiving assistance for twenty-four months may be dropped from the rolls. Second, adults, with few exceptions, are barred from receiving federally funded assistance for more than sixty months, or fewer, at state option. Although Michigan is barred from using federal funds for families after sixty months, it has chosen to support these families with state funds (as will be discussed later). Only Michigan and Vermont have no time limit.

## PRWORA's Changes to Welfare Funding and Implications for Michigan

PRWORA also changed the federal-state funding structure for cash assistance that had been in place since 1935. Instead of matching state expenditures and providing funds for states to draw down for employment and training services, TANF provides a capped block grant to each state that does not change over time. The states' block grant is based on a formula that takes into account historical federal spending on AFDC, JOBS, and the Emergency Assistance program, a joint federal-state program that helped families in short-term crises, which was also abolished by TANF.

Because of a "maintenance of effort" (MOE) provision, states must maintain their own spending at a level equal to or greater than 80% of 1994 state welfare expenditures, or risk penalties of reduced federal funding. However, states meeting the work-participation rates are allowed to drop their spending to 75% of historic expenditures.

A criticism of block grant funding is that increased welfare costs associated with population growth, economic downturns, or inflation must now be borne by the states or else by the poor—the federal contribution remains constant (Sheldon Danziger 2001). The law set aside $2 billion in a contingency fund for states experiencing growth in their low-income populations (e.g., due to a recession). However, if those funds were exhausted, states would bear any additional costs for the program. Because caseloads have fallen in most states since 1994, many states were allocated more federal funds in the first five years post-PRWORA than they would have received under the AFDC matching-grant arrangement.

From fiscal year 1997 through fiscal year 2000, Michigan was awarded $3.1 billion total in federal TANF funds. The state transferred $282 million to the Child Care Development Fund to fund child care for recipients, and $309 million to the Social Services Block Grant to fund child-abuse and child-neglect programs. The amount available for direct TANF use (i.e. for FIP) was just over $2.5 billion. Of this amount, the state spent just over $2.3 billion, leaving a TANF surplus of just under $200 million (U.S. Department of Health and Human Services 2001a). State MOE funds from fiscal year 1997 through fiscal year 2000 amounted to $469 million, which satisfies the 75% MOE requirement, as Michigan met federal work-participation requirements (U.S. Department of Health and Human Services 2001a).

### Welfare Reform in Michigan: FIP, Work First, and Project Zero

Although Michigan had been moving toward a work-based welfare system since the early 1990s, implementation of PRWORA accelerated that change. The Work First program is the central activity by which welfare clients meet federal work requirements. Most clients in Work First participate in job search and other activities designed to help them find employment quickly. However, in 1999 the state expanded Work First to include some education and training activities. This section describes the organization of Michigan's welfare system, services provided through Work First and FIP, the state's TANF program, and how the state met PRWORA's work participation requirements.

### Organization of Work First Programs

Prior to the introduction of Work First, FIA (and DSS) administered all welfare-to-work activities directly or through referrals to or local contracts with not-for-profit and public agencies. In 1994, Governor Engler created the Michigan Jobs Commission (MJC), charged with improving the state's business climate through a range of initiatives, including Work First and workforce development.

TANF funds used for Work First were passed from the FIA to the MJC. The MJC then allocated funds for employment and training services and workforce development programs among local Workforce Development Boards and their staff, called Michigan Works! Agencies (MWAs). Until 1997, MWA staff could provide services directly, or the MWA could contract out for services. In 1996, for example, MWA staff provided Work First services directly in ten of the twenty-six MWAs, while the other sixteen contracted out for services, primarily with nonprofit and school-based organizations, and a smaller number with for-profit providers (Seefeldt, Sandfort, and Danziger 1998).

In April 1999, Governor Engler dismantled the MJC and placed economic development functions in the new Michigan Economic Development Corporation (MEDC). Job training and workforce development functions and former MJC staff overseeing these programs, including Work First, were put in another new agency, the Michigan Department of Career Development (MDCD). Like the MJC, MDCD sets policy, provides guidance to localities, and administers state and federal funds, while local Workforce Development Boards and their contractors oversee program operations.

### FIP and Work First Service Delivery

Entrance into a Work First program starts when a potential welfare recipient applies for FIP, or at benefit redetermination, or upon job loss for a client receiving FIP. Families apply for assistance (or have eligibility redetermined) at a local FIA office. In most areas of the state, there is one FIA office per county. Larger urban areas have multiple district offices located throughout the county. After meeting with FIA staff (see the following for more details), the applicant/client is referred to an orientation session.

As of 1 October 1996, to be eligible for cash assistance, all recipients and applicants are required to attend this orientation session, during which the rules and regulations of the Family Independence Program and Work First are explained. Unless deferred from further participation, the client must continue to participate in Work First and find employment. As of October 1998, ties between participation in Work First and FIP program eligibility were further strengthened, with applicants now required to attend orientation and the first day of a Work First program before their FIP case is opened and receipt of benefits can begin.

In Work First programs clients typically participate in "job search readiness" activities, such as résumé and cover letter preparation and mock interviews. They are also required to search for work. During job search, clients have access to a variety of tools to help them in their search (e.g., phones to call employers, lists of job openings from newspapers and from the state employment agency) (Danziger and Seefeldt 2000). Hours of participation in Work First follow federal guidelines. Although the details of other states' program vary, most were operating "work first" programs after PRWORA went into effect (Holcomb et al. 1998).

Clients who participate in Work First and follow other eligibility rules receive a monthly FIP check. The maximum monthly benefit is between $424 and $489 (for a family of three), depending on the county of residence. Average monthly benefits in Michigan were $357 in 1999 (U.S. House of Representatives 2000). These benefit levels have not increased since 1993, although families in which only the children receive benefits (e.g., the children live with a noneligible relative) received increases in 2000 and 2001. In terms of benefit generosity, Michigan's maximum monthly FIP payment ($459 in Wayne County for a family of three) in 2000 is the sixteenth-highest in the nation and about 9% higher than the $429 benefit in the median state. However, Michigan's benefit fell from 142% of that of the median state in 1990 to 109% of that of the median state in 2000. Comparing Michigan to other Midwestern states, benefits are higher in Minnesota and Wisconsin, and lower in Illinois, Indiana, Iowa, and Ohio (U.S. House of Representatives 2000).

The goal of Work First participation is to find employment and ultimately leave the FIP rolls. Clients may take part-time work, as long as the hours fulfill the federal work participation requirement. Starting in mid-2002, some clients may be required to work forty hours per week, based on determination by their FIA caseworker. Clients who do not find employment within four weeks may stay in Work First and continue searching for work, or they may be placed in another activity, such as vocational training.

### Other Employment-Related Activities

For the first several years post-reform, participation in Work First or working in paid employment were the primary work-related activities for welfare recipients in Michigan. Beginning in October 1999, the state allowed clients to engage in some forms of education and training to satisfy the work requirement. Clients can combine ten hours of employment per week with ten hours of class and ten hours of study time (called the "10-10-10") or can attend a full-time, short-term (six months or fewer) vocational training program. Clients without a high-school diploma or GED may fulfill up to ten hours of their work requirement by participating in GED preparation activities.

According to MDCD data and reports from Work First staff, few welfare recipients participate in education or training activities—about 3% to 4% in fiscal years 2000 and 2001 (Michigan Department of Career Development 2002). This may be due to difficulties some clients have in balancing training with work and family responsibilities. Also, Work First staff reported challenges in finding employers willing to provide jobs for only ten hours per week, or training programs willing to admit clients without GEDs or high school degrees, limiting the choices for clients who lack this certificate (Seefeldt et al. 2001).

### Work First Funding

Work First is funded by a mixture of TANF, federal Welfare-to-Work program dollars, and state General Fund/General Purpose revenues. In 2001 dollars, about $43 million in federal TANF funds and $34.4 million in state funds were expended on work-related activities (primarily Work First) during fiscal year 1997 (U.S. Department of Health and Human Services 1998). By fiscal year 1999, $141.2 million federal TANF dollars and $16.7 million in state funds were spent on work activities and training (U.S. Department of Health and Human Services 2001a). During fiscal year 2000, federal funds increased to $165.3 million, while state funds fell to $6.9 million (Center for Law and Social Policy 2002a). This represents both a reduction in the welfare caseload and a shift in state dollars toward funding child care services (discussed further in the following section).

Welfare-to-Work (WTW), passed by Congress in 1997, authorized funding to states and localities to serve "hard to employ" TANF recipients and the noncustodial parents of children on TANF. Michigan received $42 million in federal WTW funds in fiscal year 1998, and $39 million in fiscal year 1999, both matched at a 50% rate with state funds. No further funds are authorized under WTW. Michigan used its WTW funds primarily to offer employment services to noncustodial parents as well as to augment Work First and pay for services for welfare recipients who fall into one of WTW's target groups (e.g., long-term recipients, recipients with poor work histories). Detroit received one of the WTW grants made directly to localities. It used its $4.9 million to subsidize the full wages of approximately 2,400 recipients placed into public- or private-sector jobs with employers recruited to participate in its project (Nightingale et al. 2000). Kalamazoo's Metro Transit Service also received $375,000 to enhance the city's public transportation service, particularly to assist welfare recipients' commute to work.

## Work Participation Rates

Michigan has had no trouble meeting the federal work-participation rates. Although the participation rates increase each year, these increases may be offset or eliminated by credits states receive for reductions in their TANF caseloads. With the caseload reduction credit, Michigan's 1997 participation rate was reduced from 25% to 13% for all families and from 75% to 47% for two-parent families. Actual participation was 41% for all families and 60% for two-parent families. Levels of participation rose in 1998 and 1999, but Michigan's required (adjusted) participation rate continued to drop due to further caseload reductions, with the state having an adjusted participation rate of 0% for all families and 15% for two-parent families in 1999 (U.S. Department of Health and Human Services 1998, 1999, 2000).

## Exemptions from the Work Requirement

Exemptions (called "deferrals") from Work First and the work requirement are limited primarily to clients who are disabled or caring for a disabled family member. Shorter-term deferrals are available to mothers with a child under three months old, victims of domestic violence, clients with temporary mental or physical illnesses or injuries, and clients experiencing a temporary crisis that limits their ability to participate. A comparison of Michigan's work requirement deferral criteria to those of other states characterized Michigan's criteria as narrower than those of many other states, in part because the definition of "disabled" is tied

to eligibility for the Supplemental Security Income (SSI) program, the federal disability program for low-income individuals (Thompson et al. 1998).

While the FIP rolls have declined, the number of deferred cases receiving assistance has grown. In December 1997, just under 33,000 cases were deferred, or 26% of the caseload (Michigan Family Independence Agency 1998a). Four years later, approximately 39,700 cases were deferred. Because the total caseload was lower in 2001 (about 71,000 cases in 2001, compared to 122,500 in 1997), deferred cases made up about 58% of FIP cases (Michigan Family Independence Agency 2002c).

## The Family Independence Specialist and Service Delivery

PRWORA also sought to "change the culture of the welfare office." For states to be successful in placing recipients into jobs, the work of welfare office staff had to be changed from primarily determining eligibility and providing cash benefits (clerical functions) to providing employment and social services with an emphasis on "case management," a term often used to describe holistic treatment of clients.

Michigan adopted a case-management philosophy in its FIA offices, and implemented the Family Independence Specialist (FIS) in April 1997. Welfare applicants and recipients are assigned to a single Family Independence Specialist. Previously, an applicant might see up to three workers to open his or her case and receive other services. The FISs perform all eligibility functions and also may visit clients in their homes, provide (as needed) counseling services, and perform other client-assessment and case-management activities.

## Project Zero

In July 1996, Michigan initiated "Project Zero" as a six-site effort to achieve zero unemployment among nondeferred AFDC/FIP recipients. Project Zero sites undertook surveys of client barriers to employment, and then sites were provided with increased resources to help alleviate those barriers. In the first six sites, these funds were primarily used for additional child care and transportation services, for example, giving funds to a day-care center to expand its hours of service (Seefeldt, Sandfort, and Danziger 1997).

In the first year of operation, one site (Ottawa County) attained the goal of zero unemployment, and all six sites showed higher rates of cases with earned income than the rest of the state. For example, in February 1997, 54% of Project Zero cases expected to work had earnings during the month, compared with 35% of cases in the balance of the state (Seefeldt et al. 1998). Project Zero was expanded to all FIA offices by October 2000. As of February 2002, all but twelve of FIA's 104 offices had reported zero unemployment at least once since implementing Project Zero.

## Work Supports for Welfare Recipients

For welfare reform to be successful in moving recipients to work, other types of assistance, besides cash and job search assistance, are needed. Child care and transportation problems are frequently mentioned hurdles for recipients attempting to enter or stay in the workforce. Many states, including Michigan, have invested funds to provide such assistance. Earnings disregards are another tool the state uses to support the work efforts of welfare recipients. Finally, the federal Food Stamp program can be an important source of income for families moving from welfare to work. This section discusses work-support programs and policies.

### Child Care

The federal government and states have greatly expanded child-care spending since 1996. PRWORA enhanced several sources of federal child-care funding (AFDC Child Care, Transitional Child Care, At-Risk Child Care, and the Child Care Development Block Grant—CCDBG), each with different eligibility rules, and consolidated them into the Child Care and Development Fund (CCDF). Consolidation has the potential to eliminate gaps in coverage that existed under the old system. For example, consider a working AFDC recipient who received child-care assistance through the AFDC system. When she left welfare, she could continue to receive assistance for up to another year through the Transitional Child Care program. However, she might have had to make a separate application, potentially going without child-care assistance while her application was processed. With the CCDF, families in Michigan fill out one application that covers all eligibility categories (Seefeldt et al. 2001).

Approximately twenty billion dollars are available to states through CCDF for the period 1997 to 2002, a 25% increase over spending prior to 1996 (U.S. House of Representatives 2000). States can increase funding further by moving TANF funds into the CCDF. Of the more than $3 billion in TANF funds allocated to it between 1997 and 2000, Michigan has transferred just under $3 million to the CCDF (U.S. Department of Health and Human Services 2001a). As with TANF, states must match federal CCDF funds.

Federal regulations specify that CCDF funds may be used only for care of children under age thirteen in families with income up to 85% of the median state income (although states can set lower age and income limits). In Michigan, employed FIP recipients and those participating in Work First are automatically eligible for child-care assistance. Other low-income families with qualifying children may receive assistance if monthly income does not exceed certain limits (188% of the poverty line in 1999 and about 56% of the median state income), although they have a co-pay. Unlike a number of other states, Michigan does not have a waiting list to receive child care assistance (Seefeldt et al. 2001).

Families can choose any type of care—a child day-care center, a nonlicensed family day-care home, a group day-care home (license required, and more children allowed than a family day-care home), a relative, or a nonrelative in-home day care provider (called a day-care aide). In-home care provided by a relative accounted for nearly half of the child-care settings receiving FIA subsidies in 1998. The next most common were center-based (18%) and in-home care by nonrelatives (16%). Eleven percent of providers that the state supported were family child-care homes, and 9% were family group homes (Public Sector Consultants, Inc. 1998).

Child-care providers are reimbursed for care. The amount up to which FIA will reimburse providers is determined by a legislatively mandated market rate survey for different types of providers in different areas of the state, with maximum reimbursement currently set at 75% of the market rate. Rates of reimbursement have not been adjusted for several years, and, as of 1 June 1999, the reimbursement rates in Michigan were based on the seventy-fifth percentile of the 1995–96 market (Seefeldt et al. 2001).

## Transportation Assistance

Both FIA and Work First can provide transportation assistance to recipients to attend Work First, look for a job, or go to work. This assistance can take the form of bus tickets, mileage reimbursement, funds to repair a personal automobile, or, under some circumstances, funds to help purchase a car. The maximum amount available for car repairs is $900 (per twelve-month period) and the maximum for car purchase is $1,200 per participant. For fiscal year 2000, FIA spent $5.4 million for car repair, $6.2 million for car purchase, and $300,000 for other transportation-related costs (Michigan Family Independence Agency 2001a).

## Earned-Income Disregards

Under AFDC, when a recipient first went to work, the first $120 and an additional 33% of the remainder of his or her earnings were not counted, or were disregarded, when calculating the grant amount. However, after four months of employment, this disregard was eliminated, and the recipient's grant would be reduced by nearly a dollar for every dollar he or she earned.

PRWORA allows states to set their own earned-income disregard policies. Three states have retained the old AFDC policy, but the rest, including Michigan, have policies that allow recipients to keep more of their earnings (Seefeldt 2002). Michigan retains its waiver policy of not counting the first $200 per month and an additional 20% of remaining earnings. Blank and Schmidt (2001) categorize the state's earned-income disregard as "medium" in terms of its generosity relative to that of other states. A low-wage working recipient would keep more money (benefits plus wages) in the Midwestern states of Illinois, Iowa, and Ohio than in Michigan.

## Food Stamps

Food Stamps is a federal food-assistance program for low-income families. Benefits are 100% federally funded, and are adjusted each year for inflation. Most program rules are set by the federal government, although states can request waivers. Food stamps are available for low-income individuals, childless families, and families with children, unlike AFDC and TANF. Nearly all (80% to 90%) welfare recipients are eligible for and receive food stamps. For most of the Food Stamp program's history, benefits were issued in the form of vouchers (stamps) that allowed families to purchase food but not other items. In the 1990s, some states received waivers to "cash out" food stamps, allowing recipients to receive benefits in the form of a check. This provided the flexibility to purchase nonfood items and eliminated the stigma of using food stamps in a grocery store. In May 1996, Michigan implemented a cash-out program for recipients who had earnings of at least $350 a month for three consecutive months.

PRWORA requires states to convert food stamps to an Electronic Benefit Transfer (EBT) system. Instead of getting stamps or checks, recipients receive a card, much like an ATM card, to use at grocery or other authorized food retailers. As of July 2001, food stamp beneficiaries in Michigan receive a "Bridge Card" through which they can access their monthly food stamp and FIP benefits.

Welfare reform's emphasis on work has major implications for the Food Stamp program. The federal government oversees a quality-control system for food stamps, whereby states must monitor the rate at which they make mistakes in eligibility or benefit issuances. States can be assessed financial penalties if they have high error rates. Between fiscal years 1996 and 2000, Michigan had food stamp error rates between 11% and 16%, above the national average of 9% to 10%, and faces up to $20 million in sanctions from the federal government (Michigan Family Independence Agency 2001b). Most of the errors resulted from overpayments, which the state has attributed to the fluctuating earnings of working recipients. While PRWORA's flexibility allows Michigan to adjust FIP benefits only when income changes by $100 or more from month to month, federal Food Stamp rules mandate that states take into account any variation in income when computing benefits.

## Welfare, Food Stamp, and Child Care Caseloads

In the media, dramatic reductions in the number of families receiving TANF have been noted as a great success of welfare reform. Between January 1993 and January 2002, the number of families on welfare was cut by 58% nationwide and by 66% in

**FIGURE 17.1**

**Changes in Michigan Caseloads, 1995–2001**

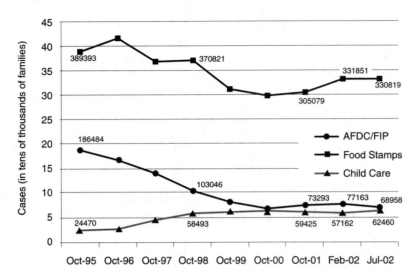

SOURCE: Michigan Department of Social Services (1995b); Michigan Family Independence Agency (1996, 1997b, 1998b, 1999, 2000b, 2001e, 2002d, 2002e).

Michigan. A variety of factors have been credited with spurring that decline, including welfare policies, other federal policy changes, and the booming economy. This section discusses welfare and related caseload trends, and the potential impact of policies and the economy on those trends.

**Caseload Trends**

In most states, including Michigan, caseload declines pre-date PRWORA. As shown in figure 17.1, just under 190,000 families received FIP (TANF) in October 1995. One year later, the FIP caseload was down to 166,000 families. The decline continued steadily until the end of fiscal year 2000, when the caseload was about 68,000 families. As the economy went into recession, caseloads grew to approximately 77,000 families in early 2002. By July 2002, that number was back down to just under 69,000.

The composition of the caseload has also changed. In fiscal year 1995, just over half (52%) of adults on FIP were African American, 43% were white, and 3% Hispanic (U.S. Department of Health and Human Services, n.d.). In 2000, nearly 57% of adults on FIP were African American and 38% were white (Michigan Family Independence Agency 2001c).

With TANF's time limits and work requirements, some caseload decline was anticipated.

Less expected, though, were the declines seen in the Food Stamp program, both nationally and in Michigan. Nationwide, the number of households receiving food assistance through this program dropped by 36% over the 1996–2000 period. In Michigan, the drop has not been as great, with Food Stamp rolls (including those who received cashed out benefits) declining by 29% and then starting to rise in late 2000. The Food Research and Action Center, a Washington, D.C.–based advocacy group, ranks Michigan as one of the top ten states with regard to the estimated proportion of Food Stamp–eligible persons receiving assistance (Food Research and Action Center 2002).

On the other hand, the caseload of the Child Day Care program has steadily increased. Figure 17.1 shows that the number of families receiving child care assistance has more than doubled since 1995 (from 24,000 cases in October 1995 to about 62,000 in July 2002). State policy makers attribute the increase in Child Day Care cases to increases in employment (Michigan Family Independence Agency 2001a). Of cases in which the adult is expected to work, the proportion with earnings grew from 37% in October 1996 to 72% by the end of 2000 (Michigan Family Independence Agency 2001d). Also, in late 1996, about 30% of FIP cases closed were due to increased earnings, but by the end of 2000, closures due to earnings accounted for almost half of all closures (Michigan Family Independence Agency 1997a; 2000a). Both working recipients and many of those whose cases were closed due to earnings are eligible for child-care assistance.

**Welfare Policies and Caseload Declines**

Federal welfare reform and state policies, such as Work First and Project Zero, have contributed to higher employment among FIP recipients and reductions in the caseload. While work is one route off welfare, other policies also have reduced the welfare rolls.

*Sanctions.* In Michigan, failure to participate in Work First and to find employment can result in sanctions. Michigan's sanction policy is fairly severe compared to those of other states. As of April 1997, recipients on FIP for fewer than sixty days who do not comply with Work First may be terminated immediately from both the FIP and Food Stamp rolls. This is an immediate, full-family sanction, in that the entire case is closed and must remain so for at least one month. Recipients who have been on FIP for at least sixty days face a 25% reduction in both FIP and Food Stamp benefits for noncompliance with Work First, with case closure occurring after four months of non-compliance. Legislation modifying the state sanction policy went into effect in mid-2002. Clients have ten days to show good cause for noncompliance. If the client is still determined to be non-compliant, the entire case is closed for at least one month.

*Time Limits.* In most states, welfare recipients can also lose TANF benefits when they reach a time limit. PRWORA requires recipients to be engaged in a work activity within twenty-four months of coming on the welfare rolls, or cash assistance can be terminated. However, Michigan's regulations specify immediate referral to Work First for new applicants and for current recipients who are unemployed, so the twenty-four-month time limit is not a factor.

Additionally, receipt of TANF benefits, with few exceptions, is limited to sixty months during one's lifetime, or less at state option. Just over half (twenty-eight) of states, including the Midwestern states of Illinois, Iowa, Minnesota, and Wisconsin, adopted the sixty-month federal policy. The other twenty-two states have policies that limit benefits for a certain number of months, followed by a period of ineligibility before the recipient can reapply (thirteen states), limit benefits to fewer than sixty months (five states), or limit assistance to adults, allowing children to continue receiving cash assistance, either up to sixty months or indefinitely (Seefeldt 2002).

Michigan must abide by the prohibition against using federal funds to provide cash assistance to adults beyond the sixty-month limit. However, it has not adopted a time limit. Only Vermont has a similar time-limit policy. In December 2001, approximately 4,500 Michigan families on FIP, or about 6% of the caseload, had exceeded the sixty-month federal limit (Michigan Family Independence Agency 2002b). The state continues to provide cash grants to these cases by using state funds.

## Caseload Trends and the Economy

While federal and state reforms put increased pressure on recipients to leave welfare for work,

the reforms were implemented during a period of unprecedented economic growth. Given the booming economy in the late 1990s, it is likely that some welfare recipients would have entered the labor force even in the absence of welfare reform.

The Council of Economic Advisers attempted to sort out the effect of welfare reform on caseloads versus the effect of the economy. By their estimates, welfare reform policies played a small role in the caseload declines between 1993 and 1996, but accounted for approximately one-third of the caseload declines between 1996 and 1998. The economy was estimated to have had a large effect (26% to 36%) on pre-PRWORA declines but much less (about 8% to 10%) between 1996 and 1998 (Council of Economic Advisers 1999). Similar analyses were undertaken to examine national Food Stamp caseload declines. Here, drops in state unemployment rates accounted for two-thirds of caseload reductions, and changes in welfare and child-care policies the other third (Jacobs et al. 2001).

Other, nonwelfare policies, primarily a 1997 increase in the minimum wage and the expansion of the Earned Income Tax Credit (EITC), have made it much more beneficial for welfare recipients to go to work, and may also account for welfare and Food Stamp caseload reductions. The EITC provides tax relief to low- and moderate-income families in the form of a refund, even if the family's earnings were so low that they did not owe income taxes. By the late 1990s a minimum-wage worker employed full–time, full-year could receive an EITC of more than $3,500 if he or she had two or more children.

As the nation's and Michigan's economy experienced a recession in 2001, the relationship between caseloads and the economy was evident. From 2000 to 2001, the total number of TANF cases nationwide declined by 4%. However, between March and December 2001, thirty-three states, including Michigan, experienced increases (Center for Law and Social Policy 2002b). With the exception of a few very small increases, Michigan's welfare caseload had declined steadily since March 1994, reaching a low of 66,715 in November 2000 (Michigan Family Independence Agency 2001c). After that, caseloads began to rise in nearly every month, reaching more than 77,000 families in early 2002, the approximate size of the caseload in December 1999 (Michigan Family Independence Agency 2000a, 2002a). Although caseloads began to fall after that, they are still higher than the November 2000 low.

**TABLE 17.3**

**Comparison of Expenditures for Welfare, Child Care, and Food Stamps, FY 1995 and 2000**

|  | FY 1995 (in millions) | FY 2000 (in millions) |
|---|---|---|
| Cash Benefits (AFDC and FIP)[a] | $636.0 (federal) | $160.9 (federal) |
|  | $482.9 (state) | $180.1 (state) |
| Education, Training, and Work Assistance[b] |  |  |
| (JOBS/MOST and Work First) | $56.3 (federal) | $165.4 (federal-TANF) |
|  | $35.9 (state) | $6.9 (state) |
| Child Care[c] | $66.0 (federal) | $197.9 (federal) |
|  | $27.4 (state) | $269.4 (state) |
| Food Stamp Benefits | $902.6 (federal) | $465.8 (federal) |
| TOTAL | $2,207.1 | $1,446.4 |

SOURCES: California Dept. of Social Services (1999); Greenberg and Richer (2002); Seefeldt et al. (1998); U.S. Department of Health and Human Services (2002).
NOTES: Amounts reported in 2001 dollars.
(a) State funds are AFDC matching funds (1995) and TANF maintenance of effort funds (2000).
(b) State funds are JOBS matching funds (1995) and TANF maintenance of effort funds (2000).
(c) Federal Child Care funds in 1995 include those from AFDC, the At-Risk Child Care Program, and the Child Care Development Block Grant. State funds for 1995 are the matches required under AFDC and the At-Risk program. Federal funds for 2000 include TANF funds expended on child care and funds spent through the Child Care Development Fund (CCDF). State funds in 2000 are CCDF matching funds and the TANF maintenance of effort funds spent on child care.

## Caseload Trends and Expenditures

Welfare caseload declines have also affected overall spending on benefits and services to welfare recipients. As shown in table 17.3, federal and state expenditures on AFDC benefit payments, education, training, and work assistance through JOBS, child care, and Food Stamp benefit payments exceeded $2.2 billion in fiscal year 1995. By fiscal year 2000, spending had dropped to slightly more than $1.4 billion. However, nearly all of the spending decline was driven by decreases in direct benefits through FIP and food stamps. The shift in the goal of welfare, from providing income support to providing work supports, is reflected in increased spending in 2000 on job-related and child-care assistance, particularly the latter. For example, in fiscal year 2000, the Family Independence Agency expended more state and federal funds on the Child Day Care program ($467 million) than it did on FIP benefit payments ($341 million).

## Welfare Recipients in Michigan, Post-Reform

The previous discussion of declining caseloads and increased employment does not provide any information on the economic well-being of families who have left welfare. The Women's Employment Study (WES), conducted by the Program on Poverty and Social Welfare Policy at the University of Michigan, surveyed about 750 women from one urban Michigan county who received FIP in February 1997. Interviews were conducted in 1997, 1998, and 1999, and the resulting data contain information on respondents' education, employment, welfare receipt, family income, physical health, mental health, and other personal characteristics. This section presents selected WES findings (see Danziger et al. 2000; Danziger and Seefeldt 2002; Danziger et al. 2002).

All WES respondents were single mothers receiving FIP in February 1997. By the fall of 1999, only 32% still received FIP. Many left welfare for work; employment rates increased (from 40% in February 1997 to 73% in fall 1999), as did hours of work. Not only has the level of work increased, but so too has the proportion of women who worked but did not receive cash welfare (FIP)—from 20% in fall 1997 to 52% in fall 1999. Median hourly wages of those who work have also increased over time, from about $6.00 per hour in 1997 to just under $7.00 per hour in 1999. However, many experienced employment instability—almost half of employed respondents reported at least one spell of unemployment during the study period. These respondents usually were fired, were laid off, or quit due to dissatisfaction with the job.

A small subset of respondents did not work at all or worked very little over the study period. Some of these women are now married or living with a partner, and rely on that person's earnings. However, some have remained on welfare, and others have cycled between welfare and work. Comparing respondents who accumulated few months of work over the study period to those with more, the former group are more likely to have various barriers to employment, such as no high school diploma or GED, few job-related skills, lack of transportation, and mental health problems, which persist over time for some respondents.

WES respondents who left welfare for work had higher net incomes and lower poverty rates than those who still relied on welfare for support. Average annual income (in 1998) of work-reliant respondents was $17,000, while those on welfare (with and without working) had incomes between $9,000 and $13,000. Just under half of the wage-reliant had annual incomes below the federal poverty line, while between 70% and 88% of those who received welfare for most of the year were below the poverty line.

## Issues for Future Consideration

Welfare reform has been hailed by many as a success, due to increased work effort on the part of current and former recipients and decreased caseloads and expenditures. However, the recession of 2001–02 and other factors may present challenges to the state. We conclude with a discussion of these issues, and suggest some policy options for consideration if it is desired to address these concerns.

## Welfare Reform and Slower Economic Growth

PRWORA and many state-level reforms were implemented during a period of unprecedented economic growth, both nationally and in Michigan. Low unemployment and the availability of jobs have helped welfare recipients meet work requirements. It is less clear how a work-based welfare system will operate during a prolonged economic slowdown. When jobs are less plentiful, Work First may need to expand the education and training component of the program and increase enrollment in those activities, or the state may need to design other options for recipients to meet the work requirement.

Also, an economic slowdown may lead to increased spending for welfare services, as caseloads grow. The experience during the slowdown in 2001 indicates that some recipients returned to the rolls and others perhaps entered welfare for the first time, since, as noted earlier, FIP caseloads

**TABLE 17.4**

**Prevalence of Selected Employment Barriers, Women's Employment Study, Fall 1999**

| Barrier | Wage Reliant | Welfare Reliant |
| --- | --- | --- |
| No HS diploma/GED | 20% | 48% |
| Reads below fifth-grade level | 16% | 24% |
| Low work experience | 10% | 25% |
| Major depressive disorder | 16% | 28% |
| Post-traumatic stress disorder | 10% | 23% |
| Generalized anxiety disorder | 7% | 14% |
| Social phobia | 5% | 18% |
| Alcohol dependence | 1% | 4% |
| Drug dependence | 1% | 8% |
| Physical health problem | 13% | 44% |
| Experienced domestic violence | 5% | 23% |
| Transportation problem | 19% | 57% |
| Child-care problem | 8% | 18% |

SOURCE: University of Michigan, Program on Poverty and Social Welfare Policy (2001).

increased throughout 2001 and early 2002. The state's current TANF surplus could disappear if caseload growth continues.

## Caseload Composition

Another factor that could affect the state's budget is the needs of current FIP recipients. With welfare caseloads declining so sharply, many speculate that those left on the rolls are increasingly "hard-to-serve," with many impediments to employment. The Women's Employment Study collected data on barriers to employment in the domains of: (a) education and work experience; (b) psychiatric disorders or substance dependence; (c) physical health problems; and (d) other barriers such as domestic violence, transportation problems, and child-care problems.

Table 17.4 compares the prevalence of some of these barriers between WES respondents who worked and did not receive welfare in the fall of 1999 survey month (wage reliant) with those who were not working and were receiving FIP (welfare reliant). Previous research has shown that these barriers negatively affect the likelihood of working (see Danziger et al. 2000). A greater proportion of welfare-reliant women had each of the barriers, and with the exception of work norms and low literacy, the differences are statistically significant.

Not only are welfare-reliant women more likely to have these barriers than wage-reliant women, the prevalence of many of these barriers among the welfare reliant are quite high. For example, between 18% and 28% meet the diagnostic screening criteria for at least one psychiatric condition, whereas national studies of women find rates of 4% to 13%. More than half of the welfare reliant have a transportation problem (compared to 8% nationally), and nearly half lack a high school diploma or equivalency certificate (national average is 13%) (Danziger et al. 2000; University of Michigan 2001).

### Possible Policy Options and Service Delivery Strategies

As welfare reform continues to evolve, Michigan might consider adopting different policies and services to deal with recipients who lose jobs, especially when unemployment increases, and with those for whom Work First has not proven an effective employment strategy, especially those with multiple barriers to work. Policies and services we will discuss in this section are: assessment and referral, community service jobs, and supported work.

*Assessment and Referral.* The kinds of personal problems documented for Michigan TANF recipients in table 17.4, particularly mental health, domestic violence, and other barriers, may not be easily observed by welfare office staff. Recipients themselves may not be aware they have a mental health problem, or they may be reluctant to talk about it with a welfare caseworker. In Michigan, as in many other states, self-disclosure is the primary means by which a caseworker finds out about a recipient's potential problems (Danziger and Seefeldt 2000; Thompson and Mikelson 2001; U.S. General Accounting Office 2001).

A few states have developed programs that use trained staff or standardized instruments to identify a wide range of problems and provide mental health, substance abuse, and other counseling/ treatment services. For example, TANF workers in Utah screen clients for a number of barriers using a standardized tool. If the results from that screening indicate a possible mental health or substance-abuse problem, the client is seen by a trained social worker, who administers further diagnostic assessment tests and makes appropriate referrals for services (Thompson and Mikelson 2001).

*Community Service Jobs.* In Community Service Jobs (CSJ), sometimes called Public Service Employment), clients work in public-sector jobs or in nonprofits in exchange for their welfare checks. A frequently mentioned benefit of CSJ is that recipients have an employment opportunity, while providing often-needed services for the community (Savner and Greenberg 1997). For example, CSJ participants might do landscaping in public parks or serve as teacher's aides in schools. Washington and Wisconsin are two states in which CSJ is a major activity for TANF recipients. Participation in CSJ can serve a dual purpose. First, clients who are unable to find regular employment because they lack work experience can gain skills and experience. Second, CSJs may be an option for clients who have lost jobs and cannot find employment due to slack labor markets.

*Supported Work.* Supported work programs have received attention as a policy option for "hard-to-employ" TANF recipients, because of their success in working with other difficult-to-employ populations, particularly the physically and developmentally disabled, as well as those with severe mental illness. In supported work programs, participants work in a job, but with more supervision and structure than in the private sector, and they also receive services to address problems that might interfere with employment. For example, participants might work in a production facility run by a nonprofit, such as a Goodwill or other vocational rehabilitation agency. While working, they are overseen by a job coach, who monitors the employees' work skills, as well as their "soft skills," such as their ability to get along with co-workers and supervisors. Case managers also provide assistance with personal and family challenges, making referrals to services as necessary (Pavetti and Strong 2001). After working successfully in this environment, many clients can move into private-sector employment. Currently, a number of supported-work programs serving TANF recipients operate throughout the country, including several in Michigan.

### Trends in Poverty

Welfare has always been the United States' most controversial anti-poverty program. Yet, cash assistance plays a relatively small role in our income-support system as a whole. For example, the typical social security recipient receives several times as much per month as the typical welfare recipient. Nonetheless, a discussion of welfare reform would not be complete without a discussion of recent trends in poverty.

Figure 17.2 shows the official poverty rate for all families in the United States and in Michigan for each year between 1980 and 1999; it also shows the Michigan unemployment rate. In 1999, the official poverty line was $16,895 for a family of four with two related children, and about half that for one person living on his or her own. The census reports pre-tax money income and thus does not include noncash income, such as Food Stamps, or tax credits, such as the Earned Income Tax Credit, and does not exclude taxes paid. The poverty line varies with family size and has been increased since the mid-1960s only to correct for inflation. Many researchers prefer an alternative measure of poverty—valuing noncash income and tax credits would lower the poverty rate, while choosing an updated poverty line would raise the poverty rate. However, Burtless and Smeeding (2002) show that in recent years trends in the official and alternative measures that take the criticisms of the official poverty rate into account are similar.

The family poverty rate (which excludes households with only one person) increased in the early

**FIGURE 17.2**

**Trends in U.S. and Michigan Poverty Rates, All Families, 1980–1999**

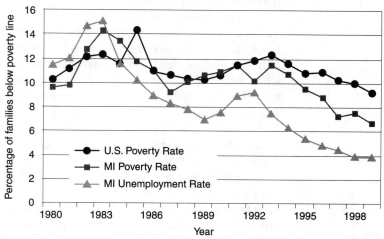

SOURCE: Professor James Ziliak, Department of Economics, University of Kentucky, based on calculations from the Census Bureau's annual March Current Population Survey.

1980s to about 14% in both the United States (1985) and in Michigan (1983) as a result of the severe recession during that period. Poverty then declined to about 10.5% in both in the late 1980s, rose some during the recession of the early 1990s, and then fell throughout the rest of the 1990s to about 9% of families in the United States and 7% in Michigan in 1999. Results are similar for the

**FIGURE 17.3**

**Trends in Michigan Poverty Rates by Race and Family Type, 1980–1999**

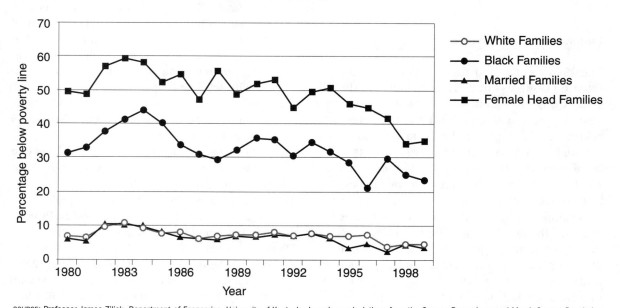

SOURCE: Professor James Ziliak, Department of Economics, University of Kentucky, based on calculations from the Census Bureau's annual March Current Population Survey.

trend in poverty for all persons. In 1999, 11.8% of all persons in the United States were poor, compared to 10.8% in Michigan.

The unemployment rate and the poverty rate in Michigan are highly correlated. For example, when unemployment in Michigan rose from 11.5 to 15.1% between 1980 and 1983, the poverty rate followed; when the state unemployment rate rose from 7 to 9.2% between 1989 and 1992, the state poverty rate rose again. This is not surprising, as earned income is the largest component of family income, and hence, changes in earnings brought about by the business cycle have a strong effect on poverty.

Data on poverty in cities is available only from the Decennial Censuses. The city of Detroit has a very high poverty rate, 26.1% in 1999, making it one of five cities among the largest fifty to have a poverty rate above 25%. However, Detroit's poverty rate fell over the 1990s from 32.4% in 1989, when it had the highest rate of any of the fifty largest cities (Metzger and Booza 2002).

Figure 17.3 shows trends in family poverty in Michigan by race—families whose head is white or black—and by family structure—families headed by married couple or an unmarried woman. Poverty rates are much higher for families headed by an African American and by an unmarried woman, but trends are similar. Between 1989 and 1999, the family poverty rate fell from 7.4 to 4.3% for white families and from 32.3 to 23.5% for black families. Poverty rates for families headed by women fell from about 51% in 1994 to 35% in 1999.

## Summary

The 1996 welfare reform act was to be reauthorized by Congress in 2002, although in late fall 2002, Congress extended the deadline into the next Congressional term. Most analysts agree that reform, in Michigan and the nation, has contributed to large reductions in welfare caseloads, large increases in work by single mothers, and small reductions in poverty. However, poverty rates remain high for many single mothers who have made the transition from welfare to work and for those who have had a difficult time finding or keeping a job, even when the economy was booming. A recent public opinion poll shows that while an overwhelming majority of Americans (85%) believe moving welfare recipients into work is a very important goal of welfare reform, just slightly fewer (74%) also think welfare

reform should result in fewer poor families (Lake, Snell, Perry, and Associates 2002). A challenge for the next decade is to raise both incomes and employment of Michigan families at the lower end of the economic ladder.

■

## REFERENCES

Blank, Rebecca. 1997. *It takes a nation.* New York: Russell Sage Foundation.

Blank, Rebecca, and Lucie Schmidt. 2001. Work, wages, and welfare. In *The new world of welfare.* Washington, D.C.: Brookings Institution Press.

Burtless, Gary, and Timothy Smeeding. 2002. The level, trend, and composition of poverty. In *Understanding poverty.* New York: Russell Sage Foundation.

California Department of Social Services. 1999. Food stamp household characteristics survey. *www.dss.cahwnet.gov/research/res/pdf/foodstamp99.pdf.* Accessed August 2002.

Center for Law and Social Policy. 2002a. Analysis of fiscal year 2000 TANF and MOE spending by states. Washington, D.C.: Center for Law and Social Policy.

———. 2002b. New data show most states had TANF caseload increases in last year. Washington, D.C.: Center for Law and Social Policy.

Council of Economic Advisers. 1999. The effects of welfare policy and the economic expansion on welfare caseloads: An update. Washington, D.C.: CEA.

Danziger, Sandra K., Mary Corcoran, Sheldon Danziger, Colleen Heflin, Ariel Kalil, Judith Levine, Daniel Rosen, Kristin S. Seefeldt, Kristine Siefert, and Richard Tolman. 2000. Barriers to the employment of welfare recipients. In *Prosperity for all?* New York: Russell Sage Foundation.

Danziger, Sandra K., and Kristin S. Seefeldt. 2000. Ending welfare through work first. *Families in Society* 81 (6): 593–604.

———. 2002. Barriers to employment and the "hard to serve": Implications for services, sanctions, and time limits. *Focus* 22 (1): 76–81.

Danziger, Sheldon. 2001. Welfare reform policy from Nixon to Clinton. In *Social science and policy making.* Ann Arbor: University of Michigan Press.

Danziger, Sheldon, Colleen M. Heflin, Mary E. Corcoran, Elizabeth Oltmans, and Hui-Chen Wang. 2002. Does it pay to move from welfare to work? *Journal of Policy Analysis and Management* 21(4): 671–92.

Food Research and Action Center. 2002. *State of the states: A profile of food and nutrition programs across the nation.* Washington, D.C.: FRAC.

Gallagher, Jerome. 1999. *A shrinking portion of the safety net: General Assistance from 1989 to 1998.* Washington, D.C.: Urban Institute.

Greenberg, Mark, and Elise Richer. 2002. Analysis of fiscal year 2000 TANF and MOE spending by states. Washington, D.C.: Center for Law and Social Policy. *www.clasp.org/Pubs/TANF/michigan.pdf.* Accessed August 2002.

Gueron, Judith M., and Edward Pauly. 1991. *From welfare to work.* New York: Russell Sage Foundation.

Henly, Julia R., and Sandra K. Danziger. 1996. Confronting welfare stereotypes: Characteristics of General Assistance recipients and post-Assistance employment. *Social Work Research* 20 (4): 217–27.

Holcomb, Pamela, LaDonna Pavetti, Caroline Ratcliffe, and Susan Riedinger. 1998. *Building an employment-focused welfare system: Work First and other work-oriented strategies in five states.* Washington, D.C.: Urban Institute.

Jacobs, Jonathan, Nuria Rodriguez-Planas, Loren Puffer, Emily Pas, and Laura Taylor-Kale. 2001. The consequences of welfare reform and economic change for the Food Stamp program: Illustrations from microsimulation, final report. Washington, D.C.: USDA.

Kaplan, Jan. 2002. TANF reauthorization and time limits. Welfare Information Network Reauthorization Notes, May 2002. *http://www.welfareinfo.org/timelimits_trn.htm.* Accessed August.

Kossoudji, Sherrie, Sandra K. Danziger, and Robert Lovell. 1993. Michigan's General Assistance population: An interim report of the General Assistance Termination Project. Ann Arbor: University of Michigan.

Lake, Snell, Perry, and Associates. 2002. Public views on welfare reform and children in the current economy. Prepared for the David and Lucile Packard Foundation, February 2002. *http://www.futureofchildren.org/usr_doc/lsp_welfare_survey.PDF.* Accessed September 2002.

Levitan, Sar A. 1985. *Programs in aid of the poor.* Baltimore, Md.: Johns Hopkins University Press.

Metzger, Kurt, and Jason C. Booza. 2002. Poverty in the United States, Michigan, and metropolitan Detroit: An analysis of Census 2000. Working paper, Center for Urban Studies. Detroit: Wayne State University.

Michigan Department of Career Development. 2002. Preliminary data from MWA extract, March 2002. Lansing, Mich.: MDCD.

Michigan Department of Social Services. 1995a. To strengthen Michigan families: Welfare reform data monitoring, August–September 1995. Lansing, Mich.: MDSS.

———. 1995b. Assistance payments data, October, 1995. Lansing, Mich: MDSS.

———. 1996. Assistance payments data, June 1996. Lansing, Mich.: MDSS.

Michigan Family Independence Agency. 1996. Assistance payments data, October, 1996. Lansing, Mich.: MFIA.

———. 1997a. Assistance payments data, December 1996. Lansing, Mich.: MFIA.

———. 1997b. Assistance payments data, October, 1997. Lansing, Mich.: MFIA.

———. 1998a. Project Zero data monitoring packet, December 1997. Lansing, Mich.: MFIA.

———. 1998b. Assistance payments data, October, 1998. Lansing, Mich.: MFIA.

———. 1999. Assistance payments data, October, 1999. Lansing, Mich.: MFIA.

———. 2000a. Assistance payments data, December 1999. Lansing, Mich.: MFIA.

———. 2000b. Assistance payments data, October, 2000. Lansing, Mich.: MFIA.

———. 2001a. 1999–2000 biennial report to the legislature. Lansing, Mich.: MFIA.

———. 2001b. Information packet, April 2001. Lansing, Mich.: MFIA.

———. 2001c. Assistance payments data, December, 2000. Lansing, Mich.: MFIA.

———. 2001d. Project Zero data monitoring packet, December 2000. Lansing, Mich.: MFIA.

———. 2001e. Assistance payments data, October, 2001. Lansing, Mich.: MFIA.

———. 2002a. Assistance payments data, January 2002. Lansing, Mich.: MFIA.

———. 2002b. Fact sheet, January 2002. Lansing, Mich.: MFIA.

———. 2002c. Project Zero data monitoring packet, December 2001. Lansing, Mich.: MFIA.

———. 2002d. Assistance payments data, February, 2002. Lansing, Mich.: MFIA.

———. 2002e. Assistance payments data, July, 2002. Lansing, Mich.: MFIA.

Michigan Jobs Commission. 1995. Work First monthly report. Lansing, Mich.: MJC. November.

———. 1997. Work First monthly report. Lansing, Mich.: MJC. November.

Nichols, Marion, and Kathryn Porter. 1995. General assistance programs: Gaps in the safety net. Washington, D.C.: Center on Budget and Policy Priorities.

Nightingale, Demetra Smith, Terri Thompson, Nancy Pindus, Pamela Holcomb, Edgar Lee, Jesse Valente, and John Trutko. 2000. *Early implementation of the Welfare-to-Work grants program: Findings from exploratory site visits and review of program plans.*

Washington, D.C.: Urban Institute.

Pavetti, LaDonna, and Debra Strong. 2001. *Work-Based strategies for hard-to-employ TANF recipients: A preliminary assessment of program models and dimensions.* Washington, D.C.: Mathematica Policy Research.

Public Sector Consultants, Inc. 1998. *Michigan in brief: 1998–99.* 6th ed. Lansing, Mich.: Public Sector Consultants, Inc.

Savner, Steve, and Mark Greenberg. 1997. *Community service employment: A new opportunity under TANF.* Washington, D.C.: Center for Law and Social Policy.

Seefeldt, Kristin S., LaDonna Pavetti, Karen Macguire, and Gretchen Kirby. 1998. *Income support and social services for low-income people in Michigan.* Washington, D.C.: Urban Institute.

Seefeldt, Kristin S., Jodi Sandfort, and Sandra K. Danziger. 1997. Project Zero: The view from the sites. Ann Arbor: University of Michigan.

———. 1998. *Moving toward a vision of family independence: Local managers' views of Michigan's welfare reforms.* Ann Arbor: University of Michigan.

Seefeldt, Kristin S., Jacob Leos-Urbel, Patricia McMahon, and Kathleen Snyder. 2001. Changes to Michigan's welfare and work, child care, and child welfare systems since 1997. Washington, D.C.: The Urban Institute.

Seefeldt, Kristin S. 2002. *Welfare reform: CQ Vital Issues series.* Washington, D.C.: Congressional Quarterly Press.

Their promises: Excerpts from the candidate's basic stump speeches, a look at what they vow to do for the nation; Clinton. 1992. Decision '92: Special Voter's guide to the Presidential Election, *Los Angeles Times,* 18 October, 4.

Thompson, Terri S., Pamela A. Holcomb, Pamela Loprest, and Kathleen Brennan. 1998. *State welfare to work policies for people with disabilities: Changes since welfare reform.* Washington, D.C.: U.S. Department of Health and Human Services, Assistant Secretary for Planning and Evaluation.

Thompson, Terri, and Kelly Mikelson. 2001. *Screening and assessment in TANF/Welfare-to-Work: Ten important questions TANF agencies and their partners should consider.* Washington, D.C.: U.S. Department of Health and Human Services.

U.S. Department of Health and Human Services, Administration for Children and Families. n.d. *Aid to Families with Dependent Children, characteristics and financial circumstances of AFDC recipients FY 1995.* Washington, D.C.: U.S. Department of Health and Human Services.

———. 1998. *TANF annual report to Congress, 1998.* Washington, D.C.: U.S. Department of Health and Human Services.

———. 1999. *TANF annual report to Congress, 1999.* Washington, D.C.: U.S. Department of Health and Human Services.

———. 2000. *TANF annual report to Congress, 2000.* Washington, D.C.: U.S. Department of Health and Human Services.

———, Office of Administration, Financial Services. 2001a. Spending under welfare reform. *http://www.acf.dhhs.gov/programs/ofs/ data/index.html,* 2001. Accessed April 2002.

———, Office of Administration, Financial Services. 2001b. Aid to Families with Dependent Children caseload data, 1977–1997. *www.acf.dhhs.gov/programs/opre/afdc/afdc.htm.* Accessed March 2002.

———, Office of Administration, Child Care Bureau. 2002. Fiscal year 2000, Child Care Development Fund grant award summary. *www.afc.dhhs.gov/programs/ccb/research/00acf696/grant.htm.* Accessed August 2002.

U.S. General Accounting Office. 2001. *Welfare reform: More coordinated federal effort could help states and localities move TANF recipients with impairments toward employment.* Washington, D.C.: GPO.

U.S. House of Representatives, Committee on Ways and Means. 1993. *1993 overview of entitlement programs.* Washington, D.C.: GPO. .

———. 1994. *1994 overview of entitlement programs.* Washington, D.C.: GPO.

———. 1996. *1996 overview of entitlement programs.* Washington, D.C.: GPO.

———. 1998. *1998 overview of entitlement programs.* Washington, D.C.: GPO.

———. 2000. *2000 overview of entitlement programs.* Washington, D.C.: GPO.

University of Michigan, Program on Poverty and Social Welfare Policy. 2001. Unpublished Women's Employment Study data.

Walsh, Edward. 1991. Michigan's welfare cut, a "social experiment"; More "able-bodied" homeless are expected. *Washington Post,* 19 November, A1.

Weaver, R. Kent. 2000. *Ending welfare as we know it.* Washington, D.C.: Brookings Institution Press.

Weissert, Carol. 2000. Michigan's welfare reform: Generous but tough. In *Learning from leaders: Welfare reform politics and policy in five Midwestern states.* Albany, N.Y.: Rockefeller Institute Press.

Werner, Alan, and Robert Kornfeld. 1997. The evaluation of To Strengthen Michigan Families: Final impact report. Cambridge, Mass.: Abt Associates.

# 18

# The Less-Skilled Labor Market in Michigan

*Rebecca M. Blank*

## 1. Introduction

For the past two decades, there has been concern over trends in the labor market for less-skilled workers in the United States. Inflation-adjusted wages among less-skilled men fell steadily from 1979 through the mid-1990s; wages among less-skilled women fell as well, although by a smaller amount. Wages among these workers rose during the hot economy of the late 1990s, but these increases still left lower-skilled workers earning less than they had two decades earlier.

With these national concerns as a backdrop, this chapter focuses on the less-skilled labor market in the state of Michigan over the past two decades. (Chapter 4 in this volume focuses on broader labor market issues.) In the next section I look at wage trends among various groups of workers, with particular attention to the characteristics of current low-wage workers in Michigan. In the third section I discuss unemployment rates and the correlation between low wages and high unemployment. In the fourth section I look at part-time work, and in the fifth section I discuss labor market participation and changes in who is working or looking for work. The final section focuses on policies that can influence these factors, particularly those policies that supplement or raise wages.

Unless otherwise noted, the data throughout the chapter are based on tabulations from the Outgoing Rotation Group (ORG) data of the Current Population Survey (CPS).[1] The CPS collects employment information on a monthly basis from a random sample of households throughout the United States, and is the country's main source of monthly unemployment numbers. Each month, individuals in the ORG sample are asked about wages, as well as employment and hours of work.

I typically compare Michigan data with U.S. data and with data from Ohio and Illinois, two nearby Midwestern states with similar histories as major manufacturing states. To get reliable annual state-specific data, I have combined the twelve monthly ORG samples in each state for each year. Between 1979 and 2000, the resulting annual samples average 6,763 observations in the state of Michigan, 7,362 in Ohio, 7,331 in Illinois, and 174,493 in the United States in total. These samples are large enough to provide reliable annual information on subgroups by gender, race, and education level, although the subgroup data are clearly noisier and bounce around a bit more from year to year.[2]

The ORG data are available from 1979 onward. While I show annual time trends in many cases, at some points I present data for only the years 1979,

**FIGURE 18.1**

**Adjusted Median Weekly Wages**

### A. Adjusted Median Weekly Wages Among All Workers

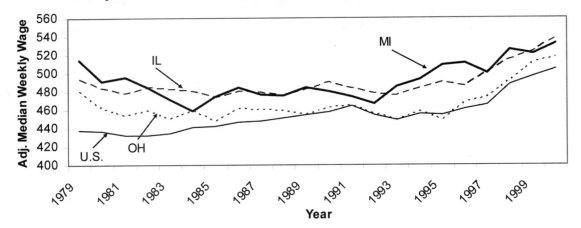

### B. Adjusted Median Weekly Wages Among Workers with Less Than a High School Degree

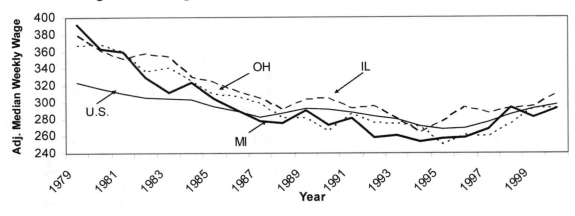

### C. Adjusted Median Weekly Wages Among Workers with Only a High School Degree

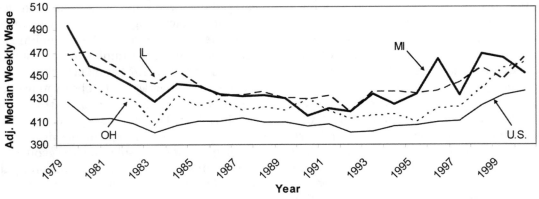

SOURCE: Author's tabulation of Current Population Survey, Outgoing Rotation Groups.
NOTE: All data reported in 2000 dollars.

1989, and 2000. Each of these represents the final year of an extended economic expansion, and thus provides comparable comparison data. On the other hand, these years do show the labor market at its best; other years (such as 1982 and 1992, for example) would show worse overall outcomes.

## 2. Who Are the Low-Wage Workers?

Michigan has historically been a high-wage state. Figure 18.1a shows how inflation-adjusted median wages among all workers in Michigan compare to median wages in the United States, Illinois, and Ohio between 1979 and 2000. I report adjusted median weekly wages because the weekly wage data are more reliable than the hourly wage data in the ORG. I adjust the data for those who report working less than full time by multiplying their weekly earnings up to a full-time equivalent.[3] Without this adjustment, some groups (such as women) would appear to have lower weekly earnings not because they are paid less for each hour of work but because they work fewer hours. (I discuss the prevalence of part-time work later in this chapter.) All wage data are reported in inflation-adjusted year 2000 dollars, using the deflator for personal consumption expenditures.[4]

Figure 18.1a verifies Michigan's status as a high-wage state, although the wage gap between adjusted median weekly wages in Michigan and those in the United States as a whole has shrunk over the past two decades. In 1979, median weekly wages in Michigan were $76 higher than in the United States. By 2000, the difference was only $28. Throughout this period, Michigan's median wages remained above median wages in Ohio and close to median wages in Illinois.

Figures 18.1b and 18.1c show adjusted median weekly wages among workers with less than a high school diploma and with only a high school diploma. Among the least skilled (figure 18.1b), the trends are quite different than the trends for the population as a whole. Michigan was a very high wage state for workers without a high school diploma in the late 1970s, with median weekly earnings $68 above the U.S. median in 1979. This advantage eroded entirely over the 1980s. By the late 1980s and throughout the 1990s, earnings among this group of workers in Michigan were usually at or below the U.S. median, and usually at or below the median among these workers in Ohio or Illinois. Among slightly more skilled workers (those with just a high school diploma), Michigan appears to have retained its wage advantage throughout the 1990s.

Table 18.1 provides more detail on adjusted median weekly wages by subgroups based on gen-

**TABLE 18.1**

**Adjusted Median Weekly Wage Levels in Michigan**

|  | 1979 | 1989 | 2000 | Percentage Change from 1979 to 2000 |
|---|---|---|---|---|
| U.S. (all earners) | $438 | $451 | $504 | 15.1 |
| Michigan (all earners) | $514 | $484 | $532 | 3.5 |
| Males | $643 | $623 | $650 | 1.1 |
| Females | $363 | $372 | $446 | 22.9 |
| Black, non-Hispanic | $506 | $456 | $464 | −8.3 |
| White and other, non-Hispanic | $515 | $491 | $557 | 8.2 |
| Hispanic | $459 | $478 | $395 | −13.9 |
| No high school diploma | $392 | $290 | $292 | −25.5 |
| High school diploma | $494 | $430 | $452 | −8.5 |
| Some college, no B.A. | $531 | $478 | $527 | −0.8 |
| B.A. or higher | $720 | $781 | $932 | 29.4 |

SOURCE: Author's tabulation of Current Population Survey data, Outgoing Rotation Groups.
NOTE: All data reported in 2000 dollars.

**TABLE 18.2**

## Determinants of Wages in Michigan versus the United States

Dependent Variable = log(hourly wages)

| | Michigan | | | United States | | |
|---|---|---|---|---|---|---|
| | 1979 | 1989 | 2000 | 1979 | 1989 | 2000 |
| Education[a] | | | | | | |
| Less than high school | −0.462** | −0.683** | −0.804** | −0.534** | −0.675** | −0.767** |
| | (0.018) | (0.018) | (0.025) | (0.003) | (0.004) | (0.005) |
| High school diploma | −0.316** | −0.511** | −0.571** | −0.343** | −0.488** | −0.536** |
| | (0.016) | (0.014) | (0.017) | (0.003) | (0.003) | (0.003) |
| Some college | −0.206** | −0.354** | −0.389** | −0.238** | −0.331** | −0.386** |
| | (0.018) | (0.015) | (0.018) | (0.003) | (0.003) | (0.004) |
| Experience[b] | 0.034** | 0.040** | 0.032** | 0.032** | 0.034** | 0.032** |
| | (0.001) | (0.001) | (0.002) | (0.000) | (0.000) | (0.000) |
| Experience squared | −0.001** | −0.001** | −0.001** | −0.001** | −0.001** | −0.001** |
| | (0.000) | (0.000) | (0.000) | (0.000) | (0.000) | (0.000) |
| Race (1 = black) | −0.006 | −0.024 | −0.107** | −0.087** | −0.113** | −0.100** |
| | (0.017) | (0.017) | (0.021) | (0.004) | (0.004) | (0.004) |
| Ethnicity (1 = Hispanic) | 0.012 | 0.037 | −0.091* | −0.093** | −0.119** | −0.121** |
| | (0.047) | (0.048) | (0.039) | (0.005) | (0.005) | (0.004) |
| Gender (1 = female) | −0.344** | −0.295** | −0.240** | −0.341** | −0.244** | −0.221** |
| | (0.011) | (0.011) | (0.014) | (0.002) | (0.002) | (0.003) |
| Hours (1 = part-time[c]) | −0.347** | −0.322** | −0.159** | −0.249** | −0.268** | −0.113** |
| | (0.014) | (0.014) | (0.016) | (0.003) | (0.003) | (0.003) |
| Constant | 2.691** | 2.656** | 2.842** | 2.651** | 2.646** | 2.751** |
| | (0.017) | (0.017) | (0.021) | (0.003) | (0.004) | (0.004) |
| Number of observations | 6,579 | 7,515 | 5,333 | 172,132 | 174,588 | 143,944 |

SOURCE: Author's tabulations of Current Population Survey data, Outgoing Rotation Groups.
NOTE: Standard errors in parentheses. All data reported in 2000 dollars.
(a) The omitted education category is those workers who hold a college diploma or higher.
(b) Experience is defined as (Age − Education − 5).
(c) Part-time workers are those who report working fewer than thirty-five hours per week.
* 5% level of significance; ** 1% level of significance

der, race, and education. Females made major gains over this period, with their median adjusted weekly wages rising from $363 in 1979 to $446 in 2000. The most skilled—those with a college degree or more—show even larger gains, from $720 to $932 during these years. The biggest losers are those without a high school diploma, whose median weekly wages fell by $100 over the period studied. Those with only a high school diploma lost about $42 in weekly wages over this time period, while wages for those with some college remained essentially the same. Hispanics also lost out, especially over the 1990s. This may, in part, be due to a decline in wages caused by increased immigration among less-skilled Hispanic workers over this period. Although my data do not allow me to separate immigrants from nonimmigrants, average education levels among Hispanics in Michigan fell from 1989 to 2000,

which is consistent with the in-migration of a large number of less-educated Hispanic adults.

Table 18.2 provides a more detailed analysis of wages, regressing the log of hourly wage levels against a standard set of variables, including dummy variables for education level, race, Hispanic ethnicity, and gender, and a variable for experience and experience squared (which allows experience to affect wages differentially over the lifecycle). Columns one to three show these regressions on Michigan data for the years 1979, 1989, and 2000, while columns four to six show these regressions on U.S. data for the same three years.

The regression coefficients reported in table 18.2 can be directly interpreted as the percentage change in hourly wages resulting from a one-unit change in a given variable, holding all other variables constant. Hence the coefficient on the dummy variable indicating "education less than a high school diploma" indicates that, all else equal, persons in this category (i.e., those with less than a high-school diploma, for whom the dummy variable equals one rather than zero) had wages 46% lower than the wages of college graduates (the omitted category in table 18.2) in 1979 in Michigan, and 80% lower in 2000. The 46% gap in Michigan in 1979 compares with a 53% gap in the United States as a whole in that year, and the 80% gap in Michigan in 2000 compares with a 77% gap in the United States as a whole.

Table 18.2 provides a way to compare how the determinants of wages in Michigan and the United States are changing over time. In most cases, the trends over time in Michigan are similar to those in the United States. The effects of additional experience on wages are about the same in the state and the nation and change little over time. Women earned about one-third less than equivalent men in 1979; by 2000 they earned about one-quarter less. The negative effect of part-time work on wage levels also declined over time. The wages received by those with lower educational levels shrank, relative to the wages earned by the college educated, holding constant other influences on wages. As we saw in table 18.1, this is both because wages among the more skilled are rising and because wages among the less skilled are falling. Both Michigan and the United States show similar trends.

The biggest Michigan/U.S. differences are with regard to race and ethnicity. In 1979 there were no significant wage differences between black and Hispanic workers in Michigan and white workers; in the United States both black and Hispanic workers received 9% lower wages on average in 1979. By 2000, there were few differences between the United States and Michigan; black and Hispanic workers received around 10% lower wages in both the state and the nation.

What happened in Michigan to significantly reduce wages for these two groups? Among Hispanics, large in-migration probably increased the share of Hispanics with lower levels of education (even beyond that controlled for in the regression) and English-language skills. Among blacks, the story is harder to understand. The growing negative effect on wages among black workers cannot be explained by declining unionization. I have data on the coverage of workers by collective bargaining agreements in the latter years of my data set. If I rerun the wage regression in 1989 or in 2000 and include this as an explanatory variable, I find that unions significantly boost wages, but including this variable has little effect on the black coefficient. Similarly, I cannot explain the effect by geographic location; controlling for location in the Detroit metro area has no significant effect on the regression. It is possible that the growing negative wage effect for black workers reflects a shift of black workers into lower-wage industries over time. It is also possible that this effect indicates a shift in the composition of the black workforce; for instance, if more productive black workers migrated out of the state

**TABLE 18.3**

**Population and Earner Shares in Michigan**

| | Share of Total Population[a] | | | Share of All Earners | | |
|---|---|---|---|---|---|---|
| | 1979 | 1989 | 2000 | 1979 | 1989 | 2000 |
| Male | 0.483 | 0.484 | 0.488 | 0.581 | 0.541 | 0.530 |
| Female | 0.517 | 0.516 | 0.512 | 0.419 | 0.459 | 0.470 |
| | | | | | | |
| Black, non-Hispanic | 0.118 | 0.135 | 0.129 | 0.108 | 0.106 | 0.121 |
| White and other, non-Hispanic | 0.869 | 0.852 | 0.845 | 0.879 | 0.881 | 0.850 |
| Hispanic | 0.013 | 0.013 | 0.027 | 0.013 | 0.013 | 0.029 |
| | | | | | | |
| No high school diploma | 0.371 | 0.257 | 0.188 | 0.247 | 0.143 | 0.115 |
| High school diploma | 0.345 | 0.366 | 0.329 | 0.395 | 0.384 | 0.320 |
| Some college, no B.A. | 0.177 | 0.224 | 0.280 | 0.218 | 0.271 | 0.319 |
| B.A. and above | 0.107 | 0.154 | 0.203 | 0.139 | 0.203 | 0.246 |

SOURCE: Author's tabulation of Current Population Survey, Outgoing Rotation Groups.
(a) Ages sixteen and over.

**FIGURE 18.2**

**Percentage of Workers Under the U.S. 20th Wage Percentile**

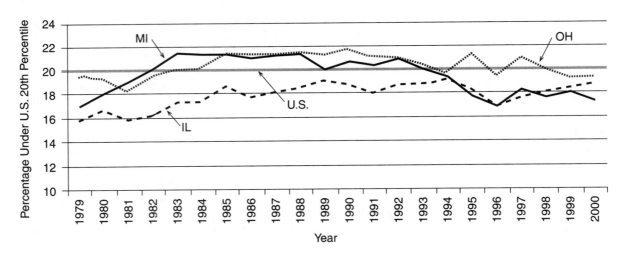

SOURCE: Author's tabulation of Current Population Survey data, Outgoing Rotation Groups.

over the 1980s one would see this effect. It is also possible that this effect indicates growing discrimination in the Michigan labor market. With the information available, it is not possible to separate these different hypotheses.

Overall wage levels are affected by the share of earners within each subgroup category, and this has been changing steadily over this time period. Table 18.3 shows the share of the total population (ages sixteen and over) in each subgroup, as well as the share of all earners in each subgroup. While the male/female population ratio does not change, women substantially increase as a proportion of earners, reflecting the ongoing rise in female labor force participation. The rise in the share of women workers pulls down aggregate wages, given women's lower earnings, but this is somewhat muted by the steady rise in women's earnings levels over this period.

There is a very large decline in the share of the population with only a high school diploma or less, from 72% of the Michigan population in 1979 to 52% in 2000. These less-educated residents are disproportionately older (retired) or not in the labor force. By 2000, those with a high school diploma or less made up only 44% of all earners, while 57% had at least some post–high school training. Hence, declining earnings among the less skilled are affecting a shrinking share of the workforce and had a smaller impact than they would have if the share of the workforce in the less-skilled categories had not fallen.

The preceding analysis has focused on overall wage levels, which may not tell us much about the distribution of very low wages among the population. To look at how many Michigan workers have very low wages, I have calculated the twentieth percentile of the U.S. wage distribution, that is, the wage level below which exactly 20% of all U.S. workers earn. The top row of table 18.4 shows how this twentieth percentile wage has changed within the entire United States, falling from $274 to $263 from 1979 to 1989, and rising from $263 to $299 from 1989 to 2000.

Figure 18.2 shows the percentage of Michigan workers falling below the U.S. twentieth wage percentile. I refer to these workers as "very-low-wage" workers. If Michigan has disproportionately more very-low-wage workers than the United States in total, it will have more than 20% of its earners below the U.S. twentieth percentile wage; if Michigan has disproportionately fewer very-low-wage workers, it will have less than 20% below this wage. Figure 18.2 indicates that the percentage of very-low-wage workers in Michigan grew rapidly between 1979 and 1983. Throughout the 1980s Michigan had disproportionately more very-low-wage workers than did the United States in aggregate. By the late 1990s, however, Michigan's workers had experienced strong wage growth and Michigan had a disproportionately smaller percentage of very-low-wage workers than in the United States, overall.[5] Illinois had a disproportionately smaller percentage of very-low-wage workers throughout these decades, while Ohio's percentage was similar to that of the entire United States.

The rows in part A of table 18.4 show the percentage of Michigan workers below the U.S. twentieth percentile wage by subgroup. The data in table 18.4 show that those subgroups with lower median wages also have disproportionately more very-low-wage workers, perhaps not surprisingly. Women are much more likely than men to have very low wages, although the differential shrinks over these two decades. Less than 20% of black and Hispanic earners had very low wages in 1979 in Michigan, but these numbers rose sharply to over 20% for both groups in 2000. Consistent with the decline in median wages among those without high school diplomas in Michigan, this group went from about one-third with very low wages in 1979 to over half with very low wages in 2000. This suggests that the incidence of very-low-wage work is borne disproportionately by women, by minorities, and by the less skilled in Michigan.

Part B of table 18.4 looks at these same data, but shows the share of all very-low-wage workers who fall within each subgroup in each year. In short, part B takes the data in part A and weights them by the share of earners in each group. For instance, even though only 9% of all men had very low wages in 1979, they comprised 30% of all those with very low wages, reflecting the larger share of men versus women who were working in 1979. Over these two decades, the share of very-low-wage workers who were female fell.

Both the population share (table 18.3) and the percentage of very-low-wage workers among blacks and Hispanics (table 18.4, part A) rose over the period studied, leading to substantial increases in their representation among all very-low-wage workers (table 18.4, part B). Interestingly, although the incidence of very-low-wage work among those without a high school diploma rose over the period, their declining representation among all earners meant that the percentage of all very-low-wage workers without a high school diploma fell from 46% to 35% from 1979 to 2000. Likewise, the share of very-low-wage workers with higher levels of education rose over the period, even though there was little change in the incidence of low-wage work among these subgroups.

My conclusion from the preceding wage data is that Michigan has lost ground relative to two decades ago, when it was disproportionately a much higher wage state. By 2000, however,

**TABLE 18.4**

### Workers in Michigan Whose Wages Fall Under the U.S. Twentieth Percentile Weekly Wage Level (Very-Low-Wage Workers)

| | 1979 | 1989 | 2000 |
|---|---|---|---|
| **Twentieth percentile of U.S. wage** | $273.57 | $262.96 | $299.10 |
| **Part A: Percentage in Michigan below this level by sub-group** | | | |
| All persons | 17.0 | 20.1 | 17.3 |
| Male | 8.8 | 12.3 | 11.8 |
| Female | 28.4 | 29.3 | 23.5 |
| Black, non-Hispanic | 16.9 | 22.1 | 21.7 |
| White and other, non-Hispanic | 17.4 | 19.8 | 16.4 |
| Hispanic | 13.9 | 28.8 | 25.1 |
| No high school diploma | 32.0 | 45.5 | 52.0 |
| High school diploma | 13.9 | 19.6 | 17.9 |
| Some college, no B.A. | 13.4 | 18.9 | 14.6 |
| B.A. and above | 4.8 | 4.5 | 4.5 |
| **Part B: Share in each sub-group among all very-low-wage workers in Michigan[a]** | | | |
| Male | 0.297 | 0.327 | 0.365 |
| Female | 0.703 | 0.673 | 0.635 |
| Black, non-Hispanic | 0.107 | 0.115 | 0.152 |
| White and other, non-Hispanic | 0.883 | 0.866 | 0.806 |
| Hispanic | 0.010 | 0.018 | 0.041 |
| No high school diploma | 0.464 | 0.324 | 0.352 |
| High school diploma | 0.324 | 0.375 | 0.322 |
| Some college, no B.A. | 0.172 | 0.255 | 0.262 |
| B.A. and above | 0.039 | 0.045 | 0.064 |

SOURCE: Author's tabulation of Current Population Survey, Outgoing Rotation Groups.
NOTE: Adjusted weekly wages, ages sixteen and over, all data reported in 2000 dollars.
(a) For example, of the 17% of all Michigan workers whose average weekly wage was below the twentieth percentile of U.S. weekly wages in 1979, 29.7% were male and 70.3% were female.

Michigan still had a relatively favorable wage outlook. Its median wage levels remained above the national average and at about the same level as neighboring states. Its share of very-low-wage workers was less than that of the United States as a whole (and also below the share in Ohio and about on par with the share in Illinois).

These statements about relative position need to be tempered by consideration of the large absolute wage losses among specific groups. Less-skilled workers in Michigan, as in the United States as a whole, faced much lower inflation-adjusted wages by 2000 than in 1979. The size of this group shrank over the decades studied, but it

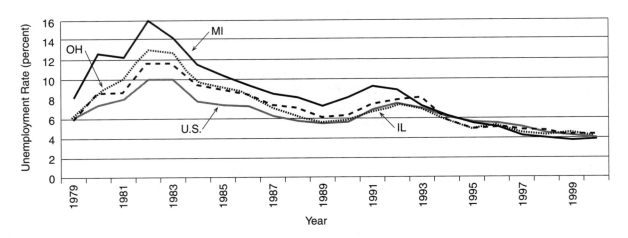

**FIGURE 18.3**

**Unemployment Rates among All Workers**

SOURCE: Author's tabulation of Current Population Survey data, Outgoing Rotation Groups.

still constituted a substantial minority among all earners in 2000. Both blacks and Hispanics lost wages over these two decades, and their population shares grew at the same time. One group that fared better was female workers, who remain a lower-wage group but markedly improved their relative position over the period studied.

Reasons for the wage losses of the 1980s and early 1990s are still being debated (see Ellwood et al. 2000). These economic changes are clearly related to changes in international competition and to changes in technology, with so-called skill enhancing technologies disadvantaging the less skilled. They are also related to the institutional changes that were driven by changes in both technology and competition. For instance, the ongoing decline in unionization clearly lowered wages among the less skilled. Michigan's changes reflect the same factors that affected the United States as a whole over the period studied, although these factors interacted with the Michigan economy. The relative changes in Michigan versus those in the United States reflect Michigan's more severe recession in the early 1980s and its faster-growing economy in the late 1990s.

The decline in unionization is particularly key for Michigan, which has a higher-than-average share of unionized workers. The percentage of workers in Michigan covered by collective bargaining agreements fell from 32% in 1983 (the earliest date for which I have data on this variable) to 22% in 2000. In the United States, these percentages declined from 23% in 1983 to 15% in 2000.

The decline in union coverage was greater for males than for females, and greater for blacks than for whites. Those without a high school diploma in Michigan went from 34% coverage in 1979 to 11% coverage in 2000, a very large decline.

One of the key questions for low-wage workers in Michigan and throughout the United States is whether the 2000s will continue the trend of the last half of the 1990s, when less-skilled and low-wage workers fared better, or whether we will return to the trend of the 1980s, when these workers steadily lost ground in the labor market.

### 3. Unemployment Rates

Low wages are not the only signal of labor market problems. Some workers are unemployed—that is, actively looking for work but not finding it. (Note that those who do not actively seek work are not considered unemployed but out of the labor market entirely. I discuss this group further in the fifth section.) Unemployed workers may be worse off than those with low wages, since they have no earnings at all.

Figure 18.3 graphs unemployment rates among all workers in Michigan, Ohio, Illinois, and the United States between 1979 and 2000.[6] In all states, unemployment peaked in the economic downturn of 1982–83. Michigan was particularly hard hit in the early 1980s and experienced unemployment rates well above the U.S. average and above those of neighboring states. Unemploy-

**FIGURE 18.4**

Michigan Unemployment Rates among All Workers by Education Level

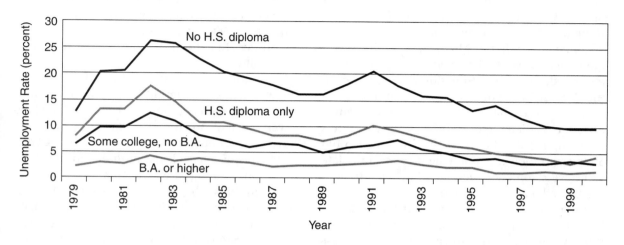

SOURCE: Author's tabulation of Current Population Survey data, Outgoing Rotation Groups.

ment fell everywhere through the last part of the 1980s, rose slightly in the more mild recession of 1990–91, and then fell throughout the 1990s. Michigan's unemployment rate fell in the 1991–93 period, while the U.S. unemployment rate actually rose slightly, and from 1993 through 2000, Michigan had essentially the same unemployment rates as the United States, Illinois, and Ohio. In short, based on unemployment rates alone, the Michigan labor market was doing much better in both relative and absolute terms in the 1990s than in the 1980s.

Figure 18.4 shows how unemployment in Michigan varied by level of education. Those with college degrees showed very few problems with unemployment over this time period. Even in the depths of the 1982–83 recession, unemployment rates for this group remained below 5%. In 2000 they had an unemployment rate of 1.4%. In Michigan, as in the United States as a whole, unemployment is concentrated among those with lower skill levels. In 1982, unemployment rates among those without a high school diploma surpassed 25% in Michigan, a shockingly high number. U.S. unemployment among this group was at 17% in 1982. In Michigan and in the United States, the unemployment rates among all less-educated groups fell throughout the 1990s. By 1999, those in Michigan with only a high school diploma actually reached parity in unemployment rates with those who had some post–high school training. While unemployment among those without a high school diploma was much lower in 2000 than at any point in the

preceding two decades, it still remained around 10%, even in the very job-rich and fast-growing Michigan economy of the late 1990s.

Unemployment rates among men and women were quite similar throughout these two decades in Michigan (as they were in the United States). Unemployment rates among Hispanics were more than five percentage points above those of whites throughout the 1980s, but fell to only two to three percentage points higher than those of whites in the 1990s. Black unemployment rates were substantially above Hispanic rates in the 1980s, but converged to the same level as those of Hispanics by the late 1990s.

If the wage data show that workers in Michigan were generally doing slightly better than in the United States as a whole, this conclusion is not offset by looking at unemployment data. In the late 1970s, Michigan was a high-wage state, but it experienced very high unemployment rates in the recession of the early 1980s, relative to the rest of the country. By the late 1990s, Michigan was still a high-wage state (although closer to the U.S. average than before), but its unemployment rates were at par with those of workers throughout the United States.

Finally, the correlation between low wages and high unemployment rates is worth a comment. When viewed by skill level, it is clear that the two are highly correlated in Michigan (as in the United States). Less-skilled workers have much greater difficulty finding jobs and are likely to find only very-low-wage jobs when they do find employment. A similar pattern occurs for black and Hispanic workers as well, as they suffer much lower wages and substantially higher unemployment. While differences in black/white and Hispanic/white unemployment rates have declined somewhat in Michigan over the 1990s, differences in wages between these groups have increased. Compared to national data, however, the Michigan labor market environment for blacks and Hispanics looks more favorable. Absolute median wage levels for these two groups were higher in Michigan than in the United States, and their unemployment rates in the late 1990s were somewhat lower in Michigan than in the United States as a whole.

The wage/unemployment rate correlation breaks down when we compare women and men. While women continue to earn substantially less than men, they experience no higher unemployment rates. Since less-skilled women remain highly gender-segregated on their jobs, this suggests that women work in occupations that pay consistently lower wages but do not experience consistently lower levels of demand or greater cyclical variability.

## 4. Part-Time versus Full-Time Work

Some workers suffer because they cannot find any work and remain unemployed. Others may suffer because they cannot find as much work as they would like, and are forced to work part time rather than full time. The majority of part-time workers, however, indicate that they are "voluntary" part-timers—that is, they are working part time for noneconomic reasons (typically this involves family-related reasons).

Women are far more likely to work part–time, and when they do, are more likely to be voluntary part-timers.[7] In 2000 in the United States, 31% of women reported working part–time, and the majority of these—91%—indicated they were voluntary part-timers. Fewer men work part–time, and of those who do, a somewhat higher share indicate they are seeking but cannot find full-time work (i.e., they are involuntary part-timers). Among men in the United States in 2000 only 16% reported part-time work, with 86% of these indicating they were voluntary part-timers. (Because of the strong economy of 2000, the overall share of part-time workers is lower in this year, and the percentage of involuntary part-timers is particularly low.)

The level of and trend in part-time work in Michigan mirrors that of the United States. In 2000, 81% of male workers were full time in both the state and the nation. Sixty percent of female workers in Michigan worked full time in 2000, slightly less than the 66% reporting full-time work nationally.

I do not show the trends in part-time work, largely because substantial data revisions create a break in the data between 1993 and 1994, making it very difficult to compare 1989 with 2000, as I have done for other labor market indicators. Part-time work is cyclical, rising in economic slowdowns and falling in expansions. Until the data break in 1994, the average long-term share of women working part time appears to have been largely constant for the past three decades. The share of men working part time appears to have risen a few percentage points in the 1980s.[8] The strong expansion of the late 1990s reduced part-time work among both men and women.

Part-time work is particularly prevalent among the less skilled. The share of those with a high school education who work part time is similar to the share of those with a college education who work part time. Yet those with less than a high school education are much more likely to work part time. In Michigan in 2000, 53% of those without a high school diploma worked part time, compared to 26% of those with only a high school diploma. This differential almost surely reflects both the nature of the jobs available to the least skilled and the family circumstances of many less-skilled individuals. For instance, single mothers with young children may find it very difficult to work full time.

## 5. Labor Force Participation

Looking only at wages and unemployment restricts us to those who are actively at work or seeking work—that is, the active labor force. If there had been no change in the propensity to work, we could stop here and ignore labor force participation rates. Indeed, among white men, there has been little change in labor force participation behavior over time. Yet for other groups, particularly women, there have been significant changes over time in who chooses to work.

Figure 18.5a shows changes in total labor force participation rates in Michigan, Illinois, Ohio, and the United States. This is the share of the population over age sixteen that is actively at work or

FIGURE 18.5

**Labor Force Participation Rates**

### A. Total Labor Force Participation Rates

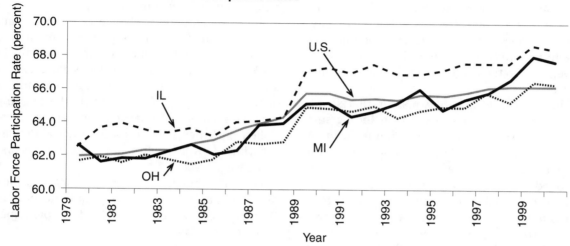

### B. Male and Female Labor Force Participation Rates[a]

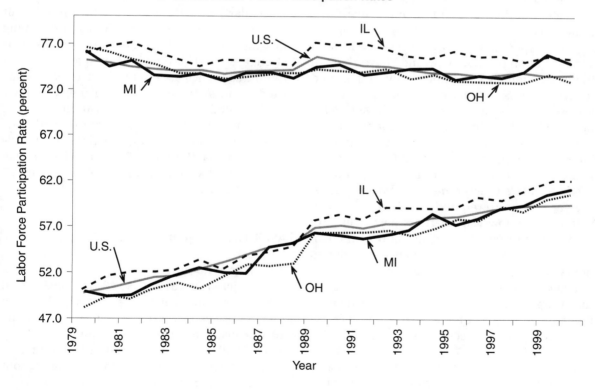

SOURCE: Author's tabulation of Current Population Survey data, Outgoing Rotation Groups.
(a) Male rates are the upper four lines; female rates are the lower four lines.

seeking work. There has been a steady increase in this share in the United States, from 62% in 1979 to 66% in 2000. Michigan shows a similar trend, with rates rising from 63% to 68% over these years.

Figure 18.5b indicates that virtually all of this increase is driven by increases in female labor force participation. Women in Michigan have increased their labor force participation rate from 50% to 61% between 1979 and 2000, similar to movements in the United States and in neighboring states.

There are multiple reasons for this steady increase in female labor supply, including such factors as rising education among women, increases in occupational choice with the enforcement of equal employment opportunity laws, reduced fertility and later age of marriage, and greater social acceptance of women's careers and employment. In the last decade, strong welfare-to-work programs have also pushed more low-skilled single mothers into the labor market. Of course, all of these factors are interactive and simultaneously reinforcing; it is therefore difficult to separate out their relative contributions.

It is useful to contrast these labor market changes with the wage and unemployment rate trends discussed previously. Many economists might have predicted that a large increase in labor supply among women would have led to increased female unemployment rates and reduced wages. As we have seen, however, female wages—in Michigan as elsewhere—have steadily improved. At least in part, this is due to the fact that women's experience and education were increasing, at precisely the time that the labor-market returns to skill were increasing rapidly. While women's wages remain well below men's, the gap has narrowed and the share of women who are very-low-wage earners has shrunk. In Michigan, the female-to-male ratio in median weekly wages, adjusted for differences in reported hours of work, has risen from 0.56 in 1979 to 0.69 in 2000. At the national level, evidence suggests that a large share (although not all) of the remaining gap can be accounted for by differences in work experience between women and men (Blau and Kahn 1997).

In contrast to women, men's labor force participation rates have been relatively steady over this time period. For Michigan the rates were 76% in 1979 and 75% in 2000. The U.S. aggregate data show similar constancy over the two decades studied.

Within Michigan, as within the United States, labor market participation among blacks and Hispanics has risen on average over these decades. Although I cannot reliably calculate Michigan data on racial groups by gender, within the United States as a whole the increase in black and Hispanic labor force participation is driven by increases in female labor force participation. In fact, national labor force participation among black men has fallen, largely due to declines in workforce participation by the less skilled (Holzer and Offner 2002). One of the labor market puzzles of the second half of the 1990s is the ongoing decline in labor force participation among less-skilled black men, despite a very strong labor market with relatively low unemployment levels and rising wage levels.

Overall, labor force trends in Michigan look quite similar to those throughout the nation. Ongoing increases in female labor force participation are the primary story.

## 6. Policies to Improve the Incentive to Work among Low-Wage Workers

Particularly over the past decade, a number of policies to increase the incentive to work among low-wage workers have been implemented or strengthened. These include increases in minimum wages, increases in the Earned Income Tax Credit, and increases in the availability of other work-related benefits. They also include the strong push to implement welfare-to-work programs among low-skilled (primarily female) welfare recipients. (I do not discuss this last change here, since it is addressed in detail in chapter 17 of this volume.)

### A. Minimum Wage Changes in Michigan

The federal minimum wage fell from $6.25 (in 2000 dollars) in 1979 to $4.40 by 1989, due to inflation erosion of an unchanged wage level. Yet four increases in the minimum wage over the 1990s caused it to rise again, ending at $5.15 by 2000. (While Michigan has a statutory minimum wage, it is below the federal minimum throughout this time period and hence was not binding.)

As the minimum wage fell and then rose, one would expect the share of workers reporting wages at or below the minimum wage would also fall and then rise.[9] Figure 18.6 shows that this is exactly what happened in Michigan. The upper

**FIGURE 18.6**

**Percentage in Michigan At or Below the Federal Minimum Wage**

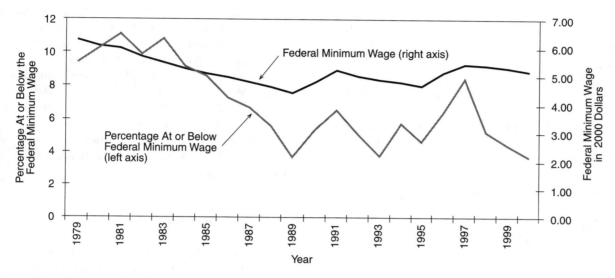

SOURCE: Author's tabulation of Current Population Survey data, Outgoing Rotation Groups.

line (graphed against the scale on the right-hand side) shows the real minimum wage. The lower line (graphed against the scale on the left) shows the percentage of workers in Michigan at or below the minimum. The percentage of workers reporting wages at or below the minimum fell from over 10% in 1980 to below 4% in 1989, and was at this same low level in 2000. Among workers with less than a high school diploma, the percentage reporting wages at or below the minimum fell from 25% in 1980 to 12% in 1989 and in 2000.

Of course, higher minimum wages can lead to higher unemployment. Most research based on the increases of the 1990s indicate that these minimum wage increases had little disemployment effect for most workers. For instance, Bernstein and Schmitt (1998) indicate no disemployment effect from the minimum wage increases in the mid-1990s. Neumark (2001) indicates only a relatively small effect on youth unemployment, with little effect on other workers. This perhaps reflects the relatively low share of workers affected by the minimum wage over the 1990s, as well as the strong increases in labor market demand fueled by an expanding economy during that decade.

**B. Changes in the Earned Income Tax Credit**

Increases in the Earned Income Tax Credit (EITC) also contributed to higher earnings among very low skilled workers. The EITC is a refundable tax credit paid to low-wage workers in low-income families. It is operated by the federal tax system; refundability means that low-income earners who do not owe any taxes can still receive a refund check from the federal government. For those who do owe taxes, the EITC will offset all or part of their tax liabilities.

The EITC is primarily available to families with children, and since 1991 has been scaled by number of children. The maximum EITC paid to parents with two children or more rose from $1,195 in 1989 to $3,888 in 2000 (in constant 2000 dollars); for parents with one child the maximum payment rose from $1,195 to $2,353. The maximum amount is available for low-income parents of two children or more earning between $12,690 and $31,152, and for parents with one child earning between $12,690 and $27,413.

The combined effects of the minimum wage increases and the EITC increases are shown in table 18.5. For a family with two children and one adult working full-time at the minimum wage, earnings (including the EITC) rose substantially from 1989 to 2000. Both the increased minimum wage and the expanded EITC were important in this change. By 2000 families with full-time working adults were no longer below the poverty line.

Table 18.6 shows the impact of these changes on the number of federal tax filers from Michigan who received the EITC. The number rose from

## TABLE 18.5

### Effects of Changing Policy on Earnings of Single Mothers

|                                                                          | 1989    | 2000     |
|--------------------------------------------------------------------------|---------|----------|
| 1. Minimum wage                                                          | $4.40   | $5.15    |
| 2. Maximum EITC subsidy                                                  |         |          |
|     Single mother (1 child)                          | $1,195  | $2,353   |
|     Single mother (2 children)                       | $1,195  | $3,888   |
| 3. Earnings and EITC (single mother working full-time at minimum wage)   |         |          |
|     Single mother (1 child)                          | $9,995  | $12,653  |
|     Single mother (2 children)                       | $9,995  | $14,188  |
| 4. Ratio of earnings (including EITC) to U.S. poverty line               |         |          |
|     Single mother (1 child)                          | 0.89    | 1.07     |
|     Single mother (2 children)                       | 0.76    | 1.02     |

SOURCE: http://www.cbpp.org/219steic.htm and http://www.census.gov.
NOTE: All data reported in 2000 dollars.

330,746 in 1990 to 547,783 in 1999. The subsidy to these families rose from $243 million ($734 per household) in 1990 to $897 million ($1,637 per household) in 1999. In 1999, just under 3% of all EITC dollars went to Michigan.

These policy changes reinforced the strong labor market of the late 1990s. Not only were jobs more available (unemployment was lower), with rising wages among lower-skilled workers, but these work incentives were strengthened further

## TABLE 18.6

### Utilization of the Earned Income Tax Credit among Federal Income Tax Filers in Michigan

|      | Total Number of Returns Receiving the EITC | Total Dollars in EITC Credit Received in Michigan[a] | Dollars/Filer in Michigan[a] |
|------|--------------------------------------------|-----------------------------------------------------|------------------------------|
| 1990 | 330,746                                    | $242,840,208                                        | $734                         |
| 1991 | 362,591                                    | $348,698,678                                        | $962                         |
| 1992 | 368,166                                    | $388,397,530                                        | $1,055                       |
| 1993 | 395,860                                    | $329,214,224                                        | $832                         |
| 1994 | 549,440                                    | $635,150,753                                        | $1,156                       |
| 1995 | 563,423                                    | $781,487,441                                        | $1,387                       |
| 1996 | 564,631                                    | $854,018,711                                        | $1,513                       |
| 1997 | 573,904                                    | $886,592,890                                        | $1,545                       |
| 1998 | 562,121                                    | $905,931,523                                        | $1,612                       |
| 1999 | 547,783                                    | $896,917,034                                        | $1,637                       |

SOURCE: IRS Statistics of Income Bulletin and http://www.irs.gov/prod/tax_stats/soi/ind_st.html.
(a) Columns 2 and 3 include both the refundable and nonrefundable portion of the Earned Income Tax Credit, and are reported in constant 2000 dollars.

by the minimum wage and EITC expansions. At the national level, the EITC expansion appears to be one cause of the increases in labor supply among single mothers (Meyer and Rosenbaum 2001). By 2000 the returns to work—especially among the lowest-paid workers—were much higher than they had been a decade earlier.

Fourteen states and the District of Columbia have chosen to implement their own state-based EITCs, typically by supplementing the federal EITC in their state income tax system. This would further raise the returns to work among very-low-wage workers in the state. Michigan has so far chosen not to pursue this tax option.

### C. Child Care Subsidies

For working families, one of the costs of employment is child care. Particularly for families with small children, finding workable child care can be difficult due to problems of cost, quality, travel logistics (depending upon the location of job and child care center), and hours of availability. For low-wage earners (who are more likely to work nonstandard hours), it may sometimes be impossible to locate usable child care. Anderson and Levine (2000) indicate that child care subsidies may have quite a large effect on the work behavior of less-skilled workers.

At the federal level, there has been a substantial increase in the number of dollars available for child care subsidies. Much of this has come through expansions in the Child Care Tax Credit (CCTC). The CCTC is a tax credit whose amount is scaled to income, so that high-income families get very few dollars. Unlike the EITC, the CCTC is not refundable. This means that families without any tax obligation (i.e., very low income families, typically those with incomes below $15,000 to $20,000) get no benefit from the CCTC.

An extended time trend on receipt of the CCTC in Michigan is not available. In 1999, 184,000 families in Michigan claimed the CCTC, receiving a total of $77.5 million dollars (in 2000 dollars) in tax offsets. This is $421 per family, somewhat lower than the $448 per family received on average throughout the United States.

Child care subsidies for low-income women, particularly those leaving welfare, have expanded substantially over the 1990s. A new federal block grant, which consolidated a variety of child care subsidy programs, allocated 25% more dollars into subsidies for the child care needs of low-income women than did previous legislation. States have also put more welfare program dollars into child care subsidies, on top of their child care block grant money. For instance, Michigan increased child care subsidies to welfare mothers who entered work from $128 million in fiscal year 1996 to $454 million in fiscal year 1999 (Seefeldt et al. 2001).

The Head Start program also provides child care to low-income preschool children. Head Start programs are typically located in high-poverty neighborhoods and provide social services to families as well as enrichment programs for young children ages three and four. In 2000, Michigan received $187 million in Head Start funds and enrolled 33,800 children. Funds for Head Start have expanded at the federal level, in an attempt to provide services to more eligible children. In Michigan over the past decade, the share of children participating in Head Start programs has grown by almost one-third.

As child care subsidies expand, this provides further incentives for less-skilled women (and particularly single mothers) to enter the workforce. For instance, Danziger, Oltmans, and Browning (2002) indicate that larger subsidies are linked to greater work participation in Michigan. The whole thrust of welfare reform in the 1990s has reinforced these incentives, by forcing welfare recipients to participate in job search and placement programs. Particularly for less-skilled women, child care subsidies and child care availability may be as important as wages or job availability in determining labor force participation.

## D. Health subsidies

Most working-age families who are covered by health insurance receive it as a benefit of employment. Low-wage workers are less likely to be covered by health benefits, which lowers their relative total compensation from employment. (Chapter 9 discusses a broader set of health care issues.)

Relative to the United States as a whole, lack of health insurance is less frequent in Michigan. In 1999, 9.8% of the nonelderly population in Michigan was uninsured, while 15.1% of the nonelderly population in the United States was uninsured.[10] This is largely due to the fact that a higher share of Michigan workers receives employer-sponsored health insurance. Particularly high rates of uninsurance occur among Hispanics and among the foreign-born (two categories with substantial overlap), and among part-time workers. Because

of the availability of Medicaid, the federally provided low-income insurance program to poor children and to some poor adults, uninsurance rates tend to be higher among the near poor than among the poor.

Public health insurance is received by 7% of the nonelderly population in Michigan. Welfare recipients and the disabled often are eligible for Medicaid. (All elderly and some of the disabled are eligible for Medicare, which is public insurance for those with a substantial work record who become disabled or elderly.) Historically, access to Medicaid has required participation in a public assistance program. If going to work reduces public assistance eligibility, families that need health insurance but cannot find covered jobs may have little reason to find employment and leave welfare. One of the big policy changes of the past two decades that addresses this issue is a substantial expansion in the insurance coverage of low-income children. Children's eligibility for Medicaid has been uncoupled from their families' participation in welfare, and eligibility has been expanded to virtually all low-income children. In 2000 in Michigan, all children in families whose income was below 100% of the poverty line were eligible for Medicaid insurance.[11] Unfortunately, many of the families of these children are unaware of their eligibility or unsure of how to access it, hence the utilization of medical services by many low-income children remains low.

In response to this concern, the federal government provided special funds to the states to subsidize children's health insurance through the Children's Health Insurance Program (CHIP). In Michigan these funds are distributed through the MIChild program. In Michigan, about 13% of children under age eighteen receive insurance through Medicaid or MIChild.

The expansions in insurance to low-income children should make low wage work more attractive, since they allow parents to continue to access public health insurance for their children, even when no longer receiving other forms of public assistance. The unavailability of health insurance to adults in low-wage jobs remains a problem in Michigan, as well as throughout the United States.

## E. What Does This Mean about Low-Wage Work?

The policy changes described in the preceding section were in part a response to the deterioration in wages and the high unemployment rates experienced by less-skilled and lower-wage workers in the 1980s. As we saw, wages and employment opportunities improved over the 1990s. These changes were clearly reinforced by policy. The rise in wages in part reflects the rise in the minimum wage, which did not appear to generate significant disemployment effects. The expansion of the EITC added to wages and made work pay more fully than it had before.

After the decade of the 1980s, when wages eroded in Michigan for many less-skilled workers, the 1990s brought a turnaround. By 2000 the returns to work had unambiguously risen for low-wage workers, in part because of the booming economy, but also because of the expanded EITC, expanded child care subsidies, and more readily available public health insurance (at least for children in low-income families). In the current economic slowdown of the early 2000s, it is difficult to tell how much of this progress will be reversed. Certainly the policy changes that expanded subsidies to lower-wage workers will continue to benefit these workers in the years ahead.

## 7. Conclusions

There is both good news and bad news for low-wage workers in Michigan. The high-wage/high-unemployment environment of the late 1970s and early 1980s has disappeared. The bad news: By 2000, wages among the least skilled were no higher in Michigan than in the United States (although wages among workers with at least a high school diploma continue to be higher in this state than in the nation as a whole.) These least-skilled workers have experienced serious wage erosion, in Michigan as in other states. The good news: Unemployment rates among lower-wage workers fell markedly over the 1990s. Hence, while Michigan workers without a high school diploma no longer earn higher wages than elsewhere in the nation, neither do they face higher unemployment rates.

In contrast, women have unambiguously improved their labor market position in Michigan over the past two decades. Their wages have increased, both in absolute terms and relative to male workers. Their unemployment rates have remained low. For low-wage single mothers, the somewhat increased availability of public health insurance for their children and the increase in child care subsidies should also increase their return from employment. Throughout the last two decades, labor force participation among women in Michigan and throughout the United States has continued to rise.

Black and Hispanic workers are disproportionately more likely to be less skilled than are white workers. Like other lower-skilled workers, they have lost wages over the past two decades. Yet also like other lower-skilled workers, their unemployment rates have declined.

In addition to a booming economy throughout the late 1990s, low-wage workers have also benefited from various policy changes. Minimum wages, which fell in real terms throughout the 1980s, were raised again in the 1990s. Increases in the Earned Income Tax Credit significantly increased the returns to work among workers in low-income families. Health insurance coverage of children in low-income families improved, although almost 10% of all nonelderly persons in Michigan remain uninsured. Furthermore, child care subsidies for low-income and middle-income families also expanded. All of these policy changes increased the returns to work, and somewhat offset wage declines among the least skilled.

Ongoing problems for low-wage workers remain. Most important, the long-term deterioration in the wages of less-skilled workers has made economic survival harder for their families. To address this problem, the state of Michigan may need to consider pursuing multiple policy approaches. On the one hand, the state needs to ensure that its public education and training system works effectively so that the share of less-skilled workers who enter the Michigan labor market continues to decline. On the other hand, the state may be concerned with those less-skilled workers who still have many years of potential labor market involvement ahead of them. A state Earned Income Tax Credit or other state-based policies (such as state-subsidized health insurance packages affordable to adults who do not receive health insurance through their employers) may need to be considered to make work pay for the least skilled. Retaining these workers in the labor force, even at low wages with subsidies, is preferable to having them drop out of mainstream employment at a young age.

The long-term unknown for low-wage workers is the state of the larger labor market. If the 2000s repeat the stellar economic performance of the late 1990s, then the need for more labor will provide employers with incentives to hire and train the less skilled. If, however, demand for labor is not as strong, then it is possible that the recent increases in wages among the less skilled will be reversed and wages will begin to decline, as they did from the late 1970s through the mid-1990s. In this case, the problems of low-skilled labor in the Michigan labor market will become an even more important focus of public concern. If this happens, Michigan's problems are likely to be mirrored in many other states throughout the nation.

■

## REFERENCES

Anderson, Patricia M., and Phillip B. Levine. 2000. Child care and mothers' employment decisions. In *Finding jobs: Work and welfare reform*, edited by David Card and Rebecca M. Blank. New York: Russell Sage.

Bernstein, Jared, and John Schmitt. 1998. *Making work pay: The impact of the 1996–97 minimum wage increase*. Washington, D.C.: Economic Policy Institute.

Blank, Rebecca. 1998. Contingent work in a changing labor market. In *Generating jobs: How to increase demand for less-skilled workers*, edited by Richard B. Freeman and Peter Gottschalk. New York: Russell Sage Foundation.

Blau, Francine D., and Lawrence M. Kahn. 1997. Swimming upstream: Trends in the gender wage differential in the 1980s. *Journal of Labor Economics* 15 (1, pt. 1): 1–42.

Bureau of Labor Statistics. 2001. *Employment and Earnings* 48(1).

Danziger, Sandra K., Elizabeth Oltmans, and Kimberly G. Browning. 2002. Child care subsidies and child care problems: Effects on the transition from welfare to work. Unpublished manuscript, University of Michigan Program on Poverty and Social Welfare Policy.

Ellwood, David T., Rebecca M. Blank, Joseph Blasi, Douglas Kruse, William A. Niskanen, and Karen Lynn-Dyson. 2000. *A working nation: Workers, work and government in the new economy*. New York: Russell Sage.

Holzer, Harry J., and Paul Offner. 2002. Trends in employment outcomes of young black men, 1979–2000. Institute for Research on Poverty, Discussion Paper 1247–02. Madison, Wisconsin.

Meyer, Bruce D., and Dan T. Rosenbaum. 2001. Welfare, the earned income tax credit, and the labor supply of single mothers. *Quarterly Journal of Economics* 116 (3): 1063–114.

Neumark, David. 2001. The employment effects of minimum wage: Evidence from a pre-specified research design. *Industrial Relations* 40 (1): 121–44.

Seefeldt, Kristin S., Jacob Leos-Urbel, Patricia McMahon, and Kathleen Snyder. 2001. Recent changes in Michigan welfare and work, child care, and child welfare systems. State Update No. 4, July. Program to Assess Changing Social Policies. Washington, D.C.: Urban Institute.

Urban Institute. 2001. *Health insurance, access, and use: Michigan. Tabulations from the 1999 national survey of America's families SP-06*. Assessing the New Federalism Project. Washington, D.C.: Urban Institute.

## NOTES

Thanks are due to Heidi Shierholz, Elizabeth Scott, and Cody Rockey for excellent research assistance.

1. These are the individuals who are rotating out of the CPS sample each month. Each month one-fourth of the CPS sample is in the ORG sample.

2. These samples are not large enough to gain information on more specific subgroups. For instance, I cannot look at wage or employment levels among black men or less-skilled women.

3. Full-time work for men is defined as the average number of hours worked by men who report full-time employment (based on the entire U.S. sample). Full-time work for women is defined equivalently.

4. This is preferable to the consumer price index (CPI). The computational methods used to construct the CPI have been much criticized, and that index is believed to show unreliably high inflation. The personal consumption deflator rises by 116% between 1979 and 2000, while the CPI rises by 137%.

5. Table 18.4 and figure 18.2 use a "relative" definition of very-low-wage workers, based on the twentieth percentile of U.S. wages (which is changing over time.) Alternatively, I could use an "absolute" definition, such as the number below $300/week in real wages. This alternative definition gives very similar results, with numbers of very-low-wage workers increasing in the early 1980s and declining in the 1990s.

6. Because the data in this chapter are based on the annual average of the monthly ORG samples, the state unemployment rates in figure 18.3 are not exactly identical to official annual state unemployment rates. They are, however, extremely close to the official numbers. I am able to use my data to

look at unemployment within the state by race or skill level, which is not possible with the official data.

7. The data in this paragraph are not tabulated from the ORG, but from Bureau of Labor Statistics (2001), table 23.

8. Blank (1998) reviews the trends in part-time work through the mid-1990s.

9. Some workers consistently report wages below the minimum wage. Some of these may be workers in family-owned businesses or others not covered by minimum wage laws; some may be working in firms that do not comply with the laws. Some of these data may be erroneously reported.

10. I have no information on health insurance in my data set. All information on health insurance in Michigan comes from Urban Institute (2001).

11. For children ages one to five, the cutoff is family income below 133% of poverty, and for infants the cutoff is family income below 185% of poverty.

# 19

# Income Replacement and Reemployment Programs in Michigan

*Stephen A. Woodbury*

G overnments in every developed industrial economy administer programs that partially replace the earnings of workers who suffer job loss or on-the-job injury. In addition, governments administer programs to help job losers gain reemployment, either through direct job placement (for those who are job-ready) or through retraining (for those who are not).

This chapter describes and discusses current policy issues surrounding the main social insurance and reemployment programs in Michigan: Unemployment Insurance (UI), which partially replaces lost earnings following loss of a job; Workers' Compensation (WC), which pays for medical treatment, vocational rehabilitation, and lost earnings following a work-related injury or illness; and the cluster of reemployment and training programs that, since 1998, has come under the Workforce Investment Act (WIA). In addition to describing these programs, a main goal of the chapter is to offer a critical view of Michigan's programs by comparing them with corresponding programs in neighboring states.

Discussion of these three programs could hardly be more timely. UI has come under attack for a range of alleged failings, and the Michigan legislature passed a bill in April 2002 that increased weekly benefits, lengthened benefit durations, and tightened the eligibility require-

ments for UI in Michigan. Also, the Workforce Investment Act of 1998 has resulted in significant changes in reemployment services nationwide, as well as in Michigan, and there is continuing debate over the effectiveness of the "work first" approach that WIA entails. Finally, WC has gone through cycles in which dramatic cost increases have been followed by efforts at cost containment. Michigan's WC law has seen only minor changes during the last twenty years because reforms instituted in the early 1980s appear to have kept both medical and wage replacement costs of WC in Michigan in line with those in other states. However, health care costs are projected to resume their growth in the near future, which would directly affect WC costs and put increased pressure on the WC system.

## Unemployment Insurance (UI)

Since 1936, UI has paid weekly benefits for a limited period of time to workers who have lost their job through no fault of their own and are actively seeking work. The UI system was established by the Social Security Act of 1935 as a federal-state system; that is, each state administers its own UI program, setting its own benefit levels and tax rates subject only to broad federal guidelines and oversight by the U.S. Department of Labor. Since April 2002, UI in Michigan has been administered by the Bureau of Unemployment & Workers' Compensation (under the Department of Consumer and Industry Services), which consolidates two former agencies: the Unemployment Agency and the Bureau of Workers' Disability Compensation.

This section describes first the eligibility requirements and benefit levels of Michigan's UI program, and then the financing of the program. Policy issues are discussed in turn, and comparisons are drawn with neighboring states. The discussion provides background both for understanding the debate that led to the April 2002 changes in Michigan's UI law and for examining the ongoing controversy over the goals of the UI system—that is, whether it should serve mainly as an income replacement program for workers with a strong attachment to the labor force, or whether it should play a more aggressive role in fighting poverty by transferring income from higher-wage to lower-wage workers.

### Eligibility and Benefits

To be eligible for UI benefits in any state, an unemployed worker must satisfy two broad sets of criteria. The first are referred to as "monetary eligibility" criteria and pertain to a worker's earnings history. The second are "nonmonetary eligibility" criteria and pertain to the conditions that led a claimant to leave the last employer and whether the claimant is now seeking work.[1]

*Monetary eligibility and weekly benefits.* In Michigan, as in other states, a worker's monetary eligibility is based on earnings in a so-called base period, which is conventionally defined as the first four of the last five completed quarters before the claim is filed. The quarter of the base period in which earnings were highest is referred to as the "high quarter." To be eligible for benefits in Michigan, a worker must have high-quarter earnings of at least $2,146 and total base-period earnings at least 1.5 times high-quarter earnings (or at least $3,219).

For workers who meet these criteria, the weekly benefit amount is calculated as 4.1% of high-quarter earnings, up to a maximum of $362 per week. For example, a worker with high-quarter earnings of $2,146 (and base period earnings of at least $3,219) would receive the minimum

weekly benefit of $88. A worker with high-quarter earnings of $8,829 or more (and base period earnings of at least $13,244) would receive the maximum of $362. (Before the April 2002 changes in the Michigan UI law, the maximum weekly benefit amount was $300.)

This basic method of calculating weekly benefits—that is, multiplying high-quarter earnings (or earnings in the two highest quarters) by some factor—is used by all but nine states.[2] In addition, Michigan workers with dependents receive a "dependents' allowance" of $6 per dependent (for up to five dependents, or $30) per week. However, the $362 maximum cannot be exceeded, so the dependents' allowance increases the weekly benefit only of workers who are below this maximum. Michigan is one of twelve states that have a dependents' allowance.

In Michigan, the minimum potential duration of benefits is 15.5 weeks (14 weeks before April 2002), and the maximum is 26 weeks. Within these bounds, potential benefit duration is determined by the following formula: Multiply total base-period earnings by a factor (43% in Michigan's case) and divide the result by the weekly benefit amount. For a worker who barely qualifies for benefits, this calculation yields a potential benefit duration of 15.5 weeks (0.43 × $3,219 ÷ $88 = 15.7, which is rounded down to the nearest half-week). For a worker who just qualifies for the *maximum* weekly benefit, this calculation also yields a benefit duration of 15.5 weeks (0.43 × $13,244 ÷ $362 = 15.7, again rounded down).

This rather arcane formula for potential duration of benefits does have a rationale. The idea is that the potential duration of benefits should be greater for workers whose earnings are more stable, as measured by the ratio of base-period earnings to high-quarter earnings. For a worker with the same earnings in all four base-period quarters, this ratio is 4; for a worker with highly variable earnings, the ratio could be as low as 1.

Under these monetary eligibility criteria and benefit levels, a worker earning the minimum wage of $5.15 for 417 hours in one quarter (that is, full time for about 11 weeks) and for 209 hours in any other base-period quarter (that is, full time for about 5 weeks), would be eligible for the minimum weekly benefit of $88 for 15.5 weeks, or up to $1,364. That is, earnings of $3,219 during 16 weeks of employment would yield benefits totaling as much as $1,364 over a 15.5-week spell of unemployment.

**TABLE 19.1**

## UI Benefits in Michigan and Neighboring States, First Quarter 2002

|  | Michigan[a] | Illinois | Indiana | Ohio | Wisconsin |
|---|---|---|---|---|---|
| Minimum weekly benefit amount[b] | $82–112 ($88–118) | $51–56 | $50 | $85 | $48 |
| Minimum duration of benefits (weeks) | 14 (15.5) | 26 | 8 | 20 | 12 |
| Earnings required for minimum benefit | $2,997 ($3,219) | $1,600 | $2,750 | $2,640 | $1,590 |
| Maximum weekly benefit amount[b] | $300 ($362) | $296–431 | $312 | $308–414 | $324 |
| Maximum duration of benefits (weeks) | 26 | 26 | 26 | 26 | 26 |
| Earnings required for maximum benefit | $10,976 ($13,244) | $17,069 | $29,200 | $10,680 | $9,390 |
| Average weekly benefit amount | $260 | $286 | $256 | $254 | $253 |
| State average weekly wage | $714 | $746 | $603 | $631 | $600 |
| Average weekly replacement rate | 36.5 | 38.3 | 42.5 | 40.3 | 42.2 |
| Average benefits per unemployment spell | $3,349 | $4,787 | $3,264 | $3,400 | $2,953 |
| Average duration of benefits (weeks) | 13.3 | 16.3 | 12.9 | 14.4 | 12.2 |
| Benefit exhaustion rate (%) | 28.2 | 37.0 | 36.6 | 27.6 | 20.6 |
| Recipiency rate[c] (%) | 57.5 | 52.6 | 48.4 | 48.6 | 66.1 |

SOURCES: Rows 1 through 6: U.S. Department of Labor (2002a) and author's calculations. Rows 7 through 13: U.S. Department of Labor (2002b).
(a) For Michigan, figures shown in parentheses indicate provisions that took effect with the April 2002 amendments to Michigan's UI law.
(b) Ranges shown for Illinois and Ohio are the result of dependents' allowances, which vary with the number of dependents.
(c) The recipiency rate is the percentage of all unemployed workers receiving unemployment insurance benefits (that is, the number of "insured unemployed" divided by the number of all unemployed workers, stated as a percentage.

How does a relatively high-wage worker fare under the program? A worker earning an hourly wage of $17.31 for forty hours a week over 32 weeks would be eligible for the maximum weekly benefit of $362 for 26 weeks. That is, earnings of $22,157 over 32 weeks of employment would yield benefits totaling as much as $9,912 over a 26-week spell of unemployment. (This example is chosen to show the lowest wage rate and hours worked that would yield the maximum benefit amount and maximum duration of benefits.)

Table 19.1 summarizes several aspects of UI benefits in Michigan and neighboring states. Michigan's minimum weekly benefit amount is somewhat higher than that of neighboring states, but the base period earnings required to qualify for those benefits are also higher. (For Michigan, the figures in parentheses show the increases that took effect following the April 2002 amendments to the Michigan UI law.)

Before April 2002, Michigan's maximum weekly benefit amount was the lowest in the region; it now exceeds Indiana's and Wisconsin's, and is in the midrange of the Illinois and Ohio maxima (these ranges exist because Illinois and

Ohio have dependents allowances, which vary with the number of dependents and can increase the maximum). The base period earnings required to qualify for the maximum benefit in Michigan are somewhat higher (post–April 2002) than in Ohio and Wisconsin, but considerably lower than in Illinois and Indiana. Note that Illinois is the only "uniform duration" state in the region—any worker who qualifies for benefits in Illinois is potentially eligible for up to twenty-six weeks of benefits.

Whereas the first six rows of table 19.1 summarize statutory UI benefit provisions, the lower seven rows show data on UI benefits actually paid. Michigan's average weekly benefit amount was lower than that in Illinois, but similar to that in the other states shown. However, Michigan's average weekly replacement rate—the ratio of average weekly UI benefits to average weekly earnings—was the lowest in the region. This occurred both because Michigan's maximum weekly benefit amount was the lowest in the region and because wages are higher in Michigan than in any neighboring state except Illinois.

Thirty-four states, including Illinois and Ohio,

automatically adjust the maximum benefit amount by linking it to the state's average weekly wage—Michigan does not. A typical approach is to set the maximum at between 50 and 60% of the average weekly wage. (Illinois, for example, sets it at 50%.) By adopting such an approach, Michigan could prevent UI replacement rates from slipping well below those in neighboring states, as they did before the April 2002 amendments. It could also avoid repeated political wrangling over the maximum benefit amount, as occurred in early 2002.

Both average benefits per unemployment spell and the average duration of benefits are similar in Michigan and three of its neighboring states; the exception is Illinois, where the twenty-six-week uniform duration of benefits leads to relatively high benefits per spell and spell durations. About 28% of UI recipients in Michigan exhausted their benefits in early 2002—higher than in Wisconsin, similar to Ohio, and well below Illinois and Indiana. (In Illinois, relatively high weekly benefits combine with long potential durations and what appears to be relatively lax enforcement of the work search test to give a relatively high exhaustion rate.) Exhaustion rates are sometimes used as a rough gauge of the adequacy of the potential duration of benefits.

Finally, Michigan's UI recipiency rate—the percentage of unemployed workers receiving UI benefits—was over 57% in early 2002, well above the national average of 48% and higher than in most neighboring states. The determinants of UI recipiency are only partially understood (Vroman 2001), but Michigan's relatively high rate is usually attributed to the relatively high proportion of workers who are union members and consequently receive assistance in claiming UI benefits. The number of workers receiving UI varies greatly over the business cycle—in 1999, only 323,015 Michigan workers received UI (a ten-year low), whereas by 2001, the number had jumped to 513,277.

*Alternative methods of qualifying.* Workers who are ineligible under the standard criteria outlined previously may be eligible under either the "alternative base period" or the "alternative earnings qualifier." Under the alternative base period, the base period is defined as the last four completed quarters (rather than the first four of the last five completed quarters). By considering relatively recent earnings to determine eligibil-

ity, the alternative base period works to the advantage of claimants who entered employment only recently and hence do not have a long history of employment. Without the alternative base period, these workers would need to wait three months to receive benefits. For details, see Woodbury (2002c).

Under the alternative earnings qualifier a worker is eligible for benefits if he or she has wages in two base-period quarters, and total base-period wages at least twenty times the state average weekly wage ($714 in 2002, so that a worker needs base period earnings of at least $14,289.20). The alternative earnings qualifier works to the advantage of seasonal workers who, like construction workers, may have high earnings in one quarter but low earnings in other quarters, so that their total base period earnings fall below 1.5 times high-quarter earnings. Weekly benefits and maximum durations are determined as under the regular formula (using high-quarter earnings).

*Nonmonetary eligibility.* To be eligible for UI benefits, a worker must also satisfy three sets of "nonmonetary" criteria. First, a worker must have left his or her last job due to lack of work and through no fault of his or her own (these are known as "separation criteria"). Accordingly, a worker who quits voluntarily or is discharged for cause is ineligible for UI. Second, a worker must be currently available for and seeking full-time work (these are known as "nonseparation criteria" or the "UI work test"). Accordingly, a worker who is unavailable for full-time work due to child care responsibilities, who decides not to search for work in the belief that jobs are unavailable, or who takes a vacation, is ineligible for UI. Third, a worker must not be receiving "disqualifying income," the definition of which varies from state to state.

The nonmonetary eligibility criteria appear straightforward, but they are difficult to implement and enforce. Consider first the separation criteria. Should all base period separations be considered in applying the separation criteria, or only the most recent? Michigan considers all base period separations, and several states—including Illinois and Ohio—consider separations in addition to the most recent under some circumstances (see table 19.2). What reasons should be included as "good causes" for quitting a job voluntarily? In Michigan, as in most states, good cause is restricted to issues directly related

**TABLE 19.2**

### Separation and Nonseparation Eligibility for UI Benefits, Michigan and Neighboring States, 2002

| Eligibility Criteria | Michigan[a] | Illinois | Indiana | Ohio | Wisconsin |
|---|---|---|---|---|---|
| **Separation** | | | | | |
| Voluntary leaving: | | | | | |
|   Only last separation considered | no | no | yes | no | yes |
|   Good cause restricted to work-related issues | yes | yes | yes | yes | yes |
|   Additional reasons allowed | 2 | 6 | 3 | 2 | 14 |
|   Earnings to requalify | 7 x WBA (12 x WBA) | WBA in 4 weeks | WBA in 8 weeks | 6 weeks of work | 4 x WBA |
| Misconduct: | | | | | |
|   Last separation only | no | no | yes | no | yes |
|   Earnings to requalify | 7 x WBA (17 x WBA) | WBA in 4 weeks | WBA in 8 weeks | 6 weeks of work | 14 x WBA |
| **Nonseparation** | | | | | |
| Able and available for: | | | | | |
|   Full-time work | yes | yes | yes | yes | yes |
|   Suitable work | yes | no | no | yes | no |
|   Usual work | yes | no | no | no | no |
| Refusing suitable work: | | | | | |
|   Disqualification period | 6 weeks (13 weeks) | duration | duration | duration | duration |
|   Benefits reduced | yes | no | yes | no | no |

SOURCE: U.S. Department of Labor (2002a); UWC (2002).
NOTE: "WBA" refers to weekly benefit amount; "duration" refers to disqualification for the duration of the current unemployment spell.
(a) For Michigan, figures shown in parentheses indicate provisions that took effect with the April 2002 amendments to Michigan's UI law.

to work or the employer, but two additional reasons are allowed in Michigan—leaving an unsuitable job within sixty days and leaving a job to accept another job that does not materialize. Some states include additional reasons; for example, leaving a job due to sexual harassment is considered good cause in eight states, including Illinois and Wisconsin, but not Michigan. As is suggested by table 19.2 ("additional reasons allowed"), Michigan is somewhat less permissive than neighboring states, particularly Wisconsin, in allowing additional "good causes" (for details, see UWC 2002).

In Michigan, a claimant who quits voluntarily or is discharged for cause cannot receive UI benefits for the duration of the current unemployment spell. To requalify, a worker who quits voluntarily must earn twelve times the weekly benefit amount, and a worker who is discharged must earn seventeen times the weekly benefit amount. (Before the April 2002 changes in Michigan's UI law, such workers needed to earn only seven times the weekly benefit amount to requalify.)

Consider next the nonseparation criteria. For most workers, satisfying the nonseparation criteria entails registering with Michigan Works! (which administers the public labor exchange in Michigan—see following), being available for "suitable" work, and actively searching for *full-time* work. Registering with Michigan Works! is unambiguous, but suitable work can be variously defined. Michigan's law defines suitable work as a job that pays 70% or more of the gross pay rate received on the pre-layoff job. (Michigan also defines suitable work as work previously performed or for which the worker is trained.) A worker who refuses to apply for or accept such work can be denied benefits. (Before April 2002, suitable work was defined in relation to a claimant's duration of unemployment. For the first twelve weeks of unemployment, a job was suitable if it paid 80% or more of the pre-layoff rate; for the next eight weeks, 75% of the pre-layoff rate; and thereafter, 70% of the pre-layoff rate.) A worker who refuses suitable work is now disqualified from receiving benefits for thirteen weeks (formerly six weeks).[3]

The requirement to seek full-time work has been controversial because of its implications for the eligibility of part-time workers. For example, a worker who worked thirty hours a week over a period of years and was laid off would very likely be monetarily eligible for UI. Such a worker would have a strong attachment to the labor force by most reasonable definitions, but unless that worker were seeking full-time employment (meaning employment of at least thirty-five hours per week), the nonseparation criteria for eligibility would not be satisfied. This problem has led some to conclude that the UI system is outmoded, in that it fails to take account of the needs of single household heads with childcare responsibilities. For example, the Advisory Council on Unemployment Compensation (1995) recommended that workers who satisfy a state's monetary eligibility criteria should not be denied benefits solely because they are seeking part-time work. Sixteen states have modified their eligibility requirements along these lines (U.S. Department of Labor 2002a); however, Michigan and its neighboring states have not (see table 19.2).

Finally, Michigan reduces the weekly benefit amount by the amount of any disqualifying income, which now includes severance pay, salary continuation, back pay, wages in lieu of notice, vacation and holiday pay, and pension income received from a base-period employer (severance pay became disqualifying income only in April 2002). Some states consider WC to be disqualifying income; Michigan does not. Supplemental Unemployment Benefits (SUB), which are important in Michigan because they are paid to many laid-off autoworkers by their employers under UAW contract, are *not* considered disqualifying income in Michigan (as in most states). Although Michigan's disqualifying income provisions are generally similar to those in other states, UI agencies throughout the country complain that these provisions are difficult to administer and enforce because they generally depend on the worker reporting the income. As a result, they appear to be a frequent source of payment errors (Woodbury 2002b).

*The waiting week.* During the debate over amending Michigan's UI law in early 2002, consideration was given to requiring a waiting week; that is, a one-week period at the beginning of a claim during which an eligible claimant does not receive benefits. Michigan is the largest of the twelve states that currently does not have a waiting week (U.S. Department of Labor 2002a). Illinois, Indiana, and Ohio have a waiting week; Wisconsin, like Michigan, does not. Ultimately, the Michigan legislature did not adopt a waiting week in 2002, but it is an issue that will almost surely recur.

The argument against a waiting week is simply that it delays the receipt of benefits by workers. However, two arguments have been made in favor of the waiting week. First, some researchers have argued that short spells of unemployment tend to be overcompensated, whereas long spells tend to be undercompensated (Davidson and Woodbury 1997; O'Leary 1998). If so, then imposing a waiting week could improve the efficiency of the UI program if the savings resulting from the waiting week allowed the potential duration of benefits to be extended. (It is worth noting that such an extension was not discussed during the debate over the Michigan UI law in 2002.) Second, in insurance terms, the waiting week acts as a deductible and reduces the possibilities for abuse of UI. (For further discussion, see Woodbury and Rubin [1997].)

**Financing UI**

In Michigan, as in nearly every other state, UI is financed by a payroll tax that is collected entirely from employers. The UI payroll tax is essential to the federal role in the UI system. The Social Security Act provides for a payroll tax (the Federal Unemployment Tax), which is currently 6.2% of at least the first $7,000 of a worker's earnings in a calendar year. (The amount of earnings taxed can be greater than $7,000, at the discretion of the state.) However, employers in states with a federally approved UI program (that is, one that meets the broad guidelines stated in the act) are credited 5.4% and as a result pay only a 0.8% federal payroll tax. This is the incentive whereby the federal government induced all of the states to adopt a UI program (see, for example, Blaustein 1993, chapter 6, for a discussion).

In Michigan, virtually all employers are required to pay the UI payroll tax. Aside from agricultural and domestic employers, any employer who has one or more workers in any twenty weeks of a calendar year, or who has payroll of $1,000 or more in a calendar year, is a "liable employer" and must pay the tax.

**TABLE 19.3**

**UI Payroll Taxes and Program Solvency, Michigan and Neighboring States, First Quarter 2002**

| | Michigan[a] | Illinois | Indiana | Ohio | Wisconsin |
|---|---|---|---|---|---|
| Taxable wage base benefit amount | $9,500 ($9,000) | $9,000 | $7,000 | $9,000 | $10,500 |
| Total wages of taxable employers (in millions) | $32,487 | $44,762 | $18,214 | $34,950 | $16,561 |
| Taxable wages (in millions) | $4,326 | $5,493 | $2,102 | $4,876 | $2,877 |
| Taxable/total wages (%) | 13.3 | 12.3 | 11.5 | 14.0 | 17.6 |
| Statutory tax rates (%) | | | | | |
| Minimum | 0.10 (0.06) | 0.60 | 0.01 | 0.10 | 0.00 |
| Maximum | 6.00 (6.30) | 6.80 | 5.40 | 6.50 | 9.75 |
| Average tax rate on: | | | | | |
| Taxable wages (%) | 2.6 | 2.1 | 1.1 | 1.9 | 1.7 |
| Total wages (%) | 0.6 | 0.4 | 0.2 | 0.5 | 0.4 |
| UI tax revenues (last twelve months, in millions) | $982 | $1,045 | $222 | $618 | $446 |
| Trust fund balance (in millions) | $2,412 | $1,109 | $1,316 | $1,852 | $1,456 |
| High-cost multiple | 0.48 | 0.22 | 0.99 | 0.42 | 0.69 |
| Average high-cost multiple | 0.65 | 0.31 | 1.31 | 0.54 | 0.92 |

SOURCES: U.S. Department of Labor (2002a); U.S. Department of Labor (2002b); author's calculations.
(a) For Michigan, figures shown in parentheses indicate changes that took effect in April 2002 under amendments to Michigan's UI law.

*Tax base.* Like any tax, the UI payroll tax has two parts: a base and a rate. In Michigan, the tax base, known as "taxable payroll," was the first $9,500 of a worker's earnings in a calendar year from 1986 through 2002. The April 2002 changes in Michigan's UI law reduced the taxable payroll to $9,000 starting in calendar year 2003. As shown in table 19.3, the tax base in three of the states neighboring Michigan is also slightly above the federally mandated minimum of $7,000. Sixteen states have a taxable wage base that changes annually in relation to the state's average weekly wage. All of these states have taxable wage bases substantially higher than Michigan's, most in excess of $20,000.

Michigan's taxable payroll is well below the average annual earnings of full-time workers in the state, which are on the order of $37,000. Hence, the taxable wage base is quite narrow and necessitates higher tax rates than would a broader base, for a given level of benefits. The taxable wage base has not always been so narrow. At the outset of the program in 1936, the wage base was the same as Social Security's and covered about 93% of earnings (Hamermesh 1977, 72). Only in the 1960s did the UI wage base start to erode significantly relative to payrolls. In the first quarter of 2002, the taxable wage base

covered only 13% of total wages paid by taxable employers in Michigan (see table 19.3), and this will clearly drop further with the reduction in the taxable wage base to $9,000 in 2003. Similarly, states neighboring Michigan have taxable wages that are a small percentage of total wages (see again table 19.3).

The low taxable wage base tends to work against the employment prospects of low-wage, high-turnover workers. Over 85% of the earnings of a full-time minimum-wage worker were taxable in Michigan in 2002 (that is, $9,000 out of roughly $10,500 earned). In contrast, less than 25% of the earnings of a full-time worker at the average weekly wage were taxable ($9,000 out of roughly $37,000).

*Tax rates.* In Michigan and every other state, UI payroll tax rates are "experience rated" at the level of the employer, meaning that each employer's tax rate depends on the extent to which that employer has laid off workers who have claimed and received UI benefits in the past. To implement a system of experience rating, it is necessary to trace UI benefits received by a worker to the employer, who is in some sense responsible for that worker's unemployment. This "charging" of benefits to employers is done in various ways. Michigan is one of eight states that charges base period employers in reverse chronological order, with the most recent base period employer charged up to 75% of the claimant's maximum benefit amount, followed by the next most recent base period employer.

In practice, experience rating applies only to employers who have been liable (that is, paying UI payroll taxes) for more than two years. In Michigan, new employers all pay a "standard rate" of 2.7% for their first two years, except for new construction employers, who pay the average construction industry rate (between 6.8 and 8.1% in recent years). In their third and fourth years, employers pay a rate that combines a standard rate (which is specific to the year in business) with a rate calculated from their layoff experience during the first two or three years of business (specifically, the Chargeable Benefits Component, as described in the following). In their fifth and subsequent years, the payroll tax is the sum of three components, all of which are specific to the employer and depend on past layoff experience.

The first component of Michigan's UI payroll tax is the "Chargeable Benefits Component" (CBC), which is calculated by summing all *UI benefits paid* to workers laid off by the employer during the past five years and dividing this by the *UI taxable payroll* of the employer during the same five years:

$$\text{CBC} = \textit{UI benefits paid} \div \textit{UI taxable payroll}$$

The CBC cannot exceed 6.0% in 2002 (this maximum increases to 6.3% in 2003). For example, an employer whose workers received $100,400 in UI benefits during the past five years and had a five-year taxable payroll of $10,000,000 would have a CBC of 1.1%. Formulas similar to the preceding "benefit-ratio" formula are used by seventeen states (including Illinois) to experience rate the UI taxes of employers.

The second component of the payroll tax rate is the "Account Building Component" (ABC), which is more involved to calculate (see Woodbury 2002c). However, it is less important (in terms of both revenues and degree of experience rating generated) because it is capped at only 2%. Michigan's ABC is similar to the "reserve-ratio" formulas that are used by thirty-five states (including Indiana, Ohio, and Wisconsin) to experience rate the UI taxes of employers. Only Michigan and Pennsylvania use *both* a reserve-

ratio formula and a benefit-ratio formula to experience rate UI payroll taxes.

The third component of the UI payroll tax rate is the nonchargeable benefits component (NBC), which is a flat rate charged to all employers who have been in business for more than four years. The NBC is either (1) 1% for employers who have incurred any benefit charges in the last five years; or (2) a lower rate for employers who have incurred no benefit charges in the last five years. The lower rate for employers who have incurred no charge in the last five years fell by statute from 0.5% in 1993–95 to 0.1% in 1999–2002. It is scheduled to fall to 0.06% in 2003.

The resulting range of tax rates in Michigan and the ranges that are currently in effect in neighboring states are shown in table 19.3. Michigan's range of 0.06 to 6.3% is similar to the ranges in Illinois, Indiana, and Ohio. Wisconsin has a substantially greater range of tax rates, from 0 to 9.75%. Recall that Wisconsin also has a larger taxable wage base, which gives it greater leverage to collect taxes from employers who frequently lay off workers. From the mid-1980s well into the 1990s, Michigan had a maximum payroll tax rate of 10%, but its taxable wage base has never exceeded $9,500.

Table 19.3 also shows that Michigan's average UI payroll tax—0.6% of total wages—is slightly higher than that of other states in the region. This is partly because Michigan's taxable wage base has been slightly higher than that of its neighboring states (except Wisconsin), and partly because Michigan's dual experience rating system (which uses both a benefit-ratio formula and a reserve-ratio formula) assigns most employers a higher tax rate than would a system that uses a single formula.

*Policy issues in UI financing.* Because the payroll tax is capped at 6.00%, Michigan's method of setting UI payroll taxes results in experience rating that is incomplete. If the payroll tax were not capped, many employers would face higher tax rates as a result of their layoff experience. This leads to the first of two issues concerning the UI payroll tax that are of longstanding concern to policy makers, employers, and UI advocacy groups— effective subsidization of high-layoff employers by low-layoff employers through the UI system.

The most recent study of cross-subsidies in Michigan, by Munts and Asher (1980), used data for 1969–1976 and found that Michigan's cross-subsidies were the highest of the twenty-one states studied. However, this study is rather out of date. More recent evidence on cross-subsidies (Woodbury 2002a) comes from firm-level data in Missouri, Pennsylvania, and Washington State during 1985–95. In Pennsylvania, which has a UI payroll tax structure similar to Michigan's, benefit payments to laid-off construction workers were twice the payroll taxes paid by the construction industry. Moreover, a firm that was subsidized in one year had a probability in excess of 50% of being subsidized five years later.

The second main concern generated by the cap on the payroll tax is that, for high-layoff employers who reach the maximum tax rate, the incentive to avoid layoffs is removed. Several studies have estimated large impacts of experience rating on temporary layoffs. For example, Card and Levine (1994) find that incomplete experience rating leads to temporary layoffs that, during a recession, are 50% higher than they would be if experience rating were complete.

As mentioned above, in April 2002, the Michigan legislature lowered the taxable wage base and widened the spread between the minimum and maximum UI payroll tax rates. The impact of these changes on cross-subsidization and employer layoff behavior is difficult to predict: The reduced taxable wage base will exacerbate the cross-subsidies and increase the incentive for employers at the maximum tax rate to lay off workers, but the reduced minimum and increased maximum tax rates will have the opposite effects. Firm-level data and a simulation model would be needed to estimate the impacts of the tax changes with any confidence. However, the legislated changes are probably too small to have significant impacts.

*Trust fund adequacy.* Unlike Social Security, UI is not a pay-as-you-go system. Rather, each state places UI payroll taxes that it collects in a trust fund from which benefits are paid. The intent is to "forward-fund" UI so that, in a recession, funds required to pay benefits will be available and UI will serve as an automatic stabilizer. The bottom four rows of table 19.3 display figures on the UI revenues and trust fund balances of Michigan and its neighboring states. During 2001, Michigan collected nearly $1 billion in UI payroll taxes, and in early 2002, it had a trust fund balance of about $2.4 billion, largest in the region.

The trust fund must be viewed in relation to the demands that may be placed on it. Two widely used measures of UI trust fund adequacy are shown at the bottom of table 19.3. The first—the high-cost multiple—is the trust fund as a percentage of state taxable wages divided by the highest ratio of benefits to wages ever paid in the state's history. This suggests the fraction of a year for which a state's existing trust fund would be adequate if benefits were paid at the highest rate ever observed in the past. The second measure—the average high-cost multiple—is (again) the trust fund as a percentage of state taxable wages, but this time divided by the *average* ratio of benefits to wages paid over the last three recessions. This latter is a less stringent measure of trust fund adequacy because it suggests the fraction of a year for which a state's existing trust fund would be adequate if benefits were paid at their average historical rate.

Standards for trust fund adequacy have been somewhat elusive. The Advisory Council on Unemployment Compensation (1995) recommended that states maintain an average high-cost multiple of 1. But Emsellem et al. (2002) consider states with a high-cost multiple of 0.75 to be adequately funded. In early 2002, the high-cost multiple for the United States as a whole was 0.54, and the *average* high-cost multiple for the United States was 0.75.

Table 19.3 shows that Michigan's average high-cost multiple was 0.65 in early 2002—below the national average and the levels that have been considered "adequate." Illinois and Ohio are also below the national average; Indiana and Wisconsin substantially exceed the average.

The April 2002 amendments to Michigan's UI law reduced the taxable wage base and the minimum payroll tax rate but increased the maximum tax rate. The Bureau of Unemployment & Workers' Compensation has referred to these changes overall as a tax cut. Yet the April 2002 amendments also increased the maximum benefit amount, which will increase benefit payments. It seems clear that the adequacy of Michigan's UI trust fund, as measured by the high-cost multiple, will fall as a result of the amendments.

## Competing Goals of the UI System

The origins of the UI program are rooted in the idea of social insurance—that it is desirable and efficient to partially replace the earnings of workers who lose their jobs through no fault of their own, and that the extent of wage replacement should be tied to a job loser's regular earnings. This goal was reiterated by the Advisory Council on Unemployment Compensation (1995, 8):

> The most important objective of the U.S. system of Unemployment Insurance is the provision of temporary, partial wage replacement as a matter of right to involuntarily unemployed individuals who have demonstrated a prior attachment to the labor force. This support should help to meet the necessary expenses of these workers as they search for employment that takes advantage of their skills and experience.

The goal, then, is to increase the stability of income and consumption of workers who have a history of labor force attachment.

An alternative view is that UI can and should serve as an essential component of an income transfer system that redistributes income to the working poor. This has been implicit in various policy discussions of UI following the growth of anti-poverty programs in the 1960s. For example, twenty years ago, Corson and Nicholson (1982) criticized one of the extended UI benefit programs as "target inefficient" because it paid "substantial" benefits to the nonpoor. Recently, interest in the potential for UI to serve as an important part of a larger anti-poverty strategy has been heightened by the welfare reforms of 1996. As former welfare recipients have flowed into the labor market following those reforms, the effectiveness of UI has been measured increasingly by its ability to provide income support for unemployed former welfare recipients, who generally had low earnings while they were employed. The U.S. General Accounting Office (2000, 7) has noted that, "few states have adjusted their UI programs to eliminate practices that may present difficulties to low-wage workers, particularly these new workers [former welfare recipients]." Other research—for example, Gustafson and Levine (1998) and Kaye (2001)—has raised specific concerns about the extent to which nonmonetary eligibility criteria prevent former welfare recipients from obtaining UI.

Clearly, the effectiveness of UI is being judged by its ability to provide income support to workers who have not traditionally been within its ambit. However, policy makers will need to be creative if the goal is to benefit former welfare recipients without abandoning the original insurance purposes of UI. It seems clear that future debate over changes in UI will be influenced by tensions between the traditional insurance goals of UI and more recent concerns that UI should serve as part of a broader anti-poverty strategy.

## Reemployment Programs

Reemployment policy in Michigan and other states has been significantly shaped by federal policy, which has funded and directed most state employment and training programs. Federal reemployment policy can be dated to the passage in 1933 of the Wagner-Peyser Act, which established the U.S. Employment Service (ES). Throughout its history, the ES has served as a free public labor exchange, registering job seekers, taking job orders from employers, and matching workers with job vacancies. Since the establishment of UI in 1935, the ES has also administered the nonseparation criteria for UI (discussed previously), which attempt to ensure that UI recipients are able to work, available for work, and seeking work. Although the ES has had other goals and functions over the years, these two—matching workers to jobs through placement and other reemployment services, and administering the UI work test—have been consistent.

The Workforce Investment Act of 1998 (WIA) has pointed federal and state policy to assist unemployed workers in a new direction. This section reviews the evolution of reemployment policy through WIA and describes how reemployment services are changing under WIA. It also discusses the activities of the Michigan Department of Career Development and its role under WIA, and poses research questions that will need to be addressed in evaluating WIA's effectiveness.

### The Employment Service

Like UI, the ES is a federal-state system; that is, each state administers its own ES program, but the U.S. Department of Labor funds and oversees the state programs. Accordingly, the role of the ES has changed as the emphasis of federal reemployment policy has changed. Until the 1960s, reemployment policy in the United States emphasized job placement and assumed that unemployed workers were job-ready and merely needed to be matched to an employer. During the 1960s, however, the Manpower Development and Training Act and the Economic Opportunity Act shifted emphasis away from job placement and toward "second-chance" training of workers who either were poorly served by the conventional system of public education or were dislocated as a result of structural economic change. The role of the ES in this shift was at first substantial, but that role dwindled with the adoption of the Comprehensive Employment and Training Act (CETA) in 1973. Under CETA, training services were administered locally, with the result, in the view of many, that reemployment services became fragmented. The diminished role of the ES continued through the 1980s and into the 1990s following adoption of the Job Training Partnership Act (JTPA) in 1982.[4]

During the 1980s, there was much dissatisfaction with the ES, and questions were raised about its role and importance. Also during the 1980s, however, convincing research (reviewed by LaLonde [1995]) became available showing that existing government training programs fell short of their hoped-for results. Moreover, a series of demonstrations using randomized trials suggested the effectiveness of relatively inexpensive reemployment services—job search workshops, interview and resume preparation classes, and other assistance—in helping unemployed workers (see the review by Meyer [1995]). As a result, the former optimism about second-chance training was replaced by an emphasis on placing workers in jobs. In short, the sentiment in favor of "training first" was replaced by a growing belief in "work first."

The reemphasis on "work first" that took hold during the late 1990s is reflected in federal funding of training programs in Michigan for disadvantaged adults, youth, and dislocated workers. As table 19.4 shows, overall funding for these programs fell by over 40% between 1994 and 2000, although it has risen slightly since. Funding for the youth program was cut more severely than was funding for the adult or dislocated worker programs. This was a response to evidence from the National JTPA Demonstration that training programs for out-of-school youths had no positive impact on earnings. (See U.S. General Accounting Office [1996] and Bloom et al. [1997] for summaries of the evidence, much of which was available as early as 1993.)

The new emphasis on "work first" is also reflected in amendments to the Social Security Act

| TABLE 19.4 |

**Funding for Adult, Youth, and Dislocated Workers Programs under the Job Training Partnership Act (JTPA) and the Workforce Investment Act (WIA), Michigan, 1993–2002 (in thousands of dollars)**

| Program Year | Adult | Youth | Dislocated Workers | Total |
|---|---|---|---|---|
| 1994 | $35,740 | $56,099 | $15,384 | $107,223 |
| 1995 | 31,310 | 56,040 | 24,554 | 111,904 |
| 1996 | 30,084 | 46,366 | 23,267 | 99,717 |
| 1997 | 21,942 | 25,358 | 26,962 | 74,262 |
| 1998 | 20,890 | 29,769 | 21,947 | 72,606 |
| 1999 | 21,705 | 29,069 | 18,768 | 69,542 |
| 2000 | 19,568 | 23,367 | 17,540 | 60,475 |
| 2001 | 24,943 | 25,958 | 15,662 | 66,562 |
| 2002 | 21,550 | 26,136 | 15,913 | 63,599 |

SOURCE: Michigan Department of Career Development (n.d.).
NOTES: Program Years run from 1 July of the preceding year through 30 June of the Program Year. The summer youth program ended as a separate allocation at the end of Program Year 1999 (that is, 30 June 1999).

that established the Worker Profiling and Reemployment Services initiative in 1993. Under profiling, UI claimants who are likely to exhaust their UI benefits are required to attend job search assistance workshops conducted by the ES, or risk losing their UI benefits. (Eberts and O'Leary [1996] discuss Michigan's profiling system; Corson and Decker [2000] offer evidence on the effectiveness of profiling.)

## The Workforce Investment Act (WIA)

The emphasis on "work first" is again clear in the Workforce Investment Act of 1998, which embodies two main changes in reemployment policy. First, it requires that states provide most federally funded employment and training services through a system of One-Stop Centers, which provide all reemployment services (or information about and referral to such services) at a single location. The intent of One-Stop Centers is to offer an attractive, logically organized office that directs any job seeker to information, assistance, or programs needed to gain employment. Moreover, One-Stop Centers encourage coordination of services by collecting the operations of various reemployment programs under a single manager.

Second, WIA has replaced the JTPA programs for economically disadvantaged and dislocated workers with programs for adults, dislocated workers, and youth that deemphasize the differences among groups needing assistance. Specifically, WIA provides three levels of services—core (including basic services such as job search assistance), intensive (including services such as assessment that require staff assistance), and training (for eligible workers). As part of this overhaul, the Private Industry Councils that existed under JTPA are replaced with Workforce Investment Boards. This latter change is significant because, whereas Private Industry Councils were concerned mainly with the provision of training under JTPA, Workforce Investment Boards have responsibility, in principle, for overseeing all reemployment services and government-funded training in their region.

The idea of "one-stop" reemployment services is hardly new: Haber and Murray (1966) referred to it as early as 1966, and a year later, the Manpower Administration issued a memorandum that discussed integrated delivery of human services at central locations. Accordingly, WIA must be viewed as an attempt to bring about what has long been viewed as desirable—the centralization of information and other reemployment services, including referral to training, to promote employment.

### Reemployment Services in Michigan

The traditional role of the ES—that of a free public employment agency—has involved provision of five main services: assessment (which may include counseling and aptitude and interest testing), job referral, job development (which is similar to job referral except that an ES interviewer contacts employers known to hire workers with the applicant's skills), referral to training, and other job search assistance services. As a result, it has been natural to make state ES agencies responsible for One-Stop Centers. Michigan's One-Stop Centers are known as Michigan Works! and are administered by the Michigan Department of Career Development.

Michigan Works! differs from One-Stops in other states in two ways. First, in 1997, Michigan dissolved the Michigan Employment Security Commission, which used to house Michigan's ES agency, and contracted out ES services rather than having those services provided by state workers. Second, at the same time, Michigan was one of a handful of states that was granted permission by the Department of Labor to allow ES applicants to serve themselves and refer them-

selves to jobs, rather than rely on ES staff for job referrals. In Michigan, then, workers register with Michigan Works! by entering information on themselves into a computerized "talent bank." They are then able to access job listings and can contact employers without the assistance of Michigan Works! staff. Research does not exist on whether this approach benefits workers more than the traditional approach (which requires staff assistance). It is clear, however, that the self-service approach has made it difficult to monitor the extent to which use of the ES results in job referrals and placements.

Table 19.5 compares the 1999 activities of Michigan Works! with those of ES agencies in neighboring states (Program Year 1999—July 1999 to June 2000—is the most recent year for which data are available). The overall level of activity of these agencies can be measured by ES applicants as a percentage of the labor force. The ES agencies of Michigan, Indiana, and Wisconsin all appear to have activity levels that are fairly close to the national average. Ohio has an unusually active ES, and Illinois has the least active ES of the states shown.

The mix of clients served by Michigan's ES differs from that in neighboring states in several respects. Mainly, a far higher percentage of Michigan Works! clients are UI claimants (who in principle must register with the ES in order to remain eligible for benefits) than is the case elsewhere. The finding suggests that Michigan makes more effort than other states to ensure that UI claimants are seeking work. This is consistent with anecdotal evidence that, when the Michigan Employment Security Commission was dissolved, efforts were made to ensure that UI claimants would register with Michigan Works!

Table 19.5 also suggests that Michigan Works! is serving fewer economically disadvantaged and disabled workers than are ES agencies in neighboring states. Whether this is actually the case is debatable. It seems likely that the conversion of One-Stop Centers to self-service in Michigan lowered the reported number of disadvantaged and disabled workers who are served by Michigan Works! Disadvantaged and disabled workers who register with Michigan Works! are not required to classify themselves as such—in fact, Michigan Works! staff may urge them not to report that they are disadvantaged or disabled, in the belief that doing so would lower their chances of getting a job. If this is the case, then these figures represent a failure to report services provided to disadvan-

**TABLE 19.5**

**Public Labor Exchange Applicants and Activities, Michigan, Neighboring States, and the United States, 1999**

| | Michigan | Illinois | Indiana | Ohio | Wisconsin | United States |
|---|---|---|---|---|---|---|
| Total applicants | 572,305 | 560,850 | 324,742 | 774,218 | 339,184 | 16,708,228 |
| as % of labor force | 11.2 | 8.7 | 10.4 | 12.7 | 11.2 | 11.9 |
| Total applicants as % of: | | | | | | |
| UI claimants | 69.74 | 48.42 | 28.12 | 34.35 | 24.92 | 36.9 |
| Veterans | 16.52 | 10.52 | 13.46 | 15.12 | 8.57 | 10.0 |
| Disadvantaged | 1.42 | 5.40 | 17.59 | 55.66 | 0.79 | 12.9 |
| Disabled | 0.88 | 1.05 | 4.45 | 2.60 | 7.25 | 2.0 |
| Farm workers | 1.99 | 0.08 | 0.01 | 0.25 | 0.23 | 1.1 |
| Percentage of all applicants receiving: | | | | | | |
| Assessment | 1.36 | 1.81 | 3.11 | 3.04 | 4.28 | 10.64 |
| Job search assistance | 12.26 | 38.54 | 50.26 | 76.15 | 5.53 | 40.13 |
| Training referral | 0.69 | 2.48 | 3.07 | 1.06 | 0.27 | 2.37 |
| Job referral | 2.30 | 29.77 | 34.36 | 35.80 | 57.89 | 40.30 |
| Job placement | 0.87 | 11.15 | 6.50 | 13.00 | 9.95 | 10.60 |
| Percentage of UI claimants receiving: | | | | | | |
| Assessment | 0.26 | 0.35 | 0.46 | 3.08 | 7.88 | 10.70 |
| Job search assistance | 2.17 | 9.66 | 36.46 | 84.90 | 12.25 | 39.38 |
| Training referral | 0.21 | 0.92 | 1.58 | 1.27 | 0.61 | 2.82 |
| Job referral | 0.31 | 13.73 | 7.80 | 26.37 | 58.52 | 26.80 |
| Job placement | 0.09 | 3.22 | 4.89 | 5.70 | 13.32 | 5.83 |

SOURCES: U.S. Department of Labor (2001); author's calculations.

taged and disabled workers. Nevertheless, it is unfortunate that the extent to which Michigan Works! potentially serves the needs of disadvantaged and disabled workers is difficult to track. The underlying problem is that the U.S. Department of Labor has not imposed uniform reporting requirements on the ES agencies of the states.

The middle panel of table 19.5 shows the percentage of ES applicants receiving various services in each state and nationally, and the bottom panel shows the percentage of UI claimants who receive various services. Michigan's rates of training referral, job referral, and job placement are far below the national average and the rates in neighboring states. This could reflect Michigan's self-service approach, discussed previously, although other states that have moved to self-service report much higher rates of service delivery. These states have devised ways of tracking the extent to which workers who serve themselves contact employers (that is, "self-refer") and obtain jobs. No research has examined the relative effectiveness of self-referrals and referrals made with ES staff assistance; this is an important question that is ripe for research.

The middle panel of table 19.5 suggests that

Michigan provides less job search assistance to workers than do other states (except Wisconsin). Job search assistance includes job search workshops, job-finding clubs, and classes in job-finding skills, all of which are important parts of UI profiling. The bottom panel shows that Michigan provides job search assistance to only 2% of UI claimants, compared with nearly 40% nationally, suggesting that Michigan is profiling relatively few UI claimants. So although Michigan is registering a higher percentage of its UI claimants than are most states (top panel of table 19.5), it is providing them with relatively few reportable services.

## Michigan's Response to Changing Federal Policy and Policy Issues

Although reemployment programs are largely federally funded, much variation exists among states in the organization and administration of reemployment services, and under WIA, these interstate differences are likely to increase. Such differences represent both politics and efforts to deliver reemployment services effectively.

Since 1999, the Michigan Department of Career Development (MDCD) has been responsible for the state's reemployment and training programs. Originally, the MDCD consisted of three agencies—the Employment Service Agency, which has already been discussed; the Office of Workforce Development, whose main responsibility is to administer Work First, the state's welfare-to-work program, but which also administers other training programs; and Michigan Rehabilitation Services, whose main responsibility is to administer the Vocational Rehabilitation component of Workers' Compensation (discussed in the following). A later executive order moved three additional agencies into MDCD—the offices of Career and Technical Education Services, Postsecondary Service, and Adult Education. These latter are essentially educational programs that are outside the scope of this chapter. MDCD currently employs about 1,100 personnel, and in 1999–2000 directed the distribution of nearly $550 million, over 95% of which were federal funds (Michigan Department of Career Development 2000). Many observers expect the organization of these agencies to change after the Engler administration ends.

WIA represents a significant change in the reemployment system, and its success will depend on whether the assumptions underlying its adoption are correct. The preceding discussion suggests the importance of the following research questions:

*1. Is WIA's "work first" approach effective?* WIA has been criticized because it emphasizes job placement over training and reduces funding for training (Bartik and Hollenbeck 2000). An essential question for reemployment policy, then, remains whether programs that encourage employment (or rapid reemployment, even in a low-wage job) are better for workers and society in the long run than are government training programs.

*2. What is the value of various reemployment services?* Of the reemployment services traditionally provided by the ES—job referral, counseling and assessment, job development, and other (intensive) services—only job referral and intensive services have been evaluated comprehensively. However, existing evidence on the effectiveness of referrals has been criticized because, unlike the most convincing evidence on employment and training policies, it has not

been based on randomized trials. Also, the intrinsic value of intensive job search assistance remains unclear. Existing experimental research suggests that job search workshops reduce unemployment duration by imposing an additional requirement on UI recipients (that is, the requirement to report for services) rather than by enhancing workers' job search abilities per se (Balducchi, Johnson, and Gritz 1997). In order for One-Stop Centers to function effectively, knowledge of what services work best for various groups of workers is essential.

*3. Do the arguments in favor of a public labor exchange—such as those made by Bendick (1989) more than a decade ago—continue to hold in a day of relatively easy Internet access?* Little is known about the value of universal access to information of the kind available through America's Job Bank, the computerized national labor exchange. Arguments for the public subsidy and provision of information on jobs depend on the value of such information and the failure of private markets to generate enough information.

*4. How is the performance of reemployment services best gauged?* The performance indicators set out in WIA have been criticized by researchers for their focus on easily measurable outcomes that are weakly related to the value of reemployment services and that may create incentives for One-Stop Centers to assist those applicants who are least in need of services (that is, to "cream"). For example, emphasis on the "entered-employment rate"—the proportion of applicants who enter employment within ninety days—can be expected to induce One-Stop Centers to focus on workers who might easily find jobs on their own rather than on workers requiring greater effort to place (U.S. General Accounting Office 2002). There is much need for research into performance measures that are easily obtained and that also gauge the benefits and costs of services provided.

WIA brings reemployment policy closer to the focus on job placement and "work first" that existed before the emergence of federally funded training programs in the 1960s, but with a twist. While attempting to retain what many view as the benefits of a reemployment system that receives substantial direction from local community interests, WIA promises to centralize the locus of information, training, and other services that help unemployed workers in One-Stop Centers. Evaluating whether WIA is effective and learning what can be done to improve the reemployment system will require data and innovative research that will occupy policy makers and researchers for years to come.

## Workers' Compensation and Vocational Rehabilitation

Every state except Texas requires virtually every employer to carry insurance that covers and compensates workers who are injured on the job or suffer work-related illness. This Workers' Disability Compensation (WC) insurance covers medical care associated with the injury or illness, occupational rehabilitation services necessary before the worker can return to work, and cash benefits that partially replace the earnings lost by the worker as a result of the injury.

Unlike UI, WC has no federal component—each state has adopted a WC system without federal incentives or mandates. All but four states adopted WC between 1911 and 1921 (Michigan's WC law dates to 1912). Before WC existed, liability for a workplace injury essentially fell on the worker. In order to recover any damages resulting from a workplace injury, a worker needed to sue the employer and show that the employer's negligence had caused the injury. Even workers who prevailed received a remedy only after great expense and long delay. In contrast, WC shifts much of the liability for workplace injuries to the employer.[5]

Every WC law has three essential features. First, WC is a no-fault insurance system—if a worker is injured on the job, he or she receives benefits that are specified in the law, regardless of who is at fault. Second, WC is intended as the exclusive remedy for workplace injuries and hence limits the employer's liability. That is, in exchange for buying WC insurance, the employer's liability is limited to providing the benefits specified in the law, and workers give up their right to sue the employer in exchange for the certainty of receiving those specified benefits in a timely manner. Third, employer participation in the system is mandatory—with few exceptions, employers are required to buy WC insurance that provides benefits specified in the law. (In Michigan and six other states, employers with fewer than three workers are exempt from

coverage. Most states have special provisions allowing exemption of some agricultural and domestic employers.)

Although the principles of WC are clear, disputes arise routinely over whether an injury or illness is compensable (for example, is the injury or illness in fact work-related?), as do questions about the adequacy of medical treatment, rehabilitation services, and earnings replacement benefits. Each state has procedures for handling such disputes, which arise in roughly 20% of Michigan's WC claims. The state provides and administers these dispute resolution procedures, which include mediation, a pretrial hearing, a trial conducted before a WC magistrate who specializes in WC cases, and an appeals process that includes review by the Workers' Compensation Appellate Commission. Claimants often employ attorneys to represent them in such procedures, and civil lawsuits are possible in unusual cases (Falaris, Link, and Staten 1995). Welch (2000) includes a useful guide to dispute resolution procedures in Michigan.

## Workers' Compensation Benefits in Michigan and Neighboring States

It is useful to begin by distinguishing between "medical only" claims and "lost-time" claims. Most WC claims are for relatively minor injuries that involve medical treatment but no wage replacement benefits. Nationally during 1996–98, these "medical only" cases have been estimated to account for 76% of all WC *claims*, but for only 6.2% of all WC *benefits paid* (Mont et al. 2002). Lost-time claims involve payment of cash wage replacement benefits. In Michigan, the number of medical-only claims is not tracked, but the number of lost-time cases has fallen sharply from about 95,000 in 1988 to under 44,000 in 2001, reflecting a general decline in workplace injury rates (Welch 2002).

WC claims that do involve payment of wage replacement benefits are of five types. "Temporary total" benefits are paid to workers who are expected to recover but are unable to work at all for some time. Some workers with a temporary disability return to work before they recover fully, taking on less work for a period of time during which they receive "temporary partial" benefits. Workers who are not expected to recover fully from an injury or illness receive "permanent" disability benefits, which may be

**TABLE 19.6**

**Workers' Compensation Benefits in Michigan and Neighboring States, 2002**

|  | Michigan | Illinois | Indiana | Ohio | Wisconsin |
|---|---|---|---|---|---|
| Medical benefits | full | full | full | 90 days[b] | full |
|   Initial physician selection | employer | worker | employer | employer | worker |
| Temporary total benefits: |  |  |  |  |  |
|   waiting period | 7 days | 3 days | 7 days | 7 days | 3 days |
|   paid retroactively after | 2 weeks | 14 days | >21 days | — | >7 days |
|   as % of worker's wage | 80 | 66.7 | 66.7 | 72 (12 weeks) | 66.7 |
|    | (after-tax) |  |  | then 66.7 |  |
|   weekly minimum | none | $101–$124 | $50 | $206 | $30 |
|   weekly maximum | $644 | $956 | $508 | $618 | $582 |
|   as % of SAWW[a] | 90 | 133.3 | na | 100 | 100 |
|   maximum duration | none | none | 500 weeks | none | none |
| Permanent partial benefits: |  |  |  |  |  |
|   Scheduled: |  |  |  |  |  |
|     hand |  |  |  |  |  |
|     (maximum) | 215 weeks | 190 weeks | $53,500 | 175 weeks | 400 weeks |
|      | ($138,460) | ($286,896) |  | ($108,150) | ($73,600) |
|     eye |  |  |  |  |  |
|     (maximum) | 162 weeks | 160 weeks | $43,500 | 125 weeks | 275 weeks |
|      | ($104,328) | ($191,264) |  | ($77,250) | ($50,600) |
|   Nonscheduled: |  |  |  |  |  |
|     as % of wage | 80 | 60 | 66.7 | na | 66.7 |
|      | (after-tax) |  |  |  |  |
|     weekly minimum | $179 | $81-97 | none | none | $30 |
|     weekly maximum | $644 | $516 | $508 | $618 | $184 |
|     as % of SAWW[a] | 90 | na | na | 100 | 66.7 |
|     maximum duration | none | none | none | none | 1000 weeks |

SOURCE: Clifton et al. (2001).

(a) SAWW is the state average weekly wage.

(b) In Ohio, a worker must be examined by the Bureau of Workers' Compensation Medical Section after ninety days of temporary total compensation to determine eligibility for continued treatment and compensation.

either "permanent partial" or "permanent total." Permanent total benefits (along with death benefits, which are the fifth type of benefit) account for just less than 1% of all WC *cases* involving wage replacement benefits, but for 11% of all WC *benefits* that involve wage replacement (Mont et al. 2002). For further discussion, see Woodbury (2002c).

Table 19.6 summarizes benefits provided by WC in Michigan and its neighboring states. Michigan and three neighboring states provide "full" medical benefits to WC recipients, meaning that all "reasonable and necessary" medical care associated with the covered injury or illness is provided or reimbursed. In Ohio (the exception), a worker must be examined by the Bureau of Workers' Compensation Medical Section after ninety days of temporary total compensation to determine eligibility for continued treatment and compensation. Ohio is unusual in this limitation (only six other states limit medical benefits under WC in some way). Nevertheless, to contain the costs of medical benefits under WC, insurers in Michigan and elsewhere have resorted to a number of expedients, such as managed care and fee schedules that specify the maximum a health care provider can charge for a given service (similar to the fee schedules that exist for Medicare and private health coverage). Also, in Michigan, Indiana, and Ohio, the employer may make the initial selection of the health care provider.

In Michigan and its neighboring states, vocational rehabilitation benefits are provided by law; hence, the employer is responsible for rehabilitation costs. In Michigan, Illinois, and

Indiana the worker is required to accept vocational rehabilitation or suffer reduced wage replacement benefits. Michigan, Indiana, and Ohio have rehabilitation units that provide rehabilitation services directly. Michigan Rehabilitation Services, in addition, provides referrals and monitors cases.

In most states, WC wage replacement benefits —temporary and permanent, partial and total— are specified as two-thirds of a worker's pre-tax, pre-injury weekly wages up to a maximum. The maximum is usually specified as a percentage of the state's average weekly wage (SAWW in table 19.6). This is the case in the states that neighbor Michigan, except for Ohio, where temporary total benefits are 72% of pre-injury wages for the first twelve weeks of payment. Wage replacement benefits are not subject to either federal or state income taxation, in contrast to UI benefits. Also, in all states, wage replacement benefits start only after a waiting period of three to seven days, although many states pay benefits for the waiting period retroactively if the disability exceeds some specified period of time. (Table 19.6 shows the waiting periods and retroactivity for temporary total benefits.)

In contrast to most other states, Michigan specifies wage replacement benefits as 80% of a worker's "spendable" (or after-tax) pre-injury weekly wages, up to 90% of the SAWW. (Five other states also determine benefits as a percentage of spendable or after-tax earnings.) To determine the worker's pre-injury wage, Michigan averages wages in the highest thirty-nine of the fifty-two weeks before the injury.

Permanent partial benefits, summarized at the bottom of table 19.6, are the most contentious category of benefits because disputes arise over both the degree of disability and whether the disability is truly permanent. Permanent partial benefits may be paid in either of two ways. First, "scheduled" benefits (called "specific loss" benefits in Michigan) are paid for specific injuries that are listed in the law, such as loss of a hand. Michigan and most states pay scheduled loss benefits as a number of weeks of benefits up to a dollar maximum. Table 19.6 shows the scheduled loss benefits paid for loss of a hand and loss of an eye in Michigan and its neighboring states. For example, a worker who loses a hand in Michigan receives 215 weeks of benefits (up to $138,460) regardless of the amount of work time lost.

Second, nonscheduled benefits are paid for injuries that are not listed in the law, such as a back injury. Determination of nonscheduled benefits can be quite complicated (Berkowitz and Burton 1987). In Michigan, an attempt is made to estimate the wage loss resulting from the disability (in many cases the wage loss is negotiated). Many other states use a level of disability expressed as a percentage to determine nonscheduled permanent partial benefits. The bottom panel of table 19.6 shows how nonscheduled permanent partial benefits compare in Michigan and neighboring states.

In 1972, the National Commission on State Workmen's Compensation published recommended standards for state WC laws (National Commission on State Workmen's Compensation 1972). Michigan's law currently meets many of the commission's recommendations, but in two areas Michigan's law falls short of both the commission's recommendations and the laws of neighboring states. First, the commission's recommendations call for maximum wage replacement benefits equal to 100% of the SAWW. Illinois, Ohio, and Wisconsin do so, but Michigan sets its maximum at 90% of the SAWW. (Indiana sets its maximum by statute, rather than in relation to SAWW, a practice that also fails the commission's recommendations.) Second, the commission's recommendations call for broader coverage provisions than does Michigan's law. In particular, Michigan does not require employers of fewer than three workers to carry WC, whereas neighboring states make coverage compulsory even for very small employers.

### Workers' Compensation Costs in Michigan and Neighboring States

During 2000, private insurance companies provided roughly 58% of the WC insurance in Michigan (Mont et al. 2002). The remaining 42% was provided by employers who self-insured— Michigan, like most states, allows companies that are large and financially sound to administer their own WC programs and provide the benefits that are specified in the law. (Also, smaller employers belonging to a trade organization may "group self-insure.")

A third option for providing WC insurance currently exists in half the states—a state-operated insurance fund. In twenty states, these funds are "competitive," meaning that they exist alongside private insurers in the state. In five

**TABLE 19.7**

**Measures of Workers' Compensation Costs in Michigan, Neighboring States, and the United States, Various Years**

| | Michigan | Illinois | Indiana | Ohio | Wisconsin | United States |
|---|---|---|---|---|---|---|
| Adjusted manual rate (per $100 of payroll, 2000) | 2.40 | 2.62 | 1.32 | 2.89 | 2.01 | 2.26[a] |
| Adjusted manual rate (per $100 of payroll, 1995) | 2.69 | 2.80 | 1.40 | 3.36 | 2.04 | 2.97[b] |

SOURCE: Row 1 from Research and Analysis Section, Oregon Department of Consumer and Business Services (2002); row 2 from Thomason, Schmidle, and Burton (2001, tables C.17 and C.18).
(a) Adjusted manual rate of the median state.
(b) Weighted mean of all states.

states, the largest of which is Ohio, the state fund is "exclusive," meaning that private insurers are not permitted to offer WC insurance in the state. Michigan had a competitive state fund until the end of 1994, when that fund was privatized (it was bought by Blue Cross Blue Shield and is now known as the Accident Fund). Michigan is the only state that has privatized a state fund. In fact, the trend nationally has been toward creating competitive state funds—Minnesota did so in 1984, and eight other states followed during the 1990s. These state funds were created mainly because regulation of WC premium rates at low levels resulted in losses for many private insurers, which caused them to pull out of those states (see following). The relative merits of state funds and the implications of the various arrangements for providing WC have been treated at length by Thomason, Schmidle, and Burton (2001).

Until the early 1980s, rates for WC premiums were set in every state by a regulatory process that generated a so-called manual rate (stated in dollars per $100 of payroll) for each of over five hundred industry-occupational classifications. (For a summary, see Woodbury 2002c.) These administered prices were charged by all insurers, with some exceptions (which required approval of the state WC bureau), usually for medium and large employers that might be experience rated.

Since 1981, most states have moved to "open competition" in setting WC premiums. Michigan and Illinois were early to do so (in 1983 and 1982, respectively), and Indiana did so in 1989. (Ohio has an exclusive state fund, and Wisconsin has maintained a system of administered pricing.) Open competition can take various forms, but in general it means that insurers can compete for business by offering employers different pre-

mium rates at the start of the policy period. Rates are still based on the employer's industry and the occupational classification of workers, but each insurer can now set his or her own rate. Most large employers are experience rated, and insurers frequently adjust their basic rates for different employers. Not surprisingly, insurers resisted the move to competition, but it is now well established in most states.

Interstate comparisons of WC costs are not straightforward. The main difficulty is the need to adjust for interstate differences in industry composition, which influence statewide averages of WC premiums paid. Difficulties also arise in obtaining comparable data across states, estimating insurers' loadings for administrative expenses and profits, and estimating the effects of experience rating and other discounts on premiums ultimately paid. Nevertheless, careful interstate comparisons of WC costs do exist, and two are summarized in table 19.7.

The first row of table 19.7 reports adjusted manual rates that have been constructed by the Oregon Department of Consumer and Business Services (2002). These are weighted averages of manual rates in fifty industry-occupation categories that account for 68% of covered payroll in Oregon. Weights applied are derived from Oregon's industry-occupational mix, rather than the industry-occupational mix of the United States, and this is their main drawback: they suggest the premium rate that the average *Oregon* employer would face if he or she moved to another state. Nevertheless, Oregon's industry-occupational mix is not so unlike that of the country generally that these rates cannot be used to give some idea of relative interstate WC rates.

The Oregon adjusted rates suggest that WC costs in Michigan are below those in Ohio and

Illinois, and above those in Wisconsin and Indiana. (Indiana's WC costs routinely come in last or close to last in such interstate comparisons, reflecting what many WC researchers believe to be an inadequate benefit structure.) Nationally, Michigan is slightly above the median state. This is in sharp contrast to Michigan's position twenty years ago, when it was one of the highest WC cost states in the nation despite having statutory benefits that (as now) are no more generous than the median state's (Burton, Hunt, and Krueger 1985; Rence 1982).

The second row of table 19.7 reports the 1995 adjusted manual rates that were constructed through a laborious process by Thomason, Schmidle, and Burton (2001, 317–92). These adjusted rates represent the premiums that the average U.S. employer would face if he or she moved to a given state. Unfortunately, 1995 is the last year for which these adjusted manual rates have been constructed, but they tell a story similar to that told by the Oregon index with respect to Michigan's position compared with its neighboring states. In addition, Thomason, Schmidle, and Burton constructed a national adjusted

manual rate, which suggests that Michigan's WC costs were slightly below the national average in the early and middle 1990s.

What accounts for the relative decline in WC costs in Michigan during the last twenty years? In the late 1970s, Michigan's business community complained that Michigan's WC costs were high by national standards, and evidence both at the time and subsequently supports this view (see figure 19.1). After several attempts, the Michigan legislature passed major changes in WC in 1981, including comprehensive coordination of benefits, a restricted definition of disability, and managed care as a way of containing medical costs (Hunt and Eccleston 1990). Also, as already noted, the legislature adopted open competition in the setting of WC rates, which became effective in 1983. These changes appear to have brought Michigan's WC costs closer to the national average from about 1982 on. Indeed, after an upward deviation during 1990–92, Michigan's costs appear to have been somewhat below the national average during the mid-1990s, and the Oregon data suggest that Michigan remains close to the average in WC costs.

**FIGURE 19.1**

**Adjusted Average Workers' Compensation Manual Rates, Michigan and the United States, 1975–95**

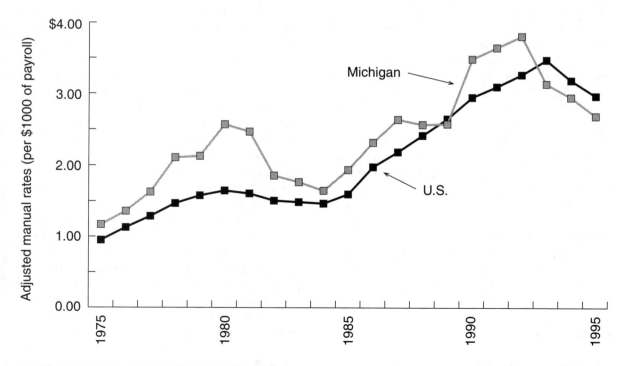

SOURCE: Thomason, Schmidle, and Burton (2001, tables C.17 and C.18).

### Workers' Compensation and Workplace Safety

The National Commission on State Workmen's Compensation (1972) made workplace safety one of the goals of WC. The WC system could improve workplace safety for at least three reasons. First, if it is less costly for employers than for workers to take steps that improve workplace safety, then WC improves workplace safety by placing the liability for workplace injuries on the employer. (This is the case in theory as long as it is costly for workers and employers to negotiate [Butler 1999; Burton and Chelius 1997].) Second, state WC agencies and WC insurance carriers (both private and public) provide employers with loss prevention services, which may include safety consulting. Third, the experience rating of WC premiums creates a financial incentive for employers to takes steps to reduce workplace accidents and injuries.

A full discussion of workplace safety policy and the relative merits of WC versus safety regulation is beyond the scope of this chapter. However, Burton and Chelius (1997) offer a thorough review of the cases for and against government intervention through direct regulation (as with the Occupational Safety and Health Act of 1970) and mandatory WC (which entails both financial incentives and various methods of managing workplace risks). Research on OSHA has been unable to show that direct regulation improves workplace safety, probably because the regulations that are enforced bear only a tangential relation to workplace risks. The evidence on WC is more mixed. Research using data from the early twentieth century suggests that workplace death rates did fall after adoption of WC. However, research on whether experience rating reduces injury rates suggests relatively small impacts (Burton and Chelius 1997). Finally, the evidence on the effectiveness of expedients like mandatory safety committees and meetings between workers and managers is difficult to interpret; often such measures are adopted along with other measures (like additional government safety inspections), making it difficult to draw convincing conclusions. In short, much remains to be done to understand the mix of policies that would deliver the optimal level of workplace safety.

### Policy Issues

Apart from privatizing its state fund, Michigan has made no major changes to its WC system since the early 1980s, reflecting a period of stable or declining costs along with benefits that were in line with those of neighboring states. Changes that have been made pertain mainly to confidentiality issues surrounding release of medical information. This period of stability contrasts with many other states, which experienced sharply increased costs during the 1980s and early 1990s, along with rates that were held by state regulators below the rates needed to cover those costs (Thomason, Schmidle, and Burton 2001, chap. 2). The combination of higher costs and low regulated rates resulted in large losses for insurers and prompted many private insurers to leave states where they were writing WC policies. The result was a series of state crises during the mid- and late-1990s in which employers could not obtain required insurance.

Michigan avoided such a "crisis" because its 1981 reforms had moved the system toward managed medical care, and because Michigan was among the early adopters of open competition in setting WC rates. Moreover, injury rates fell during the 1990s (Ruser 1999). Hence, modest increases in medical costs, premiums set by competition, and lower injury rates have created a relatively problem-free and stable environment for WC in Michigan during the past fifteen years.

The question now is whether this period of stability can continue in the face of medical costs that are projected to rise dramatically in the future. Existing evidence suggests that managed care has had a one-time effect on medical costs, and that those costs can be expected to resume a growth rate that outpaces the growth rate of prices generally (Chernew et al. 1998). How the WC system would respond to a resumption of high growth of medical costs is an open question. From an economic standpoint, the appropriate response to an increase in the cost of injuries is increased efforts to prevent injuries in the workplace, and the key for policy is to induce employers and workers to create an appropriately greater level of workplace safety. However, other responses can be imagined: attempts to restrict medical care, shifting costs to workers through deductibles and co-payments, and simply "absorbing" the increased costs (which would likely have other consequences, such as reduced employment and output). Clearly, growth in medical benefits under WC is the most likely source of future controversy and policy debate for Michigan's WC system.

## Conclusions

UI, Michigan Works!, and WC are unique among Michigan's programs because they replace lost earnings and deliver services to workers on a regular basis. Other programs that are intended to improve workers' well-being are regulatory—the Michigan Department of Consumer and Industry Services oversees workplace conditions under the Michigan Occupational Safety and Health Act, and the Michigan Department of Civil Rights investigates complaints about employment discrimination. Each requires the commitment of resources for administration, but none involves the regular payment of benefits or delivery of services to workers.

Controversy is the norm for UI, Michigan Works!, and WC. UI has become increasingly contentious in the wake of welfare reform and the first recession in a decade. The program's critics offer various suggestions for reform that follow from different views of the program's goals. Some see UI as an anti-poverty program; others see it primarily as social insurance. It is not likely that the tension between these two views will be resolved soon.

Michigan Works! has faced similar tensions: Given limited resources, should the state focus on providing second-chance training to disadvantaged workers or relatively inexpensive reemployment services for job-ready workers? Is Michigan Works! providing the best possible mix of services to assist workers in gaining employment?

WC has been relatively free of controversy during the past decade, but this period of relative calm may end soon as medical costs resume their rise. Workers' Compensation has faced such pressures in the past and has managed to adjust, albeit after a lag. The main question raised here is whether the system will respond to increased WC medical costs by attempting to improve workplace safety, or by restricting medical treatment and cutting benefits.

Controversies over these programs should not obscure the fact that each has succeeded over a period of decades in gaining widespread acceptance as essential to the efficient functioning of the labor market. Arguments over the generosity of benefits and the appropriate extent of training for disadvantaged workers are secondary compared with arguments from decades past over whether these programs should even exist.

The challenge, however, is to ensure that these programs return benefits in relation to their costs. It is here that Michigan has been less progressive than other states—notably Illinois and Wisconsin in the Midwest—that have acted on their own or cooperated with the federal government to design and encourage research that could add to the understanding of these programs and improve their operations. This is especially true of UI and reemployment programs, for which Michigan's debates have centered on the views of political interests and have often neglected the perspective that research could offer. A willingness to accept that a program may have flaws and that all the answers do not already exist is a prerequisite to admitting research as a component of policy debate. Whether Michigan will, in the new millennium, be more receptive to the role of research in debates over programs for workers is an open question.

■

## REFERENCES

Advisory Council on Unemployment Compensation. 1995. *Unemployment insurance in the United States: Benefits, financing, and coverage.* Washington, D.C.: Advisory Council on Unemployment Compensation.

Balducchi, David E., Terry R. Johnson, and R. Mark Gritz. 1997. The role of the employment service. In *Unemployment insurance in the United States: Analysis of policy issues,* edited by Christopher J. O'Leary and Stephen A. Wandner. Kalamazoo, Mich.: W. E. Upjohn Institute.

Bartik, Timothy J., and Kevin M. Hollenbeck. 2000. The role of public policy in skills development of black workers in the 21st century. Unpublished manuscript, W. E. Upjohn Institute, Kalamazoo, Mich.

Bendick, M. 1989. Matching workers and job opportunities: What role for the federal-state employment service? In *Rethinking employment policy,* edited by D. L. Bawden and F. Skidmore. Washington, D.C.: Urban Institute.

Berkowitz, Monroe, and John F. Burton Jr. 1987. *Permanent disability benefits in workers' compensation.* Kalamazoo, Mich.: W. E. Upjohn Institute.

Blaustein, Saul J. 1993. *Unemployment insurance in the United States: The first half-century.* Kalamazoo, Mich.: W. E. Upjohn Institute.

Bloom, Howard S., Larry L. Orr, Stephen H. Bell, George Cave, Fred Doolittle, Winston Lin, and

Johannes M. Bos. 1997. The benefits and costs of JTPA Title II-A programs: Key findings from the national JTPA study. *Journal of Human Resources* 32 (summer): 549–76.

Burton, John F., Jr., and James R. Chelius. 1997. Workplace safety and health regulations: Rationale and results. In *Government regulation of the employment relationship*, edited by Bruce E. Kaufman. Madison, Wis.: Industrial Relations Research Association.

Burton, John F., H. Allan Hunt, and Alan Krueger. 1985. Interstate variations in the employers' cost of workers' compensation, with particular reference to Michigan and other Great Lake States. Ithaca, N.Y.: Workers' Disability Income Systems, Inc., February.

Butler, Richard J. 1999. *The economics of social insurance and employee benefits.* Boston: Kluwer Academic Publishers.

Card, David, and Phillip B. Levine. 1994. Unemployment insurance taxes and the cyclical and seasonal properties of unemployment. *Journal of Public Economics* 53 (January): 1–29.

Chernew, Michael E., Richard A. Hirth, Seema S. Sonnad, Rachel Ermann, and A. Mark Fendrick. 1998. Managed care, medical technology, and health care costs: A review of the evidence. *Medical Care Research and Review* 55 (September): 259–88.

Clifton, Josh, Nancy Grover, Leslie Lake, and Kerry Loomis. 2001. *2002 workers' compensation year book.* Horsham, Penn.: LRP Publications.

Corson, Walter, and Paul T. Decker. 2000. Using the unemployment insurance system to target services to dislocated workers. In *Long-term unemployment and reemployment policies,* edited by L. J. Bassi and S. A. Woodbury. Stamford, Conn.: JAI Press/Elsevier.

Corson, Walter, and Walter Nicholson. 1982. *The federal supplemental benefits program: An appraisal of emergency unemployment insurance benefits.* Kalamazoo, Mich.: W. E. Upjohn Institute.

Davidson, Carl, and Stephen A. Woodbury. 1997. Optimal unemployment insurance. *Journal of Public Economics* 64 (June): 359–87.

Eberts, Randall W., and Christopher J. O'Leary. 1996. Design of the worker profiling and reemployment services system and evaluation in Michigan. W. E. Upjohn Institute Staff Working Paper 96–41, April.

Emsellem, Maurice, Jessica Goldberg, Rick McHugh, Wendell Primus, Rebecca Smith, and Jeffrey Wenger. 2002. Failing the unemployed: A state by state examination of unemployment insurance systems. New York, N.Y.: National Employment Law Project, March.

Fagnoni, C. M. 2000. Workforce Investment Act: Implementation status and the integration of TANF services. Washington, D.C.: U.S. General Accounting Office, GAO/T-HEHS-00–145, June.

Falaris, Evangelos M., Charles R. Link, and Michael E. Staten. 1995. *Causes of litigation in workers' compensation programs.* Kalamazoo, Mich.: W. E. Upjohn Institute.

Gustafson, Cynthia K., and Phillip Levine. 1998. Less-skilled workers, welfare reform, and the unemployment insurance system. National Bureau of Economic Research Working Paper 6489, March.

Haber, William, and Merrill G. Murray. 1966. *Unemployment insurance in the American economy.* Homewood, Ill.: Richard D. Irwin.

Hamermesh, Daniel S. 1977. *Jobless pay and the economy.* Baltimore, Md.: Johns Hopkins University Press.

Hunt, H. Allan, and Stacey M. Eccleston. 1990. *Workers' compensation in Michigan: Administrative inventory.* Cambridge, Mass.: Workers' Compensation Research Institute.

Kaye, Kelleen. 2001. Reexamining the potential role of unemployment insurance as a safety net for workers at risk of public assistance receipt. Paper prepared for the National Conference on Workforce Security Issues, Washington, D.C., June.

LaLonde, Robert J. 1995. The promise of public sector-sponsored training programs. *Journal of Economic Perspectives* 9 (spring): 149–68.

Meyer, Bruce D. 1995. Lessons from the U.S. unemployment insurance experiments. *Journal of Economic Literature* 33 (March): 91–131.

Michigan Department of Career Development. n.d. 1999–2000 annual report. Available at *www.michigan.gov/mdcd.*

Mont, Daniel, John F. Burton Jr., Virginia Reno, and Cecili Thompson. 2002. Workers' compensation: Benefits, coverage, and costs, 2000 new estimates. Washington, D.C.: National Academy of Social Insurance, June.

Munts, Raymond C., and Ephraim Asher. 1980. Cross-subsidies among industries from 1969 to 1978. In *Unemployment compensation: Studies and research,* vol. 2, edited by Raymond Munts. Washington, D.C.: National Commission on Unemployment Compensation.

National Commission on State Workmen's Compensation. 1972. *Report of the commission.* Washington, D.C.: U.S. Government Printing Office.

O'Leary, Christopher J. 1998. The adequacy of unemployment insurance benefits. In *Reform of the unemployment insurance system,* edited by Laurie J. Bassi and Stephen A. Woodbury. Stamford,

Conn.: JAI Press.

O'Leary, Christopher J., and Stephen A. Wandner, eds. 1997. *Unemployment insurance in the United States: Analysis of policy issues.* Kalamazoo, Mich.: W. E. Upjohn Institute.

Oregon Department of Consumer and Business Services. 2002. Workers' compensation premium report, calendar year 2000. Oregon Department of Consumer and Business Services, Research and Analysis Section, March. Available at *www.cbs .or.us.*

Rence, Cynthia. 1982. Costs of social insurance programs. In *Michigan's fiscal and economic structure,* edited by Harvey E. Brazer and Deborah S. Laren. Ann Arbor: University of Michigan Press.

Ruser, John W. 1999. The changing composition of lost-workday injuries. *Monthly Labor Review* (June): 11–17.

Thomason, Terry, Timothy J. Schmidle, and John F. Burton Jr. 2001. *Workers' compensation benefits, costs, and safety under alternative insurance arrangements.* Kalamazoo, Mich.: W. E. Upjohn Institute.

U.S. Department of Labor. 2001. U.S. employment service annual report: Program report data. Washington, D.C.: Employment and Training Administration, U.S. Employment Service, May.

———. 2002a. *Comparison of state unemployment insurance laws 2002.* Washington, D.C.: Employment and Training Administration, Office of Workforce Security.

———. 2002b. UI data summary. Washington, D.C.: Employment and Training Administration, Office of Workforce Security. Available at <workforcesecurity.doleta.gov/unemploy/ content/data.asp>.

U.S. General Accounting Office. 1996. Job Training Partnership Act: Long-term earnings and employment outcomes. Washington, D.C.: U.S. General Accounting Office, GAO/HEHS-96–40, March.

———. 2000. Unemployment insurance: Role as a safety net for low-wage workers is limited. Washington, D.C.: U.S. General Accounting Office, GAO-01–181, December.

———. 2002. Workforce Investment Act: Improvements needed in performance measures to provide a more accurate picture of WIA's effectiveness. Washington, D.C.: U.S. General Accounting Office, GAO-02–275, February.

UWC—Strategic Services on Unemployment & Workers' Compensation. 2002. Highlights of state unemployment compensation laws, January 2002. Washington, D.C.: National Foundation for Unemployment Compensation & Workers' Compensation.

Vroman, Wayne. 2001. *Low benefit recipiency in state unemployment insurance programs.* Washington, D.C.: The Urban Institute.

Welch, Edward M. 2000. An overview of workers' compensation in Michigan. Lansing, Mich.: Bureau of Workers' Disability Compensation, Michigan Department of Consumer and Industry Affairs, November. Available at *www.michigan.gov/bwuc.*

———. 2002. Bureau data. *Michigan Workers' Compensation Reporter* 12 (March): 2–3.

Williams, C. Arthur, Jr., John G. Turnbull, and Earl F. Cheit. 1982. *Economic and social security: Social insurance and other approaches.* 5th ed. New York: Wiley.

Woodbury, Stephen A. 2002a. The persistence of inter-industry and inter-firm subsidies under unemployment insurance. Manuscript, Michigan State University and W. E. Upjohn Institute for Employment Research, March.

———. 2002b. Unemployment insurance overpayments and underpayments. Testimony prepared for Hearings on Unemployment Fraud and Abuse, Human Resources Subcommittee, House Committee on Ways and Means, 11 June.

———. 2002c. Income replacement and reemployment programs in Michigan and neighboring states. W. E. Upjohn Institute Staff Working Paper 02–86, October. Available at *www.upjohninstitute.org.*

Woodbury, Stephen A., and Murray Rubin. 1997. The duration of benefits. In *Unemployment insurance in the United States: Analysis of policy issues,* edited by Christopher J. O'Leary and Stephen A. Wandner. Kalamazoo, Mich.: W. E. Upjohn Institute.

## NOTES

1. Details can be found at the Michigan Bureau of Workers' & Unemployment Compensation website: *www.michigan.gov/bwuc.* I am grateful to Robin Norton of the Bureau for clarifying several points. Useful general references on UI include Advisory Council on Unemployment Compensation (1995); Blaustein (1993); and O'Leary and Wandner (1997). See also U.S. Department of Labor (2002a) and UWC (2002).

2. Note that Michigan's 4.1% factor results in a weekly benefit slightly greater than 50% of average high-quarter earnings. Multiplying high-quarter earnings by $\frac{1}{26}$ (3.85%) would yield a replacement rate of exactly 50% because a quarter has thirteen weeks.

3. Most states are less specific than Michigan in defining "suitable" work; indeed, most simply state that a worker must be available to accept work, which is likely to exclude more workers from eligibility. As table 19.2 shows, among neighboring states, only Ohio specifies that UI claimants must be available for "suitable" work.

4. This chronology comes from Haber and Murray (1966); Bendick (1989); Balducchi, Johnson, and Gritz (1997); and Fagnoni (2000).

5. Useful general references on workers' compensation include Butler (1999); Thomason, Schmidle, and Burton (2001); and Williams, Turnbull, and Cheit (1982).

# 20

# Public Pensions and Pension Policy in Michigan

*L. E. Papke*

The purpose of this chapter is to acquaint readers with the public retirement systems in Michigan. I focus on aspects of public pensions that are of interest to Michigan taxpayers and officials in state and local government—their basic structure, financial soundness, and current matters of policy interest.[1] As the eighth-most populous state in the United States, Michigan has a large public pension sector. State plans in Michigan provide an important source of retirement income for 170,624 retirees and beneficiaries. Another 378,247 workforce members count on benefit payments in retirement. Payments from the state systems alone to pension recipients totaled $2.4 billion in 2001. Local government plans administered through the Municipal Employees' Retirement System add a covered population of almost 63,000.

Recently, Michigan has been at the forefront of public pension reform. In 1997, Michigan closed its traditional defined benefit pension plan to new state employee hires, and the state now offers individual defined contribution accounts in its place. This reform of the state's second largest pension plan altered the nature of the long-term obligation facing Michigan taxpayers and the nature of the pension promise for state workers. Further, the Michigan pension system has played a role in recent state budget balancing through the use of early retirement schemes for public employees.

In the discussion that follows, I will be focusing primarily on five plans: the Michigan State Employees' Retirement System (MSERS), the Michigan State Police Retirement System (MSPRS), and the Michigan Legislative Retirement System (MLRS), all sponsored and administered by the state, and the Michigan Public Schools Employees' Retirement System (MPSERS) and the Michigan Judges' Retirement System (MJRS), both multiemployer plans administered by the State of Michigan. Except for the MLRS, which is separately administered, the state Office of Retirement Services administers these plans.

In addition, I will be discussing local government pension plans, many of which are administered by a voluntary association created under state law: the Municipal Employees' Retirement System of Michigan (MERS). The state of Michigan has 83 counties, 1,242 townships, 273 cities, 262 villages, and an unknown number of special authorities with taxing power ranging from entities such as the Capital Area Transportation Authority to local fire districts funded by special assessments. A number of these units may be too small to have pension plans, but others will have multiple plans (separate police and firefighter plans, for example). MERS's $3.6 billion defined

## TABLE 20.1

**Michigan's State-Administered Retirement Systems and Municipal Employees Retirement System (defined benefit plans only)**

| System; Date of Valuation | Actuarial Value of Assets[a] | Actuarial Accrued Liability[a] | Number of Active Members | Number of Retirees & Beneficiaries | Average Annual Benefit ($) | Funding Ratio (%) |
|---|---|---|---|---|---|---|
| State employees (Act 240 of 1943) 9/30/01 | 10,337 | 9,474 | 44,967 | 37,111 | 7,268 | 109.1 |
| Public school employees (Act 136 of 1945) 9/30/01 | 36,893 | 37,139 | 318,538 | 130,790 | 14,859 | 99.3 |
| Judges (Act 234 of 1992) 9/30/01 | 291 | 224.7 | 380 | 546 | 29,355 | 129.5 |
| State police (Act 182 of 1986) 9/30/01 | 1,113 | 1,040.7 | 2,137 | 2,382 | 26,724 | 107.0 |
| Legislative (Act 261 of 1957) 9/30/01 | 168.4 | 138.6 | 54 | 242 | N.A. | 121.0 |
| Municipal Retirement (Act 427 of 1984) 12/31/01 | 3,787 | 4,397 | 36,856 | 16,932 | 10,664 | 86.1 |

SOURCE: Comprehensive Annual Financial Report of each system for year in column 1, and Lindquist (1992).
(a) In millions of dollars.

benefit plan has 563 participating municipalities and courts and 120 defined contribution plans. Of the non-MERS members, it is estimated that there are 130 defined benefit pension plans (Gabriel, Roeder, Smith, and Company 2000).

As an obligation of state and local residents, pension and retiree health payments are a significant current and future expense for taxpayers. It is important to note at the outset that all the state-sponsored or administered plans are extremely well funded, with several over 100% funded in the 2001 fiscal year. The MERS system as a whole has a funded ratio of over 85%. Public pension plans in Michigan, and in most states, are prefunded beginning with the first year of employment for a new hire.

While the pension benefits of the current and future retirees of these systems are well protected by these funding levels, the same may not be true of their health benefits. Just as the costs of health care for active workers and their employers are rising, so, too, do retiree health benefit costs projections describe dramatic future costs. Future retiree health obligations for the state-administered plans alone faced a $21 billion obligation in 2001, of which almost $14 billion was for the Michigan Public Schools Retirement System.

Under current law, the health benefits for retirees are paid on a cash basis as costs are incurred. This practice is known as pay-as-you-go financing, or PAYGO for short. The scope and potential impacts of the different funding practices will be discussed in detail later in this chapter.

The following section provides an overview of Michigan's major retirement systems. The third section is a pension primer that will acquaint readers with basic pension concepts and terminology. It summarizes the recent financial health of Michigan's pension systems and includes a glossary of key pension terms that are used throughout the chapter. The fourth section highlights current policy issues facing the Michigan Public School Employees' Retirement System, the Michigan State Employees' Retirement System, and the Michigan Municipal Employees Retirement System. The fifth section briefly introduces retiree health costs and finance that are also part of the various public employees' retirement programs in Michigan. There is a brief conclusion.

### An Overview of Public Retirement Systems in Michigan

The State of Michigan, through the Office of Retirement Services, administers four retirement systems covering 378,247 working and 170,624 retired members (Office of Retirement Services 2002b). It delivered pension payments totaling over $2.45 billion in 2001. The four funds cover public school employees, state employees, state police, and judges. Legislators are covered by the separate statutory Michigan Legislative Retirement System.[2] The state treasurer is responsible for all investments and cash management strategies for the funds. As of the end of their fiscal year, 30 September 2001, these Michigan public pension funds totaled about $49.9 billion, more than twice as large as total own-source tax revenue in Michigan in 2001 ($22.4 billion).

In addition, the Municipal Employees' Retirement System of Michigan (MERS) manages about five hundred separate defined benefit plans for counties, municipalities, school districts, libraries, and other small governmental units that elect to join MERS. MERS manages most of the nonstate governmental unit defined benefit plans, totaling $3.6 billion in assets and covering almost 37,000 active and 17,000 retired members.

Michigan is the eighth-largest state in terms of population in the United States, and Michigan's combined state and local pension funds also rank eighth overall in the United States, totaling about $68.4 billion in the most recent Census of Governments.[3]

Table 20.1 displays the membership, assets, and liabilities of the Michigan pension systems as of the end of the 2001 fiscal year. By far the largest single system is the Michigan Public Schools Employees' Retirement System (MPSERS), with nearly 319,000 active members, almost 131,000 retirees and beneficiaries, and assets of almost $37 billion. The second-largest system is the Michigan State Employees' Retirement System (MSERS), with assets over $10 billion, about 45,000 active members, and 37,000 retirees and beneficiaries.

As in other states, most of the public employees in Michigan are covered by a defined benefit plan. However, in 1997 Michigan dramatically reformed its MSERS plan, effectively phasing out the defined benefit plan for state employees. To help the reader understand the implications of this change and the structure of Michigan's other pension systems for the state budget, the next section is a basic pension primer. It provides background on pension systems generally as well as definitions of key pension terms. Following this, I will discuss some specifics of Michigan's defined benefit plans.

## A Pension Primer

This section describes the basics of defined benefit and defined contribution pension plans. First is an overview of pension plan types. The second section introduces financial basics about defined benefit plan funding and the third section presents recent financial statistics for Michigan's defined benefit plans. The fourth section discusses the relationship between pension reserve funds and state budgets. The final section provides a cursory glossary of key pension terms and abbreviations introduced in this section.

## Overview

There are two general types of pension plans. In a defined benefit (DB) plan, benefits are typically determined by a formula that is a function of a benefit multiplier, years of service, and final average salary. For example, in the Michigan State Employees' Retirement System, the benefit formula is the product of (0.015) times years of service times the highest salary averaged over three years (see appendix A).[4] Thus, a retiree with thirty years of service would receive 45% of salary (30 × 0.015 = 0.45). The benefit is paid in the form of an annuity, that is, a participant receives level payments over his or her lifetime, or the lifetime of a survivor.[5]

In the private sector, a defined benefit plan is often funded primarily by employer contributions (a noncontributory plan). In the public sector, employee contributions are common. All contributions are invested by the sponsor—the state in the case of public plans, or the employer in the case of private plans. The sponsor bears the investment risk of meeting the pension obligation. Unexpectedly high returns on the assets may lead to reductions in the employer's future contribution, while unexpectedly low returns may make it necessary for increased future contributions. One way that pension plans moderate the gains and losses of long-term investment performance is to smooth, or average, both gains and losses over a five-year period. This means that total valuations for the system change more gradually.

In the second type of pension plan, a defined contribution (DC) plan, the sponsor establishes an individual account for each participant. The employer typically makes a monthly or annual contribution for each individual, or may match a pretax contribution by the participant. The participant selects investments from a menu of choices established by the employer. Benefits at retirement are determined by the size of the contributions and the investment earnings on the assets. The employer bears certain administrative and fiduciary responsibilities (such as providing a sufficient number of investment options), but otherwise the employer's obligation ends with the contribution. There is no guaranteed pension benefit with defined contribution plans.

Consider the fundamental difference for taxpayers between a defined benefit and a defined contribution plan. Defined benefit plans promise a certain payment at retirement—this is a long-term obligation. The state, and ultimately, its residents, is responsible for meeting that obligation. What is uncertain is whether the assets set aside to fund the liability are sufficient. All investment risk is borne by the state and its taxpayers.[6]

The state or local government can prefund the defined benefit obligation on an actuarial basis (making contributions over long periods of time) and this should provide assets to make retirement benefit payments in the future. Yet even a fully funded DB plan may become quite poorly funded if assets fail to perform as expected, or if the actuarial assumptions that determine the path of contributions prove incorrect. If the assets are not sufficient to meet the promised pension payment, taxes may have to be increased.[7] Taxpayers can avoid this by moving to another jurisdiction, but only if those locations have a better-funded plan. Of course, it is possible that the plan assets will overperform relative to what is assumed, and the state's subsequent contributions may be reduced.

In contrast, defined contribution plans entail a certain contribution in the current year. The payment by the state government, say, is a current obligation paid by the current generation of taxpayers. This type of plan transfers all investment risk from taxpayers to the pension participant. By definition, the system is always fully funded. There are no future payments for past liabilities with a defined contribution plan.

Clearly, the worst case from the taxpayers' standpoint is a severely underfunded defined benefit plan. An unfunded defined benefit plan makes current-year benefit payments out of current-year appropriations. This method of financing is called cash funding, or pay-as-you-go (PAYGO). A pay-as-you-go system is most likely to lead to funding shortfalls, and also is ultimately more costly because there are no investment earnings to augment the sponsor's contribution. As I will discuss in the following, retiree health benefits are funded on a cash basis in Michigan.

In the private sector, if a defined plan is underfunded and the company files for bankruptcy, most pension benefits are paid by a federal agency, the Pension Benefit Guaranty Corporation (PBGC). That is, the PBGC pays benefits up to a cap. Corporations that sponsor defined benefit plans are required to pay premiums to the PBGC to ensure that most of the defined pension benefits are paid in the event of bankruptcy. In the public sector, taxpayers play the role of the PBGC. The state, through current taxes, prefunds the defined benefit obligation. However, if the fund is insufficient, the state can raise taxes to meet its obligation or can borrow, thus raising future taxes. There is no such insurance for defined contribution plans.

Defined benefit plans traditionally have dominated both the private and public sectors, but in the last twenty years defined contribution plans have become more common in the private sector (Papke 1999). The most common defined contribution plan in the private sector is the 401(k) plan that allows participants as well as employers to make pretax contributions. The Internal Revenue Code sets annual limits on contributions, and the U.S. Department of Labor sets "nondiscrimination" rules to ensure that the tax benefits are distributed among high-paid and lower-paid employees. The transition to defined contribution plans has taken several forms. In some cases, the defined benefit plan has been closed, and only a defined contribution plan has been offered to new hires. In some cases, a defined benefit plan has been retained, but it has been altered to appear like a defined contribution plan to participants. For a discussion of these so-called cash balance plans, see Gale, Papke, and Vanderhei (2002).

While defined benefit plans are still the dominant pension form in the public sector, they are often offered along with a supplemental DC plan.[8] For example, prior to the MSERS pension reform in 1997 that replaced the DB plan with a 401(k) plan for all new hires, the MSERS offered two supplemental DC plans—a 401(k) type and a 457(b) plan.[9]

Generally speaking, there are three major differences between private and public defined benefit plans. First, vesting—becoming legally entitled to a benefit at retirement—takes longer in the public sector. Forty-three percent of public plans nationwide have ten-year cliff vesting (Mitchell, McCarthy, Wisniewski, and Zorn [hereafter Mitchell et al. 2001). That is, a worker is entitled to a pension benefit at retirement once he has worked for ten years. If he terminates employment in his ninth year, for example, he is not entitled to any pension. This is the standard vesting pattern in Michigan (see appendix B). In the private sector, this vesting period is usually shorter— five years with cliff vesting or seven years with graded (partial) vesting.

Second, there are usually regular, though not perfect, inflation increases for pensions in the public sector. MSERS and MPSERS, for example, have inflation adjustment features that do not index perfectly for inflation. Few private-sector plans have automatic indexing, and some never increase benefits after retirement. Instead, private-sector plans tend to rely on ad hoc adjustments that typically make up for less than half of inflation (Hustead and Mitchell 2001).

Third, public defined benefit plans are often contributory, and therefore are often more generous than private plans. That is, employees are required to contribute some fraction of pretax salary to the plan. Nationwide, the average contribution rate is 5% (Hustead and Mitchell 2001). MSERS became noncontributory in 1974, but the other plans, as well as most municipal DB plans, are contributory to some degree.[10]

Because a defined benefit plan requires the employer or the state to pay pension benefits in the future, the state or employer prefunds this long-term debt. Given assumptions about rates of return and life expectancies, actuaries determine the plan obligation and the contributions necessary to prefund benefits over time. The remainder of this section discusses the specifics of DB funding and the financial status of Michigan's DB plans.

## Defined Benefit Plan Funding

Private plans are governed by the Employee Retirement Income Security Act (ERISA) of 1974 that established minimum coverage, participation, funding, vesting, and fiduciary requirements. ERISA mandates that private plans submit periodic, standardized reports to participants and to the U.S. Department of Labor. State and local retirement plans are governed by individual state constitutions and are generally exempt from the provisions of ERISA, but these federal requirements for private plans have influenced public plan design and administration. ERISA also established guidelines in public system litigation. In addition, public plans must comply with the Internal Revenue Code that shapes both private and public plans.

Michigan's public pension plans are governed by the state constitution and state statute in addition to the basic need to meet actuarial standards and the requirements of the Internal Revenue Code and federal pension legislation. The Michigan constitutional language creates a critical difference between public pensions in Michigan and public and private plans elsewhere. Article IX, Section 24, reads in pertinent part "the accrued financial benefits of each pension plan and retirement system of the state and its political subdivisions shall be a contractual obligation thereof which shall not be diminished or impaired thereby." The second paragraph of Section 24 requires annual funding of pension obligations:

"Financial benefits arising on account of service rendered in each fiscal year shall be funded during that year and such funding shall not be used for financing underfunded accrued liabilities." This language creates a strong level of protection for pension benefits in Michigan's public sector.

Further, governments are bound to financial measurement and reporting requirements established by the Governmental Accounting Standards Board (GASB). Since state and local plan administrators may choose different assumptions for salary growth, investment rates of return, worker turnover, and mortality rates, GASB issues guidelines for these assumptions. The current standards, as established in GASB Statement No. 25, require that beginning with fiscal year 1996 and later, assets are to be reported at "fair value" and that unfunded liabilities are to be amortized over thirty years. Fair value approximates market value by smoothing year-to-year market fluctuations over a three- or five-year averaging period. This dampens the short-term investment volatility of plan assets, and tends to stabilize the required employer contribution. The thirty-year requirement for amortization is to ensure that the current generation of taxpayers pays for the current services of public employees.

To be "actuarially sound," the employer's contribution needs to cover the annual expected benefit accrual—the pension benefits earned in the current year are called the normal costs—and to amortize (pay over time) any past unfunded pension liability. Past unfunded liabilities may arise if benefits are increased, or if past actuarial assumptions proved incorrect and resulted in underfunding when measured against actual experience. Unfunded liabilities are called actuarial accrued liabilities (AAL). So, the employer's annual contribution is the sum of normal costs and actuarial accrued liabilities.

Administrative directors set plan investment policy and hire actuaries to determine the value of the plan's assets, liabilities, and sponsor contribution. For the DB plans managed by the State of Michigan, these comprehensive financial reports are undertaken annually.[11] To determine the plan's payments to current and future retirees, actuaries combine information about: (1) the past and the future age, service, and compensation of employees, (2) demographic assumptions related to mortality, disability, and probabilities of retirement, and (3) economic assumptions regarding wage increases and long-term rates of return (Hustead 2001).

Different actuarial assumptions can be used to calculate the liability. The State of Michigan, and two-thirds of all state and local plans nationally (Zorn 1997) use the entry age normal actuarial cost method.[12] The end result is an annualized cost called the contribution rate. The contribution rate is stated as a percentage of membership payroll. It consists of the normal cost plus the annual payment required to amortize the unfunded accrued liability, divided by payroll, expressed as a percentage. This contribution rate can be thought of as a tax on wages, much like the federal Social Security tax on wages.

The plan's funding ratio is calculated from the fair value of assets and the actuarial liability (sum of normal cost and AAL). The funding ratio is equal to the fair value of assets divided by the actuarial liability. It is a useful single-year summary statistic of funding adequacy. A fully funded plan has a funding ratio at or near one. However, it is an imperfect measure for making comparisons across time or across plans, since the underlying assumptions and methods of measuring plan assets or liabilities may differ.

## Defined Benefit Plans Administered by the State of Michigan

Table 20.1 presents the actuarial value of assets and liabilities and the funding ratio for the five State of Michigan pension plans and for the separate voluntary association, the Municipal Employees Retirement System (MERS). These figures are from the 2001 fiscal year Comprehensive Annual Financial Reports for each plan. The MLRS is administered separately from the others, but since the other plans managed by the state are evaluated by the same actuarial firm with basically the same assumptions, it is possible to make meaningful comparisons across these plans. The MERS assumptions differ slightly but are similar.

As of the end of September 2001, the five nonmunicipal plans were fully or overfunded. For example, the State Employees' fund, with assets over $10 billion and liabilities over $9 billion, has a funding ratio of 109.1. MERS, while not fully funded, is in a strong funding position with a funding ratio of 86.1%, especially given that MERS's funding ratio is an aggregate over 563 or more defined benefit plans.

Michigan pensions, and state and local plans nationwide, have a strong funding status because so many invested heavily in stocks in the 1980s and 1990s (Munnell and Sunden 2001; Hustead 2001). Before the early 1980s, state and local retirement systems held most of their assets in fixed-income securities, earning relatively low rates of return. Typically, their asset choices were restricted to "legal lists" that specified types of investments and the maximum investments allowed in each type. Often investment in equities was limited to 30% or less (Mitchell et al. 2001). During the 1980s, legal lists were replaced with "prudent person" rules that allow a wide mix of investments as long as standards of prudence and diversification are met. Equities came to play a large role in investments in the 1990s.[13] For example, at the end of the 2001 fiscal year, MSERS held 40.8% of its fund in domestic equities, and 6.6% in international equities, while the corresponding percentages for MPSERS are 41.2% and 6.5%.

Table 20.2 presents historical funding ratios for the five nonmunicipal DB plans and the MERS aggregated DB plan. The funding ratios for all state-administered plans show an upward trend generally, but all declined with the drop in the stock market following the 11 September 2001 terrorist attack. For example, the MPSERS Comprehensive Annual Financial Report (CAFR) reports that the fund had 41.2% invested in domestic equities, and investment losses of $4.56 billion at the end of fiscal year 2001. This represented a decrease in total assets of 10.5% from the previous year.

Table 20.2 also illustrates the frequency with which benefits or actuarial assumptions are changed, thereby changing the funding ratio. Between 1990 and 2001, for example, MSERS and MPSERS changed benefits or assumptions, or both, four and five times, respectively. Funding ratios across time are not directly comparable for that reason. Funding ratios for MERS have changed across time for those reasons, but, in addition, less well funded DB plans have joined MERS over time, which has lowered their aggregate funding ratio.

Note that in 1997 there is a dramatic increase in the funding ratios of the state-managed plans. In 1997, the state introduced a DC plan for all new state employees and allowed most current employees to choose between the DB and the new DC plan. Along with this change, the state made a one-time change in the valuation of plan assets for all state-managed plans. The state "marked to market" to reflect the current fair value of the MSERS and MPSERS systems, and then returned

**TABLE 20.2**

**Historical Funding Ratios of Defined Benefit Plans**

|      | State Employees | Public School Employees | Judges | State Police | Legislative | Municipal Retirement |
|------|-----------------|-------------------------|--------|--------------|-------------|----------------------|
| 1970 |                 |                         |        |              |             | 63.1 |
| 1975 |                 |                         |        |              |             | 68.3 |
| 1980 |                 |                         |        |              |             | 75.7 |
| 1985 |                 | 79.7                    |        | 73.4         |             | 112.6 |
| 1990 | 92.0            | 87.2[a]                 | 92.0   | 81.8[b]      |             | 113.3 |
| 1991 | 88.0[b]         | 81.3                    | 94.6   | 78.7         |             | 107.6 |
| 1992 | 82.7            | 78.4                    | 95.8   | 75.8[b]      | 103         | 104.6 |
| 1993 | 81.7[a]         | 78.3[a]                 | 98.3[a]| 78.0[a]      | 98[a]       | 86.8 |
| 1994 | 83.5[a]         | 74.0[a]                 | 102.7  | 79.6[a]      | 93          | 80.5 |
| 1995 | 88.8            | 74.6                    | 108.8  | 77.9         | 98          | 79.0 |
| 1996 | 93.4            | 78.9                    | 115.0  | 84.8         | 101         | 80.2 |
| 1997 | 109.1[a]        | 100.9[a]                | 117.8  | 105.9[a]     | 109         | 82.0 |
| 1998 | 108.8           | 97.0[a]                 | 125.3[a]| 101.2       | 117         | 84.4 |
| 1999 | 106.9           | 99.3                    | 131.8  | 103.0        | 115         | 90.3 |
| 2000 | 109.1           | 99.3                    | 134.6  | 107.0        | 125         | 86.1 |
| 2001 | 107.6           | 96.5                    | 129.5  | 107.0        | 121         |      |

SOURCE: Annual Actuarial Valuation, selected years.
(a) Revised actuarial assumptions, revised valuation method, or both.
(b) Benefit changes.

to five-year market smoothing immediately there-after.[14] This had the effect of making both systems fully funded, and allowed reductions in required contributions for both the state and the school districts. For example, prior to the reevaluation in 1997, the funding ratio for MSERS was 91.5. This increased to 109.1 as a result of the revaluation. For the teachers' plan, the funding ratio began at 84.4 and rose to 100.9.

## State Budgets and Pension Funds

Since states regulate their own pension funds and appoint members to the boards that determine pension policy, a conflict of interest may be created between state and plan participants during times of economic distress.[15] For example, the financial health of public pensions improved dramatically during the 1980s due to improved funding practices and high investment returns. In contrast, many states faced severe budget deficits in the early 1990s, and several of them turned to their pension funds as a source of revenue.

There are two methods by which a state could use pension funds to offset budget pressure. First, a state could reduce contributions or appropriate money directly from the funds. The State of California failed to make the actuarially required contributions to its public pension plan, CalPERS, several times between 1991 and 1994. Fund administrators filed suit, and eventually the California Supreme Court ruled that workers had a right to an actuarially sound pension system and ordered the state to pay back the past revenues to the fund.

This direct use of pension funds is relatively rare (Munnell and Sunden 2001), but indirect use is more common. In the face of budget shortfalls, fund sponsors can alter actuarial assumptions in order to reduce required contributions.[16] While evidence suggests that most of the changes can be justified on economic grounds (Mitchell and Smith 1994), it can be difficult to determine what is being done to improve state budgets, and what is actuarially sound. There have been two recent cases—in New York in 1990 and in New Jersey in 1992—where obvious accounting changes were made to create a surplus and reduce state contributions to zero. In both cases, the courts in those states eventually made the state meet the contribution obligation. Of course, this payment may have required higher taxes.

This has not occurred with the Michigan pension systems, and it is unlikely to occur, given the strong constitutional language protecting pension payments. Furthermore, Michigan's sound administrative practices at the state level provide an additional level of protection. For example, the state sponsored and administered plans have reasonable investment assumptions (about 8%) for the long-term horizon of pension investing. The demographic and financial assumptions are also reasonable. In addition, every five years, the plan actuary completes a study of actual experience related to the assumptions and recommends changes as necessary. Finally, both pension boards and the state are subject to court action for self-interest.

### Glossary of Terms Used Frequently in the Text

*401(k) Plan.* A defined contribution plan in which employees may make pretax contributions. The employer often matches employee contributions, but matching is not required by statute.

*AAL.* Actuarial Accrued Liability. The long-term costs of retirement benefits.

*Amortization of Unfunded AAL.* Payments over time to pay off unfunded liabilities, usually over twenty to thirty years.

*CAFR.* Comprehensive Annual Financial Report.

*Contribution Rate.* The employer contribution rate is a ratio. The numerator is equal to normal cost plus the annual payment required to amortize the unfunded accrued liability. The denominator is payroll. The ratio is expressed as a percentage.

*Defined Benefit (DB) Plan.* A pension plan where the benefit is defined by a formula.

*Defined Contribution (DC) Plan.* An individual account-type pension plan where the benefit is determined by contribution size and investment performance.

*ERISA.* The Employee Retirement Income Security Act (ERISA) of 1974 established minimum coverage, participation, funding, vesting, and fiduciary requirements for private pension plans.

*GASB.* The Governmental Accounting Standards Board establishes accounting practices for public pension plans.

*MERS.* Municipal Employees Retirement System.

*MJRS.* Michigan Judges' Retirement System.

*MPSERS.* Michigan Public Schools Employees'

Retirement System.

*MSERS.* Michigan State Employees' Retirement System.

*MSPRS.* Michigan State Police Retirement System.

*Normal Cost.* The cost of funding benefits accrued to members in the current year.

*PAYGO.* Pay-As-You-Go or cash funding (no prefunding) of current obligations.

*PBGC.* The Pension Benefit Guaranty Corporation is a federal agency that insures private defined benefit pension plans.

*Vesting.* Becoming legally entitled to a benefit at retirement.

### Current Issues Facing Michigan Pension Systems

In this section, I discuss some recent developments in pension policy in the context of Michigan's three largest pension systems. The first section provides an overview of the Michigan Public School Employees' Retirement System. I discuss the implications of Michigan's 1994 K–12 school finance reform on the pension liabilities facing school districts. The second section focuses on the Michigan State Employees' Retirement System. This system underwent substantial reform legislated in 1996, in which the fully funded defined benefit plan was closed to new entrants and replaced with a 401(k) plan for new hires. The third section provides an overview of the Municipal Employees Retirement System. I discuss what we know, and do not know, about local government pension solvency.

### Michigan Public School Employees' Retirement System

The Michigan Public School Employees Retirement System (MPSERS) is a multiple-employer, statewide DB public employee retirement plan. Employees of K–12 public school districts, public school academies, district libraries, tax-supported community colleges, and seven universities may be members.[17] MPSERS is the largest DB pension plan in Michigan, with 716 participating employers, 318,538 active employees, 130,790 retirees and beneficiaries, and assets of about $37 billion in 2001 (see table 20.1).

There are two types of defined benefit plans in MPSERS (see appendix A). While the benefit formula is the same for both types—final salary ×

0.015 × years of service—members of the Basic Plan prior to 1987 do not contribute and do not receive inflation adjustments. New hires that began Michigan public school employment in 1990 or later are automatically enrolled in the Member Investment Plan (MIP).[18] MIP participants contribute out of their pretax salary to a reserve fund, and after retirement MIP participants receive a fixed 3%, noncompounding, annual increase in their pension benefit, based on the initial pension amount. The MIP contribution is graduated—beginning with 3.0% for the first $5,000 of salary, 3.6% of $5,001 through $15,000, and 4.3% of compensation for those with salary over $15,000.

At the end of the fiscal year in 2001, MPSERS had almost $37 billion in assets to cover $37 billion in actuarial accrued liabilities, for a funding ratio of 99.3%. As the largest defined benefit plan in Michigan, with an aging membership, liabilities are large, but the contribution rate has been relatively low, due to the large active membership and payroll. Employer contributions for pensions were 6.8% of covered payroll for the fiscal year ending 30 September 2001. Health benefits for teachers are not prefunded, so current health claims are paid on a cash basis. Health benefits are discussed in more detail later in this chapter.

A significant issue facing MPSERS is the change in its source of funding. Prior to the 1994 Michigan K–12 school finance reform, for the most part, annual payments to MPSERS came out of general state appropriations. In 1994, Michigan changed the way K–12 schools are financed (see chapter 15). In place of the local property tax, Proposal A replaced local funds with a state-level district foundation guarantee equal to per-student spending in the 1993–94 school year plus annual increases. As part of the school finance reform, pension payments made for school employees were included in the foundation grant given to school districts.

Therefore, since the reform in 1994, the state no longer makes direct payments to MPSERS, or to the federal Social Security Administration. Those payments now come from the school districts and are essentially paid out of the foundation grant. Each employer—the school district or other reporting entity—is required to contribute the full actuarial funding contribution amount to fund pension benefits, plus an additional amount to fund retiree health care benefit amounts on a cash disbursement basis. The districts are responsible for the cost of all retirement benefits, including health benefits.

If school districts feel financial pressure, they may use early retirement schemes to lower their payroll. They can do this by taking advantage of the fact that the pension system is a multiemployer system with no experience rating. In this system, employers—the school districts—are assessed a pension contribution rate following an actuarial valuation of the system as a whole. This enables a district to reduce its payroll by encouraging higher-paid teachers to retire and replacing them with less experienced, lower-paid teachers with no retirement cost penalty because the system as a whole absorbs the increased retirement cost.[19]

Consider an analogy to the financing of workers' compensation benefits. These benefits are financed almost entirely by employer premiums or self-insurance payments. Most employers are relatively small and are class rated. Class rating means all employers in the same class pay the same rate. Larger employers are subject to experience rating—the class-rated premium is adjusted upward or downward depending on the employer's loss experience. As Steve Woodbury explains in chapter 19 of this volume, incomplete experience rating in unemployment insurance gives firms an incentive to make temporary layoffs.

Because school districts are not experience rated—where individualized contribution rates would be based on the district's own retirees—there is an incentive for schools to be first to offer early-out retirement deals. This will lower current payroll for the individual school. The pension system as whole is financially sound (though future contribution rates will be higher), but the burden will be shifted in the short run from districts with the first retirees to those with later retirees.

## State Employees', Judges', and Legislative Retirement Systems in Michigan

The Michigan State Employees' Retirement System (MSERS) is a statewide defined benefit public employee retirement plan that covers the employees of many state agencies hired prior to 1997 and of certain related programs that perform quasi-public functions.[20] The defined benefit plan, referred to as Tier 1, is the second-largest defined benefit plan in the state of Michigan, and has 44,967 active members, 37,111 retirees and beneficiaries, and $10.337 billion in assets (see table 20.1). The DB plan is supplemented by two defined contribution plans: the Deferred Compensation Plan I/457 and the Deferred Compensation Plan II/401(k).[21] MSERS also administers postemployment health benefits offered to retirees, but these are funded on a cash basis.

Effective 31 March 1997, Public Act 487 of 1996 closed the fully funded defined benefit plan to new entrants. All new employees become members of a 401(k) DC plan, called Tier 2.[22] The Tier 2 DC plan is an extension of the MSERS original 401(k) plan. Employee contributions are voluntary and pre-tax. The state contributes a mandatory 4% of annual salary, and will also match up to the first 3% of the employee voluntary contribution in addition to the mandatory 4%. Vesting for retirement health, dental, and vision insurance benefits remains at ten years, as for participants that remain in the Tier 1 DB plan.

The health benefits with the new DC plan are less generous. Instead of cliff-vesting at ten years, the health plan is on a graded premium subsidy, with a ten-year employee eligible for only a 30% subsidy of the premium.

Each participant in Tier 2 is fully vested in his or her own contributions and in any funds transferred from the DB plan. A participant is gradually but quickly vested in the state's contribution, becoming 100% vested in four years. As with a 401(k) plan in the private sector, the employee's contribution, and the vested portion of the state's contribution, is available to withdraw, roll over to an IRA or another 401(k) account, or leave in the DC retirement plan upon retirement or upon pre-retirement termination of employment with the state.[23]

During fiscal year 1998, the Michigan State Employees' Retirement Act provided existing employees an opportunity to transfer to the DC plan. This transfer to the DC plan was a one-time opportunity, and the decision to transfer was irrevocable. If a participant opted to leave the DB plan, the actuarial present value of his or her DB benefit was transferred to the DC plan. Slightly over 5% (3,224 of about 58,000) of active state employees transferred to DC plan (Office of Retirement Services [1998]).

The judges' plan was also fully funded, and judges were initially allowed to opt into the DC plan as well. This transfer was delayed by legal matters, but ultimately resulted in the transfer of 172 of about 600 judges.

This legislation dramatically reassigns financial responsibilities between the state and the MSERS members. Defined benefit and defined contribution plans differ markedly in investment risk, portability, and benefit accrual.[24] First, under the Tier 1 DB plan, the State of Michigan is responsible for acquiring enough funds to pay the future pension obligation. Under the Tier 2 DC plan, the employee chooses investments for his or her contribution and for the state's contribution, and the pension benefit will be determined by the size of the contributions and the success of the investments. The state has no further obligation to the participant, beyond administering the investment options. The DB to DC switch transferred pension investment risk from the state (and therefore, from Michigan taxpayers) to the public employees.

Second, the Tier 2 plan has portability advantages for employees who plan to be short term (note that this includes, for example, all members of the term-limited legislature). Participants are 100% vested in only four years. An employee who leaves state employment before retirement may take his or her contributions (and the state's after four years) under the DC plan. In contrast, in the DB plan, participants are entitled to a deferred pension benefit only after working for ten years (that is, they are cliff vested in ten years). Furthermore, even if the DB participant is vested, he or she may not take the defined benefit pension with him or her when moving to a new employer, but must wait until age sixty to begin receiving benefits.[25] Further, the DC account continues to increase in value (or decrease) if the participant moves out of public employment, while the pension benefit from a defined benefit formula is frozen in nominal terms until retirement.

Payout options are also more flexible under the Tier 2 plan, since it sets up an individual account. The participant continues to accrue earnings in the account through retirement, and can set the distribution schedule. If needed, the fund can be a source of loan funds before retirement.

Private-sector DC plans are portable generally; that is, upon separation from service, the participant can roll over existing assets into a new employer's plan, or the assets can remain in the older employer's plan. In the case of MSERS members, however, the DC plan is fully portable, but may incur a tax penalty. The State of Michigan does not tax qualified pension plan distributions of public-sector employees. If the participant rolled the pension over to an IRA, or to a private-sector employer plan, and remained a Michigan resident, the tax exemption would cease and the benefit might be subject to state income tax as well.

Third, benefits are backloaded in a traditional DB plan, since the benefit is a function of years of service and final salary. That is, a large fraction of the total pension benefit is accrued in the final years of employment. This provides employees an incentive to remain in public employment until they are eligible to collect pension benefits. Stated another way, backloading significantly lowers lifetime pension benefits for employees who change jobs midcareer (Gustman and Steinmeier [1993]). This is not the case with the new Tier 2 plan, since the state's annual contribution is a percentage of salary.[26]

Given these plan features, we can speculate about the type of worker who would benefit from the switch from a DB to a DC plan. A worker that anticipates fewer than ten years of state employment would prefer the DC plan, since ten years of employment are required for entitlement to any future benefit under the DB plan. This would be true for an employee of any age. Yet younger workers with a longer expected career in public employment may also prefer the portability of the DC plan. Workers early in their careers with, say, a projected fifteen-year career in state employment, would be vested in the DB plan when they left. However, the Tier 1 benefit is frozen at its nominal value at job separation. If the younger worker still has about twenty years until retirement, the Tier 1 nominal benefit will lose much of its value before age sixty. Of course, the worker has to consider the probability of involuntarily layoff as well.

The ultimate size of a 401(k) pension benefit is subject to financial risk. That is, the value of the fund at retirement is determined in part by investment choices and performance. Workers with a taste for managing their own investments will find this feature attractive, but others may prefer the certainty of a formulaic benefit. Finally, defined benefit payments come in the form of an annuity—much like Social Security payments. Knowing that part of their retirement income comes from an annuity may incline workers to diversify across types of retirement income and switch to the DC plan. On the other hand, the recent discussions of privatizing all or part of Social Security may encourage workers to hang on to a vanishing breed of pension plan.

It is commonly thought that the preference for DC plans in the private sector is due to the regulatory burdens on defined benefit plans associated with ERISA, booming stock markets, and a view that portability and flexibility of DC plans are an appreciated benefit in changing labor markets (Fore 2001). Often employee choice is the reason cited for introducing a DC component. These factors must play a role in the public sector as well.

In a letter from State Treasurer Douglas B. Roberts to state employees who would be eligible to choose between the two plans (dated 2 December 1996), two aspects of the plan were highlighted. I paraphrase them here: First, more state employees would receive a retirement benefit. According to the State of Michigan actuary, only 55% of all state employees vest under the DB plan. Second, the portable retirement benefit in the Tier 2 plan "can be taken with you when you leave public service, and the assets in the DC account would continue to earn interest at a compounded rate until you retire. With the current plan, if you leave public service before 10 years, you get no retirement benefits."

Often employers that alter pension plans are motivated by cost reductions. Sometimes the new plan is less generous, or a plan may be "revenue neutral" but may be less generous to a subgroup of employees.[27] Cost stabilization and a reduction in future retirement costs are mentioned in this Office of Retirement Services (1998) summary of the new Michigan DC plan:

> The DC Plan offers several advantages to both employer and employee. . . . For the state, shorter vesting periods, benefit portability, and investment flexibility enhances recruitment in an increasingly mobile workforce. Fewer employees will be forced to stay in a position in order to vest. Retirement budget predictability should potentially improve under the DC Plan, as all liabilities are fully funded. Program proponents expect the DC Plan to stabilize and reduce future retirement costs.

There have been only a handful of reforms of this type at the state level.[28] In 1991, West Virginia closed its teachers' DB plan and created a new DC. In 1995–96, Washington, Colorado, and California set up DC plans in a hybrid or cash balance format—that is, they retained a DB plan in some form. Many more states added DC plans as supplements, but North Dakota (1999) and Florida (2002) legislated DB replacement with DC plans (Fore 2001).

Early opinion on the state employees DB to DC switch seems to be that the DC plan is generally preferred at the managerial level, since managers tend to be shorter-term employees, and the high turnover in the clerical and support staff means that they also prefer a DC plan. However, non-managerial, nonclerical employees seem to prefer formula-based benefits. Already in 2001, legislation was proposed to provide state employees with the option to choose between the DB and the DC systems.[29]

In the last several years, the state has used sweetened early retirement deals as a budget-balancing device. This may decrease current costs, since the state plans to replace only one in four retirees, but this will increase retirement-related costs in the Tier 1 plan.[30] In particular, retiree health care costs will increase, since early retirees are more likely to have full family health coverage (including children) for several years, and early retirees will require health insurance for a longer period.

Two other state-level defined benefit plans were affected by the DC legislation. These are discussed briefly in the following.

*Michigan Judges' Retirement System.* The Michigan Judges' Retirement System (MJRS) is a multiple-employer, statewide defined benefit plan. It is administered by the State Office of Retirement Services, but is not a state-sponsored plan. The system, created under Public Act 234 of 1992, consolidated the former Judges' and Probate Judges' Retirement Systems into one retirement system. There are 172 participating employers. The system also includes the governor of the state of Michigan, the lieutenant governor, the secretary of state, the attorney general, the legislative auditor general, and the constitutional court administrator.

Public Act 523 of 1996, effective 31 March 1997, closed the judges' contributory defined benefit plan to new entrants. Judges or state officials appointed or elected on or after 31 March 1997 become members of the defined contribution plan. During fiscal year 2000, following a lawsuit settled in connection with the DC legislation, 172 judges transferred to the DC plan for FY 2001, along with $77.8 million of defined benefit assets attributable to their benefits.

*Michigan Legislative Retirement System.* The Michigan Legislative Retirement System (MLRS) is a single-employer, public employee DB plan governed by the State of Michigan. The MLRS operates within the legislative branch of state government, and is administered by a separate board.

Public Act 486 of 1996 amended the MLRS enabling statute to mandate that persons elected to the Michigan legislature after 31 March 1997 participate in the statewide DC plan. Thus, the DB plan is a closed plan.

Michigan's constitutional term-limit amendment limits service in the House of Representatives to three two-year terms of office, and service in the Michigan Senate to two four-year terms of office. Almost all MLRS active members will be term-limited from office by 2002. In addition, their successors will be automatically enrolled in the DC plan, ensuring that in the next two years there will be a dramatic reduction in the number of active members in the MLRS.

**Local Government Retirement Systems**

Michigan has a strong home rule tradition. Consequently, unlike in most other states, local governments in Michigan may sponsor and administer their own pension plans. The 2001 Census of State and Local Governments reports that Michigan ranks fifth in the United States in the number of separate pension systems, with 141.[31] Only Pennsylvania (with 357), Minnesota (179), Illinois (377), and Florida (168) report more pension systems. A nationwide consolidation movement occurred in the 1980s, and many separate local systems were absorbed into state-administered systems (in Kentucky and Colorado, for example), but this did not occur in Michigan (Rajnes 2001).

It is difficult to determine exactly how many local plans exist in Michigan. Pension systems may offer more than one plan. The public retirement systems are surveyed every two years by an actuarial firm (Gabriel, Roeder, Smith & Company of Southfield, Michigan). Participation is voluntary and the survey is thought to be comprehensive but not all-inclusive. The 1999 survey (based on actuarial valuations dated 31 December 1998) reports that there were 527 MERS plans, 42 police/fire retirement system plans set up under 1937 Public Act 345 ("Act 345" plans), and 88 Independent Plans (such as section 12a county pension plans under MCL 46.12a, or city charter/ordinance pension plans).

It is even more difficult to count the number of DC plans. A DC plan may be the only municipality plan or may be a part of a municipality's plan, but DC plans typically appear only as a note in the survey. In addition, there are exclusive public-sector DC third-party administrators as well as private vendors that are not part of any comprehensive DC (401[a], 457, and 401[k]) compilation for Michigan municipalities.

The 130 estimated DB plans not in MERS are still subject to federal and state laws and generally accepted accounting principles in governing their plans. They all should be publishing comprehensive annual financial reports, and regular, if not annual, actuarial valuations. Unfortunately, these are not collected and summarized by any central agency, so they can be discussed only generally. Some large units administering their own plans include the City of Detroit, Wayne County, and Oakland County. The independence of these plans is not necessarily a cause for concern. The 2000–2001 Michigan Commission on Public Pensions and Retiree Health Benefits identified only one system with major funding problems.

Local governments may fund and administer their own pension plans, or they may join the Municipal Employees Retirement System of Michigan (MERS) that began in 1946 as a state agency.[32] MERS administers retirement, survivor, and disability benefits on a voluntary membership for retirees of its local government members. By virtue of 1996 legislation, MERS is now an independent public corporation and not part of state government. The MERS Plan Document provides local governments with the choice of a defined benefit or a defined contribution plan. As of 31 December 2001, the $3.65 billion aggregated defined benefit plan included 563 participating municipalities and courts with 36,856 active members, 16,932 retired members and beneficiaries, and 4,660 vested former members (Municipal Employees' Retirement System of Michigan 2001).[33] There were 102 plans in the relatively new Defined Contribution Plan, with assets totaling $83.3 million and 4,427 participants.[34] Effectively, this combined plan for local government employees—a covered population of 62,875 and over $3.73 billion in assets—is the third-largest public-sector defined benefit plan in Michigan.

MERS administers plans negotiated by local governments, and it offers a menu of benefit options to its members. Generally, benefits vest after ten years of service, although benefits may vest after eight or six years of service if earlier vesting is approved by the municipality's governing body. The standard retirement age is sixty years. However, members may retire with several combinations of age and years of service and receive reduced early retirement benefits. Benefits are paid monthly over the member's or survivor's lifetime, and are equal to a specific percentage of the member's final average compensation times the number of years of credited service. The specific percentage depends on the benefit plan or plans adopted by each municipality for its employees. Members contribute to the retirement system at rates that range from 0% to 10%, depending on the contribution program adopted by the municipality.

At this level of government, unlike any other level of public service or in the private sector, municipalities are adopting new defined benefit plans. Defined benefit plans remain quite popular at the local level perhaps because there is limited employee turnover below the managerial level. For example, between 1995 and 2001, MERS membership grew from 490 participating municipalities to 563. Three counties joined over this period, along with a number of cities, villages, townships, and special purpose units. Most of these additions involved adoption of MERS defined benefit programs, and conversion from prior defined contribution or 457 deferred compensation plans.

MERS administration offers several advantages to a local government. First, as a large administrator, MERS has expenses that are substantially below what smaller employers could achieve. For example, MERS's investment and administrative expenses in 2001 were 37.6 basis points (0.376%)—administrative expenses alone were only 15.4 basis points.[35] This compares quite favorably with the 100 basis points that large private-sector equity managers commonly charge their clients.[36]

Second, MERS enforces fiscal responsibility. MERS requires plans electing to participate to be at least 50% funded if past service is to be credited. Also, as a third-party administrator, MERS conducts Annual Actuarial Valuations for each participating municipality to calculate the local government's annual required contribution. If a locality wants to add a new benefit, or offer an early retirement incentive, for example, MERS requires a Supplemental Valuation to determine the immediate and long-term effect on employer and employee contributions and the plan's funding level. MERS will not implement any benefit change without a current (not less than one year old) Supplemental Valuation. This valuation provides important cost information for employees as well as employers, and the requestor of the valuation (the employer, an employee bargaining representative, or both) pays the fee for the valuation.

Third, MERS provides an essential oversight function for the state. The Michigan Constitution of 1963 (Article 9 Section 24), state law, and the MERS Plan Document all mandate that localities make required pension payments, and this is enforceable through court action. A court may order a Judgement Levy (millage under section 6093 of the Revised Judicature Act) imposed on local taxpayers to fund the delinquent contributions. The same can happen when a non-MERS member fails to fund a retirement program adequately. For example, in a 1991 Michigan Supreme Court case (*Shelby Township Police and Fire Retirement Board v Charter Township of Shelby*, 438 Michigan Reports 247, 255), involving a non-MERS municipality, the court ruled that municipalities are constitutionally mandated to actuarially fund their pension plan, including prior service liabilities.

Local governments are not required to join MERS. This is not a cause for alarm, but it does create two difficulties. First, there is only local oversight if a local entity's plan is not part of MERS. This could create an opportunity for local governments to use pension contributions to conceal general fund deficits, with little notice by the public or participants. For example, the city of Highland Park is under the control of an emergency financial manager appointed in June 2001 by the governor (under the Local Government Fiscal Responsibility Act). Only one of the city's five pension plans is in MERS, and information on the finances of the other four plans is not generally available.

Second, there is no centrally accumulated source of data for these non-MERS plans. It is hard to assess the extent of local non-MERS underfunding, but the 2000–2001 Michigan Commission on Public Pension and Retiree Health Benefits (hereafter, the Pension Commission 2001) hints that it may be significant in the following statement. "The confusion, lack of information, and in some cases, misinformation about public employee retirement systems in Michigan can hardly be overstated."

There is a risk of default at the local level, but participants may use the court system to seek an order to levy additional taxes to meet this constitutional obligation. Court action to force local payment through special assessment would occur before delinquent payments became a legal state obligation, although the state may feel a moral obligation to intervene earlier. In the extremely unlikely case that additional local taxes fail to raise enough revenue, or if the increase is judged too burdensome, then the state may intervene, since a local default on pension payments is likely to be reflected in a state's bond rating.

In part to address the potential need for another mechanism to enforce local payment obligations, the Pension Commission has embraced MERS's recommendation that state revenue sharing be withheld to make delinquent pension contributions. A bill to that effect passed the House in May 2002.[37] This may obviate the need for court action, or at least reduce the size of the special assessment needed.

An obvious change that would enhance both pension security and information availability would be to require membership in MERS. MERS requires plans to be at least 50% funded, however, and this may not be a viable option for some. A less intrusive option would be state monitoring of non-MERS local systems through the treasury's local audit function. This may be a reasonable step in the attempt catch problems before the obligations become a crushing burden to local taxpayers.

## Retiree Health Benefits

All the state sponsored and administered retirement systems, and many of the municipal systems, provide retiree health insurance benefits. Unlike pension benefits, there is only partial prefunding of medical benefits.[38] The state or local governments pay the current year's health care costs on a cash disbursement basis. There are several reasons why pay-as-you-go funding is a particularly costly way to fund health benefits. First, as with cash funding of defined benefit obligations, there are no investment earnings to reduce future employer contributions. Second, an aging workforce means there are fewer actives to support benefit payments to retired individuals in the future. Retiree health costs as a fraction of payroll have trended upward as a result.[39] Third, medical costs are volatile (as discussed in the following). It is more difficult to budget for large fluctuations in costs. Recall that the actuarial methods used in prefunding defined benefit plans smooth both investment earnings and cost shocks.

In recent years, the state has requested actuarial valuations of its postretirement health benefits. These valuations calculate the state's contribution rate *as if* the medical liability were prefunded

## TABLE 20.3

**State Contribution Rates as a Percentage of Payroll, Health Benefits Only**

| | Michigan Public Schools Employees Retirement System | Michigan State Employees Retirement System (Tier 1 & 2) | Michigan State Police Retirement System | Michigan Judges Retirement System (Tier 1 &2) |
|---|---|---|---|---|
| Actuarial accrued liability (AAL) ($ million) | $13,990.27 | $7,586.49 | $526.00 | $5.393 |
| Normal cost (% of payroll) | 6.85 | 4.19 | 9.18 | 2.61 |
| Payment required to amortize AAL (% of payroll) | 7.67 | 13.43 | 22.91 | 7.89 |
| Total employer cost (% of payroll) | 14.52 | 17.62 | 32.09 | 10.50 |
| Payroll used in deriving contribution rates ($ million) | $9,264.2 | $2,899.3 | $118.8 | $6.17 |
| Date of valuation | 9/30/2001 | 9/30/2001 | 9/30/2001 | 9/30/2001 |

SOURCE: The Segal Company letters to Christopher DeRose, director, Office of Retirement Services, "Actuarial Valuation" of the various State of Michigan Pension Plans.

using traditional methodology. These hypothetical rates are provided in table 20.3. In the followingdiscussion, I will focus on the health care costs for the largest system, the Public School Employees' Retirement System.

An aging retirement system without investment reserves for health costs puts pressure on employer contributions, since retiree benefits are rising relative to active member payrolls. In 1980, the ratio of active workers to retirees was 6.04. In 2000, the ratio had fallen to 2.48, and the prediction for 2040 ranges from 1.15 to 1.49 (Segal Company 2001a).

MPSERS's actuarial accrued potential liabilities for health benefits alone are about $14 billion as of the end of 2001—about 38% of pension costs projected for that year that are effectively prefunded. These are *potential* liabilities, since health benefits do not have the same strong constitutional guarantee that basic pension benefits do (although the political and moral promise may be as strong). The hypothetical contribution rate as a fraction of payroll would have been 14.52% in 2001 to actuarially prefund health benefits for MPSERS. That cost consists of 6.85% in normal cost and 7.67% to amortize past liabilities.

The projected MPSERS 14.52% contribution rate in 2001 increased over the 2000 and 1999 valuations (13.47% and 12.27%, respectively). This is due to the fact that there are no investment earnings from prefunding assets. Also, there was growth in the number of covered members, and payroll increased by less than the 4% assumed in actuarial calculations.

As table 20.3 illustrates, the contribution rate to prefund health benefits is also high for the Michigan State Employees Retirement System (MSERS)—15.73% in 2001. Recall that new state hires are members of the Tier 2 defined contribu-

tion plan. This further raises the retirees/actives ratio in Tier 1, raises Tier 1 accrued liabilities, and spreads the contributions over a shrinking workforce. Similarly, with an earlier retirement age, the State Police Retirement System has a high contribution rate.

It is more difficult to project health care costs than pension costs. Rates of medical inflation are difficult to predict. In the most recent valuation, the assumed rates of medical inflation (the increase in system aid claims) are 9%, 8%, 7%, and 6%, respectively, for the next four years, and remain at 5% thereafter. These assumed rates may have to be adjusted, particularly if federal legislation to address prescription drug costs fails to pass.[40]

As with pension payments, prefunding health benefits would require two payments. The normal cost—the present value of the portion of future retiree health benefits considered to be earned in the current year by current employees—and a second payment to amortize future benefits considered to have been earned prior to the current year. For the teachers' retirement system, as of 30 September 2001, the total prefunded costs would be 14.52% of payroll, or $1,345 billion (see table 20.3). For state employees, the total prefunded cost would be 17.6% of payroll, or $451.9 million.[41]

Current expenditures for postretirement health benefits are based on the cost of insurance premiums for current retirees. For fiscal year 2001, this cost was approximately 5.5% for public school employees, and 8.6% of payroll for state employees. Therefore, the increase in contribution requirements to totally prefund postretirement medical benefits would be about 9.0% of payroll for both public school employees and state retirement systems.

For the Public Schools Employees' Retirement System, this 9.0% increase in payroll costs would be paid by school districts. Prefunding may be particularly burdensome for school districts, since these costs would increase, in part, at the rate of medical inflation, while their source of funding—the dedicated School Aid Fund—grows more slowly than the costs of health care do.

K–12 school funding—the foundation grant from the state—comes from two percentage points of the sales and use tax, a portion of the cigarette tax, a six mill state education tax (on both homestead and nonhomestead property), a 0.75% real estate transfer tax, and 23% of individual income tax revenues. The basic foundation grant increases each year according to an index that equals the total statewide revenues per pupil for all taxes that are earmarked for the School Aid Fund, divided by the 1995 level. Essentially, there may be a mismatch between the rates of increase of medical costs and the sources of school funding that may put pressure on other school expenses.

In recent years, there have been several legislative proposals to prefund retiree health benefits. With the pension plan close to fully funded, this may be a good time to examine those proposals.[42] There are certain advantages to prefunding the health care costs. First, the current generation of taxpayers pays for the full package of promised benefits. The full cost of public employment is made explicit. Second, the investment earnings on the assets can reduce future contributions. Third, the volatility of medical costs will be smoothed by the accounting techniques discussed earlier, making it easier for school districts to budget for them.

The magnitude of these health care liabilities will soon become readily available. The GASB Project on Other Post-employment Benefits proposes that the long-term cost of retiree health care be determined on an actuarial basis and shown in the financial statements of governmental employers and postemployment plans. GASB will propose standards in January 2003 that will not be effective for at least one and a half years. It would be useful for policy makers in Michigan to be prepared to address these liabilities, once this information is commonly available.

While the potential state system liabilities are large, they are at least known with a great degree of certainty. The same cannot be said for municipal plans. The Pension Commission (2001) reports that many local governments also provide med-ical plans on a pay-as-you-go basis. Initially, plans were established when there were a handful of retirees and benefit use and retiree life expectancy were low. Now, however, increasing costs, higher utilization, and longer life expectancies are driving the costs of these plans well above initial calculations. It is therefore likely to become more difficult for governments to fund past promises about retiree health care. Again, a central data source for local pension and retiree health liabilities would be useful.

## Summary and Conclusion

This chapter has reviewed the workings and financial status of Michigan's public retirement systems. The major findings are:

- The state-administered defined benefit pension plans covering public school teachers, state employees, state police, and judges are prefunded, and, as of the end of fiscal year 2001, were fully funded.
- The Tier 2 defined contribution plan for state employees, judges, and legislators is fully funded by definition. Over time, the defined contribution plan will come to replace the defined benefit plan for these public employees.
- From the taxpayers' perspective, a defined contribution plan has the advantage that there are no future unfunded liabilities. Current compensation—wages plus pensions—is paid by the current generation of taxpayers. A defined contribution plan may be cheaper for the state as well—a flexibility exists that allows the state to alter its match rate during tight-budget times, as private firms do, that is not present in defined benefit formulas.
- The Michigan Public School Employees' Retirement System is the largest public employee system in the state, with a membership of about 450,000. School district contribution rates are likely to increase due to an imperfect experience-rating scheme. In addition, following the passage of Proposition A, pension, health, and Social Security payments for public school teachers are now made by the school districts directly. Shortfalls in the retirement system will compete directly for money from a school district's foundation grant.
- Defined benefit pension plans continue to be popular at the local level. Municipal pension

plans that are members of the Municipal Employees Retirement System are well funded and have administrative costs well below what these plans could achieve independently.

- The pension and health liabilities of non-MERS municipal plans are difficult to determine. There is no central source of information for plans that operate independently. Yet even if there were, it is doubtful that the public at large would be able to effectively monitor local pension finances.

- Non-MERS governmental units that fail to provide the funding needed to meet local obligations should expect financial penalties, including the witholding of state revenue to enforce payment. It may useful to allow the state treasury to monitor the status of these plans. Since severe underfunding is likely to result in a court-ordered special assessment, a state monitoring function could protect local taxpayers from burdensome taxes.

- At both the state and local government levels, retiree health benefits are funded on a pay-as-you-go basis. The lack of prefunding increases the ultimate cost of funding health benefits, results in fluctuating annual cash payments, and creates uncertainty about future health funding. With the state pension plans in a strong funding position, it may be time to phase in prefunding of these liabilities.

■

## REFERENCES

Employee Benefit Research Institute. 1997. EBRI databook on employee benefits. 4th ed. Washington D.C.: EBRI-ERF.

Fore, Douglas. 2001. Going private in the public sector: The transition from defined benefit to defined contribution plans. In *Pensions in the public sector.* Philadelphia: University of Pennsylvania Press.

Gabriel, Roeder, Smith & Company. 2000. 1999 Michigan public employee retirement systems survey. Southfield, Mich.: Gabriel, Roeder, Smith & Co.

Gale, William G., Leslie E. Papke, and Jack Vanderhei. 2002. The shifting structure of private pensions: Evidence, causes, and consequences. In *The evolving pension system: Trends, effects, and proposals for reform.* Washington, D.C.: Brookings Institution.

Gustman, Alan L., Olivia Mitchell, and Thomas Steinmeier. 1994. The role of pensions in the labor market: A survey of the literature. *Industrial and Labor Relations Review* 3 (April): 417–38.

Gustman, Alan L., and Thomas Steinmeier. 1993. Pension portability and labor mobility: Evidence from the survey of income and program participation. *Journal of Public Economics* 50: 299–323.

Hustead, Edwin C. 2001. Determining the cost of public pension plans. In *Pensions in the public sector.* Philadelphia: University of Pennsylvania Press.

Hustead, Edwin C., and Olivia S. Mitchell. 2001. Public sector pension plans: Lessons and challenges for the twenty-first century. In *Pensions in the public sector.* Philadelphia: University of Pennsylvania Press.

Kaiser Family Foundation. 2002. Trends and indicators in the changing health care marketplace: chartbook.

Lindquist, Kirk L. 1992. Michigan's public employee retirement systems. Senate Fiscal Agency Issue Paper. Lansing, Michigan, January.

Michigan Commission on Public Pension and Retiree Health Benefits, 2000–2001. Lansing, Michigan.

Michigan Legislative Retirement System. 2001. Comprehensive annual financial report for the fiscal year ended 30 September 2001. Lansing, Michigan.

Mitchell, Olivia S., David M. McCarthy, Stanley C. Wisniewski, and Paul Zorn. 2001. Developments in state and local pension plans. In *Pensions in the public sector.* Philadelphia: University of Pennsylvania Press.

Mitchell, Olivia S., and Robert S. Smith. 1994. Pension funding in the public sector. *Review of Economics and Statistics* 126 (2): 278–90.

Municipal Employees' Retirement System of Michigan. 2001. Comprehensive annual financial report, year ended 31 December 2000. Lansing, Michigan.

Munnell, Alicia H., and Annika Sunden. 2001. Investment practices of state and local funds. In *Pensions in the public sector.* Philadelphia: University of Pennsylvania Press.

Office of Retirement Services. 1998. Defined contribution plan final report. Lansing, Michigan.

———. 2002a. Michigan Judges Retirement System: Comprehensive annual report for the fiscal year ended 30 September 2001. Lansing, Michigan.

———. 2002b. Michigan Public Schools Employees Retirement System: Comprehensive annual report for the fiscal year ended 30 September 2001. Lansing, Michigan.

———. 2002c. Michigan State Employees Retirement System: Comprehensive annual financial report for the fiscal year ended 30 September 2001. Lansing, Michigan.

———. 2002d. Michigan State Police Retirement System: Comprehensive annual financial report for fiscal year ended 30 September 2001. Department of Management and Budget, Lansing, Michigan.

Papke, Leslie E. 1999. Are 401(k) plans replacing other employer-provided pensions? Evidence from panel data. *Journal of Human Resources* 34 (spring): 346–68.

Rajnes, David. 2001. State and local retirement plans: Innovation and renovation. EBRI Issue Brief Number 235, July.

Retirement Coordinating Council News for Michigan Public School and State Employees. 2001. 22 (5, March).

Segal Company. 2001a. Michigan public school employees retirement system: Projections of population, pension costs and health care expenditures. March.

———. 2001b. Michigan state employees retirement system actuarial valuation as of September 30.

U.S. Department of Commerce, Census Bureau. 2001. Government Finance Series, Employee-retirement systems of state and local government.

U.S. General Accounting Office. 1996. Public pensions: Section 457 plans pose greater risk than other supplemental plans. GAO/HEHS-96-38, April.

Zorn, Paul. 1997. 1997 Survey of state and local government retirement systems: Survey report for members of the Public Pension Coordinating Council. Chicago: Government Finance Officers Association.

## NOTES

I thank Doug Drake and Charley Ballard for helpful discussion and comments on earlier drafts, and Kristy Bies for excellent research assistance.

1. As part of a compensation package, both defined benefit and defined contribution pensions provide various work and retirement incentives for workers. There is a vast literature on the labor market effects of pensions that I will not cover here. The reader is referred to Gustman, Mitchell, and Steinmeier (1994) for an introduction to labor market issues relating to pension plans.

2. Term limits ensure that soon all legislators will be members of the newly defined contribution plan, discussed in section 4.

3. Survey data can be found in the 2001 Government Finances series, Employee-Retirement Systems of State and Local Governments, U.S. Department of Commerce, U.S. Census Bureau: *http//www.census.gov/govs/www/ retire.html.*

4. In addition, there is a 3% noncompounding in-

flation adjustment not to exceed $300 that begins one year after retirement.

5. For this plan, final average compensation is the average of the member's monthly pay during thirty-six consecutive months of credited service. Members of MSERS may retire with full benefits after age sixty with ten years of service, or after age fifty-five with thirty years of service (see appendix B). Any member with ten or more years of credited service who leaves a government job but has not reached retirement age is vested and will receive a benefit at age sixty. Note, however, that the benefit formula of a midcareer job changer is frozen at the nominal value of final average compensation until retirement. This is discussed later in this section.

6. Participants do bear default risk, but this risk is considered negligible at the state level.

7. See Fore (2001) for a detailed discussion.

8. The DB form has been predominant for full-time and part-time eligible employees throughout the 1990s (Rajnes 2001). In 1998, 98% of full-time state and local public employees participated in a retirement plan. Of those, 90% of full-time workers were in a DB plan, and 14% participated in a DC plan (some participate in both). Among part-time workers, the fractions were 59% DB and 5% DC.

9. See the U.S. General Accounting Office (1996) for a discussion of 457 plans. A second type of public-sector DC plan, the 403(b) plan, is sponsored by hospitals, churches, and public-sector colleges and universities.

10. Participants in MPSERS contribute only in order to receive an extra postretirement inflation adjustment. This will be covered more fully in the discussion of current issues later in this chapter.

11. See, for example, the Comprehensive Annual Financial Reports for the various state plans.

12. Under the entry age actuarial normal cost method, the required employer contribution is expressed as a level percentage of payroll over time. The benefit obligation is calculated by allocating the actuarial present value of the projected benefits of each individual included in the valuation as a level percentage of the individual's projected compensation between entry age and assumed exit. The projected benefit obligation is the present value of the amount the state needs to cover the total pension benefit to be received for the remaining life of that member. The portion of this actuarial present value allocated to the valuation year, the normal cost, is funded entirely in the employer's contribution for that year. The remainder, the actuarial accrued liability, is amortized—divided up among additional level contributions over a period that ranges

between twenty and thirty years.

13. Mitchell et al. (2001) discuss restrictions on certain types of investments (usually investments in South Africa) and mandates favoring certain investments (a minimum percentage of in-state holdings, for example).

14. GASB 25 requires this "marking to market" or use of the "fair" value of assets.

15. See Munnell and Sunden (2001) for a detailed discussion and examples. In Michigan, pension boards may change actuarial assumptions, with the concurrence of the Department of Management and Budget, but boards may not change investments or benefits.

16. For example, the real discount rate of pension obligations is the difference between the assumed rate of return on pension assets and the rate of assumed wage growth (the growth of the liabilities). The higher this discount rate, the lower future pension obligations will be, so that an increase in the discount rate will reduce the state's required contribution to the fund.

17. The seven universities are Eastern Michigan, Central Michigan, Northern Michigan, Western Michigan, Ferris State, Michigan Technological, and Lake Superior State. Employees who first become employed by one of the seven universities on or after January 1, 1996, become members of an alternative plan.

18. Members of the Basic Plan may also buy into MIP.

19. I thank Doug Drake for calling this to my attention.

20. Employees of the following employers are covered by this plan: American Legion, American Veterans, Disabled American Veterans, Mackinac Island State Park, Marine Corps League, Michigan Bar Association, Military Order of the Purple Heart, Commission for Independent Vendors, Third Circuit Court, Recorders Court, and Thirty-Sixth District Court. Michigan judges and elected officials, legislators, national guard members, and state police officers are covered by separate retirement plans.

21. The 457 plan was the first supplemental DC plan, but initially the 401(k) plan had higher contribution limits so most members have both plans, and some contribute to both.

22. The act allows returning employees and members who left state employment on or before 31 March 1997 to elect the DB plan rather than the DC plan.

23. The participant may leave the money in the plan until age 70.5, when he or she must begin taking benefits under IRS regulations. If the participant withdraws the money in a lump sum, he or she must pay applicable federal income tax plus a 10% penalty if he or she is not at least 59.5 years of age.

24. See Fore (2001) for an extensive discussion.

25. There is some defined benefit mobility between MSERS, MPSERS, and a few others.

26. For example, suppose an employee makes no contribution. Then, each year the state would contribute a flat 4% of salary. The flat benefit accrual pattern (that is, 4% is contributed every year) is neutral with respect to job changes. In a defined benefit plan, in contrast, the fraction of final salary accrued rises with years of service.

27. For example, under many cash balance plans, older employees fail to earn any pension benefits during the "wear away" period. See Gale, Papke, and Vanderhei (2002).

28. See Rajnes (2001) for a comprehensive survey of state and local pension systems and recent developments.

29. See the *Retirement Coordinating Council News for Michigan Public School and State Employees* ( 2001), for details about House Bill 4046 that was proposed in 2001.

30. The early-out plan offered in 2002 included a 17% improvement in benefits. About 12,000 civil servants out of 60,000 were eligible (workers whose age and years of service added up to eighty or more). Eventually, 7,857 workers opted to retire—the largest mass retirement in state history. That number represented about 12.5% of the state workforce, and nearly twice as many as expected. This was the second early retirement deal in five years—the one in 1996 reduced the workforce by 5,100. See the *Lansing State Journal*, 1 April 2002, 1.

31. See *http://www.census.gov/govs/www/retire.html*.

32. I thank Anne M. Wagner, executive director of MERS, and Michael Moquin, general counsel for MERS, for providing much of the information in this section. I alone am responsible for any errors or opinions expressed in this chapter.

33. For the year ended 31 December 2001, MERS membership is comprised of the following: 64 out of 83 counties in Michigan; 231 cities and villages; 51 townships; 55 county road commissions; 146 authorities, districts, and others; and 16 closed groups. For more information about MERS, see *www.mersofmich.com*.

34. The DC option became operative in 1997. Participating municipalities may offer current employees an opportunity to opt into the DC plan. MERS transfers the present value of such members' accrued benefit in the DB plan into the members' accounts in the DC plan.

35. See the 2001 MERS Comprehensive Annual Financial Report at *www.mersofmich.com*.

36. Mitchell et al. (2001) find that larger plans incur

substantially lower expenses on an annual basis—44 basis points as a fraction of assets, which falls to 27 basis points if dollar-weighted. Fees in this range are consistent with the lower end of institutional money management fees charged by pension investment managers.

37. See HB 5727, which passed the House on 7 May 2002 as part of a five-bill implementation package (5727–31).

38. The MSERS and MPSERS have begun a limited prefunding mechanism for health benefits. Contribution levels for pension liabilities will remain constant as a percentage of payroll, and in years in which the pension system is 100% funded, the excess assets will be credited to prefund retiree health benefits. For FY 2002, this resulted in a contribution of $112 million toward future health costs for MSERS.

39. See Segal Company (2001a) for trends and projections in pension and health care costs for MPSERS.

40. Medical inflation is difficult to measure due to quality changes over time. An alternative measure of health care costs is the increase in employer health insurance premiums. These have been volatile, ranging from 0.8% in 1996 to 18% in 1989. Recently, the rates have steadily increased, from 3.7% in 1998 to 11% in 2001 (Kaiser Family Foundation 2002). Thus, the assumed rates of increase in the valuation are on the low side.

41. These figures are from a letter from Christopher DeRose, Director of the Office of Retirement Services, to the author.

42. Several bills have been introduced in an attempt to prefund health benefits (House bills 5723 and 5724 and Senate Bill 1242 were introduced in the 1999–2000 legislative session). Recent *Retirement Coordinating Council* newsletters have expressed concern that there is no funding mechanism that guarantees that funding will be available to pay health benefits. See, for example, *http://members.aol.com/rccrcc/retirement*.

### APPENDIX A

## Defined Benefit Pension Formulas

| Plan/Group | Formula |
|---|---|
| **1. State Employees Retirement System** | |
| A. Regular | (Three-year average salary × 0.015 × years of service) + 3% annual COLA (not exceeding $300, noncompounding) |
| B. Corrections Officers | (Three-year average salary × 0.02 × years of service as Corrections Officer) + ([same three-years average salary] × [0.015 × years of service in other class]) |
| C. Conservation Officers | Two-year average salary × 0.6 |
| D. Early Retirement | Calculated pension benefit less 0.5% for each month retired before age sixty |
| **2. Public School Employees Retirement System** | |
| A. Regular | (Final five-year average salary × 0.015 × years of service) + "13th check" (when investment earnings exceed actuarial assumptions) |
| B. Regular + Member Investment Plan | (Three-year average salary × 0.015 × years of service) + 3% annual COLA beginning year two (noncompounding) |
| C. Early Retirement | Calculated pension benefit less 0.5% for each month retired before age sixty |
| **3. State Police Retirement System** | |
| A. Regular | Three-year average salary × 0.60. Troopers and Sergeants receive a 5% COLA benefit: max. of $500 (noncompounding) |
| B. Early Retirement | Two-year average salary × 0.02 × years of service |
| **4a. Michigan Judges Retirement System** | |
| A. 8–11 years of service | Final salary × 0.03 × years of service |
| B. 12+ years of service | (Final salary × 0.5) + (0.025 × final salary for each year served above twelve) (max = 0.60 × final salary) |
| C. Early retirement | Basic benefit less 0.5% for each month retired before age sixty |
| **4b. Retirees of Former Michigan Probate Judges Retirement System** | |
| A. Plan A | Final salary × .03 × years of service (max.= 0.40 × final salary or $15,000, but ≤ 0.66 of final salary when added to county pension) |
| B. Plan B | Final salary × .035 × years of service (max. = 0.66 × final salary) |
| **5. Legislative Retirement System** | |
| Basic Benefit | For members joining after 1/95, (highest salary × 0.03 × years of service) + 4% COLA, non compounding |

SOURCE: Comprehensive Annual Financial Report of each system, various years; Lindquist (1992).

## APPENDIX B

## Pension Service Requirements for Defined Benefit Regular Retirement

**Plan/Group Minimum Service Requirements**

1. State Employees Retirement System
   - A. Regular                          60 years old and 10 years of service, or age 55 with 30 years of service
     - Corrections officers           51 years old and 25 years in correction officer position
     - Conservation officers          Any age, 25 years of service
   - B. Early retirement                 55 years old and 15 years of service

2. Public School Employees Retirement System
   - A. Regular–Basic plan              60 years old and 10 years of service, or age 55 with 30 years of service
     - Member investment plan        30 and out, or age 60 and 5 years of service
   - B. Early Retirement                 55 years old and 15 years of service

3. State Police Retirement System        Any age and 25 years of service, or age 50 with 10 years of service

4. Judges Retirement System              60 years old and 8 years of service, or age 55 and 18 years of service

5. Legislative Retirement System
   - A. Regular                          55 years old and 5 years of service, or age 50 with age + service $\geq 70$

SOURCE: Comprehensive Annual Financial Report, selected years; Linquist (1992).

# 21

# Environment and Natural Resources in Michigan

*Gloria E. Helfand and John R. Wolfe*

## Trends in Environmental Protection

### Trends in Environmental Awareness and Policy

The 165-year history of Michigan has seen substantial growth in population, production, and prosperity. A by-product of this growth is the stress of increased development, resource extraction, and waste generation on the natural environment. At the same time, increasing living standards have raised our expectations and willingness to pay to protect human and ecological health. While these issues are not unique to Michigan, balancing a clean, safe environment with the costs of achieving that goal is of increasing concern as Michigan manages the industrial and environmental benefits of being the "Great Lakes State."

Many important initiatives in U.S. environmental policy have proceeded in quantum leaps in response to incidents that raised public consciousness about threats to the environment. Rachel Carson's bestseller *Silent Spring* (1962) focused public attention on risks associated with chemical pollutants, launching an environmental movement that led to creation of the U.S. Environmental Protection Agency (USEPA) in 1970 and passage of the National Environmental Policy Act (1969) and the Clean Air Act (1970). The

Clean Water Act, in 1972, was in part a response to incidents like Cleveland's Cuyahoga River catching fire in 1969 and declarations that Lake Erie was dead, choked with algae that deprived fish of oxygen. The U.S.-Canadian Great Lakes Water Quality Agreement of 1972, establishing goals for phosphorus loads to the Great Lakes, arose from the same concerns. The Resource Conservation and Recovery Act (RCRA 1976) and Comprehensive Environmental Response, Compensation and Liability Act (CERCLA 1980), known as Superfund, were responses to episodes such as Love Canal in New York, where unsafe disposal of toxic substances had exposed a neighborhood to health risks. These episodes led to better handling of hazardous substances and cleanup of hazardous waste sites.

Not all changes in Michigan's environmental quality and policies have been due to federal laws; during the last thirty years, Michigan has enacted many of its own programs. In 1968, state voters approved a $335 million bond measure for cleaning the state's waters. The year 1970 saw passage of the Michigan Environmental Protection Act (MEPA), which authorized citizens to bring suit to stop environmental damage in the state, and the Inland Lakes and Streams Act of 1972 gave the state authority over damming, dredging, and filling of lakes and streams. In 1976, state voters

FIGURE 21.1

**Michigan Appropriations for DNR (and DEQ since 1996)**

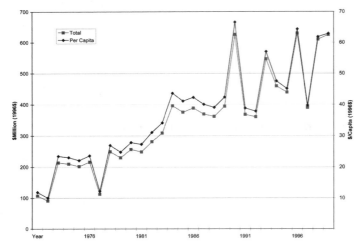

SOURCE: Legislative Service Bureau, and U.S. Bureau of Economic Analysis (for Gross Domestic Product Implicit Price Deflator).

approved a deposit-refund system for beer and soda containers, the first in a major industrial state. The following year saw a stringent limit placed on the phosphate content of laundry detergents, to reduce excess nutrients in the Great Lakes and the state's waters, and 1979 brought the Wetlands Protection Act. These and other measures, combined with the federal laws enacted during this time, led to great environmental improvements in the state.

FIGURE 21.2

**Average Annual Percentage Change in Private Pollution Control Expenditures, 1973–94**

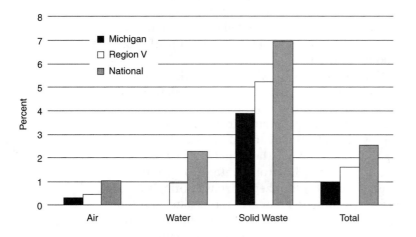

SOURCE: Analysis of data from U.S. Bureau of the Census, Current Industrial Reports and Vogan (1996).

While these and other policies have helped reduce the magnitude of identified environmental problems, previously unrecognized problems have increased in prominence. For example, the growth of algae in Lake Erie has been greatly reduced, allowing fish populations to return. With the return of fisheries, however, the bioaccumulation of toxic substances, with potential adverse health impacts on people and other predators who eat fish, has become more visible. Thus, success has both highlighted new challenges and encouraged the idea that these new problems can be solved.

Environmental policy, like any other policy, is subject to unlimited wants and limited resources. Continued improvements in environmental quality are likely to come with increasing costs, and elimination of a problem may be impossible without new technologies. A view that the costs of some cleanups may exceed their environmental benefits led to a major 1995 amendment ("Part 201") to Michigan Environmental Response Act (MERA), shifting the focus from contaminant removal to risk reduction.

Efficient environmental policy prioritizes threats by balancing the risks that they pose to human and ecological health, in the present and in the future, with the resources needed to reduce those risks. This requires monitoring trends in environmental indicators, to identify the most important risks and link them to their most important causes.

### Trends in Spending

*Public.* Until 1996, the Michigan Department of Natural Resources (DNR) managed most state environmental programs, including not only those related to forests and wildlife but also air and water quality programs. These activities ranged from supervising state forests and parks to monitoring and enforcing pollution laws. In 1996, these functions were split between the DNR (which has parks, forests, and wildlife programs) and the Department of Environmental Quality (DEQ), which handles pollution programs. Figure 21.1 shows that both total and per capita real (i.e., inflation-adjusted) spending have increased considerably since 1971. During that time, the responsibilities of these agencies increased with the new state and federal requirements and a popular commitment to Michigan's natural resources and environment. Year-to-year variation in spending increased significantly in the last decade as well. These variations appear to be due, in large part, to changing policies on where to show the appropriations for environmental protection bonds and the new clean water bonds. For example, environmental bond appropriations from existing issues were removed from the DEQ budget in FY 1997 and moved to Treasury, while a new issue was appropriated again in DEQ in FY 2001, along with Clean Michigan Initiative (CMI) bonds. Appropriations for specific programs, such as air or water quality, are almost impossible to track consistently, because the agencies have been occasionally reorganized in an attempt to find new ways to address environmental problems.

*Private.* As environmental regulation has tightened, businesses have faced increasingly costly pollution control measures. At the same time, environmental regulation has stimulated technologies that reduce the costs of pollution abatement. For instance, it is now common for manufacturers to conduct life-cycle analyses, accounting for all environmental impacts, from raw material extraction to waste disposal. These analyses sometimes lead not only to reduced pollution, but also to cost savings.

Figure 21.2 shows how total real private-sector expenditures on pollution abatement (including capital expenditures and operation/maintenance expenses by large manufacturers, mining firms, electric and gas utilities, and some petroleum companies) have changed from 1972–94, based on data from the federal Bureau of Economic Analysis. (This data series was discontinued in 1994). Expenditures in USEPA's Region V (Illinois, Indiana, Michigan, Minnesota, Ohio, and Wisconsin) increased more slowly than did national expenditures, and Michigan's expenditures increased even more slowly. Per unit of Gross State Product, Michigan expenditures are virtually the same as Region V expenditures (figure 21.3)— about 0.45 percent.

Private-sector expenditures on solid waste increased more rapidly nationally, regionally, and in Michigan than did expenditures on air and water pollution. At the national, regional, and state levels, expenditures on solid waste are now closer in magnitude to those for air and water. Figure 21.4 shows these trends for Michigan.

Environmental protection is not free; the cost of public expenditures on environment and natural resources for each resident of Michigan is

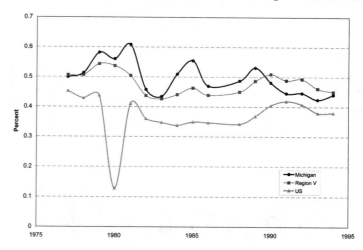

### FIGURE 21.3

**Private Pollution Control Expenditures as Percentage of Gross Product**

SOURCE: Analysis of data from U.S. Bureau of the Census, Current Industrial Reports, and U.S. Bureau of Economic Analysis, Regional Accounts Data.

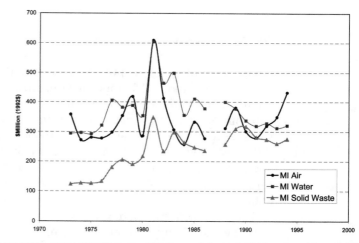

### FIGURE 21.4

**Michigan Private Sector Pollution Control Expenditures by Medium, $1992**

SOURCE: Analysis of data from U.S. Bureau of the Census, Current Industrial Reports, and Vogan (1996).

approximately $60/year (though this value does not include all local government expenditures and does include expenditures not related directly to environmental protection), and business expenditures (not all of which are paid for by Michigan residents) are less than half a percent of Gross State Product. Passage by Michigan voters of the $675 million Clean Michigan Initiative in 1998 suggests that Michigan residents do not consider state expenditures on the environment excessive. These expenditures have also improved

FIGURE 21.5

**Numbers of Fish Advisories for Region V States, 1988–98**

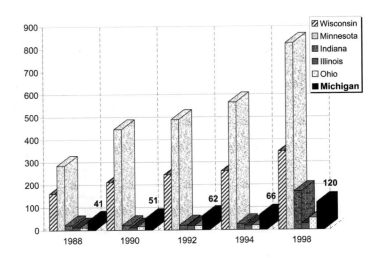

SOURCE: U.S. Environmental Protection Agency, National Water Quality Inventory, various years.

Michigan's environment in a number of ways. The following section examines some measures of environmental quality in Michigan.

## Trends in Environmental Quality

Environmental quality is not easily measured. It comprises a number of factors, including (but not limited to) air and water quality, exposure to toxic substances, habitat for plants and animals, and pleasing surroundings. Many of the variables that influence environmental quality are localized, and some are subjective. It is not possible to capture all-important local trends with statewide data.

The approach used here is to assess aggregate measures for Michigan, both to summarize environmental quality in the state and to facilitate comparisons to national and regional data. At the same time, it is important to emphasize that these aggregate data do not indicate how well every local area in the state is doing.

An important distinction must be made between pollution loadings (emissions) and environmental quality. Pollution loadings are important to monitor, because they are a key indicator of the stress we apply to the environment. However, the effect of loadings on quality is not always local or immediate. Some pollutants can be dispersed and carried long distances, as when wind scatters air pollutants. Loadings from out-

side Michigan affect environmental quality in Michigan, and Michigan's loadings affect the environment in other states. Geographic and meteorological factors affect the vulnerability of the environment to pollutant loadings; thus, two areas can have identical emissions but different ambient quality. Also, some pollutants have transient effects—they naturally degrade—while others accumulate in the biosphere and can cause problems decades after emissions have ceased. The trends that follow include information both on loadings (e.g., aggregate emissions) and on environmental quality (e.g., violations of ambient quality standards). Assessing and improving environmental quality is the ultimate goal, but information on loadings contributes to understanding how to achieve improvements.

*Surface Water Quality.* The USEPA (2000) provides a biannual report to Congress on the extent to which each state's surface waters can support beneficial uses defined by the Clean Water Act. In 1998, 97% of Michigan's river miles were fully supportive of aquatic life, 96% of fishing, and 98% of swimming. The most important cause of impairment is organic chemicals that contaminate fish. Most pollution comes from nonpoint sources, such as agriculture and combined sewers. USEPA lists "almost all" of Michigan's inland lakes as swimmable, but Michigan applies a generic fish advisory to all inland lakes, due to mercury contamination (see figure 21.5). Fish advisories in Michigan show similar patterns to those for other EPA Region V states.

While these USEPA data show that Michigan's surface waters can sustain a high level of beneficial use, they do not tell the whole story. Wet-weather discharges of raw sewage into rivers and lakes impair water quality, leading to beach closings. Fully 42% of Michigan beaches reporting in a 2000 USEPA survey were affected by storm water pollution, and 276 beach closings were reported (Natural Resources Defense Council 2001). Beaches on Lake St. Clair have been especially affected by storm water pollution.

Problems associated with the nutrients nitrogen and phosphorus also persist in some water bodies, despite decades of effort to control them. Uncontrolled discharges of nitrogen and phosphorus from agricultural runoff, sewage systems, and industrial operations can foster the growth of algae, leading to fish kills, beach closings, and taste and odor problems for water-supply systems. Some 5% of Michigan's inland lakes are listed as hypereutrophic (that is, excessively productive of algae and other plant life), although figure 21.6 shows that Michigan's lakes suffer less from overenrichment than do those of several comparison states.

Discharges of nutrients also affect the Great Lakes. The potential for algae blooms is especially great in shallow, partially contained areas of open water such as Saginaw Bay, because there is less dilution of the nutrients than in open water. Of the Great Lakes, Lakes Erie and Ontario have had the most serious problems with nutrient enrichment and algal growth, in large part because of their locations downstream of Detroit and other major metropolitan areas.

Algae require a fixed ratio of nitrogen to phosphorus for growth. Because this ratio is generally exceeded in the Great Lakes, phosphorus is the "controlling" nutrient: reducing phosphorus loadings reduces algal blooms. Thus, the 1972 Great Lakes Water Quality Agreement (GLWQA) between the United States and Canada and its 1978 Revision set phosphorus load and concentration targets for the Great Lakes and outlined a control program to meet these objectives. Michigan imposed limits for point-source phosphorus dischargers under the Clean Water Act and mandated a reduction in the phosphorus content of detergents, beginning in 1977. For Lakes Erie and Ontario and for Saginaw Bay, phosphorus concentration targets were set at levels that would represent significant water quality improvement. For the open waters of the upper lakes (Superior, Michigan, and Huron), where serious nutrient problems had not yet occurred, the targets were set to prevent water quality degradation.

By the early 1980s, phosphorus loads to each of the Great Lakes had been reduced to levels near target values; this action prevented degradation of the upper lakes and improved water quality in the lower lakes, as intended (DePinto, Young, and McIlroy 1986). The most substantial reductions in loads were from municipal wastewater treatment plants. Notably, the load to Lake Erie, to which Detroit-area treatment plants were a major contributor, dropped by more than 80% between 1972 and 1982. Nonpoint sources such as agricultural runoff now provide the bulk of the loads.

By 1980, a reduction in blue-green algae in Saginaw Bay had eliminated taste and odor problems for the Saginaw-Midland water supply intake, in the Outer Bay (Bierman, Dolan, and Kasprzyk 1984). This suggests that point-source load reductions were effective in targeting the

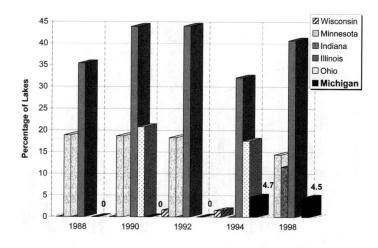

**FIGURE 21.6**

**Percentages of Hypereutrophic Lakes in Region V States, 1988–98**

SOURCE: Environmental Protection Agency, National Water Quality Inventory, various years.

phosphorus compounds that most readily support algal growth.

However, blue-green algae blooms have recently reappeared in Saginaw Bay and western Lake Erie (Vanderploeg et al. 2001). This change is probably attributable to the colonization of the Great Lakes by the zebra mussel (see discussion of "Exotic Species," following), which selectively preys on competing algal species (Limno-Tech, Inc. 1997), thus improving the ecological niche occupied by blue-green algae. As a result, Saginaw Bay water quality is now more vulnerable to loads of available phosphorus than it was in 1972, when the GLWQA was reached. This unforeseeable threat to Great Lakes water quality underscores the importance of finding an effective method to keep invasive species out of the Great Lakes. It also underscores a need to better understand the factors promoting algal growth in Saginaw Bay. This will require more intensive monitoring and study of phosphorus loads, their sources and response to management practices, and the effect of exotic species on this ecosystem.

*Drinking Water.* More than 80% of Michigan's population obtains its drinking water from surface water, with the remainder drawing upon groundwater. Currently, about 3% of Michigan's population is affected by drinking water from systems not in compliance with all health-based standards, compared to about 7% in Region V and 9% nationally (see figure 21.7); Michigan's violations relate

FIGURE 21.7

**Proportion of Population in Systems with Violations of Health-Based Drinking Water Standards, 1994–2001**

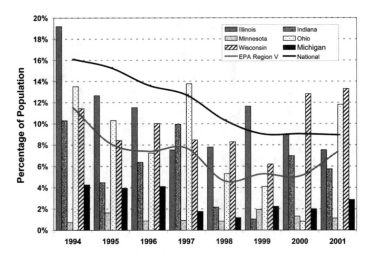

SOURCE: U.S. Environmental Protection Agency, Summary Inventory of Violations, and Government Performance and Results Act Data.

Region V is among the regions with a lower proportion of people affected by noncompliant water systems. Because standards are uniform across states, differences in compliance rates reflect different proportions of small systems, systems using treated surface water, and older distribution systems with copper and lead piping, all factors associated with greater difficulty achieving compliance.

In 2001, USEPA lowered the drinking water limit for arsenic from fifty to ten micrograms per liter, effective in 2006. This will require many water systems to install costly treatment equipment or to develop alternate supplies.

The Great Lakes provide Michigan with a plentiful source of water for drinking and other purposes. There is concern, however, that significant removals of water from the Great Lakes Basin to meet the needs of other regions could endanger this resource and threaten the Great Lakes ecosystem. One recent case involved the permitting of two high-capacity wells in western Michigan, installed to produce bottling water for nationwide sale. At issue is whether water withdrawals should be regulated, consistent with their potential environmental impacts. Currently, the Great Lakes states and provinces are exploring implementation of a directive contained in their 2001 Annex to the Great Lakes Charter. This directive sets a new standard for evaluating proposals for new water withdrawals, requiring improvements while avoiding adverse impacts to water-related resources of the Great Lakes.

primarily to coliform, a bacterial indicator of contamination, and turbidity, a measure of cloudiness. Despite an upswing in 2001 in Michigan and other Region V states, the trend in population affected by violations shows improvement since 1994 in Michigan, the region, and the nation. About 4% of Michigan's drinking water systems had violations of standards in 2001, compared to 5% in Region V and 6% nationally. Nationally, EPA's

*Air Quality.* The federal Clean Air Act of 1970 set ambient air quality standards for "criteria" pollutants. Permit limits for industrial point-source air emissions are set to meet these targets. As figure 21.8 shows, emissions of carbon monoxide (CO), ten-micron (PM10) and 2.5-micron (PM25) particulate matter, and volatile organic compounds (VOC) have dropped since the mid-1980s (PM 25 since 1990), while emissions of nitrogen oxides (NOX) have gone up and sulfur dioxide (SO2) and ammonia (NH3) emissions have shown little trend. Michigan is mostly in compliance with air-quality standards (see figure 21.9), with the exception of ozone. Ozone production is greatly enhanced by warm weather, and can occur as winds carry its precursors (including car exhaust) downwind of their source. Thus, ozone control measures need to be sufficient for warm weather episodes, and may require control of air emissions outside the state, as well as within Michigan.

FIGURE 21.8

**Emission Trends for Industrial Point-Source Pollutants, 1985–99**

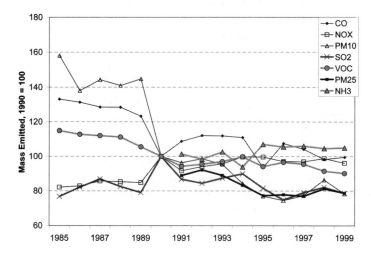

SOURCE: U.S. Environmental Protection Agency, AirData.

**FIGURE 21.9**

## Number of Pollution Violations in Michigan, 1978–2000

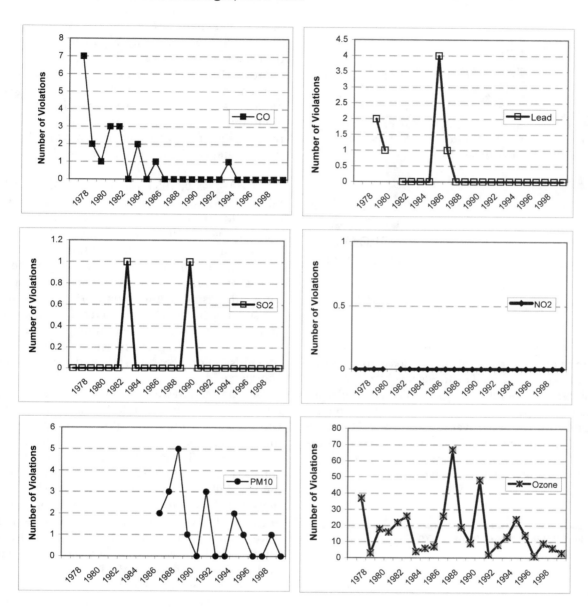

SOURCE: Michigan Department of Natural Resources, Air Quality Division.

*Toxic Substances.* The federal 1986 Emergency Preparedness and Community Right-to-Know Act established the Toxic Release Inventory (TRI), which identifies annual releases of approximately six hundred listed toxic substances to air, water, land, or to another facility, by businesses in specified industries with ten or more full-time employees. While there is no requirement for emissions reductions, the public nature of the information appears to provide an incentive for reductions (see, e.g., Hamilton 1995). Additional-ly, USEPA provides technical assistance to sources seeking to reduce their emissions. Figure 21.10 compares trends in total toxic waste managed in Michigan, in EPA's Region V, and in the United States as a whole. Total releases to the environment of these substances have dropped nation-ally, regionally, and in the state, but off-site transfers of these substances have increased dur-ing the same period. As Khanna, Quimio, and Bojilova (1998) note, these transfers are probably to waste management or recycling facilities, and

FIGURE 21.10

**Annual Percentage Changes in Toxic Substances Managed, 1991–99**

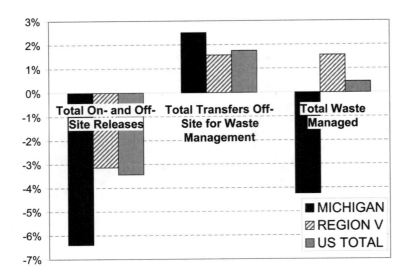

SOURCE: Analysis of data from U.S. Environmental Protection Agency, Toxic Release Inventory.

thus suggest more environmentally sound handling of these materials than release to the environment. While total toxic releases have increased slightly nationally and regionally, total releases have dropped in Michigan. Because these reductions are summed over all sources in Michigan and are, for the most part, voluntary, it is not possible to determine, without an in-depth study, why Michigan's releases have dropped.

FIGURE 21.11

**PCBs and DDT in Lake Michigan Lake Trout, 1970–92**

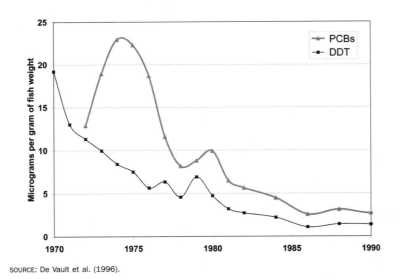

SOURCE: De Vault et al. (1996).

Some toxic substances persist in the environment (that is, they do not degrade quickly), accumulate in plants and animals, and can be passed up the food chain through consumption. Figure 21.11 shows trends for polychlorinated biphenyls (PCBs) and DDT in Lake Michigan lake trout, and figure 21.12 shows PCB trends in herring gull eggs. Legislation in the 1970s contributed to substantial reductions in PCB and DDT loads to the environment; thus, figures 21.11 and 21.12 also show the time required for the food chain to recover, due to the persistence of these contaminants.

*Solid Waste.* In 1993, Michigan banned landfilling of yard waste. This change and the growth of recycling programs have been credited with reducing the volume of solid waste from Michigan households. However, the resulting excess Michigan landfill capacity and low tipping fees may have induced an increase in imported waste from other states and Canada (Public Sector Consultants, Inc. 1998). The ability of Michigan to limit imports of solid waste is limited by the U.S. Constitution, which gives the federal government sole jurisdiction over interstate and cross-border commerce.

Data on solid waste volumes were not available until 1996, when the Solid Waste Management Act was amended to require landfills to report volumes by source. Figure 21.13 shows the trend since 1996. While solid waste generated in Michigan has increased by 32% since 1996, the total volume landfilled in Michigan has increased by even more (42%), because imports from other states and Canada to Michigan over the same period have each roughly doubled. Since 1999, two-thirds of the increase in landfilled waste has been due to increased imports. In 2001, imports accounted for about 20% of all solid waste landfilled in Michigan, from the following places: Canada 10%, Illinois 4%, Indiana 3%, Ohio 2%, and Wisconsin 1%.

A task force recently reporting to Governor Engler reflected the range of views on this issue: while the majority recommended coordination with Congress to encourage legislation to limit imports, representatives of environmental groups favored actions to further reduce waste generation, while solid-waste-industry representatives opposed regulation of trade in solid waste (Michigan Department of Environmental Quality 2000).

*Wetlands and Open Space.* While pollutants are important determinants of human and ecological health, the survival of wildlife species may depend more directly on preservation of their habitats. Wetlands provide essential habitat for migrating birds and other sensitive species. Wetlands also help to enhance surface water and groundwater quality, by assimilating solids from storm water runoff. During the first two centuries of U.S. history, the lower forty-eight states as a whole lost 53% of their wetlands (figure 21.14). Michigan lost about 50% of its wetlands during this period. Illinois, Indiana, and Ohio lost much greater percentages (85–90%) of their original wetlands, reflecting their greater intensity of drainage for farmland. Wisconsin and Minnesota lost smaller percentages of wetlands (42–46%) than did Michigan.

More recent estimates show a slowdown in wetlands loss. The U.S. Fish and Wildlife Service (2001) estimates the national rate of wetlands loss to have slowed by 80% from 1986 to 1997, compared to the preceding decade. Forested wetlands and freshwater emergent wetlands show the most losses, while open water pond acreage has been increasing, reflecting wetlands mitigation requirements imposed on developers to minimize net wetlands losses. The U.S. Department of Agriculture's Natural Resource Inventory (U.S. Department of Agriculture 2000) also shows low rates of wetland losses between 1992 and 1997. According to the USDA, Michigan is estimated to have lost about 0.1% of its wetlands during this period, with about the same loss rate for the other Region V states and the lower forty-eight states. However, Michigan's estimated loss rate of vegetated wetlands was higher, at 0.3%. The overall wetlands loss rate was suppressed by an increase in open water wetlands, equal to about 1.1% of 1992 open water acreage, between 1992 and 1997. Thus, a change in the mix of wetlands habitats is being effected, favoring open-water species over others, even as current policies now approach the goal of no net loss of wetlands.

Wetland losses to development were dwarfed by losses of agricultural and forest lands. According to the USDA, 364,100 acres of Michigan land were developed between 1992 and 1997. Some 42% of this land was previously forest, representing a loss of forest habitat to suburban landscapes. Another 33% of the land developed during this period was previously prime farmland. In 1992, a panel of experts ranked absence of land-use planning and loss of habitat as posing greater risks to the environment and quality of life in Michigan than contaminated groundwater and

sediment, hazardous waste, and solid-waste disposal (Michigan Department of Natural Resources 1992). For additional discussion, see chapter 5 of this volume, "Land Use in Michigan" and chapter 10, "Michigan's Agricultural, Forestry and Mining Industries."

*Exotic Species.* Just as economic activity and development have reduced habitat, human activ-

**FIGURE 21.12**

**PCB Levels in Herring Gull Eggs**

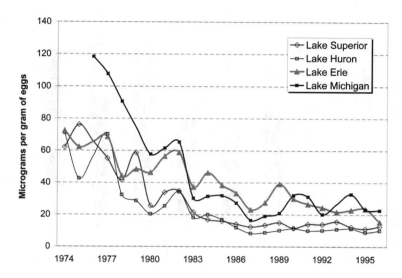

SOURCE: U.S. Council on Environmental Quality, Twenty-eighth Annual Report (1997).

**FIGURE 21.13**

**Michigan Solid Waste Trends by Source, 1996–2001**

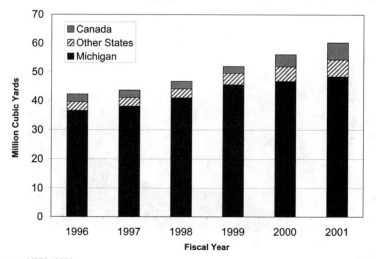

SOURCE: MDEQ (2002).

**FIGURE 21.14**

## Wetland Losses in Contiguous U.S. and EPA Region V, 1780s–1980s

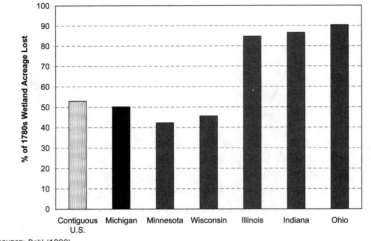

SOURCE: Dahl (1990).

ity has also modified habitat by introducing non-native species of fish, invertebrates, and plants. Numerous introduced species have been able to compete successfully with native organisms, profoundly altering the ecology of the Great Lakes themselves, and also inland habitats. The proliferation of introduced species continues to accelerate, despite efforts to cut off known invasion routes.

Documented introductions of nonnative species began in the early nineteenth century (Mills et al. 1993). Important exotics include the sea lamprey, a parasitic fish that has decimated

**FIGURE 21.15**

## Non-Native Species Introduced to the Great Lakes by Shipping

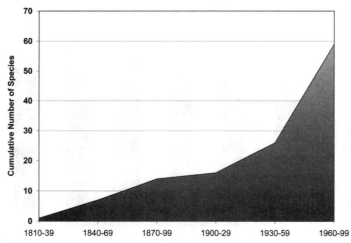

SOURCE: Mills et al., (1993).

native lake trout populations; purple loosestrife, an ornamental plant that chokes out native plants and deprives waterfowl of habitat; eurasian milfoil, a submerged plant whose beds overwhelm native plants and interfere with recreational boating; and the zebra mussel, a mollusk that clogs water intakes and promotes blue-green algae blooms by filtering other particles from lakes. Unintentional releases, such as the escape of garden plants or release of unused bait by anglers, have accounted for a large fraction of introductions in each period since the mid–nineteenth century. Intentional releases by fisheries managers have also been significant, although less so since the mid-1900s, and have profoundly impacted native fish species and habitat (Krueger and May 1991). Each stage of canal development, from the opening of the Erie Canal in 1825 to that of the St. Lawrence Seaway in 1959, has transported a new wave of exotic species to the Great Lakes, attached to the hulls of ships, in ballast, or under their own power.

Access to international shipping is one of Michigan's greatest economic assets, and it is increasingly important as commerce becomes more global. In recent decades, however, most Great Lakes exotic species introductions have been due to shipping, primarily through discharge of ballast taken on in foreign ports (figure 21.15). Most species introduced since 1985 are native to the Ponto-Caspian region (which includes the Black, Azov, and Caspian Seas), on the southern boundary of the former Soviet republics of southwestern Asia (Ricciardi and MacIssac 2000). While direct U.S. shipping trade with this region is limited, the opening in the 1990s of canal systems linking the Black Sea with northern European ports has provided a pathway to ports of origin for Great Lakes trade. The adaptability of these Ponto-Caspian species is due in part to the diversity of fresh- and brackish-water habitats in that region, which provides them with a tolerance for saltwater, enabling them to survive the required substitution of saltwater for fresh water ballast by vessels bound for the Great Lakes (Mills et al. 1993). Additional measures, such as heating or filtration of ballast, biocides, or ultraviolet light, may be needed to abate the growing invasion of nonnative aquatic species.

In summary, environmental legislation, starting in the 1970s, has reduced environmental loadings, and thus environmental damages, for air and water quality and toxic substances. At the same time, some improvements have led to identification of previously masked problems, and loss of habitat and invasion of exotic species pose serious concerns. These improvements have not come cheaply, nor have they been uniformly distributed in the state. The following section discusses some current and impending environmental issues that Michigan faces.

## Issues

Some important themes emerge from our survey of environmental quality trends:

- *Nonpoint source loads to surface water deserve more attention, relative to point sources.* Agricultural runoff, atmospheric deposition, and releases from sediments all contribute to continuing water-quality problems in Michigan, and have not been effectively controlled by implementation of the Clean Water Act.
- *Loss of habitat and competition from introduced species are very serious risks.* These two problems have been consistently identified in the scientific literature as the greatest threats to the Great Lakes ecosystem (Limno-Tech, Inc. 1993).
- *Some important environmental threats come from outside Michigan, and cannot be effectively managed through internal policies alone.* These include air pollutants and solid wastes generated in neighboring states.

In the following sections, we discuss the impact of nonpoint sources and water quality trading, one strategy that can be used to reduce it. We also address a shift in policy direction from contaminant removal to risk reduction and brownfields development, which reflects a concern with habitat preservation. We also discuss two other important issues, environmental justice and control of combined sewer overflows.

## Point Source Versus Nonpoint Source Controls

The environmental laws of the past thirty-five years have led to substantial improvements in water quality. They have focused on so-called point sources of pollution—sources that have a defined point (such as an outfall pipe) where effluent enters the receiving body (a river, lake, or groundwater). These sources, which include industrial facilities, are relatively easy to identify,

regulate, and monitor, because the source and the destination of the effluent are visible. Reductions in effluent from point sources have contributed greatly to improvements in water quality.

Relatively unaddressed are "nonpoint" sources of pollution. Nonpoint source pollution is characterized by difficulty either in observing the effluent or in identifying the source. For instance, agricultural runoff can travel via subsurface flows to the receiving body; in this case, the effluent itself cannot be observed. Additionally, because the flows could come from any farmer in the watershed, the source cannot be easily identified. Similarly, contaminated storm water is the product of accumulated runoff from businesses, public properties, and private residences. Because of these difficulties, nonpoint source pollution is not subject to the same National Pollution Discharge Elimination System (NPDES) permit requirements that point sources face, and nonpoint sources are now the leading source of water quality impairment in the United States (U.S. Environmental Protection Agency 2000).

Control of nonpoint-source pollution is especially problematic, because of the difficulty in tracing the link between the effluent and the source. This weak link means that effluent cannot easily be regulated directly. Instead, indirect control methods, such as requiring use of agricultural "best management practices" (e.g., buffer strips along waterways or runoff-reducing tillage methods) and reduced use of polluting chemicals (such as fertilizer) are often proposed. Because these methods are indirect (targeting methods rather than outcomes), some will be more effective than others, and they may have unintended consequences. For instance, Helfand and House (1995) found that reducing fertilizer use was much more costly as a way to reduce groundwater contamination in California's Salinas Valley than reduction of irrigation water. In addition, these indirect methods might lead polluters to switch to inputs that are unregulated but more polluting. These switches might also lead to much higher costs to sources that use the regulated substances but do not pollute, and they might discourage polluters from finding new and more effective ways of reducing effluent.

The complexities involved in indirect regulation suggest why nonpoint source pollution has not received the same focus or achieved the same successes as point source control. At the same time, nonpoint pollution reduction is necessary to further improve water quality. Additionally, because point sources have been regulated for thirty years, and many of the most cost-effective controls have been implemented, it is likely that reductions in nonpoint discharges will be less expensive than further reductions from point sources. Thus, even though nonpoint control measures need to be designed carefully, to avoid unintended impacts, they are likely to be an important part of future water-pollution-control strategies.

In Michigan, this importance has led to conflict between the USEPA and MDEQ over the issue of concentrated animal feeding operations (CAFOs). These facilities, where large numbers of animals are kept in confined spaces, produce enormous quantities of animal waste. Under the Clean Water Act, CAFOs cannot discharge any of this waste into waterways without an NPDES permit (U.S. Environmental Protection Agency, Region 5 Water Division 2001). Michigan law prohibits farms from discharging pollutants into waterways (Michigan Department of Agriculture 2002), and Michigan has claimed on this basis that these permits were not necessary. The USEPA and environmental groups have disagreed with that claim, citing examples of discharges from these operations into waterways (Michigan Sierra Club 2001). The state is currently proposing a plan to the USEPA to develop a permit system.

### Air and Water Quality Trading

Economists have long advocated "market-based incentive" programs—either taxing emissions, subsidizing pollution abatement, or using marketable pollution permits—for reducing air and water pollution (see, for example, Baumol and Oates 1988). In contrast to standards-based approaches to pollution control, these policies allow dischargers to choose their emissions levels in the face of costs imposed on the discharger per unit of emissions. In theory, a discharger will abate as long as the cost associated with polluting (for instance, a pollution tax or the cost of a permit for a unit of pollution) exceeds the profits or other benefits associated with polluting, but it may still emit pollution if the benefits associated with a unit of emissions are higher than the cost. In a market-based system, a high tax or permit cost will achieve high levels of cleanup, because making polluting costly gives dischargers an incentive to reduce the cost by reducing emissions. At the same time, a discharger with high

abatement costs has the flexibility to reduce its emissions less than a discharger with lower abatement costs (who has an incentive to reduce a great deal).

In the United States, marketable pollution permit programs are the primary incentive-based program in use; in fact, the term "market-based" approach is sometimes considered synonymous with permit programs, despite the existence of other methods (such as a pollution tax). Under a permit program, a discharger that reduces emissions below permitted levels can sell those reductions to a discharger with higher cleanup costs. Total emissions can be constant (or a required reduction may be part of the program), while reallocating abatement from a high-cost source to a low-cost source reduces total abatement costs. The largest use of marketable permits is for the reduction of sulfur dioxide emissions, authorized by the Clean Air Act Amendments of 1990; it is estimated to have reduced cleanup costs, compared to a standards-based approach, by $225 million to $375 million per year (Schmalensee et al. 1998).

The cost savings associated with a marketable permit program, combined with no change (or a possible reduction) in emissions, provide the advantage for this system. If the amount of total emissions is the only environmental concern, there is no disadvantage to such a system (except, perhaps, added administrative costs). In fact, though, the spatial pattern of emissions of many pollutants is as important as the total level of emissions. If emissions are reduced in an area with low pollution, so that an area with high pollution can have higher emissions, the permit system may lead to a net *increase* in health and environmental damage, by creating "hot spots" where pollution levels are very high. Marketable permit schemes are most likely to be both environmentally and financially successful if trading is limited to the area of the pollutant's impact, if spatial effects are accounted for in the trading scheme (for instance, by requiring greater payments for reductions in a low-pollution area to justify an increase in a higher-pollution area), or if the permit scheme is one aspect of an overall reduction in total emissions (Stavins 1998).

Michigan has an emissions trading program for air pollution, and is proposing a trading system for water pollution. In both cases, the reduction in emissions from the seller must be greater than the amount provided to the buyer. This provision both reduces emissions and increases the costs of the permit program. If emissions need to be reduced to meet environmental targets, the more direct way to achieve this goal is to require emissions reductions regardless of whether trading takes place. If emissions do not need further reduction, this provision primarily discourages trading. If the spatial aspects of the pollution are not a concern (for instance, if dischargers are neighbors), then this discouragement of trading is economically inefficient, because trading is made more costly for possibly unnecessary environmental gains.

Michigan's air and proposed water quality trading programs take different approaches to avoiding the exacerbation of local hot spots. The air program allows trading with little regard to geography, as long as trading regions have attained air-quality standards. The proposed water-quality trading program, on the other hand, would allow trade only within watersheds.

The air-quality program allows some banking of permits. A discharger that reduces emissions below its requirements can save credits to emit on a future date, though the credits have to be used within five years of their generation. Banking decreases current emissions, but allows emissions to increase in the future. If total emissions levels are scheduled by regulation to decrease over time, banking allows dischargers to keep emissions more constant than those standards dictate. If emissions levels are not required to decrease, pollution in the future might increase, when the banked credits are finally emitted. Table 21.1 shows trading activity as of 3 December 2001 (Michigan Department of Environmental Quality 2002). Currently the number of Emissions Reduction Credits (ERCs) generated exceeds the sum of the number used and retired because, with the current economic slowdown, the credits are not needed, and they are being banked.

In sum, marketable permit systems for air and water emissions can reduce the costs of complying with a specified level of emissions. The Michigan trading programs have some protections against hot spots, although USEPA may require additional protection before approving water-quality trading. Requirements for mandatory permit retirement for trades may increase the cost of trading, and banking programs have the potential to allow increased emissions in the future. If trading programs are implemented when good monitoring exists for ambient air and water quality, to ensure that hot spots are avoided, they can be a very useful way to reduce the costs

### TABLE 21.1

**Reductions, Benefits, and Credits Due to Trading**

| Pollutant | Emission Reduction Credits (ERCs), in tons | | | |
|---|---|---|---|---|
| | Generated | Used | Retired | for Retirement on 1/1/02 |
| CO | 5,652.37 | 74 | 342 | 5,236.78 |
| NO$_x$ | 40,419.47 | 1,749 | 33,185.81 | 14,977.51 |
| VOC | 6,332.37 | 212 | 3,253.51 | 2,334.53 |
| Pb | 0 | 0 | 0 | 0 |
| PM10 | 400 | 0 | 76 | 323 |
| SO$_2$ | 11,227.77 | 0 | 1,670.56 | 9,413.21 |

SOURCE: Michigan Department of Environmental Quality (2002a).

of clean air and water. In the absence of a monitoring network, trades for pollutants with localized effects should be geographically constrained for better assurance that environmental quality goals will be met.

### Contaminant Removal Versus Risk Management

The original objective of the Superfund law was to require polluters to bear the cost of returning the environment to an uncontaminated condition. In the same spirit, Michigan's Environmental Response Act (MERA, or Act 307) had the stated objective "to eliminate environmental contamination." To facilitate cleanups, the Act imposed strict liability on owners and operators of properties and generators and transporters of wastes, regardless of demonstrated fault.

In the early years of Superfund and the MERA, the main efforts were cleanups of historical spills to groundwater and soil. Fuels and chlorinated solvents were and continue to be a major cause of contamination, introduced to the environment by improper storage or disposal. These chemicals include numerous known or suspected carcinogens, potentially toxic at low concentrations. Many of these are sufficiently soluble to travel great distances underground with natural groundwater flow. It was estimated in the early 1990s that there were more than 300,000 groundwater contamination sites nationwide (U.S. Environmental Protection Agency 1993), and that cleanup cost ranged from about $0.5 trillion to $1 trillion. (Russell, Colglazier, and English 1991).

In addition to the large scale of the problem, elimination of contaminants from groundwater has proven to be technically challenging. Because organic chemicals tend to cling to soil particles, it is difficult to reduce their concentrations to safe levels by pumping and treating tainted groundwater. Some chemicals, such as the constituents of gasoline, can be degraded by microorganisms already present in the subsurface environment, and scientists and engineers have developed methods to speed this process. Chlorinated solvents are not very responsive to this approach, however. The complexity of the subsurface environment and the presence of pockets of undissolved contaminants further complicates cleanup. A 1994 report by a panel appointed by the National Academy of Sciences (National Research Council 1994) concluded that existing technologies were not adequate to treat groundwater to health-based standards at the majority of existing sites. In their view, the best that could be done in these cases was to contain the contamination while ongoing research seeks more effective remediation methods. Despite some technological progress since 1994, this pessimistic assessment remains largely true today.

The difficulties involved in eliminating contamination have led to a greater emphasis on managing risk. In 1995, MERA was amended and relabeled Part 201 of the Michigan Natural Resources and Environmental Protection Act. Its objective is to "eliminate unacceptable risks" based on designated residential, industrial, or commercial land uses, set by binding restrictions recorded in real-estate records. Risks may be reduced or eliminated by preventing exposure to the contaminant, blocking "reasonable and relevant exposure pathways associated with that particular site." For example, covering a site with pavement may be sufficient to satisfy Part 201's requirements, if it sufficiently reduces exposures by the pathways of importance at the site.

In the 1990s, contaminated sediments emerged as another major source of potential exposure to toxic chemicals. The major route of human and ecological exposure from sediment contamination is bioaccumulation through the food chain, especially through consumption of contaminated fish by anglers and nonhuman predators. Nationwide, USEPA (1997) has estimated that 6–12% of the sediment underlying surface water is contaminated. In Michigan, the International Joint Commission has designated fourteen harbors and other water bodies as Great Lakes Areas of Concern, each due in part to sediment contamination, and Michigan has targeted $25 million of the Clean Michigan bond author-

ized in 1998 for cleanup of areas containing as much as three million cubic yards of contaminated sediments (State of Michigan 1998). However, at a cost of $100 or more per cubic yard for removal (Romagnoli et al. 1998) (not including expenses for characterizing sites and evaluating strategies), $25 million would remove no more than 250,000 cubic yards, only 8% of the total identified volume of contaminated sediments. Clearly, the current effort is only a beginning. Additional federal funds would make it possible to increase the sediment cleanup effort, and the Great Lakes Legacy Act, authorizing funds for Great Lakes sites, has just been approved by Congress as this volume goes to press.

As with groundwater cleanups, significant technical limits exist for sediment cleanups. Most importantly, there are limits to the residual concentrations at the sediment surface that can be achieved with current environmental dredging techniques, and sediment removal at the largest sites could take decades. It may be possible and cost-effective to speed burial of contaminants, limiting exposures by capping contaminated deposits with sand or other materials. However, there is little experience to date with the permanence of burial by this method, especially under conditions of high storm-driven flows.

As with groundwater contamination, the potential cost and technical difficulty of removing all contamination from sediments is daunting, if not prohibitive. The challenge is to identify sites with the greatest risks and to find cost-effective, permanent means of reducing those risks. In some cases, this will require removing the contaminant, while in other cases monitored natural attenuation of exposures may be sufficient. Changing the focus of the issue away from risk elimination to risk management—to cost-effective ways to reduce harm from contaminants, rather than eliminating them—is likely to increase the number of sites addressed, at lower cost.

### Brownfields Development

Prior to 1995, an unintended consequence of CERCLA and MERA was that developers were reluctant to take on the potential liability associated with businesses in older urban areas. CERCLA and MERA made owners and operators strictly liable for any site contamination, regardless of responsibility. This fostered a bias toward use of undeveloped land, reducing wildlife habitat, and required construction of new public utilities and other facilities, while abandoning existing urban infrastructure.

Michigan reformed this system in 1995 with the Part 201 amendments, adopting a new causation standard that assigns liability more fairly. Prior owners responsible for a release of contaminants remain liable, but subsequent owners are not, as long as they demonstrate that a condition existed prior to purchase, by conducting a "baseline environmental assessment." New owners and operators are still obliged to exercise due care, to prevent worsening the spread of contamination and to mitigate unacceptable exposures, but they are not required to remediate the site. If a cleanup is necessary to make the property safe for future uses, the liability for this falls on the responsible previous owner, or MDEQ as the last resort. Cleanup standards were also relaxed, to make more industrial properties usable: the threshold of acceptable cancer risks was increased from one additional cancer in one million lifetimes to one in one hundred thousand, based on the property's use.

There has been considerable activity under the new Part 201 provisions and associated grant programs, and MDEQ reports that cumulative investment in brownfields properties (properties having environmental impacts from past development) has risen from about $1 billion in 1999 to about $3.5 billion in 2001 (Michigan Department of Environmental Quality and Michigan Department of Natural Resources 2001). Many counties and municipalities have only in the last few years begun their efforts to match funding of development on brownfield sites with developers, and it is too early to say whether these changes will significantly reduce sprawl and habitat loss. For more information on these issues, please see chapter 5, "Land Use in Michigan," and chapter 11, "The Economic Performance of Michigan's Cities and Metropolitan Areas," in this volume.

## Environmental Justice

Environmental policies do not lead to equal environmental quality everywhere. Even if all areas achieve the same environmental standards (e.g., for air or water quality), one area may exceed standards by a great deal, while another barely satisfies them. In other cases, the way in which environmental problems are addressed may be influenced by factors other than science. For instance, it is possible for one hazardous waste site

to be declared a Superfund site, when another, with similar risk characteristics, either is not listed as a Superfund site, is delayed in being added to the list, or is delayed in being treated (Lavelle and Coyle 1992). A variety of studies have argued that poor or minority communities face disproportionate exposure to environmental hazards (see, for example, Lavelle and Coyle 1992; Mohai and Bryant 1992; United Church of Christ Commission for Racial Justice1987; U.S. General Accounting Office 1983). In Michigan, Callewaert (1997) argues that the zip codes with the highest counts of pollution sources have disproportionately high proportions of minority residents. These disparities have led to the call for increased environmental justice—a safe environment for all.

A variety of factors may contribute to the relationship between environmental risks and concentrations of poor or minority residents. Helfand and Peyton (1999) cite four factors: (1) income (both poor people, who are disproportionately members of minority groups, and polluting facilities seek low-rent areas, and poor people might be swayed by the lure of economic activity from those facilities); (2) information (members of poor/minority communities may not have sufficient information, or the education required to understand the available information, about the risks in an area); (3) political organization or influence (poor/minority communities may not have as much political influence as wealthy or majority communities); and (4) racism (a deliberate decision to impose risks on poor/minority communities). The multiple contributing factors are likely to make it difficult to achieve environmental justice for all, but communities burdened with poverty and other problems are increasingly rebelling against environmental burdens.

A controversy over the site of an incinerator near the City of Flint demonstrates the problem of environmental justice and the difficulties in addressing it. Consumers Power Company, a major electrical utility in Michigan, got approval to build an incinerator to burn wood waste in Genesee County. Some of the wood waste contains lead, which can cause neurologic and other damage, especially to young children. Emissions from the plant could blow into Flint, whose residents already feel disproportionately affected by environmental hazards. The industrial park where the incinerator is located already has three facilities that deal with hazardous waste (two of which produce toxic air pollutants). The City of Flint, about three-fourths of whose population is not white, felt that it was receiving disproportionate harm from Genesee County, about three-fourths of whose population is white. Suit was brought to shut down the facility, claiming disproportionate impact on a minority community, and lack of consideration of the cumulative effects of exposure to a full range of contaminants, in addition to lead from incineration. The courts did not support the disproportionate impact argument, saying that the state's policy did not appear to be at fault, but did require examination of cumulative impacts before an emissions permit could be issued. Operation of the incinerator continues.

While a growing body of evidence suggests that poor or minority groups face disproportionate environmental hazards, the causes of the correlation are complex enough that remedies are difficult to develop. At the same time, adding environmental insults to the other burdens faced by poor or minority communities may lead to increased opposition to new industrial facilities in poor areas.

## Combined Sewer Overflows

Many older sewer systems, especially in Northeastern and Great Lakes states, were constructed to convey sewage and storm water in a shared network of piping, called combined sewers. During dry weather the combined sewer systems deliver sanitary flows to sewage treatment plants for treatment and discharge. During wet weather, storm water runoff from streets and rooftops also drains to the combined sewer system. Treatment facilities are sized to handle typical maximum sanitary sewage volumes. Consequently, during all but the smallest storms, and also during heavier snowmelt runoff, excess flows into the sewer systems are discharged into adjacent surface waters as combined sewer overflows (CSOs). The resulting CSO discharges are typically an unhealthy combination of urban storm water, sanitary sewage, and industrial wastewater, containing pathenogenic microbes, solids, trace metals, and other pollutants. These constituents may pose a significant threat to water quality and public health. Even communities with separate sewer systems can experience wet-weather discharges, due to infiltration of rainwater into sewers, and illegal hookups of building footing drains into sanitary sewers.

Fifty-two Michigan communities have a total of 297 known CSO discharge points. These com-munities are located throughout the state, but the greatest numbers are in the Detroit metropolitan area. Much recent attention has been focused on untreated CSO discharge from communities in the Clinton River watershed, which has contributed to Lake St. Clair beach closings (Schmitt and Askari 2001).

Other communities, like Saginaw, have made substantial investments and significantly reduced their untreated wet-weather discharges and pollutant emissions. In the Rouge River watershed, sixteen communities embarked on a National Wet Weather Demonstration Project to control discharges from 168 CSO outfalls, with federal, state, and local participation (U.S. Environmental Protection Agency 2001a). Retention of larger flow volumes within the collection system during storm events, using adjustable gates, is a key element of the control plan.

Under the Clean Water Act, USEPA requires states to formulate CSO control strategies. These strategies must establish specific levels of control over CSOs but also provide flexibility to match site-specific conditions encountered with each system. They also allow for a long-term phasing in of control implementation to avoid overtaxing the available financial resources of each community. At a minimum, CSO communities are required to implement nine technology-based controls and develop CSO Long-Term Control Plans (LTCPs).

Michigan's implementation of the federal CSO policy has been to require either elimination of CSOs or "adequate treatment." Adequate treatment is defined to be complete treatment for one-hour storms of a size to occur annually; limited treatment (settling) for ten-year frequency storms; and at least some treatment for bigger storms. Over 90% of Michigan's CSO-permitted communities have submitted and received approval for their LTCPs, and approximately twenty-five others have separated their sewers (U.S. Environmental Protection Agency 2001a).

MDEQ has undertaken enforcement actions against a number of communities to require CSO upgrades, including some Rouge River communities that fell behind schedule for the USEPA CSO demonstration project. Michigan has also provided subsidies to communities through the State Revolving Fund (SRF). Established with 83% federal funds, the SRF provides low-interest loans for system improvements. Michigan has been the most aggressive user of SRF funding for CSO control among all states, accounting for about one-quarter of all dollars loaned nationally between

1988 and 2000 (U.S. Environmental Protection Agency 2001a). Clearly, Michigan policy makers view this as a cost-effective strategy for funding CSO controls.

Whether more will need to be done after the current round of LTCPs is implemented will depend on the remaining water-quality impacts and Michigan's answer to the question "how clean is clean?." The CSO problem could be greatly reduced by requiring all communities to separate their sanitary and storm water systems, as some Michigan communities have done. For larger communities, however, eliminating CSOs is very costly compared with upgrading controls on existing systems. For example, the CSO control plan implemented in Saginaw was chosen in part because its cost was about half the cost of sewer separation, and the controls are estimated to have reduced the volume of CSOs by about three-fourths. What remain are discharges triggered by the largest storms; these are not only the most expensive to eliminate, but they involve the greatest dilution of contaminants, and occur when swimming and fishing are least likely.

The complete elimination of CSOs may be an unrealistic goal, given that controls are costly and must compete for scarce resources. The elimination of significant water-quality and public health impacts may be a more realistic standard by which to measure the effectiveness of Michigan's current CSO control strategy (or any other controls). Continual and consistent monitoring of the affected water bodies is needed to assess these benefits as the current CSO control policy is implemented.

## Conclusions

Environmental quality in Michigan has improved dramatically from the 1960s, when some waters in the state "looked like a blueberry milkshake," and the "editor of *Air Engineering Magazine* . . . said Michigan was 'disgraceful' last among states in air pollution control" (Dempsey 2001). The classic pollution problems appear to be under control, in large part due to national and state regulatory activities. There is currently insufficient information to determine whether environmental protection levels are too high or low from the perspective of balancing costs and benefits; nevertheless, the continuing support for environmental programs expressed by the people of Michigan (for instance, through passage of the

Clean Michigan Initiative) suggests that environmental programs have not gone too far, and that the costs have not been onerous.

Perhaps the most important remaining environmental issue for Michigan is loss of biodiversity. More than 50% of Michigan's eighteenth-century wetlands have been lost, and nonnative invasive species are crowding out native species. These trends are partly associated with loss of habitat due to conversion of land to residential and commercial activities (see chapters 5 and 10 of this volume). The loss of biodiversity is likely to become increasingly difficult and important to address.

As the state continues to work on its environmental programs, a few general principles should be considered in formulating policies.

*1. There are both benefits and costs to protecting the environment.* The people of Michigan benefit from improved public health, scenery, and tourism opportunities, and ecological values provided by a clean environment. At the same time, these benefits impose costs on dischargers, on their customers, and on the state's residents themselves, because avoiding environmental damages forces changes in industrial processes and human behavior. A sound environmental policy cannot ignore either these benefits or costs. For instance, the large amount of money that would be required to reduce risk from exposure to hazardous waste to zero might be better spent by reducing risk to a small but nonzero amount and using the savings for other programs. At the same time, the benefits of protecting wetlands from filling might exceed the benefits from new developments on those lands. While it is difficult to determine, in many cases, whether environmental benefits outweigh the costs associated with protection, acknowledging that tradeoff is necessary for effective management of environmental (and other) problems.

*2. Prioritizing environmental policies based on their benefits and costs can lead to increased gains to state residents.* Because environmental gains are usually costly, greater gains can be achieved if those with great benefits and low costs are tackled before those with lower gains and higher costs. As discussed earlier, for instance, eliminating all contaminated sediments in Michigan's fourteen Great Lakes Areas of Concern might cost more than $300 million, when less expensive containment measures might reduce most of the risk at substantially lower cost. The funds not spent on eliminating contamination might be spent to address other issues, such as contamination of beaches and water supplies by bacteria and other hazards, which pose more immediate health risks.

*3. Attention needs to be paid not only to the total benefits and costs but also to who bears the benefits and the costs.* Policies that might be beneficial to the people of Michigan are almost certain to be opposed by those who would bear the costs, even if the benefits outweigh the costs. Also, as discussed in the context of environmental justice, environmental problems are not distributed evenly around the state. Understanding the distributional effects of environmental policies can help to explain the political support and opposition to those policies. If the gains from a policy outweigh the costs, then, in theory, it is possible for the gainers to compensate those who bear the costs for their losses, and for everybody therefore to be better off. For instance, a developer might benefit enough from filling a particular wetland that he or she might be willing to protect, create, or enhance wetlands elsewhere sufficiently that both the environment and the developer will come out ahead. If a neighborhood is significantly harmed by a polluter, the polluter could either reduce its pollution or help people in the neighborhood to find new housing elsewhere. If win-win situations can be identified through creative means of compensation for losses, then the political opposition to policies can be reduced.

*4. Problems need to be targeted as directly as possible.* As discussed in the context of nonpoint source pollution and marketable permits, policies need to be designed carefully to avoid unintended consequences. Marketable permits work best if pollution from one source affects the same area as pollution from the source with which it is trading. If the two firms are producing the same pollutant and are adjacent to each other, this condition is likely to hold, because they are contributing to the same problem. However, if one firm is in Detroit and another is in the Upper Peninsula, the problems in those places are different, and trading should not be permitted without examining the consequences for the local areas. Similarly, if the problem is pollution, then an indirect policy, such as requiring reduced fertilizer use, needs to be evaluated carefully for effectiveness and for possible switches in behavior (such as changing the crop produced) that might exacerbate the pollution problem. Indirect policies can work, but they need to be developed in conjunction with monitoring and research on whether the policies will have their intended effect.

■

## ACKNOWLEDGMENTS

We greatly appreciate the research assistance of Michael Wagg and Ruchi Misra in collecting the data used in this chapter, and Ruth Blum's assistance in preparing the document and designing the figures. Charles Ballard, Elizabeth Gerber, Rosina Bierbaum, Paul Webb, Victor Bierman, Wendy Larson, Joseph DePinto, and John Marr provided very useful suggestions and editorial comments.

## REFERENCES AND SUGGESTED READINGS

Baumol, William J., and Wallace E. Oates. 1988. *The theory of environmental policy.* New York: Cambridge University Press.

Bierman, Victor J., Jr., D. W. Dilks, T. J. Fiest, J. V. DePinto, and R. G. Kreis. 1998. A coupled phytoplankton-zebra mussel model for Saginaw Bay, Lake Huron. In *Proceedings of the workshop on aquatic ecosystem modeling and assessment techniques for application within the U.S. Army Corps of Engineers, U.S. Army Engineers Waterways Experiment Station, Vicksburg, MS.* Misc Paper EL-98–1.

Bierman, Victor J., Jr., David M. Dolan, and Robert Kasprzyk. 1984. Retrospective analysis of the response of Saginaw Bay, Lake Huron, to reductions in phosphorus loadings. *Environmental Science and Technology* 18(1): 23–31.

Callewaert, John. 1997. Environmental injustices in Michigan: A spatial analysis of the interactions between race, income, and the distribution of environmental hazards. *http://www-personal.umich.edu/~wddrake/545_97/cal/johnfin.html.*

Carson, Rachel. 1962. *Silent spring.* Boston: Houghton-Mifflin.

Comer, Patrick J. 1996. *Wetland trends in Michigan since 1800: A preliminary assessment.* Lansing, Mich.: Michigan Department of Environmental Quality/U.S. Environmental Protection Agency.

Dahl, Thomas E. 1990. *Wetlands losses in the United States 1780's to 1980's.* Washington, D.C.: U.S. Department of the Interior, Fish and Wildlife Service.

Dempsey, Dave. 2001. *Ruin and recovery: Michigan's rise as a conservation leader.* Ann Arbor: University of

Michigan Press.

DePinto, Joseph V., Thomas C. Young, and Lyn M. McIlroy. 1986. Great Lakes water quality improvement. *Environmental Science and Technology* 20(8): 752–59.

DeVault, David S., Robert Hesselbert, Paul W. Rodgers, and Timothy J. Fiest. 1996. Contaminant trends in lake trout and walleye from the Lawrention Great Lakes. *Journal of Great Lakes Research* 23(4): 884–95.

Environment Canada, Canadian Wildlife Service, Canadian Centre for Inland Waters. 2000. Organochlorine contaminant concentrations in herring gull eggs from Great Lake colonies. Unpublished, Burlington, Ontario.

Hamilton, James T. 1995. Pollution as news: Media and stock market reactions to the toxics release inventory data. *Journal of Environmental Economics and Management* 28(1): 98–113.

Helfand, Gloria E., and Brett W. House. 1995. Regulating nonpoint source pollution under heterogeneous conditions. *American Journal of Agricultural Economics* 77 (November): 1024–32.

Helfand, Gloria E., and L. James Peyton. 1999. A conceptual model of environmental justice. *Social Science Quarterly* 80 (March): 68–83.

Khanna, Madhu, Wilma Rose H. Quimio, and Dora Bojilova. 1998. Toxics release information: A policy tool for environmental protection. *Journal of Environmental Economics and Management* 36(3): 243–66.

Krueger, C. C., and B. May. 1991. Ecological and genetic effects of salmonid introductions in North America. *Canadian Journal of Fisheries and Aquatic Sciences* 48 (Supp.1): 66–77.

Lavelle, Marianne, and Marcia Coyle. 1992. Unequal protection: The racial divide in environmental law. *National Law Review,* 21 September, S1–S12.

Legislative Service Bureau. 1970–2000. *Public and local acts of the legislature of the State of Michigan.* Lansing, Mich.: Legislative Council.

Limno-Tech, Inc. 1993. Great Lakes environmental assessment. Prepared for the National Council of the Paper Industry for Air and Stream Improvement.

———. 1995. A preliminary ecosystem modeling study of zebra mussels (*Dreissena Polymorpha*) in Saginaw Bay, Michigan.

———. 1997. Application of a coupled primary productivity-exotic species model for Saginaw Bay, Lake Huron.

Michigan Department of Agriculture. 2002. State submits plan on livestock production facilities. Lansing, Michigan. *http://www.michigan.gov/mda/*

*1,1607,7–125–1572_3628–17601—M_2002_1,00.html.*

Michigan Department of Environmental Quality. 2000. Report of Michigan solid waste importation task force. Waste Management Division. 22 November.

———. 2002. Report of solid waste landfilled in Michigan, October 1, 2000–September 30, 2001. Waste Management Division. 22 February.

Michigan Department of Environmental Quality, Air Quality Division. 1994–2000. *Annual air quality report.* Lansing, Mich.: Michigan Department of Environmental Quality.

———. 2002a. Michigan air emission trading program overview. Lansing, Michigan. *http://www.michigan.gov/deq/1,1607,7–135–3310_4103_4194–10617—,00.html.*

———. 2002b. Water quality trading. Lansing, Michigan. *http://www.michigan.gov/deq/1,1607,7–135–3313_3682_3719–13825—,00.html.*

Michigan Department of Environmental Quality and Michigan Department of Natural Resources. 2001. State of Michigan's environment 2001, first biennial report. Lansing, Michigan. Office of Special Environmental Projects.

Michigan Department of Natural Resources. 1992. Michigan's environment and relative risk. July.

———, Air Quality Division. 1979–1993 (excluding 1981). *Michigan annual air quality report.* Lansing, Mich.: Michigan Department of Natural Resources.

Michigan Sierra Club. 2001. *Sierra Club vs. River Ridge Farms et al.* Case No.: 1:101CV236, U.S. District Court for the Western District of Michigan. *http://www.michigan.sierraclub.org/riverridge.html.*

Mills, Edward L., Joseph H. Leach, James T. Carlton, and Carol L. Secor. 1993. Exotic species in the Great Lakes: A history of biotic crises and anthropogenic introductions. *Journal of Great Lakes Research* 1(19): 1–54.

Mohai, Paul, and Bunyan Bryant. 1992. Environmental racism: Reviewing the evidence. In *Race and the incidence of environmental hazards,* edited by Bryant Bunyan and Paul Mohai. Boulder, Colo.: Westview Press.

National Research Council. 1994. *Alternatives for groundwater cleanup.* Washington, D.C.: National Academy Press.

Natural Resources Defense Council. 2001. Testing the waters 2001: A guide to water quality at vacation beaches.

Public Sector Consultants, Inc. 1998. Solid waste management and recycling. *Michigan in Brief* 3 (1 April): 306–10.

Real Estate Center at Texas A & M University. 2002. State population data. *http://recenter.tamu.edu/data/pops/.*

Ricciardi, Anthony, and Hugh J. MacIssac. 2000. Recent mass invasion of the North American Great Lakes by ponto-caspian species. *Trends in Ecology and Evolution* 15(2): 62–65.

Romagnoli, R., H. M. VanDeWalker, J. P. Doody, and W. H. Anckner. 1998. The future challenges of environmental dredging. In *Proceedings of the fifteenth World Dredging Congress,* edited by R. E. Randall, 651–61. Las Vegas, N.V., 29 June–2 July.

Russell, M., E. W. Colglazier, and M. R. English. 1991. Hazardous waste remediation: The task ahead. Knoxville: University of Tennessee, Waste Management Research and Education Institute.

Schmalensee, Richard, Paul L. Joskow, A. Denny Ellerman, Juan Pablo Montero, and Elizabeth M. Bailey. 1998. An interim evaluation of sulfur dioxide emissions trading. *Journal of Economic Perspectives* 12(3): 53–68.

Schmitt, Ben, and Emilia Askari. 2001. A tide of pollution; state presses cities to stop overflows. *Detroit Free Press,* 5 April. *www.freep.com/newslibrary/.*

State of Michigan. 1998. Governor Engler details clean Michigan plan. Press Release. 2 February.

Stavins, Robert N. 1998. What can we learn from the grand policy experiment? Lessons from SO$_2$ allowance trading. *Journal of Economic Perspectives* 12(3): 69–88.

Stow, Craig A., Stephen R. Carpenter, and James F. Amrhein. 1994. PCB concentration trends in Lake Michigan coho (*Oncorhynchus kisutch*) and chinook salmon (*O. tshawytscha*). *Canadian Journal of Fisheries and Aquatic Sciences* 51: 1384–90.

United Church of Christ Commission for Racial Justice. 1987. *Toxic wastes and race in the United States: A national report on the racial and socio-economic characteristics of communities surrounding hazardous wastes sites.* New York: United Church of Christ.

U.S. Bureau of Economic Analysis. 2001. Regional accounts data, gross state product data. *http://www.bea.doc.gov/bea/regional/gsp/.*

U.S. Bureau of the Census, Current Industrial Reports. 1980, 1984, 1989, and 1993. *Pollution abatement cost and expenditures.* MA200(78), (82), (86), and (91). Washington, D.C.: U.S. Government Printing Office.

———. 1996. *Pollution abatement cost and expenditures, 1994. http://www.census.gov/econ/www/mu1100.html.*

U.S. Coast Guard. 1993. Ballast water management for vessels entering the Great Lakes. Code of Federal Regulations 33-CFR Part 151. 1510.

U.S. Council on Environmental Quality. 1986 (17th), 1987–88 (19th), 1993 (24th), and 1997 (28th). *The annual report of the council on environmental quality.* Washington, D.C.: U.S. Government Printing Office.

U.S. Department of Agriculture. 2000. Natural resources inventory, 1997. *http://www.nhq.nrcs.usda.gov/NRI.*

U.S. Environmental Protection Agency. 1984, 1986, 1988, 1990, 1992, and 1994. *National water quality inventory.* Washington, D.C.: Office of Water.

———. 1993. Cleaning up the nation's wastes: Markets and technology trends. EPA 542-R-92-012. Washington, D.C. Office of Solid Waste and Emergency Response.

———. 1997. The incidence and severity of sediment contamination in surface waters of the United States. Vols. 1–3, EPA 823-R-97-006, Washington, D.C.: Office of Science and Technology.

———. 2000. National water quality inventory: 1998 report to Congress. Washington, D.C., 2000. *http://www.epa.gov/305b/98report/toc.html.*

———. 2001a. Report to congress: Implementation and enforcement of the combined sewer overflow control policy. Office of Water, EPA 833-R-01–003, December.

———. 2001b. Summary inventory, violations and GPRA MS excel pivot tables. 1 April 2002. *http://www.epa.gov/safewater/data/pivottables.html.*

———. 2002. Factoids: Drinking water and groundwater statistics for 2001. 1 April. *http://www.epa.gov/safewater/data/getdata.html.*

———. 2002a. AirData Net Tier report. *www.epa.gov/air/data/geosel.html.*

———. 2002b. TRI Explorer. *www.epa.gov/triexplorer/chemical.html.*

———. Region 5 Water Division. 2001. Animal feeding operations. Chicago, Ill. *http://www.epa.gov/r5water/npdestek/npdcafohome.htm.*

U.S. Fish and Wildlife Service. 2001. Report to congress on the status and trends of wetlands in the conterminous United States, 1986 to 1997.

U.S. General Accounting Office. 1983. Siting of hazardous waste landfills and their correlation with racial and economic status of surrounding communities. GAO/RCED-83-168. Washington, D.C.: U.S. General Accounting Office.

Vanderploeg, Henry A., J. R. Liebig, W. W. Carmichael, M. A. Agy, T. H. Johengen, G. L. Fahnenstiel, and T. F. Nalepa. 2001. Zebra mussel (*Dreissena polymorpha*) selective filtration promoted toxic *Microcystis* blooms in Saginaw Bay (Lake Huron) and Lake Erie. *Canadian Journal of Fisheries and Aquatic Sciences* 58: 1208–21.

Vogan, C. R. 1996. Pollution abatement and control expenditures, 1972–94. In *Survey of Current Business,* September. Washington, D.C.: GPO.

# 22

# Travel, Tourism, and Recreation in Michigan

*Donald F. Holecek*

## Introduction: Should the State Care about Tourism?

Tourism is a large and growing industry globally and in Michigan, yet its scale and importance are often not well understood or fully appreciated. The key to understanding the role that the tourism industry plays in an economy is to recognize that it is an export industry. Unlike most other exported products, which are shipped for consumption elsewhere in exchange for payment received, consumers of tourism products and services must travel to tourism venues where consumption and exchange transactions take place. Although the flow of product and consumption venue are in opposite directions for tourism and most other exports, both result in income flowing into the exporting economy from the importing economies. Since economic growth is tied to achieving a positive balance between export income and import payments, tourism can be either a stimulus or a hindrance to economic growth.

Whether one's focus is on national, state, or regional economic development, it is critical to account for tourism exports and imports in framing economic development policies and strategies. Understanding the degree to which trade in tourism is negative or positive is important in deciding how to allocate legislative attention and other resources between tourism and other industries. Hence, balance of trade in tourism is an essential theme in this chapter.

Tourism is important to Michigan residents for reasons other than for the role it plays in economic development per se. Unfortunately, neither space nor adequate information allow these reasons to be considered in depth herein. However, it is useful to acknowledge two general categories of tourism's impact. The first of these relates to tourism as a stimulus for the purchase of Michigan-produced products. The demand for these products is closely linked to national and even global tourism trends; hence there is little that we in Michigan can do to influence these trends. Second, tourism can have significant positive and negative impacts on the quality of life of Michigan residents. Poorly conceived tourism development can negatively alter the character of host communities, severely stress local infrastructures and the ability to maintain them, and diminish the quality of life for resident populations. On the other hand, quality tourism development can enrich entertainment, shopping, and cultural options for residents, provide superior tourism product to Michigan residents in close proximity to where they live and work, and positively influence the location decisions of entrepreneurs that assign high priority to quality-of-life considerations in their new investment decisions.

Assessing the scope, scale, and economic importance of Michigan's tourism industry is complicated by the complex nature of travel itself and of its supporting infrastructure. Deriving relevant information from commonly available secondary data series is also problematic because tourism data are aggregated with nontourism data. Even in the relatively few tourism data series that are available, analyses are hindered by methodological differences that often limit comparability of results across data series. Despite these complications, it is possible to develop a set of reasonably objective indicators for Michigan's tourism industry, which can be drawn upon to capture the essence of its scope, scale, and economic importance.

An economic assessment of Michigan's tourism industry ultimately hinges on the fundamental question of what tourism is and is not. It is useful to introduce the central issues in defining tourism here. Detailed issues will be discussed in subsequent sections in concert with the introduction of data series employed to develop selected tourism industry indicators.

The terms "tourism," "travel," and, at times, "recreation" are used interchangeably in everyday conversation. One also finds considerable overlap among these three terms even in the technical literature. Variation in each term's specific definition across authors is common. In general, "travel" is used to describe the "nonroutine" movement of people back and forth between their residences and one or more destinations. Routine travel, such as commuting to and from work or school and work related to travel by travel industry employees (e.g., airline pilots) is excluded. The most frequent general purposes of travel that are included are: pleasure travel, visiting friends and relatives, and business. In most definitions of travel, an overnight stay or a minimum one-way travel distance are required. These restrictions are used as a convenience in empirical studies to minimize the presence of routine or intracity/ intraregion travel in the statistical findings.

The concept of "tourism" is generally associated with leisure forms of travel, including primarily pleasure trips and visits to friends and relatives. As in the case of definitions of travel, routine trips are excluded and a minimum one-way travel distance is used in empirical tourism studies. Thus, the primary difference between the definitions of travel and tourism is that the former includes business-related trips while the latter does not, unless pleasure is indicated as a joint purpose of a trip.

The definition of "recreation" closely parallels that of tourism but is unlikely to require a specific one-way travel distance. Empirical studies of recreation are most often conducted by public-sector recreation providers and thus focus on recreation activities commonly made available by tax-supported park and recreation agencies.[1] Nonetheless, selected recreation statistics can be useful in developing Michigan tourism industry indicators.

A broad assessment of the economics of Michigan's tourism industry would include considerations of both its nonmarket and market value and impacts. A relatively high proportion of economic activity associated with tourism is nonmarket in nature. For example, travelers do not pay directly to access highways or the abundant public recreation lands in northern Michigan. While economists have developed procedures for estimating values associated with nonmarket goods and services, they are complex and costly to apply. The examples of nonmarket value estimation that are available, while confirming that the nonmarket values associated with tourism can be sizeable, are too few to use to develop market-comparable overall estimates of tourism's nonmarket value.

From the preceding discussion, it should be evident that assessing the economic importance of Michigan's tourism industry is not a simple task. There is no simple way to count the number of tourists that visit Michigan each year or to estimate how much they spend on their trips in Michigan. Even if these data were available, the significant nonmarket value of tourism is not currently accessible. As will become obvious as this discussion unfolds, developing a composite picture of Michigan's tourism industry with the information currently available is akin to trying to assemble a jigsaw puzzle with some key pieces missing and with some pieces included that do not fit precisely with the others. While a perfectly clear economic image cannot be constructed from the pieces of information currently available, there is enough information to frame the importance of tourism to the Michigan economy and to identify some of the critical challenges and opportunities that confront the industry.

## National and International Scope of Tourism

### International Tourism

In 1997, the tourism industry recorded U.S. $2.1 trillion in sales (all monetary data presented in this chapter are reported in nominal terms; they have not been adjusted for inflation) and employed 262 million people, and these sales produced more than U.S. $700 billion in tax revenue for national, state and local economies (World Travel and Tourism Council [WTTC] 1997). While the jobs available in the travel and tourism industry are often perceived as being of low quality (i.e., relatively low salaried), a recent study suggests industry employees earn slightly above-average salaries if one accounts for both direct and indirect jobs associated with travel and tourism (WTTC 1997). In effect, the low-paying, entry-level positions, which are the basis for the low quality of jobs image associated with this industry, are more than offset by the less visible individuals who derive their earnings from travel and tourism. These include: (1) owners of travel and tourism businesses and their management-level employees; (2) owners and employees of a wide array of businesses that provide support services to tourism businesses, such as accounting firms, banks, and insurance companies; (3) those that design, build, and maintain hotels, golf courses, and other elements of the industry's physical infrastructure; (4) owners and employees of firms that produce products for travel and tourism businesses (e.g., furniture, technology hardware, slot machines, airplanes, and food products); and (5) owners and employees of firms that produce products and services consumed directly by tourists (e.g., boats, recreational vehicles, sporting equipment and apparel, medical services, and travel agencies).

Imbedded in the preceding discussion is a complex technical issue which is convenient to confront in brief here. The World Travel and Tourism Council (WTTC) report introduced previously is one of the first to employ satellite accounting methodology to derive estimates of sales, employment, and tax revenue collections for travel and tourism. Governments regularly collect and publish data series that track the overall performance of their economies. The most familiar statistic derived from these accounts is Gross Domestic Product (GDP), which is often featured in media reports of, for example, the vitality of the U.S. economy. These accounts include detailed information by economic sectors and subsectors (i.e., Standard Industrial Classification [SIC] codes). Since these data series are readily available and contain high-quality data, they are widely used by economists for many purposes. The economic activity associated with tourism cuts across many of the industry sectors contained in these accounts, which, in fact, do not include a tourism sector per se. Considerable research by the WTTC, the World Tourism Organisation, and economic agencies in some countries has been directed toward creating a satellite accounting system for travel and tourism that is tied to existing government economic statistical reporting systems. The basic idea involves estimating what percentage of economic activity by sector in the standard accounts is associated with travel and tourism. The results are summed across all standard sectors to provide a new composite travel and tourism sector from which various economic statistics such as employment can be readily derived.

To date, satellite tourism accounts have been developed for only selected countries and one state (Georgia), and thus the procedure remains in an experimental stage of development. If empirical issues are solved and more and higher quality calibration data become available, satellite tourism accounts are likely to become available for more regions, which will facilitate assessment of travel and tourism's economic importance and how it changes over time.

The tourism industry's relative rank among the world's leading industries is of little consequence here beyond the fact that it is very large and one of the world's most significant growth industries. Over the last ten years, international tourist arrivals have increased from 463 million persons to nearly 700 million persons per year, an average annual rate of growth equal to 4.3%. International tourism receipts over this same period have grown at an even faster rate of over 6% per year, reaching about $475 billion in 2000 (Travel Industry Association of America 2001a). Both arrivals and receipts have exhibited year-to-year growth every year over the last decade, which suggests that the industry is less cyclical than many of the world's other leading industries.

Numerous factors have been suggested as driving forces behind growth in international tourism; some of the most often cited include globalization, the end of the cold war, improved air transportation systems, and growth in the number of people who can afford to travel. The latter is largely tied to the aging populations in the United States, Germany, the United Kingdom, Japan, and France, whose residents generate over 40% of total spending on international travel. In contrast to the previous generation of older people, today's seniors are healthier, wealthier, and perceive travel as a more desirable way to spend their leisure time and discretionary earnings.

The United States is the world's leading recipient of international travelers' dollars, earning $82 billion in 2000, which was an increase of 9.8% over the previous year. It hosted over fifty million international visitors, ranking it a distant second to France, which hosted over seventy-five million visitors. Americans spent almost $60 billion outside of the United States in 1999, ranking it first among nations in international tourism spending. Over the last decade, the United States has held a significant trade surplus in travel and tourism, and, in 2000, inbound international travelers' expenditures exceeded those of outbound travelers by over $14 billion (Travel Industry Association of America 2001a).

## U.S. Domestic Tourism

Domestic travel (i.e., U.S. residents traveling in the United States) is common and is growing in popularity. Americans took about one billion person trips in 2000 in the United States and spent almost $500 billion on domestic travel, almost 5% of nominal Gross Domestic Product. Pleasure/leisure travel accounted for 74% of domestic person trips. Total domestic and international traveler spending in 2000 generated over 7.8 million jobs, or about 6% of total nonagricultural employment in the United States. Traveler spending in 2000 generated over $100 billion in tax revenue for federal, state, and local units of government (Travel Industry Association of America 2001a).

Since 1996, the volume of U.S. resident domestic person trips has grown by 3.1% (Travel Industry Association of America 2001a). Domestic travel expenditures over the last decade have grown at an annual average rate of 5.2%. Since 1991, travel-generated employment has increased by over 25%. To put employment in the travel industry in perspective, manufacturing industry employment has remained essentially unchanged, while travel industry employment has grown to equal over 42% of manufacturing industry employment (Travel Industry Association of America 2001a).

## The Michigan Tourism System

The Michigan tourism system is extensive and difficult to encapsulate in a brief discourse. It includes the full range of suppliers of products and services consumed by travelers on trips; these will be referred to as core components of the system. It also includes suppliers of products and services to these core components; these suppliers will be referred to as infrastructure components. Travelers themselves are both consumers and producers of travel experiences. This is especially true in Michigan, where packaged tours are relatively rare. The majority of Michigan tourists select their destinations, arrange their own accommodations, transport themselves by privately owned vehicle, make their own meal arrangements, and prepare their own daily activity schedules. Because of the central role tourists play in the production of their travel experiences, the tourism system includes suppliers of products and services that support tourists in their roles as travel experience producers; these components will be referred to as tourist service components.

The *core components* of the Michigan tourism system and selected examples of product or service providers in each include:

- The lodging component—hotels, motels, resorts, bed & breakfast establishments, owned and rented second homes/condos, and campgrounds.
- The food and beverage component—restaurants, convenience stores, bars, liquor stores, wineries, and agriculture product retail businesses.
- The attractions component—museums, historical sites and facilities, festivals and special events, shopping complexes, sporting events, wildlife, unique natural areas, man-made structures, and even entire communities.
- The entertainment component—casinos, theaters, and concerts.
- The transportation component—vehicle service businesses, rental car outlets, and intra- and intercity commercial transportation companies.
- The commercial recreation component—golf courses, ski facilities, marinas, charter boat operators, and recreation equipment rental outlets.
- The land and water component—over three thousand miles of Great Lakes' coastline; national, state, and local parks and recreation

areas; thousands of inland lakes; thousands of miles of rivers and streams; an extensive recreational trail system; and millions of acres of public land and private land open to the public for recreation.

The *infrastructure components* of the Michigan tourism system and selected examples of product and service providers in each include:

- The transportation component—roads and highways, rest areas, and fuel distributors.
- The business services component—financial institutions, wholesalers, insurance companies, accountants, communication companies, and equipment and furnishings suppliers.
- The public service component—police, fire, medical, and education organizations, and utilities.
- The commercial construction and maintenance component—builders, crafts persons, sanitary services, roadway construction and maintenance companies, and designers and artists.

The *tourist services components* of the Michigan tourism system and selected examples of product and service providers in each include:

- The information services component—travel agents, destination marketing organizations, auto clubs, various media, news centers and bookstores, and highway information centers.
- The vehicle dealer component—firms that sell boats, campers, snowmobiles, bicycles, and off-road vehicles.
- The clothing and equipment component—ski shops, sporting goods stores, sellers of hunting and fishing licenses and gear, and various retailers.
- The residential construction and maintenance component—builders, crafts persons, and maintenance companies.
- The public services component—police, fire, medical services, and utilities.

The Michigan tourism system is complex and extensive, with components, such as the lodging component, that exist primarily to serve the traveling public, and many others whose inclusion as part of the tourism industry may not have been expected and may be questioned by some readers. However, a full accounting of tourists' economic impact requires inclusion of all purchases

they make while on Michigan trips, as well as the indirect stimulus their expenditures have on sectors of the economy beyond those that capture tourist dollars directly. Satellite accounting, discussed in an earlier section, has recently emerged as an empirical tool for estimating the total economic impacts associated with tourism systems. To date, the procedure has not been applied in Michigan.

Were one to apply satellite accounting to Michigan's tourism system, an especially interesting decision to be made would be how to account for the economic role of privately owned vehicles, by far the dominant means of transportation used by Michigan tourists as well as all U.S. domestic tourists, play in tourism. One might distribute the annual cost of vehicle ownership between tourism-related travel and other travel purposes and credit the former to the tourism system account. Obviously, this would dramatically increase one's estimate of the economic importance of Michigan's tourism industry. Furthermore, what about applying similar logic to the vehicles produced in Michigan that are exported elsewhere? Since a significant proportion of the use of these vehicles is for tourism-related travel, might the value of this use also be ascribed to Michigan's tourism account? Since only a small percentage of the use of these vehicles is for tourism travel in Michigan, logically only that percentage is attributable to the Michigan tourism account. However, the remainder is indicative of the overall but indirect dependence of the Michigan economy on a vibrant domestic tourism industry. Thus, trends in national tourism activity directly affect the Michigan economy, both through the impact they have on Michigan's own tourism industry and through the indirect impact they have on Michigan-based companies that produce vehicles and other products used for tourism purposes outside of Michigan. These are revolutionary though not totally pointless questions. After all, sales of Michigan-produced vehicles are driven by how owners derive value from using them.

### The Geography of Michigan Tourism

The most definitive source of information about the long-distance travel of persons living in the United States (a.k.a., domestic travel) is the American Travel Survey, which is conducted by the Bureau of Transportation Statistics (BTS), U.S.

## TABLE 22.1

**Distribution of Domestic Travel to Michigan by Visitor Origin**

| State of Origin | Number of Household Trips (in thousands) | Percentage of Total Household Trips |
|---|---|---|
| Michigan | 13,561 | 61.9 |
| Illinois | 1,388 | 6.3 |
| Indiana | 1,043 | 4.8 |
| Ohio | 1,297 | 5.9 |
| Wisconsin | 748 | 3.4 |
| Florida | 388 | 1.8 |
| California | 377 | 1.7 |
| New York | 284 | 1.3 |
| Minnesota | 253 | 1.2 |
| Kentucky | 238 | 1.1 |
| Pennsylvania | 227 | 1.0 |
| Other states | 2,136 | 9.6 |

SOURCE: Bureau of Transportation Statistics, U.S. Department of Transportation (1997).

Department of Transportation. The BTS survey is scheduled to be conducted every five years. The initial survey began in April 1995 and was concluded in March, 1996 It is based upon a probability sample of all members of 80,000 households in the 50 states and the District of Columbia. Respondents were provided diaries to record information about each trip taken over the twelve-month sampling period. Quarterly interviews were conducted by the U.S. Census Bureau field staff. Rigorous survey research standards were followed to minimize all sources of potential bias. An overall response rate of 85% was achieved to the BTS American Travel Survey.

In 1995, Michigan captured nearly forty million domestic person trips (a person trip is defined as a round trip by one person of at least some specified distance [one hundred miles one-way in the BTS survey] away from home) and nearly twenty-two million household trips (a household trip refers to a trip in which one or more members of a household traveled together), which involved one-way travel of one hundred or more miles in distance. (Bureau of Transportation Statistics [BTS], U.S. Department of Transportation 1997). Michigan captured an estimated three million international person trips in that year. About 7% of tourism expenditures in Michigan in 1995 were captured from international visitors (Travel Industry Association of America 1997), primarily from Canada. The three million person trip estimate was derived using this estimate of international travelers' share of total tourism expenditures in Michigan and the assumption of equal international and domestic per person trip expenditures. About two-thirds of these trips were pleasure trips (Bureau of Transportation Statistics 1997). Nearly half of Michigan pleasure trips were taken primarily to visit friends and relatives (Bureau of Transportation Statistics 1997).

Michigan is primarily a regional travel destination, as can be seen in table 22.1. Over 80% of Michigan-destined household trips originate in Michigan, Illinois, Indiana, Ohio, and Wisconsin. Michigan residents alone account for over 60% of household trips with Michigan as the primary destination (Bureau of Transportation Statistics 1997).

In 1995, 25.4 million household trips originated in Michigan, of which 13.6 million were destined in state and 11.9 million were destined out of state. In that year, Michigan received 21.9 million household trips, 8.4 million captured from out of state. Thus, Michigan held a net deficit in travel in 1995 equal to 3.5 million household trips. The deficit in terms of person trips was 5.4 million. On a state-to-state basis, Michigan has a travel exchange deficit with thirty-seven states, led by Ohio, Illinois, and Florida, and a surplus with only eleven states, led by Indiana and Wisconsin (Bureau of Transportation Statistics 1997).

A regional survey, the Michigan Travel Market Survey (MTMS), which focuses specifically on Michigan's primary travel market (i.e., Michigan, Ohio, Indiana, Illinois, Wisconsin, Minnesota, and Ontario) is a source of additional information on the geography of Michigan's tourism industry (Holecek et al. 2000). The study region covered by this survey is estimated to be the source of 90% of Michigan's total pleasure trips. The MTMS data indicate that pleasure trips account for 85% of all Michigan-destined trips taken by residents and nonresidents, considerably more than the two-thirds reported in the 1995 American Travel Survey. The trip definition used in the MTMS is fifty miles one way, versus the one-hundred-mile distance used in the American Travel Survey, which may account for the significant difference between estimates of pleasure travel's share of total Michigan-destined trips. The distribution of Michigan-destined pleasure trips derived from the MTMS by origin is as follows: Michigan, 47%; Ohio, 13%; Illinois, 13%; Indiana, 9%; Ontario, 8%; Wisconsin, 7%; and Minnesota, 3%.

MTMS respondents' primary trip destinations

are displayed in table 22.2. Again, here it is evident that Michigan is the most popular destination for its residents, with Florida ranking as their second-most popular destination. These results may appear questionable, given the proximity of large populations of Michigan residents along borders with Ontario, Ohio, and Indiana. Yet when one recalls that only pleasure trips of at least fifty miles one way were counted in this study, the results become less confounding. Measuring tourism trips this way minimizes the inclusion of routine travel in survey results because such travel is not commonly viewed as tourism; however, this practice does present an obstacle to fully assessing the dollar flows associated with travel to and from Michigan. Unfortunately, data are not available to resolve this issue. Within the region, Michigan leads in the percentage of residents' trips retained in their home state or province, followed closely by Ontario, Wisconsin, and Minnesota. Illinois, Indiana, and Ohio are far less popular destinations for their residents.

Tourism in Michigan is often perceived as being concentrated in the state's northern counties. The reported primary destination county of Michigan pleasure trips by respondents to the MTMS between 1996 and 2001 is presented in table 22.3. Clearly, Michigan's tourism industry is not confined to northern Michigan. Five of the top ten most popular pleasure trip destinations are populous southern Michigan counties, led by Wayne county's nearly 9.5% of Michigan's pleasure trip market. While residents of popular and less populous northern county destinations are more dependent upon tourism as a source of income, the economies of all eighty-three Michigan counties are impacted by tourists' expenditures. With total direct travel expenditures in Michigan equal to about $11.5 billion in 1999 (Travel Industry Association of America 2001b), tourism expenditures are often significant in less populated rural counties with a small share of Michigan's overall tourism market.

## Tourism Expenditures in Michigan

The Travel Industry Association of America (2001b) reported that travel spending in Michigan was $11.5 billion in 1999, an increase of 9% over 1998. This includes expenditures by travelers whose travel distance was at least fifty miles (one way) away from home and thus includes expenditures by Michigan residents as well as visitors who

### TABLE 22.2

**Primary Destinations of Respondents' Most Recent Pleasure Trips, 1996–98 (percentage)**

| Destination | ORIGINS | | | | | | |
|---|---|---|---|---|---|---|---|
| | IL | IN | MI | MN | OH | WI | ON |
| Michigan | 8.2 | 8.6 | 44.0 | 2.7 | 6.9 | 6.1 | 5.2 |
| Florida | 9.9 | 12.9 | 8.4 | 4.7 | 11.0 | 6.5 | 7.7 |
| Wisconsin | 10.0 | 2.1 | 1.4 | 9.6 | 0.4 | 37.9 | 0.2 |
| Ohio | 2.0 | 6.7 | 3.9 | 0.5 | 19.4 | 0.9 | 1.8 |
| Illinois | 14.1 | 5.6 | 4.2 | 2.5 | 3.2 | 6.8 | 0.6 |
| Minnesota | 2.0 | 1.1 | 0.8 | 37.5 | 0.4 | 7.9 | 0.5 |
| Indiana | 3.7 | 19.4 | 1.8 | 0.7 | 3.7 | 1.5 | 0.2 |
| Tennessee | 1.8 | 6.5 | 2.9 | 0.7 | 5.2 | 0.5 | 0.3 |
| Nevada | 3.1 | 2.7 | 3.0 | 2.7 | 3.1 | 2.9 | 0.9 |
| Missouri | 7.3 | 2.7 | 0.9 | 1.3 | 0.7 | 1.6 | 0.3 |
| Other states | 28.8 | 26.7 | 19.9 | 29.0 | 37.3 | 20.5 | 15.6 |
| U.S. Territories | 0.3 | 0.0 | 0.2 | 0.1 | 0.3 | 0.2 | 0.2 |
| Ontario | 0.9 | 0.8 | 4.1 | 1.2 | 3.4 | 1.1 | 43.0 |
| Other Canada | 0.3 | 0.5 | 0.5 | 1.3 | 0.4 | 0.2 | 11.1 |
| Mexico | 2.3 | 0.8 | 0.6 | 1.8 | 1.1 | 1.2 | 1.9 |
| Caribbean | 1.5 | 0.9 | 0.8 | 0.8 | 1.4 | 0.9 | 1.2 |
| Overseas | 3.8 | 2.2 | 2.6 | 2.7 | 2.2 | 3.5 | 9.4 |
| TOTAL | 100.0 | 100.0 | 100.0 | 100.0 | 100.0 | 100.0 | 100.0 |

SOURCE: Holecek et al. (2000).

traveled at least fifty miles one way to reach a Michigan destination. An exact estimate of how this $11.5 billion in travel expenditures is distributed between what Michigan residents spend and what is captured from other parts of the United States cannot be directly derived from the published report. Since between 47% (Holecek et al. 2000) and 60% (Bureau of Transportation Statistics 1997) of qualifying household trips in Michigan are made by Michigan residents, and since nonresidents' trips are generally of longer duration and involve higher expenditures than do Michigan residents' trips, it seems reasonable to suggest that almost half of the $11.5 billion in travel expenditures captured in Michigan in 1999 resulted from Michigan residents' travel expenditures in Michigan.

Michigan ranked thirteenth among the fifty states and the District of Columbia in direct domestic expenditures captured, and sixteenth in international direct expenditures captured. Total direct domestic travel spending in Michigan was $10.9 billion, or about 95% of the total travel expenditures captured by Michigan's travel industry. The distribution of Michigan's direct total

## TABLE 22.3

**Estimated Michigan Pleasure Trip Market Share by County, 1996–2001**

| County | Est. Market Share (%) | County | Est. Market Share (%) | County | Est. Market Share (%) |
|---|---|---|---|---|---|
| Wayne | 9.48 | Van Buren | 1.20 | Lenawee | 0.44 |
| Grand Traverse | 6.16 | Iosco | 1.13 | Alcona | 0.42 |
| Saginaw | 4.66 | Manistee | 1.07 | Iron | 0.42 |
| Oakland | 4.43 | Oceana | 0.95 | Menominee | 0.40 |
| Mackinac | 3.95 | Clare | 0.84 | Montmorency | 0.40 |
| Kent | 3.53 | Calhoun | 0.82 | Oscoda | 0.40 |
| Chippewa | 3.07 | Crawford | 0.82 | Luce | 0.36 |
| Ingham | 2.98 | Wexford | 0.80 | Montcalm | 0.36 |
| Berrien | 2.82 | Alpena | 0.78 | Baraga | 0.32 |
| Isabella | 2.77 | Huron | 0.78 | Lapeer | 0.29 |
| Cheboygan | 2.54 | Houghton | 0.76 | Missaukee | 0.29 |
| Washtenaw | 2.54 | Antrim | 0.74 | Presque Isle | 0.27 |
| Muskegon | 1.89 | Dickinson | 0.71 | Sanilac | 0.27 |
| Ottawa | 1.83 | Cass | 0.69 | Schoolcraft | 0.27 |
| Allegan | 1.79 | Leelanau | 0.69 | Hillsdale | 0.25 |
| Kalamazoo | 1.79 | Alger | 0.65 | Kalkaska | 0.25 |
| Jackson | 1.53 | Keweenaw | 0.63 | Shiawassee | 0.23 |
| Marquette | 1.53 | Lake | 0.63 | Arenac | 0.21 |
| Emmet | 1.51 | Monroe | 0.61 | Gladwin | 0.21 |
| Gogebic | 1.45 | Bay | 0.59 | Gratiot | 0.17 |
| Charlevoix | 1.43 | Ogemaw | 0.59 | Ionia | 0.17 |
| Mason | 1.43 | Benzie | 0.57 | St. Joseph | 0.17 |
| Otsego | 1.37 | Midland | 0.55 | Barry | 0.15 |
| Genesee | 1.32 | Ontonagon | 0.55 | Eaton | 0.15 |
| Delta | 1.30 | Livingston | 0.53 | Clinton | 0.06 |
| Roscommon | 1.30 | Mecosta | 0.46 | Tuscola | 0.06 |
| St. Clair | 1.28 | Newaygo | 0.46 | Osceola | 0.04 |
| Macomb | 1.28 | Branch | 0.44 | | |

SOURCE: Michigan Travel Market Survey, Travel, Tourism, and Recreation Resource Center, Michigan State University.

## TABLE 22.4

**Distribution of Direct Total Travel Expenditures by Type of Expenditure for Selected States, 1999 (percentage)**

| | MI | IL | IN | MN | OH | WI |
|---|---|---|---|---|---|---|
| Public transportation | 26.8 | 27.4 | 17.5 | 25.1 | 24.0 | 21.4 |
| Auto transportation | 20.3 | 16.8 | 20.2 | 15.0 | 20.0 | 19.0 |
| Lodging | 15.5 | 18.5 | 17.5 | 17.5 | 15.6 | 15.9 |
| Food service | 22.5 | 22.4 | 27.2 | 25.8 | 24.4 | 26.8 |
| Entertainment/recreation | 7.0 | 7.0 | 7.9 | 6.8 | 7.5 | 7.5 |
| General trade | 7.9 | 7.8 | 9.7 | 9.8 | 8.5 | 9.4 |

SOURCE: Travel Industry Association of America (2001b).

travel expenditures by type of expenditure is presented in table 22.4.

The Travel Industry Association of America does not account for variations in populations in its reporting of tourism expenditures captured per state. Overall travel to a state is highly correlated with its population, because visiting friends and relatives, business, and personal travel all increase roughly in proportion to its population. Thus, it is not surprising that California, the most populous state, ranks first in the amount of travel expenditures that it captures. The influence of a state's population in attracting tourism expenditures can be mitigated by dividing its total direct travel expenditures by its resident population. The results of this division are presented in the last column in table 22.5. The state of Nevada's economy is clearly the most dependent on tourism, captur-

TABLE 22.5

**Direct Domestic and International Travel Expenditures Captured by State and Per State Resident, 1999**

| State | Direct Travel Expenditures Population[a] | Domestic/Int'l.[b] | Per Resident[b] | State | Direct Travel Expenditures Population[a] | Domestic/Int'l.[b] | Per Resident[b] |
|---|---|---|---|---|---|---|---|
| Nevada | 1.20 | 21,034.2 | 17,528.5 | Maine | 1.28 | 2,073.4 | 1,619.8 |
| Hawaii | 1.21 | 14,223.6 | 11,755.0 | Oregon | 3.42 | 5,460.5 | 1,596.6 |
| Washington, D.C. | 0.57 | 5,721.2 | 10,002.1 | Texas | 20.85 | 33,130.9 | 1,589.0 |
| Florida | 15.98 | 55,784.9 | 3,490.9 | South Dakota | 0.76 | 1,189.0 | 1,574.8 |
| Wyoming | 0.49 | 1,496.4 | 3,029.1 | Connecticut | 3.41 | 5,242.6 | 1,537.4 |
| Alaska | 0.63 | 1,507.5 | 2,404.3 | Mississippi | 2.84 | 4,347.5 | 1,530.8 |
| Vermont | 0.61 | 1,441.9 | 2,367.7 | Maryland | 5.30 | 8,043.3 | 1,517.6 |
| Colorado | 4.30 | 9,354.6 | 2,175.5 | Nebraska | 1.71 | 2,591.9 | 1,515.7 |
| Montana | 0.90 | 1,904.4 | 2,111.3 | North Carolina | 8.05 | 11,868.3 | 1,474.3 |
| California | 33.81 | 71,369.9 | 2,110.9 | Washington | 5.89 | 8,499.2 | 1,443.0 |
| New Mexico | 1.82 | 3,545.4 | 1,948.0 | Iowa | 2.93 | 4,171.6 | 1,423.8 |
| Massachusetts | 6.35 | 12,207.1 | 1,922.4 | Minnesota | 4.92 | 6,918.5 | 1,406.2 |
| New York | 18.98 | 36,315.2 | 1,913.3 | Delaware | 0.78 | 1,087.6 | 1,387.2 |
| New Hampshire | 1.24 | 2,347.0 | 1,892.7 | Arkansas | 2.67 | 3,659.1 | 1,370.4 |
| Arizona | 5.13 | 9,488.8 | 1,849.7 | Kansas | 2.69 | 3,412.4 | 1,268.6 |
| Louisiana | 4.47 | 8,089.6 | 1,809.8 | Kentucky | 4.04 | 5,067.5 | 1,254.3 |
| New Jersey | 8.41 | 15,053.3 | 1,789.9 | Pennsylvania | 12.28 | 14,763.3 | 1,202.2 |
| North Dakota | 0.64 | 1,148.4 | 1,788.8 | Wisconsin | 5.36 | 6,253.3 | 1,166.7 |
| Illinois | 12.42 | 22,147.2 | 1,783.2 | Michigan | 9.94 | 11,511.6 | 1,158.1 |
| Georgia | 8.19 | 14,538.2 | 1,775.1 | Alabama | 4.45 | 5,109.5 | 1,148.2 |
| Utah | 2.23 | 3,924.2 | 1,759.7 | Ohio | 11.35 | 12,748.3 | 1,123.2 |
| South Carolina | 4.01 | 7,046.3 | 1,757.2 | Oklahoma | 3.45 | 3,734.5 | 1,082.5 |
| Tennessee | 5.69 | 9,751.7 | 1,753.9 | Indiana | 6.08 | 6,057.5 | 996.3 |
| Virginia | 7.08 | 12,863.2 | 1,713.8 | Rhode Island | 1.48 | 1,425.2 | 963.0 |
| Missouri | 5.60 | 9,346.2 | 1,669.0 | West Virginia | 1.80 | 1,642.3 | 912.4 |
| Idaho | 1.29 | 2,101.7 | 1,629.2 | | | | |

SOURCE: Travel Industry Association of America (2001b).
(a) In millions.
(b) In dollars.

ing over $17,500 of direct tourism expenditures per resident. It is not surprising to see Hawaii, Washington, D.C., and Florida ranked at the top of this tourism earnings per resident listing. While Michigan ranks relatively high in direct domestic and international tourism expenditures captured, it ranks only forty-fifth with respect to expenditures captured per resident, which suggests that its residents' incomes are far less dependent upon tourism than are those of residents of most other states. Within the region, Michigan captures considerably fewer tourism dollars per resident than Illinois and Minnesota, is competitive with Wisconsin and Ohio, and outperforms Indiana.

It is evident from the preceding discussion that Michigan has a negative balance of payments in tourism, although it is difficult to estimate precisely. The American Travel Survey (ATS) indicates that the deficit in terms of household trip nights was 11.8 million in 1995. Expenditures per household trip night were not collected in the ATS. However, respondents to the Michigan Travel Market Survey (MTMS) have been asked to report their expenditures per trip night. While asking respondents to recall how much they spent on a trip taken at any time during the past year during a telephone interview is less than an ideal method for gathering this type of information, no superior expenditure data are readily available. The mean expenditure per household trip night reported by respondents to the MTMS was $132.24, which is more likely than not to be low due to recall bias. Multiplying this mean per household trip night estimate by Michigan's 11.8 million household trip night deficit results in an estimated $1.56 billion deficit in balance of trade in domestic travel.

Michigan's negative balance of trade in domestic travel could be offset by a surplus in international travel, but unfortunately, this is not the case. It has been estimated that international visitors to Michigan, about half of which are Canadians, spent about $600 million in Michigan (Travel Industry Association of America 2001b). Thus, the value of Michigan's international travel exports is available. Estimating what Michigan residents spend while visiting international destinations (i.e., travel imports) involves extrapolating information contained in the American Travel Survey and the Michigan Travel Market Survey that were also used in deriving Michigan's balance of trade in domestic travel. The resulting estimate is that Michigan residents spent $1.86 billion while visiting international destinations in 1999. Subtracting the $600 million in international travel exports (i.e., what international visitors spent in Michigan) from the $1.86 billion in international imports (i.e., what Michigan residents spent while visiting international destinations) yields an estimated international travel trade deficit for Michigan equal to $1.26 billion in 1999.

Taken all together, Michigan's total travel trade deficit in domestic and international travel is $1.56 billion (domestic) plus $1.26 billion (international), for a grand total of $2.82 billion.

While the precision of these estimates can be legitimately questioned, there is abundant evidence to support the existence of a multi-billion-dollar trade deficit in travel in Michigan. Such a large outflow of dollars from Michigan to other states and countries has a significant negative impact on Michigan's economy. However, tourism has a broader role in the quality of life of its residents, as demonstrated by the relatively high proportion of residents who choose a Michigan destination for their trips, and the significance that tourism plays in stimulating demand for Michigan-produced vehicles likely more than offsets Michigan's travel account deficit.

Why the deficit? The deficit in travel is pervasive across the region. Illinois has the largest deficit in the region, and Indiana, Ohio, and Minnesota all have substantial deficits in travel. Only Wisconsin holds a positive balance of trade in travel, and its surplus is quite small (Bureau of Transportation Statistics 1997). It is therefore likely that conditions shared across the region are factors in Michigan's weak performance in domestic tourism. Climate is surely one cause for the deficits. The region's long winters encourage residents to seek relief in warmer areas across the

world and discourage nonresident travel to the region for several months of the year. Population distribution is another likely negative factor for the region's travel trade. Sparsely populated areas to the north are a limited source of prospective travelers and stimulate only light transient north to south pass-through traffic. Geography is an especially challenging obstacle for Michigan, as the Great Lakes serve as barriers to east- and west-bound traffic, which reduces access to the pass-through traveler market. Although rich in natural resource attractions, the region and Michigan possess relatively fewer headliner tourism attractions than do many competing states. Climate here again is a factor, since locating major attractions such as a Disneyland is more risky in Michigan than in Florida or California. Public and private investment in promoting destinations such as Florida allow Michigan to be barraged by their advertising. Michigan has not been able to amass an advertising budget of the scale of Florida's, which limits the state's ability to penetrate distant markets. Finally, residents of Michigan and the region have a relatively high propensity to travel and the incomes to pursue their travel interests.

Little can be done to reduce the primary climatic and geographic obstacles that combine to create a negative environment for balancing Michigan travel exports and imports. Classical marketing theory holds that one builds a marketing strategy by adjusting one or all of the four P's (i.e., place, product, price, and promotion). In the case of Michigan, "place" is a given and on balance is more negative than positive. Michigan's tourism product offerings are generally considered to be value priced, leaving little room to manipulate the "price" element of the marketing mix. Thus Michigan would need to rely on "product" and "promotion" to stimulate more tourism activity in the state.

## Accommodations Used by Michigan Tourists

The lodging sector is a large and central component of Michigan's overall tourism system. The majority of overnight tourists' total trip expenditures are captured by lodging providers and businesses in the vicinity of where tourists spend the night. The average Michigan travel party of about three people spends about $150 per day, of which about $45, or 30%, is spent on lodging (Holecek et al. 2000). Many factors influence the distribution of this state's lodging capacity, with preexisting demand being an obvious major determinant in the attraction of lodging investment capital. Land costs, tax structures, availability of labor, and other factors often play significant roles in selection of lodging sites. In the case of lodging developments specifically targeting the pleasure travel market, preexisting demand often plays less of a role than for properties developed with the business traveler in mind. For example, resort developments including lodging have the potential to drive lodging demand in regions with limited existing tourism activity. In rural areas, resorts of this type have been developed around natural attractions such as inland lakes and along the Great Lakes shoreline, and are often augmented by developing downhill skiing facilities and golf courses. Recently, casinos have emerged as the focus of resort-type lodging developments in both Detroit and rural areas of the state. The Soaring Eagle Casino and Resort in Mt. Pleasant is an example of a casino resort development, which in addition to entertainment, has the added attraction of modern conference and spa facilities. Destinations with limited available lodging capacity are not well positioned to attract a significant share of tourists' dollars, even in cases where such tourists visit these destinations in large numbers.

Results from a recently completed survey of commercial lodging establishments conducted by the Tourism Resource Center at Michigan State University are presented in table 22.6. The state has 107,380 rooms for rent. Wayne (15,574), Oakland (11,833), Kent (6,036), and Macomb (3,973) Counties alone account for almost 35% of these rooms, almost all of which are in hotels and motels. Six counties (Barry, Cass, Gladwin, Missaukee, Osceola, and Oscoda) have fewer than one hundred rooms available for rent. Yet, this does not necessarily mean that tourism is not a significant factor in their economies, since each of these counties has a significant number of second homes. Oscoda County, for example, with only seventy-three rooms for rent and a resident population of only about 9,400, has 4,174 second homes. On any given day in the peak tourism summer months, the number of nonresidents lodging in Oscoda County exceeds the number of residents, and the influx of dollars these second-home owners bring to the area is critical to sustaining the county's economy. Second homes are not only of major importance to the tourism industry in selected counties, they are important

to Michigan's overall tourism system, numbering 233,382, or more than double the 107,380 rooms for rent in the state.

The distribution of lodging used on overnight Michigan pleasure trips is as follows:

Hotel/motel/resort ....................... 43%
With friends or relatives .................. 27%
Owned or rented second home ........... 15%
Campground ............................ 9%
Bed & breakfast ......................... 2%
Other ................................... 4%

As might be expected by Michigan's ranking among the top three states in licensed boat ownership, the most frequently mentioned lodging type in the other category is "on a boat." To round out the inventory of lodging available for tourists, the state offers about 112,000 licensed campsites in its public and private campgrounds.

## What Tourists Do on Their Michigan Pleasure Trips

As important as accommodations are within the tourism system, they are generally not what attract tourists to Michigan destinations. One might argue that an exception to this is the Grand Hotel, which offers its visitors a truly unique lodging experience. Yet, even this renowned property resides on Mackinac Island, with its rich history and outstanding natural beauty. What tourists do on their Michigan pleasure trips provides considerable insight to what attracts tourists to Michigan.

Respondents to the regional Michigan Travel Market Survey were asked whether they participate in thirteen selected activities. Results are presented in table 22.7 for the period 1996–2001 and indicate that more than half of Michigan tourists shop, tour around, and participate in some form of outdoor recreation. They are least likely to be involved in a fall color tour, but considering the short fall color season, "leaf peeping" is nonetheless an important tourist attraction in Michigan. On average, tourists participate in 4.5 of the activities listed in table 22.7, an indication that their trips have multiple purposes. This is a critical characteristic of Michigan tourism's product offering, with important marketing and product development implications.

The typical Michigan trip includes a bundle of activities provided by independent public- and

**TABLE 22.6**

## Distribution of Second Homes and Commercial Lodging Accommodations in Michigan by County

| County | No. Second Homes (2000 Census) | No. Lodging Establishments | No. Available Rooms | Hotel/Motel/Lodge/Historic Inn | Cabin/Cottage/Condo/Rental | Bed and Breakfast | County | No. Second Homes (2000 Census) | No. Lodging Establishments | No. Available Rooms | Hotel/Motel/Lodge/Historic Inn | Cabin/Cottage/Condo/Rental | Bed and Breakfast |
|---|---|---|---|---|---|---|---|---|---|---|---|---|---|
| Alcona | 5,067 | 23 | 125 | 30% | 46% | 23% | Lake | 8,235 | 14 | 115 | 83% | 17% | 0% |
| Alger | 1,842 | 44 | 631 | 67% | 30% | 3% | Lapeer | 685 | 8 | 274 | 99% | 0% | 1% |
| Allegan | 3,154 | 81 | 907 | 58% | 9% | 33% | Leelanau | 4,111 | 63 | 534 | 27% | 49% | 24% |
| Alpena | 1,658 | 22 | 485 | 90% | 8% | 2% | Lenawee | 1,911 | 16 | 367 | 91% | 2% | 7% |
| Antrim | 5,152 | 34 | 912 | 84% | 12% | 5% | Livingston | 1,553 | 12 | 684 | 99% | 0% | 1% |
| Arenac | 2,274 | 9 | 130 | 78% | 12% | 9% | Luce | 1,255 | 22 | 365 | 71% | 27% | 2% |
| Baraga | 1,014 | 12 | 220 | 81% | 19% | 0% | Mackinac | 3,945 | 123 | 3,245 | 81% | 12% | 6% |
| Barry | 1,886 | 7 | 55 | 33% | 56% | 11% | Macomb | 1,122 | 48 | 3,973 | 100% | 0% | 0% |
| Bay | 355 | 18 | 820 | 81% | 18% | 1% | Manistee | 3,488 | 45 | 703 | 55% | 39% | 5% |
| Benzie | 3,181 | 43 | 684 | 37% | 57% | 7% | Marquette | 4,225 | 47 | 1,382 | 95% | 3% | 2% |
| Berrien | 5,259 | 57 | 2,351 | 84% | 11% | 4% | Mason | 3,774 | 58 | 992 | 60% | 28% | 12% |
| Branch | 2,216 | 14 | 409 | 91% | 3% | 6% | Mecosta | 3,611 | 11 | 288 | 94% | 6% | 0% |
| Calhoun | 521 | 31 | 1,734 | 98% | 0% | 2% | Menominee | 2,374 | 9 | 148 | 95% | 3% | 3% |
| Cass | 3,031 | 6 | 53 | 19% | 53% | 28% | Midland | 547 | 11 | 795 | 100% | 0% | 0% |
| Charlevoix | 4,391 | 53 | 997 | 55% | 37% | 8% | Missaukee | 2,839 | 6 | 61 | 79% | 18% | 3% |
| Cheboygan | 4,777 | 99 | 2,919 | 89% | 11% | 1% | Monroe | 364 | 11 | 623 | 99% | 0% | 1% |
| Chippewa | 4,776 | 101 | 2,356 | 82% | 17% | 1% | Montcalm | 2,396 | 8 | 108 | 81% | 15% | 5% |
| Clare | 8,583 | 20 | 429 | 67% | 7% | 26% | Montmorency | 4,390 | 18 | 407 | 82% | 10% | 8% |
| Clinton | 94 | 6 | 125 | 100% | 0% | 0% | Muskegon | 1,379 | 43 | 1,394 | 93% | 6% | 2% |
| Crawford | 4,112 | 20 | 659 | 91% | 6% | 3% | Newaygo | 4,394 | 11 | 141 | 44% | 30% | 26% |
| Delta | 2,332 | 47 | 871 | 76% | 14% | 10% | Oakland | 3,778 | 99 | 11,833 | 100% | 0% | 0% |
| Dickinson | 1,574 | 20 | 545 | 88% | 12% | 0% | Oceana | 4,155 | 29 | 610 | 50% | 43% | 7% |
| Eaton | 257 | 26 | 2,162 | 99% | 0% | 1% | Ogemaw | 5,829 | 14 | 266 | 88% | 12% | 0% |
| Emmet | 5,039 | 54 | 2,043 | 88% | 8% | 4% | Ontonagon | 1,486 | 25 | 309 | 61% | 37% | 2% |
| Genesee | 937 | 34 | 2,701 | 97% | 0% | 3% | Osceola | 3,365 | 6 | 50 | 54% | 46% | 0% |
| Gladwin | 5,588 | 6 | 94 | 72% | 28% | 0% | Oscoda | 4,174 | 8 | 73 | 34% | 66% | 0% |
| Gogebic | 2,259 | 41 | 1,048 | 54% | 12% | 34% | Otsego | 3,804 | 39 | 1,513 | 57% | 42% | 2% |
| Grand Traverse | 3,026 | 102 | 3,500 | 67% | 27% | 6% | Ottawa | 2,087 | 66 | 1,635 | 92% | 3% | 5% |
| Gratiot | 121 | 11 | 224 | 92% | 0% | 8% | Presque Isle | 3,278 | 18 | 196 | 58% | 36% | 7% |
| Hillsdale | 1,904 | 10 | 171 | 92% | 0% | 8% | Roscommon | 11,091 | 71 | 845 | 54% | 45% | 0% |
| Houghton | 2,646 | 46 | 946 | 85% | 10% | 5% | Saginaw | 301 | 64 | 3,459 | 87% | 10% | 3% |
| Huron | 4,770 | 52 | 557 | 59% | 31% | 10% | Sanilac | 3,244 | 34 | 1,141 | 98% | 0% | 2% |
| Ingham | 519 | 21 | 1,836 | 98% | 2% | 1% | Schoolcraft | 1,720 | 20 | 564 | 91% | 2% | 7% |
| Ionia | 380 | 7 | 222 | 97% | 0% | 3% | Shiawassee | 970 | 17 | 181 | 49% | 20% | 31% |
| Iosco | 6,752 | 65 | 928 | 33% | 65% | 2% | St. Clair | 1,921 | 31 | 458 | 73% | 21% | 6% |
| Iron | 2,377 | 30 | 491 | 40% | 58% | 2% | St. Joseph | 1,676 | 11 | 211 | 93% | 0% | 7% |
| Isabella | 954 | 19 | 1,689 | 88% | 0% | 12% | Tuscola | 724 | 9 | 108 | 86% | 3% | 11% |
| Jackson | 1,887 | 19 | 774 | 97% | 0% | 3% | Van Buren | 3,857 | 40 | 586 | 58% | 21% | 21% |
| Kalamazoo | 805 | 27 | 2,283 | 97% | 0% | 3% | Washtenaw | 1,114 | 54 | 3,964 | 98% | 0% | 1% |
| Kalkaska | 3,287 | 9 | 136 | 73% | 22% | 5% | Wayne | 2,448 | 137 | 15,574 | 99% | 0% | 1% |
| Kent | 1,627 | 65 | 6,036 | 99% | 0% | 1% | Wexford | 2,202 | 27 | 663 | 74% | 25% | 1% |
| Keweenaw | 1,176 | 25 | 284 | 47% | 44% | 8% | TOTAL | 233,382 | 2,839 | 107,380 | | | |

SOURCE: U.S. Census Bureau (2001); Travel, Tourism, and Recreation Center, Michigan State University.

private-sector suppliers, many of which are relatively small businesses. The responsibility for packaging is left largely to the consumer. Contrast this tourism product with an all-inclusive ten-day Caribbean cruise on a Holland America ship. The cruise product's price is known in advance; the packaging of activities is largely handled by the cruise line; it also arranges air and on-shore transportation for cruisers and their baggage; and, as the single provider, it oversees the quality and marketing of the cruise product. Holland America is a large corporate entity with the resources to market internationally, hire and train skilled employees, conduct its own research and evaluation, and invest in new products in response to changing demand. It takes a great deal more effort on the part of the consumer to plan and execute a Michigan tourism experience than a cruise, and considerable more risk is involved. For example, the price is highly variable; first-time visitors have limited prior knowledge of the quality of the overall package and individual components; and they must rely primarily on themselves to resolve problems associated with unpredictable weather, traffic, road conditions, illness, vehicle breakdown, and so on. As an aggregation of independent organizations, Michigan's tourism industry is challenged to perform system management and planning functions such as marketing, quality control, and new product development that would enhance customer satisfaction and the economic performance of the Michigan tourism system. These challenges are, of course, not unique to Michigan. Destinations that develop policies, organizational structures, and the coping strategies that mitigate these challenges will gain advantage over competitors.

The relative popularity of outdoor recreation and the related activities of visiting state and national parks, general touring, and fall color touring support the conclusion that Michigan's tourism industry is highly dependent upon natural resources. Further evidence of this can be gleaned from the following statistics for 2000 obtained from the Michigan Department of State and Michigan Department of Natural Resources:

Registered watercraft . . . . . . . . . . . . . . . . . 829,210
Registered snowmobiles . . . . . . . . . . . . . 278,473
Hunting and fishing licenses
     sold of all types . . . . . . . . . . . . . . 4,987,048

Clearly, the future of Michigan's tourism industry is tied to maintaining the state's extensive and

---

**TABLE 22.7**

**Participation in Selected Activities by Michigan Tourists on Pleasure Trips, 1996–2001**

| Activity | Participation Rate | Trend |
|---|---|---|
| General touring or driving for pleasure | 53.0% | Down |
| Outdoor recreation | 50.9% | Down |
| Shopping | 54.9% | Stable |
| Explore small city or town | 49.7% | Stable |
| Dine at unique restaurant | 46.4% | Stable |
| Visit other attraction | 40.9% | Stable |
| Night life | 29.7% | Stable |
| Visit state or national park | 27.4% | Down |
| Visit historic site | 25.0% | Down |
| Attend festival or event | 24.8% | Up |
| Visit museum or hall of fame | 12.4% | Stable |
| Casino gaming | 11.5% | Stable |
| Fall color touring | 9.4% | Stable |
| Mean number of activities | 4.5 | Unchanged |

SOURCE: Michigan Travel Market Survey, Travel, Tourism, and Recreation Center, Michigan State University.

---

high-quality natural resource base.

The last column in table 22.7 presents the trend in participation in activities based upon comparing participation rates in 1996–97 to those for 2000–2001. Participation rates did not change significantly for most of the thirteen activities listed, but one general trend is apparent. Participation in outdoor recreation and related activities declined enough between 1996–97 and 2000–2001 to conclude that the observed change is unlikely to be associated with some type of sampling error. This trend is in line with similar trends found in other regions of the United States, which have been linked to our aging population. This is probably a causal factor in the Michigan trend as well, but it has been exacerbated by poor snow conditions in 2000–2001, which severely limited snowmobile and cross-country skiing opportunities during the winter season. Regardless of the cause, it is important for Michigan to expand its product offering to better fit the changing tastes of its tourist customer base.

## Tourism across the Seasons of the Year

Travel to and from Michigan varies markedly across the months of the year. Michigan records the most travelers in July and August, with about 45% of total visitors recorded during the warm season months of June to August. About 25% of our visitors arrive in the fall, and the remaining 30% are about equally distributed between winter and spring. The distribution of tourists across the months and seasons of the year can fluctuate significantly because of prevailing climatic conditions. Snow conditions are significant to winter tourism, as are summer temperature and precipitation patterns. More Michigan residents travel to out-of-state than to in-state destinations during all but three months of the year (exceptions are July, August, and September). The outflow of residents and their dollars peaks during March and April, with nearly 75% of residents bound for out-of-state destinations. The peaking of tourism during the summer is most evident in northern regions of the state and rural areas of southern Michigan. The westernmost counties in the Upper Peninsula, with more abundant and consistent snow conditions, typically experience pronounced summer and winter season spikes in tourism (Holecek et al. 2000).

The seasonal pattern of tourism travel has changed over the last several decades both in Michigan and in the rest of the United States. In the 1950s and 1960s, extended summer vacations were the dominant type of leisure travel and resulted in an extreme summer season peaking challenge for the industry. The general trend since that time has been toward distributing one's vacation days more evenly across the seasons and toward taking more weekend trips, especially over holidays. Michigan's tourism industry has responded to these changes in travel patterns. Even the most seasonal businesses remain open well into the fall and open earlier in the spring. However, midweek business during these shoulder seasons is often limited. Many other businesses now remain open on a year-round basis. Nonetheless, the seasonality of tourism in Michigan remains one of the industry's greatest challenges.

## Tourism Trends in Michigan

The most useful indicators of Michigan's tourism industry's performance are highway traffic statistics available from the Michigan Department of Transportation and tax collections data for hotels and motels available from the Michigan Department of Treasury. Highway traffic counts are useful indicators of the volume of tourism activity, although these data obviously contain more than just tourism traffic. Tax collection data for Michigan hotels and motels (SIC 701) are useful

indicators of the trend in tourists' expenditures. As in the case of traffic counts, hotel and motel tax data are not ideal tourism indicators, since they include the impact of sales to local residents as well as to business travelers. Hotels and motels pay a use tax to the state on their revenue from room sales, and a sales tax on their other sales, consisting primarily of food and beverages. The trends in these data series along with the trend in gasoline prices are presented in figure 22.1. Gasoline prices exhibit little change since 1985; however, traffic volume has increased at a relatively steady 4% average annual rate. Hotel and motel sales and use tax collections are more volatile from year to year, but exhibit a clear growth trend of about 6% per year. Since 1985, these trends indicate that tourism volume in Michigan has increased about 75% and tourists' spending in Michigan has increased by about 150%. These admittedly imperfect indicators of the industry's performance are consistent with international and national growth trends in tourism and with other indicator statistics.

A number of factors are commonly believed to be driving growth in tourism, with population and overall economic growth most often considered to be the dominant factors. Population increases in Michigan and other states in the region have been relatively small and thus of limited impact on tourism growth in Michigan. General economic growth is a much more likely candidate as a major driver of tourism growth. The fifteen-year period between 1985 and 2000 was one of economic prosperity, with the later years being especially prosperous. However, general economic growth is not the total answer to what is driving tourism growth in Michigan, as suggested by the steady increase in probable tourism volume regardless of prevailing economic conditions. Fluctuations in economic conditions appear to have much more impact on trip spending than on the volume of trips taken. The steady increase in the latter is probably a function of the age distribution trend in Michigan's prime tourism market region and to a lesser degree population growth itself. Propensity to travel tends to increase as one ages, up to the point where travel becomes impractical for health or other age-related reasons. This is driven by: (1) changing tastes that favor travel, (2) more leisure time, and (3) more discretionary income. Until the baby-boomer generation passes the age where travel must be stopped or severely limited, one can anticipate an extension of the recent growth trends in travel vol-

**FIGURE 22.1**

**Statewide Trends in Selected Industry Indicators, 1985–2001**

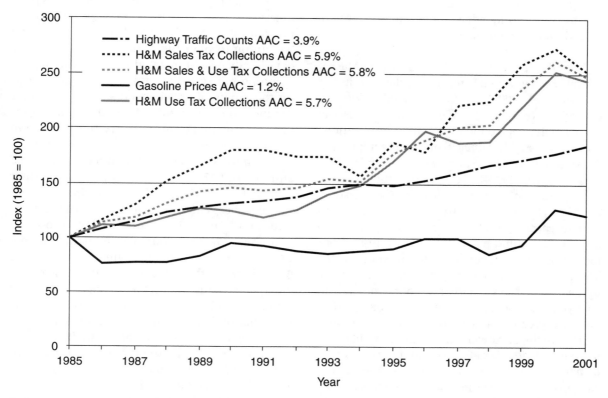

SOURCE: Michigan Department of Transportation; Michigan Department of Treasury, AAA Michigan.
NOTES: AAC means "average annual change." H&M means "hotel and motel."

ume and travel spending depicted in figure 22.1, so long as Michigan continues to capture market share equal to that it has held in recent years.

There is convincing evidence to indicate that Michigan's tourism industry has grown significantly since 1985, but also that Michigan has a significant trade deficit in travel. Is this deficit increasing or decreasing? Data are not available that would allow one to directly answer this question, but statistics reported annually in the Travel Industry Association of America's U.S. Travel Data Center series on the *Impact of Travel on State Economies* tend to indicate that the deficit has grown since 1985. Consider the relative ranking of Michigan among the fifty states and the District of Columbia in terms of direct travel expenditures captured in table 22.8.

Since 1985, these data indicate that Michigan has lost market share of both domestic and international travelers' spending in the United States, which would suggest Michigan's trade deficit in travel has been increasing over the last approximately fifteen years.

There is little hard evidence that might explain the declines in Michigan's share of the domestic and international travel markets. Likely factors that can be noted include:

- The strong U.S. dollar, especially in comparison to the Canadian dollar, which has made visiting the United States more expensive.
- The deregulation of the airlines with accompanying lower prices, which has allowed travelers

**TABLE 22.8**

**Michigan's Rank in Capturing Domestic and international Travelers' Expenditures in Selected Years**

| | Expenditure Rankings | |
|---|---|---|
| Year | Domestic | International |
| 1985 | 8 | 12 |
| 1995 | 13 | 14 |
| 1999 | 13 | 16 |

SOURCE: Travel Industry Association of America (1987, 1997, 2001b).

to travel farther in search of more exotic destinations or those perceived to offer a higher quality tourism product.

• Growth in worldwide competition for travelers and their expenditures.

Data collected via the Michigan Travel Market Survey were grouped into those collected during 1996–97 and 2000–2001 and analyzed to identify emerging trends in Michigan tourism. Several trends were revealed with potential implications for the industry. Declines in outdoor recreation as the stated primary trip purpose (15.3% in 1996–97 versus 8.7% in 2000–2001) and in participation in outdoor recreation on trips (from 57.8% to 46.6%), coupled with a decline (from 9.5% to 7.3%) in tourists camping on their overnight trips indicate a downward trend in the importance of outdoor recreation to Michigan's overall tourism industry. This trend is likely to be tied to a reported increase in mean age of travel party members from 37.7 to 39.2 years. These changes in ages of party numbers are greatest among the over-50 age categories. Michigan travel parties are more likely to include individuals older than 50. The percentage of parties with members in the 31–40-year-old category declined significantly during this period, from 65.5% to 49.8%. Yet, parties with children ten or younger increased slightly during this period, suggesting that grandparents traveling with their grandchildren may be an emerging and important tourism market niche.

Respondents in 1996–97 were more likely to report being on an overnight trip (84.7%) than were those in 2000–2001 (80.1%) and that their trips involved more nights away from home (3.6 versus 3.3 nights). The distribution of travel across seasons was somewhat less dominated by summer trips in 2000–2001 (40.0%) than in 1996–97 (44.9%). These trends track the national trend, which has prevailed for several years, of more trips of shorter duration distributed throughout the year. The most common explanation for this shift away from traditional longer vacations to more, shorter "getaway" trips is the increasing challenge households face in coordinating schedules across dual wage earners and children engaged in ever more school and nonschool activities. Finding the time rather than the money to travel is the bigger challenge in dual-wage-earner households with very active children.

It is not surprising, then, that respondents in 2000–2001 reported spending somewhat less on their shorter trips than did those contacted in 1996–97 ($524 versus $453). Trip planning horizons have also become shorter, with trip planning horizons falling from a mean of seventy days prior to travel in 1996–97 to fifty-six days prior to travel in 2000–2001. Nearly 70% of travelers reported beginning to plan their trips fewer than thirty days in advance of planned travel. Shrinking trip planning horizons have important implications for the timing of travel advertising as well as for the most relevant mode of communications for destinations marketing organizations to use in conveying information to prospective travelers.

The most striking trend between the 1996–97 and 2000–2001 groups of respondents is their reported access to and use of the Internet. Internet access increased from 35.6% of reporting households in 1996–97 to 67.1% of reporting households in. 2000–2001, and use of the Internet to obtain travel information grew from 46.5% to 69.1% between these two time periods. The recent emergence of the Internet has already had a great impact on Michigan's tourism industry, and its potential to further impact the industry is only beginning to be recognized and exploited.

A final noteworthy trend emerged from comparing these two groups of respondents. In 1996–97, 87.2% of all Michigan tourists reported that they were white/Caucasian. This percentage declined to 83.6% in 2000–2001. Statewide, the industry is overly dependent upon the white/Caucasian market, and this is problematic across most of northern Michigan, where the proportion of white/Caucasians often exceeds 95%. The minority population in Michigan's prime tourism markets is growing more rapidly than the white/Caucasian population, and a significant proportion of the minority population can afford to take pleasure trips and do so.

With the projected decline in the white/Caucasian population relative to other racial/ethnic groups in Michigan and other states in this region, Michigan's tourism industry will need to become more adept at attracting minorities or inevitably experience further decline in its share of domestic tourists' expenditures.

It seems fitting to conclude this discussion of trends with some brief commentary on the immediate and potential long-term impacts of the terrorism attacks in New York and Washington, D.C., on 11 September 2001. The short-term impacts of these attacks were widely felt across the tourism industry, with the airlines and destinations most dependent on air travel suffering the greatest amount of economic damage. Yet, by spring 2002, even the hardest hit tourism sectors and destinations were rebounding quickly from the shock of the 9/11 attacks. Their impacts on Michigan's tourism industry do not appear to have been substantial, except in the southeastern region, which is more dependent upon air travel than is the rest of the state. It is evident that, when the safety of travel becomes an issue, the public responds immediately to avoid perceived unsafe travel modes or destinations. However, the net impact is minimal because, more often than not, travelers simply substitute safer travel modes and destinations for those perceived to be less safe.

One can only speculate about the long-term impacts of the 9/11 attacks and the emergence of terrorism as an ongoing threat in the United States. We can be certain that increased security will make air travel less convenient and more costly. The fear of flying induced by the 9/11 attacks has diminished, but it is likely to persist as a factor in some people's travel choices for many years to come. Thus, terrorism incidents can disrupt "normal" travel behavior significantly in the short run but are unlikely to dampen the long-term upward growth trend of the tourism industry in America or in Michigan.

## Advertising and Promotion

The advertising and promotion infrastructure that has evolved to support tourism is a dominant feature of Michigan's tourism system. It receives the bulk of the state's general fund investment that is specifically earmarked to support the industry, and hence is the central focus of its public policy activities. What follows is a greatly condensed overview of the advertising and promotion infrastructure that exists to support the tourism industry.

Tourism is a minor focus within the federal government, and this focus is restricted primarily to promoting the United States as a travel destination. Although the federal role in the nation's transportation and outdoor recreation systems is of critical importance to tourism throughout the nation, domestic tourism per se has rarely generated much attention in Washington. A couple of exceptions are worthy of note here. The energy crisis in the 1970s, which spawned legislative interest in gasoline rationing and restrictions on pleasure travel, and the terrorism attacks last year both attracted considerable attention from federal lawmakers. However, neither appears to have produced a lasting change in the minimalist position tourism garners on the federal legislative agenda.

Tourism advertising and promotion have a more prominent role at the state and local levels. Currently, all states are engaged in promoting their state as a destination for tourists, and the trend in recent years has been toward increasing the amount of money directed toward tourism advertising and promotion. Travel Michigan, within the Michigan Economic Development Corporation, is the state agency that directs Michigan's tourism promotion program. It also manages Michigan's thirteen highway welcome centers. Most communities rely on nongovernmental chambers of commerce, convention and visitor's bureaus, and regional travel associations to promote them as tourism destinations.

All of these organizations are autonomous, without formal ties to each other. However, informal cooperation among them is common. Relations between and within these organizations, however, are not always harmonious. Conflicts arise most often in cases where missions overlap or where two or more organizations rely on common revenue sources to support their activities. Hence, a general knowledge of how these organizations are funded is useful to understanding the basis for many of the conflicts and policy issues that arise.

Travel Michigan is funded by appropriations from the state's general fund. It is the only organization that routinely receives state funding for tourism advertising and promotion, but this has not always been the case in Michigan, nor is it the universal practice across all states. Until the early 1980s, Michigan appropriated funds to support regional tourism promotion organizations in the Upper Peninsula and west, east, and southeast Michigan. The West Michigan Travel Association (WMTA) survived the loss of state funding, and now relies on member dues and advertising sales in its publications to support its activities. The Upper Peninsula Travel and Recreation Association (UPTRA) also continues to exist, with its financial support derived from regionwide room assessment and member dues.

The local-government-affiliated advertising and promotion organizations in the populous urban counties rely on state-authorized room taxes collected by these counties for their revenue bases. The legislation authorizing these room taxes includes the general provision that they should be used for "tourism" purposes; however,

**TABLE 22.9**

**State Tourism Office Total Budgets in Selected Fiscal Years**

| Fiscal Year | Average/State ($ millions) | Michigan ($ millions) | Michigan Rank | Illinois ($ millions) |
|---|---|---|---|---|
| 1984–85 | 3.80 | 9.07 | 6 | 14.40 |
| 1989–90 | 6.81 | 14.01 | 6 | 22.04 |
| 1994–95 | 8.14 | 9.04 | 15 | 30.48 |
| 1999–2000 | 12.88 | 15.45 | 11 | 55.29 |

SOURCE: Travel Industry Association of America (1985, 1991, 1995, 2000).

what is or is not a legitimate tourism purpose is a common source for debate during discussions of how to best allocate room tax revenues and has spawned considerable controversy in some jurisdictions.

The non-government-affiliated advertising and promotion organizations derive their funding from memberships and various other fund-raising activities (e.g., chambers of commerce) and legislatively authorized and self-imposed room assessments (e.g., convention and visitors' bureaus). These funding arrangements often are a source of competition and controversy. Membership-funded organizations often perceive those funded through the room assessment as obstacles to expanding their member revenue base. Within room assessment-supported organizations, the lodging and other sectors of the local tourism industry often disagree over how to best allocate room assessment revenues.

The primary and only mission of the tourism offices in most states, including Michigan's, is to sell their states as tourism destinations. Thus, total state tourism office budgets are of considerable interest to each state's overall tourism industry. Selected state tourism office budget data are presented in table 22.9. The average state tourism office budget has grown steadily from $3.80 million in the 1984–85 fiscal year to nearly $13 million in 1999–2000. Michigan's tourism office's budget has fluctuated widely over this fifteen-year period and has generally fallen in comparison to that of other states. This is especially evident when comparing Michigan's budget to that of Illinois, which has increased fourfold.

Several conclusions can be drawn from these data. First, Michigan, one of the first states to significantly boost its investment in tourism advertising and promotion, has seen its lead in this arena erode. In the 1984–85 fiscal year, Michigan's travel office budget was nearly three

times higher that the national average, but in 1999–2000 its budget was only about 25% above average. Contrast this to Illinois, one of Michigan's major competitors in this region. Its travel office budget grew significantly and steadily during this fifteen-year period. In 1984–85, Illinois invested 60% more in tourism advertising and promotion than did Michigan; in 1999–2000, it invested 260% more than did Michigan.

Second, Michigan's travel office budget has increased about 70% during this fifteen-year period, while tourism volume in Michigan has about doubled and tourists' expenditures have increased by about 150%. The state's investment in tourism advertising and promotion has fallen behind overall growth in tourism in Michigan. Furthermore, although the state's investment in advertising and promotion has increased in nominal terms, the increase is not enough to offset inflation.

Third, the significant fluctuations in Michigan's tourism office budget are problematic and indicative of a budget decision-making process that is not responsive to market conditions. This is evident in the tendency for the tourism office's budget to wax and wane with state government's fiscal conditions. More often than not, the travel office budget is reduced as the economy slows, which is a time when market conditions would indicate an increase in advertising and promotion would be beneficial.

In conclusion, a number of arguments can be made to support increasing the state's investment in tourism advertising and promotion. An increase is needed to: (1) reflect industry growth, (2) offset inflation in advertising and promotion costs, and 3) match the growth in competitors' investments in tourism advertising and promotion. More importantly, it could be argued that the state's balance of trade deficit in travel requires that this state should invest relatively more in tourism advertising and promotion than do its competitors. Investment in advertising and promotion is one of a very few tools that the state can draw upon to offset the intractable and powerful forces (e.g., climate) that underline its deficit in travel trade. However, it is important to recognize that the solution to the deficit problem is not simply to invest more state dollars in advertising and promotion. This is demonstrated in Illinois, which invests substantially more than does Michigan in tourism advertising and promotion, yet nonetheless has a travel trade deficit that surpasses Michigan's.

## Conclusions

In the preceding sections of this chapter, important indicators of the scale, scope, and economic importance of Michigan's tourism industry were introduced. Now let us turn our attention to putting these individual pieces together to form a composite picture of the overall industry.

Michigan's tourism industry is an immense system with a presence in every corner of the state. Despite its overall scope, scale, and economic importance, the production of tourism experiences rests largely in the hands of thousands of independent, very small businesses and the tourists themselves. The business of tourism fluctuates considerably across seasons and days of the week, and with weather conditions. The industry relies on a regional market for its customers, who are disproportionately white/Caucasian and travel primarily by privately owned vehicles. Michigan's outstanding endowment of natural resources provided the foundation for the early development of a Michigan tourism industry, and natural resources remain a dominant attraction for current Michigan tourists.

The industry can be characterized as a growth industry, with visitor volume and expenditures increasing at average annual rates of 4% and 6%, respectively. Furthermore, tourism plays an important role in the quality of life of residents of Michigan and the region. However, the importance of tourism to Michigan's economy extends beyond what tourists spend directly on lodging, meals, and other products and services. Nearly 75% of all U.S. domestic travel is tourism-related, and nearly 75% of total miles traveled in the United States are via privately owned vehicles (Travel Industry Association of America 2001a). This leads to the conclusion that well over half of the miles recorded on privately owned vehicle odometers each year are a result of tourism travel. With its dominant position as a supplier of this nation's privately owned vehicles, Michigan's economy is far more dependent upon tourism than probably any other state economy in the United States.

The disappointing piece of the overall Michigan tourism picture that emerges from detailed review of the data available is that Michigan has a multi-billion-dollar deficit in tourism. Michigan residents spend more on out-of-state trips than do nonresident visitors to Michigan. This trade deficit in travel appears to be expanding. Furthermore, Michigan has probably had a travel trade deficit for many years.

Since most states in the region also have a travel trade deficit, and since Michigan fares better than the others in retaining resident travelers' dollars in state, there are surely common and powerful forces across this region that underlie Michigan's travel trade deficit. These include: geographical location, population distribution, climate, and a relatively wealthy resident population. These forces are largely intractable and will persist as challenges confronting Michigan's tourism industry for the foreseeable future.

The obvious question, then, is: What, if anything, can or should be done to offset the persistent and powerful forces that are responsible for Michigan's annual travel trade deficit? This is indeed the question that should guide this state's tourism policy formulation and the tourism element within the state's overall economic development planning efforts. At the outset, it is important to acknowledge that the deficit is far too large and pervasive to be substantially reduced in the short run or via minor adjustments in current policies, marketing plans, or increases in investment in the industry. Reducing the deficit will require a coordinated long-term strategy and meaningful new amounts of public- and private-sector investment. The industry currently does not appear to be organized in a manner that can accommodate such a revolutionary expansion in tourism industry planning, management, and investment. Within state government's executive branch, travel and tourism-related functions are scattered across departments, which are not interlinked. Revolutionary tourism policy development would also be problematic, given the existing organizational structure within the legislative branch of state government. Furthermore, the private sector of the industry is not organized in a manner to participate as a full partner with the public sector in a coordinated attack on Michigan's travel trade deficit.

Let us separate and focus on recommendations related to the "what can be done" and "should be done" elements of the above question, recognizing that these come from the author's observations gained from a couple of decades of monitoring Michigan's tourism industry.

### What Can Be Done

1. State government agencies could be reorganized to better reflect the importance of tourism to the state's economy.

2. The state could be more cognizant of and pro-active in the central role it plays in the development of Michigan's tourism industry via its provision and regulation of transportation systems, public lands and waterways, and other public tourism attractions; its investments in promoting this state as a tourist destination; the incentives (and disincentives) it offers to stimulate new investment; and its investments in education and training as well as research and technical assistance to businesses. These functions should be coordinated, possibly in a separate department drawing upon a strategic tourism development plan.

3. Return on investment appears to be of little consequence in setting the level of the state's investment in promoting Michigan tourism. The state's investment in promotion fluctuates with its fiscal circumstances and politics of the day, rather than being based on a sound investment strategy. An alternative mechanism for funding tourism promotion could be developed that is more responsive to market conditions and the challenges and opportunities they present.

4. The state could reach beyond promotion to find ways to support tourism development in Michigan. The following avenues could be explored: (a) Enhance education and training opportunities for tourism businesses and their employees, (b) develop programs to encourage investment in new and improved tourism products, and (c) enhance industry access to research and technical assistance to allow it to better target development opportunities.

5. The state could take a leadership role in marshalling the resources across state government, the industry, and its educational institutions to address the economic development needs of Michigan's tourism industry.

### What Should Be Done

Implementing the above recommendations would naturally lead to an expanded role for state government in the tourism development arena, but should the state assume this role? Arguments in support of an expanded role for the state in tourism development include:

1. The economic scale of this industry and the state's multi-billion-dollar deficit in travel trade suggest that it merits greater government attention than it has received in the past.

2. The size of the deficit and its persistence and expansion over time would suggest that what we have been doing is not working. It is time to try a new approach.

3. Given the structure of Michigan's tourism industry (e.g., relatively small, unaffiliated businesses), there appears to be no alternative to the state assuming a leadership role in tourism development.

4. The expense associated with well-targeted state investments in tourism will be offset by expanded tax revenue collections. Many of these investments can be expected to yield positive rates of return.

The scale, scope, and economic importance of Michigan's tourism industry justify assigning it a higher priority on the state's economic development agenda. Continuing to ignore the massive multi-billion-dollar travel trade deficit is ill advised. While the global and national tourism markets are growing and are expected to continue to grow, Michigan does not appear to be capturing its fair share of these growth markets, so we cannot rely on growth to reduce the deficit. Thus, the travel trade deficit appears destined to expand. Unless offset by expanded exports from other sectors of the economy, its negative burden on Michigan's overall economy will grow until an effective long-term strategy for mitigating it is developed and implemented.

■

### NOTE

1. Deriving tourism-relevant indicators from recreation data sets is complicated by: (1) the limited scope of recreation activities that are generally included (e.g., travel to attend concerts or professional sporting events and to visit casinos are not included); (2) aggregation of local residents along with nonresidents in data sets; and (3) the common omission of commercially provided recreation such as camping and golf along with data for these same activities when they are provided by the public sector.

## REFERENCES

Bureau of Transportation Statistics (BTS), U.S. Department of Transportation. 1997. *1995 American travel survey.* Washington, D.C.: Bureau of Transportation Statistics, U.S. Department of Transportation.

Holecek, D. F., D. M. Spencer, J. E. Williams, and T. I. Herbowicz. 2000. Michigan travel market survey. Special report 108. East Lansing: Michigan Agricultural Experiment Station, Michigan State University.

Travel Industry Association of America (TIA). 1985. *Survey of state travel offices 1984–1985.* Washington, D.C.: Travel Industry Association of America.

———. 1987. *Impact of travel on state economies 1985.* Washington, D.C.: Travel Industry Association of America.

———. 1991. *Survey of state travel offices, 1990–91.* Washington, D.C.: Travel Industry Association of America.

———. 1995. *Survey of state travel offices, 1994–95.* Washington, D.C.: Travel Industry Association of America.

———. 1997. *Impact of travel on state economies 1995.* Washington, D.C.: Travel Industry Association of America.

———. 2000. *1999–2000 survey of U.S. state and territory tourism offices.* Washington, D.C.: Travel Industry Association of America.

———. 2001a. *The economic review of travel in America 2001 edition.* Washington, D.C.: Travel Industry Association of America.

———. 2001b. *Impact of travel on state economies 1999.* Washington, D.C.: Travel Industry Association of America.

U.S. Census Bureau. 2001. *Profiles of general demographic characteristics 2000. 2000 Census of Population and Housing. Michigan.* Washington, D.C.: U.S. Census Bureau.

World Travel & Tourism Council (WTTC). 1997. *Summit of the eight: Travel & tourism creating jobs.* London: World Travel & Tourism Council.

# 23

# Restructuring and Deregulation of the Electric Power Sector in Michigan

*Michelle F. Wilsey*

## Introduction

Michigan, like many other states in the United States as well as the federal government, is in the process of restructuring and selectively deregulating its traditional public utility industries, including natural gas, telecommunications, and electricity. Because of the inherent economic characteristics and "essential" nature of their services, these industries have been classified as natural monopolies and subject to extensive economic regulation. During the past thirty years, the principles underlying the regulated utility model have been subject to increased skepticism. In particular, the notion that the industries are "natural monopolies" has been eroded due to technological advances and market developments (such as the development of trading markets to allocate capacity and the use of financial instruments to manage risk). These developments have created opportunities for competitive entry and deregulation of utilities.

Full deregulation has occurred in such industries as airlines and motor carriers, and to a large extent in rail transport. In the telecommunications and natural gas industries there has been substantial restructuring and significant, growing deregulation. Most recently, the electric power industry has come under structural pressure. As

has been demonstrated in past efforts to reform utility sectors, there is no rapid transition from fully regulated natural and legal monopolies to alternative arrangements. New regulatory instruments and institutions are required to provide adequate oversight for restructured industries. Given the relative importance of electricity reform over the last decade and the work yet to be done, it will be the principal focus of this chapter.

It is important to note at the outset that restructuring is not equivalent to deregulation. According to Severin Borenstein and James Bushnell,

> The gains from restructuring are most likely to occur through improvement in the efficiency and prudency of long-term investment, but these benefits will be very difficult to measure. Though restructuring could have near term benefits in the efficiency of production and consumption, concerns with the efficiency of decentralized dispatch and the exercise of market power make it at least as likely that restructuring will not benefit society in the short run. We argue that electricity is especially vulnerable to the exercise of market power, even by firms with relatively small market shares, so there will be continued need for regulatory oversight in these markets, at least until there is much more

**TABLE 23.1**

**Utility Retail Sales, Revenue, and Number of Customers for the State of Michigan, 1999**

|  | IOUs | Public | Co-operative | Total |
|---|---|---|---|---|
| Number of utilities | 9 | 41 | 10 | 60 |
| Number of retail customers | 3,994,111 | 288,243 | 251,877 | 4,534,231 |
| Retail sales (thousand MWh) | 93,529 | 7,543 | 2,407 | 103,480 |
| Percentage of retail sales | 90.9 | 7.3 | 2.3 | 100.0 |
| Revenue from retail sales (million dollars) | 6,704 | 478 | 205 | 7,387 |
| Percentage of revenue | 90.8 | 6.5 | 2.8 | 100.0 |
| Average price (cents)/kWh | 7.17 | 6.34 | 8.54 | 7.14 |

real-time demand responsiveness. Thus, restructuring in electricity markets is not now, and is unlikely to be, synonymous with deregulation. (Borenstein and Bushnell 2000)

The regulatory reform model in electricity tends to follow the process set out in telecommunications and in the natural gas industry. Potentially competitive segments of the industry (generation) are structurally or functionally separated from the monopolistic segments (transmission and distribution).[1] Market entry and exit as well as prices for competitive services are gradually deregulated. Network interconnection and open access is required, and performance-based approaches are adopted for the services that remain under regulation.

Restructuring of the public utility industries has been driven by several interrelated factors. Economic growth and technological improvements have reduced the importance of scale economies, lowered the cost of raising large amounts of capital, and changed perceptions about the potential for economic efficiency in utility industries. In many cases, these changes have led to new products, new delivery systems, or new providers that selectively compete with firms in regulated industries. In addition, changing perceptions about the role of government and dissatisfaction with the performance of the regulated public utility industries have contributed to the movement toward greater reliance on markets for maximizing social welfare.[2] Restructuring of the electricity industry therefore offers the potential for more efficient production and investment, but, as has been demonstrated through recent experience, may also create the opportunity for producers to exercise market power.

The magnitude and importance of the electricity industry to the national and statewide econ-omy and the reach of the industry to all consumers will command the attention of all stakeholders to the debate on the transformation of this sector. This chapter examines the transformation of the electric utility industry nationally and in Michigan over the last decade. Michigan's electric industry is being restructured so that the generation and supply of power is now opening to competition. While it is too early in the process to know what the effects of restructuring will be, key indicators, such as the number of customers switching to competitive suppliers and retail price trends, are examined to provide some insight and a basis for future evaluation. At present, findings suggest that Michigan is achieving slow but steady progress in opening up its markets to competition. This deliberate path has allowed Michigan to avoid many of the pitfalls encountered by other states who have pursued restructuring of their electricity industries. At the same time, however, benefits in terms of retail price have been slow to accrue, especially to residential and small commercial customers. Future progress hinges a great deal on improvements in wholesale markets. Therefore, Michigan, like other restructuring states, should actively participate in the national debate and federal policy making in order to encourage progress and assure coordinated policies at the state level.

## The Organization of the Electricity Industry

### Traditional Electric Utilities

The electric utility industry in the United States includes 3,152 investor-owned, publicly owned, cooperative, and federal electric utilities. Combined, these utilities serve approximately 126 million customers (U.S. DOE Energy Information

**TABLE 23.2**

### Six Largest Utilities in Michigan Ranked by Retail Sales, 2000

| Utility (Type) | MWH Sales | Revenue | Customers |
|---|---|---|---|
| DTE Energy (investor-owned) | 48,089,315 | 3,510,985,299 | 2,117,948 |
| Consumers Energy (investor-owned) | 35,504,051 | 2,457,181,481 | 1,700,014 |
| Lansing Board of Water and Light (municipal) | 3,221,827 | 157,215,000 | 96,237 |
| American Electric Power (Indiana Michigan Power Co.) (investor-owned) | 2,907,942 | 160,412,471 | 121,435 |
| Wisconsin Electric Power (investor-owned) | 2,744,061 | 107,260,846 | 26,307 |
| Great Lakes (cooperative) | 1,028,713 | 93,415,850 | 109,383 |

SOURCE: Michigan Public Service Commission, "Statistical Data of Retail Sales Electric Utilities in Michigan Year Ended December 31, 2001" and American Public Power Association, 2001 Annual Directory & Statistical Report, "100 Largest Public Power Utilities, 2000."

Administration 2002a). Historically, investor-owned electric utilities (IOUs) have been vertically integrated companies serving large, consolidated markets where economies of scale afford the lowest prices. However, publicly owned, cooperative, and federal electric utilities also have a role in producing, transmitting, and distributing electricity to all customers. As of 1999, there were sixty utilities serving Michigan's 4.5 million customers. Of those, nine were investor-owned, forty-one were public, and ten were electric cooperatives (see table 23.1). Throughout most of the United States, investor-owned utilities account for the largest portion of the market by nearly any measure.[3] In Michigan, investor-owned utilities serve nearly 90% of retail customers (U.S. DOE Energy Information Administration 2002a). DTE Energy (through its principal operating subsidiary, Detroit Edison) and Consumers Energy are the largest utilities in the state (see table 23.2). Combined they serve over 3.9 million Michigan customers (Michigan Public Service Commission 2002f).

### Competitive Suppliers

In markets, like Michigan, that have authorized retail choice programs for electricity, power marketers or "alternative electric suppliers" may also serve customers. Alternative electric suppliers purchase electric generation service and in turn sell that service to retail customers. However, they do not physically deliver the electricity because they do not own or operate generation, transmission, or distribution facilities. Power marketers emerged after passage of the federal Energy Policy Act of 1992 (EPACT) with provisions that opened transmission lines and allowed development of a competitive wholesale market for electricity. Alternative electric suppliers are particularly active in markets where the retail rates are high, where there is sufficient transmission infrastructure, and where there is open access to the utility distribution system.[4]

In Michigan, retail open access was phased in beginning in 1998, with the market for all customers opened in 2002. Power marketers have just begun making inroads in Michigan. While small, the number and volume of customers is growing. Currently there are twenty-four alternative electric suppliers licensed to operate in the state, with four additional applications pending.[5] Eight of the twenty-four licensed alternative electric suppliers are currently serving customers. In the period from June 2001 to October 2002, the total number of customers served by competitive suppliers increased from 1,322 to nearly 5,000, representing over 1,500 megawatts (MW) of sales. As of October 2002, there were an additional 914 customers with 153 MW enrolled in the customer choice program.[6] At present, competitive activity in Michigan is concentrated in the commercial and industrial segments of the market. Only one company is presently serving residential customers.[7]

This trend is typical of states with retail choice. Competitive entry reflects the relative economics of serving the different market segments. Competitors typically target large users first because they:

- represent the best opportunity to earn profits;
- represent the best opportunity to establish a significant presence in the marketplace;
- are motivated, sophisticated energy buyers, thereby reducing the cost of customer acquisition.

## TABLE 23.3

**Percentage of Industrial Sales (MWh) in Consumers and Detroit Edison Service Territories Participating in Retail Open Access**

|                 | Consumers | Detroit Edison |
|-----------------|-----------|----------------|
| November 2001   | n/a       | 0.9%           |
| December 2001   | 4.9%      | 3.6%           |
| January 2002    | 5.7%      | 0.9%           |
| February 2002   | 6.4%      | 22.9%          |
| March 2002      | 7.7%      | 18.9%          |
| April 2002      | 9.2%      | 24.5%          |
| May 2002        | 9.2%      | 9.9%           |
| June 2002       | 10.8%     | 6.7%           |
| July 2002       | 10.7%     | 18.7%          |
| AVERAGE         | 8.5%      | 9.7%           |

SOURCE: Michigan Switch Rate Data provided by Tom Stanton, Competitive Energy Division, Michigan Public Service Commission. Compiled from EIA Form 826 (through July 2002) for Detroit Edison and Consumers Energy.

According to Michigan Public Service Commission staff reports, data for Consumers Energy from the Energy Information Administration (EIA) data (form 826) through September 2002 shows approximately 5% of commercial megawatt hours (MWh) and 0.2% of commercial customers are currently on choice service. For the industrial segment, approximately 11% of MWh and 1.1% of customers are served by competitive electric suppliers. In total, about 8.5% of Consumers's total MWh sales have migrated to competitive service.[8] Competition is more pronounced in Detroit Edison service territory, with 12.8% of commercial MWh and 1.7% of customers taking competitive supply. Similarly, 18.7% of industrial MWh and 5.3% of customers are served by alternative electric suppliers.[9] As of July 2002, total MWh migration for Detroit Edison under retail open access is 9.7%.

In Michigan, competitive supply activity in the industrial segment is relatively low, given the potential. This is primarily due to the fact that about 50% of industrial sales, including the "big three" automotive manufacturers, are under special contracts with the utilities. When special contracts are considered as part of competitive supply, over 60% of the industrial market (as measured by MWh sales) has migrated from regulated rates.

The potential for growth of competitive activity will increase over the next five years as special contracts expire and as wholesale markets improve. The outlook for competitive supply for small commercial and residential customers is less optimistic in the near term, given the costs and complexity of serving smaller, nonaggregated loads (see table 23.3).

### Competitive Generators

The profile of the U.S. electric power generation industry is also changing, with ownership shifting from regulated utilities to competitive suppliers.[10] In fewer than five years, the competitive supplier share of installed capacity has increased by more than a factor of four, rising from 70.3 gigawatts (GW) in 1997 to 319.5 GW in 2001.[11] The large increase reflects sale or transfer of a significant number of generators from utilities to nonutilities, driven by state-level restructuring policies. From 1997 to 2001, the amount of competitive generation has grown from less than 10% of total U.S. capacity to 35.6% (The changing face of U.S. power suppliers [2000]).

Competitive generation in Michigan is beginning to expand with the passage of the Electric Choice and Reliability Act of 2000 (PA 141). The Michigan Public Service Commission reports, "in 2001, 970 MW of generating capacity was completed in Michigan. In the 18 months since the passage of PA 141, construction has begun on almost 6,000 MW of new generating plants by companies not affiliated with any Michigan utility. Construction by affiliates of Michigan utilities during this same period was less than 1,000 MW" (Michigan Public Service Commission 2001a). As of the most recent MPSC report, however, a significant amount of generation has been delayed due to uncertainty in the market.[12]

While total industry production for the United States as a whole (actual sales) generally increased through the decade, the amount of generation by utilities began to decline in 1998 as more capacity, and thus production, shifted to competitive generators (see figure 23.1). Total electricity generation by the industry reached 3,799 billion kilowatthours (kWh) in 2000, compared with 3,071 billion kWh in 1991, reflecting an industry-wide increase of 23.7%. The share of total electricity output that is generated by utilities decreased by 12.6 percentage points, from 91.9% in 1991 to 79.3% in 2000. Competitive power suppliers' share of actual sales (net generation) increased to approximately 20.7% of total U.S. production by 2000. This expansion of "merchant" generation, made possible by open access policies, is spurred by the availability of smaller-scale gas-fired "peak-

**FIGURE 23.1**

**Net Electricity Generation (Sales) in the United States, 1991–2000**

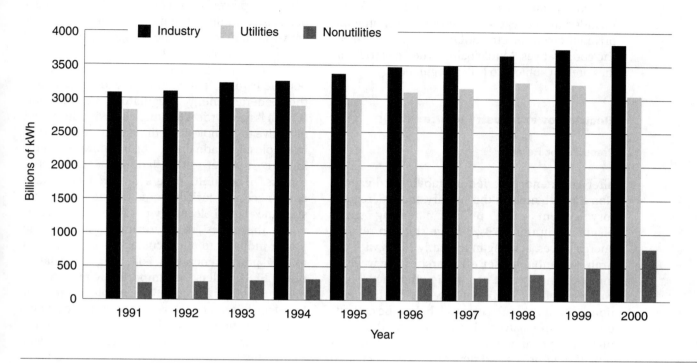

ing" units that can be brought on line to serve customers more cost effectively than base-load central generation.[13]

In 2000, Michigan ranked thirteenth nationally in electricity production, with 104 billion kWh of net generation. Of that, the utilities' share was 85.9%. Overall net generation grew by 11.4% in Michigan between 1993 and 2000, while U.S. net generation increased by approximately 15.8% during the same period.

While nationally the utilities' share of production is declining, the utility share of net generation in Michigan increased from 84.9% in 1999 to 85.9% in 2000. As more capacity shifts to competitive generators, however, production is likely to shift as well.

In Michigan, generation capacity and electricity production have been adequate to meet demand. However, recent reliability issues caused by changing market conditions, decentralization of capacity planning with deregulation, and declining reserve margins have raised concerns throughout the country about the adequacy of supply to meet increasing demand. As a result of these concerns, a substantial amount of new generating capacity is being produced. As new capacity is completed, it will alleviate some of the concern about whether enough generating capac-

ity is available. The downturn in the economy in 2001 and 2002 has slowed demand. This further diminishes the acute near-term capacity and production concerns that were experienced in several parts of the country toward the end of the 1990s. No capacity deficiencies are currently projected for Michigan.

## Electric Utility Regulation

Investor-owned utilities are principally regulated by state and federal authorities. Generally, wholesale rates (sales and purchases between electric utilities), licensing of hydroelectric facilities, nuclear safety and high-level nuclear waste disposal, and environmental regulation are federal matters. Regulation of electric distribution service territories, including approval for most plant and transmission line construction and retail rate levels are state regulatory functions. Public power utilities are not typically subject to state regulation. Approximately twenty states regulate cooperatives, and seven states regulate municipal electric utilities. Many state legislatures, however, defer this control to local municipal officials or cooperative members. In Michigan, the Public Service

Commission (MPSC)—a unit of the Department of Consumer and Industry Service, is responsible for regulation and oversight of energy utilities. Included in this regulatory responsibility are nine privately owned electric utilities and ten rural electric cooperatives. Municipally owned electric utilities are not subject to MPSC regulation.

## Electric Power Industry Restructuring

### Pressure for Reform

After an extended period of stability and expansion through most of the century, the U.S. regulatory system came under increasing stress beginning in the 1970s.[14] Large shifts in relative energy prices, starting in the early 1970s with the Arab oil embargo, set off searches for ways to improve energy and economic efficiency.[15] The commercial availability of new gas-fired generation technology, with costs well below the embedded costs of existing plants, created additional pressure to change the status quo. The combination of high prices and new technologies created opportunity and incentive for large customers to bypass—or credibly threaten to bypass—utility systems to secure lower prices. Thus, large users became a strong force in favor of electricity deregulation.

While mounting inefficiencies create forces for change in the industry, the required changes frequently conflict with the existing regulation. States began to experiment with changes in regulation to allow flexible pricing, limited entry or competition.[16] Many of these experiments led to national legislation or policy programs (such as "retail wheeling" experimental programs or "customer choice" pilot programs). As time passed, not all of these innovations proved successful. Nevertheless, changing government programs often interacted with economic forces to increase the momentum of industry restructuring and deregulation of public utility industries.

### The Competitive Policy Framework

The electric power industry is currently in the midst of a transition from a vertically integrated and regulated monopoly system to a competitive market where retail customers choose the suppliers of their electricity.[17] This process began in 1978 with passage of the Public Utility Regulatory

Policies Act (PURPA). PURPA laid the groundwork for deregulation and competition by opening wholesale power markets to nonutility producers of electricity. Competition in the bulk power market was expanded with the passage of the Energy Policy Act of 1992 (EPACT).

The intent of the act was to establish a competitive wholesale market for electricity. In 1996 the Federal Energy Regulatory Commission (FERC) issued Orders 888 and 889, with the stated objective to "remove impediments to competition in wholesale trade and to bring more efficient, lower cost power to the Nation's electricity customers." The FERC orders required open and equal access to jurisdictional utilities' transmission lines for all electricity producers, thus facilitating the states' restructuring of the electric power industry to allow customers direct access to retail power generation. Following the issuance of the FERC orders (but importantly prior to the *development* of a competitive wholesale market for electricity), state-level activity in electricity markets at the retail level increased significantly. States where electricity prices were highest began to investigate whether a competitive retail market for electricity could lower prices and spur marketing and technological innovations to benefit their customers.

### Retail Restructuring

Almost half of the states have passed major legislation or regulatory orders to restructure their electric power industries. The retail restructuring trend began in 1996, when California and Rhode Island passed landmark legislation to restructure their electric power industries and give their consumers the right to choose the supplier of their electricity. As of early 2001, the Energy Information Administration (EIA) reported that twenty-four states had taken steps to introduce retail restructuring and that most of the remaining states were actively investigating the issues, monitoring federal developments, and observing the states that had begun retail access. Restructuring momentum has slowed considerably in 2002, however, due to the compounded effects of economic uncertainty, corporate scandals, and the lack of a workably competitive wholesale electricity market.

Michigan began experimenting with retail choice as early as 1994. However, the trend toward restructuring the energy industry in Michigan began in earnest in 1997. Following recommendations from the administration,[18] the Michigan Public Service Commission (MPSC) issued order U-11290, which laid out a plan for restructuring the state's electricity industry.[19] Restructuring was driven principally by economic development concerns over the ability of the state to retain and attract industrial customers, given Michigan's higher than average industrial rates.

In January 1998, a bill was introduced in the state legislature providing a three-year phase-in for retail access, stranded cost recovery, and major customer protections. That same month, the MPSC issued a phase-in schedule for competition, requiring that 2.5% of the utility customers of Consumers Energy (Consumers) and Detroit Edison (DTE) should be eligible for retail choice by March 1998, followed by another 2.5% in June 1998, and another 2.5% every six months thereafter until January 2001 (a total of 12.5%).[20] All Consumers and DTE customers would have retail choice by 2002 under the order. Consumers and DTE filed restructuring plans to meet the Public Service Commission order's phase-in schedule in April 1998.

In November 1998, a state senate committee passed a bill that would begin restructuring by allowing electric choice for 7.5% of Michigan electric customers, and would include all the state's electric customers by 1 January 2002. The bill was not passed.

While legislative efforts stalled, the MPSC proceeded with restructuring. In March 1999, MPSC Orders U-11451 and U-11452 adopted the Consumers and DTE plans and set September 1999 as the date on which the first 2.5% of the state's customers would be allowed to choose an alternative supplier. Each successive six months, a further 2.5% of customers would be afforded electric choice under the programs until the market was fully opened on 1 January 2002.

In a key ruling in June 1999, the Michigan Supreme Court upheld a 1995 challenge to the MPSC's authority to design and implement restructuring plans.[21] Despite the ruling, Consumers and DTE proceeded on a voluntary basis with implementation of the retail access program. Following the Supreme Court decision, lawmakers, driven by the high price of electricity in Michigan relative to nearby Midwestern states, introduced a number of bills to ensure the progression of electricity restructuring.

Michigan restructuring legislation, the Electric Choice and Reliability Act (PA 141 and 142),

became law in the summer of 2000. The law opened the generation and power supply markets to competition for all customers of investor-owned utilities by 2002. It mandated a 5% rate cut and imposed a three-year rate cap for customers who continued to take "bundled" service (as opposed to purchasing from a competitive supplier) from the utility under regulated rates. Measures in the legislation allowed for the recovery of stranded costs and stranded benefits. It also directed the commission to establish customer education programs and consumer protection measures, including a code of conduct for all electric utilities and their affiliates.

The Customer Choice and Electric Reliability Act of 2000 requires the commission to determine the stranded costs created when retail open access customers purchase generation services from market-based alternative electric suppliers and thereby displace prior commitments made by the electric utility to serve those customers' generation requirements. In Michigan, qualified stranded costs that can be recovered by utilities include: (1) capital costs of nuclear power plants, (2) regulatory assets, (3) capacity costs in excess of market value that arise from power purchase agreements, (4) employee retraining costs, and (5) costs related to the implementation of restructuring.

In January 2001, the MPSC authorized DTE to securitize $1.77 billion in costs by issuing bonds, allowing the utility to recover costs it would incur as a result of the application of the mandated 5% rate cut and other restructuring measures.[22] A similar commission order allowing Consumer's to issue $468 million in bonds was upheld by the Michigan Court of Appeals, after being challenged by the state attorney general's office. A transition charge is payable by retail open access customers to provide compensation to the electric utility for net stranded costs, if any.[23] The Michigan Public Service Commission makes stranded cost determinations on an annual basis. The MPSC did not allow transition charges for Consumers in either 2002 or 2003 (Michigan Public Service Commission 2002d). Implementation costs of $27,225,289 incurred by Detroit Edison during 2000 were approved for deferred recovery (at the conclusion of the rate freeze), subject to the success of Detroit Edison's implementation efforts (Michigan Public Service Commission 2002e).

In response to the MPSC orders and the restructuring bill, Consumers Energy and Detroit Edison each established retail choice programs.[24]

Consumers Energy's "Direct Access" program allowed customers with loads of at least 135 megawatts (MW) to choose an alternative supplier, and expired as soon as tariffs were approved for the utility's main retail choice program, "Electric Customer Choice." The Electric Customer Choice retail open access program allowed for 12.5% of Consumers' load (750 MW) to be auctioned off in 2.5% portions. By 1 January 2002 all customers had the ability to choose new suppliers under the retail open access restructuring law.

Detroit Edison's Experimental Retail Access Program plan has a 90 MW limit for participation, and will run through June 2004. The Electric Choice Program, similar in design and scope to Consumers' Electric Customer Choice, is a retail open access program that will employ a five-stage bid process for a total of 12.5% of Detroit Edison's load, or 1,125 MW. The process invited bids representing the amount parties were willing to pay per kWh, through December 2001, toward the recovery of stranded costs associated with DTE's [or Consumers'] participation in the competitive electric marketplace.

Other regulated utilities in Michigan (investor-owned utilities and rural electric cooperatives) were required to formulate proposals for implementing electric choice programs for all of their customers no later than 2002.

Initially, alternative electric suppliers (AESs) experienced problems entering Michigan's market because of the constraints of the transmission grid.[25] This led to a mandated 2,000 MW capacity increase for power lines coming into the state aimed at alleviating transmission constraints to further development of competition. The inclusion of DTE and Consumers in the Midwest Independent System Operator (ISO) is also aimed at relieving some interstate congestion problems.

## Federal Restructuring

The Federal Energy Regulatory Commission (FERC) is responsible for transmission oversight. The buying and selling of electricity requires direct coordination and proactive monitoring of the electrical systems. If a problem develops in one place, it affects operations elsewhere. To handle this coordination, ten industry reliability councils were established that operate three independent electrical systems (called power grids) in the United States. (This action was taken because electrical reliability is a major responsibility of

transmission oversight.) Within each of these power grids, there are different types of equipment and facilities that are owned by many different entities. Yet, each system is operated in a coordinated and unified manner within its power grid. However, since the three power grids are not simultaneously linked together, electricity (alternating current power) cannot flow between them.

Standardizing market design and encouraging the development of new institutions to support competitive wholesale electricity trade has been a major concern of FERC. Federally owned utilities and state and municipally owned utilities are not regulated by FERC, but must follow federal regulations if they wish to buy and sell electricity in the wholesale market or use the transmission facilities of utilities under FERC jurisdiction.

Before the Energy Policy Act of 1992 authorized individual utility access to all the interstate transmission systems, each utility that wanted to move electricity across another system had to get approval, and each was charged for this service. FERC further altered the access to the transmission system under FERC Order 888/889, which opened access to power suppliers and purchasers. This reduced the ability of system owners to engage in "pancaking," under which a series of system owners add transmission charges when power is transferred across several electrical systems. FERC also allowed nonjurisdictional utilities to access jurisdictional utilities operating in competitive markets, if they would allow usage of their own transmission systems by these jurisdictional utilities.

The electric power industry has adopted a working definition of reliability of service, under which customers have power when they want it more than 99% of the time. Weather (ice storms, lightning, and natural disasters like floods) is the primary cause for 70% of outages. Initially, declining generation reserve margins resulting from efforts to reduce costs contributed to reliability problems. The recent surge in power plant construction alleviates the problem to a certain extent. However, transmission constraints remain and reliability is an ongoing concern.

Overall use of the transmission system is growing without significant new construction or upgrades. This is due primarily to siting problems and lack of financial incentives to expand transmission.

Approving new projects and acquiring new right-of-ways has been difficult. Tension exists because transmission facilities support wholesale markets but siting and approval are generally a state and local function. Many customers are not interested in having new transmission facilities built near them. Given only indirect benefits to the retail market, it is difficult for local policy makers to approve projects over strong local opposition.

Open access rules enacted by the Federal Energy Regulatory Commission in 1999 promote the independent operation of the electric transmission grid. Without that control, the incentive to own such assets diminishes. While not mandated, public policy clearly aims to speed up divestitures. Congress, for instance, is expected to reconsider a broad energy bill that will contain a provision to allow the taxes due from transmission asset sales to be amortized over six years. Another way that FERC is trying to encourage the splitting of transmission assets by vertically integrated utilities is to give others a more favorable rate structure. Recently, DTE Energy announced the sale of its transmission assets to ITC Holdings. The transaction is under review by the Michigan Public Service Commission and requires the approval of FERC. If the sale is completed, Michigan will be the first state to have virtually all electric utility customers served by a completely independent electric transmission system (Silverstein 2002).

Economic dispatch and efficient pricing of transmission usage are essential to support competitive electricity markets and widespread customer choice. As utilities are deintegrated, new markets must be designed and institutions created to support coordination and compatibility of transmission and transmission-related services across regions. To that end, FERC is creating Regional Transmission Organizations (RTOs) that will operate the transmission portion of the electrical system. These operational entities are being structured under the guidance found in FERC Order 2000.[26] In general, these new entities are intended to improve power grid reliability, reduce discriminatory transmission practices, and increase investments in transmission infrastructure.

At present, the Midwest ISO (MISO) is emerging as the primary RTO for Michigan utilities. MISO has the responsibility for regional transmission planning and has direct responsibility and authority over the process to add or expand generation connected to the MISO transmission system. The MISO covers all of Iowa, Nebraska, North Dakota, and Wisconsin, nearly all of Indiana, Kentucky, Michigan, and Minnesota, and portions of Illinois,

Kansas, Manitoba, Missouri, Montana, Ohio, Pennsylvania, South Dakota, and Virginia. (For details, see *http://www.midwestiso.org.*) Nearly all of Michigan is covered; the exceptions include a part of the northeastern Lower Peninsula, a part of the eastern Upper Peninsula, and a part of the southwestern corner of the Lower Peninsula.

Constraints in the transmission system surrounding Michigan have led the MPSC to require expansion of Michigan's transmission capacity by 2,000 MW by mid-2002 (Michigan Public Service Commission 2002g, 4). Generation can also serve as a substitute for transmission. Given technological advancements in small-scale generation technologies and significant problems in siting transmission, interest in distributed generation in Michigan and around the country is growing.

## Retail Price Trends

### United States

State-level retail electricity prices vary considerably across the United States. In 2000, prices ranged from a high of 14.0 cents per kilowatthour in Hawaii to a low of 4.1 cents per kilowatthour in Kentucky (U.S. DOE Energy Information Administration 2000b). Generally, states in New England have the highest average retail electricity prices, while states in the Northwest have the lowest. Variation in prices is caused by many factors, including access to low-cost fuels for generating power, state taxes, and the mix of power plants in the states.

Over the past forty years, U.S. retail electricity customers have seen two distinct trends in nominal electricity prices (that is, prices unadjusted for the effects of inflation): First, high construction costs and increased fuel prices contributed to increasing retail electricity prices in the 1970s and 1980s. Then, improved operating efficiencies, reduced construction costs, and other factors resulted in a leveling of nominal electricity prices in the 1990s.

Trends in real electricity prices (that is, prices from which the effects of inflation are eliminated) are somewhat different. U.S. retail electricity prices declined through the 1960s, increased through the 1970s and mid-1980s, and have been decreasing steadily since. Currently, the nation as a whole is experiencing the lowest real electricity prices it has seen since the late 1960s.

Today, many consumers in California, Illinois,

Future trends in retail electricity prices are uncertain. They will depend on capacity, weather, fuel prices, electricity use, and electricity generation, transmission, and distribution costs.

**FIGURE 23.2**

### Comparison of Annual Average Residential Real Prices for Michigan and the United States, 1990–2000

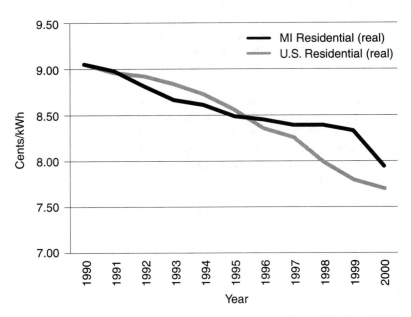

SOURCE: Compiled from U.S. DOE Energy Information Administration Electricity Databas Files, "Form EIA-826 Database Monthly Electric Utility Sales and Revenue Data" and "Current and Historical Monthly Retail Sales, Revenues, and Average Revenue per Kilowatthour by State and by Sector." Real prices are adjusted using U.S. Gross Domestic Product implicit price deflator in chained 1996 dollars (consistent with EIA approach). The deflator series used is located in EIA 2001 *Annual Energy Review*, table E1 "Population and U.S. Gross Dmoestic Product, 1949–2001."

### Retail Price Trends in Michigan

In 1990, Michigan's residential rates were moderate while commercial and industrial rates were among the highest in the nation. Inflation-adjusted residential rates of 9.05 cents per kWh in 1996 dollars (7.83 cents per kWh in nominal 1990 dollars) placed Michigan on par with the national mean price.[28] Overall, Michigan's average residential rates were the twenty-first-highest in the nation. In 2000, the average residential rate in Michigan was 7.95 cents per kWh in 1996 dollars (8.51 cents per kWh in nominal 1990 dollars). Though residential rates declined in real terms, the rate of decline in Michigan was generally less than that experienced across the country on average. Therefore, residential rates in Michigan in 2000 were the sixteenth-highest in the nation.

Average commercial and industrial rates in Michigan declined at approximately the same rate as did those across the country. The average commercial rate in Michigan declined in real terms from 9.41 to 7.38 cents per kWh. Compared to other states, Michigan's average commercial rates were twelfth-highest in the country in 1990 and 2000.

Michigan's annual average industrial rate also declined in real terms, from 6.76 to 4.76 cents per kWh. In 2000, Michigan's average industrial rates were eleventh-highest in the nation, compared to twelfth-highest in 1990.

On a regional basis, Michigan's commercial and industrial rates remain the highest overall, though the margin of difference between prices has been narrowed significantly.

It is unclear what effect the introduction of competition at the retail level will have on future retail prices in Michigan. At present, there is no compelling evidence that restructuring has improved overall price levels for most utility customers as compared to regulated rates.[29] However, retail choice is still in its infancy and institutions are still in transition. The phased-in approach to creating competitive markets may delay the full effects that competition may have on retail prices. The outlook in Michigan should improve once stranded costs are fully recovered (2007) and the wholesale market becomes more workably competitive.

Massachusetts, Michigan, New Jersey, New York, Pennsylvania, and Rhode Island may choose the company that supplies their electricity. In some cases new suppliers are able to offer lower prices or new products and services (including green power that is generated with renewable energy resources) to consumers. In many cases, however, the transitional economics of restructuring plus the high costs of customer acquisition have left potentially competitive suppliers with little incentive to enter the broad market. Instead, most competitive retail supply is targeted to the industrial or large commercial market. In Michigan, the commercial market segment is most active, since most large industrial customers are under special supply contracts with the major utilities.[27]

Because of inherent efficiencies in large-volume purchases, industrial customers generally realize lower electricity prices than do residential and commercial customers. In 1999, industrial customers paid an average of 4.43 cents per kilowatthour (kWh), while residential and commercial customers paid an average of 8.16 cents per kWh and 7.26 cents per kWh, respectively.

**FIGURE 23.3**

## Comparison of Annual Average Real Commercial and Industrial Prices for Michigan and the United States, 1990–2000

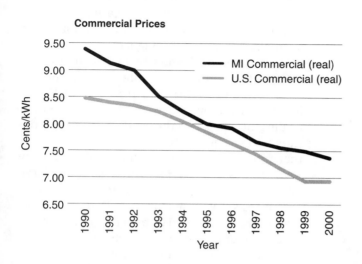
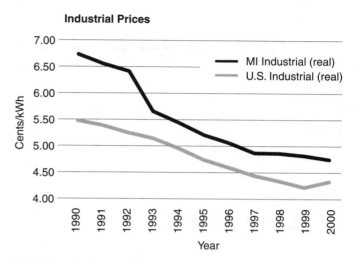

SOURCE: Compiled from U.S. DOE Energy Information Administration Electricity Databas Files, "Form EIA-826 Database Monthly Electric Utility Sales and Revenue Data" and "Current and Historical Monthly Retail Sales, Revenues, and Average Revenue per Kilowatthour by State and by Sector." Real prices are adjusted using U.S. Gross Domestic Product implicit price deflator in chained 1996 dollars (consistent with EIA approach). The deflator series used is located in EIA 2001 *Annual Energy Review*, table E1 "Population and U.S. Gross Dmoestic Product, 1949–2001."

**FIGURE 23.4**

## Regional Comparison of the Change in Real Average Annual Prices for 1990 and 2000

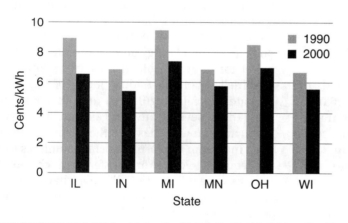
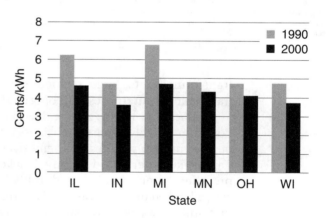

SOURCE: Compiled from U.S. DOE Energy Information Administration Electricity Database Files, "Form EIA-826 Database Monthly Electric Utility Sales and Revenue Data" and "Current and Historical Monthly Retail Sales, Revenues, and Average Revenue per Kilowatthour by State and by Sector."

## Recent Developments

The year 2000 was clearly a transition year for the electric industry, as the nation moved state by state toward restructuring. Consolidation through mergers and acquisitions was prominent as industry participants maneuvered, hoping to gain a competitive advantage. Divestiture of generating assets was common as some electric utilities exited the generation business in order to con-

centrate on the distribution of electricity. Others used the opportunity to purchase divested assets to build critical mass that many thought would be necessary to survive what was expected to be a very competitive industry. According to one observer, "The most distinctive feature of deregulation, however, has been the massive move toward greater concentration at both the national and global levels. Industries that were once considered to be localized monopolies have been

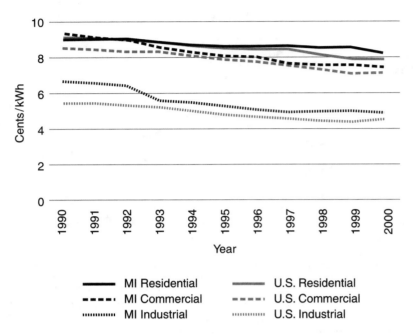

**FIGURE 23.5**

**Comparison of Real Price Movements by Sector for Michigan and the United States, 1990–2000**

Legend:
—— MI Residential      —— U.S. Residential
– – – MI Commercial      – – – U.S. Commercial
·········· MI Industrial      ·········· U.S. Industrial

SOURCE: U.S. DOE Energy Information Administration Historical Electricity Data (*http://www.eia.doe.gov/neic/historic/helectricity.htm*). Compiled from the following tables: 1990–2001 Estimated Electric Utility Monthly Average Revenue per Kilowatthour for Residential Sector by State (cents per kilowatthour); 1990–2001 Estimated Electric Utility Monthly Average Revenue per Kilowatthour for the Commercial Sector by State; 1990–2001 Estimated Electric Utility Monthly Average Revenue per Kilowatthour for the Industrial Sector by State.

transformed into large regional, national, or transnational enterprises" (Trebing 2001, 263).

Significant problems arising due to the transition from a highly regulated business into a competitive market manifested themselves in 2000. California experienced rolling blackouts, unprecedented price spikes, and utility bankruptcies, all linked to restructuring. California was the first and most aggressive state to restructure its electricity industry. It also became the first state to re-regulate the industry and take over as the major purchaser of electricity from generators. These experiences slowed the course and caused some to reconsider the idea of restructuring. During 2000, Michigan and West Virginia were the only states to enact restructuring legislation.

California's energy crisis can be grouped broadly into three interrelated problems, including (1) precipitous increase in wholesale electricity prices resulting in part from market manipulation, (2) intermittent power shortages during peak demand periods, and (3) deterioration of the financial stability of California's three

major investor-owned utilities (IOUs)—Pacific Gas and Electric (PG&E), Southern California Edison (SCE), and San Diego Gas and Electric (SDG&E) (U.S. Energy Information Administration 2002c). Retail price controls have also been cited as a contributing factor to the breakdown between retail and wholesale markets.

In addition to Enron's strategies to distort the market, recently Dynegy Inc. agreed to pay $5 million to settle a regulatory investigation into their trading practices. In the Settlement Order, the Commodity Futures Trading Commission found that from January 2000 to June 2002, "Dynegy Marketing & Trading knowingly submitted the false information to the reporting firms in an attempt to skew those indexes to Dynegy Marketing & Trade's financial benefit" (Commodity Futures Trading Commission 2002, 1).

The company is shutting down its trading business. Several other companies, including Williams Company, CMS Energy, and American Electric Power Company, have disclosed that they have found false reporting by traders. The Commodity Futures Trading Commission opened investigations of several companies in 2002. Dynegy is the first settlement so far (Hayes 2002). Locally, CMS Energy has also announced that it is exiting the speculative trading business. CMS has recently announced the sale of its wholesale gas trading book to Sempra Energy and is presently seeking a buyer for its wholesale electricity trading book (CMS sells wholesale trading book [2002]).

State officials, regulators, and analysts have pointed to several advantages that Michigan's restructured market has over the formerly deregulated market in California. Michigan utilities were not required to divest or transfer so much generation (as were utilities in California) that providing electricity for customers at times of peak demand would require heavy reliance on purchased power. Even if a reliance on purchased power were to become necessary, utilities in Michigan are free to purchase contracts for power, whereas California utilities relied on the spot market, where prices were unpredictable. In regard to the rate caps, Chairman Chappelle of the Michigan Public Service Commission explains,

Michigan's new electric restructuring law allows the Public Service Commission to gradually loosen the regulations on utilities and provides incentives to the utilities to get out from under the rate cap imposed by the law. This rate cap, like the one the Commission instituted 3 years ago for natural gas prices, is one that recognizes the need to protect customers who may not be ready for a customer choice program, while at the same time recognizing the needs of the utilities to respond to market conditions. In contrast, California's rate cap has been vitiated because California's electric utilities were required to buy power on the spot market and were unable to control their supply portfolios. Michigan's gas and electric utilities are able to purchase power or natural gas through long-term contracts in order to hedge against dramatic increases in market prices. (Chappelle 2001)

Because wholesale markets are not sufficiently developed, they remain subject to manipulation. The lack of transparency remains a concern for regulators as they attempt to introduce competition at the state level.

The uncertainty in the economy, corporate scandals, and the lack of a workably competitive wholesale electricity market will be formidable challenges to the future success of retail restructuring efforts in Michigan and elsewhere. Further concerns are raised by the significant consolidation of investor-owned electric utilities. Since 1995, the FERC has approved fifty mergers between investor-owned utilities, including the acquisitions of MCN Energy by DTE Energy (2001), Panhandle Eastern/Trunkline Gas by CMS (1999), and Upper Peninsula Energy by WPS Resources (1998), among others. These mergers are undertaken in order to gain operating efficiencies usually achieved by a larger company, which utilities believe are necessary to remain competitive in the industry. More mergers are expected over the next few years, resulting in further consolidation of the industry.

Reliability will continue to be a concern in a decentralized power industry. However, participation in a well-structured, independent Midwest ISO and active performance monitoring at the state level should provide an appropriate framework for assuring the adequacy of supply to Michigan as well as reducing the potential for market abuses. The success of Michigan's retail restructuring is largely dependent on wholesale developments. Participation by the state in the design of a workable wholesale market is critical to the interests of Michigan.

In July 2001, the Federal Energy Regulatory Commission issued the landmark "Standard Market Design and Structure Notice of Proposed Rulemaking" (RM01-12-000), in which it proposed new market rules to standardize the struc-ture and operation of the competitive wholesale power markets nationally. The Standard Market Design, prompted by the severe market dysfunctions in California, is an attempt to eliminate discriminatory transmission practices.[30] According to FERC, "the absence of standardization with respect to market rules and practices within and between regional markets" allows discrimination to continue and hinders establishment of an efficient competitive wholesale marketplace.[31] The main purpose of the proposed rules is to assure adequate generation resources and establish a standard platform for the exchange of electricity and transmission services.

Elements of the plan include active monitoring and mitigation to prevent market abuses, a well-organized central spot-power market that complements a decentralized contract-based market for long-term power supplies, and price discovery and market transparency.

Among the many issues of concern for state regulators is the assertion of federal authority over bundled transmission. In the proposed rules, FERC would require all transmission users to be under the network tariff, thus preempting state regulators' traditional role in determining the rates of return for wholesale transmission service "bundled" into state-regulated retail power sales.

At the state level, energy policy will continue to be driven by economic development considerations. Michigan's NextEnergy Initiative, announced in April 2002, seeks to position Michigan as a world leader in the research, development, commercialization, and manufacture of alternative energy technologies, focusing principally on hydrogen fuel cells.[32] The energy plan is fundamentally an economic development strategy designed to preserve Michigan's competitiveness in the automotive sector and to leverage the advanced manufacturing capabilities of the state into new energy technologies. "NextEnergy includes consumer and business tax incentives for new alternative energy investments. The plan also features a 700-acre, tax-free zone designed to attract new alternative energy business developments. The zone will include the NextEnergy Center, an alternative energy research, development and educational facility" (Michigan Economic Development Corporation 2002a). The focus, according to former governor John Engler, is "on long term growth and job creation in the alternative energy industry." Other states, such as Ohio, are pursuing similar strategies.[33]

While regulatory changes are not required to

implement the NextEnergy initiative, certain actions may be needed to eliminate barriers to the development of distributed generation sources such as renewables. Michigan currently lags behind several other states in the development of renewables. According to the Great Lakes Renewable Energy Association, "Pennsylvania's solar resource is only 2% better, but Philadelphia alone deployed more solar systems in 2001 than all of Michigan. Oregon has less sunshine, but seventeen times as many solar systems deployed. These greater market penetrations can be directly traced to state policies." They suggest action by the commission or legislature in areas such as tariffs and pricing, systems benefits incentive programs, low-interest financing programs, and property taxes (Great Lakes Renewable Energy Association 2002, 8).[34]

The outlook for distributed energy improves as interconnection standards are developed. Recently the Institute of Electrical and Electronics Engineers, Inc. (IEEE)—a leading authority in technical areas ranging from computer engineering, biomedical technology, and telecommunications to electric power, aerospace, and consumer electronics, among others—adopted a draft standard for interconnecting distributed resources with electric power systems. This marks a major milestone toward IEEE publication of a body of standards for interconnection of distributed resources.[35] Michigan, several other states, and FERC are currently formulating interconnection rules and standards.

## Future Outlook

In the wake of the California crisis, the Enron collapse, and the general decline in the economy, some are questioning the future of competitive markets in electricity. There is evidence that markets are slowing, and the outlook is uncertain. However, despite these generally negative developments, new entrants are continuing to enter commercial retail markets where growth in energy demand is projected to be most significant. Accent Energy, for example, was recently approved to serve retail commercial and industrial accounts in Ohio and has applied for a retail electric license in New York (Newest Ohio retail marketer has 20 years' experience [2002]). The trend in Michigan is similar, as demonstrated by the recent approval of a license for Constellation NewEnergy, Inc. as an alternative electric supplier,

bringing the 2002 year-end total of approved competitive suppliers to twenty-five (Michigan Public Service Commission 2002c). The present commission remains committed to furthering competition and developing a supportive policy framework at both the state and federal levels.

Infrastructure is the engine of growth and productivity in society. The rationale for reforming these sectors is to expand opportunities for productivity growth across the economy. Michigan is among the states cutting a careful path toward competition. The transition requires sustained effort that is continually assessed against the relative gains or losses to society. Progress, in terms of material outcomes, will likely be measured in decades rather than years. Clearly, deregulation has introduced a number of new institutions, new markets, and new players. However, their development is still in its infancy. The complex challenges involved in this process will demand on-going attention to the rules, laws, and policies governing these industries. They will also require adequate resources for oversight and participation in the marketplace to assure that Michigan consumers benefit from the restructuring of the electric power sector.

■

## REFERENCES

Bauer, Johannes M. 1997. Regulatory reform in the U.S. electricity sector, presented at the Conference on Electricity Restructuring hosted by the Public Utility Authority of Israel, Jerusalem, 15 December 1997.

Blumstein, Carl, L. S. Friedman, and R. J. Green. 2002. The history of electricity restructuring in California. Center for the Study of Energy Markets, Working Paper 103. University of California-Berkeley.

Borenstein, Severin, and James B. Bushnell. 2000. Electricity restructuring: Deregulation or reregulation? Program on Workable Energy, Working Paper 074.

The changing face of U.S. power suppliers. 2000. *Electric Power Supply Association Industry Review.* November.

Chappelle, Laura. 2001. State is positioned to offer consumer choice. *Lansing State Journal*, 25 March, 11A.

Citizens Research Council of Michigan. 1991. An analysis of selected issues regarding the regulation of public utilities in Michigan. Report No. 302.

CMS sells wholesale trading book. 2002. *Gas Daily* 19 (245): 1, 5.

Commodity Futures Trading Commission. 2002. Order instituting proceedings pursuant to sections 6(c) and 6(d) of the Commodity Exchange Act, making findings and imposing remedial sanctions. CFCT Docket No. 03-03. 18 December.

ConnectOhio. 2001. Ohio third frontier fuel cell initiative, web site document located at *http://www.connectohio.com/pdf/Fuel_Cell.pdf.*

Federal Energy Regulatory Commission. 1999. Docket No. RM99-2-000, Order No. 2000. Regional Transmission Organizations. 20 December.

Federal Energy Regulatory Commission Staff. 2001. Concept discussion paper for an electric industry transmission and market rule. 17 December.

Great Lakes Renewable Energy Association. 2002. Barriers to renewable energy deployment in Michigan. September.

Hall, George R. 2000. Consumer benefits from deregulation of retail natural gas markets: Lessons from the Georgia experience. Report prepared for AGL Resources, Inc.

Hayes, Kristen. 2002. Dynegy agrees to pay $5 million to settle CFTC probe. Associated Press, 20 December.

Hogan, William W. 2002. Electricity market design and structure: Avoiding the separation fallacy. Comments submitted to the Federal Energy Regulatory Commission. Docket No. RM01-12-000. 12 March.

Jess, Margaret. 1997. Restructuring energy industries: Lessons from natural gas. *Natural Gas Monthly* (May): vii–xxi. Energy Information Administration.

Michigan Economic Development Corporation. 2002a. Michigan Economic Development Corporation CEO addresses U.S. House Subcommittee on NextEnergy initiative plan to develop Michigan into a world alternative energy leader presented to congressional leaders. Press Release. 26 June.

———. 2002b. NextEnergy announces permanent location: Center to be housed within the Woodward Technology Corridor SmartZone. Press Release. 16 September.

———. 2002c. NextEnergy powering Michigan's future: Blueprint includes NextEnergy center, national program, tax-free zone, incentives, steps to spur demand, demonstration microgrids. Press Release. 18 April.

Michigan Public Service Commission. 1997. In the matter, on the commission's own motion, to consider the restructuring of the electric utility industry. Case. No. U-11290. 5 June.

———. 2000. MPSC staff investigation of Detroit Edison Company retail open access program customer enrollment and supplier support systems and processes. December.

———. 2001a. 2001 annual report, electric division. *http://www.cis.state.mi.us/mspc/reports/annual/2001/electric.htm.*

———. 2001b. Staff report of Consumers Energy ROA program customer enrollment and supplier support systems and processes. 5 July.

———. 2002a. In the matter of the application of the Detroit Edison Company to recover implementation costs for the 12-month period. Case No. U-12892. 23 July.

———. 2002b. Merchant power plants in Michigan. *http://www.cis.state.mi.us/mpsc/electric/restruct/merchantplants.htm.* Updated 15 July 2002.

———. 2002c. MPSC grants constellation NewEnergy, Inc. a license as an alternative electric supplier. Press Release. 20 December.

———. 2002d. MPSC sets Consumers Energy stranded cost charge for 2003 for retail access customers. Press Release. 20 December.

———. 2002e. Order U-12892. 23 July.

———. 2002f. Statistical data of retail sales, electric utilities in Michigan, year ended December 31, 2001.

———. 2002g. Status of electric competition in Michigan. 1 February.

Newest Ohio retail marketer has 20 years' experience. 2002. *Restructuring Today.* 6 September.

Penn, David W. 2002. The future of the electric utility industry—Post California and Enron. Annual Meeting of the Florida Municipal Electric Association, Palm Beach.

Phillips, Jr., Charles F. 1988. The regulation of public utilities: Theory and practice. Arlington, Va.: Public Utiltities Reports.

Public Sector Consultants, Inc. 2002. Michigan in Brief 2002–03, 7th ed., Lansing, Mich.

Silverstein, Ken. 2002. DTE energy: A mind of its own. *UtiliPoint Issue Alert.* 5 December.

Smith, Douglas W. 2000. The FERC's rule on regional transmission organizations. Presentation at the American Bar Association Conference, FERC Order 2000: Status of Regional Collaboration and Hot Issues. 8 June.

Trebing, Harry M. 2001. On the changing nature of the public utility concept: A retrospective and prospective assessment. In *Economics broadly considered: Essays in honor of Warren J. Samuels,* edited by J. E. Biddle, J. B. Davis and S. G. Medema. London and New York: Routledge.

U.S. DOE Energy Information Administration. 2002a. *Electric power annual, volume I.* Electric sales and revenue 2000.

———. 2002b. *Electric power annual, volume I.* Table A21. Retail sales of electricity, revenue, and average revenue per kilowatthour (and RSEs) by U.S. electric utilities to ultimate consumers by census division, and state, 2000 and 1999—All sectors.

———. 2002c. Status of the California electricity situation.

U.S. Federal Energy Regulatory Commission. 2002a. Remedying undue discrimination through open access transmission service and standard electricity market design. Notice of Proposed Rulemaking, Docket No. RM01-12-000.

———. 2002b. SMD 101. *http://www.ferc.gov/Electric/ rto/Mrkt-Strct-comments/nopr/SMD101.pdf.*

## NOTES

1. Within the transmission and distribution functions the degree of monopoly is not clear. With further unbundling of distribution, services such as metering and billing, load management, or maintenance may be separated from the monopoly function. Likewise, with separation of competitive generation from regulated transmission and system control, the functions required to meet time-varying customer loads and ensure a control area is able continuously to balance generation to load (referred to as ancillary services) may be separated from the monopolistic transmission function.

2. The deregulation movement is driven in large part by the neoclassical argument that deregulated market forces would put the most efficient industry structure in place with minimum government intervention. For a complete discussion see Trebing (2001, 261–62).

3. Nebraska, a public power state, is a notable exception.

4. This allows import and export of power to the state.

5. This is the status reported on the MPSC web site (*http://www.cis.state.mi.us/mpsc/electric/restruct/es p/*) as of December 2002.

6. Enrolled means that a contract for service has been executed with a competitive supplier but service has not yet begun. It usually takes approximately forty-five days to transfer service from the utility to the competitive supplier.

7. According to current data filed in U.S. DOE Energy Information Administration Report 862, only eight companies are currently actively serving customers. Michigan Public Service Commission (MPSC) staff reports indicate that fewer than fifty residential customers are participating in the program at the present time.

8. Compiled data for Consumers provided in personal correspondence with Tom Stanton, Competitive Energy Division, Michigan Public Service Commission. Original source is EIA form 826 for Consumers Energy.

9. U.S. DOE Energy Information Administration EIA Form 826 data for Detroit Edison through July 2002.

10. The approximately 2,110 nonutility power producers in the United States include: facilities that qualify under the Public Utility Regulatory Policies Act of 1978 (PURPA); cogeneration facilities that produce steam and electricity but that are engaged in business activities other than the sale of electricity; independent power producers that produce and sell electricity on the wholesale market at nonregulated rates but do not have franchised service territories; or exempt wholesale generators under the Energy Policy Act of 1992 (EPACT).

11. This is total generator capability as opposed to production. This large shift from utility to competitive generation was driven in part by large states such as California requiring utilities to sell off their generating units as a condition of restructuring. State restructuring legislation has either required or encouraged the divestiture of generation assets (1) to encourage competition among generating companies, (2) to prevent a few companies from dominating the marketplace, and (3) as a condition for the recovery of costs incurred by utilities for power plants and contracts under a regulated environment that may not be recoverable in a competitive market for generation. At the end of 2000, approximately 16% of all electric utility generating capacity had been sold to unregulated companies or transferred to unregulated subsidiaries that sell their power in competitive markets rather than under cost-of-service regulation. In some regions of the nation, such as New England, almost all generating plants have been sold to private companies.

12. Approximately 7,660 MWH of announced capacity was delayed beginning in January 2002. See Michigan Public Service Commission 2002b.

13. "Base load" generation is generally provided by very large power plants that provide energy needed around the clock to meet the consistent energy demands of the community served. Except for maintenance, these plants run virtually all of the time. In Michigan, these plants are primarily fueled by low-cost coal. Peaking units are smaller (than base load) generators designed for limited run times when demand rises above base load levels, for example, late on a hot summer afternoon. These units are generally fueled by natural gas.

14. The U.S. regulatory system expanded significantly during the era of the New Deal in the 1930s and again during the 1970s, as new environmental concerns strongly influenced public policy.

15. Both publicly and privately owned systems had great difficulty coping with volatile fuel prices, high capital costs due to high inflation rates, and cost overruns, especially for nuclear plants.

16. Flexible pricing typically came in the form of special contracts to limit bypass of the utility system.

17. Most observers anticipate transmission and distribution will—for the foreseeable future—remain regulated.

18. On 8 January 1996 Governor John Engler forwarded to the commission recommendations from the Michigan Jobs Commission report entitled "A Framework for Electric and Gas Utility Reform." This report suggested moving the electric industry in Michigan to competitive markets for the power supply component of electricity service. Transmission and distribution would remain the function of a regulated utility monopoly; and new commercial and industrial loads would be allowed to purchase electrical generation from anyone willing to supply this service.

19. The 5 June 1997 Commission Order (U-11290) set forth the commission's framework for electric industry restructuring in Michigan. The order was based on the December 1996 Staff Report, information presented at the public hearings, and the utility filings of March 1997.

20. Detroit Edison is a principal operating business of DTE Energy.

21. The challenge was brought by Detroit Edison, Consumers Energy, the Michigan Attorney General's office, and ABATE.

22. Securitization is a form of refinancing of utility debt using state secured bonds. This lowers the utility's financing costs and allows the costs to be taken out of the rate base. They are paid with a nonbypassable surcharge on customer bills.

23. In Michigan, stranded costs are based on actual contract costs and netted against the savings from securitization.

24. Detroit Edison's programs were the Experimental Retail Access Program (ERAP) and the Electric Choice Program (ECP). The Consumer's Energy programs were the Direct Access Program (DA) and the Electric Customer Choice Program (ECC).

25. Generally these were associated with "right of first refusal," under which a party who has reserved capacity on the grid can refuse another's request for that capacity.

26. FERC Order 2000 Rule on Regional Transmission Organizations (RTOs) set out a new market framework to allow for the development of regional electric transmission system operators that were consistent with FERC's open-architecture market design. RTOs are intended to ensure the compatibility of transmission and transmission-related services, including short-run market functions, transmission operations, and reliability functions across regions. FERC did not prescribe the specific approach or design of the new entities, but they had to satisfy minimum characteristics and functions of RTOs, including that they be independent of power market participants (e.g., sellers of electric energy). The institutions created as a result of the RTO rule are referred to by various names such as independent system operators (ISOs), regional transmission organizations (RTOs), and so on. While not synonymous, they all fall under the FERC RTO framework.

27. Contracts for Chrysler, Ford, and GM were ten-year contracts executed in 1996. They are presently scheduled to end in 2006.

28. Real prices are adjusted using U.S. Gross Domestic Product Implicit Price Deflator in chained 1996 dollars. The deflator series used is located in EIA 2001 Annual Energy Review, Table E1 "Population and U.S. Gross Domestic Product, 1949–2001."

29. This is particularly true of "bundled" customers. Bundled consumers are those provided electric service by a single utility who did not select an alternate competitive energy supplier in state retail choice programs.

30. Examples of discrimination include transmission owners favoring their own generation, inconsistent rules governing transmission that limit some transactions while lowering costs for others, the existence of seams between regions that raise costs for interregional power flows, and the practice by many vertically integrated utilities of interrupting their competitors' transactions to address reliability problems while protecting their affiliated generation and its flows.

31. SMD 101 document located on FERC website at *http://www.ferc.gov/Electric/rto/Mrkt-Strct-comments/ nopr/SMD101.pdf.*

32. These technologies include mobile applications to power cars and trucks, stationary uses for homes and factories, and portable applications such as laptop computers, cell phones, and personal digital assistant devices.

33. See "Ohio Third Frontier Fuel Cell Initiative," *http://www.connectohio.com/pdf/Fuel_Cell.pdf.*

34. System benefits incentive programs are designed to preserve services with a societal benefit, such as low-income programs, energy efficiency programs, renewable resources, and research and development, that might be reduced or eliminated in the transition to more competitive structures. Funding for system benefits programs is generated through

some form of nonbypassable, competitively neutral surcharge. A charge on the use of the electricity distribution system is a common approach. The universal service or 911 charges are comparable examples from telecommunications.

35. E-mail memorandum sent to P1547 Work Group and Ballot Group Colleagues from Tom Basso; Secretary SCC21, P1547, P1547.2, and P1547.3 IEEE, dated Friday, 27 September 2002, 1:14 P.M.

# 24

# Issues in Crime and Criminal Justice in Michigan

*Sheila Royo Maxwell, David Martin, and Christopher D. Maxwell*

## Introduction

Safety and the prevention and control of crime is one of America's primary concerns. Surveys show that both fear of crime and exposure to crime are widespread, and reducing crime and alleviating its effects on victims is a major public concern (Schulman 1999; Maguire and Pastore 2001). Michigan residents share this concern. One in two Michigan residents fears becoming a victim of a household burglary, one in five fears a physical assault, and one in five fears a sexual assault (Polsenberg 1995). Yet, societal institutions that are responsible for preventing crime and controlling offenders face enormous challenges. Their challenges include fiscal issues, identifying interventions that efficiently prevent and control crime, and identifying effective law enforcement practices that strengthen the trust of citizens, among others (Clark 1997; Tonry and Farrington 1995).

Meeting the challenges of preventing and controlling crime both efficiently and effectively is complicated by the complex and intertwined medley of constitutionally and statutorily interdependent agencies that are collectively known as the *criminal justice system*. This term was coined more than thirty years ago by the President's Commission on Law Enforcement and the Administration of Justice (LEAA) at the beginning

of the sharpest increase in crime in the United States in the twentieth century (Fagan 1997). This system of multiple agencies was depicted at one point by a presidential commission as convoluted (Welford 1997), and with good reason. For instance, while law enforcement agencies are governmental entities that represent citizens, their jurisdictions differ, at times they compete for the same resources, and authority over a criminal incident is sometimes at issue. Take, for example, the Greater Lansing area: the Lansing Police Department serves the City of Lansing, with citizens living in three counties. Meanwhile, the Ingham County sheriff and the Ingham County prosecutor also represent some Lansing citizens as well as more than 200,000 other citizens across the county. Likewise, elected or politically appointed criminal justice leaders who are voted in or hired are supported by different tax bases, enforce many but not a totally identical set of criminal and civil codes, and receive most of their compensation from agencies that are not directly responsive to the citizens who voted them into their leadership positions.[1]

Estimates of the cost of combating crime in the United States for the police, the courts, and the prisons totaled $147 billion in 1999, according to the Bureau of Justice Statistics. This figure is four times the amount the criminal justice system

**TABLE 24.1**

**Expenditures for Corrections, the Judiciary, and State Police in Michigan (in millions of dollars)**

| Department | FY90 | FY91 | FY92 | FY93 | FY94 | FY95 | FY96 | FY97 | FY98 | FY99 | FY00 | FY01 | FY02 | 13-Year Total | Avg. Annual Increase |
|---|---|---|---|---|---|---|---|---|---|---|---|---|---|---|---|
| Corrections | 757 | 807 | 897 | 1,005 | 1,082 | 1,206 | 1,297 | 1,318 | 1,335 | 1,454 | 1,582 | 1,704 | 1,682 | 16,125 | 6.96 |
| Judiciary | 153 | 152 | 164 | 173 | 196 | 199 | 211 | 187 | 205 | 210 | 223 | 237 | 241 | 2,551 | 4.03 |
| State police | 230 | 234 | 253 | 259 | 273 | 291 | 321 | 350 | 347 | 354 | 364 | 428 | 407 | 4,112 | 5.04 |
| Total criminal justice expenditures | 1,140 | 1,194 | 1,314 | 1,436 | 1,551 | 1,697 | 1,828 | 1,856 | 1,887 | 2,017 | 2,168 | 2,369 | 2,331 | 22,787 | 6.20 |
| Other agencies | 17,181 | 18,193 | 19,393 | 20,940 | 22,622 | 26,199 | 18,822 | 29,081 | 29,701 | 30,636 | 32,367 | 34,629 | 35,402 | 312,378 | 7.57 |

SOURCE: State of Michigan, Senate Fiscal Agency.

spent in 1982 ($36 billion).[2] Federal, state, and local expenditures for the police, courts, and prisons increased every year during the 1990s, even as crime rates fell. Nearly 2.2 million people now work in the U.S. criminal justice system, including 1 million police officers, 717,000 prison and jail guards, and 455,000 court personnel. On average, criminal justice spending accounts for about 8% of all state and local government spending (Bureau of Justice Statistics 2002b).

## Crime and Justice in Michigan: An Overview of Issues

For more than two decades, Michigan has ranked among the top ten states in the nation in numbers of incarcerated offenders (Bureau of Justice Statistics 2002a; Beck and Harrison 2001). The number of prisoners under state jurisdiction has increased from 13,372 in 1982 to 48,920 in the spring of 2002. Expenditures have also increased for policing, the courts, and corrections. Table 24.1 shows that over a period of ten years, from 1992 to 2002, expenditures for corrections increased nearly 88%; from about $897 million in 1992 to $1.68 billion in 2002. Expenditures for the judiciary increased by 47% within the same period, and expenditures for the state police increased by 61%. These expenditures exclude agencies that also provide services to individuals within criminal justice system, such as the Office of Drug Control Policy, the Crime Victims Services Center, the Domestic Violence Prevention and Treatment Board, or the State Psychiatric Hospitals and Mental Health Services, among many others.

Criminal justice–related spending represents a significant portion of Michigan's budget. In 2001, about one of every ten dollars in general fund spending went toward public safety and corrections. Total spending for public safety and corrections ($2,155.7 million), however, was less than general fund spending for education ($2,930.9 million) and for family independence services ($3,596 million) (Department of Management and Budget 2002).

Within the past thirty years, several major reforms have been enacted in Michigan that have directly affected the workings of the criminal justice system. In 1978 and in subsequent years, several changes in the rules regarding good time for prisoners were enacted. In 1988, the Community Corrections Act established the Office of Community Corrections to implement and coordinate community sanctions. In 1994, truth-in-sentencing laws were enacted that required offenders convicted of violent crimes to serve their full minimum sentence imposed and established a system of disciplinary "bad time" that potentially extended the minimum time to be served by an inmate for committing infractions. Also in 1994, the Michigan Sentencing Commission was established to examine and evaluate felony-sentencing practices throughout the state, develop sentencing guidelines for the legislature's consideration, and monitor the impact of the guidelines, once enacted.[3] Still further in 1994, the Violent Crime Control and Law Enforcement Act, (a.k.a. the 1994 crime bill), which is the largest grant program ever administered by the U.S. Department of Justice, provided Michigan with resources to enhance and reform policing, possibly affecting the flow of cases into the criminal justice system. In 1997, the juvenile justice code was revised to include parameters for transferring juveniles to adult prisons, establishing juvenile boot camps, and enhancing penalties for offenses committed with firearms.

The specific effects of these reforms have yet to

be uncovered. Yet, as the Michigan legislature and policy makers consider ways to address the social and fiscal challenges posed by crime and the complexities of the criminal justice system, relevant information is needed. In this chapter, we provide an overview of crime and justice issues in the state. Specifically, we discuss trends in crime, policing, sentencing, and corrections in the state within the last fifteen years. This information is designed to provide legislatures, policy makers, academics, and citizens with a rich array of data that will provide useful background in framing criminal justice policies that will best serve Michigan residents in the coming years.

We attempt to present, whenever possible, comparisons between Michigan and similar states. These comparisons allow an assessment of how Michigan fares relative to similar jurisdictions and the rest of the United States, and enables detection of worrisome patterns that may need further investigation. Current literature on trends in crime and costs of crime do not often compare trends between states. This is because raw data about trends in crime are often not sufficiently standardized to enable comparisons over time or across states. Likewise, information on crime-related expenditures do not often come with other pertinent information about crime, court processing, or other related information, again making comparisons concerning crime trends and expenditures difficult.

The data that we used in this chapter were derived by combining several data sources and aggregating these data into state-level measures. Databases used here include: (a) the Federal Bureau of Investigation's (FBI) Uniform Crime Reports (UCR),[4] an annual report of crimes reported to and arrests made by police agencies across the United States; (b) the UCR Supplementary Homicide Report, a database containing more detailed information about all reported homicides; (c) the State Court Statistics database, containing information on the number of cases filed and disposed by states; (d) the U.S. Census and their adjusted annual estimate for population figures; (e) the National Corrections Reporting Program database; (f) the Criminal Justice Employment and Expenditures database; (g) The National Prison Population Program database; and (h) the Michigan Department of Corrections's database containing information on the types and lengths of felony sentences. Each of these databases has limitations, particularly the Uniform Crime Reports, whose shortcomings have been well documented

(Maltz 1999). However, these databases provide the most comprehensive sources of information available about the topics they cover. Combining these databases and standardizing measures for this project allowed us to construct a comprehensive set of data about crime and the criminal justice system throughout the United States.

This chapter has five parts. It begins with an overview of the criminal justice process, particularly highlighting information gathered from various federal and state agencies that describe the number and nature of criminal cases processed. The second section discusses crime trends in Michigan compared to the rest the nation, with an analysis of the implications of these trends. The third section discusses trends in policing. The fourth section discusses incarceration and sentencing trends for violent, drug, and nonviolent crimes, and the fifth section discusses correctional costs and alternatives. Trends in Michigan are compared with trends within the Great Lakes region and the rest of the United States, when possible.[5]

## 1. The Criminal Justice Process

The American criminal justice system is a complex set of governmental and sometimes non-governmental units that collectively function to prevent and control crime. This complexity can be illustrated by a simplified version of how the criminal justice system functions from the time a crime is reported to the time a convicted offender is placed in the custody of a correctional official.

When a citizen decides to report an incident that he or she believes is a crime, this person typically calls 911 to report it to the local city or municipal police department. This law enforcement agency may then dispatch a police officer to the crime scene or the complainant's address to investigate whether a crime has indeed occurred. If the officer finds probable cause that a crime has occurred, the officer may arrest the suspect, if present, or seek a warrant for the suspect's arrest, as well as complete an incident report documenting the nature of the crime. If an arrest is secured, the officer will then turn the suspect over to the custody of the county sheriff and forward the arrest and citizen complaint to the county prosecutor's office for review.

A representative of the county prosecutor will then assess the merits of the case by using a variety of information as well as legal and administrative

FIGURE 24.1

**Rate of Index (Part I) Crime Reports**

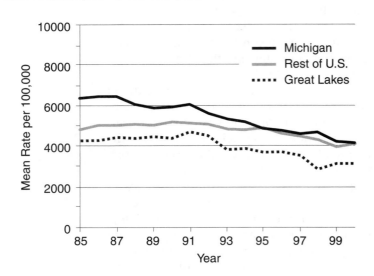

SOURCE: UCR County Level File, prepared by the National Archives of Criminal Justice Data.

**FIGURE 24.2**

**Rate of Property Crime Reports**

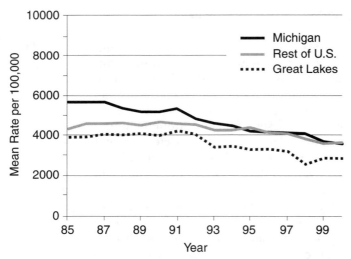

SOURCE: UCR County Level File, prepared by the National Archives of Criminal Justice Data.

doctrine, and decide whether to authorize and prosecute the incident as a violation of Michigan's criminal or juvenile code or a violation of a county's ordinances committed inside the county (Prosecuting Attorneys Coordinating Council 2002). If the prosecutor decides to go forward with the complaint, the prosecutor will notify the district court to arrange a hearing to review the evidence and address other pretrial motions.[6] If statutorily necessary, the case will be turned over

to the circuit court for felony prosecution.[7] After a number of pretrial steps and motions to dismiss the case, a jury or judge will determine the suspect's guilt or innocence, or the prosecutor and the suspect will arrange a plea bargain. If a case is not dismissed and is disposed by a finding of guilt, the judge, after consulting with a probation officer and the state's sentencing guidelines, will sentence the offender. All adults and juveniles sentenced as adults who are convicted of felonies for which the statutory maximum is more than one year can be sentenced to the state's prison system, which is under the jurisdiction of the Michigan Department of Corrections. If given a sentence of one year or less, the adult or juvenile is sent to a county jail.

The exact number or percentage of cases processed through the entire criminal justice system remains unknown. Nationally, as well as in Michigan, there is no systematic way to track cases from the time they are reported to the police to their final disposition.[8] Nevertheless, a variety of data sources collected nationally provide estimates of the number of cases processed through the criminal justice system. According to the National Crime Victimization Survey, victimizations were reported to the police in more than 40% of violent crimes and in over 30% of property crimes in 1999. Robbery was the violent crime most often reported (61%), while sexual assault was least often reported (28%). Police were notified in approximately a quarter of personal thefts like purse snatching and pocket picking. Motor vehicle theft continued to be the most commonly reported property crime (84%), while theft was the least often reported to the police (27%). The percentages of crimes reported to the police in 1999 was similar to that reported in 1998, with three exceptions. The percentage of thefts reported to the police fell significantly between 1998 and 1999, while reporting of all crimes and of property crime overall fell somewhat (Rennison 2000). Besides those reported by citizens, an unknown percentage of crimes are directly detected by the police.

Among those crimes known to the police, only a fraction result in an arrest. In 1999, the clearance rate for the Modified Crime Index total was 21%.[9] Crimes against persons (murder, forcible rape, and aggravated assault), which are often given more investigative efforts than property crimes, had a 50% clearance rate compared to 18% for property crimes (excluding arson). Among violent crime offenses, the clearance rate for murder was 69%; that for aggravated assault was 59%; for forcible rape, 49%; and for robbery, 29%. Among property crimes, 19% of larceny-theft was cleared by the police, 15% of motor vehicle thefts, and 14% of burglaries (Federal Bureau of Investigation 2000).

## 2. Crime Trends in Michigan

Crime rates (computed as the number of crimes reported to the police per 100,000 residents) are important social indicators, providing assessments of the nature, extent, and fluctuations of crime. In figures 24.1 through 24.3, we compare crime trends in Michigan to trends in the Great Lakes region and the rest of the nation.

After a decade of growth during the 1980s, crime rate in America began to drop in the early 1990s. Explanations for this include a strong economy, changing demographics, changes in markets for illegal drugs and firearms, expanded imprisonment, policing innovations, and a growing cultural intolerance for violent behavior (Blumstein and Wallman 2000). A study by the Urban Institute estimates that a decline in juvenile offenses (offenders under age eighteen) and offenses among older youth (offenders aged eighteen to twenty-four) accounted for 51% of the drop in the violent crime rate between 1995 and 1999 (Butts 2000).

We see in figures 24.1 and 24.2 that the declines in both Michigan's reported Part I (Index)[10] and property offenses closely mirrored the national trends, for which rates declined steadily between 1992 and 2000. Michigan's rates are higher than the national average or the average for the Great Lakes states; however, these rates had been declining precipitously within the last fifteen years. Michigan's rates since 1995 are at the national average for both Part I and property offenses.

What is markedly different from the comparison regions is Michigan's rate for reported violent crimes, shown in figure 24.3 (includes murder, forcible rape, robbery, and aggravated assault), which is significantly higher than the national average or the average for the Great Lakes region. Per 100,000 violent crimes reported, Michigan has 710, compared to 416 for the Great Lakes region and 481 for the nation as a whole.[11] It should be noted, however, that even though Michigan's rates for violent offenses are significantly higher than those in the other regions, these rates have declined since 1991, and the speed of decline appears more pronounced in Michigan than in

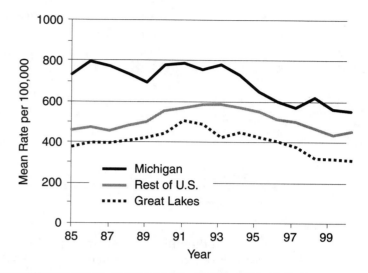

**FIGURE 24.3**

**Rate of Violent Crime Reports**

SOURCE: UCR County Level File, prepared by the National Archives of Criminal Justice Data.

the comparison regions. In 2000, Michigan's violent crime rate was at its lowest level since 1969, and Michigan's property crime rate was at its lowest level since 1967. Michigan's homicide rate in 2000 was also at its lowest level since 1967.

### Big City Crime in Michigan

Big cities account for a disproportionate share of crime in Michigan. Crime rates for urban areas such as Detroit, Flint, Grand Rapids, Warren, and Lansing (the five largest in Michigan) remain higher than rates in Michigan's smaller communities. In 2000, these cities, which had a total of 15.5% of Michigan's population, accounted for about one in every three serious crimes in the state (including murder, rape, robbery, aggravated assault, burglary, larceny, auto theft, and arson). With regard to violence, they accounted for about 70% of all murders and robberies in Michigan in 2000. Table 24.2 shows the population distribution throughout the state, and relative to this population distribution, show the distribution of serious crimes and homicides within the state.

### Drug Crimes

The period from the mid-1980s through the 1990s was characterized by enormous increases in drug arrests and convictions throughout the country in

**TABLE 24.2**

**Distribution of Crime in Michigan's Big Cities, 2000**

| | Detroit | Flint | Grand Rapids | Lansing | Warren | Other Communities | State Total |
|---|---|---|---|---|---|---|---|
| Population | 951,270 | 124,939 | 197,846 | 119,128 | 138,276 | 8,406,985 | 9,938,444 |
| | 9.6% | 1.3% | 2.0% | 1.2% | 1.4% | 15.4% | 84.6% |
| Part I (Index) Crime | 97,776 | 11,187 | 13,056 | 6,958 | 4,094 | 133,071 | 268,327 |
| | 24% | 3% | 3% | 2% | 1% | 33% | 67% |
| Homicide | 396 | 36 | 17 | 14 | 3 | 466 | 203 |
| | 59% | 5% | 3% | 2% | 0% | 70% | 30% |
| Robbery | 7,868 | 492 | 594 | 171 | 110 | 9,235 | 4,179 |
| | 59% | 4% | 4% | 1% | 1% | 69% | 31% |

SOURCE: Y2000 population figures from the State of Michigan, Michigan Information Center. Crime data is from the Michigan State Police. Index crimes include murder, rape, robbery, assault, burglary, theft, motor vehicle theft, and arson.

response to the influx of crack-cocaine in drug markets (Belenko 1990). Threatened by the insidious effects of crack-cocaine, criminal justice systems in many states, but particularly in large metropolitan areas like New York and California, have waged war on the use and sale of illicit drugs (particularly crack and powdered cocaine). Drug arrests resulting from this "war" fueled court congestions (Belenko 1990), and drug convictions are partially responsible for the increases in incarceration rates in state prisons. Figures from the Bureau of Justice Statistics estimate that incarceration for drug offenses accounted for about 20% of the increase in the prison population between 1990 and 1999 (Beck 2001).[12] In Michigan (see figure 24.4), the arrest rates for drug crimes increased by approximately 127% between 1986 and 2000, while arrest rates for property crimes decreased markedly within this period.[13] Arrests for violent crimes continued to increase until the early 1990s before beginning a modest decline in 1994. It appears from these trends that drug crimes comprise the largest proportion of increases in arrests since the early 1990s. To examine these trends further, figures 24.5 and 24.6 separately show the arrest rates for drug possession and drug selling in Michigan. These rates are juxtaposed with the rates for the Great Lakes region and the rest of the United States.

As seen in figure 24.5, the trend in arrest rates for drug possessions in Michigan tracks the national trend but is significantly lower on average than the national trend. However, the trend in arrest rates for drug selling (see figure 24.6) is higher in Michigan than in the Great Lakes region or the rest of the United States. Since 1995, arrest rates for drug possession in Michigan have been higher than those for drug selling; however, when compared to other regions, it appears that Michigan puts greater priority on arresting drug sellers than the other regions do (higher arrest rates for drug selling in Michigan). The fact that the arrest rate for drug selling is higher in Michigan than in the comparison regions is important to note, given that the Michigan sentencing guidelines impose one of the lengthiest prison terms for drug selling in the country (see section on sentencing and corrections and note 15). Fiscal costs for incarcerating drug sellers, therefore, may be more pronounced in Michigan than in other states. This issue is dealt with in greater detail in the last section of this chapter.

**FIGURE 24.4**

**Michigan's Rate of Violent, Property, and Drug Arrests**

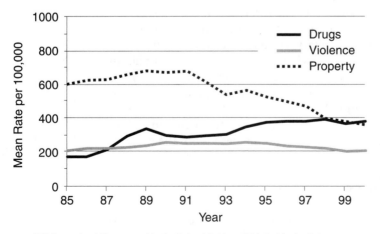

SOURCE: UCR County Level File, prepared by the National Archives of Criminal Justice Data.

## 3. Policing

Increased federal funding for community policing and crime prevention has supplemented state spending in recent years. The enactment of the Public Safety Partnership and Community Policing Act of 1994, Title I of the Violent Crime Control and Law Enforcement Act, (a.k.a. the 1994 Crime Bill) established the largest grant program ever administered by the U.S. Department of Justice. The Community Policing Act authorized $8.8 billion for fiscal years 1995 to 2000 to enhance public safety. This piece of legislation directed hundreds of millions of dollars at enhancing law enforcement through the hiring of more police officers and crime prevention programs targeting violence against women, youth gangs, and gun violence, among other issues.

Since 1995, Michigan has received nearly $200 million through the Federal Office of Community Oriented Policing Services (COPS) to support the hiring of 3,460 new police officers. In all, discretionary and formula grants from the U.S. Department of Justice to Michigan have amounted to more than $100 million annually in recent years. About 75% of these funds support policing and law enforcement efforts.

Many Michigan police departments have embraced the concept of community-oriented policing.[14] Community policing, as discussed in the following, is a policing philosophy that promotes and supports organizational strategies to address the causes and reduce the fear of crime and social disorder through problem-solving tactics and community-police partnerships. A fundamental shift from traditional, reactive policing, community policing stresses the prevention of crime before it occurs. Community policing is an integral part of combating crime and improving the quality of life in the nation's cities, towns, and rural areas. Core components of community policing include partnering with the community; problem solving; and transforming policing agencies to support and empower frontline officers, decentralize command, and encourage innovative problem solving (Definition of Community Policing 1999).

In addition to increasing the number of police officers, recent federal funding has helped Michigan police departments upgrade their technology, including computerized methods for crime analysis, such as crime mapping. Figure 24.7 illustrates the impact of federal funding for community policing in Michigan. Evident in the

**FIGURE 24.5**

**Rate of Drug Possession Arrests**

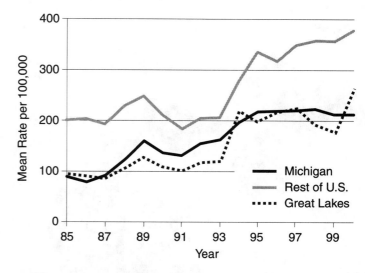

SOURCE: UCR County Level File, prepared by the National Archives of Criminal Justice Data.

**FIGURE 24.6**

**Rate of Drug-Selling Arrests**

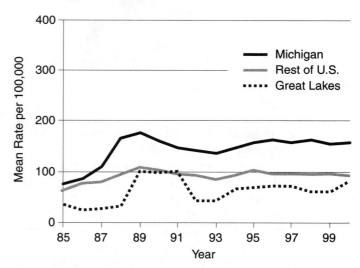

SOURCE: UCR County Level File, prepared by the National Archives of Criminal Justice Data.

map is both a wide distribution of funding throughout the state and a focus on urban areas.

## 4. Sentencing and Corrections

Over the last few years, researchers of criminal justice processes have asserted that sentencing and correctional policies in the United States have shifted from a generally *rehabilitative* model, a model that was predominant in the 1960s

**FIGURE 24.7**

**Federal Funding for New Officers by County, 1995–2000**

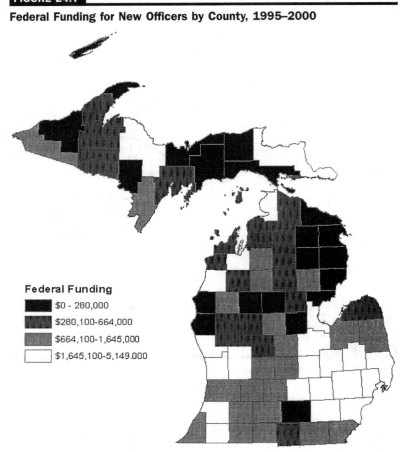

Federal Funding
- ■ $0 - 280,000
- ▨ $280,100-664,000
- ▨ $664,100-1,645,000
- □ $1,645,100-5,149.000

SOURCE: Office of Community Oriented Policing, U.S. Department of Justice.

(Andenaes 1975; Beattie 1989; Palmer 1992), to a *deterrence*-based model beginning in the 1980s and on up through the present (Palmer 1992; Tonry 1996; Wichiraya 1996; Wilson 1983). Observers have noted that increasingly, sentencing and correctional policies have shifted away from a general emphasis on treatment, education, and vocational programming to an emphasis on punishments, particularly in making punishments severe and certain so as to instill the fear of sanctions on both the offenders being punished and on potential offenders (Tonry 1996).

The most commonly cited evidence of this general shift in policy is the initiation in many states of mandatory sentencing policies or truth-in-sentencing statutes since the early 1980s (Tonry 1996; Wichiraya 1996). Broadly, mandatory sentencing statutes provide *fixed* (little or no judicial discretion) and often *augmented* prison terms for specific types of offenses. Among the most common of these are drug offenses, offenses committed with firearms, murder, rape, and offenses

committed by those who have had prior serious felony convictions (i.e., three strikes and you're out laws). By 1994, every state had adopted mandatory sentencing laws, often for several types of offenses (Maxwell 2000). Many state legislatures have also restricted the release of those serving their mandatory sentences (Wichiraya 1996), effectively restricting parole and making offenders serve their entire prison term. These enhanced penalties are designed not only to punish those who have committed crimes but also to deter potential offenders from committing crimes. By passing mandatory sentencing laws, legislators wanted to convey the message that certain crimes are deemed especially grave and that people who commit them deserve, and should expect, harsh sanctions.

Michigan has one of the toughest mandatory sentencing laws for drug offenders in the nation. The *650 Lifer Law* was enacted in 1978.[15] It provides that offenders convicted of possessing 650 grams or more of cocaine (about 1.4 pounds) are given mandatory life terms (Michigan Department of Corrections 2000). This law was revised in 1992 and then again in 1998, making parole possible after offenders have served a minimum of twenty years in prison. Offenders convicted of possessing at least 50 grams of cocaine or heroin are mandated to serve at least ten years in prison. Besides mandatory drug laws, Michigan's statutes also mandate enhanced penalties for offenses committed with firearms, and in 1998, a truth-in-sentencing statute was passed that mandated that offenders convicted of certain crimes serve their minimum sentence before becoming eligible for parole. Prior to 1998, when the truth-in-sentencing began, parole could be granted to prisoners before they had served their minimum sentence.[16] Because Michigan met the federal standard for truth-in-sentencing, the Michigan Department of Corrections received over $109 million in federal funds between 1996 and 2001 from the Violent Offender Incarceration/Truth-In-Sentencing Incentive Grant Program. The program assists states in developing additional capacity for violent offenders through the construction or lease of prison beds.[17]

In this section we examine criminal processing and incarceration in Michigan, with comparisons to other states when data is available. The overview of crime trends presented in the preceding section provides the context by which we examine how criminal justice resources are used in Michigan for punishment and rehabilitation, and the extent by which incarceration versus community sanctions are used for different types of crimes. Do increased penalties for drug crimes, for example, generally increase new court commitments to state prisons for drug crimes? Do increased penalties actually lengthen prison terms? How do incarceration trends for crimes not included in the enhancements compare with those under enhanced penalties?

We first examine criminal court filings in the state, as this trend provides a good baseline for the numbers of cases processed in criminal courts, and provides an indication of the extent of caseload facing the criminal justice system. Given the trends shown earlier of decreasing arrest rates for property and violent offenses, do these decreases also translate to decreases in criminal court filings? We see in figures 24.8 and 24.9 that, on the contrary, criminal court filings in Michigan increased by about 58% within a period of thirteen years (from a rate of 2,756 per 100,000 residents in 1985 to a rate of 4,354 in 1998), though Michigan's rates are lower than those of the Great Lakes region or the rest of the United States. Felony court filings (see figure 24.9) increased modestly by about 36% (from 177 per 100,000 residents in 1985 to 241 in 1998), coinciding mostly with increases in drug arrests during this time, which also coincide with increases in federal funding for anti-drug law enforcement activities. As shown in the figures, however, the increase in Michigan's rate is modest and substantially lower than in the other regions.

What happens to cases that are criminally processed? As indicated at the beginning of this chapter, several court decisions are made from the point that a case is brought to court for evidentiary hearing until it is disposed with a sentence (not dismissed for lack of evidence).[18] We outline in the succeeding paragraphs those cases disposed with a community sanction (such as probation, electronic monitors, or a combination of community sanctions and jail) versus new commitments to state prisons.

In most states, the largest proportion of criminal court cases is disposed with community sanctions. Often, less than a third of criminal court dispositions result in new commitments to state prisons. However, average prison populations for most states at any given time are influenced by more than new court commitments. Three key elements commonly factor into the size of a state's prison population. These are: *new commitments; length of incarceration;* and, *incarceration for pro-*

**FIGURE 24.8**

**Rate of Criminal Court Filings**

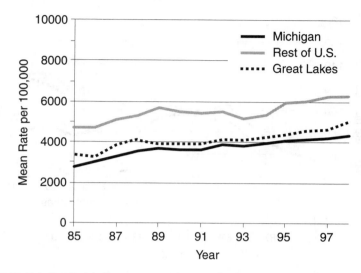

SOURCE: State Court Statistics Program, prepared by the National Archives of Criminal Justice Data.

**FIGURE 24.9**

**Rate of Felony Court Filings**

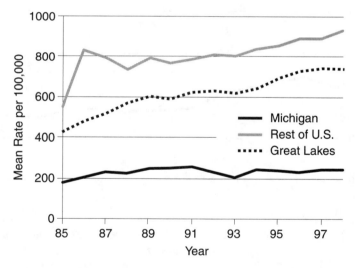

SOURCE: State Court Statistics Program, prepared by the National Archives of Criminal Justice Data.

*bation violations.* Although the number of new court commitments in a given state may be low, this does not necessarily translate into a small prison population, given that length of time per commitment may be long, or a state may have large proportions of probation violators sent to prison.

We now examine disposition patterns and prison populations in Michigan, paying particular attention to the three elements outlined

## FIGURE 24.10

**Rate of New Court Committments**

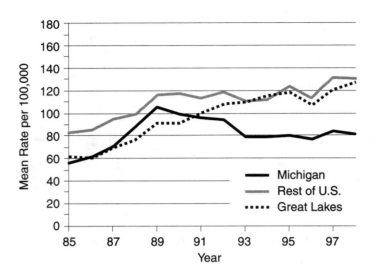

SOURCE: National Prison Statistics Program, prepared by the Bureau of Justice Statistics.

## FIGURE 24.11

**Prison Dispositions**

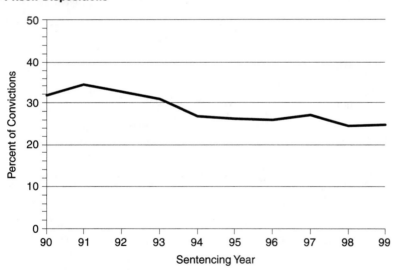

SOURCE: Michigan Department of Corrections.

increases from 1995 to 1997. This is in stark contrast to the Great Lakes region, where new prison commitments have increased dramatically since 1988. It appears from this trend that dispositions for many of the criminal court cases in Michigan since 1989 have increasingly used community sanctions or a combination of some jail time (less than one year in prison) and community sanctions.

Using the Michigan Department of Corrections database, figure 24.11 shows the trend of prison dispositions for felony cases in Michigan since 1990 (the reverse of this figure represents community sanctions, which include probation, halfway houses, electronic monitors, and probation + jail). This figure attests to the increasing use of community sanctions in Michigan over the last decade. The rate of increase in the use of community sanctions is especially pronounced for less serious felonies like obstruction of law enforcement or escape from custody, where the rate of community sanctions has increased by approximately 52% (from 53% in 1990 to 81% in 1999). Community dispositions for drug selling and personal crimes (such as assault) also increased by approximately 22% during this time period.

As mentioned earlier, however, a state's prison population at any given time is only partly due to new court commitments. We see in the following that even with decreases in new court commitments to prisons and the increasing use of community sanctions, Michigan's prison population remains significantly larger than those of the rest of the Great Lakes region and the rest of the nation, and has been increasing (see figure 24.12). This appears to be driven mainly by lengths of incarceration in Michigan, where, as shown in figure 24.13, the average length of time served by incarcerated offenders is substantially higher than in the other Great Lakes states and the nation as a whole.[19] The average time served in Michigan is thirty-three years, compared to twenty-two years for the other Great Lakes states and twenty-three years for the national average.

Several factors may be affecting Michigan's long prison terms such as mandatory sentences or local legal cultures. However, direct connections have yet to be drawn in Michigan as well as in many states, between specific policies and their effects on actual lengths of incarceration. Research is lacking in this regard. In Michigan, the decline in prison dispositions (see Figure 24.11) suggests that prisons are increasingly used only for serious offenders. This selective policy

previously. Incarceration patterns per type of crime are also examined.

Figure 24.10 shows the rate of new court commitments (per 100,000 population) to prisons in Michigan, the Great Lakes region, and the rest of the country as a whole. We can see that while numbers of new commitments have increased steadily for the other regions, Michigan's rates have declined steadily since 1989, with only minor

could subsequently raise the average length of imprisonment since the sentenced offender has committed a more serious crime. This possibility partly explains the disparities in time-to-serve shown in Figure 24.14. Other analyses conducted that compared sentencing trends between Michigan and other regions, however, suggest that sentence lengths in Michigan are generally longer than many other regions of the country per type and severity of offenses (Maxwell and Bynum 2002).

In figure 24.13, we examine the average length of incarceration by type of crime (murder is excluded here, to avoid pronounced skewing of the data). As shown, lengths of incarceration are highest for drug selling and for personal crimes. Increases in sentence lengths are discernable for drug selling, property crimes, and personal crimes toward the end of the decade.

It is clear from the preceding figures that Michigan's prison population is substantially larger than the national average or the average for the Great Lakes region. It also appears that this is *not* due to increasing prison commitments or the lack of use of community sanctions. On the contrary, increasing numbers of felony cases are disposed with community sanctions and new prison commitments have been decreasing. The large prison population in Michigan appears to be fueled more by length of incarceration (time served). Time served is longer in Michigan than the average for the Great Lakes region and the United States, and this trend is at an upward swing for crimes like drug selling, personal crimes, and property crimes. Given that the number of felony filings increased in the last decade and that a proportion of these filings will result in a prison disposition, there is potential that the prison population in Michigan will remain large or even increase in the coming years if lengths of incarceration remain high.

With a large prison population come resource needs for such elements as prison maintenance, security, programming, and capital outlays, among others. Health care costs, particularly with an aging population, are also a concern. The Michigan Department of Corrections has taken several measures within the last ten years to contain heath costs.[20] However, with a potentially increasing proportion of aging inmates (given lengthy sentences imposed), this issue will remain a major concern for the future. Using the Michigan Department of Corrections data, figure 24.15 shows the proportion of offenders who will

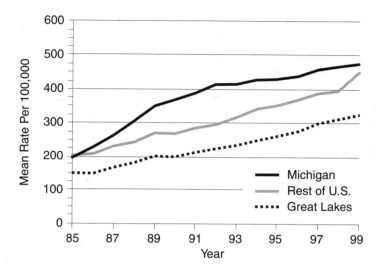

**FIGURE 24.12**

**Prison Population per 100,000 Residents**

SOURCE: National Prison Statistics Program, prepared by the Bureau of Justice Statistics.

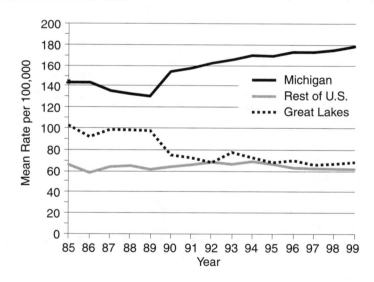

**FIGURE 24.13**

**Estimated Time-to-Serve**

SOURCE: National Corrections Reporting Program, prepared by the National Archives of Criminal Justice Data.

potentially still be serving prison time after age fifty-four. The figure shows a pronounced increase (43% increase) over the decade in the proportion of offenders who will likely still serve prison time after age fifty-four. This trend implies that unless individuals are released earlier than their sentences dictate, Michigan will be facing significant increases in their population of elderly inmates over the next few decades.

FIGURE 24.14

**Estimated Years Incarcerated by Conviction Charge Category**

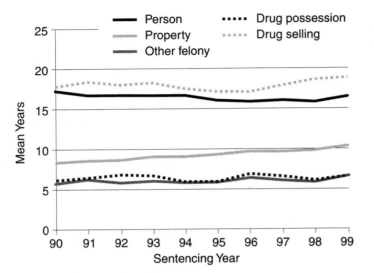

SOURCE: Michigan Department of Corrections.

FIGURE 24.15

**Inmates Scheduled for Release after Age 54**

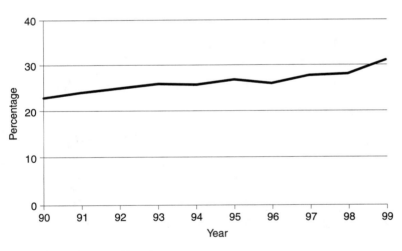

SOURCE: Michigan Department of Corrections.

## 5. Correctional Expenditures, Costs, and Alternatives

Given the preceding trends, the next line of inquiry is reasonably the costs associated with Michigan's prison population. It is estimated that the average yearly cost of keeping an offender in Level II (medium) security prison in Michigan is about $21,000. Since Michigan ranks among the highest in the nation in numbers of incarcerated individuals, correctional expenditures in Michigan are presumably also large relative to those of other states.

Using data compiled by the U.S. Census Bureau on expenses for correctional operations per state, figure 24.16 shows per capita expenditures for correctional operations (excludes capital outlays) for Michigan, the Great Lakes region, and the rest of the United States. As seen in figure 24.16, Michigan's per capita expenditure on corrections exceeds those of the Great Lakes region and the nation as a whole, and is in an upward trend. While it took roughly $29 per capita to fund correctional operations in Michigan in 1985, this cost increased to about $130 per capita in 1999. Rates in other states were at about $60–$70 per capita in 1999.[21] Michigan's high and rising costs are attributed mainly to the increasing prison population and the costs associated with operating safe prison facilities to house this increasing prison population. About 66% of Michigan's correctional budget is spent on operating correctional facilities, followed by approximately 15% on medical and health care costs (Michigan Department of Corrections 2000).

As shown at the beginning of this chapter, correctional appropriations in Michigan over the last thirteen years (1990–2002) have increased by about 88%. Public protection expenditures that include corrections, the judiciary, the state police, and the attorney general's office have increased overall by about 80%, and this does not reflect the totality of criminal justice expenditures, since many other agencies, like the Office of Drug Control Policy or Crime Victim Services also contribute resources in preventing and controlling crime. Given such large outlays, are there better ways of managing offenders?

Alternatives-to-incarceration measures are a favorite topic of consideration in assessments of better and more cost-effective ways to manage offenders. This is because community sanctions cost only a fraction of prison expenses (estimated at around $1,600 for probation supervision in Michigan in 2000), though costs for boot camps and correctional centers rival prison costs, at around $26,000. Whether community sanctions are better alternatives to prison, however, cannot be determined without comparing the recidivism rates (and other measures of criminal activity) of offenders sentenced to prison and offenders sentenced to probation who have comparable criminal histories. Little effort has been made to conduct such studies, though they have marked implications toward more efficient use of criminal justice resources. While community sanctions may be initially cheaper, if large proportions of violators are resentenced to prison, it could possibly nullify the initial savings in community corrections. Estimates of prison commitments due to revocations in Michigan are at about 35–40% yearly since the mid-1990s (Maxwell, Maxwell, and Zhang 2001).

A recent study conducted by Maxwell (Maxwell 2000) that examined probationer recidivism in Michigan indicates that often probation officers give probationers leeway before recommending resentencing due to probation violations. In most large counties in Michigan, technical violations are meted out only after two or more probation violations, and typically for new crimes committed or for multiple violations. This implies that returns to prison are typically only for more serious violations. However, more still needs to be done to examine better and more efficient sentencing alternatives and more efficient ways to address violations, to compare the effectiveness of corrections centers and boot camps with prisons, or to more fully examine the typical lengths of sentence given to technical violators.

## Conclusions

In this chapter we have presented trends in criminal justice costs, crime, policing, sentencing, and corrections in Michigan and have compared them to trends in other states in the nation. The information presented can serve as a backdrop in crafting future policies and assessing future needs. As a state that has consistently ranked among the top ten in the nation with respect to the rate of crimes and the number of incarcerated offenders, Michigan presents a complex challenge for policy makers who want to more efficiently prevent and control crime. Combating crime remains high on both the national and local agendas, especially since crime rates remain high in many urban areas. Recent concerns about terrorism and homeland security will likely keep crime and public safety in close competition with other pressing budgetary needs in the state.

Despite the good news with respect to declining crime trends in Michigan, rates for reported violent crimes remain considerably higher in Michigan than in the Great Lakes region and the rest of the United States. This trend needs to be

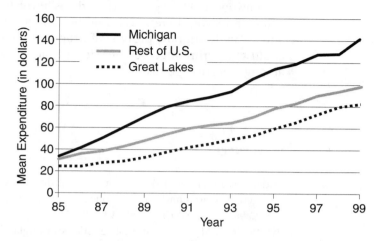

**FIGURE 24.16**

**Correctional Operations Expenditure per Capita**

SOURCE: U.S. Census Bureau, prepared by the National Archives of Criminal Justice Data.

examined more carefully, particularly the types of crimes being committed, the victims of such crimes, and the resources that can be appropriately dispersed to address the problem. Also, while rates for felony court filings in the state are considerably lower than those in the comparison regions and have seen comparatively modest increases compared to the other regions (a good indicator that fewer cases are being processed through the criminal justice system), Michigan is faced with the challenge of a large number of offenders serving prison terms and an increasing number of older inmates. Increases in felony court filings that result in prison dispositions would only worsen the state's already overburdened correctional system. Although the use of community sanctions has increased since 1990, the number of incarcerated offenders in Michigan continues to increase—primarily because of longer prison terms and the increasing number of years before an inmate is paroled. The enactment of the truth-in-sentencing policy in 1998 makes tracking the trend of the prison population even more crucial, particularly in forecasting the proportion of aging inmates, since increases in this population could substantially raise prison costs.

As it stands, Michigan appears to spend more per capita than the other regions on correctional operations, and perhaps justifiably so, given the large number of inmates in Michigan's prisons. With limited resources, legislators should look into ways of curbing the prison population for the long run, and enhancing crime prevention measures. It is acknowledged that crime prevention is more cost-effective than expending resources on the processing and incarceration of offenders (Greenwood 1999; Nagin 2001). Perhaps a worthwhile endeavor, therefore, would be to identify and strongly support promising programs that could curb criminogenic behavior, particularly among high-risk groups.

■

## REFERENCES

Andenaes, Johannes. 1975. General prevention revisited: Research and policy implications. *Journal of Criminal Law & Criminology* 66(3): 338–65.

Beattie, John M. 1989. Criminal sanctions in England since 1500. In *Sanctions and rewards in the legal system*, edited by Martin L. Friedland. Toronto, Ont.: University of Toronto Press.

Beck, Allen J. 2001. *Prisoners in 2000.* Bulletin no. 188207. Washington, D.C.: Bureau of Justice Statistics, Office of Justice Programs, U.S. Department of Justice.

Beck, Allen J., and Paige M. Harrison. 2001. *Prisoners in 2000.* Tech. Rept. no. NCJ 188207. Washington, D.C.: Bureau of Justice Statistics, Office of Justice Programs, U.S. Department of Justice.

Belenko, Steven. 1990. The impact of drug offenders on the criminal justice system. In *Drugs, crime and the criminal justice system,* edited by Ralph Weisheit. Cincinnati, Ohio: Anderson Publishing Co.

Blumstein, Alfred, and Joel Wallman. 2000. The recent rise and fall of American violence. In *The crime drop in America,* edited by Alfred Blumstein and Joel Wallman. New York: Cambridge University Press.

Bureau of Justice Statistics. 2002a. Bureau of Justice Statistics Prison Statistics *http://www.ojp.usdoj.gov/bjs/prisons.htm* Washington, D.C..

———. 2002b. *Justice expenditure and employment in the United States 1999.* Washington, D.C.: U.S. Department of Justice, NCJ 191746.

Butts, Jeffrey. 2000. *Youth crime drop.* Washington, D.C.: Urban Institute Justice Policy Center.

Clark, Edna McConnell. 1997. *Seeking justice: Crime and punishment in America.* New York: Edna McConnell Clark Foundation.

Corrections Program Office. 2002. Michigan's Violent Offender Incarceration and Truth-in-Sentencing (VOI/TIS). In State-by-State Grant Activities *http://www.ojp.usdoj.gov/cpo/mapfiles/mi.htm* Washington, D.C.. Accessed 12 June 2002.

Definition of Community Policing. 1999. 8 September *http://www.usdoj.gov/cops/more/gen/history/definition.htm.*

Department of Management and Budget. 2002. *Fiscal year 2000–2001: Michigan financial focus.* Lansing, Mich.: Michigan Department of Management and Budget.

Fagan, Jeffrey A. 1997. Continuity and change in American crime: Lessons from three decades. In *The challenge of crime in a free society: Looking back; looking forward.* Symposium on the 30th Anniversary of the President's Commission on Law Enforcement and Administration of Justice. Washington, D.C.: Office of Justice Programs, U.S. Department of Justice.

Federal Bureau of Investigation. 2000. *Crime in the United States 1999.* Criminal Justice Information Service Division. Washington, D.C.: U.S. Government Printing Office.

Greenwood, Peter W. 1999. *Costs and benefits of early childhood intervention.* OJJP Fact Sheet 94. Washington, D.C.: U.S. Department of Justice, Office of Justice Programs, Office of Juvenile Justice and Delinquency Prevention.

Maguire, Kathleen, and Ann L. Pastore, eds.. 2001. *Sourcebook of criminal justice statistics, 2000.* Tech. Rept. no. 190251, 688. Albany, N.Y.: Hindelang Criminal Justice Research Center, State University of New York at Albany.

Maltz, Michael. 1999. *Bridging the gaps in police crime data.* Discussion paper from the BJS Fellows Program. Washington, D.C.: Bureau of Justice Statistics, Office of Justice Programs, U.S. Department of Justice.

Maxwell, Christopher. 2000. The trends and nature of violence in Michigan. Paper presented at Violence Prevention: What Works, What Doesn't, What's Promising, Michigan State University. East Lansing: Michigan Department of Community Health.

Maxwell, Christopher D., Sheila Royo Maxwell, and Yan Zhang. 2001. The impact of sentencing reform on the trends and nature of revocations throughout the United States. Paper presented at the annual meetings of the American Society of Criminology, Atlanta, Georgia.

Maxwell, Christopher D., and Tim Bynum. 2002. *Sentencing practices in Michigan during the 1990s.* School of Criminal Justice. East Lansing: Michigan State University.

Michigan Department of Corrections. 2000. *Michigan Department of Corrections, 2000 annual report.* Lansing, Mich.: Michigan Department of Corrections.

Nagin, Daniel S. 2001. Measuring the economic benefits of developmental prevention programs. *Crime and*

*Justice: A Review of Research* vol. 28. Chicago: University of Chicago Press.

One Court of Justice, Michigan Courts. 2002. Trial Courts *http://courts.michigan.gov/trialcourts/trial .htm,* Lansing, MI. Accessed 10 June 2002.

Palmer, Ted. 1992. *The re-emergence of correctional intervention.* Newbury Park, Calif.: Sage Publications.

Parent, D., T. Dunworth, D. McDonald, and W. Rhodes. 1997. *Transferring serious juvenile offenders to adult courts.* Washington, D.C.: National Institute of Justice.

Pifer, Rosemarie. 2000. Reorganization expands role of the Criminal Justice Information Center. In *The Source,* Criminal Justice Information Center, Michigan State Police no. 00-3. Lansing, Mich.: Michigan State Police.

Polsenberg, Christina. 1995. *Criminal victimization and fear of crime in Michigan.* No. 95–09. East Lansing: Institute for Public Policy and Social Research.

Prosecuting Attorneys Coordinating Council. 2002. Prosecuting Attorney Duties *http://www.michigan-prosecutor.com/PA-duty.htm.* Accessed 10 June 2002.

Rennison, Callie Marie. 2000. *Criminal victimization 1999.* National Crime Victimization Survey no. 182734. Washington, D.C.: Bureau of Justice Statistics, Office of Justice Programs, U.S. Department of Justice.

Schulman, Ronica. 1999. *What do we want (and what are we getting) from the criminal justice system? Comparing the general public's expectations and perceptions with crime victims' experiences, general overview.* Eastern Regional Conference. Council of State Governments.

Senate Fiscal Agency. 2002. *Senate Fiscal Agency, State of Michigan, fiscal year 2002–2003 budget status summary.*

Tonry, Michael. 1996. *Sentencing matters.* Studies in Crime and Public Policy. New York: Oxford University Press.

Tonry, Michael, and David P. Farrington. 1995. Strategic approaches to crime prevention. In *Building a safer society: Strategic approaches to crime prevention,* edited by Micheal Tonry and David P. Farrington, vol. 19, *Crime and justice: A review of research,* 1–20. Chicago: University of Chicago Press.

Welford, Charles F. 1997. Changing nature of criminal justice system responses and its profession. In *The Challenge of crime in free society: Looking back; looking forward.* Symposium on the 30th Anniversary of the President's Commission on Law Enforcement and Administration of Justice, 58–73. Washington, D.C.: U.S. Department of Justice.

Wichiraya, T. 1996. *Simple theory, hard reality: The impact of sentencing reforms on courts, prisons, and crime.* Albany, N.Y.: State University of New York Press.

Wilson, James Q. 1983. *Thinking about crime.* Rev. ed. New York: Vintage Books.

## NOTES

1. Michigan's district court judges are elected for six-year terms on nonpartisan ballots, under the same requirements as circuit judges. The legislature sets their salaries, which may be supplemented by local governments (One Court of Justice 2002).

2. This expenditure data was not adjusted for inflation to maintain consistency with the Bureau of Justice Statistics reporting. However, expenditure on all justice functions across government levels increased at a rate greater than inflation. Using the Consumer Price Index (CPI) reported by the Bureau of Labor Statistics for the years between 1982 and 1999, price level should have increased at an annual rate of 2.9%, for a total of 166.6% (Bureau of Justice Statistics 2002b). If justice expenditure increased at the rate of inflation after 1982, expenditure in 1999 would have been $59.7 billion instead of the actual $146.6 billion (Bureau of Justice Statistics 2002b).

3. Legislation (HB 5419), which embodied the commission's recommended sentencing guidelines, was passed by the House on 16 June 1998, and by the Senate on 2 July 1998. The governor signed the bill on 28 July 1998. It was assigned Public Act No. 317 of 1998.

4. Only data up to 2000 are publicly available. There is at least a two-year lag between the time when data is put together by the FBI and the time when it becomes publicly available. Standardization procedures are performed by the Bureau of Justice Statistics to correct for underreporting and missing cases. For the purposes of this chapter, further standardization procedures were performed by the investigators to enable comparisons over time.

5. For the purposes of this chapter, the Great Lakes region includes Illinois, Indiana, Minnesota, Ohio, and Wisconsin.

6. Michigan's district courts have jurisdiction over all civil litigation up to $25,000 including landlord-tenant proceedings, land contract forfeitures, small claims, and other summary proceedings. In the criminal field, the district court handles all misdemeanors where punishment does not exceed one year, including the arraignment, setting and

acceptance of bail, trial, and sentencing. The district court also conducts preliminary examinations in felony cases. District judges may appoint magistrates to set bail and accept bond in criminal matters; accept guilty pleas; and sentence for traffic, motor carrier, and snowmobile violations and dog, game, and marine law violations. The magistrate may also issue search warrants, and arrest warrants authorized by the prosecutor or municipal attorney (One Court of Justice 2002).

7. The circuit court has jurisdiction over all actions except those given by state law to another court. The circuit court has original jurisdiction in all criminal cases where the offense involves a felony or certain serious misdemeanors, civil cases over $25,000; family division cases; appeals from district court, probate court, and administrative agencies; and drain code condemnation cases. In addition, the circuit court has superintending control over other courts within the judicial circuit, subject to final superintending control of the Supreme Court. The state is divided into judicial circuits along county lines. The number of judges within a circuit is established by the legislature to accommodate required judicial activity. In multicounty circuits, judges travel from one county to another to hold court sessions. The circuit court is the trial court of general jurisdiction in Michigan because of its very broad powers. Circuit judges are elected for terms of six years in nonpartisan elections. The legislature sets salaries for circuit judges, which may be supplemented by counties (One Court of Justice 2002).

8. The Michigan State Police are developing the *Automated Incident Capture System* (AICS). AICS is a record management system that will provide a mechanism for capturing incident-based information using an on-line central database. AICS integrates all the police reporting and record-keeping functions so that a police officer need only make one computerized entry of an incident, an arrest, or related reporting data, which is then automatically routed to booking, criminal history records, criminal intelligence files, and other criminal justice systems. By October 2000 there were five county sheriff's offices, eleven police departments, one county prosecutor, and all Michigan State Police posts participating in the AICS program (Pifer 2000).

9. Crimes "cleared" typically means crimes where an arrest was made by the police.

10. UCR Part I offenses (also referred to as Index Crimes) include criminal murder, forcible rape, robbery, aggravated assault, burglary, larceny-theft,

motor vehicle theft, and arson. Part II offenses include simple assault; forgery and counterfeiting; fraud; embezzlement; buying, receiving, or possessing stolen property; vandalism; carrying or possessing weapons; prostitution; sex offenses not involving forcible rape; drug abuse violations (UCR does not have a separate category for drug crimes such as selling or possession); gambling; offenses against the family and children; driving under the influence; liquor laws violations; drunkenness; disorderly conduct; vagrancy; curfew and loitering laws; runaways; suspicion but not charged; and all other offenses violating a state or local law except traffic offenses (Federal Bureau of Investigation 2000).

11. Rates in Michigan are significantly higher than in the other regions (statistically significant at $p < .001$ in ANOVA) for all four violent crimes: murder, rape, robbery, and aggravated assault.

12. According to Beck (2001), the largest growth in the number of state inmates between 1990 and 1999 was among violent offenders. During the 1990s, the number of violent offenders increased by 241,100, while the number of drug offenders increased by 101,500 and the number of property crime offenders increased by 70,000.

13. As opposed to reported crimes, which may or may not end up in an arrest, examining arrest trends provides a clearer portrait of the flow of cases that will potentially go through the criminal justice system.

14. The National Center for Community Policing at the School of Criminal Justice at Michigan State University assisted in and facilitated many of the organizational changes in police agencies to enable adoption of community policing standards.

15. Since this writing, Michigan passed changes to its mandatory sentencing laws for drug offenders. The law eliminates mandatory minimums and allows judges to consider individual factors in a case. The law also allows persons currently serving mandatory drug sentences to be eligible for parole, and eliminates lifetime probation. The law took effect 1 March 2003. At this point it is premature to estimate the likely impact of this law on the prison population or prison costs.

16. Judges select a minimum sentence within the range indicated by the guidelines, unless they have a "substantial and compelling" reason to depart.

17. The Michigan Department of Corrections used its FY 2000 award for the following projects: (1) lease of beds at the 450-bed Youthful Offender Facility; (2) construction of a 1,500-bed secure prison; and, (3) a 480-bed expansion at the Cooper Street Faci-

lity. In FY 2001 the Department of Corrections used the award money for the 480-bed expansion at the Cooper Street Facility and for the lease of beds at the 450-bed Youthful Offender Facility (Corrections Program Office 2002).

18. A disposition often means a guilty finding, a guilty plea, or a *nolo contendere* plea. The term is also often used to mean the type of sanction given an offender, such as prison, probation, jail, fine, or a combination of these sanctions.

19. This difference is statistically significant at $p < 0.01$.

20. Currently, MDOC is generally charging inmates a co-payment of $3.00 when they request routine medical care, to help defray costs; has used a managed care vendor to more efficiently negotiate large, cost-effective health contracts; and has begun to consolidate housing and services to prisoners with special medical needs in one geographic location, among other trends (Michigan Department of Corrections 2000).

21. We have presented comparison figures with other states only up to 1999, as data are not yet available from more recent years to enable sufficient comparisons across states.

# 25

# Overview of Michigan's Revenue System

*Charles L. Ballard*

A variety of policy issues have been discussed in the earlier chapters of this volume. Many of these issues are associated with significant government expenditures. The remaining chapters deal primarily with the government revenues that finance those expenditures. The purpose of this chapter is to provide an overview of the revenue system. The specific parts of the revenue system, such as income taxes and property taxes, will be considered in more detail in subsequent chapters.

I begin by looking at the dollar totals for state and local revenues in the fiscal year 1999–2000. I then consider the ways in which the revenue system has changed over time, and provide comparisons between the Michigan revenue system and the systems used in other states. Next, I focus on the details of some of the more important revenue sources. The goal is to provide a framework for evaluating the effectiveness of the Michigan revenue system, and to indicate some of the possibilities for reform.

## Sources of Revenue for State and Local Governments in Michigan

The state government, local governments, and public schools in Michigan raise revenues from a very wide variety of sources. Figures 25.1 and 25.2 provide a quick look at the revenue sources for state and local governments for the 1999–2000 fiscal year, and table 25.1 includes considerably more detail.[1]

## State Government Revenues

As seen at the top of the second column of table 25.1, total revenue for the State of Michigan in 1999–2000 was about $49.5 billion. In the census data, this total is broken down into a variety of categories. About $9.2 billion come from the federal government. (Intergovernmental fiscal relations are discussed in detail in chapter 31.) In the middle of the column, it can be seen that another $7.4 billion fall into the category of "Charges and Miscellaneous General Revenue." The largest part of this category are the tuition and fees charged by institutions of higher education. At the bottom of the column, table 25.1 shows that about $9.5 billion, or about one-fifth of the state's total revenues, come from insurance trusts for unemployment compensation, employee retirement, and workers' compensation. (These programs are discussed in detail in chapters 19 and 20 of this volume.) However, it should be understood that the insurance trust revenues are not available for

**FIGURE 25.1**

**Major Sources of State Government Revenue in Michigan, 1999–2000**

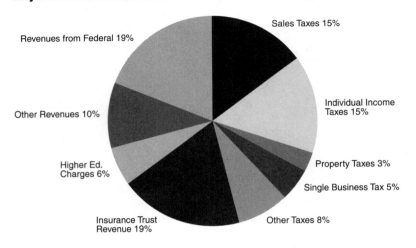

SOURCE: U.S. Bureau of the Census, *www.census.gov/govs/estimate00sl23mi.html.*

**FIGURE 25.2**

**Major Sources of Local Government Revenue in Michigan, 1999–2000**

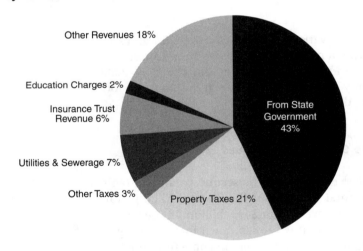

SOURCE: U.S. Bureau of the Census, *www.census.gov/govs/estimate00sl23mi.html.*

general government purposes. Consequently, in the rest of this chapter, most of our attention will be focused elsewhere.

If we begin with the total state revenues of $49.5 billion, and then subtract intergovernmental revenues, charges and miscellaneous revenues, and insurance trust revenues, we are left with the revenues that come in the form of taxes. As shown by table 25.1 and figure 25.1, taxes accounted for about $22.8 billion of the revenues of the State of Michigan in 1999–2000, which is about 46% of total revenues. The largest of these

are the general retail sales tax, which is discussed in chapter 27, and the individual income tax, which is discussed in chapter 26. Substantial amounts of state tax revenue are also generated by property taxes (discussed in chapter 28), the Single Business Tax (discussed in chapter 29), taxes on motor fuels (discussed in chapter 16), and taxes on alcohol and tobacco (discussed in chapter 32).

**Local Government Revenues**

Local governments in Michigan receive revenues from many of the same sources as the state government, but the percentage distribution of revenues across the various sources is quite different.[2] As seen in the third column of table 25.1 and in figure 25.2, local government revenues are dominated by aid from the state government. State aid to local governments (including counties, municipalities, and public schools) was about $15.6 billion in 1999–2000, which was fully 43% of the total revenue for the local governments.

Local governments in Michigan collected about $8.7 billion of taxes in 1999–2000. The revenues from the property tax were about $7.8 billion, and thus were far larger than the revenues from any of the other taxes levied by local governments in Michigan. In Michigan, local governments do not collect any general retail sales tax, and they collect only modest amounts of income tax revenue.[3] Thus, the two largest sources of tax revenue for the *state* government are relatively unimportant at the *local* level.

In addition, local governments in Michigan rely relatively more on fees than does the state government. Local governments receive revenue from tuition at community colleges, payments to public hospitals, airport fees, fees for use of county and municipal parks, fees for sewerage and garbage disposal, charges for water and electricity, bus fares, payments for parking in government-owned parking garages and parking lots, parking tickets, library fines, and a host of other fees and charges.

Before going on, it is important to emphasize two implications of the data shown in table 25.1 and figures 25.1 and 25.2. First, because the state government sends so much revenue to the local governments, the distinction between state government revenues and local government revenues is inherently somewhat arbitrary. In much of the

**TABLE 25.1**

## State and Local Government Revenues in Michigan, 1999–2000 ($thousands)

| | State & Local Government Amount[a] | State Government Amount | Local Government Amount[a] | | State & Local Government Amount[a] | State Government Amount | Local Government Amount[a] |
|---|---|---|---|---|---|---|---|
| Revenue[a] | 70,111,672 | 49,511,464 | 36,411,119 | Hospitals | 1,367,894 | 799,835 | 568,059 |
| General revenue[a] | 56,415,159 | 39,490,569 | 32,735,501 | Highways | 97,526 | 17,199 | 80,327 |
| Intergovernmental revenue[a] | 10,330,841 | 9,370,103 | 16,771,649 | Airports | 248,089 | 1,120 | 246,969 |
| From federal government | 10,330,841 | 9,167,840 | 1,163,001 | Parking facilities | 70,310 | 0 | 70,310 |
| From state government | (a) | 0 | 15,608,648 | Sea and inland port facilities | 806 | 0 | 806 |
| From local governments[a] | (a) | 202,263 | (a) | Natural resources | 58,283 | 53,340 | 4,943 |
| General revenue from own sources | 46,084,318 | 30,120,466 | 15,963,852 | Parks and recreation | 135,276 | 4,552 | 130,724 |
| Taxes | 31,474,162 | 22,756,403 | 8,717,759 | Housing & community develop. | 40,331 | 17,542 | 22,789 |
| Property | 9,498,688 | 1,702,501 | 7,796,187 | Sewerage | 1,238,596 | 0 | 1,238,596 |
| Sales and gross receipts | 9,905,560 | 9,784,723 | 120,837 | Solid waste management | 128,338 | 0 | 128,338 |
| General sales | 7,666,399 | 7,666,399 | 0 | Other charges | 1,388,669 | 160,547 | 1,228,122 |
| Selective sales | 2,239,161 | 2,118,324 | 120,837 | Miscellaneous general revenue | 5,960,465 | 3,180,963 | 2,779,502 |
| Motor fuel | 1,074,816 | 1,074,816 | 0 | Interest earnings | 2,597,814 | 1,510,767 | 1,087,047 |
| Alcoholic beverage | 136,399 | 132,648 | 3,751 | Special assessments | 94,285 | 0 | 94,285 |
| Tobacco products | 604,672 | 604,672 | 0 | Sale of property | 66,063 | 7,457 | 58,606 |
| Public utilities | 66,902 | 12,303 | 54,599 | Other general revenue | 3,202,303 | 1,662,739 | 1,539,564 |
| Other selective sales | 356,372 | 293,885 | 62,487 | Utility revenue | 1,413,543 | 0 | 1,413,543 |
| Individual income | 7,729,539 | 7,190,407 | 539,132 | Water supply | 710,152 | 0 | 710,152 |
| Single business | 2,382,496 | 2,382,496 | 0 | Electric power | 641,120 | 0 | 641,120 |
| Motor vehicle license | 817,078 | 816,160 | 918 | Gas supply | 11 | 0 | 11 |
| Other taxes | 1,140,801 | 880,116 | 260,685 | Transit | 62,260 | 0 | 62,260 |
| Charges & misc. general revenue | 14,610,156 | 7,364,063 | 7,246,093 | Liquor store revenue | 567,312 | 567,312 | 0 |
| Current charges | 8,649,691 | 4,183,100 | 4,466,591 | Insurance trust revenue | 11,715,658 | 9,453,583 | 2,262,075 |
| Education | 3,875,573 | 3,128,965 | 746,608 | Unemployment compensation | 1,256,112 | 1,256,112 | 0 |
| Institutions of higher ed. | 3,536,228 | 3,128,965 | 407,263 | Employee retirement | 10,432,065 | 8,169,990 | 2,262,075 |
| School lunch sales (gross) | 201,258 | 0 | 201,258 | Workers' compensation | 27,481 | 27,481 | 0 |

SOURCE: U.S. Bureau of the Census, *www.census.gov/govs/estimate00sl23mi.html.*
(a) Duplicative intergovernmental transactions are excluded.

rest of this chapter, the focus will be on the combined state and local revenues.

Second, it is appropriate to recognize that governments can substitute between taxes and fees. Changes in taxes can be offset, at least in part, by changes in fees and other charges. In other words, a tax cut does not necessarily translate into a reduction in overall government revenues, and a tax increase does not necessarily imply an increase in overall government revenues.

For example, as of this writing, reductions in tax revenues at the state level are expected to lead to reductions in funding for state departments, as well as reductions in state government aid to universities, local public schools, and local governments. Yet a reduction in tax-financed state funding for state parks may be offset by an increase in entry fees for those parks. A reduction in state funding for state universities may lead to increased tuition. A reduction in state funding for local public schools may lead to increased use of a variety of activity fees for students. A reduction in state revenue sharing for local governments may lead to higher fees for local parks, higher fees for garbage collection, higher fines for parking and traffic violations, and so on. Ultimately, the change in total revenues may be much smaller than the original change in taxes. The size of the offset will depend on the decisions of state agencies, local governments, and the individual families that use government-provided services and facilities.

## TABLE 25.2

**Trends in State and Local Tax Revenues in Michigan, 1981–82 to 1999–2000**

| Year | Real Per Capita Tax Revenues in 2000 Dollars | Tax Revenues Per $1,000 Personal Income |
|------|------|------|
| 1982 | $2120 | $115.07 |
| 1987 | 2528 | 120.88 |
| 1992 | 2496 | 115.50 |
| 1993 | 2687 | 120.63 |
| 1994 | 2834 | 124.48 |
| 1995 | 2656 | 111.28 |
| 1996 | 2732 | 108.72 |
| 1997 | 2859 | 111.79 |
| 1998 | 2986 | 112.75 |
| 1999 | 3098 | 113.60 |
| 2000 | 3167 | 113.81 |

SOURCE: For tax revenues 1992–2000: U.S. Bureau of the Census, *www.census.gov/govs/estimate.html* (various years). For tax revenues before 1992: U.S. Bureau of the Census, *Census of Government*, vol. 4, Government Finances, various years. For inflation adjustments: U.S. Bureau of Economic Analysis, *www.bea.gov/bea/dn/nipaweb/selectTable.asp?Selected=N#ST*.

### Relative Comparisons of Revenues

For many revenue categories, the totals shown in table 25.1 amount to billions of dollars, or even tens of billions. When the numbers are this large, they may be difficult to comprehend fully. Therefore, it makes sense to provide some comparisons, to put the raw data into context.

Perhaps the most popular comparison involves dividing by population, so as to obtain measures of per capita revenues. According to the estimates of the U.S. Bureau of the Census, Michigan's population was just under ten million in the year 2000.[4] Dividing the revenue numbers from table 25.1 by the population estimate, we find that total state and local revenues were more than $7,000 per person in 1999–2000. If we then exclude intergovernmental grants from the federal government, utility revenue, liquor store revenue, and insurance trust revenue, we have a measure of general revenue from own sources, which was more than $4,600 per capita in 1999–2000. Finally, if we exclude charges and miscellaneous general revenue, we have a measure of taxes, which amounted to more than $3,100 per capita.

Another way to gain perspective on the size of the revenue system is to divide by the number of workers. Since about half the population is work-ing, per worker revenues are approximately twice as great as per capita revenues. Thus, in 1999–2000, Michigan taxes were more than $6,000 per worker. See Ballard (2002) for more discussion.

It is natural to ask whether this amount of revenue per capita is "too much," "too little," or "just right." For better or worse, there is no easy answer to that question. The optimal amount of tax-financed government expenditure is difficult to identify precisely, even in theory.[5] No attempt will be made here to give a definitive answer to the question of whether Michigan governments spend and tax too much or too little. However, we can get a richer understanding of the nature of Michigan's revenue system by looking at how Michigan's revenue levels have changed over time, and how they compare with the revenue levels of other states.

To make meaningful comparisons over time, it is necessary to adjust for changes in population and price level.[6] The best-known price index is the Consumer Price Index (CPI), which is calculated by the U.S. Bureau of Labor Statistics. However, the CPI is badly flawed. Because of a number of technical problems, the inflation rate calculated according to the CPI tends to overstate the true increase in the cost of living. (For discussion, see Boskin et al. [1998].) Instead of the CPI, we use the deflator for Personal Consumption Expenditures, which is calculated by the U.S. Commerce Department's Bureau of Economic Analysis.[7]

Table 25.2 shows some of the changes over the last few decades in real (inflation-adjusted) per capita tax revenue in Michigan, in 2000 dollars.[8] The level rose a bit in the 1980s, and again in the late 1990s.

It is interesting to see that real per capita taxes increased during the second half of the 1990s, at a time when the rates of the individual income tax and Single Business Tax were declining. This can be understood in terms of the robust economic expansion that occurred during the late 1990s. The Michigan economy was growing so rapidly that revenues were increasing, even though some tax rates were falling. However, the national economy began to show signs of weakness in the late summer of 2000, and a recession was underway by March 2001. The economic slowdown, combined with continued reductions in tax rates, meant that revenues for the State of Michigan were lower in 2000–2001 than they had been in 1999–2000, and lower again in 2001–2.[9] When more complete data on local government revenues become available, it is quite likely that the

**TABLE 25.3**

## Rankings of State and Local Tax Revenues in the United States, 1999–2000

| | Per-Capita Taxes | Ranking | | Taxes per $1,000 of Personal Income | Ranking |
|---|---|---|---|---|---|
| District of Columbia | $5621.97 | 1 | District of Columbia | $156.86 | 1 |
| Connecticut | 4595.15 | 2 | New York | 141.04 | 2 |
| New York | 4577.79 | 3 | Maine | 139.10 | 3 |
| New Jersey | 3902.77 | 4 | Alaska | 131.57 | 4 |
| Massachusetts | 3786.75 | 5 | Wisconsin | 128.93 | 5 |
| Minnesota | 3694.43 | 6 | New Mexico | 127.09 | 6 |
| Alaska | 3687.08 | 7 | Hawaii | 125.92 | 7 |
| California | 3544.74 | 8 | Minnesota | 123.72 | 8 |
| Wisconsin | 3457.60 | 9 | California | 120.69 | 9 |
| Maryland | 3453.53 | 10 | Vermont | 120.66 | 10 |
| Hawaii | 3384.17 | 11 | Utah | 120.05 | 11 |
| Maine | 3342.86 | 12 | Connecticut | 119.69 | 12 |
| Delaware | 3340.09 | 13 | North Dakota | 119.10 | 13 |
| Rhode Island | 3256.06 | 14 | Rhode Island | 118.70 | 14 |
| Illinois | 3241.49 | 15 | Wyoming | 117.05 | 15 |
| Washington | 3178.46 | 16 | West Virginia | 116.36 | 16 |
| **Michigan** | **3167.05** | **17** | Delaware | 115.11 | 17 |
| Vermont | 3079.71 | 18 | Idaho | 113.87 | 18 |
| Colorado | 3072.82 | 19 | **Michigan** | **113.81** | **19** |
| Wyoming | 3045.87 | 20 | New Jersey | 113.70 | 20 |
| Ohio | 3015.83 | 21 | Ohio | 112.44 | 21 |
| Pennsylvania | 2978.67 | 22 | Kentucky | 111.67 | 22 |
| Virginia | 2978.24 | 23 | Iowa | 110.96 | 23 |
| Nevada | 2915.33 | 24 | Arizona | 110.88 | 24 |
| Nebraska | 2906.47 | 25 | Massachusetts | 110.88 | 25 |
| Georgia | 2840.65 | 26 | Mississippi | 110.67 | 26 |
| Kansas | 2833.46 | 27 | Montana | 110.00 | 27 |
| Iowa | 2765.05 | 28 | Louisiana | 109.92 | 28 |
| North Dakota | 2754.07 | 29 | Nebraska | 109.84 | 29 |
| Oregon | 2751.18 | 30 | Maryland | 109.36 | 30 |
| Indiana | 2691.35 | 31 | Kansas | 108.87 | 31 |
| North Carolina | 2663.69 | 32 | Georgia | 108.77 | 32 |
| New Hampshire | 2652.41 | 33 | Illinois | 107.76 | 33 |
| New Mexico | 2639.13 | 34 | Washington | 107.47 | 34 |
| Utah | 2630.15 | 35 | Pennsylvania | 106.82 | 35 |
| Florida | 2623.99 | 36 | Oklahoma | 106.51 | 36 |
| Arizona | 2598.64 | 37 | Arkansas | 106.44 | 37 |
| Missouri | 2558.33 | 38 | North Carolina | 105.75 | 38 |
| Idaho | 2545.78 | 39 | Oregon | 105.65 | 39 |
| Kentucky | 2516.68 | 40 | Indiana | 105.63 | 40 |
| Texas | 2504.63 | 41 | Nevada | 105.27 | 41 |
| Louisiana | 2436.21 | 42 | South Carolina | 104.58 | 42 |
| West Virginia | 2412.78 | 43 | Colorado | 103.10 | 43 |
| Oklahoma | 2391.02 | 44 | Virginia | 102.88 | 44 |
| South Carolina | 2378.59 | 45 | Missouri | 99.50 | 45 |
| Montana | 2363.46 | 46 | Florida | 98.74 | 46 |
| South Dakota | 2298.85 | 47 | Texas | 96.83 | 47 |
| Arkansas | 2230.20 | 48 | South Dakota | 94.49 | 48 |
| Mississippi | 2214.20 | 49 | Alabama | 93.65 | 49 |
| Tennessee | 2185.13 | 50 | Tennessee | 88.09 | 50 |
| Alabama | 2117.18 | 51 | New Hampshire | 88.00 | 51 |

SOURCE: U.S. Bureau of the Census, *www.census.gov/govs/estimate00.html.*

overall level of state and local government taxes will be seen to decrease after 2000.

Another way to understand the relationship between tax rates and tax revenues is to consider the right column of table 25.2, which shows state and local tax revenues in Michigan, per $1,000 of personal income. This shows that the proportion of personal income going to state and local tax revenues did not increase very much during the late 1990s. In fact, as a percentage of personal income, state and local taxes were lower in 2000 than they had been in 1994, even though real per capita tax revenue increased over this period. In other words, because of economic growth, it is possible for the *level* of tax revenues to rise in real terms, even though there is no increase in the *percentage* of income that is devoted to taxes.

Table 25.3 shows some rankings of the fifty states and the District of Columbia, for 1999–2000.[10] Table 25.3 indicates that, in terms of per capita taxes, Michigan ranked sixteenth (or seventeenth if we include the District of Columbia). Michigan's ranking has been in this general vicinity for many years.[11] One part of the reason for Michigan's high ranking in terms of per capita government revenues is that Michigan is a relatively high-income state. Thus, it is possible for Michigan residents to pay more taxes per person than are paid by the residents of some other states, even if Michigan's taxes are not any higher as a proportion of income. Thus, when we measure on the basis of personal income, rather than on a per capita basis, Michigan's ranking is somewhat lower. Michigan's state and local taxes are eighteenth-highest as a percentage of personal income (or nineteenth if we include the District of Columbia).

The data in table 25.3 are for taxes. If we include all of the other types of revenue from own sources, Michigan was the thirteenth-highest state in terms of per capita own-source revenues (or fourteenth if we include the District of Columbia). Michigan is the twenty-second-highest state in terms of state and local own-source revenues as a percentage of personal income (or twenty-third if we include the District of Columbia).

Thus, overall, Michigan tends to be somewhat above average in terms of government revenues. However, it is important to keep this in perspective. Michigan residents tax themselves substantially more than do the residents of Tennessee and Alabama, but the residents of New York and Minnesota tax themselves much more than Michiganians do.

In terms of the individual components of the tax system, Michigan is above the median for property taxes, individual income taxes, and sales taxes. Michigan ranks near the bottom in terms of taxes on motor fuels. On the other hand, Michigan is among the top four states in the nation in terms of taxes on tobacco products.[12]

## Description of Major Taxes in Michigan

This section provides a basic description of some of the most important features of Michigan taxes.[13] Much more detail is available in chapter 16, which deals with motor-fuels taxes, chapters 26, 27, 28, and 29, which deal with the income tax, the sales and use tax, the property tax, and the Single Business Tax, and chapter 32, which is concerned with taxes on alcohol and tobacco, lottery revenues, and inheritance taxes.

### Property Taxes

The most important change in Michigan's tax system in recent decades was the implementation in 1994 of Proposal A, under which the taxes on retail sales and cigarettes were increased and the taxes on income and property were decreased. In spite of the tax reductions brought about by Proposal A, however, property taxes remain the largest single source of revenue for Michigan's state government, local governments, and public schools. In 1999–2000, property taxes raised about $9.5 billion. The property tax is the only tax that raises revenue for jurisdictions at every level, including the State of Michigan, counties, cities, townships, villages, and school districts. Property taxes are especially important for local governments (including public schools), providing nearly half of the own-source revenues for these jurisdictions, and nearly 90% of their tax revenues. (However, since Proposal A, local school districts rely much less on property taxes than before.)

A detailed process ensures that *property assessments* are kept uniform throughout the state. However, this does not mean that the actual *property taxes* are uniform. First of all, personal property is taxed only at the business level. Second, special arrangements and exemptions exist for utilities, forestland, iron mines, mobile homes in mobile home parks, and certain industrial facilities.[14]

Moreover, Michigan's system of property taxes was made much more nonuniform and discriminatory by Proposal A. As a result of Proposal A, which exempted homesteads from paying school operating millages, there has been an increase in the share of the property tax burden that is borne by rental housing, second homes, and business property. Another feature of Proposal A is a cap on the amount by which the taxable value of a property can increase from year to year. The cap is removed when the property is sold. (An important exception is made for agricultural property, which is not "uncapped" even when sold, if the property is kept in agricultural use.)

By reducing local property taxes, and replacing them with a state property tax, an increased state sales tax, and other revenue sources, Proposal A was instrumental in a centralization of Michigan's revenue system.

### The Individual Income Tax

Michigan is one of forty-three states (in addition to the District of Columbia) that levy an individual income tax.[15] A taxpayer's computation of Michigan taxable income begins with federal adjusted gross income. As a result, it is said that Michigan's income tax "piggybacks" upon the federal tax.

Once the taxpayer's income is calculated, the next step is to subtract personal exemptions, which were $3,000 for each person in 2002. Additional amounts are exempted for senior citizens, children age eighteen and under, and persons who suffer from certain physical disabilities. Because of the exemptions, low-income residents pay very little Michigan income tax.

Senior citizens are allowed to deduct Social Security benefits, retirement and pension benefits, dividends, interest, and capital gains. Thus, senior citizens also pay very little Michigan income tax. After these and some other adjustments to income, tax is calculated by applying a flat tax rate, which was 4.1% in 2002, and dropped to 4.0% on 1 January 2003. Currently, the tax rate is scheduled to decrease to 3.9% in 2004.[16]

After the tax rate is applied, the taxpayer's liabilities may still be reduced by the use of any of twelve tax credits. A tax credit provides a direct reduction in the tax bill, regardless of the tax rate. The largest credit is the Homestead Property Tax Credit, which reduces the effective burden of property taxes for households with incomes below $82,650. Senior citizens are eligible for larger Homestead credits than are the rest of the population. The Homestead credit is *refundable*, which means that if the amount of credit is greater than the tax liability before the credit, the taxpayer will receive a refund check.

Because of the various deductions, exemptions, and credits, it is said that the tax base of the individual income tax is *eroded*. It would be possible to raise the same amount of income-tax revenue with a significantly lower income tax rate, if the tax base were less eroded.

In recent decades, there has been an increase in the proportion of the population that is aged sixty-five and over. Thus, there has been an increase in the revenue loss associated with the tax preferences for the elderly. Because of the aging of the Baby Boom generation, this issue is likely to become much more significant in the future.

### The Sales and Use Tax

Michigan is one of forty-five states (in addition to the District of Columbia) that raise revenue from a "general retail sales tax."[17] The term "general" might be interpreted as meaning that the tax applies to *all* retail sales. In fact, however, a very large portion of retail sales is not subject to the tax. The tax is not collected on food purchased for home consumption. Even more important is the fact that the tax does not apply to most services, such as the services of accountants, appliance repairpersons, barbers, doctors, lawyers, and others.

In Michigan, for most of the items that are taxed, the tax is levied at a rate of 6%. (The rate had been 4% since 1960, but was raised as part of the tax changes associated with Proposal A in 1994.)

When a purchase is made from a mail-order service or over the Internet, the buyer is supposed to pay tax. However, these taxes are widely evaded. Internet sales have grown rapidly in recent years, and are expected to continue to grow.[18] This poses an ongoing challenge for the state's revenue system, and Michigan is one of a large number of states that have been attempting to set up a nationwide system for online retailers to collect sales taxes. (For discussion of the taxation of electronic commerce, see Bruce and Fox [2000] and McLure [1999].)

In recent decades, there has been a strong increase in the proportion of consumer expenditure that is devoted to services. Much of this increase would probably have occurred in any case, but it is likely that the growth of services has also been stimulated by the favorable tax treatment. The revenue loss associated with nontaxation of services has increased over time, and it is likely to continue to increase, unless the laws are changed.

### The Single Business Tax

The Single Business Tax (SBT) was enacted in 1975, as a replacement for several taxes on businesses. (Hence the name "Single" Business Tax.)[19] The SBT is levied on all business enterprises, and not just on corporations.[20]

Michigan's Single Business Tax is unique in the United States, in that it is a form of value-added tax. It is thus similar to the value-added taxes that are used by all of the countries of the European Union, although the SBT and the European value-added taxes are implemented differently. The tax base of the SBT includes profits (exclusive of dividends, interest, and royalties), labor costs, depreciation, and interest expenses. For most of the years of its existence, the SBT allowed deductions for capital expenditures. The deduction was replaced by a small investment tax credit in 1999.

Corporate profits tend to rise rapidly during economic expansions, and fall rapidly during recessions. This means that a tax on corporate profits is likely to generate a revenue stream that is highly variable over time. Chapter 29 of this volume presents evidence that the revenue collected from the SBT appears to change less over the business cycle than the revenue that would be collected from a corporate profits tax.

The SBT has been the subject of much controversy throughout the quarter-century since its enactment. This is partly due to the difficulties of taxing businesses that operate in other states. One especially vexing problem has to do with the tax treatment of investments made by multistate firms. On the one hand, it is desirable to avoid discouraging investment, and this provides a rationale for granting deductions or credits for investments. On the other hand, there is concern that SBT deductions would be given for investments that are ultimately located outside Michigan. Over the years, this problem has led to a large number of changes in the SBT. A detailed description of this history can be found in chapter 29.

Currently, the SBT is scheduled to be eliminated in 2010 (although there is an active debate over whether the phase-out should be com-

pleted). Regardless of whether the phase-out continues, the contentious debate over the SBT has led to a large amount of base erosion over the years.

### Taxes on Alcohol, Tobacco, Motor Fuels, and Gambling

Michigan, like every other state, as well as the federal government and the District of Columbia, levies taxes on sales of alcoholic beverages and tobacco products. Consumption of tobacco and alcohol is associated with a variety of negative external effects. For example, secondhand smoke harms the health of nonsmokers, and sober people are injured or killed by drunk drivers. If no correction is made for these negative effects, the amount of tobacco and alcohol consumption can be greater than the optimal amount. These external effects provide a justification for high taxes on these commodities. The evidence presented in chapter 32 suggests that the optimal taxes on alcohol and tobacco may be quite large. Taxes on motor fuels are sometimes justified along similar lines, because vehicle exhaust contributes to air pollution. In addition, motor fuel taxes are often considered (at least in part) to be fees for the use of highways.

For the most part, these taxes take the form of *unit taxes*. A unit tax is levied in terms of dollars per unit. The current tax on cigarettes in Michigan is $1.25 per pack. Beer is taxed at $6.30 per barrel, wine at about 51 cents per gallon, and fortified wine at about 76 cents per gallon. Gasoline is taxed at 19 cents per gallon, diesel fuel at 15 cents per gallon, and aviation fuel at 3 cents per gallon. These unit taxes stand in contrast to most other taxes, which are levied on an *ad valorem* basis, which means that the tax is a percentage of some dollar value.

One problem with unit taxes is that their potential to raise revenue will be reduced over time as a result of inflation, unless the tax rate is explicitly increased. Thus, the cigarette tax was established in 1947 at a rate of 3 cents per pack. The tax rate was raised in 1959, 1961, 1962, 1970, 1982, and 1987. By 1987, the tax rate had climbed to 25 cents per pack, but its inflation-adjusted revenue was only about twice as great as it had been when it was first established. The cigarette tax was raised to 75 cents per pack in 1994, as part of the set of tax changes in Proposal A. It was raised to $1.25 per pack in 2002. These increases were substantially larger than the rate of inflation, so that the real tax revenues from cigarettes have increased.

The gasoline tax was established in 1925 at a rate of 2 cents per gallon, and it has been increased nine times since then, most recently from 15 cents per gallon to 19 cents per gallon in 1997. On the other hand, the beer tax has been increased only twice in its history, most recently in 1962. The tax on wine has been increased only once, in 1981. Consequently, the tax revenues from beer and wine have fallen in real terms for the last forty years.

The issues discussed in the preceding paragraphs do not arise in the case of *ad valorem* taxes. Since *ad valorem* taxes are expressed in terms of percentages, the revenue raised by an *ad valorem* tax is much more likely to keep up with inflation, even if the rate is not changed.

The State of Michigan also collects substantial amounts of revenue from the lottery, although the lottery tax is implicit. The tax rate can be inferred by comparing the total receipts of the lottery with the amounts paid out in prizes. As reported in chapter 32, Michigan's implicit lottery tax rate is above 60%, which is far higher than any of the other tax rates in the Michigan revenue system.

### Changes in the Composition of Taxes in Michigan

As shown in table 25.4, Michigan has had a long-term trend of stability in the percentages of total state and local taxes that were collected from different sources. Throughout the 1970s, 1980s, and early 1990s, the property tax tended to account for about 40% of state and local taxes. Individual income taxes tended to account for about 20% of total taxes, and the sales tax tended to account for about 18%. The passage of Proposal A brought about the first major changes in these percentages in a generation. As can be seen in table 25.4 and figure 25.3, the share of both income taxes and sales taxes rose to about 25% after 1994, and the share of the property tax fell to about 30%.

### Evaluation of the Revenue System of Michigan Governments

We have now established some of the basic facts about the system of state and local government revenues in Michigan. With these facts in mind, the next step is to move toward an evaluation of

**TABLE 25.4**

**Composition of State and Local Taxes in Michigan, 1971–72 to 1999–2000**

| Year | Property Taxes as % of Total | Sales Taxes as % of Total | Income Taxes as % of Total | Other Taxes as % of Total |
|------|------|------|------|------|
| 1972 | 40.0 | 18.8 | 16.5 | 24.7 |
| 1977 | 37.5 | 17.6 | 20.7 | 24.2 |
| 1982 | 42.5 | 16.1 | 21.2 | 20.1 |
| 1987 | 37.7 | 17.3 | 21.9 | 23.1 |
| 1992 | 42.7 | 18.2 | 18.1 | 21.0 |
| 1993 | 41.3 | 15.5 | 23.4 | 19.8 |
| 1994 | 41.1 | 18.7 | 20.1 | 20.1 |
| 1995 | 28.0 | 25.0 | 25.1 | 21.8 |
| 1996 | 28.6 | 26.5 | 23.7 | 21.2 |
| 1997 | 29.0 | 26.8 | 24.1 | 20.2 |
| 1998 | 30.1 | 24.4 | 24.1 | 21.4 |
| 1999 | 29.5 | 24.2 | 25.0 | 21.4 |
| 2000 | 30.2 | 24.4 | 24.6 | 20.9 |

SOURCE: For 1992–2000: U.S. Bureau of the Census, *www.census.gov/govs/estimate.html* (various years). For years before 1992: U.S. Bureau of the Census, *Census of Government*, vol. 4, Government Finances, various years.

the system. In order to perform such an evaluation, it is necessary to have some criteria against which to judge the tax system. Some possible criteria for a desirable tax system are discussed in the next few paragraphs.

Before beginning that discussion, however, it is important to emphasize that the goal is *not* to

**FIGURE 25.3**

**Property Taxes and General Retail Sales Taxes as Percentage of Total State and Local Taxes in Michigan, 1991–92 to 1999–2000**

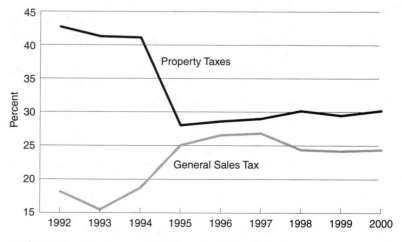

SOURCE: U.S. Bureau of the Census, *www.census.gov/govs/estimate.html* (various years).

identify an "ideal" tax system. Several criteria are discussed in the following, and they are often in conflict with one another. Therefore, a tax system that is most favored by someone with one set of values may not be favored by someone with a different set of values. Nevertheless, it is hoped that this discussion will provide a framework within which individuals will be able to make sounder judgments about the tax system.

### Raising Revenue (But Not Necessarily from Michigan Residents)

The first requirement of any revenue system is that it raise revenue. If not for the necessity to finance government expenditures, there would be little justification for most taxes.[21] However, there is no requirement that the taxes raised by state and local governments in Michigan have to be paid by Michigan residents.

If a government can arrange its tax system so that residents of other jurisdictions pay some of the taxes, it is said that the government is engaging in *tax exporting*. While tax exporting may not be a good thing for the nation as a whole, it can be an attractive alternative for a state or local government.

One example of tax exporting is that tourist destinations may rely heavily on retail sales taxes, in order to export a portion of their tax burden to nonresidents. For example, Florida, Hawaii, and Nevada are all tourist destinations. In each of these states, the general retail sales tax accounts for more than 35% of total state and local revenues, compared to about 24% in Michigan, and about 25% for the United States as a whole. However, Michigan is not a leading tourist destination.[22] Thus, in practice, it will be difficult to export a very large share of Michigan's tax burden to tourists.

However, there is another type of tax exporting that is readily available to state and local governments in any state, including Michigan. This second type of tax exporting arises from the fact that state and local income taxes and property taxes are deductible under the federal individual income tax. Thus, for Michigan residents who itemize deductions on their federal income tax returns, state and local income taxes and property taxes lead to a reduction in federal tax liability. Effectively, this leads to tax exporting.

Before the Tax Reform Act of 1986, federal income tax deductions were given for state and local

sales taxes, as well as for income and property taxes. However, the sales tax deduction was eliminated by the Tax Reform Act. This gave states the incentive to increase their reliance on income taxes and property taxes, and decrease their reliance on sales taxes. Ironically, Michigan has chosen to go in precisely the opposite direction. As a result of Proposal A and subsequent changes in Michigan tax law, Michigan has increased its sales tax and reduced its taxes on income and property. Because of the tax changes in Michigan during the last decade, the federal tax payments of Michigan taxpayers are greater than they would have been, by several hundred million dollars per year.

### Minimizing Administrative and Compliance Costs

*Administrative costs* are the costs incurred by government agencies, in order to collect tax revenues. Administrative costs include the expenses of operating the Bureau of Revenue in the Michigan Department of Treasury, as well as the revenue agencies of local governments. *Compliance costs* are the costs incurred by households and businesses, in order to obey the tax laws. These include the time costs of keeping records and filling out forms, as well as the money costs of buying tax software, hiring accountants and attorneys, and so on.

Administrative and compliance costs are true costs of the tax system. In other words, the real burden of the tax system on society includes not only the actual tax revenue raised, but also the administrative and compliance costs. Thus, all else equal, a reasonable goal of a tax system is to minimize these costs.

Several studies have attempted to estimate compliance costs, and they indicate that compliance costs may be as much as 5% or 10% of revenues. (For example, see Blumenthal and Slemrod [1992, 1993] and Slemrod and Sorum [1984].) In many cases, it is difficult to separate the compliance costs of federal taxes from the compliance costs of state and local taxes, since the record-keeping requirements are similar. Nevertheless, it is relatively safe to say that the tax system in Michigan generates administrative and compliance costs that are at least a few percent of revenues.

As mentioned earlier in this chapter, the Michigan individual income tax is "piggybacked" upon the federal individual income tax.[23] The starting point for the calculation of Michigan income tax is the taxpayer's Adjusted Gross Income, from the federal form 1040. Since taxpayers have to collect much of the same information to comply with the federal tax, the additional record-keeping burden of the Michigan tax is relatively small. However, the Michigan individual income tax does require several adjustments, so its compliance costs are not as low as they could be.

As discussed previously, when a tax has special exemptions, deductions, exclusions, and credits, we say that the tax suffers from base erosion. The net result of these tax preferences is to make the tax system substantially more complicated. Base erosion is therefore associated with high costs of administration and compliance. In other words, if we were to adopt a simple, more uniform tax structure, it would be possible to raise the same amount of revenue for a lower total cost to society, because the costs of administration and compliance could be reduced.

In the next section, we will see that base erosion is also costly in other ways.

## Minimizing Excess Burden

In the language of the public-finance economist, most taxes are *distortionary*, because they have an adverse effect on the allocation of resources. Distortionary taxes lead to an extra cost of the tax system, which is called *excess burden* or *deadweight loss*. The phrase "excess" burden indicates that the true cost of a tax is greater than the amount of revenue collected by the government. In this way, excess burden is similar to administrative costs and compliance costs. In the case of each of these, the true cost of taxes is greater than the actual tax revenue.

In the last few decades, economists have devoted a lot of attention to estimating the excess burden of the tax system. (For example, see Ballard, Shoven, and Whalley [1985a and 1985b].) The estimates cover a wide range, but it is very likely that the excess burdens are at least 5 or 10% of revenues, and perhaps far more. Thus, if we include administrative and compliance costs as well as excess burdens, the true cost of the tax system is substantially greater than the amount of tax revenue collected.

In the next few paragraphs, we will mention several issues associated with the excess burden of the state and local tax system in Michigan. The most important point is that the major taxes are badly eroded. Base erosion creates a discriminatory tax system, and this almost certainly means that the excess burden of the tax system is significantly larger than necessary.[24]

The Michigan Department of Treasury produces an explicit calculation of the amount of revenue that is lost as a result of the tax preferences in the state and local revenue systems. These revenue losses (State of Michigan, Department of Treasury [2002]) are called *tax expenditures*. The term "tax expenditures" indicates that, from the point of view of the budget deficit, there is no difference between a tax preference and an explicit expenditure.

The estimates of tax expenditures are not extremely precise, but they are probably good enough to give us a fair idea of the magnitude of the revenues that are lost because of tax preferences.[25] The Michigan Treasury Department's Tax Expenditure Appendix lists twenty-one tax expenditures associated with the property tax. The revenue loss from these tax preferences in fiscal year 2003 is estimated to be about $8.8 billion. No fewer than fifty-two tax expenditures are associated with the sales-and-use tax, and the estimated revenue loss from these tax preferences is about $8.2 billion. The individual income tax is associated with thirty-six tax expenditures, totaling about $5.8 billion. The Single Business Tax has twenty-eight tax expenditures, for a total revenue loss of about $1.4 billion.

When we add all of these together, along with assorted other tax expenditures associated with other parts of the tax system in Michigan, the treasury estimates a total tax expenditure of about $24.6 billion, from some 165 separate tax preferences.

The largest tax expenditures are shown in table 25.5. This table includes the thirty tax expenditures that are estimated to lead to revenue losses of at least $100 million each. Together, these thirty tax expenditures account for more than 80% of total estimated tax expenditures. In table 25.5, the tax expenditures are ranked by the size of the estimated revenue loss. The largest is the exemption of services from the sales tax.

As shown in table 25.1, the state government collected about $22.8 billion of taxes in 1999–2000, and local governments collected about $8.7 billion, for a total of about $31.5 billion. The estimated tax expenditures are about three-fourths as large as the revenues collected. If even a portion of the tax preferences were removed, it would be

## TABLE 25.5

**State and Local Tax Expenditures in Michigan, FY 2003 (Ranked by Size)**

| Tax Expenditure Item | Estimated Revenue Loss ($ millions) |
| --- | --- |
| Services exemption (sales tax) | 4,806 |
| Tax-exempt property (property tax) | 3,028 |
| Taxable value cap (property tax) | 2,380 |
| Adjustments to income (income tax) | 2,074 |
| Personal exemption (income tax) | 989 |
| Food exemption (sales tax) | 868 |
| Industrial processing exemption (sales tax) | 769 |
| Exclusion of employer contributions to pension plans (income tax) | 601 |
| Exclusion of employer contributions to insurance (income tax) | 594 |
| Homestead Property Tax credit (income tax) | 540 |
| Exemption for prescription drugs (sales tax) | 415 |
| Investment Tax Credit (SBT) | 397 |
| Exemption for industrial facilities development (property tax) | 330 |
| Tax-increment financing (property tax) | 270 |
| Exclusion of Social Security benefits (income tax) | 225 |
| Excess compensation reduction (SBT) | 188 |
| Exemption for nonprofit organizations (sales tax) | 181 |
| Nonresident reduced rate (city income tax) | 178 |
| Exemption for government and Red Cross (sales tax) | 163 |
| Gross receipts reduction (SBT) | 134 |
| Compensation exemption (SBT) | 132 |
| Individual Retirement Accounts (income tax) | 131 |
| Exemption for horticultural and agricultural products (sales tax) | 130 |
| Homestead exemption for farm property (property tax) | 130 |
| Exemption for vehicles and aircraft transfers (sales tax) | 125 |
| Exemption of air and water pollution control property (property tax) | 120 |
| Exclusion of gain on sale of primary residence (income tax) | 115 |
| Small Business Credit (SBT) | 115 |
| Exemption for residential utilities (sales tax) | 108 |
| Exclusion of interest on life-insurance savings (income tax) | 106 |
| TOTAL OF THESE ITEMS | 20,341 |
| TOTAL FOR ALL ESTIMATED TAX EXPENDITURES | 24,639 |

SOURCE: Michigan Department of Treasury, Executive Budget Tax Expenditure Appendix, Fiscal Year 2003.

possible to cut tax rates substantially, while raising just as much revenue as before. This could make for a more efficient tax system, that is, the excess burden of the tax system could be reduced. Depending on the details of the tax reform, the reduction in excess burden could be quite substantial.[26]

This is especially relevant in the current environment, in which the Single Business Tax is scheduled for elimination. The revenues raised by the SBT are much smaller than the tax expenditures associated with either the property tax, the income tax, or the sales tax. Thus, even modest progress in reducing tax expenditures would make it possible to eliminate the SBT, while still preserving the overall level of revenues, without raising any tax rates. A tax reform of this type would undoubtedly be associated with a substantial reduction in excess burden.

It would also be possible to *increase* the amount of tax revenue raised, even while tax rates are being *decreased*. If policy makers desire to increase tax revenues, it would be much more efficient to do so through the elimination of tax expenditures, rather than through raising tax rates.[27]

Another important efficiency issue is the choice between income taxes and consumption taxes. This is relevant for tax policy in Michigan, since the state government uses an income tax, and it also uses two broad taxes that could potentially be considered to be consumption taxes, namely, the general retail sales tax and the Single Business Tax.

The choice between income taxation and consumption taxation has been the subject of one of the most prominent debates in public economics in the last generation. Most research studies indicate that a *pure* consumption tax is more efficient than a *pure* income tax. In other words, these studies indicate that the excess burden of a pure consumption tax is less than the excess burden of a pure income tax that raises the same amount of revenue.[28]

However, it is difficult to render a clear judgment about the relative efficiency of the income tax, the sales tax, and the SBT. All three have numerous tax preferences. No comprehensive study has ever measured the excess burden of the extremely messy taxes that are actually used in Michigan. We can be certain that the income tax, the sales tax, and the SBT all have higher excess burdens than they would have if they were more uniform. Because of all of the tax preferences, it is not clear whether any of these taxes has an efficiency advantage over the others.

### Fairness

There is nearly universal agreement that, all else equal, it would be good for taxes to be distributed among the population in a way that is "fair." The difficulty is that different people may have dramatically different ideas about what is fair, and economists do not have any ironclad way to resolve these differences. However, we can provide a vocabulary for thinking about the issue, and we can make some statements about the distributional effects of different taxes.

*Horizontal Equity.* One notion of fairness is that similarly situated people should pay similar amounts of tax. If a tax system has this quality, it is said that the tax system is characterized by *horizontal equity*. Of course, no two individuals are identical in every way, so our judgments about horizontal equity must ultimately be based on some ideas about which distinctions are appropriate for tax policy, and which are not. Perhaps the best way to discuss horizontal equity is to give examples of tax laws that have been criticized on grounds that they are not horizontally equitable.

The property tax in Michigan is associated with several forms of horizontal inequity. First, Proposal A instituted a cap on the amount by which the taxable value of a property can increase in any one year. However, when the property is sold, it is reassessed at full market value. Thus, if one house has just been sold, but the house next door has been under the same ownership for many years, the house that has just been sold can have a significantly higher property tax assessment, even if the two houses have exactly the same market value.

The individual income tax in Michigan is also a source of horizontal inequity. The largest source of such inequity is the tax treatment of the elderly. Elderly persons receive additional exemptions and a more favorable Homestead Property Tax Credit. In addition, elderly persons are exempt from Michigan income tax on dividends, interest, Social Security income, and pension income.

This brief discussion has highlighted only a very few of the many instances of horizontal inequity in the Michigan revenue system. In fact, whenever there is erosion of the tax base, there is potential for horizontal inequity. By their very nature, tax preferences give favored treatment to some groups and not to others.

*Vertical Equity.* Horizontal equity has to do with the idea that similarly situated people should pay similar amounts of tax. On the other hand, *vertical equity* has to do with the idea that different people should pay different amounts of tax. Specifically, vertical equity is usually associated with the idea that those with higher incomes should pay higher taxes, because they have greater ability to pay.

Vertical equity is usually discussed in terms of the percentages of income that are paid in taxes by people at different income levels, rather than the absolute dollar amounts of taxes paid. When an increase in income is associated with an increase in the percentage of income that is paid in tax, it is said that the tax is *progressive.* When an increase in income is associated with a *decrease* in the percentage of income paid in tax, it is said that the tax is *regressive.* Finally, if the percentage of income paid in tax is constant across income levels, it is said that the tax is *proportional.*

*Distribution of the Property Tax across Income Groups. Tax incidence* is the phrase used by economists to describe who really bears the burden of a tax. The true economic burden of a tax is not necessarily borne by the group that has legal responsibility for paying the tax. For example, the true burden of the sales tax is probably borne mostly by consumers, even though the tax is collected from retail stores. Ultimately, tax incidence depends on the way in which buyers and sellers adjust to the tax.

The incidence of the property tax has been the subject of debate for many decades. One view is that the property tax acts like an excise tax on housing. As a result, according to this theory, the property tax is regressive, because the share of housing in the budget is larger for those with lower incomes. A competing view is that the property tax acts like a tax on capital. If so, then the property tax is progressive, because higher-income people have larger holdings of capital. The idea that the property tax acts as a tax on capital is probably the predominant view within the economics profession today. If this view is correct, then the property tax is a progressive source of revenue, at least over the short to medium run. Therefore, the reduced reliance on property taxes as a result of Proposal A would have the effect of reducing the overall progressivity of the Michigan revenue system, or increasing its overall regressivity.

*Distribution of the Income Tax across Income Groups.* The federal individual income tax has graduated marginal tax rates (that is, the tax rate on an additional dollar of taxable income is higher for those with higher incomes). Because of the graduated rates, the federal income tax is substantially progressive over a very wide range of incomes. Michigan's individual income tax does not have graduated marginal rates, and this puts limits on the progressivity of the Michigan income tax.

However, even though the Michigan income tax has a single flat rate on taxable income, the tax is *not* proportional. In fact, the Michigan income tax is quite progressive in the lower- and middle-income ranges, for two reasons. First, because of the personal exemptions, those with very low incomes do not pay any income tax at all. (However, the threshold at which low-income families begin to pay income tax is lower in Michigan than in most other states that levy an income tax. See Johnson et al. [2002].) Second, the Homestead Property Tax Credit is refundable, as is the smaller Home Heating Credit. Because of refundability, many low-income taxpayers actually receive a refund check from the State of Michigan. In other words, the net income tax payments by these taxpayers are negative.

Thus, on balance, the individual income tax in Michigan is progressive at low and middle incomes. Above incomes of $60,000 or so, the Michigan income tax is only slightly progressive. At higher incomes, the tax becomes nearly proportional.

Before we conclude our discussion of the distributional effects of the income tax, it is necessary to make one qualification. The individual income tax is levied on the income received during a particular year, and the discussion in the preceding paragraphs has been based on the one-year perspective. However, over the course of a lifetime, most individuals move through several different income classes. For example, most workers have large increases in their incomes from the beginning of their career through late middle age. In addition to this long-term variation in incomes, there is also short-term variation: In any year, some people have temporarily high incomes, and some people have temporarily low incomes. Over the course of a lifetime, these sources of variation tend to average out. As a result, if we take a lifetime perspective, the income tax is still progressive, but much less progressive than if we perform the calculations with annual data.[29]

*Distribution of the Sales Tax across Income Groups.* The retail sales tax is officially collected from retailers. However, the consensus among economists is that consumers ultimately bear the burden of retail sales taxes, in the form of higher prices.

A *uniform* general retail sales tax would be somewhat regressive. The reason for this is that a sales tax does not apply to saving. Since the percentage of income saved is higher for higher-income people, such a tax would be somewhat regressive.[30] However, the general retail sales tax is not a uniform tax on all retail sales. In Michigan, as in many other states, food purchases for home consumption are not subject to the sales tax. Since food is a larger share of the budget for those with lower incomes, the exclusion of food from the tax base will reduce the regressivity of the tax. However, it should be noted that the food exclusion is an inefficient method of reducing the regressivity of the sales tax. The high-income person's steak and artichokes are given the same favorable treatment as the poor person's ground beef and potatoes. An alternative would be to tax food, but to offset the regressivity in some other way, such as through more generous exemptions and credits in the income tax.

Services are also excluded from the sales tax base. Many services are more important to the budgets of higher-income individuals than to the budgets of those with low incomes. Therefore, the exclusion of services does *not* mitigate the regressivity of the sales tax in the same way as the exclusion of food. Overall, most studies suggest that the general retail sales tax is somewhat regressive.

*Distribution of the Single Business Tax across Income Groups.* A pure value-added tax is basically a tax on consumption. As such, a pure value-added tax (like a general retail sales tax) would be somewhat regressive, especially when viewed from an annual perspective. When viewed from a lifetime perspective, such a tax would still be slightly regressive, although it would be fairly close to proportional. Yet the Single Business Tax is not a pure value-added tax by any means. The actual SBT exempts small businesses. The distributional effect of this provision is difficult to assess, since it depends on whether people in different income classes consume the outputs of small businesses and large businesses in different proportions. The SBT is also eroded by a variety of other provisions. The SBT is probably not very far from proportional, but it is difficult to have great confidence in this assessment.

Before we leave the subject of the SBT and its effects on the distribution of income, one more point deserves emphasis. The SBT was born as a replacement for several taxes that were levied on businesses. Today, when the SBT is scheduled for elimination, there are some discussions of resurrecting a corporate income tax, or of replacing the SBT with some other constellation of business taxes. As a result, one could easily conclude that Michigan simply must have a business tax.

Indeed, the debate sometimes includes references to "business's fair share of the tax burden." However, from an economic perspective, these statements are meaningless. Only people pay taxes: Ultimately, the burden of business taxes must be borne by people. The burden may be borne by consumers, in the form of higher prices; by workers, in the form of lower wages; or by stockholders and other business owners, in the form of lower returns on investment.

In fact, there is substantial evidence that some business taxes are ultimately borne by workers. (For example, see Fullerton, King, Shoven, and Whalley [1981].) If a tax on business income leads to a reduction in the rate at which capital is accumulated, then there will eventually be less capital per worker. Less capital per worker will ultimately be reflected in lower wages. Thus, today's workers bear part of the burden of the business taxes that were levied a generation ago, in terms of lower wages. Similarly, the next generation of workers will bear a part of the burden of today's business taxes.

*Distribution of Other Taxes across Income Groups.* When a tax is levied on a specific activity, the distribution of the burden across income classes will depend on how the demand for that activity changes as we move up the income scale. Thus, cigarette taxes are fairly regressive, because cigarettes take up a larger share of the budgets of low-income households, on average. Taxes on alcoholic beverages are approximately proportional, because the percentage of income devoted to alcoholic beverages is fairly constant across income classes. On the other hand, the lottery tax is highly regressive, because lottery purchases are a much larger share of the budget for low-income people, on average.

Even if the tax on cigarettes were an *ad valorem* tax, it would be somewhat regressive. However, the tax is a unit tax, and this introduces another element of regressivity. A unit tax is a larger percentage of the sales price of a discount brand, and a smaller percentage of the sales price of a premium brand. Thus, the tax imposes a relatively larger burden on cheap cigarettes, and a relatively smaller burden on expensive cigarettes. Since higher-income smokers are more likely to buy premium brands, and low-income smokers are more likely to buy discount brands, this imparts a further element of regressivity to the tax. The same argument also applies to the unit taxes on alcoholic beverages. A unit tax is a larger percentage of the sales price of cheaper beers and wines,

and a smaller percentage of the sales price of fancier beers and wines. This additional element of regressivity would disappear if the taxes were levied on an *ad valorem* basis.

*Changes in the Distribution of the Tax Burden over Time.* The most progressive element of the state and local revenue system is the individual income tax. The most regressive elements are the taxes on consumption, including the general retail sales tax, the tobacco taxes, and the implicit tax on lotteries. In recent years, Michigan (like many other states) has reduced its reliance on income taxes and increased its reliance on the regressive sources of revenue. Thus, Michigan has moved in a more regressive direction.[31]

## Revenue Stability

Federal tax revenues tend to increase rapidly during an economic expansion, but they tend to fall during a recession. Macroeconomists have long admired this feature of the federal tax system. When tax revenues shrink during a recession, the economy receives a stimulus. Thus, the business cycle is cushioned, and it is said that the federal tax system provides an "automatic stabilizer."

The federal government's tax system is able to function as an automatic stabilizer because there is no requirement of a balanced federal budget. When federal taxes shrink during a recession, there is an increase in the federal deficit (or, less commonly, a decrease in the federal surplus). However, most states, including Michigan, have a constitutional requirement of a balanced budget. Thus, while fluctuating revenues are an advantage for the federal government, they can cause serious problems for a state government. If state revenues are falling, then it is usually necessary to cut spending or increase taxes. Neither of these is a painless alternative. Consequently, it may be desirable to have revenue sources that are relatively stable.

Two aspects of the Michigan revenue system are notable in this regard. First, the Single Business Tax is more stable than the corporate income tax that it replaced in 1975 (see chapter 29). The fiscal difficulties that the State of Michigan is currently experiencing might well be even worse if we still had a corporate income tax.

Second, as mentioned previously, the individual income tax in Michigan is levied as a flat percentage of taxable income. In most other states that have an individual income tax, there are graduated marginal tax rates. In a state with a system of graduated marginal income-tax rates, people are pushed into higher tax brackets when their incomes increase, and they fall into lower tax brackets when their incomes fall. Under this type of graduated income tax structure, revenues will be less stable than under the flat rate used in Michigan.[32]

### Earmarking

In the preceding paragraphs, we have discussed the issue of revenue stability. A related issue is the degree to which revenues are dedicated, or "earmarked," for specific purposes. An important trend in recent years in Michigan has been an increase in earmarking. Several of the tax changes in Proposal A involved earmarking. The recent increase in the tobacco taxes produced additional earmarking. The rate reductions in the individual income tax also involve earmarking. On the other hand, the intangibles tax, the estate tax, and the Single Business Tax are among the few taxes with no earmarking, but these either have been repealed or are scheduled for repeal.

When one set of funds is earmarked, it may still be possible to offset the earmarking by using other funds for other purposes. However, when larger and larger shares of state revenues are earmarked, there may be a reduction in the government's flexibility. The recent increases in earmarking may have led to a situation in which it is difficult for the state government to respond flexibly to changing circumstances. See Drake (2002) for discussion of some issues relating to earmarking.

### Conclusions

In this chapter we have introduced some of the broad features of the system by which revenues are generated for governments in Michigan. All told, the state and local governments received more than $70 billion in revenues 1999–2000. Even if the revenues from insurance trusts are excluded, the total is still about $58 billion. About $10 billion of these revenues came in the form of grants from the federal government. About $16 billion came from a remarkably wide variety of charges, fees, and miscellaneous revenues. The remaining revenues were in the form of taxes. The state government collected about $22.8 billion in taxes in 1999–2000. The individual income tax and the sales tax are the largest sources of tax revenue for the state government. Local governments collected about $8.7 billion in taxes in 1999–2000. The overwhelming majority of these local tax revenues are from property taxes.

In recent years, the taxes collected by state and local governments in Michigan have amounted to more than $3,000 per person, or a bit more than 11% of personal income. These amounts put Michigan somewhat above the average tax level for the fifty states.

In many ways, Michigan's tax system is fairly similar to the tax systems used in most other states. Most state governments, like Michigan's, rely a great deal on income taxes and sales taxes, and the local governments in most states rely heavily on property taxes. However, Michigan's tax system does have some features that are not commonly found in other states. For example, Michigan's individual income tax is levied at a flat rate on taxable income, whereas most states have a system of graduated marginal tax rates. Another unusual feature of the income tax in Michigan is its extraordinary generosity toward the elderly. Because of special exemptions, special credits, and special exclusions, elderly people pay very little income tax in Michigan.

Yet another unusual feature of Michigan's tax system is the Single Business Tax. Most other states have a corporation income tax, but Michigan's corporation tax was among several taxes that were replaced by the Single Business Tax in 1975. In principle, the SBT is a kind of value-added tax. In practice, however, the SBT is complicated by a wide variety of exclusions, credits, and special computations. One advantage of the SBT is that it generates a revenue stream that is less variable over time than a corporation income tax would be. In any event, however, the SBT is currently scheduled to be eliminated in 2010.

In the 1990s, the tax system in Michigan underwent a number of important changes. The two biggest events were the implementation of Proposal A in 1994, and the passage in 1999 of a series of rate cuts in the individual income tax and the Single Business Tax. As a result, there have been decreases in property taxes, income taxes, and the Single Business Tax. Some of those revenue reductions have been offset by increases in retail sales taxes and cigarette taxes. (Michigan's cigarette taxes are now among the highest in the nation.)

A common theme of most of these changes is that they have moved the tax system in a more regressive direction. The trend toward regressivity also includes the state lottery. The lottery is the most regressive revenue source of all. As a result of these changes, the portion of the state and local tax burden that is borne by high-income households has been reduced, and the burden on low-income households has been increased.

During the last few decades, another theme in Michigan's tax system has been the increase in tax preferences, which are sometimes called tax expenditures. The system has dozens of exclusions, deductions, and credits. Many of these tax preferences are the result of good intentions. Nevertheless, they create a tax system that is deficient in several ways, when compared with a more uniform tax system. The current tax system is more inefficient, more costly to comply with, and more costly to administer than it would be if it were more uniform. The current system also discriminates among taxpayers in a variety of ways: It favors the old over the young; it favors agriculture over other sectors of the economy; it favors those who buy services over those who buy goods; and it favors homeowners who have lived in the same place for many years over those who have recently moved. These are only a few of the ways in which the tax system concentrates its burden on certain groups, while excusing others.

On the basis of the issues raised in this chapter, it is possible to consider a variety of tax reforms. One of the simplest reforms to consider would be to change the taxes on tobacco products and alcoholic beverages from unit taxes to *ad valorem* taxes. This would reduce the regressivity of the taxes, and it would relieve the necessity to make frequent changes in the tax rates in order to offset the effects of inflation.

Another possibility would be to export more of the Michigan tax burden onto the residents of other states. This could be accomplished by increasing the income tax and property tax, which are deductible from the federal individual income tax. Of course, this change is exactly opposite to the changes that have actually been undertaken in recent years. Based on recent experience, it appears that the people of Michigan are sufficiently eager for reductions in the income tax and the property tax that they are willing to send hundreds of millions of additional tax dollars to the federal government each year.

The tax-reform issue that has emerged most often in this chapter has to do with the erosion of the tax base. Virtually all of the important sources of tax revenue in Michigan are eroded by deductions, exclusions, and credits. As mentioned previously, many of these tax expenditures are well intentioned. In many instances, however, the net effect of the tax breaks is to make the tax system more complicated, more inefficient, and more inequitable.

The rallying cry for generations of tax economists has been "broaden the base and lower the rates." If taxes were applied more uniformly, it would be possible to reduce the tax rates while still collecting the same amount of revenue as before. This is especially noteworthy in light of the scheduled phase-out of the Single Business Tax. If policy makers desire to replace the revenues that were previously collected by the SBT, they should consider closing some of the tax preferences that exist elsewhere in the tax system, rather than raising tax rates. Even if the SBT is not replaced, it is worth considering a program of base-broadening tax reforms.

The obstacles to tax reform are primarily political, rather than economic. The groups that benefit from tax preferences tend to be acutely aware of their fortunate situation, and they are often well organized and determined to resist any tax reform. On the other hand, average taxpayers (who end up footing the bill for the tax preferences) tend to be organized poorly.

It remains to be seen whether it is possible to muster the political will to reform the tax system. For more details on many of the issues raised in this chapter, the reader is invited to read on to chapters 26 through 33.

■

### REFERENCES

Atkinson, Anthony B., and Nicholas H. Stern. 1974. Pigou, taxation, and public goods. *Review of Economic Studies* 41:119–28.

Auerbach, Alan J., and Laurence J. Kotlikoff. 1987. Dynamic fiscal policy. Cambridge, England: Cambridge University Press.

Ballard, Charles L. 1990. On the specification of simulation models for evaluating income and consumption taxes. In *Heidelberg Congress on taxing consumption*, edited by Manfred Rose. Berlin: Springer-Verlag.

———. 2002. Michigan's tax climate: A new perspective. Prepared for the Michigan Chamber Foundation.

Ballard, Charles L., and Don Fullerton. 1992. Distortionary taxes and the provision of public goods. *Journal of Economic Perspectives* 6:117–31.

Ballard, Charles L., John B. Shoven, and John Whalley. 1985a. General equilibrium computations of the marginal welfare costs of taxes in the United States. *American Economic Review* 75:128–38.

———. 1985b. The total welfare cost of the United States tax system: A general equilibrium approach. *National Tax Journal* 38:125–40.

Blumenthal, Marsha, and Joel Slemrod. 1992. The compliance cost of the U.S. individual income tax: A second look after tax reform. *National Tax Journal* 45:185–202.

———. 1993. The compliance costs of the U.S. corporate income tax for large corporations. *Proceedings of the 86th annual conference of the National Tax Association*. Washington, D.C.: National Tax Association.

Boskin, Michael J., Ellen R. Dulberger, Robert J. Gordon, Zvi Griliches, and Dale W. Jorgenson. 1998. Consumer prices, the Consumer Price Index, and the cost of living. *Journal of Economic Perspectives* 12:3–26.

Bruce, Donald, and William F. Fox. 2000. E-commerce in the context of declining state sales tax bases. *National Tax Journal* 53:1373–90.

Citizens Research Council of Michigan. 2003. Outline of the Michigan tax system. Available at *http://www.crcmich.org/TaxOutline/index.html.*

Davies, James, France St.-Hilaire, and John Whalley. 1984. Some calculations of lifetime tax incidence. *American Economic Review* 74:633–49.

Diamond, Peter A., and James A. Mirrlees. 1971. Optimal taxation and public production I: production efficiency and II: tax rules. *American Economic Review* 61:8–27 and 261–78.

Drake, Douglas C. 2002. A review and analysis of Michigan tax policies impacting K–12 finances. Report prepared for Michigan Association of School Administrators, Michigan Association of School Business Officials, and Michigan Association of School Boards. Available at *http://www.gomasa.org/Executive_Summary.pdf.*

Fullerton, Don, and Diane Lim Rogers. 1993. *Who bears the lifetime tax burden?* Washington, D.C.: Brookings Institution.

Fullerton, Don, A., Thomas King, John B. Shoven, and John Whalley. 1981. Corporate tax integration in the United States: A general equilibrium approach. *American Economic Review* 71:677–91.

Illinois Tax Foundation. 2002. 2002 Michigan tax climate. 6th ed. Springfield, Ill.: Illinois Tax Foundation.

Johnson, Nicholas, Kevin Carey, Michael Mazerov, Elizabeth McNichol, Daniel Tenny, and Robert Zahradnik. 2002. State income tax burdens on low-income families in 2001. Center on Budget and Policy Priorities. Available at *http://www.cbpp.org/2–26–02sfp.htm.*

McIntyre, Robert S., Robert Denk, Norton Francis, Matthew Gardner, Will Gomaa, Fiona Hsu, and Richard Sims. 2003. Who pays? A distributional analysis of the tax systems in all 50 states, 2d ed. Washington, D.C.: Institute on Taxation and Economic Policy.

McLure, Charles E., Jr. 1999. Electronic commerce and the U.S. sales tax: A challenge to American federalism. *International Tax and Public Finance* 6:193–224.

Menchik, Paul L., and Martin David. 1983. Income distribution, lifetime savings, and bequests. *American Economic Review* 83:672–90.

Poterba, James M. 1989. Lifetime incidence and the distributional burden of excise taxes. *American Economic Review* 79:325–30.

Samuelson, Paul A. 1954. The pure theory of public expenditure. *Review of Economics and Statistics* 36:387–89.

Shoven, John B. 1976. The incidence and efficiency effects of taxes on income from capital. *Journal of Political Economy* 84:1261–83.

Slemrod, Joel. 1990. Optimal taxation and optimal tax systems. *Journal of Economic Perspectives* 4:157–78.

Slemrod, Joel, and Nikki Sorum. 1984. The compliance cost of the U.S. individual income tax system. *National Tax Journal* 37:461–74.

State of Michigan, Department of Treasury. 2002. Executive budget: Tax expenditure appendix, fiscal year 2003. Available at *http://www.michigan.gov/treasury.*

State of Michigan, Department of Treasury, Office of Revenue and Tax Analysis. 2001. Tax revenue loss estimates for consumer remote sales. Available at *www.michigan.gov/documents/RemoteSales_2001_3174_7.pdf.*

State of Michigan, Senate Fiscal Agency. 2003. Michigan state government taxes, FY 1985–86 to FY 2001–02. Updated January 2003. Available at *http://www.senate.state.mi.us/sfa/Revenue/MichiganStateGovernmentTaxes.PDF.*

State of Michigan, Senate Fiscal Agency. Various years. Monthly revenue report. Available at *http://www.senate.state.mi.us/sfa/Publications/EconIndMonthRev/econindmonthrev.html.*

U.S. Department of Commerce, Bureau of Economic Analysis. 2003. Chain-type quantity and price indexes for personal consumption expenditures by major type of product. Table 7.4 of national income and product accounts tables. Revised 30 January 2003. Available at *http://www.bea.gov/bea/dn/ nipaweb/SelectTable.asp?Selected=N#S7*.

U.S. Department of Commerce, Bureau of the Census. 2002a. State and local government finances by level of government and by state: various years. Revised 12 December 2002. Available at *http://www.census .gov/govs/www/estimate.html*.

——. 2002b. State population estimates: April 1, 2000 to July 1, 2002. Revised 27 December 2002. Available at *http://eire.census.gov/popest/data/ states/tables/ST-EST2002-01.php*.

——. 2002c. Time series of intercensal estimates by county. Revised 23 May 2002. Available at *http://eire.census.gov/popest/data/counties/tables/ CO-EST2001-12.php*.

U.S. Department of Labor, Bureau of Labor Statistics. 2003. Consumer price index: All urban consumers. Available at *http://stats.bls.gov/cpi/home.htm*.

Wedeland, Mike. 2003. Net shoppers' tax-free days nearly gone. *Detroit News and Free Press*. 8 February, 1A.

## NOTES

The author thanks Doug Drake, Ron Fisher, and Liz Gerber for helpful comments on an earlier draft. In addition, the author thanks Paul Courant, Scott Darragh, Naomi Feldman, Sue Fino, Jeff Guilfoyle, Mark Haas, Howard Heideman, Jim Hines, Tricia Kinley, Larry Martin, Paul Menchik, Joel Slemrod, Rich Studley, and Jay Wortley, all of whom provided valuable information and insightful discussions. However, any errors are the sole responsibility of the author.

1. These data include virtually all of the funds that flow into the treasuries of state and local governments, with the exception of bond proceeds. For a discussion of bonds, see chapter 30.

   The data shown in table 25.1 and figures 25.1 and 25.2 were compiled by the Bureau of the Census, and were taken from *http://www.census .gov/govs/estimate/00sl23mi.html*. The advantage of the Census data is that they are available in the same format for all fifty states and the District of Columbia, which greatly facilitates interstate comparisons. Also, they bring together information for states and information for local governments in a single consistent data set. Not surprisingly, however, one disadvantage of the census data is that it usually takes more than two years for them to be made available. Thus, figures 25.1 and 25.2 and table 25.1 include data for 1999–2000, whereas data

for Michigan's *state* government (but not for local governments as a group) are available for 2000–1 and 2001–2. There were no fundamental changes in the *structure* of the Michigan revenue system between 1999–2000 and 2001–2. However, the fiscal situation changed considerably over this period, partly because of tax-rate reductions, and partly because of a pronounced slowdown in the economy. It should also be noted that there are minor differences between the data presented here, and the data available from the State of Michigan. However, those differences are sufficiently small that they do not change the interpretation of the data.

2. It is noteworthy that the "Other Revenues" categories are rather substantial, both in figure 25.1 and figure 25.2. This is an indication of the fact that the state and local governments generate revenue from a very wide range of sources. See table 25.1 for some additional detail.

3. Only twenty-two cities in Michigan have a city income tax. More than 60% of the revenue from these taxes is collected in the City of Detroit. (See State of Michigan, Department of Treasury [2002].)

4. A wealth of information is available at the census web site, *www.census.gov*. The population estimates for recent years for the fifty states and the District of Columbia were taken from *http://eire .census.gov/popest/data/states/tables/ST-EST2002-01 .php*.

5. Many economists have wrestled with the question of the optimal level of government expenditure. A famous example is Paul Samuelson (1954), but Samuelson did not consider the effects of distortionary taxes. Anthony Atkinson and Nicholas Stern (1974) were among the first to expand the theory to consider the effects of taxes in a systematic way. Their results indicate that the optimal level of expenditure is often (but not always) reduced when we take distortionary taxes into account. For a discussion of some related issues, see Charles Ballard and Don Fullerton (1992). In practice, it is difficult to calculate the optimal level of government expenditure with precision. Thus, reasonable people can disagree about the optimal amount of government expenditure.

6. For the per capita calculations, we use the updated population estimates for states, for 1 July of each year except 2000, for which data for 1 April were used. For the 1990s, these are slightly different from earlier population estimates. This is because the 2000 census data reveal that the population had grown more rapidly than had previously been thought. The Census Bureau has now gone back

and adjusted the population estimates for the "intercensal" years between 1990 and 2000. These figures were found at *http://eire.census.gov/popest/data/counties/tables/CO-EST2001-12.php.*

7. From 1972 to 2000, the national Consumer Price Index rose by 312%, and the Detroit CPI rose by 304%. The Personal Consumption Expenditures deflator rose by only 255% over the same period. Thus, the rate of increase of the CPI was greater than the rate of increase of the PCE deflator by more than one-half of one percentage point per year.

8. The full-scale Census of Governments is taken every five years. From 1981–82 to 1991–92, the data are shown for the years that correspond to a Census of Governments. The data are then shown annually for the years from 1991–92 to 1999–2000.

9. For details, readers are referred to the Senate Fiscal Agency web site. For example, *http://www.senate.state.mi.us/sfa/Revenue/MichiganStateGovernment Taxes.PDF,* and *http://www.senate.state.mi.us/sfa/Publications/EconIndMonthRev/econindmonthrev.html.*

10. The government of the District of Columbia performs a number of functions that are typically handled by state governments, as well as a number of functions that are typically handled by local governments. Thus, the only appropriate comparison is with the combined level of state and local taxes for the other states, and that is the comparison provided here. Nevertheless, the District of Columbia is obviously unusual in several respects, and comparisons should be made with caution.

11. See Ballard (2002) for more comparisons of this type.

12. This trend is very likely to continue. The data presented here were collected *before* Michigan raised its tax rate on cigarettes from $0.75 per pack to $1.25 per pack in 2002.

13. A very thorough description of the revenue trends and historical background for state and local revenue sources can be found in the "Outline of the Michigan Tax System," by the Citizens Research Council of Michigan, at *http://www.crcmich.org/TaxOutline/index.html.* In addition, "2002 Michigan Tax Climate," published by the Illinois Tax Foundation, includes many detailed comparisons among Michigan and other states. Other excellent sources of data and information on the Michigan tax system include the Senate Fiscal Agency, which provides data tables at *http://www.senate.state.mi.us/sfa/Revenue,* as well as the Michigan Department of Treasury, at *http://www.michigan.gov/treasury.*

14. See chapter 28 for a detailed discussion of these special rules.

15. The following states have no individual income tax: Alaska, Florida, Nevada, South Dakota, Texas, Washington, and Wyoming.

16. The recent changes in the tax rate are nothing new. When Michigan's individual income tax was established in 1967, the rate was 2.6%. It was raised to 3.9% in 1971 and to 4.6% in 1975. During the fiscal crisis of the early 1980s and its aftermath, the rate was changed five times, finally returning to 4.6% in 1986. In 1994, the rate was reduced to 4.4%, as part of the package of tax changes contained in Proposal A.

17. The following states have no sales tax: Alaska, Delaware, Montana, New Hampshire, and Oregon. Among the states that do have a sales tax, many allow counties and/or municipalities to collect some sales tax, in addition to the state sales tax. However, this practice is not followed in Michigan.

18. The Office of Revenue and Tax Analysis of Michigan's Department of Treasury (2001) estimates that the tax revenue losses from consumer remote sales (including mail-order and Internet sales) were about $187 million in 1999–2000, and that they will grow to about $349 million by 2004–05. The portion associated with electronic commerce is expected to grow rapidly. However, in 2003, several large retailers announced that they would begin to collect state sales tax on their online sales. See Mike Wedeland (2003).

19. The SBT replaced a corporate income tax, a local personal property tax on business inventories, a corporate franchise "fee" based on the net worth of the corporation, and several smaller taxes.

20. From the standpoint of economic efficiency, this is a major advantage for the SBT, when compared to a tax on corporate income. Economists have long recognized that a great deal of damage can be done to the economy when a tax discriminates by applying only to the corporate sector and not to the rest of the economy. (For example, see Shoven [1976] and Fullerton, King, Shoven, and Whalley [1981].) By applying to both corporations and other enterprises, the SBT has the potential to avoid this damage. Unfortunately, much of the potential efficiency advantage of the SBT is probably lost because of the many special provisions that have eroded the SBT over the years.

21. Most taxes do damage to the allocation of resources in the economy. As a result, most taxes generate "excess burden" or "deadweight loss," which means that the true cost to society of these taxes is greater than the amount of revenue collected for the government. Without a requirement to raise revenue, it

is difficult to justify taxes that generate deadweight loss (such as individual income taxes, sales taxes, business taxes, and property taxes). However, some taxes may actually improve the allocation of resources in the economy. (In other words, they may have negative excess burden.) Examples include taxes on tobacco products and alcoholic beverages. Thus, the case for corrective taxes on alcohol and tobacco does not rest quite so heavily upon the need to raise revenue. A similar argument can be made for taxes on industrial pollution, although these have not been used nearly as widely as taxes on alcohol and tobacco.

22. See chapter 22 for a detailed discussion of Michigan's tourism industry.

23. Some form of piggybacking is used by all of the states that levy an income tax. However, the details differ from state to state. The simplest procedure is to assign state income tax liability as a percentage of federal liability, but this is used in only North Dakota, Rhode Island, and Vermont.

24. The theory of optimal taxation indicates that uniform taxes are not necessarily the best. (For example, see Diamond and Mirrlees [1971] and Slemrod [1990].) However, Michigan's highly discriminatory tax system does not appear to be motivated by optimal tax theory. Rather, the system has grown up in piecemeal fashion over the years, in response to political pressures.

25. The tax-expenditure calculations in Michigan use the same assumptions that are employed by the federal government in its tax-expenditure budget. First, it is assumed that the removal of a tax expenditure would not lead to any changes in behavior. Second, it is assumed that the various tax expenditures are independent of each other. Finally, it is assumed that the elimination of tax expenditures would not have any effects on overall macroeconomic conditions. The first of these assumptions is the most problematic, and yet, even though the tax-expenditure budget uses assumptions that are not quite realistic, it probably provides a good first approximation.

26. However, it should be noted that some of the items that are classified as tax expenditures actually enhance efficiency. For example, deductions or credits associated with business investment in the Single Business Tax help to offset the tendency of the tax system to retard economic growth. Also, in the retail sales tax, taxes on business-to-business sales will tend to harm the efficiency of the tax system. For discussion of these issues, see chapters 27 and 29.

27. See Drake (2002) for a discussion of base erosion of the revenue sources that are used to finance public schools in Michigan.

28. For comparisons of income taxes and consumption taxes, see Auerbach and Kotlikoff (1987). However, it is important to note that the efficiency advantage of a consumption tax is not necessarily huge. The streets won't be paved with gold under either tax system. See Ballard (1990).

29. For discussion of these issues, see Davies, St.-Hilaire, and Whalley (1984) and Fullerton and Rogers (1993).

30. In the previous section, it was pointed out that things tend to average out over the course of a lifetime. Consequently, the income tax is less progressive when we take a lifetime perspective than when we look at annual data. The same argument applies (in reverse) to a tax on consumption, like a retail sales tax. The sales tax is less regressive when we take a lifetime perspective. For more discussion of this issue, see Poterba (1989). However, even over the course of a lifetime, the sales tax is not likely to be completely proportional. See Menchik and David (1983).

31. McIntyre et al. (2003) provide comparisons of the distributional effects of the tax systems in the fifty states. Their results should be treated with caution, because some of their assumptions appear to overstate the regressivity of state and local tax systems. Nevertheless, it is interesting to note that their calculations show Michigan to be one of the ten most regressive states in the country.

32. This does not imply that the income tax is an especially stable source of revenue. Its revenues do vary over the business cycle. The point is merely that a tax with a flat rate is less volatile than one with graduated rates.

# 26

# Michigan's Personal Income Tax

*Paul L. Menchik*

## Introduction

Michigan's personal income tax, along with the state's retail sales tax, represents the strongest financial pillar in Michigan's state revenue system (see table 26.1). The income tax generated $7.3 billion in fiscal year 2001, which amounts to over 32% of state tax revenues.[1] The income tax supplies approximately 50% of General Fund revenues. This far outstrips the number two general revenue source—the Single Business Tax—which provides 20% of General Fund revenues. (The retail sales tax, which is largely earmarked for the School Aid Fund, provides only 14% of General Fund revenues). It is interesting that something as important as the income tax is in fiscal terms something of a "Johnny-come-lately" tax for Michigan, having been adopted only in 1967, as compared, say, to the retail sales tax, which dates back to 1932. The growth in importance of Michigan's income tax mirrors a national trend, one in which forty-three states and the District of Columbia have adopted some type of income tax.[2] One possible reason for the growth in importance of the income tax among states is that it is viewed as an "equitable" tax, since income is a measure of a household's ability to pay taxes.[3] Another possibility is that the presence of the federal income tax has had the indirect effect of spawning growth of state income taxes. Two reasons for this could be (a) the relatively low administrative cost of adding a state income tax which "piggybacks" (by employing a similar tax base) on the federal tax, and (b) the deductibility provision that enables federal income tax payers to "export" part of their state income tax obligation to Washington, D.C.

In any case, in this chapter we analyze Michigan's income tax, starting with a statement of the three general principles of taxation. Next we focus on the actual details of the income tax, keeping in mind the possible trade-off among these principles. Michigan, unlike most states, employs a "flat-rate," not a graduated, income tax. Michigan's income tax is made mildly "progressive" by its personal exemptions and its credits. However, some of the factors that augment progressivity create other problems, such as inefficiencies, inequities, and complexities. Using panel data provided by the Michigan Department of Treasury, we analyze the distribution of the burden of Michigan's income tax across taxpayers. Next we consider a host of policy issues connected with Michigan's income tax, such as erosion of the tax base over time, the implications in tax design of federal deductibility, interstate comparison of state income taxes, and finally relative tax treatment of senior citizens. While many states have instituted some form of preferential treatment of sources of income

**TABLE 26.1**

**Income Taxes as Percentage of Total Taxes and Total Revenue in Michigan, 1990–2000**

|                                | FY 1990 | FY 1991 | FY 1992 | FY 1993 | FY 1994 | FY 1995 | FY 1996 | FY 1997 | FY 1998 | FY 1999 | FY 2000 |
|--------------------------------|---------|---------|---------|---------|---------|---------|---------|---------|---------|---------|---------|
| Income tax as % of total taxes | 35.3%   | 35.1%   | 34.9%   | 35.4%   | 31.8%   | 29.5%   | 30.1%   | 31.3%   | 31.3%   | 32.2%   | 31.9%   |
| Income tax as % of total revenue | 24.1%  | 22.3%   | 21.7%   | 21.5%   | 20.0%   | 19.8%   | 19.8%   | 20.8%   | 21.2%   | 21.9%   | 21.2%   |

SOURCE: State of Michigan (2001) Executive Budget, Fiscal Year 2001.

received by seniors, Michigan has done so to an exceptional degree and appears to be out of step with the rest of the nation. This practice has created a host of inequities, inefficiencies, and complexities and will become increasingly difficult to maintain as the population of the state ages.

## Principles of Taxation

Tax economists have come to view the trinity of equity, efficiency, and simplicity as the standards for the evaluation of tax systems.

## Equity

Equity has two stripes, horizontal and vertical. The former deals with the question of whether "equals are treated equally," that is, whether those taxpayers equally able to pay taxes are required to do so, or whether there are there gross disparities in their tax obligations. While it seems obvious that a fair tax system would avoid large disparities in treatment, it is not obvious how one would conclude that two taxpayers are, in fact, equally able to pay. Measured income certainly could be employed, but so could other indicators of financial well-being. Second, if income is to be used, what is the appropriate accounting period over which it is to be measured? Should it be measured by monthly income, annual income, the average of multiyear income, or even lifetime income? Furthermore, income is a measure of outcome, and one could argue that the effort required to earn one's income should also be taken into account. Concerns about horizontal inequity can be a useful bar to certain types of egregious discrimination, such as that between taxpayers of different eye colors or skin colors. However, this standard becomes less clear when it comes to differences in tax treatment according to the choices of goods consumed, or by differences in age.

The concept of vertical equity addresses the

notion of fairness in tax obligation across income categories. Economists in their role as economists are not qualified to conclude that one tax system is more vertically equitable than another. We are, however, qualified to present distributional analyses of how a tax falls across income groups. Distributional analyses of tax systems often include the terms *progressive, proportional,* and *regressive.* These terms refer to the change in the ratio of tax paid to an appropriate tax base, usually income, as we compare it across income levels. If the ratio, generally referred to as *average tax rate* (or ATR), rises with income, the tax is said to be progressive.[4] Alternatively, if ATR remains constant, the tax is said to be proportional, and if the ATR falls with increasing income, it is considered regressive. Hence, a tax in which every taxpayer remits the same absolute amount-the so-called poll or head tax-would be highly regressive, since the tax as proportion of income would fall markedly as one moved up the income scale.

The conventional wisdom is that the retail sales tax is regressive, since the proportion of one's income consumed tends to vary inversely with income. This conventional wisdom needs elaboration, however, for two reasons. First, while general consumption falls as a share of income as income increases, general consumption is not what is subject to tax under retail sales taxation. Only certain goods, and no services, are included in Michigan's retail sales tax base, so the tax is distributed proportionally to consumption of taxed goods. The study completed many years ago by Blume (1982) found that in Michigan the share of taxed goods falls with income, which therefore implies a degree of regressivity. Second, many economists like to consider tax incidence over a longer period of account than a one-year "snapshot"; that is, they favor a "time-exposure" or multiyear approach to the snapshot. Their view is that income averaged over several years is a more meaningful representation of a taxpayer's economic position than is a one-year reading. The time-exposure approach would tend to mute to some degree the regressivity of the retail sales tax (see, for example, Fullerton and Rogers 1994 and Poterba 1989).[5] Whether or not consumption taxation approaches proportionality in the limiting case of the lifetime is very much an open question and hinges, in part, on the share of one's earnings bequeathed to one's heirs. If rich taxpayers bequeath a larger proportion of their lifetime resources to their heirs than others, even a lifetime accounting period will not make consumption taxation proportional.[6]

The income tax is often thought of as a progressive tax, with the tax share increasing with ability to pay. However, this view requires elaboration as well. The incidence of an income tax by income level depends on three characteristics: the rate structure, the personal exemption level, and other subtractions-deductions, exclusions, exemptions, and credits incorporated in the tax. The federal government and most states employ a graduated rate structure, with the rate of tax on the last dollar of income—the so-called marginal tax rate (MTR)—increasing with income. This feature most certainly results in an ATR that increases with income, which fits the definition of progressivity. However, an income tax can have a constant MTR and still be progressive, if some amount of income is exempt from taxation. That is because the proportion of income subject to the constant (or *flat*) tax rate rises with income, and so must the average tax rate.

Michigan's income tax is such a tax. It features a constant marginal tax rate (in 2001 it was 4.2%) and rather generous personal exemptions ($2,900 per person in 2001), which impart progressivity. Note that if there were no personal exemptions (or other subtractions) the constant MTR would result in a proportional income tax, rather than a progressive one. Hence, the smaller the personal exemption levels, other things being the same, the less progressive the tax.

As an example, consider three families of four persons, one with an income of $11,600, the second with an income of $35,000, and the third with an income of $100,000. With personal exemptions of $2,900 per person, a family of four would have total exemptions of ($2,900 × 4) = $11,600, so that any such family with an income equal to $11,600 or less would pay no tax. Under a flat rate tax of 4.2%, modified by only the personal exemptions, the average tax rates paid by the three families would be 0%, 2.8%, and 3.7%, respectively. This is clearly a progressive tax structure. If the exemptions were halved, the ATRs would be 2.1%, 3.5%,

and 3.95%, respectively. In the second case, the income tax remains progressive, to be sure, with the ATRs increasing with income, but the increase is far more gradual than in the first case. Finally, consider the limiting case in which the exemption is zero. In that case, all three ATRs are constant, and the income tax would be proportional rather than progressive.

The distributional effects of an income tax are also influenced by all subtractions from income-exemptions, deductions, and exclusions, as well as tax credits. An exclusion is a component of one's income that is never counted as *taxable* income. A deduction is an expenditure chosen by the taxpayer that reduces his or her taxable income. Exemptions are amounts by which certain taxpayers are allowed to reduce their taxable income (often based upon family size and composition). The distributional effects of each of these depend on how they vary as a proportion of income as one moves up the income scale. If the subtraction as a proportion of income falls with increasing income, as it does in the case of personal exemptions, the effect is progressive. Alternatively, if the proportion rises, the effect is regressive and if the proportion is constant, the effect is proportional. As an example, a deduction for milk expenditures would likely impart a progressive tilt to the income tax, while a deduction for caviar would probably impart a regressive tilt.

Tax credits differ from subtractions, such as exemptions and deductions, in the following way: a one-dollar credit directly reduces one's tax obligation by a dollar, whereas a one-dollar exemption, exclusion, or deduction reduces only a person's *taxable income* by the dollar, and thus reduces the tax liability by only the applicable marginal tax rate. If a taxpayer takes a deduction of $100, the value to the taxpayer (in terms of reduced tax payments) is equal to $100 times the marginal tax rate. For many Michigan taxpayers, the marginal tax rate is 4.2%, so that the taxpayer's liability would be reduced by $4.20 as a result of a $100 deduction. Consequently, there is a relationship between a subtraction from income and a tax credit. (These two concepts are related by the mathematical equivalence $C = mX$, with $C$ the amount of the tax credit, $X$ the amount of the subtraction, and $m$ the marginal tax rate.) For example, a $100 exemption is equivalent to a $4.20 credit if the marginal tax rate is 4.2%.

An additional distinction between a credit and an exemption occurs if the credit is designated as *refundable*. In some cases, the credit cannot be used fully because the amount of the credit exceeds the taxpayers' income tax obligation. If the credit is refundable, the excess is remitted to the taxpayer as a kind of negative tax payment, while if the credit is not refundable its full value may go unused by the taxpayer. Although this is a distinction which makes no difference for most taxpayers, it can make a great deal of difference for low-income taxpayers, or for taxpayers who are so preferentially treated by other provisions of the income tax that they have no tax obligation. One refundable credit that adds considerable progressivity to Michigan's income tax system is the property tax credit.

### Efficiency

Economists use the term *efficiency* to convey how well an economy is utilizing its resources to provide goods and services to its members. Note that, for an economy to be efficient, it is not sufficient to provide the greatest quantity of goods and services. Rather, efficiency requires producing the right mix of these goods and services, and this requires that production proceed in the correct manner. Taxes generally have efficiency costs for several reasons. Their imposition changes the prices of goods and services and, as a consequence, can alter the amount produced and consumed. Taxes can also alter the mode of production, and decisions regarding saving and investment. Consequently, taxes are said to have "efficiency costs" that can make an economy poorer. The efficiency costs of a general income tax, a tax on all sources of income, result from distortion in two markets. First, an income tax will distort the labor market by reducing the after-tax wage rate, which will alter the decision to work and earn in the marketplace, as compared to spending time engaged in nonmarket activities, including leisure. Second, the income tax will distort the capital market, because it will reduce the after-tax returns to saving and investment. This will alter the amount saved and invested, and change the pattern of future output and consumption.

A general consumption tax will distort only one market, the labor market. Since taxpayers work and earn in order to spend, if spending is taxed, working in the market is taxed as well. It is important to note that although an income tax distorts two markets and a consumption tax distorts only one, it does *not* follow that a consumption tax will be less distortionary than an income tax. It is not the *number* of markets distorted that matters but

rather the *size* of the distortions (see, e.g., Atkinson and Sandmo 1980, 529). If consumption is less than total income (the difference being saving), the consumption tax rate required to raise a given amount of revenue would need to exceed the income tax rate. Consequently, with the higher tax rate, the consumption tax would distort the labor market more than would the income tax. Hence the "winner" (in terms of having the lower efficiency cost) between the two taxes is unclear in theory: it would depend on the damage done to capital markets by the income tax, versus the additional damage to the labor market by the consumption tax as compared to the income tax. The professional jury is still out on which tax distorts more, and a review of the matter by the Congressional Budget Office finds the issue to be a close call.[7] Actually, the consumption tax we have in Michigan, the retail sales tax, is not comprehensive, and creates additional distortion by not taxing some goods, and by not taxing most services. Although the problem is not as severe with the state income tax, it is also less than fully comprehensive (see discussion following).

While economists do not yet know which tax, income or consumption, is more efficient, we do know that higher tax rates result in a greater efficiency cost per dollar raised than do lower rates. Consequently, the general refrain of tax reformers has been to broaden the tax base (that is, define the tax base comprehensively, to include most goods and services in the consumption tax base, and to include most sources of income in the income tax base) so that tax rates can be set as low as possible. Exempting certain forms of consumption or certain forms of income requires higher tax rates on what is left in the base, and invites larger than necessary efficiency costs. Therefore it follows that the presence of personal exemptions in the modern income tax system can create a trade-off between efficiency and vertical equity, and the same can be said for some credits and deductions.

One remaining point relating to the efficiency cost of taxation should be noted. Cross-jurisdictional tax rules may significantly affect the cost of taxation within a jurisdiction. I am referring to the issue of tax exporting, a process by which one jurisdiction can transfer the cost of raising public funds to another jurisdiction. If one state tax is deductible on the federal income tax while another state tax is not, raising one dollar using the first tax costs the residents of the state less in terms of net income sacrificed than raising the one dollar with the second tax. Michigan's income tax is deductible on the federal income tax return, while the retail sales tax is not. Therefore, Michigan can, in principle, raise more revenue with a lower cost to residents by marginally raising the income tax rate and lowering the sales tax rate. Whether Michiganians choose to do this is another story, but federal deductibility provides a financial reason to make the swap.

## Simplicity

An additional cost of taxation is the resources used up in complying with and enforcing a tax. The simpler the tax, the less time and money must be spent by taxpayers to comply with it, and by the government to administer it. Since the federal government employs an income tax, Michigan, by choosing to *piggyback* by employing a similar tax base (adjusted gross income), keeps compliance costs low. Alternatively, since at present there is no national retail sales tax, states must provide their own administrative and accounting superstructure to operate state sales taxes.

Which tax costs more to enforce and administer, Michigan's income or sales tax? The organizational structure of the Michigan Department of Treasury is such that it is difficult, if not impossible, to allocate the costs of the individual taxes precisely. However, even though we may not be able to make a precise calculation, the costs of administration and compliance for Michigan's income tax are probably lower than those for the state's retail sales tax. First, businesses already must withhold federal income taxes from the paychecks of their employees. Second, the record-keeping requirements for individual taxpayers are very similar for the federal income tax and the state income tax. Third, the administration of the state income tax is greatly facilitated by a program of electronic exchange of filing and audit data with the Internal Revenue Service. There is no such overlap for the sales tax. In fact, the compliance costs for multistate businesses can be significant, since the sales tax base differs from state to state. In addition, the state sales tax administration must maintain its own audit and enforcement mechanism.

## Michigan's Income Tax

Michigan employs a flat, or single rate, tax on the income of Michigan residents and the income earned in Michigan by nonresidents. The income tax was originally instituted in 1967 at a rate of 2.6% of federal adjusted gross income (AGI), after exemptions of $1,200 per person. The birth of the income tax was a difficult one. Michigan instituted the income tax relatively late as compared to other states. Starting with Wisconsin in 1911, the number of states with an income tax rose steadily over the years, so that by the end of the 1930s, thirty-one states used this tax. Amendments to the Michigan constitution that would have established a state income tax were proposed and defeated repeatedly at the polls. In addition, there were many failed attempts by state legislators to establish the tax by statute. In 1957, popular governor G. Mennen Williams, who served six terms in the office, proposed a graduated income tax in order to address a fiscal crisis. However, it was argued that Michigan's 1908 constitution proscribed such a tax under the "uniformity" clause, and his proposal failed. The structure of a possible income tax was hotly debated at the state's Constitutional Convention in 1961–62, with the lines drawn between those who sought rate graduation and "flat-raters." In the end the flat-raters won, and Michigan's 1963 constitution proscribed institution of "an income tax graduated as to rate or base" by the state or any of its subdivisions.[8]

When George Romney became governor in 1963 he proposed a flat-rate income tax, but it took the prospect of a state deficit to get it established in 1967, and then only after five and one-half months of debate. It is important to note that although the 1967 income tax bill and all revisions since are flat-rate (not graduated), the original legislation established a tax that is effectively progressive as a consequence of two important provisions, the personal exemptions and the property tax credit.

The Michigan income tax has changed considerably over the years. The rate rose to 3.9% in 1971, to 4.6% in 1975, and to 5.6% in 1982, fell to 4.6% later in 1982, rose again to 6.35% in 1983 (due to continued budget shortfalls caused by the recessions in the early 1980s), then fell to 6.1% later in 1983, to 5.35% in 1984, to 5.1% in 1985, and to 4.6% in 1986. In 1994, the rate fell to 4.4% as part of the voter-approved Proposal A, which swapped income—and property—tax reductions for a sales tax increase and a package of other tax increases. In 1999, a series of phased reductions commenced, with the rate falling to 4.3% in 2000, to 4.2% in 2001, and to 4.1% in 2002. Further

**TABLE 26.2**

**Michigan Income Tax Personal Exemption Allowance**

| Year | Personal Exemption | Real Personal Exemption[a] |
|------|-----|-----|
| 1967 | $1,200 | $1,200.0 |
| 1968 | $1,200 | 1,152.0 |
| 1969 | $1,200 | 1,092.0 |
| 1970 | $1,200 | 1,033.0 |
| 1971 | $1,200 | 989.6 |
| 1972 | $1,200 | 958.9 |
| 1973 | $1,500 | 1,128.0 |
| 1974 | $1,500 | 1,016.0 |
| 1975 | $1,500 | 931.2 |
| 1976 | $1,500 | 880.5 |
| 1977 | $1,500 | 826.7 |
| 1978 | $1,500 | 768.4 |
| 1979 | $1,500 | 690.1 |
| 1980 | $1,500 | 608.0 |
| 1981 | $1,500 | 551.2 |
| 1982 | $1,500 | 519.2 |
| 1983 | $1,500 | 503.0 |
| 1984 | $1,500 | 482.2 |
| 1985 | $1,500 | 465.6 |
| 1986 | $1,500 | 457.1 |
| 1987 | $1,600 | 470.4 |
| 1988 | $1,800 | 319.3 |
| 1989 | $2,000 | 538.7 |
| 1990 | $2,100 | 536.6 |
| 1991 | $2,100 | 515.0 |
| 1992 | $2,100 | 499.9 |
| 1993 | $2,100 | 485.4 |
| 1994 | $2,100 | 473.3 |
| 1995 | $2,400 | 526.0 |
| 1996 | $2,400 | 510.9 |
| 1997 | $2,500 | 520.2 |
| 1998 | $2,800 | 519.3 |
| 1999 | $2,800 | 561.3 |
| 2000 | $2,900 | 562.5 |
| 2001 | $2,900 | 546.9 |
| 2002 | $3,000 | |

SOURCE: Prepared by the Office of Revenue and Tax Analysis, Michigan Department of Treasury and the authors.
(a) Adjusted for changes in the Consumer Price Index.

decreases are scheduled, to 4% for 2003 and to 3.9% for 2004. If one looks at the history of these rate changes, they are obviously driven largely by revenue shortfalls and surpluses. The 1999 legislation is interesting because the phased-in rate reductions were based upon both current (1999) and anticipated future surpluses. In fact, however, the anticipated surpluses were not realized.

One rationale for personal exemptions is that they insure a minimum level of subsistence income that cannot be subjected to income taxation. They allow for differences in ability to pay for reasons other than income, such as family size. They also result in vertical equity effects, since they lead to average tax rates rising with income. The personal exemption level of the Michigan income tax has changed considerably over time (see table 26.2). Originally set at $1,200 per person, it was increased to $1,500 in 1973, to $1,600 in 1987, to $1,800 in 1988, to $2,000 in 1989, to $2,100 in 1990, to $2,400 in 1995, and to $2,500 in 1997, and thereafter has been linked to inflation. While the exemption has steadily increased in nominal terms, its value in purchasing power has not kept up with inflation. The exemption is now worth less than half of its original value in 1967 (table 26.2).[9] This halving of the real value of the personal exemption clearly reduces the progressivity of the Michigan income tax.

Although the real value of the personal exemption has not been maintained over time, there has been growth in other, "special" exemptions. Michigan provides a number of $1,900 exemptions, one for each person in a taxpaying unit who is deaf, blind, hemiplegic, paraplegic, quadraplegic, or totally and permanently disabled; one for each person aged sixty-five or older; and finally one exemption for unemployed people (more correctly, those for whom unemployment insurance amounts to 50% or more of adjusted gross income for the tax year). Of these special exemptions, 90% of the revenue impact is accounted for by the age exemption. Finally, an additional $600 exemption for each child aged eighteen or younger is provided as well as an exemption, of up to $1,500, for taxpayers who file their own returns but are claimed as dependents on another taxpayer's return. While these special exemptions certainly add to the progressivity of the income tax, they raise interesting questions regarding horizontal equity, and their base-narrowing effect does have its associated costs.

The Michigan income tax is less than comprehensive. The underlying tax base is federal adjusted gross income. There are obvious simplicity benefits in basing an income tax on the federal income definition that the taxpayer must adhere to anyway. However, since federal AGI is not fully comprehensive, Michigan inherits an income tax base that is narrowed by current federal exclusions and is vulnerable to future federal exclusions.[10] Economists have analyzed a number of important omissions from the federal base, and have studied the effects of these omissions. Examples of major omissions include interest income on state and local bonds, capital gain income—particularly deferral of taxation until realization of the capital gain, exclusion of the capital gain on home sales, and forgiveness of capital gains at death.[11]

Other important omissions include the exclusion of employer contributions for medical insurance premiums and the exclusions of contributions to and earnings of saving and pension plans. The preferential tax treatment of benefits results in a distortion of the composition of compensation between earnings and benefits—a source of inefficiency. This creates a situation in which employers have an incentive to pay one dollar of compensation in the form of fringe benefits, even though those fringe benefits might be valued at only 90 cents by the employees, while if benefits were taxed like wages no such incentive would be present. Preferential tax treatment of benefits creates horizontal inequities, since those with the same total compensation face different tax bills, depending on their benefit package. Finally, if the share of compensation in benefits varies across the income spectrum, preferential treatment of benefits can create vertical inequities as well. Another quantitatively important omission is the exclusion of most Social Security benefits.

Additional but smaller omissions result from the accelerated depreciation of certain assets and the omission of workers' compensation and veterans' benefits. The forgone revenues associated with omissions from the tax base or other forms of preferential treatment are referred to as *tax expenditures*. Both direct public expenditures and indirect support via tax subsidies can advance public policy initiatives. Since direct expenditures are subject to scrutiny and evaluation by government entities in Washington, such as the Congressional Budget Office and the Office of Management and Budget, indirect support through tax expenditures should be scrutinized as well. Both direct expenditures and tax expenditures ought to be subject to cost-benefit analysis, taking into account the efficiency costs associated with their provision, including (in the case of a narrowed tax base) the efficiency costs resulting from higher tax rates. The federal government has been estimating the size of federal tax expenditures since 1974. Michigan, to its credit, has been measuring tax expenditures since 1979.[12]

We have seen that Michigan's state income tax base is not comprehensive, because it piggybacks on the federal definition of income. In addition, the Michigan state income tax base is not comprehensive due to its own omissions. Michigan allows "subtractions" for some income sources that are subject to federal tax. In other cases Michigan provides tax credits for certain activities. For example, Michigan taxes neither Social Security benefits nor most of the retirement or pension benefits that *are* federally taxable. Indeed, most retirement or pension benefits are not taxed here. Michigan also excludes a portion of interest and dividend income received by the elderly. Some, but not all, out-of-state property income received by Michigan residents is excluded by Michigan. Examples include the income from an out-of-state business, and rents, royalties, and capital gains on properties located out of state. However, the dividends or gains from corporate stock in a company incorporated outside of Michigan are fully taxable, along with interest paid by an out-of-state bank. One consequence of the failure to tax all of a taxpayer's out-of-state capital income is measurement error in computing average (or effective) tax rates. Use of tax data from only Michigan understates the total amount of the taxpayer's income tax obligation, assuming income tax is paid to the other state. This measurement problem is symmetric. Say an out-of-state taxpayer has Michigan property income. Utilizing only the income tax paid to Michigan will yield a misleadingly low measure of the average tax rate (income tax paid to Michigan divided by federal AGI) for this taxpayer. If the likelihood of out-of-state property income rises with AGI, studies of the distribution of state income tax structures will tend to understate the progressivity of the income tax due to this measurement error.

Michigan compensation received by active-duty military personnel is not taxed. There is also no tax on income earned by those living or working in a state renaissance zone. (Renaissance zones were established to stimulate economic growth in these zones.) Starting with tax year 2001, Michigan allows up to $5,000 ($10,000 for a joint return) to be subtracted for contributions into the Michigan Education Savings Program, which can be used to support a student's future expenditures on tuition, fees, and books at institutions of higher learning. Since the value of these contributions is not taxed as income when withdrawn (assuming the withdrawal is not in the year of the deposit), this provision would amount to quite a large subsidy for postsecondary school attendance. With a 4.2% tax rate, a family can save $420 (plus the savings on the nontaxed interest income) for one year's contribution. The key question, of course, is the degree to which this program induces increased college attendance, as compared to simply providing a windfall to families in which students would be attending college anyhow. A careful benefit-cost analysis of the program would measure both its benefits and its costs to state taxpayers. There are no data yet on how much this program is costing, in terms of forgone revenue, or on the distribution of usage by AGI, but such a study would be enlightening. Another subtraction related to higher education is for expenditures made to purchase Michigan Education Trust contracts.

While Michigan does not allow itemized deductions, as the federal income tax does, beginning with tax year 2001 a taxpayer may subtract a distribution from a pension plan contributed to a charitable organization. There are restrictions on these subtractions; for example, the donor cannot take both a pension deduction and a charitable deduction, but this new provision marks a departure from Michigan's historical reluctance to allow elements of itemized deduction on its state income tax return. Additional subtractions are allowed for political contributions, $50 on an individual and $100 on a joint return.

## Tax Credits and the Michigan Personal Income Tax

Tax credits are equivalent to deductions from income (related in amount by the reciprocal of the tax rate) and have been a part of Michigan's income tax from the beginning. The original income tax law in 1967 allowed for two tax credits, one a credit to offset income taxes paid to other states and the other a credit for property taxes paid directly by owners and implicitly paid by renters. By 1979 there were six credits, and currently there are twelve. The ten credits added to the original law are for income taxes paid to Michigan cities, for public contributions (formerly this credit was allowed only for contributions to Michigan colleges and universities), for contributions to community foundations, for contributions to homeless shelters/food banks, the Michigan Historic Preservation credit, the college tuition and fees credit, the farmland preser-

vation credit, a credit for qualified adoption expenses, a home heating credit, and finally a Holocaust survivor credit. In addition, in 2001 Michigan had a prescription drug credit, but eliminated it in favor of a direct outlay program.

The largest tax credit program is the property tax credit, which (along with the home heating credit and the farmland preservation credit) is a "refundable" credit. These are called refundable credits because if they exceed the tax liability, the excess is refunded to the taxpayer. As a consequence, taxpayers can pay "negative" amounts of income taxes. The property tax credit (formally known as the Homestead Property Tax credit) is by far the largest credit, amounting to $483.6 million in fiscal year 2001, with 50.4 % of the benefits going to general taxpayers, 47.3% going to senior citizens, and the remaining 2.3% going to veterans and blind and disabled persons. The Michigan property tax credit, claimed by over 1.1 million Michigan taxpayers in 2001, merits detailed analysis. (Note that while this chapter treats the property tax credit as an important facet of the income tax, an alternative approach would be to treat it as an administrative detail of the property tax system. Since this credit significantly affects the marginal income tax rate, discussion of the credit deserves a place in this chapter.)

The property tax credit works to offset the amount of property taxes that exceed certain thresholds of income. If property taxes paid by homeowners or renters exceed 3.5% of income, the credit takes effect. (While homeowners pay the property tax directly, renters pay the tax indirectly, through higher rental rates than would exist in the absence of the property tax, and the rules impute 20% of rent to be payment of property taxes.) Taxpayers who are elderly receive 100% of the excess, and the nonelderly receive 60% of the excess, up to a limit of $1,200.[13] The credit is targeted to nonwealthy taxpayers, and phases out over the range of $73,650 to $82,650 in household income.

As an example, assume a taxpayer household has four members, two of whom are dependent children, and pays $1,800 per year in property taxes (or is a renter and pays $7,500 in rent). If the taxpaying household had an income of $30,000, they would be liable for income taxes of $722.40 *prior* to consideration of the credit.[14] Since the property taxes paid exceed 3.5% of income, the taxpayer is eligible for the credit, which amounts to $450.[15] Thus, after accounting for the property tax credit, the family's net income tax payment would be $(722.40 – 450) = $272.40. If the same family fell on harder times and its income fell to $20,000, the credit ($660) would exceed the income tax ($302.40) and the household would receive a net refund of $357.60 from the state. Conversely, if the family's income were to rise from $30,000 to $52,000 (perhaps due to an additional member being employed) the family would no longer be eligible for the credit, because the family's property tax payments would now be less than 3.5% of income.

Given the obvious income test, not to mention the explicit income cap, associated with the property tax credit, it is no surprise that the credit lowers average income tax rates more for lower- than for higher-income taxpayers. Consequently, studies of the property tax credit show it to significantly increase the progressivity of Michigan's income tax.[16]

While the homestead property tax credit may advance *vertical* equity goals, it can be criticized on grounds of horizontal inequity, inefficiency, and complexity. This credit has the effect of treating taxpayers with the same income very differently, by providing more income tax relief to those with more expensive homes or apartments. Indeed, the taxpayers who choose to spend relatively less money on housing and more on other forms of consumption are clearly disfavored by the tax code. This treatment also has an efficiency effect promoting demand for housing as compared to other forms of consumption. In addition, the means testing nature of the credit implicitly increases the tax rate on earning income, since the credit received for a given level of property tax payments falls with rising income. One can compute the implicit increase in the income tax rate as simply the product of 3.5% and 0.60, or 2.1% for the nonelderly. For the elderly, the increase in the income tax rate is 3.5% for seniors with incomes of $6,000 or more, and lower amounts for those with incomes lower than $6,000. Consequently, for those receiving the property tax credit, the actual marginal tax rate on income is not 4.2% but 6.3% among the nonelderly, and 7.7% for (most of) the elderly. For those in the $73,650 to $82,650 phaseout interval, the implicit tax can be much more than that. For taxpayers within that interval, every additional $1,000 in income, or part of $1,000 in income, reduces the credit by 10%. Therefore, for those receiving the maximum of $1,200, an additional $1,000 in income costs the taxpayer $120 in forgone credit, plus an increased tax obligation of $420, yielding

a net state marginal income tax rate over this interval of 16.2%. If understood by taxpayers, this (when combined with the federal income tax rate) can be expected to result in a significant work disincentive.[17]

There is also a cost in terms of simplicity associated with the property tax credit. In order to qualify for the credit, one must fill out a complicated form with fifty-eight entries. While the income tax computation is based on federal adjusted gross income, the property tax credit requires the detailed computation of a much more comprehensive income concept. Although entirely laudable from the viewpoint of a truly comprehensive tax design, this approach does add significant complexity to the system. Although there are no available data on this issue, I would surmise that the time it takes a taxpayer to fill out the tax credit form exceeds the time needed for the income tax form.

To summarize, the homestead property tax credit adds significantly to the progressivity of Michigan's flat income tax structure, but at the same time this creates horizontal inequities, and it creates inefficiencies in terms of distorting consumption choice and labor supply, and adds to the complexity of the income tax system. While the possible improvement in vertical equity may be worth these other drawbacks, a tax reformer may well ask about the availability of an *alternative* progressivity-enhancing provision resulting in vertical equity without the drawbacks. One possible provision that Michigan does not have (but several other states do) that might provide equity with a lower cost would be an earned income tax credit (see, e.g., *National Tax Journal* 2000 and Neumark and Wascher 2001). Such a policy change replaces the incentive to live in more expensive housing than a family would otherwise choose with an increased incentive to earn wage income in the labor market; that is, it replaces an incentive to consume with an incentive to produce. Depending on the scope and the degree of refundability of the credit, the increased wage income that results may alleviate problems associated with low-income status, and increased job experience may lead to future wage growth as well. (For additional discussion of the earned income tax credit and related policies, see chapters 17 and 18 of this volume.)

The Michigan Home Heating Credit is a refundable credit intended to help pay the home energy bills of low-income households. The program is funded largely by a grant from the federal

## TABLE 26.3

### Individual Income Tax Expenditures (in $ thousands)

| Tax or Tax Expenditure | FY 2001 | FY 2002 |
|---|---|---|
| **State income tax** | | |
| Adjustments to income | $1,871,500 | $1,883,200 |
| Adoption credit[a] | 0 | 1,100 |
| Child deduction | 56,200 | 55,700 |
| City income tax credit | 38,600 | 39,200 |
| College savings accounts[a] | 7,700 | 8,500 |
| Community foundation credit | 2,300 | 2,400 |
| Dependent exemption[a] | 28,900 | 28,800 |
| Farmland credit | 17,900 | 25,900 |
| Higher education/public contributions credit | 24,500 | 25,700 |
| Historic preservation credit | 200 | 200 |
| Holocaust survivor subtraction | n.a. | n.a. |
| Home heating assistance credit | 1,400 | 1,400 |
| Homeless/food bank credit | 13,100 | 13,900 |
| Homestead property tax credit | 483,600 | 498,100 |
| Military pay and pensions | 19,100 | 19,500 |
| Personal exemption[a] | 940,000 | 958,000 |
| Prescription drug credit | 16,100 | 16,400 |
| Renaissance zones | 300 | 300 |
| Special exemption[a] | 64,000 | 64,600 |
| Tuition credit | 8,500 | 32,700 |
| TOTAL STATE | $3,593,900 | $3,675,600 |
| **Federal adjustments** | | |
| Accelerated depreciation | $69,469 | $70,910 |
| Employer contributions to insurance | 603,787 | 633,243 |
| Employer pension plans | 709,627 | 696,955 |
| Federal adjustments to income | 6,680 | 7,345 |
| Fellowships and scholarships | 10,592 | 10,496 |
| Income maintenance benefits | 3,972 | 3,901 |
| Individual retirement accounts | 183,383 | 180,109 |
| Interest on life insurance savings | 123,214 | 130,295 |
| Medical savings account | 219 | 215 |
| Railroad retirement benefits | 2,955 | 2,938 |
| Social security benefits | 303,804 | 298,379 |
| Student loan deduction | 2,932 | 3,251 |
| Veterans' benefits | 35,710 | 35,073 |
| Workers' compensation | 41,804 | 44,483 |
| TOTAL FEDERAL | $2,098,148 | $2,117,593 |
| TOTAL STATE AND FEDERAL | $5,692,048 | $5,793,193 |

SOURCE: State of Michigan 2002a. Executive budget, Tax expenditure appendix. Fiscal Year 2002.
(a) Denotes a new tax expenditure or an existing tax expenditure that was expanded or modified.

government but is administered by the Michigan Department of Treasury. The number of Michigan households receiving the credit in 1999 was about 306,000, with the average credit being $164. About 83% of the credit is received in the form of an energy draft that can be used only to pay energy bills, and the remaining 17% is provided as a check to the recipients. Since the amount of the credit is determined on the basis of need, there is a phaseout range in which an increase in the household's earning results in a reduction in the size of the credit. This benefit reduction process results in an implicit tax rate of 3.5% over the phaseout range. Consequently, the total marginal Michigan income tax rate faced by a nonelderly household receiving *both* the property tax and heating credits would be 9.8% (4.2% + 2.1% + 3.5%), and for an elderly household it would be 11.2% (4.2% + 3.5% + 3.5%).

### Revenue Cost of the Noncomprehensive Tax Base

By utilizing a less-than-comprehensive income tax base, Michigan must levy higher rates on what remains in the base. While it is difficult to know the actual magnitude of this loss in revenue, Michigan fortunately requires an estimate of the revenue cost of some of the omitted income in its tax expenditure budget. According to the tax expenditure report, the magnitude of tax expenditure associated with the state income tax is estimated to be $3.67 billion, approximately 52% of projected income tax revenues.[18] While this seems like an enormous exclusion, the consumption tax expenditure figure is far greater, amounting to $8.33 billion for the combined retail sales and use taxes.

The tax expenditure for the sales and use tax is actually larger (by 2%) than the revenue raised by those taxes. The tax expenditure estimates in table 26.3, like the federal tax expenditure estimates, rely on somewhat crude assumptions, such as zero behavioral responses to tax incentives, and the tabulation itself is less than comprehensive.[19] Furthermore, analyses of provisions of the income tax would be aided if a breakdown of "adjustments to income" were provided (currently, these are lumped together in a single category, amounting to a whopping $1.87 billion). Finally, one might well quibble with listing personal exemptions as a tax expenditure item, a clear departure from federal practice.

### The Distribution of the Michigan Income Tax

In determining how income taxes are distributed among taxpayers, economists have argued that a longer (or "time exposure") look is more meaningful than a shorter (or "snapshot") view. The

**TABLE 26.4**

**Effective Tax Rates from Three-Year Panel of Michigan Taxpayers, All Returns for Tax Years 1998–2000**

| | All Taxpayers | | Resident Taxpayers | |
|---|---|---|---|---|
| Three-Year Average AGI | Number of Returns | Average Tax Rate | Number of Returns | Average Tax Rate |
| ≤ $0 | 126,890 | | 126,310 | |
| $1–$5,000 | 233,050 | –5.3% | 228,800 | –5.5% |
| $5,001–$10,000 | 322,850 | –0.4% | 315,210 | –0.5% |
| $10,001–$15,000 | 303,220 | 0.5% | 295,150 | 0.5% |
| $15,001–$20,000 | 279,750 | 1.4% | 271,830 | 1.4% |
| $20,001–$25,000 | 252,700 | 2.0% | 245,490 | 2.0% |
| $25,001–$30,000 | 225,410 | 2.4% | 219,450 | 2.4% |
| $30,001–$35,000 | 200,430 | 2.6% | 194,620 | 2.6% |
| $35,001–$40,000 | 182,860 | 2.7% | 177,540 | 2.7% |
| $40,001–$45,000 | 167,720 | 2.8% | 162,740 | 2.8% |
| $45,001–$50,000 | 157,000 | 3.0% | 152,310 | 3.0% |
| $50,001–$60,000 | 281,600 | 3.1% | 273,720 | 3.1% |
| $60,001–$70,000 | 229,820 | 3.2% | 223,140 | 3.2% |
| $70,001–$80,000 | 180,360 | 3.3% | 175,110 | 3.4% |
| $80,001–$90,000 | 134,680 | 3.4% | 130,780 | 3.5% |
| $90,001–$100,000 | 98,500 | 3.5% | 95,670 | 3.5% |
| $100,001–$125,000 | 143,640 | 3.6% | 138,970 | 3.6% |
| $125,001–$150,000 | 66,430 | 3.7% | 63,690 | 3.7% |
| > $150,000 | 117,700 | 3.1% | 108,770 | 3.9% |
| | 3,704,610 | 2.9% | 3,599,300 | 3.1% |

SOURCE: Office of Revenue and Tax Analysis, Michigan Department of Treasury.

NOTE: Estimates are based on a panel created by matching returns based on a 10% random sample for each year 1998–2000. The panel represents 80.9% of the 1998 returns, 80.1% of the 1999 returns, and 78.6% of the 2000 returns.

argument is equally valid for Michigan's income tax. The time exposure measure of income is seen as more valid because income in any one year is a less reliable indicator of permanent economic position than income over several years. Consequently, table 26.4 presents the distribution of income tax payments in a three-year period (1998–2000), based upon a matched sample of Michigan taxpayers.[20] Taxpayers were matched across a three-year panel of data, and the average income and tax rate were computed. (The three-year panel is the longest data panel available for research purposes.) At very low income levels the ATR is negative, a consequence of the refundable credits. ATR rises steadily with income, as might be expected with a flat tax, but surprisingly falls at the top income interval. I believe this is due to measurement error associated with the computation of ATRs for nonresidents. As mentioned earlier, if the bulk of one's income is taxed in another state, the part taxed in Michigan divided by federal AGI computes to a misleadingly small number. A better measure of income taxes paid would

be obtained either by prorating federal AGI across states or by fully including in the numerator the non-Michigan income tax obligation. However, neither adjustment can be easily done easily, so an alternative strategy is pursued on the right side of table 26.4, which presents the distribution of the income tax for only those taxpayers who are Michigan residents. While not a perfect remedy for the problem, the resident distribution provides a more realistic portrayal of the progressivity of Michigan's income tax than does the overall distribution.[21]

The pattern of average tax rates over the income distribution conveys the distribution of the burden of an income tax. Alternatively, analysts may focus on the pattern of marginal tax rates to determine where in the income spectrum the greatest work disincentives arise. Figure 26.1 portrays the average and marginal tax rates for a nonelderly Michigan family of four. Two of the lines in figure 26.1 show the rates that this family would face under a hypothetical income tax with a flat rate of 4.2% (with personal exemptions but

FIGURE 26.1

**Marginal Tax Rates (MTR) and Average Tax Rates (ATR) under Hypothetical Income Tax with Flat Rate of 4.2% and Exemption of $12,800, and under Actual Michigan Law for Family of Four with Two Children, Receiving the Property-Tax and Home Heating Credits**

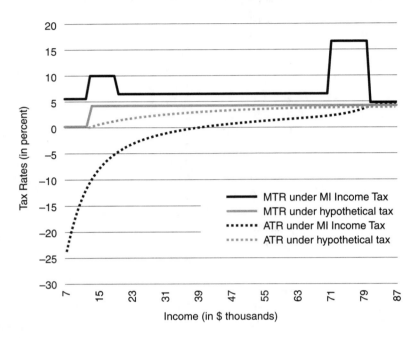

SOURCE: Author's calculations.

rates over parts of the income spectrum, with higher rates creating a possible loss of economic efficiency.

## Other Policy Issues

### Tax Base Erosion

A virtue of a comprehensive flat income tax is that under a broad and inclusive tax base, the rates could be kept relatively low, while raising the same amount that is generated from an eroded tax base. However, the Michigan income tax base has been narrowing in recent years as legislators incorporate special provisions in the code. These provisions add complexity, necessitate higher rates to raise equivalent revenue, and raise questions about the equity of the code.

One obvious question is, "Who benefits from base narrowing?" Table 26.5, which employs the "snapshot," or one-year, approach, uses the Office of Revenue and Tax Analysis data to examine the distribution of some of the deductions and credits across income groups. The most striking result from this table is the distribution of refundable credits, which are very heavily weighted toward the lower income groups. On the other hand, the distribution of subtractions appears to be U-shaped, with subtractions enjoyed by the top income groups amounting to a very large proportion of both income and total subtractions. It would be useful to have a detailed breakdown of these subtractions, but the data are not immediately available. The base-broadening additions to the income tax base, largely non-Michigan state and local bond interest, out-of-state property losses, and the deduction for the self-employment tax on the federal return are much smaller than the subtractions, and are also U-shaped.

While the use of tax expenditures is growing in Michigan, it appears that we are not alone. The federal tax code increasingly is using this method of indirect expenditure, instead of direct outlays (see Sammartino, Toder, and Maag 2002). According to a data set provided to me by the Office of Revenue and Tax Analysis, Michigan, as compared to other states, appears to be in the middle of the pack when measured by the by degree of comprehensiveness of its taxable income measure—as shown in table 26.6. Perhaps politicians find tax expenditures to be more attractive than direct expenditures as ways of promoting favored activities, because they can be sold as tax cuts so polit-

no credits). The other two lines show the more complex set of tax rates that this family would face under Michigan's actual income tax (with the home heating credit and the property tax credit, as well as personal exemptions). Under the hypothetical tax with no credits, the average tax rate is zero at low income levels, and it eventually rises, trending toward the 4.2% marginal rate. For the actual Michigan income tax, including credits, the average and marginal tax rates are both quite different. The average tax rates are significantly lower as a result of the credits, and they are negative at lower income levels. For most income levels, the marginal tax rates are higher under the actual Michigan income tax than under the hypothetical tax system with no credits. In addition, under the actual Michigan income tax, the marginal tax rates spike in two places. The first spike is due to the home heating credit phaseout, and the second to the property tax credit phaseout. Comparison of the two profiles illustrates an equity-efficiency tradeoff engendered by Michigan's income tax. While the refundable credits result in more progressivity than a strict flat tax would provide, they also elevate marginal tax

**TABLE 26.5**

## Distribution of Michigan Income Tax Deductions and Credits, Tax Year 2000

| Adjusted Gross Income Range | City Income Tax Credit | | Public Contribution Credit | | Income Tax Paid to Other States Credit | |
|---|---|---|---|---|---|---|
| | % of Tax before Credits | Total Amount | % of Tax before Credits | Total Amount | % of Tax before Credits | Total Amount |
| ≤ $0 | 0.7 | 50,207 | 0.6 | 45,367 | 0.6 | 41,870 |
| $1–$10,000 | 2.3 | 1,729,241 | 0.5 | 352,885 | 0.5 | 384,147 |
| $10,000–$20,000 | 1.6 | 3,594,058 | 0.4 | 854,126 | 0.4 | 928,542 |
| $20,000–$30,000 | 1.2 | 4,476,015 | 0.3 | 1,194,354 | 0.3 | 1,259,164 |
| $30,000–$50,000 | 0.8 | 7,745,164 | 0.3 | 2,957,564 | 0.3 | 3,204,201 |
| $50,000–$75,000 | 0.6 | 8,207,597 | 0.3 | 4,407,445 | 0.4 | 5,545,529 |
| $75,000–$100,000 | 0.5 | 5,226,836 | 0.4 | 4,021,468 | 0.5 | 4,922,787 |
| > $100,000 | 0.2 | 7,547,539 | 0.4 | 10,725,988 | 0.5 | 15,492,968 |
| | 0.6 | $38,576,656 | 0.4 | $24,559,197 | 0.5 | $31,779,208 |

| Adjusted Gross Income Range | Total Nonrefundable Credits | | Homestead Property Tax Credits | | Home Heating Credits | |
|---|---|---|---|---|---|---|
| | % of Tax before Credits | Total Amount | % of Tax before Credits | Total Amount | % of Tax before Credits | Total Amount |
| ≤ $0 | 0.2 | 13,177 | 1,133.9 | 79,226,282 | 386.6 | 27,024,669 |
| $1–$10,000 | 0.9 | 700,665 | 142.9 | 106,727,117 | 33.0 | 24,672,001 |
| $10,000–$20,000 | 2.6 | 5,738,461 | 53.3 | 119,386,780 | 3.0 | 6,787,695 |
| $20,000–$30,000 | 2.0 | 7,561,122 | 18.7 | 71,216,776 | 0.1 | 515,392 |
| $30,000–$50,000 | 1.7 | 15,657,790 | 7.9 | 73,937,880 | 0.0 | 93,867 |
| $50,000–$75,000 | 1.6 | 21,129,912 | 3.3 | 43,006,088 | 0.0 | 34,994 |
| $75,000–$100,000 | 1.6 | 17,132,534 | 0.4 | 3,883,439 | 0.0 | 12,922 |
| > $100,000 | 1.4 | 41,444,258 | 0.0 | 177,909 | 0.0 | 15,619 |
| | 1.6 | $109,377,918 | 7.1 | $497,562,271 | 0.6 | $59,157,159 |

| Adjusted Gross Income Range | Income Tax Subtractions (1) | | Income Tax Additions (2) | |
|---|---|---|---|---|
| | % of Tax before Credits | Total Amount | % of Tax before Credits | Total Amount |
| ≤ $0 | 216.8 | 15,146,799 | 846.4 | 59,136,657 |
| $1–$10,000 | 41.4 | 30,890,339 | 2.3 | 1,723,299 |
| $10,000–$20,000 | 44.5 | 99,615,742 | 1.1 | 2,429,472 |
| $20,000–$30,000 | 25.5 | 96,724,044 | 0.6 | 2,327,198 |
| $30,000–$50,000 | 20.4 | 189,833,819 | 0.5 | 5,068,811 |
| $50,000–$75,000 | 16.6 | 217,176,641 | 0.5 | 6,264,086 |
| $75,000–$100,000 | 13.5 | 141,661,706 | 0.5 | 4,985,302 |
| > $100,000 | 39.4 | 1,198,300,044 | 2.4 | 72,859,743 |
| | | $1,989,349,133 | | $154,794,569 |

SOURCE: TA12720 report, Michigan Department of Treasury. PREPARED BY: Office of Revenue and Tax Analysis, Michigan Department of Treasury.
NOTES: The totals for subtractions and additions represent the total adjustments for each income group multiplied by the 2000 tax rate, 4.2%.

ical coalitions are more readily established. In any case, the narrowing of the tax base is costly.

## The Federal Deductibility Issue

The state income tax is deductible by taxpayers on their federal income tax returns. Taxpayers who itemize their deductions can reduce their taxable income, and therefore their tax obligation, as a consequence of making state income tax payments. The amount they save per tax dollar is their marginal federal income tax rate (assuming their other itemized deductions brought them up to the itemization threshold level). Consequently, taxpayers who itemize their deductions receive federal tax benefits for paying the state income tax and the property tax, while they do not receive

**TABLE 26.6**

### Income Subject to Tax as Percentage of Broad-Based Income (dollar amounts in millions)

| State | Tax Year | Total Taxable Income | | | Resident Taxable Income | | |
|---|---|---|---|---|---|---|---|
| | | Income | As % of AGI | As % of Personal Income | Income | As % of AGI | As % of Personal Income |
| Arkansas | 1999 | | | | $32,634 | 86.5% | 57.5% |
| Arizona | 1999 | | | | $55,443 | 60.9% | 46.1% |
| California | 1998 | | | | $522,600 | 78.9% | 56.6% |
| Colorado | 1997 | | | | $50,594 | 63.0% | 46.5% |
| Deleware | 1998 | | 85.0% | | | | |
| Georgia | 1998 | $93,023 | 64.3% | 46.6% | $88,192 | 60.9% | 44.2% |
| Iowa | 1999 | $49,967 | 95.8% | 68.0% | $36,177 | 69.3% | 49.3% |
| Illinois | 1998 | $235,442 | 88.5% | 65.0% | $223,579 | 84.1% | 61.7% |
| Maine | 1999 | $14,600 | 65.3% | 47.4% | $15,500 | 69.3% | 50.3% |
| Michigan | 1999 | $158,748 | 76.6% | 57.3% | $154,539 | 74.6% | 55.7% |
| New Jersey | 1999 | | | | $197,882 | 85.6% | 68.2% |
| New York | 1998 | $392,879 | 96.7% | 67.1% | $283,807 | 69.8% | 48.4% |
| Ohio | 1999 | $236,982 | 107.2% | 77.5% | | | |
| Oregon | 1999 | $51,875 | 79.7% | 58.0% | $48,024 | 73.8% | 53.7% |
| Pennsylvania | 1999 | $224,102 | 90.9% | 65.3% | $213,631 | 86.6% | 62.2% |
| South Carolina | 1999 | $33,015 | 49.9% | 36.1% | $30,910 | 46.7% | 33.8% |
| Utah | 1999 | $31,307 | 83.4% | 63.2% | $28,685 | 76.4% | 57.9% |
| Virginia | 1998 | | | | $106,842 | 73.2% | 55.5% |
| Vermont | 1999 | $14,838 | 128.8% | 96.7% | $6,990 | 60.7% | 45.6% |
| Wisconsin | 1999 | $93,598 | 85.5% | 65.1% | | | |
| West Virginia | 1999 | $19,385 | 79.3% | 51.3% | $20,102 | 82.2% | 53.2% |

SOURCE: Office of Revenue and Tax Analysis, Michigan Department of Treasury.
NOTES: (1) Federal AGI is taken from the IRS Statistics of Income, Expanded Unpublished Version of State Estimates, for 1997–99. (2) Personal income is taken from the Survey of Current Business, September 2001, U.S. Department of Commerce. (3) Taxable income was either received over the listserve maintained by the Federation of Tax Administrators, or taken from statistics published by the tax agency in the state. (4) Michigan resident taxable income is the state total for 1999 less the amount mailed from an out-of-state address.

such benefits for paying the state retail sales tax, since it is no longer deductible.

How important is this treatment? According to specialists at the Michigan Office of Revenue and Tax Analysis, approximately 20% of Michigan's state income tax is "exported," meaning that the average income-tax dollar costs Michigan taxpayers only eighty cents, and the federal treasury (the nation's taxpayers) pay the other twenty cents.[22] While not deductible, the retail sales tax is, in part, exported to individuals living in other states who make taxable purchases in Michigan. Although a recent estimate of the importance of this effect is not available, Blume (1982) found that 3% of the revenue raised by Michigan's retail sales tax is exported to tourists.

If these numbers are correct, we can come up with the first-order approximation that Michigan residents gain seventeen cents for every tax dollar shifted from the state sales tax to the state income

tax. Note that this computation takes into account only the financial effects of such a shift, and does not consider the resulting equity, efficiency, or simplicity effects, which, if taken into account, might strengthen the case for such a shift.[23]

Federal deductibility could also be considered in relation to both the design and the reform of state income taxation. One can liken the financial benefit of itemizing to the receipt of a matching grant from the federal government, with the rate of match dependent upon the taxpayer's marginal federal income tax rate. For example, if a taxpayer has a marginal federal tax rate of 30%, each dollar in state income payments actually has a net cost to him or her of seventy cents, with the difference exported to (or "granted" by) the federal treasury. Similarly, if the marginal tax rate is 15%, the federal "grant" is fifteen cents, and the grant is zero if the taxpayer does not itemize. Consequently, the amount of federal dollars "granted" to state taxpayers depends upon the distribution of income tax liabilities among taxpayers in the following ways: (a) the greater the share paid by those who itemize on their federal return, the greater the grant, and (b) among itemizers, the greater the share paid by high versus low marginal tax rate taxpayers, the greater the grant. The likelihood of itemizing is not randomly associated with income. Data provided by the Internal Revenue Service reveal the likelihood of itemizing on the federal return by income category, and the data for Michigan shows that the proportion itemizing clearly increases with income.[24] For example, about 8% of those at the $10,000 to $20,000 income level itemize, while the itemization rate is 38% at the $30,000 to $50,000 income level, 84% at the $75,000 to $100,000 income level, and 95% at income levels above $150,000. Since the graduated nature of the federal income tax means that marginal tax rates also rise with income, the presence of federal deductibility leads to a surprising result: a proportional income tax leads to a *smaller* degree of exporting (a smaller federal "grant") than does a progressive tax of equal yield. Hence, the presence of deductibility suggests an independent rationale for progressive income taxation at the state (or local) level.[25]

Deductibility also has an implication concerning the manner of future income tax reform, in Michigan and other states. In recent years, Michigan's income tax rates have declined, and are scheduled to continue to fall (to 3.9% in 2004), while the personal exemption is growing only at the rate of inflation. It may seem that a dollar of revenue forgone as a consequence of rate reductions and a dollar lost due to increases in exemptions are fiscally equivalent, since they have the same effect on state solvency. However, federal income tax deductibility makes this untrue. Since an increase in the personal exemption directs a larger proportion of the tax savings to those who do not itemize than does a rate reduction, the rate reduction has a higher associated opportunity cost, measured in federal dollars lost, than the exemption increase. Hence, increasing exemptions instead of reducing rates, given an equivalent cost in state revenue, actually makes Michiganians richer by retaining more income in Michigan, rather that sending it to Washington, D.C.[26]

One final point to make about deductibility pertains to the distribution of the state income tax, taking federal exporting into account. Since both the probability and the benefit of itemization increase with income level, the average or effective rates net of the deductibility do not rise as much with income as they would when deductibility is ignored. Table 26.7 shows the average tax rates by 2000 income for Michigan residents. Note that average rates rise monotonically after all credits (column 5) but level off at the $30,000 to $50,000 level once the "federal offset" (the effect of deductibility on state income tax liability) is taken into account. Hence, the net effect of deductibility is to make Michigan's income tax less progressive than it would be absent deductibility.[27]

**TABLE 26.7**

**Michigan Income Tax: Effective Tax Rates for Michigan Residents, 2000**

| Adjusted Gross Income Range | Tax Rate before Credits | Tax Rate after Non-refundable Credits | Tax Rate after Non-refundable Credits and Federal Offset | Tax Rate after All Credits | Tax Rate after All Credits and Federal Offset |
|---|---|---|---|---|---|
| $1–$10,000 | 1.7 | 1.6 | 1.6 | –0.9 | –0.9 |
| $10,000–$20,000 | 2.1 | 2.0 | 2.0 | 0.9 | 0.9 |
| $20,000–$30,000 | 2.7 | 2.6 | 2.6 | 2.1 | 2.0 |
| $30,000–$50,000 | 3.0 | 2.9 | 2.7 | 2.7 | 2.5 |
| $50,000–$75,000 | 3.2 | 3.2 | 2.7 | 3.0 | 2.6 |
| $75,000–$100,000 | 3.4 | 3.3 | 2.6 | 3.3 | 2.6 |
| $100,000–$200,000 | 3.6 | 3.6 | 2.6 | 3.6 | 2.6 |
| >$200,000 | 3.8 | 3.8 | 2.5 | 3.8 | 2.5 |
| OVERALL TOTAL | 3.3 | 3.2 | 2.6 | 3.0 | 2.4 |

SOURCES: Michigan income tax data are from the Income Tax Simulation, Office of Revenue and Tax Analysis. The probability of claiming itemized deductions for each income group was estimated from the 1999 Statistics of Income for Michigan returns, available at *www.irs.gov*. The marginal federal tax rate for each income group was estimated using Table 2 from Individual Income Tax Rate and Tax Shares, 1998, available at *www.irs.gov*.
PREPARED BY: Office of Revenue and Tax Analysis, Michigan Department of Treasury.

**TABLE 26.8**

### State Individual Income Taxes for FY 2000 Per Person and as Percentage of Personal Income

| State | Per Person Individual Income Taxes | Rank | Income Taxes as a % of Personal Income | Rank |
|---|---|---|---|---|
| Alabama | $465 | 37 | 2.00% | 35 |
| Alaska | No Tax | N/A | No Tax | N/A |
| Arizona | 444 | 38 | 1.84% | 38 |
| Arkansas | 549 | 34 | 2.56% | 26 |
| California | 1,164 | 5 | 3.79% | 4 |
| Colorado | 841 | 15 | 2.72% | 18 |
| Connecticut | 1,165 | 4 | 2.95% | 14 |
| Delaware | 933 | 9 | 3.13% | 13 |
| Florida | No Tax | N/A | No Tax | N/A |
| Georgia | 773 | 17 | 2.88% | 15 |
| Hawaii | 878 | 11 | 3.22% | 11 |
| Idaho | 743 | 18 | 3.25% | 9 |
| Illinois | 614 | 30 | 1.99% | 36 |
| Indiana | 616 | 29 | 2.35% | 33 |
| Iowa | 646 | 26 | 2.51% | 29 |
| Kansas | 692 | 23 | 2.59% | 25 |
| Kentucky | 667 | 25 | 2.87% | 16 |
| Louisiana | 354 | 39 | 1.56% | 40 |
| Maine | 843 | 14 | 3.40% | 8 |
| Maryland | 869 | 12 | 2.69% | 21 |
| Massachusetts | 1,422 | 1 | 3.95% | 3 |
| Michigan | 723 | 21 | 2.51% | 30 |
| Minnesota | 1,125 | 6 | 3.66% | 6 |
| Mississippi | 353 | 40 | 1.73% | 39 |
| Missouri | 634 | 27 | 2.40% | 32 |
| Montana | 572 | 32 | 2.62% | 23 |
| Nebraska | 685 | 24 | 2.52% | 27 |
| Nevada | No Tax | N/A | No Tax | N/A |
| New Hampshire | 53 | 42 | 0.17% | 42 |
| New Jersey | 855 | 13 | 2.40% | 31 |
| New Mexico | 484 | 36 | 2.27% | 34 |
| New York | 1,221 | 2 | 3.72% | 5 |
| North Carolina | 879 | 10 | 3.41% | 7 |
| North Dakota | 310 | 41 | 1.29% | 41 |
| Ohio | 725 | 20 | 2.65% | 22 |
| Oklahoma | 618 | 28 | 2.69% | 20 |
| Oregon | 1,195 | 3 | 4.45% | 1 |
| Pennsylvania | 551 | 33 | 1.92% | 37 |
| Rhode Island | 789 | 16 | 2.79% | 17 |
| South Carolina | 608 | 31 | 2.61% | 24 |
| South Dakota | No Tax | N/A | No Tax | N/A |
| Tennessee | 32 | 43 | 0.13% | 43 |
| Texas | No Tax | N/A | No Tax | N/A |
| Utah | 737 | 19 | 3.25% | 10 |
| Vermont | 709 | 22 | 2.71% | 19 |
| Virginia | 961 | 8 | 3.21% | 12 |
| Washington | No Tax | N/A | No Tax | N/A |
| West Virginia | 534 | 35 | 2.52% | 28 |
| Wisconsin | 1,108 | 7 | 4.05% | 2 |
| Wyoming | No Tax | N/A | No Tax | N/A |
| U.S. average | $689 | | 2.43% | |
| U.S. average for states w/ general income tax | $853 | | 2.97% | |

SOURCES: Census Bureau and Bureau of Economic Analysis, U.S. Department of Commerce.

## Interstate Comparison of State Income Taxes

A comparison of Michigan's income tax with other state income taxes in terms of revenue yield has been assembled by the U.S. Bureau of Census and is presented in table 26.8. According to these figures, Michigan is not a relatively high income tax state. Michigan ranks at or below the median in the terms of revenue per person and as a percentage of income, ranking twenty-first and thirtieth, respectively, among the forty-three states with income taxes (see State of Michigan, Department of Treasury 2001, 21).

Another way to compare tax obligations across states is to compare the potentially highest rates to which a taxpayer can be subject.[28] Since most states employ graduated income tax structures and Michigan does not, it would seem that high-income Michiganians would fare rather well. A comparative study done by the Wisconsin Legislative Fiscal Bureau in 1999 confirms this conjecture. Among the forty-three states (plus Washington, D.C.) that levy an income tax, there are only three states with a lower top marginal rate than Michigan (see column 3 in table 26.9). The tradeoff to this favorable treatment for high-income taxpayers is higher rates at the bottom end of the income scale. When compared to the other states with income taxation, it appears that most of these have a lower bottom rate than does Michigan (table 26.9, column 2).

## Michigan's Income Tax Treatment of Seniors

Many state income taxes preferentially tax sources of income received by seniors (see table 26.10). Michigan employs preferential taxation to an exceptional degree: in addition to taxing no Social Security income, the state taxes no public pension income (local, state, or federal, including military pensions) and the state exempts private pension or IRA income up to the allowable exemption of $36,090 for a single filer and $72,180 for a married couple (in 2001).[29] These allowances are indexed to inflation. In addition, Michigan allows seniors (as measured by those taxpayers claiming an age sixty-five exemption) an indexed exemption for investment income (interest, dividends, and capital gains) of $8,048 for a single person and $16,095 for a couple. Furthermore, Michigan allows special senior exemptions of $1,900 per person (indexed) and an enhanced property tax credit.[30] Consider the following

**TABLE 26.9**

## Tax Rates and Brackets by State (Tax Year 1999)

| State | Marginal Tax Rates | | | Top Marginal Tax Rate Begins at: | |
|---|---|---|---|---|---|
| | Lowest Tax Rate | Top Tax Rate | Number of Brackets | Single Bracket | Married, Filing Jointly Bracket |
| Alabama | 2.0% | 5.0% | 3 | $3,000 | $6,000 |
| Arizona | 2.87 | 5.04 | 5 | 150,000 | 300,000 |
| Arkansas | 1.0 | 7.0 | 6 | 25,400 | 25,400 |
| California | 1.0 | 9.3 | 6 | 34,548 | 69,096 |
| Colorado | 4.75 | 4.75 | Flat Rate | — | — |
| Connecticut | 3.0 | 4.5 | 2 | 10,000 | 20,000 |
| Delaware | 0.0 | 6.4 | 7 | 60,000 | 60,000 |
| District of Columbia | 6.0 | 9.5 | 3 | 20,000 | 20,000 |
| Georgia | 1.0 | 6.0 | 6 | 7,000 | 10,000 |
| Hawaii | 1.6 | 8.75 | 9 | 40,000 | 80,000 |
| Idaho | 2.0 | 8.2 | 8 | 20,000 | 40,000 |
| Illinois | 3.0 | 3.0 | Flat Rate | — | — |
| Indiana | 3.4 | 3.4 | Flat Rate | — | — |
| Iowa | 0.36 | 8.98 | 9 | 51,660 | 51,660 |
| Kansas | 3.5 | 6.45 | 3 | 30,000 | 60,000 |
| Kentucky | 2.0 | 6.0 | 5 | 8,000 | 8,000 |
| Louisiana | 2.0 | 6.0 | 3 | 50,000 | 100,000 |
| Maine | 2.0 | 8.5 | 4 | 16,500 | 33,000 |
| Maryland | 2.0 | 4.85 | 4 | 3,000 | 3,000 |
| Massachusetts[a] | 4.0 | 12.0 | Flat Rate | — | — |
| Michigan | 4.4 | 4.4 | Flat Rate | — | — |
| Minnesota | 5.5 | 8.0 | 3 | 56,680 | 100,200 |
| Mississippi | 3.0 | 5.0 | 3 | 10,000 | 10,000 |
| Missouri | 1.5 | 6.0 | 10 | 9,000 | 9,000 |
| Montana | 2.0 | 11.0 | 10 | 70,400 | 70,400 |
| Nebraska | 2.51 | 6.68 | 4 | 26,500 | 46,750 |
| New Hampshire | 5.0 | 5.0 | Flat Rate | — | — |
| New Jersey | 1.4 | 6.37 | 5/6 | 75,000 | 150,000 |
| New Mexico | 1.7 | 8.2 | 7 | 65,000 | 100,000 |
| New York | 4.0 | 6.85 | 5 | 20,000 | 40,000 |
| North Carolina | 6.0 | 7.75 | 3 | 60,000 | 100,000 |
| North Dakota[b] | 2.67/14.0 | 12.0/14.0 | 8/% of Fed. | 50,000 | 50,000 |
| Ohio | 0.716 | 7.228 | 9 | 200,000 | 200,000 |
| Oklahoma | 0.5 | 6.75/10.0 | 8/11 | 16,000 | 24,000 |
| Oregon | 5.0 | 9.0 | 3 | 5,900 | 11,800 |
| Pennsylvania | 2.8 | 2.8 | Flat Rate | — | — |
| Rhode Island | 26.5 | 26.5 | % of Fed. | — | — |
| South Carolina | 2.5 | 7.0 | 6 | 11,700 | 11,700 |
| Tennessee | 6.0 | 6.0 | Flat Rate | — | — |
| Utah | 2.3 | 7.0 | 6 | 3,750 | 7,500 |
| Vermont | 25.0 | 25.0 | % of Fed. | — | — |
| Virginia | 2.0 | 5.75 | 4 | 17,000 | 17,000 |
| West Virginia | 3.0 | 6.5 | 5 | 60,000 | 60,000 |
| Wisconsin | 4.77 | 6.77 | 3 | 15,240 | 20,320 |

SOURCE: "Individual Income Tax Provisions in the States," State of Wisconsin, Legislative Fiscal Bureau, January 2001.
(a) Massachusetts has three flat tax rates, each of which is applied to different sources of income.
(b) Most taxpayers use the method that imposes state tax equal to 14% of adjusted federal tax liability.

**TABLE 26.10**

**State Tax Exclusion for Pension/Retirement Income (Tax Year 1999)**

| State | Private | State and Local | Federal Civilian | Military |
|---|---|---|---|---|
| Alabama | None | Most exempt | Exempt | Exempt |
| Arizona | None | $2,500 | $2,500 | $2,500 |
| Arkansas | $6,000 | $6,000 | $6,000 | $6,000 |
| California | None | None | None | None |
| Colorado | $20,000 | $20,000 | $20,000 | $20,000 |
| Connecticut | None | None | None | None |
| Delaware | $2,000/$5,000 | $2,000/$5,000 | $2,000/$5,000 | $2,000/$5,000 |
| District of Columbia | None | $3,000 | $3,000 | $3,000 |
| Georgia | $13,000 | $13,000 | $13,000 | $13,000 |
| Hawaii | State Calculation | Exempt | Exempt | Exempt |
| Idaho | None | $16,788/$25,182[a] | $16,788/$25,182[a] | $16,788/$25,182[a] |
| Illinois | Exempt | Exempt | Exempt | Exempt |
| Indiana | None | None | $2,000 | $2,000 |
| Iowa | $5,000/$10,000 | $5,000/$10,000 | $5,000/$10,000 | $5,000/$10,000 |
| Kansas | None | Exempt | Exempt | Exempt |
| Kentucky | Up to $35,700 | Exempt | Exempt | Exempt |
| Louisiana | $6,000 | Exempt | Exempt | Exempt |
| Maine | None | None | None | None |
| Maryland | $16,100 | $16,100 | $16,100 | $16,100 |
| Massachusetts | None | Exempt[b] | Exempt[b] | Exempt |
| Michigan | $34,170/$68,340 | Exempt | Exempt | Exempt |
| Minnesota | None | None | None | None |
| Mississippi | Exempt | Exempt | Exempt | Exempt |
| Missouri | $3,000 | $6,000 | $6,000 | $6,000 |
| Montana | $3,600 | $3,600 | $3,600 | $3,600 |
| Nebraska | None | None | None | None |
| New Hampshire | Exempt | Exempt | Exempt | Exempt |
| New Jersey | $7,500/$10,000 | $7,500/$10,000 | $7,500/$10,000 | $7,500/$10,000 |
| New Mexico | None | None | None | None |
| New York | $20,000 | Exempt | Exempt | Exempt |
| North Carolina | $2,000 | $4,000 | $4,000 | $4,000 |
| North Dakota | None | None/$5,000[a] | None/$5,000[a] | None/$5,000[a] |
| Ohio | $200 credit | $200 credit | $200 credit | $200 credit |
| Oklahoma | $3,300 | $5,500 | $5,500 | $5,500 |
| Oregon | 9% credit | 9% credit | Pre-1991 exempt | 9% credit |
| Pennsylvania | Exempt | Exempt | Exempt | Exempt |
| Rhode Island | None | None | None | None |
| South Carolina | $3,000/$10,000 | $3,000/$10,000 | $3,000/$10,000 | $3,000/$10,000 |
| Tennessee | Exempt | Exempt | Exempt | Exempt |
| Utah | $4,800/$7,500 | $4,800/$7,500 | $4,800/$7,500 | $4,800/$7,500 |
| Vermont | None | None | None | None |
| Virginia | None | None | None | None |
| West Virginia | None | $2000 | $2,000 | $2,000 |
| Wisconsin | None | Pre-1964 Exempt | Pre-1964 Exempt | Pre-1964 Exempt |

SOURCE: "Individual Income Tax Provisions in the States," State of Wisconsin, Legislative Fiscal Bureau, January 2001.
(a) reduced by amount of social security received.
(b) only contributory pension income is exempt.

**TABLE 26.11**

**Effective Tax Rates from Three-Year Panel of Michigan Resident Taxpayers, 1998 Senior Returns for Tax Years 1998–2000**

| Three-Year Average AGI | Senior Returns | | | Nonsenior Returns | | |
|---|---|---|---|---|---|---|
| | Number of Returns | Average AGI | Average Tax Rate | Number of Returns | Average AGI | Average Tax Rate |
| ≤ $0 | 86,120 | –$442 | | 40,190 | –$5,592 | |
| $1–$5,000 | 42,320 | 2,430 | –30.2% | 186,480 | 3,159 | –1.1% |
| $5,001–$10,000 | 45,530 | 7,626 | –7.9% | 269,680 | 7,461 | 0.8% |
| $10,001–$15,000 | 45,530 | 12,425 | –4.3% | 249,620 | 12,462 | 1.4% |
| $15,001–$20,000 | 32,550 | 17,347 | –2.8% | 239,280 | 17,484 | 1.9% |
| $20,001–$25,000 | 20,800 | 22,319 | –1.8% | 224,690 | 22,478 | 2.4% |
| $25,001–$30,000 | 14,350 | 27,379 | –1.2% | 205,100 | 27,440 | 2.6% |
| $30,001–$35,000 | 10,230 | 32,420 | –0.8% | 184,390 | 32,449 | 2.8% |
| $35,001–$40,000 | 7,640 | 37,473 | –0.5% | 169,900 | 37,453 | 2.9% |
| $40,001–$45,000 | 6,580 | 42,403 | –0.4% | 156,160 | 42,468 | 3.0% |
| $45,001–$50,000 | 4,630 | 47,435 | –0.1% | 147,680 | 47,456 | 3.1% |
| $50,001–$60,000 | 7,340 | 54,615 | 0.3% | 266,380 | 54,885 | 3.2% |
| $60,001–$70,000 | 4,420 | 64,892 | 0.5% | 218,720 | 64,820 | 3.3% |
| $70,001–$80,000 | 2,700 | 74,617 | 0.7% | 172,410 | 74,779 | 3.4% |
| $80,001–$90,000 | 1,460 | 84,369 | 1.5% | 129,320 | 84,733 | 3.5% |
| $90,001–$100,000 | 520 | 93,889 | 2.0% | 95,150 | 94,714 | 3.5% |
| $100,001–$125,000 | 540 | 110,145 | 2.0% | 138,430 | 110,921 | 3.6% |
| $125,001–$150,000 | 150 | 135,101 | 2.5% | 63,540 | 135,698 | 3.7% |
| > $150,000 | 330 | 269,270 | 3.3% | 108,440 | 338,740 | 3.9% |
| | 333,740 | $14,220 | –3.4% | 3,265,560 | $51,662 | 3.3% |

SOURCE: Office of Revenue and Tax Analysis, Michigan Department of Treasury.

NOTE: Estimates are based on a panel created by matching returns based on 10% random sample for each year 1998–2000. The panel represents 80.9% of the 1998 returns, 80.1% of 1999 returns, and 78.6% of 2000 returns.

example. A senior couple with $100,000 in income (e.g., $64,000 in private pension, $19,000 in Social Security income, and $17,000 in property income) would pay no Michigan income tax. If the couple's income was somewhat lower, $70,000, and the couple paid $3,600 per year in property tax or $1,500 per month in rent, they would actually be paying a negative tax (receive a subsidy) of $1,200 for the year, due to the refundable nature of the property tax credit. Table 26.10 shows that, among the forty-three states (plus the District of Columbia) with an income tax, Michigan's preferential income tax treatment for seniors is among the most generous in the nation.

The Office of Revenue and Tax Analysis in the Michigan Department of Treasury has provided, for scientific purposes, some tabulations based upon the 567,937 federal income tax returns filed from Michigan for 1999 in which at least one exemption for age sixty-five or over was taken. These data reveal $7.8 billion in total federally taxable pension and IRA income. The share of that

total exempt from the Michigan income tax is $7.3 billion, or 93%. Furthermore, if we compute for each of these tax returns the ratio of Michigan taxable income (prior to personal and senior exemptions and all credits) to federal adjusted gross income, the mean is 18% (which compares to 81% for nonseniors). Among the seniors who report any adjusted gross income on their federal income tax return, the proportion having to pay any Michigan income tax is approximately 13%.

Table 26.11 presents the distribution of average income tax rates, including the effects of all credits, among the population of senior and nonsenior taxpayers in Michigan. One striking finding is that while some seniors do make a net positive contribution to income tax revenues, taken as a whole, seniors on net pay no income tax. Indeed, the net amount contributed by all seniors is a *negative* 3.4%. Second, adjusted gross income among seniors is quite low on average. Hence, generous treatment of seniors does augment the progressivity of the income tax. However, such an indirect approach to augmented vertical equity has other unfortunate effects on horizontal equity, efficiency, and simplicity.

The comparison of effective tax rates between seniors and nonseniors reveals that seniors face significantly lower rates than nonseniors within the same income bracket. For example, at the $20,000 to $25,000 income level, the ATR for seniors is −1.8%, as compared with 2.4% for nonseniors. As a tax analyst, it is hard to understand or justify such horizontal inequity.[31] Looking back at the history of this favorable treatment, it appears that initially state employees received the right to have tax-free pensions, and then a "me-too" argument ultimately persuaded the state to grant tax-free status to an increasing portion of private pensions, followed by tax-exempt status for some property income.

While it is true that seniors may face higher expenses, such as unreimbursed health care outlays, the best policy is to allow a deduction for such expenses, as the federal income tax does and many state income systems do. After all, some younger taxpayers have high health care costs as well, while some elderly have low costs. A point relevant to the efficiency cost of this provision arises when we compare the tax treatment of a senior trying to supplement his Social Security payments (for example, by taking a job as a grocery store employee) with his neighbor living off a comfortable pension. While the pensioner need not pay any income tax, the wages received by our friend in the grocery are fully taxable. Besides the obvious inequity of this differential treatment, the state is providing an incentive for wage earners to retire from the labor force in favor of living off their pensions. The income tax treatment of private pension income adds complexity to the system. While most pension income is potentially exempt, certain pension income resulting from contributions that are unmatched by one's employer is taxable, and determining which pension streams are or are not taxable is not altogether obvious to the taxpayer. (For further discussion of issues related to pensions, see chapter 20 in this volume.)

Given the long-term demographic trend faced by this and other states (see Menchik 2002), the cost of this preferential tax treatment is sure to grow.[32] The share of Michigan's personal income accruing to seniors (including their Social Security income) is currently 13.1%. With both the number and the proportion of seniors forecasted to markedly increase by 2025, this proportion is likely to increase significantly. Unless state income tax policies or the sources of income change in the future, the evolving demography interacting with the preferential income tax treatment of seniors is likely to contribute to fiscal stress in the long run. Although it may be unrealistic to expect a rollback in these preferential policies, one more modest strategy would be to freeze the exemption levels in current dollars (as the property tax credit is currently being handled) to limit the magnitude of the tax preference.

## Conclusion

Michigan's income tax has become an increasingly important source of revenue for the state. Unlike most other states, Michigan has a flat-rate tax that is made mildly progressive by its personal exemptions and many credits. However, some of the factors that augment progressivity create other problems, such as inefficiencies, horizontal inequities, and complexity. In addition, the flat-rate nature of the tax limits the amount of matching revenue, specifically the benefits of federal deductibility, that *could* be realized with a graduated tax of equal yield. The preceding analysis suggests that an equal yield movement to a graduated income tax rate structure would provide a net benefit to Michigan's citizens. However, such a change would require amending the state constitution, and is probably a political impossibility. Indeed, Michigan's voters have defeated previous attempts to amend the constitution to allow graduation. A feasible reform proposal might be to combine exemption increases with rate increases, while limiting the loss of revenue associated with the credits. If such increases in the personal exemptions are regarded as providing too much relief for households with children as compared to those without, implementing a standard deduction or a nonrefundable earned income tax credit might be an alternative policy worthy of consideration.[33]

Michigan appears to be out of step with the rest of the nation in the degree to which income sources received by seniors are favored under its income tax. Such a large degree of preferential treatment raises important equity, efficiency, and simplicity concerns. Given predicted long-term demographic trends, such policies are very hard to justify, and will be very hard to afford in future years.

■

## REFERENCES

Atkinson, A.B., and A. Sandmo. 1980. Welfare implications of the taxation of savings. *Economic Journal* 90: 529–49.

Blume, L. 1982. The sales and use taxes. In *Michigan's fiscal and economic structure*, edited by Harvey E. Brazer, with Deborah S. Laren. Ann Arbor: University of Michigan Press.

Congressional Budget Office. 1997. Comparing income and consumption tax bases. July.

Dunbar, W., and G. May. 1995. *A history of the wolverine state*. Grand Rapids, Mich.: Eerdmans.

Fullerton, D., and D. L. Rodgers. 1994. *Who bears the lifetime tax burden?* Washington, D.C.: Brookings Institution.

Menchik, P. 2002. Demographic change and fiscal stress on states—The case of Michigan. *National Tax Association Proceedings* 90–98.

Menchik, P., and M. David. 1983. Income distribution, lifetime savings, and bequests. *American Economic Review* 83: 672–90.

*National Tax Journal,* Special Issue The Earned Income Tax Credit. 2000. 53(4).

Neumark, D., and W. Wascher. 2001. Using the EITC to help poor families: New evidence and a comparison with the minimum wage. *National Tax Journal* 54: 281–317.

Poterba, J. 1989. Lifetime incidence and the distributional burden of excise taxes. *American Economic Review papers and proceedings* 79: 325–30.

Sammartino, F., E. Toder, and E. Maag. 2002. Providing federal assistance for low-income families through the tax system: A primer. Urban-Brookings Tax Policy Center, Discussion Paper No. 4.

State of Michigan. 2002a. *Executive budget-Tax expenditure appendix, Fiscal Year 2002.*

———. 2002b. Michigan's Individual Income Tax, July.

State of Michigan, Michigan Department of Treasury, Office of Revenue and Tax Analysis. 2001. Michigan's Individual Income Tax, May.

## NOTES

I owe special thanks to the Michigan Department of Treasury's Office of Revenue and Tax Analysis, and to Mark Haas, Howard Heideman, and especially Scott Darragh for assistance in the preparation of this chapter.

1. Computed before refundable credits. The net amount raised by the income tax after the refundable credits are subtracted is $6.7 billion, which accounts for 30.1% of taxes raised. Computed as a share of all revenues, including grants-in-aid, the income tax before credits amounts to 20.2%, or 18.8% after credits are subtracted.

2. However, New Hampshire and Tennessee employ income taxes only upon property income, exempting taxation of labor earnings.

3. An alternative measure of ability to pay would be levels of wealth and consumption.

4. Sometimes the term *effective*, rather than *average*, is used to convey the same concept.

5. This is due to the fact that some taxpayers may only temporarily be in a low-income position, due perhaps to a layoff. Given their longer-run prospects, they will rationally dip into their savings to maintain consumption standards based on their permanent situation. Consequently, for these cases the one-year ATR may lie above their longer-run ATR, and the measured ATRs at lower incomes will be higher than they would be using a longer accounting period. In this chapter I used a three-year accounting period (the longest period matched panel data set available for research purposes) when I could. In tabulations requiring more detailed data, like tax credit information, the one-year "snapshot" period was used.

6. Menchik and David (1983) found this to be the case in a sample of Wisconsin taxpayers, but more recent data on this topic are sorely needed.

7. See Congressional Budget Office 1997. Based on computer simulation of the Fullerton-Rogers general equilibrium model, efficiency gains at the national level from moving from the income tax to a consumption tax, figured as a percentage of lifetime income, would be approximately zero (chapter 5, footnote 28) and could even be negative. Given the uncertainties of the model and around key parameters, economists just do not yet know which tax is more efficient.

8. Note that this constitutional language does *not* prohibit progression because it does not rule out subtractions such as exemptions or refundable credits. For a history of the establishment of the Michigan income tax see Dunbar and May 1995.

9. If the real value of the original $1,200 exemption was preserved, the exemption per person for tax year 2001 would be $6,360.

10. An exception would be Michigan's use of "additions" into its tax base.

11. The treatment of capital gains under an income tax has inspired quite a lot of animated discussion and debate. At the federal level, capital gains are treated preferentially in four ways—deferral (often defended on simplicity grounds), exclusion on home sale gains, forgiveness of gains at death, and

reduced rates on long-term gains—and capital gains are treated harshly in one way, through taxation of nominal (not inflation-adjusted) gains. The state of Michigan does not tax long-term gains at reduced rates, but follows federal practice on the other four matters.

12. See, most recently, State of Michigan 2002.

13. For senior taxpayers, or those with certain disabilities, who have low incomes, the income threshold is gradually reduced from the 3.5% level down to zero. For example, a senior taxpayer with an income of $4,500 would receive as a credit the amount of property taxes paid in excess of 2% of income, or $90 for the year.

14. The total amount of personal exemption is $10,600 (= $2,900 × 4), plus there would two $600 child exemptions, adding to a total of $12,800 in exemptions. Subtracting that from the $30,000 income yields $17,200 in taxable income, which, when multiplied by the 4.2% tax rate, yields $722.40.

15. Multiply the $30,000 by 3.5%, which yields $1,050. The excess of the $1,800 over $1,050 is $750, which when multiplied by .6 equals $450.

16. See, e.g., State of Michigan, Michigan Department of Treasury, Office of Revenue and Tax Analysis 2001.

17. This analysis may *understate* the disincentive. The way the phaseout actually works can be characterized as a "notch." Over the income interval $73,650 to $82,650, an additional 10% loss of credit is triggered when income is equal to or greater than a sum ending with the digits 651 (e.g., 74,651; 75,651; etc.). This means that the last amount of earnings that vaults a taxpayer to $*xx*,651 (with *xx* representing any number between 73 and 82) results in a severe financial cost. If the last $100 in earnings loses the taxpayer $120, the implicit tax rate on earnings is 120%. To the extent that the taxpayer understands these rules, we could expect a severe work disincentive to result.

18. See State of Michigan 2002.

19. For example, in the federal tax expenditure budget, the cost in forgone income tax revenue of the federal practice of step-up of cost basis at death in computing capital gains ranks as the ninth largest item, estimated to cost $28.7 billion in fiscal 2003. For some reason, the prorated value of this tax expenditure is missing from Michigan's tax expenditure report.

20. In this table, as with all panel data, there was attrition, since some taxpayers were not represented in all three years, due to interstate migration and death. Therefore, the aggregate number of returns falls short of statewide totals.

21. Recall that the income taxes paid to other states by Michigan residents on certain kinds of out-of-state property income goes unreported as a Michigan tax obligation. If this income source is positively correlated with in-state income, measured progressivity has been understated.

22. This figure is obtained from Internal Revenue Service data using the proportion of taxpayers itemizing at alternate income intervals across the income spectrum and the marginal tax rates over these intervals. The 20% figure is in agreement with the estimate made independently by Joel Slemrod in his chapter on sales taxation (chapter 27) in this volume.

23. Recall that it was pointed out that the CBO study of the efficiency of comprehensive consumption versus income taxation finds there to be a toss-up, and the cost in simplicity of a piggyback state income tax is rather low. Consequently, if the income tax is to be favored over the sales tax on equity grounds, the analysis favoring the shift would be compelling.

24. See Internal Revenue Service web page, *www.irs.ustreas.gov/tax/stats/display*. I used 1999 tax year data from table 99IN23MI.XLS.

25. An unexpected corollary would be that in order to increase the federal matching grant deductibility provides, Michigan should income tax most harshly those with a large amount expended on categories that could be itemized deductions on the federal return, like mortgage interest and property tax expenses, because they would likely itemize. Michigan, with its sizeable property tax credit provision, does just the opposite.

26. This result is subject to the caveat that the higher marginal tax rate on state income tax payers may result in a higher efficiency cost.

27. One possible remedy to counteract this erosion in progressivity would be an equal yield swap, larger exemptions for a higher rate. Such a swap would also have the virtue of leading to increased federal tax exporting.

28. State officials concerned with losing as residents the highest income and the potentially most mobile taxpayers may be particularly concerned with the top rates.

29. It should be pointed out that if a taxpayer has both public and private pension income, the amount of the exempt public pension income reduces the effective private pension exemption.

30. Seniors receive the credit based upon 100% of the excess of 3.5% of income paid in property taxes, while nonseniors receive a credit of 60% of the excess. In addition, low-income taxpayers who are seniors face a reduced threshold in order to qualify for the credit.

31. Regarding income tax, the federal government is far less generous than Michigan in its treatment of seniors.

32. The number of Michiganians sixty-five and older in 2025 is forecasted to grow by 50%, while the number aged twenty-five to sixty-four is expected to decline.

33. A nonrefundable credit is far less costly than a refundable credit and would lead to average income tax rates rising with income and at the same time would stimulate work effort instead of consumption of expensive living quarters, as the property tax credit does. If a limited refundable earned income tax credit program is desired, that, too, could be included in the income tax code.

# 27

# Michigan's Sales and Use Taxes: Portrait and Analysis

*Joel Slemrod*

## Background

As of 1931, no state levied a retail sales tax (RST). Until that time, states had relied mostly on property taxes, business taxes, excise taxes, and, in a few states, income taxes. By the 1930s, though, state revenue was under pressure, both because of the Depression and because of the movement to transfer the property tax to local governments. In 1932, Mississippi adopted a retail sales tax at a rate of 2% as a replacement for a business tax. Michigan was one of nine states that introduced a RST (at a rate of 3%) soon after, in 1933.

Seventy years later, at the turn of the new millennium, sales and use taxes now account for 32% of state government tax collections nationwide, trailing only the individual income tax as a source of revenue. They are imposed by forty-five states and the District of Columbia, as well as over 7,500 local jurisdictions. In fiscal year 2001, the Michigan retail sales tax and the complementary use tax raised $7.7 billion, compared to individual income tax revenues of $6.8 billion.

By the standard of generating tax revenue, the Michigan RST is clearly a success. Yet is it a success by the criteria of public finance—equity, efficiency, and simplicity—relative to alternative ways of generating revenue? Furthermore, can the RST be improved so as to make it a more success-

ful tax? This chapter addresses these two questions. It does so by first reviewing the arguments for and against an idealized RST. It next addresses Michigan's RST, warts and all, and places it in the context of a federal tax system dominated by the national income tax.

## The Pros and Cons of the RST

Economists are accustomed to analyzing any tax system against the criteria of equity, efficiency, and simplicity, and to applying formal models of excess burden and incidence to make these analyses. The political reality from which the RST emerges is far removed from this kind of analysis, and is well summarized in the following appraisal of the RST from the widely cited treatise on the RST by Due and Mikesell (1995):

> Support for a sales tax in most states has come mainly from the state administration, which has sought additional revenue to meet expenditure demands in the face of inadequate revenues from other sources. Support has also come from business groups (other than retailers) fearing higher income and property taxes, from farmers seeking property tax relief, and from school officials and teachers seeking additional funds for schools. Institutional

opposition has come primarily from labor groups objecting to the regressivity, and from retailers concerned about compliance costs and adverse reactions from customers. (4)

Due and Mikesell's characterization of the political context surrounding the RST raises some important issues. First, the desirability of raising revenue with a RST should be evaluated relative to the alternatives, which may be some other tax, reduced expenditures, or some combination of both. In Michigan, one principal revenue alternative is the state personal income tax. Another is the single business tax, which is in many ways akin to an RST. Yet another is the property tax; as part of its 1994 school finance reform, Michigan shifted toward less reliance on property taxes and more reliance on the RST. Second, political attention centers on the distribution of the tax burden and compliance costs, rather than on another traditional focus of economists—economic efficiency.

The Cliff's Notes assessment of the RST is that it is a simple, efficient tax that unavoidably imposes a regressive distribution of the tax burden. According to that assessment, the RST does well on the simplicity and efficiency criteria of a good tax, but falls short on the equity criterion. All three of these judgments need elaboration.

### Equity

The case that the RST is regressive rests largely on the observation that, on average in any given year, those with lower income spend a much higher percentage of their income than do higher-income households. Thus, it is reasoned, any tax that is proportional to consumption must impose a regressive burden. However, a large body of literature (Poterba 1989; Lyon and Schwab 1995; Casperson and Metcalf 1994; Fullerton and Rogers 1994) suggests that incidence analysis based on a snapshot of annual income and consumption overestimates the regressivity of sales taxes. This is because over a lifetime (and ignoring transfers from the government as well as bequests and inheritances) the present value of consumption must equal the present value of labor income—in other words, eventually all income is spent. The fact that, in any given year, those with low income exhibit high spending-income ratios generally means that these people have transitorily low incomes and set their consumption based on

their permanent expectation of income. The conclusion is that the burden of a uniform consumption tax is not much different than the burden of a flat-rate tax on labor income. This conclusion must be modified if the consumption tax base is not all-inclusive and instead includes goods that figure more heavily in the total expenditures of particular income groups. In this case the distributional effect of the tax depends on the propensities of different income groups to consume exempted goods. In this context, the exemption of food is undoubtedly an attempt to render the sales tax burden more progressive than otherwise. To the extent that exempted goods are consumed disproportionately by higher-income households, the sales tax burden is less progressive than otherwise.

If the principal alternative to the Michigan RST is the personal income tax, a few of the attributes of the income tax are notable. First, it is a flat-rate tax with an exempt level of income based on marital status (and the number of dependents), so it is more progressive than a proportional tax with no exemptions, which characterizes the Michigan RST as a first approximation. Second, it is a comprehensive income tax, not a tax only on labor income. The fact that the income tax base includes capital income suggests that it is even more progressive than otherwise. This is certainly true for the Michigan personal income tax, the base of which is all capital income, regardless of source. Finally, the effective progressivity of the RST versus an income tax also depends on the fact that only the latter is deductible from federal taxable income. Deductibility makes the income tax less progressive than the state rate schedule suggests, because the deduction is more likely to be available to, and is worth more at the margin for, high-income taxpayers. I return to this issue in section 2.

The mobility of capital and labor across states raises the general question of whether state governments should, or even *can*, redistribute. The conventional wisdom is that redistribution should primarily be the responsibility of the national government, because individual mobility will undermine any state attempts to redistribute. Feldstein and Wrobel (1998) conclude that differences in the effective progressivity of state income taxes are offset by changes in gross wages, so that the net distribution of income is unchanged, and state attempts to achieve a progressive distribution of the tax burden are thereby thwarted. This is, however, a controversial conclusion. For example,

Chernick and Reschovsky (1996) argue that mobility of high-income individuals is an issue only for states that are in close geographic proximity. The case that states *cannot* redistribute is not compelling, leaving open the question of whether they *should*.

## Efficiency

The efficiency question is whether the RST raises revenue with a lower cost to the economy than the likely alternative. Comparing a pure, uniform RST to a pure, comprehensive proportional income tax, the essential difference is the treatment of capital income. The RST, or any consumption tax, does not tax capital income and therefore does not distort individuals' and firms' decisions regarding saving and investment. An income tax does tax capital income and therefore does distort these decisions. Whether an optimal tax system *certainly* avoids this kind of distortion—and thus favors consumption taxes—is highly controversial and remains an unsettled issue.

The theoretical evaluation of pure tax types is not directly relevant, however. Because the actual RST does not exempt all business-to-business sales, it is not a clean consumption tax at all, and has elements of a source-base tax on capital. As Zodrow (1999) says, "it is quite possible that capital income is taxed more heavily under the state sales tax than under the state corporate tax, although this would have to be determined on a state-by-state basis" (38).

The efficiency analysis of the RST must also confront the fact that its base is by no means comprehensive, taxing few services and exempting various goods on distributional and administrative grounds. Here again, the theory of optimal taxation offers little guidance. According to this theory, there is no compelling case for a comprehensive base taxed uniformly, and the most efficient tax system might offer differentially high rates to goods and services that are especially complementary to leisure and low rates to especially substitutable goods and services. However, the empirical evidence needed to pin down these deviations from uniformity is not readily available, and it is not at all clear that the efficiency gains from deviating from uniformity would outweigh the costs of administering the deviations from uniformity and opening up the system to politically motivated rate differentials. The valu-

able policy implication of this body of literature is that, when administrative and political realities are confronted, a broader base of tax levied at a lower rate of tax is likely (but not assuredly) to be more efficient than a higher rate applied to a narrower base.

## Simplicity

Although generally addressed as a separate criterion, simplicity of a tax matters only to the extent that it affects the cost of raising revenue (efficiency) or how the tax burden is assigned (equity). With regard to the RST, much more is known about the former.

Individuals and businesses try, to varying degrees, to avoid paying sales tax (and most other kinds of taxes, for that matter). The amount of tax owed must be calculated, the tax must be collected, and the accounts must be audited, and all of this costs money. The more exemptions to the sales tax a state has, the more expensive it is for a firm to comply with the tax. Firms must keep track of which sales are taxable and which sales are not. They may have to buy new cash registers, or at least spend time and money to reprogram their existing ones, every time the tax laws are changed.

While states can piggyback on the federal income tax to reduce the compliance costs and the enforcement costs of state income taxes, no such luxury is possible for the sales tax. Income tax piggybacking is due not only to federal enforcement, but also to piggybacking on the federal definition of income, record keeping, and so on.

Due and Mikesell (1995) report that in 1991–93 the administrative cost of an RST, as a percentage of revenue, ranged from 0.4 to 1.0 percent in a sample of eight states. Compliance costs borne directly by the taxpayers—retailers in this case—account for the bulk of collection costs. Peat, Marwick, Mitchell, and Company (1982) did the most complete study of compliance costs to retailers. They estimated the cost to retailers in seven states in 1982 to range from 2.0% of tax due in Missouri to 3.75% in Arizona. They found that the main element in compliance costs was the cost of distinguishing between taxable and nontaxable items. A *Tax Administrators News* survey in 1993 combined the results of several studies since 1990 and found an average cost for all retailers in all states of 3.18% of total sales tax collected. The lowest-cost state was Florida (2.69%), and the highest-cost state was Colorado (4.52%). A more recent study by Ernst & Young in 1999 estimates that it costs a small retailer (defined as having less than $250,000 in sales) 87% of the tax to collect and remit it, but this estimate is way out of the range of other estimates.

Adding the estimates for administrative and compliance costs suggests a range of collection costs between 2.4 and 4.8% of revenue collected. Is this high or low, relative to alternative ways of raising revenue? This is difficult to say, for a number of reasons. First, unless the policy under consideration is eliminating either the sales tax or the income tax, what is relevant is the *marginal* cost of raising revenue, about which little is known. Second, most of what we know about the collection costs of income taxes is based on the federal income tax; Slemrod (1996) suggests that it is about 10% of revenues collected. However, because all states, including Michigan, piggyback on the federal income tax system, both in terms of the definition of the tax base and in terms of enforcement, it is almost certainly true that the incremental collection costs imposed on the taxpayers, relative to revenue raised, are lower for the Michigan income tax than for the RST.

## Stability

Tax policy debates at the state (and local) level often add a fourth criterion—stability of revenue—to the well-known troika of equity, efficiency, and simplicity. The case for stability as an independent criterion depends on two assumptions. The first assumption is that a stable source of revenue minimizes the extent to which government services must fluctuate or additional revenues must be raised in bad economic times, given that balanced budgets are required and borrowing capacity is limited in most states. The second is that the cost of these alternatives is high, a claim that is widely accepted but not well documented.

On the first question, Dye and McGuire (1991) conclude that the relative stability of sales tax revenue depends upon the precise composition of the sales tax base. In particular, variability increases when food is exempt from the base, as in Michigan, both because food has a low income elasticity and because its absence puts more weight on business-cycle-sensitive consumer durables. Furthermore, the business purchases part of the base may be quite sensitive to eco-

nomic fluctuations. Also, states like Michigan with a virtually flat individual income tax structure have less revenue variability than states with progressive tax structures.[1] All in all, Dye and McGuire conclude that a narrow sales tax base can be *more* variable than a flat individual income tax. This challenges the conventional wisdom that a sales-tax-based tax structure will certainly reduce cyclical variations in revenue—the structure of each tax matters a lot. Sobel and Holcombe (1996) criticize Dye and McGuire's methodology, but their own analysis also concludes that the retail sales and personal income taxes have similar cyclical variability; they do not, though, examine the importance of the narrowness of actual sales tax bases or the progressivity of the income tax.

### Two Folk Theorems and a Real Theorem

The theory of optimal taxation has embarrassingly little to say definitively about tax structures. It does not resolve definitively whether consumption taxes or income taxes are superior, or whether a consumption tax should have a comprehensive base taxed at uniform rates.

There are, though, two folk theorems that are very influential in practice. The first is that tax bases (consumption or income) should be as broad as possible, thus allowing a relatively low, uniform, tax rate for any given amount of revenue need. This approach does not certainly minimize the excess burden of raising taxes. But, according to the proof of the first folk theorem, political systems cannot differentiate between legitimate and illegitimate claims to tax preference, and a presumption against *any* preferences keeps the tax system from descending the slippery slope to a narrow tax base that is susceptible to political manipulation and the incentives of special interest groups to pursue self-serving legislation.

The second folk theorem is that revenue needs should be spread across more than one kind of tax. The gist of the proof of this theorem is that all taxes have strengths and weaknesses, and they have different strengths and weaknesses, and thus diversification of revenue sources is a good thing.[2] (I said it was a folk theorem). There have been some formal attempts to address this, notably Boadway, Marchand, and Pestieau (1994).

The idea of revenue balance as a criterion, sometimes defined as equal weight between sales and income taxes, has been taken up in the state and local tax literature. The Advisory Commission on Intergovernmental Relations advocates this as an objective of state policy. Shannon (1987) agrees, calling it a "truism" that there is no such thing as an ideal tax, and arguing that revenue diversification strikes a realistic political balance between conservative and liberal views of tax equity, revenue adequacy, and political accountability. Ladd and Weist (1987) express some skepticism about revenue balance as an independent criterion; in their view, the choice of tax policy should reflect the balancing of competing policy goals rather than of revenue totals.

The real theorem is due to Diamond and Mirrlees (1971a, 1971b). This seminal theoretical investigation establishes a strong presumption that tax policy should preserve production efficiency, such that outputs are produced without wasting resources.[3] The underlying intuition is that, for any tax system that disturbs production efficiency, there is another tax system that preserves production efficiency and generates the same distribution of resources among taxpayers, and thus is superior. This real theorem is important because, although a pure RST preserves production efficiency, in practice all states' RSTs, and certainly Michigan's RST, violate it by not comprehensively exempting business-to-business sales. By taxing many transactions between businesses, the RST provides a tax incentive for firms to consolidate when, absent taxes, doing so would not be profitable; distorts production decisions; and gives rise to multiple taxation of inputs, known as cascading.

## The Devil Is in the Details

The standard case for the RST, compared to the income tax, depends on the details of things like what the tax base covers and the extent to which business-to-business sales are exempt. It also depends on the context of the RST existing in a federal system dominated by an income tax. In what follows I review the details of the Michigan RST, and stress why the context matters.

## The Michigan Sales and Use Tax

The Michigan sales tax is imposed at a rate of 6% on retail sales of goods in Michigan, unless a particular category of good—such as most foods at grocery stores—is specifically exempted from the tax. The use tax, which is applied in coordination with the sales tax, is imposed on the use (or storage) in Michigan of goods bought outside of Michigan or from vendors with no physical presence in Michigan. The use tax is imposed at the same 6% rate as the sales tax. Because the sales and use taxes are designed to complement each other, the use tax is not imposed on transactions that are subject to the sales tax.

In fiscal year 2001, Michigan's sales tax collected $6.36 billion in revenues, which amounted to 29.2% of Michigan's total tax collections of $21.8 billion.[4] When use tax revenue amounting to $1.34 billion is included, the sales and use taxes together accounted in FY 2001 for 35.3% of Michigan's yearly revenues, making these taxes comparable to the income tax as the largest revenue generator for the state government.

Michigan's reliance on sales and use taxes rose substantially when, as of 1 May 1994, the tax rate was increased from 4% to 6% due to the passage of Proposal A. Between fiscal years 1993 and 1995, the two taxes' share of total taxes went from 26.7% to 33.4%, and the proportion has stayed fairly steady since then. As a result of Proposal A, since 1994, 73.3% of Michigan's sales tax revenue has gone to the School Aid Fund, which pays for Michigan's public K–12 schools. Proposal A decreased the property tax burden in the state substantially.[5]

Table 27.1 provides some summary information about the Michigan sales and use taxes in comparison to those of other states. To highlight how Michigan's RST stacks up to relevant comparison groups, table 27.1 presents simple averages for both the United States as a whole and a set of six neighboring or nearby states—Illinois, Indiana, Minnesota, Ohio, Pennsylvania, and Wisconsin. Michigan's sales tax rate is, along with that of seven other states, 6%, which is above the national average rate of 5.28% and the average tax rate for the six reference states of 5.63%. Nine states have higher rates, thirty-eight have lower rates, and five states have no sales tax at all. However, two of the seven states with higher rates have no state personal income tax. Michigan does not allow local sales taxes, although thirty-three states do.[6] Alaska has only local sales taxes (Due and Mikesell 1995).

### Broadness of Base

According to the first folk theorem and the Diamond-Mirrlees theorem, an efficient sales tax base should be broad, but not too broad. It should apply to all sales from businesses to consumers, and

## TABLE 27.1

### Sales and Use Taxes in Michigan, Neighboring States, and the United States

| State[a] | Sales Tax Collections, 2000 ($ thousands)[d] | Ratio of Sales Tax Revenue to Total Revenue[f] | Basic Sales Tax Rate, 2000[e] | Revenue as % of Personal Income[f] | % of Personal Income per 1% of Rate[f] |
|---|---|---|---|---|---|
| Michigan | 7,666,399 | 0.34 | 6.00 | 2.76 | 0.46 |
| U.S. average | | 0.35 | 5.28 | 2.48 | 0.49 |
| Reference state average[b] | | 0.30 | 5.63 | 2.18 | 0.39 |
| Alabama | 1,701,885 | 0.26 | 4.00 | 1.69 | 0.42 |
| Arizona | 3,832,686 | 0.47 | 5.60 | 3.18 | 0.64 |
| Arkansas | 1,706,645 | 0.35 | 7.25 | 3.01 | 0.59 |
| California | 23,457,385 | 0.28 | 7.25 | 2.37 | 0.34 |
| Colorado | 1,849,305 | 0.26 | 2.90 | 1.45 | 0.50 |
| Connecticut | 3,419,939 | 0.34 | 6.00 | 2.65 | 0.44 |
| Florida[c] | 15,010,888 | 0.60 | 6.00 | 3.58 | 0.60 |
| Georgia | 4,630,179 | 0.34 | 4.00 | 2.17 | 0.54 |
| Hawaii | 1,536,276 | 0.46 | 4.00 | 4.70 | 1.18 |
| Idaho | 747,134 | 0.31 | 5.00 | 2.61 | 0.52 |
| Illinois | 6,393,080 | 0.28 | 6.25 | 1.69 | 0.27 |
| Indiana | 3,579,416 | 0.35 | 5.00 | 2.30 | 0.46 |
| Iowa | 1,722,836 | 0.33 | 5.00 | 2.34 | 0.47 |
| Kansas | 1,743,835 | 0.36 | 4.90 | 2.45 | 0.50 |
| Kentucky | 2,171,609 | 0.28 | 6.00 | 2.36 | 0.39 |
| Louisiana | 2,060,822 | 0.32 | 4.00 | 2.06 | 0.52 |
| Maine | 847,358 | 0.32 | 5.00 | 2.75 | 0.55 |
| Maryland | 2,498,184 | 0.24 | 5.00 | 1.49 | 0.30 |
| Massachusetts | 3,565,267 | 0.22 | 5.00 | 1.62 | 0.32 |
| Minnesota | 3,723,638 | 0.28 | 6.50 | 2.53 | 0.39 |
| Mississippi | 2,333,384 | 0.50 | 7.00 | 4.07 | 0.58 |
| Missouri | 2,787,531 | 0.33 | 4.23 | 1.93 | 0.46 |
| Nebraska | 1,027,940 | 0.34 | 5.00 | 2.28 | 0.46 |
| Nevada[c] | 1,941,674 | 0.52 | 6.50 | 3.46 | 0.53 |
| New Jersey | 5,508,046 | 0.30 | 6.00 | 1.90 | 0.32 |
| New Mexico | 1,502,319 | 0.40 | 5.00 | 3.95 | 0.79 |
| New York | 8,563,323 | 0.21 | 4.00 | 1.39 | 0.35 |
| North Carolina | 3,361,189 | 0.22 | 4.50 | 1.69 | 0.42 |
| North Dakota | 330,269 | 0.28 | 5.00 | 2.24 | 0.45 |
| Ohio | 6,263,251 | 0.32 | 5.00 | 2.05 | 0.41 |
| Oklahoma | 1,441,670 | 0.25 | 4.50 | 1.87 | 0.42 |
| Pennsylvania | 7,057,309 | 0.31 | 6.00 | 2.06 | 0.34 |
| Rhode Island | 621,066 | 0.31 | 7.00 | 2.13 | 0.30 |
| South Carolina | 2,458,308 | 0.39 | 5.00 | 2.69 | 0.54 |
| South Dakota[c] | 487,897 | 0.53 | 4.00 | 2.66 | 0.66 |
| Tennessee[c] | 4,446,160 | 0.57 | 6.00 | 3.17 | 0.53 |
| Texas[c] | 14,012,165 | 0.51 | 6.25 | 2.60 | 0.42 |
| Utah | 1,423,234 | 0.36 | 4.75 | 2.87 | 0.60 |
| Vermont | 215,423 | 0.15 | 5.00 | 1.40 | 0.28 |
| Virginia | 2,471,938 | 0.20 | 4.50 | 1.21 | 0.27 |
| Washington[c] | 7,739,014 | 0.62 | 6.50 | 4.42 | 0.68 |
| West Virginia | 917,050 | 0.27 | 6.00 | 2.42 | 0.40 |
| Wisconsin | 3,506,696 | 0.28 | 5.00 | 2.46 | 0.49 |
| Wyoming[c] | 368,779 | 0.38 | 4.00 | 2.91 | 0.73 |
| MAXIMUM | 23,457,385 | 0.62 | 7.25 | 4.70 | 1.18 |
| MINIMUM | 215,423 | 0.15 | 2.90 | 1.21 | 0.27 |
| STANDARD DEVIATION | 4,393,394.93 | 0.11 | 1.02 | 0.80 | 0.16 |

(a) Five states have no sales tax. These are Alaska, Delaware, Montana, New Hampshire, and Oregon.
(b) Reference states are Illinois, Indiana, Minnesota, Ohio, Pennsylvania, and Wisconsin.
(c) These states, along with Alaska and New Hampshire, have no personal income tax.
(d) From *State Government Tax Collections: 2000*, www.census.gov/govs/www/statetax00.htm.
(e) From *State Sales Tax Rates*, www.taxadmin.org/fta/rate/sales.html.
(f) Calculated by author.

it should apply *only* to those final sales. Actual sales tax bases differ from this ideal in two directions, with distinctly different efficiency implications.

One type of deviation from this efficient sales tax base is to exempt particular categories of retail sales from the base. This may be justified on the grounds of improving progressivity. (This is the argument usually used to justify the exemption of food sales from the tax base.) Another justification for exemptions is that some categories of retail sales, such as some services, are too difficult administratively to get into the tax base. In both cases the issue is that tax policy must trade off among competing objectives. In the first case, efficiency is sacrificed to vertical equity, and in the second case efficiency is sacrificed to simplicity. Efficiency is sacrificed because any deviation from a comprehensive consumption base provides an incentive for consumers to shift their purchases from taxed goods to untaxed goods.

On the other hand, the tax base may also deviate from the efficient base in the other direction. In particular, the tax base may be too big to the extent that it does not successfully exempt business-to-business sales from the base. As discussed previously, this is a violation of production efficiency.

Thus, from an efficiency standpoint, the base may be both too small *and* too large. This is a useful perspective to keep in mind when evaluating a commonly used measure of the broadness of a sales tax base—per capita annual sales tax collections as a percentage of personal income per 1% of the sales tax rate. This measure, which I will call sales tax yield, isolates the yield from other factors such as the per capita income of the state.[7] The last column of table 27.1 shows that Michigan's RST yield is 0.46%. To put this figure in perspective, the national average yield is slightly higher, 0.49%, but the reference state average is significantly less, at 0.39%. This comparison suggests that Michigan has a sales tax base that is very comparable to the national average, but one that is significantly broader than those of adjacent states. Yet, as argued previously, the factors underlying this figure are crucial to a policy evaluation—the tax base may be too broad, or too narrow. Further investigation is needed.

## Statutory Exemptions and Exclusions

There are many different statutory exemptions that can affect the broadness of a state's sales tax base. The Executive Budget of the State of Michi-

gan includes a tax expenditure appendix compiled by the Office of Revenue and Tax Analysis (ORTA) of the Michigan Department of Treasury. In principle, a tax expenditure budget puts a dollar value on all narrowing deviations from a comprehensive tax base. According to this budget, in FY 2000, sales and use tax expenditures totaled $7.10 billion, or 91.4% of the revenue actually collected and 47.8% of potential tax liability, defined as actual revenues plus tax expenditures. What are the sources of this total?

*Food and Drugs.* Michigan, along with every other state, allows some retail items to be exempt from sales tax. The two biggest of these exemptions are (1) food that is not for immediate consumption and (2) prescription drugs. These exemptions were created by voter approval of an initiative petition that placed it, effective as of January 1975, in the State of Michigan Constitution, Article IX, Section 8. According to the ORTA tax expenditure budget, the food exemption cost $880 million in FY 2000, and the prescription drug exemption cost $199 million. As table 27.2 shows, Michigan is by no means an outlier in its RST exemption of food: twenty-four other states exempt food from sales tax, and three other states levy reduced but nonzero rates for food. Of the states that have a sales tax, all except Illinois provide an exemption for prescription drugs; Illinois taxes them at 1%. Michigan is not one of the eleven states that exempt nonprescription drugs (Federation of Tax Administration web site).

The overriding objective of exempting food and drugs is to increase the progressivity of the sales tax. Many economists, however, call into question the validity of these exemptions. For example, Due and Mikesell (1995) write that the "food exemption is perhaps the largest mistake the states have made in their sales tax structures, costing substantial revenue, adding administrative and compliance problems, and deviating from the basic rule of uniformity of treatment of all consumption expenditures." Unquestionably, a food exemption to an RST is a very blunt instrument for increasing tax progressivity. It applies to all food purchased, be it staples by low-income households or caviar by high-income households. Moreover, food purchased using Food Stamps is already exempted from all state sales taxes.

Michigan taxes some other goods that are commonly exempt in other states, such as motor fuel. Motor fuel is taxed in Michigan under the RST and

**TABLE 27.2**

**Factors Related to Sales Tax Yield**

| State[a] | % of Personal Income per 1% of Rate[f] | Consumers' Share[g] | EXEMPTIONS Food[d] | EXEMPTIONS Non-prescription Medicines[e] | EXEMPTIONS Professional & Personal Services[d] | % of Returns Audited[h] |
|---|---|---|---|---|---|---|
| Michigan | 0.46 | 0.58 | Y | N | Y | 0.89 |
| U.S. average | 0.48 | 0.59 | | | | 2.23 |
| Reference state average[b] | 0.39 | 0.62 | | | | 1.01 |
| Alabama | 0.42 | 0.73 | N | N | Y | 7.50 |
| Arizona | 0.64 | 0.50 | Y | N | Y | n/a |
| Arkansas | 0.59 | 0.60 | N | N | Y | 8.10 |
| California | 0.34 | 0.53 | Y | N | Y | 2.00 |
| Colorado | 0.50 | 0.60 | Y | N | Y | 0.95 |
| Connecticut | 0.44 | 0.58 | Y | Y | N | 2.40 |
| District of Columbia | | 0.44 | Y | Y | Y | |
| Florida[c] | 0.60 | 0.50 | Y | Y | Y | 5.50 |
| Georgia | 0.54 | 0.64 | Y | N | Y | n/a |
| Hawaii | 1.18 | 0.28 | N | N | N | n/a |
| Idaho | 0.52 | 0.62 | N | N | Y | 0.63 |
| Illinois | 0.27 | 0.68 | N | N | Y | 1.70 |
| Indiana | 0.46 | 0.54 | Y | N | Y | 1.07 |
| Iowa | 0.47 | 0.59 | Y | N | N | 0.78 |
| Kansas | 0.50 | 0.67 | N | N | Y | 1.90 |
| Kentucky | 0.39 | 0.54 | Y | N | Y | 4.60 |
| Louisiana | 0.52 | 0.51 | N | N | Y | 1.70 |
| Maine | 0.55 | 0.57 | Y | N | Y | 1.30 |
| Maryland | 0.30 | 0.60 | N | Y | Y | 1.10 |
| Massachusetts | 0.32 | 0.62 | Y | N | Y | 2.80 |
| Minnesota | 0.39 | 0.56 | Y | Y | Y | 0.88 |
| Mississippi | 0.58 | 0.66 | N | N | Y | 9.03 |
| Missouri | 0.46 | 0.64 | N | N | Y | n/a |
| Nebraska | 0.46 | 0.60 | Y | N | Y | 0.53 |
| Nevada[c] | 0.53 | 0.44 | Y | N | Y | 5.50 |
| New Jersey | 0.32 | 0.62 | Y | Y | Y | 1.20 |
| New Mexico | 0.79 | 0.50 | N | N | N | 0.45 |
| New York | 0.35 | 0.66 | Y | Y | Y | 0.76 |
| North Carolina | 0.42 | 0.62 | N | N | Y | 1.90 |
| North Dakota | 0.45 | 0.60 | Y | N | Y | 2.10 |
| Ohio | 0.41 | 0.66 | Y | N | Y | 0.65 |
| Oklahoma | 0.42 | 0.66 | N | N | Y | 2.90 |
| Pennsylvania | 0.34 | 0.64 | Y | Y | Y | 1.20 |
| Rhode Island | 0.30 | 0.59 | Y | Y | Y | 2.40 |
| South Carolina | 0.54 | 0.61 | N | N | Y | 1.20 |
| South Dakota[c] | 0.66 | 0.61 | N | N | N | 1.02 |
| Tennessee[c] | 0.53 | 0.63 | N | N | Y | 3.20 |
| Texas[c] | 0.42 | 0.53 | Y | Y | Y | 2.55 |
| Utah | 0.60 | 0.63 | N | N | Y | 2.20 |
| Vermont | 0.28 | 0.56 | Y | Y | Y | 0.49 |
| Virginia | 0.27 | 0.70 | N | Y | Y | n/a |
| Washington[c] | 0.68 | 0.49 | Y | N | Y | 2.20 |
| West Virginia | 0.40 | 0.89 | N | N | Y | 1.08 |
| Wisconsin | 0.49 | 0.62 | Y | N | Y | 0.56 |
| Wyoming[c] | 0.73 | 0.54 | N | N | Y | 0.30 |

(a) Five states have no sales tax: These are Alaska, Delaware, Montana, New Hampshire, and Oregon.
(b) Reference states are Illinois, Indiana, Minnesota, Ohio, Pennsylvania, and Wisconsin.
(c) These states, along with Alaska and New Hampshire, have no personal income tax.
(d) From *Michigan's Sales and Use Taxes: 2000,* www.michigan.gov/documents/SalesandUset2000_3167_7.pdf.
(e) From Commerce Clearing House, Inc.
(f) Calculated by author.
(g) Prescription drugs are exempt in all states except Illinois. Medical services are exempt in all states except Hawaii and New Mexico.
(h) From Ring (1999).
(i) From Due and Mikesell (1995). Data from 1989–1992.

also under a separate state gasoline tax of nineteen cents per gallon. Only nine other states do this (Due and Mikesell 1995). Seven states tax motor vehicles at a lower rate; Michigan taxes them fully. Eight states exempt some clothing; Michigan does not.

*Services.* The Michigan sales and use taxes are levied on gross proceeds from retail sales of tangible personal property, and generally are not imposed on the sale of services. The use tax is, however, levied on certain transactions that involve services, such as telephone, telegraph, and other leased wire communications; sales of used autos between individuals; monthly vehicle lease payments; and transient hotel and motel charges. Some transactions involve both services and property, and the Michigan Department of Treasury has issued guidelines for determining whether a transaction is the sale of property and is therefore subject to sales tax or instead is the sale of services and is therefore exempt. The guidelines codify a judicial doctrine known as the "real object test." This test is used to distinguish between the sale of a nontaxable service and the taxable sale of personal property by ascertaining whether, from the perspective of the purchaser, the purpose of the transaction is the transfer of an end product or the acquisition of services (Research Institute of America 2001).

As mentioned previously, in principle a tax expenditure budget should list and put a dollar value on all narrowing deviations from a comprehensive tax base. Furthermore, when the base is inappropriately expanded, that should be noted as well. The Michigan sales and use tax expenditure list does not conform to this ideal. Of the forty-six separate items in the FY 2000 budget, as many as eighteen relate to categories of business purchases, which would not be part of a conceptually correct sales and use tax base. Many of these are small, but for one—the industrial processing exemption—the estimated revenue impact is $660 million.

According to the tax expenditure budget, by far the biggest tax expenditure arises because of the exclusion of services from the tax base, an exclusion that accounts for $4.26 billion in foregone revenue. Of this total, $1.88 billion is from health services and $0.69 billion is from business services. The estimated revenue impact of excluding services from the tax base amounts to 55.8% of actual collections of the sales and use tax. Put another way, if all services were added to the tax base, the tax rate needed to raise the same amount of revenue could fall from 6.00% to 3.85%.[8]

The importance of excluding most services from the tax base has steadily grown over time as the (U.S. and Michigan) economy has moved toward having a much more dominant service sector. For example, in the United States as a whole, services represented 45.4% of gross domestic product in 1980, and 65.9% in 2000. In response, many states have attempted to impose the sales tax on some services (such as repair or installation services) in order to maintain their revenue streams. Although Michigan's General Sales Tax Act of 1933 has since been amended to include utilities, such as residential utilities and telephone service (but not water), most services remain outside the retail sales tax base. Note, moreover, that in 1994 Proposal A exempted residential energy utilities from the 2% increase that applied to most other taxed goods and services.

There is no compelling economic reason, other than the cost of collection, to exclude services purchased by consumers from the tax base.[9] Excluding them from the base introduces a presumptively inefficient bias against consumption of tangible goods in favor of services.

The most serious issue has to do with collection costs. For service retailers who are already registered because they also sell tangible goods, the marginal compliance cost is probably not large. In this case the exemption for services may even complicate administration by requiring a distinction between taxable sales of tangible goods and nontaxable sales of services. In other cases, though, adding services to the tax base is more than a matter of reprogramming the cash register, as it entails adding a new class of retailers into the tax net. Fox and Murray (1988) report that when Florida added many services to its sales tax base (discussed further in the following), the estimated increase in sales tax vendors amounted to 36% of active vendors. This makes the marginal collection costs higher than otherwise, although there is no compelling quantification of how large this cost might be.

The Florida sales tax episode is often brought up as an example of the administrative complexities that arise in adding services to the tax base. Florida enacted a sales tax on services on 1 July 1987, only to see it repealed effective 1 January 1988 (along with a 1 percent increase in the sales tax rate), and this episode is often characterized as an administrative nightmare. What is not clear is whether the administrative and compliance difficulties were due to Florida's particular scheme for expanding the tax base, or whether they are unavoidable for any extension of the base to include sales taxes. Some argue that the administrative issues were not instrumental to this episode. For example, Francis (1988) ascribes the repeal of the law entirely to political factors specific to Florida. Hellerstein (1988) does admit that "difficulties encountered by taxpayers who sought to comply with it added to the swell of public indignation" (15), although six months is hardly enough time to judge the long-run collection cost of a new tax measure. It is also worth noting that Hawaii's general excise tax applies with limited exceptions to all services performed within the state.

After reviewing all the evidence on this issue, Fox and Murray (1988) concluded that the total costs of collecting revenues under expansion of the base to services may be greater than the total costs of collecting a similar amount of revenue from a rate increase on an existing base. This is not definitive, because expansion of the base to include services provided to consumers would almost certainly reduce the costly tax-induced distortion of consumer purchases toward services.[10]

### The Tax Treatment of Business-to-Business Sales

Theoretically, the retail sales tax should apply to retail sales only. If business inputs are taxed, then that tax will be imbedded in the price of the final good. Failure to exempt input purchases introduces a host of production inefficiencies into the economy, including providing an incentive for firms to make things themselves instead of buying them, even when the latter would be cheaper, excluding tax considerations. Stated simply, the case for the RST as being more efficient than the income tax is rendered moot by the fact that, in practice, it arguably introduces large production inefficiencies.

States differ widely in the effectiveness of their attempts to exempt producer purchases from the sales tax base. All states except Hawaii exempt inventory bought for resale. Every state except Hawaii and Connecticut, which tax them at lower rates, exempts raw materials that become part of the final product. Twenty-four states, including Michigan, have specific exemptions for products that are used or consumed in industrial processing, sometimes referred to as "consumables." Six

others provide limited exemptions for these (Due and Mikesell 1995). The exemptions for consumables are typically part of a broader manufacturing or (as in Michigan) industrial processing exemption, under which sales to manufacturers or processors are not subject to tax if the property purchased becomes part of the product that is ultimately sold at retail. For example, under this exemption a manufacturer of washing machines does not have to pay sales tax on the steel used to make the washing machines, because retail consumers will pay sales tax on the entire machine.

Another class of goods that receives mixed sales tax treatment is industrial machinery and equipment. When states first began adopting sales taxes, they taxed machinery and equipment even though it was used to produce taxable goods. Because of their large manufacturing industries, Michigan and Ohio were the first two states to exempt these types of inputs from tax. States that adopted the tax after World War II usually exempted this machinery, and since then other states have added the exemption. As of 1993, thirty states fully exempted industrial machinery and equipment from the sales tax base (Due and Mikesell 1995).

Michigan is one of eleven states that exempt virtually all purchases for farm use. This group also includes Indiana, Ohio, and Pennsylvania. Other states exempt some farm inputs. These exemptions vary widely. Some states exempt only seed and fertilizer, while some exempt anything used to produce food for human consumption, and one state (Hawaii) taxes livestock feed at a lower rate, while any other farm input is taxed fully. Twenty-six states, including Michigan and all six of the reference states, fully or partially exempt farming machinery and equipment.

For the purpose of assessing the efficiency of an RST, the proper perspective is not the extent to which business-to-business sales are exempt; it is the extent to which business-to-business sales are *not* exempt, for in principle (and with an exception noted in the following) all such sales should be exempt. The distinction in many states' RST codes between inputs that are "used up" in production and those that are not is irrelevant for this argument. As discussed previously, the Michigan tax expenditure budget does not provide the information needed to estimate how much of the sales and use tax base is due to nonexempt business purchases. The most commonly cited sources of state-by-state estimates of this are two papers by Ring (1989, 1999). These papers estimate the consumers' share of the retail sales tax in each state using data on the number of households from the U.S. Census, average spending by households in eight income classes from the Consumer Expenditure Survey (CES), and information on how each state defines its sales tax base. Ring (1999) calculates that in 1989, Michigan's consumer share was 58%, just slightly below the national average of 59%, and compared to a maximum of 89% in West Virginia and a minimum of 28% in Hawaii (which has the least exemptions for business, as noted previously). The reference state average share was 62%. Because it is based on national household spending rather than state-specific data, and because the CES is known to underreport consumer spending, these estimates are imperfect. Note also that the implied producers' share (100 minus the numbers reported here) includes sales to governmental and nonprofit entities. Nevertheless, Ring's work, and other similar studies, make clear that the base of the average state RST is far from simply retail sales, and that Michigan's RST taxes business-to-business sales about as much as does the average state.[11] More than 40% of tax revenue comes from business-to-business sales. The burden of the haphazard sales taxation of business purchases "varies across industries, and distorts a variety of business production decisions" (Zodrow 1999, 115).

Ring argues that when states raise their sales tax rates, the consumers' share tends to go up, because the higher rates give businesses more incentive to avoid the tax, and they are better at avoiding it than consumers are. In particular, Ring argues, when a state raises its sales tax rates, multistate business entities move more heavily taxed activities from that state to places that tax that activity less heavily. Since Michigan raised its rate in 1993 from 4 to 6%, one might suspect that the consumers' share might now be higher than the 58% reported for 1989.

One argument for taxing inputs would be that it is a second-best substitute for directly taxing retail commodities that are exempt. There is, though, no systematic evidence that the taxation of business-to-business sales is concentrated in sectors that produce inputs used in the production of consumption goods whose final sales are likely to be tax-exempt. It is true, though, that in many states, including Michigan, businesses that are service providers are not allowed to receive the sales tax exemption on their purchases that is available to other businesses. This may not offer much offset, to the extent that services are more labor-intensive, and thus subject to less cascading, than goods.

## Evasion

Patterns of noncompliance with the sales and use tax follow the remittance responsibilities under the law. Retail businesses evade these taxes by underreporting sales, while consumers evade them by underreporting purchases made out of state but consumed in the state, and therefore subject to use tax. There is no hard evidence about the size and nature of sales and use tax noncompliance in Michigan, nor is there any evidence about the yield of enforcement efforts, either on an average or a marginal basis. The final column of table 27.2 lists some data from Due and Mikesell (1995) on the fraction of sales tax returns audited. Michigan's 0.89% places it well below the national (2.23%) average and slightly below the reference state (1.01%) average.

There is some evidence about the magnitude of noncompliance in other states. A Washington study estimated noncompliance as a share of total tax liability to be 1.7% for sales tax and 40.3% for use tax, or 6.2% for the two together. A Tennessee study estimated the sales tax gap to be 4.5% of total tax liability, excluding the revenue loss from unreported transactions and use tax. A 1990 Florida study estimated the sales tax gap to be 8.5% of potential tax receipts. Based on potential (i.e., including uncollected liability) Michigan sales and use tax collections of about $8 billion, if sales and use tax evasion in the state is in the same ballpark with that of Florida and Washington (I exclude Tennessee because of the limited coverage of the aforementioned study), then the annual revenue loss from evasion of sales and use tax would be between about $500 million and $700 million.

## Collection Costs

There are no data available that shed light on the collection costs, either the administrative cost or the compliance cost component, of the Michigan RST. As an incentive for prompt payment, and as an offset to compliance costs, Michigan allows retailers to deduct 0.75% of the first 4% of their tax liability if payment for the preceding month is remitted before the seventh day of the month. Large taxpayers (those with more than $720,000 in annual tax liability) can deduct 0.5% of the first 4% of total tax liability.

## Exporting and Federal Deductibility

The possibility that a significant fraction of the state's RST burden might be "exported" to out-of-state residents (primarily tourists) if they buy products within Michigan is unlikely.[12] A more likely form of tax exporting occurs via the deductibility of state taxes against federal taxable income.

Before 1986, both sales tax and income tax were deductible. The Tax Reform Act of 1986 (TRA86) eliminated the deductibility of state sales tax, leading many observers to predict a shift away from sales tax. This did not occur, though, either in Michigan or in the country as a whole. A study done by Citizens for Tax Justice (1991) noted that, in the period 1986 to 1991, twenty-six states increased their sales tax, and only two reduced it. During the same period, the personal income tax was increased in eleven states and reduced in twenty-eight states.

On the surface, this appears to contradict the predictions made at the time by many observers. Pollock (1991) argues that the response was not so surprising. He claims that, in 1986, 90% of state income tax payments were deducted against an average federal income tax rate of 33.7%, while only 22.2% of state sales tax payments were deducted against an average federal rate of 28.8% (largely because the IRS sales tax tables used by most itemizers understated true sales tax liability). In addition, TRA86 lowered tax rates and the number of itemizers, effectively increasing the price of both sales and income taxes. He argues that the tax price of the state income tax increased on average by 15%, compared with only 8% for the average state sales tax.

The current policy issue is the relative exportability via federal deductibility of the RST, compared to its principal alternative, the personal income tax. Table 27.3 provides some information on this, based on the public-use database of federal tax returns that the IRS Statistics of Income Division makes available to researchers (after removing any identifying information). This database identifies the state of residence for all taxpayers that have adjusted gross income of less than $200,000. Based on these data, I estimate that 20.7% of deductible Michigan income tax payments are exported to all American taxpayers through the deductibility.[13] (Details of the methodology used are explained in the notes to table 27.3.) Moreover, the fraction of the tax burden that

**TABLE 27.3**

**Value of Federal Tax Deductibility of Michigan Income Taxes**

| AGI Class ($000) | All Taxpayers | | Itemizers | | | | Non-Itemizers | | | Est. Fed. Inc. Tax Reduction as % of Total State & Local Taxes |
| | No. of Returns | Total AGI | No. of Returns | Total AGI | State & Local Income Tax | Est. Fed. Inc. Tax Reduction | No. of Returns | Total AGI | Est. State & Local Income Tax | |
|---|---|---|---|---|---|---|---|---|---|---|
| 0–10 | 1,119,252 | 5,105 | 5,608 | 29.2 | 1.39 | 0.19 | 1,113,645 | 5,076 | 29.12 | 0.006 |
| 10–20 | 792,360 | 11,480 | 45,657 | 679.9 | 18.72 | 1.92 | 746,703 | 10,800 | 171.50 | 0.010 |
| 20–30 | 564,750 | 13,980 | 98,956 | 2,492 | 85.07 | 11.52 | 465,794 | 11,490 | 312.30 | 0.029 |
| 30–40 | 432,351 | 15,110 | 140,682 | 4,945 | 185.80 | 35.23 | 291,669 | 10,160 | 314.40 | 0.070 |
| 40–50 | 367,280 | 16,420 | 170,383 | 7,659 | 307.60 | 64.06 | 196,897 | 8,763 | 289.00 | 0.107 |
| 50–75 | 639,788 | 38,410 | 420,752 | 25,490 | 1,056.00 | 249.60 | 219,036 | 12,920 | 457.20 | 0.165 |
| 75–100 | 246,573 | 21,280 | 211,100 | 18,150 | 744.10 | 207.40 | 35,473 | 3,126 | 120.50 | 0.240 |
| 100–125 | 76,834 | 8,484 | 61,578 | 6,777 | 298.50 | 84.61 | 15,256 | 1,707 | 68.70 | 0.230 |
| 125–150 | 37,523 | 5,199 | 36,856 | 5,110 | 223.90 | 67.60 | 667 | 89.0 | 3.69 | 0.297 |
| 150–200 | 35,574 | 6,127 | 34,069 | 5,890 | 240.50 | 77.41 | 1,506 | 238 | 9.82 | 0.309 |
| >200 | 54,994 | 28,993 | 51,239 | 27,053 | 1,485.00 | 550.01 | 3,753 | 1,938 | 87.00 | 0.350 |
| TOTAL | 4,367,279 | 170,588 | 1,276,877 | 104,275.3 | 4,646.7 | 1,349.5 | 3,090,401 | 66,307 | 1,863.23 | 0.207 |

SOURCE: The numbers are based on a weighted tabulation of Michigan residents' tax returns in the 1996 public-use file of individual tax returns from the Statistics of Income Division of the IRS. State is not identified for returns with over $200,000 of AGI, so for that group it is assumed that Michigan residents are the same proportion of all taxpayers, and are otherwise similar to all U.S. residents in that group. For nonitemizers, deductible state and local income taxes are estimated based on a regression of these taxes on income for itemizers and applying that equation to the income of nonitemizers.

NOTE: All numbers are in millions except for number of returns.

is exported increases monotonically by income class, rising to as high as 35.0% for those with adjusted gross income exceeding $200,000. Thus, the income tax is significantly less burdensome to Michiganders than the rate structure implies, and is significantly less progressive, as well.

The estimates of table 27.3 have important implications for an evaluation of the right balance between sales and income tax use. If the marginal alternative to the RST is a proportional magnification of the personal income tax, the results of table 27.3 apply directly. If, however, the marginal alternative is some other revenue-raising alternative, the results will be different.

## Cross-Border Sales and the Use Tax

Conceived of as a tax on the consumer, for the most part the Michigan sales tax relies on the remittance of tax revenue by retail businesses. When the seller fails to collect the sales tax (seen most often in interstate commerce), it is then the duty of the buyer to file a use tax return or remit the use tax with the income tax return. While this situation is quite rare inside the stores of the "brick and mortar" businesses of America, it is a growing issue in the world of e-commerce as well as mail-order businesses.

According to a ruling made by the Supreme Court in its 1992 *Quill v. North Dakota* decision on mail-order sales, a business cannot be required to collect and remit sales tax on a good it sells if it is purchased in a state where the business does not have a "physical presence." Due to this ruling, which reinforced the rulings from numerous earlier cases, if a good is purchased from a company that does not reside in the state where the purchase was made, the company is *not* required to collect a sales tax on the purchase. Instead, it is the duty of the buyer to fill out a use tax form that includes the amount owed in sales tax on the purchase. However, due to an overall lack of enforcement,[14] the actual amount of use tax received is extremely small when compared to the amount that *should* be collected.

In principle, and putting aside the cost of collection, an RST should tax consumption in Michigan regardless of the location of the seller; this is uncontroversial among economists. Failing to do so is a violation of production efficiency according to Diamond-Mirrlees, because it favors out-of-state retailing, one stage of the production and distribution process, over in-sate retailing.

ORTA (2001a) estimates that use tax revenue losses from consumer remote sales were $186.7 million in FY 2000, and that they will grow to $348.7 million in FY 2005. The fraction of this that is due to e-commerce is predicted to grow markedly.[15] In FY 2000, $37.3 million out of the $186.7 million, or 19.9%, is e-commerce. By FY 2005, $160.3 million of the $348.7 million, or 45.9%, is projected to be due to e-commerce. Put another way, revenue loss from traditional mail order is predicted to grow by 26.1% between FY 2000 and FY 2005, while revenue loss from e-commerce is expected to grow by 329.8%. Although the projected growth rate is striking, in the near term the estimated revenue loss is a small fraction of the loss erosion due to the exclusion of services from the tax base.

Beginning with tax year 1999, Michigan added a line on its personal income tax form to "remind" taxpayers of any use tax due and to facilitate the calculation and remittance of tax liability. Taxpayers are given the option of reporting actual use tax due or instead using a table that estimates use tax liability based on income.[16] In tax year 1999, 64,650 taxpayers submitted $2.9 million of use tax with their income tax forms. Several other states have attempted to collect use tax via the income tax collection process.

Some states have pursued other strategies. A 1999 North Carolina law ordered state agencies not to buy from out-of-state vendors that fail to collect sales tax. In 2000, North Carolina passed a law saying that if out-of-state vendors do not collect and remit use tax on sales to North Carolina residents, they will not be allowed to sue in North Carolina courts to collect bad debts. Whether this will be upheld in court is unclear. North Carolina also has a line on its income tax return related to use tax, from which it collected $2.9 million in 2000.

The projected revenue loss from remote sales has not settled comfortably with some governors, legislators, and tax administrators in Michigan, as well as in the other forty-four states (plus the District of Columbia) that currently have a state sales tax. Their focus is mostly on revenue loss, but there is also an efficiency argument for being concerned about the effective exemption of remote sales. In the words of Michigan Senate Majority Floor Leader Joanne Emmons, because of the nontaxation of the Internet, e-commerce retailers have a "6% advantage," which she describes as an unfair playing field.

With over 7,500 different taxing jurisdictions in the United States, both local and state, figuring out the tax rate and tax base for each "district" is arguably a costly and time-consuming task.[17] As discussed earlier, there are estimates from Ernst & Young that purport to show that the cost to a small business of collecting sales tax from every state and district would be as high as 87% of the sales taxes collected, and 14% for large companies. However, with the help of Vertex and Taxware International, software has now been produced that contains "databases that can calculate the amount of tax to be collected if given the address of the purchaser and the amount of the purchase" (Goolsbee and Zittrain 1999, 421). This "solution" is not as simple as it seems, however. The problem of distributing this software to every single retailer in America, programming it to interface with the software already in use by the sellers, and keeping it up to date as tax systems change is not trivial.

Former Michigan governor John Engler encouraged the state legislature to allow Michigan to join the Streamlined Sales Tax Project (SSTP), a project made up of representatives from over thirty states dedicated to simplifying sales tax systems so as to address the problem of taxing Internet sales. The Equitable Sales and Use Tax Administration Act passed the Michigan Senate in May 2001, and passed the House in October, allowing Michigan to become a participating member of the SSTP. The goal of the SSTP is to get a critical mass of states to operate under similar sales and use tax rules and to cooperate with each other in sales tax administration and enforcement, possibly with the help of sales tax software systems. The prospect that there will be enough harmonization and simplification to persuade the Congress or the Supreme Court to require use tax collection by out-of-state vendors is highly unclear, however.

### Conclusions

The second folk theorem of tax policy suggests that Michigan should levy both an income tax and a retail sales tax. The first theorem holds that Michigan's RST should cover as broad a base of retail sales as possible, while exempting business-to-business sales.

Based on what can be learned from publicly available data, the Michigan retail sales tax is both about as good and about as bad as the average American state's RST. It covers a restricted class of retail sales by providing several exemptions, including for most services; given the growing

importance of services as a share of consumption, this source of erosion is likely to grow in importance. It introduces production inefficiency and cascading by not exempting many business-to-business sales. Compared to the nontaxation of services, the effective exemption of remote sales is currently a relatively small source of base erosion, but is likely to grow in relative importance.

In the context of the U.S. federal tax system, collecting state revenue through an RST rather than an income tax forgoes a nontrivial subsidy that operates through federal deductibility of state income taxes, but not state sales tax. The fact that this subsidy to the income tax is highly regressive undermines the standard argument that the state income tax is more progressive than the state sales tax.

I believe that (and hope that some day it will be recognized as the third public finance folk theorem) tax administration is as important as the design of the tax code. Given available data, however, it is impossible to evaluate how well the Michigan RST is administered relative to other states' sales tax systems, or relative to the Michigan state income tax and single business tax. No data are available on either the cost of administration (or compliance) or the success of the administration in stemming noncompliance.

What does the future hold for the Michigan sales and use tax, in light of base erosion due to services and remote sales that is likely to grow as a share of the potential base? This erosion is not a threat to the revenue potential of the RST, as it can be offset by increases in the tax rate applied to the narrowing base. Yet a narrow-base, high-rate RST probably raises revenue more inefficiently than a broad-base, low-rate RST does, and so the erosion, if not stopped, implies that over time the RST will become a less attractive way to raise revenue. Whether that means it should be cut back depends on whether it will become *relatively* less attractive than alternative revenue sources, and therefore whether these other revenue sources are subject to forces that portend to make them even more inefficient than the RST.

Traditional tax theory suggests, though, that the base erosion should not be dealt with by adding more business inputs into the base; that will make the RST *less,* rather than more, efficient. Modern tax theory stresses that how efficient a tax is depends not only on the composition of the tax base but also on the administration and enforcement of tax collection. For this reason the success of efforts—including but not limited to multistate initiatives—to collect use tax will affect whether the RST deserves to maintain its place as a principal revenue raiser. Finally, overcoming the mainly political but also administrative obstacles to extending the base to include services will be critical to whether the sales and use tax of the future can be an efficient part of Michigan's tax structure.

■

## REFERENCES

Boadway, Robin, Maurice Marchand, and Pierre Pestieau. 1994. Towards a theory of the direct-indirect tax mix. *Journal of Public Economics* 55: 71–88.

Bohm, Robert A., and Eleanor D. Craig. 1987. The stability of revenues from state sales taxes. In *Proceedings of the seventy-ninth annual conference.* Columbus, Ohio: National Tax Association–Tax Institute of America.

Casperson, Erik, and Gilbert Metcalf. 1994. Is a value-added tax progressive? Annual versus lifetime incidence measures. *National Tax Journal* 47: 731–46.

Chernick, Howard, and Andrew Reschovsky. 1996. The political economy of state and local tax structure. In *Developments in local government finance: Theory and policy,* edited by Giancarlo Pola, George France, and Rosella Levaggi, 253–72. Cheltenham, U.K.: Elgar.

Citizens for Tax Justice. 1991. Major tax changes by state, 1985–91. *A Far Cry From Fair* (April): 74–80.

Cline, Robert J., and John Shannon. 1986. Characteristics of a balanced and moderate state-local revenue system. In *Reforming state tax systems,* edited by Steven B. Gold. Denver: National Conference of State Legislatures.

Diamond, Peter A., and James A. Mirrlees. 1971a. Optimal taxation and public production I: Production efficiency. *American Economic Review* 61: 8–27.

———. 1971b. Optimal taxation and public production II: Tax rules. *American Economic Review* 61: 261–78.

Due, John F., and John L. Mikesell. 1995. *Sales taxation.* Washington, D.C.: Urban Institute Press.

Dye, Richard F., and Therese J. McGuire. 1991. Growth and variability of state individual and general sales taxes. *National Tax Journal* 44: 55–66.

Ernst and Young. 1999. Sales and use tax system in need of simplification? *CPA Journal* 69: 12.

Federation of Tax Administrators. 2002. *State sales tax rates. www.taxadmin.org/fta/rate_stru.html#Sales.*

Feldstein, Martin, and Marian Vaillant Wrobel. 1998. Can state taxes redistribute income? *Journal of Public Economics* 68: 369–96.

Florida Department of Revenue, Office of Tax Research. 1990. *The Florida tax gap: Evidence and issues.* Tallahassee, Fla.: Florida Department of Revenue, 25 September.

Fox, William F., ed. 1992. *Sales taxation.* Westport, Conn.: Praeger.

Fox, William F., and Matthew Murray. 1988. Economic aspects of taxing services. *National Tax Journal* 41: 19–36.

Francis, James. 1988. The Florida sales tax on services: What really went wrong? In *The unfinished agenda for state tax reform,* edited by Steven Gold. Denver: National Conference of State Legislatures.

Fullerton, Don, and Diane Lim Rogers. 1994. *Who bears the lifetime burden?* Washington, D.C.: Brookings Institution Press.

Gentry, William M., and Helen F. Ladd. 1994. State taxes and multiple policy objectives. *National Tax Journal* 47: 747–72.

Goolsbee, Austan. 2000. In a world without borders: The impact of taxes on Internet commerce. *Quarterly Journal of Economics* 115: 561–76.

Goolsbee, Austan, and Jonathan Zittrain. 1999. Evaluating the costs and benefits of taxing Internet commerce. *National Tax Journal* 52: 413–28.

Hellerstein, Walter. 1988. Florida's sales tax on services. *National Tax Journal* 41: 1–18.

Joulfaian, David, and James Mackie. 1992. Sales taxes, investment, and the Tax Reform Act of 1986. *National Tax Journal* 45: 89–105.

Ladd, Helen F., and Dana R. Weist. 1987. State and local tax systems: Balance among taxes vs. balance among policy goals. In *The quest for balance in state-local revenue structure,* edited by Frederick D. Stocker. Cambridge, Mass.: Lincoln Institute of Land Policy.

Lyon, Andrew B., and Robert M. Schwab. 1995. Consumption taxes in a life-cycle framework: Are sin taxes regressive? *Review of Economics and Statistics* 37: 389–406.

Metcalf, Gilbert E. 1994. The lifetime incidence of state and local taxes: Measuring changes during the 1980s. In *Tax progressivity and income inequality,* edited by Joel Slemrod. Cambridge: Cambridge University Press.

Michigan Department of Treasury. 2002. *Annual report of the state treasurer, fiscal year 2000–2001.* Lansing, Mich.: Michigan Department of Treasury.

Michigan Department of Treasury, Office of Revenue and Tax Analysis. 2001a. *Michigan Sales and Use Tax.* Lansing, Mich.: Michigan Department of Treasury.

———. 2001b. *Tax revenue loss estimates for consumer remote sales.* Lansing, Mich.: Michigan Department of Treasury.

Peat, Marwick, Mitchell, and Company. 1982. *Report to the American Retail Federation on costs to retailers of sales and use tax compliance.* New York: Peat, Marwick, Mitchell, and Co.

Pollock, Stephen. 1991. Mechanisms for exporting the state sales tax burden in the absence of federal deductibility. *National Tax Journal* 44: 297–310.

Poterba, James M. 1989. Lifetime incidence and the distributional burden of excise taxes. *American Economic Review Papers and Proceedings* 79: 325–30.

Research Institute of America. 2001. *Guide to sales and use taxes.* New York: Research Institute of America.

Ring, Raymond R., Jr. 1989. The proportion of consumers' and producers' goods in the general sales tax. *National Tax Journal* 42:167–79.

———. 1999. Consumers' share and producers' share of the general sales tax. *National Tax Journal* 52: 79–90.

Shannon, John. 1987. State revenue diversification: The search for balance. In *The quest for balance in state-local revenue structure,* edited by Frederick D. Stocker. Cambridge, Mass.: Lincoln Institute for Land Policy.

Slemrod, Joel. 1996. Which is the simplest tax system of them all? In *The economics of fundamental tax reform,* edited by Henry Aaron and William Gale. Washington, D.C.: Brookings Institution Press.

Sobel, Russell S., and Randall G. Holcombe. 1996. Measuring the growth and variability of tax bases over the business cycle. *National Tax Journal* 49: 535–52.

Vendor collection of state sales and use tax. 1993. *Tax Administrators News* 57:88.

Washington State Department of Revenue. 1990. *Washington state excise tax noncompliance sudy.* Olympia, Wash.: Washington State Department of Revenue, August.

Zodrow, George R. 1999. *State sales and income taxes: An economic analysis.* College Station: Texas A & M University Press.

## NOTES

I am grateful to Naomi Feldman, David Lenter, Julie Skelton, Mark Soskolne, and Jeff Sukatch for research assistance. Extremely valuable comments on an earlier draft were received from Howard Chernick, William Fox, Walter Hellerstein, Therese McGuire, John Mikesell, George Zodrow, and the project editors. Howard Heideman assisted in locating and interpreting Michigan data. Responsibility for any remaining errors is mine alone.

1. As discussed in chapter 26 of this volume, Michigan's income tax is somewhat more progressive than it might appear, because of some large refundable tax credits.

2. Note that this folk theorem is *not* restating the argument that, because excess burden is a function of the square of a given tax rate, to minimize total excess burden revenue should be raised from a broad base. The folk theorem refers to how to choose among different taxes that affect the *same* relative prices. For example, both an income tax and a sales tax reduce the real wage in terms of all taxed goods, so the choice between them is not addressed by the arguments for a broad base of tax. I ignore here the fact that a sales tax and an income tax have different effects on the relative price of consumption across time.

3. For example, a tax levied on some inputs more than others would violate production efficiency, because it would induce firms to produce their products with a mix of inputs that does not minimize the true cost of production. For the same reason, a tax on business-to-business transactions would violate production efficiency, because it would distort production toward vertical integration even when it is more cost-effective to operate with many smaller firms. On the other hand, a tax on a final product, whether uniform or selective, does not violate production efficiency. Although it will in general distort the mix of products consumed, whatever products are produced are still produced efficiently.

4. Michigan Department of Treasury, *2000–2001 State Treasurer's Annual Report.*

5. *Proposal A: A Retrospective. http://www.treas.state .mi.us/revedata/reports/propa.pdf.* Further discussion of Proposal A can be found in several other chapters in this volume, including chapters 26 and 28.

6. This ban is not in the state constitution, but the attorney general has consistently ruled in this way.

7. It is an imperfect measure to the extent that the consumption-to-income ratio varies across states.

8. The calculation finds the rate that solves the equation $s \times (7632.9 + 4256.0) = 0.06 \times 7632.9$.

9. Bohm and Craig (1987), using the 1984 Consumer Expenditure Survey, conclude that adding services to the sales tax base, in particular medical services, insurance, and personal services, would be regressive. However, because their analysis compares annual consumption to annual income, it does not speak to the more appropriate question of the burden relative to lifetime income.

10. Expanding the base by including both services

provided to consumers and services provided to businesses would have much more ambiguous implications for efficiency.

11. Of interest is Ring's claim that, on average, states that exempt more consumer purchases also tend to exempt more business purchases, so that there is no clear relationship across states between the consumers' *share* of the RST and the extent of consumer good exemptions.

12. Such an argument would depend on the absence of reasonable substitutes for Michigan's tourist attractions, which seems implausible. Thus, the apparent ability to export the tax burden via sales taxes paid by nonresidents is largely illusory, because any revenue so collected is offset by lower net-of-tax prices received by the Michigan purveyors of tourist services.

13. Zodrow (1999, 113) estimates 15% for a comparable calculation for Texas.

14. It is undoubtedly true that many residents are simply unaware of their use tax obligations. This explanation is becoming less persuasive as the use tax obligations are made explicit in the income tax forms and information booklet, discussed in the following.

15. ORTA (2001b) argues that because of business tax audits, direct tax payment agreements between Michigan businesses and the state of Michigan, voluntary compliance with tax laws, and tax exemptions for business production inputs, the current revenue loss from business-to-business remote sales is "small." ORTA cautions, though, that it could rise if Internet business-to-business sales increase and use tax is not strongly enforced.

16. For any single purchase over $1,000, the actual use tax must be reported.

17. In some states, local jurisdictions that levy a sales tax must do so at a standard rate. For example, in Georgia, any county with a local option sales tax simply has a 1% rate added to the state rate.

# 28

# The Property Tax
# in Michigan

*Naomi E. Feldman, Paul N. Courant, and Douglas C. Drake*

## The General Property Tax in Michigan

The State of Michigan enacted the General Property Tax, as we know it today, via Public Act 206 of 1893. As of Fiscal Year 2000, it was the single largest tax in the state, accounting for 9.6 billion dollars, 30.8% of all state and local taxes. In second place is the personal income tax, generating 6.79 billion dollars, or 21.8% of all state and local taxes, and third is the sales tax, which accounts for 6.39 billion dollars, or 20.5% of the total.[1] Table 28.1 reports total property tax collections in Michigan, by unit of government, in calendar year 2001, and demonstrates that even after the major school property tax reductions of Proposal A, local school property taxes are the largest single use of property taxes in Michigan. In addition, the State Education Tax (SET) is one of the revenue sources supporting the State School Aid Fund. Table 28.1 includes taxes levied for both operations and debt.

The tax rate on property in Michigan is generally expressed as the number of mills levied, or the millage rate.[2] Both state and local governments tax two types of property—real and personal. The tax rate is identical within each jurisdiction for both real and personal property. Real property includes land plus the buildings and fixtures permanently attached to it. Personal property generally is interpreted to be that property not permanently affixed to land: for example, equipment, furniture, tools, and computers. In addition, electric transmission and distribution equipment, gas transmission and distribution equipment, and oil pipelines are all considered personal property. In Michigan, only businesses pay the personal property tax (PPT); household personal property has been exempt since the 1930s. Total property tax collections for a given parcel equal the tax base (the taxable value) multiplied by the tax rate (that is, the number of mills). The total tax rate, in turn, is the sum of the tax rates levied by all of the overlapping levels of government in which a property is located.

## The Michigan Property Tax: Constitutional Basis

The constitutional basis of the Michigan property tax is found in Article IX, Section 3 of the Michigan Constitution:

> The legislature shall provide for the uniform general ad valorem taxation of real and tangible personal property not exempt by law except for taxes levied for school operating purposes. The legislature shall provide for the determination of true cash value of

**TABLE 28.1**

**Michigan Property Tax Collections, 2001**

|  | 2001 Levy ($1000s) | Percent of Total Collection |
|---|---|---|
| School | 4,525,182 | 44.14% |
| City | 1,923,619 | 18.77% |
| County | 1,612,237 | 15.73% |
| Township | 564,489 | 5.51% |
| Village | 79,095 | 0.77% |
| State (SET) | 1,546,273 | 15.08% |
| Total Levy | 10,250,893 | 100.00% |

SOURCE: Michigan Department of Treasury, Office of Revenue and Tax Analysis and Michigan State Tax Commission.

such property; the proportion of true cash value at which such property shall be uniformly assessed, which shall not, after January 1, 1966, exceed 50 percent; and for a system of equalization of assessments. For taxes levied in 1995 and each year thereafter, the legislature shall provide that the taxable value of each parcel of property adjusted for additions and losses, shall not increase each year by more than the increase in the immediately preceding year in the general price level, as defined in section 33 of this article, or 5 percent, whichever is less until ownership of the parcel of property is transferred. When ownership of the parcel of property is transferred as defined by law, the parcel shall be assessed at the applicable proportion of current true cash value. The legislature may provide for alternative means of taxation of designated real and tangible personal property in lieu of general ad valorem taxation. Every tax other than the general ad valorem property tax shall be uniform upon the class or classes on which it operates. A law that increases the statutory limits in effect as of February 1, 1994 on the maximum amount of ad valorem property taxes that may be levied for school district operating purposes requires the approval of $\frac{3}{4}$ of the members elected to and serving in the Senate and in the House of Representatives.

Two recent amendments made major changes to the Michigan property tax system. The first was the Headlee Amendment, which was passed in 1978 (Michigan Constitution, Article IX, Sections 25–34). Section 31 of this amendment places limitations on the growth rate of property taxes on a unitwide basis. The second major change came with the adoption of Proposal A school finance reform in 1994 (Michigan Constitution, Article IX, Section 3). Proposal A affects property

tax revenues in several ways: by constraining the growth rate of taxable value on individual parcels (commonly known as the "assessment cap"), by authorizing nonuniform treatment of homestead property for school operating taxes, and by requiring a three-fourths vote of the legislature to authorize any future increases in the maximum allowable rates for school operating purposes. Each of these amendments will be discussed in detail in the following.

## The Michigan Property Tax: Key Statutory Provisions

Public Act 206 of 1893 as amended is found in Sections 211.1–211.157 of the Michigan Compiled Laws. Real property is defined in Sections 211.2–211.6b; the personal property definition is at 211.8-8c. Assessment requirements are spelled out in Sections 211.10-23a. Equalization by counties is at Sections 211.34-34e, and the role of the State Tax Commission is found at Sections 211.146-154.

## Administration of the Property Tax: Assessment and Equalization

The requirement for the uniform taxation of property specified in the Section 3 language quoted previously has been in the Michigan Constitution since 1850. Under the uniformity requirement, each parcel of property and all classes of property are to be assessed at the same percentage of true cash value throughout the state. Also, the property tax rate applied to each parcel and class of property is to be uniform throughout each jurisdiction. Michigan has about 1,500 local assessing jurisdictions and over 2,500 taxing jurisdictions.

Michigan has a market value–based system of assessing property. The legislature has provided by law that all property is to be assessed annually at 50% of its true cash value or the usual selling price. As rerquired by the constitution, the legislature also has provided for the equalization of assessments made by local assessors within each county, and for the equalization of assessments among the eighty-three counties by the state. This three-step process of local assessment, county equalization, and state equalization is designed to ensure both that all property is uniformly assessed and that uniformity results in the State

Equalized Value (SEV) of each parcel being equal to 50% of its true cash or current market value.

In the subsequent discussion, we pay a good deal of attention to the determination of both the tax rates (which vary by jurisdiction within the state) and the tax base. Prior to the passage of Proposal A, the tax base for most taxable property was SEV. Subsequent to the passage of Proposal A, the tax base is equal to Taxable Value (TV), which can equal SEV but can never exceed it, and, under many circumstances, is less than SEV due to the assessment cap that was part of Proposal A. SEV is still an important construct in Michigan's system of property taxes, so our discussion of assessment and equalization begins with SEV.

While SEV is no longer the tax base upon which millage is levied, it is still computed for all parcels, and it is the tax base for newly constructed properties or properties where ownership is transferred, per the constitutional provisions. SEV is generated in three steps, as noted previously: local assessment and county and state equalization. Following the local assessment, the county determines whether the assessed value (AV) of the units of government within the county corresponds to the state requirements of uniformity and of 50% of true cash value.[3] If, for example, the county finds that commercial property in township X is assessed, on average, at 40% of true cash value, and all other units and classes of property are assessed at 50%, the county will equalize the assessments in the commercial property class by multiplying AV in township X by a factor of 1.25, yielding 50% of true cash value. State equalization performs essentially the same function across the counties.

### Why Is Equalization Necessary?

The drafters of the constitution realized that if there were no equalization at the county and state levels, local assessors could reduce or redistribute local tax burdens by deliberately manipulating the assessment of property in their jurisdictions. This practice could be used to increase state aid to local schools, and would also reduce county taxes or the taxes of other overlapping jurisdictions for residents of municipalities where property was underassessed. Both county and state equalization are designed to assure that residents of all jurisdictions are treated equitably, on average.

Since 1981, equalization has been done separately for each class of real property. The equal-

---

**TABLE 28.2**

**Equalization Changes, 2002 State Equalization**

| | |
|---|---|
| Counties with net increase of SEV over AV | 22 |
| Counties with net decrease of SEV over AV | 12 |
| Total number of counties with changes | 34 |

SOURCE: Authors' calculations from data supplied by the Office of Revenue and Tax Analysis and the State Tax Commission, Michigan Department of Treasury.

---

ization director at the county level presents his or her recommendations to the County Board of Commissioners for approval and transmittal to the State Tax Commission (STC). The STC then reviews the county equalized valuations for each separately equalized class of property.

Table 28.2 summarizes changes made in the state equalization process for 2002. Some 40.96% of all Michigan counties had a net change in the process of going from local AV to SEV. In dollar terms, the largest change to assessed values came in Mackinac County, which was up $42.0 million, or 4.68%. Only three other counties were increased by more than 1.00%. In three of these four counties, the overwhelming bulk of the change was in the residential class, although Mackinac had significant changes in agricultural, commercial, industrial, and timber cutover as well.

### Administration of the Property Tax: The Tax Collection Process

The Michigan system of tax collection is as fragmented as the assessing system, with each township or city usually collecting its own tax levies as well as those for overlapping taxing jurisdictions. For example, the City of Lansing will collect its taxes, the taxes for the Lansing Public Schools, the taxes for the portion of the Lansing Community College district within the city borders, and the Ingham County taxes for the portion of the county within the city borders. Lansing will also collect for the Capital Area Transportation Authority and any other special taxing authority within its borders. In addition, a number of school districts collect their own tax levy in the summer, usually in township areas that do not otherwise have a summer tax collection. Each tax-collecting treasurer is then responsible for distributing the taxes to each taxing jurisdiction (including the State School Aid Fund for the SET of six mills on all property and certain specific taxes levied in lieu of the general property tax). Michigan allows each local tax-collecting unit the option of adopting a 1% tax administration fee in addition to its general-purpose taxes.

In general, property taxes may be billed once or twice a year, on 1 July and/or on 1 December. Taxes billed on 1 July are usually due on 14 September, and taxes billed on 1 December are due and payable without penalty or interest by 14 February. Some cities may specify alternate due dates, or even installment payment plans in their city charters. Beginning 1 March, any unpaid taxes due on real property are normally turned over to the county for delinquent collection, as will be discussed in the following. Cities and more urbanized townships collect taxes either twice a year or once a year in July. More rural townships often bill only in December, and county taxes are always billed in December only. Of the total dollar volume of property taxes, a little over 50% is now collected on July bills, and slightly under 50% on December bills. This percentage will be further weighted to July billings beginning with 1 July 2003, when 100% of the six-mill SET will be levied in July. For July 2003 only, the tax will be reduced to five mills to offset any negative cash flow impact on taxpayers who must pay earlier than normal.

### Delinquent Tax Revolving Funds

Every year some portion of the property tax levy remains uncollected, varying by local unit. In most communities unpaid delinquent taxes on real property are turned over to the county treasurer on 1 March of each year. Through a mechanism known as the Delinquent Tax Revolving Fund (DTRF), the county treasurer issues bonds or notes and pays the city, township, school district, or other taxing unit the amount of their delinquent tax. The taxing jurisdictions thus are able to benefit from receiving the full amount of their tax levy. When property owners subsequently pay the delinquent tax and penalties and interest, those funds are used to retire the notes or bonds. After three years, if the taxes remain delinquent, the county treasurer bills the city, township, school district, or other taxing unit for a return of payments made by the DTRF. These bill backs are normally very small, due to the further penalty of the tax sale process discussed below. Most counties have a DTRF for two primary reasons: first, by aggregating the collection of delinquent taxes, the collection rate improves; and second, counties using the DTRF tool have been able to turn a profit

on the DTRF because the penalties and interest on the delinquent taxes are generally higher than the interest costs of the notes or bonds.

### The Delinquent Property Tax Foreclosure Process (Tax Sales)

Under Michigan law, owners of real property who fail to pay property taxes lose ownership of the property after receiving notice of the proceedings as described in the following. As of this writing, Michigan is in transition to a new tax sale system. Under the system that is being phased out, tax lien buyers could pay the delinquent taxes on another's property and receive interest of up to 50% of the delinquent taxes. If the property owner failed to repay the lien buyer, the lien buyer could go to court and obtain clear title to the property. If no lien buyer paid the taxes, the state would eventually either sell the property or deed it to a local government. This process is still in effect through December 2006 for property taxes levied before 1999. A significant objection to it is that it can take up to six years to be able to provide clear title to a new owner.

A new tax foreclosure system, enacted by Public Act 123 of 1999, simplifies and expedites the process. The legislation establishes a three-year process that applies to property taxes levied after 1998. Annual tax lien sales have been eliminated in favor of an annual forfeiture and judicial foreclosure process. The new law permits counties to exercise significant control over the handling of tax-delinquent property within their boundaries, with minimal involvement by the state. As under the former process, county treasurers are responsible for collecting delinquent taxes and for sending notices prior to forfeiture. The owner can redeem property forfeited to the county treasurer during the next year by payment of the taxes, penalties, and interest. If a county has elected not to participate in the foreclosure and sale of the property, the state will be responsible for those portions of the tax foreclosure process.

One goal of the new process is to ensure that purchasers of tax-foreclosed property will receive marketable title, for which title insurance can be obtained. However, it now appears that title insurance will not be offered until the courts uphold the new system, which could take five to ten years.

Another goal of the new system is to shorten the time required for abandoned property to return to productive use, particularly in urban areas. For example, under the old system, Wayne County foreclosed on only about one-third of an estimated fifteen thousand eligible parcels. The impact of the new tax foreclosure process will deserve careful review.

## Administration of the Property Tax: Appeals of Assessments and Other Issues

Appeals of local assessments may be made informally to the local assessor if the issue is simply one of clarifying the accuracy of the description of a property. Formal appeals of disputed valuations are made to an appointed Board of Review. Board of Review actions may be appealed to the State Tax Tribunal. Tax Tribunal decisions may be appealed to the Court of Appeals and then to the State Supreme Court, but not simply on an appeal of the value. An appeal must assert that it demonstrates application of wrong principles of law. Besides property tax appeals, the tribunal also hears appeals of all other Michigan tax issues.

One consequence of the passage of Proposal A is that assessment appeals where the value of the property is being contested have drastically declined. This follows from the fact that any increase in assessed value is now less contentious because what matters for an individual's tax burden is TV, which can be no more than, and is usually less than, AV. However, assessment appeals having to do with a parcel's "status" under Proposal A have increased. Property owners now appeal when their property is classified as having been transferred, when their assessments are uncapped, or when their property is classified as nonhomestead property. One other source of these "status" appeals would be removal of property from the agricultural class on the grounds that it was no longer being farmed (it is then taxed at the higher nonhomestead rate).

## Selected Exceptions to the General Property Tax in Michigan

Not all property is taxed according to the General Property Tax. There are a number of cases in which property receives different treatment. In some cases the differential treatment is due to the practical difficulties of assessing certain types of property. In other cases the desire to provide some degree of preferential treatment has driven the alternative tax policy. Recall the language of

Article IX, Section 3, requiring the uniform treatment of all property "not exempt by law." All of these alternative treatments are thus preceded by exemption from the general property tax.

## State Utility Property Tax

The State Utility Property Tax is a special version of the general case of differential taxation. It was created by Article IX, Section 5 of the Michigan Constitution, and dates to 1905. This tax applies to the taxable value of all property of telephone and telegraph, railroad, car loaning, sleeping car, and express car companies used in connection with doing business in Michigan. The companies subject to this tax report the value of all of their Michigan property to the state, and pay the utility property tax based upon the average millage rate for the state as a whole during the prior year. This procedure recognizes the practical difficulty of accurate assessment of property such as rail and telephone lines extending statewide across multiple assessing and taxing jurisdictions. The funds collected are deposited to the General Fund, General Purpose revenues of the state. Railroads receive a credit against their tax liability equal to 25% of expenditures for maintenance and improvement of rights-of-way in Michigan, if certain conditions are met. This essentially reduces the tax for railroads to zero in many cases. State collections of the utility property tax in FY 2001 were $152.5 million.[4]

## The Commercial Forest Specific Tax (CFT)

The Commercial Forest program provides a property tax reduction to private landowners as an incentive to retain and manage forestland for long-term timber production. Landowners participating in this program are exempted from the general property tax and pay the CFT tax of $1.10 per acre listed in the program. The State of Michigan pays an additional $1.20 per acre annually to each county where land is listed in the program. The total of $2.30 an acre is distributed by local treasurers to taxing jurisdictions in the same proportion as local general property tax millage levies (the 1993 pre-Proposal A school millages are used for this calculation). That portion of the $2.30 attributable to school operating taxes is returned to the State School Aid Fund for the support of the Proposal A foundation grants. As of

2001, there were approximately 2.2 million acres listed in this program under the ownership of nearly 1,300 private landowners. Landowners in this program agree to develop, maintain, and manage the land as commercial forest through planting, natural reproduction, or other silvicultural practices.[5] Relative to the potential taxes due on vacant recreational land in those parts of the state where the CFT is in wide use, this alternative taxation provides a significant incentive to keep these private lands in their forest status in recognition of the provision for public access rights and the difficulty in setting a value on their future use in timber production.

### The Severance Tax

In recognition of the difficulty of assessing the value of resources utilized by extractive industries, oil and gas production in Michigan is subject to the Severance Tax in lieu of the general property tax, and iron ore mining activities are subject to the Iron Ore Specific Tax. The severance tax is levied on the value of oil and gas at the point of extraction—the wellhead. The tax rate is 6.6% of the wellhead value of oil (4.0% if the well is a very low volume "stripper" well), and 5.0% for natural gas. The severance tax raised $61.8 million in Fiscal Year 2001, but varies considerably with the world price of oil. When market prices decline, the low-profit "stripper" wells are often shut down completely.

### The Iron Ore Specific Tax

The Iron Ore tax dates to Public Act 77 of 1951. "Low grade" iron ore mining properties are exempted from the general property tax and instead pay this tax based on the annual production of the mine. Both iron mines remaining in production in Michigan are in Marquette County. The iron mining industry has been struggling for some time. Public Act 249 of 2001 provided a credit against the Single Business Tax for low-grade pelletized hematite, which is also produced at one of the mines. Subsequently, Public Act 443 of 2002 provided for a 32% effective reduction in the Iron Ore Specific Tax for six years.

### The Mobile Home Specific Tax

The Mobile Home Specific Tax is another example of a tax in lieu of the general property tax, but it is hardly an extractive industry issue. Created in an era when mobile homes were very inexpensive housing options that often depreciated rapidly, it continues today as one of Michigan's more curious examples of differential taxation. A mobile home located on an individual parcel of real property is taxed under the general property tax just as any traditionally built home would be. On the other hand, a mobile home located in a mobile home park is exempt from the general property tax and instead pays a fee of $3.00 per month, which is distributed to local taxing jurisdictions: $2.00 is now returned to the State School Aid Fund under the reforms of Proposal A, $0.50 goes to the county, and $0.50 to the city or township in which the mobile home park is located. By virtue of paying lot rent, of course, the mobile home owner also pays some portion of the park owner's property taxes. The manufactured housing park is considered to be nonhomestead property for purposes of assessment, so it is subject to generally higher millage rates than homestead property. In addition, the purchaser of a mobile home pays sales tax on the full purchase price.

### Payments in Lieu of Property Taxes

Certain tax-exempt housing properties pay a fee in lieu of property taxes to the general purpose government in which they are located to address the costs of public services to the tax-exempt property. The most common are payments for housing constructed by or with financing from the Michigan State Housing Development Authority (MSHDA), or the federal Housing and Urban Development program. Housing owned by municipal housing corporations also will make payments in lieu of taxes.

### Alternative Taxes Based on the General Property Tax

The best and most widely known example is Michigan's Industrial Facilities Property Tax Abatement program (PA 198). A number of other economic development incentives are structured identically or nearly identically. PA 198s are Michigan's largest tax abatement program for economic development incentives. A PA 198 certificate effectively exempts a property from the general property tax (recall Article IX, Section 3). A new building is then taxed at one-half of the millage rate of the general property tax. A rehabilitation project is taxed at the value of the old facility only, no matter how much value is added. Once the PA 198 certificate is granted by a local unit of government and approved by the state, the only nonautomatic reduction would apply to the six-mill SET that can be exempted only by approval at the state level by the president of the Michigan Economic Development Corporation. These exemptions are discussed in more detail in chapter 14 of this volume.

## Special Assessments on Property

While not an exception or an "in lieu of property tax" situation, Michigan allows fairly widespread use of special assessments based on property value in addition to the general property tax. Many citizens will be aware of the use of special assessments to finance local services such as street improvements or sewers. These special assessments are normally levied on property owners based on the "front footage" of their property along the street or sewer line, not upon the value of the property itself.

Far different are special assessments authorized to finance services such as police, fire, trash collection, or lighting districts. These special assessments are usually levied on a millage basis, but only on the value of real property. They may be levied *without* voter approval and are not subject to any of the constitutional limits on property taxes, including the "Headlee" millage rollbacks to be discussed in the following.

## Michigan Property Taxes Compared to Those of Other States

In the interstate comparisons of state and local tax burden, we look at tax revenue on a per capita basis, or as a percentage of state personal income.[6] The personal income benchmark is preferable in most cases because it accounts for differential income levels across the states. This measure divides total state and local taxes paid by state personal income for the fiscal year. Using this measure, the total state and local tax burden includes all taxes, even business taxes, because generally these are ultimately paid by individuals, although in a multistate national environment individual states may seek to tax businesses more heavily if they feel that the business will increase

**FIGURE 28.1**

**State and Local Government: Property Taxes as a Share of Personal Income**

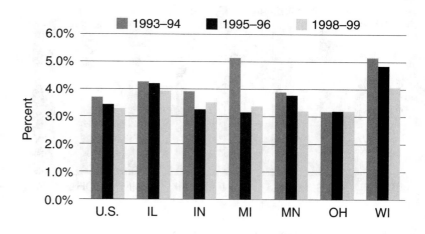

SOURCE: United States Census Bureau: State and Local Government Finances.

its prices and "shift" the final tax burden primarily to residents of other states who buy its products.

Prior to Proposal A, Michigan stood out when compared to the other Midwestern states. As figure 28.1 illustrates, prior to 1994, Michigan had a much higher state and local effective property tax rate than most of its neighbors (except for Wisconsin), and also a much higher rate than the United States average. However, this changed with the passage of Proposal A, with Michigan then ranking just above the U.S. average of 3.25% and above the 3.1% average in Ohio, the Midwestern state with the lowest measured state and local property tax burden.

Proposal A was passed in a climate in which many people believed that Michigan property taxes were excessive.[7] It had the intended consequence that the Michigan tax system now more closely resembles the "typical" state tax system. In Fiscal Year 1993, Michigan had a relatively low sales and use tax burden and a relatively high property tax burden compared to the national average.

## The Changing Nature of the State-Local Fiscal Relationship in Michigan

Another consequence of Proposal A was the shift of the property tax burden attributed to the state relative to local jurisdictions. Even prior to Proposal A, Michigan levied some "property"

**FIGURE 28.2**

**Local Property Taxes as a Share of Total Local and State Property Taxes**

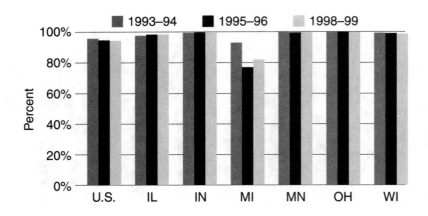

SOURCE: United States Census Bureau: State and Local Government Finances.

taxes at the state level (e.g., the State Utility Property Tax and the Intangibles Tax) in contrast to other states in the region that collected very little. After 1994, this locally collected percentage decreased even more, as figure 28.2 shows. For all state and local taxes, Michigan collects less at the local level than do its neighbors. As shown in figure 28.3, by 1999 Michigan was collecting 26.9% of its taxes locally, while the U.S. average was 38.7%. Part of the explanation for this is that Michigan does not allow local sales taxes; allows

**FIGURE 28.3**

**Local Taxes as a Share of Total State and Local Taxes**

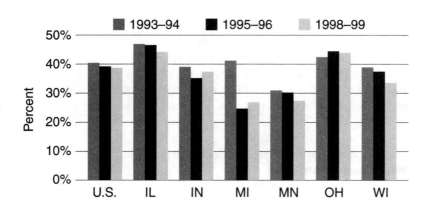

SOURCE: United States Census Bureau: State and Local Government Finances.

but has limited use of local income taxes; and has one of the larger programs of state-collected, locally shared taxes in the country. Chapter 31 of this volume discusses Michigan's state-local fiscal relationships in greater detail.

While virtually all systems of local finance involve a mixture of locally raised funds and transfers from higher levels of government, the variation in shares reflects a philosophical difference regarding local government finance. At one end of the spectrum (Tiebout [1956]; Fischel [1992]) is a highly decentralized system. Local governments offer a wide menu of alternative packages of local public services, and each individual household selects a community of residence based on its preferred combination of public outputs. In such a setting, local public finance takes on marketlike qualities, where households "vote with their feet." In choosing a residential jurisdiction, they effectively "purchase" their preferred level of public services, with taxes functioning analogously to prices in a market setting. Residents then determine changes in output through local decisions. These decisions tend to be efficient because the benefits and costs of local programs will be capitalized into local property values. In this world, local taxes are an essential element of local finance: they are the prices that guide individuals to make efficient decisions.

At the other end of the spectrum is a much more centralized system of local government. States are more important actors, and they constrain local government taxation and expenditure decisions in order to facilitate their own goals. In this model, a premium is placed on equal access to local services, and local governments may take on basic redistributive functions on behalf of the state governments. Greater reliance is placed on central finance, with intergovernmental grants providing the lion's share of local revenues.

Within a relatively centralized system, the case for local taxation is based primarily on the desire for local government autonomy and economic efficiency in making fiscal decisions. This position does not require complete financing at the local level. Some fraction of funds may come in the form of grants, as long as these funds do not distort economic decisions. The crucial element here is that when decisions are being made at the margin to expand or contract local services, local tax finance must play a decisive role so that the economic costs and benefits of such decisions are a driving force in the deliberative process.

**TABLE 28.3**

**Millage Rates**

| | Average Millage Rates,[a] Calendar Year | | | | | | | | | Change 1993–2001 | |
| | 1993 | 1994 | 1995 | 1996 | 1997 | 1998 | 1999 | 2000 | 2001 | Mills | Percent |
|---|---|---|---|---|---|---|---|---|---|---|---|
| County | 6.22 | 6.27 | 6.28 | 6.36 | 6.32 | 6.30 | 6.28 | 6.27 | 6.26 | 0.04 | 0.64% |
| Township | 3.36 | 3.56 | 3.68 | 3.74 | 3.87 | 4.02 | 3.99 | 4.09 | 4.06 | 0.70 | 20.83% |
| City | 15.45 | 15.75 | 15.95 | 16.06 | 16.18 | 16.23 | 16.17 | 16.36 | 16.23 | 0.78 | 5.05% |
| Village | 11.94 | 12.13 | 12.34 | 12.54 | 12.57 | 12.22 | 12.37 | 12.2 | 12.15 | 0.21 | 1.76% |
| Total Non-School | 15.89 | 16.13 | 16.23 | 16.37 | 16.40 | 16.41 | 16.30 | 16.37 | 16.22 | 0.33 | 2.08% |
| | | | | | | | | | | | |
| Local School Operating | 33.91 | 9.26 | 9.26 | 9.28 | 8.79 | 8.74 | 8.59 | 8.41 | 8.35 | −25.56 | −75.38% |
| Local School Debt[b] | 2.54 | 2.56 | 3.03 | 3.27 | 3.57 | 3.63 | 3.8 | 4.01 | 4.28 | 1.74 | 68.50% |
| ISD/Community College[c] | 4.30 | 4.24 | 4.36 | 4.40 | 4.48 | 4.48 | 4.47 | 4.51 | 5.01 | 0.71 | 16.51% |
| State Education Tax | 0 | 6 | 6 | 6 | 6 | 6 | 6 | 6 | 6 | 6 | n/a |
| Total School (includes SET) | 40.75 | 22.06 | 22.65 | 22.95 | 22.85 | 22.86 | 22.86 | 22.95 | 23.64 | −17.11 | −41.99% |
| | | | | | | | | | | | |
| TOTAL MILLS | 56.64 | 38.19 | 38.88 | 39.32 | 39.25 | 39.27 | 39.16 | 39.32 | 39.86 | −16.78 | −29.63% |

SOURCE: May 2002 Property Tax Report, Michigan Department of Treasury, Office of Revenue and Tax Analysis (ORTA), Exhibit 35, p. 50, and current data supplied by ORTA.
(a) All property, does not include special assessments
(b) Includes sinking fund mills for all years. Includes 1993 building and site mills.
(c) Includes intermediate school district and community college debt mills.

In comparison, the case for reliance on intergovernmental grants has several aspects. First, one can argue that a tax system that relies heavily on central government revenues will be better able to engage in redistribution. Higher levels of government can make more effective use of progressive taxes, because people cannot easily avoid the tax by moving across jurisdictional lines. Centrally levied taxes tend to avoid locational distortions caused by local tax differentials. A second and related argument is that competition among jurisdictions leads to a "race to the bottom." The claim is that state and local governments, in their enthusiasm to attract new investment and jobs, tend to keep tax rates below efficient levels, resulting in a level of public services that is too low. Third is the issue of fiscal disparities. Under a system of centralized revenues, funds can be distributed in an egalitarian way to local governments, so that fiscal opportunities across jurisdictions become more equal. One could, for example, envision a system in which state governments collect revenues and then distribute them on an equal per-pupil basis to local school districts, perhaps adjusted for cost differentials (Oates 2001).

As figures 28.2 and 28.3 show, Michigan had a relatively centralized system prior to 1994, and has shifted to an even more centralized tax system since the passage of Proposal A. While there has been some slight movement in recent years back toward local taxation, the state as a whole collects a much lower share of its taxes at the local level (and hence a higher share at the state level) than most of the other Midwestern states. This can be seen in the changing levy rates by unit of government as displayed in table 28.3.

This table shows very clearly that property tax reform in Michigan was accomplished in large part through centralization of school finance, discussed in more detail in chapter 15. From an ideological perspective, centralization is generally more liberal than conservative, more Democrat than Republican. Yet, Proposal A was very strongly supported by conservative Republicans in coalition with Democrats. One would not have expected, a priori, these individuals to be champions of a program in which state taxes were substituted for local taxes, and in which local school spending levels are determined in large part at the state level.

**The California Experience**

This section will turn briefly to an examination of California's experience with a property tax system very similar to Michigan's. California's system resembles Michigan's, particularly in terms of their common "modified acquisition systems."[8] California has a long experience under this system, dating to June 1978, when California voters led the era of taxpayer revolts by amending their constitution with the citizen-initiated Proposition 13.

As with Michigan's Proposal A, California's Proposition 13 places a cap on the increase in assessed value of property. Two neighboring properties, similar in every way, can have very different taxable values solely as a function of the last date of transfer.[9] In California, the assessed value of property cannot increase by more than 2% per year until the property is sold, at which time the property is reassessed at its full market value, usually the selling price. This has created a statewide tension between those who have owned their homes for many years and those who have purchased properties in more recent years. There will always be some disparity, simply because some homeowners have lived in the same home for two decades or more. Nonetheless, a study done by the Public Policy Institute of California found that the gap between assessed value and market value for properties sold after 1980 is not much different from that found in states that do not have Proposition 13–type legislation (Lyon 1995).

Because of the limits on property tax revenue growth established by the passage of Proposition 13, local governments in California have turned to alternative sources of revenue to finance the infrastructure necessary for new residential development—including developer impact fees to finance expanded capacity in utilities, roads, lighting, and schools. Unlike bonds, these fees are often invisible because the home buyer does not know what kinds of fees were levied against the builder or how much of the cost has been passed on to the buyer in the form of higher home prices. A study conducted on development fees in Contra Costa County found that government fees imposed on new construction were significant—typically in the range of $20,000 to $30,000 per dwelling. In one community, fees and bond assessments accounted for 19% of the mean sales price of a new home. However, the degree to which the fees were passed on varied widely over the county, primarily due to disparate economic conditions. In softer housing markets, the developer absorbs most of the cost. In stronger markets, he or she can pass it on to the buyer (Lyon 1995). This seemingly negative reliance on fees may have a positive consequence relative to allocating a larger share of the cost of new development to those properties that will most directly benefit.

It is important to note that a major difference between the California legislation and Michigan's is that California does not have the double restriction imposed by the per parcel cap of Proposal A and the jurisdictional level cap on tax revenue growth imposed by Headlee. There is no equivalent of the Headlee Amendment in California.

## Tax Limitations before Headlee and Proposal A

The basic legal citation of the General Property Tax, Public Act 206 of 1893, as amended, provides a critical clue to the long history of the property tax in Michigan governmental finance. For decades, two key lynchpins of that history were the fifteen/eighteen-mill limitation and the overall fifty-mill limitation.

Among its many other impacts, Proposal A has significantly changed both of these key features. The fifteen/eighteen-mill limitation applied to the aggregate local tax rates that can be levied on property without further voter approval. Where there were exceptions to the constitutional limits, separate statutes set those specific limits. This long-standing language was carried over into the new constitution that took effect after voter approval on 1 January 1964 (Article IX, Section 6).

Prior to 1994–95, the Allocation Board in each county distributed either the fifteen or the eighteen mills to each taxing jurisdiction in the county. The local school district was generally granted between six and eleven mills of fifteen/eighteen-mill taxing authority. This was referred to as the district's "allocated millage." Under Proposal A, school districts no longer receive any "allocated millage." The fifteen or eighteen mill limit in each county has been reduced by the number of mills formerly allocated to local school districts (Addonizio 2001).

While the constitutional limits allow local taxpayers to vote to exceed the fifteen- or eighteen-mill limits, they also apply an aggregate limitation of fifty mills. All three of the millage limits, however, apply only to operating tax rates and exclude taxes levied for debt service. The fifteen (or eighteen) and fifty-mill limits also do not apply to cities, villages, charter townships or charter authorities. These units of government, as well as a number of other charter entities, are limited instead by specific state laws granting the charter, or by their own voter-approved charters, which in turn must conform to state-level limitations on the amount of millage levied. For example, city charters are limited by state law to a maximum of twenty mills for general operating purposes.

Because of the exemption of charters for cities and other local units, as well as the exemption of millage levied to repay debt, it is not quite correct to think of either the fifteen- (or eighteen-) or the fifty-mill limits as absolute. Indeed, the average total statewide millage rate from 1973 to 1993 was over fifty mills. Even in today's post–Proposal A world, the average rate on nonhomestead property is above fifty mills.

## The "Headlee" Amendment to the Michigan Constitution

In November 1978, Michigan voters approved the so-called Headlee Amendment (Michigan Constitution, Article IX, Sections 25–33).[10] Section 31 pertains to local government taxation in two key ways. First, it requires that voters approve the future levy of taxes not authorized by law or charter prior to November 1978. That is, current residents must approve any local taxes not already authorized. This provision is in the first and second sentences of Article IX, Section 31 as quoted here. The second key provision of Section 31, known as the "millage rollback" provision, begins with the third sentence.

Units of Local Government are hereby prohibited from levying any tax not authorized by law or charter when this section is ratified or from increasing the rate of an existing tax above that rate authorized by law or charter when this section is ratified, without the approval of a majority of the qualified electors of that unit of Local Government voting thereon. If the definition of the base of an existing tax is broadened, the maximum authorized rate of taxation on the new base in each unit of Local Government shall be reduced to yield the same estimated gross revenue as on the prior base. If the assessed valuation of property as finally equalized, excluding the value of new construction and improvements, increases by a larger percentage than the increase in the General Price Level from the previous year, the maximum authorized rate applied thereto in each unit of Local Government shall be reduced to yield the same gross revenue from existing property, adjusted for changes in the General Price Level, as could have been collected at the existing authorized rate on the prior assessed value.

The limitations of this section shall not apply to taxes imposed for the payment of principal and interest on bonds or other evidence of indebtedness or for the payment of assessments on contract obligations in anticipation of which bonds are issued, which were authorized prior to the effective date of this amendment.

The phrase "If the assessed valuation of property . . . increases by a larger percentage than the increase in the General Price Level . . ." effectively applies a unitwide cap on the growth of local taxes for each taxing unit, implemented by automatically reducing the number of mills that can be levied. This limits the amount of increased revenues a local government can extract from property taxes on existing property, over the whole taxing unit, to an inflationary increase plus the taxes generated by any new construction. The Headlee Amendment's unitwide cap is quite different in its effect than the assessment cap under Proposal A, as will be discussed in the following.

For example, given an inflation rate in consumer prices of 2.5%, if the tax base increased from $1,000,000 to $1,100,000 (excluding new construction), and if the tax rate were one mill, the millage would have to be reduced to 0.932 mill so that the yield would be the same as that generated by the one mill on the original tax base adjusted for inflation—$1,025. The millage reduction in this example is called a "Headlee Rollback."

Section 31 has had a significant restraining effect on local revenue and has caused local government units to roll back millage rates so as to offset assessment increases, especially during the 1980s, and continuing into the early 1990s, when real estate values were rising in many jurisdictions. A unit's total tax base is measured against the Section 31 standard each year.

The Headlee millage rollbacks themselves are automatic. However, the governing body of the local unit may place the question of a full or partial "override" of the millage on the local ballot. Voter approval by simple majority is required to replace the reduced millage. The original implementing statutes for the Headlee Amendment provided for a "pop-up" option without voter approval. If the total tax base of a unit (excluding new construction) increased by less than the Consumer Price Index (CPI) in a year after its tax rate had been rolled back, the rate could automatically be adjusted up to yield the amount allowed by the CPI trigger. This "pop-up" feature was removed from the property tax statute by the same act that led to Proposal A, Public Act 145 of

1993, which banned property taxes for school operating purposes.

The Headlee millage rollback provision had significant impacts on the growth of total property taxes at the unitwide level from 1979 to 1993. While these rollbacks have diminished in frequency since Proposal A, they continue to play a role because Proposal A's implementing legislation considers the increase in taxable value resulting from a property transfer to be an increase in the value of existing property, not "new construction" or an "addition." Because Proposal A allows taxable value (TV) to grow no faster than the rate of inflation (or 5%) until the point the property is sold, at which point TV jumps to SEV, this increase in value can cause a Headlee rollback to occur in units with sufficient appreciation and property turnover.

## Major Changes Due to Proposal A

Prior to the passage of Proposal A, Michigan relied much more heavily than most other states on local property taxes to finance its public schools. Typical of the period prior to Proposal A, in the 1990–91 school year, Michigan, with a slightly above average level of state taxation overall, was third among states in the share of school spending financed locally (65.2%), behind only New Hampshire, which has virtually no state taxes, and Oregon, which also has since changed its school financing in recent years. Michigan property tax revenues had risen from 4.3% of personal income in 1978 to 5.1% in 1991, while the national trend was one of reduced dependence on property taxes. The national average of property tax revenues as a percentage of personal income in 1991 was 3.7%.[11]

Whether or not the differences between Michigan and national norms should have warranted what seemed to be a perpetual property tax rebellion, they clearly did so. Between 1973 and 1993, reformers placed more than ten property tax–related initiatives on the statewide ballot. Only one of these ballot initiatives, the 1978 Headlee Amendment, actually passed prior to Proposal A, but the fervor for property tax cuts was sufficiently strong that in some cases new ballot initiatives for cutting property taxes were developed even as the old ones were going down to defeat. Property tax cuts, rather than reform of the school financial system itself, had been a dominant statewide political issue for decades.

In July of 1993, the Michigan Senate was deliberating a property tax cut bill. Somewhat unexpectedly, an amendment was offered that simply abolished, with no source of revenue replacement specified, all use of local property taxes for school operating expenditures. The amendment was adopted, the bill passed, and the terms of the property tax debate were forever changed. In this one act, the state imposed a local tax cut of over six billion dollars for the school year to start 1 July 1994, with no offsetting tax increase.

In the early morning hours of 24 December 1993, both houses passed, and the governor signed, a reform financing package of bills that contained two options. The 1994 referendum differed from its predecessors in the previous two decades in at least one critical way: voters did not have the option to reject major reform—that is, the status quo was no longer an option. The options differed greatly, but each had the essential features of radically changing the system of school finance in Michigan and replacing nearly all of the lost revenue to local school districts (Courant, Gramlich, and Loeb 1994).

Three features of Proposal A contributed to its success in addition to apparent voter preference for the sales tax that was the major component of the new financing system. First, it cut homestead millage rates more than the competing Statutory Plan did. Second, it increased the cigarette tax more than the Statutory Plan did, and voter sentiment was anti-tobacco. Third, the Ballot Plan placed a constitutional cap on property tax assessment increases, while the Statutory Plan did not. Given that the impetus for the 1993–94 tax reforms was property tax reform and not necessarily school finance reform, tax relief, in the form of a limitation on the maximum annual increase in assessments on each parcel of property (commonly known as an "assessment cap"), was highly popular.

## Property Tax Millage Rates in the Post–Proposal A World

For property owners, the most noticeable impact of Proposal A was the immediate reduction in millage rates. From 1993 to 1995, average statewide millage rates for all property (a weighted average of homestead and nonhomestead property) decreased 17.76 mills, a 31.4% reduction. This decline was attributable solely to the reduction in local school operating millage rates. For homeowners, the reduction was even more dramatic, from a state effective average of 34 mills for school operating purposes to 6 mills paid via the SET, a drop of 82.35%. Smaller reductions were experienced in the fifty-two "hold-harmless" school districts that were authorized to levy higher millages to support their preexisting higher-than-guaranteed spending levels.[12] The effect of Proposal A is striking, as illustrated in both table 28.3 and figure 28.4.

While average millage rates have increased slightly since 1994 (except for local school operating mills), the upward trend is especially noticeable for local school debt and sinking fund mills, all of which finance purchases of capital for schools.[13] From 1993 to 2001, the average effective rate for debt mills climbed from 2.54 mills to 4.28 mills.[14]

## The Taxable Value Limitation (Assessment Cap)

As noted previously, the limit on taxable value growth, or assessment cap, feature of Proposal A may have been critical to its approval by the voters. This cap on taxable value has created an ever-widening gap between SEV and TV and has resulted in a dramatic reduction in property taxes paid relative to what would have happened in the absence of Proposal A.

Since 1994, the growth in taxable value of parcels that have not changed hands has been held to the inflation rate because annual inflation, as measured by the CPI, has been less than 5%. Housing values, on average, have appreciated more rapidly than has the CPI. Figure 28.5 and table 28.4 illustrate this fact.

In 2002, SEV was $343 billion and TV was $275 billion, a roughly 20% reduction from what taxable value would have been on the old SEV base. Classes of property have been affected in varying degrees by this new system of assessment and local units have experienced varying effects based on their shares of the different classes of property and their own differing property turnover rates.[15]

With an average tax rate of 39.3 mills, the divergence of SEV and TV resulted in a total statewide tax yield in 2002 of about $2.7 billion less than would have been the case had SEV been used as the tax base. However, because more Headlee rollbacks would have most likely occurred with SEV as the tax base, this $2.7 billion is the maximum of the tax yield difference. In addition, the existence of higher values may well

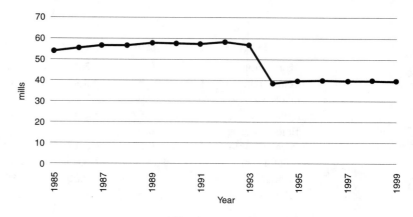

**FIGURE 28.4**

### Statewide Average Millage Rate, All Property, 1985–1999

SOURCE: State Tax Commission: All property rates, 1985–93, 1995–2000; Office of Revenue and Tax Analysis: All property rate and homestead and non-homestead rate estimates, 1994.

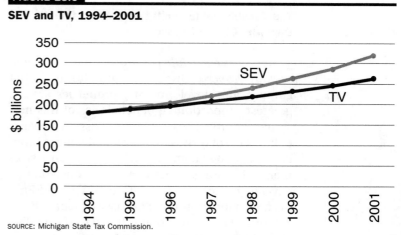

**FIGURE 28.5**

### SEV and TV, 1994–2001

SOURCE: Michigan State Tax Commission.

**TABLE 28.4**

### Applicable Inflation Limit on Taxable Value Growth

| | |
|---|---|
| 1995 | 2.50% |
| 1996 | 2.80% |
| 1997 | 2.80% |
| 1998 | 2.70% |
| 1999 | 1.60% |
| 2000 | 1.90% |
| 2001 | 3.20% |
| 2002 | 3.20% |
| 2003 | 1.50% |

SOURCE: Michigan Department of Treasury, Office of Revenue and Tax Analysis.

**TABLE 28.5**

**Differences between TV and SEV, 1994 and 2002, by Class of Property ($ billions)**

|  | 1994 | | 2002 | | | | |
|---|---|---|---|---|---|---|---|
|  | SEV | % of Total | TV | % of Total | SEV | % of Total | TV as % of SEV Statewide |
| Agricultural | 6.80 | 3.87 | 7.91 | 2.88 | 13.38 | 3.89 | 59.12 |
| Commercial | 24.52 | 13.97 | 37.63 | 13.68 | 46.47 | 13.52 | 80.98 |
| Industrial | 12.98 | 7.39 | 18.08 | 6.57 | 20.55 | 5.98 | 87.98 |
| Residential | 109.57 | 62.42 | 180.64 | 65.68 | 231.99 | 67.49 | 77.87 |
| Timber cutover | 0.32 | 0.18 | 0.15 | 0.05 | 0.31 | 0.09 | 48.39 |
| Developmental | 0.28 | 0.16 | 0.34 | 0.12 | 0.63 | 0.18 | 53.97 |
| Total real | 154.47 | 88.00 | 244.75 | 88.99 | 313.34 | 91.16 | 78.11 |
| Personal | 21.07 | 12.00 | 30.29 | 11.01 | 30.37 | 8.84 | 99.74 |
| TOTAL | 175.54 | | 275.04 | | 343.72 | | 80.02 |

SOURCE: Michigan Department of Treasury, Office of Revenue and Tax Analysis.

have contributed to keeping rates somewhat lower, also impacting the actual tax differential.

### The Taxable Value Limitation ("Assessment Cap") by Class of Property

*Agriculture, Timber Cutover, and Developmental Property.* Owners of agricultural, timber cutover, and developmental properties are the greatest proportionate beneficiaries of this new system of property assessment. Possibly because of low rates of turnover in ownership, these properties tend to remain subject to the cap on assessments for longer periods and consequently develop greater gaps in the TV to SEV ratio. Moreover, starting with the 2001 assessment roll, PA 260 of 2000 provides that a transfer of qualified agricultural property is *not* a "transfer of ownership" and therefore subject to uncapping, provided that the property remains qualified agricultural property after the transfer. The person to whom the property is transferred files an affidavit with the assessor and the register of deeds. The signer of the affidavit must attest that the qualified agricultural property shall remain qualified agricultural property. In 1994, these three classes of property constituted 4.3% of the total statewide tax base. In 2002, their TV constituted 3.2% and their SEV 4.2% (see table 28.5).

*Commercial and Industrial Property.* Commercial and industrial property has the narrowest gaps between TV and SEV of all classes of property. Although these types of property remain closest to full assessment, they now constitute a

smaller percentage of the total statewide tax base than they did in 1994. Most growth in these classes is from new construction. Commercial properties are usually assessed by the income method of valuation, and industrial properties are usually assessed by replacement or reproduction costs adjusted for depreciation due to low turnover in these industries.[16] In 1994, these two classes of property constituted 21.4% of the total statewide tax base. In 2002, their TV constituted 20.3% and their SEV 19.5%.

*Residential Property.* The TV of residential property was 77.9% of SEV in 2002. Unlike the other classes of property, residential property constituted a larger portion of the total statewide tax base in 2002 at 65.7% than it did in 1994 at 62.4%. The growth in the portion of the total tax base would have been even larger had SEV continued as the tax base, in which case residential property would have been 67.5% of the total statewide tax base.

*Local Government Differences.* The change in the relationship between TV and SEV has varied among individual counties, ranging from Midland County (with TV equal to 93.0% of SEV in 2002) to Luce County (with TV equal to 65.0% of SEV in 2002). While the state as a whole had a ratio of TV to SEV of 80.0% for all property in 2001, the ratio was 81.8% for all cities as a group, and 78.6% for townships as a group. The ratio for classes of property ranged from a low of 43.6% for agricultural property in cities to a high of 99.9% for personal property in cities. Local units that are experiencing new growth, additions to existing property, and a rapid turnover of properties will tend to have TV that is keeping pace with the growth in SEV, although never equaling the level of SEV. Conversely, local units with lower investment rates and slower turnover of properties have seen the gap between SEV and TV growing more rapidly.

### The Proposal A Homestead Exemption

Section 380.1211 of the Michigan Compiled Laws states that the board of a school district shall levy not more than eighteen mills or the number of mills levied in 1993 for school operating purposes, whichever is less. Homesteads and qualified agricultural property are generally exempt from the mills levied under this subsection except in the case where the school district levies "hold-harmless" mills (see chapter 15 of this volume).

Creation of differential tax rates for homestead and nonhomestead property, as part of Proposal A, was a major departure from the Michigan tradition of taxing all property at the same rate within an individual taxing jurisdiction. Homestead property is about 90% of the total residential class statewide, and the combination of the assessment cap and the exemption from school operating taxes has made homeowners the major beneficiary of the significant property tax cuts created by Proposal A.

### The Three-Fourths Vote Requirement to Raise Maximum Rates for School Operating Purposes

Proposal A established a three-fourths supermajority requirement for the legislature to increase the maximum rate of any property tax for school operating purposes. This requirement applies to the six-mill state school tax on all property and the eighteen-mill local school tax on nonhomestead property. It also applies to the additional taxing authority under which some school districts may levy hold-harmless mills, and to the local enhancement millage option for ISDs (Addonizio 2001; Michigan Constitution, Article IX, Section 3).

### New Property Tax Levies under Proposal A: The Michigan State Education Tax (SET)

Public Act 331 of 1993, in conjunction with the passage of Proposal A, established the SET to be levied on all property in the state. The six-mill rate of the SET was established when voters approved Proposal A. Because the SET is a state tax and not a local tax, it does not require local voter approval, nor is it subject to Headlee rollbacks. All revenue from the SET is earmarked for the School Aid Fund to help finance public K–12 education. Uncollected SET taxes are subject to the same delinquent tax collection process detailed earlier in this chapter (Single Business Tax Division 2002).

### Additional Taxes under Proposal A: The Eighteen-Mill Levy on Nonhomestead Property

Nonhomestead property includes essentially all property that is *not* the principal residence of a homeowner, or qualified agricultural property. Examples of nonhomestead property are rental housing, second homes, and business property. Beginning in 1994, local school districts could levy a basic operating millage equal to the lesser of eighteen mills or their 1993 local school operating millage. In some respects, this levy may be thought of as the "admission ticket" for Proposal A: districts meeting this levy test then receive the full foundation amount provided by Proposal A, with state School Aid Funds supplementing the locally raised revenue to reach the full foundation. If a district levies less than eighteen mills (or its own rate, if less), it simply receives that much less of its total foundation rather than completely losing eligibility. The state share of the foundation remains the same whether or not the local district levies its full eighteen mills, or indeed any of its eighteen mills. Of the 556 local school districts existing in 1994, 536 of them levied eighteen mills of basic school operating millage. Thirteen of the remaining 20 had levied less than eighteen mills in 1993, and the final 7 levied fewer than eighteen mills either by choice or because their levy had been reduced because of a Headlee rollback (Michigan Department of Treasury 2002).

### Additional Taxes under Proposal A: Hold-Harmless Millage Rates

Under Proposal A, hold-harmless mills permit the highest pre–Proposal A spending school districts to raise additional local revenue to maintain that level, but not to increase it. Altogether, there are fifty-two high-revenue school districts that are authorized to levy "hold-harmless" mill-ages in order to avoid substantial per pupil revenue losses under the 1994 reforms (see chapter 15 of this volume). The hold-harmless millage is first levied on homestead property up to eighteen mills. If more millage is needed, additional hold-harmless millage is levied upon both homestead and nonhomestead property such that the millage is uniform on all classes of property. Of the fifty-two school districts authorized to levy these millages, thirty-four actually need to do so as of this writing.

Hold-harmless millages are subject to three limitations. First, these district-specific rates may not exceed the maximum rates certified by the Michigan Department of Treasury for the 1994–95 fiscal year. Second, the revenue per pupil raised by this millage may not exceed the amount authorized to be raised by this millage for 1994–95. This is the revenue in excess of the maximum foundation (or baseline) level that is determined by the statewide school aid formula (see chapter 15 of this volume). Third, the hold-harmless millage rate must be reduced if local taxable value growth results in per pupil revenue growth that exceeds the lesser of the dollar increase in the state basic foundations allowance or the increase in the CPI (Addonizio 2001).

## Additional Taxes under Proposal A: Individual School District "Enhancement" Millages

The Proposal A legislative package authorized individual local school districts to seek voter approval for the levy of up to three mills of local operating "enhancement" millage. This levy was created to allow the option of seeking additional but temporary funding to address any unforeseen transitional issues created by Proposal A. The levies were authorized for the 1994–95, 1995–96, and 1996–97 school years only (the 1994, 1995, and 1996 property tax years). An option still exists for up to three local "enhancement" mills, but, now they may be levied only by Intermediate School Districts (ISDs), with the funds distributed on a per-pupil basis to all the local member districts of the ISD. Local districts representing a majority of the pupils within an ISD may request that the question be put before the voters, and the tax must be approved by a majority of the voters in the ISD as a whole. To date only one Intermediate District, Monroe, is levying a voter-approved enhancement millage.

## Property Tax Incidence: Who Pays the Property Tax?

As a general matter, the ultimate payer of a tax can differ from the initial payer. The determination of who pays once all of the economic effects are accounted for is called tax incidence. There are currently two competing theoretical views of the property tax as a local tax. The first view is the so-called benefit view of the tax. In this view, the assignment of the tax liability accords with the benefits received from the associated local public services. In other words, the property tax approximates a benefit tax that encourages efficient fiscal decisions by local residents. People get what they pay for from local government, much as they do in the private marketplace. Economists who take this view believe that the benefits from local public programs and their costs in terms of property tax liabilities tend to be "capitalized" into local property values. For example, the benefits that accrue to communities with good local schools, nice parks, little crime, and low tax rates will manifest themselves in the form of high prices for dwellings. People are willing to pay more to live in communities with comparatively good services and low taxes. This, in turn, gives local residents a powerful incentive to undertake those public projects that provide a net benefit to the community and promote the value of the local property, up to the point where the marginal benefits equal the marginal costs. Various authors (Hamilton 1975; Fischel 1992) show that residential zoning laws can be used to turn the property tax into a lump-sum tax (or benefit tax) assessed as payment for local public services provided.

The competing conceptual approach to understanding local property taxation is called the "new view," which sees the tax as a levy on capital that leads to certain kinds of distortions, both in housing markets and in local fiscal decisions. Because the tax base includes improvements to land and other structures, the tax on property discourages building and other activities by increasing their cost. This leads to an underutilization of land, and the amount of capital used per unit of land is less than the efficient amount.

Each view—and both in combination—has its proponents, and both contribute in important ways to the understanding of how the property tax works. The balance of the two views has important implications for "incidence"—who pays the tax. Early writers such as Netzer (1966) argued that the property tax was primarily a tax on housing, and therefore regressive. This argument maintains that because the tax is essentially a flat or proportional tax on the value of a dwelling unit, and since lower-income families tend to spend a higher proportion of their wealth on housing, it follows that property tax liabilities constitute a larger fraction of the incomes of families with lower incomes. However, modern general equilibrium analysis—the basis for the "new view" of the property tax—finds that the average rate of the tax across all jurisdictions functions essentially as a tax on all capital. The basic idea is that because nearly all communities are taxing local capital, the average rate of tax essentially becomes a national tax on capital. Because higher-income people tend to disproportionately be the owners of capital, the property tax is more apt to be progressive. Zodrow (2001) points out that empirically, it is quite difficult to differentiate the two models, due to their similar predictions (that is, both theories imply that the benefits and costs of local programs are borne locally and give rise to capitalization).

The initial incidence of a tax may not necessarily equal the final incidence of the tax. This differential is most easily seen in the example of business taxation. It is true of all taxes, including the property tax. The initial incidence of the property tax and other taxes is certainly on the business, and the business also clearly receives at least some of the benefits of the property tax, such as police and fire and other public services and the inherent value of an educated local workforce resulting from school property taxes. While initially paying the property tax or any other tax themselves, businesses actually "shift" the final incidence to the owners of the capital supporting the businesses, in the form of lower profits; to the vendors supplying the businesses, in the form of pressure to reduce their prices; to the employees of the business, in the form of lower wages; or to the customers of the business, in the form of higher prices.

In the real world all four likely bear the final incidence of the tax in varying proportions, depending on the pricing power of the business in its market and the relative strengths of its employees, suppliers, and customers. The degree of "forward shifting" to customers is relevant in a discussion of business taxes at the state level to the extent that the final incidence of any tax can be shifted to customers in other states or other countries. As a major exporting state, this issue

has significance for an overall evaluation of taxes in Michigan.

## The Michigan Circuit-Breaker Property Tax Credit

Michigan has a generous homestead property tax credit or "circuit-breaker," which reduces the net property tax burden on households with incomes under $82,650 whose taxes exceed more than 3.5% of their income.[17] Households with residents who are under age sixty-five receive a refundable tax credit of 60% of the taxes paid in excess of 3.5% of income. Households with residents who are over age sixty-five receive a credit of 100%, and also benefit from a lower threshold, or circuit breaker, if their incomes are extremely low (under $6,000). All are subject to a cap of $1,200 in tax credits, and the credit is gradually phased out for annual incomes between $73,650 and $82,650. Renters are allowed to claim 20% of their rent as estimated property taxes under the law. While Proposal A's dramatic reduction of school operating taxes also reduced the total amount of credits, the circuit breaker still provides very significant relief for those whose property taxes are very high relative to their income. The credit is claimed on state income tax returns, and for a more complete discussion of the credit, please see chapter 26 of this volume.

## Exemptions from the General Property Tax

Institutions, such as federal, state, or local governments, and charitable and religious organizations, own much of the property exempt under state law. Article IX, Section 4 of the Michigan Constitution states, "Property owned and occupied by non-profit religious or educational organizations and used exclusively for religious or educational purposes, as defined by law, shall be exempt from real and personal property tax." Moreover, certain types of property are exempt no matter who owns them. Notable examples of this type of exemption in Michigan are agricultural personal property, household personal property, and business inventories.[18] Over time, the tax base has become more and more circumscribed due to frequent legislation that exempts either types of property owners or types of property, and legislation rarely adds new classes of property to the tax base.

The very nature of tax-exempt property means that there is little or no actual data available to

## TABLE 28.6

### Real and Personal Property by Class, 2001

| | Taxable Value (millions) | | | Personal as |
| | Real | Personal | Total | % of Total |
|---|---|---|---|---|
| Agriculture | $7,685.70 | $0.50 | $7,685.70 | 0.01% |
| Timber cutover | 184.70 | 0 | 184.70 | 0.00% |
| Developmental | 310.50 | 0 | 310.50 | 0.00% |
| Commercial | 35,303.00 | 10,637.10 | 45,940.10 | 23.15% |
| Industrial | 17,011.70 | 11,570.50 | 28,582.20 | 40.48% |
| Residential | 167,456.20 | 194.60 | 167,650.80 | 0.12% |
| Utility | 0 | 7,535.40 | 7,535.40 | 100.00% |
| TOTAL | $227,951.80 | $29,938.00 | $257,889.80 | 11.61% |

SOURCE: State Tax Commission and Office of Revenue and Tax Analysis, Michigan Department of Treasury.

measure its value. However, as a general matter, it should be recognized that tax exemptions provide subsidies to the activities that receive the exemptions. As a result, the exempt user will use more real resources (and increase the tax burden on other classes of property) than if there were no exemption. Estimates of the value of tax-exempt property are provided in the annual editions of the Tax Expenditures Report, prepared by the Michigan Department of Treasury's Office of Revenue and Tax Analysis (ORTA).

While some exemptions, such as those for federal and state government property, are firmly grounded in the constitution and the traditions of fiscal federalism, many exemptions do not have such a natural justification. Given that all exemptions explicitly mean that the current level of the tax burden must then be borne by others, it is appropriate that policy makers should routinely evaluate them in the same way that a direct subsidy program is evaluated. For example, it is important to revisit exemptions and reaffirm that the original public purpose that justified the exemption still exists. In the case of exempt property, such an evaluation is complicated by the fact that if property of a given type or owned by a given class of user is exempt, it will be exempt statewide, while the costs of exemption will be borne largely by localities.

The largest exemptions from the general property tax are Proposal A–related: the exemption of homesteads and qualified agriculture from school operating taxes and the savings from the assessment cap. These are followed by tax-exempt personal property owned by public, nonprofit, and private entities; real property owned by schools and colleges; real property owned by nonprofits;

federal property; local governmental property; and state property. Public Act 198 industrial development exemptions provide over $310 million in reduced taxes, with Tax Increment Financing Authorities utilizing over $250 million for their public-private economic development programs. For details on these and other exemptions, see the State Tax Expenditure Report.[19] For more information on PA 198s and TIFs, see chapter 14 of this volume.

## Current and Future Issues for Property Taxation

Predictions based on current issues do not always hold true, but the long history of the property tax and of some of these issues in Michigan indicates that the following will see on-going debate. First is the taxation of personal property. Second is the "welcome stranger," or reassess on sale, feature of the assessment cap. Third is the eventual stabilization of valuation growth, and fourth are the potential overlapping effects of the Proposal A assessment cap and the Headlee unitwide tax revenue cap.

### Personal Property Taxation in Michigan

In Michigan, only businesses pay the personal property tax (PPT); household personal property has been exempt since the 1930s. Personal property taxes on business inventories were eliminated in 1975 with the creation of the Single Business Tax, but personal property such as machinery and equipment was not exempted. Table 28.6 shows the relative differences in the value between real and personal within each class. All personal property subject to tax is taxed at the same rate as real property in a given jurisdiction. By reducing millage in general, Proposal A substantially reduced the PPT. The average nonhomestead (including business property) rate fell from 56.6 to 48.17 mills, a 15% decline.[20]

Unlike real property, personal property is self-reported by firms. Each year, every business must provide the local assessor with a form itemizing each type of personal property and its age. The assessor then assigns a value, using depreciation schedules published by the state, to each item. This self-reporting of taxable property may lead to substantial underreporting, and any auditing done is at the discretion of individual local assessors.

There are currently two public policy issues regarding personal property taxation (PPT) on the table in Michigan. First, a number of business groups have called for the elimination of the personal property tax, either immediately or through a multiyear phase out. They have argued that this step is necessary to continue improving the competitive position of Michigan businesses. Opponents of repeal argue that the resulting financial impact on local government would be devastating without development of a replacement source of revenue, as was done when the tax on inventory was repealed as part of the Single Business Tax package in 1975.

The second issue devolves from a partial response to the business community's desire for complete repeal or substantial reform of the PPT. One of the key arguments for repeal beyond the general difficulty of administration has been the unfairness of the outdated depreciation schedules that are used in the valuation and assessment of personal property. These schedules have been argued to be especially out of date relative to the valuation of rapidly depreciating technology property, such as computers and software systems.

In 1997, in partial response to the demands for updated depreciation schedules, the Michigan State Tax Commission (STC) partnered with an outside contractor to update the depreciation schedules used for assessing the value of personal property. The STC then reviewed the work of the contractor, revised a number of proposed tables up and down, and added others to address what it felt were omissions in both the current tables and the work of the contractor. These multiplier tables are applied against the original cost of the property and reflect both appreciation and depreciation. Appreciation occurs when the replacement costs of original equipment increase, and depreciation is applied to recognize losses from wear and tear.

Published in 1999 for use by assessors, the net result of the new schedules was overall faster depreciation and thus lower valuations of personal property, although certain types of property, such as oil and gas pipelines and vending machines, increased substantially in value. A major challenge to the tables for valuation of public utilities has been raised by a number of local units of government. Pipeline and vending machine owners are challenging from the other side.

This litigation raises some very complex issues regarding valuation. However, they center on two core concepts. First, what is the value of individual pieces of property located in various communities relative to their value as part of the business as a whole? This argument bears remarkable similarity to the economic justification for the application of the Utility Property Tax to telephone, telegraph, and railroad property, and perhaps the road to a solution of this portion of the argument lies in this direction. The second core issue also strikes at the heart of valuation theory: while accepting the concept of physical depreciation, the sides differ over whether or not to recognize the concept of economic obsolescence or economic depreciation as reflected by market prices of used and similar new equipment. If this concept is to be recognized, it appears that there also are differences over the degree of recognition. While these arguments sound academic, there is considerable money involved for businesses and taxing jurisdictions. On net, the potential refunds to businesses could run to hundreds of millions of dollars by the time the litigation is finally resolved.

Whatever the result of the litigation, the pressure to eliminate, reform, or simply reduce the personal property tax will continue. Because the PPT base varies widely across the state, the effect of reducing or eliminating the tax would be much greater in some places than in others. With the exception of the six-mill SET levy created with Proposal A, the tax is a *local* tax that would be changed or eliminated by *state* law. This fact would likely lead to discussions about state reimbursement to locals for lost revenue, as was done with the Single Business Tax and the repeal of business inventory taxation. Beyond the issue of reimbursement from an as yet unidentified source (and the business community support for a multiyear phaseout argument that no reimbursement would be necessary as local governments could absorb the lost revenue through the future growth of all taxes), there are significant administrative questions.

In Michigan, the tax rates on real and personal property always have been identical. However, creation of a statutory distinction between the two will become very important if personal property comes to be taxed at a reduced or zero rate compared to real property. In that event there will be significant incentives on the part of businesses to seek a broad definition, and incentives for local governments to seek a narrower definition for the exemption. Even under current law there are frequent disagreements between local assessors and businesses over just what should be considered real or personal property. If personal property

**FIGURE 28.6**

TV/SEV Ratio (Stabilized); CPI = 2.47%; Housing Appreciation Rate = 4.91%

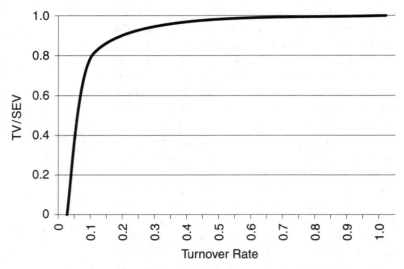

SOURCE: Authors' calculations as described in text.

were completely exempt such disagreements could be expected to increase in both frequency and intensity.[21]

**Reassessment upon Sale ("Welcome Stranger")**

In the spring of 2002, eight years into the Proposal A system, Michigan began to see media coverage

**FIGURE 28.7**

TV/SEV Ratio (Stabilized); CPI = 2.47%; Property Turnover Rate = 10%

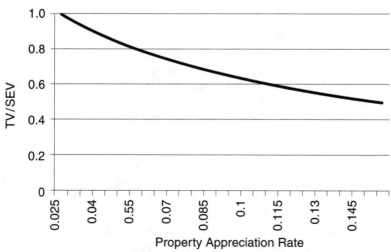

SOURCE: Authors' calculations as described in text.

of complaints about the reassess on sale feature of Proposal A. While many properties obviously had turned over in the prior seven years, it seemed that there were finally enough sales of long-held property that the new assessments were becoming very noticeable and very objectionable to the new owners. Whatever the cause, it seemed that for the first time the issue was drawing noticeable (but not widespread) media attention, especially in southeast Michigan.

While many new homeowners objected to the reassessments, they are clearly mandated by the State Constitution as amended by Proposal A. Also, as noted previously, the U.S. Supreme Court has upheld the very similar practice in California as not being a violation of the U.S. Constitution. It thus seems clear that the system meets the test of legality. The practice also immediately becomes a benefit to the new owner of a home by applying the assessment cap to future growth in value until the time of the next sale. A certain level of objection is likely to continue, but any major change now will require amending the state constitution, not an easy task under any circumstances, and overall the assessment cap is still very popular with most homeowners.

**Stabilization over Time**

Over time, the different growth rates of TV and SEV arising from the Proposal A cap mechanism are likely to narrow and could disappear. The percentage difference between TV and SEV should eventually stabilize, with the ratio of TV to SEV varying by community and class of property. As figure 28.6 shows, stabilization should occur at levels less than one as long as the turnover rate is less than 100%. When properties are sold or new properties are placed on the tax rolls, their TV is adjusted upward to equal SEV, and the cap mechanism begins anew with the next year's assessment on that parcel. Figure 28.7 shows how the average appreciation rate affects this stabilization ratio.

Assumptions on the CPI, turnover, and appreciation rates determine the length of time until stabilization. Generally, the shorter the turnover period of property sales, the sooner the stabilization of the ratio of TV to SEV will occur. Areas or property classes with relatively little sales activity will take longer to stabilize than will areas with considerable in- and out-migration and the associated higher frequency of property sales. Moreover, the greater the proportion of new property that

**TABLE 28.7A**

**Example of Pre-1978, Millage Rate = 30 Mills, Both Houses Have SEV of $100,000**

| | Value ($) in: | | | | |
|---|---|---|---|---|---|
| | Year 1 | Year 2 | Year 3 | Year 4 | Year 5 |
| House A (market value appreciates at 10%) | $100,000 | 110,000 | 121,000 | 133,100 | 146,410 |
| House B (market value appreciates at 0%) | 100,000 | 100,000 | 100,000 | 100,000 | 100,000 |
| Average house value | 100,000 | 105,000 | 110,500 | 116,550 | 123,205 |
| Sum | 200,000 | 210,000 | 221,000 | 233,100 | 246,410 |
| Increase value of house by CPI (3%) | 100,000 | 103,000 | 106,090 | 109,273 | 112,551 |
| **No legislation—neither Headlee nor Proposal A** | | | | | |
| House A tax payment | 3,000 | 3,300 | 3,630 | 3,993 | 4,392 |
| (A's share of tax burden) | (0.5) | (0.524) | (0.548) | (0.571) | (0.594) |
| House B tax payment | 3,000 | 3,000 | 3,000 | 3,000 | 3,000 |
| (B's share of tax burden) | (0.5) | (0.476) | (0.452) | (0.429) | (0.406) |
| Total property tax revenue | 6,000 | 6,300 | 6,630 | 6,993 | 7,392 |

**TABLE 28.7B**

**Headlee Only**

| | Year 1 | Year 2 | Year 3 | Year 4 | Year 5 |
|---|---|---|---|---|---|
| Revenue increases by rate of inflation | $6,000 | 6,180 | 6,365 | 6,556 | 6,753 |
| Millage rate under Headlee rollback | 30 | 29.4 | 28.8 | 28.1 | 27.4 |
| House A tax payment | 3000 | 3237 | 3485 | 3744 | 4012 |
| (A's share of tax burden) | (0.500) | (0.524) | (0.548) | (0.571) | (0.594) |
| House B tax payment | 3000 | 2943 | 2880 | 2813 | 2741 |
| (B's share of tax burden) | (0.500) | (0.476) | (0.452) | (0.429) | (0.406) |
| Total property tax revenue | 6,000 | 6,180 | 6,365 | 6,556 | 6,753 |

**TABLE 28.7C**

**Proposal A Only**

| | Year 1 | Year 2 | Year 3 | Year 4 | Year 5 |
|---|---|---|---|---|---|
| **House A** | | | | | |
| Taxable value | $100,000 | 103,000 | 106,090 | 133,100 | 137,093 |
| State equalized value | 100,000 | 110,000 | 121,000 | 133,100 | 146,410 |
| **House B** | | | | | |
| Taxable value | 100,000 | 100,000 | 100,000 | 100,000 | 100,000 |
| State equalized value | 100,000 | 100,000 | 100,000 | 100,000 | 100,000 |
| House A tax payment | 3,000 | 3,090 | 3,183 | 3,993 | 4,113 |
| (A's share of tax burden) | (0.500) | (0.507) | (0.515) | (0.571) | (0.578) |
| House B tax payment | 3,000 | 3,000 | 3,000 | 3,000 | 3,000 |
| (B's share of tax burden) | (0.500) | (0.493) | (0.485) | (0.429) | (0.422) |
| Total property tax revenue | 6,000 | 6,090 | 6,183 | 6,993 | 7,113 |

SOURCE: Authors' calculations as described in text.

comes onto the tax rolls of SEV, the faster the stabilization of the ratio of TV to SEV will occur.

The average yearly statewide housing price appreciation rate from 1980 to 2001 in Michigan was 4.91%.[22] Since the passage of Proposal A, the average CPI growth has been 2.47%. Using these numbers and assuming a yearly turnover rate for residential property of 10%, TV/SEV will be at 95.0% of its stabilized ratio within roughly eleven years. In comparison, with a turnover rate of 5.0% the time to stabilization is thirty years, and with a turnover rate of 15.0%, the time is approximately six years. The early 1980s and the post–Proposal A 1990s saw unusually rapid growth in house values. If house values were to rise at something closer to overall inflation, the ratio of TV to SEV would stabilize more quickly and at a higher ratio. Other classes of property will have different turnover rates and different stabilization periods, making estimates of stabilization difficult for individual units. Moreover, property appreciation rates vary widely among classes of property, not to mention from unit to unit.

The ability of TV to grow even while SEV is decelerating can be thought of as a reservoir of untapped tax base. Much as a rainy day fund provides additional funds that allow a unit of government to avoid cuts in services during economic slowdowns, this reservoir of untapped tax base provides a stable source of revenues during recessions. There is a certain irony in the fact that under Proposal A assessments can continue to rise (albeit within the limits of CPI change, or reassessment via turnover) even as property values overall may be stable.

## The Overlapping Effects of the Headlee Amendment and Proposal A

Proposal A's assessment cap and Headlee millage rollbacks can interact, and the net effect on the level of local government revenues and the distribution of tax payments is not easy to calculate. Consider the following simple example. Suppose a unit of government existed in Michigan with only two residential properties. Both houses are valued at $100,000 at the beginning of the period. Suppose further that neither house changes ownership from years one to three, but then House A is sold at the end of year three. The millage rate is set at thirty mills and the two houses, House A and House B, appreciate at 10% and 0%, respectively. The rate of inflation (CPI) is 3%. Table 28.7a shows the change in value of the houses and the tax burden imposed on each house before the imposition of both the Headlee Amendment and Proposal A. This example illustrates how the property tax system operated in Michigan prior to 1978. Keep in mind that this is a "simple" example, and the illustration can quickly become more complicated if slower-growing residential or nonresidential properties are added to this two-factor equation, as they would be in the real world.

Table 28.7b shows how the tax revenue and millage rates change under the Headlee Amendment. Recall that Headlee dictates that total tax revenue cannot increase by more than the rate of inflation. Because Headlee is applied unitwide, both parcels benefit by the same percentage (but not the same dollar amount) and there is no change in aggregate tax burden. Because House A has an increasing fraction of the value in the jurisdiction, its share of taxes rises, but is reduced relative to the pre-Headlee world. This is the property tax system as it existed from 1979 through 1993, assuming no voter approval of rollback "overrides."

Table 28.7c shows how tax revenues and burdens change when Proposal A is introduced (assume for now that there is no Headlee Amendment). Under Proposal A, the TV of each house can increase by at most the CPI (or 5%, whichever is less).

Thus, when the inflation rate is a binding constraint on the increase in the value of property, Proposal A shifts a slightly greater share of the property tax burden to households whose property is growing relatively slowly in the long run. Also, note that total tax revenue collected is higher than that under the Headlee revenue cap.

Now assume that we have the current property tax system with both Headlee and the taxable value cap of Proposal A (the system in place in Michigan since 1995).

The current system, with both the Headlee Amendment and Proposal A, constrains revenue the most (see table 28.7d). This is because there are two restricting effects taking place: Proposal A restricts the tax base by capping growth in TV per parcel, and Headlee caps growth in unitwide aggregate tax collections. As long as the growth rate of aggregate TV, excluding new construction, does not exceed the CPI, Headlee rollbacks will not occur. However, the uncapping that results from a transfer of ownership may cause a Headlee rollback, as in this example. This is because a transfer of ownership is considered to create an increase in the value of existing property.

**TABLE 28.7D**

**Headlee plus Proposal A**

|  | Year 1 | Year 2 | Year 3 | Year 4 | Year 5 |
|---|---|---|---|---|---|
| Millage rate with Headlee rollback | 30 | 30 | 30 | 27.3 | 27.3 |
| **House A** | | | | | |
| Taxable value | 100,000 | 103,000 | 106,090 | 133,100 | 137,093 |
| State equalized value | 100,000 | 110,000 | 121,000 | 133,100 | 146,410 |
| **House B** | | | | | |
| Taxable value | 100,000 | 100,000 | 100,000 | 100,000 | 100,000 |
| State equalized value | 100,000 | 100,000 | 100,000 | 100,000 | 100,000 |
| | | | | | |
| House A tax payment | 3,000 | 3,090 | 3,183 | 3,636 | 3,745 |
| (A's share of tax burden) | (0.500) | (0.507) | (0.515) | (0.571) | (0.578) |
| House B tax payment | 3,000 | 3,000 | 3,000 | 2,732 | 2,732 |
| (B's share of tax burden) | (0.500) | (0.493) | (0.485) | (0.429) | (0.422) |
| Total property tax revenue | 6,000 | 6,090 | 6,183 | 6,368 | 6,477 |

SOURCE: Authors' calculations as described in text.

These examples are highly dependent upon the fact that SEV is larger than TV and that there are residential units where market prices are growing faster than the CPI so that Proposal A is binding. In the real world the two-house examples would be greatly complicated in a community with many houses individually growing or declining at different rates and with other classes of property growing on average much less than residential property. During a recession, where SEV growth slows (or theoretically declines), but still grows faster than TV for the typical parcel, or in very high turnover communities, uncapping of properties under Proposal A could result in the total TV of the community rising at a rate greater than the CPI, and thus could trigger a unitwide rollback under Headlee.

While Proposal A works at the level of the individual parcel, limiting the growth of taxable value, the Headlee Amendment restricts the growth of tax revenue at the jurisdictional level—via rolling back the overall millage rate. Assuming that property values are growing sufficiently rapidly, as they have in at least two periods of each of the last two decades, the constraint that Proposal A places on the growth of tax revenue dominates the restriction imposed by the Headlee Amendment. Figure 28.8 illustrates how this restriction may affect tax revenue growth for a single class of property where the turnover rate is 10%, the CPI grows on average at 2.47%, and there is a distribution of property growth rates between the CPI and 4.91%. This figure shows how over time, as the difference between TV and SEV grows, tax revenue growth under Proposal A alone would accelerate and then grow at the same rate as SEV (although from a lower starting point) as turnover occurs. At some point in this process, the Headlee Amendment's restriction that tax revenue cannot grow more than the rate of the CPI becomes the constraining effect. Once the Headlee Amendment begins to bind, tax revenue will continue to grow at a rate equal to inflation.

**FIGURE 28.8**

**Percent Growth in Tax Revenue**

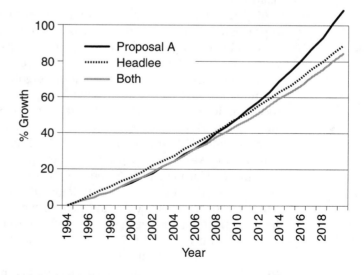

SOURCE: Authors' calculations as described in text.

In combination, Proposal A and Headlee rollbacks could reduce tax revenue overall, below the amount that would have obtained under either alone. Once the Headlee Amendment begins to take effect, the initial base under both constraints is less than the initial base in the case of only Headlee. The time until Headlee begins to bind and the difference between tax revenue under the current system and that under only Headlee depends on the difference between the housing appreciation growth rate and the CPI. As the former gets closer to the latter, this period of time is longer and the reduction in the amount of revenue relative to what would have been collected under Headlee alone is greater.

## Conclusion

The visibility of the property tax is both its greatest strength and its greatest weakness, especially for homeowners, and this has probably contributed to a great deal of the long-standing contention about both its level and its fairness. The system itself contributes to the visibility, with frequent reminders coming from annual assessment notices, frequent millage elections for overlapping levels of government, annual or semi-annual bills for large lump sums for taxpayers making direct payment of taxes, and with annual recalculations of escrow account requirements for taxpayers paying as part of mortgages or land contracts. Somewhat perversely, we all seek magical appreciation in the value of our own homes without appreciation in their value for property taxation purposes.

Michigan has made numerous administrative improvements to address the basic issues of fairness and accuracy in the administration of the tax, largely through increasingly stringent requirements for assessor certification and ongoing training. Michigan first addressed complaints about the level of property tax burdens through the creation of the "circuit-breaker" in 1973. The 1978 "Headlee" Amendment to the Michigan Constitution was a demonstration that the public perception of fairness and burden was still a dominant political issue. Even the millage rollback provisions of the Headlee Amendment proved to be unsatisfactory, however, as the period between its voter approval in 1978 and Proposal A's approval in 1994 saw numerous proposals for property tax reduction and reform. The parcel by parcel assessment cap established by Proposal A

was a powerful attraction for homeowners who faced dramatic increases in their own assessments that at best were only partially offset by Headlee rollbacks that often were not triggered at all, as slow or no growth in some areas of a community or another class of property offset faster growth in certain neighborhoods or classes. As we have seen here, the future interaction of Headlee rollbacks and the Proposal A assessment cap will likely result in greater constraint on the growth of property taxes than either constitutional feature would generate on its own.

Can we see what the future holds for property taxation in Michigan? Yes, but as always, through a glass darkly. The current degree of reasonable fairness in administration and limits on growth will still likely prove to be insufficient for many taxpayers. We know that pressures for continuing current public service levels in the face of inflationary pressures, and the pressure for expansion of services will likely continue to gradually push millage rates higher. We do have the assurance that this will happen only with local voter approval, but the low turnouts common in such elections in the past will likely continue. This will exacerbate the contention between those who seek more public services and those who for whatever reason either fail to vote in such elections, or continually find themselves in the minority in their community even if they do vote regularly. Such persons can, of course, apply to themselves Tiebout's classic theory and "vote with their feet" to move to a community whose service and tax burdens are more to their liking. In the real world, however, such mobility may not universally exist. The resulting community contention will probably continue, and the ongoing dialogue ultimately will remind those seeking services that all members of the community participate in paying for them, and also remind those that do not wish to pay that other members of the community may find such services desirable or even necessary.

■

## REFERENCES

Addonizio, M. 2001. Public school finance programs of the U.S. and Canada: 1998–99. National Center for Education Statistics, Pub. Number 2001309.

Courant, P., E. Gramlich, and S. Loeb. 1994. A report on school finance and educational reform in Michigan. In *Proceedings of the 87th annual conference of the National Tax Association*, 29–36.

Fischel, W. 1992. Property taxation and the Tiebout model: Evidence for the benefit view from zoning and voting. *Journal of Economic Literature* 30:171–77.

Hamilton, B. 1975. Zoning and property taxation in a system of local governments. *Urban Studies* 12(2): 205–11.

Lyon, David W. 1995. Representation without taxation: Proposition 13 and local government in California. San Francisco: Institute for Public Policy of California

Michigan Department of Treasury, Office of Revenue and Tax Analysis. 2002. The Michigan property tax: Real and personal. May.

Netzer, D. 1966. *Economics of the property tax.* Washington, D.C.: Brookings Institution.

Oates, W. 2001. Property taxation and local government finance: An overview and some reflections. In *Property taxation and local government finance*, edited by Wallace E. Oates. Cambridge, Mass.: Lincoln Institute of Land Policy.

Tiebout, C. 1956. A pure theory of local expenditures. *Journal of Political Economy* 64: 416–24.

Zodrow, G. 2001. Reflections on the new view and the benefit view of the property tax. In *Property taxation and local government finance*, edited by Wallace E. Oates. Cambridge, Mass.: Lincoln Institute of Land Policy.

## NOTES

Special thanks also to Howard Heideman and Thomas Patchak-Schuster, Michigan Department of Treasury.

1. Wayne State University State Policy Center, "Michigan State Government Revenues," Research Resources Series, *www.culma.wayne.edu/spc/publications.html*; U.S. Census and Office of Revenue and Tax Analysis; and State of Michigan Comprehensive Annual Financial Reports for years subsequent to 1998.

2. A monetary unit equal to $\frac{1}{1000}$ of a dollar; millage is the tax rate on property—the number of mills assessed against the property's taxable value. For example, a tax rate of 30 mills equals $30 per $1000 of taxable value.

3. MCL 211.27.

4. Wayne State University State Policy Center, "Michigan State Government Revenues," Research Resources Series, *www.culma.wayne.edu/spc/publications.html* and State Michigan Compre-

hensive Annual Financial Reports for years subsequent to 1998.

5. As specified by the Michigan Department of Treasury, Michigan Department of Natural Resources.

6. Michigan personal income is defined as any type of income received by Michigan residents, including wages and salaries, business income capital gains, rent, interest, dividend and royalty income, and any transfer payments.

7. A few cautionary notes regarding tax burden measures should be noted. It is not possible to address the issue of whether Michigan taxes are "too high" or "too low" without also considering the spending side of the equation. For example, how were tax revenues spent? Was the purchase a "good" or "fair" buy? A simple comparison of tax burdens across states does not take into consideration the goods and services residents receive in return.

8. An "acquisition system" is the term used to describe how the value of property is updated. In this case, the property assessment is changed when the property is transferred. A "modified acquisition system" describes the current system in Michigan and California, where the value is updated yearly but the property tax owed does not fully reflect this updated value until the property is transferred.

9. The U.S. Supreme Court upheld Proposition 13 in *Nordlinger v. Hahn*, Opinion No. 90-1912, 18 June 1992. The Court ruled that the Proposition 13 acquisition-value system did not violate the Equal Protection clause despite the fact that it created vast disparities in the taxes paid by households owning similar properties. The Court held that Proposition 13 did not discriminate between newer and older owners with respect to the tax rate or the annual rate of adjustment in assessments. Owners were treated differently on one factor only—the initial assessment value.

10. This amendment is commonly known as the Headlee Amendment after its primary author, Richard Headlee, who was later an unsuccessful candidate for governor. See chapter 33 for an extended discussion of the Headlee Amendment. Here we discuss only its effects on property tax rates and its considerable interactions with Proposal A.

11. Census of Governments, *http://www.census.gov/govs/estimate/92censusviewtabss.xls*.

12. Hold-harmless mills permit the highest-spending school districts to raise additional local revenue by levying supplemental millages. This topic is addressed in further detail later in this chapter.

13. Sinking fund millages are a way for a local unit to collect extra taxes to make capital purchases.

Rather than making a purchase and paying off the costs with interest, the sinking fund allows the unit to save until it has sufficient funds to make the purchases in cash.

14. These numbers include community college debt and Intermediate School District (ISD) debt.

15. Assessors continue to record, and the state continues to compute, the SEV of each parcel of property for purposes of assigning a taxable value upon transfer equal to 50 percent of the true cash value.

16. Assessment by the income method estimates the value of a parcel of property by the cash flow it generates. Assessment by the replacement method measures the value of a parcel of property by the reproduction cost of real and personal property adjusted for estimated depreciation and inflation. The adjustments are controversial and we will discuss them later in the chapter.

17. The income to which this 3.5% limitation applies is similar to taxable income but excludes some per-

sonal exemptions and includes other exempt types of income, most importantly social security.

18. See Michigan Compiled Laws, Sections 211.7 et.seq. for most real property exemptions, and 211.9 et.seq. for most personal property exemptions. Another source is at www.crcmich.org in the General Property section of Citizens Research Council's "Outline of the Michigan Tax System."

19. Tax Expenditure Appendix to the Executive Budget, various years, Michigan Department of Treasury, Office of Revenue and Tax Analysis.

20. State Tax Commission and Office of Revenue and Tax Analysis.

21. Personal interviews with Mark Hilpert, former chair, State Tax Commission, Michigan Department of Treasury. Any misinterpretations or omissions are the fault of the authors.

22. Office of Federal Housing Enterprise Oversight (OFHEO), *http://www.ofheo.gov/house.*

# 29

# Michigan's Flirtation with the Single Business Tax

*James R. Hines, Jr.*

## Introduction

The State of Michigan requires significant tax revenue in order to finance government expenditures, but is reluctant to impose taxes at high rates on economic activity that might thereby be reduced or encouraged to relocate. In this, Michigan encounters the same dilemma that all taxing jurisdictions face. The problem is most severe with business taxes, since business enterprises are notoriously mobile between states and countries, frequently very sensitive to their tax situations, and always crucial to the economic performance of a state. Michigan rose to this challenge in 1975 by adopting the Single Business Tax (hereafter abbreviated SBT), an innovative form of business taxation that resembles a value-added tax and thereby differs from the corporate income taxes used by other states. The SBT is a major source of Michigan tax revenue, raising $2.2 billion, or approximately 10% of state tax revenues, in fiscal year 2001. This is not, however, likely to persist, since under current law the SBT is being gradually reduced, and will be eliminated altogether by 2010. What, if any, business taxes will replace the SBT in 2010 is not yet clear.

The purpose of this chapter is to analyze Michigan's thirty-five-year flirtation with the Single Business Tax, its motives in first embracing the Single Business Tax, its motives in first embracing and later moving toward abandoning the tax, and the implications of Michigan's SBT experience for the future of business taxation in Michigan and other states. The original concept behind the SBT was to impose a form of value-added taxation that would permit firms to deduct 100% of investment expenditures from taxable income, thereby encouraging business investment. It was also hoped that the SBT would offer a more stable source of revenue than did its corporate income tax predecessor in Michigan, that the SBT would simplify and broaden business taxation in Michigan, and that it would provide a revenue windfall to address Michigan's short-term fiscal needs. While the evidence suggests that the SBT has generated a more stable revenue stream than that produced by the corporate income taxes of other states, investment incentives under the SBT differ significantly from those produced by textbook value-added taxes. The SBT also has the vexing property of imposing significant taxes on firms that lose money. In the wake of multiple tax reforms, the SBT became sufficiently unattractive to enough of the state that legislation (passed in the summer of 2002) mandated its removal by 2010.

Problems with the Single Business Tax emerged in the 1990s due to the multistate nature of many of Michigan's businesses. Michigan legislators were understandably concerned that investment incentives under Michigan's Single Business Tax might reward Michigan firms for investing outside of Michigan. The SBT was designed to minimize the extent to which firms could obtain Michigan tax deductions for out-of-state investment expenditures, but this design feature came under increasing fire from those who maintained that such provisions violate the interstate commerce clause of the U.S. Constitution. The Single Business Tax was amended in 1995 (effective starting in 1997) to permit favorable treatment only for assets put in place in Michigan, but legal challenges to this provision prompted the elimination of capital acquisition deductions in 1999 (effective starting in 2000), and their replacement with a new system of investment tax credits. Among the costs of these frequent changes, however, were political compromises that ultimately led to phased elimination of the Single Business Tax by 2010.

The second section of the chapter reviews state practices in taxing business income, and the estimated effects of such taxation. The third section offers a history of business taxation in Michigan, culminating with recent reforms to the Single Business Tax. The fourth section analyzes the incentives created by SBT provisions. The fifth section compares the stability of revenue collections under the SBT to those of the corporate income taxes used by other states, finding that Michigan's SBT revenue source is considerably less sensitive to cyclical fluctuations. The sixth section draws implications for the future of business taxation in Michigan, and final section is the conclusion.

## Business Taxation in American States

The modern U.S. corporate income tax was introduced following passage of the Sixteenth Amendment to the U.S. Constitution in 1913, but business taxation by American states (who face no federal constitutional prohibition) has a much longer history. In the early years states struggled with the appropriate design of business taxes, though state governments were small enough, and revenue needs sufficiently modest, that low rates of taxation meant that poor tax design did little to impede economic activity.[1] The modern era in state business taxation followed the introduction of the federal corporate tax in 1913.

## State Business Taxation in Modern Times

The corporate income tax is the primary business tax in all U.S. states other than Michigan that tax business income.[2] State corporate income taxes generally follow the classic pattern established by the federal corporate income tax. A classic corporate income tax is a tax only on incorporated businesses. The base of the tax is corporate income, defined as the difference between revenues and deductible expenses. Deductible expenses include labor expenses, materials and services purchased from other firms (other than investment in plant and equipment), interest expenses, depreciation of capital, and other costs. The effect of the corporate income tax is to extract revenue from corporations at the cost of discouraging investment in plant and equipment, unless such investment is financed entirely with debt (for which interest payments are tax-deductible).[3] The corporate income tax does not directly discourage the use of labor or material inputs, since the cost of such inputs is deductible from taxable income. The importance of deductibility is illustrated by the fact that a rational firm considering the purchase of $220 worth of labor and materials, and anticipating that the use of these inputs will generate more than $220 worth of final sales, will make the purchase in spite of corporate profit taxation. A corporate profit tax reduces the profitability of labor and materials expenditures that the firm will undertake in any case, but does not change the actions of a profit-maximizing enterprise. The situation is rather different in the case of plant and equipment investment, since firms are not entitled to deduct their capital investment outlays, instead depreciating such expenditures over typically long horizons. As a result, higher rates of corporate taxation can be expected to reduce investment spending by corporations.

In the modern era all but six U.S. states tax corporate income, the exceptions being Nevada, South Dakota, Texas, Washington, and Wyoming, which have no corporate income tax, and, importantly, Michigan, which imposes the Single Business Tax in lieu of a corporate tax. Corporate tax rates change over time; table 29.1 presents tax rates for 2002, along with some description of the rate structure. Individual income tax rates are typically progressive, meaning that tax rates rise with income, while progressivity is less commonly a feature of business taxes. In thirty-one of forty-four states, corporate income is subject to tax at a constant rate, while in thirteen states tax rates increase as taxable corporate income rises. The first column of table 29.1 reports the highest and lowest tax rates at which each state taxes corporate income; the second column of table 29.1 indicates the number of tax brackets a state uses, and the third column indicates the income level at which the lowest tax rate bracket ends, and that at which the highest tax rate bracket begins. The highest corporate tax rate is 12% (Iowa), while the lowest top-bracket corporate tax rate is 4% (Kansas).

One of the important design features of a corporate tax is its treatment of business enterprises located in more than one jurisdiction. A New Jersey company that also operates in California earns income that is potentially subject to taxation by both states, so it is necessary to determine what part of the firm's income and expenses is properly attributable to New Jersey, and what part is attributable to California. When firms have entirely separate operations that simply happen to be owned by the same entity (for example, a New Jersey electronics plant and a California restaurant chain), they calculate profits separately for each business component and pay appropriate taxes to the state in which each is located.

Matters become considerably more complicated when firms have what is known as "unitary" businesses, meaning that there are close connections between activities located in different states. For example, a publishing firm might have editorial offices in New York, a printing facility in Wisconsin, and a distribution arm in Ohio. In principle, one could determine the profitability of operations in each state by requiring the use of separate accounting, with exchanges between related parties conducted under the terms of contracts using arm's-length (market) prices. Such arm's-length pricing is routinely used to determine the location of taxable incomes of multinational firms with operations in multiple countries. Since separate accounting for the operations of American companies located in different states would require considerable compliance and enforcement effort in return for modest amounts of tax revenue, American states instead use simple formulas to determine what fraction of a company's total U.S. income they will tax.[4] A common formula is one in which a state requires taxpayers to apportion half of their U.S. income on the basis of sales location, one-quarter on the basis of business property, and one-quarter on the basis of payroll. A taxpayer with U.S. income of $10 million, and 20% of its sales, 10% of its property, and

## TABLE 29.1

### State Corporate Tax Rates, 2002

| State | Tax Rate(s) (%) | # Brackets | Low/High Brackets (Taxable Income) |
|---|---|---|---|
| Alabama | 6.50 | 1 | Flat Rate |
| Alaska | 1.0–9.4 | 10 | $10,000 $90,000 |
| Arizona | 6.97 | 1 | Flat Rate |
| Arkansas | 1.0–6.5 | 6 | $3,000 $100,000 |
| California | 8.84 | 1 | Flat Rate |
| Colorado | 4.63 | 1 | Flat Rate |
| Connecticut | 7.50 | 1 | Flat Rate |
| Delaware | 8.70 | 1 | Flat Rate |
| Florida | 5.50 | 1 | Flat Rate |
| Georgia | 6.00 | 1 | Flat Rate |
| Hawaii | 4.4–6.4 | 3 | $25,000 $100,000 |
| Idaho | 8.00 | 1 | Flat Rate |
| Illinois | 7.30 | 1 | Flat Rate |
| Indiana | 7.90 | 1 | Flat Rate |
| Iowa | 6.0–12.0 | 4 | $25,000 $250,000 |
| Kansas | 4.00 | 1 | Flat Rate |
| Kentucky | 4.0–8.25 | 5 | $25,000 $250,000 |
| Louisiana | 4.0–8.0 | 5 | $25,000 $200,000 |
| Maine | 3.5–8.93 | 4 | $25,000 $250,000 |
| Maryland | 7.00 | 1 | Flat Rate |
| Massachusetts | 9.50 | 1 | Flat Rate |
| Minnesota | 9.80 | 1 | Flat Rate |
| Mississippi | 3.0–5.0 | 3 | $5,000 $10,000 |
| Missouri | 6.25 | 1 | Flat Rate |
| Montana | 6.75 | 1 | Flat Rate |
| Nebraska | 5.58–7.81 | 2 | $50,000 |
| New Hampshire | 8.00 | 1 | Flat Rate |
| New Jersey | 9.00 | 1 | Flat Rate |
| New Mexico | 4.8–7.6 | 3 | $500,000 $1 million |
| New York | 8.00 | 1 | Flat Rate |
| Ohio | 5.1–8.5 | 2 | $50,000 |
| Oklahoma | 6.00 | 1 | Flat Rate |
| Oregon | 6.60 | 1 | Flat Rate |
| Pennsylvania | 9.99 | 1 | Flat Rate |
| Rhode Island | 9.00 | 1 | Flat Rate |
| South Carolina | 5.00 | 1 | Flat Rate |
| Tennessee | 6.00 | 1 | Flat Rate |
| Utah | 5.00 | 1 | Flat Rate |
| Vermont | 7.0–9.75 | 4 | $10,000 $250,000 |
| Virginia | 6.00 | 1 | Flat Rate |
| West Virginia | 9.00 | 1 | Flat Rate |
| Wisconsin | 7.90 | 1 | Flat Rate |

SOURCE: Author's compilation from state web sites and published sources.

## TABLE 29.2

### American States and Their Business Taxes

| State | Corporate Income Tax | | | | Financial Institutions Tax | Corporate Franchise Fee | Savings & Loan Association Fee | Domestic Insurance Company Privilege Fee | Local Government Property Tax on Inventories | Intangibles Tax on Businesses |
|---|---|---|---|---|---|---|---|---|---|---|
| | C-Corp | S-Corp | Partnership | LLC | | | | | | |
| Alabama | √ | | | | √ | √ | | | | √ |
| Alaska | √ | | | √ | | | | | √ | |
| Arizona | √ | | | | | √ | | | | |
| Arkansas | √ | | | √ | | | | | √ | |
| California | √ | √ | | √ | | | | | | |
| Colorado | √ | | | | | | | | | |
| Connecticut | √ | | | | | | | | | |
| Delaware | √ | | | √ | √ | √ | | | | |
| District of Columbia | | | √ | √ | | | | | | |
| Florida | √ | | | √ | | | | | | |
| Georgia | √ | | | √ | √ | √ | | | √ | |
| Hawaii | √ | | | | √ | | | | | |
| Idaho | √ | | | | | | | | | |
| Illinois | √ | | √ | | | | | | | |
| Indiana | √ | | | | √ | | | | √ | |
| Iowa | √ | | | | | √ | | | | |
| Kansas | √ | | | √ | | | | | | |
| Kentucky | √ | | | | | √ | | | √ | |
| Louisiana | √ | √ | | | | | | | √ | |
| Maine | √ | | | | √ | √ | | | | |
| Maryland | √ | | | √ | | √ | √ | | √ | |
| Massachusetts | √ | | | | | √ | √ | √ | √ | |
| Michigan | | | | | | | | | | |
| Minnesota | √ | | √ | | | | | | | |
| Mississippi | √ | | | | | | | | √ | |
| Missouri | √ | | | | | √ | | | | |
| Montana | √ | | | | | | | | | |
| Nebraska | √ | | | | | | | | | |
| New Hampshire | √ | √ | √ | | | | | | | |
| New Jersey | √ | √ | | | √ | | | √ | | |
| New Mexico | √ | | | | √ | √ | | | | |
| New York | √ | √ | | | | | | | | |
| North Carolina | √ | | | | | √ | | | | √ |
| North Dakota | √ | | | | √ | √ | | | | |
| Ohio | √ | | | | | | | | √ | |
| Oklahoma | √ | | | | | √ | | | √ | |
| Oregon | √ | | | | | | | | | |
| Pennsylvania | √ | | | | √ | √ | | | | |
| Rhode Island | √ | | | | | | | | √ | |
| South Carolina | √ | | | | √ | √ | √ | | | |
| South Dakota | | | √ | | √ | | | | | |
| Tennessee | √ | √ | √ | | | √ | | √ | | |
| Texas | | | | | | | | | √ | |
| Utah | √ | | | | | √ | | | | |
| Vermont | √ | | | | √ | | | √ | √ | |
| Virginia | √ | √ | | | √ | | | | | |
| Washington | | | | | | | | | | |
| West Virginia | √ | √ | | | | √ | | | √ | |
| Wisconsin | √ | √ | | | | | | | | |
| Wyoming | | | | | | | | | | |

SOURCE: Author's compilation from state web sites and published sources.

NOTES: LLC: √ denotes states that do not follow federal treatment of LLCs. Partnership, C-Corp, S-Corp: √ denotes that this business organization income is taxable.

40% of its payroll in a state using such a formula would then owe taxes on apportioned income of $2.25 million. Since apportionment formulas differ, it is possible for taxpayers to owe state taxes on more or less than their total U.S. income. The use of formulary apportionment to allocate taxable income between states distorts investment and employment decisions by encouraging particularly profitable firms to establish new activities in low-tax states and avoid high-tax states,[5] but persists, due mostly to its simplicity.

There are states in which business entities other than C corporations are subject to corporate income taxes, oppressive though that may seem. The left panel of table 29.2 offers a quick summary of such expansive taxation. Checkmarks in table 29.2 indicate the presence of taxation, so a check in the "C-corp" column indicates that a state taxes the incomes of subchapter C corporations (the same type of corporation that is subject to the U.S. federal corporate income tax). A check in the second column of the left panel of table 29.2 indicates that a state also taxes the income of subchapter S corporations, which are small corporations subject to a number of ownership restrictions and whose income is untaxed by the federal government. A check in the third column indicates that a state taxes the income of local business partnerships, while a check in the fourth column indicates that a state taxes the income of Limited Liability Companies (LLCs). Neither partnerships nor LLCs are subject to federal taxes, their income instead being attributed to their owners and then taxed under the federal individual income tax (if owned by taxable individuals). States likewise tax individual residents on their income derived from S corporations, partnerships, and LLCs, but some states also subject S corporations, partnerships, and LLCs to separate taxation at the entity level.

The right panel of table 29.2 presents information on state business taxes other than corporate income taxes. Fourteen states impose special taxes on financial institutions, eighteen collect corporate franchise fees, five collect savings and loan association fees, two have special insurance company fees, fifteen have local government property taxes on business inventories, and two impose taxes on intangible business assets.[6] The most sizable revenue raiser among these supplemental taxes is believed to be the local government property tax on business inventories, though the available evidence suggests that its revenue impact is modest.[7] Consequently, the pri-mary source of state tax revenue from business income is the corporate tax.

Michigan imposes neither a corporate income tax nor the dizzying array of supplemental taxes displayed in table 29.2.[8] Instead, the SBT is levied at a (current) rate of 1.9% on adjusted gross receipts, which is the sum of business profits, labor compensation, depreciation, and interest expenses. It is therefore not meaningful to compare Michigan's tax rate with the corporate tax rates of other states, since the tax rates are applied to very different tax bases. Furthermore, noncorporate entities such as partnerships, S corporations, and LLCs are required to pay the SBT, while only selected other states tax such businesses. It is, however, possible to identify the portion of each state's revenue that comes from taxing corporations, and to compare appropriately scaled measures of the tax burden on corporations.[9]

Figures 29.1 and 29.2 depict two such calculations for Michigan and for averages of other U.S. states (excluding those without corporate taxes) from 1977 to 1996. Figure 29.1 plots ratios of state corporate tax collections to Gross State Product, and by this measure, Michigan's corporate tax burdens are much heavier (typically exceeding 50% greater) than the average burdens of other states. Figure 29.2 plots ratios of state corporate tax collections to total state tax collections, and once again, it is clear that Michigan relies much more heavily on corporate tax collections than is typical of American states. In the 1990s approximately 8% of Michigan's tax revenue came from taxing corporations, while other American states with corporate income taxes collected less than 6% of their revenue from corporations. These patterns are consistent with the Michigan Department of the Treasury (2002, 54–55) finding that Michigan would have needed an average corporate income tax rate of 14.3% (thereby making it the highest in the country) over the 1977–98 period in order to replace the revenues obtained from the Single Business Tax.

## Impact of State Business Taxes

Business taxation has the potential to discourage business formation and expansion, for the obvious reason that firms often have opportunities to relocate or refocus their activities in competing locations based on potential after-tax returns. Until relatively recently, there was a widely held view that business tax rate differences had little

**FIGURE 29.1**

**State Corporate Net Income Tax Share of State GSP, 1977–96**

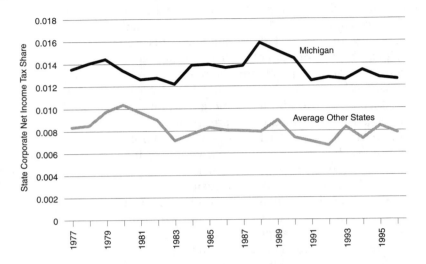

**FIGURE 29.2**

**State Corporate Net Income Tax Share of Total State Taxes, 1977–96**

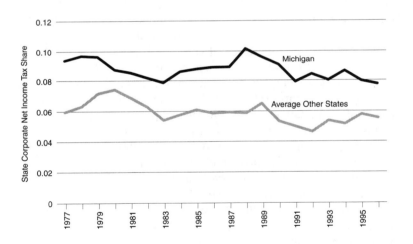

impact on business location within the United States. Since state tax rates are rather low, differences between them tend to be rather modest. Furthermore, state tax payments are deductible from taxable income at the federal level, so any tax savings associated with locating in a low-tax state is reduced by the federal tax rate. Most importantly, so the thinking went, business location is the product of many considerations, of which taxation is just one. Firms need to be profitable in order for tax considerations to matter to them, and profitability is affected by the cost

of local inputs, government regulations, transportation costs, and a host of other factors. While the fact that there are many important considerations in business location does not imply that any one of them is unimportant, it seemed intuitive that the impact of taxation might be sufficiently minor as not to produce noticeable effects.

The view that state taxation has little impact on business location was reinforced by early studies finding little or no effect. An example is Carlton's (1983) study of the determinants of new firm location, in which high tax rates appear not to discourage new firms. Others, including Newman (1983), Bartik (1985), and Leslie Papke (1987, 1991) present evidence that taxes significantly influence the location choices of new businesses, but many of the studies surveyed in Wasylenko (1981, 1991) report little support for the view that state taxes importantly affect business location within the United States. Wasylenko (1995) subsequently revisits these surveys, noting that more recent studies that use sophisticated econometric techniques or innovative estimation strategies tend to find important effects of tax rate differences on business location. An example is Hines (1996), which compares the location of foreign investment in the United States from firms resident in countries that tax foreign income with investment by firms resident in countries that exempt foreign income from tax. The mechanics of the foreign tax credit system are such that firms in the first group should be largely unaffected by U.S. state tax obligations (since taxes paid to American states generate offsetting foreign tax credits in their home countries), while those in the second group have the usual incentives to avoid state taxes. The evidence indicates that investment from countries that exempt foreign income from tax tends to be concentrated in low-tax states, which suggests that taxes significantly influence business location patterns in the United States.

The responsiveness of investment to state taxation implies that states can have strong incentives to lower their business tax rates in order to attract additional investment that stimulates their economies and in the process replaces some or all of the tax revenue lost from lower tax rates. Much of the additional business activity attracted by lower tax rates comes at the expense of other states.[10] In a setting with perfect business mobility, competitive pressures become so strong that the only stable configuration is the absence of any state taxation of business income.[11] While this is an unrealistic scenario, the significant degree of observed business mobility does have a chilling effect on any intention to finance state governments primarily with business taxes, and has the potential to initiate downward spiraling of state business tax rates.

## History of Business Taxation in Michigan

Business taxation in Michigan, and, indeed, the use of a type of value-added taxation in Michigan, long predates the 1975 adoption of the Single Business Tax. The first Michigan business tax, introduced in 1953, was its Business Activities Tax (BAT).

### Michigan up to BAT

The BAT was the product of a political compromise, as are all major tax initiatives. Michigan had growing state revenue needs in the early 1950s, and at the time did not tax personal or business income. Democratic governor G. Mennen ("Soapy") Williams was eager to introduce a state personal income tax and a state corporate income tax to finance greater expenditures, but his plans to do so encountered significant political opposition. In that era state-level income taxes were considerably less common than they are a half-century later: in 1953 only thirty-one states taxed corporate income, and only twenty-seven states taxed personal income. Furthermore, nearby Midwestern states such as Illinois, Indiana, and Ohio taxed neither corporate nor individual income. The Michigan business community was concerned that, once the state legislature introduced a corporate income tax, the rate of tax could easily be increased, and that a corporate tax would particularly discourage investment in the manufacturing activities upon which the Michigan economy depended. Consequently, the business community reluctantly acquiesced to the BAT as an alternative to the looming prospect of corporate profit taxation.

The BAT was a variant of what would now be called a source-based, subtraction-method, income VAT. What this sequence of qualifiers means is that the BAT was a kind of value-added tax (VAT), so firms were taxed on differences between their revenues and the expenses incurred to other firms. The BAT rate was initially 0.40% of taxable value added, though it rose to 0.65% in 1955 and was 0.75% of taxable value added by the time of its repeal in 1967. The BAT was imposed on value added by activities in Michigan, regardless of the destination of final products, giving the tax a source basis, and in that way distinguishing it from destination-based VATs currently used in Europe and elsewhere. Corporations and unincorporated businesses alike were subject to the tax, which was one difference between the BAT and many of the corporate income taxes used by other states.[12] A second difference was that Michigan firms might incur BAT liabilities despite being unprofitable, since taxpayers were not entitled to deduct labor expenses and certain other expenses in calculating their tax base under the BAT.

The BAT permitted firms to deduct depreciation expenses for real property investments (typically in commercial and industrial structures), which is characteristic of "income VATs."[13] Yet one curious feature of the BAT was that no tax deduction was permitted for expenditures on personal property (primarily equipment) or for depreciation of personal property. As a result, the BAT strongly discouraged equipment investment while taxing returns to investments in structures. This very odd—and highly distortionary—feature of the BAT reflected concern over the mobility of equipment, and in particular, the possibility that firms might claim depreciation deductions for property purchased in Michigan but actually used in other states. Concern over proper attribution of depreciation deductions continues to influence the design of Michigan tax policy throughout the SBT era.

The BAT contained a number of other features designed to improve its political attractiveness at the possible expense of neutral treatment of taxpayers in different situations. Financial institutions were exempt from the BAT. Firms had the option of deducting half of their gross receipts (instead of actual expenses incurred to other firms, plus depreciation on real property) in calculating their taxable incomes under the BAT. Firms with high ratios of payroll expenses to gross receipts were entitled to a "labor intensity deduction," and others with low profit rates could claim net income credits to offset part of their BAT liabilities. In addition, all firms were entitled to exemptions of $10,000.[14]

## Michigan Drops the BAT: Corporate Income Taxation, 1968–75

Growing state government expenditures in the 1960s led to rising income and corporate tax rates

## TABLE 29.3

**Michigan Corporate Income Tax Collections, 1968–75**

| Fiscal Year | Corporate Income Tax Collections | |
| --- | --- | --- |
| | Current dollars | Constant 2001 dollars |
| 1968 | $38.5 | $204.4 |
| 1969 | 210.4 | 1,047.1 |
| 1970 | 188.0 | 864.5 |
| 1971 | 151.2 | 649.1 |
| 1972 | 259.0 | 1,049.6 |
| 1973 | 357.8 | 1,346.6 |
| 1974 | 299.5 | 1,014.9 |
| 1975 | 235.7 | 783.1 |

SOURCE: Michigan Department of Treasury (2002).
NOTE: Dollar amounts in the second column are millions of current dollars; dollar amounts in the third column are millions of constant 2001 dollars.

around the country, thereby encouraging Michigan to expand the scope of government activity and to finance this expansion by introducing personal income taxation. Other Midwestern states, such as Illinois, introduced personal income taxation during the same period. There was a strong feeling in some circles, particularly among organized labor, that the imposition of state personal income taxation should be accompanied by state corporate income taxation. The Business Activities Tax was riddled with inefficiencies, notably the differing treatment of equipment and structures investments. Consequently, few rued its passing when, in 1967 (though taking effect in 1968), Michigan replaced the BAT with a corporate income tax. The Michigan corporate income tax was introduced at a 5.6% rate on taxable profits, though the tax rate was increased to 7.8% in 1971. Taxable profits were defined for Michigan tax purposes much the same as they were for federal tax purposes, meaning that firms deducted their labor expenses in calculating taxable income, and were permitted to deduct depreciation costs for capital investments in real and personal property.

The Michigan corporate income tax quickly proved unpopular. In addition to firms that felt unduly burdened by the tax, many others in Michigan were concerned about the instability of revenues collected by the corporate tax. There were two U.S. economic recessions in the early 1970s (1970–71 and 1974–75) that severely impacted the profitability of Michigan's manufacturing-intensive corporate sector. As a result, Michigan corporate tax collections fluctuated

sharply from year to year. Table 29.3 presents tax collection figures for Michigan's corporate tax from its inception during the 1968 fiscal year to its last year in 1975. Full-year corporate tax collections started in 1969 at $210 million, fell to $151 million by 1971, rose to $358 million by 1973, and fell again to $236 million by 1975. Not only did corporate tax collections fluctuate sharply over this period, they did so in a procyclical pattern that contributed to the state's budgetary problems during difficult economic times.

By 1975 Michigan faced a fiscal crisis in which its general fund budget was projected to have a shortfall of at least $200 million due to the economic recession. Since the state customarily increased business taxes during times of acute revenue needs, it was natural to consider higher corporate profit tax rates in response to the 1975 situation. At this time, however, reformers advocated a more systematic tax policy response that might reduce the need for emergency tax increases by attenuating the effect of business cycle fluctuations on business tax collections. The Single Business Tax, introduced in this environment, was thought to offer four advantages over the corporate income tax that it replaced. The first advantage was that the SBT could be designed to raise an additional $200 million in tax revenue upon inception, thereby eliminating Michigan's budget shortfall.[15] The second, and longer-run, benefit was that the SBT was believed to provide a more stable source of tax revenue than the corporate income tax. The third advantage was that the SBT promoted economic efficiency by encouraging capital investment and not distinguishing between incorporated and unincorporated businesses. The fourth advantage was that the SBT was easier to administer than the taxes it replaced. These arguments proving compelling, the SBT was adopted in 1975.

### Michigan Embraces the Single Business Tax.

The Single Business Tax replaced the corporate income tax and six other taxes, including local property taxes on business property.[16] (Thus the name "single" business tax.) The SBT rate was a flat 2.35%. The SBT is a form of source-based value-added tax, and therefore shares many of the features of the BAT. Incorporated and unincorporated businesses are obliged to pay the SBT, subject to various deductions and credits. In particular, as a gesture toward tax simplification and small-business tax relief, firms with annual gross receipts under $34,000 were exempted from the SBT and were not required even to file an SBT form.

The tax base under the SBT is determined by addition. Specifically, taxpayers calculate taxable value added as the sum of profits (as defined for federal tax purposes), labor costs, depreciation, and interest expenses. Firms then deduct the cost of capital expenditures as well as interest receipts, dividend and royalty receipts, and any income received from partnerships. There are also various small additions and subtractions to the SBT base. The concept behind the SBT is to tax business receipts minus purchases from other firms, excluding financial transactions. Since business profits as defined for federal tax purposes include financial income and subtract depreciation and interest expenses, it is necessary to make some adjustments in calculating taxable value added under the SBT.

Business investments in real property (commercial and industrial structures) located in Michigan were fully deductible from SBT value added. The Michigan portion of investments in personal property (consisting primarily of business equipment) were also fully deductible from taxable value added, but the determination of Michigan location was different for personal property than for real property. Firms located entirely in Michigan deducted all expenditures on both real and personal property. Multistate firms engaged in unitary businesses were entitled to deduct against Michigan value added an allocated portion of total U.S. expenditures on personal property. The formula used to determine the Michigan portion of personal property expenditures was 50% based on the location of business property and 50% based on the location of payroll. Thus, a firm with 30% of its U.S. employment and 60% of its U.S. property located in Michigan would be entitled to a Michigan tax deduction equal to 45% (half of 30% plus half of 60%) of its total U.S. expenditures on business equipment.

Michigan did not apply the same formula to apportion other income and expenses of unitary businesses. These other items instead were allocated based one-third on the location of business property, one-third on the location of payroll, and one-third on the location of sales. The reason for the difference is that other states permitted taxpayers to depreciate expenditures on equipment and structures rather than deduct capital spending as it occurs, so Michigan's SBT offered a more generous treatment of investment expenditures than did the tax system of any other state. Since state formulas apply to investment expenditures undertaken anywhere in the United States, Michigan legislators were concerned that the SBT might reward firms investing in capital projects outside Michigan with generous Michigan tax deductions. In the case of real property, this problem could be addressed by permitting deductions only for investments in structures located in Michigan. In the case of personal property, much of which can be easily moved between states, the location of investment was thought to offer a potentially misleading guide to the ultimate location of use. Instead, the application of equally weighted property and employment factors to apportion the capital acquisition deduction for personal property seemed like a reasonable approximation to actual use. The effect of this rule for apportioning deductions for personal property expenditures was to encourage investments by firms with significant production in Michigan.

The SBT contained a number of provisions that reduced tax liabilities for small firms and those with low profit rates. Firms with adjusted gross receipts below $34,000 were exempt from the SBT and its filing requirements. Firms with value added exceeding $34,000 were entitled to claim a $34,000 exemption, but its value was reduced by $2 for every dollar of value added above $34,000, until declining to zero at value added of $51,000. The base exemption was scheduled to increase to $36,000 by 1977, but new rules adopted in 1977 instead raised it to $40,000; the exemption was subsequently increased to $45,000 by legislation enacted in 1988. In 1991 firms with gross receipts less than $100,000 were exempted from filing SBT returns; this exemption was increased to $250,000 in 1994, and to $350,000 in 2002.

Taxpayers were entitled to choose between two alternative methods of reducing value added subject to the SBT. The gross receipts deduction has the effect of reducing taxable value added to 50% of adjusted gross receipts, regardless of the magnitude of actual expenses. This deduction is of most value to taxpayers with high ratios of receipts to SBT value added. The excess compensation deduction is designed to reduce the tax base of firms for which labor compensation represents unusually large fractions of their SBT value added. Firms are eligible to reduce taxable value added by any fraction that compensation exceeds 65% of taxable value added, up to a maximum of 35%. Suppose, for example, that a firm's total compen-

**TABLE 29.4**

**1998–99 Tax Liability Breakdown**

| Michigan Tax Base Class | # of Firms | % of Firms | Cumulative % | Tax Liability | % of Liability | Cumulative % |
|---|---|---|---|---|---|---|
| $100,000,000 and over | 92 | 0.07% | 0.07% | $658,785,505 | 27.85% | 27.85% |
| $50,000,000–$99,999,999 | 129 | 0.09 | 0.16 | 140,451,466 | 5.94 | 33.78 |
| $10,000,000–$49,999,999 | 1,597 | 1.13 | 1.29 | 499,620,252 | 21.12 | 54.90 |
| $5,000,000–$9,999,999 | 2,311 | 1.63 | 2.92 | 249,735,200 | 10.56 | 65.46 |
| $2,000,000–$4,999,999 | 6,769 | 4.79 | 7.71 | 311,628,596 | 13.17 | 78.63 |
| $1,000,000–$1,999,999 | 9,768 | 6.91 | 14.61 | 189,535,488 | 8.01 | 86.64 |
| $500,000–$999,999 | 15,843 | 11.20 | 25.82 | 136,179,006 | 5.76 | 92.40 |
| $100,000–$499,999 | 56,239 | 39.77 | 65.58 | 141,381,742 | 5.98 | 98.38 |
| $50,000–$99,999 | 13,433 | 9.50 | 75.08 | 6,400,335 | 0.27 | 98.65 |
| $1–$49,999 | 13,415 | 9.49 | 84.57 | 1,553,940 | 0.07 | 98.71 |
| $0 or less | 21,825[a] | 15.43 | 100.00 | 30,482,124 | 1.29 | 100.00 |
| TOTAL | 141,421 | 100.00% | | $2,365,753,654 | 100.00% | |

SOURCE: Michigan Department of the Treasury, Office of Revenue and Tax Analysis (2002).
(a) Includes gross receipts short-method filers who do not report their Michigan Tax Base (recorded as zero).

sation were equal to 75% of its value added. Then that firm would be entitled to reduce its SBT tax base by 10% (75 – 65 = 10). The excess compensation reduction could not, however, be applied if taxpayers also used the gross receipts deduction. In 1977 the value of the excess compensation reduction was increased by permitting firms to reduce their SBT liabilities by any differences between compensation and 63% of value added.

Unincorporated businesses and S corporations are obliged to pay the Single Business Tax, but are also eligible to claim credits to reduce their liabilities. These entities other than C corporations are entitled to credits that reduce their SBT liabilities by 10%. Small unincorporated businesses and S corporations can claim larger credits: firms with less than $20,000 of taxable value added are eligible for 20% credits, and those with value added between $20,000 and $40,000 can claim 15% credits. Various other smaller credits are also available.[17]

SBT provisions were frequently amended subsequent to introduction of the SBT in 1975. In 1977 value added from agricultural production was exempted from the SBT. In the same year Michigan adopted the small business credit for firms with gross receipts under $3 million, business income under $300,000, and individual shareholder and officer income under $60,000. The effect of the small business credit is to replace SBT liabilities with obligations based on taxing adjusted business income at a higher rate.[18] Taxes after credits equal the product of adjusted business income, the ratio of the SBT rate and 0.45, and the fraction by which the tax base under the

SBT is reduced by deductions and exemptions. For firms not claiming the capital acquisition deduction, the statutory exemption, or the excess compensation or gross receipts deduction, and otherwise subject to an SBT rate of 2.35%, the small business credit changes their tax obligation to 5.22% of adjusted gross income. Firms that are able to benefit from additional exemptions or deductions reduce their tax liabilities proportionately. Eligibility for the small business credit subsequently expanded in 1982, 1992, and 1995, so that firms are now eligible if they have gross receipts less than $10 million, adjusted business income less than $475,000, and individual shareholder and officer income below $115,000.

For taxpayers unsatisfied with the small business credit, Michigan introduced the alternative tax rate calculation method in 1988. Firms with gross receipts below $7.5 million were entitled to claim an SBT obligation equal to 4% of adjusted business income. The small business credit cannot be used together with the alternative tax rate calculation. The alternative tax rate was subsequently reduced to 3% in 1992, and to 2% in 1994. The Single Business Tax rate itself was reduced to 2.3% in 1994.

Large companies account for the bulk of taxable value added under the SBT, and SBT collections, so small business tax provisions have little impact on total state revenues. Table 29.4 presents information on SBT liabilities in 1998–99 by tax base of SBT filer. In that year there were ninety-two firms with taxable Michigan value added exceeding $100 million; these firms, repre-

**TABLE 29.5**

## Tax Adjustments as a Percentage of Michigan Tax Base, 1998–99

| Michigan Tax Base Class | Net Capital Acquisition Deduction[a] | Business Loss Deduction | Statutory Exemption[a] | Gross Receipts Reduction | Excess Compensation Reduction | Small Business Credit[b] | Other Business Credits[c] |
|---|---|---|---|---|---|---|---|
| $100,000,000 and over | 7.04% | 1.14% | 0.00% | 4.32% | 4.84% | 0.00% | 2.03% |
| $50,000,000–$99,999,999 | 5.53 | 5.41 | 0.01 | 11.91 | 7.89 | 0 | 1.25 |
| $10,000,000–$49,999,999 | 4.52 | 3.94 | 0.02 | 9.59 | 8.87 | n.a. | 2.47 |
| $5,000,000–$9,999,999 | 5.15 | 2.82 | 0.05 | 8.54 | 10.22 | 0.95 | 3.03 |
| $2,000,000–$4,999,999 | 5.83 | 2.87 | 0.12 | 6.83 | 11.52 | 1.78 | 3.21 |
| $1,000,000–$1,999,999 | 5.37 | 3.6 | 0.28 | 7.23 | 12.11 | 3.48 | 3.03 |
| $500,000–$999,999 | 6.42 | 4.88 | 0.7 | 6.56 | 11.23 | 6.06 | 2.76 |
| $100,000–$499,999 | 7.56 | 6.32 | 4.56 | 5.53 | 7.75 | 7.86 | 3.01 |
| $50,000–$99,999 | 9.45 | 10.55 | 33.4 | 1.14 | 5.23 | 5.02 | 2.42 |
| $1–$49,999 | 5.85 | 18.38 | 57.7 | 1.18 | 2.22 | 2.17 | 1.74 |
| TOTAL | 5.93% | 3.52% | 0.89% | 7.25% | 8.86% | 2.58% | 2.67% |

SOURCE: Michigan Department of the Treasury, Office of Revenue and Tax Analysis (2002).
(a) Effective deductions and exemptions only.
(b) Claimed credits were divided by the tax rate (0.023) to allow for a comparison to other deductions, exemptions, and reductions.
(c) Other credits include unincorporated, public utility, community foundation, college, homeless, and other credits.

**TABLE 29.6**

## Single Business Tax, 1998-99

| Business Sector | # of Firms | % of Firms | Tax Liability | % of Liability |
|---|---|---|---|---|
| Agriculture, forestry, and fishing | 2,016 | 1.4% | $8,511,091 | 0.4% |
| Mining | 500 | 0.4 | 6,422,628 | 0.3 |
| Construction | 14,430 | 10.2 | 117,784,450 | 5.0 |
| Manufacturing | 14,436 | 10.2 | 924,413,544 | 39.1 |
|    Other durable manufacturers | 5,098 | 3.6 | 182,661,011 | 7.7 |
|    Nondurable manufacturers | 3,497 | 2.5 | 208,251,644 | 8.8 |
|    Primary metals | 543 | 0.4 | 48,382,640 | 2.0 |
|    Fabricated metals | 2,284 | 1.6 | 79,137,028 | 3.3 |
|    Machinery, except electrical | 2,328 | 1.6 | 77,812,457 | 3.3 |
|    Transportation equipment | 686 | 0.5 | 328,168,764 | 13.9 |
| Transportion | 3,956 | 2.8 | 47,366,083 | 2.0 |
| Communications and utilities | 1,426 | 1.0 | 166,482,764 | 7.0 |
| Wholesale trade | 5,262 | 3.7 | 110,029,943 | 4.7 |
| Retail trade | 34,428 | 24.3 | 332,019,018 | 14.0 |
| Finance, insurance, and real estate | 15,699 | 11.1 | 129,293,255 | 5.5 |
| Services | 41,474 | 29.3 | 429,293,774 | 19.4 |
| Not elsewhere classified/misc. | 7,794 | 5.5 | 64,137,104 | 2.7 |
| All businesses | 141,421 | 100.0% | $2,365,753,654 | 100.0% |

SOURCE: Michigan Department of the Treasury, Office of Revenue and Tax Analysis (2002).
NOTE: Liability figures represent tax years ending December 1998 or from January through November 1999.

senting 0.07% of SBT filers, had total SBT liabilities of $659 million, or 27.9% of total Michigan collections. More than half of all SBT collections came from the 1.29% of SBT filers with value added exceeding $10 million.

Table 29.5 illustrates the impact of deductions and credits on SBT collections from taxpayers of different sizes in 1998–99. The capital acquisition deduction is used by taxpayers of all sizes, accounting for roughly 6% reductions in value

**TABLE 29.7**

## Michigan SBT Filing Methods, 1998–99

| Business Sector | Excess Compensation Filing Method | | | Gross Receipts Reduction Methods | | | Alternate Tax Method | | | Straight Percentage Method | | |
| --- | --- | --- | --- | --- | --- | --- | --- | --- | --- | --- | --- | --- |
| | # of Firms Claiming | % of Firms in Sector Claiming | Reduction in SBT Liability | # of Firms Claiming | % of Firms in Sector Claiming | Reduction in SBT Liability | # of Firms Claiming | % of Firms in Sector Claiming | Final Tax Liability | # of Firms Claiming | % of Firms in Sector Claiming | Final Tax Liability |
| Agriculture, forestry, fishing | 558 | 27.68 | $1,284,288 | 152 | 7.54 | $946,548 | 740 | 36.71 | $919,759 | 566 | 28.02 | $1,439,643 |
| Mining | 100 | 20.00 | 360,937 | 43 | 8.60 | 889,023 | 75 | 15.00 | 75,859 | 282 | 56.40 | 3,294,205 |
| Construction | 4,709 | 32.63 | 26,556,939 | 695 | 4.82 | 4,840,582 | 4,985 | 34.55 | 6,577,702 | 4,014 | 28.00 | 19,106,086 |
| Manufacturing | 7,301 | 50.57 | 93,172,873 | 1,149 | 7.96 | 36,521,384 | 2,468 | 17.10 | 3,666,556 | 3,518 | 24.37 | 296,646,374 |
| Other durable manufactures | 2,561 | 50.24 | 25,296,870 | 367 | 7.20 | 5,790,339 | 829 | 16.26 | 1,146,651 | 1,341 | 26.30 | 44,623,204 |
| Nondurable manufacturers | 1,674 | 47.87 | 19,803,990 | 200 | 5.72 | 12,596,744 | 599 | 17.13 | 885,221 | 1,024 | 29.28 | 71,448,079 |
| Primary metals | 304 | 55.99 | 6,534,720 | 37 | 6.81 | 1,553,751 | 72 | 13.26 | 110,903 | 130 | 23.94 | 12,310,459 |
| Fabricated metals | 1,229 | 53.81 | 9,494,642 | 234 | 10.25 | 5,762,152 | 421 | 18.43 | 667,130 | 400 | 17.51 | 19,460,710 |
| Machinery, except electrical | 1,195 | 51.33 | 12,338,722 | 263 | 11.30 | 4,528,288 | 472 | 20.27 | 758,597 | 398 | 17.10 | 18,188,397 |
| Transportation equipment | 338 | 49.27 | 19,703,929 | 48 | 7.00 | 6,290,109 | 75 | 10.93 | 98,054 | 225 | 32.80 | 130,615,525 |
| Transportation | 1,298 | 32.81 | 8,015,912 | 316 | 7.99 | 5,334,273 | 790 | 19.97 | 898,629 | 1,152 | 39.23 | 10,007,874 |
| Communications and utilities | 360 | 25.25 | 4,716,980 | 152 | 10.66 | 15,683,926 | 185 | 12.97 | 283,916 | 729 | 51.12 | 131,877,298 |
| Wholesale trade | 2,493 | 47.38 | 13,821,488 | 199 | 3.78 | 2,397,826 | 806 | 15.32 | 1,120,029 | 1,764 | 33.52 | 40,422,299 |
| Retail trade | 11,690 | 33.95 | 56,184,113 | 772 | 2.24 | 9,117,280 | 10,814 | 31.41 | 12,110,207 | 11,152 | 32.39 | 76,346,049 |
| Finance, insurance, and real estate | 1,395 | 8.89 | 14,056,445 | 3,245 | 20.67 | 34,809,657 | 2,208 | 14.06 | 2,980,299 | 8,851 | 56.38 | 44,617,617 |
| Services | 13,647 | 32.90 | 83,453,160 | 8,707 | 20.99 | 121,271,143 | 8,964 | 21.61 | 11,541,426 | 10,156 | 24.49 | 56,521,886 |
| Misc. | 1,076 | 13.81 | 4,193,021 | 1,367 | 17.54 | 18,294,402 | 1,013 | 13.00 | 1,222,235 | 4,338 | 55.66 | 26,844,342 |
| All businesses | 44,627 | 31.56% | $305,816,155 | 16,797 | 11.88% | $250,106,043 | 33,048 | 23.37% | $41,390,617 | 46,949 | 33.20% | $707,123,673 |

SOURCE: Michigan Department of the Treasury, Office of Revenue and Tax Analysis (2002).

added. Deductions for business loss carryforwards from earlier years are concentrated among taxpayers with lower value added, as is the small business credit and the application of statutory exemptions. The gross receipts reduction reduces the Michigan tax base by 7.25%, while the excess compensation reduction reduces the Michigan tax base by 8.9%. Both methods are used extensively by taxpayers of all sizes, though firms with very little value added tend to use these reduction methods less frequently, presumably due to the availability of more attractive alternatives.

Table 29.6 offers an industrial breakdown of the population of SBT filers in 1998–99. Manufacturing firms account for 10% of SBT filers, but 39% of aggregate SBT revenues. Firms in service industries provide 19% of SBT revenues, followed by retail trade, at 14% of SBT revenues, and communication and utilities, at 7%. Table 29.7 indicates the use of tax calculation methods by firms

in different industries. Manufacturing firms made extensive use of the excess compensation deduction, thereby reducing their aggregate SBT liability by $93 million, or approximately 10% of the total $924 million SBT liabilities of manufacturing firms. The gross receipts deduction was less valuable to manufacturing firms, accounting for an aggregate tax reduction of only $37 million. Firms in service industries reduced their SBT liabilities by $83 million using the excess compensation deduction and by $121 million using the gross receipts deduction. Retail trade establishments used the excess compensation deduction to reduce SBT liabilities by $56 million, while those in finance, insurance, and real estate were able to use the gross receipts deduction to reduce their SBT liabilities by $35 million.

Information is also available on the distribution of SBT liability by ownership form, as presented in table 29.8. C corporations had $1.75

**TABLE 29.8**

### Single Business Tax by Type of Firm, 1998-99

| Business Sector | Individuals | | S-Corporations | | Corporations | | Other[a] | |
|---|---|---|---|---|---|---|---|---|
| | # of Firms | Liability | # of Firms | Liability | # of Firms | Liability | # of Firms | Liability |
| Agriculture, forestry, and fishing | 346 | $740,801 | 720 | $2,251,316 | 644 | $4,081,484 | 306 | $1,437,490 |
| Mining | 32 | 70,375 | 128 | 675,819 | 228 | 3,859,054 | 112 | 1,815,380 |
| Construction | 2,037 | 3,160,205 | 5,034 | 43,857,176 | 6,402 | 66,088,384 | 957 | 4,678,685 |
| Other durable manufacturing | 163 | 239,625 | 1,422 | 25,120,086 | 3,244 | 152,261,463 | 269 | 5,039,837 |
| Nondurable manufacturing | 122 | 234,417 | 963 | 19,496,404 | 22,228 | 179,588,076 | 184 | 8,932,747 |
| Primary metals | n.a. | n.a. | 145 | 6,308,532 | 368 | 40,562,024 | 22 | 1,481,367 |
| Fabricated metals | 36 | 71,155 | 773 | 24,996,300 | 1,418 | 51,955,984 | 57 | 2,113,589 |
| Machinery, excluding electrical | 60 | 86,685 | 686 | 14,950,635 | 1,501 | 61,494,494 | 81 | 1,310,643 |
| Transportation equipment | n.a. | n.a. | 179 | 7,964,055 | 462 | 318,333,995 | 35 | 1,856,102 |
| Transportaion | 328 | 375,281 | 1,339 | 7,231,758 | 2,000 | 36,323,457 | 289 | 3,435,587 |
| Communications, utilities | 42 | 106,541 | 338 | 2,706,761 | 851 | 149,856,150 | 195 | 13,813,312 |
| Wholesale trade | 212 | 300,934 | 1,565 | 21,206,308 | 3,257 | 83,929,018 | 228 | 4,593,683 |
| Retail trade | 4,201 | 4,355,138 | 13,581 | 83,564,085 | 14,553 | 231,628,640 | 209 | 12,471,155 |
| Finance, insurance, real estate | 1,650 | 5,076,188 | 2,902 | 13,347,611 | 3,257 | 86,686,243 | 7,890 | 24,183,213 |
| Services | 4,611 | 15,076,593 | 12,140 | 86,862,332 | 14,969 | 242,816,579 | 9,754 | 114,538,270 |
| Not elsewhere class./misc. | 1,024 | 2,352,294 | 1,869 | 7,742,497 | 2,333 | 42,018,655 | 2,568 | 12,023,658 |
| All businesses | 14,882 | $32,293,561 | 43,784 | $368,251,675 | 57,715 | $1,751,483,700 | 25,040 | $213,724,718 |

SOURCE: Michigan Department of the Treasury, Office of Revenue and Tax Analysis (2002).
(a) Includes fiduciary companies, professional corporations, partnerships, and limited liability companies.

billion of SBT liabilities in 1998–99, representing 74% of total SBT collections. S corporations accounted for $368 million of SBT collections, while other business organizations, such as partnerships and LLCs, accounted for $213 million. Retail trade and service industries are more intensively populated with business organizations other than C corporations than is characteristic of manufacturing industries, and SBT collections reflect this pattern.

### Creeping Capital Taxation: Caterpillar and Its Aftermath

The apportionment formula used to determine the Michigan tax bases of multistate unitary businesses differed from the formula used to determine the capital acquisition deduction for personal property, thereby encouraging Michigan investment and disadvantaging taxpayers in particular situations. In the 1980s *Caterpillar v. Michigan Department of Treasury* challenged the constitutionality of this application of formulary methods, arguing that it discriminated against interstate commerce by discouraging capital investments outside of Michigan relative to capi-

tal investments in Michigan. The Michigan Court of Claims in 1989 ruled that the formula used to apportion the capital acquisition deduction was unconstitutional, and this finding was upheld by the Michigan Court of Appeals in 1991. In 1992 the Michigan Supreme Court overturned these decisions, ruling narrowly that the system of determining capital acquisition deductions was constitutional.

Concern over the constitutionality of the capital acquisition deduction, and fear that courts might impose major changes, drove the Michigan legislature to revise the capital acquisition deduction.[19] Legislation passed in 1991 provided that multistate firms apportion total U.S. expenditures on real and personal property based on the same three-factor formula used for other elements of the tax base. At the same time, the Michigan three-factor formula was amended to apportion 40% of the tax base of multistate unitary businesses according to sales, 30% according to property, and 30% according to payroll. The formula was revised in 1993 to a set of 50% sales, 25% property, and 25% payroll weights; it was subsequently revised in 1997 to 80% sales, 10% property, and 10% payroll, and, in 1999, the formula became 90% sales, 5% property, and 5% payroll.

The Michigan legislature became concerned in the mid-1990s that Michigan's generous treatment of investment expenses might, under the new apportionment rules, inadvertently subsidize firms investing in other states. Legislation adopted in 1995 permitted capital acquisition deductions only for investments in Michigan (except for certain categories of mobile property, which were eligible for Michigan tax deductions when used in Michigan); investment expenses were then apportioned according to the same formula that Michigan uses for the rest of its tax base. This system removed any subsidy to out-of-state investment, at the expense of also reducing the tax benefits associated with in-state investments. Concern over the possible legal ramifications of this change is reflected in the 1995 law's provision that, should the courts find the Michigan-only aspect of this change unconstitutional, the capital acquisition deduction would revert to pre-1995 rules. In 1999 the Michigan Court of Claims held in *Jefferson-Smurfit v. Michigan Department of Treasury* that the 1995 capital acquisition deduction rules represented an unconstitutional barrier to interstate trade, though this finding was overturned by the Michigan Court of Appeals in 2001.[20]

In the meantime the Michigan legislature again changed the tax treatment of capital expenditures. In 1999 the capital acquisition deduction was replaced by an investment tax credit (effective starting in 2000) for purchases of immobile assets located in Michigan, and an apportioned fraction of mobile assets located anywhere in the United States. The apportionment formula used for mobile assets is the same formula used for other elements of the tax base. For firms with adjusted gross receipts over $5 million, the investment tax credit rate is 0.85% of investment expenditures; the rate is 1.0 percent for firms with receipts from $2.5–5.0 million, 1.5% for firms with receipts of $1.0–2.5 million, and 2.3% for firms whose gross receipts are under $1 million. The effect of replacing the capital acquisition deduction with an investment tax credit at a rate below the SBT rate is to reduce the tax benefits associated with investment.

The 1999 political compromise that replaced the capital acquisition deduction with the investment tax credit also included a phased elimination of the Single Business Tax over the succeeding twenty-two years. The legislation reduced the SBT rate to 2.2% for 1999, to 2.1% for 2000, and successively reduced the rate in annual increments of one-tenth of one percentage point until its elimination in 2021. The investment tax credit rate is reduced along with the SBT rate, so the investment tax credit rate was 0.776% for large firms in 2000, 0.739% in 2001, 0.702% in 2002, and so on.[21] As a gesture toward revenue stability and fiscal responsibility, the 1999 legislation provided that annual reductions in the SBT rate would be suspended in any year in which the state's Budget Stabilization Fund (ironically known in Michigan as its "rainy day" fund) falls below $250 million. Such a suspension would not change the SBT's sunset date of 31 December 2020, but would increase the SBT rate by 0.1% (relative to what it would have been in the absence of such a suspension) in all succeeding years until the tax was eliminated at yearend 2020.

The 1999 legislative reforms were prompted by widespread recognition that Michigan's very generous treatment of capital expenditures under the Single Business Tax created problems in taxing multistate firms. Attempts to distinguish investments in Michigan from those outside Michigan seemed destined either to distort the behavior of taxpayers or to run afoul of constitutional requirements not to impede interstate trade, and possibly both. The introduction of an investment tax credit was thought to address these problems, but its rate (0.85% for large taxpayers) was considerably lower than the rate necessary to make the investment tax credit equivalent to capital expense deductions. In order to muster the political support necessary to enact this reform, business interests—many of whom had grown weary of incurring SBT liabilities in unprofitable years—were given the concession of the gradual elimination of the Single Business Tax.

A weakening Michigan economy in 2001 and 2002 impaired tax collections and produced fiscal strains for the state government budget. As a consequence, the balance in the Budget Stabilization Fund threatened to fall below the $250 million cutoff necessary to trigger suspension of the SBT rate reduction. Since the state budget is under the control of the legislature, it has the authority to enact tax and spending measures necessary to maintain the Budget Stabilization Fund above $250 million and thereby preserve scheduled SBT rate reductions, though doing so can be difficult and costly in a recession. The political compromise reached in the summer of 2002 was that the Budget Stabilization Fund would be permitted to fall below $250 million, and the SBT rate, which was 1.9% in 2001, would be maintained at that rate for 2002. In return, the date at which the SBT is scheduled for elimination was changed to 31 December 2009, and the filing threshold for the SBT was increased to $350,000. While these changes do not affect the SBT rate in the years between 2002 and 2009, they were sufficiently attractive to the business community that they were considered adequate compensation for the loss of the scheduled SBT rate reduction.

## Incentives Created by the Michigan Single Business Tax

As originally designed in 1975, the Michigan Single Business Tax closely approximated a classic value-added tax, in which costs incurred to other businesses, including the cost of acquiring capital, are deductible from taxable income. Such a system does not discourage capital investment in the way that an income-based tax does, despite collecting significant revenue. This counterintuitive feature of a value-added tax stems from its taxation of cash flows as they occur. In the absence of any taxation, a firm will undertake an investment if the discounted net present value of future returns to the investment equals or exceeds the cost of the investment; otherwise the firm does not invest. A value-added tax reduces the cost of investment by permitting investment expenditures to be deducted against taxable income, so the net cost falls by a fraction equal to the tax rate. The tax similarly reduces the after-tax return to investment by a fraction equal to the tax rate. Since the cost of investment and the return to investment fall by exactly the same fraction, the effect of a value-added tax is to reduce the magnitude of the difference between cost and returns, without changing the sign of this difference. Consequently, the imposition of value-added taxes does not change investment decisions, since projects that would generate positive net returns in the absence of taxation also generate positive (albeit smaller) net returns in the presence of taxation.

The 1975 Michigan Single Business Tax differed from an idealized value-added tax in several respects. Small firms, unincorporated firms, and S corporations were entitled to special exemptions and credits that favor small businesses relative to large businesses. Tax benefits for small firms implicitly tax capital investments that cause them to grow beyond a size at which they stop being eligible for favorable tax treatment. Tax benefits for

unincorporated firms and S corporations discourage the formation of C corporations (relative to alternate business forms), and discourage growing firms from reorganizing as C corporations. The gross receipts deduction permits firms to replace their SBT liabilities with taxes on 50% of adjusted gross receipts. Use of this deduction converts the SBT to something that is equivalent to a 1.175% (half of 2.35%) tax on gross receipts. Since firms electing to use the gross receipts deduction do not deduct capital acquisition costs, or any other costs, against taxable value added, it follows that the SBT implicitly taxes the use of capital or other inputs at a rate of 1.175% for these firms. If firms anticipate that use of the gross receipts deduction is transitory, so returns to investment today are received in subsequent years in which the firm is subject to the regular SBT, then investments are implicitly taxed at 2.35%. The gross receipts deduction is valuable in years in which firms are especially profitable relative to their gross receipts, so the availability of the deduction increases the taxation of investment undertaken in years of high profitability relative to years in which firms are less profitable. This feature encourages investment that runs counter to the business cycle.

Firms using the excess compensation deduction are taxed lightly on returns to labor expenditures and taxed heavily on returns to other expenditures. Consider the case in which firms are eligible to reduce taxable bases by the fractions that compensation expenses exceed 63% of taxable value added. Denoting compensation expenses as $c$, taxable value added as $y$, and the tax rate as $t$, it follows that a firm's SBT obligation in the absence of the excess compensation deduction would be $ty$. The excess compensation deduction reduces this obligation by $t(c - 0.63y)$. Hence firms using the excess compensation deduction pay taxes equal to $t(1.63y - c) = t1.63(y - c) + t0.63c$. The effect of the excess compensation deduction is to lower the effective tax rate on labor inputs from $t$ to $0.63t$ for labor expenditures in excess of 63% of SBT value added, and to raise the effective tax rate on everything else from $t$ to $1.63t$. Since new investments are effectively untaxed by the regular SBT, they remain effectively untaxed for firms electing to use the excess compensation deduction, unless taxpayers anticipate discontinuing use of the excess compensation deduction in the future. Transitory use of the excess compensation deduction implies that investment expenses are deducted against taxable value added when subject to a tax rate of $1.63t$, and investment returns are subsequently taxed at rate $t$. Consequently, the tax system effectively subsidizes investment (at rate $0.63t$) in years in which taxpayers claim the excess compensation deduction, which are years in which profitability is low relative to compensation. Investment expenses of taxpayers paying the regular SBT but anticipating future use of the excess compensation deduction are deducted against a tax rate of $t$, while the income they generate is taxed at $1.63t$, thereby effectively taxing such investment at rate $0.63t$. Hence the excess compensation deduction more heavily taxes investment in years in which firms are highly profitable than it does in years in which they are less profitable, thereby encouraging countercyclical investment activity.

Firms with unitary business operations in more than one state are affected by the apportionment of SBT income and (prior to 1999) apportionment of the capital acquisition deduction. The apportionment formula converts the SBT into a profit-based tax on sales, property, and payroll. Taxpayers for whom Michigan payroll and property represent larger fractions of their respective national totals than do Michigan sales benefited from the allocation formula used for the capital acquisition deduction, and as a result, faced lower effective tax rates on capital investment than they would have faced otherwise. Since capital investment is effectively untaxed in the case in which sales, property, and payroll are all the same fraction of national totals, it follows that firms with relatively few Michigan sales have their Michigan investments actually subsidized by the SBT, meaning that Michigan investment levels are higher than they would be in the absence of state taxation. The Michigan allocation fractions themselves further encourage both capital investment and employment by rewarding firms with greater capital acquisition deductions.

Changes to the capital acquisition deduction in the aftermath of the *Caterpillar* and *Jefferson-Smurfit* court cases greatly reduced incentives to invest in Michigan. The 1995 change restricting capital acquisition deductions to investments located in Michigan, and permitting taxpayers to claim deductions only for apportioned fractions of investment expenses, effectively reduced the value of investment expense deductions by the fraction of out-of-state economic activity. One could imagine a state restricting capital acquisition deductions to in-state investments, or, if that were infeasible or unconstitutional, approximat-

ing such a restriction with a formula based on the fraction of total economic activity; but the post-1995 Michigan capital acquisition instead *combined* these methods, thereby greatly reducing the tax deductions available to Michigan investors. Incentives to invest in Michigan (and incentives for Michigan firms to invest in other states) were thereby significantly reduced, though, as events transpired, this system was in place for only a few years.

The investment tax credit system introduced in 1999 offers significantly lower investment incentives than those produced by the SBT during most of its history. For a system with unchanging tax rates and tax provisions, an investment tax credit equal to the rate at which value added is taxed produces the same tax benefits and investment incentives as would full deductibility of investment expenses. The current investment tax credit rate for firms with gross receipts over $5 million is only 0.702%, while the SBT rate is 1.9%, so the investment tax credit system appears to be significantly less generous than would be immediate deductibility of investment expenses with unchanging tax provisions. This conclusion must, however, be tempered with recognition that the planned future reduction in SBT rate reduces the rate at which future returns to current investments will be taxed. The appropriate comparison is therefore the current investment tax credit rate (0.702%) with the present discounted value of future tax rates associated with returns to new investments.

In order to calculate the present discounted value of tax rates over the lifetime of a new Michigan investment, it is necessary to incorporate expected statutory tax rate changes and to apply a discount rate that reflects capital depreciation as well as the time value of money. Using a 7.7% annual depreciation rate based on calculations for aggregate U.S. business capital reported by Auerbach and Hines (1988) and adding the 2.3% current real interest rate on inflation-indexed U.S. government bonds produces a convenient 10% discount rate. Taking the SBT rate to be 1.9% in 2002 and 2003, and assuming that it will decline linearly to 1.2% by 2009 and become zero thereafter, permits calculation of a sequence of effective lifetime average tax rates on new investments. The present discounted value of tax rates on new investment in 2002 is, by this calculation, 0.966%. The present discounted value of tax rates on new investment in 2003 is 0.862%, for investment in 2004 it is 0.747%, for investment in

2005 it is 0.630%, for investment in 2006 it is 0.511%, and it continues to decline, to 0.13% in 2009, and to zero thereafter.

Investment tax credit rates decline over this period, but do so more slowly than the present value of tax rates. The investment tax credit rate in 2002 and 2003 is 0.702%, in 2004 it is 0.665%, in 2005 it is 0.628%, in 2006 it is 0.591%, and the rate declines linearly to 0.480% in 2009. The comparison of investment tax credit rates with the present discounted values of tax rates suggests that, for the years 2002–4, new investment will be taxed somewhat more heavily than it would be under immediate expensing, since the present discounted value of future tax rates exceeds the investment tax credit rate in those years. Investment in 2005 will be taxed roughly as it would be under immediate expensing, and investment in years 2006–9 will be subsidized relative to a system of immediate expensing (or no taxation at all). While these calculations rely on investor anticipation that currently legislated tax changes will actually transpire, which is hardly guaranteed, they illustrate the reasonability of the tax credit rates in the years around 2005. With the passage of time, however, investment incentives grow (which is inevitable, given that the decline in the investment tax credit rate is tied to current tax rates and not the present value of current and future tax rates), as a consequence of which firms have incentives to delay investments in order to benefit from more favorable future tax treatment.

### TABLE 29.9

**Single Business Tax Revenue History**

| Fiscal Year | SBT Revenue ($ Millions) | SBT Revenue ($ Millions, 2001) | % of Total State Taxes[a] | % of State Personal Income[b] |
|---|---|---|---|---|
| 1980 | $1,225 | $2,594 | 20.0 | 1.30 |
| 1981 | 1,053 | 2,028 | 17.0 | 1.04 |
| 1982 | 1,047 | 1,894 | 16.4 | 1.06 |
| 1983 | 1,143 | 1,980 | 15.6 | 1.06 |
| 1984 | 1,384 | 2,295 | 16.5 | 1.15 |
| 1985 | 1,495 | 2,386 | 16.7 | 1.14 |
| 1986 | 1,675 | 2,600 | 18.1 | 1.19 |
| 1987 | 1,638 | 2,438 | 17.1 | 1.12 |
| 1988 | 1,873 | 2,706 | 18.2 | 1.20 |
| 1989 | 1,922 | 2,682 | 17.7 | 1.15 |
| 1990 | 1,877 | 2,505 | 17.0 | 1.07 |
| 1991 | 1,750 | 2,271 | 14.9 | 0.97 |
| 1992 | 1,863 | 2,373 | 15.2 | 0.99 |
| 1993 | 1,979 | 2,458 | 15.4 | 0.98 |
| 1994 | 2,230 | 2,699 | 14.8 | 1.04 |
| 1995 | 2,344 | 2,757 | 13.4 | 1.02 |
| 1996 | 2,393 | 2,752 | 12.9 | 1.01 |
| 1997 | 2,407 | 2,699 | 12.4 | 0.97 |
| 1998 | 2,492 | 2,747 | 12.1 | 0.96 |
| 1999 | 2,560 | 2,743 | 11.7 | 0.94 |
| 2000 | 2,517 | 2,585 | 11.0 | 0.88 |
| 2001 | 2,224 | 2,224 | 9.9 | 0.76 |

SOURCE: Michigan Department of the Treasury, Office of Revenue and Tax Analysis (2002). Data from State of Michigan Comprehensive Annual Financial Reports and Bureau of Economic Analysis.
NOTE: Includes Insurance Company Retaliatory Taxes.
(a) Does not include fees, permits, or licenses.
(b) Based on Bureau of Economic Analysis State Personal Income Data, 23 April 2002 release.

## Revenue Stability

This section considers the impact of the Single Business Tax on Michigan tax collections. In order to evaluate the impact of the SBT it is necessary to consider specific tax or spending alternatives, since the loss of SBT revenue would have to be recouped either by raising other taxes, cutting spending, or running smaller state surpluses. The most natural alternative to the SBT is a corporate income tax, and other states' experiences with corporate taxation offer obvious comparison points to Michigan's SBT experience.

Corporate taxation is no more perfect in practice than is the value-added approach embodied in the SBT. States raise and lower their corporate tax rates, and they change their allocation formulas, depreciation allowances, loss carryforward and carryback provisions, and a host of other features that affect the stability of tax collections. No doubt some of these changes are designed to stabilize tax collections, while others (intentionally or not) destabilize tax collections. In comparing the actual stability of SBT collections to the stability of corporate income tax collections by other states, discretionary tax changes as well as automatic features of tax systems are implicitly included.

The most notable feature of Michigan's SBT is the very large revenue that it collects, relative both to state income and to other revenue sources for the state government. Figures 29.1 and 29.2 depict patterns of state revenue collections from corporations, illustrating the relatively higher tax burden imposed by Michigan. Table 29.9 offers a recent history of total SBT revenues (plus insurance retaliatory taxes, which are reported together with SBT revenues). In fiscal year 2001 the SBT collected $2.2 billion, representing 9.9% of total Michigan taxes and 0.76% of Michigan

TABLE 29.10

## Means and Variances of State Corporate Tax Collections, 1977–97

| | Per Capita Corporate Net Income Taxes | | | | Corporate Income Tax as Share of Total Taxes | | | |
|---|---|---|---|---|---|---|---|---|
| | Standard Deviation | Variance | Mean | Coefficient of Variation | Standard Variation | Variance (x 1000) | Mean | Coefficient of Variation |
| Alaska | 555.000 | 308,025.000 | 680.431 | 0.816 | 0.010 | 0.109 | 0.173 | 0.060 |
| Alabama | 11.361 | 129.071 | 39.716 | 0.286 | 0.009 | 0.081 | 0.044 | 0.204 |
| Arkansas | 15.823 | 250.358 | 50.572 | 0.313 | 0.010 | 0.110 | 0.056 | 0.187 |
| Arizona | 19.961 | 398.456 | 54.445 | 0.367 | 0.010 | 0.108 | 0.044 | 0.234 |
| California | 26.636 | 709.496 | 110.864 | 0.240 | 0.010 | 0.105 | 0.076 | 0.135 |
| Colorado | 8.614 | 74.202 | 36.997 | 0.233 | 0.011 | 0.113 | 0.034 | 0.312 |
| Connecticut | 59.459 | 3,535.410 | 154.044 | 0.386 | 0.017 | 0.277 | 0.093 | 0.178 |
| District of Columbia | 114.987 | 13,222.010 | 158.536 | 0.725 | 0.033 | 1.059 | 0.046 | 0.712 |
| Delaware | 70.647 | 4,990.962 | 138.212 | 0.511 | 0.021 | 0.449 | 0.084 | 0.252 |
| Florida | 13.434 | 180.484 | 45.571 | 0.295 | 0.008 | 0.072 | 0.044 | 0.194 |
| Georgia | 18.340 | 336.352 | 61.827 | 0.297 | 0.011 | 0.119 | 0.059 | 0.185 |
| Hawaii | 20.295 | 411.900 | 53.196 | 0.382 | 0.010 | 0.093 | 0.031 | 0.315 |
| Iowa | 12.903 | 166.494 | 55.845 | 0.231 | 0.009 | 0.079 | 0.047 | 0.188 |
| Idaho | 25.945 | 673.143 | 57.615 | 0.450 | 0.013 | 0.159 | 0.055 | 0.231 |
| Illinois | 27.148 | 736.993 | 75.400 | 0.360 | 0.010 | 0.101 | 0.059 | 0.171 |
| Indiana | 46.680 | 2,178.990 | 60.365 | 0.773 | 0.020 | 0.393 | 0.049 | 0.404 |
| Kansas | 16.667 | 277.776 | 71.805 | 0.232 | 0.014 | 0.209 | 0.064 | 0.227 |
| Kentucky | 16.523 | 273.018 | 61.612 | 0.268 | 0.010 | 0.105 | 0.058 | 0.175 |
| Louisiana | 12.249 | 150.031 | 48.985 | 0.250 | 0.013 | 0.169 | 0.049 | 0.266 |
| Masachusetts | 45.392 | 2,060.434 | 139.324 | 0.326 | 0.015 | 0.236 | 0.089 | 0.173 |
| Maryland | 14.381 | 206.819 | 50.339 | 0.286 | 0.006 | 0.034 | 0.036 | 0.162 |
| Maine | 15.055 | 226.661 | 49.278 | 0.306 | 0.010 | 0.099 | 0.041 | 0.241 |
| Michigan | 36.400 | 1,324.931 | 119.456 | 0.305 | 0.007 | 0.049 | 0.087 | 0.081 |
| Minnesota | 23.793 | 566.112 | 96.833 | 0.246 | 0.016 | 0.255 | 0.064 | 0.248 |
| Missouri | 15.162 | 229.888 | 38.682 | 0.392 | 0.006 | 0.034 | 0.039 | 0.150 |
| Mississippi | 17.837 | 318.175 | 42.658 | 0.418 | 0.005 | 0.021 | 0.045 | 0.103 |
| Montana | 20.894 | 436.560 | 65.666 | 0.318 | 0.011 | 0.128 | 0.058 | 0.195 |
| North Carolina | 30.066 | 903.949 | 77.981 | 0.386 | 0.009 | 0.078 | 0.069 | 0.128 |
| North Dakota | 26.967 | 727.244 | 70.551 | 0.382 | 0.014 | 0.198 | 0.061 | 0.230 |
| Nebraska | 16.211 | 262.782 | 45.762 | 0.354 | 0.005 | 0.027 | 0.040 | 0.130 |
| New Hampshire | 27.213 | 740.543 | 81.826 | 0.333 | 0.020 | 0.418 | 0.098 | 0.208 |
| New Jersey | 28.951 | 838.170 | 90.262 | 0.321 | 0.012 | 0.143 | 0.059 | 0.201 |
| New Mexico | 19.360 | 374.797 | 48.343 | 0.400 | 0.009 | 0.076 | 0.039 | 0.222 |
| Nevada | — | — | — | — | — | — | — | — |
| New York | 43.925 | 1,929.414 | 117.030 | 0.375 | 0.005 | 0.024 | 0.060 | 0.081 |
| Ohio | 10.690 | 114.278 | 51.562 | 0.207 | 0.016 | 0.247 | 0.050 | 0.317 |
| Oklahoma | 8.667 | 75.112 | 36.473 | 0.238 | 0.010 | 0.102 | 0.035 | 0.289 |
| Oregon | 15.957 | 254.613 | 60.403 | 0.264 | 0.016 | 0.259 | 0.054 | 0.298 |
| Pennsylvania | 25.743 | 662.710 | 91.256 | 0.282 | 0.012 | 0.138 | 0.075 | 0.156 |
| Rhode Island | 15.278 | 233.428 | 64.542 | 0.237 | 0.015 | 0.218 | 0.052 | 0.282 |
| South Carolina | 9.836 | 96.738 | 50.409 | 0.195 | 0.017 | 0.283 | 0.054 | 0.314 |
| South Dakota | 20.040 | 401.609 | 28.083 | 0.714 | 0.016 | 0.244 | 0.027 | 0.580 |
| Tennessee | 15.269 | 233.138 | 48.565 | 0.314 | 0.007 | 0.054 | 0.054 | 0.135 |
| Texas | — | — | — | — | — | — | — | — |
| Utah | 18.804 | 353.577 | 40.512 | 0.464 | 0.006 | 0.035 | 0.036 | 0.163 |
| Virginia | 7.715 | 59.521 | 36.198 | 0.213 | 0.008 | 0.061 | 0.033 | 0.235 |
| Vermont | 14.088 | 198.475 | 55.670 | 0.253 | 0.012 | 0.146 | 0.047 | 0.259 |
| Washington | — | — | — | — | — | — | — | — |
| Wisconsin | 16.403 | 269.072 | 69.059 | 0.238 | 0.008 | 0.068 | 0.049 | 0.168 |
| West Virginia | 35.865 | 1,286.327 | 52.128 | 0.688 | 0.021 | 0.435 | 0.041 | 0.509 |
| Wyoming | — | — | — | — | — | — | — | — |
| Average of other states | 35.154 | 7,463.410 | 79.052 | 0.352 | 0.012 | 0.170 | 0.055 | 0.230 |

SOURCE: Author's calculations from U.S. Census of Governments data.

personal income. Relative SBT collections have declined since 1980, when they provided 20% of state tax revenues and represented 1.3% of state personal income.

Business tax revenues fluctuate over time with business cycle conditions. Corporate income tax collections are typically quite sensitive to business cycle influences, for the simple reason that corporate profits are among the most procyclical of economic variables. Since the SBT base is not corporate profits, but instead a variant of value added, it follows that Michigan's business tax collections have the potential to respond much less dramatically to business cycle fluctuations than do the tax collections of other states.

Table 29.10 presents statistics describing state corporate income tax collections (including the Michigan SBT) over the 1977–97 period. For the purpose of the calculations reported in table 29.10, state corporate tax collections are adjusted in the same way that they are in constructing figures 29.1 and 29.2, meaning that tax revenues from sources other than C corporations are removed from reported revenues. The four left-most columns describe variances, means, standard deviations, and coefficients of variation (ratios of standard deviations to means) of state per capita income tax collections. Income tax collections are measured in 1997 dollars. Thus, the 119.456 figure for Michigan's mean indicates that, over this twenty-year period, Michigan collected an inflation-adjusted annual average of $119 per resident from taxing corporations with the SBT. Michigan's collections are quite high compared to those of other states, whose corporate tax collections average only $79 per resident.[22] Only four states (Alaska, Connecticut, Delaware, and Massachusetts) and the District of Columbia have per capita corporate tax collections that exceed Michigan's over this time period.

The variance, presented in the second column of table 29.10, is the sum (over the twenty years of the sample) of squared differences between a state's corporate tax collections and that state's average for the sample period. Hence the variance is a measure of the extent to which average tax collections fluctuate around their mean. The standard deviation, presented in the first column, is simply the square root of the variance. It is a bit difficult to compare standard deviations of tax collections between states, since standard deviations are almost guaranteed to be greater for states with higher corporate tax collections. The coefficient of variation, presented in column 4 of table 29.10, is a commonly used measure of variability in such situations. The coefficient of variation equals the ratio of the standard deviation and the mean, thereby implicitly controlling for the magnitude of tax collections. Michigan's coefficient of variation is 0.305, which is typical of American states. The national average is 0.352, though this average is dominated by a few states (such as Alaska and Indiana) with particularly large values. There are twenty-five states with coefficients of variation that exceed Michigan's, while twenty states have coefficients of variation less than Michigan's.

The right four columns of table 29.10 evaluate the properties of corporate income as a share of state tax collections. Michigan's mean share over the sample period is 8.7%, which is high among American states: the national average is 5.5%, and only three states (Alaska, Connecticut, and Massachusetts) collect higher fractions of state revenue with corporate taxes than does Michigan. Despite its high mean, Michigan's fraction of state revenue represented by corporate tax collections varies quite little: only six states have smaller variances than Michigan's. Michigan's coefficient of variation for this variable is 8.1%, which is considerably smaller than the national average of 23.0%; only Alaska has a smaller coefficient of variation.

From this evidence it appears that Michigan's SBT collections from corporations consistently mirror Michigan's tax collections from other sources. This finding makes sense, given that the tax base of the Michigan SBT includes items such as labor compensation that are major sources of state revenue through other taxes. Measured as a fraction of per capita state income, Michigan's SBT corporate collections exhibit roughly average variability. It is difficult, however, to interpret these coefficients of variation as indicators of cyclical responsiveness, since they capture long-run trends and do not necessarily indicate whether variability stems from fluctuations with or against business cycle movements.

In order to evaluate the responsiveness of Michigan tax collections to business cycle fluctuations, it is instructive to use the statistical technique of multiple regression to identify the extent to which corporate tax collections are affected by business cycle indicators. Doing so not only indicates the impact of the business cycle on SBT collections, but also produces simple tests of the comparability of Michigan's experience and that of other states. Table 29.11 presents estimated

### TABLE 29.11

**Corporate Tax Sensitivity to Business Cycles**

*Dependent Variable: Log of State Net Corporate Income Tax Per Capita*

| | | | | | | |
|---|---|---|---|---|---|---|
| Constant | 4.66307 | 4.71607 | 4.37705 | 4.7582 | 4.3787 | 4.2987 |
| | (0.84145) | (0.07766) | (0.05788) | (0.08333) | (0.08303) | (0.05376) |
| State unemployment rate | −0.085388 | −0.01671 | −0.03489 | −0.02084 | | |
| | (0.00911) | (0.00938) | (0.00652) | (0.00834) | | |
| State unemployment rate x MI dummy | 0.085612 | 0.016712 | 0.066228 | 0.067165 | | |
| | (0.01249) | (0.00935) | (0.008399) | (0.00796) | | |
| National unemployment rate | | | | | −0.036318 | −0.023424 |
| | | | | | (0.007900) | (0.005133) |
| National unemployment rate x MI dummy | | | | | 0.085946 | 0.084597 |
| | | | | | (0.01740) | (0.01124) |
| Year dummies? | N | Y | N | Y | N | N |
| State dummies? | Y | Y | Y | Y | Y | Y |
| State growth dummies? | N | N | Y | Y | N | Y |
| R-squared | 0.6349 | 0.8097 | 0.8452 | 0.8715 | 0.6115 | 0.8456 |
| Number of obs. | 934 | 934 | 934 | 934 | 934 | 934 |

NOTE: The dependent variable is State net corporate income tax per capita. The table represents estimated coefficients from OLS regressions; heteroskedasticity-consistent standard errors are in parentheses.

coefficients from regressions in which the dependent variable is the natural logarithm of per capita corporate tax collections, and the independent variables include unemployment rates, year dummy variables, state dummy variables, and trending variables for each state.[23] Data for all fifty states and the District of Columbia, for years 1977–96, are included in the regression sample. The table reports heteroskedasticity-consistent standard errors in parentheses.

The −0.085388 coefficient in the first column of table 29.11 indicates that, over this time period in the country as a whole, an increase in the state unemployment rate of one percentage point (e.g., the difference between unemployment rates of 4.5% and 5.5%) is associated with a reduction of 8.54% in per capita corporate tax collections.[24] The regression includes Michigan's unemployment rate interacted with a dummy variable that takes the value one for Michigan observations, thereby permitting the effect of unemployment on corporate tax collections to differ between Michigan and other states. The 0.085612 coefficient in the third row of the first column indicates that, indeed, the responsiveness of per capita tax collections in Michigan differs from that in other states. The estimated effect of higher unemployment in Michigan is the sum of −0.085388 and 0.085612, or almost exactly zero.

Hence this specification suggests that SBT collections from incorporated businesses respond little, if at all, to business cycle fluctuations as captured by state unemployment rates, which is quite different from the experience of other states.

The results reported in column one of table 29.11 reflect the effect of long-term trends in corporate tax collections and unemployment, in addition to their short-term variation. Column two of table 29.11 reports estimated coefficients from specifications that add year dummy variables to capture year effects that are common across states. The −0.01671 coefficient in the second row implies that an increase in the state unemployment rate of one percentage point reduces per capita corporate tax collections by 1.7%, after controlling for year effects. Once again, the coefficient on unemployment in Michigan interacted with a Michigan dummy variable almost perfectly offsets the general effect of unemployment, implying that Michigan corporate tax collections are unaffected by Michigan unemployment.

Column three of table 29.11 reports estimated coefficients from a regression that adds a variable that trends separately for each state, while removing year dummy variables.[25] The effect of including the trend variable is to remove any effects of state-specific trends, in order to test whether

**TABLE 29.12**

**Variability of Corporate Tax Shares**

*Dependent Variable: Net Corporate Income Tax Share of Total State Taxes*

| | | | | | | |
|---|---|---|---|---|---|---|
| Constant | 0.055517 | 0.054537 | 0.06121 | 0.579174 | 0.05547 | 0.056642 |
| | (0.00406) | (0.004918) | (0.003832) | (0.005886) | (0.003871) | (0.003575) |
| State unemployment rate | −0.00120 | −0.00197 | −0.002173 | −0.001948 | | |
| | (0.0044) | (0.000594) | (0.000431) | (0.000587) | | |
| State unemployment rate x MI dummy | 0.004376 | 0.004570 | 0.004762 | 0.004609 | | |
| | (0.00060) | (0.000593) | (0.000556) | (0.0005631) | | |
| National unemployment rate | | | | | −0.001141 | −0.001329 |
| | | | | | (0.000366) | (0.00339) |
| National unemployment rate x MI dummy | | | | | 0.005615 | 0.005634 |
| | | | | | (0.000813) | (0.00075) |
| Year dummies? | N | Y | N | Y | N | N |
| State dummies? | Y | Y | Y | Y | Y | Y |
| State growth dummies? | N | N | Y | Y | N | Y |
| R-squared | 0.5867 | 0.6288 | 0.6703 | 0.6882 | 0.5665 | 0.6665 |
| Number of obs. | 940 | 940 | 940 | 940 | 940 | 940 |

NOTE: The dependent variable is net corporate income tax share of total state taxes. The table represents estimated coefficients from OLS regressions; heteroskedasticity-consistent standard errors are in parentheses.

Michigan's corporate tax collections continue to exhibit business cycle patterns that differ from those of other states. The results confirm that they do: the estimated effect of an increase in the unemployment rate of one percentage point in other states is to reduce corporate tax collections by 3.5%, while the effect of an increase in the unemployment rate of one percentage point in Michigan is to *increase* corporate tax collections by 3.0%! Given that most economic variables, particularly tax collections, are procyclical, this countercyclical feature of SBT tax collections is striking. Certainly it reflects the fact that the SBT base includes not only profits but also other important cost components. Column four of table 29.11 reports estimated coefficients from a regression that adds year dummy variables but is otherwise the same as that reported in column three. The results imply that an increase in the state unemployment rate of one percentage point increases corporate tax collections by 4.6% in Michigan, and reduces corporate tax collections by 2.1% elsewhere.

Columns five and six of table 29.11 report the results of regressions that omit year dummy variables and use national unemployment rates as business cycle indicators in place of state-specific unemployment rates. The results are similar to those reported in columns three and four. For example, the specification reported in column five implies that an increase in the national unemployment rate of one percentage point is associated with 3.6% lower tax collections outside of Michigan and 5.0% higher tax collections in Michigan.

Table 29.12 reports the results of regressions in which the dependent variable is the ratio of corporate tax collections to total state government revenue, and the independent variables are identical to those in the regressions reported in table 29.11. The results reported in table 29.12 are similar to those reported in table 29.11: corporate tax collections decline as a fraction of total tax revenues as unemployment rises in states other than Michigan, while corporate tax collections rise as a fraction of total tax collections at higher unemployment rates in Michigan. The regression reported in column two of table 29.12 indicates that an increase of one percentage point in the unemployment rates in states other than Michigan is associated with 0.2% lower fractions of total tax receipts accounted for by corporate taxes. The same regression implies that an increase of one percentage point in the unemployment rate in Michigan increases the fraction of total tax revenue represented by SBT collections from corporations. Similar results appear in other specifications in table 29.12.

There is evidently something quite different about the Michigan SBT experience as compared to the experiences of other states. Michigan's tax collections under the SBT have been if anything countercyclical, thereby providing important revenue cushions in years in which the state government has most needed revenues. Other states have found their corporate tax collections moving with the business cycle, thereby exacerbating revenue shortfalls in recession years.

### Implications for Michigan Policy

In spite of the attractive features of value-added taxation, Michigan has struggled to find a long-run answer to the question of how it wants to tax businesses. The Business Activities Tax was replaced by corporate income taxation, which in turn was replaced by the Single Business Tax, and the SBT is itself now slated for elimination by 2010 and presumptive replacement by something else. There are many reasons why a state might want to change its tax policies over time, including changing economic conditions and revenue needs, intensified competition from other states and foreign countries, legal difficulties with existing policies, changing political winds, and the adoption of new and better ideas. Michigan's history reflects all of these forces.

The Single Business Tax is a simple and efficient tax.[26] The SBT also has the virtue of generating a revenue stream that is not procyclical in the way that corporate income taxes are, so the SBT provides revenue when the state government most needs it. The value-added tax model on which the SBT is based has the feature that new investment is effectively untaxed, which adds to the attractiveness of the SBT by raising the possibility that its use might not compromise the competitiveness of Michigan industry.

Practical considerations have led to changes over time in the design of the SBT that have undermined its efficiency. Small and unprofitable firms felt unduly burdened by the requirement that they pay taxes on the basis of business activities rather than profits, so in order to address their concerns the value-added structure of the SBT was modified to include the small business credit, the excess compensation deduction, and numerous other credits and deductions. These features of the SBT mildly penalize firm growth and introduce other small distortions. The use of formulary methods to apportion the taxable

incomes of multistate firms has made it difficult to distinguish for tax purposes investments in Michigan capital from investments in capital used outside of Michigan. The unwillingness of the Michigan legislature to extend the generous tax treatment of investments under the SBT to capital used outside Michigan sparked a sequence of changes that led ultimately to the abandonment of capital acquisition deductions and their replacement with investment tax credits. This change, together with the phased elimination of the SBT, creates investment incentives that change over time and encourage inefficient delay of investment in Michigan assets.

One lesson of the SBT experience is that efficient design features are readily sacrificed at the altar of practical politics. A second lesson is that the remaining efficient properties of the tax system encourage legislators to impose taxes at high rates on business activities. Michigan taxes its corporations more heavily with the SBT than does any other state with corporate income taxes, and Michigan also subjects unincorporated businesses and S corporations to the SBT. While it is difficult to know how heavily Michigan would tax businesses in the current environment if relying exclusively on corporate income taxes, it is unlikely that Michigan would tax corporations at a rate significantly exceeding the highest current rate in the country, and apply the same tax rate to other businesses, as it does currently with the SBT.

Since new investments are taxed lightly, if at all, by the SBT, it follows that the burden of the tax is borne either by owners of old investments, by existing laborers, by consumers, or by someone else. To the extent that labor is mobile between states, wages in Michigan are determined by a national labor market, and therefore are affected very little by the SBT. Most consumer goods are priced on national and even international markets, so Michigan prices are unlikely to reflect SBT burdens—except for goods sold by multistate firms subject to formula apportionment of income for SBT purposes, the prices of which will be somewhat elevated. The bulk of the SBT burden instead falls on sources of economic rent located in Michigan: the excess profitability of local manufacturing, high-technology, and other firms; the value of Michigan land; and the extent to which Michigan wages exceed competitive levels.

The Single Business Tax as originally conceived offered efficient investment incentives, a countercyclical revenue stream, and tax burdens that fell on economic rents. While in practice the SBT does not promote efficiency as cleanly as it does in theory, the attractive features of the SBT compare favorably to those of leading corporate income tax alternatives. The primary sticking point for the SBT in the last decade has been the difficulty of taxing multistate firms without either providing generous incentives for investments in other states or discriminating against interstate commerce. This is a problem that is likely to be surmountable if Michigan is serious about continuing to use the SBT, particularly since the problem stems solely from the use of formulary apportionment rather than arm's-length accounting for state income. In particular, the very recent adoption of investment tax credits for site-specific investments offers a promising method of maintaining many of the benefits of the SBT without running afoul of interstate commerce concerns. Rather than abandon the SBT altogether, as is currently planned for 2010, Michigan would be well advised to consider alternatives that maintain the SBT in slightly modified form.

## Conclusion

The Michigan Single Business Tax has proven to be a sizable and stable source of tax revenue since its introduction in 1975. The Single Business Tax is now, however, slated for elimination after 2009, a victim of complications that arose from successive reforms.

The Single Business Tax represents America's closest approximation to a broad-based tax on value added. Such taxes encourage business investment, do not distort financial and operating decisions, and offer more stable revenue streams than do the alternatives among classic corporate income taxes. These desirable properties of value-added taxes disappear, however, when tax rates and other tax provisions change frequently. Michigan was compelled to change its treatment of capital expenditures when it became clear that provisions designed to maintain investment benefits only for in-state capital investments might run afoul of constitutional requirements not to impede interstate trade. Normal politics likewise intruded in the form of growing deductions from taxable income, expanding numbers of credits available against SBT liabilities, and other benefits sought and received by influential taxpayers.

The Michigan experience with the Single Business Tax serves as a reminder that a tax system with properties that would be very desirable if universally adopted and never changed need not maintain those properties in the world in which we live. What the Michigan legislature will do to replace the revenues lost by the Single Business Tax as its rate falls during the 2000–2010 decade, and following its scheduled elimination in 2009, is not clear. The choice of a replacement for the SBT will hopefully be guided by wise anticipation of some of the practical difficulties that tax policies encounter.

■

## REFERENCES

Anderson, Theodore A. 1960. Recommended changes in Michigan's tax structure, in *Taxes and economic growth in Michigan,* edited by Paul W. McCracken. Kalamazoo, Mich.: Upjohn.

Auerbach, Alan J. 2002. Taxation and corporate financial policy, in *Handbook of public economics,* vol. 3, edited by Alan J. Auerbach and Martin Feldstein. Amsterdam: North-Holland.

Auerbach, Alan J., and James R. Hines Jr. 1988. Investment tax incentives and frequent tax reforms. *American Economic Review* 78 (2): 211–16.

Barlow, Robin, and Jack S. Connell Jr. 1982. The Single Business Tax, in *Michigan's fiscal and economic structure,* edited by Harvey E. Brazer and Deborah S. Laren. Ann Arbor: University of Michigan Press.

Bartik, Timothy J. 1985. Business location decisions in the United States: Estimates of the effect of unionization, taxes, and other characteristics of states. *Journal of Business and Economic Statistics* 3 (1): 14–22.

Berry, Charles H., David F. Bradford, and James R. Hines Jr. 1992. Arm's-length pricing: Some economic perspectives. *Tax Notes* 54 (6): 731–40.

Buehler, Alfred G. 1960. The state and local tax structure and economic development, in *Taxes and economic growth in Michigan,* edited by Paul W. McCracken. Kalamazoo, Mich.: Upjohn.

Carlton, Dennis W. 1983. The location and employment choices of new firms: An econometric model with discrete and continuous endogenous variables. *Review of Economics and Statistics* 65 (3): 440–49.

Diamond, Peter A., and James Mirrlees. 1971a. Optimal taxation and public production, I: Production efficiency. *American Economic Review* 61 (1): 8–27.

———. 1971b. Optimal taxation and public production, II: Tax rules. *American Economic Review* 61 (3): 261–78.

Ely, Richard T. 1888. *Taxation in American states and cities.* New York: Crowell.

Goolsbee, Austan, and Edward L. Maydew. 2000. Coveting thy neighbor's manufacturing: The dilemma of state income apportionment. *Journal of Public Economics* 75 (1): 125–43.

Gordon, Roger H., and James R. Hines Jr. 2002. International taxation, in *Handbook of public economics,* vol. 4, edited by Alan J. Auerbach and Martin Feldstein. Amsterdam: North-Holland.

Gordon, Roger H., and John D. Wilson. 1986. An examination of multijurisdictional corporate income taxation under formula apportionment. *Econometrica* 54 (6): 1357–73.

Hassett, Kevin A., and R. Glenn Hubbard. 2002. Tax policy and business investment, in *Handbook of public economics,* vol. 3, edited by Alan J. Auerbach and Martin Feldstein. Amsterdam: North-Holland.

Hines, James R., Jr. 1996. Altered states: Taxes and the location of foreign direct investment in America. *American Economic Review* 86 (5): 1076–94.

———. 1999. Lessons from behavioral responses to international taxation. *National Tax Journal* 52 (2): 305–22.

———. 2001. Corporate taxation, in *International encyclopedia of the social & behavioral sciences,* vol. 4, edited by Neil J. Smelser and Paul B. Baltes. Oxford, U.K.: Elsevier.

Hines, James R., Jr., and Eric M. Rice. 1994. Fiscal paradise: Foreign tax havens and American business. *Quarterly Journal of Economics* 109 (1): 149–82.

Kenyon, Daphne A. 1996. A new state VAT? Lessons from New Hampshire. *National Tax Journal* 49 (3): 381–99.

Michigan Department of the Treasury, Office of Revenue and Tax Analysis. 2002. *The Michigan Single Business Tax, 1998–99,* July.

Newman, Robert J. 1983. Industry migration and growth in the South. *Review of Economics and Statistics* 65 (1): 76–86.

Papke, James A. 1960. Michigan's value-added tax after seven years. *National Tax Journal* 13 (4): 350–63.

Papke, Leslie E. 1987. Subnational taxation and capital mobility: Estimates of tax-price elasticities. *National Tax Journal* 40 (2): 191–204.

———. 1991. Interstate business tax differentials and new firm location: Evidence from panel data. *Journal of Public Economics* 45 (1): 47–68.

Seligman, Edwin R. A. 1914. *The income tax.* New York: Macmillan.

Wasylenko, Michael. 1981. The location of firms: The role of taxes and fiscal incentives, in *Urban government finance: Emerging trends,* edited by Roy Bahl. Beverly Hills, Calif.: Sage.

———. 1991. Empirical evidence on interregional business location decisions and the role of fiscal incentives in economic development, in *Industry location and public policy,* edited by Henry W. Herzog Jr. and Alan M. Schlottmann. Knoxville: University of Tennessee Press.

———. 1995. Has the relationship changed between taxes and business location decisions? *Proceedings of the National Tax Association* 87:107–12.

## NOTES

I thank Alexia Brunet for superb research assistance, and the editors for many helpful comments on an earlier draft.

1. Ely (1888) and Seligman (1914), among others, describe early state efforts at business taxation. Hines (2001) reviews the history of federal efforts to tax corporations prior to passage of the Sixteenth Amendment.

2. Even New Hampshire, whose Business Enterprise Tax has some features in common with a value-added tax of the income type (see Kenyon 1996), relies much more heavily on its Business Profits Tax (which is effectively a corporate profits tax) than its Business Enterprise Tax.

3. Auerbach (2002) reviews evidence of the effect of taxation on corporate financial policies, and Hassett and Hubbard (2002) review evidence of the effect of corporate taxation on patterns of investment in plant and equipment.

4. Separate accounting with arm's-length pricing generally produces more efficient incentives than do formula apportionment methods, but can entail additional compliance and incentive costs. For analysis and estimates of the difficulties of enforcing the arm's-length standard internationally, see Berry, Bradford, and Hines (1992) and Hines and Rice (1994). Hines (1999) reviews empirical estimates of behavioral responses to arm's-length pricing rules in the presence of international tax rate differences.

5. See, for example, the analysis in Gordon and Wilson (1986).

6. Corporate franchise fees are taxes imposed on rights to establish corporations. Franchise fees commonly include small fixed payments plus a very small fraction of a corporation's capital stock.

7. Property taxes on business inventories are declining sources of government revenue. In 1966, forty-four states taxed business inventories, whereas by 1999 only fifteen states did so. Furthermore, of the

fifteen states with inventory taxes as of 1999, four have enacted legislation phasing them out over time. Appendix A describes state property taxes on business inventories, including revenue collections for the four states for which it is possible to obtain data. Of these states, only Ohio collects significant revenue from property taxes on business inventories.

8. There is one additional tax omitted from this table. Since 1987, Michigan has imposed a "retaliatory tax" on insurance companies from outside of Michigan. Most states require insurance companies to pay taxes based on premiums received, while Michigan simply subjects insurance companies to the SBT. Insurers whose home states impose more burdensome taxes on Michigan insurance companies than does Michigan with the SBT are subject to "retaliatory taxes" equal to the difference, so those insurers pay to Michigan in total what they would have paid to their own states on the same activity. The purpose of the "retaliatory tax" is to discourage other states from imposing heavy taxes on Michigan insurance companies, while raising additional revenue for Michigan. The revenue consequences of the "retaliatory tax" are quite modest, however: in 2000, the tax raised $155 million.

9. In recent years 74% of Michigan's SBT collections have come from corporations (Michigan Department of the Treasury 2002), the remainder from other business entities. The revenue adjustment used to calculate the ratios depicted in following figures 29.1 and 29.2 (and also used to calculate the dependent variables in the regressions reported in tables 29.11 and 29.12) is to multiply Michigan's SBT collections by 0.74. Revenue figures of states other than Michigan that tax S corporations, partnerships, or other business entities are adjusted by assuming that each business type that a state taxes contributes revenue in the same proportion to the total as such types do in Michigan.

10. See, for example, Goolsbee and Maydew (2000), who estimate the effects of changing components of apportionment formulas. They report that manufacturing employment increases by 3% when a state reduces the payroll weight in its apportionment formula from one-third to one-quarter, and that this employment gain is perfectly offset by employment reductions in other states.

11. See Diamond and Mirrlees (1971a and 1971b) for a general analysis, and Gordon and Hines (2002) for a critical survey of the literature on the effects of interstate tax competition.

12. During the same era Michigan also imposed a corporate franchise tax on the net worth of corporations, but its rate was quite low and its revenue yield correspondingly modest (Anderson 1960, 20).

13. An "income VAT" is a value-added tax in which taxpayers deduct from the tax base the cost of capital depreciation, while with a traditional, or "consumption VAT," capital expenditures are instead immediately expensed. An "income VAT" effectively taxes the income earned from business investments, while a "consumption VAT" does not, since immediate expensing generates a tax deduction equal in present value to the taxable income produced by marginal investments.

14. See James Papke (1960) for further description of BAT provisions and analysis of their effects.

15. The additional $200 million was not a permanent increase but instead a one-time tax windfall for the state, created by the overlap of final annual payments on some of the repealed taxes and the quarterly estimate structure of the SBT.

16. The SBT replaced the corporate income tax, the corporate franchise fee (which was based on corporate net worth), the financial institutions income tax, the savings and loan association privilege fee, the domestic insurance company privilege fee, local government property taxes on business inventories, and the intangibles tax on business. Local governments were compensated for the loss of revenue with roughly equivalent state revenue sharing, which Barlow and Connell (1982, 717) note is approximately 15% of SBT revenues.

17. As originally enacted the Single Business Tax included credits for owners of utility property and contributors to Michigan colleges and universities, public libraries, and public broadcasting stations. There are now many minor credits available toward SBT liabilities, including renaissance zone and brownfield credits; MEGA credits for payroll and business activity expansion; credits for contributions to food banks, community foundations, and homeless shelters; credits for historic rehabilitation; credits for employers of youth apprentices; and a credit for firms engaged in the extraction and processing of low-grade iron ore.

18. Adjusted business income for the purpose of calculating the small business credit equals business income plus compensation and director fees of active shareholders and officers.

19. This fear was well founded: the Michigan Court of Claims ruling initially struck all capital acquisition deductions, thereby imposing a $500 million additional obligation on Michigan taxpayers.

20. As of this writing, the *Jefferson-Smurfit* case is still pending before the Michigan Supreme Court.

21. The investment tax credit rate for large firms equals the product of 0.85 and the ratio of the current SBT rate to 2.3%.

22. This U.S. average would be significantly smaller except for the inclusion of Alaska, whose $680 mean per capita tax collection vastly exceeds that of the next highest state. Alaska obtains this tax revenue almost entirely by taxing oil drilling and related activities, making its situation difficult to compare to those of other states.

23. The dependent variable is expressed as a natural log in order to use simple specifications of state and year dummy variables, and in order to facilitate interpretation of the estimated coefficients.

24. State corporate tax collection data are reported by the Census of Governments. State and national unemployment rates are reported by the Bureau of Labor Statistics. Since states report tax collection data on a fiscal year (commonly, 1 July–30 June, though Michigan is 1 October–30 September) basis, and unemployment figures are reported on a calendar year basis, some adjustment is necessary in order to make these series comparable. For the purpose of the regressions reported in tables 29.11 and 29.12, all series were estimated on a fiscal year basis. This entailed adjusting the unemployment series by constructing average unemployment rates for the current and preceding years. Mathematically, the fiscal year unemployment rates were calculated as: $u_t^{FY} = \frac{1}{2}(u_t^{CY} + u_{t-1}^{CY})$, in which $u_t^{FY}$ is the unemployment rate attributed to fiscal year $t$, and $u_t^{CY}$ is the (reported) unemployment rate in calendar year $t$.

25. Specifically, the state growth variable is the interaction of a trending variable that equals zero in 1977, one in 1978, two in 1979, and so on, with fifty-one dummy variables that take the value one for each state, and zero otherwise.

26. The SBT is efficient in the sense of creating efficient economic incentives for taxpayers, particularly compared to the alternative of corporate income taxation. Administrative and compliance costs associated with the SBT are more difficult to assess; the Michigan Department of the Treasury (2002, 4) notes that the SBT eased administrative burdens by consolidating seven prior taxes into one state office, and replacing taxes collected by multiple local governments with a single state tax. Barlow and Connell (1982, 703) maintain that compliance costs are greater with the SBT than with a corporate profits tax, since the SBT must be paid by many more business units.

## APPENDIX A

### State Taxation of Business Inventory Property

| | State | Inventory Tax (in millions) | Elimination Status |
|---|---|---|---|
| 1 | Alaska | — | — |
| 2 | Arkansas | — | — |
| 3 | Georgia | — | — |
| 4 | Indiana | 400 | Passed HB1001 on 7/28/02. Phasing out inventory tax in 5 years |
| 5 | Kentucky | 130 | — |
| 6 | Louisiana | 160 | Phased out inventory tax in 5 years, beginning in 1997 |
| 7 | Maryland | — | — |
| 8 | Massachusetts | — | — |
| 9 | Mississippi | — | — |
| 10 | Ohio | 820 | Passed HB283. Phases out inventory tax in 25 years, beginning in 2002 |
| 11 | Oklahoma | — | — |
| 12 | Rhode Island | — | Passed HB8478 on 6/25/98. Phasing out inventory tax in 10 years |
| 13 | Texas | — | — |
| 14 | Vermont | — | — |
| 15 | West Virginia | — | — |

SOURCE: Author's compilation from unpublished data provided by state tax agencies.
NOTE: The table lists states taxing business inventory property as of 2001.

# 30

# Borrowing by Michigan Governments

*Jay B. Rising and A. Thomas Clay*

## Introduction

In a 1968 advisory opinion on the constitutionality of the Michigan State Housing Development Authority Act the Michigan Supreme Court stated, in examining the state's borrowing powers, "[t]he framers of the 1963 Constitution created a pay-as-you-go government for the State of Michigan."[1] Today that vision of the constitution's framers contrasts with a new and expansive world of revenue bonds, lease-supported appropriation debt, special-purpose revenue bonds, and a smorgasbord of municipal debt alternatives. Over the last thirty years, Michigan public debt issuers, with the encouragement of the Michigan legislature and the support of the courts, have creatively and purposefully redefined the role of debt in Michigan. In so doing, Michigan governments, on both the state and local levels, have utilized debt to make public improvements and support private investment.

This chapter will review historical trends in issuance of bonds and notes by Michigan governments and discuss the major changes in state public finance and federal tax laws and regulations that have affected the volume and timing of publicly issued debt in Michigan. It will examine the substantive policy and procedural processes that influence the issuance of state and local debt.

A survey of the processes and alternative means used by the state and local units to finance public projects and purposes will follow.

## Types of and Alternatives to Debt Issuers and Issuances in Michigan

### State Long-Term and Short-Term Financing Techniques

The state has limited constitutional authority to directly finance its own capital and operating needs with a general revenue pledge. Such "general obligation" bonds are regularly issued by the state only for financing its School Bond Loan Fund program. General obligation notes that mature in the fiscal year in which they were issued have long been used by the state to fund its annual cash needs. Other state long-term, general obligation debt requires voter approval. Currently almost $1.6 billion of general obligation bonds remain to be issued under voter authorizations approved in 1988, 1998, and 2002.

Bonds commonly classified as special-obligation bonds, because of the limited source of state-generated revenues available to be pledged for their repayment, are also commonly issued by the State Transportation Commission for highway

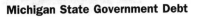

## Michigan State Government Debt

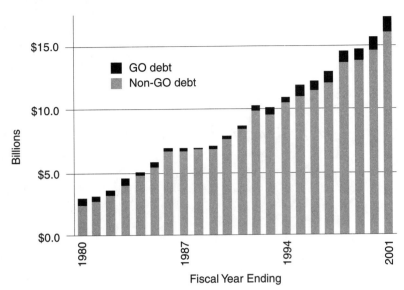

SOURCE: Annual Report of the State Treasurer, various years.

increased more rapidly than local government debt in the past two decades. Of the two broad categories, general obligation (GO) debt and non-general obligation (non-GO) debt, general obligation debt is a relatively small fraction of non-general obligation debt and has grown at a much smaller rate. Over the period from 1980 through 2001, outstanding GO debt increased from $439 million to $998 million, a gain of 127%. By 30 September 2002, that level had increased to $1.081 billion. During the period from 1980 through 2001, non-GO debt grew from $2.269 billion to $16.097 billion, an increase of 609%. Figure 30.1 depicts the two-decade trends in state government debt.

Much of the change in general obligation debt volume can be explained by new uses for debt as a method of financing programs. Table 30.1 displays the categories of general obligation debt for several years during the period from 1980 through 2002. Two categories accounting for nearly half of all outstanding GO bonds in 1980 are fully retired. In 2002, more than half of the outstanding GO bonds had been issued for environmental protection and remediation purposes, an area that did not have any bonds outstanding in 1980.

In recent years another significant form of financing has become a popular method for acquiring new state buildings. In transactions in which the state has contracted to make lease payments to a developer, the developer has certificated the state's lease payments and marketed those certificates as an appropriation-risk tax-exempt obligation. During the term of the lease the developer owns the building and, at the end of the lease term, the state is entitled to purchase the building for a nominal payment. The principal amount of capital leases outstanding as of 30

and comprehensive transportation purposes, by the State Building Authority for buildings and equipment for use of the state and institutions of higher education, and by the Michigan Underground Storage Tank Financial Assurance Authority (MUSTFAA) to assist in financing the cost of remediation for leaking underground storage tanks. Only the special-obligation bonds of the State Building Authority, which totaled $2,582,134,000 as of 30 September 2002, utilize state general fund revenues, payable as lease payments from the state to the State Building Authority, to support its debt.

State debt issued by state government has

## General-Obligation Bonds Payable by Fiscal Year (in thousands)

|  | 1980 | 1985 | 1990 | 1995 | 2002 |
|---|---|---|---|---|---|
| School loans | $56,100 | $26,700 | $9,725 | $180,000 | $448,000 |
| Water resources | 172,000 | 144,000 | 78,000 | 19,000 | 0 |
| Public recreation | 41,000 | 6,000 | 0 | 0 | 0 |
| Environmental protection | 0 | 0 | 89,998 | 386,876 | 453,816 |
| Recreation | 0 | 0 | 10,000 | 120,130 | 34,750 |
| Vietnam veteran bonus | 170,000 | 65,000 | 0 | 0 | 0 |
| Clean Michigan Initiative | 0 | 0 | 0 | 0 | 144,420 |
| Total | $439,100 | $241,700 | $187,723 | $706,006 | $1,081,276 |

SOURCE: Annual Report of the State Treasurer, various years.

## TABLE 30.2

**Non-General Obligation Bonds and Notes Payable by Fiscal Year (in thousands)**

| | 1980 | 1985 | 1990 | 1995 | 2001 |
|---|---|---|---|---|---|
| **Special Obligation Issues** | | | | | |
| Department of Transportation tax dedicated bonds | $203,180 | $409,905 | $500,711 | $888,058 | $1,081,119 |
| Department of Transportation grant anticipation notes | | | | | 400,000 |
| Joint venture tax dedicated highway bonds | 28,765 | | | | |
| DNR state park revenue bonds | 13,415 | 10,045 | 5,635 | | |
| Public building corp. bonds (Mason building) | 1,746 | 1,046 | 346 | | |
| Michigan State Building Authority | 89,450 | 539,535 | 1083600 | 1,453,388 | 2,159,314 |
| SUBTOTAL: SPECIAL OBLIGATION ISSUES | $349,971 | $950,631 | $1,590,292 | $2,341,446 | $3,540,433 |
| **Special Authorities** | | | | | |
| International Bridge Authority | $9,645 | $7,850 | $7,850 | $7,850 | |
| Mackinac Bridge Authority | 32,429 | 3,285 | | | |
| Mackinac Island State Park Commission | 255 | 480 | 1,477 | 2,625 | 2,725 |
| Michigan State Housing Development Authority | 1,182,470 | 1,949,430 | 2,091,879 | 1,985,947 | 2,010,900 |
| Michigan State Hospital Finance Authority | 647,034 | 1,698,959 | 1,819,730 | 2,467,726 | 3,751,233 |
| Michigan Higher Education Facilities Authority | 3,430 | 69,015 | 70,025 | 151,380 | 293,575 |
| Michigan Higher Education Student Loan Authority | 128,000 | 192,982 | 206,645 | 557,939 | 929,365 |
| Michigan Job Development Authority | 28,020 | | | | |
| Michigan Municipal Bond Authority | | | 712,044 | 1,469,051 | 2,883,835 |
| Michigan Strategic Fund | | 614,175 | 1,115,814 | 1,881,278 | 2,432,279 |
| Michigan Underground Storage Tank Financial Assurance Authority | | | | 206,100 | 152,520 |
| Michigan Family Farm Development Authority | | 4,884 | 3,696 | 1,843 | 181 |
| SUBTOTAL: SPECIAL AUTHORITIES | $2,031,283 | $4,541,060 | $6,029,160 | $6,029,160 | $12,456,613 |
| TOTAL | $2,367,839 | $5,501,591 | $7,619,452 | $11,073,185 | $16,097,046 |

SOURCE: Annual Report of the State Treasurer, various years.

September 2002 was $461.4 million, as increased from $254.8 million on 30 September 2001.

For short-term financing of general operating expenses, the state has intermittently utilized the constitutionally authorized power to issue general obligation notes. The limit translates to about $1.3 billion, and the loans, usually tax-exempt notes, must be repaid before the end of each fiscal year. From FY 1980 to FY 1984, the state issued as much as $500 million in notes at one time during each fiscal year. The amounts declined to $450 million in FY 1985 and $350 million in FY 1986, as the state's cash position improved. From FY 1987 through FY 1990, the state did not issue notes. The issuance of notes commenced again in FY 1991, and continued every year through FY 1998 except FY 1994. The largest amount issued in any one year was $900 million, which was issued in FY 1996. No notes were issued from FY 1998 to FY 2002.

A prevalent, although more costly mechanism for managing the short-term cash needs of the state's general and school aid funds has been interfund borrowing, also called common cash fund borrowing. The state manages its cash assets in a single fund, the common cash fund. The state's Common Cash Fund is a cash management and investment tool that allows the state treasurer to invest the cash on hand of nearly every fund.

With the approval of the state administrative board, the state treasurer is allowed to transfer cash on hand and on deposit between the various funds in order to offset negative cash balances in other funds, with the exception that bond funds and debt service funds may not be transferred in that manner. Every fund with a negative cash balance, other than the school aid fund, is charged interest equal to the average interest rate earned by the common cash investments during the period the fund has a negative balance. Since the investments of the Common Cash Fund are in short-term taxable instruments, a fund with a negative fund balance is charged with interest

**TABLE 30.3**

## State Government Per Capita Debt: National Rankings

|  | 1980 | 1990 | 2000 |
|---|---|---|---|
| California | 32 | 33 | 31 |
| Georgia | 40 | 47 | 46 |
| Illinois | 21 | 21 | 16 |
| Indiana | 49 | 40 | 36 |
| Michigan | 36 | 36 | 22 |
| Minnesota | 25 | 38 | 39 |
| New Jersey | 13 | 11 | 10 |
| New York | 6 | 10 | 8 |
| North Carolina | 41 | 49 | 38 |
| Ohio | 29 | 29 | 33 |
| Pennsylvania | 23 | 35 | 34 |
| Texas | 44 | 48 | 45 |
| Wisconsin | 24 | 23 | 18 |

SOURCE: Calculations by Senate Fiscal Agency from data on total state government debt from the U.S. Bureau of the Census.

**TABLE 30.4**

## State Government Outstanding Debt Per Capita

|  | 1980 | 1990 | 2000 |
|---|---|---|---|
| California | $353 | $970 | $1,688 |
| Georgia | 257 | 481 | 866 |
| Illinois | 550 | 1,335 | 2,321 |
| Indiana | 111 | 747 | 1,298 |
| Michigan | 315 | 887 | 1,957 |
| Minnesota | 508 | 860 | 1,139 |
| New Jersey | 886 | 2,446 | 3,439 |
| New York | 1,346 | 2,567 | 4,143 |
| North Carolina | 215 | 463 | 1,160 |
| Ohio | 372 | 1,033 | 1,593 |
| Pennsylvania | 535 | 920 | 1,514 |
| Texas | 174 | 463 | 922 |
| Wisconsin | 520 | 1,251 | 2,135 |
| United States | 540 | 1,283 | 1,951 |

SOURCE: Calculations by Senate Fiscal Agency from data on total state government debt from the U.S. Bureau of the Census.

higher than it would otherwise have paid if tax-exempt notes could have been issued to fund the cash flow deficit of that fund. Since 1990, the state's general fund common cash earnings have been negative in every fiscal year except 1999, 2000, and 2001.

**TABLE 30.5**

## Comparison of General Fund Supported Debt Positions

|  | GFS Debt/ Capita | GFS Debt/2001 Personal Income | Debt Service as % of FY 01 General Fund Expenditures |
|---|---|---|---|
| California | $838.4 | 2.5 | 3.3 |
| Georgia | 637.7 | 2.2 | 3.3 |
| Illinois | 629.1 | 1.9 | 4.4 |
| Indiana | 480.5 | 1.7 | 0.7 |
| Michigan | 122.8 | 0.4 | 1.9 |
| Minnesota | 525.8 | 1.6 | 3.8 |
| New Jersey | 1,084.1 | 2.8 | 4.3 |
| New York | 1,581.7 | 4.4 | 8.6 |
| North Carolina | 371.2 | 1.4 | 1.3 |
| Ohio | 688.0 | 2.4 | 1.5 |
| Pennsylvania | 740.9 | 2.4 | 2.4 |
| Texas | 290.5 | 1.0 | 1.2 |
| Wisconsin | 745.0 | 2.6 | 2.2 |

SOURCE: Merrill Lynch Global Securities Research & Economic Group; Municipal Credit Research.

### Non-General Obligation and State Authority Debt

Most non-GO debt is issued by special authorities of the state. Special authorities accounted for 91% of outstanding non-GO debt in FY 2001. Significant changes have occurred in the mix and amount of non-GO debt in recent years.

Table 30.2 displays the categories of non-GO debt for selected years during the period from 1980 through 2001. Two authorities that did not exist in FY 1980, the Municipal Bond Authority and the Strategic Fund, accounted for $5.3 billion of the outstanding debt in FY 2001. Other areas of significant growth are the State Building Authority, which increased by nearly $2 billion over the period, and the State Hospital Finance Authority, which increased by $3.1 billion. Three other areas added around $800 million during the period: Department of Transportation tax dedicated bonds, the State Housing Development Authority, and the Higher Education Student Loan Authority. The seven areas mentioned here accounted for $13 billion of the increases in outstanding debt during the period, 95% of the total increase in non-GO debt. Since 2001, a new authority, the Michigan Broadband Authority, has been created, and it has privately issued a $50 million bond, which was secured with a moral obligation pledge of the state, to the State Housing Development Authority in 2002.

## Trends in the Volume of Government Debt in Michigan

Like most states, Michigan and its local governmental units experienced rapid increases in the amount of outstanding debt in the past two decades. This section compares Michigan's experience with that of other states.

The U.S. Bureau of the Census collects data on total state and local outstanding debt each year. From these data, rankings of state debt per capita are prepared and distributed by many agencies monitoring state financial affairs. The data on state debt include state university debt and are not strictly comparable to the Michigan state government debt figures from the annual report of the state treasurer. Michigan's public universities are significantly more independent from state government than the public universities of most other states. State university debt amounted to only about 10% of all reported state debt as reported by the Census Bureau for the last five years when comparisons could be made.

### State Debt

In Michigan, the Senate Fiscal Agency has published interstate comparisons and rankings for many years. Tables 30.3 and 30.4 contain state rankings and per capita state debt outstanding for 1980, 1990, and 2000 for the thirteen major industrial states. Although about the U.S. average for 2000 and ranking twenty-second-highest of the fifty states, Michigan has exhibited the greatest movement toward higher per capita debt load of any of the thirteen industrial states (moving fourteen places in the ranking), followed by Indiana (moving thirteen places). Over the twenty-year period, Michigan has moved from less than 60% of the U.S. average to slightly above that average.

Viewing General Fund–supported debt only, including capital lease obligations such as certificates of participation, a different picture emerges. Table 30.5 compares the same thirteen states for fiscal years ending in 2001.

### Local Government Debt

Local government debt in fiscal year 1999 constituted about 63% of government debt in Michigan. In 1980, the local government share was 75%. Although rising at a rate significantly slower than

---

**TABLE 30.6**

**Long-Term Michigan Debt: Michigan's State and Local National Rankings, Fiscal Year 1998–99**

|  | Per Capita | Per $1,000 Personal Income |
|---|---|---|
| State general obligation | 33 | 36 |
| State nongeneral obligation | 24 | 23 |
| Total state debt | 26 | 30 |
|  |  |  |
| Local full faith and credit | 13 | 13 |
| Local nonguaranteed | 29 | 34 |
| Total local debt | 17 | 19 |
|  |  |  |
| State and local full faith and credit | 18 | 19 |
| State and local nonguaranteed | 30 | 30 |
| Total state and local debt | 27 | 35 |

SOURCE: U.S. Bureau of the Census, State and Local Government Finances.
NOTE: Fifty states and District of Columbia are included in the rankings.

---

state debt, local debt increased by 223% in the period from 1980 through 1999. Figure 30.2 depicts the increase in local debt over the nearly two-decade period.

### National Rankings—State and Local Debt

Data from the U.S. Bureau of the Census permit an examination of how Michigan ranked in several categories of debt both on a per capita basis and per $1,000 of personal income. The personal income calculation is made to adjust for the

---

**FIGURE 30.2**

**Total Local Government Debt**

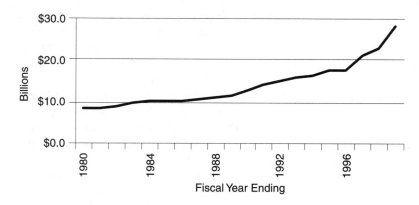

SOURCE: Annual Report of the State Treasurer, various years, and U.S. Bureau of the Census, Census of Governments, State and Local Finances by level of government.

financial capacity of the states in issuing and paying for debt. Table 30.6 contains the rankings for fiscal year 1998–99.

In most categories Michigan had debt levels lower than those of more than half of the states. There were some exceptions, however. State nonguaranteed debt levels were slightly above those of the median state, and Michigan ranked thirteenth in both per capita and debt per $1,000 personal income in local full faith and credit debt. Total state and local debt ranked barely below the median in per capita debt and just into the lower third on debt per $1,000 of personal income.

## State and Local Debt Powers

The powers of the State of Michigan and its political subdivisions to borrow money and extend their credit are specifically addressed and limited by the Michigan Constitution. Article IX, § 12 and Article IX, § 18 of the Michigan Constitution, which have been interpreted to apply to the state and its political subdivisions,[2] set forth the general rules proscribing the state and its political subdivisions from incurring debt unless authorization is otherwise found in the constitution.[3] The purpose of Article IX, § 18 is "to make certain that the State, which itself cannot borrow, except as authorized, does not accumulate unauthorized debts by endorsing or guaranteeing the obligations of others."[4]

The exceptions specified by the Michigan Constitution for the state are found in Article IX, §§14, 15, and 16 of the Michigan Constitution, which provide that the state may issue its full faith and credit notes to meet obligations incurred by appropriation in any fiscal year; that allow the legislature, by two-thirds vote of each house, to submit a question to the electors requesting authorization to borrow funds for a specific purpose; and that allow the state to issue its full faith and credit obligations to make loans to school districts under the state's School Bond Loan Fund Program.[5]

In addition to these constitutional authorizations for issuing debt, the Michigan Supreme Court has enabled the state and various legislatively created authorities to issue obligations that are not considered state indebtedness for purposes of Article IX, §§ 12 and 18 of the Michigan Constitution. Most closely tied to the state's credit are obligations pledging state-generated revenues that are issued by the State Transportation Commission for transportation purposes and the State Building Authority for public facilities and equipment. Initially included in this court-created exception, but now specially authorized by Article IX, § 9 of the Michigan Constitution, were obligations of the state issued for funding transportation purposes and secured by specially dedicated revenues. Of the other obligations issued by state authorities, the majority have been issued on a conduit basis, with the issuing state authority borrowing for the purpose of loaning the proceeds of its debt to a third party and solely pledging loan repayments promised from the third-party borrower.

With respect to political subdivisions other than the state, the Michigan Supreme Court has found both that validity of a borrowing is measured by the corporate purposes of the public corporation, as contained in its charter or as established by law,[6] and that the power to borrow must be conferred explicitly and is not inherent in general powers of public corporation that may have been granted to the public corporation under its charter or by law.[7]

## Types of Municipal Obligations

Generally speaking, there are two fundamental types of municipal bonds, general obligation bonds and revenue bonds. General obligation bonds, which are paid or payable from a municipality's general funds, carry a full-faith-and-credit pledge, and, if voter approved, are supported by additional taxing power. This pledge, however, does not preclude the utilization of any other moneys lawfully available to the issuer to pay the debt (e.g., using sewer charges to pay debt service on general obligation sewer bonds). Revenue bonds, which are not payable from taxes, are instead payable solely from the revenues of an enterprise, such as the water or sewer system.

*General Obligation Bonds.* The 1978 amendments to the Michigan Constitution that are commonly referred to collectively as the "Headlee Amendment" had a direct impact on the nature of general obligation bonds in Michigan. In part, the Headlee amendment revised Article IX, Section 6, of the Michigan Constitution of 1963 to limit the rate of *ad valorem* taxation. Under that provision the exception to the fifteen- and fifty-mill constitutional limitations was revised to require voter approval for taxes imposed for the payment of principal and interest on bonds, evidences of indebtedness, and other assessments or contract obligations in anticipation of which loans are issued.

As revised by the Headlee Amendment, debt service millage may not be levied over and above statutory and charter millage limits unless the obligation for which such debt service millage is levied has been approved by the voters.[8] Bonds so authorized are often referred to as "unlimited tax bonds" or "unlimited tax general obligation bonds." In contrast, a "limited tax" bond or other obligation is a bond or obligation that is payable from taxes levied within existing applicable constitutional, statutory, and if a charter municipality, charter tax limitations. Commonly, limited tax bonds are payable as a first budget obligation from the millage a municipality is already otherwise authorized to levy.

Many bonding statutes contain authorization to pledge a municipality's full faith and credit—either as primary or secondary security. In some instances the statutes even contain authorization to levy taxes without limitation as to rate or amount to pay debt service. Article IX, §6, as amended by Headlee, is an "override" or limitation to these statutory provisions. While the pledge for full faith credit may still be authorized, the pledge may be an "unlimited tax" pledge only if voter approval is received for the specific project. Issuance of either voted or nonvoted general obligation bonds will remain, however, subject to the statutory (or constitutional) limitations on the aggregate amount of debt a municipality may incur.

*Revenue Bonds.* Public improvements that are self-supporting through the imposition of use or service charges may be financed through the issuance of self-liquidating revenue bonds. Although revenue bonds may be authorized by a number of acts, the most frequently used authority for the issuance of such bonds is the Revenue Bond Act of 1933 (Act 94, Public Acts of Michigan, 1933, as amended). Pursuant to Act 94, revenue bonds may be issued for a variety of public improvements, including housing facilities, garbage and refuse disposal facilities, transportation systems, sewer and water systems, electric and gas utilities, parking facilities, recreational facilities, auditoriums, hospitals, airports, cable television systems, and museums. Generally, such bonds are payable solely from the revenues generated by the facility. Unless a municipality's general obligation pledge is made under the limited circumstances permitted by law, revenue bonds

are not considered as a debt of the municipality. Instead, revenue bonds are a debt of the system whose revenues support repayment of the bonds.

*Refunding Bonds.* The primary purpose of a "refunding bond" is to save money.[9] To take advantage of lower interest rates, Michigan law authorizes municipalities to reduce their debt service payments by refinancing existing bonds. Under the Revised Municipal Finance Act and without a vote of its electors, a municipality may issue bonds to fund all or any part of its outstanding obligations, whether those outstanding obligations are callable on the date the refunding obligations are issued or at some later date.

### Types of Municipal Issuers

As noted previously, municipalities have no inherent power to borrow money and must rely on statutory authorization from the legislature. Different bonding statutes provide municipalities with different tools. Each one addresses a specific need, and no one tool is right for every job. A few of the major types are noted in table 30.7.

### State Regulation of Municipal Finance

The process and terms governing the issuance of most general obligation municipal debt have been established under a single statutory enactment. From 1943 through 2002, that statute was the Municipal Finance Act.[10] In 2002 that act was repealed and replaced with the Revised Municipal Finance Act.[11]

Since 1979, the Municipal Finance Act and its successor, the Revised Municipal Finance Act, have undergone consistent legislative review and transformation. The law has, in this period, evolved from a statute designed to principally regulate the issuance of debt to a system that also regulates those municipal issuers considered to have suspect financial practices.

With the objective of simplification, in 2000 the legislature began a review of the Municipal Finance Act and the hundreds of other statutes that authorized the issuance of specific types of municipal debt or debt for a particular municipal purpose. The initial and principal product of this review was the Revised Municipal Finance Act ("Act 34"). Act 34 repealed the Municipal Finance Act, 1943 PA 202, MCL 131.1 et seq., and incorporated many of its provisions. More significantly,

## TABLE 30.7

## A Summary of Michigan's Municipal Borrowing Provisions

### DIRECT ISSUANCE

#### Special Assessment Bonds

ISSUERS: Any municipality.

PURPOSE: Generally public improvements that specially benefit assessed properties.

SECURITY: Primary security is the special assessment. General obligation of municipality may be pledged without vote.

LIMITATIONS: GO pledge on SA Bonds limited to principal amount of 5% of SEV each year, unless otherwise approved by voters. Aggregate SA Bonds with GO pledge cannot exceed 12% of issuers' SEV.

#### Public Share Bonds

ISSUERS: Cities; Villages; Charter Townships.

PURPOSE: Public Improvements.

SECURITY: General Obligation of the city, village, or charter township. Nonvoted.

LIMITATIONS: City can issue only for share of cost of a special assessment project. Village share bonds limited to 40% of cost of project.

#### Michigan Transportation Fund Bonds

ISSUERS: Cities; Villages.

PURPOSE: Street and highway improvements.

SECURITY: Primary security is Michigan Transportation Fund distributions; General obligation permitted as secondary security without vote.

LIMITATIONS: Issuance limitation by requirement that principal and interest on bonds may not exceed 50% of MFT funds received in state's last fiscal year.

#### Water Resources Commission and Court-Order Bonds

ISSUERS: Counties; Villages; Cities; Townships.

PURPOSE: Wastewater treatment facilities, sewage disposal systems, solid waste facilities, and wastewater systems.

SECURITY: General obligation bonds without vote.

LIMITATIONS: Must be obligated to make the improvements by court or Michigan Department of Environmental Quality order or pursuant to a Natural Resources and Environmental Protection Act permit requirement.

#### Rehabilitation Bonds

ISSUERS: Counties; Villages, Cities; Townships.

PURPOSE: Costs of projects under Blighted Areas Act, such as land acquisition, demolition, site improvements.

SECURITY: General obligation bonds without vote.

LIMITATIONS: Amount limited by statute. Ability to issue tax-exempt limited if improvements are for sale to private parties.

#### Capital Improvement Bonds

ISSUERS: Any municipality.

PURPOSE: Capital improvements.

SECURITY: Limited tax general obligation bonds.

LIMITATIONS: Must publish notice of intent and vote bonds if referendum petitions filed. Subject to a 5% debt limitation.

#### Judgment Bonds

ISSUERS: Any local unit of government.

PURPOSE: To defray cost of a court judgment entered against the local unit.

SECURITY: Limited tax general obligation bonds unless voted.

LIMITATIONS: Exempt from debt limitations.

### CONTRACT BONDS

#### Municipal Building Authority Bonds

ISSUERS: Authority created by a county, city, village, or township, or jointly by one or more municipalities.

PURPOSE: Acquire, furnish, equip, improve, enlarge, operate, and maintain public buildings, parking lots or structures, recreational facilities, stadiums, and necessary sites.

SECURITY: Authority bonds security by lease with incorporating municipality. Lease may be limited tax obligation or, with approval of electors, unlimited tax obligation.

LIMITATIONS: Lease obligation is considered debt for statutory debt limitations of municipality. Lease may also pledge payments received under a sublease without general obligation pledge of the municipality.

#### Department of Public Works Bonds

ISSUERS: County Board of Public Works created by a county.

PURPOSE: Water supply systems, sewer disposal systems, refuse systems, and lake improvement systems undertaken for a village or township.

SECURITY: Board of Public Work bonds secured by general obligation contractual obligation of municipality. County limited tax general obligation pledge may secure the bonds if approved by a $\frac{3}{5}$ vote of County Board of Commissioners.

LIMITATIONS: Board of Public Works may either maintain responsibility to build and manage the project or leave all or part of those responsibilities with the contracting municipality. After bonds are paid, project is conveyed to the contracting municipality.

#### Act 342 Bonds

ISSUERS: Either County Road Commission, Drain Commission, or Board of Public Works, as designated by County Board of Commissioners.

PURPOSE: Sewer systems, water supply, and garbage or rubbish collection facility systems.

SECURITY: Bonds secured by general obligation contractual obligation of municipality. County limited tax general obligation pledge may secure the bonds if approved by a majority vote of County Board of Commissioners.

LIMITATIONS: Referendum rights exist on municipal contract.

### Sewage and Water Authority Bonds

ISSUERS: Authority created by two municipalities (counties, villages, cities, and townships).

PURPOSE: Sewage disposal system, solid waste management system, water supply system.

SECURITY: Bonds may be secured by rates and charges for services or contract with constituent municipalities.

LIMITATIONS: Contract obligations of a municipal may be secured with a tax pledge.

### Drain Bonds

ISSUERS: Counties.

PURPOSE: Drains, sewers, pumping equipment, bridges, culverts, board, structures, devices to purify flow or drains and for flood control.

SECURITY: Bonds secured by general obligation contractual obligation of municipality. County limited tax general obligation may be pledged.

LIMITATIONS: Contract obligations of a municipality are full faith and credit obligations of the municipality.

### TAX/REVENUE SHARING NOTES

### Tax Anticipation Notes

ISSUERS: Municipalities and certain municipal authorities.

PURPOSE: Operating expenses (such as unforeseen expenses, expenditures for which budgeted revenues have been delayed in receipt or not yet received); debt service charges; capital improvements.

SECURITY: Secured by taxes in anticipation of which notes are issued. Must pledge to set aside certain portion of tax collections.

LIMITATIONS: Notes may be issued in anticipation of taxes to be collected for current or next fiscal year, or both if levied in the same calendar year. Tax Anticipation Notes for operating purposes is limited to 75% of net operating levy in current year or 50% of levy for next fiscal year.

### Revenue Sharing Notes

ISSUERS: Municipalities and certain municipal authorities.

PURPOSE: Payment of operating expenditures.

SECURITY: State revenue-sharing payments. Set aside required to revenue-sharing receipts.

LIMITATIONS: Limited to 50% of revenue-sharing received in last fiscal year.

### Bond Anticipation (BAN) and Grant Anticipation Notes (GAN)

ISSUERS: Municipalities and certain municipal authorities.

PURPOSE: Any purpose for which the bonds or grants may be used.

SECURITY: Any taxes or revenues of the municipality and the bonds in anticipation of which the BAN or GAN is issued by be pledged to secure a BAN or GAN.

LIMITATIONS: BAN cannot exceed 50% of amount of proposed bonds. GAN cannot exceed 50% of remaining amount of grant to be received.

### OTHER OBLIGATIONS

### Installment Purchase Contracts

ISSUERS: Cities; Villages; Townships.

PURPOSE: Purchase of land, property, or equipment for public purposes.

SECURITY: Limited tax general obligations. No vote of electorate required.

LIMITATIONS: Payable in installments over not a period to exceed fifteen years. Limited to 1.25% of taxable value of issuer.

### Tax Increment Bonds

ISSUERS: Downtown Development Authorities (DDAS); incorporating unit of a DDA; Tax Increment Financing Authorities (TIFAs); Local Development Finance Authorities (LDFAs); Brownfield Redevelopment Authorities (BRAs).

PURPOSE: Varied purposes generally related to public infrastructure and improvements.

SECURITY: Tax increment revenues and, with approval of incorporating unit, limited tax general obligation of the incorporating local unit. Voter approval permitted for unlimited tax pledge.

LIMITATIONS: Bonds excluded from debt limits. School and state tax levies are part of tax increment revenues in limited circumstances.

---

Act 34 took another step in limiting the role of the Department of Treasury in approving the issuance of municipal debt.

The system of prior approval orders and exceptions from prior approval established in 1982 (itself an evolution from a system of prior authorization by a commission created to protect the credit of the state and its municipalities[12]) was replaced with an annual prequalification procedure. Under this procedure a municipal issuer files an audit and "qualifying statement" within six months after the end of its fiscal year. If accepted by the Department of Treasury, the municipality is exempt from having to obtain prior approval of any issuance of its securities until its next audit is due. Failure to obtain qualifying status subjects the municipality to a prior approval process for each issuance of its securities. The criteria utilized for acceptance of a qualifying statement is similar to that previously used to grant an exception from the prior approval prerequisite for the issuance of debt. That criteria seeks verification of the soundness of a municipality's fiscal condition and financial practices.

Consistent with the simplification objective and in line with the trend toward liberalization and modernization of municipal finance statutes that took place in the 1980s and 1990s, Act 34 made four significant modifications. Those modifications included:

- Authorization for a municipality to sell its securities at a negotiated sale so long as the reasons for utilizing a negotiated sale are stated in the bond authorizing resolution of the issuing municipality.
- Authorization to issue Bond Anticipation Notes.
- Authority to issue Grant Anticipation Notes.
- Creation of a new type of obligation, Capital Improvement Bonds, that a municipality can issue directly to finance the costs of capital improvement items. Previously capital improvements could be financed only by installment purchase contracts, through the creation of a local building authority, or by issuance by a county of an obligation secured by a contract with the municipality.

Even while conferring new powers upon municipalities that, by their terms, provided significant discretion to municipalities in decisions of structure and security, Act 34 targeted certain municipal finance practices for greater scrutiny and regulation. Two of these targeted practices had been consistently criticized by members of the legislature and had received previous legislative attention.

The first of these targets was capital appreciation or deep discount bonds that had been first authorized under the Municipal Finance Act in the 1980s. In 1993, school districts had been specifically prohibited from issuing their bonds for capital purposes at a discount or with an accretion rate of greater than 10%. These types of bond issues were favored by school districts for a short period in the 1980s in order to restructure outstanding debt service. With the deferral of debt service through issuance of refunding bonds in the form of capital appreciation bonds, the school districts were often successful at persuading local voters to increase operating millages and thereby increase their state school aid. Act 34 continued the restrictions imposed in 1993 by restricting discounts on

municipal securities to 10% unless the Department of Treasury made certain determinations necessary to allow use of this bond structure technique.

The second target of Act 34 was municipal refundings. While these had been restricted by administrative rules since the early 1980s, Act 34 incorporated a statutory presumption against issuing refunding obligations unless a net present value savings could be obtained by the refunding. Exceptions could be granted by the Department of Treasury if the refunding was required by law, was necessary to reduce or eliminate restrictions applicable to the refunded obligation, or was necessary to avoid a potential default.

Act 34 continued authorization of a variety of finance techniques that the legislature had previously approved. Among those are the 1984 authorizations of advance refunding bonds and variable rate obligations that were payable on demand or prior to maturity. Advance refunding obligations enabled municipalities to take advantage of falling interest rates and lower debt service on obligations that would mature or be callable years in the future. Prior to 1984, the law had limited the purposes for which refunding bonds could be issued and required that the refunding bonds be issued within six months of the maturity date of the bond to be refunded (a "current refunding").

The authorization of variable rate demand obligations conferred upon all municipalities a power that had been previously granted to counties and county treasurers for delinquent tax anticipation notes. Variable rate demand obligations were required to be additionally secured to assure that funds would be available to pay the obligation when made payable prior to maturity by demand of the issuer (a "call") or holder (a "put") if a remarketing of the obligation at that time failed.

Other changes incorporated into Act 34 included the authority to issue obligations to pay premiums or establish funds for losses of a municipal self-insurance pool and interest rate swap agreements.

## The School Bond Loan Fund

One of the more innovative and perhaps least understood Michigan school support programs has been the School Bond Loan Fund Program (SBLF). This program was embodied in a constitutional amendment proposed by the legislature and adopted by the electors on 4 April 1955 and is now contained in a somewhat different form in the 1963 Michigan Constitution as Article IX, §16.

## Background

Before 1932 Michigan school bonds were issued as full faith and credit unlimited tax obligations of a school district, which meant the district could levy taxes in the amount necessary to pay debt service with no constitutional or statutory limit on the amount of taxes levied. In November 1932, the electors amended the Michigan Constitution to create a constitutional limit on property taxes levied for all purposes (including debt service). The limit was that property taxes could not exceed fifteen mills of assessed valuation of the property, with an overall limit of fifty mills (the 15–50 mill limitation). This limitation could be increased for a period of not more than five (5) years to not more than fifty mills (including the automatically allowed fifteen mills) by a two-thirds vote of the electors or when provided by charter of a municipal corporation. The Michigan Supreme Court subsequently construed this limitation to apply to school districts, counties, and regular townships, but not to those governmental units with charter tax rate limits such as cities and villages and later charter townships.

This constitutional provision was amended in 1948 to increase the number of years the limitation could be increased from five (5) to twenty (20) and reduce the vote required to a majority vote. Since the 15–50 mill limitation applied to debt service taxes, it was necessary that the limitation be increased each time bonds were proposed by an amount and for a number of years necessary to pay the debt service on the bonds.[13] Before the 1948 amendment, it was almost impossible to issue bonds in any significant amount because of the two-thirds vote requirement and the five-year limit on the number of years the increase could be voted. As a result only a few small school bond issues were sold, and very few school facilities were financed by debt issuance.

Pressure to change the limitation grew during and after World War II, in part because Michigan's population increased due to migration into the state and the postwar increase in the birth rate. These demographic changes and the exodus of people from larger cities to the suburbs began to create a serious shortage of school facilities in many communities, and initially led to the 1948 amendment.

## The Constitutional Provisions

Even with the 1948 changes, it became obvious in the early 1950s that many school districts still would be unable to issue bonds to build new facilities and provide the additional operating costs needed to serve the burgeoning school enrollment. To address these problems, Article X, § 27, the first of the school bond loan constitutional amendments, was adopted. It gave the state power to borrow funds not to exceed $100,000,000 (SBLF bonds) for the purpose of making loans to school districts for the payment of debt service on school bonds.[14] The amendment further provided that if the debt service tax levy necessary in any year on bonds qualified to participate in the SBLF exceeded thirteen mills of the state equalized valuation of the district, the state must loan the amount of excess to the district, provided all loans so made did not exceed an aggregate of $100,000,000. After a school district received a loan, it was required to levy thirteen mills until its qualified bonds were retired and SBLF loans repaid. Further, the amendment removed the 15–50 mill limitation on taxes levied for the payment of school bonds with at least a twenty-five-year last maturity. This made Michigan school bonds into obligations paid from taxes levied in whatever amount necessary to pay principal and interest without application of any statutory or constitutional tax rate limitation. These school bonds thus became unlimited tax bonds.

After adoption of the SBLF amendment, most school bonds were issued under that provision as unlimited tax bonds.[15] As the SBLF program developed, it became apparent that serious flaws existed. Since the program was immensely popular, the $100,000,000 limitation on state borrowing and lending was soon consumed or committed. Further, the thirteen-mill levy before a subsidy loan could be obtained was deemed to be too high in certain districts where, because of rapid enrollment growth, large millage increases were required to provide additional operating expenses. Finally, the twenty-five-year maturity requirement was unnecessarily long in some cases and resulted in longer bond issues with higher interest costs.

As a result, another constitutional amendment was proposed and approved by the electors in 1962. This amendment removed the $100,000,000 state bonding limitation and authorized the state to borrow whatever amount was necessary to meet program requirements. It continued the thirteen-mill limitation threshold for subsidy borrowing, but authorized the legislature to reduce the amount of the levy to something less than thirteen mills. The loan provisions were strengthened by requiring that the state lend and a school district borrow the amount necessary, making it a duty on the part of each that could be enforced by legal action brought to compel performance of these obligations. The new provision continued the exception from the 15–50 mill limitation on taxes levied for school debt service and provided that taxes levied for the payment of school bonds were to be without limitation as to rate or amount, once again resulting in unlimited tax bonds.

The 1962 amendment was repeated almost verbatim in the new 1963 Michigan Constitution. In addition, the constitutional 15–50 mill tax rate limitation was removed by the 1963 constitution for taxes levied to pay debt service on obligations including those of schools, cities, villages, counties, and townships.

## The SBLF Program in Operation

The Michigan SBLF program now has been in existence for approximately forty-seven years. The program is designed to accomplish two goals. First, it provides the equivalent of a state guaranty for the prompt payment of debt service on all qualified school bonds, thus ensuring the qualified school bonds against a default. Second, the SBLF program subsidizes tax levy requirements for debt service for certain districts where the debt service levies were expected to be greater than acceptable norms. There has been only one loan by the state from the SBLF for payment of debt service on bonds which otherwise might have defaulted and no default in repayment of SBLF monies loaned to school districts.[16]

Many districts that do not need debt service subsidies still take advantage of the SBLF to obtain the state guaranty for bond marketing purposes, which reduces the interest rate on the borrowing. In each case the school district's obligations are considered "qualified" school bonds. Participating districts are also guaranteed a floor millage for debt service in case of a future major reduction in the district's state equalized valuation.

It is now widely understood in the financial markets that a qualified Michigan school bond is in effect guaranteed by the state. With the state's full faith and credit behind them, qualified Michigan school bonds carry ratings equal to the state's.[17] This results in significant interest cost savings for most school districts in Michigan, since few districts carry a rating equal to or higher than the state's.

The SBLF program has been widely, but not universally, used within the state. Some districts, after a cost analysis, have determined that the increase in construction costs required by compliance with the state prevailing wage act was greater than the savings produced by qualifying the bonds, and accordingly did not use qualified bonds.[18] In addition, in those few districts with credit ratings equal to or greater than that of the state, qualification of their bonds was not advantageous, and the SBLF program was not used.

Critics of the SBLF program in the early 1990s contended that the program encouraged profligate borrowings by school districts and exposed the state to a future liability for school districts that had little likelihood of ever repaying the loans it received from the SBLF. While the state constitution permitted state statutes to require up to thirteen mills be levied by a local school district for repayment of its qualified bonds prior to borrowing from the state, state law had set this threshold at a substantially lower rate. School districts with more stagnant taxable valuations and larger capital needs were able to issue more and more qualified school bonds even though they were unable, in the foreseeable future, to levy sufficient taxes at the reduced threshold to repay even the interest accruing each year on the past SBLF loans to the school district.

Amendments to the 1961 PA 108 in 1991 substantially revised the threshold millage level requirements for school district qualified bond issues sold after 1 October 1991. Under these new requirements school districts are required to levy the maximum thirteen mills permitted under the state constitution unless the state treasurer determined that a lower millage level, not less than seven mills, would allow the school district to repay both its qualified bonds and loans from the SBLF within sixty months from the final maturity date of all outstanding qualified bonds. In conjunction with these 1991 amendments, the Department of Treasury also revised its requirements for qualification for school district bonds to require that a school district exhibit the ability to repay any borrowing from the SBLF within sixty months of final bond maturity at a millage rate of not more than thirteen mills. In assessing compliance with this requirement, the Department of

Treasury utilizes a taxable value growth rate equal to the prior five-year average over the first five years after issuance of the bond and to the lesser of 3% or the prior five-year average for the remaining years of the bond. These limitations, coupled with need assessment criteria that base facility needs upon enrollment projections over the next five years, serve to limit the size of a school bond issue eligible for qualification under the SBLF program.

Even with the 1991 amendments, a risk remains that dramatic declines in taxable valuations and increases in school tax collection delinquencies could produce defaults on qualified bonds, forcing the state to make payments on those school district obligations. Because the SBLF is designed as a revolving loan program, the essence of these criticisms is that the state may suffer a significant mismatch in the debt service requirements of the state on its general obligation bonds issued to fund loans to school districts and in the repayments scheduled from school districts on those loans.

In a different vein, the program continues to inadequately address the needs of school districts with stagnant property values, aging facilities, and growing student populations. Under current law, some school districts in these circumstances will be incapable of participating in the SBLF program because of their inability to levy, at the rates required, sufficient taxes to annually repay even the interest due on the state loans to the district.

## State Debt Burden Issues with the SBLF

The SBLF program has been funded through SBLF borrowings by the state. At 31 December 2002, the state had outstanding $480,670,000 of bonds and notes issued to fund loans to school districts. As a greater and greater percentage of school bond proposals are successful, this amount will likely increase in coming years.

As of 31 December 2002, local school districts had outstanding bonds in a principal amount of $12,202,395,000 that had been qualified for participation in the SBLF. One hundred and fifty-five school districts, as of 31 December 2002, were either receiving or repaying loans from the SBLF. Outstanding principal and interest amount of loans from the SBLF as of 31 December 2002 equaled $608,119,330.

These statistics point up two significant issues relative to the state's financial condition and debt

burden. First, the operation of the SBLF fund produces more than a $100 million mismatch between the amount of state obligations outstanding that were issued to fund loans to school districts in the SBLF program and the receivable owing from school districts. A similar mismatch occurred in 1991. At that time the state provided a monetary incentive for school districts to refinance their qualified bonds debt owing to the state and use their refunding bond proceeds to pay off their outstanding loans from the state. With these repayments the state was able to defease its outstanding SBLF bonds and retain the excess as realized unreserved fund balance.

The second issue presents a greater risk factor for the state. To date the City of Detroit School District has not been a borrower from the SBLF. In 2003, however, the Detroit School District has issued the last series in its current $1.5 billion bond authorization. With that series, the Department of Treasury anticipates that the Detroit School District will reach the thirteen-mill level of levies necessary to be eligible to borrow from the SBLF for debt service that collections from the thirteen mills will not cover. Significant capital needs remain for the Detroit School District, and voter authorization may be sought for up to $5 billion in improvement. If such an authorization is approved, allowed to be qualified under the SBLF program, and subsequently issued over a ten-year period, Department of Treasury preliminary projections show that all debt service on the new bond issues would be borrowed from the SBLF for over thirty years. In addition, the Detroit School District would have a balance owing to the SBLF of over $29 billion in 2047, and that amount would continue to rise for years thereafter. This means that Detroit not only would not be able to repay the principal of such a large borrowing within thirty years, but also that it would in fact have an increasing balance because the interest costs would increase faster than its ability to repay.

## Federal Tax Law Changes

A final note is appropriate relative to the impact of federal tax law upon state debt issuance. Changes in federal tax laws and regulations have affected the volume of bonds issued in Michigan by imposing substantive regulations upon the issuance of tax-exempt bonds. However, these changes have primarily affected the amount of private activity bonds issued rather than publicly supported debt.

Although there had been a longtime assault on tax-exempt bonds, and questions as to whether they should exist at all, the debate finally shifted in the 1960s from whether tax-exempt municipal bonds should exist to how to control the issuance of municipal bonds that benefited private industry.[19] This debate, fueled by the sheer volume of corporate bonds issued, sparked a response from the U.S. Department of Treasury in early 1968. The IRS announced its intent to refuse tax exemption to bonds for which a private corporation would use "a major portion" of the proceeds.[20] Congress responded by passing the first federal restrictions on Industrial Development Bonds (IDBs), the Revenue and Expenditure Control Act of 1968. The act was the first attempt to define "public purpose" and the first restriction on issuance for private corporations. The private-use test defined by the statute deemed bond interest taxable if more than 25% of the proceeds were to be used to benefit private business. The Revenue and Expenditure Control Act of 1968 caused IDB volume to drop from $1.6 billion to $24 million in the year following the bill.[21]

Further limitations were enacted in 1979 and 1982. In 1979 Congress limited the size of each IDB to $10 million. Any manufacturer who benefits from an IDB is prevented from making any capital investments exceeding $10 million for three years prior to and following the issuance of the IDB.[22] The Tax Equity and Fiscal Responsibility Act of 1982 (TEFRA) imposed new restrictions on IDBs, including but not limited to public approval and reporting requirements.[23] In an effort to control the volume of IDBs issued, Congress included in TEFRA differential treatment of IDBs and governmental bonds

The 1984 Deficit Reduction Act went further and placed limits on the amount of private-purpose tax-exempt bonds states can issue. The first three years for which the limits were in place, states could issue a total of $150 times the state's population or $200 million, whichever was larger. Starting in 1987, the maximum was lowered to $100 per capita or $200 million.[24] The 1986 Tax Reform Act decreased the cap to $50 per capita or $150 million from 1988 through 2000. In 2000, legislation raised the cap back to $62.50 per capita or $187.5 million per state in 2001 and $75 per capita or $225 million in 2002. The caps now are set to increase with the rate of inflation, starting in 2003.[25]

These volume caps have had the greatest impact of any regulation on the volume of private activity tax-exempt bonds issued. Although there have been alterations made to the various categories of deals that are allowable as tax-exempt private activity bonds, the full allocation under the volume cap is issued by most states each year. By definition, the volume cap defines the maximum amount of tax-exempt private activity bonds that can be issued, and thus the regulations subordinate to the volume cap may affect the ratio of certain types of bonds within the cap, but do not actually alter the volume of bonds issued.

## Conclusions and Future Policy Issues

Data relative to Michigan's debt position as compared to that of other states is difficult to assess. Variables unique to each state's fund structure, constitutional debt limitations, and local funding responsibilities hinder an accurate assessment of one state's debt position as compared to another's. However, even a cursory review of the statistical evidence available leads to the general conclusion that Michigan is below average in the amount of tax-supported debt outstanding, particularly with respect to direct general fund-supported debt. Perhaps the most significant evaluation of whether the state's debt burden is in pace with its financial capacity are the relatively high ratings assigned to the state by Moody's and Standard & Poor's.

On a municipal level, constitutional and statutory limitations act to constrain municipal debt issuance. Recent legislative actions have modernized Michigan statutes and allow municipal issuers to take full advantage of contemporary debt structures with minimal supervision. It remains too early to determine whether this unregulated approach will serve the objective of protecting municipal credit as well as it was served by former law.

On the state's horizon looms a serious challenge to evaluate and manage its School Bond Loan Fund program. The current inability of certain school districts to access the program penalizes schools, often in developed urban areas, with limited tax base growth, costly facility needs, and a stable school age population. However, if these school districts are permitted to issue qualified school bonds without limitation, the demand upon the state for loans to repay school bond debt service and the need for the state to issue more and more bonds to fund these loans will result in a substantial increase in the state's general obligation debt, requiring that the state dedicate a greater and greater percentage of a limited pool of general fund revenues to debt service.

∎

## NOTES

Acknowledgement and appreciation is extended to the members of the Public Finance Practice Group of Miller, Canfield, Paddock & Stone, P.L.C as a whole, and to Joel Piell, Stratton Brown, and Bree Popp Woodruff in particular, whose collective expertise and individual assistance is reflected in the efforts of this chapter. All should share any credit for this chapter while any mistakes or misstatements are purely of our own doing.

1. In the Matter of the Request of the Governor for an Advisory Opinion on the Constitutionality of Act No. 346 of the Public Acts of 1966, 380 Mich. 554, 563–64 (1968).
2. *County Drain Commissioner of Oakland County v. City of Royal Oak*, 306 Mich. 124, 142; 10 NW2d 435, 441 (1943).
3. "No evidence of state indebtedness shall be issued except for debts authorized pursuant to this constitution" (Article IX, Section 12). "The credit of the state shall not be granted to, nor in aid of any person, association or corporation, public or private, except as authorized in this constitution" (Article IX, Section 18).
4. In re Request for Advisory Opinion on Constitutionality of 1986 PA 281, 430 Mich 93, 119; 422 NW2d 186 (1988) (quoting Advisory Opinion re Constitutionality of 1966 PA 346, 380 Mich 554, 564; 158 NW2d 416 [1968]).
5. Sec. 14. To meet obligations incurred pursuant to appropriations for any fiscal year, the legislature may by law authorize the state to issue its full faith and credit notes in which case it shall pledge undedicated revenues to be received within the same fiscal year for the repayment thereof. Such indebtedness in any fiscal year shall not exceed 15% of undedicated revenues received by the state during the preceding fiscal year and such debts shall be repaid at the time the revenues so pledged are received, but not later than the end of the same fiscal year.

   Sec. 15. The state may borrow money for specific purposes in amounts as may be provided by acts of the legislature adopted by a vote of two-thirds of the members elected to and serving in each house, and approved by a majority of the electors voting thereon at any general election. The question submitted to the electors shall state the amount to be borrowed, the specific purpose to which the funds shall be devoted, and the method of repayment.

   Sec. 16. The state, in addition to any other borrowing power, may borrow from time to time such amounts as shall be required, pledge its faith and credit and issue its notes or bonds therefore, for the purpose of making loans to school districts as provided in this section.
6. *In re Advisory Opinion on Constitutionality of Act No. 346 of Public Acts of 1966*, 380 Mich. 554, 158 N.W.2d 416 (1968).
7. "It is of interest to note that article 8, § 20 [now Mich. Constitution Article 7, § 21], in directing the legislature to provide by general law for the incorporation of cities and villages, provides that such law shall *restrict their powers of borrowing money and contracting debts. . . .* [It does not] follow from the express power conferred upon defendant to acquire and improve its utility that a power is to be implied to borrow for the purpose." *Sebewaing Industries Inc. v. Village of Sebewaing*, 337 Mich 530, 544–45 (1953).
8. The Unlimited Tax Election Act, 189 P.A. 1979, also authorizes municipalities to make unlimited tax pledges and levy taxes over and above statutory and charter limitations if such pledges have been approved by the municipalities' electors.
9. Section 611(1) of the Revised Municipal Finance Act precludes the issuance of refunding oblations unless there is a net present value interest savings resulting from the issuance. The Department of Treasury has some discretion over whether this provision may be waived upon the showing of certain statutory exceptions.
10. PA 202, MCL 131.1 et seq.
11. PA 34, MCL 141.2101 et seq.
12. PA 202; Ch II,§2; MCL 132.2.
13. At the time, state law required that when a unit of government subject to the 15–50 mill limitation issued voted bonds it had to vote an increase in the proposed tax rate limitation. County and township bonds issues at this time had the same characteristics, and all were called "limited tax bonds."
14. The $100,000,000 was a limitation on the borrowed amount and not debt that could be outstanding, so that as SBLF bonds were repaid, the borrowing power did not recharge.
15. Soon after the program commenced, a New York bond counsel raised questions as to the validity of the constitutional amendment. The Michigan Supreme Court upheld in all respects the SBLF constitutional provision.

16. This occurred where the assessed valuation of a major taxpayer was being contested and through a court order debt service taxes were paid by the taxpayer and deposited in escrow. The taxpayer ultimately lost the case and paid the taxes to the school district.

17. The difference between the state's ratings and most school districts' ratings without qualification should be as much as two steps. This could result in a 0.25% to 0.50% lower interest rate for qualified bonds.

18. The prevailing wage act applies where state funds are involved. It has been determined that the SBLF guarantees are equivalent to state funds for purposes of that act.

19. Joan Pryde, "The Ongoing Battle: Almost 70 Years of Assaults on Tax-Exempt Municipals," *Bond Buyer*, 26 September 1991, 84.

20. Ibid.

21. Ibid.

22. Ola Kinnander, "IDB Issuance Plummets: Survey Blames Investment Limit, Economy," *Bond Buyer*, 3 June 2002.

23. Walter A. Abernathy, Editorial, "Tax Reform Unfair to Airports," *Bond Buyer*, 23 September 1986, 2.

24. Mark Fury, Mary G. Gotschall, and Kent Pierce, "Most States Find 1984 IDB Limits Easy Going but Scurry for Reserves," *Bond Buyer*, 18 December 1984, 1.

25. Kinnander, "IDB Issuance Plummets."

# 31

# Fiscal Relations among the Federal Government, State Government, and Local Governments in Michigan

*Ronald C. Fisher and Jeffrey P. Guilfoyle*

The structure of government in Michigan and the fiscal interrelationships among those governments are the topics explored in this chapter. Four issues seem particularly relevant. What is the governmental structure in Michigan, in terms of types, number, and size of governments, and how are fiscal responsibilities divided among those jurisdictions? What are the economic or fiscal rationale for and implications of the variation in types and sizes of governments? How are grant funds distributed from the federal government to governments in Michigan and from the state government to the various local governments, and does that distribution reflect or advance particular policy objectives? Finally, are the intergovernmental aid system and the fiscal structure of government consistent with each other?

## The State-Local Governmental Structure

### Types, Numbers, and Sizes of Governments

Individuals in Michigan are members of at least four subnational governments. Individuals are residents of the State of Michigan, obviously, and of one of the eighty-three counties that fully cover the state. In addition, each individual is a member of at least one general-purpose local government, either a city or township, and one special-purpose local government, a school district.[1] Beyond this, township residents may also be members of a village, as villages are established within township areas as a means to enhance public services beyond those provided through the township. Finally, individuals also may be members of additional special-purpose governments, such as community college districts, planning and development regions, airport authorities, mass transit authorities, and water districts, among many others.[2]

Counties are the largest local governments in Michigan. Although counties with functioning governments do not exist in every state, the structure of counties in Michigan is fairly typical of the substate governmental structure in most states. For instance, Michigan's county structure is compared to that in Illinois and Ohio in table 31.1. The size of counties is relatively consistent among these three states, although in Michigan there is somewhat less variation in county size than in Illinois but somewhat more variation than in Ohio.

Within each county, all area not part of an incorporated city is part of some township, so the cities and townships also fully cover the area of the state. Yet the structure of cities and townships is quite different, as shown in table 31.2. Cities are

**TABLE 31.1**

## County Governments in Selected Great Lakes States

|          | # of Counties | State Area     | Average County Population | Average County Area | Average County Density   |
|----------|---------------|----------------|---------------------------|---------------------|--------------------------|
| Michigan | 83            | 56,809 sq. mi. | 116,769                   | 686 sq. mi.         | 183 persons per sq. mi.  |
| Illinois | 102           | 55,593 sq. mi. | 117,105                   | 546 sq. mi.         | 178 persons per sq. mi.  |
| Ohio     | 88            | 40,953 sq. mi. | 126,748                   | 466 sq. mi.         | 280 persons per sq. mi.  |

SOURCE: U.S. Bureau of the Census (1999).

**TABLE 31.2**

## Cities and Townships in Michigan, 2000

|                                             | Cities         | Townships      |
|---------------------------------------------|----------------|----------------|
| Number                                      | 273            | 1,242          |
| Total Population                            | 5,146,791      | 4,789,634      |
| Percentage of state population              | 51.8%          | 48.2%          |
| Average population size                     | 18,853         | 3,856          |
| Coefficient of variation for population size| 3.3            | 1.9            |
| Total area                                  | 1,867.8 sq. mi.| 54,886 sq. mi. |
| Average area                                | 6.8 sq. mi.    | 44.2 sq. mi.   |

SOURCE: Author compilation based on data provided by the Michigan Department of Management and Budget.

**TABLE 31.3**

## Distribution of Cities and Townships by Size, 2000

|                 | City           |                | Township       |                |
|-----------------|----------------|----------------|----------------|----------------|
|                 | Population     | Area (sq. mi.) | Population     | Area (sq. mi.) |
| Maximum         | 951,270        | 138.8          | 95,648         | 592            |
| 80th percentile | 19,661         | 7.2            | 4,264          | 38.6           |
| 60th percentile | 8,233          | 4.2            | 2,464          | 35.7           |
| Median          | 5,536          | 3.3            | 1,929          | 35.4           |
| 40th percentile | 3,933          | 2.7            | 1,562          | 34.9           |
| 20th percentile | 1,988          | 1.6            | 870            | 32.1           |
| Minimum         | 326            | 0.5            | 10             | 0.1            |

SOURCE: Author compilation based on data provided by the Michigan Department of Management and Budget.

less numerous than townships (273 vs. 1,242), and each individual city on average is smaller in area than typical townships. However, because cities tend to have been established in the more urban or densely populated regions of the state, cities tend to serve larger populations than do townships. Despite having one-sixth the area on average, the average city has a population more than four times as great as the average township. To put this in perspective, although cities occupy only a very small fraction of Michigan's land area (3.3%), nearly 52% of Michigan residents reside in a city.

More detailed information about the sizes (by both population and area) of cities and townships is shown in table 31.3. It is apparent that there is substantial variation in sizes of both cities and townships, especially in population. The city with the largest population and land area is Detroit, with more than 18% of all city residents and about 10% of the state's population. The largest 20% of cities, fifty-five of them with population of approximately 20,000 or more, account for nearly 73% of total population in cities and nearly 38% of the entire population of the state. The substantial degree of concentration of population in cities is reflected by the relatively small size of the median-sized city, with a population of only about 5,500 residents.

As noted, townships tend to be substantially larger than cities geographically but with much smaller populations. As a consequence, townships tend to have much lower population density than cities. However, the highest-population township, Clinton Township in Macomb County, would rank as the tenth-largest city in the state and has a density comparable to those of cities in the top ten. Similarly, there are forty townships with population of at least 20,000 people, which is comparable to the top 20% of cities. Yet even in these larger townships, population density is lower than that for the average city in almost every instance. Still, if the fifty-five cities and forty townships with population of 20,000 are combined, these ninety-five municipalities account for more than 51% of the state's residents (but only about 6% of localities).

The overall local government structure in Michigan—involving subdivision into counties, municipalities, and special-purpose districts including schools—is fairly typical of that in many areas of the United States.[3] The large number of localities, the great variation in local government size, and the resulting concentration of population in a relatively few localities similarly is not unusual. A Citizen's Research Council analysis (1999) reports that Michigan ranks fourteenth among the states in terms of the number of local units of government. Michigan is the eighth-largest state by population and the twenty-second-largest state by land area, so the state's rank in terms of number of localities seems consistent with our relative population and area. Even among metropolitan areas there often is substantial variation in the number and thus size of localities. As illustrations, Fisher and Wassmer (1998) report that there are substantially more municipalities in the Chicago, Philadelphia, St. Louis, and Pittsburgh metropolitan areas than in the Detroit region, while there are substantially fewer localities in such places as Boston, San Francisco, and Washington, as compared to Detroit.

There seem to be two obvious conclusions and one important implication from these data. First, the governmental structure in Michigan is characterized by relatively few, large municipalities and by many quite small ones. In essence, about 100 larger cities and townships represent slightly more than half of the state's residents, with the other half of the population spread among the other 1,400 cities and townships. Second, the

**TABLE 31.4**

### Distribution of School Districts by Size

| | School District Enrollment | School District Area (sq. mi.) |
|---|---|---|
| Average | 2,910 | 105 |
| Coefficient of Variation | 2.4 | 1.2 |
| Maximum | 149,348 | 1,742 |
| 80th Percentile | 3,547 | 151 |
| 60th Percentile | 2,101 | 90 |
| Median | 1,636 | 73 |
| 40th Percentile | 1,309 | 58 |
| 20th Percentile | 707 | 23 |
| Minimum | 1 | 1 |

SOURCE: Author compilation of data provided by Michigan Department of Education.
NOTE: 544 school districts.

largest townships are very similar in both population and population density to the largest cities. Thus, an important policy perspective may be that the distinction between "large" and "small" municipalities (however defined precisely) may be more meaningful economically and fiscally than the political distinction between "cities" and "townships."

As with cities and townships, the size distribution for school districts reflects the existence of a few relatively large districts and many smaller ones, as shown in table 31.4. Obviously, the Detroit School District is a major outlier, with enrollment more than five times greater than the second-largest district (149,000 in Detroit compared to Utica at about 28,000). In total, there are twenty-six school districts with enrollment at 10,000 or greater. Yet enrollment levels fall off quickly after that, as the district at the eightieth percentile of the distribution has an enrollment of about 3,550. Even more telling, the median district enrollment size is about 1,600. There is a similar but less pronounced pattern for district area. An important characteristic of school districts in Michigan is that their boundaries are in many cases not consistent with city, township, or even county boundaries. Thus, the school district of median area is larger than the median area township, and much larger than the city of median size. As with townships, because there are many school districts with large area but low enrollment, pupil density is very low in these cases.

For some issues, the size of the school district may be less important than the size of individual schools within those districts. For districts with multiple elementary schools, which is quite common, or for larger districts with multiple middle or high schools, issues of cost and scale economies relate more to the size of each individual school building than to the size of the district. This potentially important policy issue is considered later in the chapter.[4]

## Fiscal Responsibilities of Local Governments

The legal and political distinctions among counties, cities, townships, and villages—the set of general-purpose localities in Michigan—are presented in the 1999 Citizen's Research Council report and in chapter 13 of this volume. Briefly, counties were established initially to serve as agents or extensions of state government, and indeed many county functions continue as illustrations of that intent. Included here are recording and record-keeping functions, public safety and criminal justice activities, as well as public health, welfare, and highway responsibilities. Beyond these broad functions, however, counties also are authorized to provide park and recreation services; water and air transportation facilities; local public safety services; utility services such as water, sewer, and waste disposal; and libraries. In theory, then, county services can serve either as substitutes for or as complements to services provided by municipalities.

In practice, however, the fiscal activity of county governments in Michigan is concentrated heavily toward those functions that represent administrative extensions of state government. As reported in chapter 13, county direct general expenditure is allocated to the following functional categories, in order of magnitude: health and hospitals (29.4%), judiciary and corrections (13%), highways (13%), public welfare (8.3%), police (4.1%), sewerage (4.1%), natural resources (3.7%), and air transportation (2.8%). It seems clear, therefore, that while counties can and do provide some services that are of local benefit in nature, the great bulk of spending by county governments goes for functions that represent broader, state responsibilities and benefits.

The Citizen's Research Council (1999) reports that initially it was similarly intended that townships would provide a set of state-mandated services, while cities would provide those services in addition to local services intended to benefit local residents. Yet under current policy in Michigan, cities, townships, and villages all have authority to provide essentially the same broad set of public services, including police and fire protection, roads, parks and libraries, water and sewer systems, and waste collection, as well as authority to adopt planning and zoning restrictions. So, by public service authority at least, there is little substantive difference between cities and townships (especially charter townships) at present.

The actual fiscal practice of cities and townships does indeed reflect spending in all of these functional areas, although expenditure by cities is more than five times as great as aggregate spending by townships, even though each type of municipality has about half of the state population as residents. Thus, city governments account for nearly 85% of public spending by these two classes of municipalities. Although cities and townships have similar fiscal authority, the relative importance of the different functions varies between cities and townships. Cities spend a substantially larger fraction of their budgets on police protection, roads and highways, and parks than do townships, while townships allocate a substantially larger share of their budgets to fire protection and sewer systems than do cities. More detail about spending by cities and townships may be found in chapter 13.

Cities and townships also differ in their legal authority and limitations for generating tax revenue. One major distinction is that cities (but not townships) may levy local income taxes, and twenty-two cities currently do so. In addition, cities are constrained by different property tax rate limitations than are townships. Generally, cities are limited to twenty mills for property tax rates, plus limited additional mills for garbage collection, libraries, services for the aged, and public safety employee pensions. In contrast, charter townships are limited to ten mills for property tax rates, while other (general law) townships are constrained by the overall state constitutional rate limits (and average less than three mills per township).

Villages occupy a unique role in the structure of local government in Michigan. When a village is incorporated, the land area remains a part of the surrounding township and the village residents also remain residents of the township (participating in both township and village elections as well as paying taxes to and receiving benefits from both jurisdictions). Thus, villages are a way for residents to augment or supplement the public services provided through the township. For instance, a village may have a separate police force in addition to township police, a village might provide professional fire protection while the township has a volunteer service, or a village might provide water service while other township residents rely on wells. There are 262 villages in Michigan, all relatively small in population, area, and public spending. It seems appropriate, therefore, to think of villages as "official" types of voluntary community associations for the purpose of jointly providing some specific community services or facilities. In that sense, villages share some characteristics with condominium or neighborhood associations, although they enjoy official municipality status and do have limited taxing authority.

## Optimal Government Structure Theory

The type of governmental structure in Michigan and most other states, with four separate but overlapping layers of jurisdictions—the state, counties, municipalities, and special-purpose governments—naturally raises questions about design and efficiency. Would it be preferable to have fewer layers of government or at least a clear division of functional responsibility among the layers? Within any layer—say municipalities—would it be preferable to have fewer, larger (or more, smaller) jurisdictions? To put it differently, what are the advantages and difficulties of the somewhat complicated structure that is in place?

One simple way to think about an "ideal" structure for government is to imagine a set of services whose benefits are confined to specific geographic areas. Services whose benefits cover a very large area might be provided by states, those whose benefits are more limited in area might be provided by large, substate regions (such as counties), and those services whose benefits are very limited in geographic scope might be provided by localities (such as cities). This simple view suggests that the size of a government should correspond to the geographic area of benefits. Yet there are three obvious difficulties with this simple notion. First, it is often not feasible to identify a fixed geographic area for benefits of a government service, particularly if there is substantial mobility of residents, consumers, and businesses.[5] Second, even if benefits are confined to fixed areas, the concept could require a great many different layers or levels of government if the benefit area for different services varies widely. One might imagine one government for defense, one for welfare, one for education, one

for police protection, one for utilities, and so on. Finally, individuals may desire different amounts or qualities of specific services, which would require that there be a number of governments at each level to allow for variation in the quantity or quality of service provided.

The most common complaint or reaction to the typical structure of state-local government is to ask whether it makes sense to have a great number of localities, many of which are quite small. The answer may be yes, if the type, amount, or quality of public service demanded by individuals varies substantially. The greater the variations in what individual consumers want from government, and the more consumers with similar wants can be grouped together, the stronger the case for having many small local governments. If all consumers desire the same amount and type of service, then there is no reason for more than one government. Conversely, if a single government serves consumers with different demands for government service, many will be dissatisfied because the amount or quality of service provided by the government will be different than the amount or quality desired.

There is evidence that this factor has contributed to the observed structure of local government in different states and metropolitan areas. For instance, Fisher and Wassmer (1998) report that for large metropolitan areas there is strong evidence that there are more (smaller) local governments in areas with greater variation in incomes, ages, and races, suggesting that different demands for public services contribute to a more decentralized governmental structure. Gramlich and Rubinfeld (1982), Nelson (1990), and Martinez-Vazquez, Rider, and Walker (1997) have reported similar results.

This perspective suggests directly why the opportunity to establish villages to augment services provided by large townships may make perfect sense. It also helps us understand why it might be efficient to have several hundred cities and townships in the Detroit metropolitan area and a very large number across the state, even though those numbers imply that some or even many of the localities will be small.

Having many small localities does create other problems, however, that must be balanced against the opportunity to satisfy diverse consumer desires. Chief among these is the issue of spatial externalities (often called spillovers), which arise when the spatial distribution of the costs or benefits of government services is not confined to the jurisdiction boundaries of the providing governments. Nonresidents thus either pay part of the costs or enjoy part of the benefits of a government's service. Spatial externalities can cause a government's choices about taxes and spending to be inefficient from the viewpoint of the entire society. If there is a spillover of costs, residents underestimate the true social cost and demand too much of the good or service. Likewise residents often do not consider the benefits of their public services to those living outside the jurisdiction. As a result, too little of the service is provided from the viewpoint of the entire society. It follows that the smaller the local governments, the more likely that these types of externalities or spillovers will arise.

The possibly conflicting objectives of having governments big enough to avoid cost or benefit spillovers but small enough to allow uniform desired amounts of public service suggests a trade-off between those two factors. Another possibility is to address the externality or spillover problem through a set of appropriately designed intergovernmental grants, as discussed in the following section. In contrast, if jurisdictions are exporting part of the costs of local services to others, then taxes may be called for.

Another aspect of benefit spillovers, separate from efficiency, is a fairness concern, because nonresidents of a local jurisdiction may benefit from services provided and funded by residents of those localities. If the local public services are subject to any congestion, so that nonresident use reduces the possibility of resident use (such as might be the case for roads, parks, or some other services), then it seems fair that nonresidents pay for the services they consume (and prevent residents from consuming). This potential problem created by many small localities is also an issue that might be resolved by appropriate intergovernmental grants.

A second potential problem with having many small localities or with having multiple levels of local government is that it may create additional political costs for citizens and additional administrative overhead, as well as make understanding of the fiscal system more difficult. Administrative costs might include the costs of elected and appointed officials and the overhead (buildings, supplies, utilities) to support those officials. Costs to citizens include becoming informed on issues and candidates, attending hearings, and voting in various elections. As the number of governments increases, either because there are multiple levels

or because jurisdictions are small at any given level, these types of costs can rise. In addition, if there are many small localities as well as different levels of government providing a given service (say, police protection), individuals may find it more difficult to determine which jurisdiction is responsible for a particularly good or poor resulting level of service (i.e., public safety). Conserving on these types of costs and improving understanding and accountability are additional factors that must be considered.

A third concern raised by having small-sized localities is the possibility that the cost *per person* for a given amount of public service may be greater than if provided by larger units. Reasons most often given for potential economies of scale include the elimination of duplication of inputs, increased coordination, and economies in purchasing. Evidence for the existence of economies of scale for the goods and services usually provided by state and local governments is not conclusive, however. For services with capital-intensive production, such as water, sewer, electric, and gas utilities, substantial economies seem to exist. In those instances public- or private-sector consolidation to produce those services is common to avoid duplication of expensive capital structures. Economies of scale may be difficult to obtain for other very labor-intensive local government services. Hirsch (1970) suggests that traditional services such as police and fire protection are examples of horizontally integrated services, with many production "plants" under control of one government. He concludes that scale economies appear to be unimportant for such horizontally integrated services.[6]

Even in those instances where scale economies are important, cost savings often can be achieved without changing the number and size of localities. Governments too small to achieve all economies of scale on their own often can arrange to purchase the desired good or service for their residents from governments or private firms that are large enough to exhaust all economies. By contracting with private firms or other governments and through joint purchasing agreements, governments can provide the amount and type of services desired by a small population *and* enjoy the cost advantage of scale economies in production. In other instances, only those aspects of a service where large-scale cost advantages exist may be centralized. The common 911 emergency dispatching service is an example. To the extent that such opportunities exist, scale economies are removed as an economic issue for the optimal size and structure of government.

## Intergovernmental Grants in Michigan

Intergovernmental grants are an important component of the finances of Michigan's state government and the governments of Michigan's local units. In FY 1999, 22.7% of state government general revenue in Michigan came from the federal government, while 48.2% of aggregate local government revenue came from state government grants. Relatively little local government revenue (3.2%) came from the federal government, and only 1.1% of state revenue resulted from payments by local units of government.[7]

## Roles for Intergovernmental Aid

Intergovernmental grants can serve a number of different functions in a federal system of government, some of which offset the difficulties created by a decentralized governmental structure.[8] First, by substituting the granting government's tax structure for that of the recipient government, intergovernmental grants can be used to take advantage of more efficient tax systems and economies of scale in tax collection. If the tax structures used by the granting government are more efficient than the ones that would be used by recipient governments, this tax substitution improves governmental efficiency. This could happen if mobility is much greater among local jurisdictions than among states, so that a tax levied statewide might generate fewer inefficiencies than a set of similar local taxes. Furthermore, the administrative cost of a statewide tax may be far lower per dollar collected than if all local governments in a state levied their own separate taxes. Therefore, it is often beneficial for the state to collect a particular tax and return the proceeds to local governments, rather than allowing the local governments to collect or administer individual taxes themselves. This is at least part of the rationale for revenue-sharing programs.

Second, properly structured grants can offset the effects of spatial externalities on government fiscal decisions by covering some production or provision costs. For instance, if jurisdictions are providing services that generate substantial benefits for nonresidents (police protection or road maintenance, for example), then aggregate benefits may be underestimated and too little of the service may be provided. An intergovernmental grant can be used to induce the local government to provide more of that specific service, as efficiency requires. Grants for this purpose should be matching grants that reduce the *marginal* cost of the service to the providing government, with the grant share of *marginal* cost equal to the nonresident share of *marginal* benefits. In addition, however, because the grant funds are generated from taxes collected by the granting (state) government, those nonresidents who benefit from the service end up paying for part of the cost. Thus, the grant serves a fairness purpose, as well.

Third, intergovernmental grants can be used to redistribute resources between regions or local units. Thus, intergovernmental grants sometimes are suggested as a method of explicit income redistribution for equity or political reasons. Taxes collected by the state government may be allocated to local governments in amounts inversely proportional to income or property value, resulting in an implicit transfer from taxpayers in higher-income jurisdictions to governments (and implicitly taxpayers and service beneficiaries) in lower-income jurisdictions.

Finally, redistribution among jurisdictions through grants can also serve an efficiency goal. Individuals may move among local communities to avoid taxes or gain services. Yet if the new residents pay less than the average cost of services they consume, existing residents face either service reductions with constant taxes or higher taxes to maintain services. The potential migrants have no incentive to include those costs imposed on other residents in their decision about whether to relocate, so the distribution of population among localities may become inefficient. Again, intergovernmental grants may be used to resolve this difficulty. Grants to high-tax-rate or low-service localities may forestall some of the migration in search of lower taxes or more services and contribute to a more efficient structure of local government.

As we shall see, federal aid to Michigan seems designed to offset externalities, encouraging spending on roads, education, and especially health care provision for low-income individuals. Unrestricted aid from Michigan's state government to local units of government is paid from the state's sales tax. While this aid does take advantage of economies of scale in tax collection, the program's primary goal seems to be redistribution of resources among localities.

### Federal Aid to Michigan State Government

As noted, federal aid provides more than one-fifth of Michigan's state government revenue. Michigan's state government received $9.5 billion in federal aid in 2000, ranking eighth among the states. On a per-capita basis, however, the $955 in federal aid per person ranked Michigan thirty-third among the states. Federal aid to Michigan was equal to 3.3% of personal income, ranking thirty-second among the states. This disparity in ranking is a result of the fact that a substantial component of federal aid to states is distributed in a manner inversely proportional to state per capita personal income.

The aid the state government receives from the federal government almost exclusively consists of funds earmarked for specific purposes. Funds for Medicaid spending represent the largest component of federal aid by far, accounting for 41% of federal aid to Michigan. Other important programs include federal funds for highways (9%), family support programs (8%), food and nutrition services (6%), housing (6%), and elementary and secondary education (5%). This is illustrated in figure 31.1.

Federal aid to Michigan state government has

grown at an annual rate of 5.9% since 1984, almost twice the rate of inflation. Over this time period, grants for Medicaid spending have grown at an average annual rate of 9.7%, with Medicaid's share of overall federal aid rising from 23.4% to 41.0%. Annual growth has also been strong in funds for elementary and secondary education (12.4%), housing programs (8.6%), and highway spending (8.1%). Grants for spending on family support payments have trailed inflation, growing at an annual rate of just 0.8% since 1984. As a result, the share of total federal aid spent on family support payments has fallen by half, from 17.1% in 1984 to just 7.1% in 2000.[9]

Medicaid is a joint federal and state program that provides health care services to low-income individuals. More than 10% of the state's population currently receives health care coverage through Medicaid. Medicaid procedures and funding are discussed in detail in chapter 9. However, Medicaid deserves mention in this chapter as it is by far the largest source of federal aid to the state, accounting for over 41% of federal aid to Michigan.

The federal share of Medicaid costs for each state is based on the state's relative per-capita income, with lower-income states receiving a higher federal matching rate. The federal matching rate ranges between 50% and 83%, with Michigan receiving reimbursement for just over half of its expenditures. Although the matching grant reduces the marginal cost to states of providing medical services, no attempt is made to adjust the matching rate to the marginal cost or benefit of service provision.

Between 1990 and 2000, Michigan's expenditures on Medicaid grew an average of 10.2% per year, far exceeding the 5.9% growth in total state expenditures.[10] As a result, Medicaid's share of total state spending in Michigan increased from 14% to 19%. Medicaid expenditures will grow in coming years and thus to consume a large portion of the state's marginal budget dollars. For instance, one estimate suggests that expenditures on prescription drugs, a substantial factor in increased costs, are expected to grow at an average annual rate of 12.7% over the next ten years.[11]

Like many states, Michigan has attempted to minimize the impact of growing Medicaid expenditures by using a number of special financing techniques. These techniques take advantage of imprecise definitions of health care expenditures in Medicaid's regulations in order to increase the federal matching dollars that flow into the state.

**FIGURE 31.1**

Distribution of Federal Aid to Michigan State Government

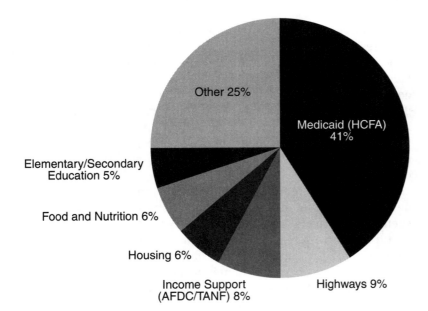

Source: U.S. Bureau of the Census (2001a).

**TABLE 31.5**

**State Aid to Local Governments, Michigan and the United States, 1996–97**

|  | State Aid as a Percentage of General Revenue | State Aid Excluding Education as a Percentage of General Revenue | State Aid as a Percentage of Taxes | State Aid Excluding Education as a Percentage of Taxes |
|---|---|---|---|---|
| **Michigan** | | | | |
| All localities | 49% | 29% | 192% | 99% |
| County | 35% | 35% | 175% | 175% |
| City/village | 24% | 24% | 67% | 67% |
| Township | 23% | 23% | 62% | 62% |
| All general purpose local governments | 29% | 29% | 99% | 99% |
| **U.S.** | | | | |
| All localities | 35% | 25% | 91% | 35% |
| County | 33% | 27% | 94% | 75% |
| City/village | 21% | 15% | 49% | 36% |
| Township | 20% | NA | 33% | NA |
| All general purpose local governments | 26% | NA | 65% | NA |

SOURCE: U.S. Bureau of the Census (2002).

Although total Medicaid expenditures grew at an average annual rate of 10.2% between 1990 and 2000, the state General Fund expenditure for this function rose by just 4.4% per year. The *FY 2003 Executive Budget* notes that these special financing arrangements have generated more than $14 billion for Michigan since 1991. Changes in the federal regulations may greatly reduce Michigan's ability to leverage federal dollars in the future. As a result, Michigan will have to either dedicate significantly more resources to Medicaid or reduce benefits.

## State Aid to Local Governments

Michigan utilizes state aid to local units of government to a substantially greater degree than do most other states. In 1997, aid from the state government accounted for 49% of local government revenue in Michigan, ranking Michigan second-highest among the fifty states. Among all states, state aid as a percentage of local revenue ranges from a high of 51% (New Mexico) to a low of 12% (Hawaii) and averages 35% for all states (see table 31.5). The state aid share of local revenue in Michigan is relatively high partly due to the unusually large state role in funding local K–12 public schools. Even excluding education funding, however, the share of local government rev-

enue accounted for by state grants was 29% in FY 1997, ranking Michigan fifth among all states. Among other states, the state aid share of local revenue (excluding education) ranged from 5% (West Virginia) to 33% (Wisconsin and California), with an average of 25% and a median value of 15%.[12] This reliance on state grants by local units of government is possibly both a result of the fact that and a reason why Michigan is one of only eleven states whose local units do not raise any revenue via local sales taxes.[13]

Focusing only on general-purpose localities, state grants accounted for about 35% of general revenue for counties, 24% for cities and villages, and about 23% for townships, as shown in table 31.5. Yet this aggregate perspective is a bit deceiving because state aid importance varies by the population size of the locality, especially among cities (table 31.6). State grants represent one-third of general revenue for the City of Detroit, but only about 20% of revenue for the remainder of cities and villages. Looking at the aggregate picture from table 31.6, excluding Detroit it appears that state grants account for a slightly greater share of revenue in smaller communities.

Intergovernmental aid payments to local governments also comprise a substantial share of the state government budget. The Citizen's Research Council of Michigan (2000, 2) estimates that almost three-fifths of all state-levied taxes, fees,

TABLE 31.6

**Distribution of Local Government Revenue by Type of Jurisdiction and Population, 1996–97**

| | Municipalities | | | | | | Townships |
|---|---|---|---|---|---|---|---|
| | All | Detroit | 100,000–200,000 | 25,000–100,000 | 10,000–25,000 | < 10,000 | All |
| Number of units | 534 | 1 | 7 | 36 | 46 | 444 | 1242 |
| State grants | 23.8% | 33.3% | 21.2% | 18.6% | 18.4% | 20.6% | 22.7% |
| Federal grants | 6.1% | 11.5% | 4.0% | 4.6% | 2.0% | 3.7% | 1.6% |
| All own-source funds | 69.1% | 53.8% | 74.7% | 75.6% | 78.6% | 74.9% | 74.7% |
| Taxes | 35.4% | 32.2% | 31.8% | 40.2% | 38.9% | 35.1% | 36.6% |

SOURCE: U.S. Bureau of the Census, Government Finances, 1997.
NOTE: Municipalities includes both cities and villages, as defined by the Bureau of the Census.

and other charges are returned to local units of government. The primary reason for this magnitude of state aid is the substantial aid to local school districts, which is by far the most important component of state aid to local governments. As a result of the school finance reforms of 1994, the bulk of public K–12 financing in Michigan is provided by the state government, with aid for local education representing roughly two-thirds of all state aid to local units of government (see figure 31.2). The share of the state budget distributed to local governments remains above the level that is constitutionally mandated (see chapter 33).

FIGURE 31.2

**Distribution of State Aid to Local Governments, 2000**

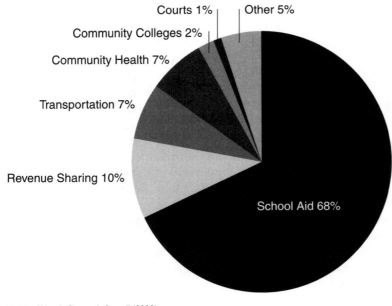

SOURCE: Citizen's Research Council (2000).

Unrestricted aid from the state government to counties, cities, villages, and townships under the State Revenue Sharing Act is the next-largest category of state aid, amounting to 10% of total state aid. In FY 2001, $1,555.4 million in aid under this program was distributed to local units of government, with $228.7 million (15% of the total) paid to county governments, $381.3 million (24% of the total) to townships, and $945.4 million (61% of the total) to cities and villages. Other important categories of state aid to Michigan's local governments include funds for transportation spending (7%), community health programs (7%), community colleges (2%), courts (1%), and miscellaneous other programs that distribute funds to local units of government (such as funds from the convention facility tax, the Health and Safety Fund, the airport parking tax, and the mobile communications fee).

*State Revenue Sharing.* The $1,555.4 million distributed as unrestricted aid to cities, villages, townships, and counties as revenue sharing funds in FY 2001 represented 4.0% of the state's budget and 6.9% of the state's revenue from taxes. Revenue sharing payments have increased by about 172% since 1980, which translates to average annual increases of about 8%. Yet because revenue sharing is tied to state tax collections, revenue sharing grants actually decreased in four of those years. In FY 1997, these payments represented approximately 13% of city and village revenue, 21% of township revenue, and 3% of county revenue.

Michigan's unrestricted revenue sharing program began in the 1930s with the redistribution of revenue collected from liquor license taxes. Over the years the program has been expanded, sometimes to replace revenue lost to local units due to state tax changes, and sometimes simply to increase aid to local units of government. For example, when the single business tax (SBT) was enacted in 1975, a share of SBT revenue was returned to local units to make up for the revenue lost from the prior local property tax on business inventories. When the state income tax was enacted in 1967, 11.5% of the revenue from the new tax was returned as aid to local units of government.[14]

Today, revenue sharing payments are made only from state sales tax revenue but arise from two separate legal sources. Constitutional payments are required under Article IX, Section 10 of the State Constitution, which specifies that 15% of the 4% state sales tax be distributed on a per capita basis to cities, villages, and townships. Because the aggregate state sales tax rate is now 6%, the constitutional provision effectively redistributes 10% of aggregate state sales tax revenue. Additional statutory revenue sharing payments are made based on formulas defined in the revenue sharing statute. Prior to 1998, statutory revenue sharing payments were made using funds from the state's income, sales, intangibles, and single business taxes, with distribution to counties, cities, villages, and townships based on population and a "relative tax effort" formula.[15] The statutory provisions for revenue sharing to localities were changed substantially in 1998. These grants are now based entirely on state sales tax revenue and are distributed by new formulas that are gradually being phased in, as explained in detail in the following. Revenue sharing to counties was, and is still, distributed on a per capita basis. Counties also still receive payments for the reimbursement that was enacted when the SBT eliminated the property tax on inventories.

Since 1998, the statutory portion of state revenue sharing has been paid using 21.3% of revenue from the 4% portion of the state sales tax. Combined with the constitutional provision, then, 36.3% of the 4% portion of the sales tax, or 24.2% of total sales tax revenue generated at a 6% rate, is allocated to revenue sharing.[16] Cities, villages, and townships receive 74.94% of statutory revenue sharing. The remaining 25.06% of statutory revenue sharing is distributed to counties on a per-capita basis.[17]

The 1998 revision of the statute established new formulas for distributing the statutory portion of revenue sharing funds. Three new formulas—one based on population weighted by relative taxable property value, one based on population adjusted by type of locality, and one

designed to provide a minimum guaranteed property tax yield—are being phased in over ten years beginning in FY 1999. The gradual phase-in is intended to moderate the impact of the change. For 1999, 90% of statutory revenue sharing funds were to be distributed based on the local unit's percentage share of total statewide statutory revenue sharing payments distributed in 1998 under the old relative tax effort formula, and the remaining 10% using the three new formulas. In each subsequent year, the share of revenue sharing distributed using the 1998 percentage shares from the old formula declines by 10 percentage points and the share distributed under the new formulas increases by 10 percentage points. Therefore, statutory revenue sharing payments will be based fully on the new distribution formulas in FY 2008.[18]

It is important to note that the language in the statute establishing the new revenue sharing allocation formulas seems to apply only through 2007, the end of the ten-year phase-in period. Thus, it is not clear whether the provisions actually "sunset" at that time, whether the general allocation system will continue without some of the special aspects, or whether the issue will have to be acted upon again by the legislature. One issue of particular interest is the fixed revenue sharing allocation amount to the City of Detroit (explained in the following). If the separate provision expires, the magnitude of grant to the city could decrease substantially without other action.

There are also two special provisions in the new procedure. First, the growth in revenue sharing that any local unit receives from one year to the next is capped at 8%. Any revenue made available as a result of the 8% growth limit is distributed to the local units receiving the least growth, creating a minimum growth rate. An exception to the 8% cap is made for local units for which the 2000 Census shows population growth of more than 10%. Second, the total revenue sharing payment to the City of Detroit, including both the constitutional and statutory amounts, is frozen for ten years at its FY 1998 level of $333.9 million.[19]

The 1998 changes made to revenue sharing have greatly increased the complexity of this primary state grant program. The combination of having three new formulas, a ten-year phase-in, and a payment growth limit of 8% applying only to units with population growth under 10% makes it difficult to make broad generalizations about the impact of these changes. Two aspects seem clear, however. One long-run impact is to reduce

**TABLE 31.7**

**Revenue Sharing Population Weights**

| Unit Type | Population | Weight |
|-----------|-----------|--------|
| Township | 5,000 or less | 1.00 |
| Township | 5,001 to 10,000 | 1.20 |
| Township | 10,001 to 20,000 | 1.44/3.60 |
| Township | 20,001 to 40,000 | 4.32 |
| Township | 40,001 to 80,000 | 5.18 |
| Township | More than 80,000 | 6.22 |
| | | |
| Village | 5,000 or less | 1.50 |
| Village | 5,001 to 10,000 | 1.80 |
| Village | More than 10,000 | 2.16 |
| | | |
| City | 5,000 or less | 2.50 |
| City | 5,001 to 10,000 | 3.00 |
| City | 10,001 to 20,000 | 3.60 |
| City | 20,001 to 40,000 | 4.32 |
| City | 40,001 to 80,000 | 5.18 |
| City | 80,001 to 160,001 | 6.22 |
| City | 160,001 to 320,000 | 7.46 |
| City | 320,001 to 640,000 | 8.96 |
| City | More than 640,000 | 10.75 |

SOURCE: Citizen's Research Council of Michigan (2002).

reliance on relative tax effort in determining distributions and to increase the impact of population. Second, the phase-in, growth limit, and City of Detroit provision clearly have minimized the immediate distributional impact. Still, it is important to understand the details of the distribution system as it now exists.

The first of the new formulas is the so-called taxable value formula, which creates a set of population weights based on a locality's relative taxable property value. A locality's share of the relevant portion of state revenue sharing, $_{Ri}$, is determined by $[V_s/V_i][POP_i/POP_s]$, where $V_i$ is per capita taxable property value in locality $i$, $V_s$ is per capita taxable property value for the state, $POP_i$ is population in locality $i$, and $POP_s$ is state population.

Thus, a local unit with a per capita taxable value equal to one-half the state's per capita taxable value would receive twice as much money per person as a unit with per capita taxable value equal to the state average.

The "unit type and population formula" distributes funds on a per capita basis, with population weights determined by the type of local unit and its population. Local units with larger populations are given greater weights (as shown in

**FIGURE 31.3**

**FY 2001 Revenue Sharing Distribution**

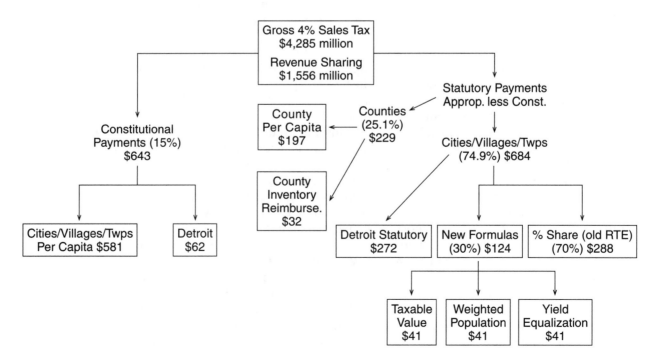

SOURCE: Author compilation.

table 31.7). In addition, for a given population, cities are given a greater weight than villages, which in turn are given a greater weight than townships. The spread in the weights is substantial, so that larger cities may receive as much as ten times per person what small townships receive. For distribution purposes in this formula, large townships are treated like cities. If a township has a population greater than 10,000 and provides a minimum level of police, fire, water, and sewer services, the city population weights are applied.

The final new formula is designed to guarantee a "minimum yield per capita" from each mill of local property tax effort, up to a maximum of twenty mills. A guaranteed tax base is calculated based on the maximum combined state and local per capita taxable value that could be supported if all of the statutory revenue sharing for cities, villages, and townships were distributed to units below the guaranteed base. The full yield equalization payment would equal the local tax rate times the difference between the guaranteed per capita tax base and the per capita taxable value for the local unit and thus apply only to units with per capita property value below the guarantee. Typically, about one-half of the local units qualify for a yield equalization payment.

This complicated distribution of revenue sharing funds for FY 2001 is summarized in figure 31.3. Sales tax revenue generated from the four percentage-point rate totaled $4,285 million, and $1,556 million was distributed as revenue sharing.[20] Constitutional revenue sharing comprises 15% of the sales tax revenue, or $643 million.

Counties received 25.1% of the statutory payments, $229 million in FY 2001, with the great majority of that amount distributed on a per-capita basis (and a small amount distributed for inventory reimbursement). The remaining 74.9% was distributed to cities, villages, and townships. Revenue sharing for the City of Detroit is fixed at $334 million per year. Because Detroit received $62 million in constitutional revenue sharing payments in FY 2001, its statutory payment was set equal to $272 million.

The remaining statutory payments are split between the percentage share allocation derived from the relative tax effort formula that existed prior to 1998 and the three new distribution formulas. In FY 2001, 70% of the revenue sharing allotment was distributed to cities, villages, and townships based on their share of the FY 1998 RTE payments and the remaining 30% was distributed

through the new formulas. Thus, only about 8% of aggregate revenue sharing payments in FY 2001, about $124 million, was distributed based on the three new formulas.

*Transportation Grants.* Another important component of aid between different governmental levels in Michigan is transportation revenue. An in-depth discussion of transportation-related issues in Michigan is provided in chapter 16. However, the importance of intergovernmental aid in the funding of transportation services merits a brief discussion in this chapter as well.

All state fuel taxes and vehicle registration fees, which totaled over $1.9 billion in FY 2000, are deposited into the Michigan Transportation Fund (MTF). Resources from this fund are distributed among city, county, and state transportation agencies for the construction, maintenance, and operation of Michigan roads. Transportation revenues are distributed under the Michigan Transportation Fund Act. In FY 2000, more than $900 million in MTF revenue was distributed to cities, villages, and counties. These funds represented approximately 10% of general revenue for most counties, and in some counties more than 30% of general revenue.[21] These transportation funds in counties are managed by the county road commissions, which operate with a degree of independence from the rest of county government.

The transportation fund procedures result in revenue to local units being distributed through a set of formulas based on the local unit type, population, and miles of roads. Deductions are made from the MTF for public transportation (approximately $160 million) and a number of other specific purposes (approximately $200 million). The balance of the fund is distributed as follows: 39.1% to the state trunkline fund, 39.1% to the county road commissions, and 21.8% to the cities and villages of the state. Townships do not receive state road money.

Distributions to counties are made for primary (75%) and secondary (25%) roads. The primary road distribution is based on the share of motor vehicle registration taxes collected in the county and on the miles of primary roads. The secondary road dollars are based on the relative size of the nonurban population residing in the county. The city and village distribution is based on the population of the city and village relative to the state's urban population and the miles of road in the municipality.[22]

## TABLE 31.8

### Source of Local Transportation Revenue

| Year | State Aid Amount | State Aid Share | Locally Raised Amount | Locally Raised Share | Federal Aid Amount | Federal Aid Share | Other Revenue Amount | Other Revenue Share | Total Amount | Total Share |
|------|------|------|------|------|------|------|------|------|------|------|
| **County Revenues** | | | | | | | | | | |
| 1990 | $360.5 | 55% | $96.8 | 15% | $51.0 | 8% | $142.0 | 22% | $650.2 | 100% |
| 1991 | $358.3 | 57% | $75.8 | 12% | $54.2 | 9% | $144.3 | 23% | $632.6 | 100% |
| 1992 | $382.1 | 56% | $85.1 | 13% | $61.6 | 9% | $148.1 | 22% | $677.0 | 100% |
| 1993 | $431.4 | 58% | $88.9 | 12% | $72.9 | 10% | $156.1 | 21% | $749.3 | 100% |
| 1994 | $449.4 | 56% | $92.6 | 12% | $88.8 | 11% | $170.3 | 21% | $801.2 | 100% |
| 1995 | $472.5 | 57% | $94.5 | 11% | $93.7 | 11% | $171.5 | 21% | $832.2 | 100% |
| 1996 | $446.6 | 55% | $111.3 | 14% | $72.8 | 9% | $186.1 | 23% | $816.8 | 100% |
| 1997 | $472.8 | 55% | $111.5 | 13% | $72.3 | 8% | $209.1 | 24% | $865.7 | 100% |
| 1998 | $560.7 | 57% | $168.9 | 17% | $67.6 | 7% | $181.7 | 19% | $979.0 | 100% |
| 1999 | $578.8 | 57% | $152.5 | 15% | $72.0 | 7% | $209.7 | 21% | $1,013.0 | 100% |
| **City and Village Revenues** | | | | | | | | | | |
| 1990 | $204.4 | 51% | $152.0 | 38% | $15.1 | 4% | $28.6 | 7% | $400.0 | 100% |
| 1991 | $202.5 | 51% | $142.8 | 36% | $13.7 | 3% | $41.5 | 10% | $400.6 | 100% |
| 1992 | $211.9 | 51% | $159.5 | 38% | $14.5 | 3% | $30.5 | 7% | $416.3 | 100% |
| 1993 | $233.1 | 57% | $139.3 | 34% | $14.6 | 4% | $21.3 | 5% | $408.3 | 100% |
| 1994 | $249.7 | 56% | $144.7 | 33% | $28.4 | 6% | $22.1 | 5% | $444.9 | 100% |
| 1995 | $256.0 | 52% | $168.8 | 35% | $24.2 | 5% | $39.6 | 8% | $488.6 | 100% |
| 1996 | $250.9 | 50% | $168.0 | 33% | $41.1 | 8% | $46.8 | 9% | $506.9 | 100% |
| 1997 | $258.6 | 51% | $184.9 | 36% | $32.4 | 6% | $35.0 | 7% | $510.9 | 100% |
| 1998 | $314.9 | 55% | $198.5 | 35% | $27.5 | 5% | $27.7 | 5% | $568.7 | 100% |
| 1999 | $325.9 | 54% | $222.2 | 37% | $24.7 | 4% | $28.8 | 5% | $601.6 | 100% |

SOURCE: Michigan Department of Transportation (2001).

Local governments also receive some transportation funds directly from the federal government, and in addition, localities can collect local revenues and issue debt. A recent history of local unit transportation revenue by source is presented in table 31.8.

The distribution formulas of PA 51 have been under review in recent years due to a sunset provision in the law. Various groups are seeking an increased share of state transportation funds. For example, the Michigan Township Association has proposed that townships should have control over some local roads and receive a share of the MTF distribution. Universities have also lobbied for a share of the MTF to assist in the maintenance of roads under their jurisdictions.[23]

Michigan also receives substantial federal aid for transportation purposes. Michigan received $766 million from the federal government for highway construction in FY 1999. Federal highway dollars received by Michigan increased substantially in the 1990s, rising by 105% between 1992 and 1999, compared to a 61% increase for the country as a whole.

The relatively large increase in federal transportation support to Michigan was the result of two factors. First, in 1997 Michigan increased the state tax on gasoline from $0.15 to $0.19 per gallon, allowing the state to leverage more federal matching dollars. Second, the federal Transportation Equity Act of the 21st Century (TEA 21) of 1998 provided Michigan with relatively more federal dollars than it had received under the old federal law.

Traditionally, Michigan has been a "donor" state, receiving fewer federal highway grant funds than its residents paid in federal motor fuel taxes. TEA 21 is more generous to donor states than its predecessor had been. In 1992, Michigan received approximately $0.54 in federal highway dollars for each dollar of federal excise tax paid. By 1999, this ratio had increased to almost $0.63 for every dollar of tax, a 17% increase. Over this time period Michigan's ranking among the states in terms of federal dollars received per dollar of federal tax paid increased from forty-first to thirtieth.

## Analysis of Governmental Structure and Intergovernmental Aid

### Intergovernmental Structure

Michigan has a substantial number of local units of government of varying sizes that provide, in theory, the opportunity for widely differing demands for local government services to be accommodated. That opportunity is restricted in practice, however, by the limited fiscal autonomy of those localities. First, about 30% of the revenue for general-purpose local governments in Michigan comes directly from the state government. State aid for these localities is essentially of the same magnitude as local taxes. Furthermore, as discussed in the following, revenue sharing grants (which mainly comprise state aid) are generally not closely related to either the fiscal responsibility of a locality or the cost of providing public services.

Second, the opportunity to levy additional local taxes is substantially constrained—by property tax rate limits, by constitutional provisions requiring voter approval for property tax changes within the rate limits, by the restricted local income taxes available only to cities, and by the absence of local sales tax options that are common in many other states. In a sense, then, Michigan has a very centralized governmental structure for generating revenue but a very decentralized structure for providing public services.

Third, important legal distinctions are drawn between cities and townships that have significant fiscal implications despite the fact that the variation *within* each local unit category may be more substantial that the differences between them. Even the largest-population townships, which tend to be charter townships, have different legal expenditure and tax authority than do cities, even very small cities. Yet state revenue sharing treats large townships the same as cities. Indeed, the largest townships are very similar in both population and density to the largest cities. The one hundred or so largest cities and townships (about sixty cities and forty townships, all with population of around twenty thousand or larger) represent slightly more than half of the state's residents. Thus, the state might want to consider several policy options. One is for the largest townships to be treated as, or even converted to, cities generally (as is done now with revenue sharing). Another, more radical, option is to set fiscal authority based on jurisdiction size rather than type (so that the largest cities and townships might be given equivalent fiscal authority as a distinctive group of localities).

### Revenue Sharing

Based on the distribution of revenue sharing funds among cities and townships for 2001, shown in tables 31.9 and 31.10, state revenue sharing provides a much larger share of revenue for smaller than for larger localities (excluding

---

**TABLE 31.9**

### Revenue Sharing Distribution to Cities and Townships

| Population | Number of Units | Per Capita Revenue Sharing Payments | Per Capita Taxable Value | Total Local Taxes Per Capita | Revenue Sharing as a Percentage of Taxes |
|---|---|---|---|---|---|
| Detroit | 1 | $351.00 | $7,620 | $665 | 0.53 |
| 20,000 or more | 91 | $124.39 | $26,300 | $354 | 0.35 |
| 8,000 to 19,999 | 127 | $110.07 | $27,803 | $277 | 0.40 |
| 4,000 to 7,999 | 178 | $94.09 | $25,185 | $161 | 0.58 |
| 2,000 to 3,999 | 365 | $87.49 | $26,602 | $129 | 0.68 |
| Less than 2,000 | 765 | $83.33 | $30,224 | $108 | 0.77 |
| TOTAL | 1526 | $134.02 | $24,942 | $308 | 0.44 |

SOURCE: Author compilation.

NOTES: 1. Total local taxes are the sum of property taxes levied by the local unit and income taxes levied by the local unit. Income tax total includes the Detroit Utility tax. 2. Revenue sharing information is for FY 2001. Taxable value information is for taxes levied in 2000.

## TABLE 31.10

**Revenue Sharing Allocations, Townships Compared to Cities**

| Population | Number of Units | Per Capita Revenue Sharing Payments | Per Capita Taxable Value | Total Local Taxes Per Capita | Revenue Sharing as a Percentage of Taxes |
|---|---|---|---|---|---|
| **Townships** | | | | | |
| 20,000 or more | 38 | $94.43 | $29,644 | $244 | 0.42 |
| Less than 20,000 | 1,204 | $80.38 | $28,119 | $94 | 0.86 |
| TOTAL | 1,242 | $84.68 | $28,586 | $134 | 0.63 |
| **Cities** | | | | | |
| Detroit | 1 | $351.00 | $7,620 | $665 | 0.53 |
| 20,000 or more | 53 | $138.30 | $24,748 | $415 | 0.33 |
| Less than 20,000 | 231 | $136.54 | $25,474 | $416 | 0.33 |
| TOTAL | 285 | $177.21 | $21,754 | $461 | 0.38 |

SOURCE: Office of Revenue and Tax Analysis, Michigan Department of Treasury.
NOTES: 1. Total local taxes are the sum of property taxes levied by the local unit and income taxes levied by the local unit. Detroit's total includes the local utility tax.
2. Revenue sharing information is for FY 2001. Taxable value information is for taxes levied in 2000.

Detroit). *Per capita* revenue sharing allocations rise with population and with per capita local taxes, although these two factors are highly correlated (i.e., localities with larger populations and greater population densities also tend to have higher per capita taxes). Yet the increase in per capita revenue sharing allocations is not proportional to the increase in local taxes. For instance, among the 91 cities and townships with population of at least twenty thousand (excluding the City of Detroit), revenue sharing represents about 35% of local taxes on average. Revenue sharing represents a much larger share of taxes for all of the identified locality groups with smaller populations. For instance, among the 178 cities and townships with population between four thousand and eight thousand (which is close to the median-sized locality), revenue sharing amounts to 58% of local taxes, on average.

Second, despite the fact that on average cities receive larger per capita revenue sharing allocations than do townships of similar population, revenue sharing allocations represent a smaller share of local taxes in cities (about 33%) compared to townships (42% to 86%). This occurs because cities collect greater amounts of local taxes and spend more on a broader range of local public services than do townships. It also seems clear that the differences among localities in per capita local taxes reflect differences in demand for local public services or differences in production costs for those services, rather than merely

differences in local property tax bases. Again, excluding Detroit, there are very small differences in per capita property tax bases among localities in the population size groups, but much larger differences in per capita local taxes.

Third, the City of Detroit is a special case with respect to revenue sharing (as it is in other aspects as well). Detroit's per capita allocation of $351 in 2001 is three to four times larger than that for other localities and amounts to more than 20% of total revenue sharing payments to all localities. Yet, per capita local taxes are also substantially higher in Detroit and the per capita property tax base much lower than in those other localities. Therefore, the revenue sharing allocation to Detroit is about 53% of local taxes, a share greater than for the other large cities in Michigan but about equal to that for the median-sized cities. From another perspective, Detroit would have had to levy more than forty-six mills in local property taxes just to collect an amount equal to its revenue sharing payment.

Recall that the current (2001) distribution of state revenue sharing reflected in tables 31.8 and 31.9 results from a blend of the previous allocation formula, which weighted local tax effort substantially, and the new formulas, which tend to focus more on property tax value and type of locality. Proponents of relative tax effort allocation formulas argue that tax effort illustrates a funding need for a local unit by illustrating either a desire for a higher service level, an inadequate tax base, or some combination of the two. However, many people are opposed to allocation based on local tax effort, arguing that these formulas reward local units for raising taxes and encourage an inefficient size of government.

Over time, therefore, it seems likely that the distribution of revenue sharing funds will tend to become skewed toward localities with smaller populations and less provision of local public services even more so than currently. Although per capita revenue sharing amounts are larger in localities with larger populations, the share of total revenue provided by revenue sharing is smaller in localities with larger populations. Once the new allocation system is dominant, the differences in per capita revenue sharing amounts among localities with different populations should become much smaller than now, as the allocation amounts to smaller, lower-spending localities increase relatively. Thus, the differences in the percentage of revenue provided by revenue sharing are expected to become larger. It seems hard to escape the conclusion, therefore, that the change in revenue sharing distribution formulas will provide a relative advantage to those localities with relatively smaller populations, which tend to be those located in rural areas.

From a policy perspective, it is not clear what fiscal or economic goal revenue sharing is designed to accomplish. For instance, if the goal of revenue sharing is to replace local taxes with state taxes on the presumption that state taxes are more efficient economically and administratively, then revenue sharing should be allocated proportionally to local tax bases or to local taxes collected. If the goal of revenue sharing is to redistribute resources to localities with lower tax bases or lower-income residents, then grants might be distributed inversely proportional to property value or per capita income. If the goal of revenue sharing is simply to provide equal support for public services to all citizens of the state, then presumably distribution should be based entirely on population (equal per capita amounts). If the goal of revenue sharing is to offset costs of providing public services that might be higher in some localities than others, then revenue sharing grants need to be distributed based on some measure of costs or on some factor associated with costs, such as population density.

In fact, of course, the revenue sharing allocation system in Michigan includes some aspects of all of the above, reiterating the point that the objective is not clear. This notion seems rein-

forced by the mechanisms used to implement the new allocation formulas, with phase-in over ten years, a limit on the degree to which grants can grow, and a special, fixed allocation to Detroit. Policy makers seeking big changes to the system and those who preferred the status quo ended up compromising by changing the distribution system, but not too much. It might be preferable to approach revenue sharing from the point of view of two questions. What primary objective does the state want to achieve with revenue sharing? And given that goal, are there explicit economic or fiscal reasons why Detroit's situation is substantially different, requiring a separate allocation system for that city?

## Annexation and Conditional Land Transfer Agreements

While the boundaries of Michigan's local units are relatively stable, they can change over time. Cities in Michigan can expand their territories by annexing land from neighboring townships. Petitions for annexation by a city are filed with the State Boundary Commission in one of three ways: (i) a city's legislative body can pass a resolution, (ii) landholders controlling 75% or more of the property to be annexed can petition, or (iii) a petition can be filed by 20% or more of the registered voters in the land being considered for annexation. Upon approval of the petition for areas with fewer than one hundred residents, the annexation is automatic and is not subject to referendum. If the area has more than one hundred residents, residents of the territories affected can petition to have the annexation order put on the ballot.[24]

The current annexation process can lead to strained relations between local units of government. Cities can annex contiguous vacant township land at the request of a landowner without township approval. Proponents of the current annexation process argue that it is important for economic development. Cities often provide services such as water and sewerage that are needed for certain types of development and are often not available in townships. By expanding these services to a wider geographic area, increased economic development may occur. Critics contend that the annexation options make it difficult for townships to conduct land use planning. A landowner whose development proposal is rejected by a township may petition a city to annex the land and grant the proposal or threaten the township with an annexation petition to get the rejection overturned.

Local governments in Michigan also have an option to engage in a more cooperative development approach under the 1984 Conditional Land Transfer Act.[25] Local units can enter into agreements that allow for the "conditional transfer" of land from one local unit to another for economic development purposes. The land does not need to be contiguous to the recipient government's boundaries, and land covered by an agreement is not subject to annexation. The agreements cannot exceed fifty years but can be renewed. The transferred land is subject to all of the taxes of the recipient government (usually a city). In addition, residents of the transferred land receive the services of the municipal government and may be subject to the recipient government's zoning and ordinances. In exchange for the conditional transfer, the transferring unit (usually a township) generally receives some form of revenue sharing from the recipient government.

For example, a city may be home to a company that wishes to expand on land in a neighboring township. With a land transfer agreement, the business could relocate to the neighboring township, and the city would extend any needed services to the land where the business relocated. The land would be subject to city taxes. A portion of these taxes would be shared with the township, with the exact sharing arrangement to be negotiated.

These agreements allow local units of government to engage in a more cooperative economic development process. However, the process is relatively new and thus new issues continue to arise. For example, because land covered by an agreement is not subject to annexation, some townships appear to have reached agreements with each other for the sole purpose of protecting land from potential annexation by neighboring cities.

## Contracting and Joint Provision

Joint purchasing and service contracting are other options that mitigate some of the potential problems associated with having many (small) localities. Joint purchasing opportunities, including traditional purchasing agreements as well as bond pooling, assist small localities in taking advantage of discounts from quantity purchases. Service contracting, either among governments or with private producers, can help small units achieve economies of scale in production, but can also be a way for small localities to have access to specialized services that may apply to only a subset of citizens.

One common example is agreements among local police and fire agencies to assist neighboring jurisdictions. Such agreements permit peak load demands to be met without permanent increases in the size or capacity of the local agency. These agreements also allow communities to provide specialized types of police and fire protection services—such as certain types of specialized investigative services, access to fire fighting equipment for high-rise buildings, access to equipment necessary for specific hazardous materials, and so on. Such services may simply be uneconomic for all units to acquire, given the costs and amount of expected use.

One challenge and opportunity for local officials and analysts is to discover or create new and innovative contract or service sharing opportunities similar in concept to the police and fire protection cases. For instance, one possibility that has not been used very extensively to date involves joint provision of certain educational services among school districts. As discussed previously in this chapter, school district sizes vary considerably, with 20% of districts in Michigan having fewer than seven hundred students. Even more importantly perhaps, about thirty public high schools in Michigan have fewer than two hundred students (or fifty per grade) and about seventy-five have three hundred students or less (seventy-five per grade). It is very difficult for districts with such small high schools to offer a full program of academic and co-curricular opportunities at reasonable cost. Multiple foreign languages, multiple tracks for academic subjects, advanced placement classes, and even certain athletic opportunities may be examples of programs that would be difficult to fund and operate in such small high schools. Joint provision may offer one possible solution (without the need for consolidating school districts). Indeed, joint provision among districts already occurs in spirit through programs offered by intermediate school districts, colleges and universities, and other similar institutions.

In the high school case, there are at least two ways in which joint provision might be implemented. The more limited option is for neighboring schools to agree to offer some specialized services for each other. Thus, one high school might offer Spanish for students in both schools while the other offers French classes for both. In this way students in both schools would have expanded academic options without requiring exceptionally small (and thus expensive) classes and without consolidating districts. A more extensive option is for the districts to operate one high school together. In this case, the districts could remain independent and operate separate elementary and middle schools; only the high school would be jointly operated. Rather than having two separate high schools of perhaps three hundred students each, for instance, there would be one school of six hundred, which again might permit a fuller academic and co-curricular program with the same total expenditure. This latter option would require some type of joint operating agreement that would specify the financial commitments of each district and a mechanism for reaching operating decisions.

These joint provision or contracting examples from education are not meant to be exhaustive or exclusive in any way. They are merely intended to illustrate the types of public service options that might be considered broadly given the highly decentralized structure of local government that exists in Michigan coupled with the highly centralized public financing system.

## Conclusion

This chapter has explored the structure of government in Michigan and the fiscal interrelationships among those governments. The governmental structure in Michigan is characterized by a relatively few, large municipalities and by many quite small ones. About one hundred larger cities and townships contain half of the state's residents, with the other half residing in the remaining fourteen hundred cities and townships. Spending on services tends to be concentrated in the more urban areas, with the state's cities spending five times as much on services as townships, despite having only half of the state's population.

Intergovernmental grants are an important component of public finance in Michigan, with federal grants accounting for 23% of state government revenue and state grants accounting for 48% of local revenue. Aid to local school districts is the largest component of state aid (68%) to local governments, followed by unrestricted aid to general-purpose governments (10%).

Michigan has a very centralized governmental structure for collecting revenue, but a very decentralized structure for providing services. Michigan

distributes aid to general-purpose local governments on the basis of complex formulas that were the result of political compromise. As a result, there is no clear policy goal being addressed by the state's revenue sharing program. This chapter suggests two questions for policy makers seeking to reform the system. First, what primary objective does the state want to achieve with its revenue sharing system? Second, given that goal, are there explicit economic and fiscal reasons to treat the City of Detroit separately from all of the state's other local units?

■

## REFERENCES

Carver, J. 2002. *House Bill analysis: House Bills 4720–4725.* Lansing, Mich.: House Fiscal Agency.

Citizen's Research Council of Michigan. 1997. Michigan highway finance and governance. Report No. 321. Lansing, Mich.: May.

————. 1999. *A bird's-eye view of Michigan local government at the end of the twentieth century.* Report No. 326. Lansing, Mich.: August.

————. 2000. *Michigan's unrestricted revenue sharing program: Retrospect and prospect.* Report No. 330. Lansing, Mich.: September.

*Facts and figures on government finance, 35th edition.* 2001. Washington, D.C.: Tax Foundation.

Fairgrieve, William. 2000. *Medicaid special financing payments and intergovernmental transfers.* Michigan House Fiscal Agency Forum, 6(1).

Fisher, Ronald C. 1996. *State and local public finance.* Chicago: Richard D. Irwin.

Fisher, Ronald C., and Karen Krastev. 1997. *Grand Rapids Metro Rebate project: Analysis of the cost and demand factors influencing local government expenditures.* East Lansing: Michigan State University, Report to the Grand Rapids Metropolitan Area Council.

Fisher, Ronald C., and Robert W. Wassmer. 1998. Economic influences on the structure of local government in U.S. metropolitan areas. *Journal of Urban Economics* 43:444–71.

Gramlich, Edward M., and Daniel L. Rubinfeld. 1982. Micro estimates of public spending demand functions and tests of the tiebout and median-voter hypotheses. *Journal of Political Economy* 90:536–60.

Hamilton, William. 2000. *Rewriting Act 51 funding transportation in Michigan: Present and future.* Michigan House Fiscal Agency Report. Lansing.

Harvey, Lynn R., and Gary D. Taylor. 2000. Conditional land transfer agreements: Michigan's alternative to annexation. Agricultural Economics Staff Paper 00–32. East Lansing: Michigan State University.

Hirsch, Werner Z. 1970. *The economics of state and local government.* New York: McGraw-Hill.

Lipson, Debra J., Michael Birnbaum, Susan Wall, Marilyn Moon, and Stephen Norton. 1997. *Health policy for low-income people in Michigan.* Washington, D.C.: The Urban Institute.

Martinez-Vazquez, Jorge, Mark Rider, and Mary Beth Walker. 1997. Race and the structure of local government. *Journal of Urban Economics* 41:281–300.

Michigan Department of Transportation. 2001. *Michigan transportation facts and figures—Finance.* Michigan Department of Transportation web page, *www.michigan.gov.*

National Association of State Budget Officers. 2001. *2000 state expenditure report.* Washington, D.C.: National Association of State Budget Officers.

———. 2002. *NASBO analysis: Medicaid to stress state budgets severely in fiscal 2003.* Washington, D.C.: National Association of State Budget Officers.

Nelson, Michael A. 1990. Decentralization of the subnational public sector: An empirical analysis of the determinants of local government structure in metropolitan areas of the U.S. *Southern Economic Journal* 57:443–57.

U.S. Bureau of the Census. 1999. *Government organization.* Vol. 1 of *1997 census of governments.* Washington, D.C.: GPO.

———. 2000a. *Compendium of government finances.* Vol. 4 of *1997 census of governments.* Washington, D.C.: GPO.

———. 2000b. *Finances of county governments.* Vol. 4 of *1997 census of governments.* Washington, D.C.: GPO.

———. 2000c. *Finances of municipal and township governments.* Vol. 4 of *1997 census of governments.* Washington, D.C.: GPO.

———. 2001a. *Federal aid to states for fiscal year 2000.* Washington, D.C.: GPO.

———. 2001b. *State and local finances by level of government: 1988–99. http://www.census.gov/govs/www/estimate.html.*

## NOTES

Fisher gratefully acknowledges the able research of Adam Pavlik. His work in collecting and tabulating information about the government structure in Michigan was invaluable. The findings and conclusions reported in this chapter do not necessarily represent the views of the Michigan Department of Treasury or the State of Michigan. Guilfoyle gratefully acknowledges Mark Haas and Constance Ross for their assistance in reviewing and editing drafts.

1. In addition to local school districts, Michigan also has "intermediate school districts," which provide services to the local school districts as well as some specialized services directly to individuals as a substitute for local schools. These intermediate school districts are coterminous either with counties or with multicounty groups.

2. The range of special-purpose districts is described more fully in Citizen's Research Council of Michigan (1999). See also chapter 13 in this volume. Some directly finance and provide services, while others serve as planning or coordinating bodies.

3. Of course, there is no official or required local government structure, so there are special features in some states. For instance, counties have few if any fiscal or functional responsibilities in the New England states, while counties are the dominant form of local government in Maryland, which has few functioning municipalities.

4. For information about other types of special districts in Michigan, see Citizen's Research Council of Michigan (1999).

5. Part of the issue here is defining what "benefit" means. In at least one sense, for instance, an individual might benefit from the existence of another county's parks even if that person does not visit those parks at present. The option to use those parks at some point in the future can be a very real benefit.

6. For instance, providing fire or police protection to a larger city simply requires having more fire or police stations, so cost per person does not change much.

7. These calculations are based on data from the U.S. Bureau of the Census (2001b).

8. For a more in-depth explanation of intergovernmental grants see Fisher (1996).

9. Unpublished data from the U.S. Bureau of the Census.

10. Figures are from the National Association of State Budget Officers (2000) and Lipson et al. (1997).

11. National Association of State Budget Officers (2002).

12. Compilation of data from U.S. Bureau of the Census (2000a).

13. Based on data from U.S. Bureau of the Census (1999).

14. Citizen's Research Council of Michigan 2000. This

publication provides an excellent history of the Glen Steil Revenue Sharing Program.

15. The tax effort of a local unit of government was defined as its total local tax collections (from property plus city income tax) divided by its taxable property value. A locality's relative tax effort (RTE) was defined as the local tax effort divided by the state tax effort. Statutory revenue sharing was distributed to cities, villages, and townships on a weighted per-capita basis, with the RTE ratio for the weights. A local unit with an RTE two times the state total received twice as much statutory revenue sharing per capita as a local unit with an RTE equal to the state average.

16. The total amount to be paid as state revenue sharing is appropriated based on the Consensus Revenue Estimate for sales tax collections. This amount acts as a cap on total revenue sharing payments. If the actual sales tax collections for revenue sharing exceed this amount the excess is returned to the state's General Fund. Because the legislature cannot statutorily restrict the amount of revenue sharing to be paid out under the constitutional provisions, if sales tax collections are greater than estimated, the constitutional amount of revenue sharing is increased to reflect actual collections and the statutory amount is decreased so that total revenue sharing payments do not exceed the appropriation. Any reductions to the statutory amount are made only to the amount to be paid out under the new formulas. The amount to be paid out under the old percentage share formula is not reduced.

17. As noted earlier, counties also receive inventory reimbursement payments for the funds they lost when the Single Business Tax replaced the property tax on inventories.

18. The actual amounts paid out under the new formula were less than these statutory amounts due to other provisions in the Revenue Sharing Act that divert money from the new formulas to the old formulas and to constitutional payments under certain circumstances. These provisions are explained in the text.

19. Detroit's level includes both the statutory and constitutional revenue sharing components. Because the statute cannot change the constitutional component, the constitutional component is calculated first. The statutory payment is then calculated by subtracting the constitutional amount from Detroit's total payment.

20. Note, the 4% sales tax total for revenue sharing cannot be calculated by strictly taking two-thirds of the total sales tax collected at 6%. Revenue sharing is computed using sales tax collections on a cash basis and the collections used to determine payment are slightly lagged from the state's fiscal year. In addition, an adjustment must be made for residential utilities that pay tax at only the 4% rate.

21. Total county general revenue for FY 1997 was compared with MTF distributions for counties for FY 1999. The transportation revenue averaged 15.5% of general revenue for counties, with a maximum value of 40%. Ten counties did not report general revenue and are not included in the totals.

22. For a more in-depth explanation of the formulas, see Citizen's Research Council of Michigan (1997).

23. Hamilton (2000, 15–16).

24. Procedures for annexation were taken from Carver (2002).

25. Much of this discussion is taken from Harvey and Taylor (2000).

# 32

# Miscellaneous Taxes in Michigan: Sin, Death, and Recreation

*Lawrence W. Martin*

## Introduction

This chapter discusses various revenue sources that have escaped consideration in the rest of this volume. Among them are taxes on tobacco products and liquor, gambling revenues, the inheritance tax, and some other charges, such as hunting and fishing licenses and the snowmobile tax or "registration fee," that fall mostly on recreational activities. The plan is to acquaint the reader with the main currents of economic thinking about each tax, briefly discuss the taxes themselves, and consider some potential reforms.

The first three taxes (on tobacco, liquor, and gambling) are often referred to as "sin taxes," with the implication that the taxed behaviors differ significantly from other more virtuous types of consumption expenditures, and that these behaviors merit special, higher taxes. The revenue yield from these sin taxes is substantial, amounting to nearly $1.5 billion, up more than 60% (23% in constant dollars) since 1990.

The traditional analysis of these taxes adopts the rational addiction model, in which "sinners" understand the consequences of their actions and, rationally, choose the alternative that best suits their preferences. According to this theory, there would be little reason to pick out these activities for extra taxation. On average, the share of expen-

diture that households devote to tobacco, alcohol, and gambling falls with income, and therefore economists criticize these taxes for their regressivity. True, some extra tax can often be justified by an appeal to the damage that they do to others via the externality argument, which can be applied to secondhand smoke, for example. Recent economic analysis of cigarette taxes in particular has taken a different approach, challenging the traditional rational addiction model. These new ideas have important implications for the setting of tax policy in this area. The third section of this chapter focuses on these revenue sources.

If smoking, drinking, and gambling are sins, then the inheritance tax might be said to fall upon the wages of sin. This tax is sometimes called the "death tax," in that it makes dying a taxable event. Precisely opposite to the sin taxes, inheritance taxes are, on the face of it, highly progressive, with the vast majority of taxes paid by the highest income groups. There is a large economic literature about this tax at the federal level, however, and it reveals some uncertainty about its incidence. Issues particular to taxing estates at the state level, on the other hand, have received little analysis. The most important fact about the inheritance tax, however, is that national policy is in a state of flux. Recent legislation has reduced the allowable state credit and scheduled the federal tax for elimination in 2010 (and, amazingly, restoration in 2011!). Michigan's options for this tax are the topic of the fourth section.

Finally, there are revenue sources that are paid by citizens for the use of certain publicly provided goods. For example, chapter 16 of this volume considers gasoline taxes, which can be seen as a user charge on those who travel on highways. This chapter picks up some of the remaining user charges, chiefly those that fall on recreational activities. There are some interesting issues in the application of user charges, including whether users of the good (i.e., snowmobile trails) should pay the full cost of the trial and whether the fee should be paid when using the service (riding the trail) or purchasing equipment (buying the snowmobile). These issues will be discussed in the fifth section.

Such a diverse list of taxes requires some common framework. In the next section I outline the key elements of optimal tax theory as they apply to these taxes. The final section concludes the article with a summary of recommendations.

## Optimal Taxation

Over the last three decades, economists have developed the theory of optimal taxation, which explains how to design the tax system so as to balance appropriately the government's revenue needs, the incentive effects of the taxes, and the citezen's ability to pay. Although much of this writing is quite complex, the substance reduces to a few maxims. The key ideas for his chapter involve the various reasons why particular activities should be taxed at different rates.

If everyone were identical, then the optimal tax system would be quite simple. As there would be no reason to treat identical households differently (the principle of horizontal equity), the best tax system would raise the needed revenue while minimizing the disruption to economic activity. Taxes should ideally fall on those goods for which the demand is relatively unresponsive to tax-induced price changes. A famous maxim is the inverse elasticity rule, which counsels the setting of tax rates inverse to the elasticity of demand.

Because households do differ in their earning power, their ability to pay taxes is unequal. This fact leads many economists to support a progressive tax structure, one in which those households that are better off pay a larger fraction of income in taxes. The best way to proceed, however, is not some complicated system of higher tax rates on goods consumed by upper-income people (say, jewelry and yachts), but rather a broad-based, progressive income tax. All other goods should be taxed at the same rate. In effect, a single tax, the tax on income, bears the entire burden of progressivity. There is nothing to be gained by taxing individual goods that cannot be achieved through the income tax rate schedule. Note especially that the inverse elasticity rule falls away. Individual demand elasticities play no role: all goods receive identical tax treatment.

The optimal level of progressivity depends upon how much we care about economic inequality and how costly it is to reduce. The costs include the behavior that is changed to avoid paying the taxes. Specifically, households may reduce their labor supply and savings in response to taxes, and these "distortions" would show up in the form of reduced economic activity, lost employment, lower investment, and less robust business formation. Moreover, because states are in competition with each other for business investment and other economic activity, and economic activity is more mobile across state boundaries than across national boundaries, a state-level tax has a greater burden than a comparable tax at the federal level. States with progressive tax structure risk losing capital investment and high-income households to other states. These potential consequences of income tax progressivity imply that states can make only limited progress in reducing economic inequality through the tax system.

While it may be too costly to reduce it further, it is especially important that the tax system not exacerbate economic inequality. Goods that are consumed in greater proportion by low-income households make especially bad candidates for higher taxes. The fact that the previously listed sins fall into this category lies at the heart of many criticisms of sin taxes.

Another important related idea is that taxes should be ad valorem taxes (that is, a fixed percentage of price), not unit taxes (a fixed dollar amount per item). The reason is that as households earn more income, they substitute higher-quality goods. Rather than buying more wine, for example, the higher-income household buys better wine. A household that buys a case of wine at $20 per bottle spends four times as much as one that pays $5 per bottle, but a unit tax assesses exactly the same tax burden on these two households. This implies that the higher-income household pays a lower tax rate. On the other hand, an ad valorem tax rises exactly in proportion to expenditure and assesses the same tax rate on each household.

There are three key exceptions to the principle of equal taxation of all goods. The first concerns the fact that work and savings are discouraged by the income tax. If the consumption of any particular good affects significantly the supply of labor or savings, then it should receive different tax treatment. Goods that are complementary with work (say, child care) are taxed at a lower rate; goods that reduce work effort (say, alcohol and gambling) are taxed at a higher rate.

Externalities are another reason to tax goods at different rates. The basic idea that prices should reflect the full cost of consuming additional units of a good or service implies that those goods whose consumption imposes extra costs on others should be taxed at a rate equal to the marginal spillover cost. For example, smoking has often been criticized for the health consequences of secondhand smoke. An optimal tax system would increase the tax on cigarettes in order to face smokers with this cost when they choose to smoke.

Finally, there is the case of merit goods. Although most economics stresses the competence of rational consumers, an old strand of thinking emphasizes that certain goods have special merit (or demerit). This approach has reappeared in a new guise with recent work on self-control problems. According to this work, individuals discount the future at an excessive rate and underestimate the consequences of current actions. The smoker places too little weight on the future health risks. In this context a tax can help the smoker to resist temptation by standing as a clear current cost and acting as a proxy for a hazy future cost. A simple way to think about this issue is that one's current smoking imposes an external cost on one's future self, but that one's current self lacks the self-discipline needed to refrain.

To sum up, optimal tax theory tells us to use the progressive income tax in order to assign appropriately the tax burden on those most able to pay (the vertical equity argument). Other goods should be taxed at the same percentage ad valorem (not unit) tax rate, with the following exceptions: When increased consumption of a particular good can be shown to reduce work effort or savings, the tax rate on that good should be higher. When the good creates external costs, the tax should reflect those spillovers. (De)merit goods, perhaps those consumed as a result of self-control problems, merit higher tax rates. Finally, it is best not to worsen the problem of economic inequality with high taxes on goods consumed disproportionately by lower-income households, which would lead to vertical inequity, or by minorities, which would lead to horizontal inequity.

## TABLE 32.1

### Sin Tax Revenues (in thousands of current dollars)

| Tax | 1990 | 2000 | 2001 |
|---|---|---|---|
| Cigarette taxes | $255,339 | $604,212 | $596,082 |
| Beer and wine taxes | $52,105 | $50,036 | $50,357 |
| Liquor taxes | $62,428 | $82,612 | $86,234 |
| Liquor purchase revolving fund | $63,518 | $127,369 | $127,393 |
| Horse race wagering | $20,627 | $13,493 | $12,520 |
| Casino gaming | $0 | $53,100 | $75,415 |
| Lottery | $490,365 | $626,515 | $597,386 |
| TOTAL | $944392 | $1,557,337 | $1,535,387 |

SOURCE: State of Michigan, Comprehensive Annual Financial Reports, various years.

## TABLE 32.2

### State Excise Tax Rates on Cigarettes

| State | Tax Rate (cents per pack) | Rank |
|---|---|---|
| Illinois[a] | 98 | 10 |
| Indiana | 55.5 | 21 |
| Iowa | 36 | 27 |
| Michigan | 75 | 15 |
| Minnesota | 48 | 24 |
| Ohio | 55 | 22 |
| Pennsylvania | 31 | 33 |

SOURCE: Compiled by Federation of Tax Administrators from various sources.
NOTE: Effective 1 August 2002, Michigan's cigarette tax rate was increased an additional $0.50 to $1.25 per pack by Public Act 503 of 2002.
(a) Counties and cities may impose an additional tax on a pack of cigarettes in Illinois, 10¢ to 15¢.

## Sin Taxes

Taxes on tobacco, alcohol, and gambling account for substantial revenues in Michigan. Table 32.1 shows that the most important revenue sources are cigarettes and lotteries.

## Tobacco Products

Taxes on the consumption of tobacco products significantly exceed those on other items. While the sales tax in Michigan is 6%, the current tax

## TABLE 32.3

**Tobacco Expenditure Shares**

| Expenditure quintile | All | 1 (lowest 20%) | 2 | 3 | 4 | 5 (highest 20%) |
|---|---|---|---|---|---|---|
| Budget share for tobacco products | 0.8 | 1.4 | 1.2 | 1.1 | 0.8 | 0.4 |

| Income quartile | | 1 | 2 | 3 | 4 | |
|---|---|---|---|---|---|---|
| Income share for tobacco products | | 3.2 | 1.4 | 0.9 | 0.4 | |

SOURCE: Data on consumption from Consumer Expenditure Survey; data on income from Current Population Survey.

rates on the "sins" are $1.25 per pack for cigarettes and 16% on smokeless tobacco, and the sales tax is applied on top of the cigarette tax. Table 32.2 shows considerable variation among cigarette tax rates across states as of July 2002, when the state's tax of 75 cents ranked fifteenth. For example, New York has a tax of $1.50 per pack; Virginia's tax is 2.5 cents. Like more than a dozen others, Michigan's rate has been increased since that time. Further, these taxes are on top of the federal cigarette tax of 39 cents per pack. What justifies the high tax rates on cigarettes?

Tobacco products are addictive. Economists have traditionally begun their analysis of tobacco taxes with the model of rational addiction (Becker and Murphy 1988). According to this view, competent individuals can foresee and weigh the future consequences of tobacco use today. As this model predicts, many studies have shown that individuals do respond not only to current but also to future price changes (Becker, Grossman, and Murphy 1995; Gruber and Koszegi 2001). Of course, taxes will raise prices and discourage consumption. According to the rational addiction model, this distortion of demand is a cost that must be balanced against the government's revenue needs, just the same as with any other good.

With the rational addiction model's denial of any special normative status for tobacco, the regressive nature of high taxes becomes especially troublesome. Table 32.3 shows the fraction of the household budget spent on tobacco products by income quintile. Although the average household spends 0.8%, those in the bottom quintile spend 1.4%. The share declines until those in the upper fifth consume only 0.4%, less than one-third of those at the bottom. Gruber and Koszegi (2001) report data for income share (also in table 32.3) and find considerably more regressivity, with the share falling from 3.2% to 0.4 %.[1]

While tobacco taxes are certainly regressive on average, the regressivity may be overstated somewhat, however, when we consider the impact of an *increase* in tobacco taxes. The reason is that lower-income households are significantly more responsive to price changes than are those at the upper end of the income scale. A 1990 Congressional Budget Office study found that due to their lower rates of quitting, those in the third and fourth quintiles would pay more of the tax increase than those in the first two.[2]

On the other hand, while the tax on smokeless tobacco is an ad valorem tax, users of cigarettes pay a unit tax. Because higher-income smokers tend to choose higher-quality, more expensive cigarettes, they implicitly face a lower tax rate. (A tax of $1.50 is a 100% tax on a pack with a tax-inclusive price of $3, but only a 50% tax on a pack with a tax-inclusive price of $4.50.) For this reason, unit taxes are inherently regressive. Switching to an ad valorem tax will mitigate, to some extent, the regressivity. Inflation presents another difficulty with unit taxes, because as the price level rises over time, the effective tax rate declines. Repeated increases are necessary to maintain the real value of tax collections. Ad valorem tax revenues, by contrast, rise automatically with inflation.

Several studies have looked into the externality issue, for smokers not only injure themselves but also affect others. These impacts can include health effects on those outside the family from smoking at work and in restaurants, for example, and effects within the family. When buying a pack of cigarettes, the smoker pays for only the cigarettes consumed, while the additional costs are borne by others. The standard correction for this example of poor incentives is to place a tax equal to the marginal external damage. How much might this be?

To give a flavor of the studies, consider Manning et al. (1989), who found negative externalities (net of budget savings from smoking-related premature deaths) of 33 cents. (The dead do not require Social Security, Medicaid, or anything else.) To this number we can add the costs of secondhand smoke (19–70 cents per pack) and low birth weight (42–72 cents per pack). Taking the middle of the ranges, we get about $1.35 in 1995 dollars, which is $1.60 in current dollars. Thus it is possible to justify quite high taxes on cigarettes by adding up their external costs. It should be pointed out, however, that most of the damages (secondhand smoke and low birth weight) fall upon family members and may not truly be external.

If this chapter were written five years ago, that would be the end of the story. We would conclude that the optimal tobacco tax of somewhere between 50 cents and $1.50 corrects for the externality, and that the tax itself is quite regressive. Some very interesting recent work on self-control problems among smokers and the implications of these problems, however, casts doubt on the traditional criticism of high cigarette taxes. See Gruber (2001) for a good discussion. This work begins with some evidence that smokers behave in a time-inconsistent manner. First, many experiments show that people use much lower discount rates between future periods than between the current period and the future. Second, there is the use of self-control devices, such as drugs to sicken the smoker. These indicate that the smoker does not trust himself to refrain in the future. Finally, there is the sad history of failures to quit. This evidence is not necessarily convincing, but it does suggest that smokers place too little weight on their future addiction costs, that they know this, and that they try to tie their hands in the future.

This new approach, called hyperbolic discounting, emphasizes that smokers discount excessively the future and regret their past smoking when the future arrives. This model of smoking stands in opposition to the rational addiction model, and it gives a rationale for tobacco taxes as a self-control aide. Smokers may be made better off by a tax. Although they have not the self-control to refrain from current smoking, the tax gives them the incentive. A further way to look at this issue is to consider the future self of the smoker as the victim of external costs resulting from smoking by the current self. Seen this way, the tax is like the tax on an externality. It should be set equal to the marginal future damage of addiction. Gruber and Koszegi (2002) calculate the optimal tax in this model and find that it is equal to the astounding figure of $35 per pack!

Note that both models imply that the tax discourages current smoking both because it raises the current price and also because it raises the future price borne by the addict. If both models predict the same behavior, how can we distinguish which model is a better description? To date there is only one paper that addresses this question, by Gruber and Mullainathan (2001). They observe that according to the rational addiction model, smokers are made worse off by the tax, while the self-control model implies that they are better off when the tax is higher. The authors use cigarette tax data along with data on self-reported happiness. After controlling for other relevant variables, they find, significantly, that the population of likely smokers is happier with higher cigarette taxes. In other words, the cigarette tax helps some smokers quit, something they would like to do but could not without the tax. Those who quit are better off; those who still cannot are worse off. On average, the population of likely smokers has higher well-being.

If cigarette taxes raise revenue and make the taxpayers better off, then they make an ideal tax. How revenue changes when cigarette taxes are increased, of course, depends upon how responsive smokers are to price increases. A plethora of studies have looked at this issue in the United States, in other developed countries, and, more recently, in developing countries. These studies use a variety of data sources and econometric techniques. Most estimates cluster around an elasticity of –0.3 to –0.5, indicating that a tax-induced 10% increase in price brings about a fall in demand of 3% to 5% (Chaloupka 1991). The resulting net change in tax revenue is an increase of approximately 5% to 7%. These are shorter-run magnitudes. This parameter has been estimated repeatedly in the U.S. context, with a consensus estimate of –0.4 to –0.5 (Chaloupka and Warner 1998), but with recent estimates at 0.6 (Gruber and Koszegi 2001 and 2002; Yurekli and Zhang 2000).

For teenage smokers, however, the demand seems to be significantly more responsive to price, with estimates around –1.4% (Chaloupka 1991). In other words, if a tax were to increase the price of a pack of cigarettes by 10%, teenagers would decrease consumption by 14%. The main locus of impact is on the decision to begin smoking. With fewer teenage smokers maturing to become adult smokers, the long-run response is, of course, more elastic. Estimates of long-run elasticities range nearer –0.8%, indicating that there is more rev-

**TABLE 32.4**

**State Tax Rates on Beer and Wine**

| State | Beer Tax Rate ($ per gallon) | Wine Tax Rate ($ per gallon) |
|-------|------------------------------|------------------------------|
| Illinois | 0.185 | 0.73 |
| Indiana | 0.12 | 0.47 |
| Iowa | 0.19 | 1.75 |
| Michigan | 0.20 | 0.51 |
| Minnesota | 0.15 | 0.30 |
| Ohio | 0.18 | 0.32 |
| Pennsylvania | 0.08 | (a) |

SOURCE: Federation of Tax Administrators web site.
(a) Sold through state stores.

enue to be raised from further increases in tax rates but that the maximum level of tax revenue is near. (Expenditure on a good is maximized when the elasticity of demand equals −1.)

One final issue concerns cigarette tax evasion. A tax increase in Michigan increases the difference between prices here and in neighboring states and gives an incentive to purchase cigarettes in other states and bring them back to Michigan. States with low taxes near Michigan include Ohio, with 24 cents, Pennsylvania, with 31 cents, and Kentucky, with a rate of 3 cents per pack. These neighbors make an inviting source for potential cross-state smuggling. In the United States there does seem to be a modest level of cross-state smuggling (3–4% of consumption in the 1970s as estimated by Thursby and Thursby [2000], and 6% of tax revenues in 1995 [Yurekli and Zhang 2000]). Significantly higher cigarette taxes, however, might promote the growth of smuggling, as occurred in Canada in the early 1990s. Between 1989 and 1993, excise taxes at the federal and provincial levels rose sharply, from an average of $1.90 per pack to $3.50 per pack. In response to these large tax increases, there was an enormous increase in smuggling in Canada through legal export and illegal reimport. Indeed, smuggled cigarettes represented roughly one-third of all domestic cigarette consumption at the peak of taxation. Then, in the face of enormous smuggling, federal and provincial taxes were halved in 1994 (Gruber, Sen, and Stabile 2002).

In summary, good arguments exist for higher cigarette taxes. The external costs are substantial. There is evidence of self-control problems among smokers. Higher taxes reduce smoking, especially among the young. Cigarette taxes are regressive,

however, and the idea that the state will solve its budget problems by taxing lower-income smokers is troublesome. One possibility is to offset higher cigarette taxes with progressive income tax reductions, such as an increase in the personal exemption. At any rate, consideration should be given to shifting from the current unit tax structure to an ad valorem tax as a minimum first step in reform.

### Alcohol Taxes

The tax on beer in Michigan is about $0.20 per gallon, and it is $0.51 per gallon ($0.76/gallon for alcohol content over 16%) for wine. Further, like eighteen other states, Michigan controls the sale of hard liquor, generating substantial revenues (See table 32.1.) These modest tax rates contrast with the much higher rates on the other sins (tobacco and gambling). Together, these taxes raised $1.3 billion in 2000. Table 32.4 shows the corresponding tax rates in other nearby states. Michigan is slightly above the median in beer taxation and slightly below in the taxation of wine. Why is alcohol singled out for special tax treatment and are the current rates appropriate?

As with cigarettes, alcohol is addictive, and alcohol consumption has costly consequences not only in terms of health but also with certain destructive behaviors such as drunk driving and crime. These facts may justify higher taxes to discourage consumption. Unlike cigarettes, however, alcohol taxes are not necessarily regressive; thus they do not bring out the same objections on vertical equity grounds.

Drinking alcohol is, of course, quite common. Roughly one-half of adults report drinking within the past month, two-thirds within the past year. Self-reported drinking declines in middle age; it increases with income and education; and it is slightly lower for blacks than for whites. Consumer expenditure data, however, show a fairly constant fraction of expenditures (about 1%) devoted to alcoholic beverages (see table 32.5). Consumption of alcohol is concentrated in the population. For example, out of a representative sample of ten adults, three are nondrinkers, three drink less than 1 gallon, and the others drink 1.5, 3, 6, and 15 gallons annually.

While alcohol taxation need not be regressive, in Michigan it is. Table 32.5 shows that the budget share for alcohol does not change as income increases. This means that expenditures rise

## TABLE 32.5

### Alcohol Expenditure Shares

| Expenditure quintile | All | 1 | 2 | 3 | 4 | 5 |
| --- | --- | --- | --- | --- | --- | --- |
| | | (lowest 20%) | | | | (highest 20%) |
| Budget share for alcoholic beverages | 1.1 | 1.2 | 0.9 | 1.1 | 1.1 | 1.0 |

SOURCE: Consumer expenditure survey.

roughly with income. The volume of alcohol consumed, however, falls as income rises. The reason is that high-income households consume higher-quality beverages. Yet the unit tax falls on the volume. This makes the tax on beer and wine unnecessarily regressive.[3] It is no different than placing a higher tax rate on lower-quality alcoholic beverages.

Estimates of the responsiveness of alcohol consumption to price range widely, but there are certain patterns. First, the demand for beer is less elastic than that for wine, with the demand for spirits most elastic. One study found elasticities of –0.35 for beer, –0.68 for wine, and –0.98 for spirits.[4] Second, the elasticity has a U-shaped pattern when compared with relative consumption. It is zero for nondrinkers, rises to –1.2 at the median of the distribution, and then falls to near zero for the heaviest drinkers. (Cook and Moore 2000)

The case for high alcohol taxes rests on the ability of the tax to increase price, discourage drinking, and reduce the bad health and behavior associated with consumption of alcoholic beverages. Some studies try to estimate directly the external costs associated with alcohol consumption. Others take a reduced form approach, estimating the overall impact of tax or price increases on various measures of negative consequences. These include drinking and driving, disease, crime and domestic violence, and lower educational attainment.

A great deal of work shows that drinking and driving and the associated traffic accidents and fatalities do respond to changes in the tax rate. Three studies (Saffer and Grossman [1987], Chaloupka, Saffer, and Grossman [1993], and Ruhm [1996]) find evidence that the beer tax significantly reduces fatality rates, especially among youth and at night. Cook and Moore, (1994) estimate a fatality elasticity of –0.1 overall and –0.2 for youths. This means that a 10% increase in the total tax on alcohol would bring about 1% fewer fatalities, 2% fewer for youths. Self-reports of drinking and driving in the last

twelve months are found to be lower in the presence of higher prices by two studies, Kenkel (1993) and Sloan, Reilly, and Schenzler (1995). In their work on youth drinking Cook and Moore (1994) estimate that a tax increase of one cent per twelve-ounce can reduces consumption by 3.4% and the probability of drinking by 2.6%.

Excessive drinking contributes to health problems, the costs of which are external in that the rest of society pays for them through higher insurance premiums. Cirrhosis mortality is affected by changes in price of alcohol. Cook (1981) and Cook and Tauchen (1982), in a longitudinal study of state cirrhosis mortality rates, find that higher liquor taxes lead to a significant drop in death rates. The drop occurs quickly, due to the fact that reduced drinking delays mortality for heavy drinkers.

Crime, including criminal homicide, aggravated assault, robbery, and rape, is found by Cook and Moore (1993a) to be somewhat lessened by higher alcohol taxes. They estimate that a 10% increase in the beer tax would result in declines of 0.3% for murder, 0.3% for assault, 1.3% for rape, and 0.9% for robbery. Another study, by Markowitz and Grossman (2000) finds that higher alcohol prices are associated with a lower likelihood of domestic violence, and even lower rates of severe violence.

Education also depends upon alcohol taxation. Students who spend their high school and college years in high alcohol tax states graduate more often from college. Cook and Moore (1993b) find that an increase from $0.10 to $1.00 per case increases the probability of graduation from a four-year college by 4.2%.

All of this work shows quite convincingly that higher alcohol taxes do have significant effects. They reduce fatalities, drinking and driving, and crime and domestic violence. They improve health, and increase years of schooling. Another study, by Kenkel and Ribar (1994), even shows that marriage rates respond positively.

How high should the alcohol tax be? Taking the externality argument, the tax rate should reflect the external costs of drinking. Effects such as lost earnings by the drinker (although there is very little evidence that alcohol consumption reduces productivity) are borne by the drinker himself and should not be considered to be external costs. Other factors, however, such as medical and disability costs reimbursed by insurance for motor-vehicle injuries to others, are external. A well-known and comprehensive study by Manning et al. (1989) found external costs per ounce of ethanol (one drink) of 48 cents, which translates to 73 cents in current dollars. This is much higher than current tax rates in Michigan. Miller and Blincoe (1993) estimate an external cost of $0.63 per drink due to increased automobile crashes alone.

At present, there has been little convincing work on self-control problems. In principle, the same arguments made about cigarette taxation apply to alcohol. Here again the alcohol tax can help individuals to refrain from drinking, an action they could not perform on their own.

To sum up, there are strong reasons to advocate higher alcohol taxation. The externality argument is powerful, and the taxes will certainly reduce the external costs associated with alcohol consumption. Furthermore, self-control problems may further increase the optimal level of alcohol taxation. Finally, because the share of expenditure devoted to alcohol is fairly constant across income groups, alcohol taxes can be raised without unduly burdening lower-income households. Clearly, however, unit taxes on beer and wine should be replaced by an ad valorem tax on alcohol.

## Gambling Taxes

Gambling represents the third of the sins that receive special tax treatment in Michigan. There are three main revenue sources: the casino gambling tax, the tax on horse racing, and lottery revenues. The state-run lottery implicitly taxes gambling by returning only a fraction of revenues in prizes. If we think about lotteries as a business with costs and revenues, then the costs include prizes and administration. Table 32.6 shows lottery revenues and costs nationally. The last column gives the implicit tax rate. In Michigan, for example, revenues of $1.6 billion generate $0.6 billion in profits, which is a 61.3% tax rate, which lies near to the top among the Great Lakes states, but falls short of Pennsylvania's 80%. (The implicit

tax rate is profits divided by administration costs plus prizes.) This is ten times the sales tax rate that applies to virtuous expenditure, and it certainly requires some justification.

Why do people gamble, or perhaps more precisely, what reasons do economists advance to explain gambling? The usual economic approach to choice under uncertainty assumes that risk-averse people maximize expected utility. While this explains investment portfolios and insurance well enough, it implies that no one would gamble. One can argue that for sporting events (such as horse racing, for example) disagreements about the likely winner are the reason people participate in gambling, but lotteries allow no such disagreement. The winner is selected randomly, and all contestants have an equal (and low) probability of winning.

The traditional model about gambling was determined by Friedman and Savage (1948), who suppose that people are risk averse for small gambles but will voluntarily accept unfair gambles if the payoff is sufficiently large. One modern update (Quiggin 1991) uses the rank-dependent expected utility model, in which people place too much weight on very high and very low probabilities. (There is much experimental evidence that this conjecture is true.) The author goes on to analyze the optimal lottery, which includes a few large prizes and many small ones, which is the structure of the Michigan lottery.

Who plays the lottery? While most adults have played the lottery at least once, and about a third play each week, the most active 10% of players account for 50% of total expenditures and the top 20% account for nearly two-thirds (Clotfelter and Cook 1990). Thus the lottery market is quite concentrated among a small portion of the population. Lottery play decreases significantly among more educated households. The pattern with respect to income, however, is less clear. Most early studies (e.g., Clotfelter and Cook 1987, 1989) found that households in all income groups spent approximately the same amount on the lottery. Some later work (Scott and Garen 1994; Stranahan and Borg 1998) finds that lottery expenditure rises with income up to just below the median and then falls off. Both of these results imply, however, that the *share* of expenditures on lottery games clearly declines with income. Thus, this commodity is consumed disproportionately by lower-income households, and it has a tax rate ten times higher than the general sales tax rate. The lottery is thus a highly regressive source of revenue.

**TABLE 32.6**

**Lottery Revenues and Implicit Tax Rates (in thousands of dollars)**

| State | Ticket Sales[a] | Prizes | Administration | Proceeds | Tax Rate |
|---|---|---|---|---|---|
| Illinois | 1,369,434 | 798,866 | 62,205 | 508,363 | 59% |
| Indiana | 530,861 | 336,659 | 32,430 | 166,772 | 45% |
| Iowa | 158,269 | 98,392 | 23,088 | 36,789 | 30% |
| Michigan | 1,616,295 | 920,800 | 81,458 | 614,037 | 61% |
| Minnesota | 370,152 | 241,157 | 71,385 | 57,250 | 18% |
| Ohio | 2,155,789 | 1,272,979 | 95,456 | 785,354 | 57% |
| Pennsylvania | 1,589,307 | 828,691 | 56,502 | 704,114 | 80% |

SOURCE: 2000 Survey of Government Finances: U.S. Census Bureau, Governments Division (created 18 July 2002, last revised 23 July 2002).
(a) Excluding commissions.

Beyond the incidence of lottery taxation across the income spectrum, there is the issue of horizontal equity, or how the tax payments vary among various population groups. Here, the evidence is disturbing. Among households with the same income, minority households spend significantly more on lottery tickets and thus pay more of the tax. Stranahan and Borg (1998) studied lottery purchases in Florida, Virginia, and Colorado and found that African Americans pay approximately twice as much in lottery taxes as whites, and Hispanics pay about 50% more as a percentage of income. Further, the difference is exacerbated by advertising, which seems more effective in increasing demand among African Americans. Another work, by Price and Novak (1999), looked at three lottery games in Texas and found similar patterns. More lottery purchases are made by minorities, and more still are made among the particular games that are most heavily advertised. Heavily taxing goods consumed disproportionately by minorities seems to be questionable tax policy.

Many studies estimate the responsiveness of demand to changes in the implicit tax. Most (see, e.g., Forrest, Gulley, and Simmons 2000) find elasticities close to one, indicating that revenues are approximately at their maximum. Since the extra administration cost of selling more tickets is negligible, this implies the state's profits are nearly maximized.

There are two directions to move so as to increase revenues. First, there is a great deal of evidence of economies of scale in the lottery market. Demand rises as the jackpot grows, even though the probability of winning falls proportionately (see Clotfelter and Cook 1990). This argues for merging the state's lottery program with that of other states. A second idea is that the payout rate need not be constant, as the jackpot rolls over in weeks where there is no winner. Beenstock, Goldin and Haitovsky (2000) find that the optimal payout rate should be reduced as the jackpot rolls over. The logic here is that when the jackpot rolls over, playing the lottery has more value to customers, and the price should reflect this additional value.

There is little or no work in the economics literature on the problem of externalities caused by gambling addiction, but the phenomenon of pathological gambling is real enough. Volberg (1998) reports that about 3% of gamblers have sought help for problems related to gambling addiction. Obviously, this is a lower bound on the fraction of the population of gamblers who experience difficulties.

The consequences commonly attributed to problem gambling may be quite extensive. The report to the National Gambling Impact Study Commission notes that many families of pathological gamblers suffer from a variety of financial, physical, and emotional problems, including divorce, domestic violence, child abuse and neglect, and a range of problems stemming from the severe financial hardship that commonly results from problem and pathological gambling (Gerstein et al. 1999). The report also notes the existence of a number of costly financial problems related to problem or pathological gambling, including crime, loss of employment, and bankruptcy.

Table 32.7 is adapted from data in their report, and it gives some idea of the extent of the problem. They grouped the population into five classes, ranging from those that never gamble to those with symptoms of pathology. Table 32.7

**TABLE 32.7**

**Social Consequences of Gambling**

|  | Non-gambler | Low risk | At risk | Problem gambler | Pathological gambler |
|---|---|---|---|---|---|
| Percentage of population | 15% | 75% | 7.5% | 1.5% | 1.25% |
| Job loss in last year | 2.6 | 4.0 | 5.6 | 10.8 | 13.8 |
| Filed bankruptcy ever | 4.2 | 5.5 | 4.7 | 10.3 | 19.2 |
| Arrested | 4.5 | 11.1 | 20.7 | 36.3 | 32.3 |
| Divorce | 18.2 | 29.8 | 36.3 | 39.5 | 53.5 |
| Mental health expenses | 6.9 | 6.5 | 5.8 | 12.8 | 13.3 |

SOURCE: Gerstein et al. (1999).

shows a consistent increase in a sample of social problems associated with additional gambling or gambling problems. We see that increased gambling activity is associated with job loss, bankruptcy, legal troubles, divorce, and mental health problems.

As of now, there are no estimates of the external cost per gambling incident; nevertheless, gambling is clearly an activity with significant external costs. It is true that much of the cost of divorce and job loss falls upon the immediate family and may not be considered as an external cost by those who see the gambler as a rational head of household acting in the interest of the family. Even if this dubious proposition is accepted, however, other costs, such as those related to crime, bankruptcy, and health care, have substantial consequences upon the community at large.

Although there has of yet been no economic work on the subject, we could, in principle, apply the self-control model discussed in the cigarette tax section to this issue. The parallel is nearly exact. Gamblers experience a current thrill with long-term negative consequences. Since the action of gambling has negative expected costs, there are the expected future financial losses. To this add the consequences of potential addiction. The gambler who places too little weight on the future will have difficulty controlling the urge to play. A wise tax policy can raise the price of gambling high enough to assist in the struggle for self-control.[5]

In summary, lottery profits are essentially a tax on gambling operations. Gambling itself is an activity, like smoking and drinking, that generates external costs. Gamblers may be troubled by problems of self-control. Good tax policy places higher tax rates on activities like gambling, and current implicit tax rates, at least on lottery play, are quite high. Unlike the other sins taxes, the lottery tax is a percentage of revenues. One troubling aspect is the regressivity and horizontal inequity of the tax.

## Inheritance and Estate Taxes, or Death Taxes

In 1993, the Michigan State Inheritance Tax was changed to a simple, unobjectionable "pick-up" tax. Federal law allows for a credit against federal estate tax liability for state estate and inheritance tax payments, up to a specified amount that varies with the size of the estate. As in thirty-seven other states, Michigan's tax equals the maximum allowable credit against federal estate taxes. The state inheritance tax imposes no additional burden on Michigan taxpayers. It is similar to revenue sharing, in that it merely transfers tax payments from the federal government to Michigan. Inheritance tax revenues exceeded $185 million in 2000. Due to the nature of the tax, these revenues are raised with little additional administrative burden placed upon the taxpayer.

The current situation, however, is somewhat jumbled. The federal tax cut package adopted in 2001 calls for a staged elimination of the federal estate tax, leading to its abolition in 2010. However, if Congress does not act in the interim, the tax will return the following year. Over the next decade, federal estate tax rates are scheduled to fall, which will not affect Michigan, but also the federal tax base will shrink as the unified credit increases. This latter provision exempted estates smaller than $675,000, a number that grew to $1 million in 2002 and is scheduled to increase further to $1.5 million in 2004, $2 million in 2006, and $3.5 million in 2009. This will reduce the number and size of taxable estates. Finally, the allowable state credit is reduced by 25% each year, beginning in 2002, leading to elimination after 2005. In the years following 2005, Michigan's inheritance tax will raise no revenues (until 2011, of course, when the tax changes expire and the entire system returns to the current law).

No longer having the option of the pick-up tax, Michigan must decide whether and how to tax inheritances. The question divides into two: what to do in the short term as the uncertainty about the federal estate tax resolves itself, and what to do in the longer term, should the federal tax be abolished. In the short run one attractive alternative is to decouple the state tax from the disappearing federal tax. Rhode Island, Minnesota, and Wisconsin have already done this. A report by the Center on Budget and Policy Priorities estimates that Michigan would collect $51 million in 2003 by decoupling, and a total of $689.3 million over the period of the phaseout, from 2003 to 2007. The main reason that this is good tax policy is that the distortions due to the inheritance tax have, for the most part, already occurred. Also, there is little additional administrative burden. This would not change the number of estates subject to tax, and all taxpaying estates must file returns anyway.

Taxation of estates falls upon those who save in order to bequeath monies to their heirs. It is a partial tax on savings, exempting those who save for their own later consumption. Anticipating the tax burden, households change their behavior in a variety of ways, including reducing their asset accumulation, giving before death, giving to charities, and pursuing legal tax avoidance through trusts and other means. These are actions that involve careful planning over the life cycle and are already available to wealthy individuals, although not everyone who is eligible takes advantage of these strategies. The retention of inheritance taxation for this four- or five-year period will likely induce little additional distortion. In effect, this decoupling is an ideal form of tax, falling chiefly upon upper-income households and inducing little change in behavior.

In the longer run the argument for estate taxation is less convincing. Unless the federal estate tax is restored, Michigan would have to create new law to institute its own tax, as opposed to the current pick-up tax on federal law. There is little or no work in economics on the effects of state-level inheritance taxation, and an evaluation of the policy is beyond the scope of this chapter.

## User Fees

Unlike taxes, which are imposed upon transactions between private buyers and sellers, user fees are assessed (directly or indirectly) for the use of particular goods that are publicly provided. Direct charges include occupational licensing fees, motor vehicle permit feess, charges for entrance to public parks, bridge tolls, hunting and fishing licenses, college tuition, and many others. Gasoline taxes and the snowmobile tax, on the other hand, are examples of user fees that are indirectly assessed.

When the state provides a good to a particular group of users, a case can be made for user fees. There are two considerations involved. First, there may be a direct user charge. Consider issuing a hunting license that gives the right to kill, say, one deer. The state maintains the deer herd and decides how many licenses to issue. Presumably, this decision balances the costs and benefits of marginal changes in the deer herd. The hunter imposes a cost by hunting (namely, the deer that he kills is not available for another hunter) and should pay a price equal to the opportunity cost. Here the reason for the user charge is to allocate resources, in particular to allocate the limited number of opportunities to hunt deer. The state should set the fee to clear the market. If there are too many hunters, it should raise the fee; if too few, it should lower it. The user fees may or may not pay the full costs of maintaining the herd.

The second rationale for user fees is different, however. That is to have those who benefit from public goods pay the costs. The issue here is not the allocation of resources, but rather the raising of funds to provide the good. Indirect user fees can be a good way to finance public goods. A good example is the snowmobile tax. The snowmobile user is required to register and pay a fee ($22 for three years). A portion of the registration receipts ($1,872,000 in 1999–2000) is appropriated to the Department of Natural Resources for planning, construction, maintenance, and acquisition of trails for snowmobile use. This tax is, in a sense, indirect in that the user does not pay per use of the trail, but rather pays one fee for any number of trail uses. The reason that the fee is imposed only once is that the snowmobile user imposes no costs on the economy when he rides. The costs are for the availability, not the use. Gasoline taxes similarly are an efficient means of financing the roads. This argument ignores other potential external costs, however, such as noise and congestion.

The third element of efficient user fees concerns external costs and benefits. When use of the public good imposes costs on others, the fee should reflect these costs; when there are external benefits, the funds should come from general revenues, not from the users. According to this logic, student tuition covers only a fraction of college costs because each student captures only a fraction of the benefits. External benefits include the better overall economic performance that goes along with an educated workforce, and better political decisions.

## Conclusions

There are good reasons for high taxes on tobacco, alcohol, and gambling. Each of these commodities is associated with external costs. Each is addictive, and users are likely troubled by self-control problems. In each case there is significant responsiveness to tax-induced price increases. That is to say, higher taxes will increase prices, reduce consumption, and reduce the external costs. Those thinking about good social policy will certainly want to consider higher sin taxes.

Tobacco and gambling are consumed disproportionately by lower-income and minority groups, and this makes these revenue sources quite regressive. Increasing these taxes, even for good reasons, makes the tax system more regressive and argues for an accompanying change to offset this increased regressivity. In other words, a tax system that relies on tobacco and gambling taxation for a large chunk of revenues is one that requires more progressivity in other areas. Increases in the personal exemption for the income tax make good candidates for the offsetting reform. Alcohol taxation, however, is not regressive. (Perhaps coincidentally, it has the lowest tax rates.) This implies that higher alcohol taxes need no offsetting change elsewhere in the tax system.

Finally, policy makers should consider making each sin tax an ad valorem tax. Unit taxes make bad tax policy because they unnecessarily exacerbate the problem of regressivity and limit tax yields.

The state should consider decoupling the inheritance and estate tax from the federal estate tax. This would preserve substantial revenues in the next few years with little distortion of economic behavior. Unless current laws are changed, the inheritance/estate tax will eventually be elim-

inated. This implies that the state's tax system will grow more regressive and might require some offsetting change in other taxes, most likely the income tax. User fees for recreation are in line with good tax policy in Michigan.

■

## REFERENCES

Becker, G., M. Grossman, and K. M. Murphy. 1995. An empirical analysis of cigarette addiction. *American Economic Review* 84(3): 396–418.

Becker, G. S., and K. M. Murphy. 1988. A theory of rational addiction. *Journal of Political Economy* 96(4): 675–700.

Beenstock, Michael, Ephraim Goldin, and Yoel Haitovsky. 2000. What jackpot? The optimal lottery tax. *European Journal of Political Economy* 16:655–71.

Chaloupka, F. J. 1991. Rational addictive behavior and cigarette smoking. *Journal of Political Economy* 99(4): 722–42.

Chaloupka, F., H. Saffer, and M. Grossman. 1993. Alcohol-control policies and motor-vehicle fatalities. *Journal of Legal Studies* 22:161–86.

Chaloupka, F. J., and K. E. Warner. 1998. The economics of smoking, in *The handbook of health economics,* edited by J. Newhouse, and A. Culyer. Amsterdam: Elsevier Science.

Clements, K.W., W. Yang, and S. W. Zheng. 1997. Is utility additive: The case of alcohol. *Applied Economics* 29:1163–67.

Clotfelter, Charles T., and Philip J. Cook. 1987. Implicit taxation in lottery finance. *National Tax Journal* 40:533–46.

———. 1989. *Selling hope: State lotteries in America.* Cambridge: Harvard University Press.

———. 1990. On the economics of state lotteries. *Journal of Economic Perspectives* 4:105–19.

Cook, P. J. 1981. The effect of liquor taxes on drinking, cirrhosis and auto fatalities, in *Alcohol and public policy: Beyond the shadow of Prohibition,* edited by M. Moore and D. Gerstein. Washington, D.C.: National Academy of Sciences.

Cook, P. J., and M. J. Moore. 1993a. Economic perspectives on alcohol-related violence, in *Alcohol-related violence: Interdisciplinary perspectives and research directions,* edited by S. E. Martin, NIH Publication n. 93–3496. Rockville, Md.: National Institute on Alcohol Abuse and Alcoholism.

———. 1993b. Drinking and Schooling. *Journal of Health Economics* 12:411–29.

———. 1994. This tax's for you: The case for higher beer taxes. *National Tax Journal* 47:559–73.

———. 2000. Alcohol, in *Handbook of health economics*, vol. 1, edited by A. J. Culyer and J. P. Newhouse. Amsterdam: Elsevier Science B.V.

Cook, P. J., and G. Tauchen. 1982. The effect of liquor taxes on heavy drinking. *Bell Journal of Economics* 13:379–90.

Forrest, David, David Gulley, and Robert Simmons. 2000. Elasticity of demand for UK national lottery tickets. *National Tax Journal* 53:853–63.

Friedman, Milton, and L. J. Savage. 1948. The utility analysis of choices involving risk. *Journal of Political Economy* 56:279–304.

Gerstein, Dean et al. 1999. Gambling impact and behavior study. National Gambling Impact Study Commission.

Gruber, J. 2001. Tobacco at the crossroads: The past and future of smoking regulation in the U.S. *Journal of Economic Perspectives* 15(2): 193–212.

Gruber, J., and B. Koszegi. 2001. Is addiction rational? Theory and evidence. *Quarterly Journal of Economics* 116(4): 1261–1305.

———. 2002. A theory of government regulation of addictive bads: Optional tax levels and tax incidence for cigarette excise taxation. NBER working paper 8777.

Gruber, J., and S. Mullainathan. 2001. Do cigarette taxes make smokers happier? Mimeo, Massachusetts Institute of Technology.

Gruber, J., Anindya Sen, and Mark Stabile. 2002. Estimating price elasticities when there is smuggling: The sensitivity of smoking to price in Canada. NBER working paper 8962.

Kenkel, D. S. 1993. Drinking, driving and deterrence: The effectiveness and social costs of alternative policies. *Journal of Law and Economics* 36:877–913.

Kenkel, D. S., and D. Ribar. 1994. Alcohol consumption and young adults' socioeconomic status, in *Brookings Papers on Economics Activity-Micro*.

Manning, W. G., E. B. Keeler, J. P. Newhouse, E. M. Sloss, and J. Wasserman. 1989. The taxes of sin: Do smokers and drinkers pay their way? *Journal of the American Medical Association* 261(11): 1604–9.

Markowitz, S., and M. Grossman. 2000. Alcohol regulation and violence towards children. *Journal of Health Economics* 19(2): 271–82.

Miller, T. R., and L. J. Blincoe. 1993. Incidence and costs of alcohol-involved crashes in the United States. *Accident Analysis and Prevention* 26:583–92.

Quiggin, John. 1991. On the optimal design of lotteries *Economica* 58:1–16.

Price, Donald, and Shawn Novak. 1999. The tax incidence of three Texas lottery games: Regressivity, race and education. *National Tax Journal* 52:741–51.

Ruhm, C. J. 1996. Alcohol policies and highway vehicle fatalities. *Journal of Health Economics* 15:435–54.

Saffer, Henry, and Frank Chaloupka. 1994. Alcohol tax equalization and social costs. *Eastern Economic Journal* 20:33–43.

Saffer, Henry, and Michael Grossman. 1987. Beer taxes, the legal drinking age and motor vehicle fatalities. NBER working paper, 1914.

Scott, Frank, and John Garen. 1994. Probability of purchase, amount of purchase and the demographic incidence of the lottery tax. *Journal of Public Economics* 54:121–43

Sloan, F. A., B. A. Reilly, and C. Schenzler. 1995. Effects of tort liability and insurance on heavy drinking and drinking and driving. *Journal of Law and Economics* 38:49–77.

Stranahan, H. A., and Mary Borg. 1998. Horizontal equity implications of the lottery tax. *National Tax Journal* 51:71–82.

Thursby, Jerry G., and Marie C. Thursby. 2000. Interstate cigarette bootlegging: Extent, revenue losses, and effects of federal intervention. *National Tax Journal* 53(March): 59–78.

U.S. Congressional Budget Office. 1990. *Regulation of tobacco, alcoholic beverages and motor fuels*. Washington, D.C.: Government Printing Office.

Volberg, R.A. 1998. Gambling and problem gaming in Oregon: A report to the Oregon gambling addiction treatment foundation. Northhampton, Mass.: Bemini Research, Ltd.

Yurekli, A., and P. Zhang. 2000. The impact of clean indoor-air laws and cigarette smuggling on demand for cigarettes: An empirical model. *Health Economics* 9(2): 159–70.

## NOTES

1. The income share measure shows a more regressive incidence. This is because consumption varies less than income. Higher-income households save more for a variety of reasons, including the fact that relatively more of their income is transitory as compared to lower-income households.

2. Of course, these are average effects, calculated over a large number of individuals. The impact upon any one individual will depend upon that person's particular response to the tax increase.

3. In Michigan spirits are taxed on an ad valorem basis.

4. See Clements, Yang, and Zheng 1997. In other words, a 10% increase in price would bring about a

3.5% decrease in consumption of beer, a 6.8% decrease in consumption of wine, and a 9.8% decrease in demand for spirits.

5. Remember that in this context, the profit taken from lottery ticket sales is essentially a tax by another name.

# 33

# Tax Limitation in the Michigan Constitution: The "Headlee Amendment"

*Susan P. Fino*

## Introduction

This chapter will read differently from the others in this volume. Here the reader is invited to step back from the economic analyses to consider the history and meaning of one of the constitutional foundations of Michigan's fiscal policy, in addition to some of its practical impacts. The chapter will focus on Michigan's state constitutional constraints on raising revenue at the state and local levels, which come primarily in the form of the so-called Headlee Amendment. Other chapters of this volume will touch on additional limitations such as the balanced budget and related requirements and the constitutional ban on a graduated income tax as well as the constitutionally capped sales tax rate. The Headlee Amendment, Michigan's manifestation of the taxpayers' revolt of the late 1970s, is actually a package of changes in Article IX, the taxation section of the Constitution. The core of the Headlee Amendment is found in Sections 25 to 34 of Article IX, but it also amended Section 6 of the same article. Among other things, the Headlee Amendment: provides that local property and other taxes may not be raised without local voter approval; it creates both a state revenue and a spending limit; it prevents the state from shifting the burden of state programs to local government through the use of unfunded man-

dates; and it prohibits the state from reducing its share of aid to local government, or shifting a tax burden to local government.

This chapter will review the course of the Headlee Amendment in order to show how Michigan's legislature and courts have struggled to interpret and implement it. This chapter will also place the amendment in context: How does the amendment fit with public opinion on taxation policy? How does the amendment fit within Michigan's state constitutional history? How does Michigan's approach to restraining government compare with efforts in other states?

## The Political Context: Understanding the Taxpayer's Revolt of the late 1970s

The "tax revolt"—a series of initiatives to restrict taxing and spending—was seen by some as the "most important political economic event of the 1970s."[1] What was the revolt about? Contemporary observers saw the phenomenon as a "genuine and effective revolt against spiraling taxes and profligate government spending, the renunciation of big-government politicians, a reaffirmation of free-enterprise priorities, and the return of control of government to the people."[2]

Why exactly it occurred has been a source of

much reflection and debate. Everett Carll Ladd noted that Americans have long had qualms about the taxes that they pay; he found 1947-vintage survey data showing that even then about two-thirds of Americans thought their federal income taxes were too high.[3] By 1978, Ladd found that only 20% of respondents in one poll thought their taxes "reasonable," while in another poll over two-thirds thought that the amount of taxes they paid had "reached the breaking point."[4] Something else was happening to the perceptions of taxpayers in the late 1970s: most taxpayers came to believe that the nation's tax system was simply not fair. Over half the respondents to an April 1978 *New York Times* poll labeled the distribution of taxes as "unfair," and a whopping 89% of respondents to a 1977 Harris Poll thought "the big tax burden falls on the little man in this country."[5]

While social scientists are certain that the American public has serious reservations about the amount and fairness of taxation, they have not been able to explain how voters came to feel this way, or what touched off the "tax revolt" of the late 1970s. Lowery and Sigel explored eight explanations offered in the literature for the tax revolution.[6] Some scholars believe individual self-interest determines a person's attitude toward taxes: The higher the income, the greater the taxes, and the smaller the need for the services that taxes fund. Others see the tax revolt as an expression of the sense that government had grown too large, or as the manifestation of a profound lack of trust in government. A fourth set of explanations focuses on the public's perception that government is wasteful and inefficient. Still others find the origins of the revolt in the taxpayers' belief that the distribution of the burdens of taxation is unfair. There is also a subset of researchers who explain public attitudes toward taxation in terms of general anxiety over personal finances and the state of the economy. The final two explanations concern voters' ideology and intelligence. Support for the tax revolt is at bottom a function of whether a person is a New Deal liberal or a small-government conservative. Furthermore, of course, people might simply be naïve and not grasp the implications of their decisions. Yet, in the end, Lowery and Sigelman found no single explanation to be fully satisfactory.

There is one other point worth noting about the sources of the 1970s tax revolt. Ladd believes that political leaders played a "critical" role in sparking the anti-government backlash that began in California with Proposition 13. Charismatic leaders behaved and spoke as if there had been a sudden and marked increase in the public's resentment of taxes that required immediate redress.[7] The public statements of political leaders capitalized on the public's latent resentment of taxes, which then translated into state constitutional initiatives.

Americans' reservations about taxes are paradoxically coupled with an enthusiasm for spending. Public opinion research on government spending since the 1960s has consistently shown wide support for all manner of public programs: schools, parks, police, roads, and so forth. Is it possible that the majority of American voters believe that there is such a thing as a free lunch? Some researchers have answered in the negative. Ladd et al. believe that the paradox is explained by public perceptions of government inefficiency and waste.[8] These voters probably believe that they could secure the same level of services for less money if government were run more efficiently. Susan Welch's research found a relatively small number of what she termed "free lunchers," voters who had unrealistic ideas of taxes and expenditures.[9] All told, she found about 75% of the public willing to provide somehow, some way for the services they desire.

William G. Jacoby's research took a novel approach in his attempt to explain why it is that many voters seem to endorse all manner of government spending while simultaneously favoring decreases in taxation.[10] Jacoby believed that most people have "very limited outlooks on the political world," so that it may be "inappropriate to regard all of the program specific responses as equally valid representations of citizens' spending preferences."[11] Therefore, Jacoby used surveys with open-ended questions that allowed the respondent first to identify government spending programs, and then to consider appropriate levels of funding for each. He found that Americans think in terms of two different kinds of spending: spending for social welfare programs (on which they believed government spends too much), and spending for everything else (on which they believed that government spends the right amount or too little). Jacoby reasoned that when voters are confronted with a generic question on government spending, most voters translate this question in their minds to "government spending that could benefit the poor, blacks and other disadvantaged groups."[12] Americans are enthusiastic spenders—regardless of ideology—on programs such as those for the environment or crime prevention, but they are much more divided on social welfare spending. For some, reservations about social welfare spending are a function of ideology, while, for others, the doubts arise from perceiving social welfare programs as emblematic of government waste and inefficiency.

Michigan's tax revolt manifested itself in the form of the Headlee Amendment to the state constitution in 1978, which came after a similar (but arguably more draconian) amendment had been defeated in 1976. It was also the less restrictive of two proposed fiscal amendments on the 1978 ballot. The Headlee Amendment began life as an initiative petition (Proposal E), which was ultimately ratified by the voters at the 7 November election. While there was latent discontent over the amount and fairness of taxes throughout the United States in the 1970s, the catalyst to the revolt in Michigan was probably local property taxes. Indeed, in a series of articles following up on the petition filings, the *Detroit Free Press* headlined one article "Irate homeowners spark the drive."[13] The content and effect of the Headlee Amendment will be reviewed later in this chapter.

## Legal Context: State Constitutions

The U.S. Constitution has been amended only twenty-seven times in over two hundred years. At any given time there are few serious proposals circulating for tinkering with the nation's charter. Each state in the Union has its own constitution, but no state has treated its fundamental charter with the same kind of reverence as the federal Constitution. Every state has had more than one constitutional convention. The Michigan Constitution itself requires that the question of general constitutional revision be put to the people every sixteen years, and in fact, the question of calling a constitutional convention was on the 1978 ballot with the proposed Headlee Amendment.[14]

When John Marshall delivered the opinion in *McCulloch v. Maryland,* he took the time to discuss the appropriate content and form of a constitution.[15] The structure, powers, and processes of government should be presented such that, "only [their] great outlines should be marked, [their] important objects designated, and the minor ingredients which compose those objects be deduced from the nature of the objects themselves."[16] Unless a constitution is but a simple framework, it "would partake of the prolixity of a legal code, and could scarcely be embraced by the

human mind."[17] Crafters of state constitutions—including Michigan's—have taken almost the opposite view: constitutions should be like legal codes.[18] While the federal Constitution contains about 7,300 words, the Michigan constitution contains over 20,000, placing it just about at the average for the states.[19]

There are reasons why state constitutions differ so profoundly from their federal counterpart. The first state constitutions were framed during the Revolution, and they have a revolutionary character. There was faith in representative democracy and a deep mistrust of strong executives. Such was this faith in democracy that early state constitutions "instituted annual elections, eschewed checks and balances, stripped the executive of meaningful powers, and/or concentrated almost all power in the legislature."[20] The delegates to the federal constitutional convention in Philadelphia in 1787 found the states' constitutions almost frightening, and deliberately rejected the idea of using them as models. The people of the states saw, and do see, their constitutions as works-in-progress or grand experiments in the art of governing. If the experiment fails, then it can be run anew after reconsideration and revision. Historian Morton Keller has argued that the frequent change in the content of state constitutions reflects two attitudes, "a dissatisfaction with the performance of state government and an optimism that tinkering with its institutional machinery can correct its deficiencies."[21]

One of the most frequently recurring problems for the states has been fiscal policy. Michigan's experience with state constitutions, economic cycles, business regulation, and state spending patterns is typical of many states. Michigan's first constitution in 1835 approximates the ideal of the minimalist constitution that speaks only to fundamentals, such as the rights of the people and the structure of government. What the constitution did not include—provisions for coping with private corporations—would soon create serious problems for the state economy. Another clause that the constitution did include—a "miscellaneous clause" requiring the state to encourage "internal improvements"—would add to the havoc. Just as Michigan entered the Union, the entire United States experienced a deep economic depression that lasted from about 1837 until 1843. A key cause in the collapse of businesses and banks was massive government and private debt.

By 1837, the national and state governments were burdened by heavy debts. Between 1841 and

1842, eight states went into default on their debt payments and another two repudiated part of their debt.[22] One of the responses to the crisis was a revision in state constitutions. New York, Louisiana, Iowa, Texas, and Missouri had all created new constitutions by 1847 that placed restrictions on the economic power of the state legislature.[23] Historian Samuel Reznick points out two typical constitutional restraints: prohibitions against the state lending its credit to private corporations or holding stock in them; and limits on the state's ability to incur new debt without popular approval.[24] Michigan had been particularly lax in regulating the establishment and operation of banks. One observer of Michigan banking, circa 1839, wrote that the situation was such that "every village plot with a house . . . if it has a hollow stump for a vault, was the site of a bank."[25] Michigan joined the wave of constitutional revision in 1850. This second constitution for the state would have an article, dedicated to corporations and their regulation, which would make corporate officers personally liable for all debts incurred by the corporation.[26]

Michigan government took a very aggressive view of the 1835 constitutional mandate to encourage internal improvements.[27] The state built public utilities, invested in private corporations, or made loans or grants to private corporations to do so. Such extravagance relied on Michigan's ability to borrow money, and borrow Michigan did: the state was so crushed by debt in the early 1840s that it repudiated part of the principal of its debt.[28] Furthermore, it was not just the state legislature that was guilty of such profligate spending—local government also participated in the development frenzy.[29] Michigan began to repair the damage to the state and its credit before the end of the depression of 1837. An amendment to the constitution was proposed in 1843 (and approved by the people in 1844) that required a public referendum on every law authorizing government borrowing or the issuance of state stock. This limited provision for direct democracy predates the progressive reforms of the initiative and referendum by over sixty years and foreshadows the active citizen involvement in state fiscal policy to come. Complete renovation of Michigan's financial house came in the Constitution of 1850. A new article was devoted to taxation and finance, and it emphasized extinguishing state debt and balancing the state budget.

The Constitution of 1908 was essentially a reworking of the 1850 charter because the conservative Republicans that dominated the convention resisted wholesale change. The 1908 constitution included limitations on state indebtedness so as not to repeat the financial fiascos of the past.[30] A 1932 constitutional amendment, which began as an initiative petition, placed a limit on property taxes.[31] In 1946, another amendment, which also came by way of the initiative, provided for a state sales tax that helped fund local government and schools.[32]

There is one more thing necessary to understand the Headlee Amendment's place in Michigan constitutional law and tradition: the Progressive Era reforms of direct democracy. Muckrakers of the turn of the twentieth century saw state legislatures as "corrupt" and "beholden to special interests," disdainful of the legitimate needs of the people.[33] An academic commentator was more polite but just as damning is his assessment of state legislatures: "Representative assemblies have not proved senates of unfailing wisdom."[34] The solution to the problems posed by state legislatures came in the form of direct democracy. Lawmaking power would be returned to the people themselves through the initiative (the power to "propose legislative measures, resolutions and laws") and the referendum (the power to "approve or reject any act passed by the legislature").[35] The initiative and the referendum, which were added to the 1908 constitution in 1914, were retained in the Constitution of 1963. Article XII, Section 2 provides a mechanism for the constitution to be amended through the initiative. The constitutional initiative allowed Richard Headlee and his supporters to bring the tax revolt directly to the people.

**Part Two: A Headlee Amendment Primer**

The Headlee Amendment is actually a package of changes made to Article IX of the Michigan Constitution of 1963. Table 33.1 summarizes the major components of the Headlee Amendment.

Given the significant ways in which this amendatory language to the Michigan Constitution has influenced public policy over the last two decades, it is interesting to note that the 1982 precursor to this volume, written shortly after the amendment's adoption, found it to have a slight impact at the time. Its namesake, Richard Headlee, was quoted as being "disappointed" in its efficacy.[36] The Section 31 millage rollbacks were judged unlikely to occur.[37] The Section 30

**TABLE 33.1**

**A Summary of Major Provisions of the Headlee Amendment**

| | |
|---|---|
| Section 25 | General outline of the Headlee system of state and local tax limitations. |
| Section 26 | State revenue limited to 9.49% of the personal income of Michigan. |
| Section 27 | Declared emergencies may occasion temporary lifting of revenue limit. |
| Section 28 | Prohibition against deficit spending. |
| Section 29 | Prohibition against state reducing its share of support to local government for required services or activities; prohibition against state imposition of unfunded mandates on local government. |
| Section 30 | Prohibition against state reducing proportion of state funds to local government (calculated at 41.61% of state budget). |
| Section 31 | Prohibition against new or increased local taxes without voter approval; property tax increases capped at the inflation rate or the increase in property valuation, whichever is less. |
| Section 32 | Authorization of taxpayers' suits in the state Court of Appeals to enforce Headlee. |
| Section 33 | Definitions of the terms "total state revenues," "personal income of Michigan," "local government," and "general price level." |
| Section 34 | Requirement that the legislature implement the Headlee Amendment. |

NOTE: This table is based on the one that appears on page 127 of The Headlee Amendment: A Study Report by the Michigan Law Revision Commission, 1998. The Headlee Amendment also added words to Article IX, Section 6 to accommodate the new provisions of Sections 25 to 34.

provisions requiring the state to maintain the total proportion of its budget spent on local government programs was judged to be a significant constraint at the time,[38] but is less so today, largely because of the Proposal A school finance reforms to be discussed in the following. Somewhat prophetically, however, the precursor of this chapter did note that such amendments "are likely to become more or less stringent in ways that cannot possibly be foreseen at the time the limitation measure is first passed."[39]

## Interpretation and Implementation of the Headlee Amendment

It is beyond the scope of this chapter to review in detail all the statutes, court decisions, and attorney general opinions related to each section of the Headlee Amendment.[40] However, this chapter will look at some of the key issues of interpretation and implementation of the amendment and in the process touch on just a few of the key court decisions and implementing statutes.

## Section 25: Summary and Statement of Purpose

Section 25 simply sets forth the goals of the Headlee changes to the constitution.

## Section 26: State Revenue Limit

This section of the Headlee Amendment limits the total amount of state taxes that can be imposed in any year by the state legislature except under emergency conditions specified in Section 27. The revenue limit is a function of total state revenues in 1978–79 and the total income received by all persons from all sources, in calendar year 1977, a lag that would prove to have significant impacts, as discussed in the following.[41] The Headlee Blue Ribbon Commission's report (1995) notes that until 1986 there was no official calculation of the revenue limit required by Section 26. Until that year, the state relied on rough estimates provided by the governor in budget messages.[42] The Michigan Law Revision Commission indicates that there is some evidence to suggest that the prescribed revenue limit might have been surpassed in FY 1984–85, before the official recalculation of the limit discussed in the following.[43] Executive and legislative neglect of the technical requirements of Section 26 ended with the passage of M.C.L. §§ 18.1350 et seq., which requires the Department of Management and Budget to calculate the revenue limit and, along with the state treasurer, submit annual reports on compliance with Section 26. The official revenue limit set in 1986 was 9.49% of the personal income of the state for the prior calendar year.

The revenue limit has proven to be problematic for state government at least five times in the

**TABLE 33.2**

**Summary History of State Compliance with Article IX, Section 26, the State Revenue Limit (dollar amounts in thousands)**

|  | FY 1979 Base Year/Audited | FY 1980 Estimated | FY 1981 Estimated | FY 1982 Estimated | FY 1983 Estimated |
|---|---|---|---|---|---|
| State Receipts to General & Special Revenue Funds | $11,090.1 | $11,953.1 | $11,706.3 | $11,764.6 | $12,469.7 |
| *Less: Interfund Transfers:* | | | | | |
| General & Special Revenue Funds | ($1,987.0) | ($2,221.3) | ($1,604.5) | ($1,352.5) | ($1,094.2) |
| Federal Aid | ($2,129.7) | ($2,452.4) | ($2,602.5) | ($2,577.9) | ($2,768.8) |
| Net Statutory Adjustments | ($415.7) | ($448.1) | ($469.8) | ($497.7) | ($520.1) |
| *Plus:* | | | | | |
| Tax Credits Not Related to Liabilities | $40.5 | $38.8 | $13.6 | $12.3 | $16.8 |
| Total State Revenues | $6,598.2 | $6,870.1 | $7,043.0 | $7,348.8 | $8,103.4 |
| Applicable CY Personal Income | $69,554 | $77,943 | $86,572 | $92,339 | $99,314 |
|  | **CY 77** | **CY 78** | **CY 79** | **CY 80** | **CY 81** |
| Percentage Change Personal Income | 12.06% | 11.07% | 6.66% | 7.55% | 0.67% |
| Section 26 Base Ratio | 9.49% | 9.49% | 9.49% | 9.49% | 9.49% |
| Section 26 Revenue Limit | $6,598.2 | $7,396.8 | $8,215.7 | $8,763.0 | $9,424.9 |
| Actual Revenue Subject to Limit | $6,598.2 | $6,870.1 | $7,043.0 | $7,348.8 | $8,103.4 |
| Percentage Change Revenue | 4.12% | 2.52% | 4.34% | 10.27% | 14.07% |
| Amount (Over)Under Limit | $0.0 | $526.7 | $1,172.6 | $1,414.2 | $1,321.5 |
|  | FY 1991 Audited | FY 1992 Audited | FY 1993 Audited | FY 1994 Audited | FY 1995 Audited |
| State Receipts to General & Special Revenue Funds | $20,482.3 | $22,086.5 | $23,432.9 | $26,360.4 | $29,125.6 |
| *Less: Interfund Transfers:* | | | | | |
| General & Special Revenue Funds | ($1,946.2) | ($1,852.6) | ($2,197.9) | ($2,039.8) | ($2,036.8) |
| Federal Aid | ($4,733.9) | ($5,289.4) | ($5,831.6) | ($6,273.1) | ($6,442.0) |
| Net Statutory Adjustments | ($1,508.8) | ($2,426.0) | ($1,989.5) | ($2,596.1) | ($2,083.4) |
| *Plus:* | | | | | |
| Tax Credits Not Related To Liabilities | $18.9 | $22.1 | $21.4 | $21.8 | $22.0 |
| Total State Revenues | $12,311.9 | $12,540.2 | $13,435.4 | $15,473.2 | $18,585.4 |
| Applicable Cy Personal Income | $161,764 | $171,003 | $174,750 | $185,713 | $194,687 |
|  | **CY 89** | **CY 90** | **CY 91** | **CY 92** | **CY 93** |
| Percentage Change Personal Income | 5.77% | 5.71% | 2.19% | 6.27% | 4.83% |
| Section 26 Base Ratio | 9.49% | 9.49% | 9.49% | 9.49% | 9.49% |
| Section 26 Revenue Limit | $15,351.4 | $16,228.2 | $16,583.8 | $17,624.2 | $18,475.8 |
| Actual Revenue Subject To Limit | $12,311.9 | $12,540.2 | $13,435.4 | $15,473.2 | $18,585.4 |
| Percentage Change Revenue | 1.85% | 7.14% | 15.17% | 20.11% | 6.53% |
| Amount (Over)Under Limit | $3,039.5 | $3,688.0 | $3,148.4 | $2,151.0 | ($109.6) |

SOURCE: Official State of Michigan Compliance Reports, Various Years. Summary compiled by Wayne State University State Policy Center.

last two decades (see table 33.2 and figure 33.1). In 1986, preliminary data on the revenue for the state fiscal year that ended 30 September 1985 (Fiscal 1985) indicated that the limit was likely to present a problem. Further review of the situation revealed that the state had never established an official procedure in statute, administrative rule, or formal practice for making this annual calculation. It was also found that the official limit had never been formally calculated for the base year (Fiscal 1979) established by the amendment.

In part, this lack of a formal process reflected the belief at the adoption of the amendment that it was unlikely that the Section 26 revenue limitation would ever be surpassed. In part, this neglect situation was the product of complicated legislation coming from the people rather than the government. Section 33 proposed the following definition

| FY 1984 Estimated | FY 1985 Audited | FY 1986 Estimated | FY 1987 Estimated | FY 1988 Audited | FY 1989 Audited | FY 1990 Audited |
|---|---|---|---|---|---|---|
| $14,142.3 | $15,473.6 | $15,295.9 | $15,873.5 | $16,834.7 | $17,537.2 | $18,750.0 |
| ($1,211.9) | ($1,715.4) | ($1,145.6) | ($1,194.2) | ($1,287.5) | ($1,196.0) | ($1,602.4) |
| ($3,161.9) | ($3,194.4) | ($3,498.6) | ($3,613.4) | ($3,714.7) | ($3,861.8) | ($4,136.4) |
| ($557.4) | ($746.1) | ($212.0) | ($208.8) | ($397.2) | ($443.4) | ($700.9) |
| $32.3 | $43.9 | $44.2 | $34.8 | $37.0 | $51.8 | $52.8 |
| $9,243.5 | $9,861.6 | $10,483.9 | $10,891.9 | $11,472.3 | $12,087.8 | $12,362.9 |
| $99,980 | $103,980 | $114,408 | $123,673 | $135,113 | $141,618 | $152,934 |
| **CY 82** | **CY 83** | **CY 84** | **CY 85** | **CY 86** | **CY 87** | **CY 88** |
| 4.00% | 10.03% | 8.10% | 9.25% | 4.81% | 7.99% | |
| 9.49% | 9.49% | 9.49% | 9.49% | 9.49% | 9.49% | 9.49% |
| $9,488.1 | $9,867.7 | $10,857.3 | $11,736.6 | $12,822.2 | $13,439.5 | $14,513.4 |
| $9,243.5 | $9,861.6 | $10,483.9 | $10,891.9 | $11,472.3 | $12,087.8 | $12,362.9 |
| 6.69% | 6.31% | 3.89% | 5.33% | 5.37% | 2.28% | |
| $244.6 | $6.1 | $373.4 | $844.7 | $1,350.0 | $1,351.7 | $2,150.5 |

| FY 1996 Audited | FY 1997 Audited | FY 1998 Audited | FY 1999 Audited | FY 2000 Audited | FY 2001 Audited |
|---|---|---|---|---|---|
| $30,309.3 | $31,122.5 | $32,930.6 | $34,727.5 | $36,941.5 | $38,465.9 |
| ($1,564.2) | ($1,269.0) | ($1,499.6) | ($1,842.0) | ($1,802.3) | ($1,910.7) |
| ($7,379.9) | ($7,653.5) | ($7,679.5) | ($7,902.7) | ($8,571.6) | ($9,383.9) |
| ($1,589.4) | ($1,529.5) | ($1,702.6) | ($1,800.3) | ($2,232.1) | ($3,289.5) |
| $23.0 | $23.8 | $23.4 | $25.9 | $27.3 | $27.3 |
| $19,798.8 | $20,694.3 | $22,072.3 | $23,208.5 | $24,362.9 | $23,909.2 |
| $210,559 | $228,369 | $239,330 | $244,329 | $255,039 | $277,296 |
| **CY 94** | **CY 95** | **CY 96** | **CY 97** | **CY 98** | **CY 99** |
| 8.15% | 8.46% | 4.80% | 2.09% | 4.38% | 8.73% |
| 9.49% | 9.49% | 9.49% | 9.49% | 9.49% | 9.49% |
| $19,982.0 | $21,672.2 | $22,712.4 | $23,186.8 | $24,203.2 | $26,315.4 |
| $19,798.8 | $20,694.3 | $22,072.3 | $23,208.5 | $24,362.9 | $23,909.2 |
| 4.52% | 6.66% | 5.15% | 4.97% | –1.86% | |
| $183.2 | $977.9 | $640.1 | ($21.7) | ($159.7) | $2,406.2 |

of revenue subject to the limit. "'Total State Revenues' includes all general and special revenues, excluding federal aid, *as defined in the budget message of the governor for fiscal year 1978–1979.* Total State Revenues shall exclude the amount of any credits based on actual tax liabilities or the imputed tax components of rental payments, but shall include the amount of any credits not related to actual tax liabilities" (emphasis supplied).

Unfortunately, neither the governor's budget message for that year, nor the complete budget, both issued before the passage of the Headlee Amendment, contained any definitions of state revenues. The amendment drafters apparently were referring to a particular table of data, which represented estimated revenues for budgetary purposes and was a common feature of the budget message. State officials at the time used

**FIGURE 33.1**

**Section 26 Revenue Percentage Margin ± Limit**

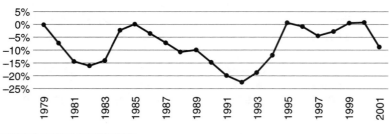

SOURCE: Calculations from Table 33.2.

the estimates contained in that table to also estimate the revenue limit. In the 1986 reviews, which were audited by the legislative auditor general, the table was found to contain many items that were not revenues under either the general language of the amendment itself or according to generally accepted accounting principles, such as interfund transfers and gross lottery sales before payment of prizes. The actual review went to an account-by-account examination of each state revenue source. The ultimate result of the review was an audited recalculation of both the base year (Fiscal 1979) and Fiscal 1985, which produced an official limit of 9.49%, and a determination that Fiscal 1985 had just barely missed exceeding the constitutional limit. These new procedures were subsequently enacted into law in 1988 and now result in a formal annual audited calculation of the revenue limit.[44]

In summary form, the calculation of "total state revenues" for purposes of the Section 26 revenue limit includes the following steps. First, pursuant to the definitional language of the amendment itself, federal revenues, revenues supporting debt service on general obligation bonds, and tax credits based on actual liability are subtracted from gross revenues. Second, to avoid double counting of revenue, interfund transfers (such as the General Fund-General Purpose appropriation to the School Aid Fund) are subtracted. Third, the proceeds of any general obligation bonds sold during the year are subtracted. Finally, a number of other subtractions are made to adjust for what may be termed technical accounting entries, such as the need to record the net increase in asset value attributable to capital lease acquisitions on state property.

As can be seen in table 33.2, and figure 33.1, in addition to nearly exceeding the revenue limit under the formal audited calculations that estab-

lished the limit at 9.49% of the prior calendar year personal income of the state, the limitation has been a factor in four other years: in 1995, 1999, and 2000, in which the limit was exceeded but not the 1% trigger discussed in the following; and in 1996, in which total revenue came in just under the limit. Two factors were responsible for causing the state to exceed, or nearly exceed, the revenue limit. First, the state made a conscious decision to not adjust the state revenue limit for the transfer of K–12 funding responsibility from local to state taxes that was a major feature of Proposal A.[45] This was done in order to count clearly the higher state spending for K–12 as part of the state's Section 30 obligation (discussed in the following), and, as some would argue, to limit the amount of room for any future state tax increases. The second factor that contributed to exceeding the limit in 1999 and 2000—after a cushion had developed in 1997 and 1998—is related to the structure of the amendment itself. Fiscal 1999, for example, was a very strong revenue growth year, but it was measured against 9.49% of total Michigan personal income for calendar year 1997, in which very weak growth was officially reported. This built-in time lag, measuring a given fiscal year against a base almost two years old, could create problems in any strong revenue growth year following a recession or slow growth period. This second factor was one of the primary causes of the close approach to the limit in Fiscal 1985.

Figure 33.1 shows the percentage margin below, or above, the revenue limit, beginning with the base year of Fiscal 1979. Fiscal 1979 was a very strong revenue growth year, measured against a weaker personal income growth in calendar year 1977, which set the limit at a moderately stringent level. By Fiscal 1985, however, the strong economic growth of that year, which included revenues from a major tax increase, was measured against a very weak 1983 calendar year personal income figure. That produced results that were essentially right at the limit. As the figure shows, the state stayed well under the limit for a decade, until the major state tax increases of Proposal A (partially impacting Fiscal 1994 and fully in place for Fiscal 1995) were measured against very weak 1992 and moderate 1993 personal income levels. The result was the first case of exceeding the limit in 1995, even after a preemptive tax reduction. The very strong economy of the late 1990s generated exceptionally strong revenue growth that pushed collections above the limit for both Fiscal 1999 and 2000.

Section 26 requires a refund to payers of the state income tax or the single business tax if the revenue limit is exceeded by more than one percentage point. If the excess is less than 1%, the moneys *may* be transferred to the State Budget Stabilization fund. The Blue Ribbon Commission saw this permissive language as a "gray area," since it is unclear what would happen if the overage were not transferred to the State Budget Stabilization Fund or refunded to the taxpayers. The Blue Ribbon Commission believes that the "spirit" of the Headlee Amendment requires either the transfer or the refund.[46]

As indicated in table 33.2 and figure 33.1, the one percentage point cushion has been a factor three times since the adoption of the amendment: in Fiscal Years 1995, 1999, and 2000. In 1995, the state enacted a "preemptive" tax credit to be paid on state income tax returns filed in 1996 for 1995 taxes in an attempt at least to stay under the 1% cushion, if not also to stay below the limit itself. The constitutional phrasing "may be transferred to the State Budget Stabilization Fund" has indeed been proven to be a somewhat gray area. While funds were put into the Budget Stabilization Fund in all three years, the Fiscal 2000 transfer was somewhat controversial because the funds so transferred were immediately withdrawn. To date there has been no legislative consideration of the Blue Ribbon Commission's recommendation to make the deposit mandatory or to require that it be refunded to taxpayers by some mechanism if no deposit is made.

The constitutional language regarding the mandatory refund provisions for exceeding the one percentage point cushion may prove to be unworkable in practice if it must be used. There can be serious questions of fairness and significant delay in implementing the required refund. The potential for delay comes from the requirement that refunds be paid *pro rata* based on liabilities reported on the annual returns filed by income tax and single business taxpayers. Both individuals and businesses with large tax liabilities routinely file extensions to obtain more time to file complete annual tax returns. Filing for extensions is routine with larger businesses reporting their single business tax liability. Such extensions mean that all the tax returns necessary to calculate the refund will not be available until the end of the next calendar year, or even later. Thus the cost of a refund could be borne by a budget two years or more after the limit was exceeded, unless the funds were reserved pending

final calculation of refunds, a procedure that is not now in law or policy.

The fairness question centers on the requirement to make refunds based upon income tax and single business tax liability. The combination of the mechanical difficulties of refunding coupled with the fairness question almost requires the state to develop accurate estimates of state revenues and the ability to enact a quick tax reduction. Policy makers may wish to examine the creation of a permanent mechanism in state law for a retroactive tax credit such as the one utilized in 1995.

Section 26 allows the revenue limit to be adjusted if responsibility for funding a program is transferred from one level of government to another. Any such adjustment cannot result in an increase in the total revenue collected by state and local government. In the recent case of the transfer of a major portion of the responsibility for K–12 funding from local to state sources under Proposal A, no adjustment was made, although it was considered, as discussed previously, and also in the following Section 30 discussion.

Finally, Section 26 provides for two exceptions to the revenue limit. First, the limit does not apply to taxes imposed to pay the principal and interest on bonds authorized under Article IX, Section 15. Section 15 requires a supermajority of both houses of the state legislature and approval by the voters before the state can float bonds. This preexisting constitutional provision for incurring indebtedness is consistent with the Headlee Amendment's purpose of requiring voter approval for new taxes. Second, the limit does not apply to loans to school districts authorized under Article IX, Section 16. Section 16 permits the state to issue bonds for making loans to school districts and provides ways for local school districts to repay the loan. This section specifically creates an exception to other constitutional provisions on taxes by authorizing school districts to tax for repayment of the loans "without limitation as to rate or amount" with local voter approval of the underlying bonds themselves.

There have been relatively few controversies regarding implementation of Section 26 since the state revenue limit was formally calculated. Two opinions of the attorney general have addressed aspects of this section. In the first, the attorney general opined (1986) that Section 26 "does not preclude the imposition of new state taxes, provided that the projected revenue there from, together with all other state revenues, does not exceed the limit."[47] The attorney general indicated that it was permissible for the legislature to rely on revenue projections to aid the decision on the imposition of a new tax. Moreover, not every form of state revenue counts toward the Headlee limit of Section 26. Proceeds from the sale of the State Accident Fund do not count toward the limit since they are neither taxes nor fees paid to the state.[48] While this (1995) opinion was controversial at the time, it was never taken to court, leaving the attorney general's opinion as the guiding legal standard on this issue.

Given recent experiences, it now seems much more likely than it did in the early 1980s that the state revenue limit will affect Michigan fiscal policy. As noted previously, the built-in time lag of the revenue limit formula itself makes this possible. Any significant state tax increase could also increase the likelihood of a trigger. At least for the short term, the scheduled current law reductions in state income tax and single business tax rates should provide some breathing room relative to the limit, whatever their impact on the funding of public services. Finally, any future state assumption of an entire program or a substantial increase in the state share of financing of a local program will need a very careful consideration of whether to make an accompanying decision to adjust the limit as provided in the constitution.

### Section 27: Exceptions to the Revenue Limit

Section 27 spells out the conditions under which an exception can be made to the revenue limit. The governor must declare a tightly defined emergency, and the legislature must accept that declaration with a two-thirds vote of approval. Such an emergency can last for only one fiscal year at a time, and the need to make a Section 26 refund cannot be considered an emergency. Since the adoption of the amendment, there has been no use of this provision, or even any public consideration of its use.

### Section 28: Expenditure Limit

Section 28 is a corollary to Section 26, but on the expenditure side. It creates an expenditure limit equal to the revenue limit plus expenditures from federal aid and any accumulated prior year surpluses. Balances in the Budget Stabilization Fund have been considered prior year surpluses. As

with Section 27, this section has not been an issue to date.

### Section 29: State Support of Local Government

Section 29, also known as the "mandates section," has been the locus of considerable controversy and litigation. It is designed to "forestall any attempt by the Legislature to shift responsibility for services to the local government, once its revenues were limited by the Headlee Amendment, in order to save the money it would have had to use to provide the services itself."[49] Section 29 "does not guarantee that local units' spending levels will not increase from the 1978 level. Increased levels of local spending attributable to other causes, e.g., inflation or the greater utilization of a program by the public, are not addressed by this provision of the Headlee Amendment."[50] The first part of Section 29 prohibits the state from reducing its proportion of the necessary costs of any existing activity or service required of units of local government by state law. The second part prohibits the state from requiring local governments to perform a new activity or service, or increase the level of an activity or service, without paying for it.

One of the questions associated with Section 29 concerns the meaning of the words "state law." The Michigan supreme court has held that the words "state law" refer only to state statutes and the rules promulgated by state administrative agencies. The requirements of the state constitution itself are separate and apart from the "state law" of Section 29, and are therefore not subject to the Headlee Amendment.[51] For the supreme court, it is "clear that the voters' concern with the possibility of the state 'shifting responsibility' without adequate state funding would not extend to constitutional provisions . . . [since] the voters themselves determine any constitutional requirements and are fully in control of what will be mandated by the constitution through the ratification process."[52]

A related question is what is meant by the word "required" in Section 29. For the supreme court, the word "required" means only "those services and activities that state law mandated in the first instance."[53] The court emphasized that the Headlee Amendment was designed to prevent the state legislature from expanding state programs or services at the expense of local government. If a unit of local government undertakes to provide a service of its own volition (such as operating a fire department or a sanitary landfill), it must absorb the costs of any new state requirements or regulations without any increased funding from the state. The supreme court reasoned that "[w]hile the state can, and sometimes does, mandate higher standards, benefits, and so forth, it does not necessarily profit from increasing these standards, and, therefore, the kind of escape hatch for the state that the Headlee Amendment was intended to close is not created."[54] The court acknowledged the concerns of the *amici curiae* that excluding optional local activities could defeat one of the purposes of the Headlee Amendment by forcing on local governments expensive new state regulations. However, the court believed that its reading of Section 29 was also consistent with the Headlee principle that each unit of government—state or local—should live within its means and fund the programs it undertakes. For the court, if Section 29 applied to optional activities or services, the local government "could look to all state taxpayers for the cost of upgrading a voluntarily assumed, quasi-governmental function."[55] The requirements of Section 29 also do not apply to increased costs that arise from federal law.[56] Nor does Section 29 apply to new state regulations whose burden falls primarily on private persons or corporations.[57]

What frame of reference should be used to determine the state's obligation of support to local government? As the Michigan supreme court put it: "[T]he underlying question [is]: does Section 29 address mandated activities that are new or required at an increased level from the perspective of a particular local unit or from the perspective of local units collectively?"[58] For the court, Section 29 was designed to prevent the state from creating "loopholes" around the Headlee Amendment's limitations on state spending by shunting burdens on local government or decreasing the state's share of support for local government. Actions of the legislature that do not attempt to create such loopholes, therefore, do not implicate Section 29. The supreme court recognized that Section 29 also must be interpreted to strike a balance between "preserving the Legislature's ability to enact necessary and desirable legislation in response to changing times and conditions and guaranteeing a predictable level of minimum funding" to local government.[59] Accordingly, the supreme court has held that the "statewide-to-local" ratio for "calculating the state's funding obligation for existing services and activities

under Section 29 preserves voter intent by securing a minimum funding guarantee while simplifying calculations and avoiding inequitable anomalies."[60]

What is the meaning of "necessary costs," and when does state law impose a new or expanded obligation on local government? The most controversial, convoluted, and protracted debate on the mandates provision and necessary costs is contained in the *Durant* litigation.[61] *Durant* refers to a series of cases in which the court of appeals and the supreme court considered the "maintenance of support" provision, the definition of a state requirement, and the meaning of "necessary costs." *Durant* began in 1980 when taxpayers filed suit in the court of appeals claiming that the state had decreased its level of support for education in a school district.[62] The school districts contended that Section 29 should apply to the state constitutional obligation of a free education.[63] The plaintiffs took advantage of Section 32 of the Headlee Amendment, which grants taxpayers standing to sue in the court of appeals to enforce the provisions of the amendment. The court of appeals, however, chose not to hear the case, ruling that the plaintiffs should seek first an administrative remedy through the Local Government Claims Review Board (LCRB), which is discussed in the following. The court of appeals, whose work normally involves deciding questions of law and reviewing the actions of trial courts, was reluctant to consider a case that required extensive fact-finding. The plaintiffs appealed to the Michigan supreme court, which then returned the case to the court of appeals, directing the appellate panel to consider the merits of the case.[64]

The court of appeals complied in part with the supreme court's directive. The appellate court chose to decide only the questions of law presented in the case. The court made the following conclusions of law: (1) "education" is too broad and indefinite a concept to be considered an existing activity or service required by state law; (2) only those specific and identifiable programs that the state requires school districts to provide by state statute or state agency regulation fall within the scope of Section 29; (3) "necessary costs" of a required service or activity are those costs which are essential to fulfill the state-required activity, and "they must be determined on a statewide basis, computed according to the actual cost to the state, were it to provide the required activity or service"; (4) the state is not required to maintain the current level of unrestricted state school aid;

and (5) the state is required to maintain the level of funding of categorical aid for the necessary costs of programs required of school districts by state statute or state agency regulation."[65] Yet without an evidentiary record to review, the court of appeals could not resolve the taxpayers' claim. The case was dismissed and once again, the court suggested that the plaintiffs avail themselves of the services of the LCBR.[66]

Once again, the case was appealed to the state supreme court. Again, the plaintiffs contended that Section 29 requires maintenance of support for the constitutional obligation of free public education. The state countered that Headlee applies only to specific requirements imposed on the school districts by state statutes and state agencies. The supreme court sided with the state, ruling that it "was not the intent of the voters to include in Section 29 any obligations that may be imposed upon local governmental units by [the state constitution] and that unrestricted state aid is not funding for an 'existing activity or service required of units of Local Government by state law.'"[67] The supreme court further found that the state statute requiring 180 school days per year did not implicate Headlee because of the "extensive local control over all other aspects of the educational process," and the "vast authority" of local school districts "to determine the necessary academic and administrative matters."[68] The high court also adopted part of the legislature's definition of "necessary costs," which defines "necessary costs" as the net actual cost to the state if the state were to provide the activity or service itself.[69] However, the supreme court took issue with a particular element of the definition of "necessary costs" used by the legislature and the court of appeals. The statutory definition of "necessary costs" excludes costs to the school district "recoverable from a federal or state categorical aid program, or other external financial aid."[70] The supreme court found that this element of the implementing legislation "clearly violated" the intent of the Headlee Amendment, which "unambiguously forbids" the reduction of state support below 1978 levels, and was, therefore, unconstitutional.[71]

All this legal analysis was still insufficient to resolve the case, since the court of appeals refused to engage in fact-finding. The supreme court found that Section 32 clearly gives taxpayers standing to sue in the court of appeals. The court noted that the LCBR was not yet ready to adjudicate claims, and that, even if it was, it was given jurisdiction only over appeals by units of local government. The supreme court "reminded" the court of appeals that state statutes and court rules allow the appeals court to appoint fact finders or special masters to hear the presentation of disputed facts and report their findings to the appellate judges.

In April 1986, the court of appeals appointed a fact finder, and his findings were submitted to the court of appeals in September 1989. By this time, plaintiffs had amended their complaint to address only a handful of specific programs that they believed were required by state law—special education, special education transportation, bilingual education, drivers' education, and the school lunch program.[72] The state countered with the argument that these special education programs were required by federal, not state, law and were thus not subject to the strictures of Section 29. Finally, in November 1990, the court of appeals made its ruling.[73] The appellate court noted that both federal and state statutes address special education. When the federal and state laws were compared, the court found that "Michigan law imposes a substantive standard prescribing the level of education to be accorded disabled children where federal law does not," which meant that special education was a requirement of state law governed by Section 29.[74] The court offered two justifications for its conclusions. First, Michigan law is written to "maximize the potential of each disabled student," while federal law imposes only an "obligation to provide a basic floor of opportunity;" thus, "it cannot be said that compliance with the lesser federal obligation satisfies the more demanding state requirement."[75] Second, federal law establishes only broad goals and procedures and leaves the state and local governments free to create and implement the actual programs. Therefore, special education as it exists in Michigan is a function of state—rather than federal—law. The court of appeals, however, disagreed with the fact finder's calculations of necessary costs of the state-mandated programs. The case was remanded to the fact finder to recompute the dollar amounts and the state's underpayment to the units of local government.[76]

By 1997, the *Durant* case had bounced repeatedly between the court of appeals and the supreme court. In a decision that has become popularly known as *Durant I*, the supreme court sought to answer finally five questions that formed the heart of this lengthy litigation. The court announced the essence of its ruling in this catechism:

1. Are special education and special education transportation state-mandated activities or services within the meaning of Section 29? Yes.
2. Are payments that are required of the state by Section 29 "funds constitutionally dedicated for specific purposes" and exempt from executive order reduction? Yes.
3. Are plaintiffs' attorney fees in this case part of the costs that may be recovered under Section 32? Yes.
4. What is the appropriate remedy for the violation of Section 29 in this case? A money judgment for plaintiff school districts for the full amount of underfunding for 1991–92, 1992–93, and 1993–94, to use for refunds for taxpayers, tax relief, or other public purposes.[77]

The toughest matter for the supreme court in *Durant III* was the appropriate remedy. Section 29 is silent on how exactly Michigan courts are to enforce the amendment. In *Durant III*, the supreme court found that substantial monetary damages were appropriate, given the state's "prolonged recalcitrance" in this case.[78] The supreme court expressed the hope that monetary damages would not be necessary in future cases. Instead, "the court of appeals would give a declaratory judgment on the obligation of the state, [and] [i]f there was such an obligation," the supreme court expected that the state would comply with that obligation in the next fiscal year, unless it obtained a stay from the court, or eliminated the mandate.[79] The supreme court also believed that in the future better use of the implementation legislation would expedite the resolution of mandates disputes.[80]

Section 34 of the Headlee Amendment authorizes the legislature to adopt legislation to implement various provisions of the amendment. In adopting such implementing legislation, the legislature recognized that there would likely be disputes between the state and local governments over the existence of new or expanded mandates and the computation of costs for reimbursement claims. The implementing legislation took two different tacks to try to forestall some of these problems, neither of which has worked well, as illustrated by the *Durant* odyssey.

First, the legislature itself was to adopt joint rules establishing a process to try to identify potential mandates and estimate the costs to local governments before legislation was adopted. It was apparently assumed that new mandates either would then not be adopted or would be funded.[81] These rules were never adopted. Instead, the legislature has relied upon its staff to identify potential mandates in bill analyses and the fiscal notes prepared on pending legislation. Thus, there are no special procedures to resolve a dispute over the existence of a new or expanded mandate. It should, however, be noted that the issue of whether or not a proposed law creates a new mandate is a frequent topic of legislative debate.

Second, the implementing legislation also provided for the creation of a Local Government Claims Review Board (LCRB).[82] It is clear from reviewing the language of 21.240 that the LCRB was intended to resolve disputes involving the proper amount of reimbursements for activities already determined to be mandates by the legislature or the courts. In practice, the LCRB's potential was frustrated by the absence of an unambiguous legal definition of a mandate. The board was flooded with claims from school districts during the 1980s, alleging that they were entitled to additional funding for special education. Unfortunately, the state's position was that special education was not a mandate, and the board was thus in no position to determine accuracy of a payment that was not considered a mandate.[83] The LCRB remains in existence today, and meets occasionally, but in practice has little or nothing to do, given its limited original charge and the claimants' tendencies to resort to the courts to establish first whether or not a mandate exists.[84] The Blue Ribbon Commission has recommended that the LCBR be given jurisdiction under the state administrative procedures act to hear Section 29 cases on an expedited basis.[85]

## Section 30: State Allocations to Local Government

As the Law Revision Commission puts it, Section 30 is a "corollary" to Section 29, which guarantees that the "percentage of total state budget earmarked for local government spending will not decline from the FY 1978–79 level."[86]

The requirement to meet a fixed share of the total budget for local government purposes, taken as a group, in effect created a requirement for a budget balanced internally between the state and local shares, in addition to the long-standing constitutional requirement for being balanced in total between revenues and expenditures. Under Section 30, the state must always maintain or

**TABLE 33.3**

**Section 30: History of Compliance with Constitutional Local Share of State Expenditures Requirement**

|                      | 1979        | 1980        | 1981        | 1982        | 1983        |
|----------------------|-------------|-------------|-------------|-------------|-------------|
| *Summary Calculations* |             |             |             |             |             |
| Required Local Share | 41.61%      | 41.61%      | 41.61%      | **41.61%**  | **41.61%**  |
| Actual Percentage    | 41.61%      | 41.62%      | 41.71%      | **41.34%**  | **41.25%**  |
| Total State Spending | $6,645,314  | $6,948,356  | $6,985,960  | **$7,195,646** | **$7,708,285** |
| Required Local Share | $2,765,115  | $2,891,211  | $2,906,858  | **$2,994,108** | **$3,207,417** |
| Actual Local Share   | $2,765,115  | $2,891,989  | $2,913,805  | **$2,974,744** | **$3,179,893** |
| Over (Under)         | $0          | $778        | $6,947      | **–$19,365** | **–$27,525** |

|                      | 1990        | 1991        | 1992        | 1993        | 1994        |
|----------------------|-------------|-------------|-------------|-------------|-------------|
| *Summary Calculations* |             |             |             |             |             |
| Required Local Share | 41.61%      | 41.61%      | 41.61%      | **48.97%**  | 48.97%      |
| Actual Percentage    | 42.88%      | 44.20%      | 43.36%      | **48.25%**  | 50.00%      |
| Total State Spending | $12,806,278 | $12,799,003 | $12,450,926 | **$13,462,626** | $14,948,761 |
| Required Local Share | $5,328,692  | $5,325,665  | $5,180,830  | **$6,592,648** | $7,320,408  |
| Actual Local Share   | $5,490,873  | $5,657,615  | $5,399,207  | **$6,496,010** | $7,474,244  |
| Over (Under)         | $162,181    | $331,950    | $218,377    | **–$96,638** | $153,836    |

SOURCE: Official State of Michigan "Statement of Proportion of Total State Spending from State Sources Paid to Units of Local Government—Legal Basis," various years.

NOTE: Years in which the requirement was not met shown in **bold**. Dollar amounts in thousands; totals may not add due to rounding.

exceed the proper balance between state spending and local spending. In the early years following adoption of the amendment, this was often a significant challenge for budget development. For example, if one assumes that the 41.61% share (prior to the recalculation required by the Oakland County litigation settlement) was the standard, and the budget at or near this level as it was in practice, and it was deemed necessary and desirable to add $1 of state spending for corrections, or higher education, or human services, the mathematics dictated that total spending had to increase by a total of $1.7126 ($1 + (41.61 ÷ 58.39 = 0.7126)). The new, post–Oakland County standard makes this test $1.9596 ($1 + (48.97 ÷ 51.03 = 0.9596)). For the near future, the significant increases in local spending created by Proposal A mean that this internal balance requirement is not an immediate problem.

Table 33.3 and figure 33.2 present the history of state compliance with the Section 30 requirement. From the base year 1978–79, when the share was determined to be 41.61%, meeting the requirement was nearly an annual challenge. This difficulty resulted from the funding calculations outlined in the preceding paragraph, and the fact that pressure for increased spending on "state side" programs was particularly intense coming out of the recession of the early 1980s. Indeed, the

state failed to meet the requirement in 1982 and 1983, falling short respectively by $19.4 million and $27.5 million. The Section 30 implementing legislation required that these shortfalls be added to the next year's spending for local government in order to make the collective total for all units of government whole over time. This constraint continued until Fiscal 1986, when the state determined that counties should be responsible for the cost of care for county residents in state mental health facilities. The state negotiated agreements with eighty-two counties to implement this practice and provided funding to cover the costs. This funding was then counted as local spending for purposes of the Section 30 calculation, resulting in a small but workable cushion for the next several years.

While Section 30 compliance became a little less of an issue in subsequent years, it never entirely went away. Also, Oakland County never signed an agreement with the state to implement the aforementioned treatment of mental health spending and engaged in a protracted dispute with the state over its propriety. The complexities of this issue are too involved for a lengthy discussion here, but Oakland County sued the state over this issue. This litigation was ultimately settled by the Engler administration and resulted in a recalculation of the required state expenditure share

| 1984 | 1985 | 1986 | 1897 | 1988 | 1989 | 1990 |
|---|---|---|---|---|---|---|
| 41.61% | 41.61% | 41.61% | 41.61% | 41.61% | 41.61% | 41.61% |
| 41.63% | 41.92% | 42.89% | 43.91% | 43.87% | 42.60% | 42.88% |
| $8,588,453 | $9,561,990 | $10,252,799 | $10,729,434 | $11,435,764 | $11,896,499 | $12,806,278 |
| $3,573,655 | $3,978,744 | $4,266,190 | $4,464,518 | $4,758,421 | $4,950,133 | $5,328,692 |
| $3,575,106 | $4,008,520 | $4,397,635 | $4,711,355 | $5,017,114 | $5,067,658 | $5,490,873 |
| $1,450 | $29,777 | $131,445 | $246,837 | $258,693 | $117,525 | $162,181 |

| 1995 | 1996 | 1997 | 1998 | 1999 | 2000 | 2001 |
|---|---|---|---|---|---|---|
| 48.97% | 48.97% | 48.97% | 48.97% | 48.97% | 48.97% | 48.97% |
| 58.55% | 59.24% | 60.77% | 62.43% | 60.93% | 61.68% | 62.77% |
| $19,525,399 | $20,011,897 | $20,399,562 | $21,569,700 | $22,791,301 | $23,451,766 | $24,686,013 |
| $9,561,588 | $9,799,826 | $9,989,666 | $10,562,682 | $11,160,900 | $11,484,330 | $12,088,741 |
| $11,431,457 | $11,855,398 | $12,397,206 | $13,466,028 | $13,887,556 | $14,465,853 | $15,494,806 |
| $1,869,869 | $2,055,572 | $2,407,540 | $2,903,346 | $2,726,656 | $2,981,523 | $3,406,065 |

for locals. This changed the share requirement from 41.61% to 48.97%, and was to take effect beginning with Fiscal 1993. As table 33.3 shows, Fiscal 1993 thus fell short of meeting its required Section 30 level of expenditures for local governments by some $96.6 million, which became an obligation of the next budget year. Fiscal 1994 met and exceeded the required level of spending, thanks to the first partial implementation of increased state expenditures for K–12 schools. Since Fiscal 1995, state support of K–12 education under Proposal A has created a substantial Section 30 spending cushion that is likely to continue for some time. (However, note that as discussed under Section 26 previously, the related decision to not adjust the state revenue limit for this transfer of funding has contributed to compliance issues for that limitation.)

It is important to note here that Section 30 does not guarantee any individual local unit of government, or indeed any type of local unit (all cities, for example), that they will always get the same

**FIGURE 33.2**

**Section 30 State Payments to Locals: Percentage ± Requirement**

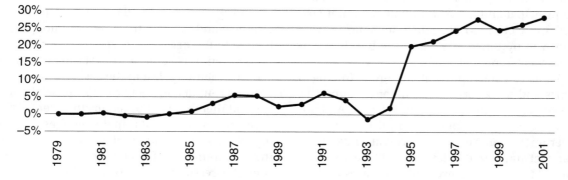

SOURCE: Calculations from Table 33.3.

number of dollars as the year before or even the same share of state dollars. Rather, it looks to total state expenditures to all types of local government taken as a group. Indeed, the state could constitutionally (if not politically) reduce spending to one type of unit and increase spending to another type (for example, by shifting a service responsibility from cities, villages, and townships to counties). This is why the Proposal A shift—from a primarily locally funded school finance system to one primarily financed from the state budget—seems to have eliminated the Section 30 problem, beginning with the partial year of Proposal A funding in Fiscal 1994

The data in table 33.3 and figure 33.2 certainly seem to indicate that there will be few short-term problems in continuing to meet the Section 30 requirements. In the long term, the most likely circumstance that could put this to a severe test would be a very major expansion of a program funded on the "state side" of the budget (perhaps a massive investment in a new statewide transportation system operated by a newly developed alternative energy source) or a long, protracted recession that forces state spending cuts to all areas of the budget, including K–12 education and local revenue sharing in order to meet immediate needs for major expansion of human services programs.

### Section 31: Local Voter Approval of New Taxes

There are four key features to Section 31: (1) voter approval is required for any new or increased local tax; (2) if a tax base is broadened, the tax rate must be decreased such that the total revenue raised by the tax is the same; (3) if property values (minus new construction and improvements) increase at a rate greater than the inflation rate, the property tax rate must be decreased to yield the same revenue from the property; (4) taxes used to repay the principal and interest on bonds are not covered by Section 31, because such taxes were approved by the voters when the bonds themselves were approved.

When is voter approval required? Michigan courts and the attorney general have found this clause easy to interpret: "The Headlee Amendment requires voter approval only if a unit of local government wants to impose taxes at a rate higher than that authorized by law at the time of its adoption."[87] The "Headlee exemption of taxes authorized by law when the [amendment] was ratified permits the levying of previously authorized taxes even where they were not being levied before."[88]

The removal of a tax exemption does not qualify as an increase in taxes that requires voter approval. According to the attorney general, "[T]he broadening of a tax base [that comes from elimination of an exemption] does not require voter approval. What is required is the adjustment of the tax rate to compensate for the addition to the tax base so that the tax revenues realized as a result of the change will be identical to those realized prior to the broadening of the tax base."[89]

What is a local tax? For the Michigan courts, the key question in determining the nature of a tax is the entity responsible for levying the tax.[90] A local tax is "collected by local government, administered directly by that local government and spent by the local government according to local fiscal policy."[91] The supreme court discussed some of the questions that go to the distinctions between state and local taxes in evaluating the application of Section 31 to a state excise tax on airport parking that works to return moneys to local government: How is the tax styled and structured? Does it serve a state purpose? Was the tax passed by the state legislature and administered by the state? Are the funds deposited in the state treasury and accounted for in the state budget? Are the funds from the tax distributed by the state, according to state statute? Does the state retain interest and penalties that flow from delinquent taxes?

When is a "user fee" really a tax? This issue is important to the Headlee Amendment because an increase in taxes requires voter approval, while the imposition of a user fee does not. The Michigan Supreme Court has recognized that there is no "bright line" distinction between a tax and a user fee.[92] Therefore, the court uses three criteria to distinguish between the two. The first criterion goes to purpose: true user fees serve a regulatory purpose, while taxes raise revenue. The second criterion looks to the relationship between a service and its cost: true user fees are proportionate to the necessary costs of the service. The third criterion is voluntariness. Payment of taxes is never voluntary; but in the case of a user fee, a person is entitled to decline or limit use of a service, and thereby avoid or reduce the user fee.[93]

Special assessments, like user fees, are not regarded as taxes and are therefore exempt from the requirements of Section 31. Unlike a tax, a special assessment is apportioned on an *ad valorem* basis and paid by only those persons who benefit from a service.[94]

The Blue Ribbon Commission found user fees and special assessments problematic for proper implementation of Section 31. A majority of the commission found that local government labeling an exaction a "mandatory user fee" rather than a tax was "one of the most frequent abridgements of the spirit, if not the letter, of the Headlee Amendment."[95] The majority of commissioners recommended that the legislature enact a law that defines clearly what constitutes a tax, a user fee, and a special assessment. The majority further urged that such a statute place the "burden of proving a new charge is not a tax on the unit of local government."[96] Unless such action was undertaken by the legislature, the majority believed that Section 31's voter-approval requirement for new taxes would be rendered "effectively meaningless."[97]

The third provision of Section 31 is generally referred to as the "millage rollback" provision. It was one of the key features highlighted in the campaign for voter approval in 1978, and while it has produced significant impacts over the years, it has sowed the seeds of voter dissatisfaction. How can these conflicting results both be true?

Millage rollbacks and elections to overturn the rollbacks (known as "override" elections) were common in the 1980s and early 1990s.[98] Millage rollbacks placed significant constraints on local governments who either chose not to seek annual overrides or encountered voter opposition and defeat of override attempts. For voters, however, the rollback based on the total valuation of the taxing jurisdiction often meant at best only a very marginal reduction in their own taxes in the face of annual increases in their assessment levels. This could and did occur because significant increases in residential property values in desirable neighborhoods drove up the total value of property in a community, while other residential and business property values grew more slowly or not at all. Under the unitwide millage rollbacks, all properties received a millage reduction, even if they had not contributed to the growth, and as a result, the faster-growing properties had a smaller proportion of their increased taxes rolled back. Further, even in the cases where voters did refuse to authorize the override of these rollbacks, the near-annual frequency of these elections in some communities probably contributed to voter perception that property taxes were on a never-ending upward trajectory. Some of this voter frustration finally found relief in the assessment cap provision of Proposal A. The cap placed limits on assessment increases for each individual parcel of property. The millage rollback provisions of Section 31 remain in effect, and, while currently significantly less common than before, there are circumstances in which they can still occur.[99]

### Section 32: Taxpayers' Suits to Enforce Headlee

Section 32 empowers any taxpayer with the right to sue in court to enforce the amendment and receive compensation from the unit of government at fault if successful. Headlee provides for the Michigan Court of Appeals to exercise original jurisdiction over such taxpayers' suits despite the fact that the court of appeals was designed to function as an appellate court. The framers of the Headlee Amendment chose the court of appeals in the belief that this would "streamline" the process of resolving the dispute. A retrospective look at the choice of the court of appeals reveals that this choice was wrong.[100] The Blue Ribbon Commission found that the drafters of Section 32 failed to appreciate the differences in the work of trial and appellate courts and thereby failed to recognize that a trial court is the appropriate forum for fact-finding. The time for a case to be heard and resolved by the court of appeals runs to about two years, which is certainly not "streamlined." The commission saw the protracted *Durant* litigation as "judicial pettifoggery at its worst."[101] To remedy the fundamental problem with Section 32, the commission recommended that "the Local Government Claims Review Board should be given jurisdiction to hear [Headlee enforcement cases] by amending the Administrative Procedures Act," and to limit the role of the courts to appellate review.[102]

### Conclusions

As foreseen by the author of the 1982 chapter on the Headlee Amendment, the amendment has in some ways been more stringent and in some ways less stringentthan foreseen at the time of its passage. It is likely that still more unforeseen impacts will develop in the coming decade. It does appear that the fundamental issues of Section 26 and Section 30 compliance have been resolved at the procedural level. Section 30 seems to be a nonissue for at least the short term due to the Proposal A funding shift, but there is no guarantee that this situation is permanent. Section 26 will probably continue to generate periodic compliance problems, largely due to the time lag built into the constitutional formula. If a Section 26 issue does arise, the state would be better prepared if there were in place some type of automatic refund mechanism—such as that used in 1995—to minimize the chances that the Headlee limit and the one percentage point cushion are not exceeded. The serious technical issues of implementing mandatory refunds under Section 26 suggest that such a situation should be avoided. The problems a Section 26 refund would create also mean that more than ever, care and forethought need to be taken in the debate over significant new state programs and the taxes to fund them. We can say with some confidence that we still face some litigation and uncertainty over alleged Section 29 mandates and their proper level of funding. We can also anticipate future issues over defining new taxes requiring voter approval at the local level.

There are ways of improving the process of identifying mandates if the legislature should persist in its reluctance to create an internal process by which mandates can be clearly identified and their costs estimated. The LCRB can be empowered to hear taxpayers' suits. Administrative agencies in federal and state government routinely adjudicate complicated claims, making findings of fact and reaching conclusions of law. Formal adjudications before administrative law judges closely resemble trials before judges. The administrative approach will also offer the advantages of expertise and experience. Administrative law judges of an invigorated LCRB will be specialists in the law of the Headlee Amendment and will become familiar with the complex computations needed to determine the state's underpayment in the case of an unfunded mandate. Any decision of an administrative law judge would be subject to review. An initial appeal could go to the LCRB, with a subsequent appeal to the court of appeals or the supreme court. Alternatively, the appeal could run from the administrative law judge to the court of appeals. In any event, the courts would have the benefit of a complete record along with the administrative law judge's written decision with relevant findings of fact and conclusions of law.[103] Given the backlog of cases pending before the state courts, the administrative alternative at least offers the prospect of quicker review of claims.

If revitalization of the LCRB proves to be unworkable or undesirable, there are two other ways to improve the process of identifying state unfunded mandates and hearing Headlee Amendment cases. First, should an essential question of law that requires early determination arise in a Headlee Amendment case pending in the circuit court or the court of appeals, the court hearing the case can certify the question to the supreme court.[104] Second, either house of the legislature or the governor can ask the supreme court for an advisory opinion on the constitutionality of legislation, as provided for in Article III, Section 8 of the 1963 constitution. There are some drawbacks to the use of the advisory opinion. There is a narrow window of opportunity within which to ask the supreme court for an advisory opinion. The request must come after a bill has been enacted into law but before its effective date. Moreover, the Michigan Supreme Court has traditionally been reluctant to grant advisory opinions, and, when the court does grant an advisory opinion, the resulting advice is often not unanimous.[105]

The Michigan legislature made a wise decision in implementing the Headlee Amendment when it excluded from the definition of "state requirement" in Section 29 obligations placed on local government by a citizen-initiated statute or constitutional amendment, or a ballot proposal approved by the voters.[106] As of today, twenty-four states provide for the initiative, and citizens in those states are making frequent use of the process. When the initiative is coupled with state constitutional caps on taxation and spending, the results can be catastrophic to the state's economy. For example, Coloradoans approved constitutional limitations on taxation and spending in one year, then approved a law that required guaranteed annual increases in education spending a few years later.[107] As of March 2002, the state of Colorado had a $700 million deficit. In Washington, the people voted to cut taxes in one year, then, in the next year, approved an $800 million spending package to increase teachers' salaries and reduce class size. Again, by March 2002, Washington had accumulated $1.6 billion in debt. Writer Timothy Egan has termed such laws "unfunded mandates from the people."[108] On top of this, research has shown that the initiative tends to "shift expenditure to local governments and away from state government." The legislature's foresight in crafting the Headlee implementation legislation just might help Michigan avoid the budgetary problems found in sister states.[109]

■

## NOTES

The author would like to express her sincere gratitude to Douglas C. Drake, Wayne State University State Policy Center, for the financial analysis and tables that appear in this chapter, especially for Sections 26 and 30 of the Headlee Amendment. Without his contributions, support, and encouragement, this chapter would not have been possible.

1. David Lowery and Lee Sigelman, "Understanding the Tax Revolt: Eight Explanations," *American Political Science Review* 75, no. 4 (1981): 963, citing Charles H. Levine, "The New Crisis in the Public Sector," in *Managing Fiscal Stress* (Chatham, N.J.: Chatham House, 1980).

2. Richard Boeth, Gerald C. Lubenow, Martin Kasindorf, and Rich Thomas, "The Big Tax Revolt," *Newsweek*, national edition, 19 June 1978, 20–25.

3. Everett Carll Ladd Jr., Marilyn Potter, Linda Basilick, Sally Daniels, and Dana Suszkiw, "The Polls: Taxing and Spending," *Public Opinion Quarterly* 43, no. 1 (1979): 128.

4. Ibid., 126–27.

5. Poll results have been taken from ibid., 127.

6. Lowery and Sigelman, "Understanding the Tax Revolt." These researchers also note that there are methodological problems associated with much tax revolt research. For example, some studies use county- or precinct-level data to attempt to explain individual attitudes. Other studies were based on voting on tax initiatives in elections where two different proposals competed against one another, leading to the question of whether voters really preferred one proposal to the other or were simply voting against what they saw as a more drastic alternative.

7. Ladd, et al., "The Polls," 128.

8. Ibid., 133–34.

9. Susan Welch, "The 'More for Less' Paradox: Public Attitudes on Taxing and Spending," *Public Opinion Quarterly* 49, no. 3 (1985): 310–16. Welch found 8% national government free lunchers, 14% state free lunchers, and 7% local free lunchers. There were more persons in a related category of "probably unrealistic revenue raisers": 14% national, 14% state, and 7% local.

10. William G. Jacoby, "Public Attitudes toward Government Spending," *American Journal of Political Science* 38, no. 2 (1994): 336–61.

11. Ibid., 338. Jacoby illustrates the problem with an example: When asked about spending for food stamps, people will give an answer whether or not they have any knowledge about, or concern for, the program.

12. Ibid., 354.

13. *Detroit Free Press*, 4 July 1978, A3.

14. Michigan Constitution of 1963, Article XXII, section 3. Each of Michigan's four constitutions has provided for the calling of state constitutional conventions. The 1835 constitution allowed the state legislature to recommend to the people the calling of a convention. Beginning in 1850, Michigan constitutions have required that the people consider calling a convention every sixteen years. See Susan P. Fino, *The Michigan State Constitution: A Reference Guide* (Westport, Conn.: Greenwood Press, 1996), 239.

15. U.S. 316 (1819).

16. McCulloch at 407.

17. Ibid.

18. This point is made by G. Alan Tarr in *Understanding State Constitutions* (Princeton, N.J.: Princeton University Press, 1998), 9. Tarr gives two good examples of the prolix propensity of state constitutions. The New Jersey Constitution, which is seen as a model, is over three times the length of the federal Constitution. The Louisiana Constitution of 1921 "ballooned to over 250,000 words before it was finally replaced in 1974."

19. Albert L. Sturm, "The Development of American State Constitutions," *Publius* 12 (1982): 57–98. These figures are somewhat dated. If anything, the Michigan constitution is longer now than when Sturm assessed it. If either of the ballot proposals presented to the people at the 2002 November election had been approved, the constitution's length would have been significantly above average.

20. Tarr, *State Constitution*, 65.

21. Quoted in Tarr, *State Constitution*, 30.

22. Samuel Reznick, "The Social History of an American Depression, 1837–1843," *American Historical Review* 40 (July 1935): 662–87.

23. Ibid., 681.

24. Ibid.

25. Ibid., 675.

26. Michigan Constitution of 1850, Article XIV.

27. Michigan was not alone in its enthusiasm for internal improvements. James Clingermayer and Dan Wood point out that debt financing was common in the nineteenth century for infrastructure such as bridges, dams, roads, railways, and sewer and freshwater supply systems. Michigan was also not alone in its problems with repayment of debt. States as a whole suffered a reputation for fiscal

irresponsibility. Clingermayer and Wood, "Disentangling Patterns of State Debt Financing," *American Political Science Review* 89 (1995): 108.

28. Carter Goodrich, "The Revulsion against Internal Improvements," *Journal of Economic History* 10 (1950): 154. The most common forms of internal improvements were railroads and canals.

29. Ibid., 150.

30. Constitution of 1908, Article 10, Section 10.

31. Constitution of 1908, Article 10, Section 15.

32. Constitution of 1908, Article 10, Section 23.

33. Joseph G. Lapalombara and Charles B. Hagen, "Direct Legislation: An Appraisal and a Suggestion," *American Political Science Review* 45 (1951): 403.

34. Ibid.

35. The Michigan Constitution of 1908, Article V, Section 1. The initiative and referendum were added as amendments to the constitution in 1914.

36. Harvey E. Brazer, with Deborah S. Laren, *Michigan's Fiscal and Economic Structure* (Ann Arbor: University of Michigan Press, 1982), 453.

37. Ibid., 455.

38. Ibid.

39. Ibid., 447.

40. For an in-depth exploration of the Headlee Amendment, the reader is referred to the following sources: Cynthia B. Faulhaber, "'No New Taxes': Article IX Section 31 of the Michigan Constitution Twenty Years after Adoption," *Wayne Law Review* 46 (2000): 211–57; and Kevin C. Kennedy, "The First Twenty Years of the Headlee Amendment," *University of Detroit Mercy Law Review* 76 (1999): 1031–78.

41. Article IX, Section 33 of the Michigan constitution provides definitions of some of the terms used through the Headlee Amendment. The state legislature has supplemented Section 33 in implementing legislation.

42. *Headlee Blue Ribbon Commission Report*, page 9, hereinafter, "Blue Ribbon Commission." The Blue Ribbon Commission was charged with determining "whether the amendment ha[d] been properly implemented and, whether the amendment ha[d] accomplished what was expected of it by the electorate."

43. *The Headlee Amendment: A Study Report by the Michigan Law Revision Commission*, 31 December 1998, found at *www.milegislativecouncil.ogr/mlrc/1998/headlee.html*.

44. The implementation legislation for this section may be found at: M.C.L. § 18.1350c.

45. "Proposal A" refers to a 1994 ballot proposal in which the legislature asked Michigan voters to approve a plan for funding operating expenses for local schools. Voters chose a 2% increase in the sales tax over the alternative, which was an increase in the individual income tax rate. For a summary of Proposal A see: *http://www.metropolicy.org/pdfs/TAX%20REFORM%20IN%20MICHIGAN.pdf*. For a 1998 retrospective on Proposal A prepared by the Michigan Department of Treasury, see: *http://www.metropolicy.org/pdfs/Proposal-A-Michigan-Tax-Reform.pdf*.

46. Blue Ribbon Commission, 11.

47. Attorney General Opinion No. 6332, 1986 Mich. AG LEXIS 79.

48. Attorney General Opinion No. 6856, 1995 Mich. AG LEXIS 38.

49. *Durant v. State Board of Education*, 424 Mich. 364 (1985) at page 379.

50. *Judicial Attorneys Association v. State*, 460 Mich. 590 (1999) at 598.

51. *Durant* (1985) at page 380. The issue addressed by the court in this phase of the *Durant* litigation was whether the state constitutional requirement of a free public elementary and secondary education (Constitution of 1963, Article VIII, Section 2) is an "activity or service required by state law."

52. Ibid.

53. *Livingston County v. Department of Management and Budget*, 430 Mich. 635 (1988)

54. Ibid. at page 639.

55. Ibid. at page 646.

56. Attorney General Opinion No. 6330, 1986 Mich. AG LEXIS 80.

57. Attorney General Opinion No. 6548, 1988 Mich. AG LEXIS 67.

58. *Judicial Attorneys Association*, at page 598.

59. Ibid. at page 608.

60. *Schmidt v. Department of Education*, 441 Mich. 236 (1992) at page 243.

61. Michigan courts had defined necessary costs before *Durant* as: the costs that are "essential or indispensable" to fulfillment of the state-mandated activity. See *Waterford School District v. State Board of Education*, 130 Mich, App. 614 (1983).

62. *Durant v. State Department of Education*, 110 Mich. App. 351 (1981).

63. Concern for education has been embedded in Michigan's fundamental law since the Northwest Ordinance of 1787. The Constitution of 1835 required the legislature to provide a system of common schools (Article 10, Section 3); the 1850 constitution required the creation of free public primary schools (Article 13, Section 4); the 1908 constitution continued the system of free public primary schools (Article 11, Section 9); and the

Constitution of 1963 required that the legislature maintain and support free elementary and secondary schools.

64. *Durant v. State Department of Education*, 413 Mich. 862 (1982), (*Durrant I*).

65. *Durant*, 1982 at page 534.

66. *Durant v. State Department of Education*, 129 Mich. App. 517 (1983).

67. *Durant v. State Department of Education*, 424 Mich. 364 (1986) at page 378, (*Durant II*).

68. *Durant II* at page 387.

69. M.C.L. 21.233(6).

70. M.C.L. 21.233(6)(a-d). The statutory definition of necessary costs excluded the cost of a state requirement if one or more of the following conditions are met: (a) the state requirement does not exceed a de minimis cost; (b) the state requirement results in offsetting savings; (c) the state requirement imposes duties on local government that can be performed at a de minimis cost; (d) the state requirement imposes a cost that is recoverable from a federal or state categorical aid program or other external financial aid. A 'de minimus cost' is defined by Michigan statute as a net cost to a local unit of government resulting from a state requirement that does not exceed $300.00 per claim. MCL 21.232(4); MSA 5.3194(602)(4).

71. *Durant* at page 392.

72. The *Durant* case was ultimately limited to special education programs. This chapter will focus on only the special education component of the case.

73. *Durant v. State*, 186 Mich. App. 83 (1990).

74. Mich. App. 83 at page 104.

75. Mich. App. 83 at pages 104–5.

76. In the meantime the Michigan Supreme Court decided *Schmidt v. Department of Education*, 441 Mich. 236 (1992), in which the court created additional guidelines for the calculation of the state-financed proportion of necessary costs.

77. *Durant v. State Board of Education*, 456 Mich. 175 (1997) at page 182. (*Durant III*). The discussion of the school lunch program is omitted for the purposes of this chapter.

78. The supreme court described the state's "prolonged recalcitrance" in the following terms: "Despite a judicial determination that the services were state-mandated, the state continued to evade its obligation to fund these services after 1990." *Durant III* n. 33.

79. *Durant III* at page 206.

80. Michigan's trial courts of general jurisdiction, the circuit courts, can now hear Section 29 cases. See: M.C.L. 600.308a.

81. M.C.L. 21.237, Public Act 101 of 1979.

82. M.C.L. 21.240, Public Act 101 of 1979.

83. The state's insistence that special education was not a mandate—even after Michigan courts had ruled otherwise—is the "prolonged recalcitrance" noted by the supreme court in *Durant I*.

84. On 19 November 2002, the Michigan supreme court denied plaintiffs leave to appeal. See *Durant v. State Department of Education*, 251 Mich. App. 185 (1999) and *Durant v. State Department of Education*, 251 Mich. App. 297 (2002). These cases involve the relationship between Proposal A and the Headlee Amendment with respect to school finance. However, on 18 December 2002, the Michigan supreme court did grant leave to appeal in a group of cases originally known as *Adair*, with similar issues and plaintiffs. See *Adair v. State Department of Education*, 467 Mich. 919; SC Docket Number 121536; decision below: *Adair v. State Department of Education*, 250 Mich. App. 691 (2002).

85. Blue Ribbon Commission, 47.

86. Law Revision Commission, 158.

87. *Saginaw County v. Buena Vista School District*, 196 Mich. App. 363; 493 N.W.2d 437 (1992).

88. *American Axle and Manufacturing, Inc. v. City of Hamtramck*, 461 Mich. 352, 361; 604 N.W.2d 330 (2000).

89. Attorney General Opinion 6572, 1989 Mich. AG LEXIS 15.

90. *Airlines Parking v. Wayne County*, 452 Mich. 527 (1996) at pages 536–37.

91. *Airlines Parking*, at page 537.

92. *Bolt v. City of Lansing*, 459 Mich. 152 (1999).

93. Ibid., 161–62. The legal distinction of voluntarism in the payment of user fees relative to the mandatory nature of taxation in general certainly works for this case. It is, however, not necessarily always an economic distinction, in the sense that taxpayer behavioral choices may also allow the avoidance of all or a portion of most taxes.

94. Attorney General Opinion No. 5562, 1979 Mich. AG LEXIS 59.

95. Blue Ribbon Commission, 26.

96. Ibid., 31.

97. Ibid., 27.

98. Unfortunately, there has been no statewide compilation of either the frequency or results of these elections.

99. See the chapter on property taxes in this volume for a discussion of the interaction of Section 31 and the assessment cap.

100. Blue Ribbon Commission, 45.

101. Ibid., 46.

102. Ibid.

103. Article VI, Section 28 of the Constitution of 1963 already provides for judicial review of adjudications conducted in administrative agencies. Section 28 also sets the standard of review for the appellate courts.

104. The procedure for the certification of questions to the supreme court is set forth in Michigan court rules, M.C.R. 7.305 (2002).

105. See, for example, *Request for Advisory Opinion on Constitutionality of 1977 PA 108,* 402 Mich. 83 (1977).

106. M.C.L. Section 21.234(5).

107. The examples and figures given here are taken from "They Give, but They Also Take: Voters Muddle States' Finances," *New York Times,* 2 March 2002, A-1.

108. Ibid.

109. John G. Marsusaka, "Fiscal Effects of the Voter Initiative: Evidence from the Last 30 Years," *Journal of Political Economy* 103, no. 3 (1995): 620.

# About the Editors and Contributors

**Charles L. Ballard** is Professor of Economics at Michigan State University. He has been on the faculty at MSU since 1983, when he received his Ph.D. from Stanford University. His research interests include using computer simulation models to assess the efficiency and distributional effects of policy instruments, such as income taxes, consumption taxes, tariffs, wage subsidies, credits for health insurance, and environmentally motivated taxes. He has served as a consultant with the U.S. Department of Agriculture and the U.S. Department of Treasury, and with research institutes in Australia, Denmark, and Finland. His previous books include *A General Equilibrium Model for Tax Policy Evaluation*, with Don Fullerton, John B. Shoven, and John Whalley (1985) and *Real Economics for Real People* (2d ed. 2001).

**Timothy J. Bartik** is senior economist at the W. E. Upjohn Institute for Employment Research, a non-profit research organization in Kalamazoo. He received his Ph.D. in Economics from the University of Wisconsin in 1982. Dr. Bartik's research focuses on state and local economic development, local labor markets, and poverty. He has written two books, *Who Benefits from State and Local Economic Development Policies?* (1991), and *Jobs for the Poor: Can Labor Demand Policies Help?* (2001), as well as numerous scholarly articles.

**Dale L. Belman** is Associate Professor in the School of Labor and Industrial Relations at Michigan State University and a Research Associate at the Economic Policy Institute. His areas of research include labor market regulation, collective bargaining, and employment relations in the public sector.

**Rebecca M. Blank** is Dean of the Gerald R. Ford School of Public Policy at the University of Michigan and Henry Carter Adams Collegiate Professor of Public Policy. She is also co-director of the National Poverty Center, funded by HHS to provide research on the causes and consequences of poverty and the effects of anti-poverty policies. Prior to coming to Michigan, she served as a Member of the President's Council of Economic Advisers and was a faculty member at Northwestern University and Princeton University. Her recent work includes the books *It Takes A Nation: A New Agenda for Fighting Poverty* (1997), *Finding Jobs: Work and Welfare Reform*, edited with David Card (2000), and *The New World of Welfare*, edited with Ron Haskins (2001).

**Richard N. Block** is Professor in the School of Labor and Industrial Relations at Michigan State University, East Lansing, Michigan. He is the author of numerous articles and books on labor-management relations, labor and employment law, the relationship between law and practice in industrial relations, industrial relations and structural economic change, and international labor standards, among other topics. His two most recent books are *Labor Standards in the United States and Canada*, with Karen Roberts and R. Oliver Clarke (2003) and *Bargaining for Competitiveness: Law, Research, and Case Studies*, edited (2003). He has been a visiting faculty member at Columbia University, the University of Toronto, and the London School of Economics and Political Science.

**Kenneth D. Boyer** is Professor of Economics at Michigan State University. He is past president of the Transportation and Public Utilities Group of the American Economic Association and is the author of the nation's leading textbook in transportation economics. He has chaired, or been a member of, numerous National Academies of Sciences committees concerning transportation economics.

**A. Thomas Clay** is a Senior Research Associate with the Citizens Research Council of Michigan. He joined the Research Council staff in November 1997. In 1997, he took early retirement after thirty years with the State of Michigan, serving as Deputy State Treasurer from 1991 to 1997 and Director of the State's Executive Budget Offices for fifteen years prior to joining the Treasury staff. He has degrees in economics from Miami University (Ohio) and Michigan State University.

**Paul N. Courant** is Professor of Economics and Public Policy, Faculty Associate in the Institute for Social Research, and Provost and Executive Vice President for Academic Affairs at the University of Michigan. He has held numerous leadership positions at UM since he joined the faculty in 1974, and has served as a Senior Staff Economist at the Council of Economic Advisers. Courant has authored half a dozen books and over sixty monographs and papers covering a broad range of topics in economics and public policy, including tax policy, local economic development, gender differences in pay, housing, radon and public health, and relationships between economic growth and environmental policy. He holds a B.A. in History from Swarthmore College (1968); an M.A. in Economics from Princeton University (1973); and a Ph.D. in Economics from Princeton University (1974).

**David B. Crary** is Associate Professor of Economics at Eastern Michigan University, with research and teaching specialties in macroeconomic and regional economic forecasting and policy. During the late 1980s and early 1990s, he regularly produced economic forecasts for the United States, Michigan, and metropolitan areas in Michigan.

**Joan P. Crary** is an assistant research scientist at the University of Michigan's Research Seminar in Quantitative Economics, where she is a principal co-author of econometric models of the national and Michigan economies. She is a specialist in economic forecasting, focusing on the economy and finances of the State of Michigan.

**Julie Berry Cullen** has been Assistant Professor of Economics at the University of Michigan since she received her Ph.D. in 1997 from MIT. Her primary research interests are the economics of education, intergovernmental relations, and social insurance. Recent publications include "Does Unemployment Insurance Crowd Out Spousal Labor Supply?" (*Journal of Labor Economics*) and "Crime, Urban Flight, and the Consequences for Cities" (*Review of Economics and Statistics*).

**Sandra K. Danziger** is Associate Professor of Social Work, Director, Michigan Program on Poverty and Social Welfare Policy, and Associate Research Scientist, The Gerald R. Ford School of Public Policy at the University of Michigan. Her primary research interests are the impact of public programs on the well being of low-income families, poverty policy, trends in child and family well-being, gender issues across the life course, program evaluation, and qualitative research methods. Dr. Danziger's current projects address the implementation of welfare-reform policies and their impacts for low-income families and children.

**Sheldon Danziger** is Henry J. Meyer Collegiate Professor of Public Policy and Co-Director of the National Poverty Center at the Gerald R. Ford School of Public Policy at the University of Michigan. His research focuses on trends in poverty and inequality and the effects of economic and demographic changes and government social programs on disadvantaged groups. He is the co-author of *America Unequal* (1995) and *Detroit Divided* (2000) and co-editor of numerous books, including *Child Poverty and Deprivation in the Industrialized Countries, 1945–1995* (1997), *Economic Conditions and*

*Welfare Reform* (1999), *Coping with Poverty: The Social Contexts of Neighborhood, Family and Work in the African-American Community* (2000), *Securing the Future: Investing in Children* (2000), and *Understanding Poverty* (2002). He is currently studying the effects of the 1996 welfare reform on the economic well-being of single mothers.

**Kenneth Darga** is Michigan's State Demographer, based at the Library of Michigan in Lansing. He is a graduate of Boston College, and he holds graduate degrees in Social Policy and in Economic Demography from the University of Michigan. He is the author of two books on the census.

**Alan V. Deardorff** is John W. Sweetland Professor of International Economics and Professor of Economics and Public Policy at the University of Michigan. He received his Ph.D. in economics from Cornell University in 1971. Since 1970, he has been on the faculty at the University of Michigan, where he served as Economics Department Chair from 1991 to 1995. He is co-author, with Robert M. Stern, of *The Michigan Model of World Production and Trade* and *Computational Analysis of Global Trading Arrangements,* and he has published numerous articles on aspects of international trade theory and policy, including theories of the patterns and effects of trade, and, with Professor Stern and with Drusilla K. Brown, computable general equilibrium models of trade policy.

**Douglas C. Drake** is Associate Director of the State Policy Center at Wayne State University. Mr. Drake had a long career in state government prior to joining Wayne State, beginning with the Michigan Department of Treasury in 1968. He has previously served as Director, Office of Education and Infrastructure, in the Michigan Department of Management and Budget, and Director of the Office of Revenue and Tax Analysis. Mr. Drake also worked for the Michigan Legislature for over a decade, serving as Staff Director for the House Taxation Committee and Co-Director of the House Majority Policy Staff.

**Peter Eisinger** is Professor of Urban Affairs and Director of the State Policy Center in the College of Urban, Labor and Metropolitan Affairs at Wayne State University. Before coming to Wayne State, he taught at the University of Wisconsin, where he was Director of the La Follette Institute of Public Affairs from 1991 to 1996. He is the author or co-author of seven books and numer-

ous articles and monographs on urban politics, economic development, and hunger in America.

**George A. Erickcek** is the Senior Regional Analyst for the W. E. Upjohn Institute for Employment Research. His research focuses on analyzing issues in regional economics and regional public policy. He also writes the *Business Outlook for West Michigan,* the Institute's quarterly report, which examines economic conditions in West Michigan. He joined the Institute in 1987.

**Abel Feinstein** is an independent economic consultant specializing in the Michigan economy and economic data systems. Among other projects, Mr. Feinstein has co-authored *Michigan: The High-Technology Automotive State,* produced by the Center for Automotive Research, Altarum, and *Employment Stability Analysis for the Michigan Economy,* in affiliation with the Institute of Labor and Industrial Relations at the University of Michigan. Mr. Feinstein was formerly a labor market research manager at the Michigan Employment Security Commission, with primary responsibility for industry-occupation forecasts and special projects. Mr. Feinstein supervised development of the 1996 edition of the *Michigan Statistical Abstract.*

**Naomi E. Feldman** is a Ph.D. candidate in Economics at the University of Michigan. She holds a B.S. in Economics and French from the University of Illinois at Urbana–Champaign and a M.A. in Economics from the University of Michigan. She is a research assistant at the Office of Tax Policy Research at the University of Michigan Business School.

**John N. (Jake) Ferris** is Professor Emeritus in the Department of Agricultural Economics at Michigan State University. His professional career focused on agricultural marketing, outlook, and economic development (domestic and international), with responsibilities in extension, teaching, and research. He developed and maintains AGMOD, an econometric/simulation model of U.S. agriculture with a satellite model on Michigan, which generates year-to-year forecasts for the following ten years. His textbook, *Agricultural Prices and Commodity Market Analysis,* was published in 1997.

**Susan P. Fino** is Professor of Political Science at Wayne State University. She received her B.A. from

Johns Hopkins and her M.A. and Ph.D. from Rutgers University. Professor Fino has a special interest in state supreme courts and state constitutional law. She has authored two books and numerous articles in this area.

**Ronald C. Fisher** is Professor in the Department of Economics and the Department of Accounting at Michigan State University, where he also serves as Director of the Honors College. Professor Fisher specializes in the study of government finance and taxation, particularly regarding state and local governments. He has authored the leading textbook in the field, *State and Local Public Finance,* and has written more than seventy-five professional articles, research reports, and books on public finance topics. He also has served as Deputy Treasurer for the State of Michigan, as research economist for the U.S. Advisory Commission on Intergovernmental Relations, as Visiting Fellow at the Federalism Research Centre at the Australian National University, and as a consultant to a number of states and several federal government agencies.

**George A. Fulton** is a senior research scientist at the University of Michigan's Institute of Labor and Industrial Relations, where he is director of labor market research. In addition, he holds an appointment as senior research scientist in the Research Seminar in Quantitative Economics, Department of Economics. He is a specialist in economic forecasting and regional economic development, focusing on the state of Michigan and its local governments. His research also explores the regional economic effects of national policies, particularly those directed at the automotive, trucking, and tobacco industries.

**Elisabeth R. Gerber** is Professor of Public Policy and Director of the Center for Local, State, and Urban Policy (CLOSUP) at the University of Michigan's Gerald R. Ford School of Public Policy. Her research focuses on the policy consequences of electoral laws and state and local political institutions. Her current research involves studies of local land use policy, intergovernmental cooperation, local political accountability, and the dynamics of local ballot initiatives. Professor Gerber received her Ph.D. in Political Science from the University of Michigan in 1991. Before joining the Ford School faculty in 2001, she held faculty appointments at Caltech (1991–94) and University of California, San Diego (1994–2001).

**John H. Goddeeris** is Professor of Economics at Michigan State University. He holds a bachelor's degree from the University of Michigan and a Ph.D. from the University of Wisconsin. He has been a member of the MSU Economics Department since 1980, serving as Director of Graduate Programs from 1988–1992 and Department Chair from 1996–2001. In 1993, he was a Visiting Scholar at the Congressional Budget Office. Dr. Goddeeris's research interests primarily involve the economics of health care.

**Allen C. Goodman** received his A.B. from the University of Michigan in 1969 and his Ph.D. from Yale University in 1976. Since 1986, he has been Professor of Economics at Wayne State University, where he specializes in urban economics and in health care economics.

**Donald R. Grimes** is a senior research associate in the Institute of Labor and Industrial Relations at the University of Michigan. He also works as a consultant with Michigan Future, Inc., and the Employment Research Corporation. His work includes forecasting economic activity in the metropolitan areas and counties of Michigan, analysis of economic development programs, including a study of the effectiveness of business incubator programs, and identification of labor shortage occupations.

**Jeffrey P. Guilfoyle** is an economist for the Office of Revenue and Tax Analysis in the Michigan Department of Treasury. His responsibilities include forecasting and tracking state tax receipts, estimating the impact of legislation on state revenues, and providing economic research support. He received his B.A. in economics from the University of Michigan and his M.A. and Ph.D. in economics from Michigan State University. His dissertation on the tax incidence and housing market effects of Michigan's 1994 school finance reforms received an honorable mention in the National Tax Association's Outstanding Doctoral Dissertation competition.

**Gloria E. Helfand** is Associate Professor of Environmental Economics in the School of Natural Resources and Environment at the University of Michigan since 1996; previously she was an Assistant and Associate Professor of Agricultural and Resource Economics at the University of California at Davis. Her research expertise includes the effects of different regulatory approaches to pollution policy, environmental policy analysis, environmental justice, and nonpoint source pollution policy. She teaches undergraduate and graduate courses in environmental and resource economics and environmental policy analysis. She holds a bachelor's degree from Swarthmore College, a master's degree from Washington University, and a Ph.D. in Agricultural and Resource Economics from the University of California at Berkeley.

**James R. Hines, Jr.,** is Professor of Economics, Public Policy, and Business Economics at the University of Michigan, and serves as research director of its Office of Tax Policy Research. Not surprisingly, his specialty is taxation. He is a research associate of the National Bureau of Economic Research, taught previously at Princeton and Harvard, and was once an economist at the U.S. Department of Commerce.

**Donald F. Holecek** is a professor in the Department of Park, Recreation, and Tourism Resources at Michigan State University. He is also Director of Michigan State University's Travel, Tourism and Recreation Resource Center and its World Travel and Tourism Tax Policy Center. He is a past president of the Central States Chapter of the International Travel and Tourism Research Association and has served on the Board of Directors of the International Travel and Tourism Research Association.

**Saul H. Hymans** is Professor of Economics and Statistics and Director of the Research Seminar in Quantitative Economics at the University of Michigan. Professor Hymans has been on the University of Michigan faculty since 1964, and his research focuses on macroeconometric modeling and forecasting. In 1984, and again in 1987, Professor Hymans received the national Blue Chip Annual Economic Forecasting Award, in recognition of "accuracy, timeliness and professionalism" in economic forecasting. Professor Hymans has been the U.S. forecaster for the Pacific Economic Outlook Project of the Pacific Economic Cooperation Council since 1988. The author of numerous journal articles and research papers, Professor Hymans traveled to the (former) Soviet Union on a U.S. scientific exchange delegation, and has been a visiting scholar in Israel, Stockholm, and Hong Kong.

**George E. Johnson** is Professor of Economics at the University of Michigan. He has written on a variety of labor market issues since he joined the University of Michigan faculty in 1966. He was also Director of the Office of Evaluation of the U.S. Department of Labor and a senior staff economist at the Council of Economic Advisers.

**Arlen Leholm** is Professor of Agricultural Economics at Michigan State University. He is an Extension specialist in product agriculture and international development, and the former state director of Michigan State University Extension. He has held university positions in North Dakota, Nebraska, Wisconsin, and Michigan.

**Susanna Loeb** is Assistant Professor in the School of Education at Stanford University. Her work addresses education policy issues, including school finance reform and teacher labor markets. She received her Ph.D. in Economics from the University of Michigan in 1998. She has been writing about school finance in Michigan since the implementation of Proposal A in 1994.

**Eric W. Lupher** is Senior Research Associate at the Citizens Research Council of Michigan, where he has been on staff since 1987. He holds degrees from Michigan State University and Wayne State University.

**David Martin** is a researcher with Wayne State University's College of Urban, Labor and Metropolitan Affairs. He possesses expertise in the use of geographic information systems (GIS) for public policy analysis and crime mapping. His academic research focuses on the spatial distribution of crime in Detroit and its implications for law enforcement and community approaches to preventing and controlling crime. He is the author of *Crime in Metropolitan Detroit,* and has published several articles and book chapters on GIS and crime policy. Dr. Martin helped develop GIS capabilities within the Detroit Police Department. His current research includes a spatial analysis of gun violence patterns in Wayne County, Michigan, and a community GIS initiative. Dr. Martin has developed a professional development seminar course entitled "Data-Driven Decision-Making: Introduction to Theory and Practice," for the WSU Department of Political Science. Dr. Martin was also a recent workshop scholar at the Center for Spatially Integrated Social Sciences.

**Lawrence W. Martin** received his Ph.D. from the University of Maryland in 1982. Since then he has served on the faculty at Michigan State University. A specialist in Public Economics, Economic Theory, and Law and Economics, he has published papers on illegal pollution, smuggling, tax incidence, search unemployment, unemployment insurance, and welfare economics. He has also served as consultant to the U.S. Department of Labor and the States of Vermont, Minnesota, and Michigan. He teaches a wide range of courses, including Principles, Law and Economics, and Public Economics at both the undergraduate and graduate levels.

**Christopher D. Maxwell** is Assistant Professor in the School of Criminal Justice at Michigan State University. His research interests include the social control and criminal justice processing of intimate partner violence, the efficacy of aggression and delinquency prevention programs, and the impact of social and ecological contexts on patterns of delinquency, crime, and criminal justice decision making. Dr. Maxwell is a graduate of Rutgers University (Ph.D., 1998, M.A., 1994) and Indiana University–Bloomington (B.A., 1990).

**Sheila Royo Maxwell** is Associate Professor in the School of Criminal Justice at Michigan State University. She obtained her doctorate degree at Rutgers University in 1994, and joined Michigan State University the same year. Before coming to MSU, Dr. Maxwell was a research fellow at the National Institute on Drug Abuse in New York City. She is currently pursuing research on the effects of policies regarding illicit drug use in Michigan and neighboring states, and court processing and decision-making. Other research interests include cross-cultural patterns of delinquency and victimization, behavioral responses to sanctioning, and the efficacy of correctional interventions.

**Paul L. Menchik** is Professor of Economics at Michigan State University and received his Ph.D. from the University of Pennsylvania. His research interests are in public economics, public policy, and income distribution. He previously was on the faculty at the University of Wisconsin-Madison, and has served in Academic Visitor positions at the London School of Economics, University College London–Institute for Fiscal Studies, University of Pennsylvania, and Stanford University. Dr. Menchik has advised or worked for both state and federal agencies, and has served as Visiting Scholar at the Congressional Budget Office, and as Senior Economist for Economic

Policy at the Office of Management and Budget–Executive Office of the President, working on a range of issues.

**Gary S. Olson** was appointed as Director of the Michigan Senate Fiscal Agency, by the Senate Fiscal Agency Governing Board, effective 1 January 1991. As Director of the Senate Fiscal Agency, he is the principal fiscal advisor to the Michigan Senate. Mr. Olson directs a staff of thirty-four people whose primary responsibilities are state budget analysis and analysis of all proposed legislation being considered by the Senate. Prior to his appointment as Senate Fiscal Agency Director, he served as Deputy Director of the Agency for five years. Previously, Mr. Olson had served as Senior Economist to the Senate Fiscal Agency and Chief Committee Aide to the Taxation Committee of the Michigan House of Representatives. Mr. Olson has twenty-four years of service with the Michigan Legislature. Mr. Olson has a Bachelor's Degree in Economics from the University of Michigan and a Masters Degree in Economics from Michigan State University.

**L. E. Papke** is Professor of Economics at Michigan State University. Her research interests in public economics include tax-deferred saving and individual saving behavior, 401(k) pension plans features and participation, the composition of pension coverage, and pension fund finance. Her research interests in state and local public finance include business taxation and economic development, inter-jurisdictional tax competition, and state enterprise zone programs. She has served on the board of the National Tax Association. She is currently a Research Fellow of the Employee Benefit Research Institute. She received her B.A. in economics from Wellesley College in 1982 and her Ph.D. in economics from the Massachusetts Institute of Technology in 1987.

**Jay B. Rising** was appointed State Treasurer by Governor Jennifer Granholm, effective 6 January 2003. Prior to his appointment, Mr. Rising practiced law with Miller, Canfield, Paddock and Stone, P.L.C. His practice areas included Public Law, State and Municipal Finance, Public Securities, and Development Finance. Mr. Rising also served the citizens of Michigan as Deputy State Treasurer for Policy Development and Finance and as Chief Deputy State Treasurer between 1983 and 1991. Mr. Rising holds a law degree from Wayne State University and an undergraduate degree from the University of Michigan.

**Earl M. Ryan** is President of the Citizens Research Council of Michigan. He was President of the Indiana Fiscal Policy Institute from 1987 to 1994 and President of the Public Affairs Research Council of Louisiana from 1984 to 1987. He holds degrees in political science from the University of Michigan and Wayne State University.

**Gary J. Sands**, AICP, is Associate Professor in the Graduate Urban Planning Program at Wayne State University. He received a Master of Urban Planning degree from Wayne and a doctorate in Housing and Public Policy from Cornell University. He is a member of the Executive Advisory Committee of the Victor Institute for Responsible Land Development and Use.

**Kristin S. Seefeldt** is a Research Investigator at the University of Michigan's Poverty Research and Training Center in the Gerald R. Ford School of Public Policy. For more than ten years she has conducted research on a variety of social policy issues, specifically, policies related to welfare and employment and training programs for low-income people. She is the author of numerous articles and reports on these topics.

**Joel Slemrod** is the Paul W. McCracken Collegiate Professor of Business Economics and Public Policy at the University of Michigan Business School, and Professor of Economics in the Department of Economics. He also serves as Director of the Office of Tax Policy Research, an interdisciplinary research center housed at the Business School. Professor Slemrod received the A.B. degree from Princeton University in 1973 and a Ph.D. in economics from Harvard University in 1980. He joined the economics department at the University of Minnesota in 1979. In 1983–84 he was a National Fellow at the Hoover Institution, and in 1984–85 he was the senior staff economist for tax policy at the President's Council of Economic Advisers. He has been at the University of Michigan since 1987.

**Raymond D. Vlasin** is a University Distinguished Professor Emeritus in the Department of Resource Development at Michigan State University. He has devoted his professional career to community and economic development in Michigan, Wisconsin, Minnesota, and nationally.

He has served the Federal government as director of the Natural Resource Economics Division of the Economic Research Service of the U.S. Department of Agriculture; and Congress as Staff Economist for the House Public Works Committee.

**Michelle F. Wilsey** is a utility consultant specializing in strategic business issues, including utility service unbundling and restructuring for competitive markets, as well as regulatory issues and public policy trends affecting the energy and telecommunication industries. Prior to establishing her independent consulting practice, she was the Associate Director (1996–2002) of the Institute of Public Utilities, Michigan State University. She led the Institute's research program and managed the publication of "Public Utilities in Japan: Past, Present and Future," by the Japan Society of Public Utility Economics; "Letting Go: Deregulating the Process of Deregulation," by Alfred Kahn; and "Promoting Competition in Michigan Telecommunications Markets Through Innovative Legislation," by Werner Sichel and Donald L. Alexander. Prior to joining the Institute, she served as the Assistant Director of the Columbia Institute for Tele-Information (C.I.T.I.), Columbia Business School. She holds a B.S. (economics, political science, international studies) and M.A. (telecommunications) from Michigan State University.

**John R. Wolfe** is Senior Project Engineer and Economist at Limno-Tech, Inc., where he is also Manager for Engineering and Science. He is a member of the American Academy of Environmental Engineering, and was previously Associate Professor of Economics at Michigan State University. His areas of expertise include surface water quality modeling, including contaminated sediments; wastewater treatment and permitting; groundwater protection; and environmental economics. He holds a bachelor's degree from Brown University, a Master of Science in Environmental and Water Resource Engineering from the University of Michigan, and a Ph.D. in Economics from the University of Pennsylvania.

**Stephen A. Woodbury** is Professor of Economics at Michigan State University and a Senior Economist at the W. E. Upjohn Institute. He has also held appointments at Pennsylvania State University and University of Stirling (U.K.), and was Deputy Director of the Advisory Council on Unemployment Compensation (U.S. Department of Labor) during 1993–94. His books include *Search Theory and Unemployment,* co-edited with Carl Davidson (2002); *Employee Benefits and Labor Markets in Canada and the United States,* co-edited with William Alpert (2000); *Reform of the Unemployment Insurance System,* co-edited with Laurie Bassi (1998); and *The Tax Treatment of Fringe Benefits,* co-authored with Wei-Jang Huang (1991). He received a Ph.D. in Economics from the University of Wisconsin–Madison in 1981.